AF593609

THE NATURAL HERITAGE OF THE WORLD

The most beautiful national parks, protected areas and biosphere reserves on Earth

According to the UNESCO Convention

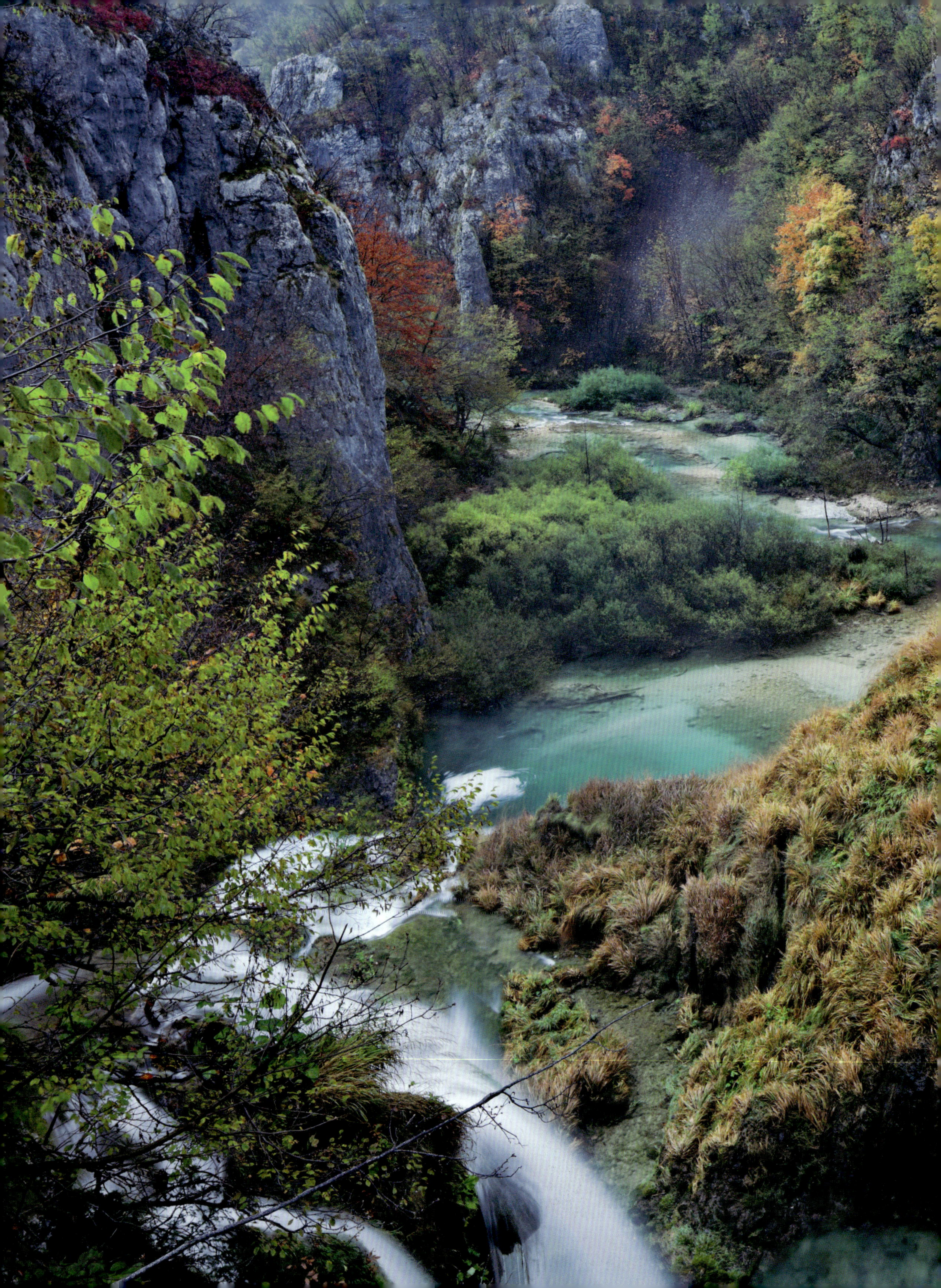

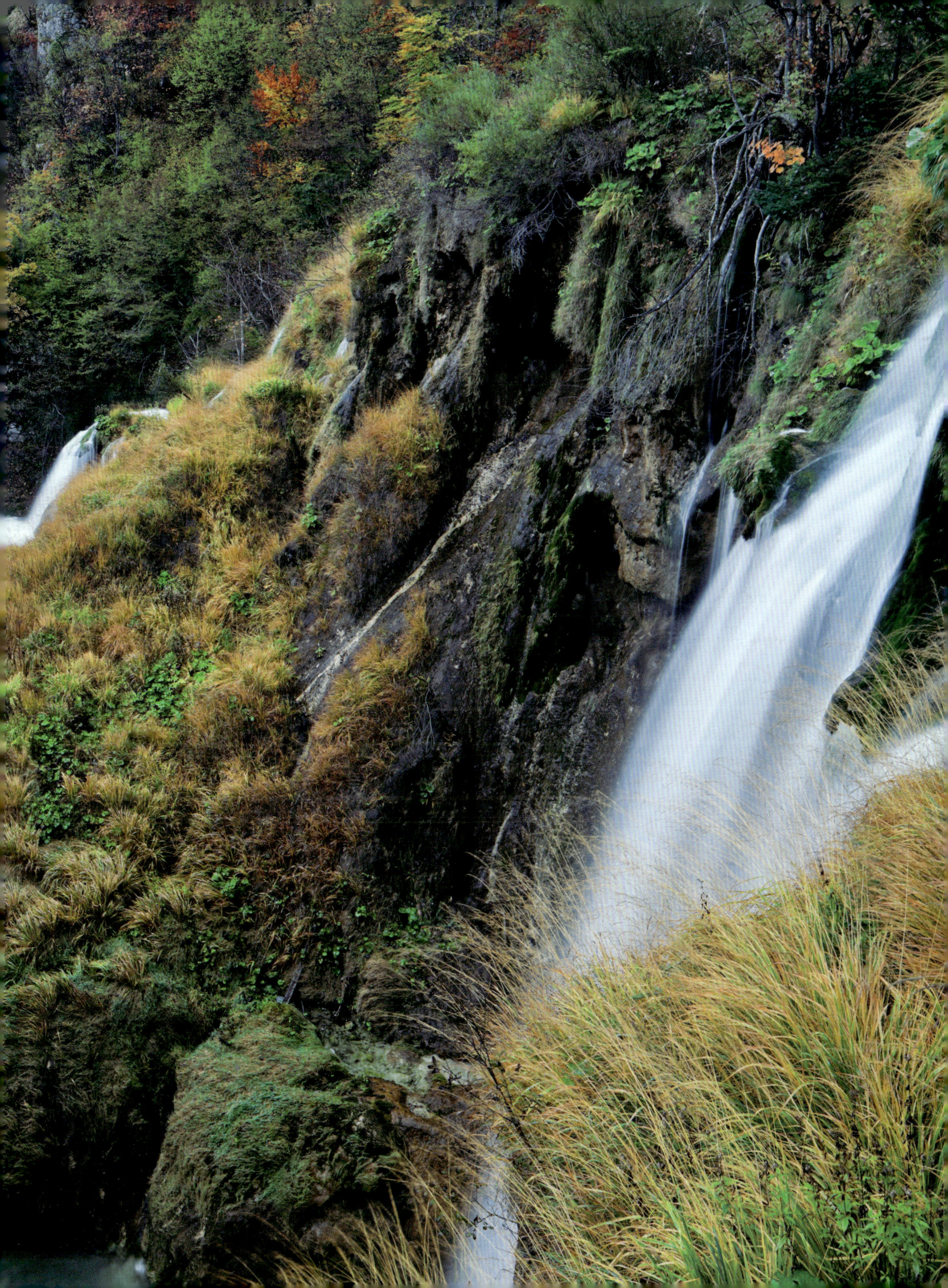

INTRODUCTION

The last remaining European primeval beech forests in the Carpathians, the impenetrable jungle of Sumatra, the Golden Mountains of Altai, the national parks of East Africa where big game flourish, the rocky moon-like landscape of the Tassili N'Ajjer in Algeria, gigantic glaciers in Patagonia, geysers and hot springs in Yellowstone National Park, the Great Barrier Reef off the east coast of Australia –

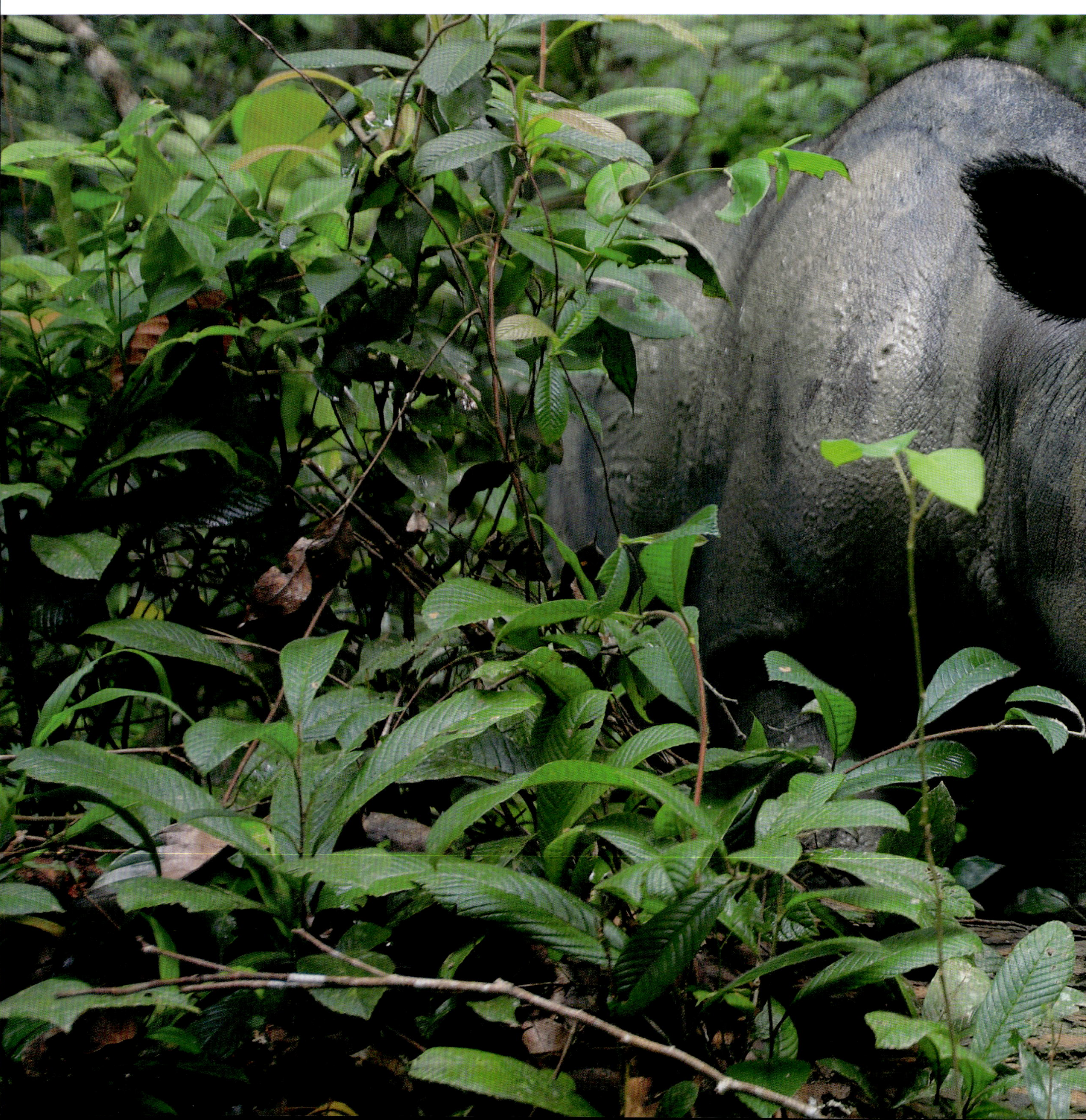

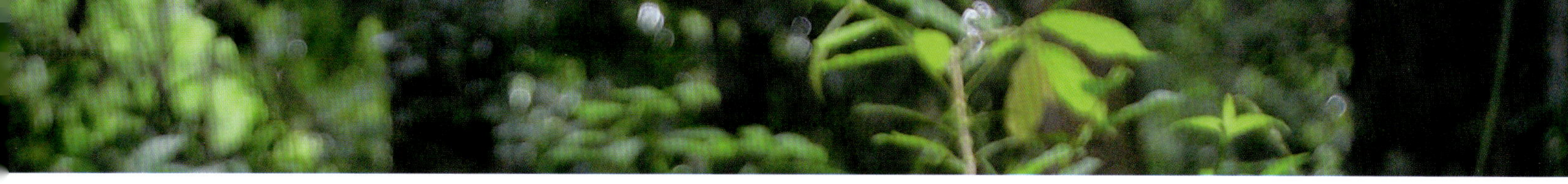

such dreamlike, paradisiacal, untamed places can still be found, where nature has created amazing "artworks" of a unique grace and beauty which have largely escaped human interference. To preserve this situation in the face of continuing worldwide destruction of the natural environment, UNESCO (the United Nations Educational, Cultural, and Scientific Organization), together with the International Union for Conservation of Nature (IUCN), and the International Council on Monuments and Sites (ICONOS), has to date designated 229 natural monuments as World Heritage Sites – of which 32 are also designated World Cultural Heritage Sites.

To receive World Natural Heritage Site status, a site must be of "universal value," and particularly worth preserving, because of its aesthetic attraction, its scientific importance, or its status as a habitat for rare species of animals and plants. The integrity and authenticity of sites are also important, and a conservation plan must be in place. In many cases, the areas will already be protected by having National Park status, as for example the Serengeti in Tanzania or the Everglades in Florida.

The UNESCO listing of World Natural Heritage Sites is designed to emphasize the fact that the preservation of our natural environment is not merely a national matter, but is a concern for all humanity – so that unique and vital ecosystems can survive, but also so that our descendants are able to enjoy these spectacular beauties of nature.

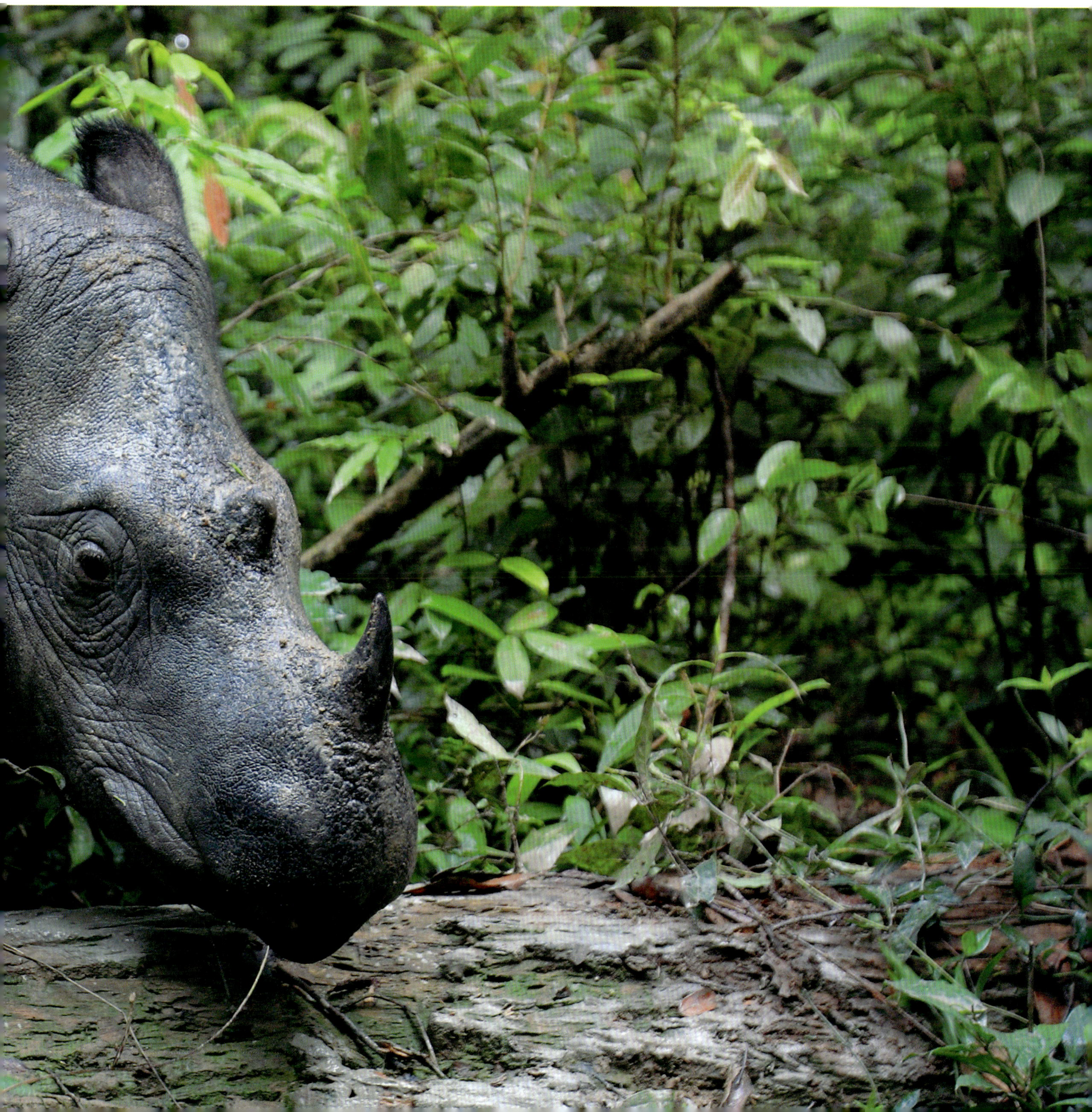

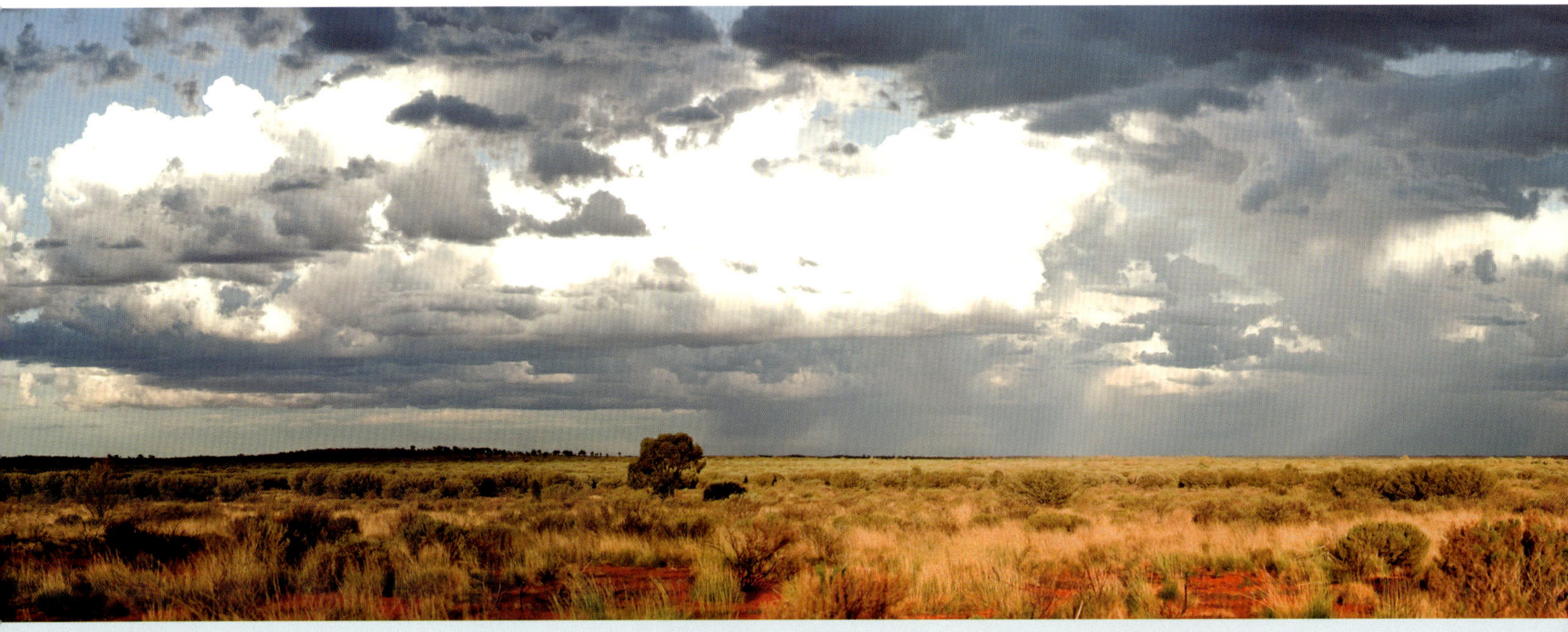

CONTENTS

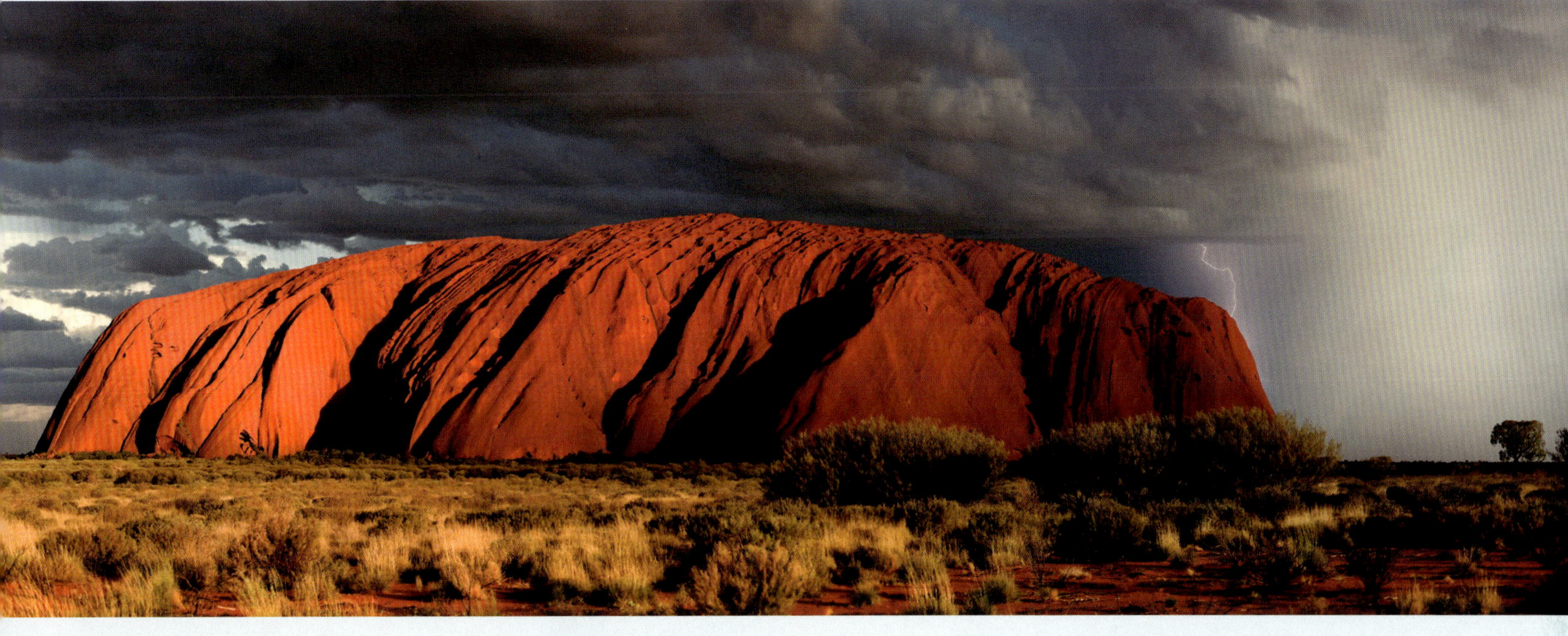

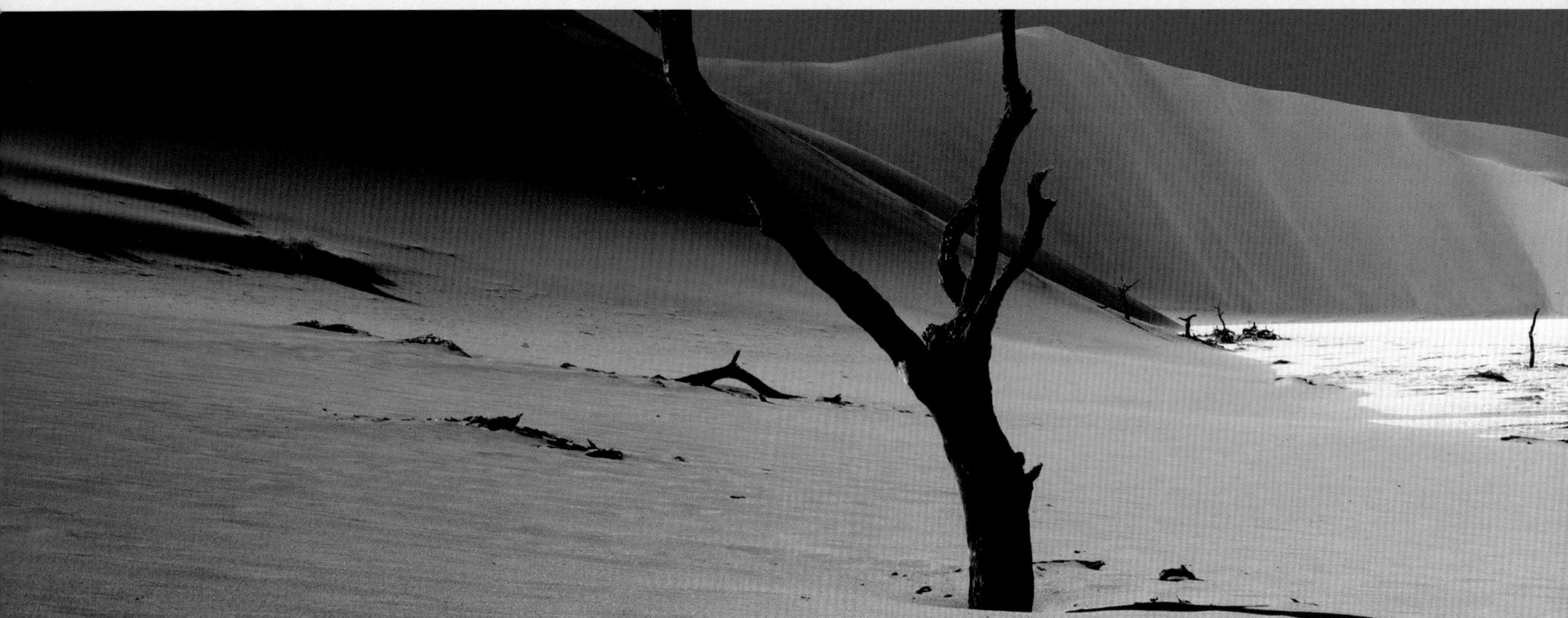

CONTENTS

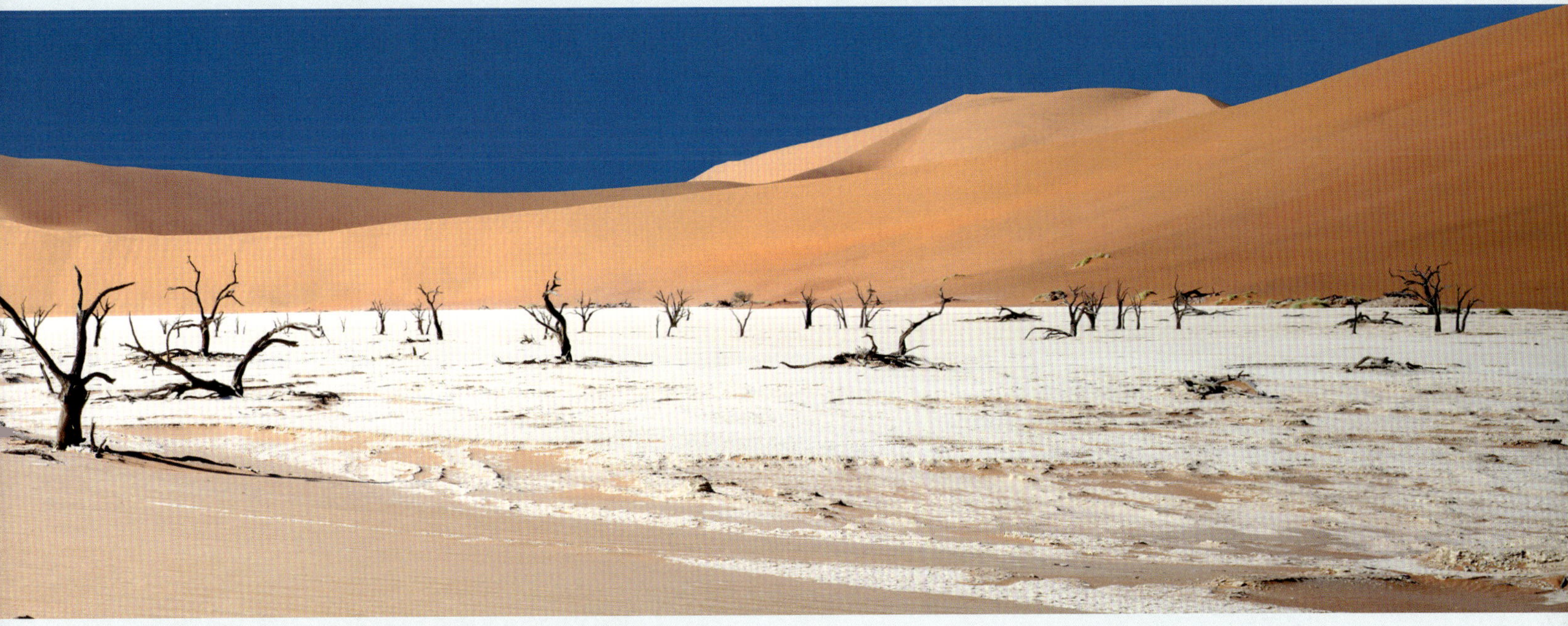

There was a time when people venerated the Eurasian brown bear (right) and when the year's seasons reflected its life and its sleep patterns. There followed many years when the bear was hunted and persecuted, but now it is once more protected in most parts of Europe. Below: The Krkonoše mountain range in Poland enjoys UNESCO protection as a national park and a biosphere reserve.

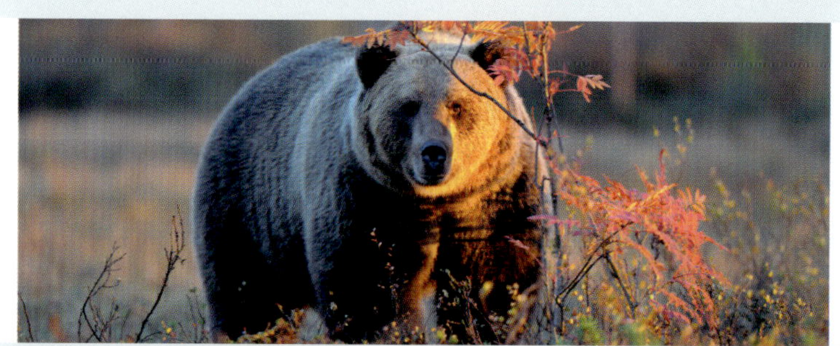

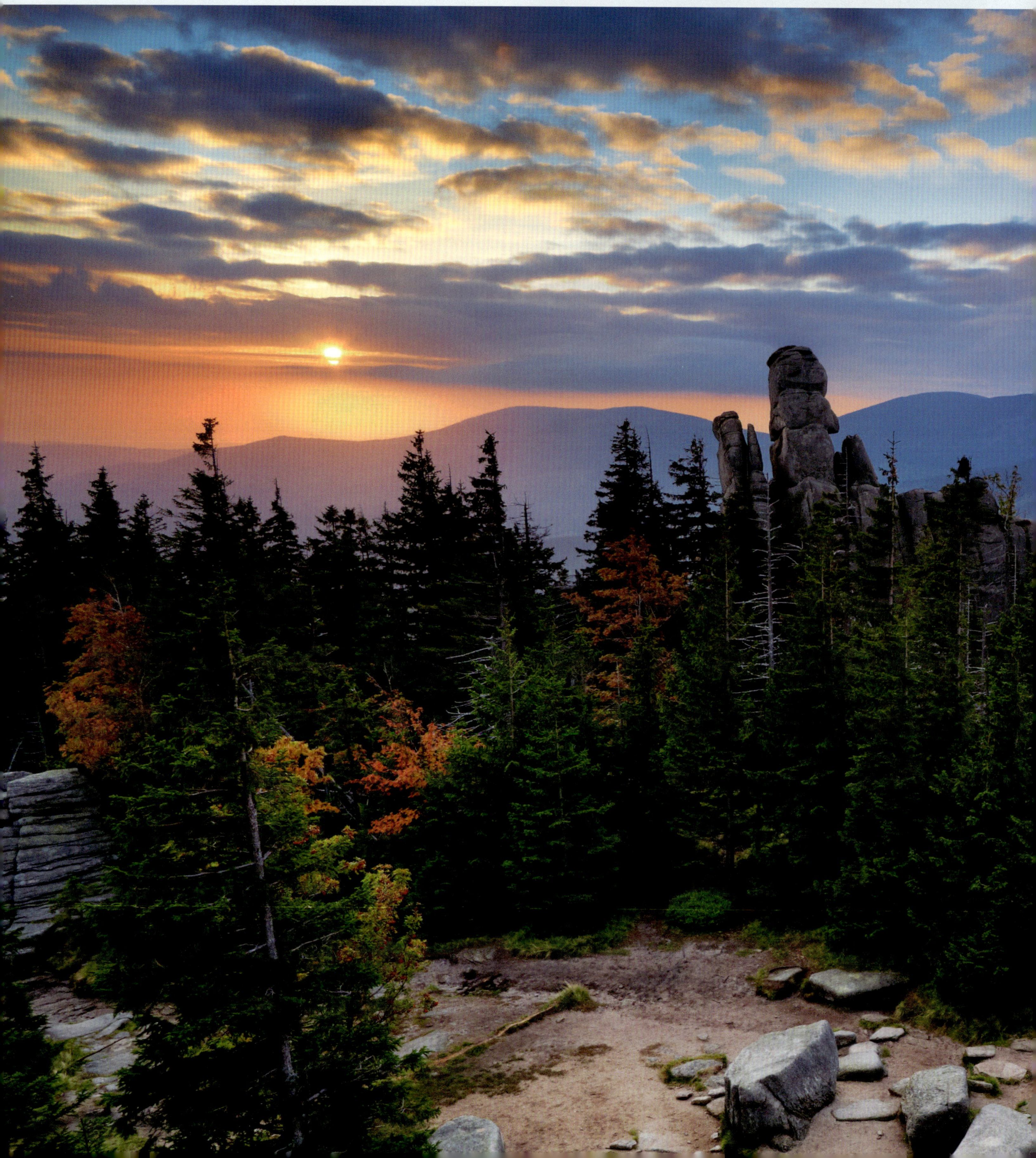

EUROPE

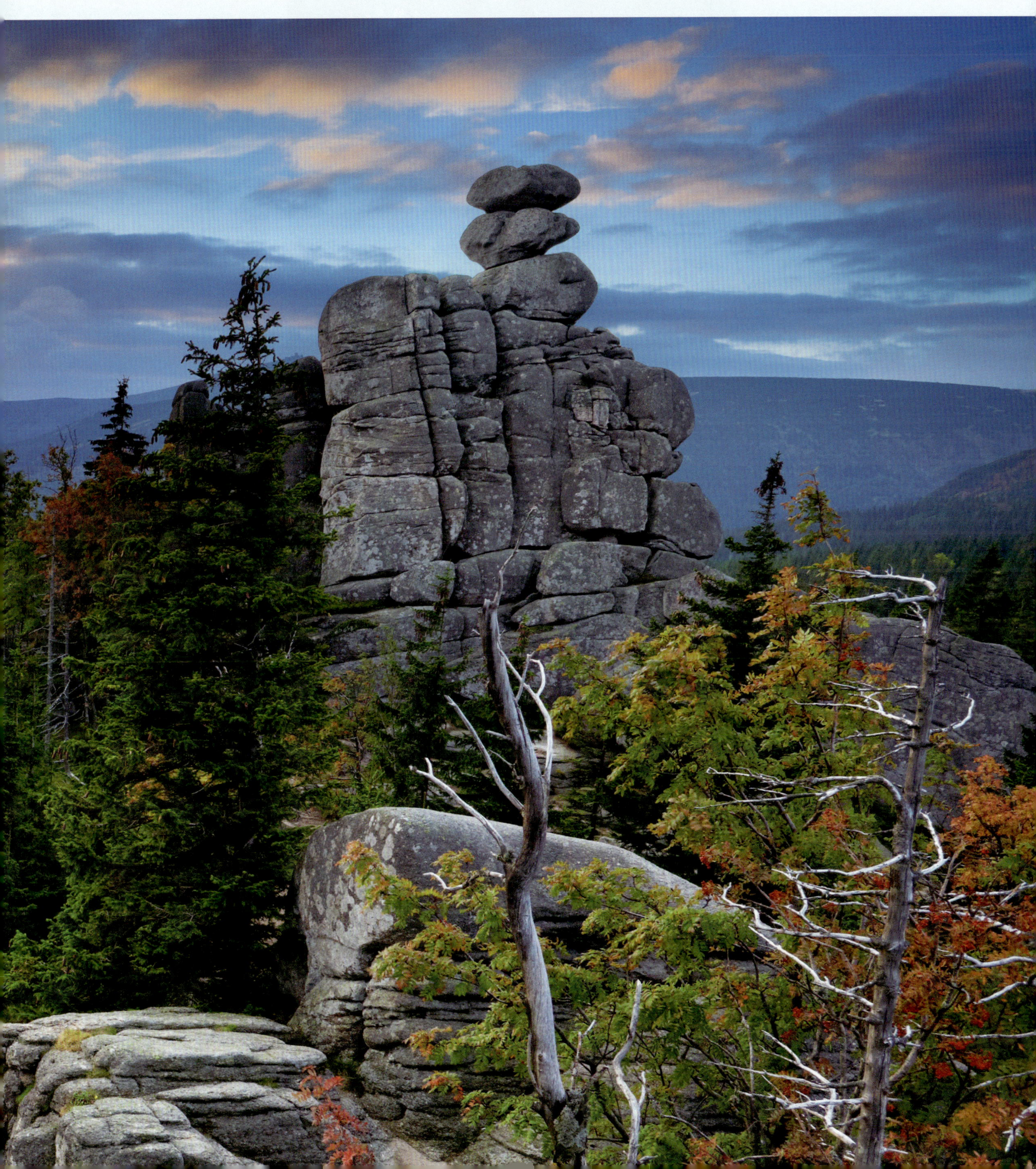

THE VOLCANIC ISLAND OF SURTSEY

Date of inscription: 2008

This island, 32 kilometers (20 miles) off the southern coast of Iceland, was the result of submarine volcanic activity. Reserved for research by the Icelandic government, it is an open air laboratory for the observation of natural colonization behaviour.

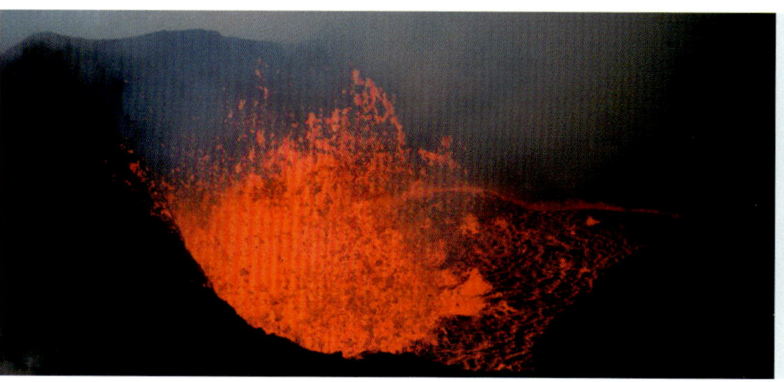

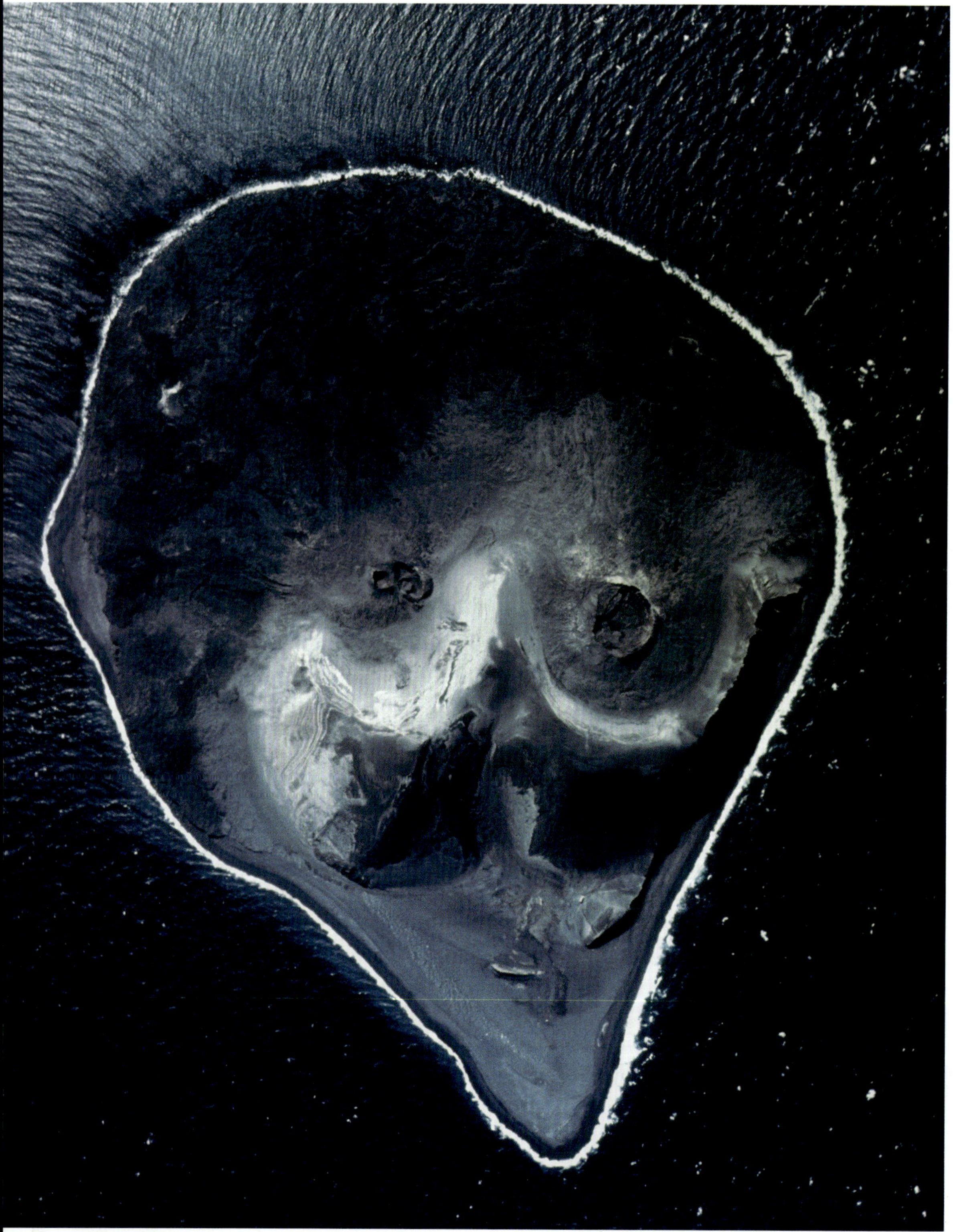

The island of Surtsey is off-limits to casual visitors. Surtsey has been reserved for scientific study since its creation, to ensure that the study of its flora and fauna is undisturbed by human intervention. The island, named after the Nordic fire giant, Surtr, was declared a wildlife reserve as early as 1965, while it was still being formed. Mosses and lichen were documented a year later,

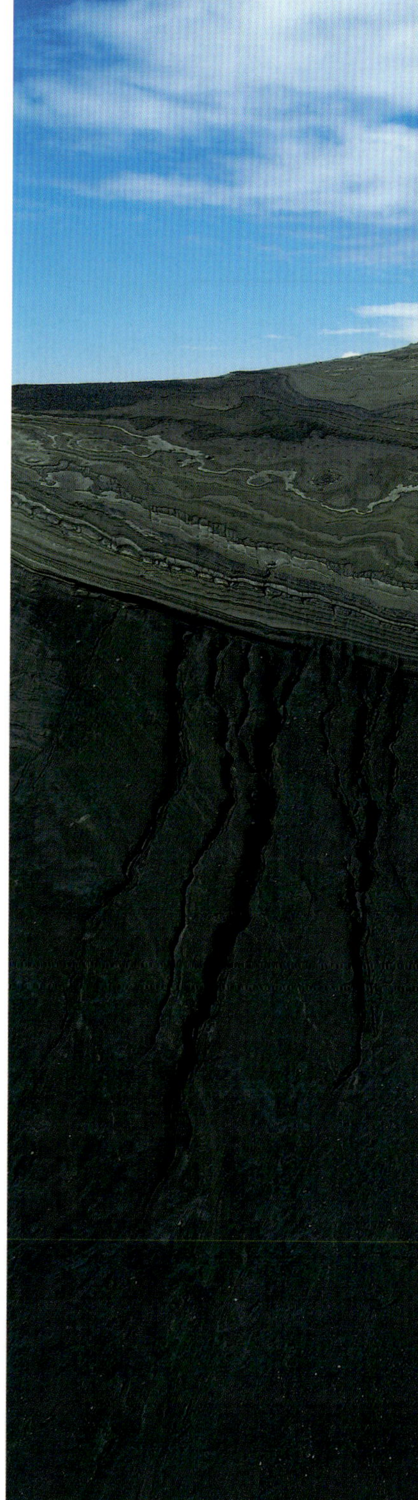

and these were followed by higher plants such as searocket, beach grass, and oyster plants, whose seeds had been blown across the sea from the bay some 20 km (12 miles) away. Birds and insects also reached the island in its first year of existence, and it is now home to 335 species of invertebrate and 89 kinds of bird. However, time and tide have not waited for Surtsey. Rough seas, wind, and rain have eroded ever greater amounts of material and the compaction of the island's sediments and base material mean that its surface area is constantly shrinking. Once covering 2 sq. km (just over a square mile), Surtsey has now shrunk to 1.4 sq. km (three-quarters of a square mile) and the highest point has dropped from 173 m (567 feet) above seal level to 154 m (505 feet). Scientists have estimated that the island will lose most of its land mass over the next century, but Surtsey will not disappear beneath the waves; the island's core will remain as a bare rock in the ocean.

Surtsey, the southernmost of the Vestmannaeyjar Islands off the coast of Iceland, is a giant open air laboratory (below right). Violent eruptions under the Atlantic (right) led to its creation in 1963. The island consists of lava and pyroclastic material and has provided an opportunity for scientists to study the "undisturbed" development of animal and plant life

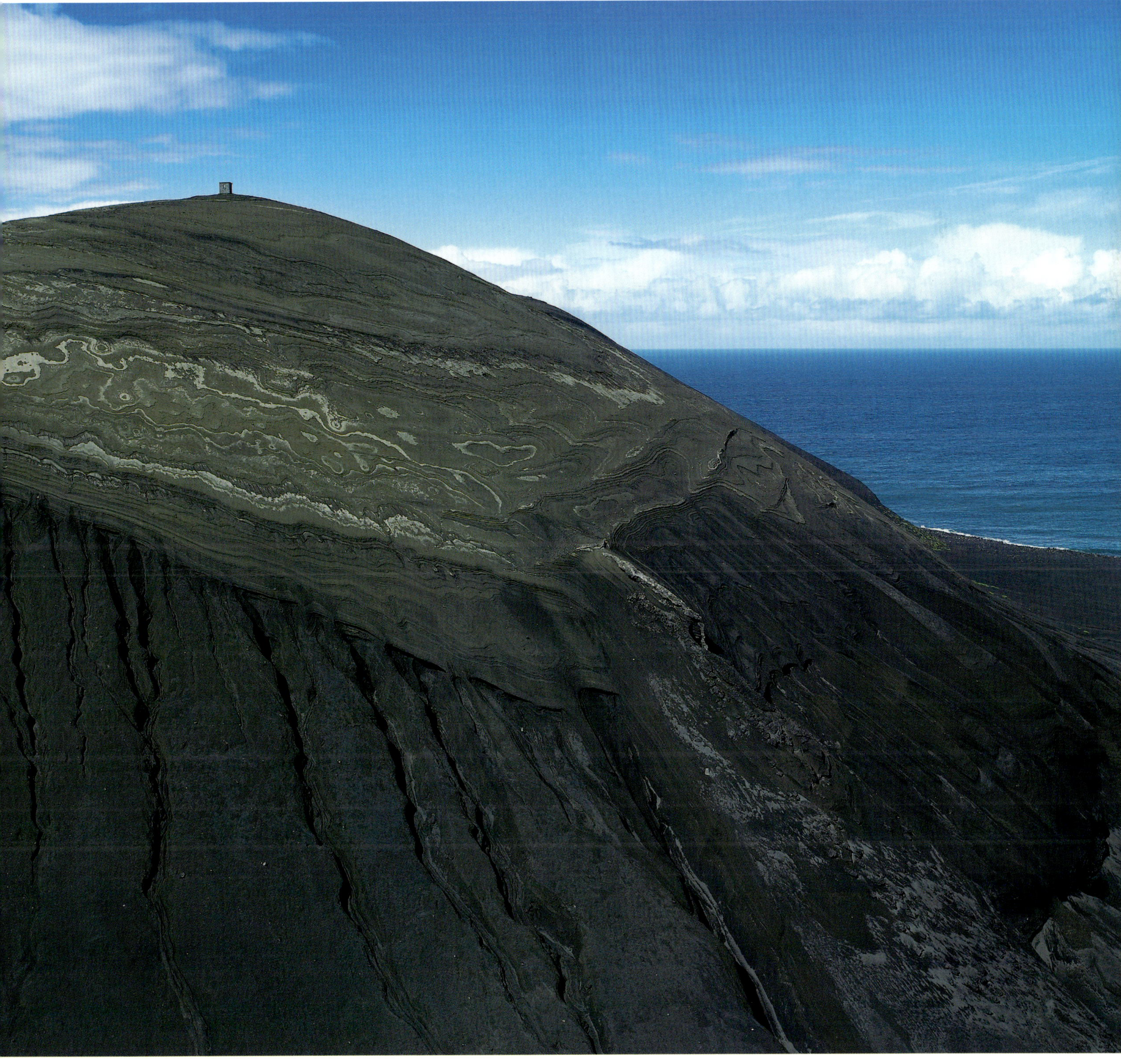

THE WEST NORWEGIAN FJORDS: GEIRANGERFJORD AND NÆRØYFJORD

Date of inscription: 2005

Norway is a land of fjords. Two of the longest, deepest, and most beautiful examples are Geirangerfjord and Nærøyfjord, both located in the south-west of the country.

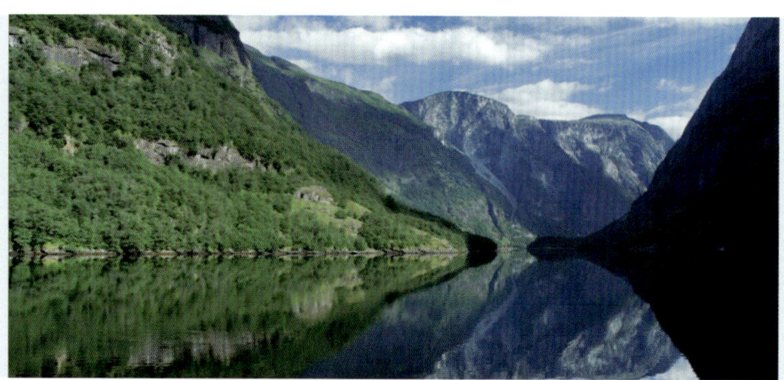

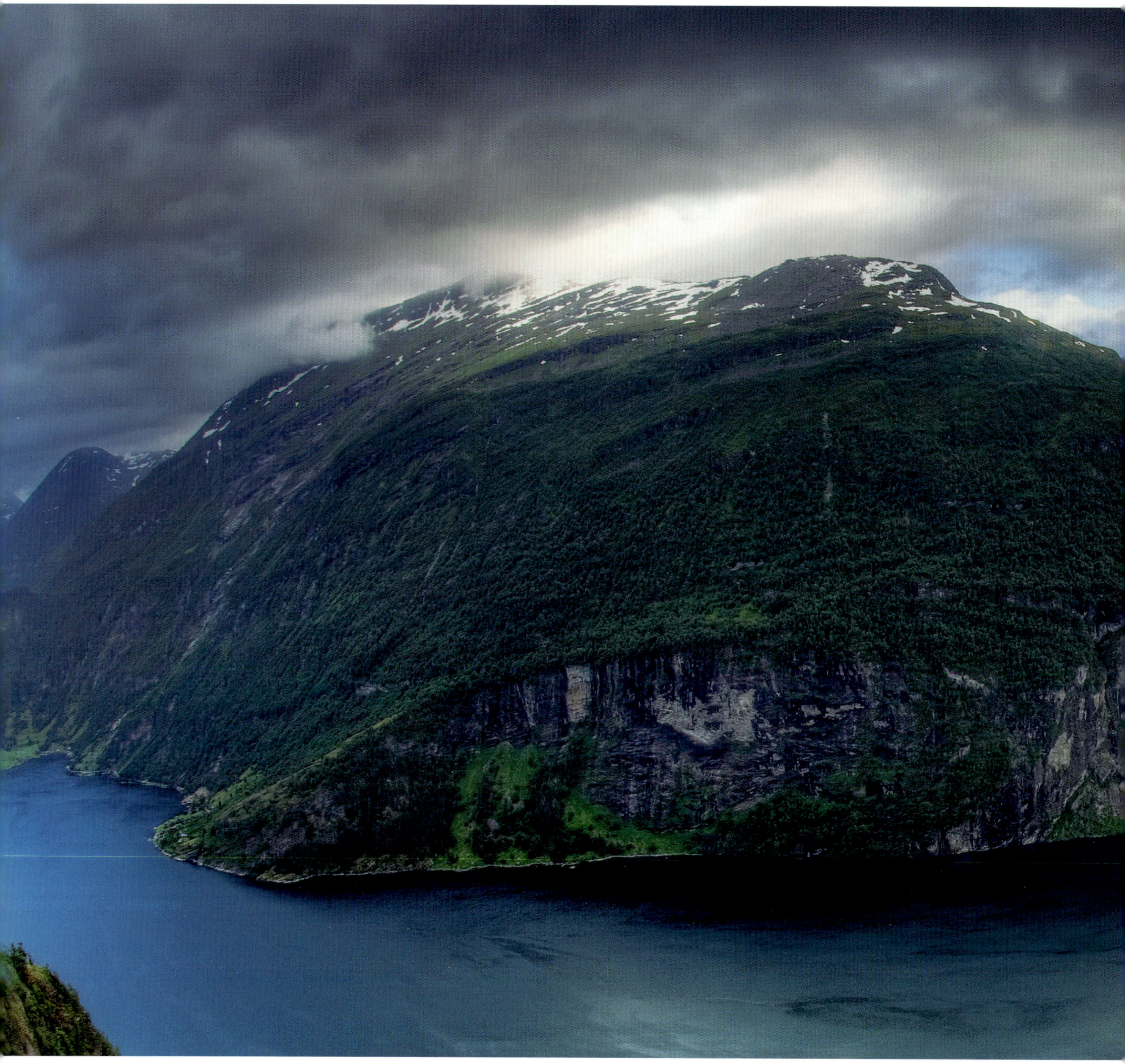

"Fjord" is a Norwegian word describing a valley originally created by rivers, and subsequently shaped by huge glaciers during the ice age. These U-shaped valleys cut deep into the coastal rocks. At the end of the ice age, rising sea levels caused the fjords to flood and so penetrate deep inland. Fjords are typified by their steep, often vertical walls, which have been polished by the movement of ice masses across their surfaces. Glacial detritus is found at the bottom of the fjords.

Geirangerfjord and Nærøyfjord are about 120 km (75 miles) apart. The ice masses that created them penetrated some 1,900 m (6,230 feet) deep into the mountains, and the bottom of the fjord walls are as much as 500 m (1,640 feet) below sea level. The estuaries are 1–2 km (0.5–1 mile) wide. Both fjords boast impressive mountain ranges that rise up behind the sheer coastal cliffs. Above Geirangerfjord, the Torvløysa mountain is 1,850 m (6,070 feet) high, and the Stiganosi mountain over Nærøyfjord reaches some 1,761 m (5,778 feet). While the Nærøyfjord mountains have rather flatter tops, the Geirangerfjord range is more alpine in character. Streams from the nearby mountains flow into the fjord from hanging valleys, often falling down the cliffs as waterfalls. At Geirangerfjord and Nærøyfjord, these streams – unlike those at most other fjords – have not yet been used to generate power. Both Geirangerfjord and Nærøyfjord run parallel to the coastline, each opening out into a further fjord.

Cruise ships pass the Seven Sisters waterfall (large picture), which drops some 300 m (984 feet). At certain points, Nærøyfjord, a branch of the Sognefjord, is only 250 m (820 feet) wide (left).

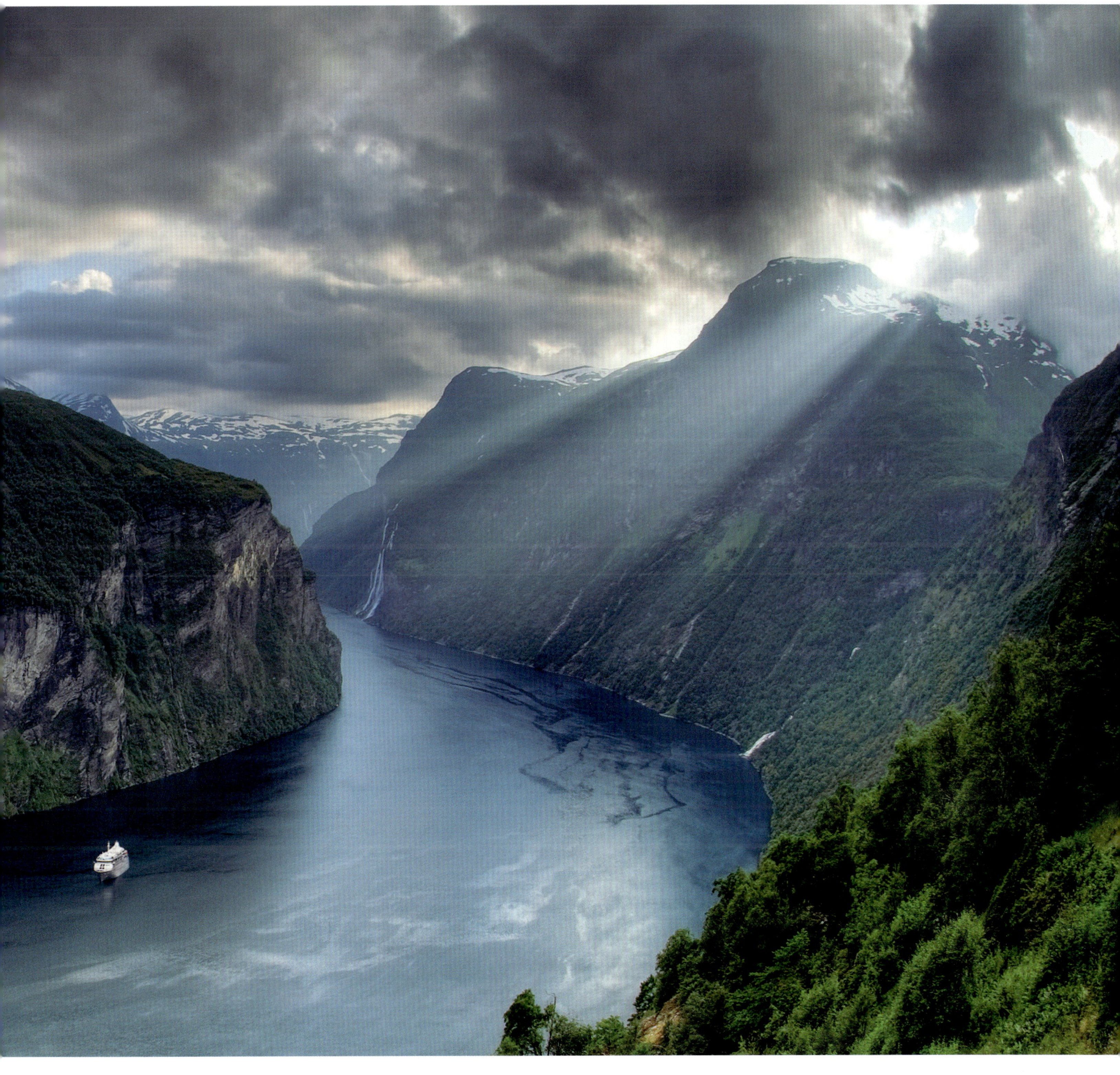

THE ARCTIC CULTURE OF LAPLAND

Date of inscription: 1996

The vast plateaus of northern Sweden are home to the Lapp or Sámi people and their culture. The nomadic Sámi way of life makes the most of the landscape's sparse natural resources.

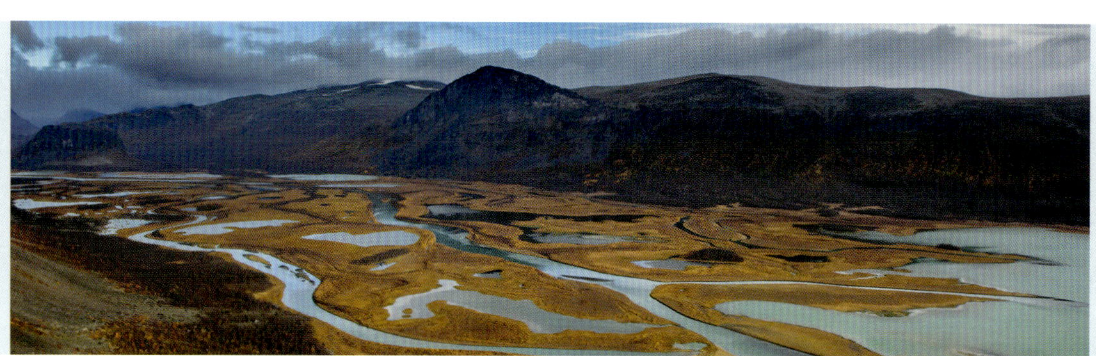

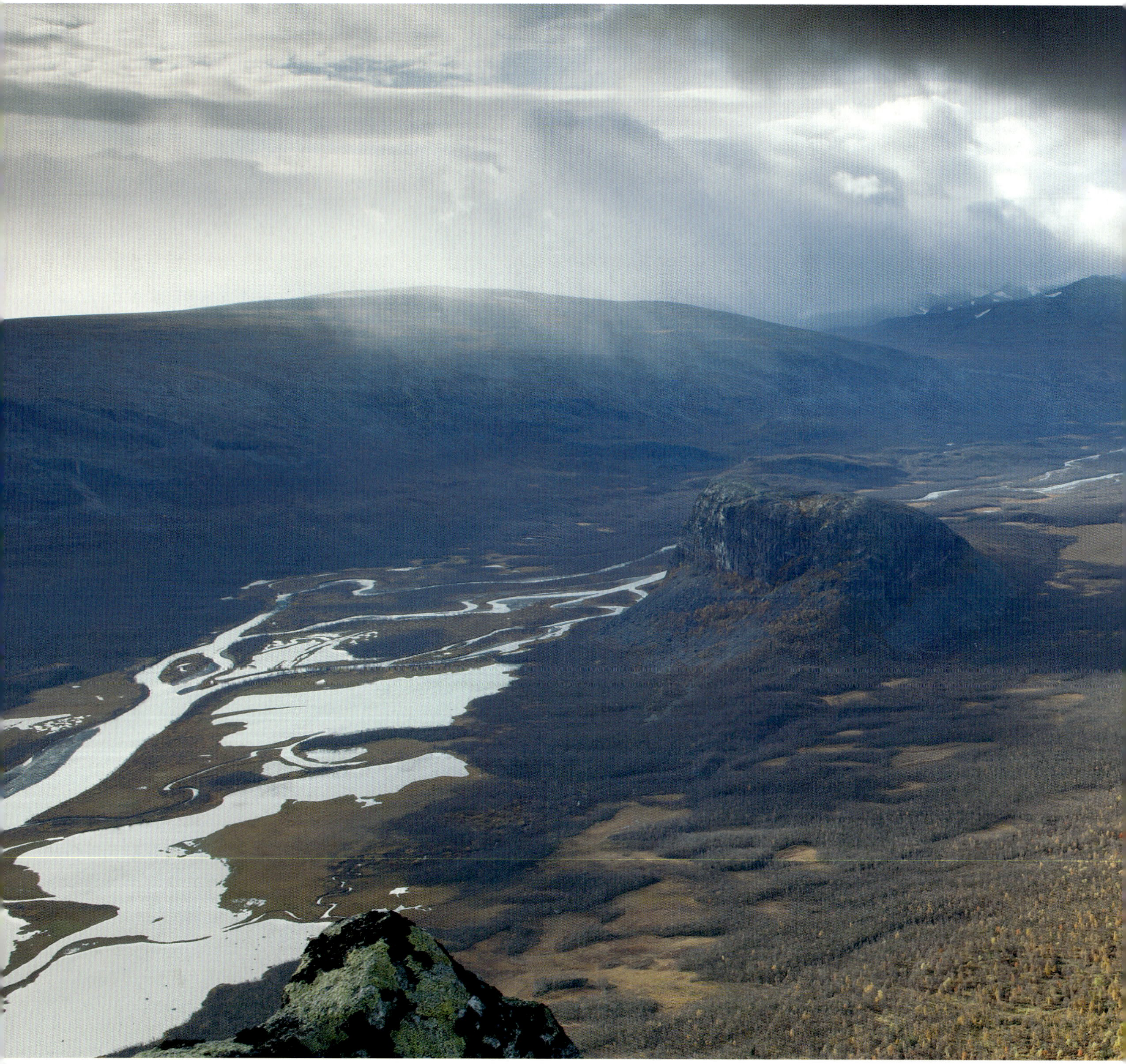

The Sámi or – as the Lapps term themselves – Samek ("bog people") have inhabited the northern regions of Scandinavia for over two thousand years. Throughout their history, these people have roamed the barely populated landmass with their giant reindeer herds, covering vast distances every year. Today, many Sámi remain true to their traditional way of life, even if they can no longer make their living from fishing and reindeer breeding alone. Tourism and conservation work have become important additional income sources. Sámi crafts, meanwhile, continue to flourish, notably in the form of lavish textiles, wood and bone carvings, and animal furs. Traditional, bright Sámi clothing is also as popular as ever. The areas of Lapland between the edge of the forests and the north sea coast are dominated by tundra vegetation, and are not used for agriculture. They are home to brown bears, as well as wolves, elk, and a wide variety of birds.

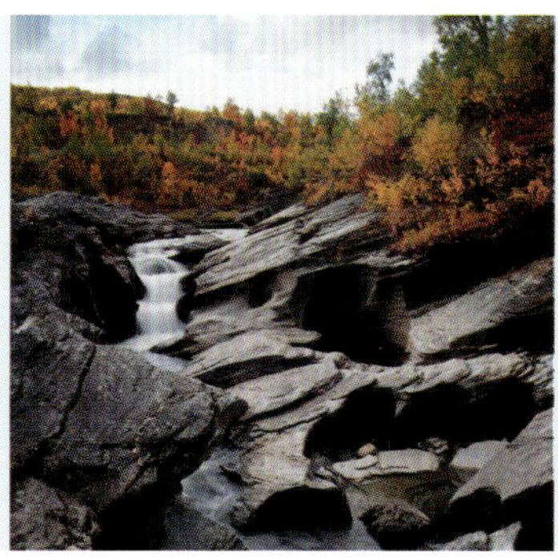

Mountains, fjords, and fields of geological boulders typify the Lapland landscape The Rapa River (below) is the biggest river of the Nationalpark.

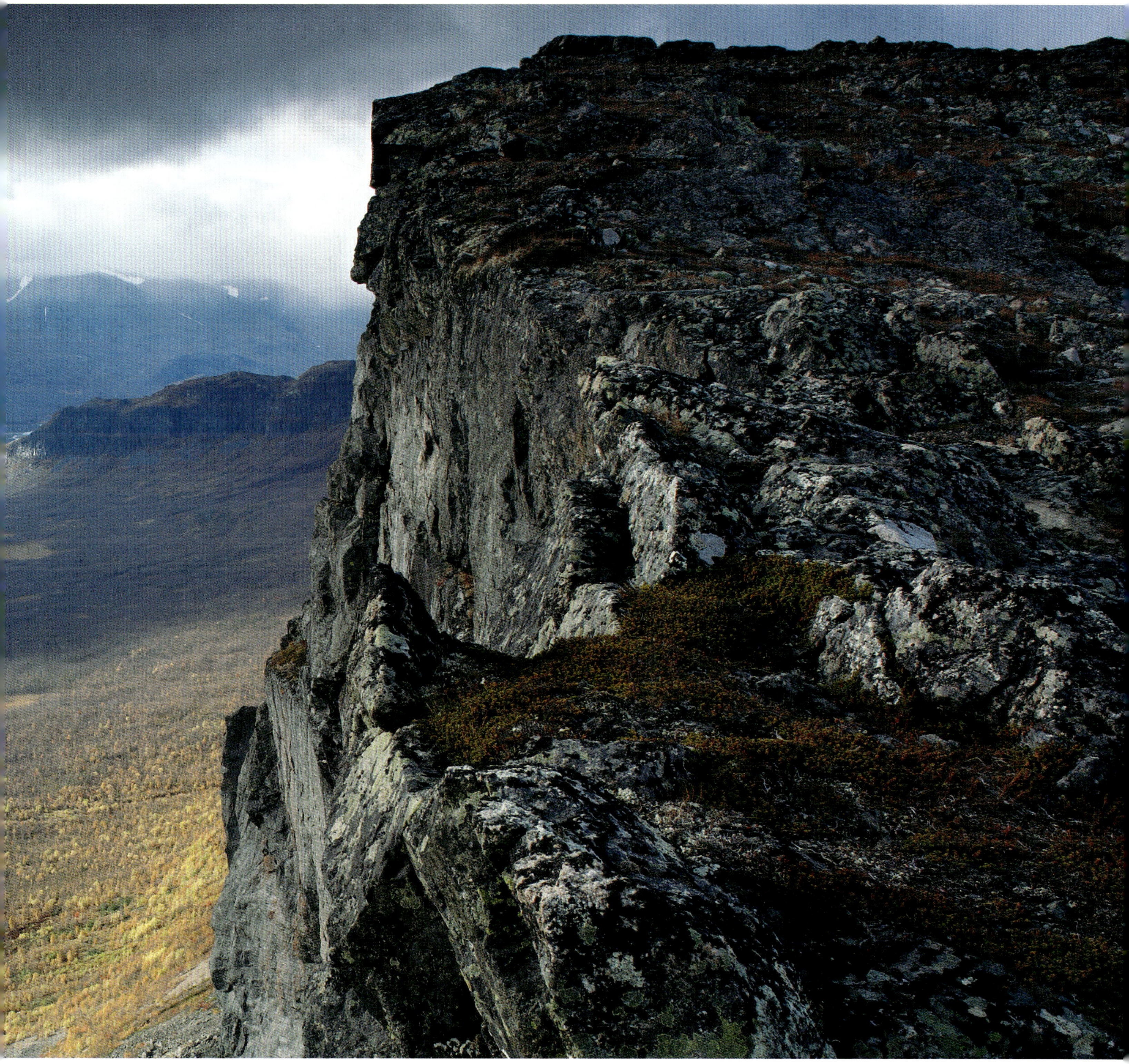

HIGH COAST / KVARKEN ARCHIPELAGO

Date of inscription: 2000
Extended: 2014

Situated in the Gulf of Bothnia, the High Coast is a fascinating archipelago landscape shaped by the glaciers of the last ice age. The addition of the Finnish part of Kvarken Archipelago has turned this into a transnational site.

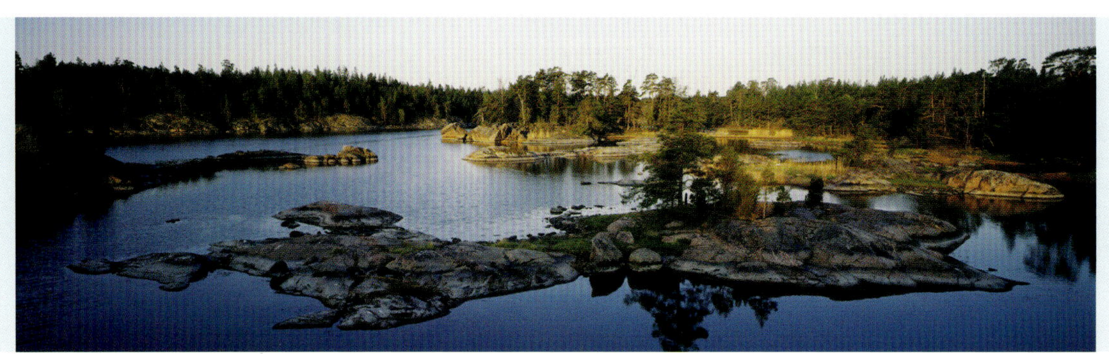

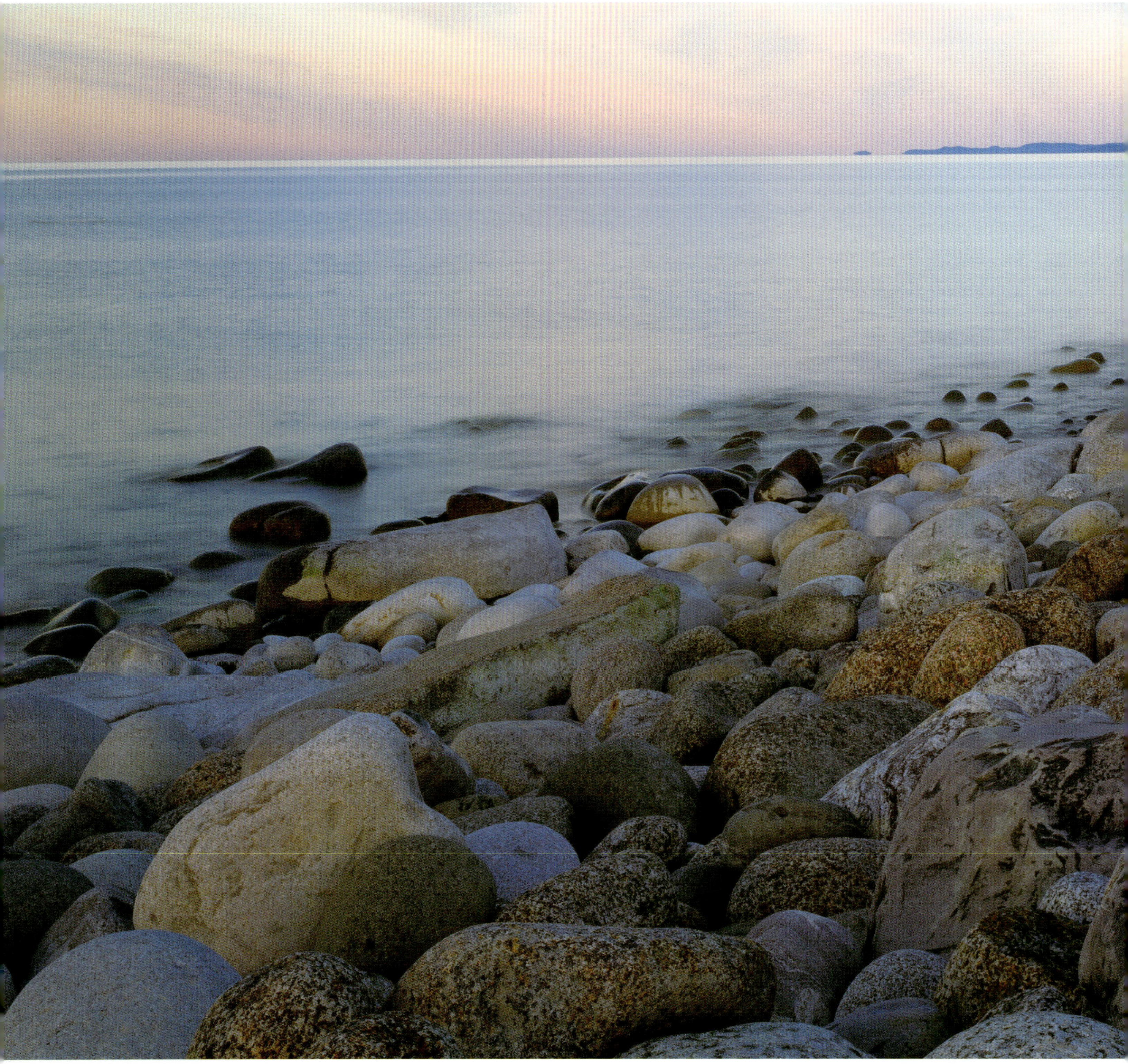

These whaleback landforms in the Gulf of Bothnia were shaped by the last ice age, which began around 80,000 years ago and ended in Scandinavia about 9,600 years ago. When the giant ice sheets melted, sea levels rose by some 115 m (380 feet). As a result, large swathes of land were left below sea level. Freed from the weight of the glaciers bearing down upon it, the land gradually rose, and skerries (rocky islands) emerged from the sea. To date, the region has risen by 285 m (935 feet), and the process is still continuing. In fact, the subsoil is rising at a rate of around 93 cm (37 inches) every century. The hills of the hinterland are up to 350 m (1,150 feet) high. It is a very attractive and largely untamed landscape, boasting rich, chalky soil and numerous lakes – all left behind by the ice age. These freshwater lakes, together with the brackish water area of the flat estuaries and coastal islands, and the open waters of the Baltic, mean that the High Coast encompasses three geologically and biologically significant water systems in one small area.

The smooth surfaces of stones and rocks polished by the glaciers and water are typical of the skerries (below). The play of nature's autumn hues is particularly charming (left).

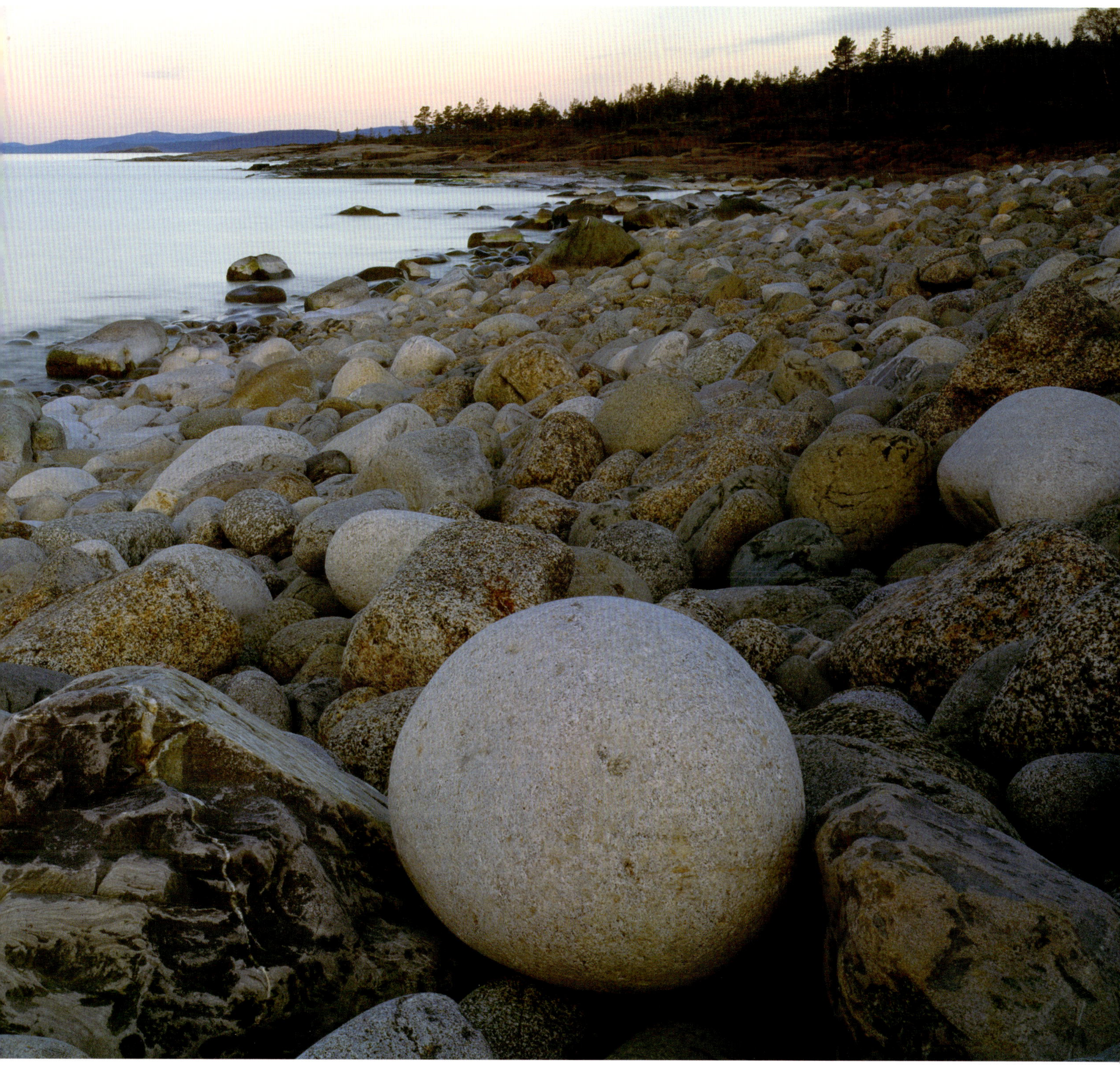

WADDEN SEA (VADEHAVET)

Date of inscription: 2014

First inscribed in 2009, the UNESCO World Natural Heritage site of the Wadden Sea was extended in 2014 to include the Danish wadden sea and areas offshore from the East Frisian islands, creating the largest protected contiguous wetland and wadden sea island system in the world.

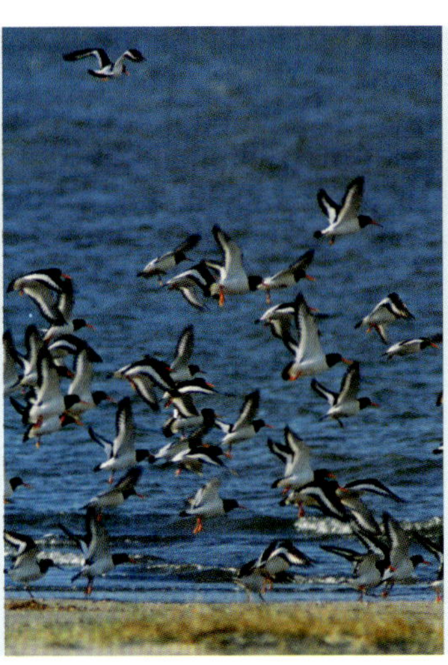

Featuring on the UNESCO list of World Natural Heritage sites since 2009, the Wadden Sea site was enlarged in 2014 to include the Danish Wadden Sea, or Vadehavet, and areas off the East Frisian Islands, making it the largest contiguous Wadden Island area in the world that is entirely protected. Aside from the Danish Wadden Sea Conservation Area, the East Frisian islands of Norderney, Langeoog, Spiekeroog and Wangerooge and northwest of Neuwerk, an offshore area situated in Germany's Lower Saxony region, were also newly added. The entire World Heritage area now covers an area of 11,500 sq km (4,440 sq miles) and extends over a distance of more than 450 km (280 miles) of coastline from the Danish town of Blåvandshuk in the north to the German coastal protected areas and down to the Dutch city of Den Helder in the south-west.

The Wadden Sea, one of the last original natural landscapes of Central Europe, is spawning ground, birthplace and home to millions of animals. Left: oystercatchers off the East Frisian Islands; below: a creek finds its path through the mudflats

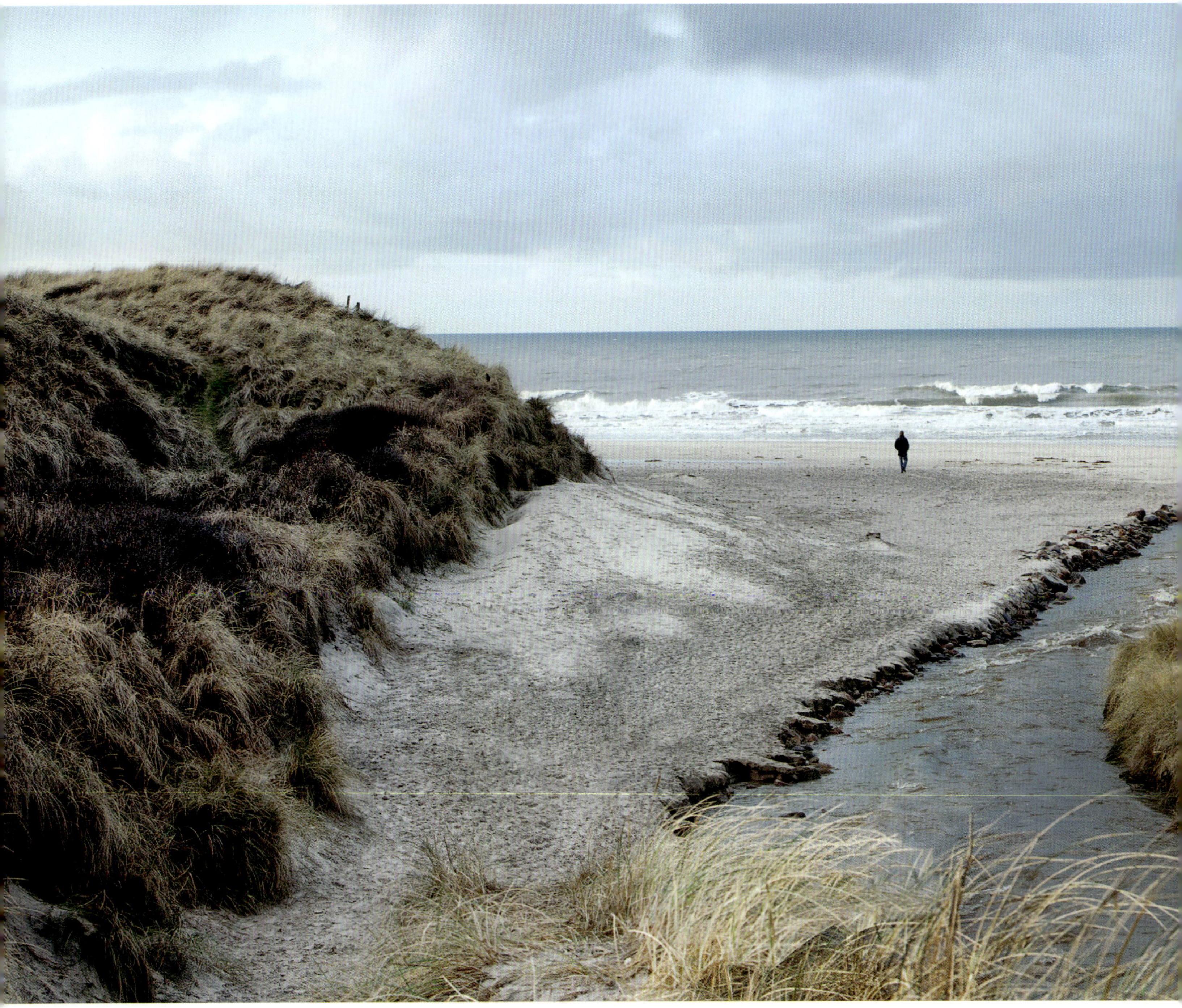

STEVNS KLINT

Geologically speaking, there is a significant break in the transition between the cretaceous period and the Paleogene (previously known as the Tertiary). As a narrow band in the sequence of layers it marks the transition from the Mesozoic to Cenozoic. Geologists recognize in the narrow ribbon that separates the older cretaceous layers from the tertiary limestone the apocalyptically seeming story of a giant meteorite impact hit, which some 65 million years ago killed more than half of all living creatures on Earth, including probably the dinosaurs. Traces of the impact were discovered as early as the 1970s. It was not until 1991, however, that the remains of a crater from this time, measuring 300 km (186 miles) in its outer circle, were discovered on satellite images of the Gulf of Mexico as well as on the adjacent Yucatan Peninsula. It was named Chicxulub.

The cliffs of the steep Stevns Klint coastline (right) extend over a total length of about 15 km (9 miles). The rich local fossil finds are known as "fish clay" among the Danish population.

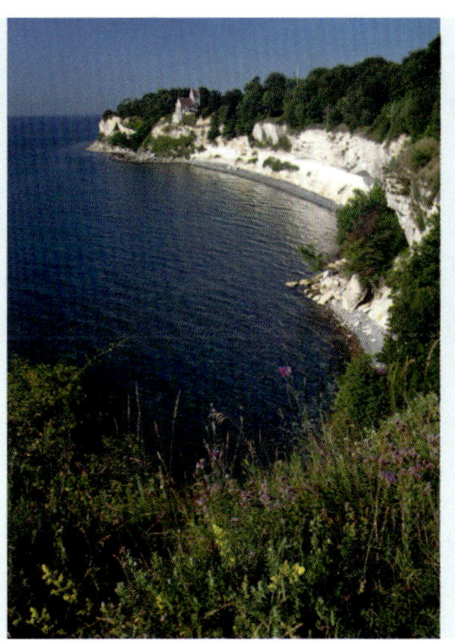

Date of inscription: 2014

The around 15-km- (9-mile-) long and up to 41-m- (134-foot-) high cliffs of Stevns Klint in the south-east of the Danish Baltic Sea, on the Seeland island, bear testimony to one of the most dramatic events in Earth's history – a mass dying around 65 million years ago.

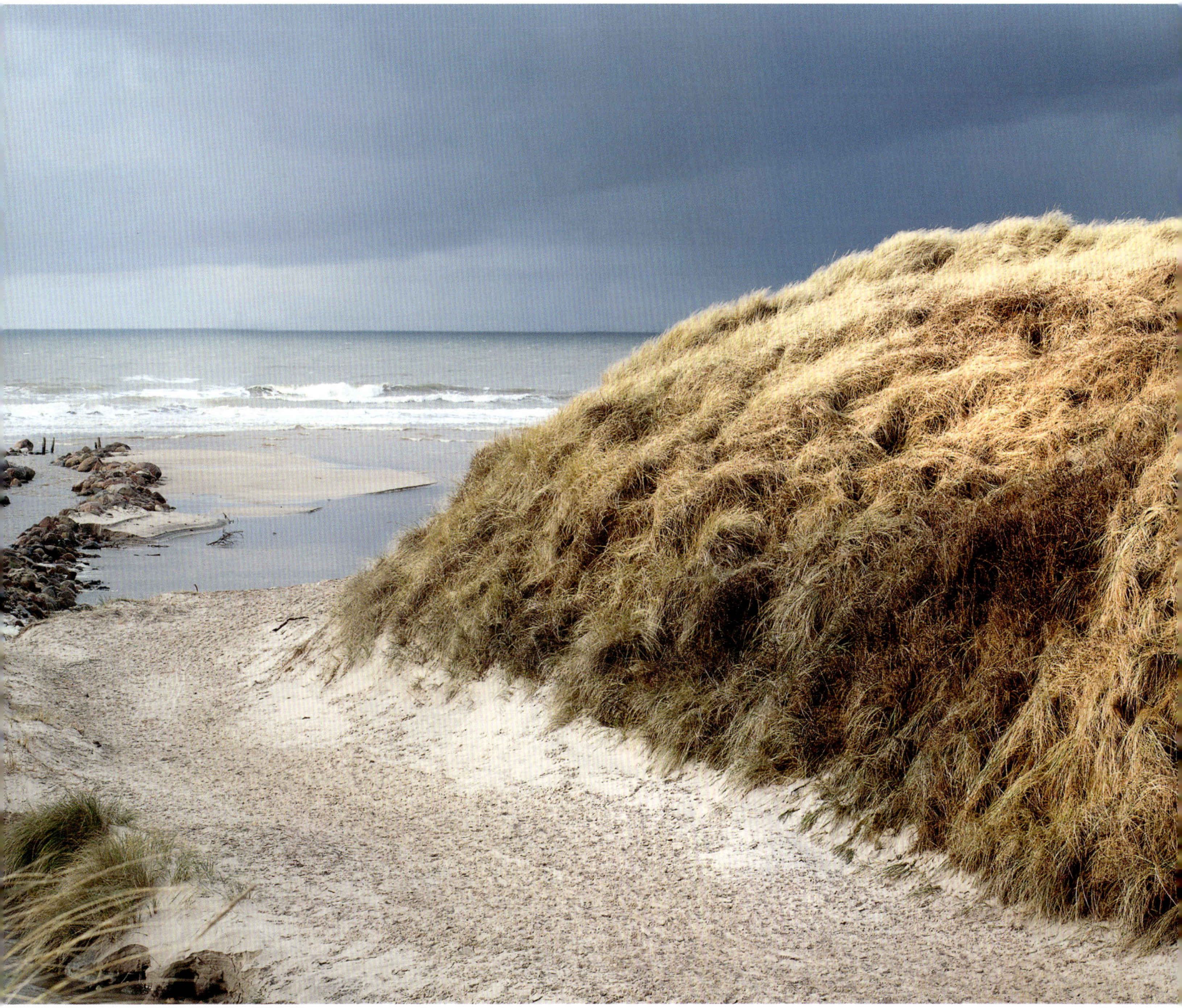

ILULISSAT ICE FJORD

Date of inscription: 2004

The ice of the Sermeq Kujalleq glacier is transported from the Greenland interior and reaches the sea at the Ilulissat ice fjord. The glacier "calves" there and releases large numbers of icebergs into the North Atlantic.

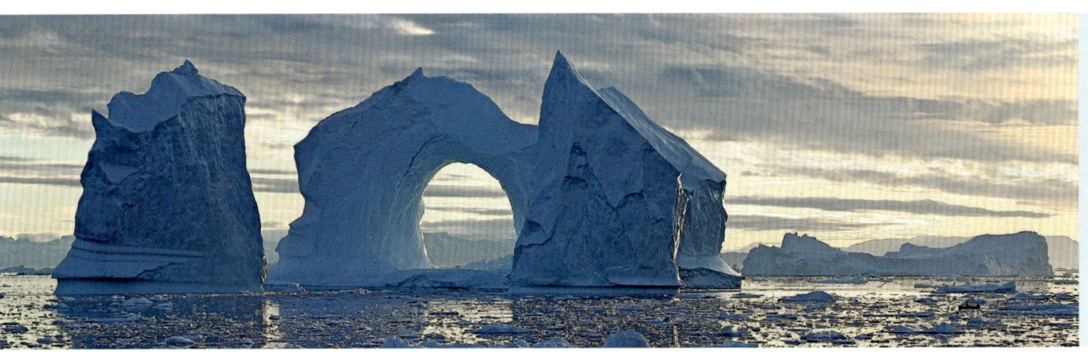

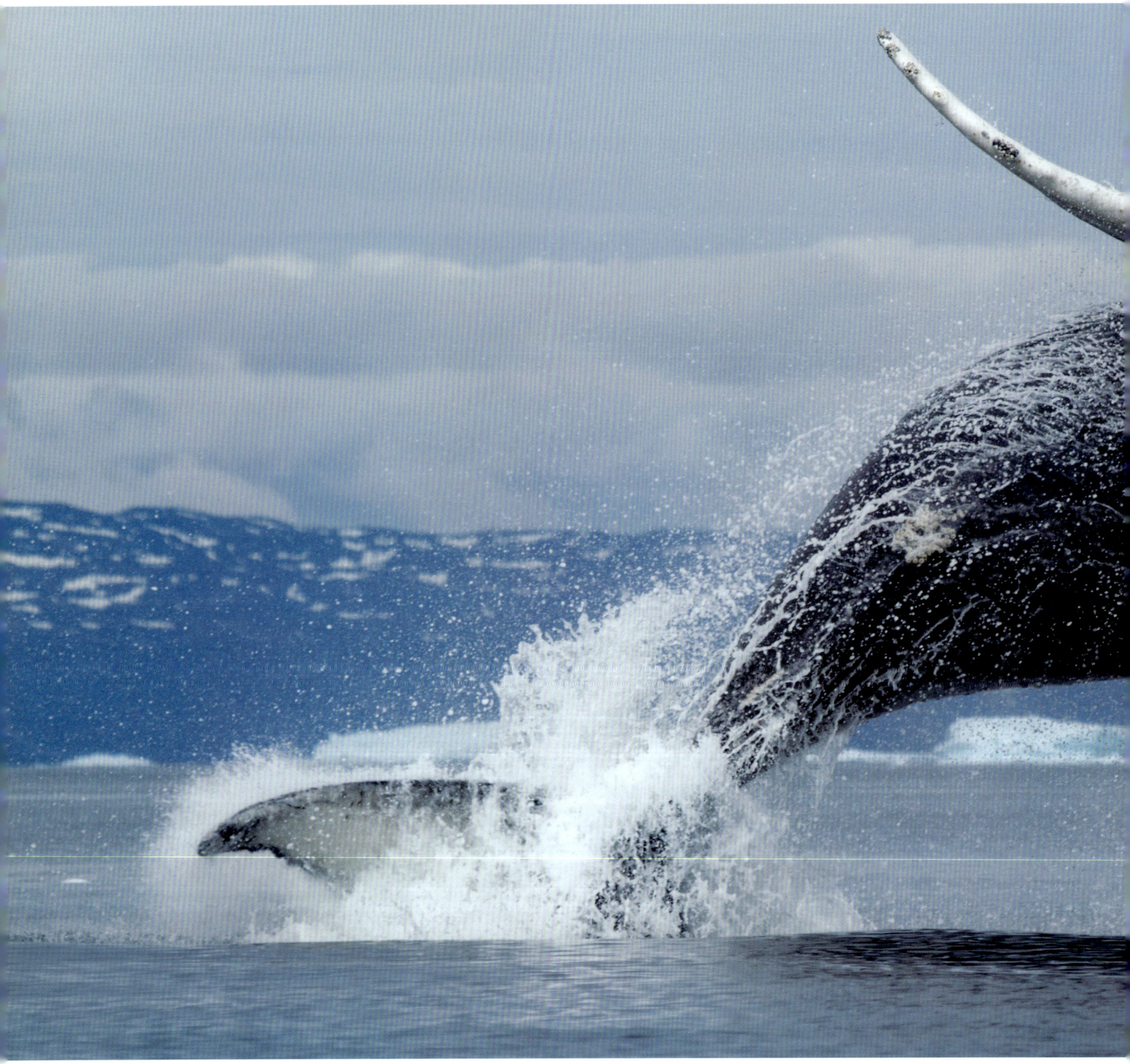

The Sermeq Kujalleq glacier flows from the Greenland ice cap, in places reaching up to 3,000 m (9,900 feet) thick, into the North Atlantic Ocean. With a daily flow rate of between 19 and 22 m (63–72 feet), the Sermeq Kujalleq is one of the fastest and most active glaciers in the world. As it reaches the sea, giant blocks of ice break off with a dramatic and deafening sound and crash into the water. These icebergs then slowly float south, where they become a danger to shipping.

The Sermeq Kujalleq "calves" 35 sq. km (14 sq. miles) of ice every year and is thus responsible for 10 percent of Greenland's total iceberg production, far more than any other glacier outside the Antarctic. The Ilulissat and its glacier have been the subject of scientific investigation for more than 250 years and have yielded copious data regarding local geomorphology, glaciology, and general climate change. The calving glacier and the tall icebergs in the fjord are a fascinating sight. Because of the icebergs, the trip to the glacier is not without its dangers. Many of these ice giants melt only just north of New York.

The cold sea is extraordinarily rich in fish; giant humpback whales can also be observed here (large picture). Left: Off the Greenland coast, the icebergs can reach a height of 100 m (330 feet) above the water.

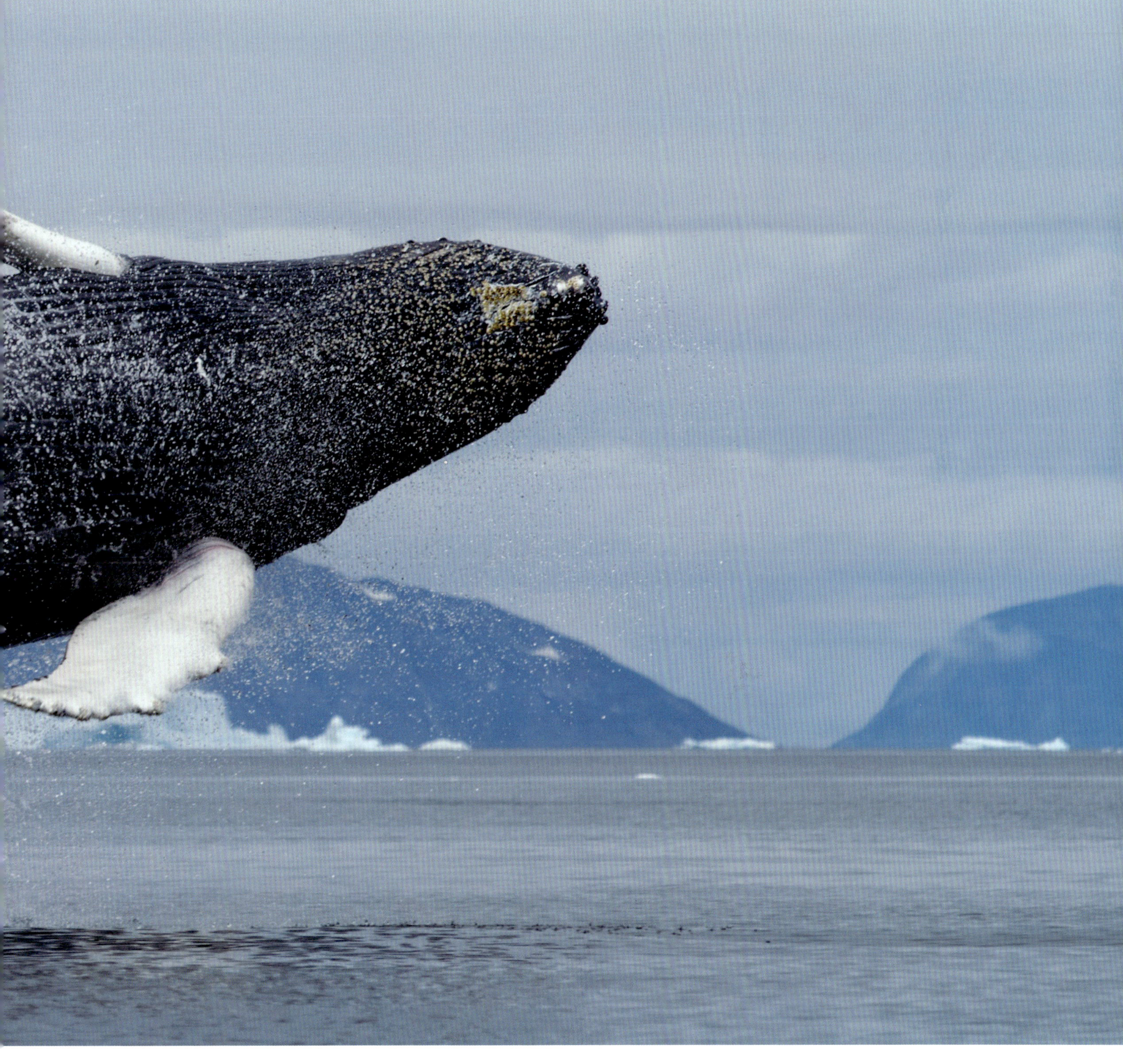

ST. KILDA

Date of inscription: 1986
Extended: 2004, 2005

Located around 175 km (110 miles) off the west coast of Scotland, Britain's most isolated and remote archipelago provides an ideal nesting place for the world's largest colony of Northern gannets.

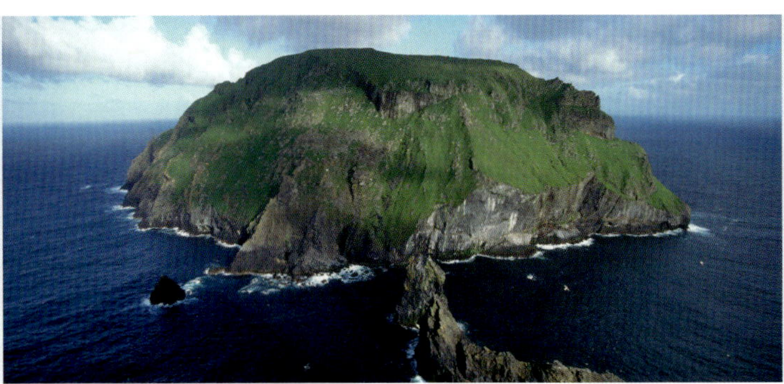

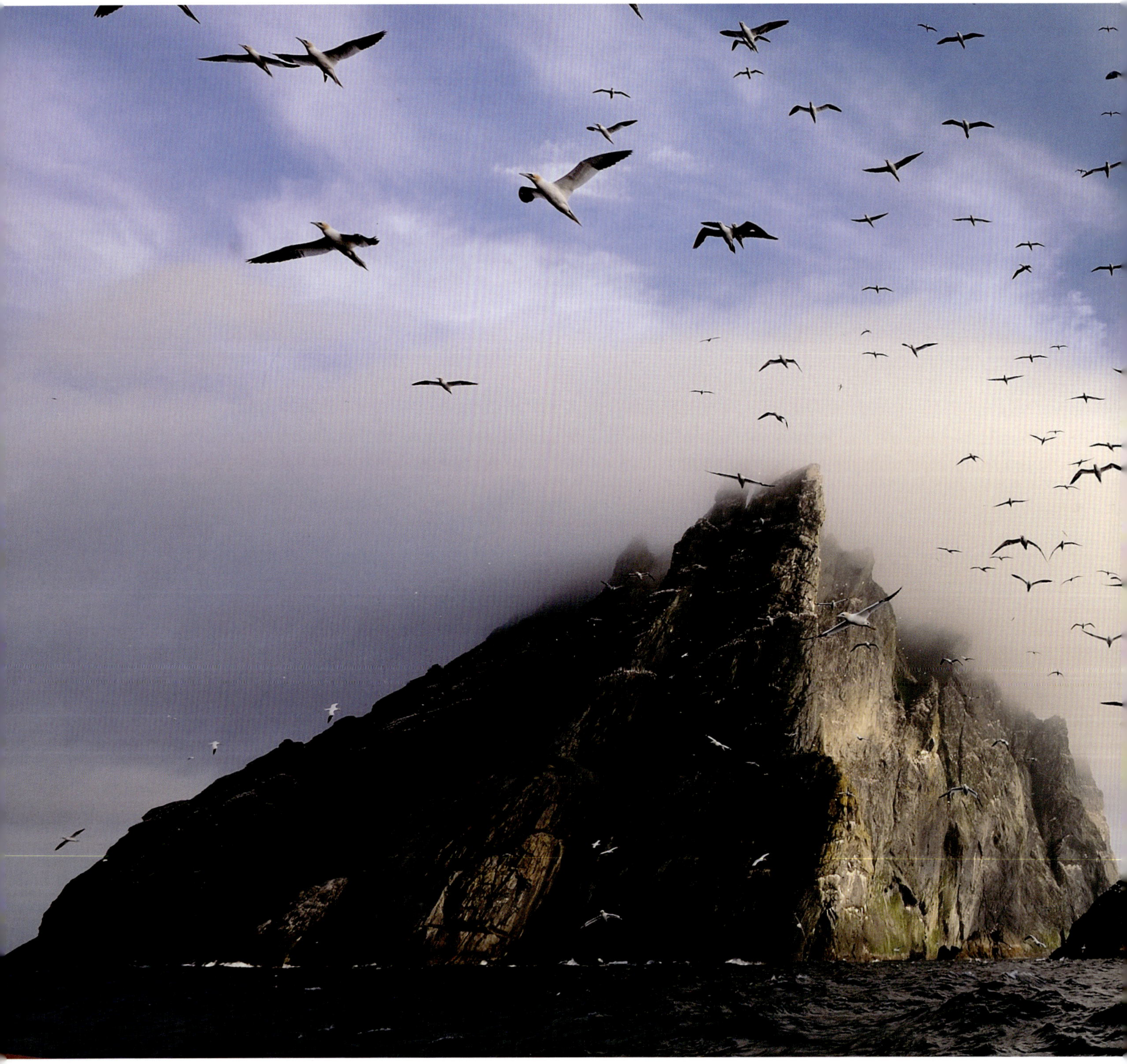

Spared from glaciation during the last ice age, this volcanic archipelago has retained its characteristic landscape. The group of islands "at the end of the world" comprises Dun, Soay, Boreray, and Hirta. The residents of Hirta were resettled in 1930, and the island has been uninhabited ever since – given over entirely to nature. Its impressive, steep cliff faces provide optimal nesting conditions for rare birds, notably for the huge numbers of gannets who have taken refuge here. For the northern gannet, the archipelago is the world's most important breeding ground. Despite the islands' harsh climate, they were first settled some two thousand years ago. The settlers' most notable buildings are the so-called cleits, of which there are 1,260 on Hirta alone, and over 170 more on the other islands. These are small structures formed of drystone walls with a grassed earth roof. Sometimes individual cleits are joined together. The position of the door varies, but common to all the stone huts is their primary purpose as storage rooms – the lack of mortar in the walls guaranteeing the constant circulation of fresh air. They were mainly used to store birds' eggs, feathers, peat, and turf.

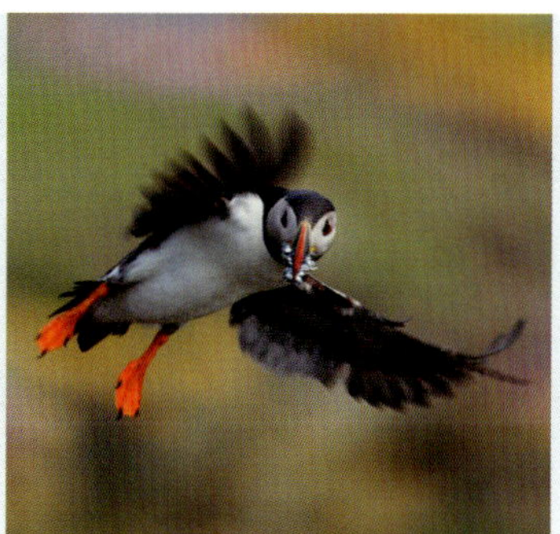

St Kilda's typical cliff formations are known as "stacks" (far left). The archipelago is a popular refuge for Atlantic puffins (left) and Northern gannets (below).

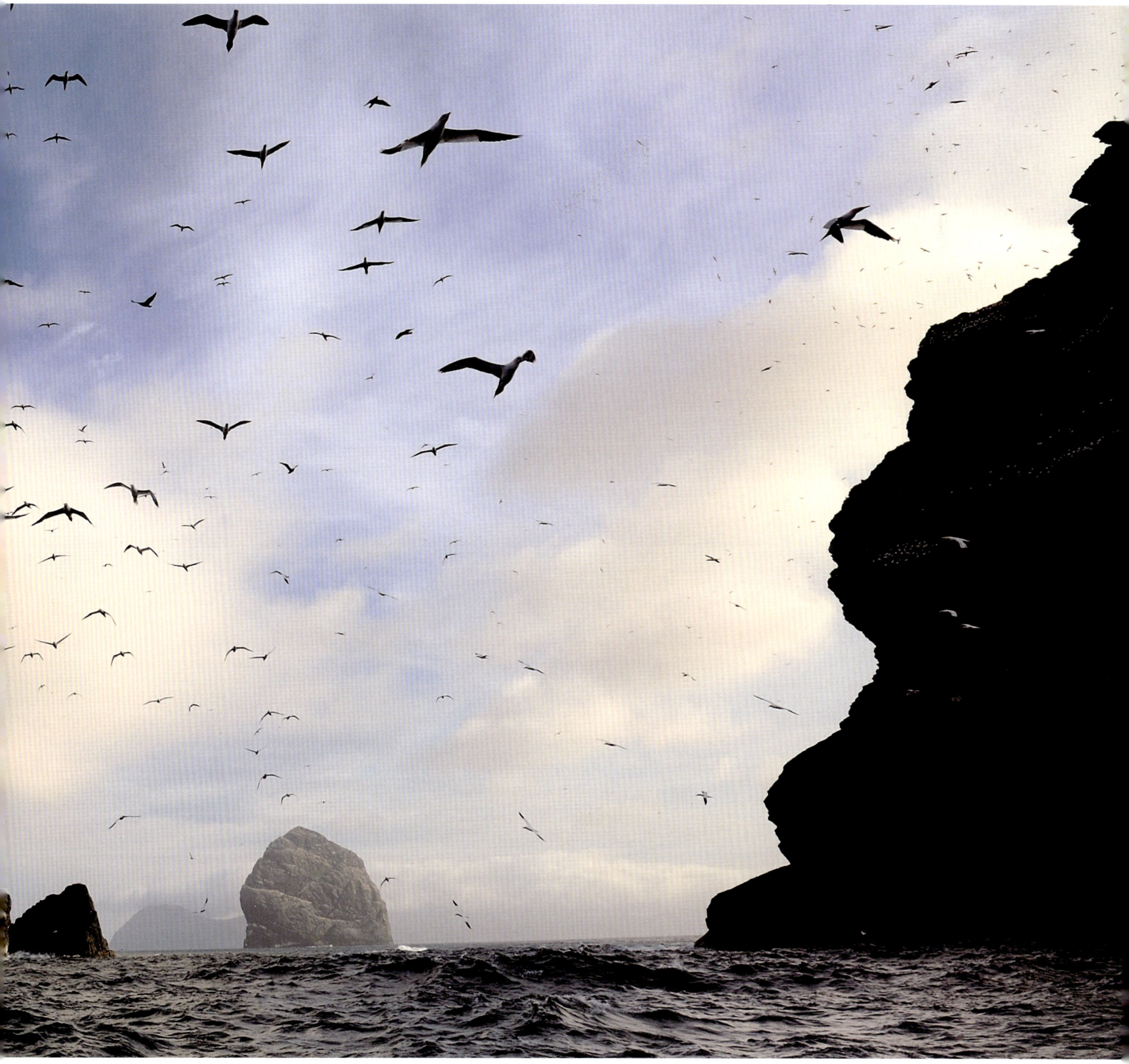

GIANT'S CAUSEWAY AND CAUSEWAY COAST

Date of inscription: 1986

The basalt columns of the Giant's Causeway span 5 km (3 miles) of the Northern Irish coastline, and are the stuff of numerous legends.

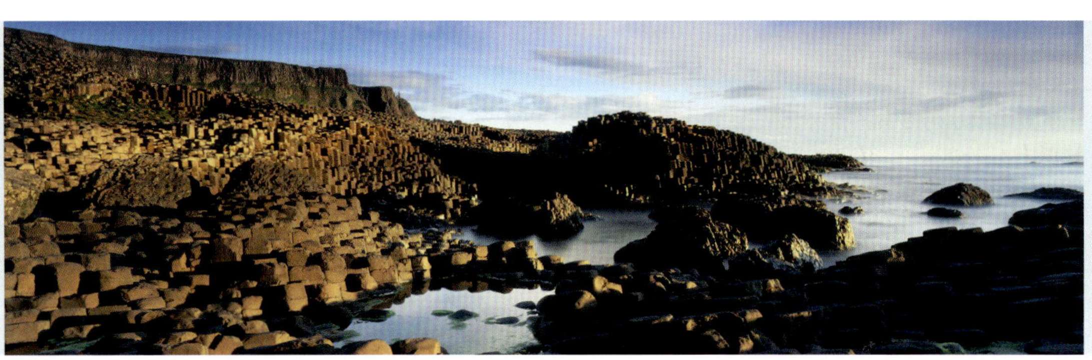

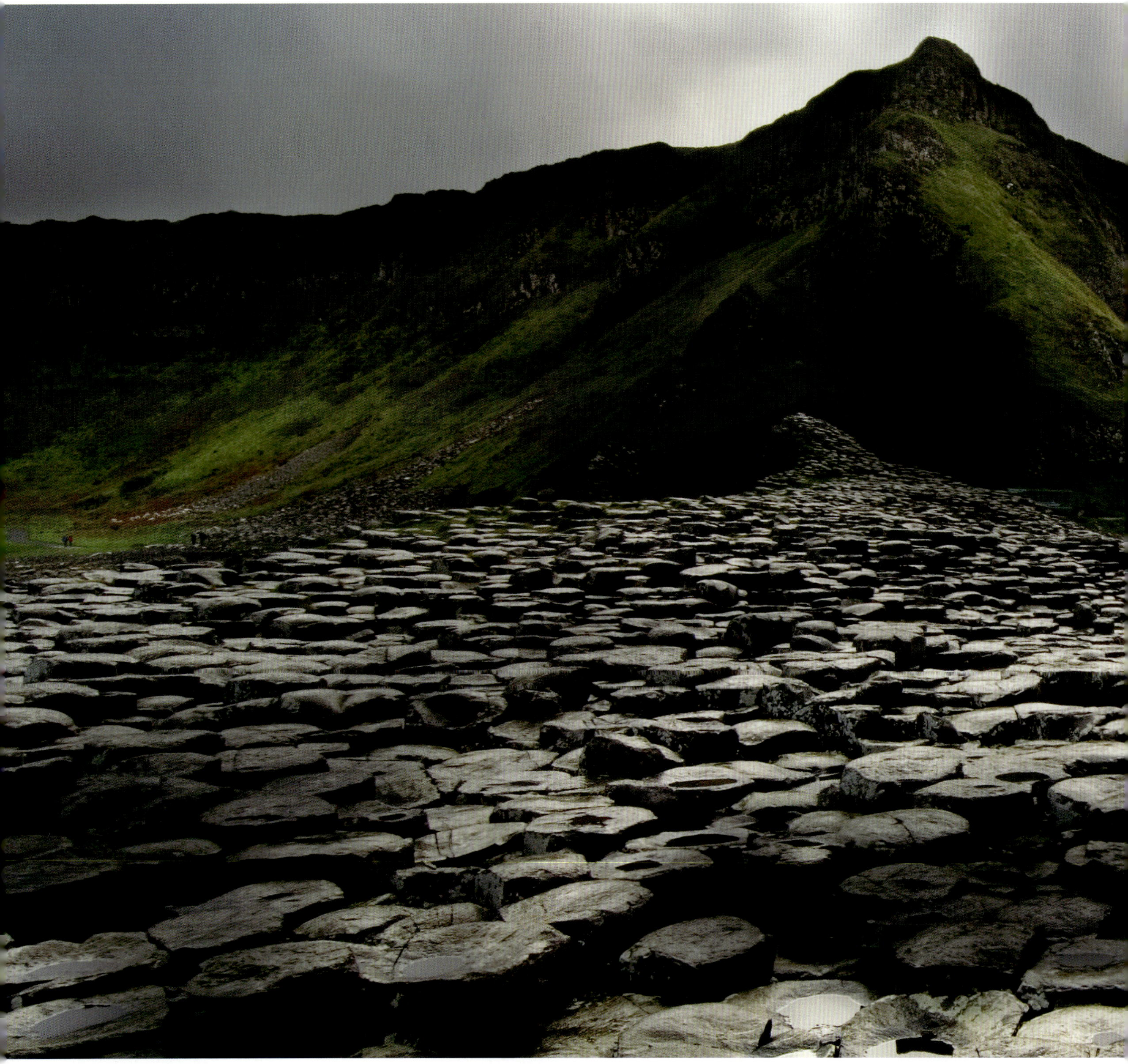

Not far from the fishing town of Ballycastle in Country Antrim, some 40,000 basalt columns rise out of the sea. Mostly hexagonal, the columns are believed to be approximately 60 million years old. Together, they create a 5-km (3-mile) path along the rocky coastline. They were formed by the crystallization of molten lava in the cold seawater.

The tallest columns are up to 6 m (20 feet) high. The name "Giant's Causeway" derives from one of the many legends to which this wonder of the natural world has given rise. According to the story, the Irish warrior Finn MacCool, challenged by his Scottish rival, the giant Benandonner, built the stone causeway to cross the Irish Sea to Scotland.

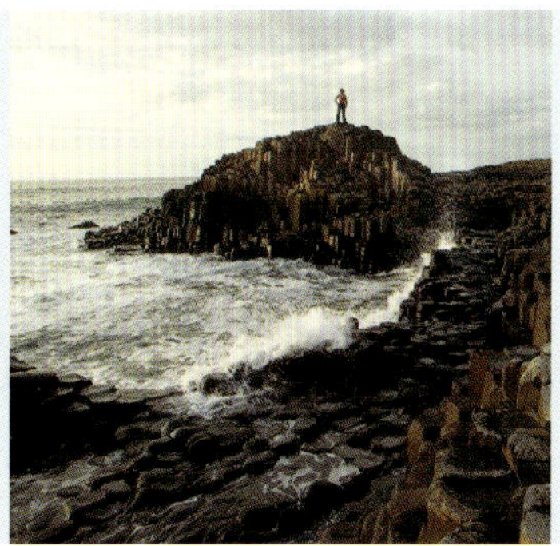

The Giant's Causeway looks like a huge, man-made staircase. Fenced off in the 19th century, it is now freely accessible again. Though most of the basalt columns are six-sided, closer inspection reveals stones with four, five, seven, and even eight edges.

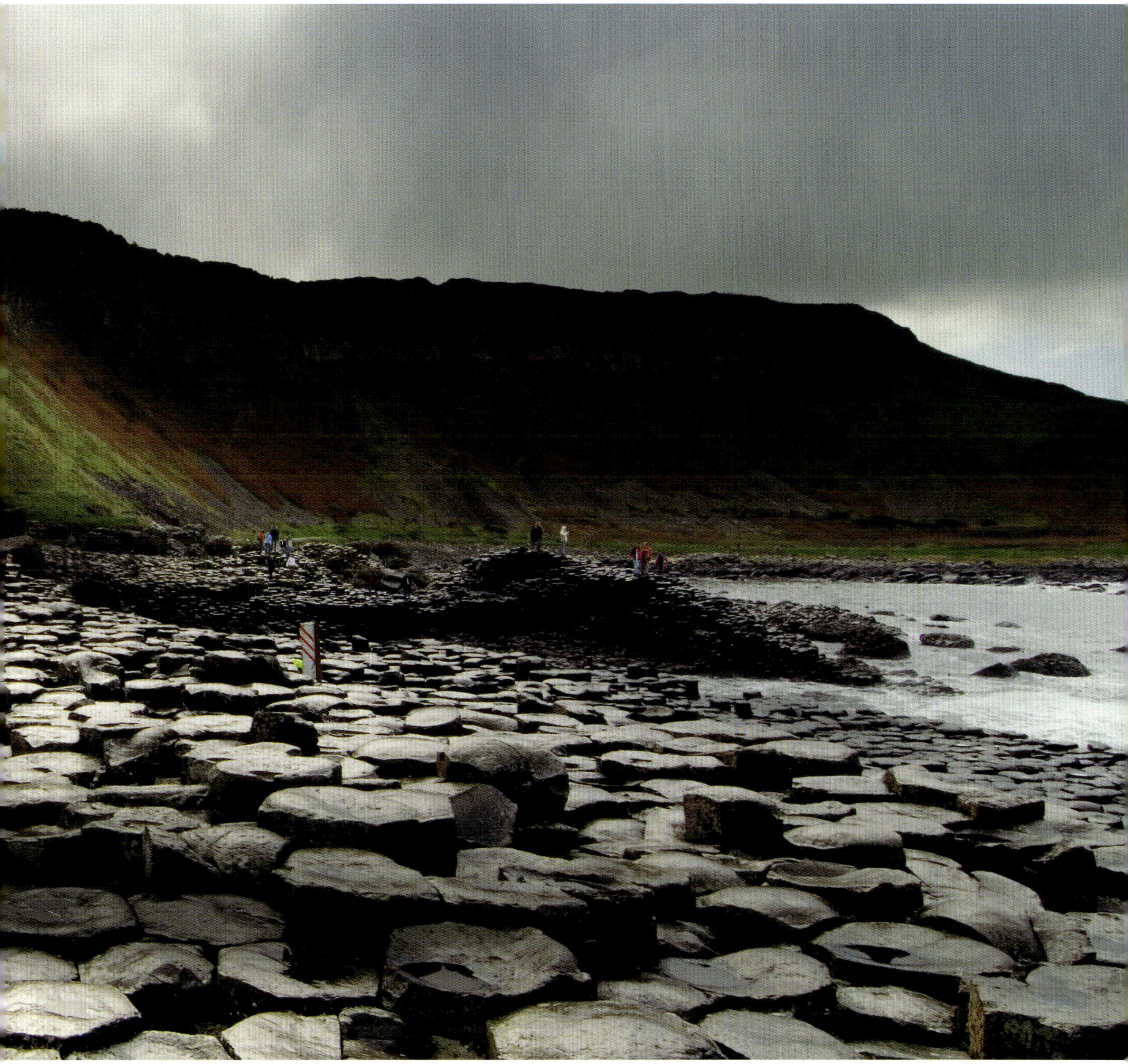

THE DORSET AND EAST DEVON COAST

Date of inscription: 2001

The cliff formations along England's "Jurassic coast" bear witness to 185 million years of geological history. Fossils from the Triassic, Jura, and Cretaceous periods have all been found here.

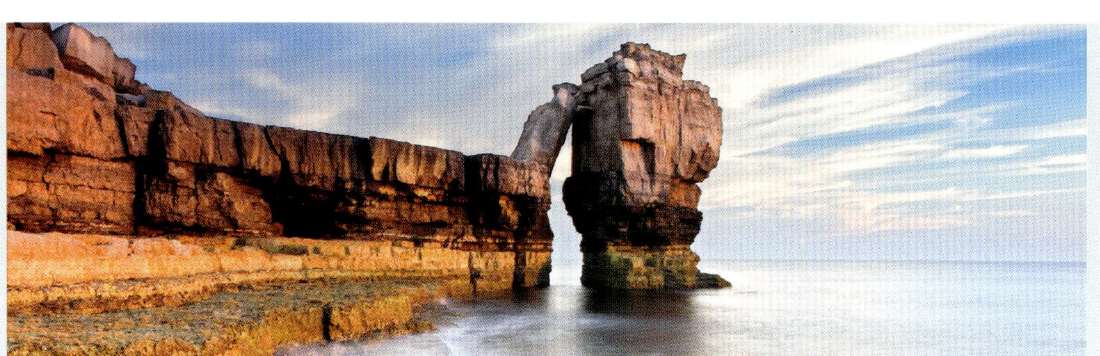

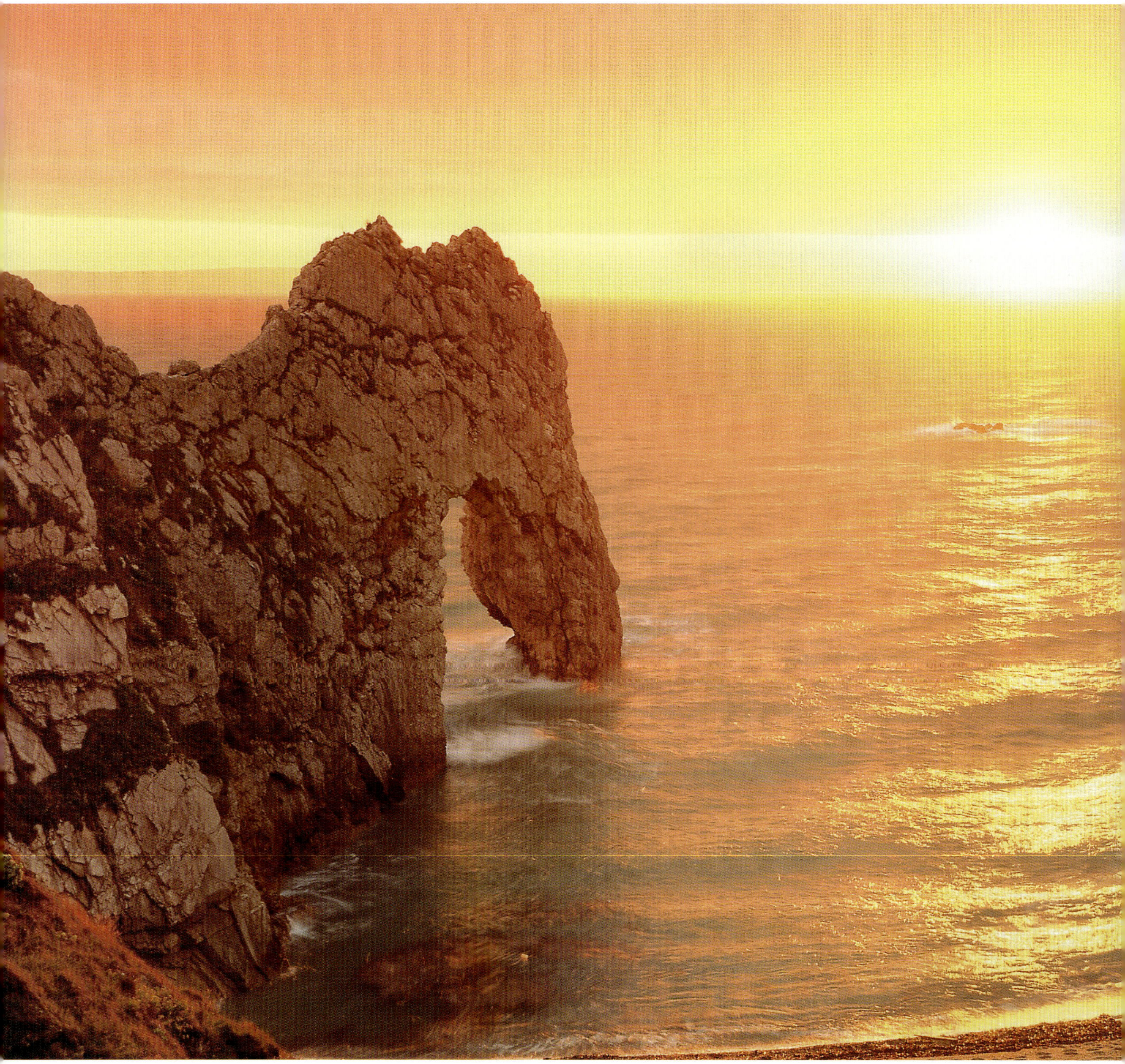

The 150-km (90-mile) long coastline between Old Harry Rocks near Swanage in Dorset and Orcombe Point in Devon is known locally as the "Jurassic coast." The geology in this area spans the entire Mesozoic era. Rock formations from the Triassic, Jura, and Cretaceous periods are displayed like the layers of a sandwich, allowing visitors to clearly view these three sections of the Mesozoic era in an uninterrupted sequence. Geomorphologists across the world first became aware of the importance of this piece of coastline in 1810, when an 11-year-old girl by the name of Mary Anning came across what she described as a "dragon" in the cliffs near the fishing village of Lyme Regis in Dorset. What she had discovered was in fact the first complete fossil of an ichthyosaur. It looked like a cross between a giant fish and a lizard, and gave rise to quite a sensation.

The ongoing erosion of the cliffs means that the landscape here is changing at a breathtaking pace, and fossils can therefore be found without the need to excavate. After a storm, a stroll along the beach or the land behind it quickly becomes a journey of discovery through the different stages of our evolution and geological history. In the interests of conservation, the National Trust has acquired around half of the world heritage coastline.

Strange rock formations like Pulpit Rock at the southern tip of the Isle of Portland (left) and the rock arch of Durdle Door (below) are two of the sights.

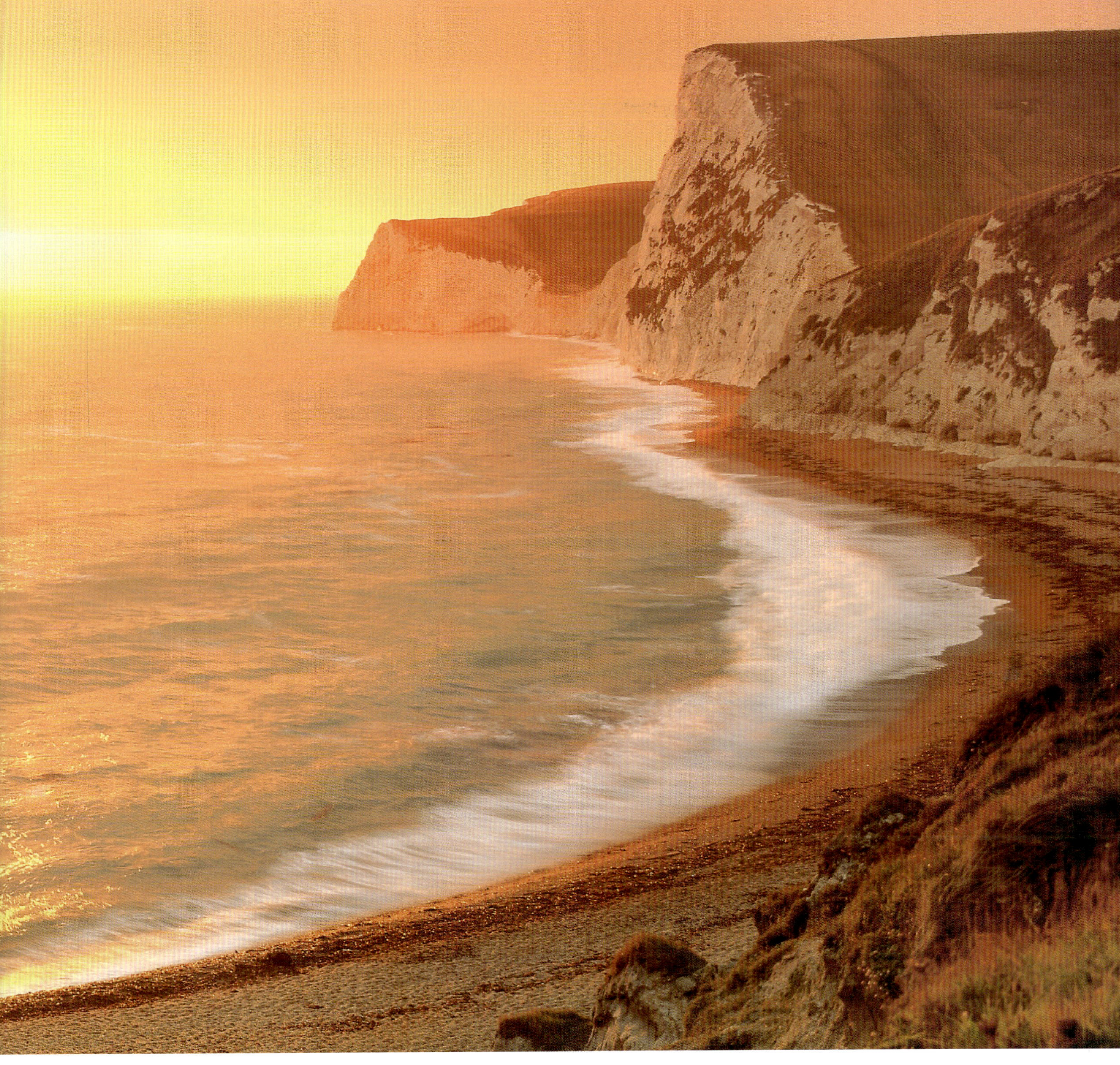

GOUGH AND INACCESSIBLE ISLAND

Date of inscription: 1995
Extended: 2004

The largely undisturbed volcanic Gough Island in the South Atlantic, belonging to the Tristan da Cunha island group, is the habitat of one of the world's largest seabird colonies. Nearby Inaccessible Island is also part of the World Heritage Site.

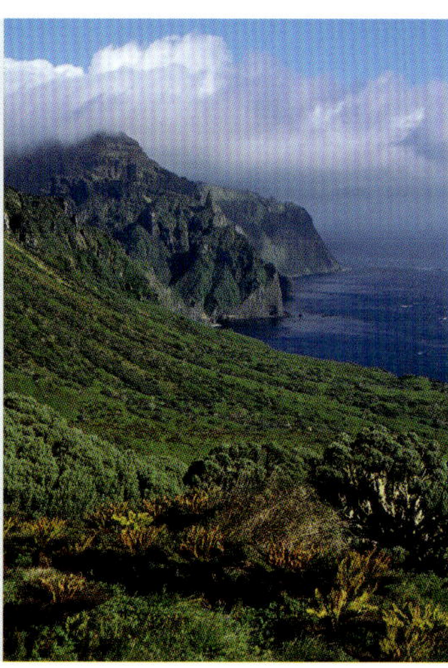

The island, part of the Tristan da Cunha archipelago, was discovered in the 16th century by Portuguese sailors. Apart from a weather station, the island is uninhabited. Gough Island's especial importance resides in its undisturbed flora and fauna; the steep cliffs are a nesting place for great colonies of seabirds. Two species of birds and 12 varieties of plant are endemic here. In 2004 the World Heritage Site was expanded to include the volcanic Inaccessible Island, which lies to the south-west of Tristan da Cunha.

Its lush vegetation, thunderous waterfalls and rich fauna make this island a veritable natural paradise.

Gough Island in the South Atlantic is a paradise for yellow-nosed albatrosses and terns (below), macaroni and rock penguins and fur seals.

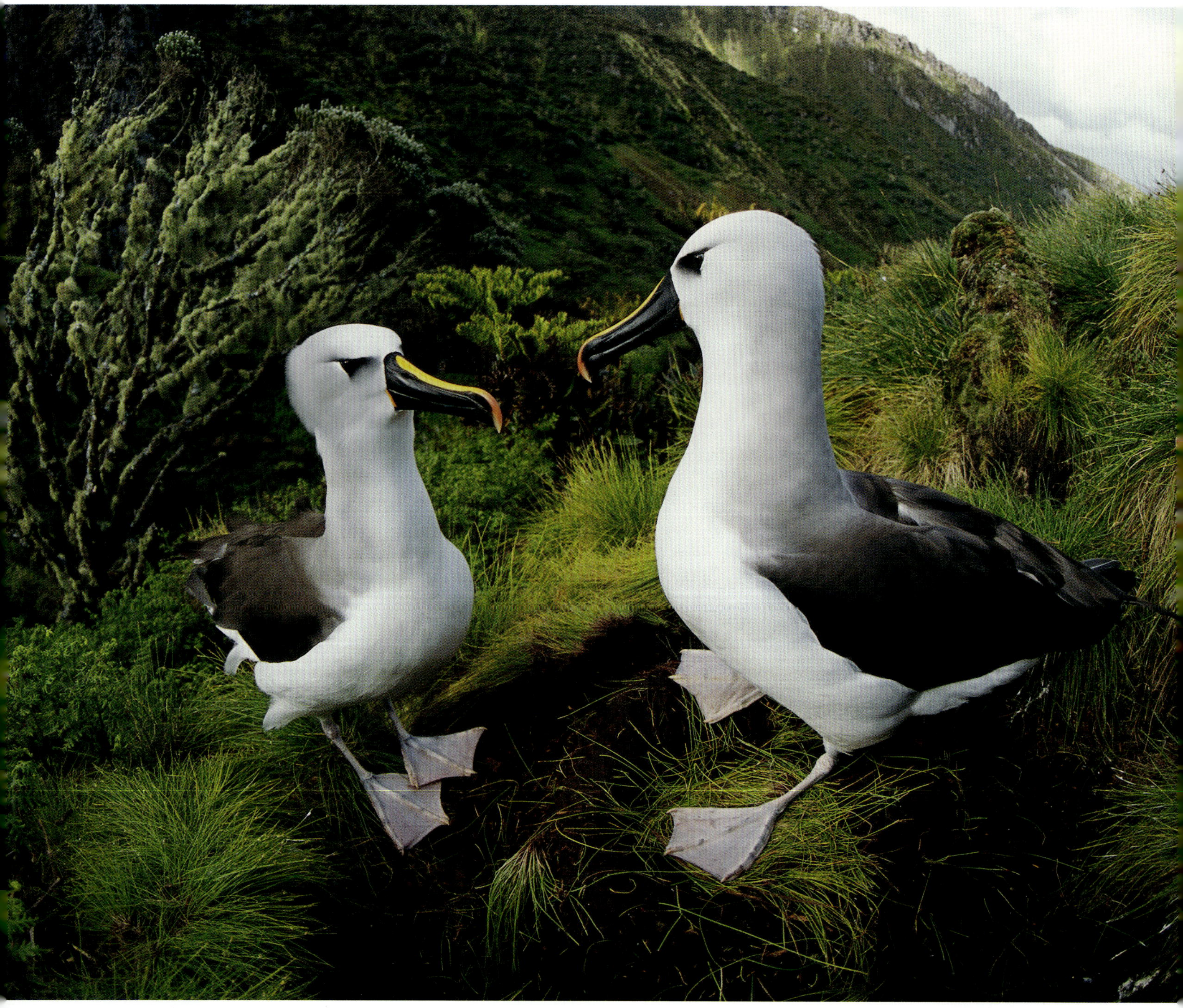

HENDERSON ISLAND

Until the 18th century, this remote island was largely spared from human influence. The animal and plant life on this towering atoll with its steep cliffs was thus undisturbed. Thus, flora and fauna on the tall coral atoll with its steep coast have managed to remain largely undisturbed. Ten plant species were discovered in the dense undergrowth which occur only on Henderson Island, among them a special type of sandalwood. Of the more than 24 bird species that are represented here, four species of land birds are endemic and so are around one-third of the numerous insect and snail species, many of which are not as yet named or researched. Thanks to its isolated location, Henderson Island offers ideal conditions for the scientific exploration of biological processes, such as natural selection and the development of species on the island.

Henderson Island is a paradise for many plants, some of which are endemic, and a habitat for rare birds like the fairy tern with its white plumage and black ring around its eyes (large picture).

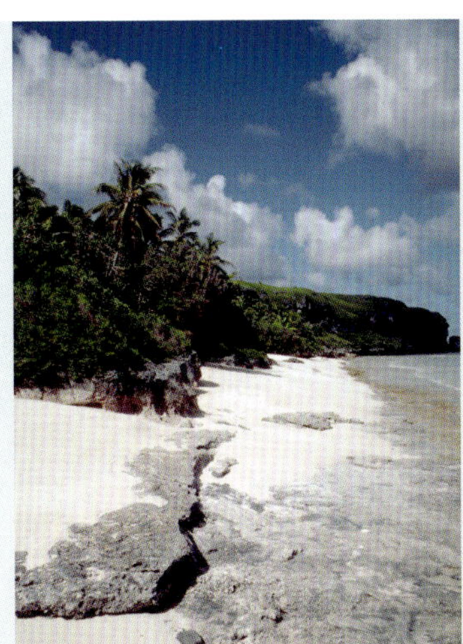

Date of inscription: 1988

At 10 km (6 miles) in length and 5 km (3 miles) in width, the island is the largest in the British Overseas Territory of the Pitcairn Islands and has remained largely undisturbed.

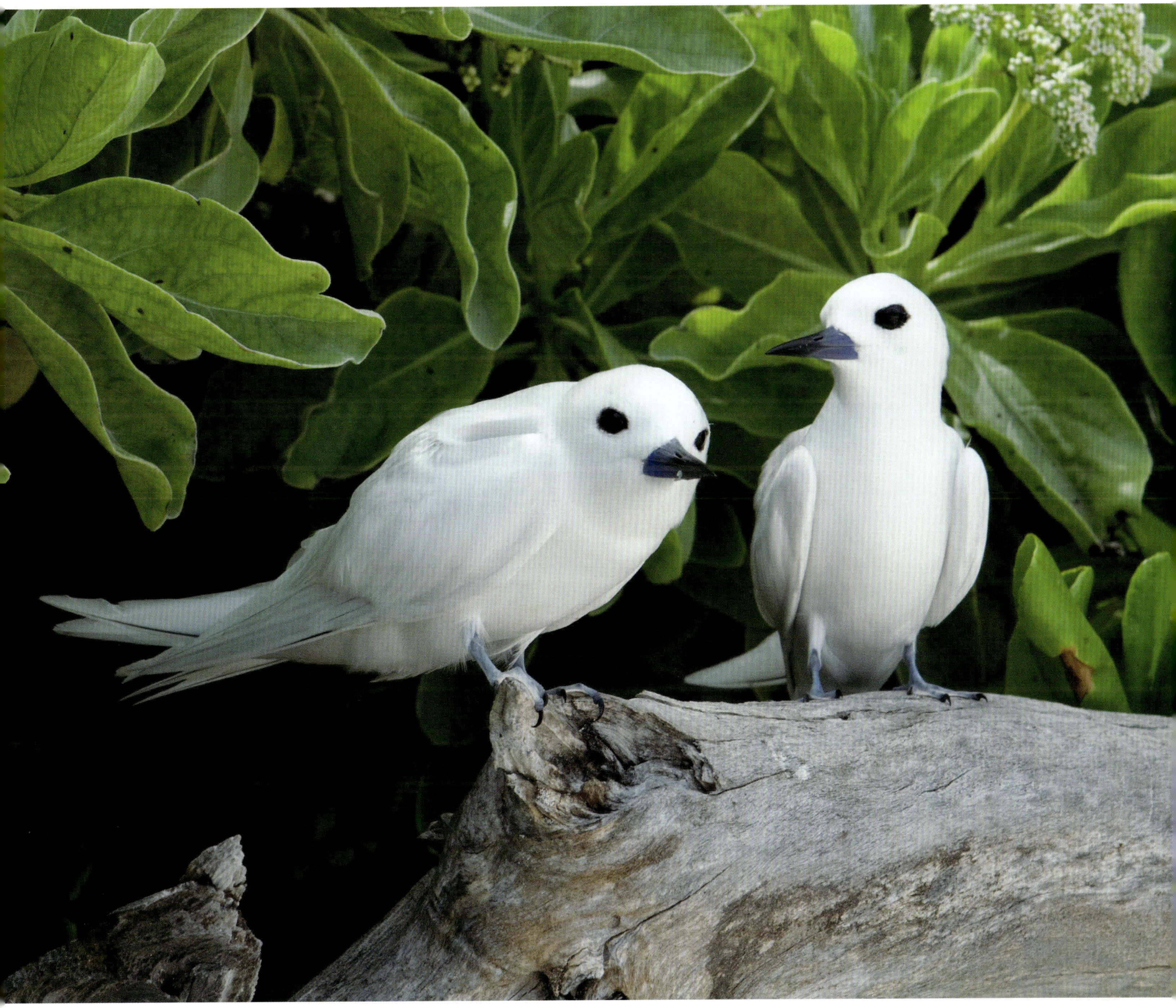

WADDEN SEA (WADDENZEE)

Date of inscription: 2009
Extended: 2011, 2014

The Dutch section is the westernmost part of the Wadden Sea World Natural Heritage site. Together with the German and the Danish Wadden Seas, it is one of the last intact ecosystems of the northern coastal regions.

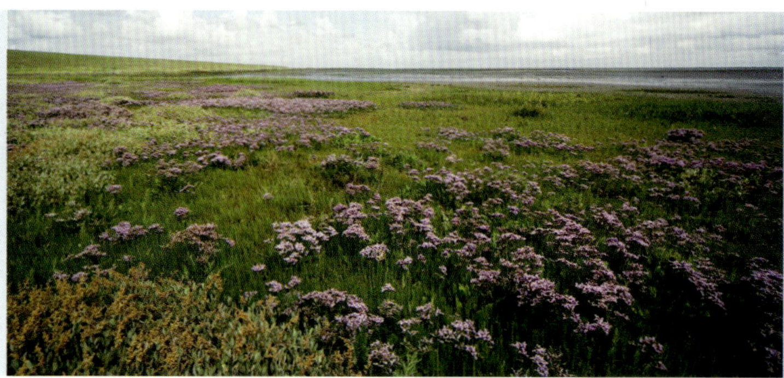

The northern end of North Sea's Wadden Sea is located near Blåvandshuk in Denmark. From there, the site extends south over a distance of more than 450 km (280 miles) along the coast, in places 40 km (25 miles) wide, ending near the Dutch city of Den Helder. About one-third of the landscape formed after the last ice age is under the administration of the Netherlands.

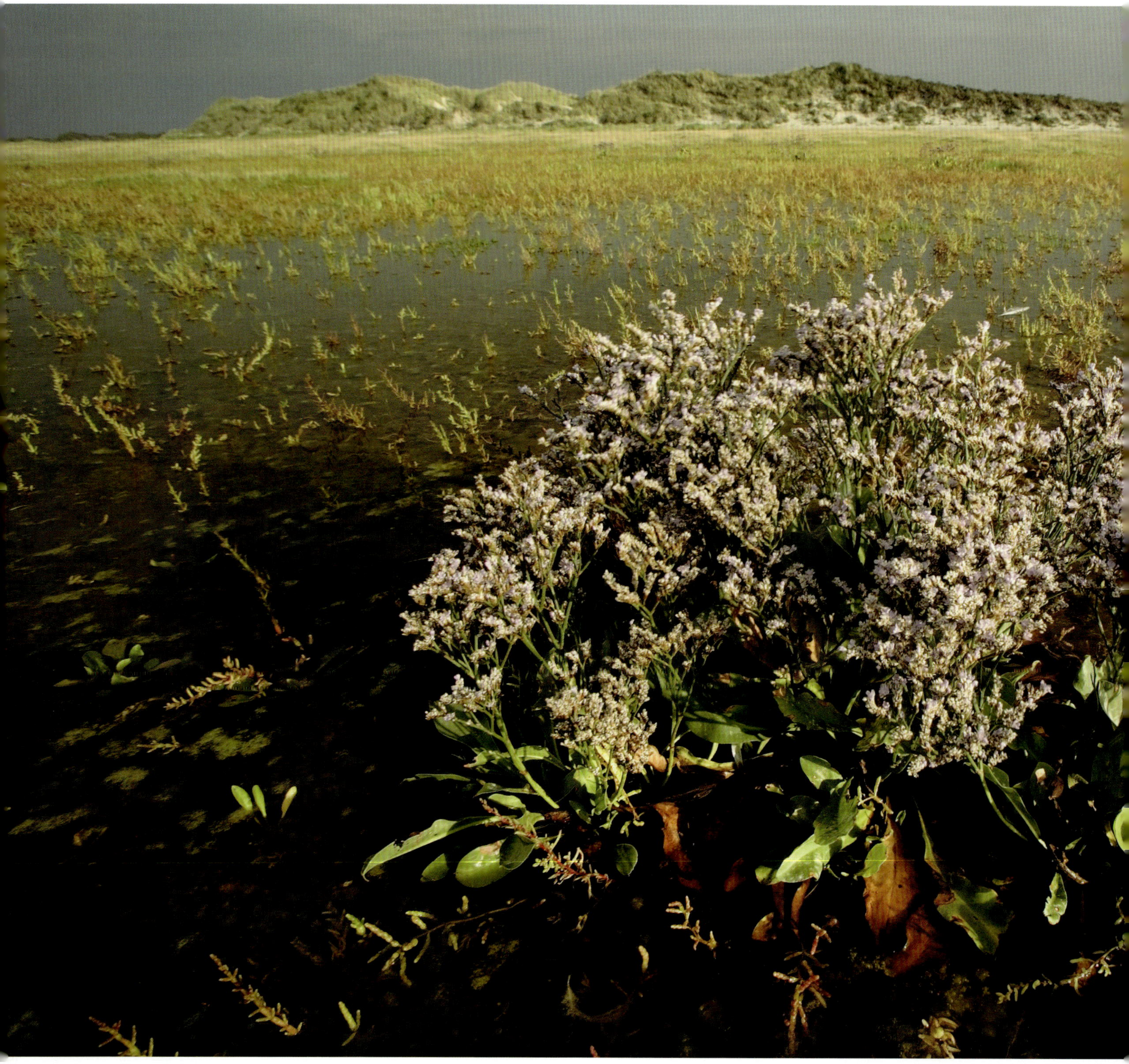

Its most striking elements are the five large West Frisian Islands of Texel, Vlieland, Terschelling, Ameland and Schiermonnikoog. Characteristic of the entire landscape at the transition between land and sea are dunes, salt marshes and richly stocked mussel beds. Creeks carry water even at low tides. In this rich area live up to 10,000 plant species and the most diverse of animal species, from the lugworm to the grey seal. Year after year, millions of migratory birds also stop over in the Wadden Sea. The Wadden Sea, defined by the tides, is one of only a few large natural landscapes on the densely populated continent of Europe where important ecological processes can still take place largely undisturbed.

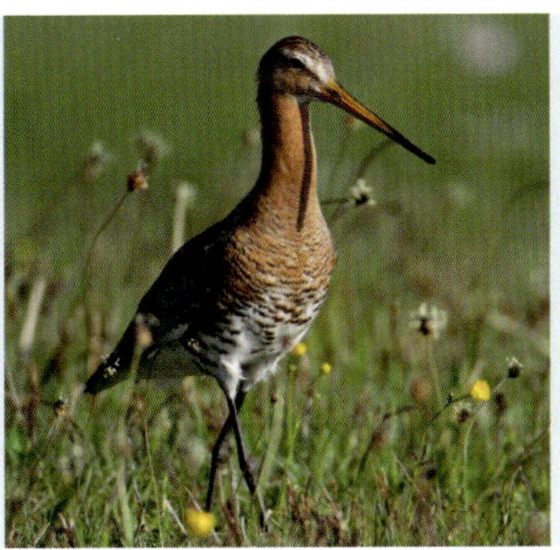

On the salt marshes you can observe black-tailed godwits (left), and the rich variety of flowers includes musk mallow, musk thistle, sea-buckthorn (below, from the top) and the widespread sea aster (far left).

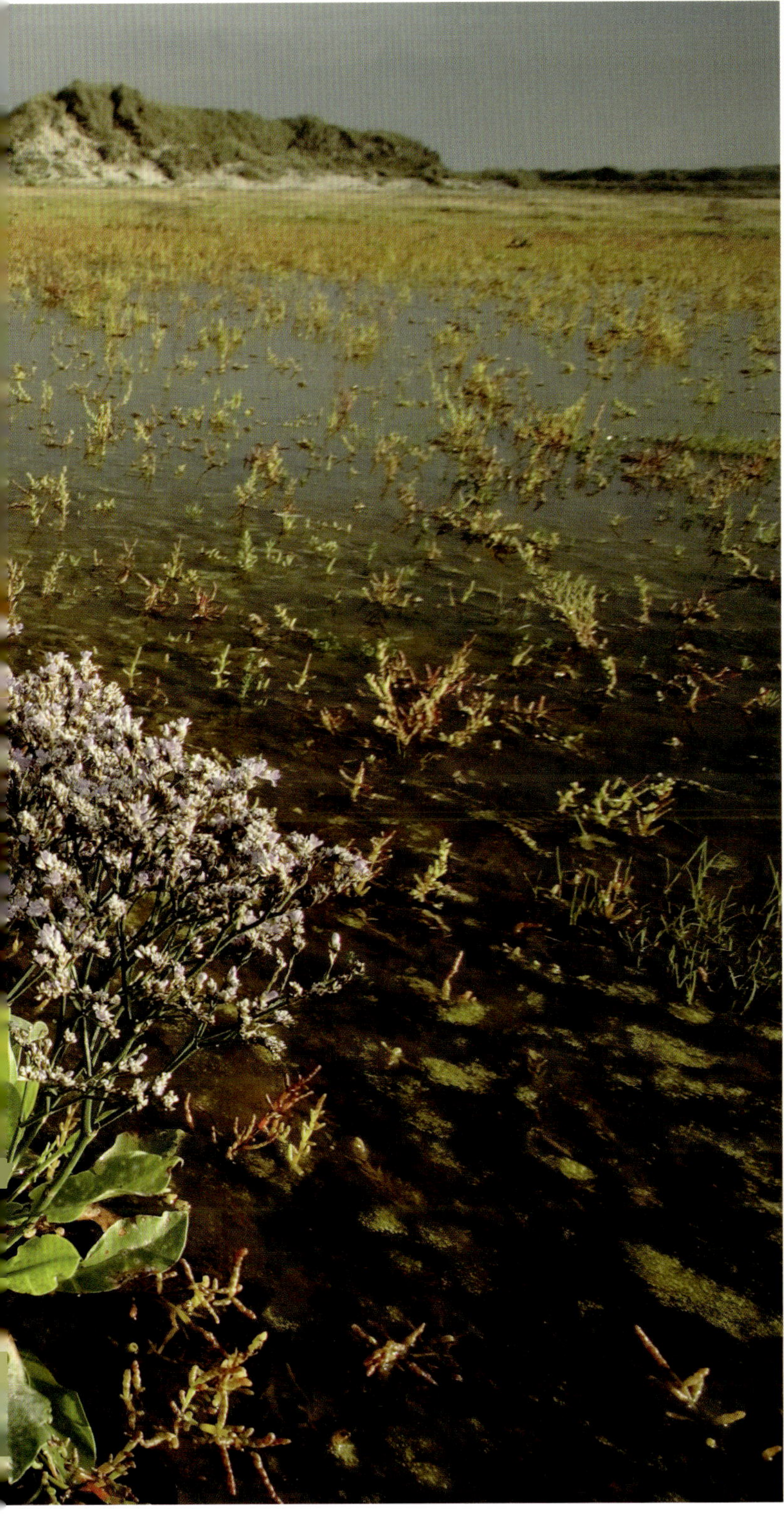

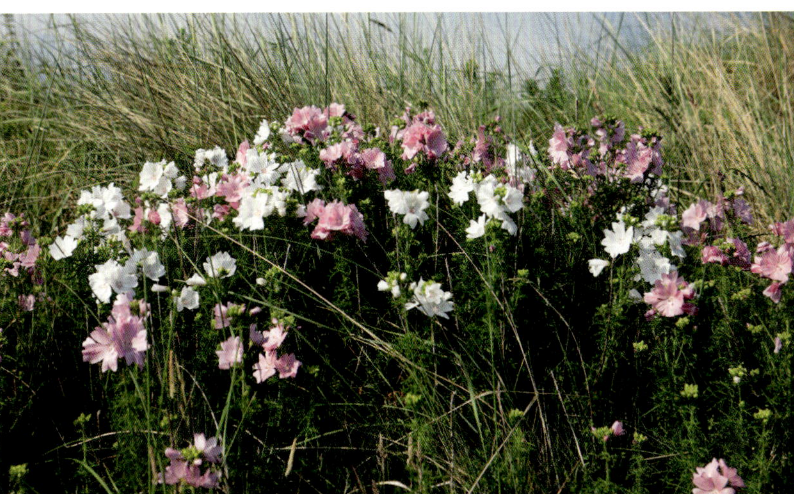

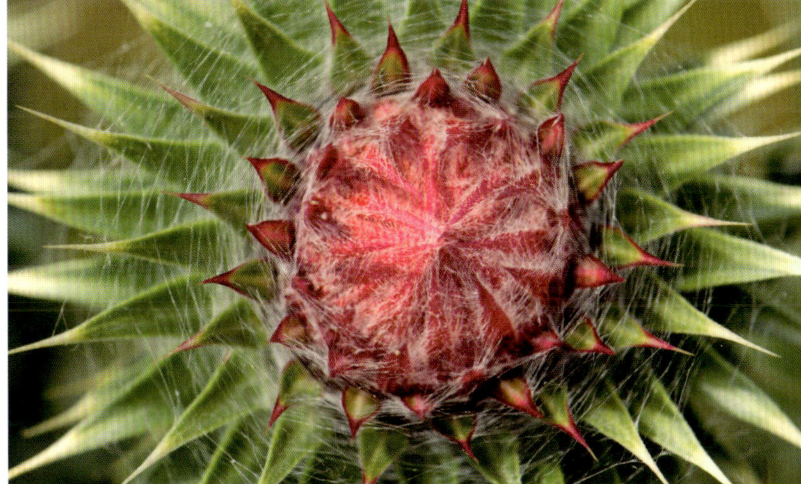

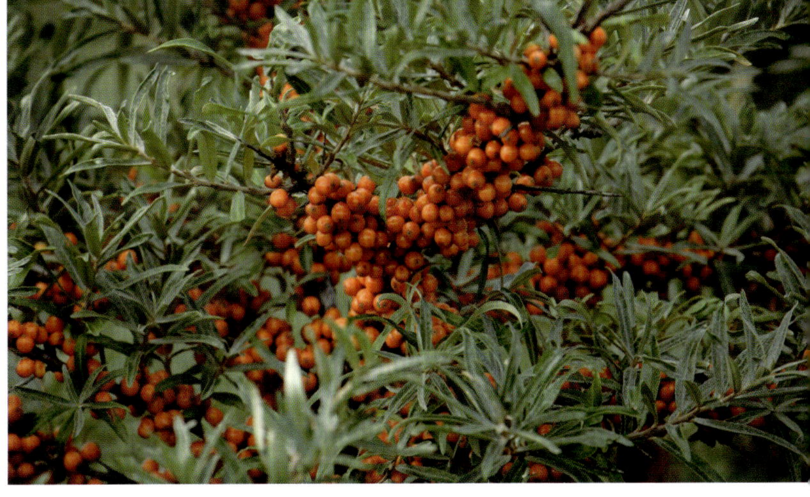

PYRÉNÉES: MONT PERDU (MONTE PERDIDO)

Date of inscription: 1997
Extended: 1999

The extraordinary mountainous landscape around Monte Perdido – or, to give it its French name, Mont Perdu – stretches across both the French and Spanish sides of the Pyrénées, and features some impressive geological formations.

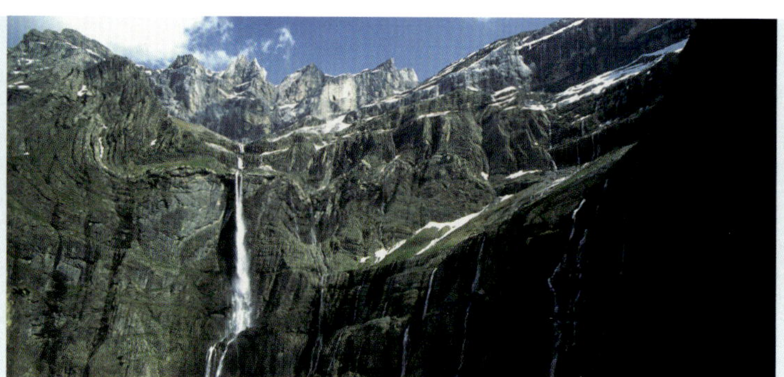

At a height of 3,352 m (10,997 feet), Monte Perdido lies on Spanish territory. The 30 sq. km (11.5 sq. mile) world heritage site around it, however, includes parts of the Spanish Parque Nacional de Ordesa y Monte Perdido and the French Parc National de Pyrénées. In 1999, the site was extended to include the French commune of Gèdre. Caught in the interplay of the Atlantic and

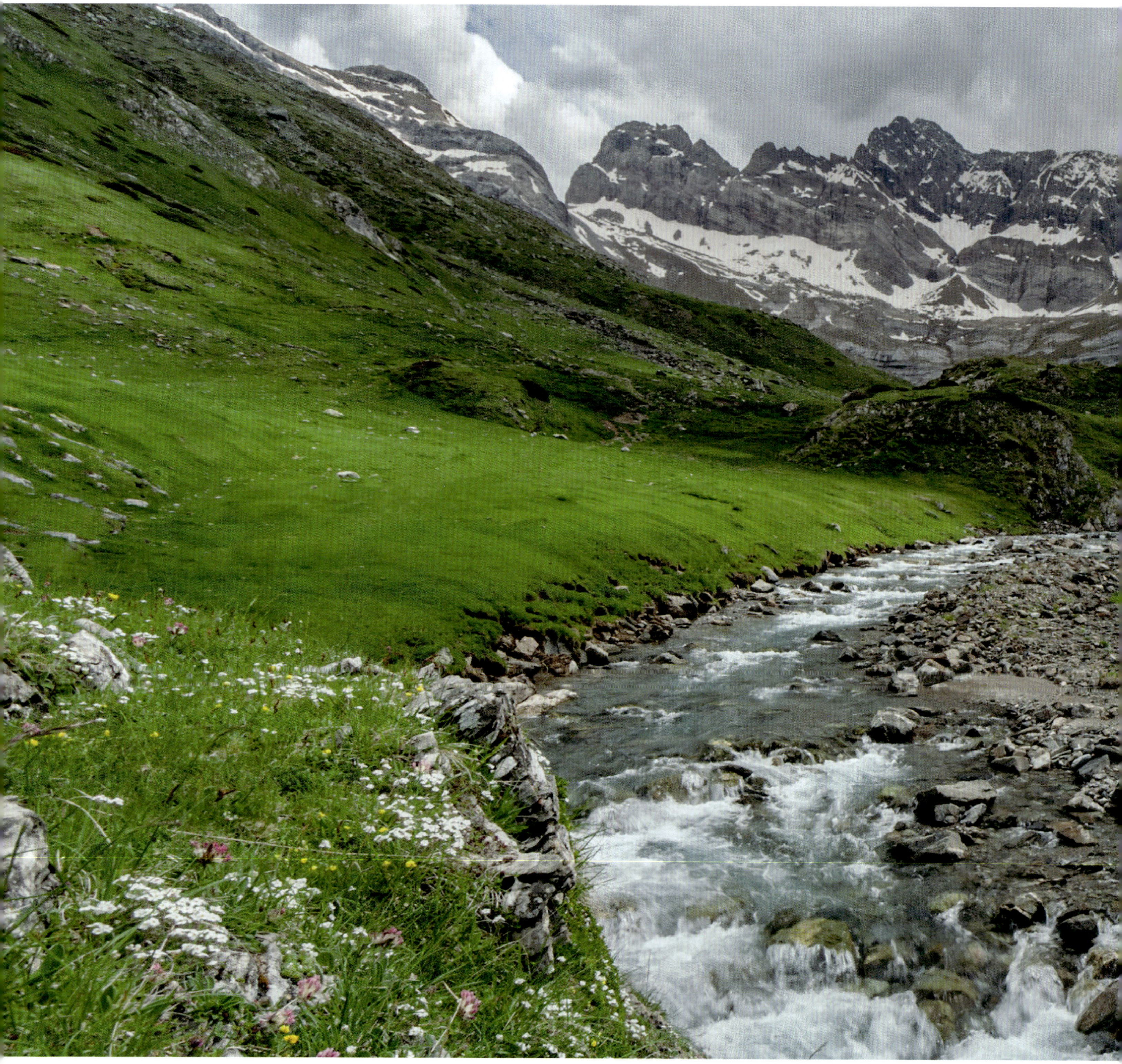

Mediterranean climates, the region's special geomorphology has produced some particularly striking rock formations. The Añisclo and Ordesa canyons – two of Europe's biggest – are the main attractions on the Spanish side of the border. The three valleys of Troumouse, Estaubé, and Gavarnie, meanwhile, belong to the French administrative department of Hautes-Pyrénées.

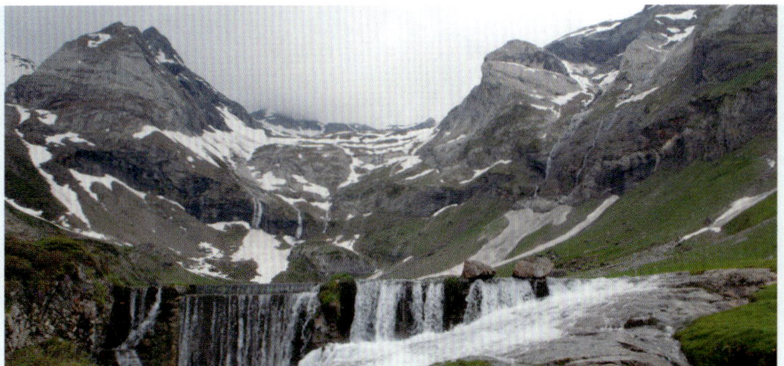

Focused on pastoral farming, life here has remained almost unchanged for centuries, and the trappings of modern living have failed to leave any real mark on the villages, farms, and fields.

Waterfalls like this one near Cirque de Gavarnie (far left) are another typical feature of the mountain landscape. Below: Cirque d'Estaubé.

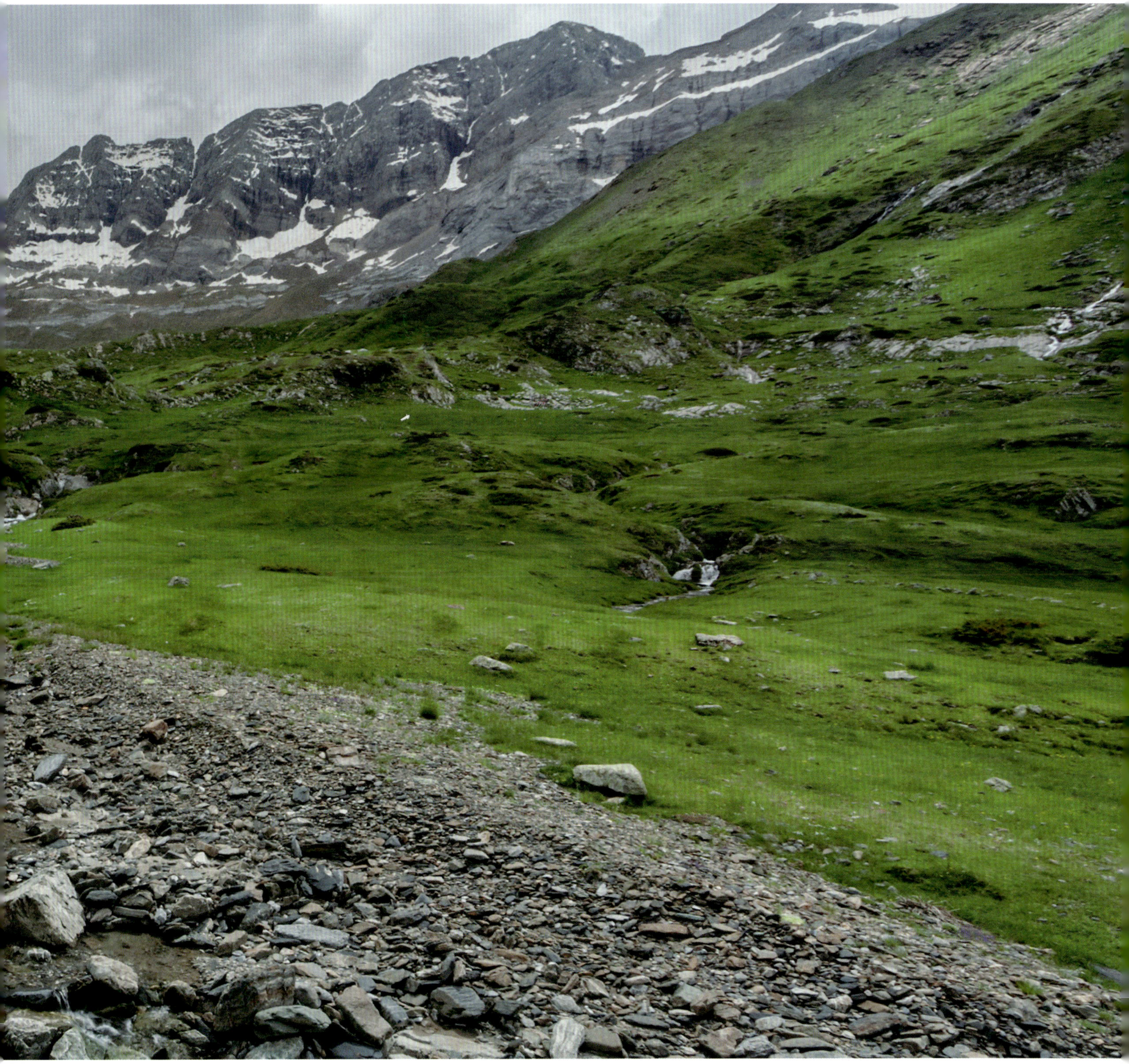

GULF OF PORTO

Date of inscription: 1983

The World Natural Heritage Site along the middle of the west coast of Corsica includes the coastal region around the Gulf of Porto, local underwater habitats, and the islands of Elbo and Gargallo.

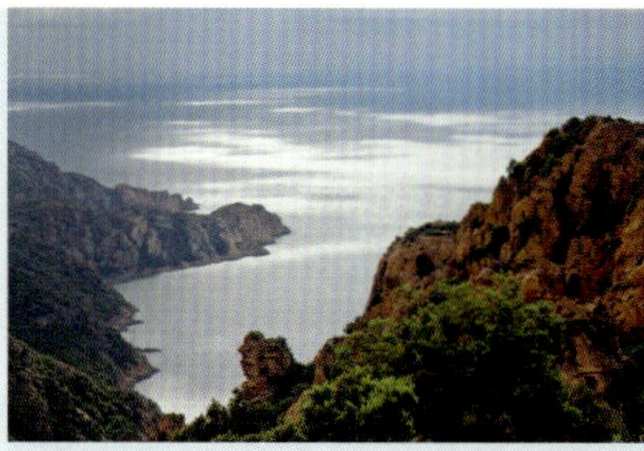

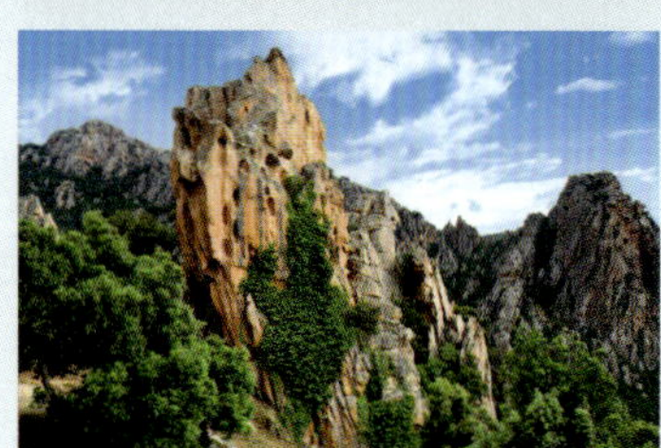

In 2006, the official name of this site was changed to "Gulf of Porto: Calanche of Piana, Gulf of Girolata, Scandola Reserve." The inclusion of the names of the two bays and peninsulas reflected the full extent of the land covered by this protected area. It was listed not only for the beauty of its landscape, but also for its flora and fauna, and the traditional methods of agricultural and pasture management used by its inhabitants. The nature reserve is part of a larger Corsican regional park. It provides an ideal nesting and breeding ground for many different seabirds, including seagulls, cormorants, and the now rare sea eagle. The rocky peninsula of La Girolata is largely given over to wild forests, and there are large areas of typically Mediterranean maquis. Dense eucalyptus forests line the sandy, yellow beaches, and the waters around the bays are alive with flora and fauna which are hard to find anywhere else.

Both rough and smooth rock formations can be found on the Scandola peninsula. This remote region is only accessible on foot, crossing terrain overgrown with maquis.

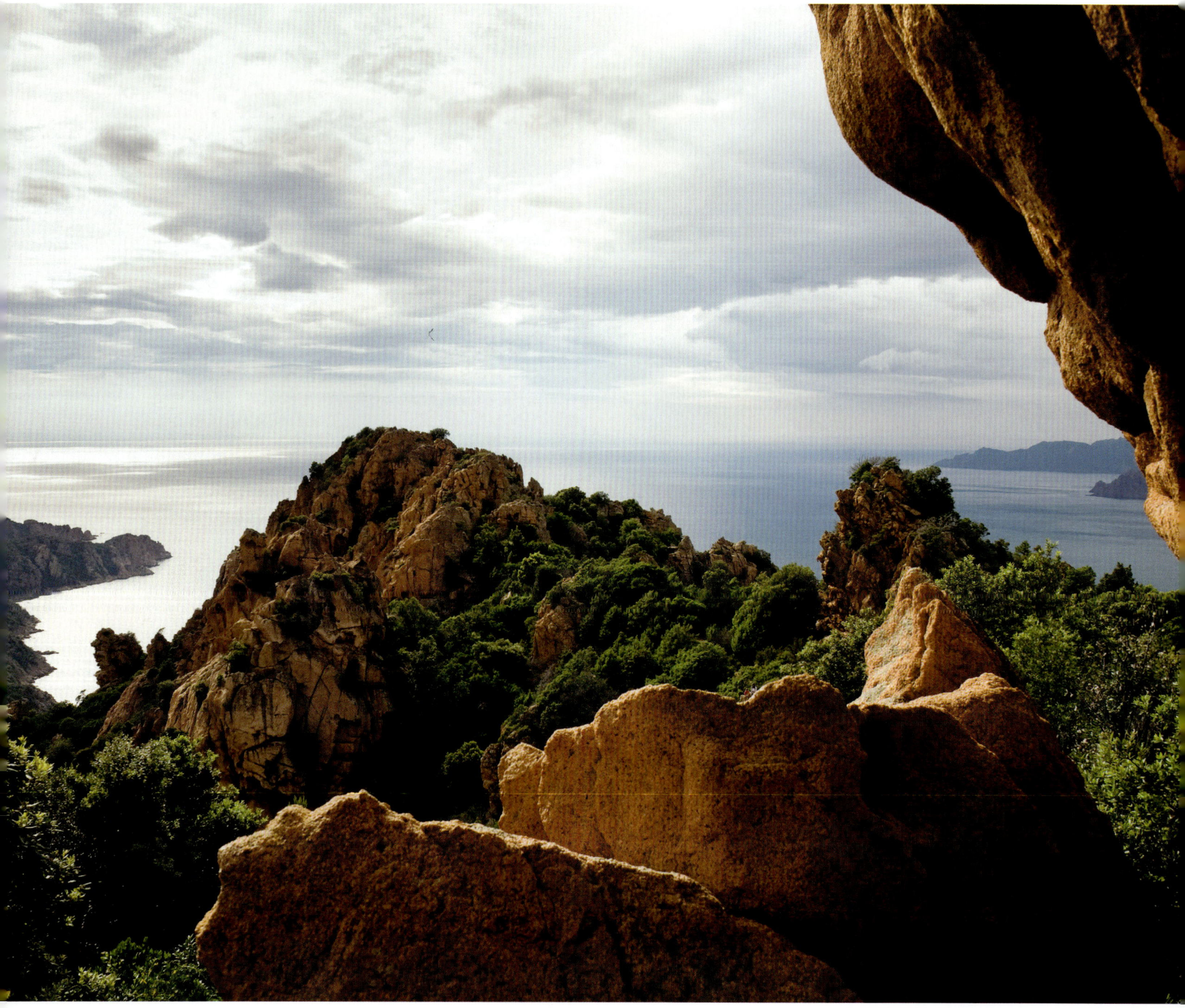

RÉUNION ISLAND

La Réunion, which together with the neighbouring islands of Mauritius and Rodrigues forms the Mascarene Islands (or Mascarenhas Archipelago), originated about two million years ago during the interplay of fire and water, when the Piton des Neiges volcano rose from the Indian Ocean. Today, this volcano is the highest peak in a volcanic chain extending across the island. The volcanic landscape which was declared a World Heritage site also includes the cirques of Cilaos, Salazie and Mafate – three valleys located in the centre of the island, and so named for their circular shape. The new reserve largely corresponds to the core based around the Piton des Neiges, which had become the Parc National de la Réunion as early as March 2007. Located in the east of the island is the Grand Etang, a mountain lake created by the waters that were damned by the cooled lava flows of the Piton des Neiges.

The steep Trou de Fer ("iron hole") Canyon (right) offers spectacular views of the Cirque de Salazie. Sunny mountain slopes and rugged cliffs characterize the Cirque de Cilaos (large picture).

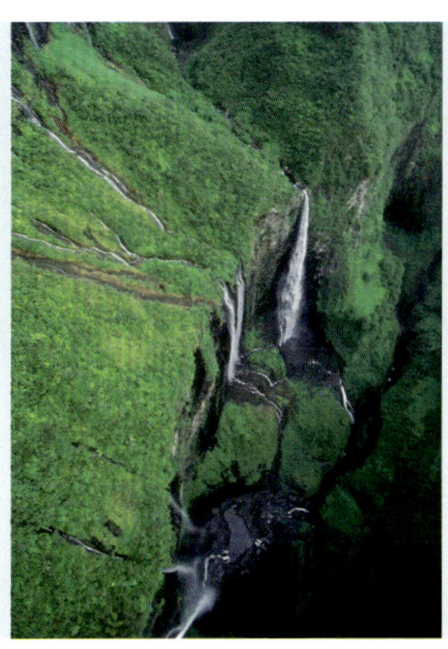

Date of inscription: 2010

The volcanic landscape of the island of La Réunion ("The Meeting"), located some 800 km (497 miles) east of Madagascar in the Indian Ocean and politically a French overseas territory, is a refuge for a rich, often endemic flora and fauna.

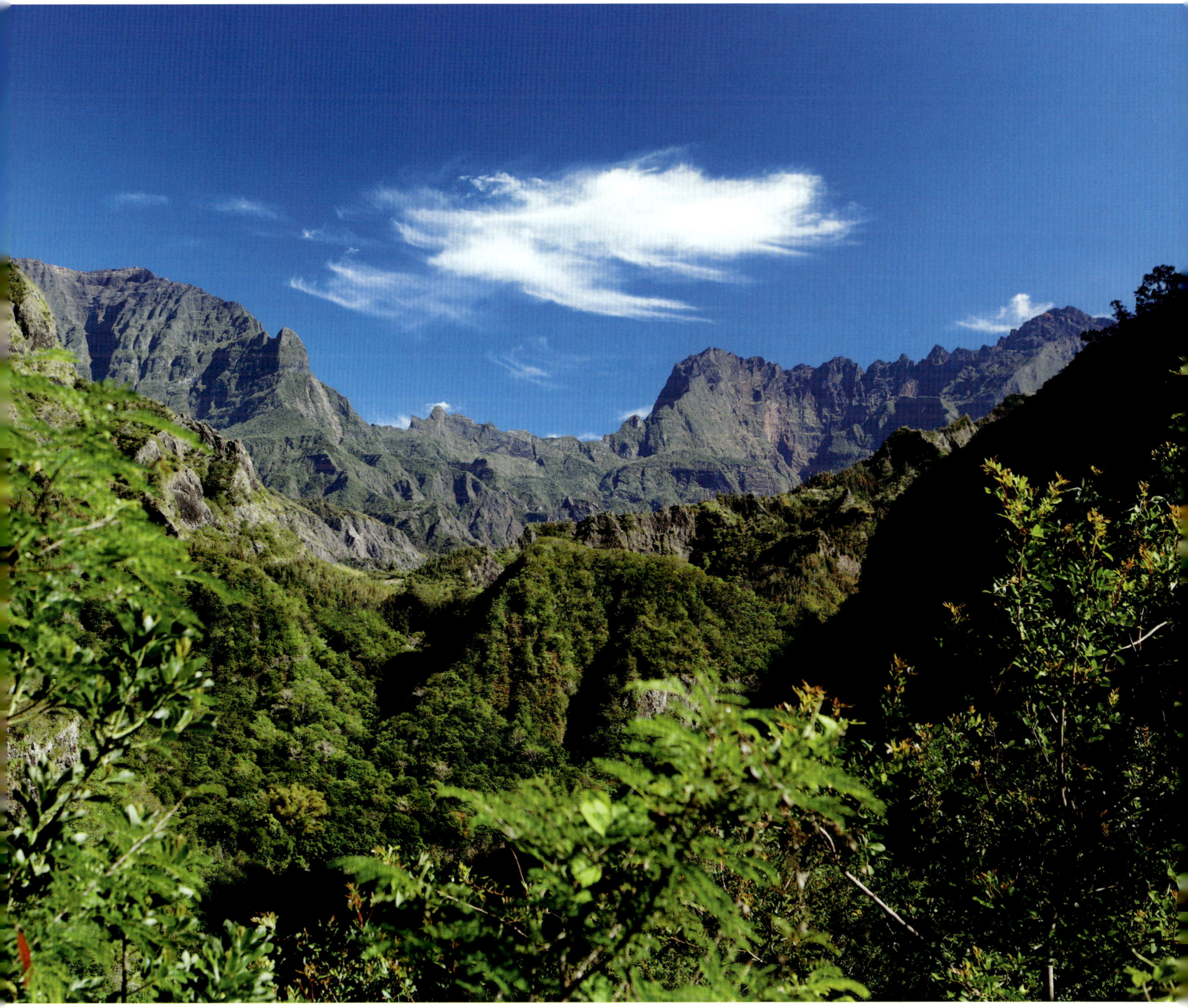

THE LAGOONS OF NEW CALEDONIA

Date of inscription: 2008

Between clumps of marine grass there are reefs which are quite unique and not to be found nowhere else in the world, offering a habitat for endangered species of fish, turtles, and mammals. The World Heritage Site encompasses six ecosystems.

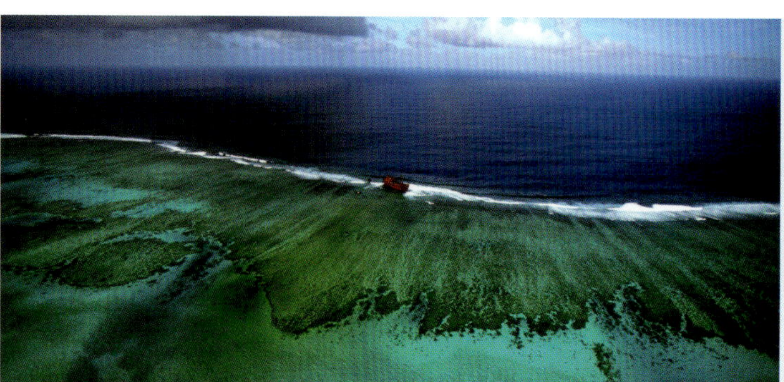

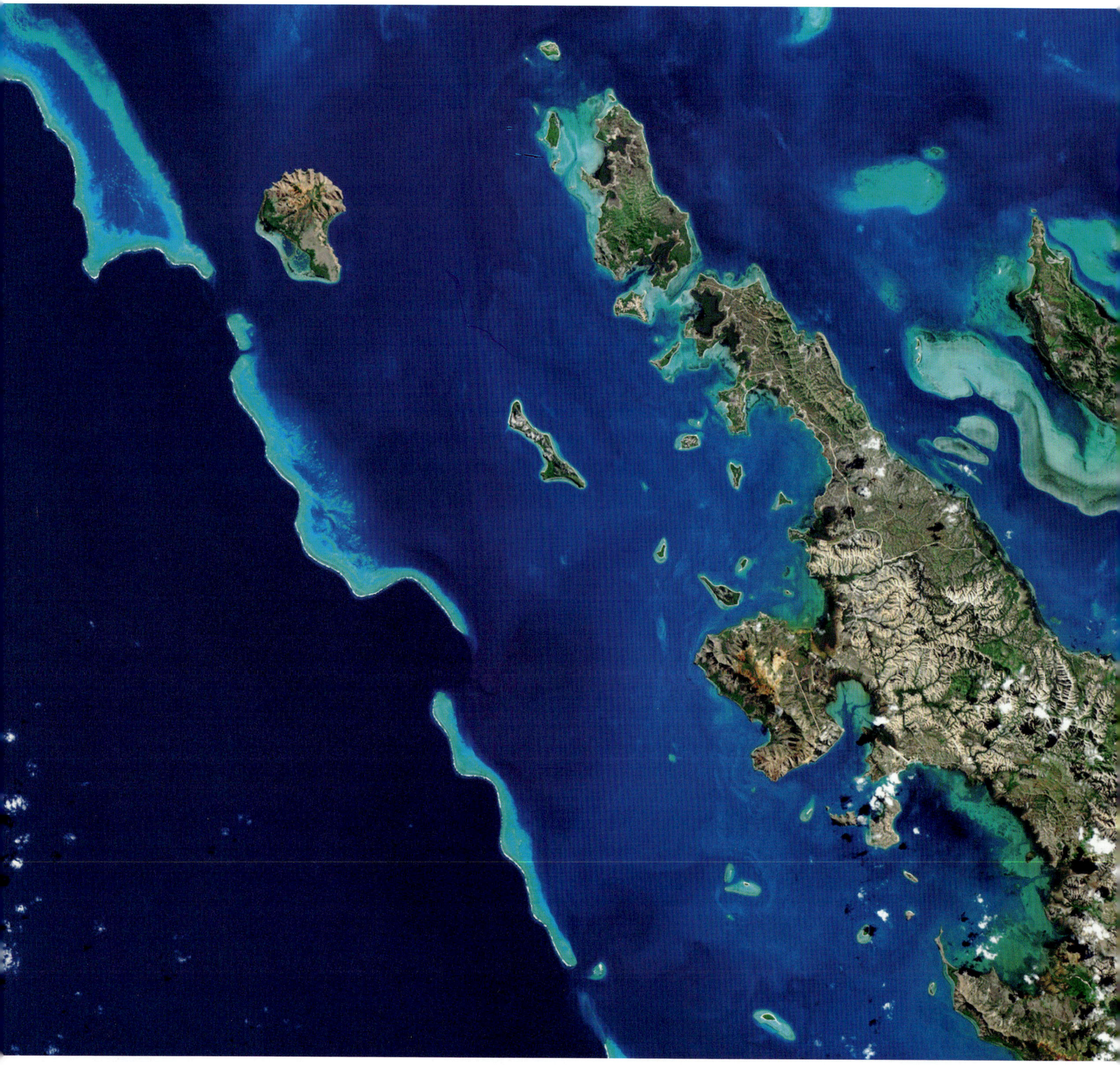

New Caledonia covers an area of some 18,600 sq. km (7,240 sq. miles) and includes the eponymous main island and several smaller coral and volcanic islands. The island group came under French rule in 1853 and is now a French Overseas Territory. The main island and the islands to its south are surrounded by a coral reef which, along with the Australian Great Barrier Reef, is one of the biggest reef systems in the world. The untouched mangrove forests are home to a variety of animal life and lush vegetation, and numerous species of fish, including parrotfish, leopard rays, reef sharks, and a species of lobster native to New Caledonia, the popinée, are to be found in the largely intact lagoon ecosystems. The shallow coastal waters are also home to the Indo-Pacific tarpon, an ancient bony fish, whose ancestors swam in the tropical seas of the Cretaceous period. Extensive meadows of sea grass provide sustenance for the world's third-largest population of sea cows. Since the extinction of their cousins in the Bering Sea in 1768, these animals, which can weigh up to 500 kilos (1,200 pounds), are amongst the last remaining dugongs. There are also ancient fossil remains of reefs in the lagoons, providing a rich source of information for researchers of the natural history of the Pacific.

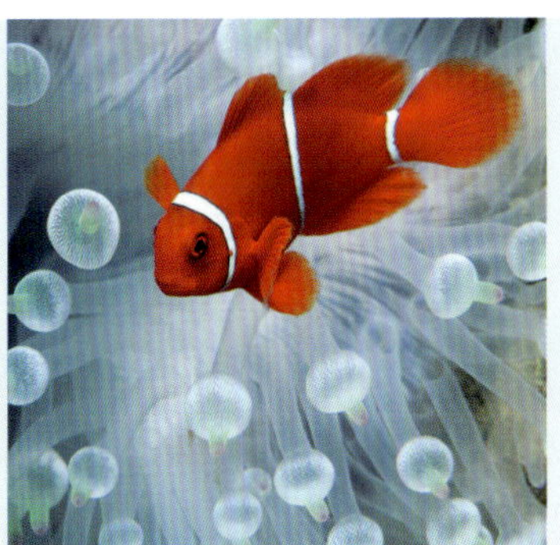

The New Caledonian Barrier Reef is home to numerous species of fish such as the clownfish (left). A satellite image illustrates the reef's amazing size (below).

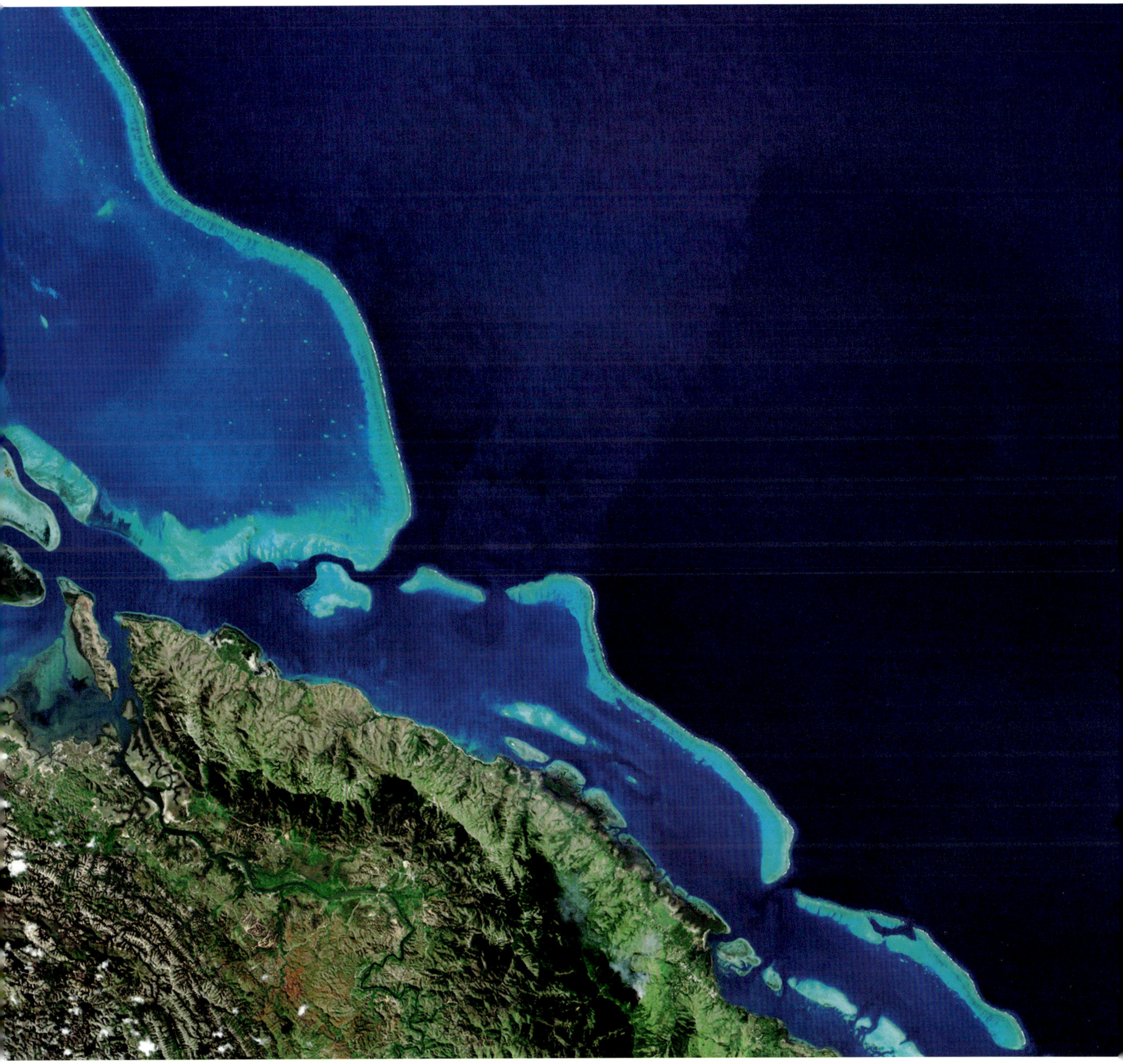

WADDEN SEA (WATTENMEER)

Date of inscription: 2009
Extended: 2011, 2014

The Wadden Sea is one of the largest coastal, tide-dependent wetlands on Earth, a unique ecosystem. In 2011, UNESCO also included the Hamburg Wadden Sea National Park in the transnational World Heritage site.

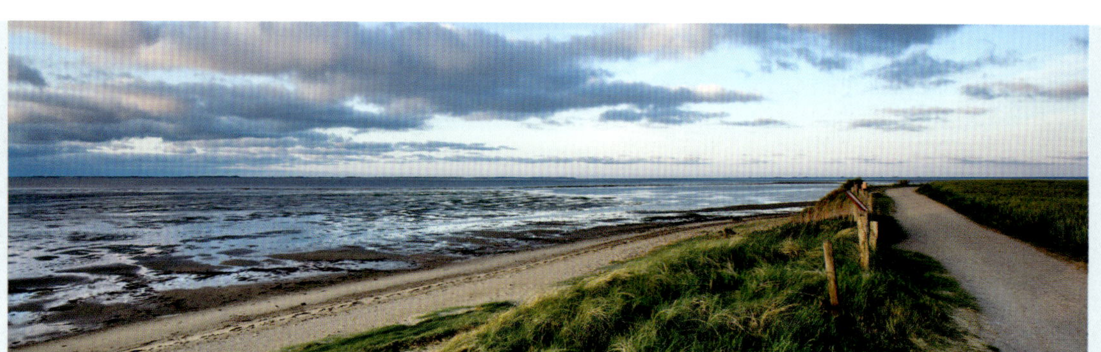

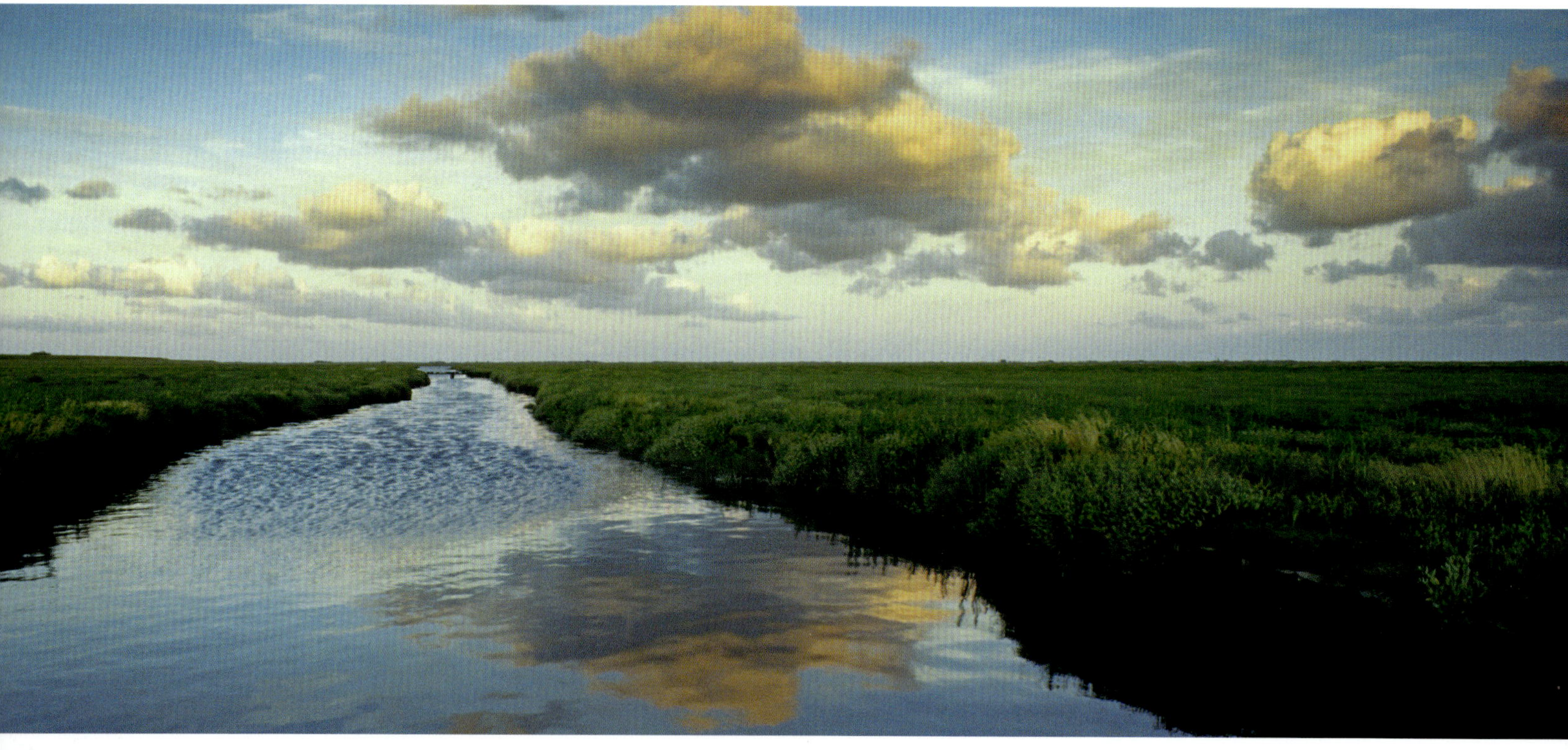

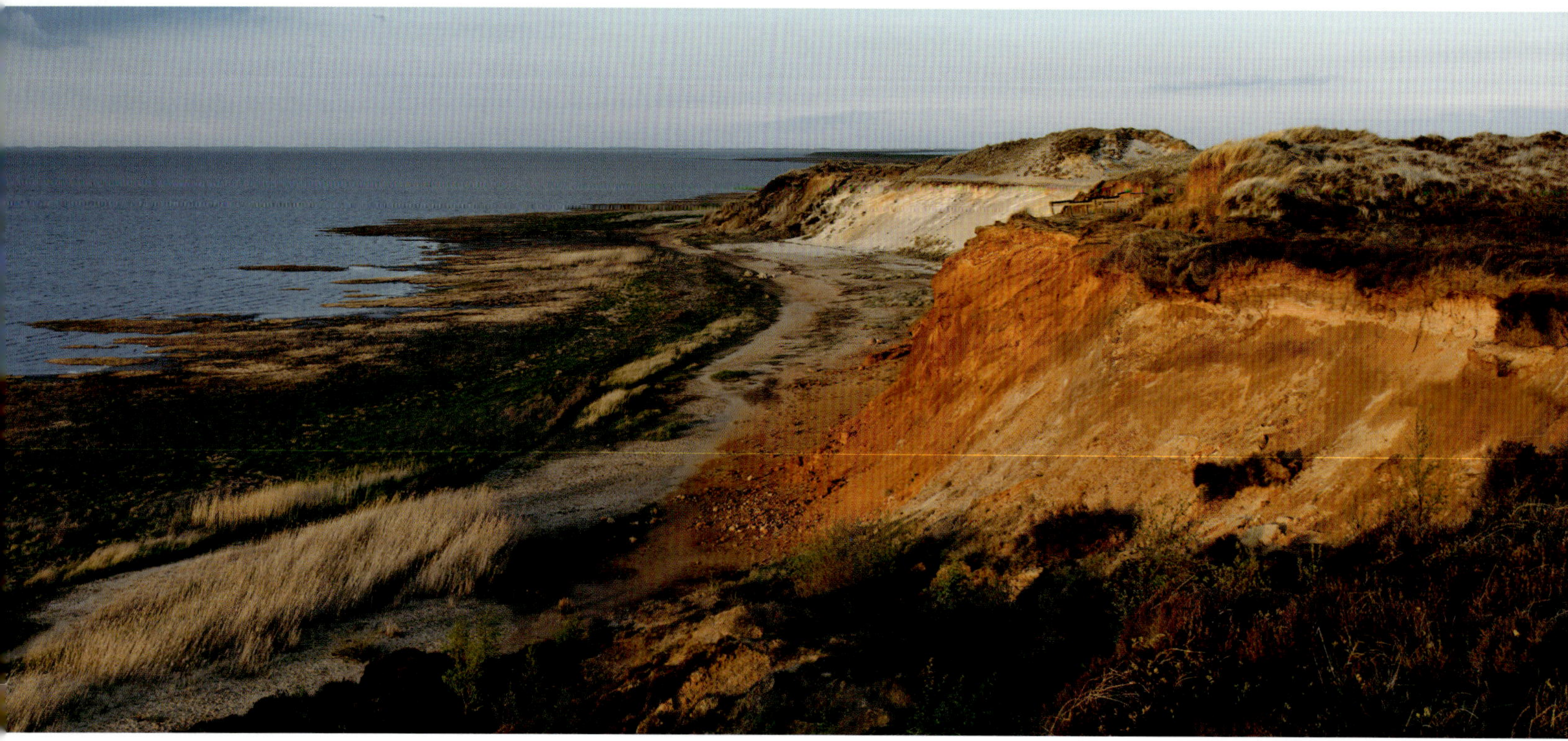

About 450 km (280 miles) long and up to 40 km (24 miles) wide, the Wadden Sea extends along the North Sea coast between the Danish town of Blåvandshuk and the Dutch town of Den Helder, a unique habitat for plants, animals and humans determined by the tides. Around two-thirds of the entire landscape are included in the World Heritage site. These comprise in the German section the Schleswig Holstein Wadden Sea, the Lower Saxon Wadden Sea and the Hamburg Wadden Sea national parks. Dotted offshore are the North Frisian and East Frisian Islands, from Sylt in the north to Borkum in the west. Besides the islands, the landscape is dominated by sandbanks, sea grass beds and mudflats.

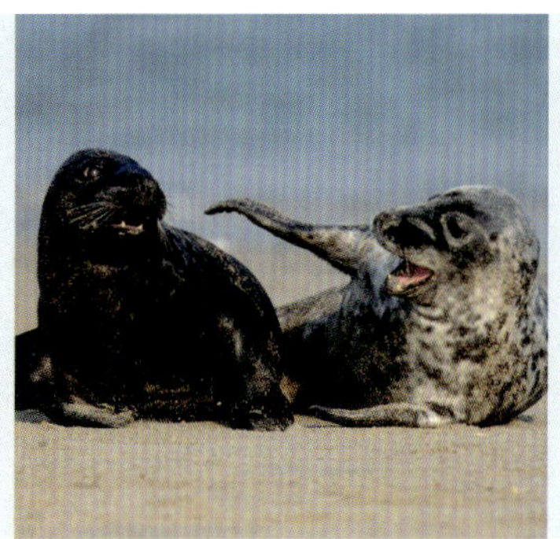

Grey seal (left) are abundant in the Wadden Sea. Far left: the Wadden Sea near Amrum. Below, clockwise: List Elbow on Sylt; quay wall on Amrum; Morsum Cliff near Morsum; Eiderstedt Peninsula.

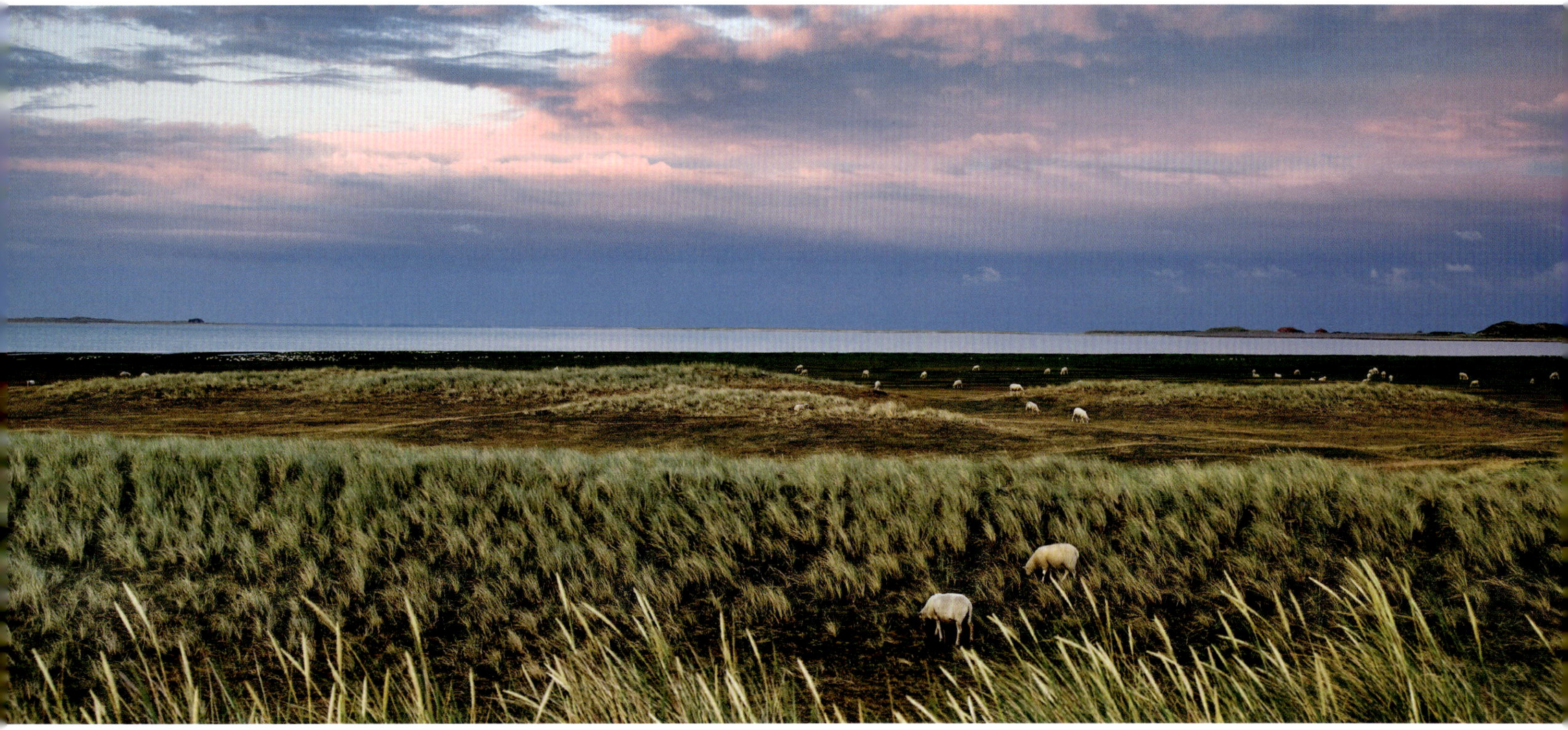

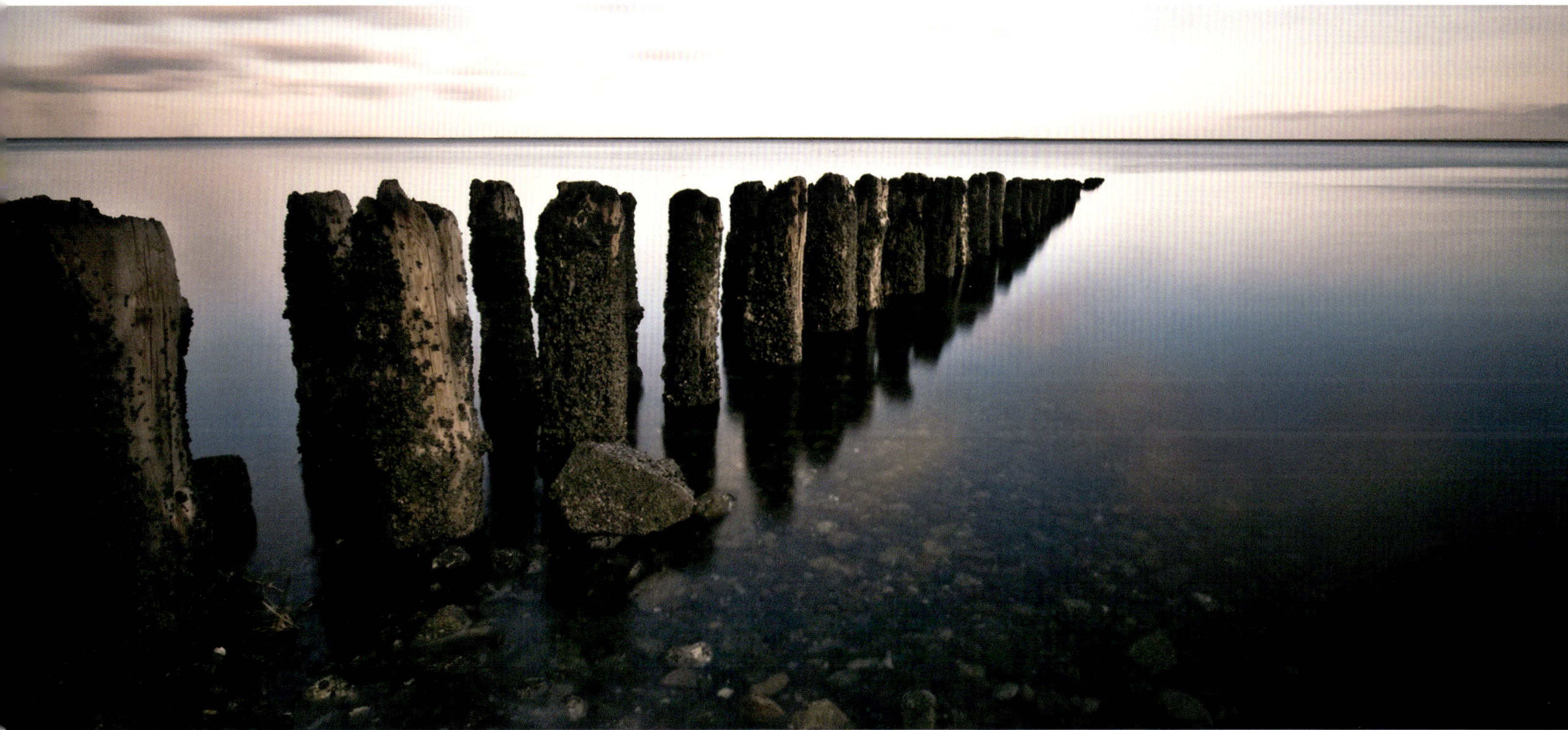

PRIMEVAL BEECH FORESTS

Date of inscription: 2007/2011

The trans-border World Natural Heritage site known as the "Primeval Beech Forests of the Carpathians", was listed by UNESCO in 2007, and expanded in 2011 to include five primeval beech forests in Germany; it was renamed accordingly.

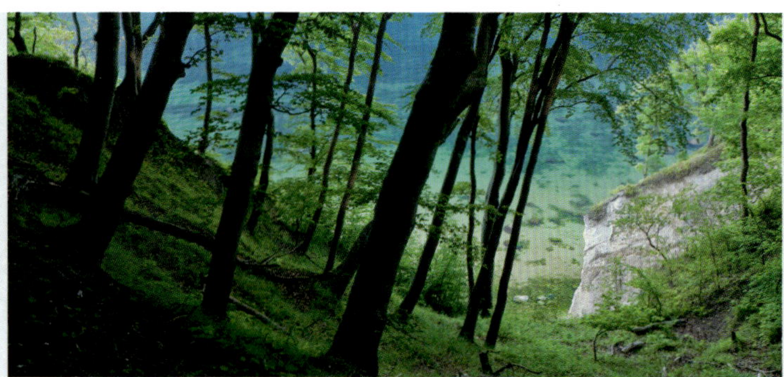

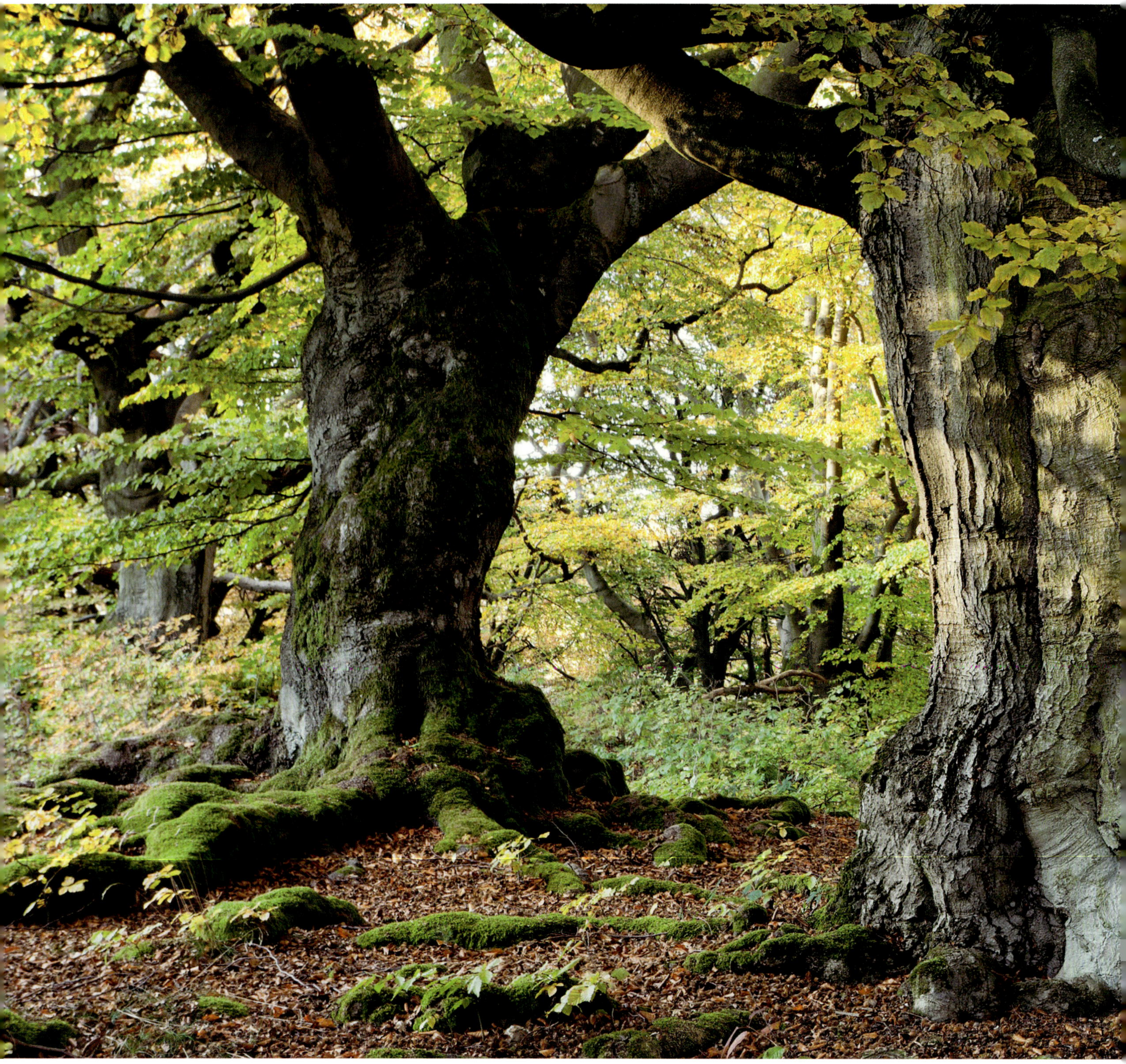

Specifically, after expansion the site now incorporates the Grumsin Forest in Brandenburg, the Kellerwald-Edersee National Park in Hesse, the Jasmund National Park and the beech forest of Serrahn in the Müritz National Park, both located in Mecklenburg-Vorpommern, as well as the Hainich National Park in Thuringia. Each of these regions is unique in its own way and thus also irreplaceable. Together the areas that make up the World Heritage site represent the most valuable relics of large areas of natural beech forests in Germany.

In the selected forest areas, the post-glacial spread of the beech from north to south, and from west to east, and from the lowlands to the high altitudes can be documented; of its original spread, only about seven per cent are still extant in Germany.

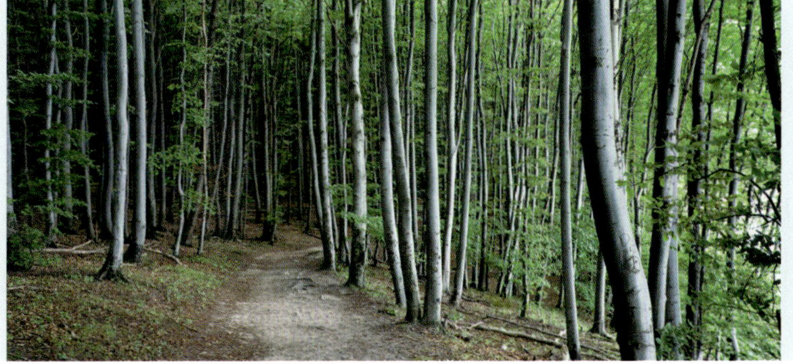

Luminous white chalk cliffs and light-flooded beech forests characterize the island of Rügen (left and far left), while the beech forest near Edersee glows a golden yellow in late summer (large picture).

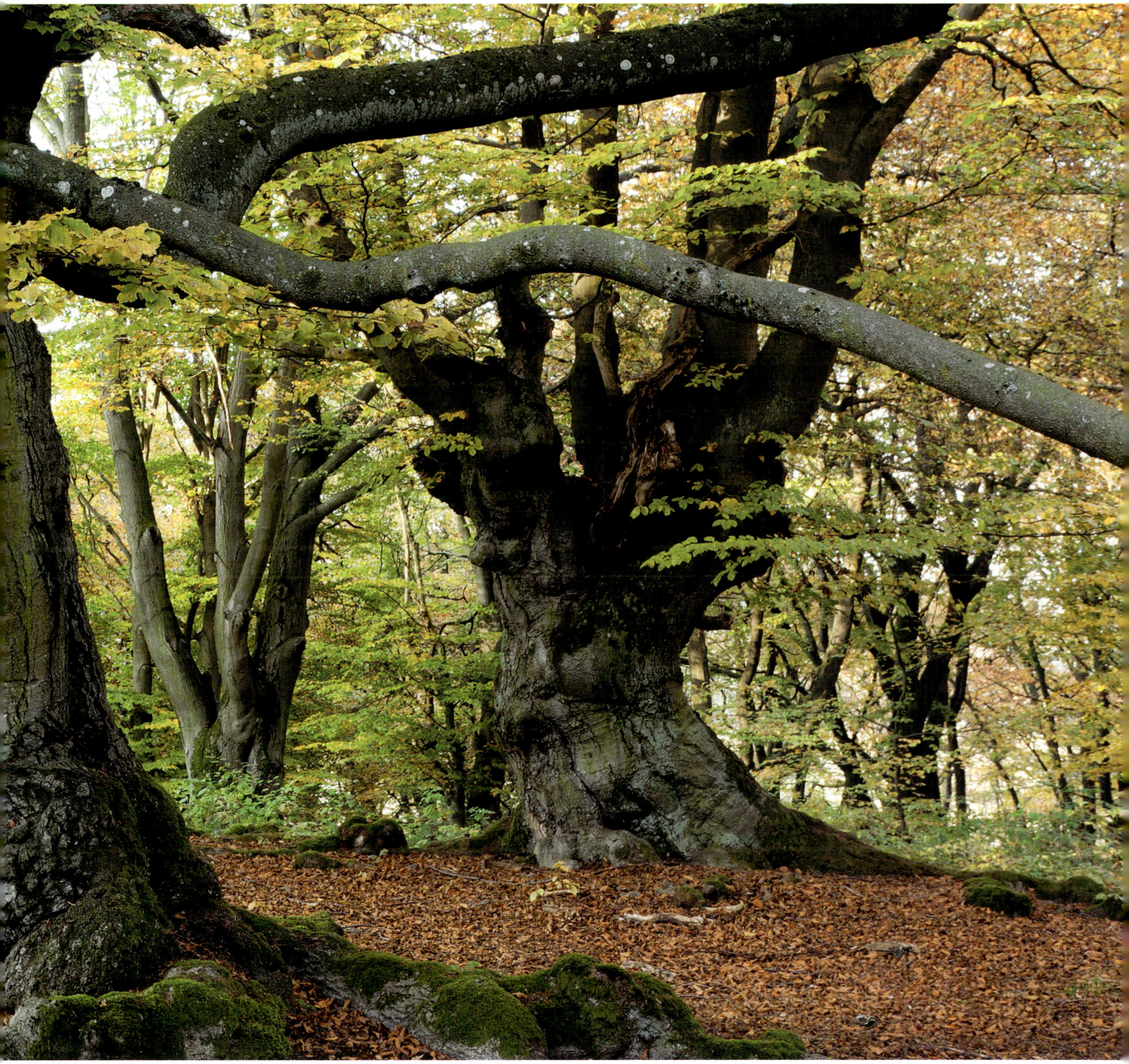

MESSEL PIT FOSSIL SITE

Date of inscription: 1995

Messel Pit is considered to be one of the world's most important fossil sites. The sedimentation and lack of oxygen in the water-filled volcanic crater have led to the preservation of fossils dating back some 50 million years.

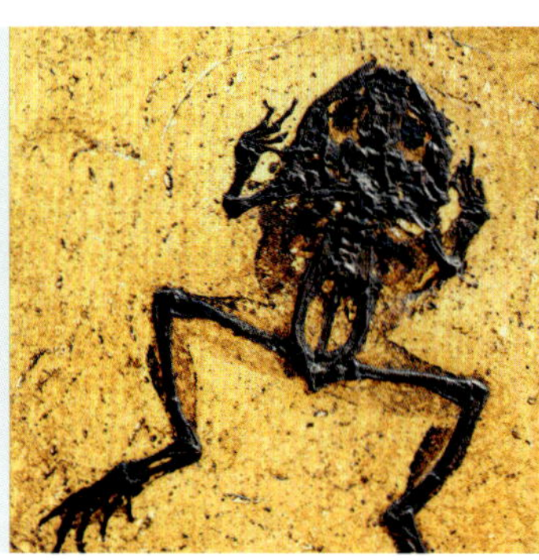

This 65-hectare (161-acre) pit near Darmstadt was, for several years, threatened with transformation into a landfill site. At the last minute, it was placed under special protection. The layers of oil shale at the site contain many well-preserved fossils, which together provide an almost complete picture of the climate, biology, and geology of this area during the Eocene epoch – a period of natural history between 60 and 36 million years ago, when, after the dinosaurs had become extinct, plants and animals gradually started to develop into the flora and fauna we know today. As such, the Messel pit provides a unique insight into the early evolution of mammals.

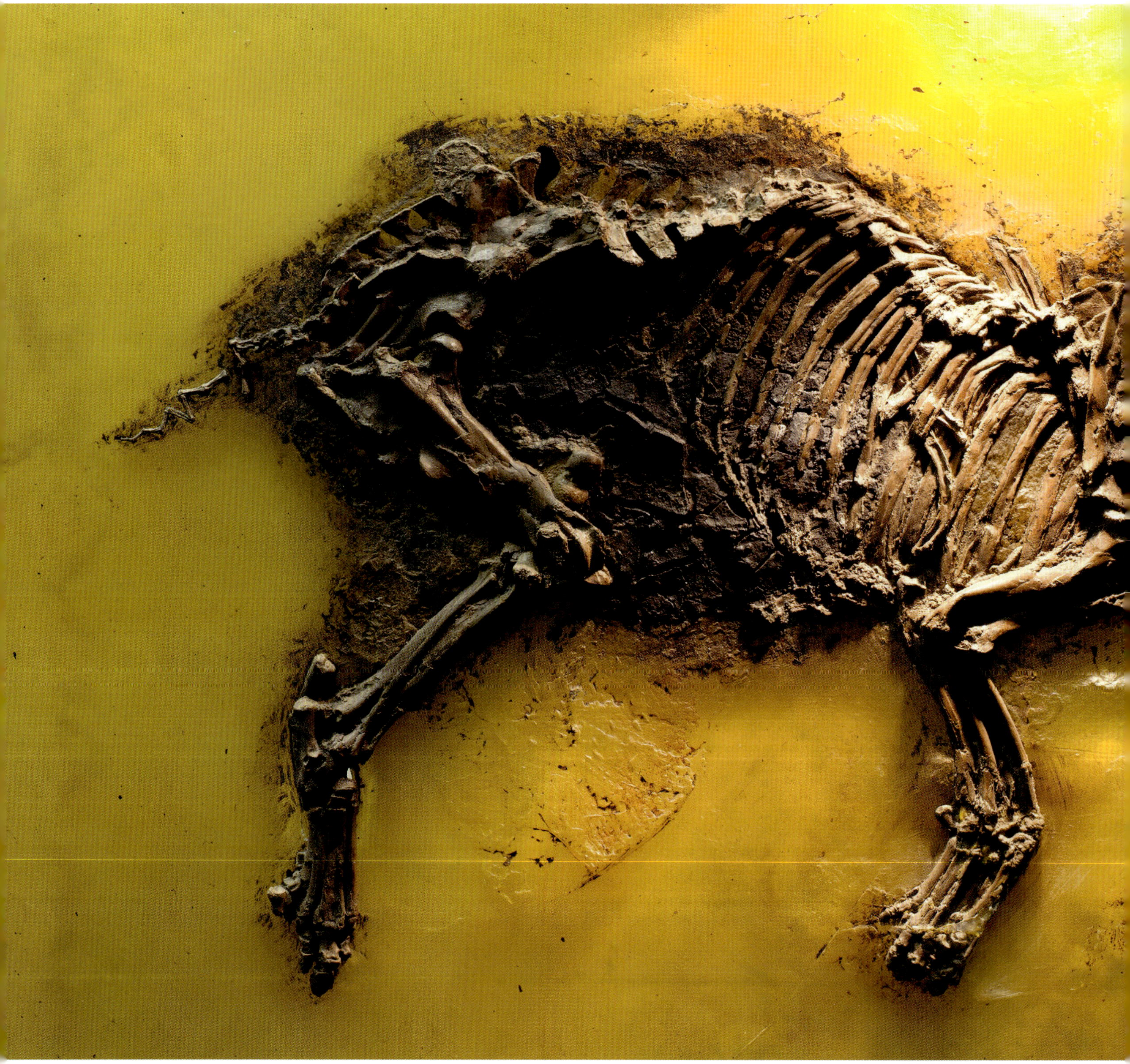

Among the most spectacular finds were the remains of over 70 early horses, including more than 30 complete skeletons. The skeletons of other vertebrates, meanwhile, were preserved with some soft body parts and the contents of the animals' stomachs intact. The finds also allowed scientists to draw conclusions about phenomena such as continental drift, land bridges, sedimentation, and the evolution of the biosphere.

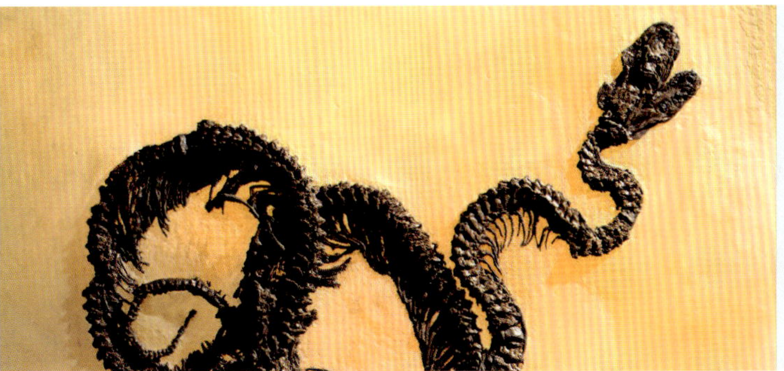

Preserved in the oil shales, the Messel fossils include primeval insects, reptiles, birds, and mammals. Below left: a prehistoric horse; far left: a frog; left a giant snake; below right: an extinct rodent.

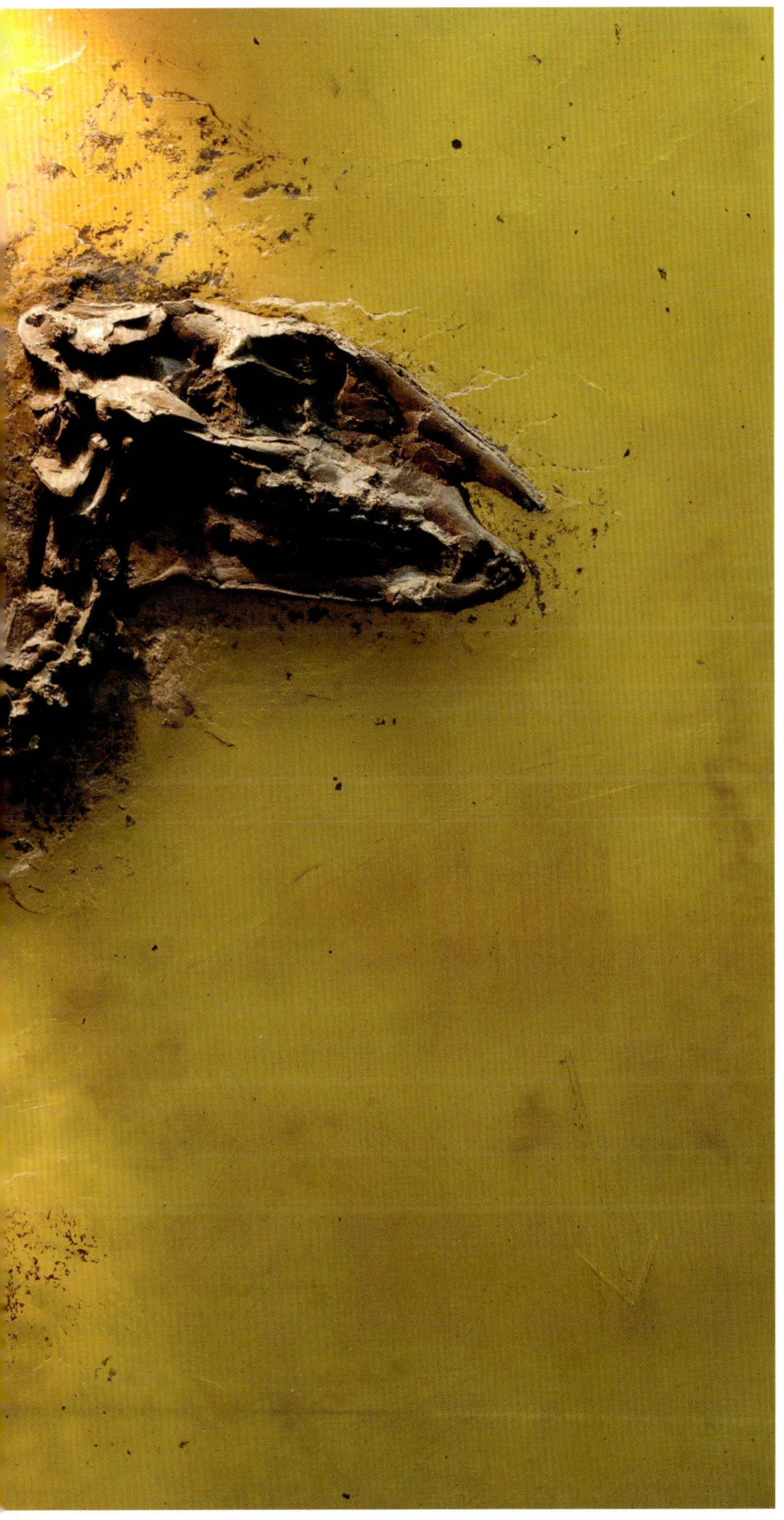

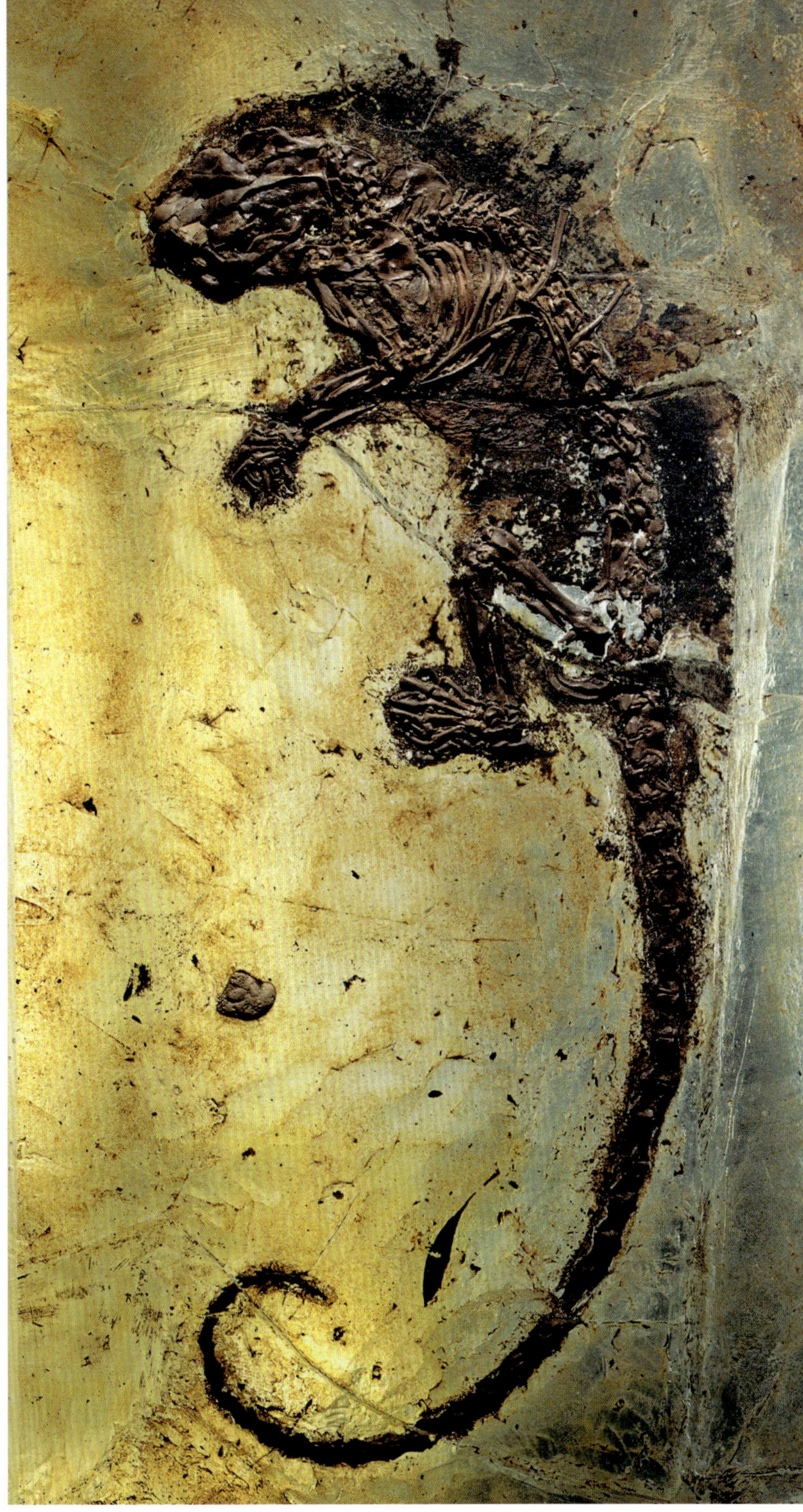

SWISS ALPS: JUNGFRAU-ALETSCH-BIETSCHHORN

Date of inscription: 2001
Extended: 2007

The Jungfrau-Aletsch-Bietschhorn region is the first part of the Alps to be added to the list of World Natural Heritage Sites.

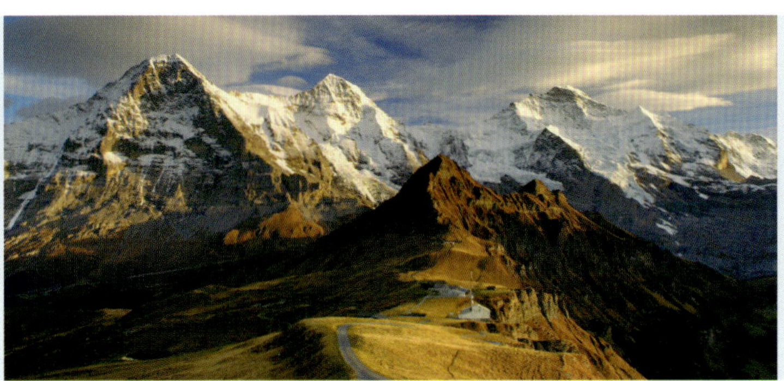

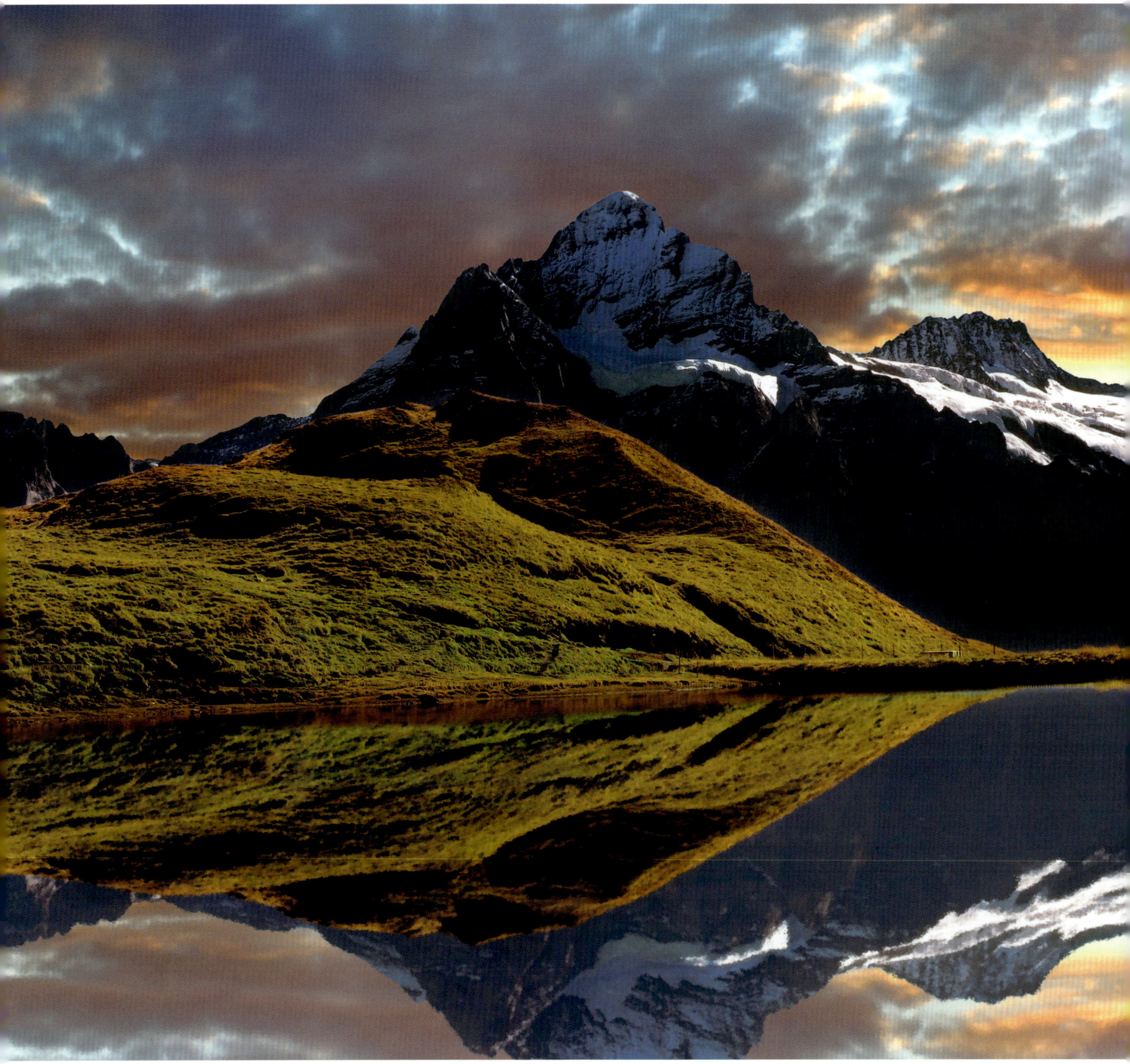

The Jungfrau, Mönch, and Eiger mountains form the heart of this dramatic mountain range. A rack railway takes visitors to the ridge of the Jungfrau mountain, terminating at an altitude of some 3,500 m (11,500 feet). The glass dome of the observatory is a well-known landmark. The only way up the north face of the Eiger, however, is by climbing. Located in the Bernese Alps, south-west of Grindelwald, the Eiger rises to a height of 3,970 m (13,025 feet). Its north face was first climbed in 1938, and – rising 1,800 m (5,900 feet) above the valley below – it has become the most famous climb in the Alps.

The region and its snowfields feed the magnificent Aletsch glacier, formed by the combination of the Aletsch névé, Jungfern névé, and Ewigschneefeld névé, which all come together at the so-called Konkordiaplatz – close to the Jungfraujoch. Spanning some 23 km (14 miles), this is still Europe's biggest glacier, although due to global warming it is slowly melting. A diverse range of flora and fauna can be found on the moraine surfaces around the ice flow. The Aletsch forest, for example, is a protected nature reserve that is home to the arve – a type of tree that can live for more than eight hundred years.

The Bietschhorn stands out for the dry, sunny valleys on its southern side, stretching out like fingers as far as the Rhône valley to the south and Lötschen valley to the north. The dry grassland of the rocky Walliser steppe is not farmed, and instead provides a home for rare plants and animals.

Located above Grindelwald is the flattened peak of First. The idyllic Bachalpsee mountain lake boasts a perfect mirror surface to reflect the surrounding majestic mountain summits (large picture). From the peak of the Männlichen (left), you can enjoy fantastic views of the famous Eiger, Mönch and Jungfrau mountains.

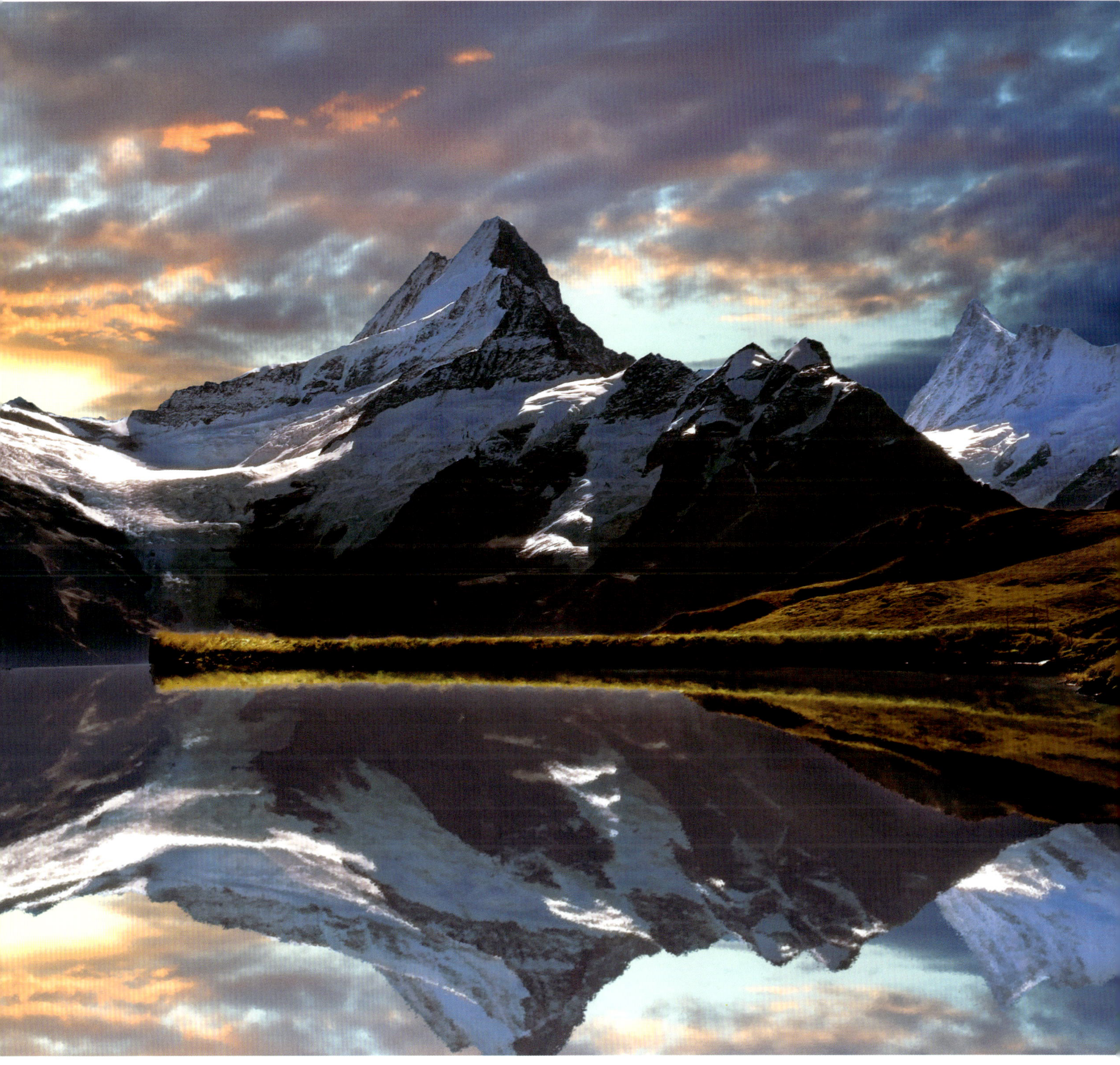

SWISS TECTONIC ARENA SARDONA

Date of inscription: 2008

The Swiss Tectonic Arena Sardona is a mountainous region of 328 ha (810 acres) including seven peaks above 3,000 m (9,900 feet). The region is composed of biotopes and geotopes housing a variety of plant and animal life and is also the location of the Glarus Overthrust, a unique exposed feature which reveals its own geomorphological history.

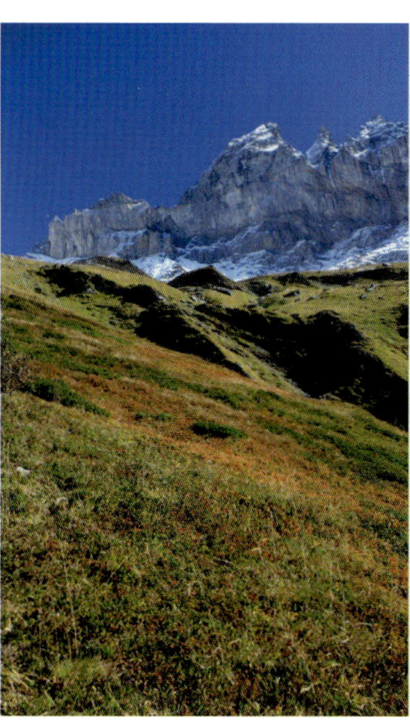

The mountainous region around the 3,056-m (10,026-foot) high Piz Sardona on the borders of the cantons of St Gallen, Glarus, and Graubünden is an example of orogeny resulting from the collision of continental plates and the release of tectonic forces. The area has been an important source of information concerning the origins and composition of the Alps since the 19th century. Visible for miles around, the Glarus Overthrust is the central feature of the protected area. Some 20 or 30 million years ago, a layer of rock up to 15 km (9 miles) thick was pushed up from the Anterior Rhine Valley over younger rock strata; along the thrust line, 250 to 300 million-year-old green and brown verrucano rock is lying on top of 35 to 50 million-year-old brownish-grey flysch. The overlap begins in the valley of the Anterior Rhine and finally culminates in the 3,000-m (9,900-feet) high Hausstock, Sardona and Ringelspitz chain of peaks before sinking away to the north. The Tectonic Arena Sardona also comprises several important biotopes, including high moorland and flood plains as well as the oldest colony of resettled ibexes in Switzerland.

The striking rock lines at the Glarus thrust contributed to the fact that UNESCO decided to protect the area.

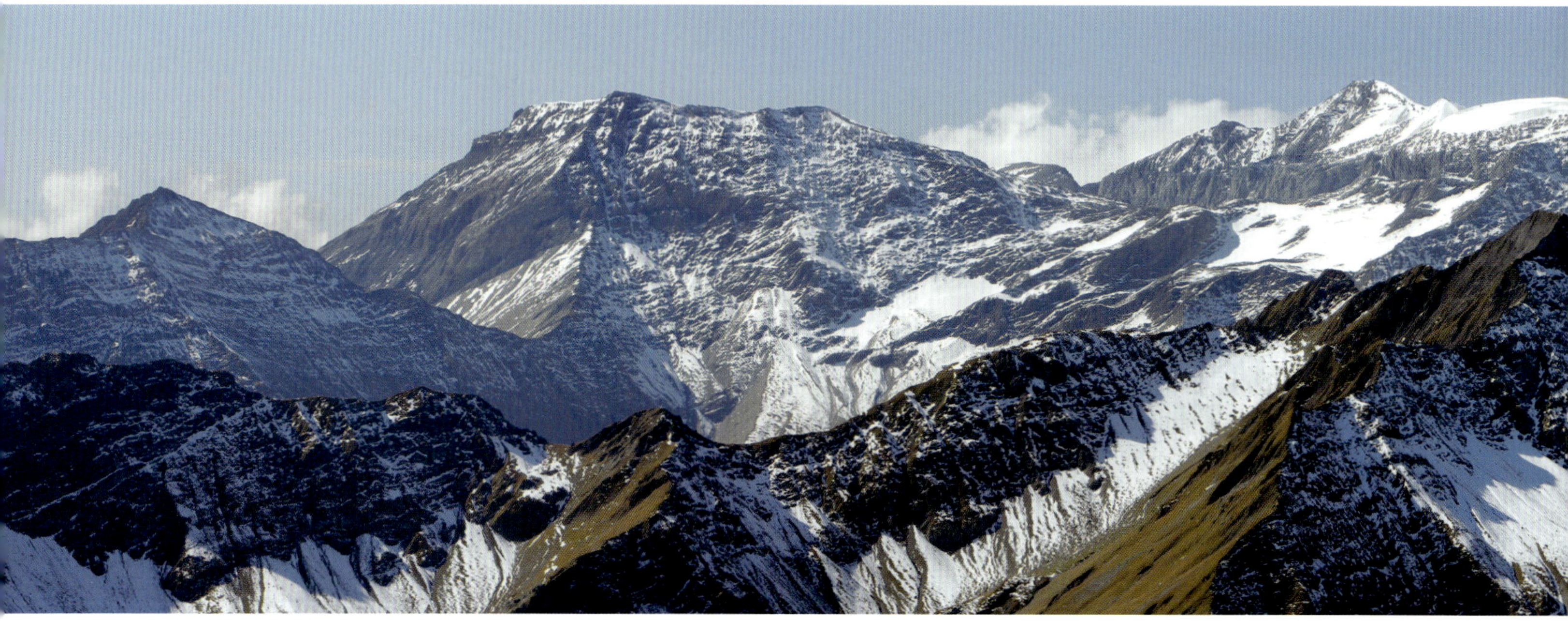

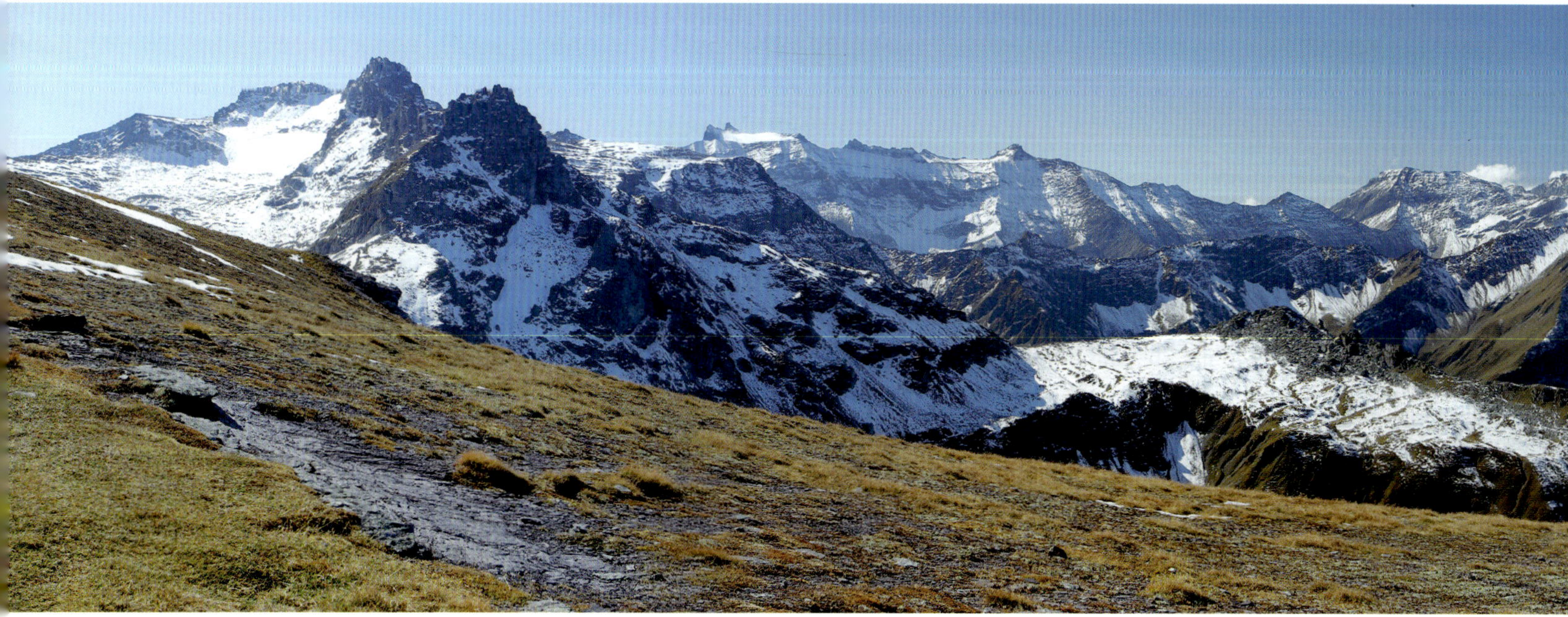

MONTE SAN GIORGIO

Monte San Giorgio lies at the southern end of Lake Lugano, and is therefore still relatively cut-off. Very few parts of the landscape of southern Switzerland have remained so unspoilt. For many years now, the forest on the 1,096-m (3,596-foot) high mountain has been allowed to grow wild. But the mountain's main claim to fame is as a significant fossil site. Nowhere else in Switzerland have such well-preserved fossils been found as in this region. The most spectacular finds are predominantly marine reptiles such as the Ticinosuchus and Ceresiosaurus ("Ceresio" being the local name for Lake Lugano). To date, the remains of 80 species of fish, 40 reptiles, and several hundred vertebrates have been found. Because the lagoon in which these animals lived was separated from the open sea by a reef and also located near to the mainland, Monte San Giorgio has also yielded fossils of land-based plants and animals. Furthermore, the fossils are completely intact and exceptionally well preserved. Some of the most beautiful examples are on display in the small museum at Meride town hall.

Around 20 cm (8 inches) long, this Pachypleurosaurus (right), a Triassic sea saurian, is just one of the specimens found at Monte San Giorgio.

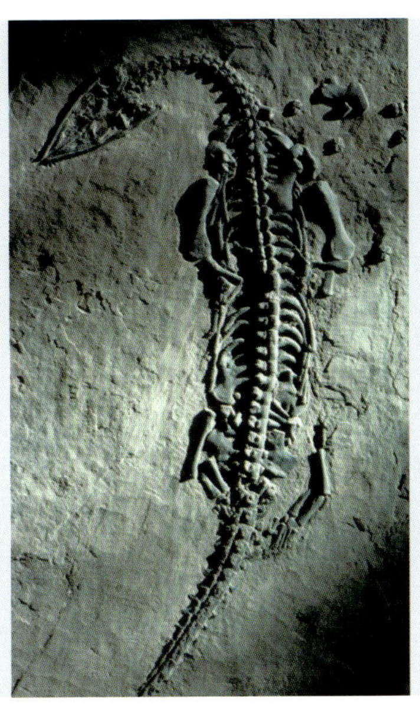

Date of inscription: 2003
Extended: 2010

The pyramid-shaped Monte San Giorgio is considered to be the world's richest depository of fossils from the Triassic period, dating back 245–230 million years. The fossilized remains of numerous marine animals have been found here, among them saurians measuring up to 6 m (20 feet) long. In 2010, the protected area was extended to include the Italian section.

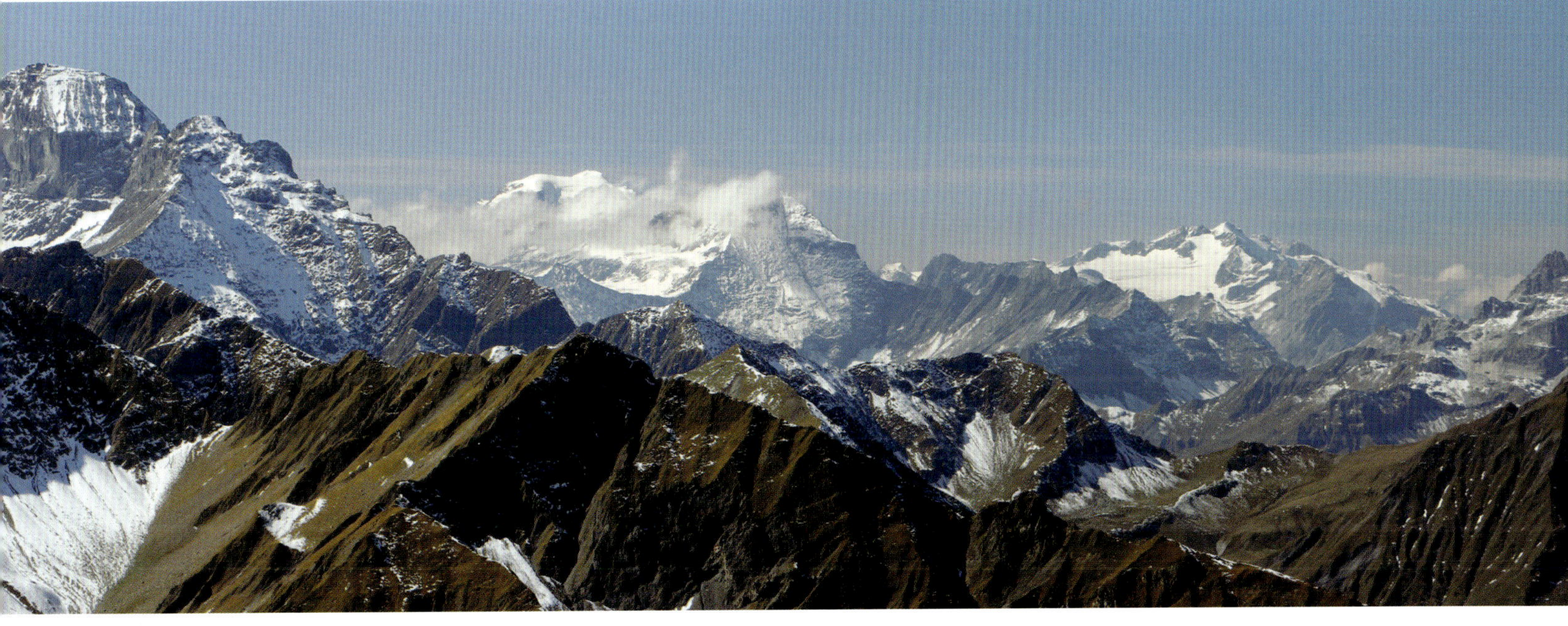

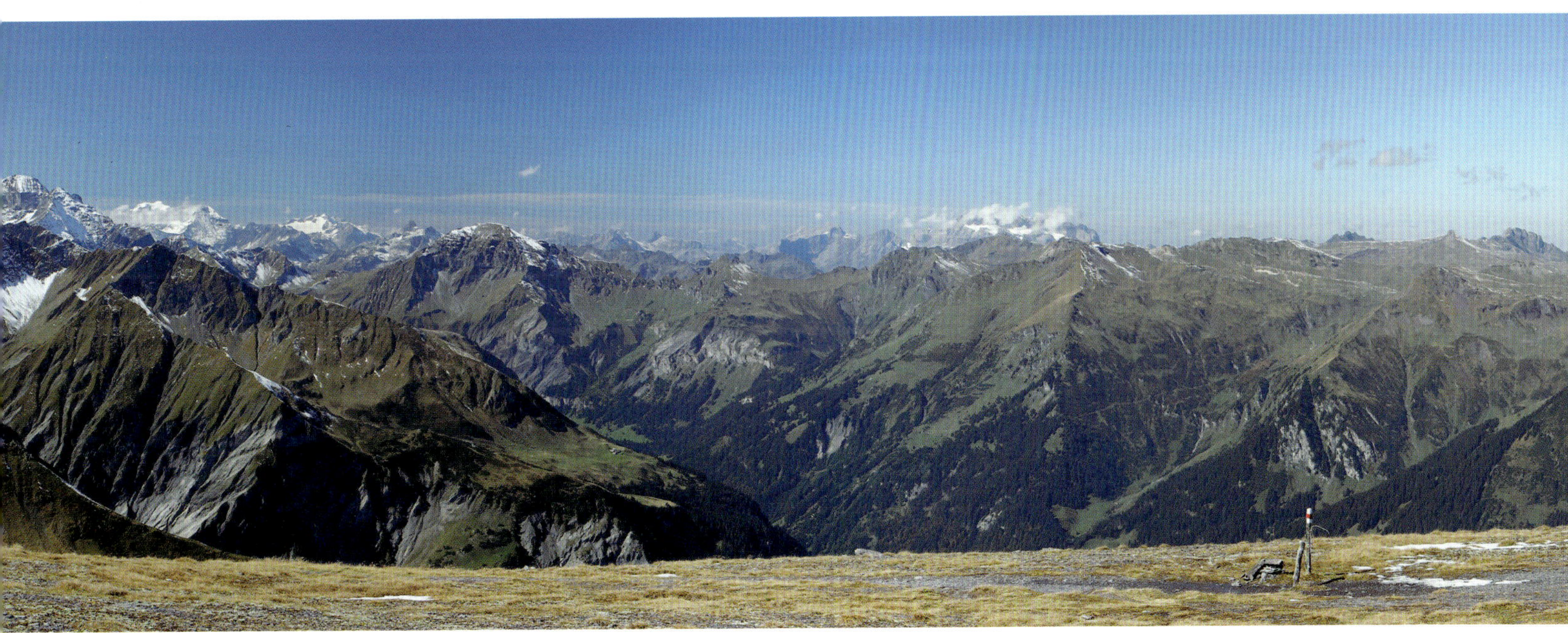

BIAŁOWIEŻA NATIONAL PARK/ BELOVEZHSKAYA PUSHCHA

Date of inscription: 1979
Extended: 1992, 2014

One of Europe's last primeval forests runs along the Polish-Byelorussian border. It is home to some unique flora and fauna.

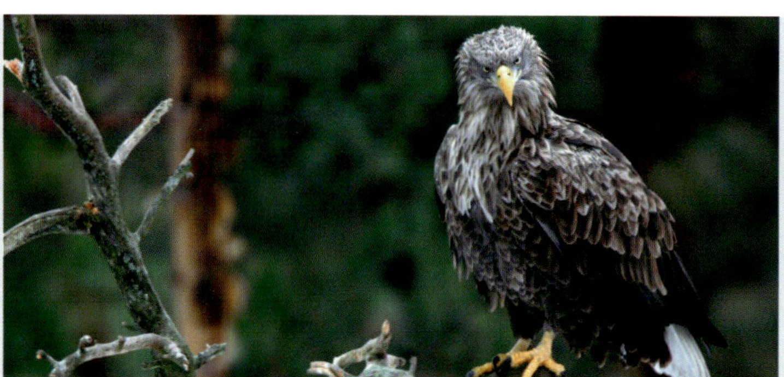

Initially, only the Polish Białowieża National Park was designated a World Heritage Site, and the larger Byelo-russian portion of the current heritage area – Belovezhskaya Pushcha – was only added in 1992. Together, they cover some 1,000 sq. km (386 sq. miles), making this the largest transnational UNESCO World Heritage Site. It was recognized primarily for its mixed virgin forest –

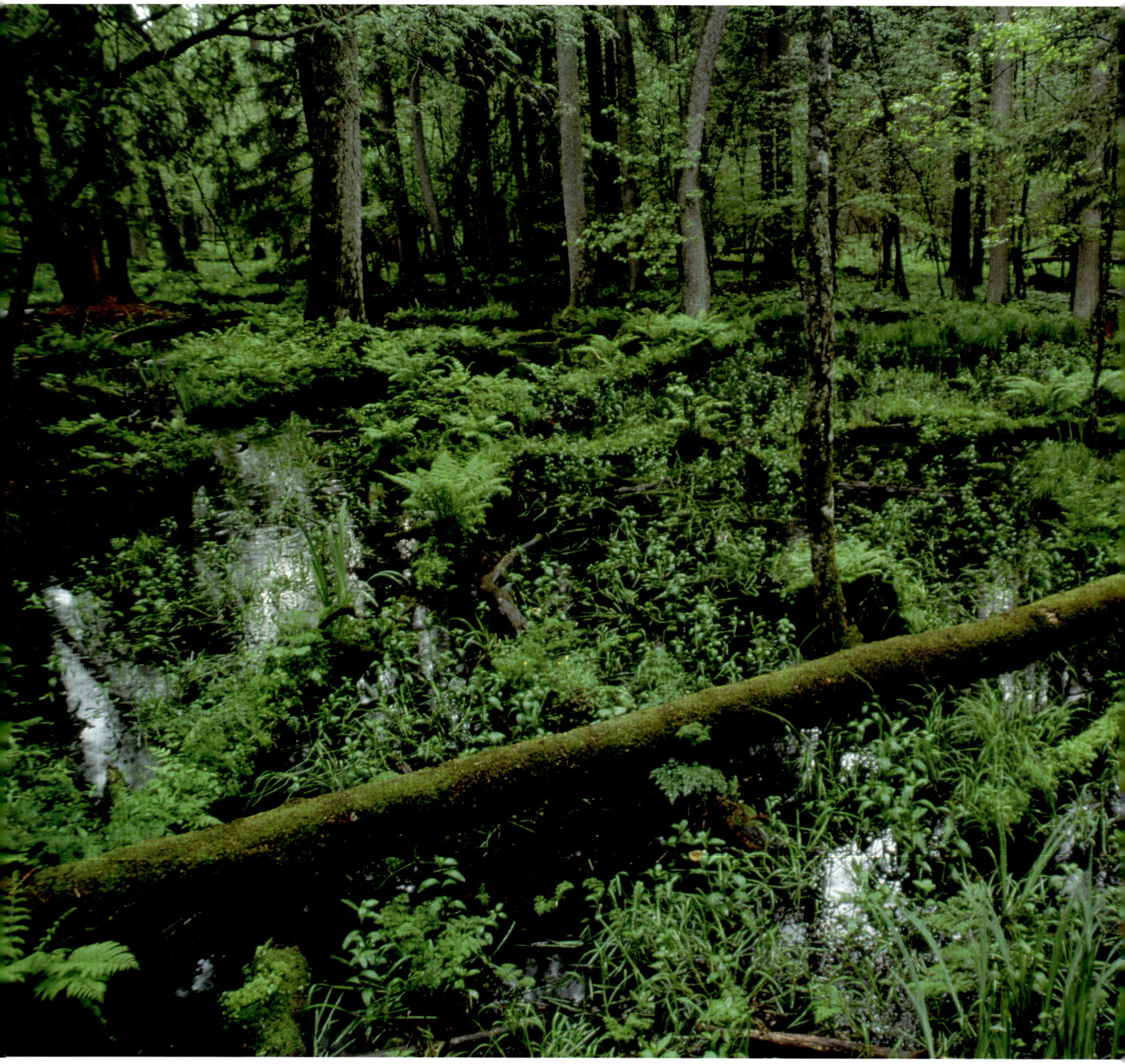

the only woods of their kind in Europe. The heavily protected core of the park is home to spruce, pine, black alder, hornbeam, oak, birch, ash, lime, maple, and poplar, and some trees are natural monuments in their own right. There are also hundreds of species of fungi, lichen, and vascular plants.

The park is most famous, however, for its bison. The animals – cousins of the North American bison – came close to dying out, but were reintroduced to the wild in 1952 using zoo stock bred in the 1920s. Today, around 900 bison roam the vast forest once more. Bears, elk, wolves, lynx, and otters are further examples of the rare mammals found here, and there are also more than 250 species of bird, including the black stork.

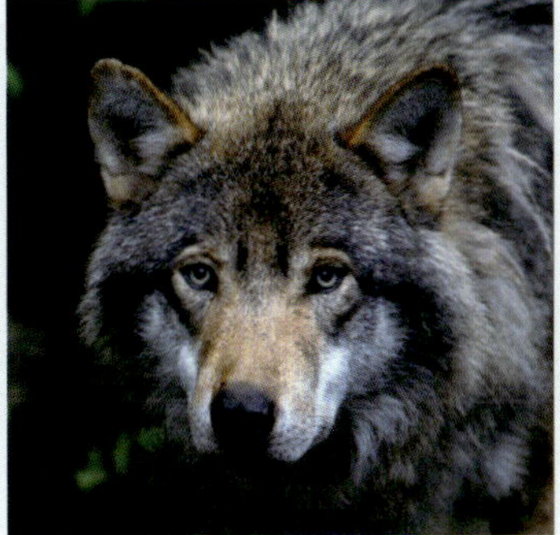

Europe's last significant wild bison population lives in the Belovezhskaya Pushcha Park, on the Polish-Byelorussian border (below). The park's vast mixed forests are also home to wolves and sea eagles (left and far left).

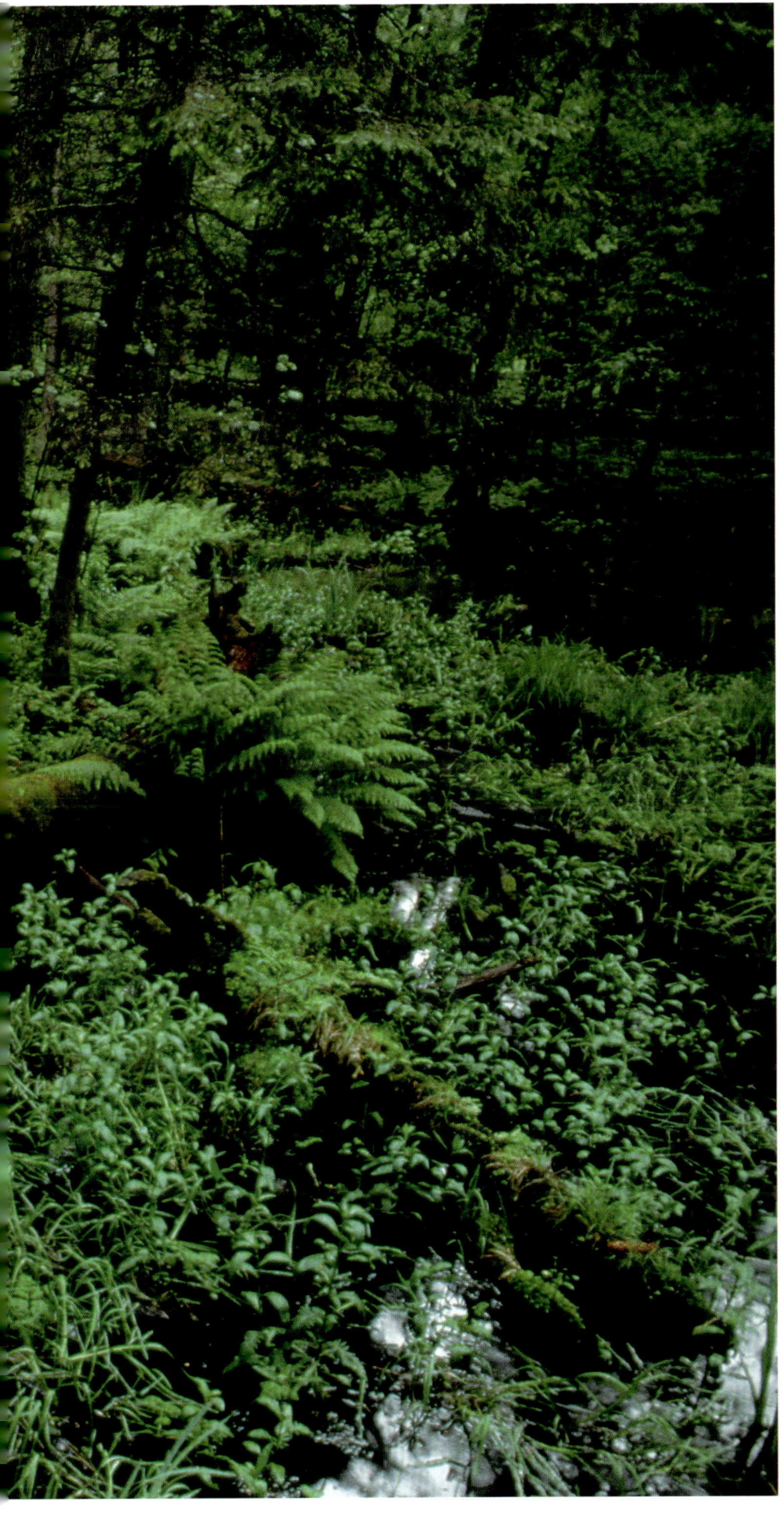

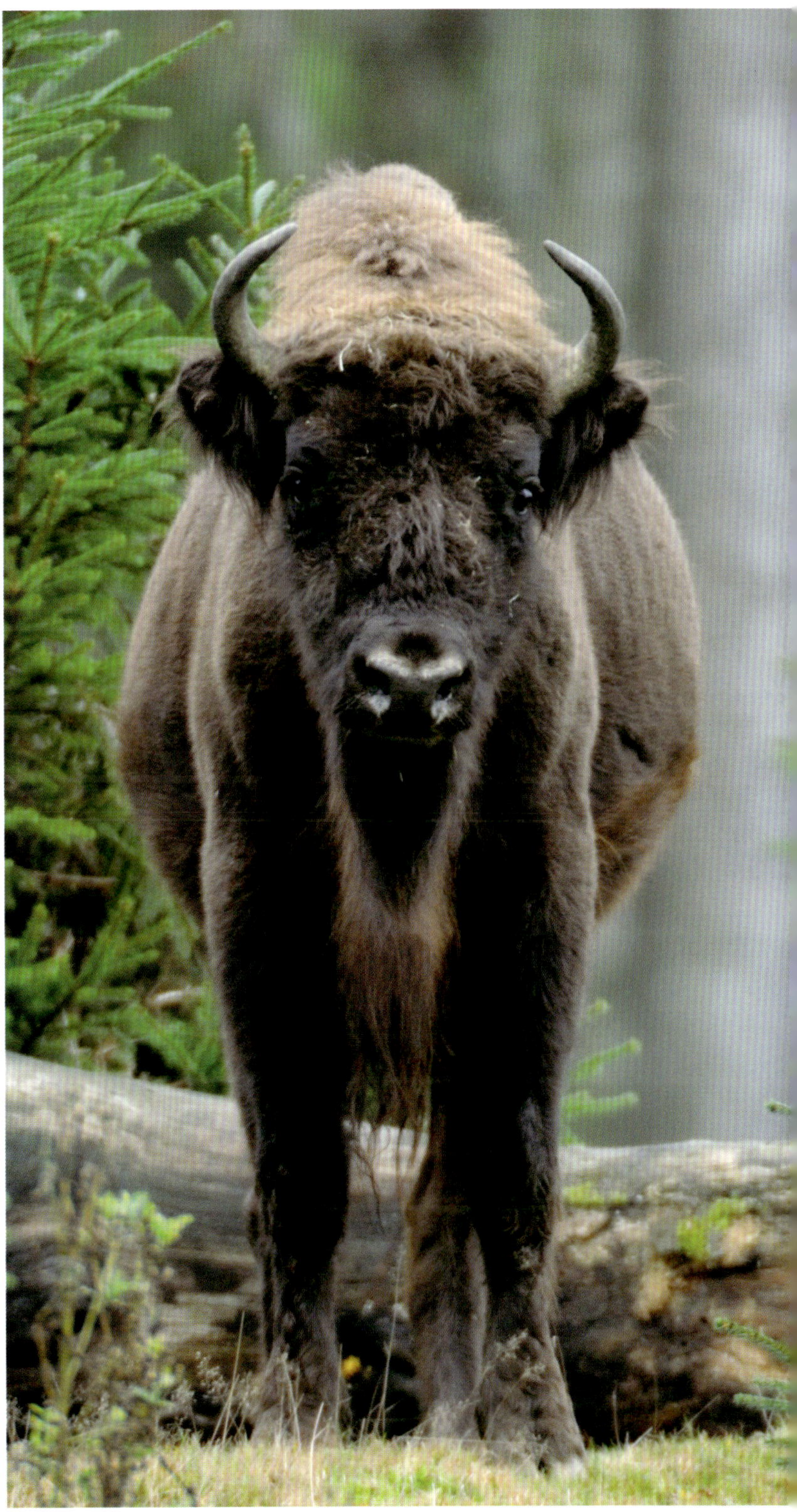

PRIMEVAL BEECH FORESTS OF THE CARPATHIANS

Date of inscription: 2007
Extended: 2011

The most beautiful beech forests in Europe, and the least impacted by humans, are located in the border region between Slovakia and the Ukraine. A total of ten protected areas on the southern slopes of the Carpathian forests make up this World Heritage site. In 2011, the site was extended to include the German beech forest regions.

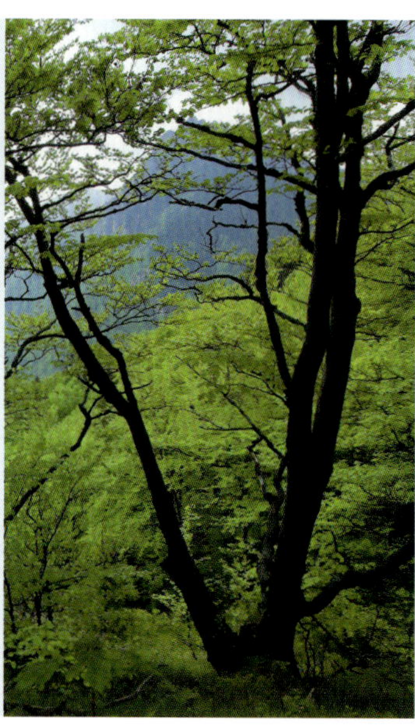

Central Europe was once mostly covered by deciduous and mixed deciduous forest, with the beech tree playing a pivotal role. Beech is able to adapt to very different environmental conditions and has a unique strategy for survival: it constantly increases its spread, displacing other species in the process. Unlike other tree species, the beech does not allow succession – that is, no sequential occurrence of different habitats in one place –, but remains in the same place over countless generations. Unspoiled beech forests therefore often have the appearance of monocultures: forests with tall beeches and very few other woody species. The Carpathians are an ancient refuge of the beech and, besides the Dinaric Alps, the only region of Europe where the beech has survived since the Ice Age. The protected site includes ten areas, which extend along a 200-km (124-mile) axis from the Rakhiv and Chornohora massifs in Ukraine via the Polonina ridge to the Bieszczady Mountains and the Vihorlat Mountains in Slovakia.

The fomes fomentarius, or tinder fungus (large picture), is a type of fungus whose habitat are mostly weak or dead trees – especially beech.

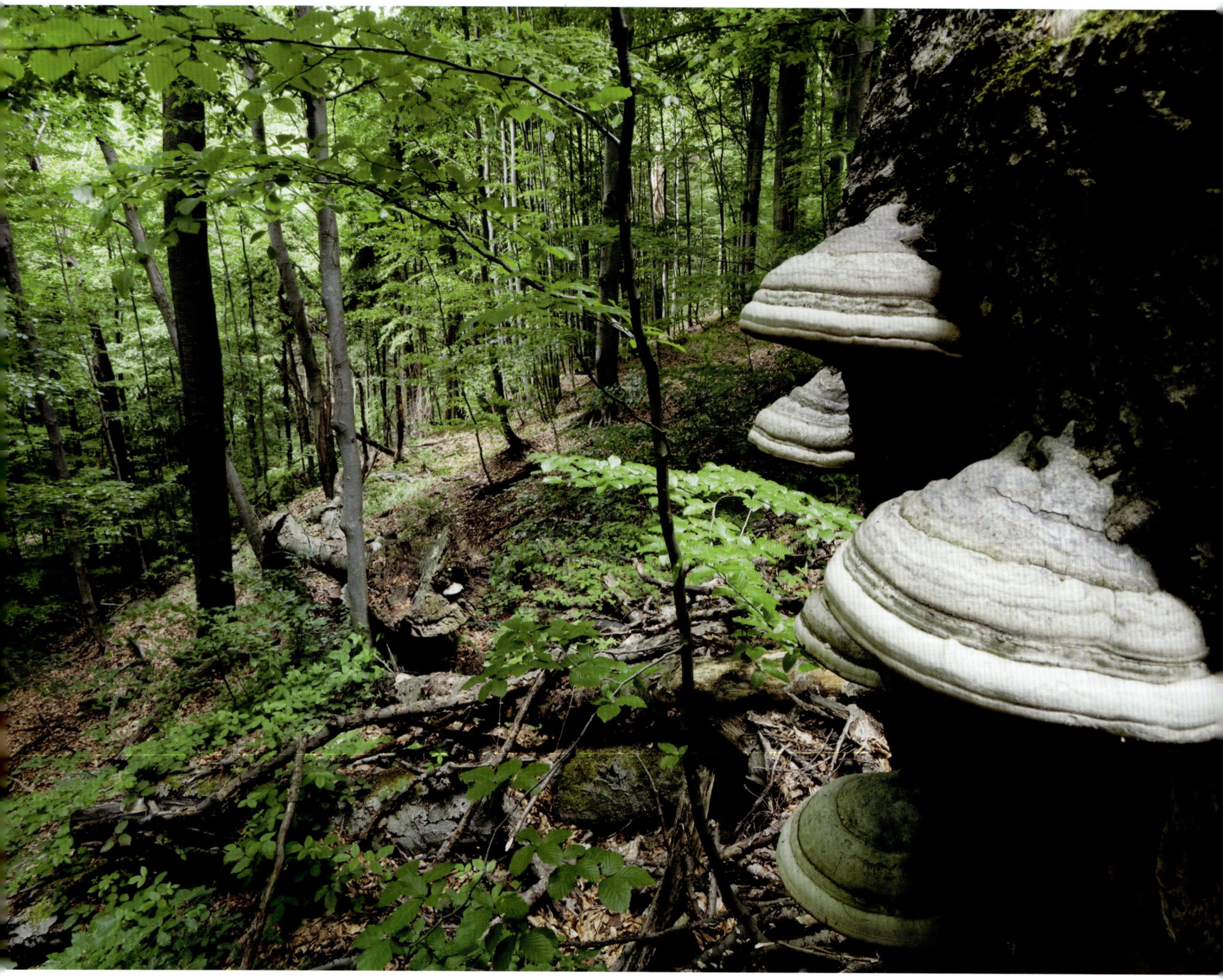

CAVES OF AGGTELEK KARST AND SLOVAK KARST

About 600 m (1,970 feet) above sea level, Aggtelek National Park is located in the karst region of the low mountain ranges of northern Hungary. The mountains reach into Slovakia, and the World Heritage Site takes in parts of both countries. Alongside the extensive cave network, it also boasts many rare plants and animals.

The many caves go down several hundred meters below ground, and can be accessed via several entrances. Joining a guided tour really makes the caves' geology tangible. The highlight of the tour is the huge Baradla Cave – an incredible landscape of stalactites and stalagmites. In some of the other chambers, meanwhile, fossils and evidence of the caves' Paleolithic inhabitants have been found. In 1965, the Béke Cave – the second biggest in the Aggtelek karst – was officially declared a "healing cave." Its atmosphere is particularly beneficial for asthma sufferers, and it is also used as a concert hall.

The network of dripstone caves in the Hungarian part of the Aggtelek karst region is 17 km (11 miles) long. Visitors are rewarded with the sight of a fascinating world of limestone columns, stalactites and stalagmites, streams, rock halls, and artificial lakes.

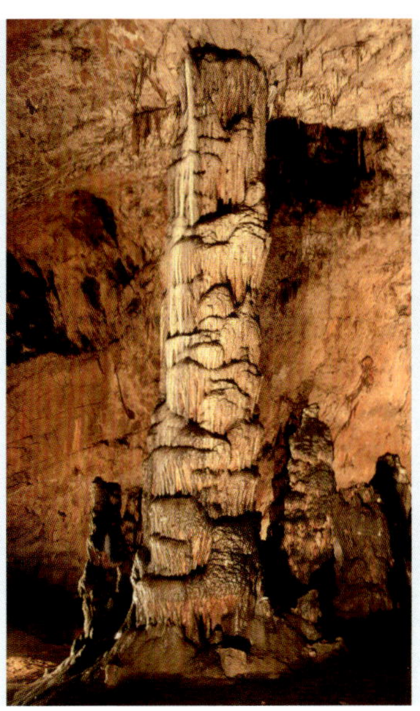

Date of inscription: 1995
Extended: 2000

The Hungarian karst region lies in the foothills of the Slovakian Erz mountains. The area's many hundreds of caves, with their striking stalactites and stalagmites, are spread across both sides of the border.

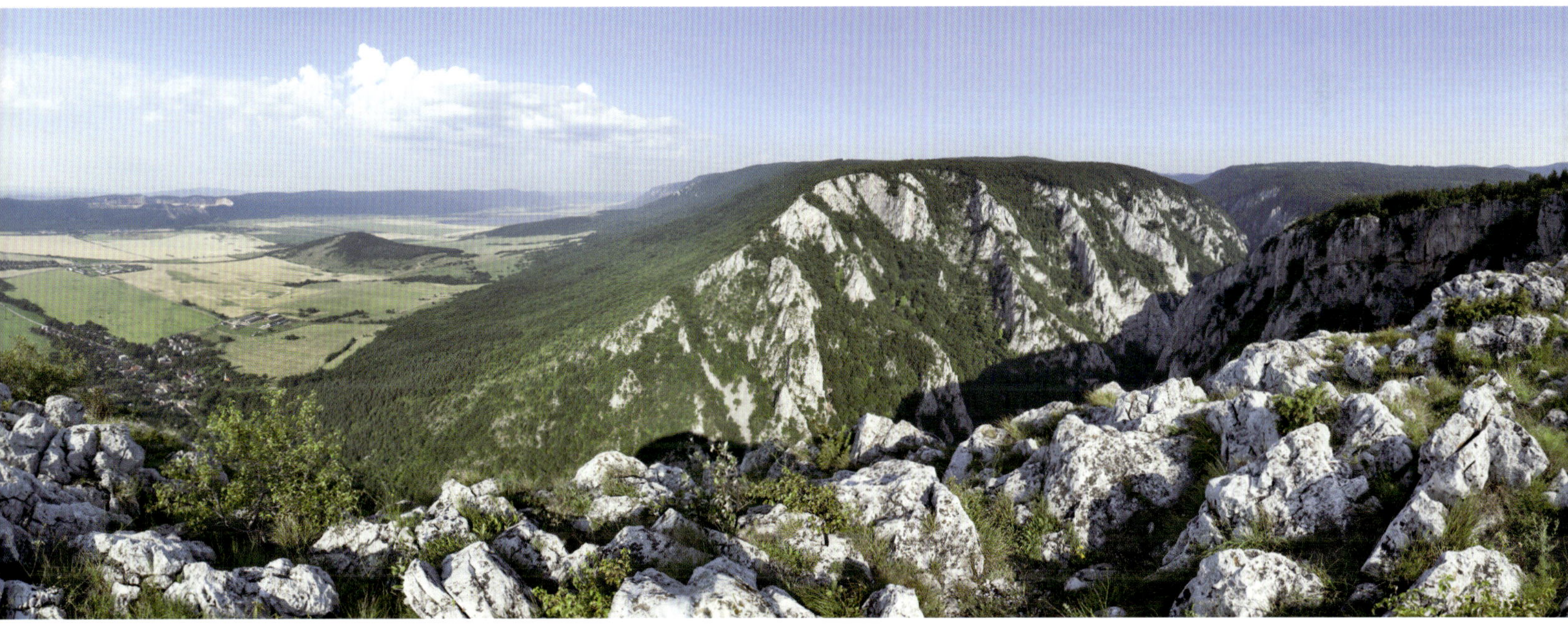

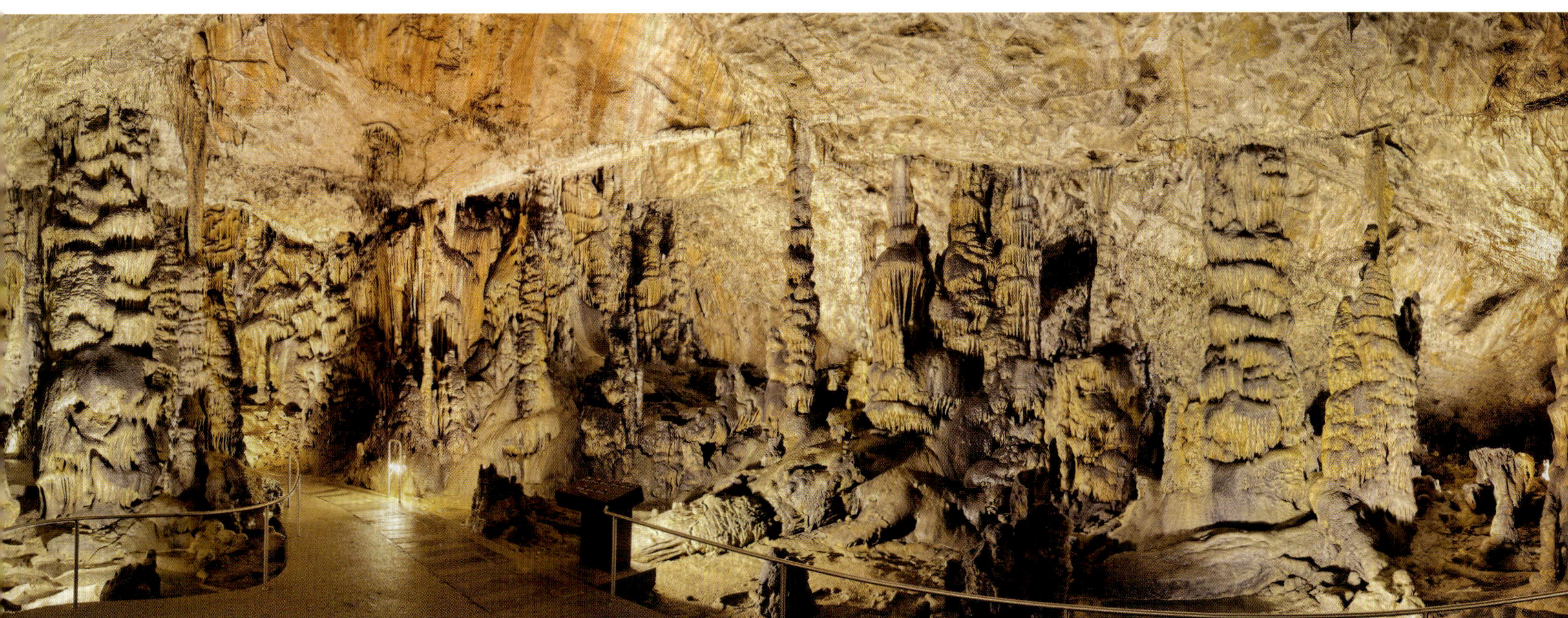

VIRGIN KOMI FORESTS

Date of inscription: 1995

On the edge of north-east Europe, the Virgin Komi Forests are one of the last remaining areas of boreal vegetation. These vast woodlands are dominated by conifers, aspen, and birch.

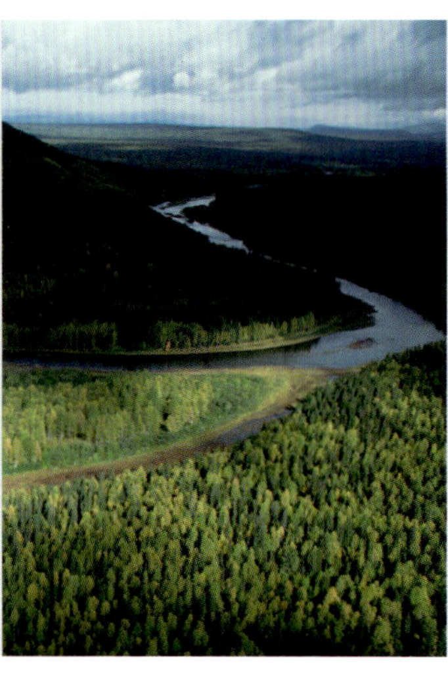

The area protected by world natural heritage status covers 32,800 sq. km (12,660 sq. miles) of Russia's Komi Republic. Large parts of the forests have barely been touched by humans, and are therefore an extremely valuable resource for natural historians. The protected area stretches from the endless plains of the Taiga, before rising high into the Ural mountains. It comprises the Pechora-Ilych Nature Reserve and biosphere reserve, which was founded as early as 1930 and is only accessible to scientists, as well as the Yugyd Va National Park, which was created in 1994 and is freely accessible, aside from a few protected zones. Its landscape takes in rivers, moors, and hundreds of lakes, alongside alpine and subalpine pastures, which melt into the tundra. The forests are home to a wide variety of both European and Asian animal species, notably bears, wolves, polar foxes, deer, reindeer, elk, beavers, otters, and squirrels.

At a height of 1,820 m (5,971 foot), Manaraga Peak (large pictures) is the tallest mountain in the Urals. The Pechora River Valley (left) is home to numerous birds.

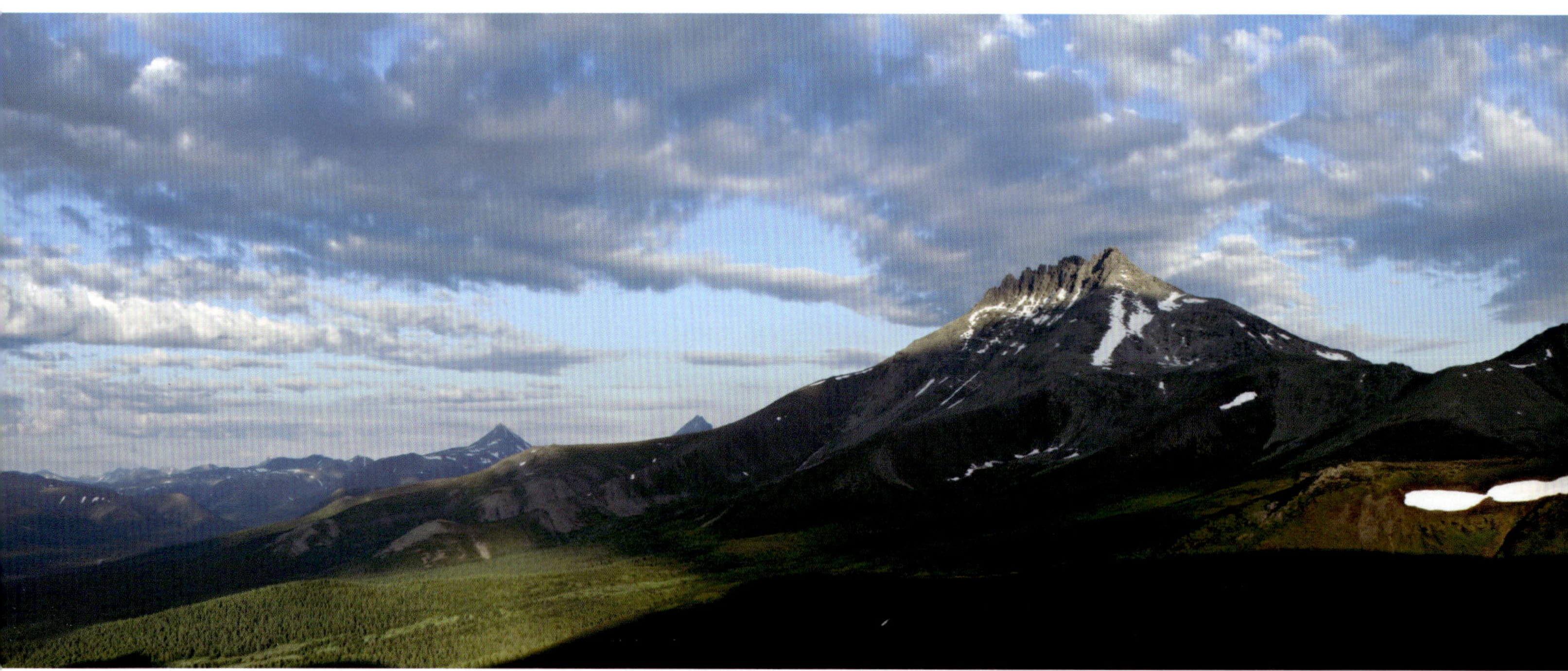

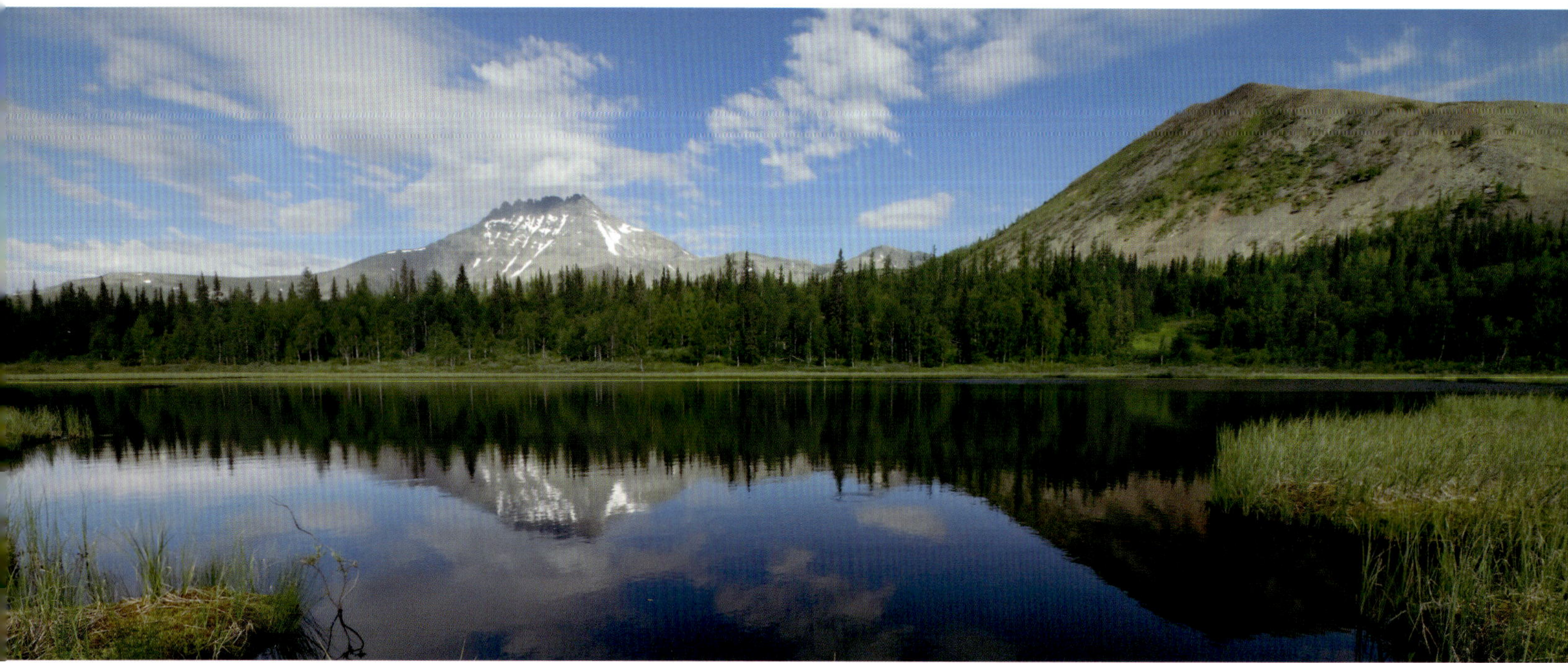

WESTERN CAUCASUS

The western Caucasus lies about 50 km (30 miles) from the Black Sea coast, and covers an area of nearly 3,000 sq. km (1,200 sq. miles). It stretches some 130 km (80 miles) from west to east, and some 50 km (30 miles) from north to south. The core of the natural heritage site is made up of large areas of the Caucasus biosphere reserve and its buffer zone, alongside the Sochi National Park and several smaller nature reserves. The landscape ranges from lowland areas to the pastures and forests of the site's subalpine zones, and on into its mountainous regions, whose highest peaks reach altitudes of over 3,000 m (9,800 feet). The site is home to numerous endemic and threatened plant and animal species.

The western Caucasus is home to a wide range of animal life, including around 60 mammals and 250 bird species. Many – like the Eurasian eagle owl (right) and West Caucasian ibex – are endemic to the area.

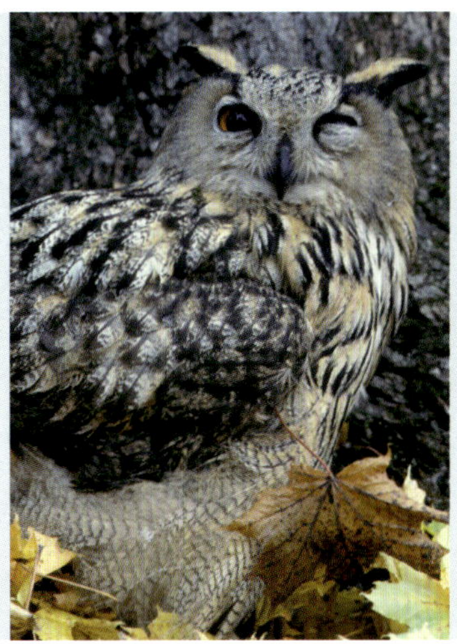

Date of inscription: 1999

On the border of Europe and Asia, the western Caucasus encompasses a multitude of ecosystems that have so far been spared large-scale human intervention.

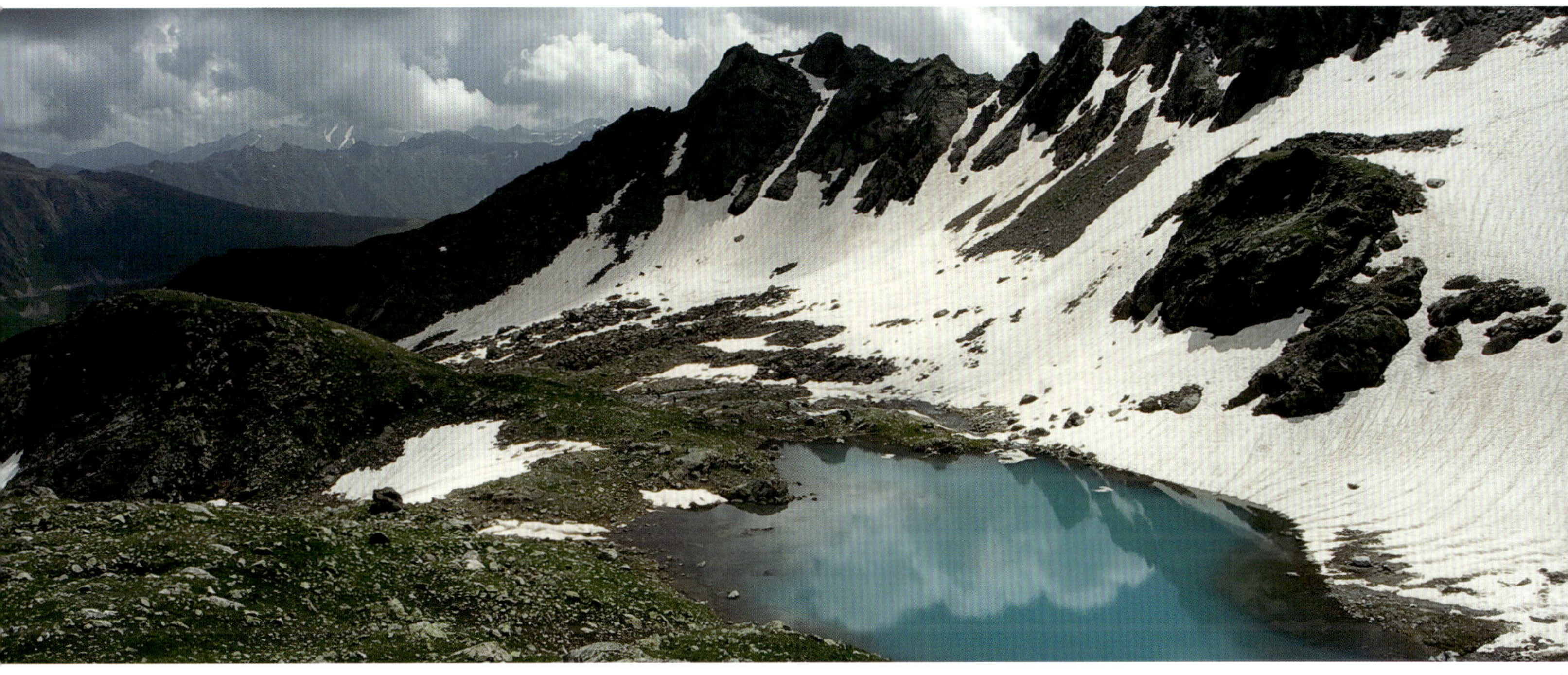

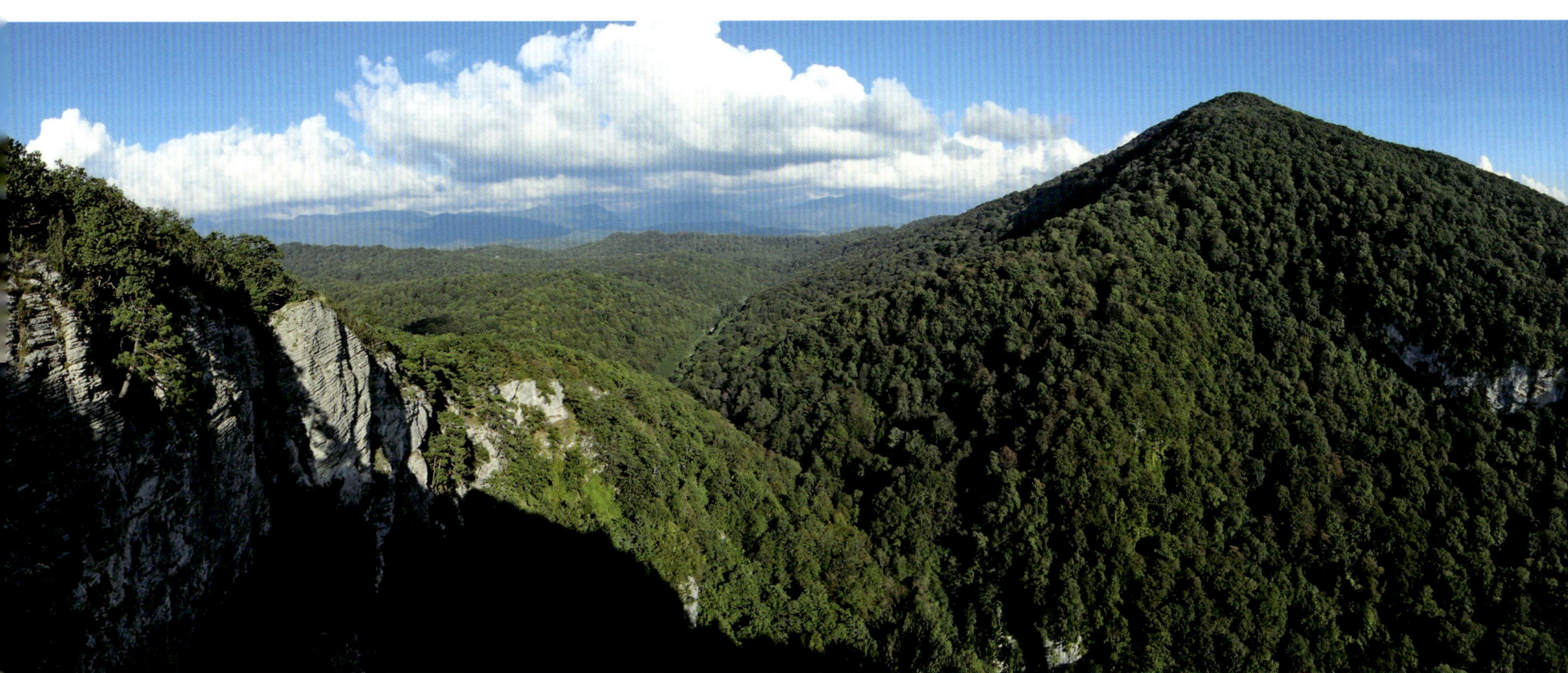

PYRÉNÉES: MONTE PERDIDO (MONT PERDU)

Date of inscription: 1997
Extended: 1999

The Pyrenees mountain landscape around Mont Perdu (or Monte Perdido) either side of the Franco–Spanish border features impressive geological formations and grants a glimpse into the traditional way of life of its inhabitants.

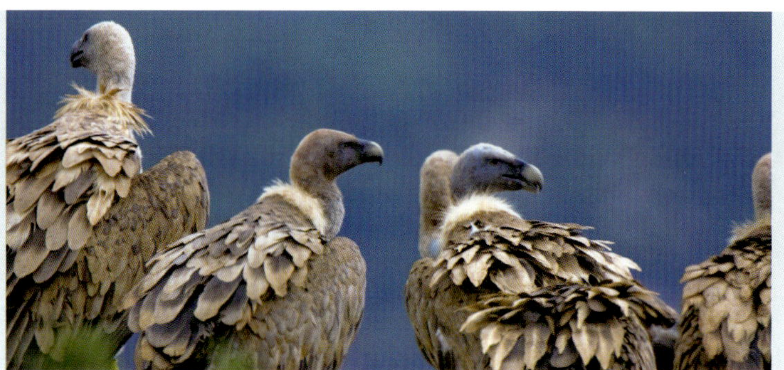

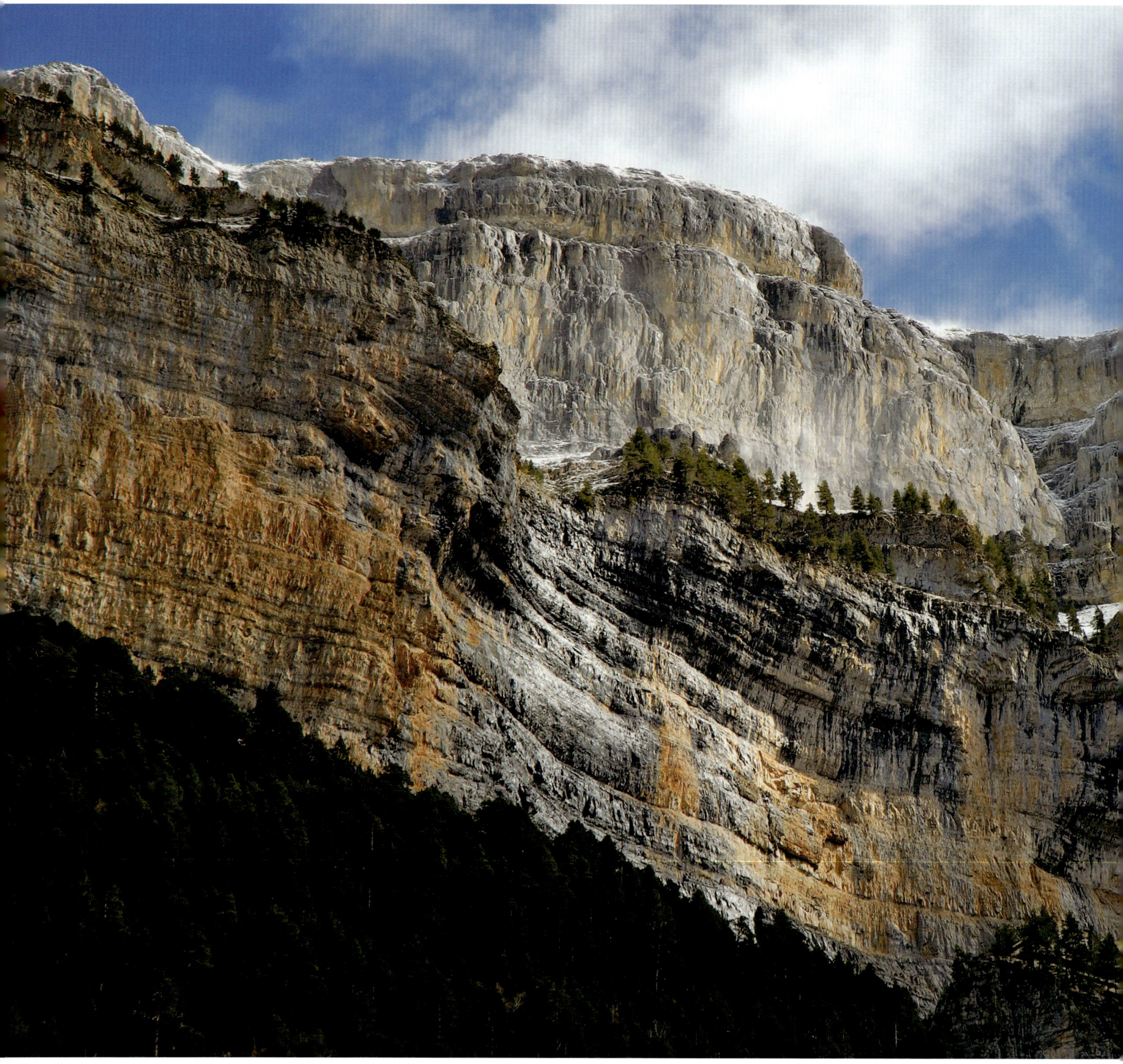

The trans-boundary protected area encompasses a breathtakingly beautiful landscape. On the Spanish side it includes two of Europe's deepest gorges. On the French side, where the slopes are even steeper, three U-shaped cirques were ground out by glacier movements; they are among the most impressive examples of this geological formation in Europe. Perhaps the strongest impression created by the imposing mountainscape, however, is its serene and untouched tranquillity. UNESCO honoured its geological uniqueness and beauty and the diversity if its nature, as well as traditional ways of life that have become rare in Europe, such as alpine dairy farming, and the extraordinary role played by the Pyrenees in the art and culture of Europe. Thus, this fascinating cultivated landscape is today still a largely undisturbed idyll. And this is how it earned an inscription not only as Natural but also Cultural Heritage site.

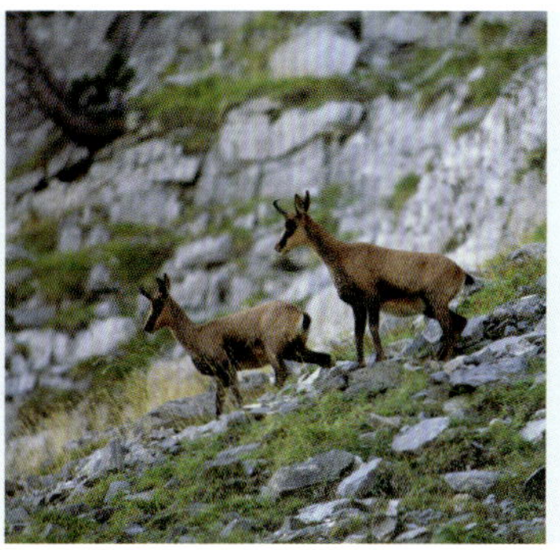

Although related to the chamois, the Pyrenean chamois (left) is a separate species that lives mainly in the French, Spanish and Central Italian mountain regions. Griffon vultures are also at home in the national park (far left).

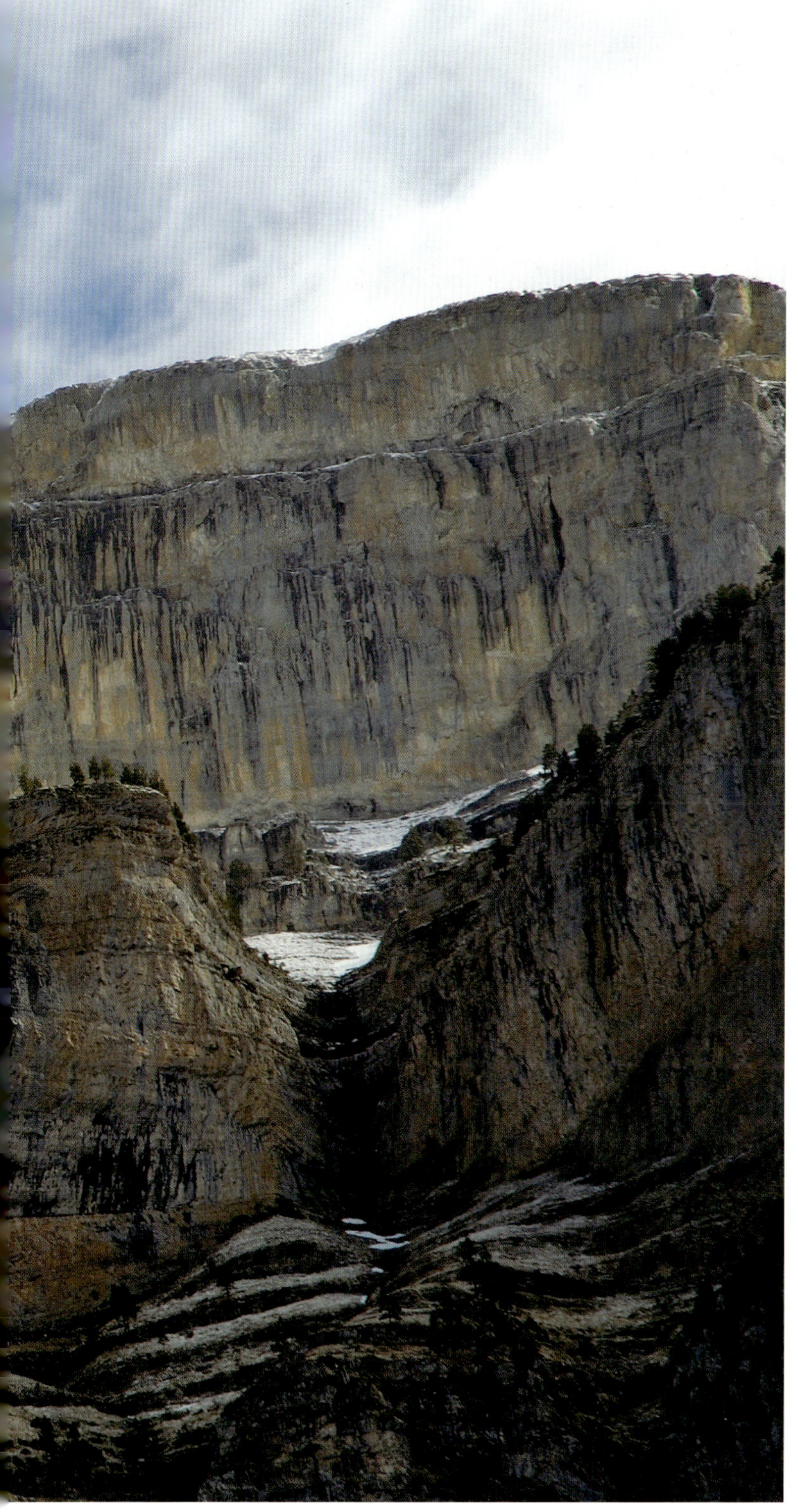

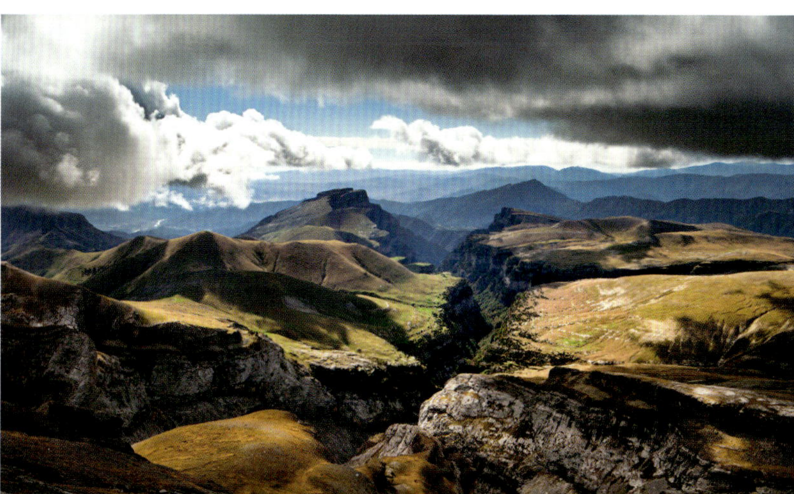

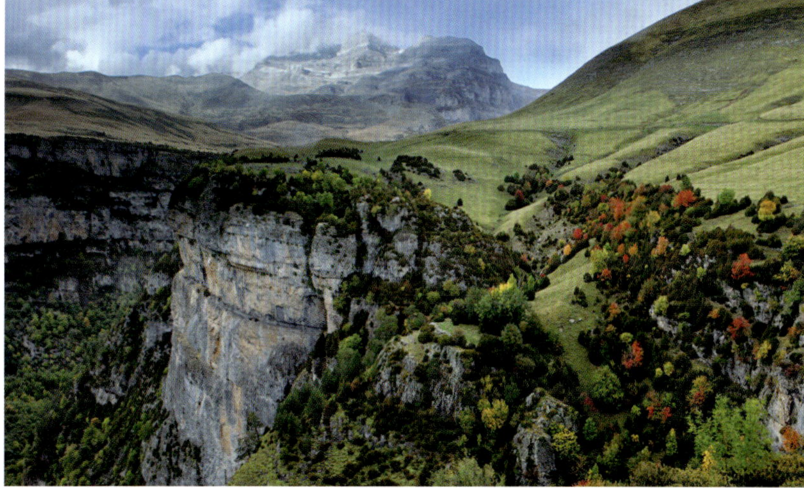

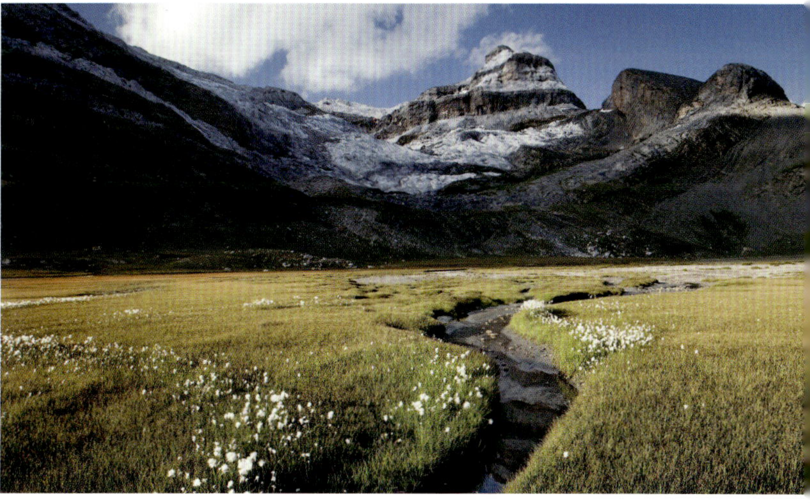

DOÑANA NATIONAL PARK

Date of inscription: 1994

Doñana National Park in Andalucia is Spain's biggest national park. Once a royal hunting ground, these extensive wetlands at the delta of the Guadalquivir river are now an important stop for many migratory birds on the journey to Africa.

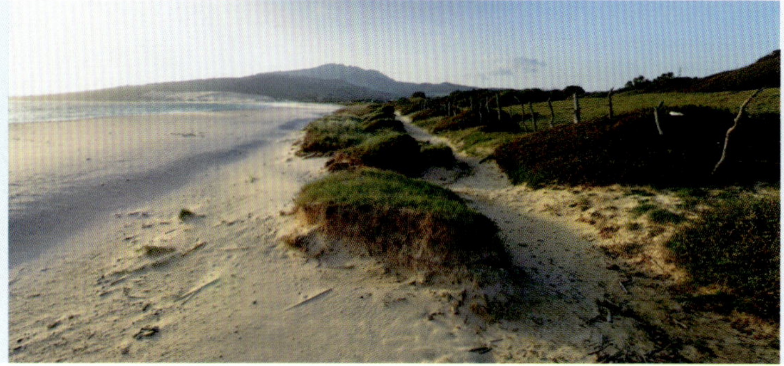

Following its extension, the Doñana National Park – also known as Coto de Doñana – covers an area of some 540 sq. km (210 sq. miles). It is the diversity of its landscape that makes it so special. Alongside large expanses of marshland complete with lagoons and boggy areas, the park also features dry areas whose character is more akin to a heath or savannah. Here, 40-m (131-

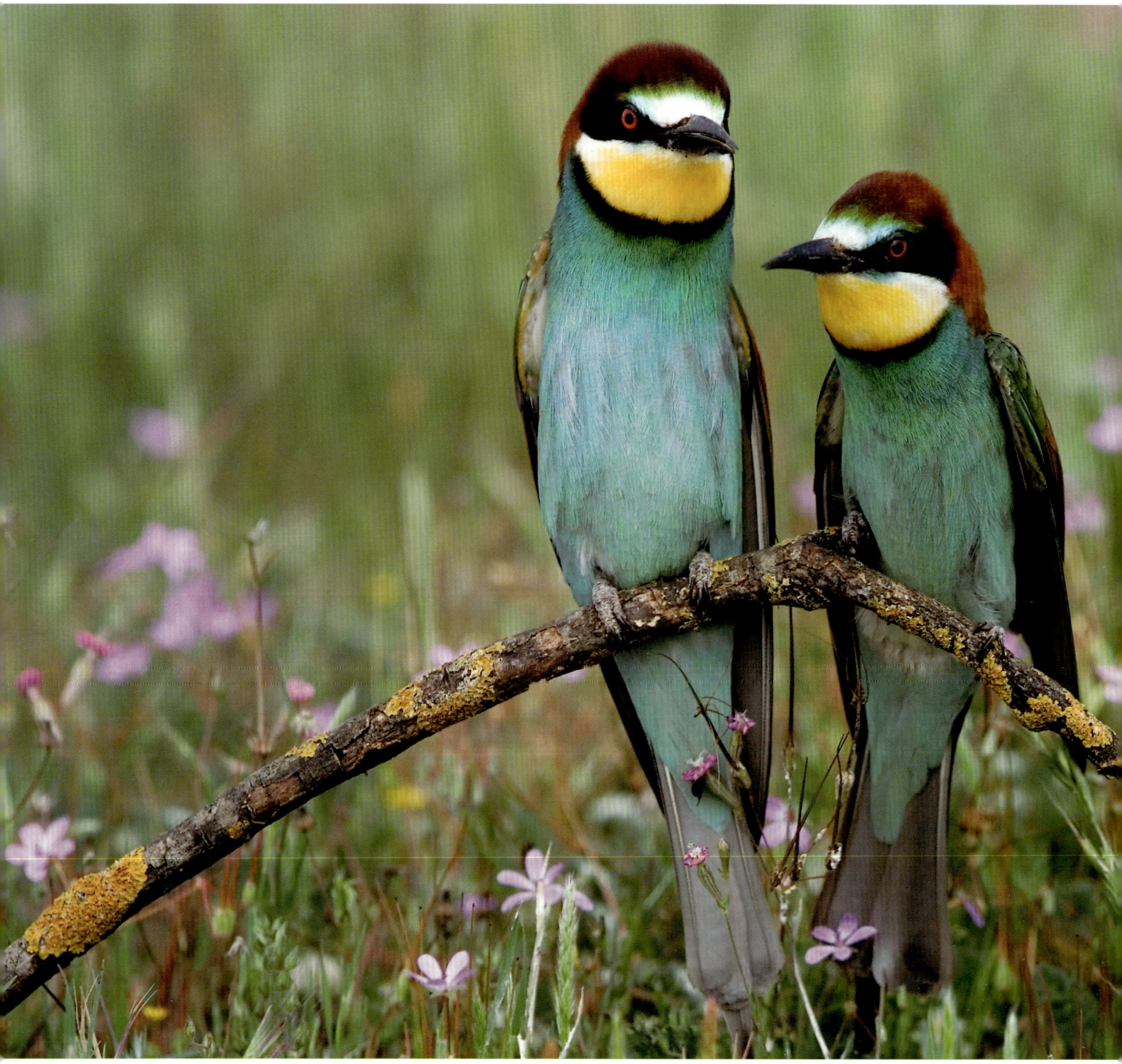

foot) sand dunes give way to bushy Mediterranean vegetation that includes rare plants like white thyme. There are also forests of cork oak, umbrella pine, and stone pine trees. The wetlands, meanwhile, provide a nesting place for numerous species of bird. The area's large flamingo population is particularly noteworthy, but grey herons, storks, and cranes also come here to nest. The lagoons within the protected area attract wild boar and red deer. Other animals found in the national park include the Iberian lynx – which is now entirely absent from the rest of Spain – and the all-but-extinct imperial eagle. The Montpellier snake, white spoonbill, ichneumon (a type of mongoose), and monk vulture are equally rare.

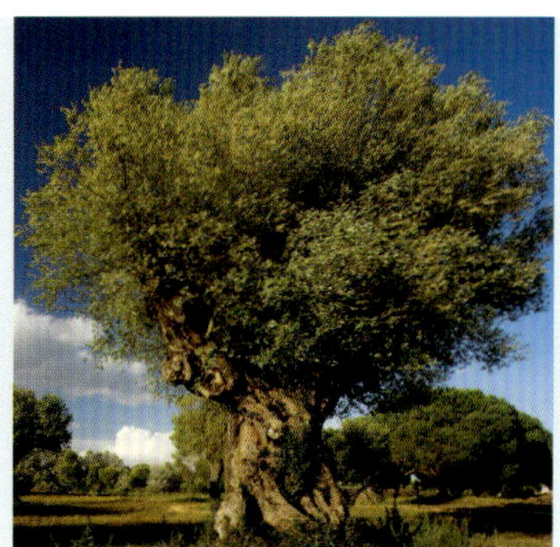

A paradise for animals: bee-eaters (large picture), as well as red deer, Iberian lynx, sandpiper and pied avocet (picture series from the top) all find ideal living conditions and a protected habitat here.

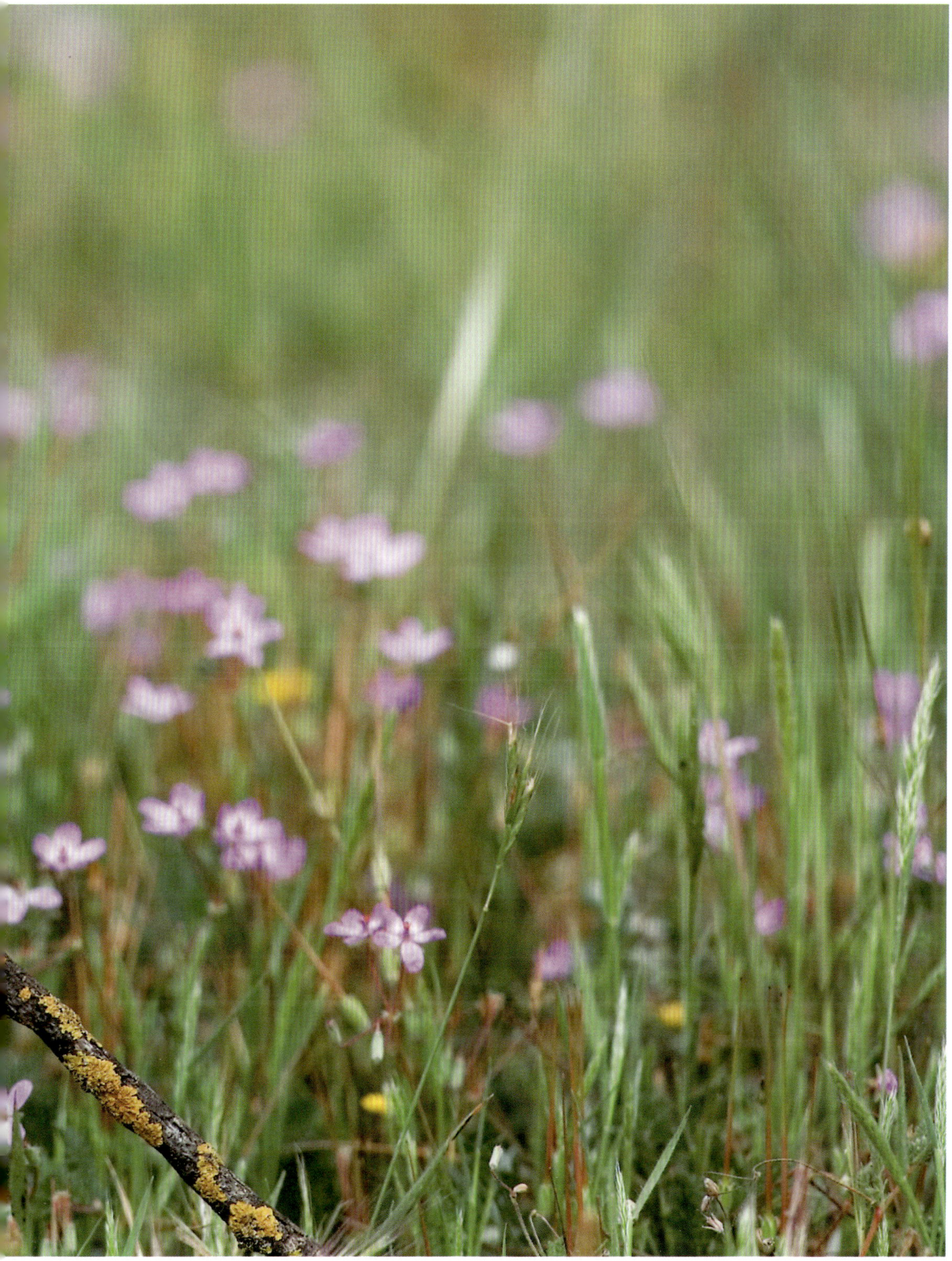

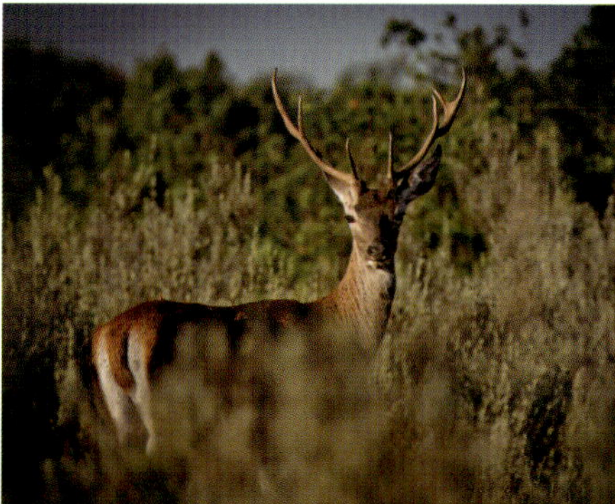

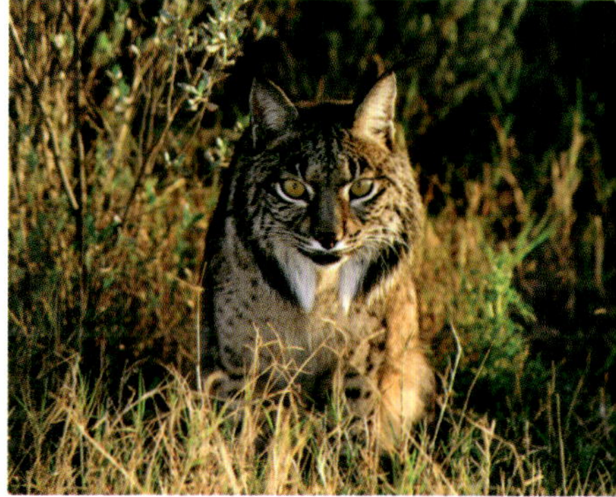

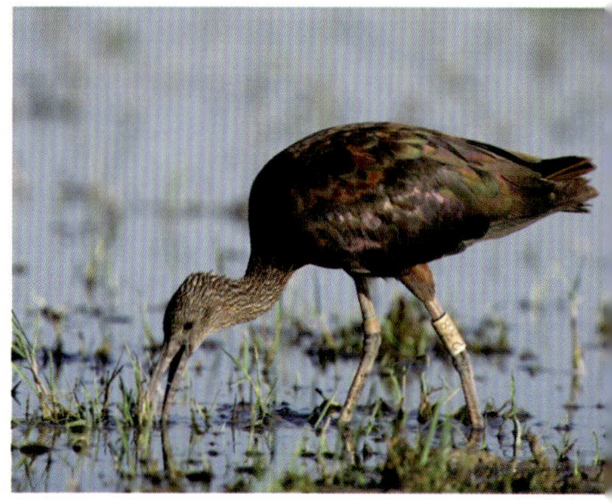

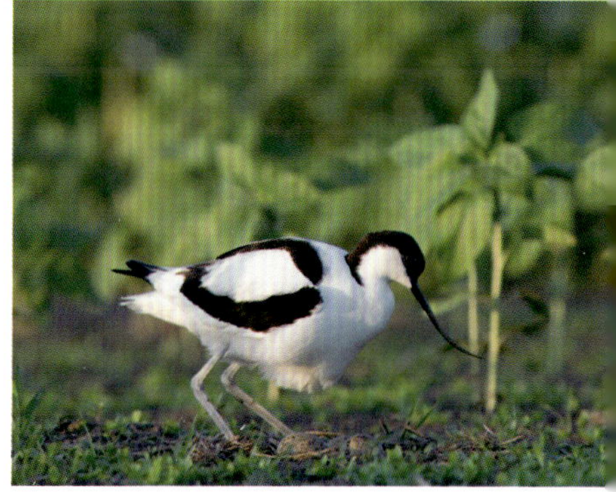

THE BIODIVERSITY AND CULTURE OF IBIZA

Date of insription: 1999

Its claim to world natural heritage status is founded upon posidonia, a grassy marine weed that plays an important role in the ecosystem. The island's significant architecture and archeological sites, meanwhile, confirm its cultural importance.

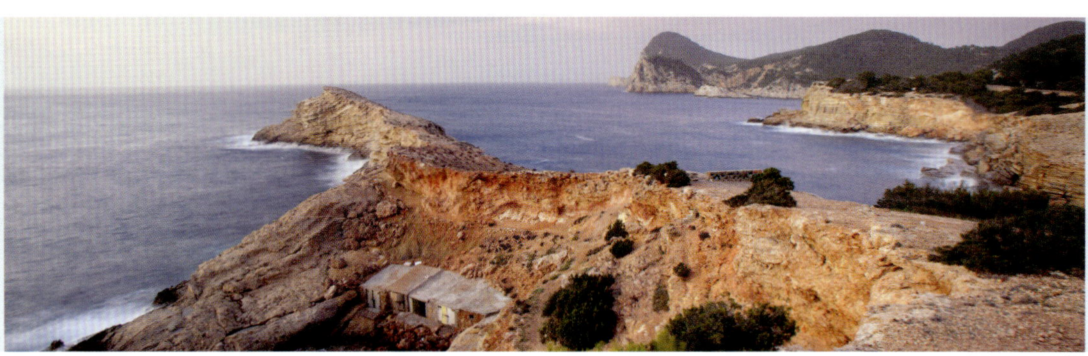

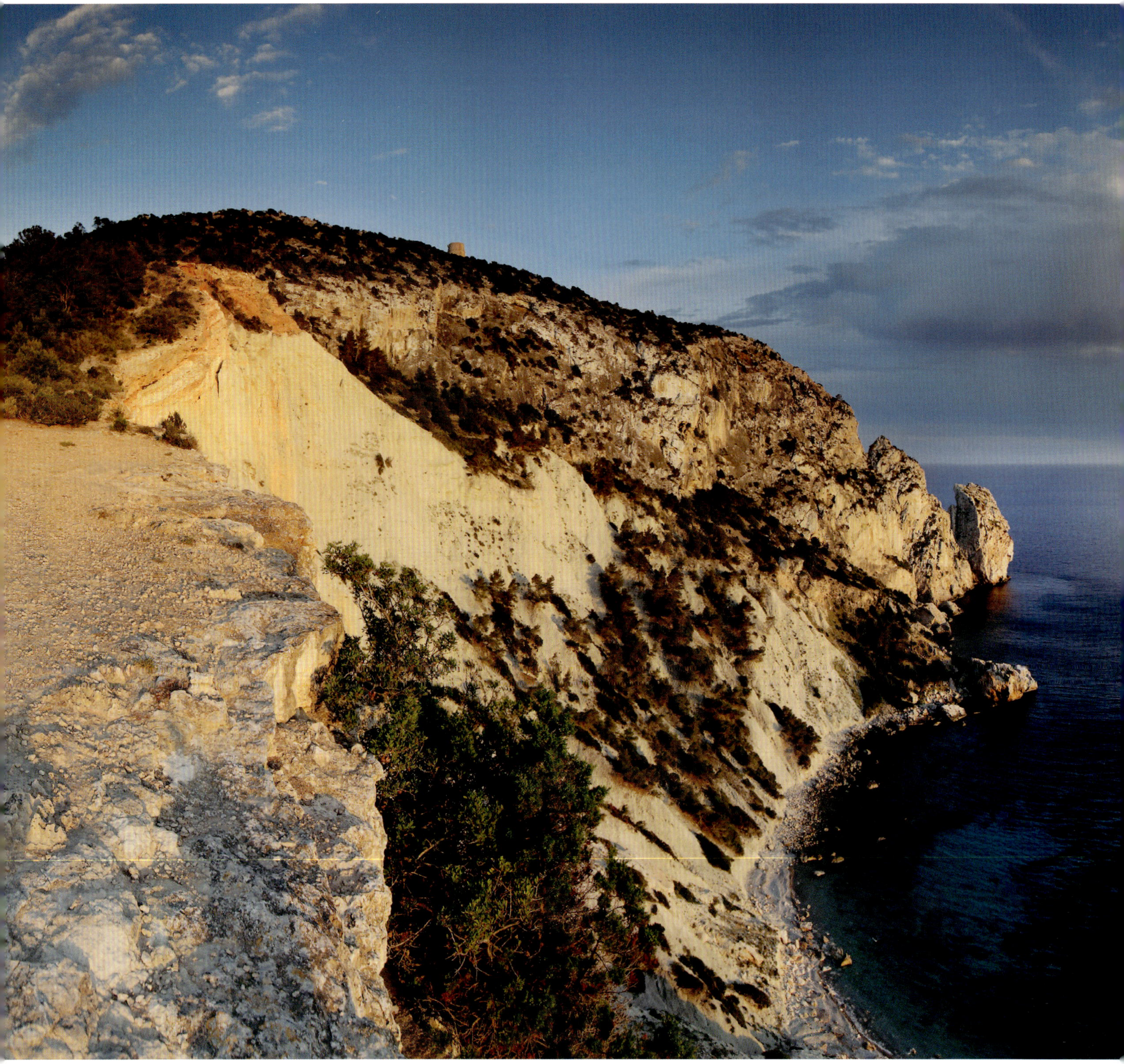

Like nearby Formentera, Ibiza belongs to the Balearic archipelago. Together, the two islands are also known as the Pityuses (or Pine Islands) – a name whose roots go back to the Greeks.
Ibiza's long history can be traced back to the 2nd millennium bc, and significant evidence of island life at this time has been preserved. Two archaeological excavations in particular – the Phoenician Sa Caleta settlement (700 bc) in the south-west of the island and the Punic necropolis Puig des Molins (5th century bc) – underline Ibiza's significance during the Phoenician-Carthaginian era. It was the Phoenicians who, some 2,600 years ago, founded the fortified upper town ("Dalt Vila") of Ibiza Old Town. Occupied without interruption ever since, it is one of the oldest towns in Europe. Posidonia is a bit like a sea grass. It is only found in the Mediterranean, but even here is increasingly under threat. The posidonia off the coast of Ibiza provides shelter for a wide variety of marine life, in particular protecting the coastal waters and coral reefs from storms. In fact, 1 hectare (2.5 acres) of posidonia produces 21 metric tons of organic substances every year.

Punta de sa Galera in Sant Antoni de Portmany (left). Below: The uninhabited islets of Es Vedrà and Es Vedranell, located offshore from Ibiza, are home to a nature reserve.

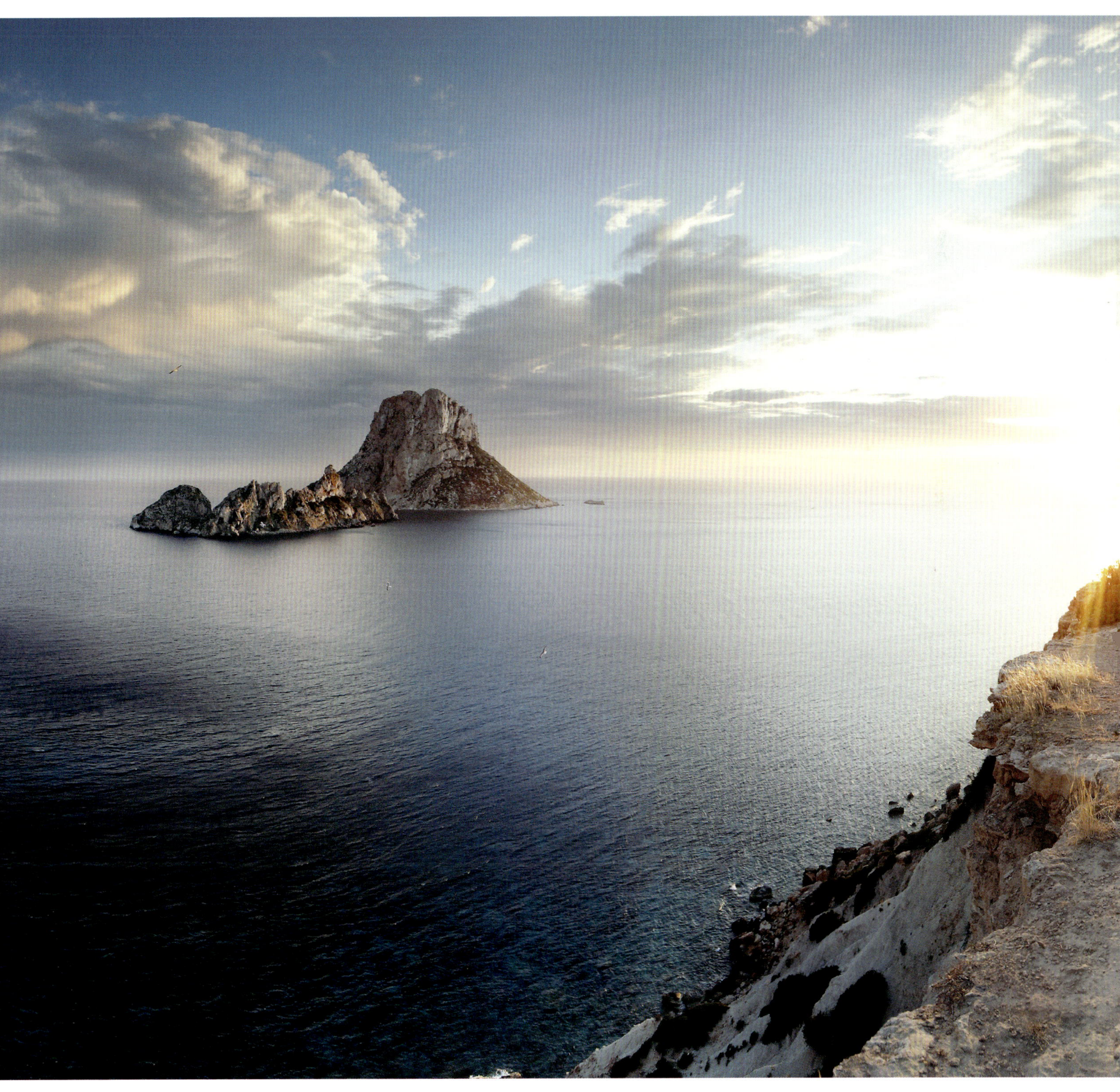

TEIDE NATIONAL PARK, TENERIFE

Date of inscription: 2007

The natural heritage site takes in the fascinating volcanic landscape of the 3,718-m (12,198-foot) high Pico del Teide – Spain's highest mountain – along with the area's characteristic flora and fauna.

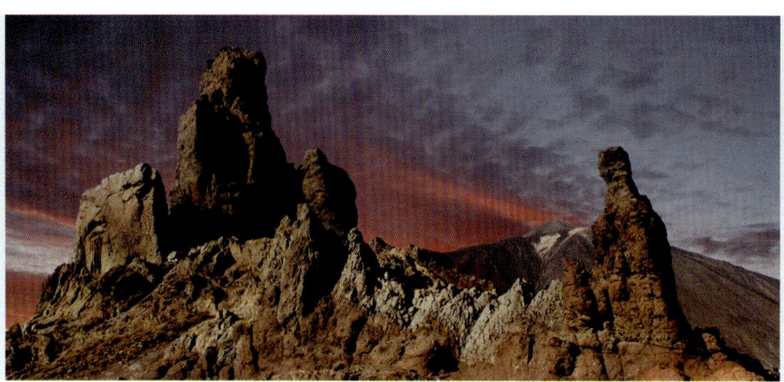

Most of the national park is an inhospitable, volcanic landscape, dominated by the Pico and its caldera, whose diameter measures some 17 km (11 miles). The ever-changing climate and frequent mists lend the scenery a very special atmosphere.

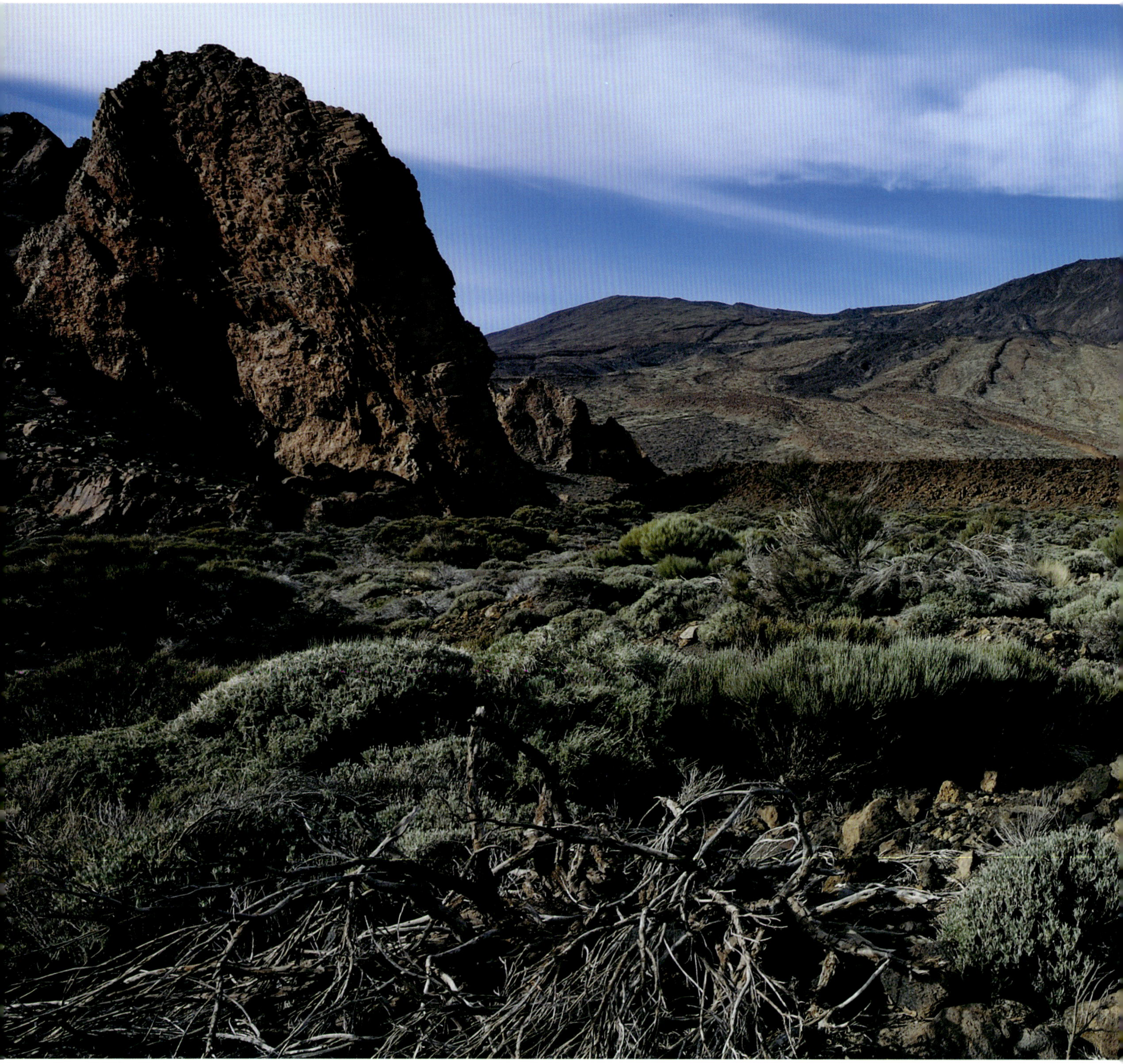

The Teide is too barren an environment to support a really diverse vertebrate life, but it is home to three endemic species. One of them, the blue-throated lizard (Gallotia galloti), has come to symbolize the park. The Teide blue chaffinch, at home in pine forests, is also found in the park. The Teide's rich insect life, meanwhile, encompasses 700 different species, most of them endemic to the Canaries. The area's flowering plants have adapted to the climate by adopting a cushion-like form, reducing the surface area of their leaves, and growing waxy coatings and thick coverings of hair – all of which help to reduce water loss through transpiration. There are 168 different types of flowering plants in the park, 58 of which are endemic. Among the most striking plants is the viper's bugloss, which belongs to the boraginaceous family. The pyramid-shaped inflorescence of the red-flowered Echium wildpretii can grow as tall as 3 m (10 feet). The park's dominant plant, however, is the Teide broom (Spartocytisus supranubius), whose white or pink flowers produce a very special honey. The bushes of Teide marguerite (Argyranthemum teneriffae), meanwhile, lend the park a unique character.

Towering above the clouds, the 3,718-m (12,198-foot) high Pico del Teide rises up out of a caldera (above) that was probably created by a powerful landslide.

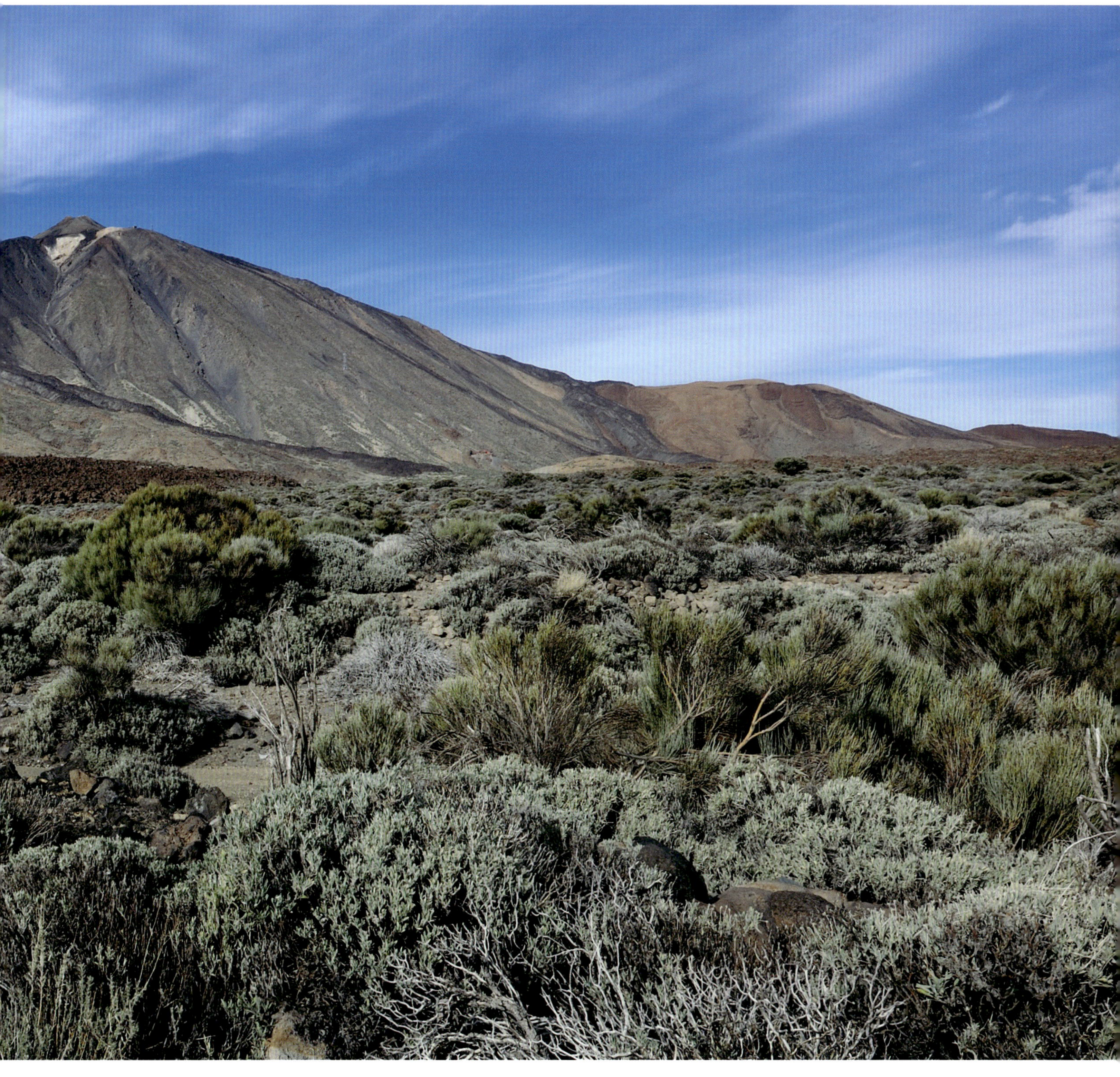

GARAJONAY NATIONAL PARK

Date of inscription: 1986

The volcanic mountains of Gomera, Canary Islands, reach altitudes of up to 1,487 m (4,879 feet). The trees that cover them form Europe's last remaining subtropical primeval forest.

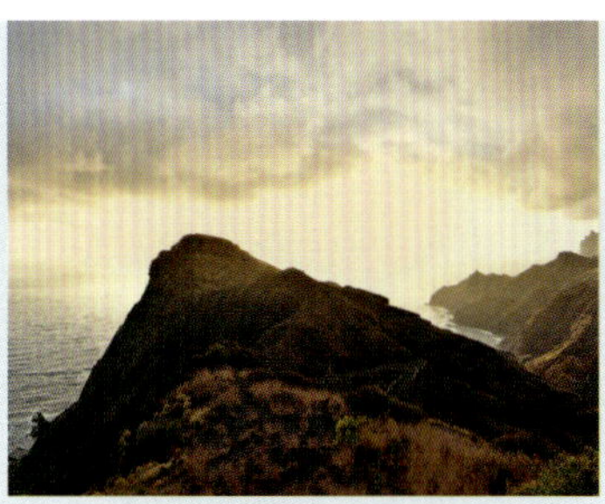

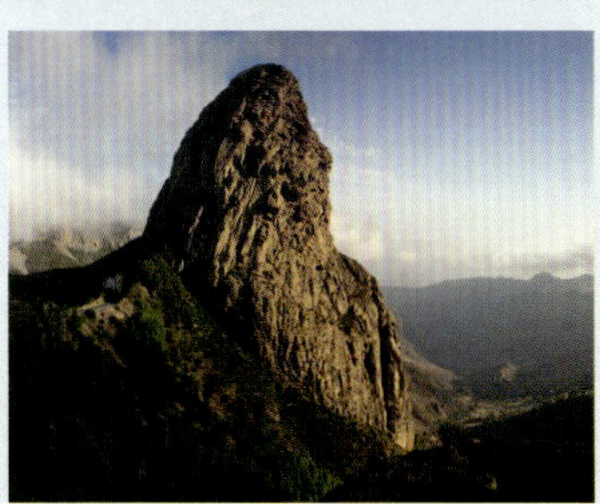

Occupying an area of almost 40 sq. km (15 sq. miles), Garajonay National Park covers almost a tenth of the island of Gomera and crosses all six of its administrative regions. The park's unique ecosystem has earned it the status of a World Natural Heritage Site under UNESCO protection. Thick forest covers the slopes of the Alto de Garajonay, the island's highest mountain. It is the last remaining subtropical primeval forest in southern Europe, including the world's only closed laurel forest dating back to the Tertiary period.

Millions of years old, the forest's position in the middle of the ocean enabled it to survive the deteriorating climatic conditions that developed during the ice age. Many of the park's plants and animals are only found here. Half a million people visit the national park every year. Some join guided tours, while others explore the designated walking trails independently.

In the Garajonay National Park on the island of Gomera, the mist almost always reaches the floor of the laurel forests, creating what is often termed horizontal rain. This ancient ecosystem allows visitors to get a good idea of how forests might have looked some 65 million years ago.

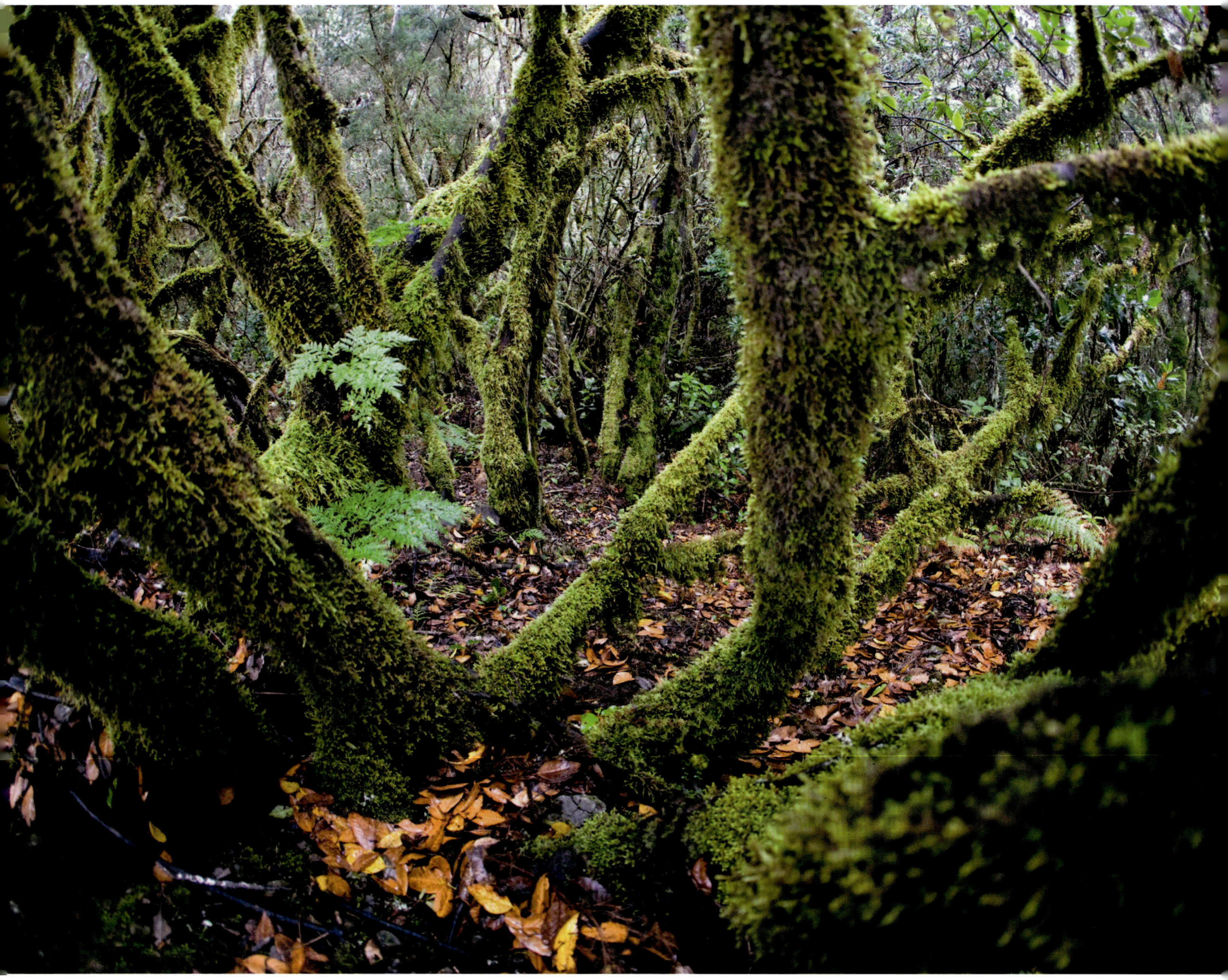

THE LAURISILVA LAUREL FOREST OF MADEIRA

The Madeiran laurel forests lie between 600 and 1,300 m (1,970 and 4,270 feet) above sea level. Along with the forests of the Garajonay National Park on Gomera, Canary Islands, they are all that is left of the extensive laurel forests once found throughout the Mediterranean. The key historical forces behind the decimation of the laurel forests were what is known as slash-and-burn agriculture and deforestation, which became a widespread method of creating new arable land and collecting firewood from the 15th century onward. Along with overgrazing and forest fires, the introduction of new plants from distant regions has further contributed to the ever-increasing threats to the forest. The result is that the forests on the steep north coast slopes of Madeira are almost all that remains of the original laurel forests. Here, the forest plays an important part in the provision of the island's water. The tree leaves "collect" water from the clouds, and this water is then retained in the understorey before finally being stored in the rocks. The laurel forests also help to significantly reduce soil erosion.

The forest covers an area of 22 hectares (54 acres), comprising species as diverse as the Madeira laurel, stinkwood laurel, and Canary Island laurel. Right: the majestic candelabra or krantz aloe.

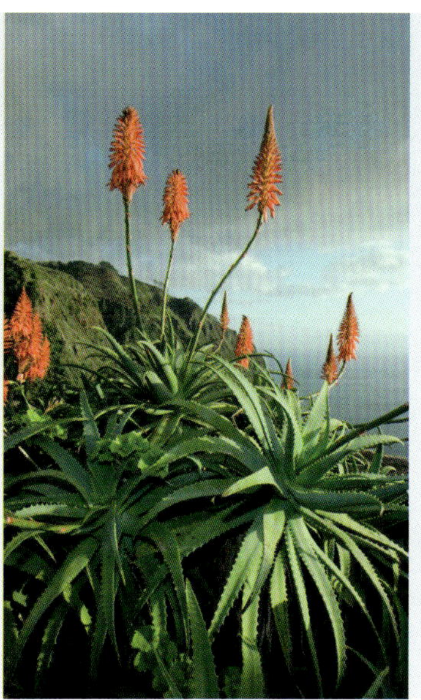

Date of inscription: 1999

Madeira was once covered in thick forests, but they have long since been decimated by clearing. Today's laurel forest is largely primary forest.

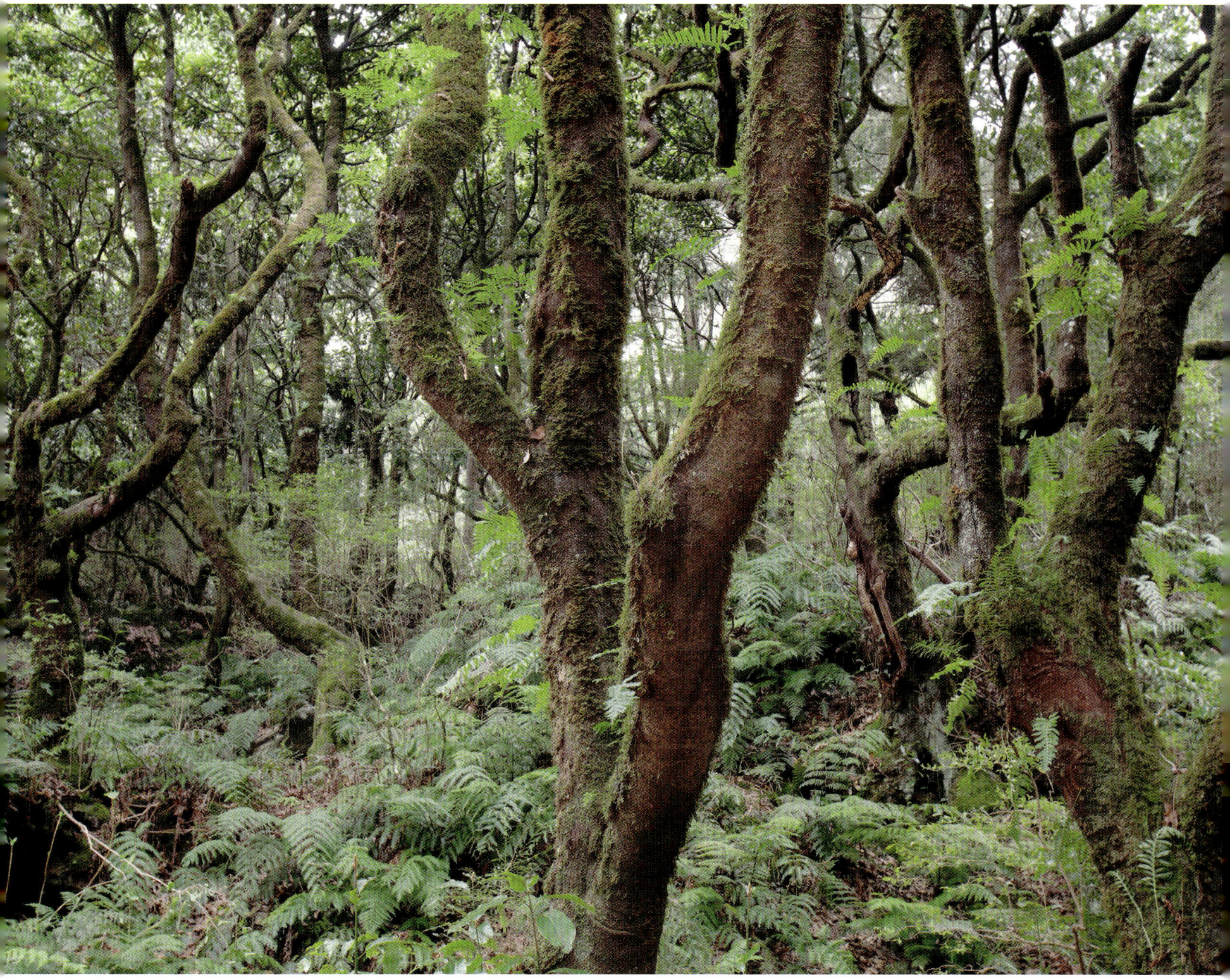

THE DOLOMITES IN SOUTH TYROL, IN THE PROVINCES OF TRENT AND BELLUNO

Date of inscription: 2009

The Dolomites are located in the north-east of the Italian Alps. Eighteen of the peaks boast an altitude of more than 3,000 m (9,843 ft). The landscape features impressively steep cliffs and narrow valleys.

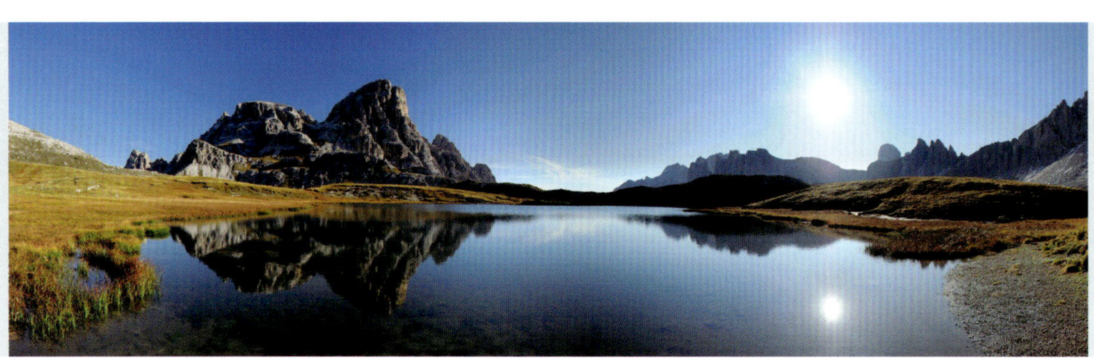

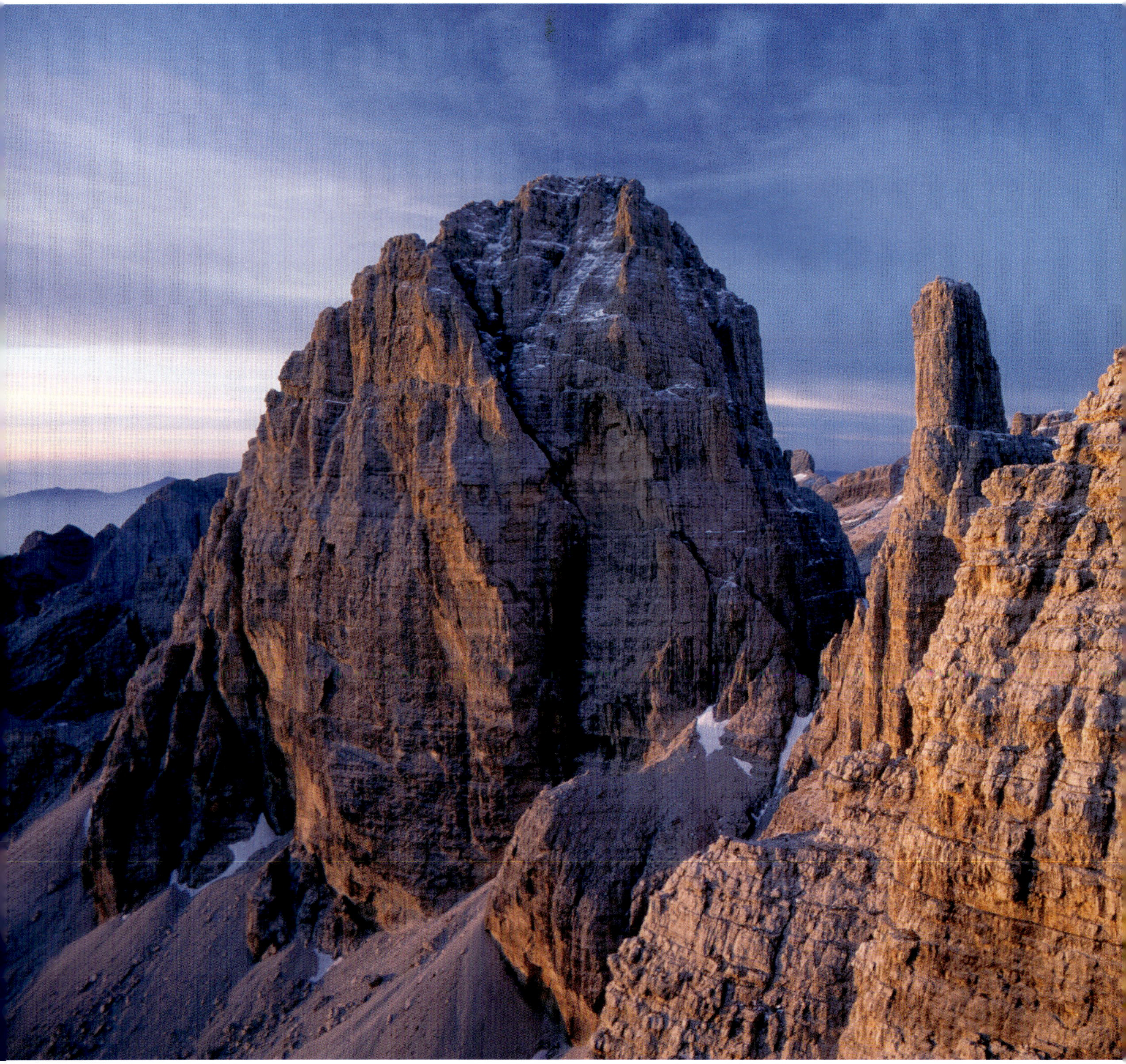

The Dolomites extend over a total area of nearly 142,000 hectares. At 3,343 m (10,968 ft), the Marmolada is their highest peak, but the Tre Cime di Lavaredo (2,999 m/9,839 ft) and the Rosengarten group, whose highest summit is the Kesselkogel (or Catinaccio d'Antermoia; 3,004 m/9,856 ft) are equally well known for their rugged charm. The Dolomites are a region of contrasts: rich meadows alternate with rugged crags and areas filled with scree from erosion. Responsible for this are the different geological histories of partial landscapes, which are documented by fossilized and uplifted coral reefs and rocks of volcanic origin. In the Dolomites areas created by glaciers can be found as well as the karst formations typical of limestone. Thus, the Dolomites are an outstanding example of a landscape, which allows us to read essential stages of our planet's development, also in its fossils. However, the story does not stop there. Its continuing dynamic evolution is evident in floods, landslides and avalanches that constantly reshape the surface.

Magnificent peaks with famous names gleam in the evening sun: the Campanile Basso pinnacle peak (large picture), the Pala Group, the striking Tre Cime and the Marmolada (picture series from the top). Far left: the sparkling Lago dei Piani near the Tre Cime.

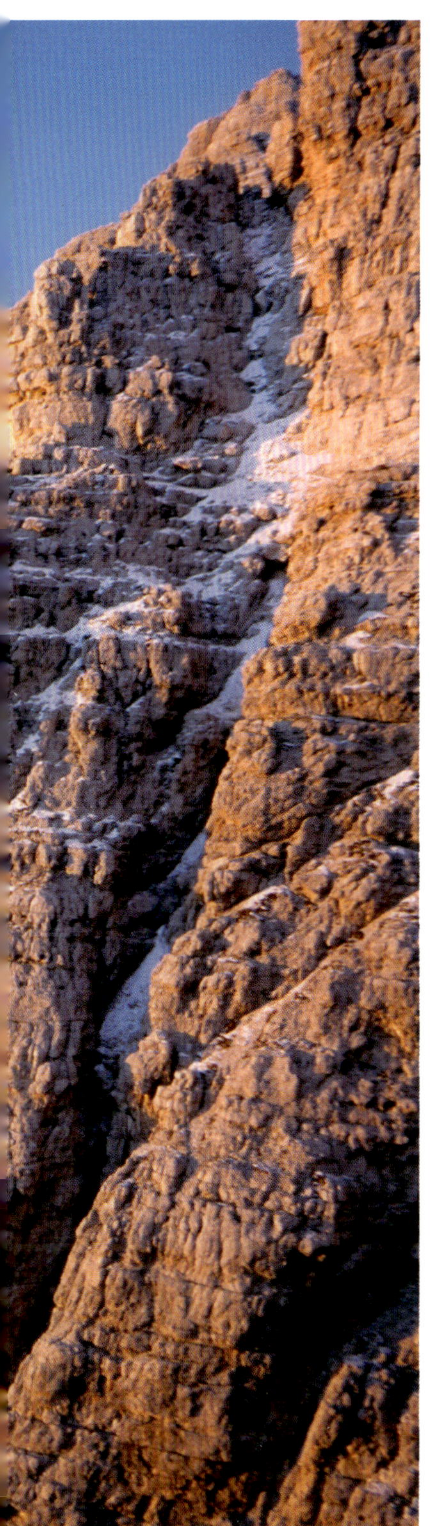

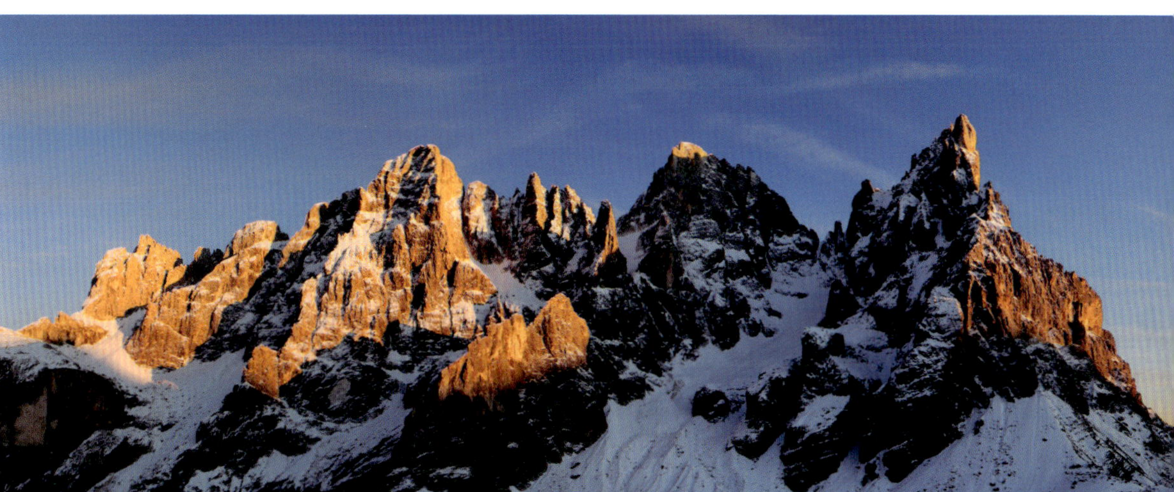

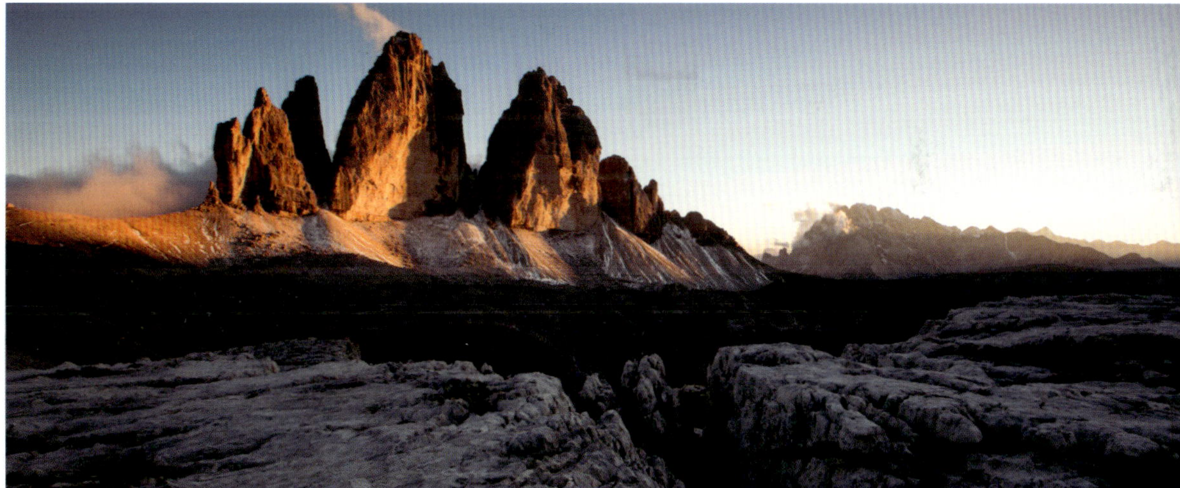

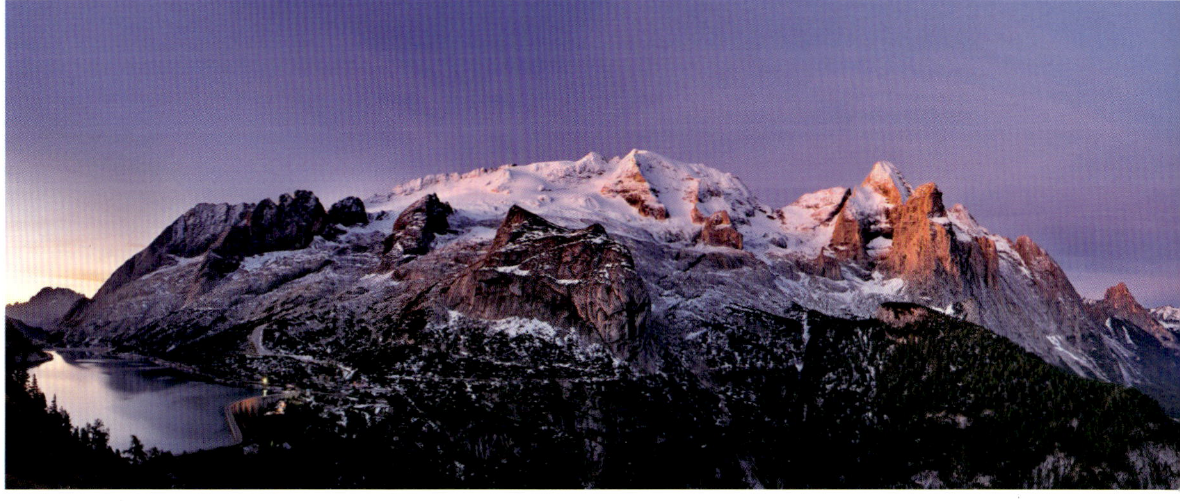

THE DOLOMITES IN SOUTH TYROL AND IN THE PROVINCES OF TRENT AND BELLUNO

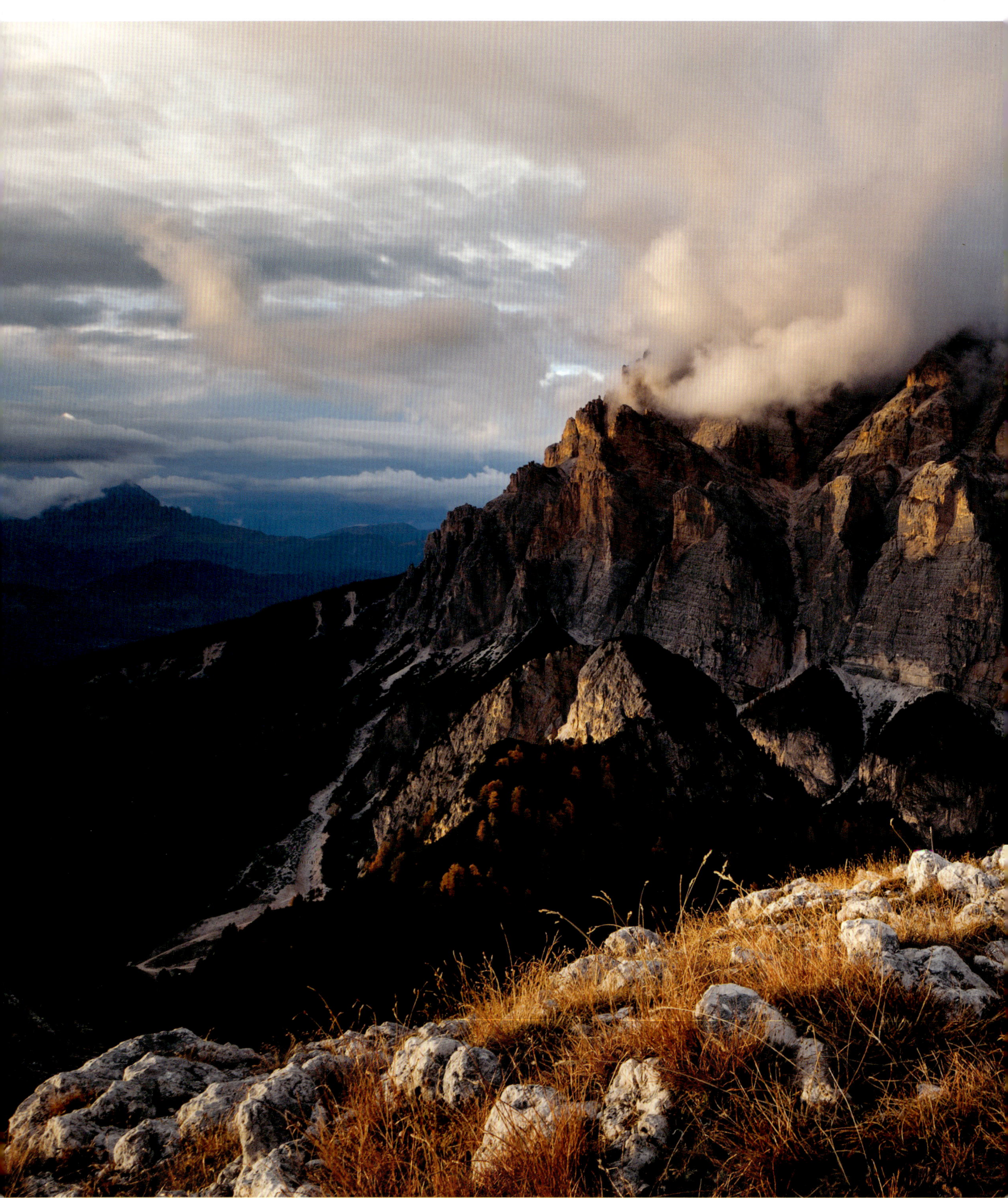

A dramatic mood on the southern Fanes Sennes Braies Natural Park in the Dolomites, overlooking the Piz dles Conturines in the light of the setting sun. This region of the Dolomites especially impresses with its colossal, massive peaks. Since the mountains are not crowned by sharp spikes, this part of the national park is a popular climbing area.

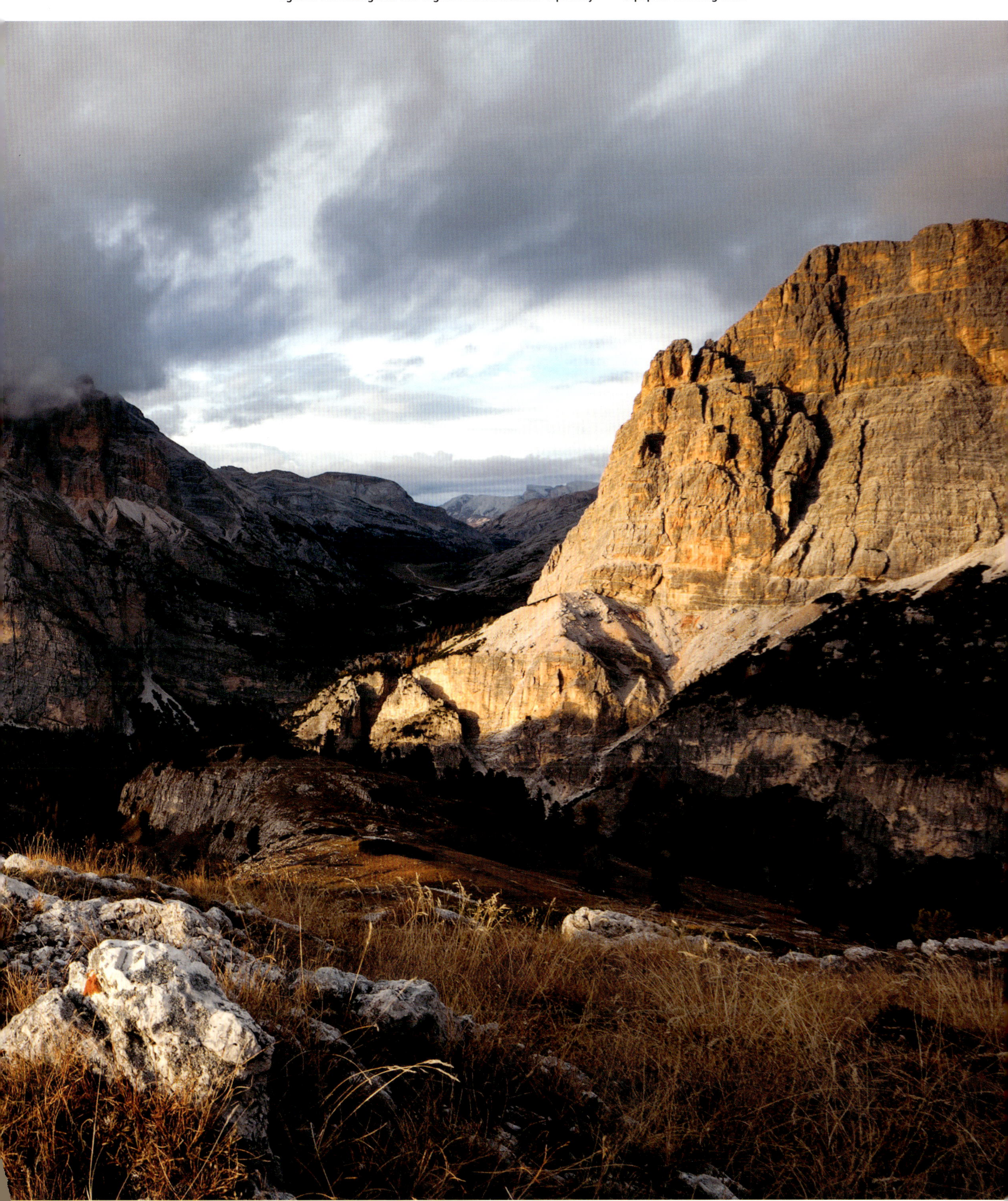

ETNA

Date of inscription: 2013

Mount Etna, on the island of Sicily, is at 3,323 m (10,902 ft) one of the highest active volcanoes on the European continent and one of the most active strato-volcanoes on Earth. It originated around 600,000 years ago, at a place where the bay extended far inland.

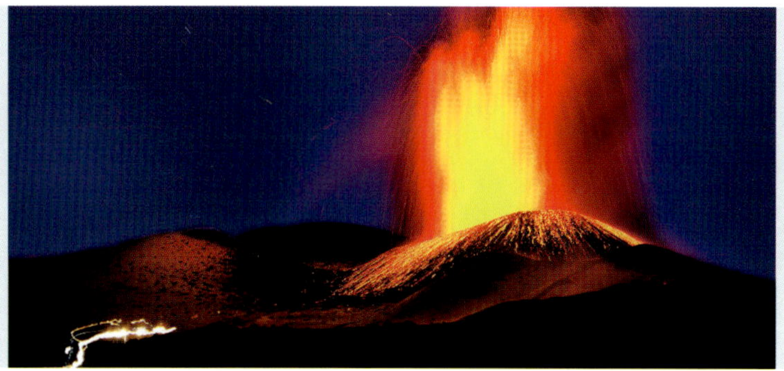

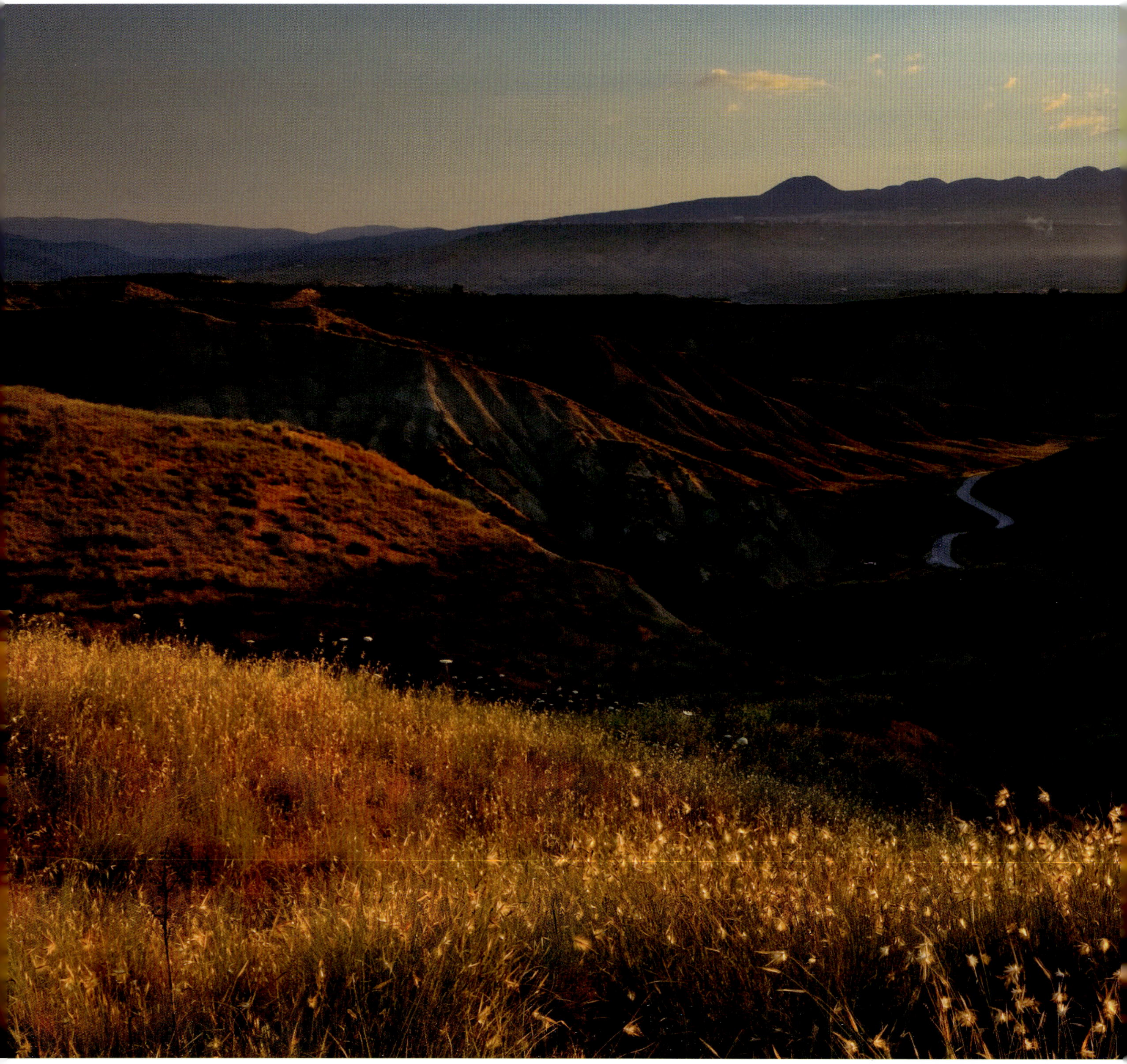

The massif of Mount Etna occupies a vast area of around 1,250 sq km (482 sq miles), and its circumference is about 250 km (155 miles). Geologically it can be divided into two regions. The lowest level up to around 1,100 m (3,609 ft) height only consists of lava flow. It is continually impacted by humans. Above that is the high mountain stage, of which approximately 192 sq km (74 sq miles) are defined as a World Heritage Site. On the surface, it is not solidified lava, but ejected ashes (pyroclastic) of different grain sizes that dominate, ranging from sands to large lava bombs. In the upper reaches of Etna lives a plant community that is otherwise dominant in Central Asian mountains, the Sicilian milk vetch (Astragaletum siculi). The most striking animals at these altitudes are black beetles, which may occur by the hundreds. Mount Etna, which has been almost constantly active for many thousands of years, is one of the best fields of experimentation for geoscientists of all specializations. Most eruptions are an exciting natural spectacle for locals and visitors alike.

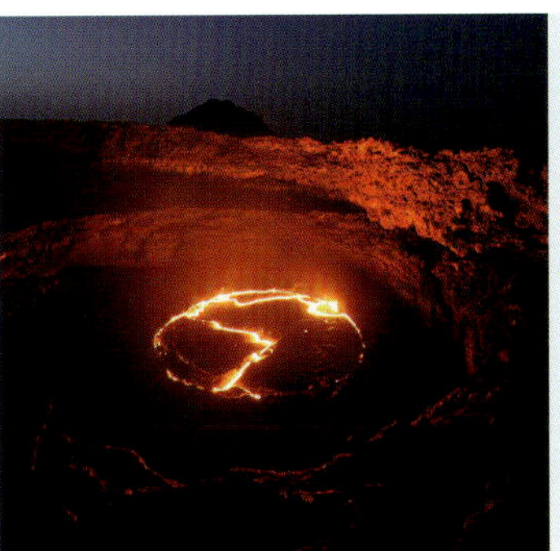

On Etna, you can find almost all geomorphological phenomena typical of volcanoes, such as cinder cones, various types of lava and datable lava flows. Large picture: view of Etna from Calanchi di Pietralunga.

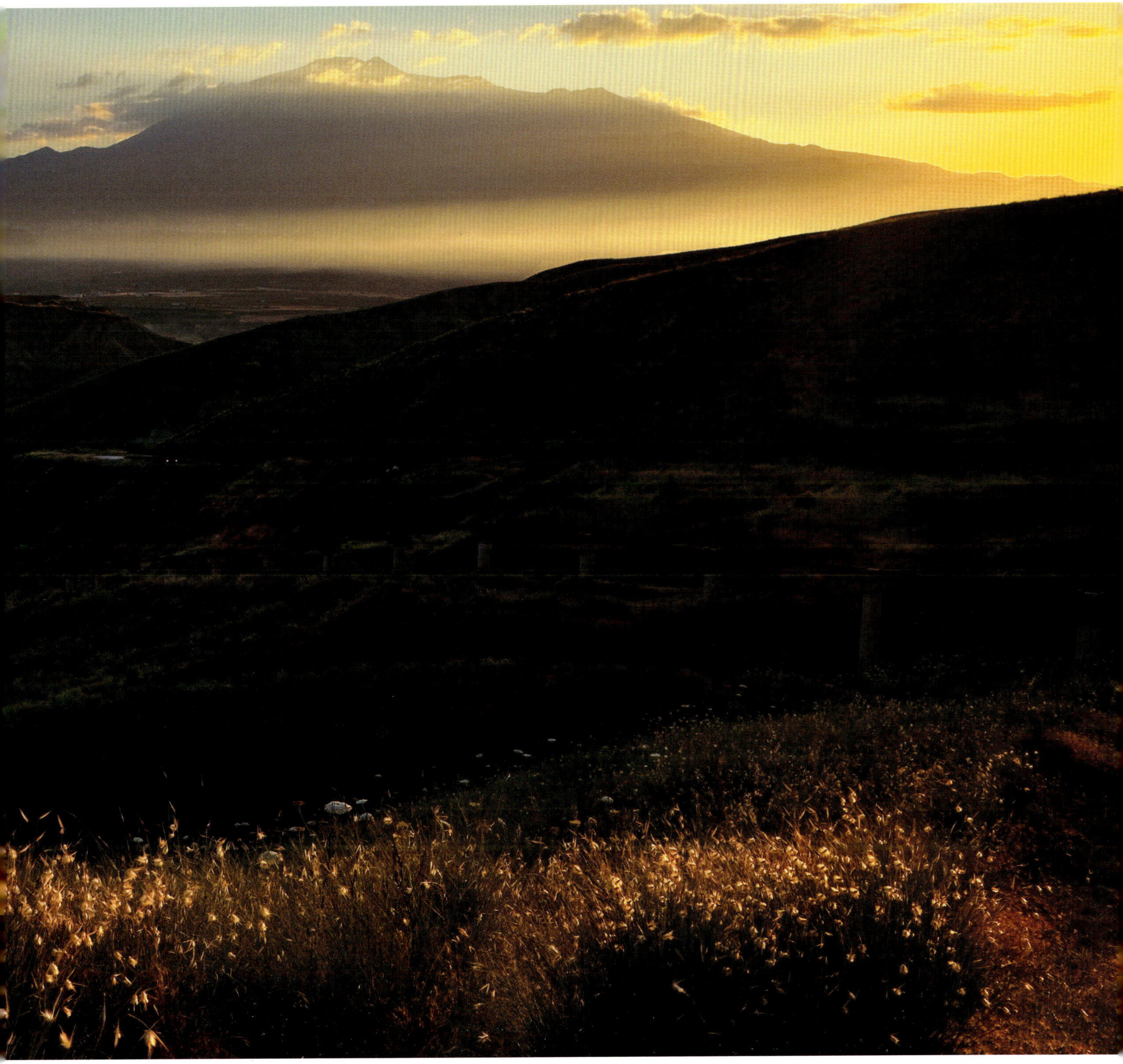

AEOLIAN ISLANDS

Date of inscription: 2000

Situated around 40 km (25 miles) off the north coast of Sicily, the Aeolian Islands owe their inclusion on the world heritage list to their volcanic activity. The islands' geology and geophysics makes them of great scientific interest to volcanologists all over the world.

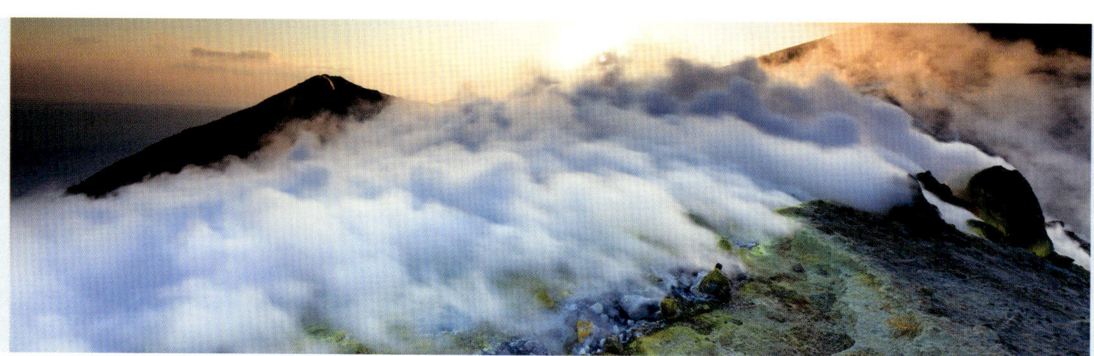

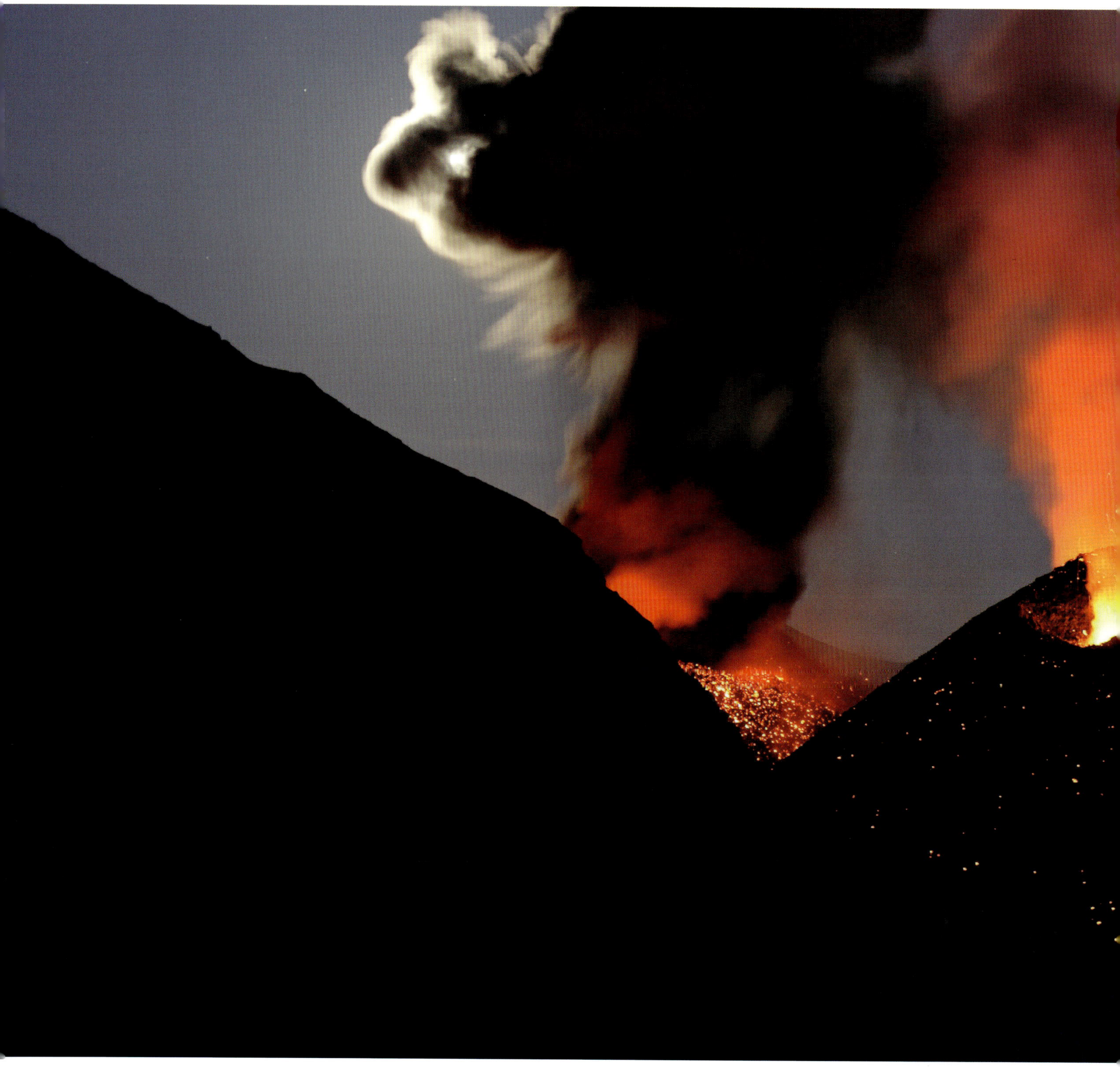

The Aeolian Islands, sometimes known as the Lipari Islands, comprise Vulcano, Lipari, Alicudi, Filicudi, Salina, Panarea, and Stromboli. The tectonic basis of the archipelago's creation was the subsidence of the Tyrrhenian Sea during the Pliocene period. New studies have revealed that volcanic activity on the islands only began in the Pleistocene epoch, and the seven islands were subsequently created over three distinct periods of volcanic activity. Today, only Stromboli and the Grande Fossa volcano on Vulcano are still active, although there are also fumaroles and solfatara on Lipari.

The most spectacular of the islands is Stromboli. It consists solely of the volcano of the same name, which rises to an altitude of almost 1,000 m (3,300 feet) above sea level. There has been volcanic activity here for some forty thousand years, and pieces of lava and incandescent cinders are constantly being spat out around the openings in the crater – accompanied by quite significant explosions. In fact, Stromboli is one of the most active volcanoes in the world that can be observed at such close quarters.

If sulphur gases along with water vapour are the dominant component in a natural volcanic vent, as here on Vulcano Island, they are known as solfataras (left). Stromboli (large picture) is an active volcano, presenting a great natural spectacle.

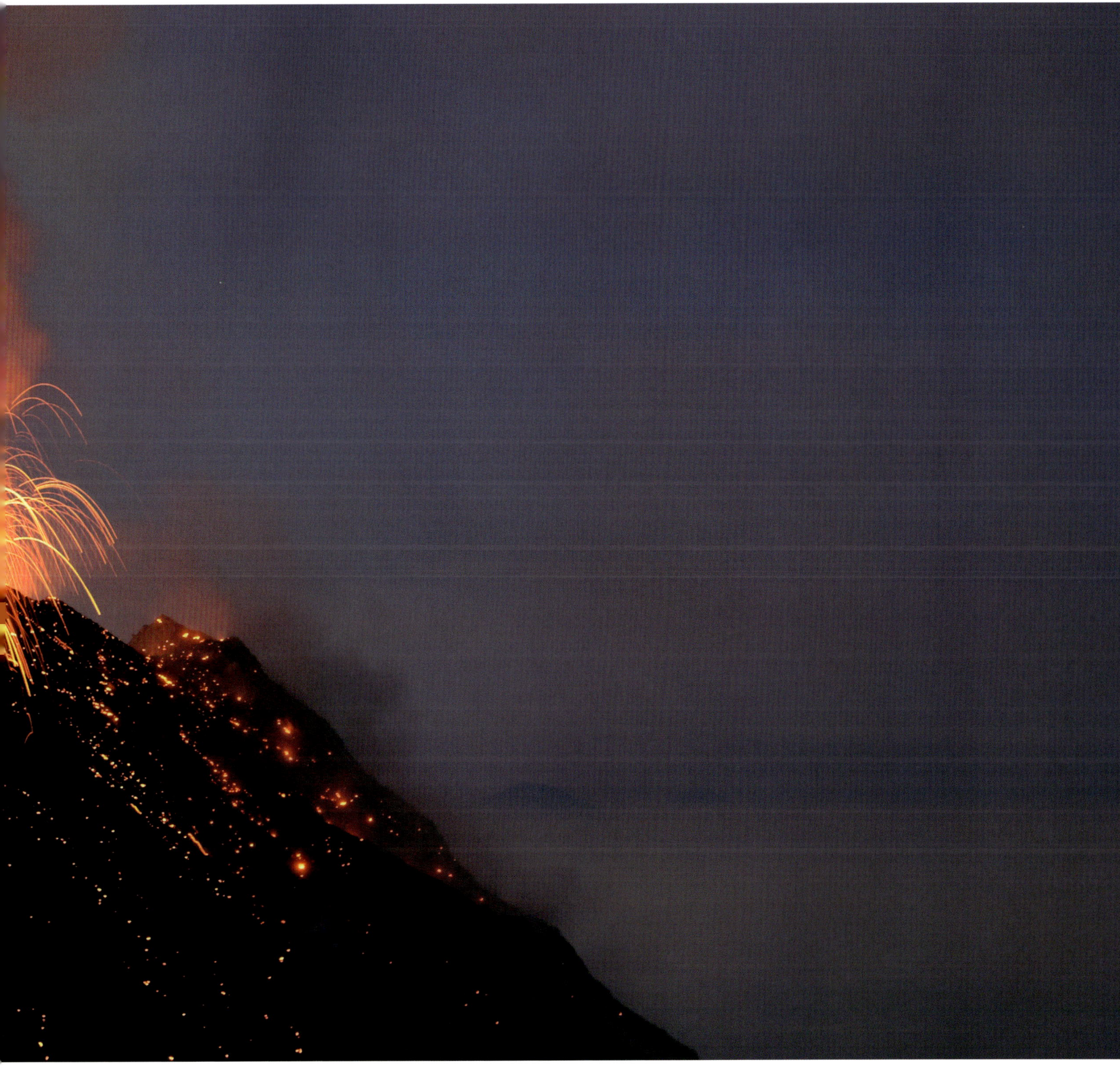

ŠKOCJAN CAVES

Date of inscription: 1986

The Škocjan caves are located in the karst mountains of Slovenia, to the east of Trieste. Nearly 6 km (4 miles) long, this is one of the largest cave systems in Europe. They are home to numerous rare plants and animals.

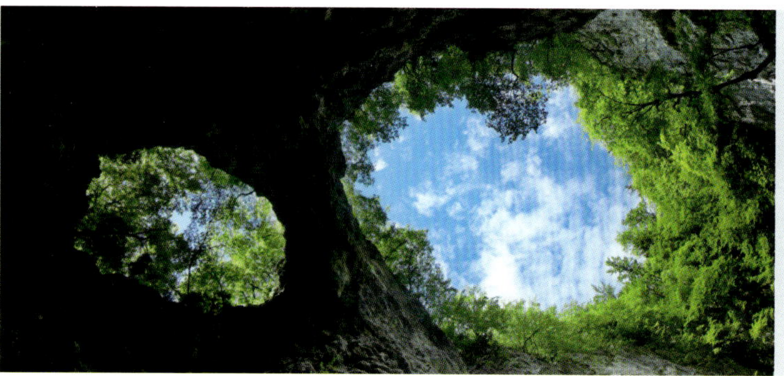

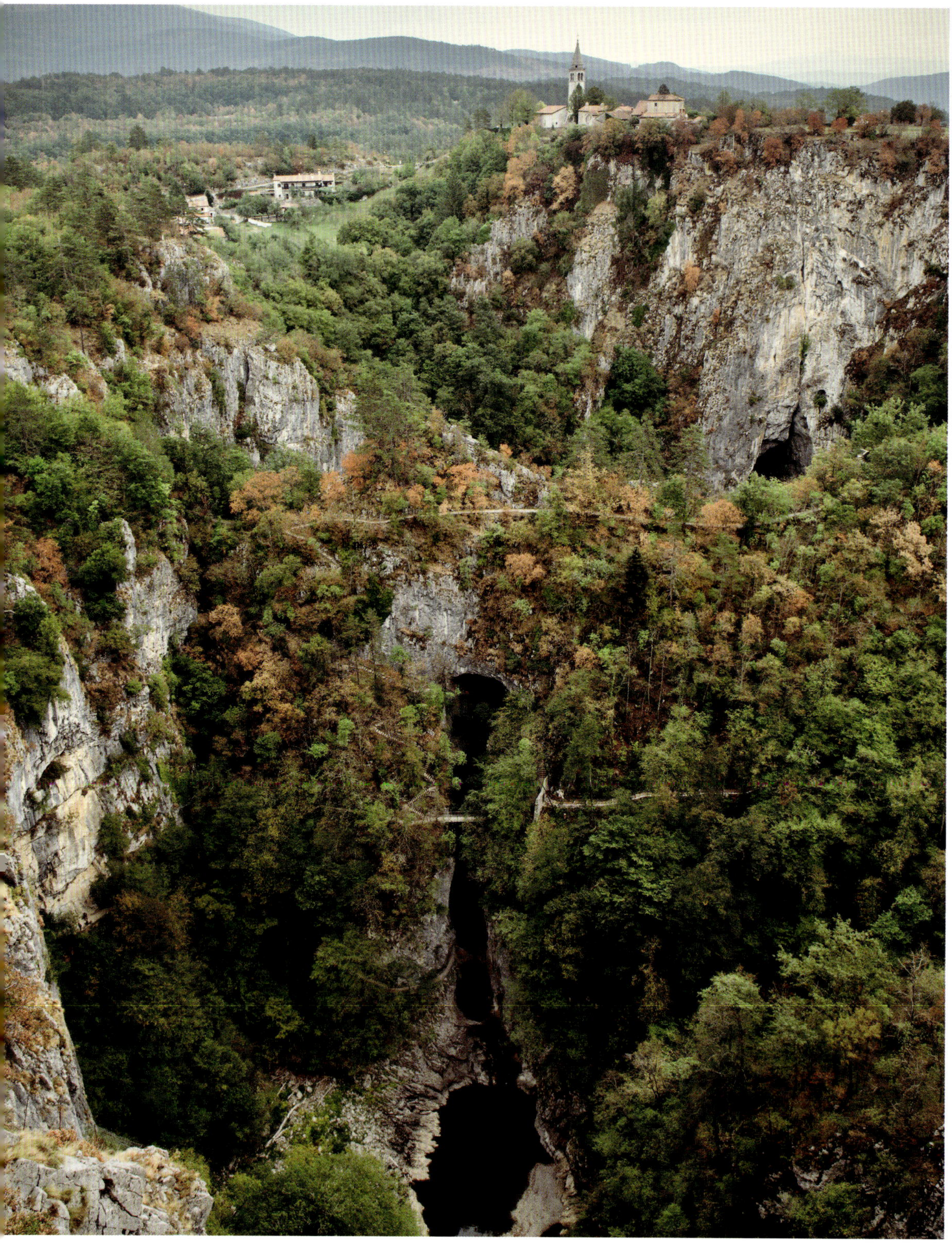

At Škocjan, the river Reka disappears underground. It flows for some 40 km (25 miles) before finally resurfacing near the Adriatic coast. In between, it creates a subterranean karst landscape that looks almost primeval – complete with all the typical signs of thousands of years of limestone erosion, namely crevices, gorges, shafts, sinkholes and basins, lakes, waterfalls, narrow pas-

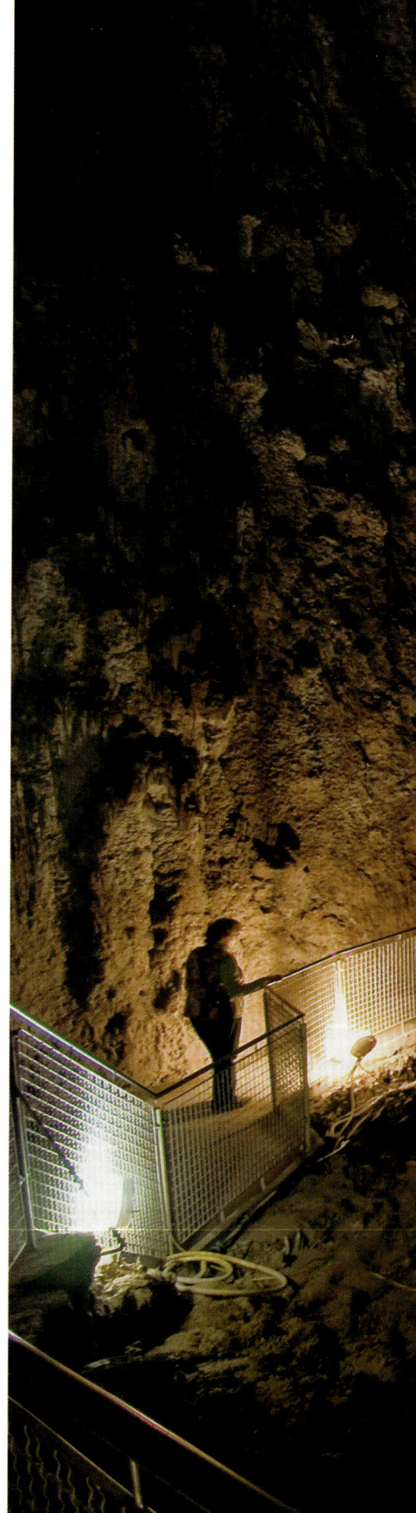

sages, and chambers. The Martelova dvorana is the largest chamber, with a length of 308 m (1,010 feet), width of 123 m (404 feet), and height of up to 146 m (479 feet). When the snow melts, the water level in the 148-m (486-foot) deep Reka underground canyon can, within a short space of time, rise dramatically. Even in summer, the 25 roaring cascades in the "murmuring cave" are still a fantastic natural spectacle. The stalactites and stalagmites in the "silent cave," meanwhile, include both mighty and more delicate formations with names like the "giant" or the "organ."

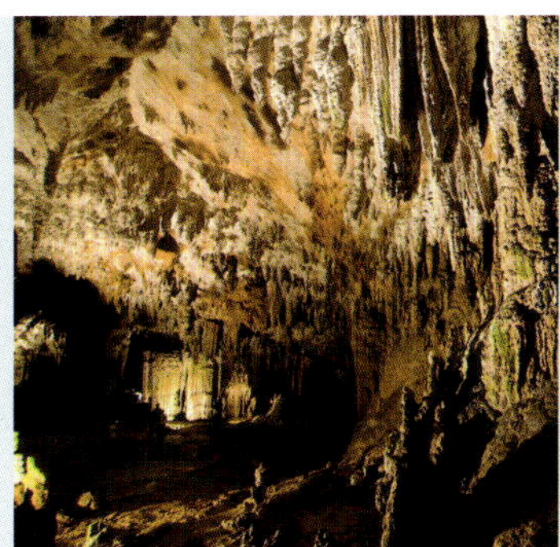

The two openings of the Zelške Jame Cave are clearly visible (far left). Once you've seen these subterranean canyon routes and caves you'll believe that an underground river can do the work of a great civil engineer.

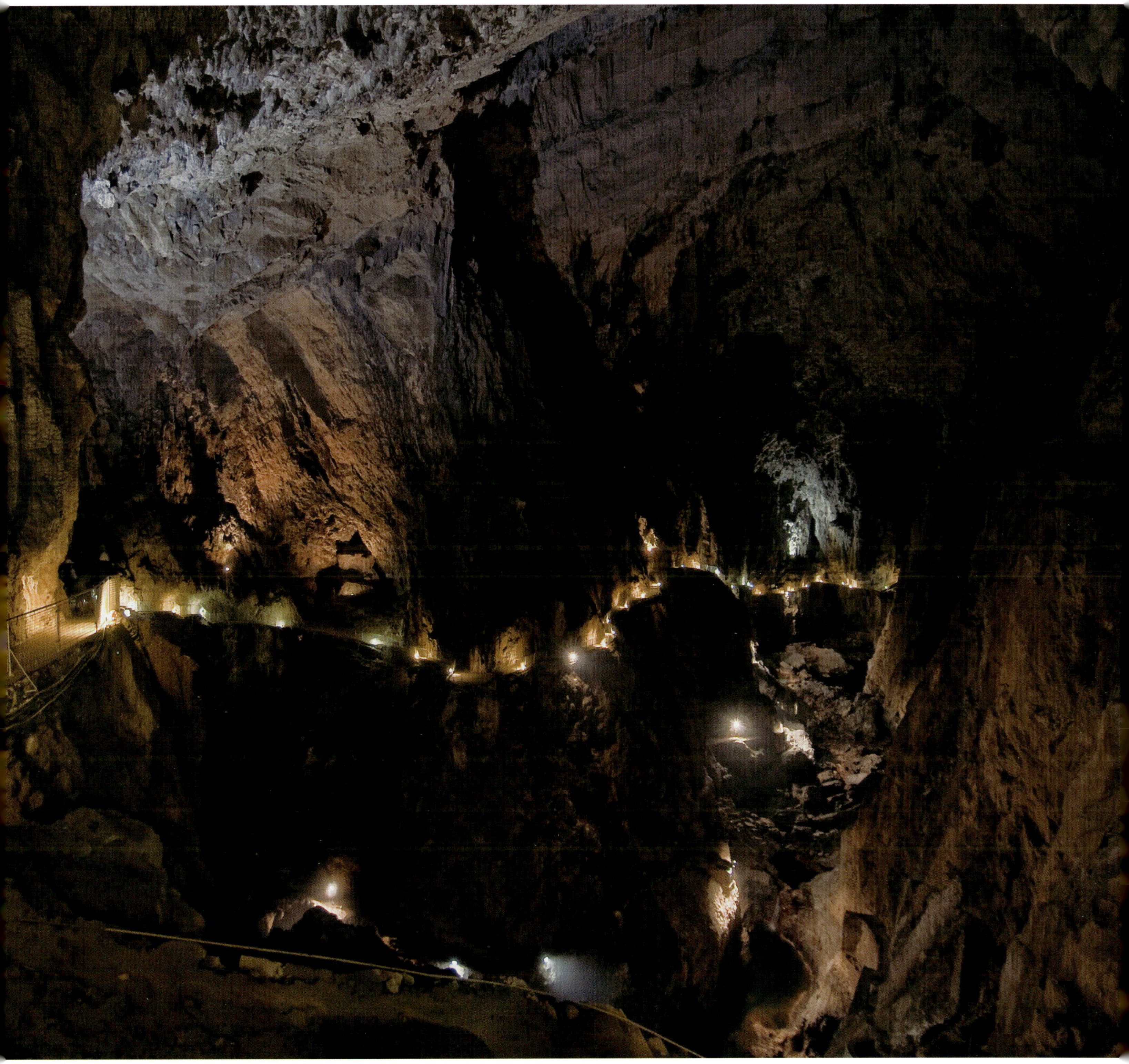

PLITVICE LAKES NATIONAL PARK

Date odf inscription: 1979
Extended: 2000

In the Croatian karst, not far from the border with Bosnia and Herzegovina, the 16 lakes of Plitvice Lakes National Park form an ever-changing, unspoiled natural panorama.They are connected by a number of cascades and waterfalls.

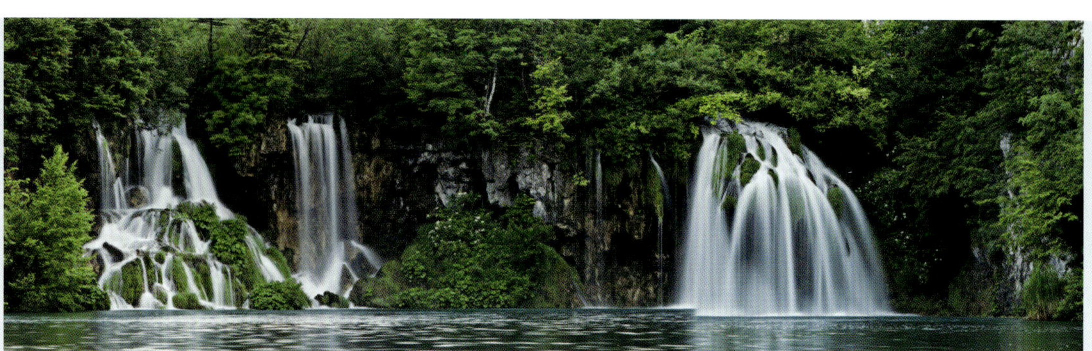

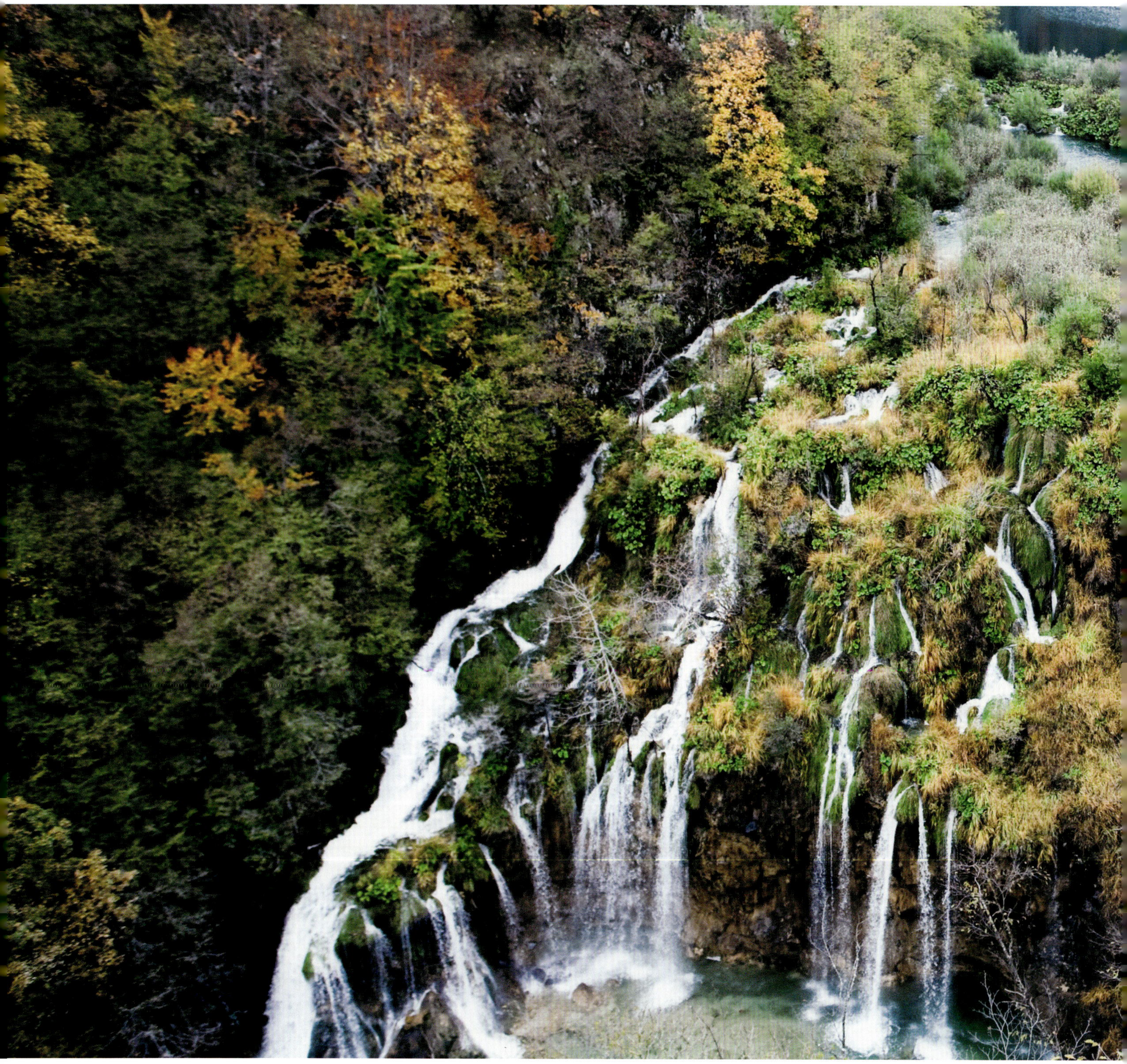

Spanning some 7 km (4 miles), this series of lakes is the result of a combination of limestone deposits and tectonic movements. The build-up of calc-sinter over millennia created the natural dams and barriers that capture the water. The lakes' bluish-green shimmer, meanwhile, is due to algae and mosses. The most impressive of the park's waterfalls are as high as 76 m (249 feet) and are found around the four lower lakes. The Plitvice river joins the water at the end of the chain of lakes, forming the source of the river Korana. Declared a national park in 1949, the region at the feet of the Mala Kapela mountains is home to a diverse range of flora and fauna. Deer, wolves, brown bears, and some 120 species of bird are all found in its dense forests.

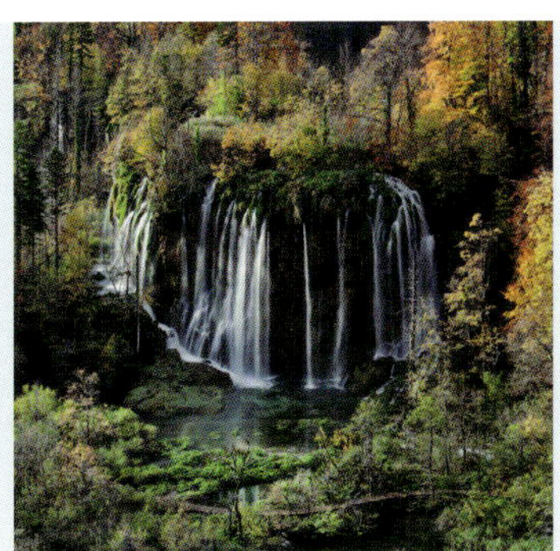

The contours of the terraces created by the flow of calcareous water through the lakes is constantly changing. Paths and bridges allow visitors to discover the park on foot, and it can also be explored by boat.

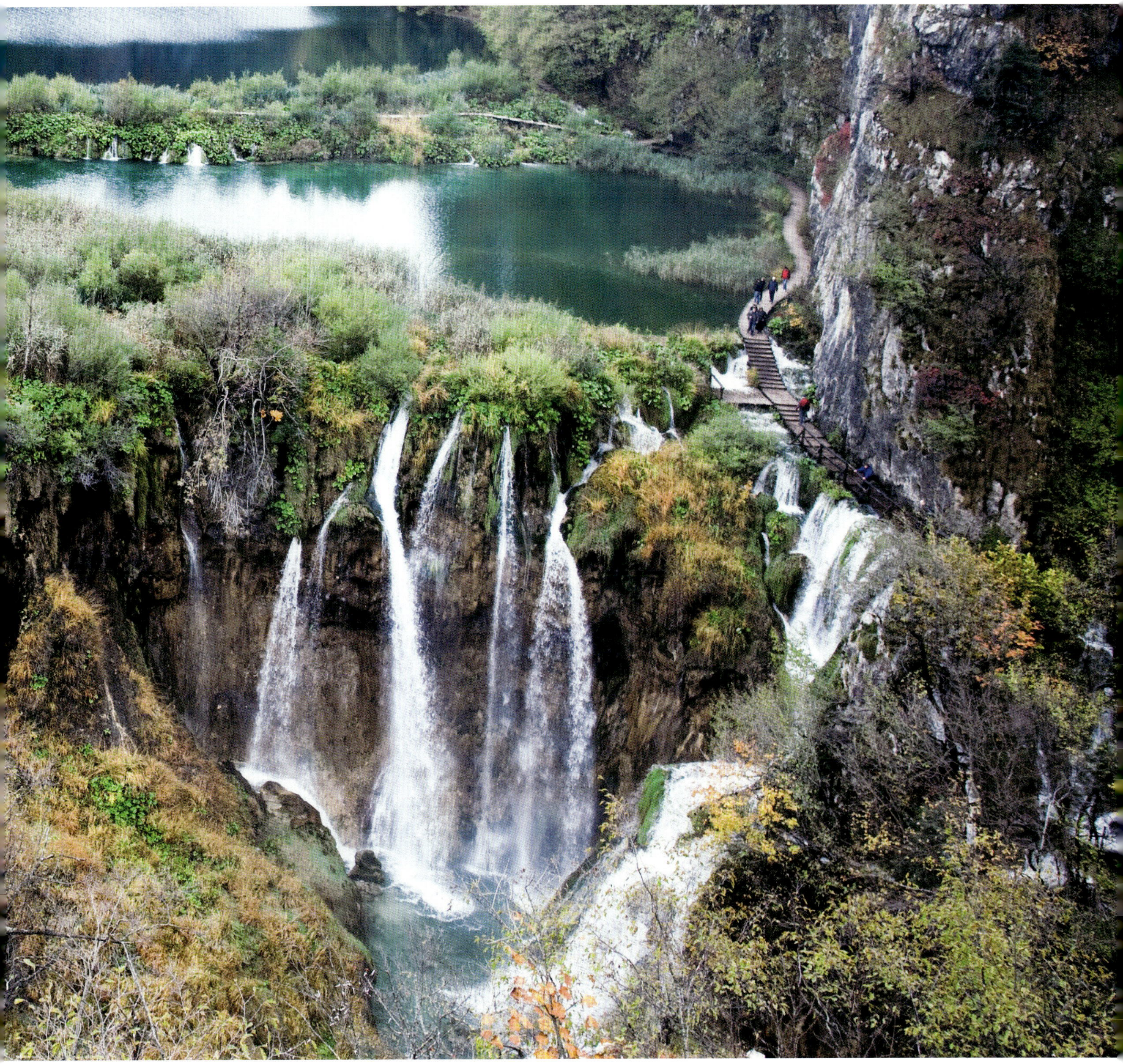

DURMITOR NATIONAL PARK

Date of inscription: 1980
Extended: 2005

Formed by the glaciers of the last ice age, the Durmitor mountains were declared a national park in 1952. There are 18 lakes within the region's mountains and forests, and the area also boasts Europe's deepest gorges.

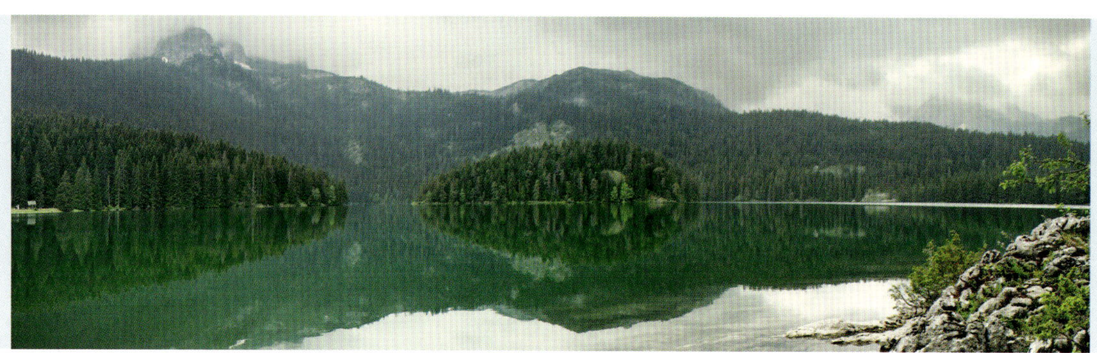

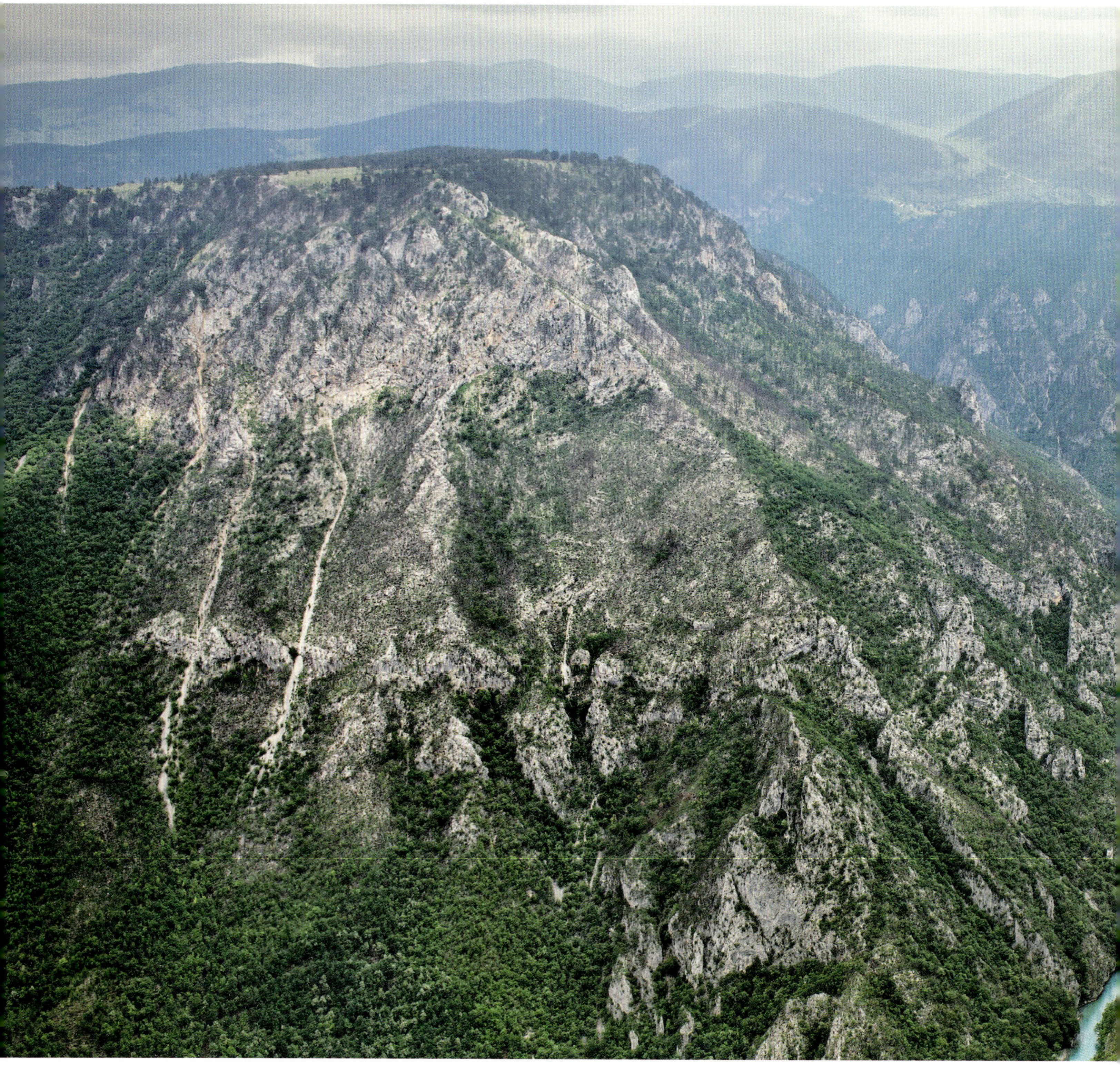

Raging through the dense coniferous forests, past the clear mountain lakes, the Tara is one of the last great, untamed whitewater rivers of the Balkan peninsula. In its wake, the gorges of the Dinaric karst are up to 1,300 m (4,265 feet) deep. With the exception of the skiers and mountain walkers around the Z˘abljak plateau, most of the Durmitor mountains have been spared human intervention. Alongside deer and chamois, the park is also home to a number of animals that have become very rare in Europe, namely brown bears, wolves, wildcats, eagles, black grouse, and capercaillies. About three-quarters of the mountain flora are endemic. The black pines – which constitute some of Europe's last primeval forests – are also noteworthy.

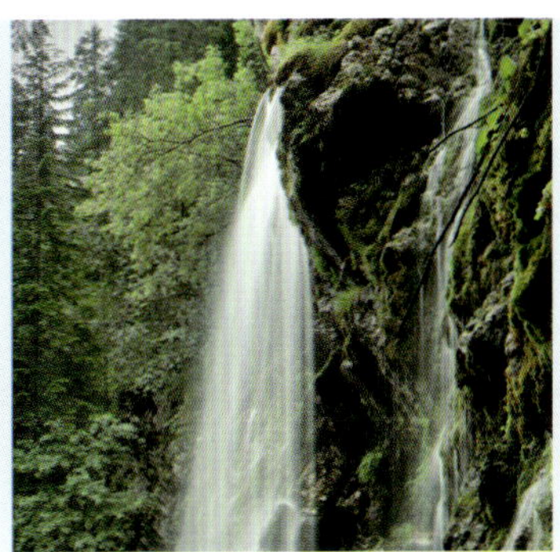

The Tara Canyon has dug itself up to 1,300 m (4,265 foot) deep into the mountains (below). The Black Lake (Crno jezero) is located near Z˘abljak and is easily accessible on foot (far left). It is up to 49 m (161 feet) deep and lies at an altitude of 1,416 m (4,646 feet).

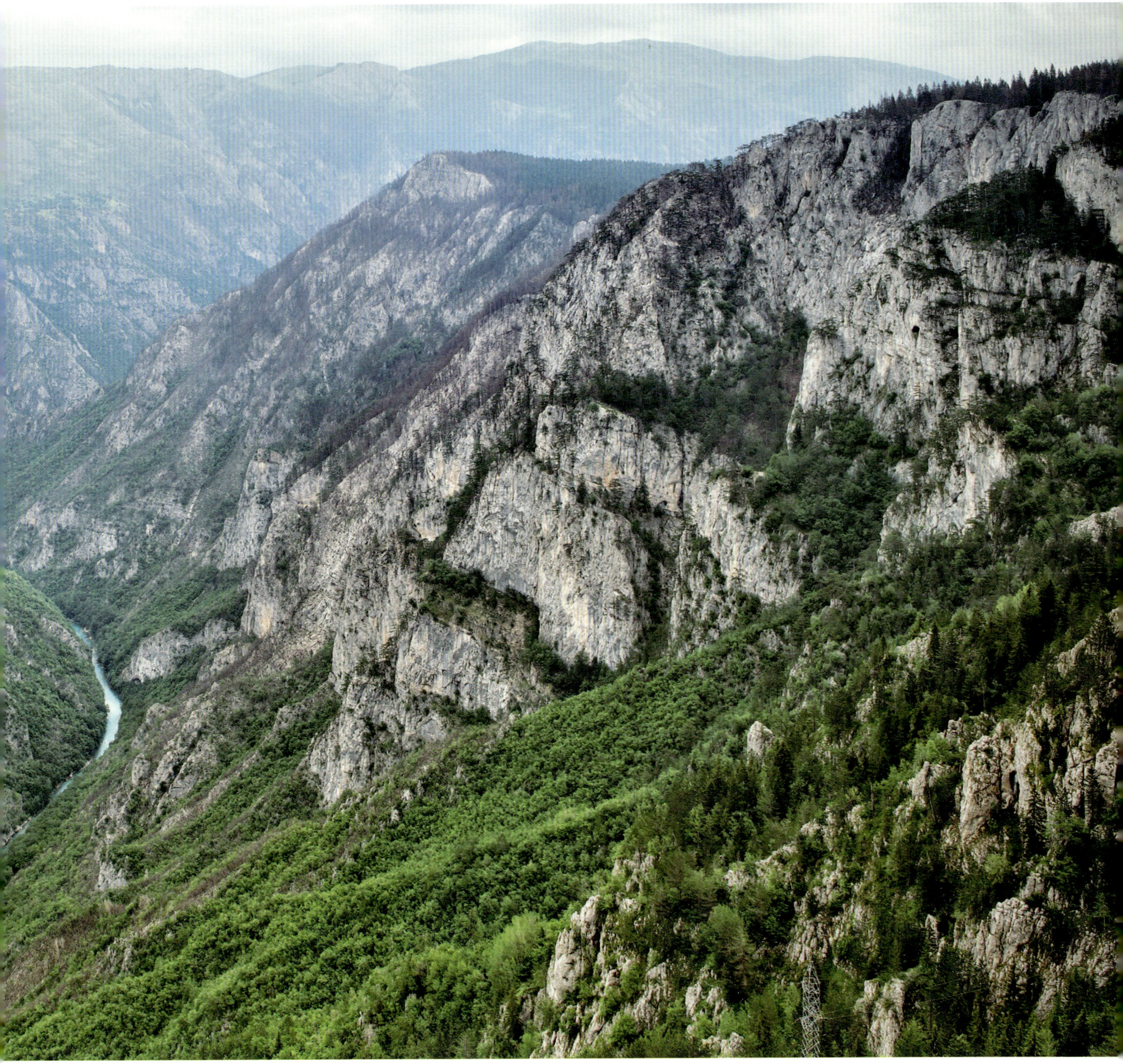

NATURAL AND CULTURAL HERITAGE OF THE OHRID REGION

Date of inscription: 1979
Extended: 1980

In the 9th and 10th centuries, Ohrid, in south-west Macedonia, was an important spiritual and cultural hub of orthodox Christianity.

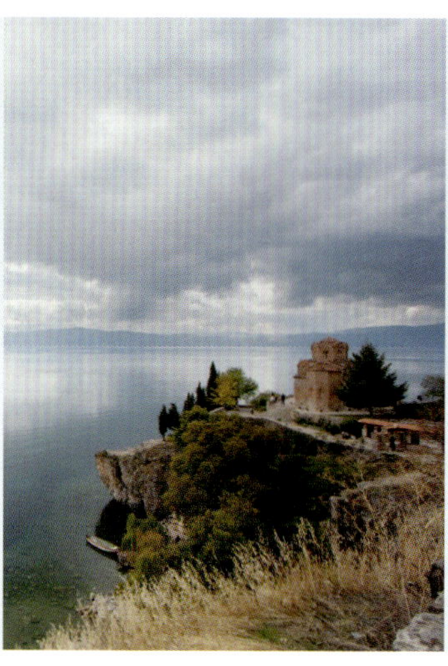

Founded by the Illyrians as Lychnidos, Ohrid's advantageous location was not lost on the Romans. Positioned on the Via Egnatia – the main road between Byzantium and the Adriatic – the town became an important strategic base.

Ohrid became a diocesan town in the 4th century. In the 9th century, Clement and Naum, disciples of the Slav apostles Cyril and Methodius, founded the monasteries here. The town became the focal point of orthodox Christianity in the Balkans. The 11th-century church of St Sophia was built under archbishop Leo, but converted to a mosque by the Turks – thus losing its impressive dome, bell tower, and internal galleries. The conversion also saw the whitewashing of the church's frescoes, which date from the 11th–14th centuries. They were finally uncovered in the course of restoration work in the 1950s. There are more Byzantine frescoes and icons in the church of St Clement.

Lake Ohrid is the largest lake in Macedonia, one of the oldest and deepest lakes in the world, and is home to several species of endemic fish. The church of St John at Kaneo (left) stands high above the water.

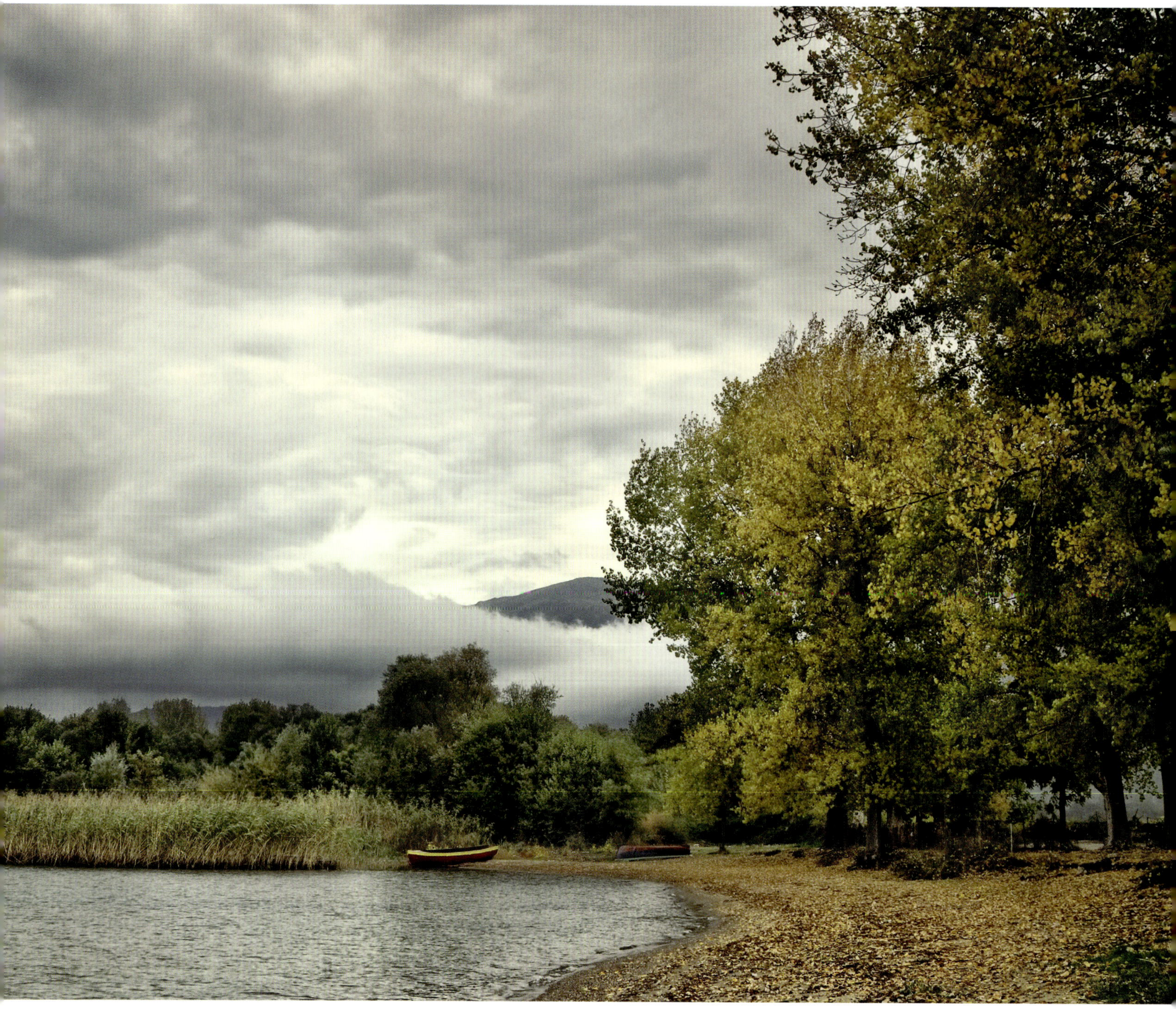

MOUNT ATHOS

The first monastery on Hagion Oros – the "Holy Mountain" – was built in 963. The monastic republic's autonomy dates back to the Byzantine period. Men under the age of 21 and women are not allowed to enter the monasteries, which are currently home to about 1,400 monks. Mount Athos has been a focus of Orthodox Christianity since 1054. In the 14th century some 3,000 peasants were employed by Athos to farm the republic's 20,000-hectare (49,500-acre) lands.The style of icon painting practiced at Athos plays an important role in the history of Orthodox Christian art, while the influence of the monasteries' characteristic architecture can be seen as far away as Russia. Of the 20 monasteries, 17 are Greek, one Russian, one Serbian, and one Bulgarian. Each monastery courtyard contains a domed church with three apses. The monastic cells and other buildings are positioned around the courtyard.

Poised on the edge of a wooded ravine, the perimeter buildings of the Dionysiou monastery cling to the ramparts like swallows' nests.

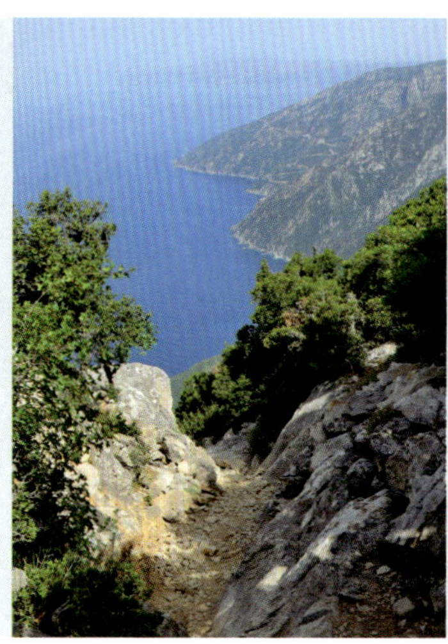

Date of inscription: 1988

A total of 20 monasteries make up the autonomous monastic state on the Khalkidiki peninsula. It is one of the most important places in the Orthodox Christian world.

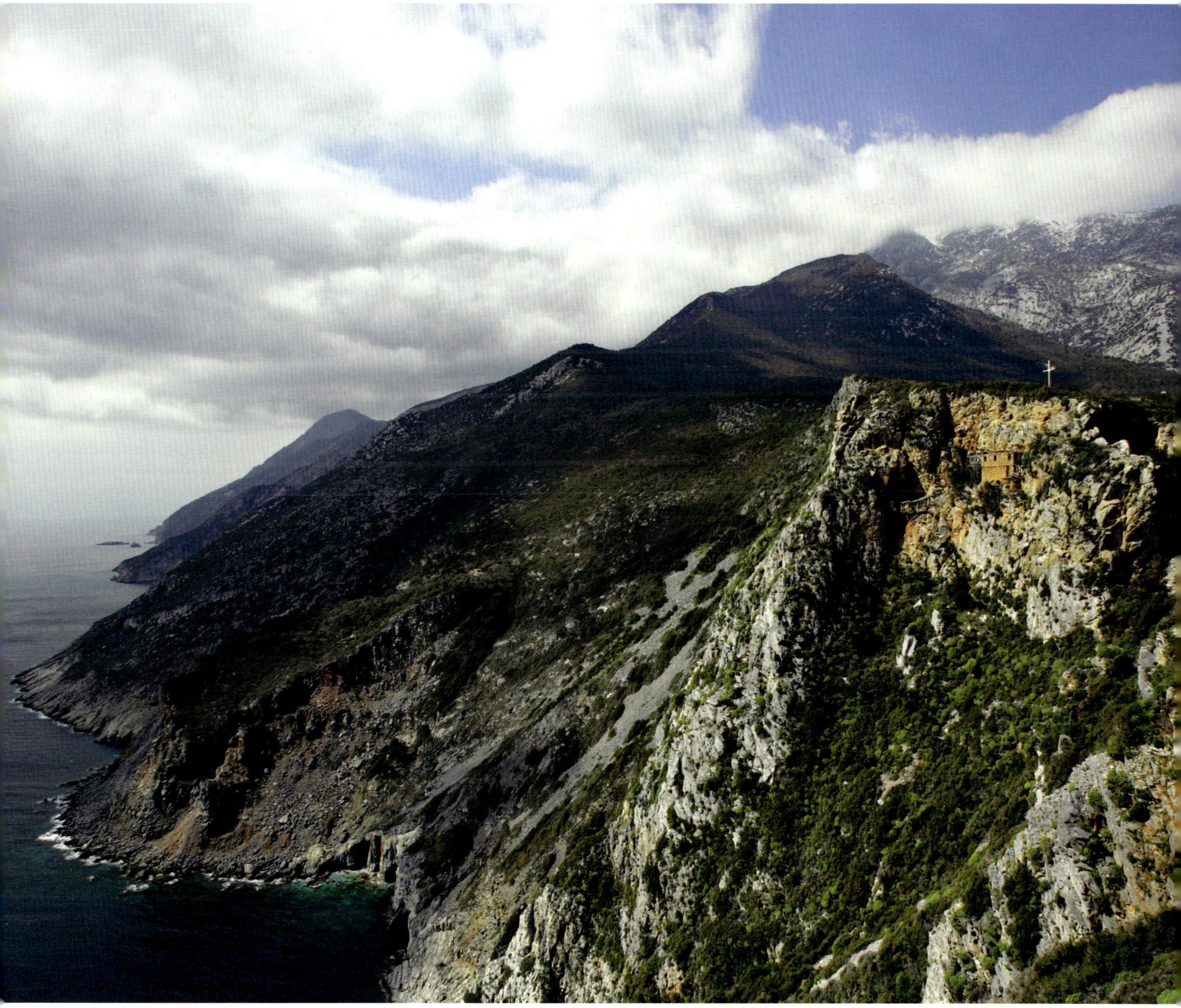

METEORA MONASTERIES

Date of inscription: 1988

Meteora's 24 monasteries were built on steep, rocky peaks that raise them high above the world below. Most of the monasteries date as far back as the 14th century.

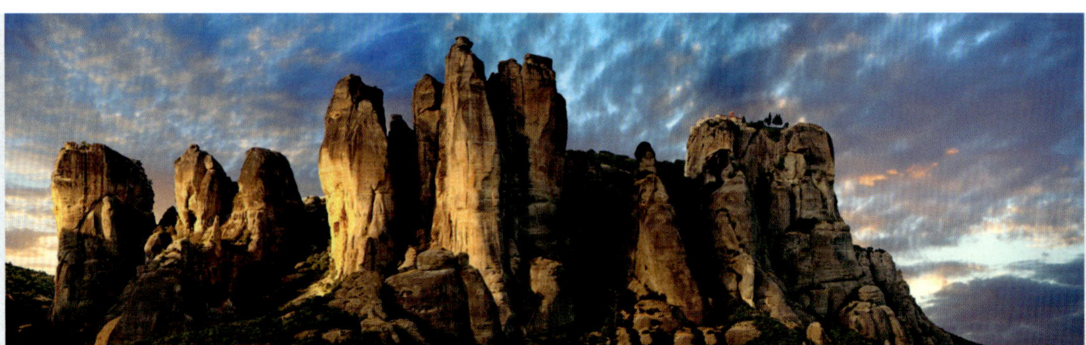

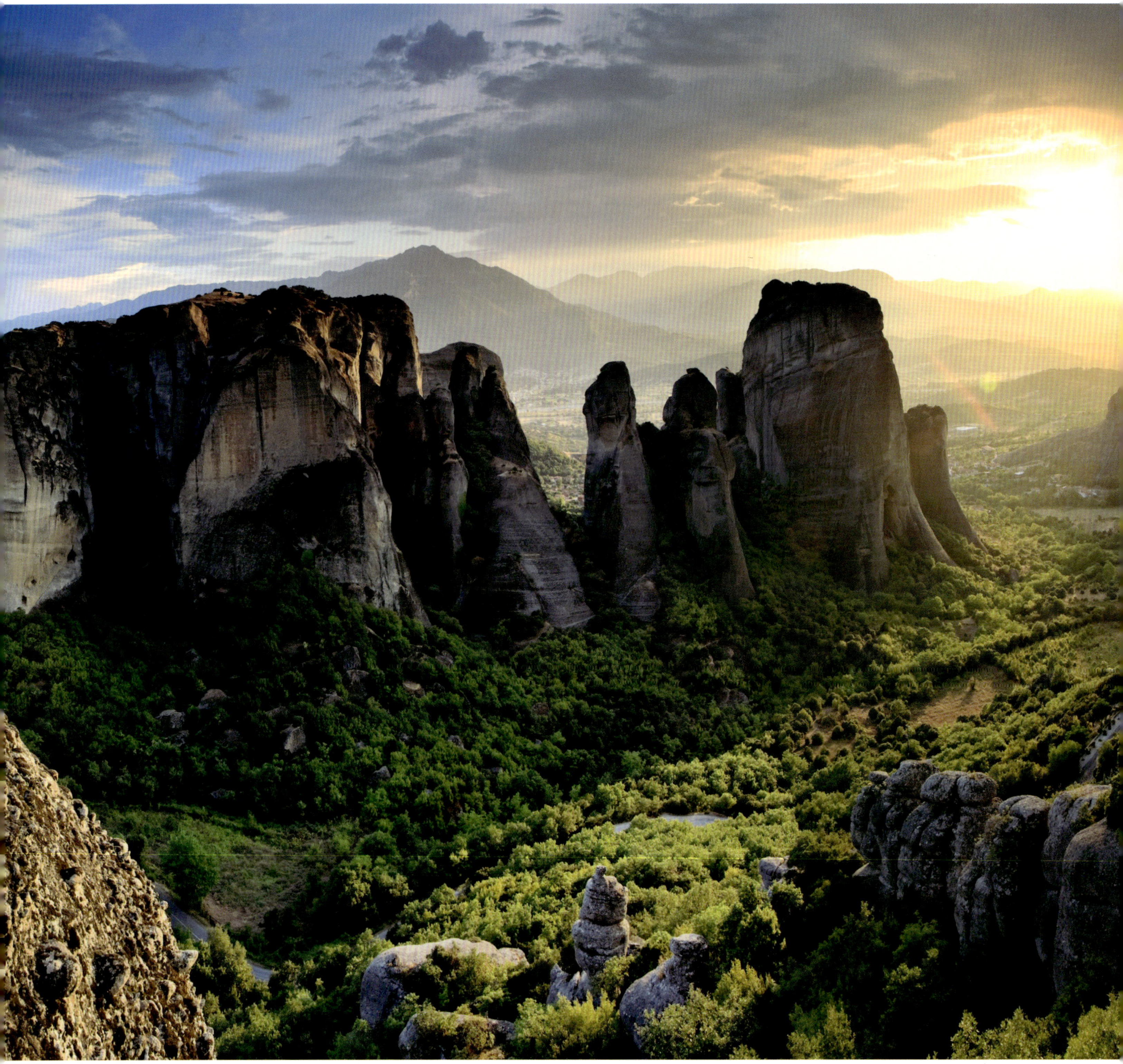

The Meteora valley is located north of the town of Kalambaka. Its 24 monasteries – five of which are still occupied today – were built over time on a series of rocky peaks that tower over the valley. For visitors, it is a truly breathtaking sight.The monastery situated at the highest altitude is Megalo-Meteoro. Founded around 1360 by the holy Athanasius, bishop of Alexandria, it was granted special privileges in 1362 and exempted from the local jurisdiction in the 15th century by Euthymius, patriarch of Constantinople. The other monasteries were placed under the authority of Megalo-Meteoro in 1490. The Monastery of St Nicholas Anapausas, meanwhile, sits on top of one of the other high mountain peaks. Founded around 1388, the monastery's late Byzantine frescoes by the influential Cretan painter Theophanes Bathas date from 1527. They were restored in 1960. Varlaam monastery was founded in 1517 and was rebuilt between 1627 and 1637. It takes its name from the 14th-century hermit who first constructed a church here.

Meteora loosely translates as "floating in the air," and it offers correspondingly fine views across the Thessalian plain. The rocks are around 30 million years old. At that time, they would have been in the middle of the sea. They owe their curious shapes to erosion by the sea water and – as the sea level dropped – also to wind and rain.

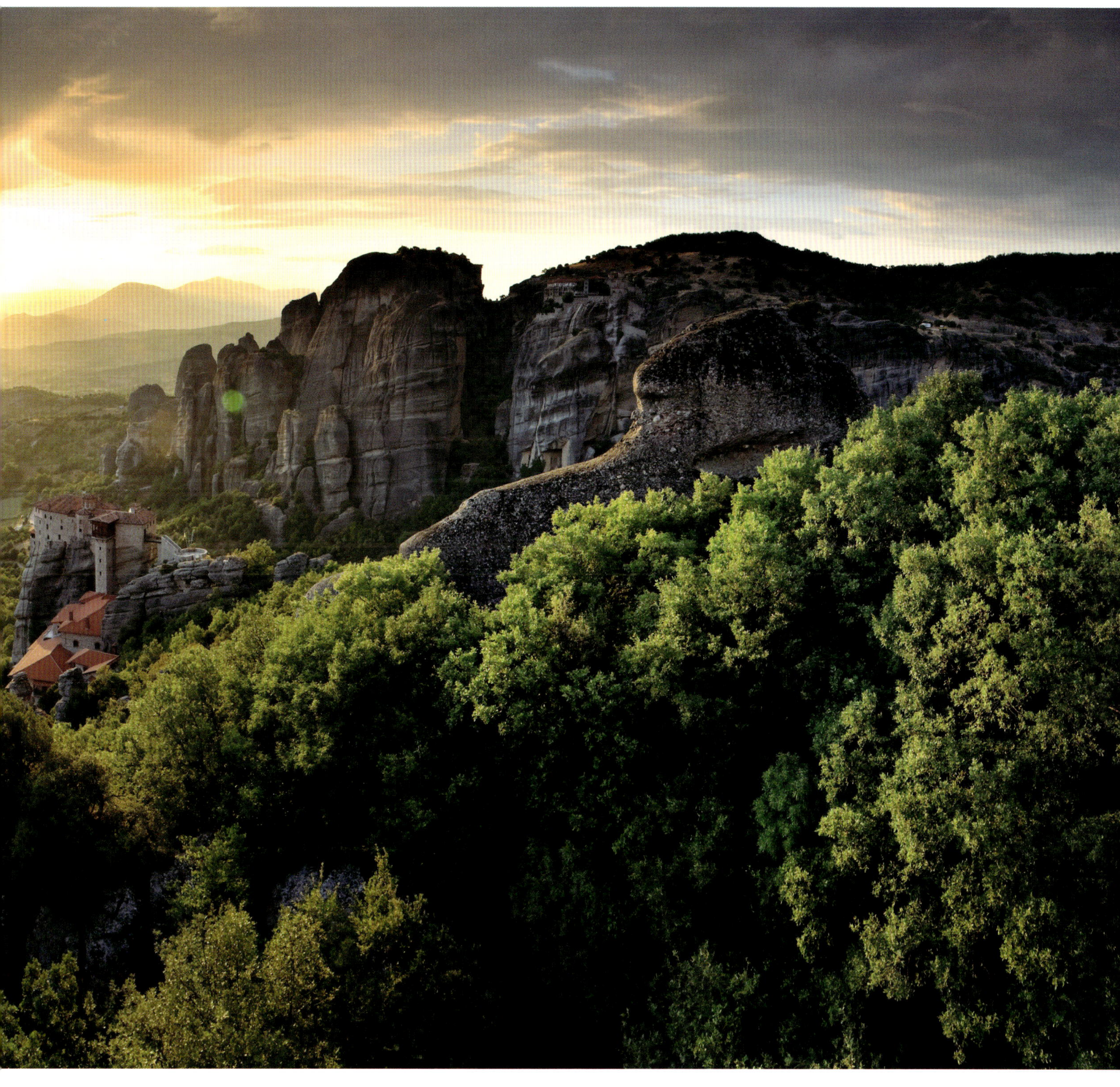

THE DANUBE DELTA BIOSPHERE RESERVE

Date of inscription: 1991

The area where the Danube flows into the Black Sea is a tapestry of tributaries, channels, lakes, woodland, bogs, reed islands, marshes, and sand dunes that provides a habitat for some 300 species of bird, 45 types of fish, and 1,150 varieties of plant.

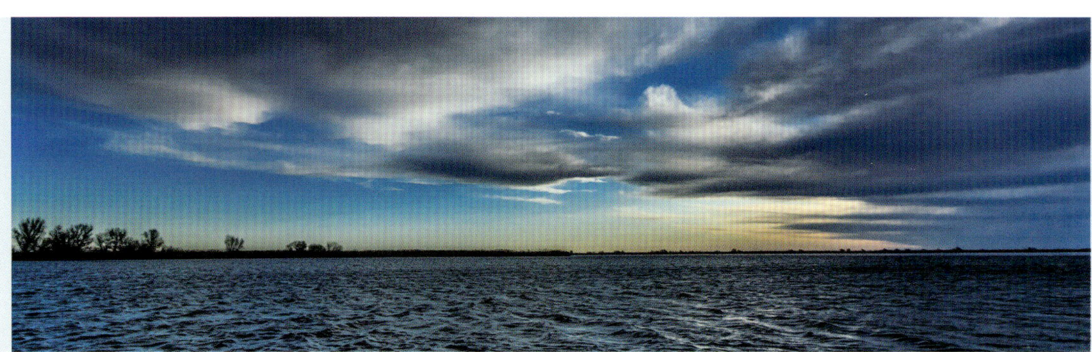

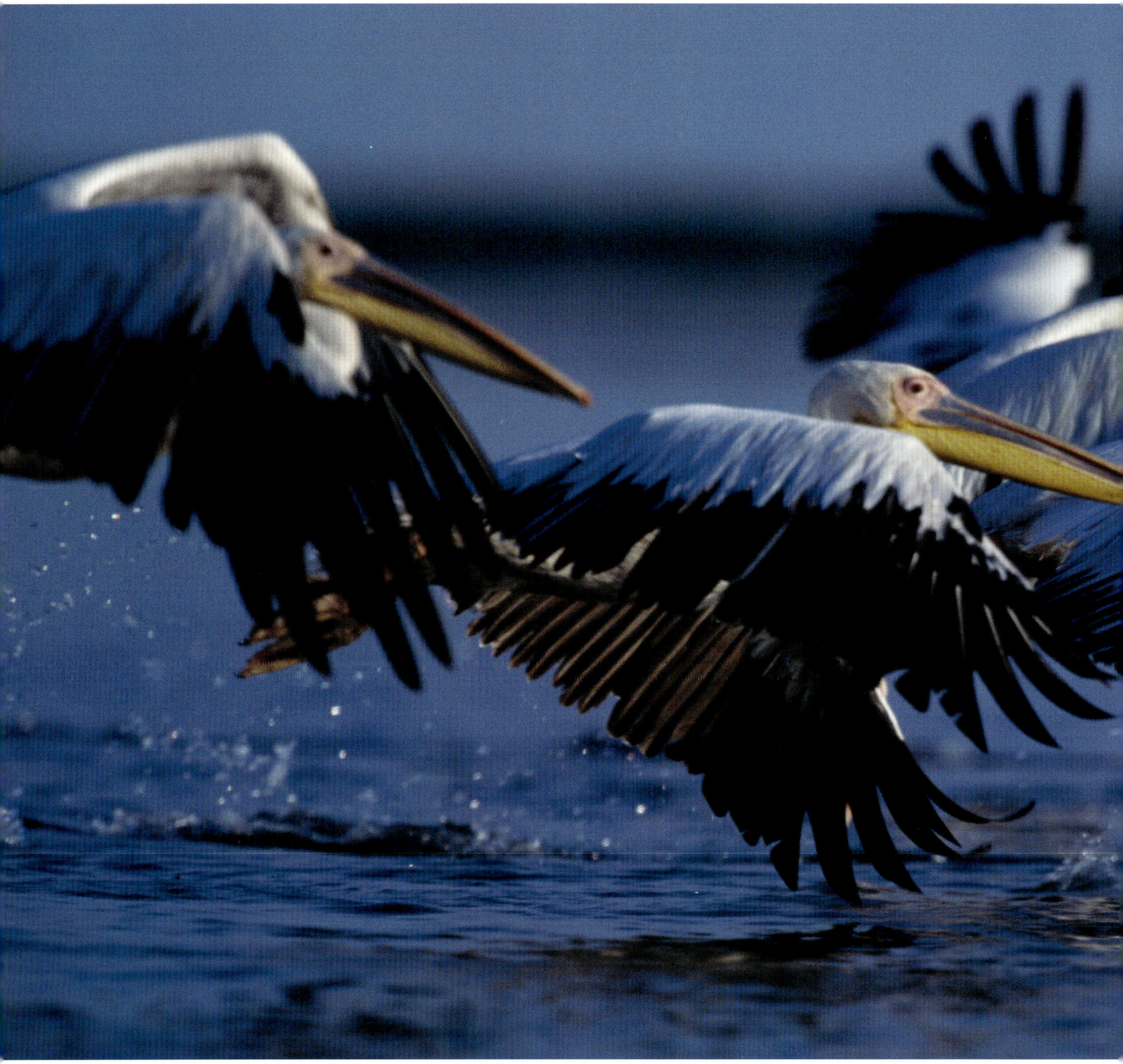

Interrupted only by floating reed islands and the wooded dry land areas, the marshy delta landscape is one of the world's largest and most important biosphere reserves. Its wetland areas are home to rare plants and countless varieties of insects. Swans, geese, herons, pelicans, glossy ibis, and spoonbills are just some of the large birds found here.

Including the Razim-Sinoie lagoon system, the delta covers an area of some 5,600 sq. km (2,200 sq. miles), and is an important resting place for migratory birds. There are also large stocks of fish in the protected waters, including the now rare sturgeon. However, the biosphere reserve is threatened by both water pollution and the commercial exploitation of its reed beds.

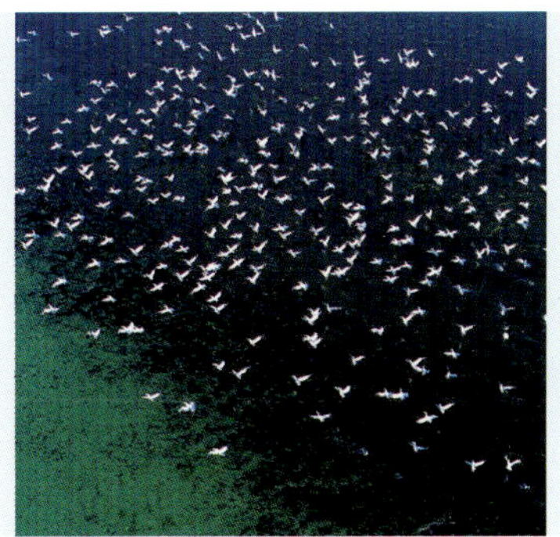

Pelicans usually appear in large flocks and they also catch their fish as a common activity (large picture and left). On the riverbanks live hobby, night heron, squacco heron and little egret (picture series from the top).

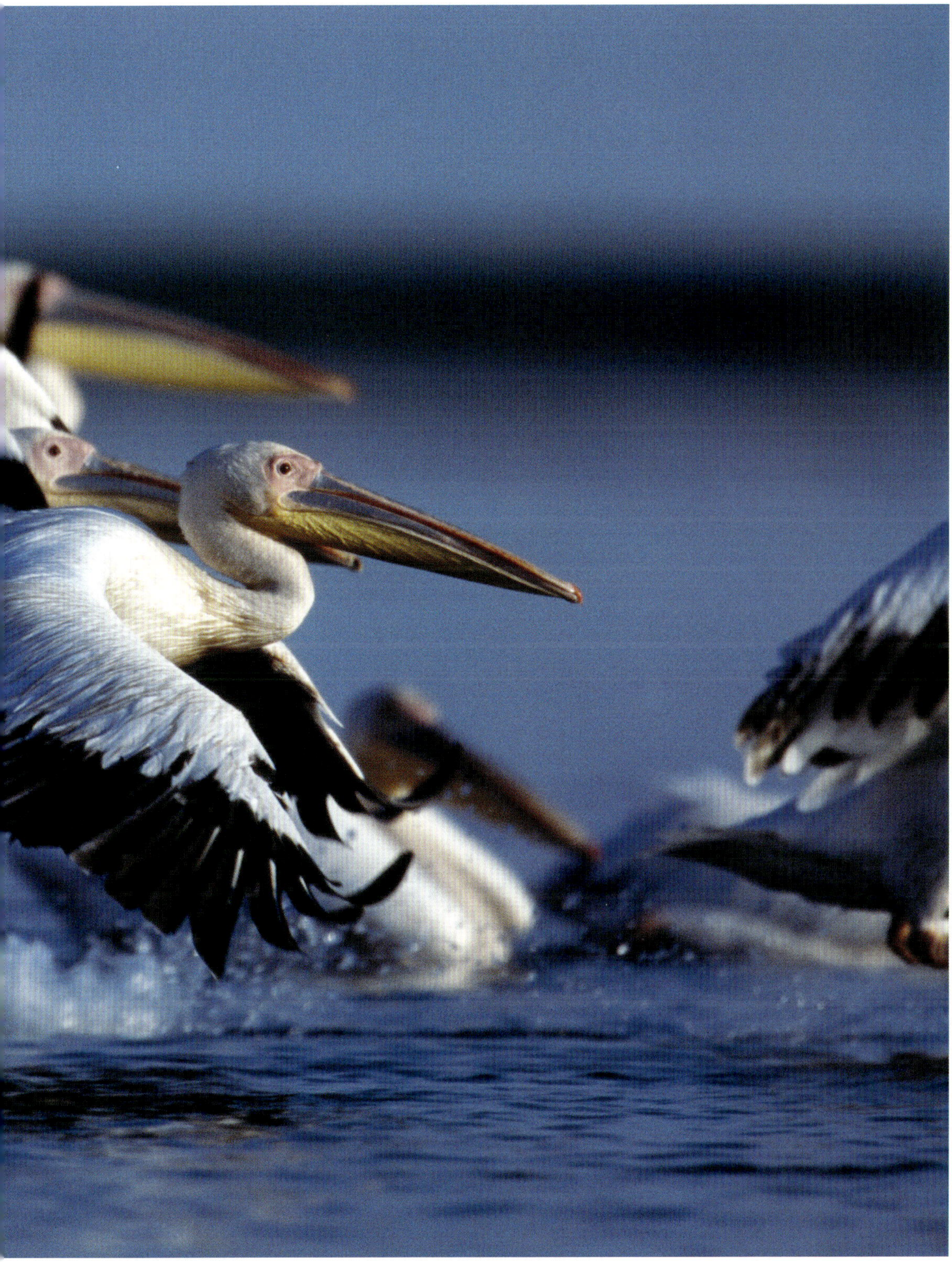

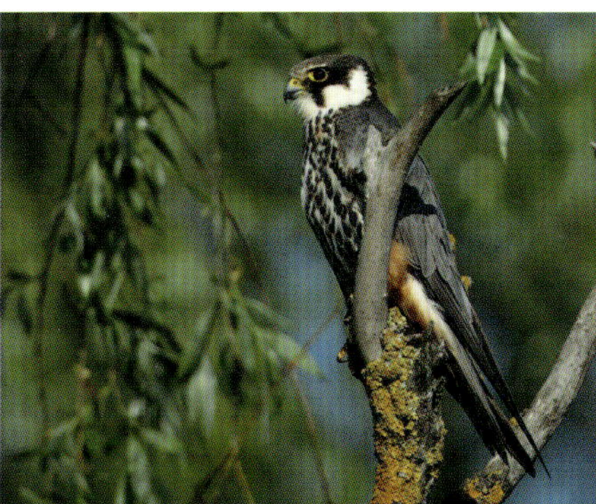

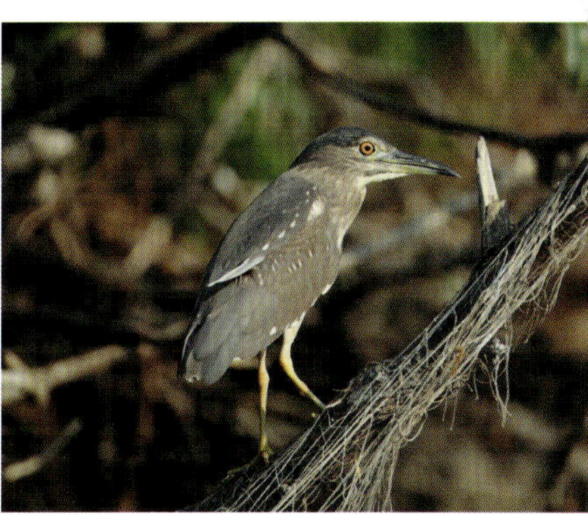

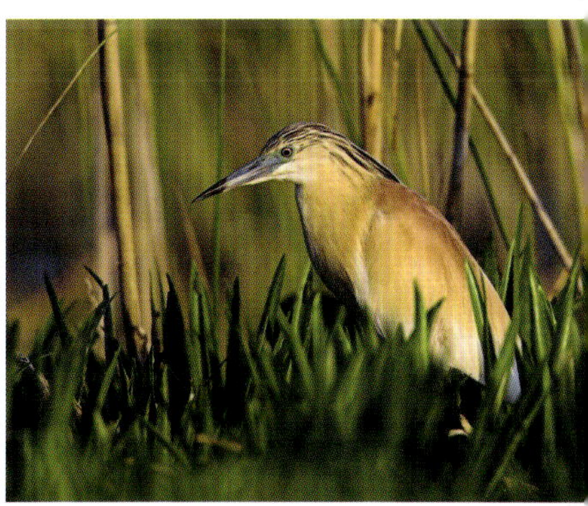

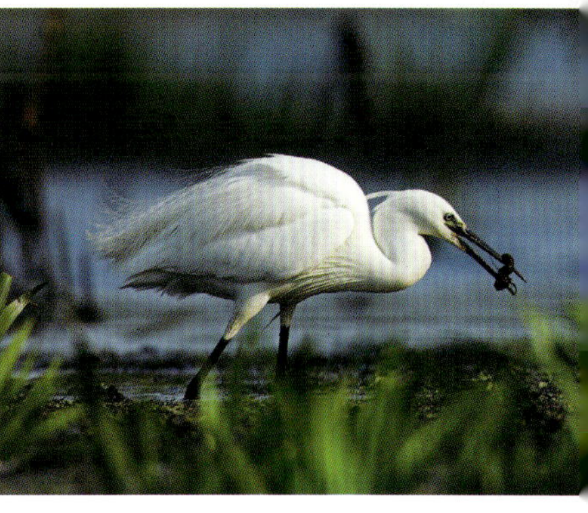

SREBARNA NATURE RESERVE

Date of inscription: 1983

Covering an area of 9 sq. km (3 sq. miles), the Lake Srebarna nature reserve is home to a wide range of water birds – many of them endangered species. During the migration season, flocks of geese, cranes, and storks take to the skies above the reserve.

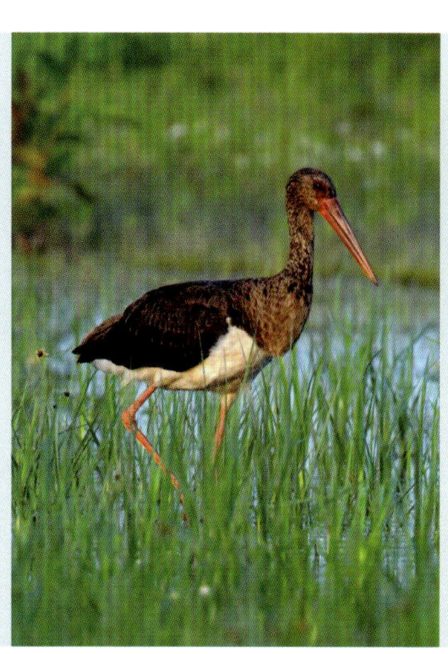

This ornithological paradise is located west of Silistra, not far from the Danube. Around 80 different types of bird visit the reed-covered lake every year – some just passing through, others spending the winter, and others – like the great egret and the rare Dalmatian pelican – raising their young here. The total number of bird breeds found on the reserve and the three Danube islands within it stands at 233.

Srebarna was designated a protected nature reserve in 1948, but between 1982 and 1994 a combination of flood prevention measures and droughts caused the region to literally dry out. The lake was connected to the river again in 1994, and, thanks to regular flooding, has now been almost completely regenerated.

Lake Srebarna may only be an average of 2 m (7 feet) deep, yet it still boasts examples of around half the plant species found in all of Bulgaria's wetland areas. Some 400 hectares (990 acres) of the lake's surface are covered by reeds. The reserve is also home to great egrets below) and black storks (left).

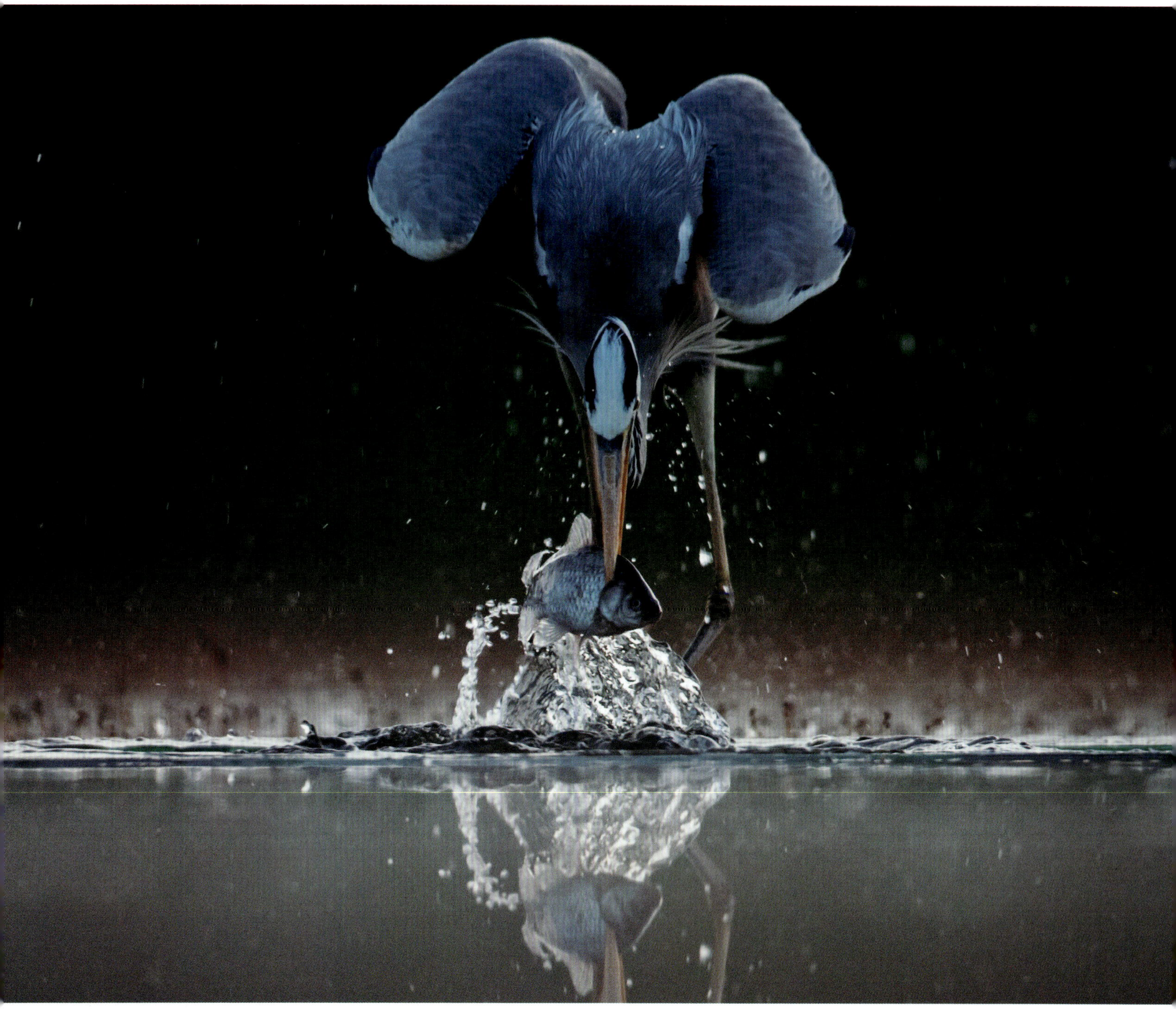

PIRIN NATIONAL PARK

The Pirin mountains lie at the north-western edge of the Rhodope mountains, about 100 km (62 miles) south of Sofia. They span about 40 km (25 miles) from north-west to south-east, flanked by the valleys of the Struma and Mesta rivers. Pirin National Park occupies the northern half of this heavily fissured mountain terrain, with 45 of its peaks reaching an altitude of over 2,600 m (8,500 feet). Towering above them all, the 2,914-m (9,560-foot) high Vihren is the third highest mountain in the entire Balkans. The Bayuvi Dupki reserve is the heart of the park. Some 70 glacial lakes are remnants of the last ice age, and – along with the park's waterfalls and caves – are typical of this limestone landscape. There are also numerous hot springs in the valleys. The park is home to a wide variety of flora, including species typically associated with central Europe and the Balkans as well as alpine plants..

The Glacial Lake Zabecko shimmers serenely in front of the Hvoinat Peak (below). The Pirin mountains are also a refuge for brown bears (right).

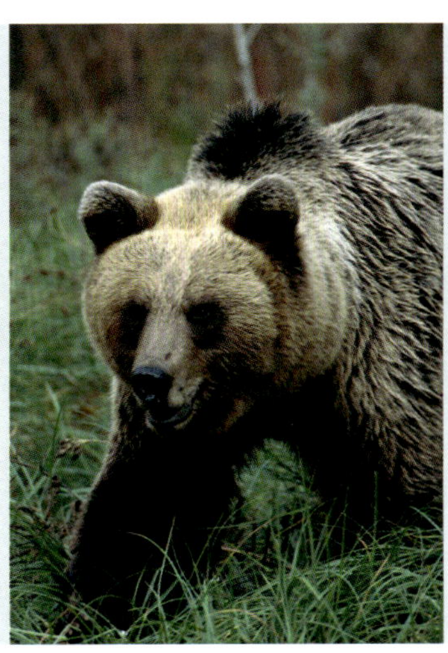

Date of inscription: 1983
Extended: 2010

Pirin National Park covers approximately 270 sq. km (104 sq. miles) of south-west Bulgaria. The coniferous forests that lie beneath its impressive mountain peaks contain some very rare plant species. Many, like the Macedonian pine, are only found in this area.

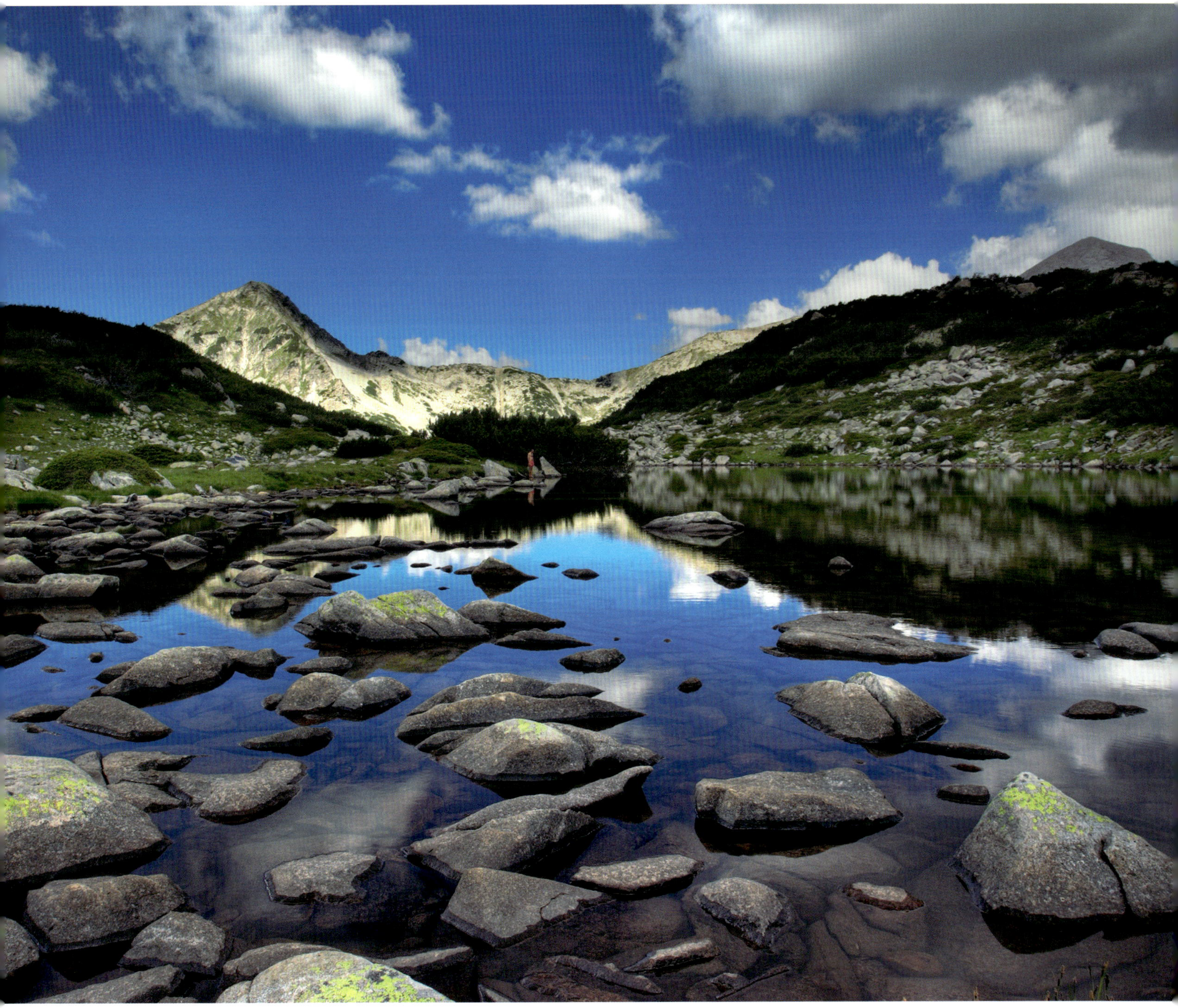

The Sundarbans mangrove forest, around the delta of the Ganges, Brahmaputra, and Meghna rivers on the border of India and Bangladesh, provides a safe haven for several hundred Bengal tigers who are threatened by hunters and decreasing habitats. The tigers playfully practice fighting for an emergency. The green sea turtle (right) is now one of the protected animal species.

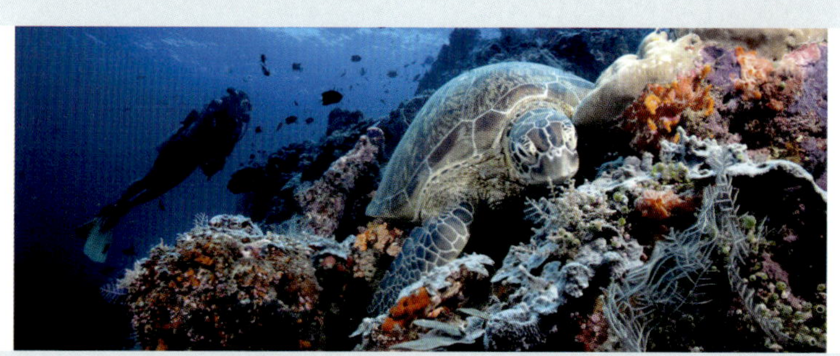

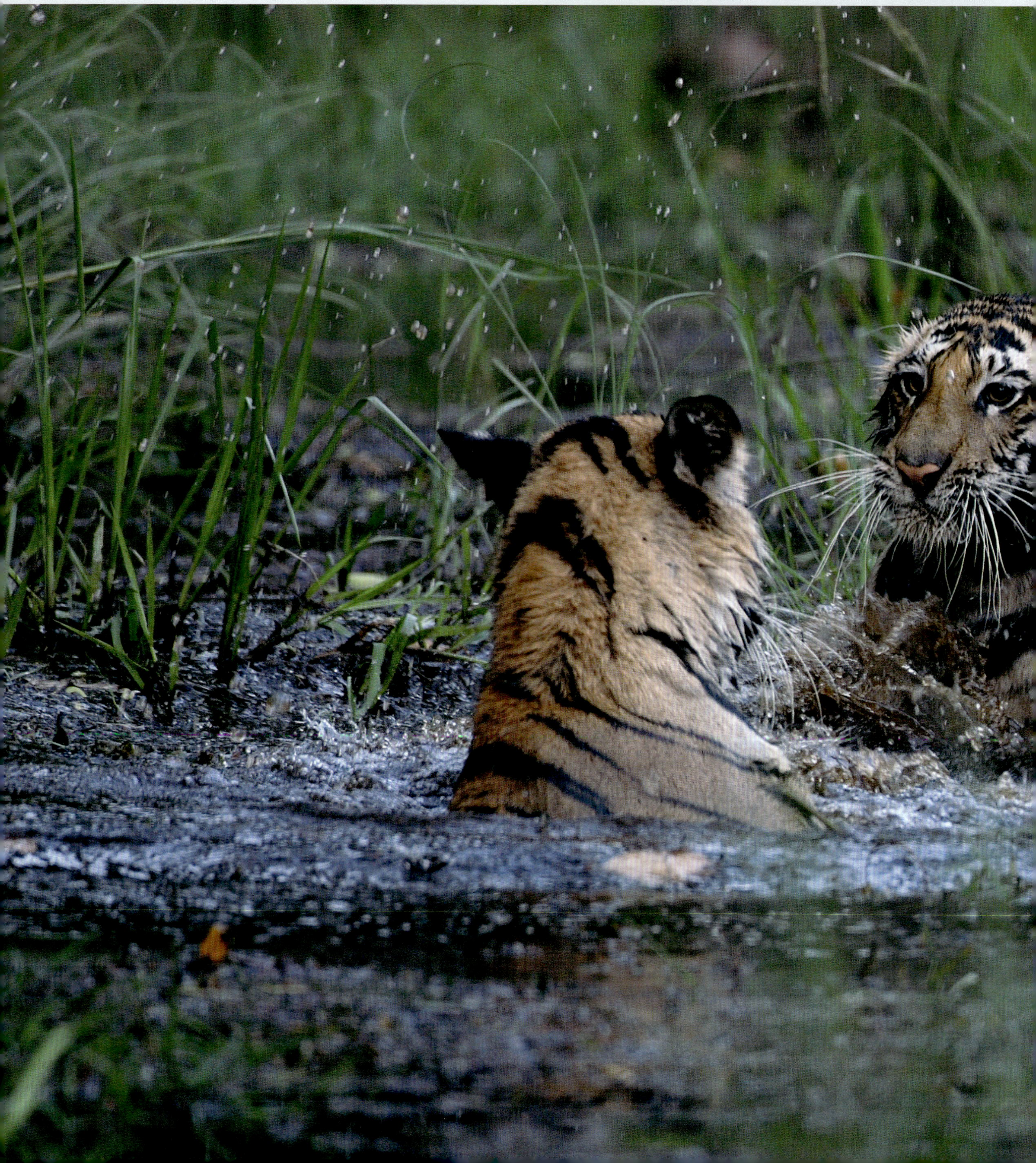

ASIA

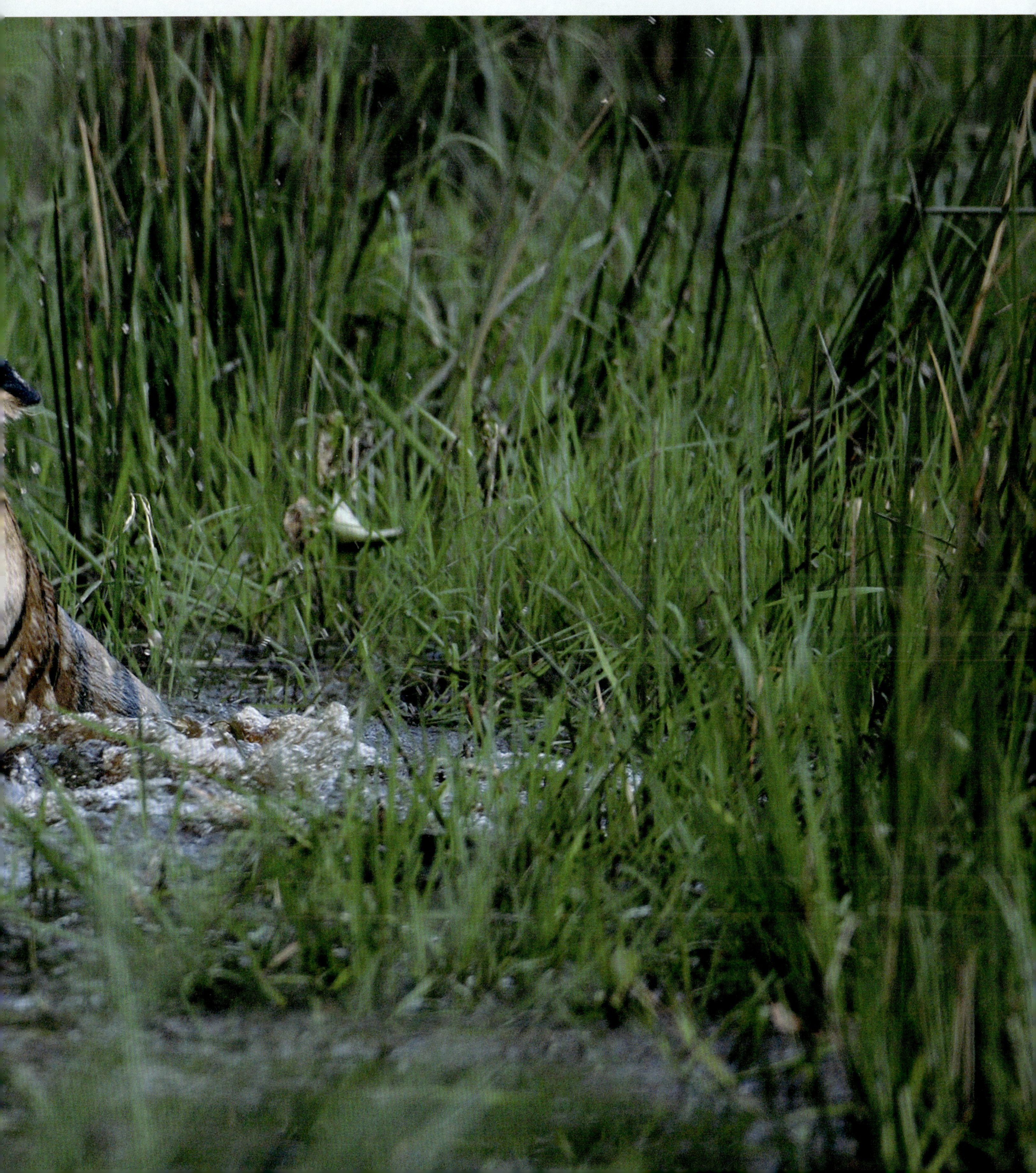

PUTORANA PLATEAU

Date of inscription: 2010

Located in an isolated mountain landscape in northern Central Siberia, the reserve is a combination of arctic and subarctic ecosystems featuring taiga and tundra vegetation and a unique animal population.

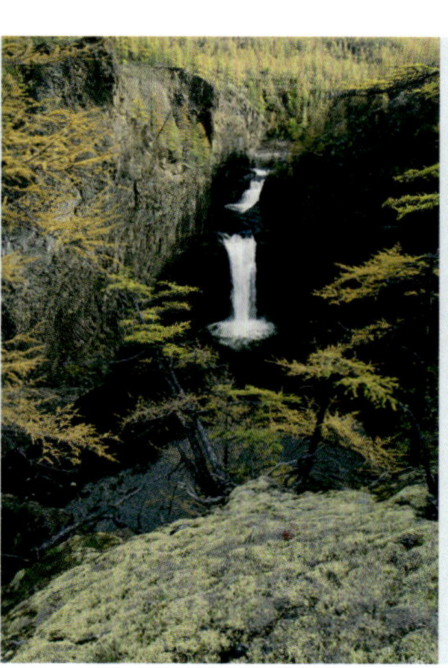

The plateau covers an area of over 18,770 sq km (7,247 sq miles) and is a largely untouched natural landscape of harsh beauty. The sparsely populated region above the Arctic Circle was declared a nature reserve as early as 1988. Its highest peak, the 1,700-m- (5,577-ft-) tall Kamen rises above the basalt plains. Striking features are the up to 400-m- (1,312-ft-) deep and more than 100-km- (62-mile-) long lakes. The two predominant forms of vegetation are taiga, covered with larch, and mountain tundra. Some 500,000 reindeer cross the plateau in their search for food. A subspecies of snow sheep, the Putorana snow sheep, was able to develop around 15,000 years ago in the remote region. In addition, 140 species of birds live here, including the rare white-tailed eagle.

In the language of the indigenous peoples, putorana means "land of lakes and steep slopes". The plateau extends to the southern Taymyr Peninsula (below). Bottom: view of the Lena River.

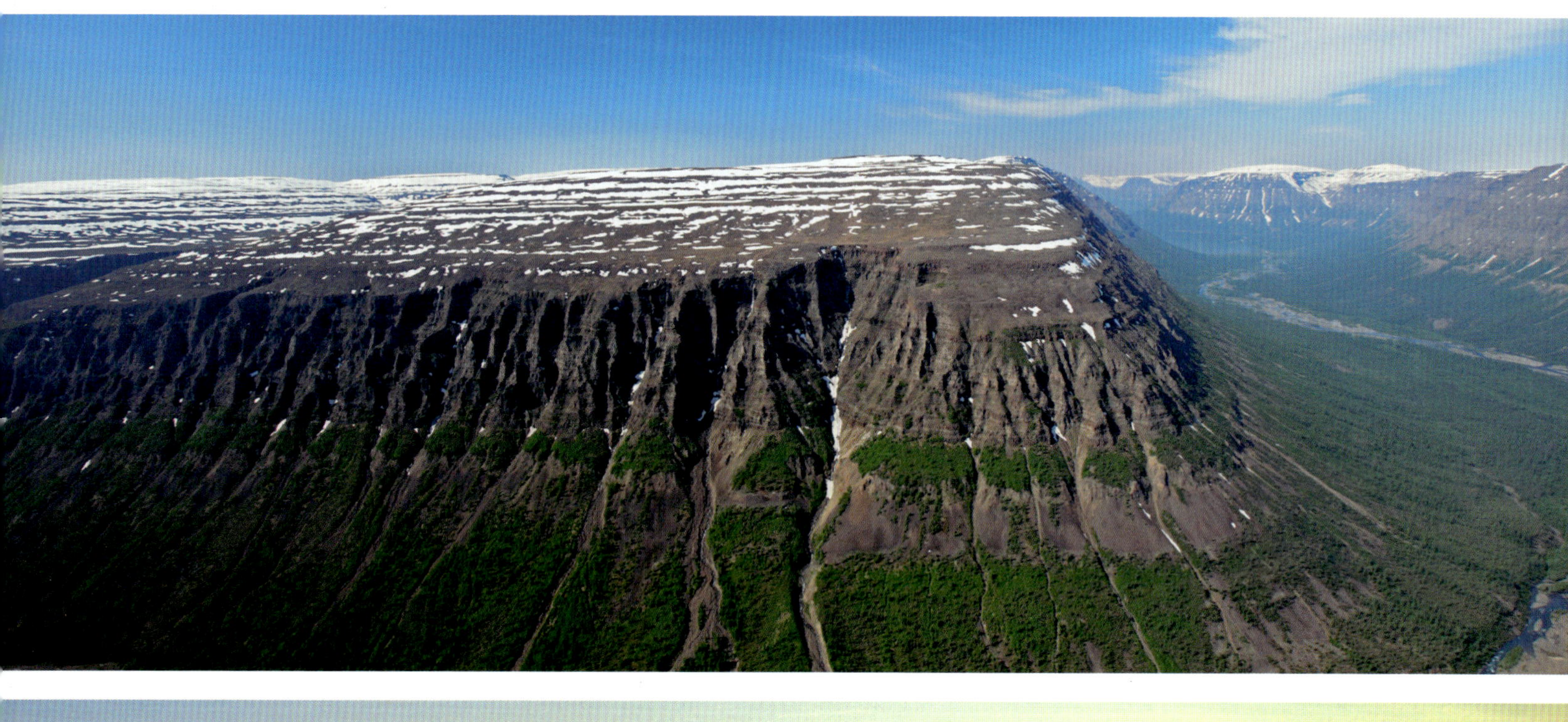

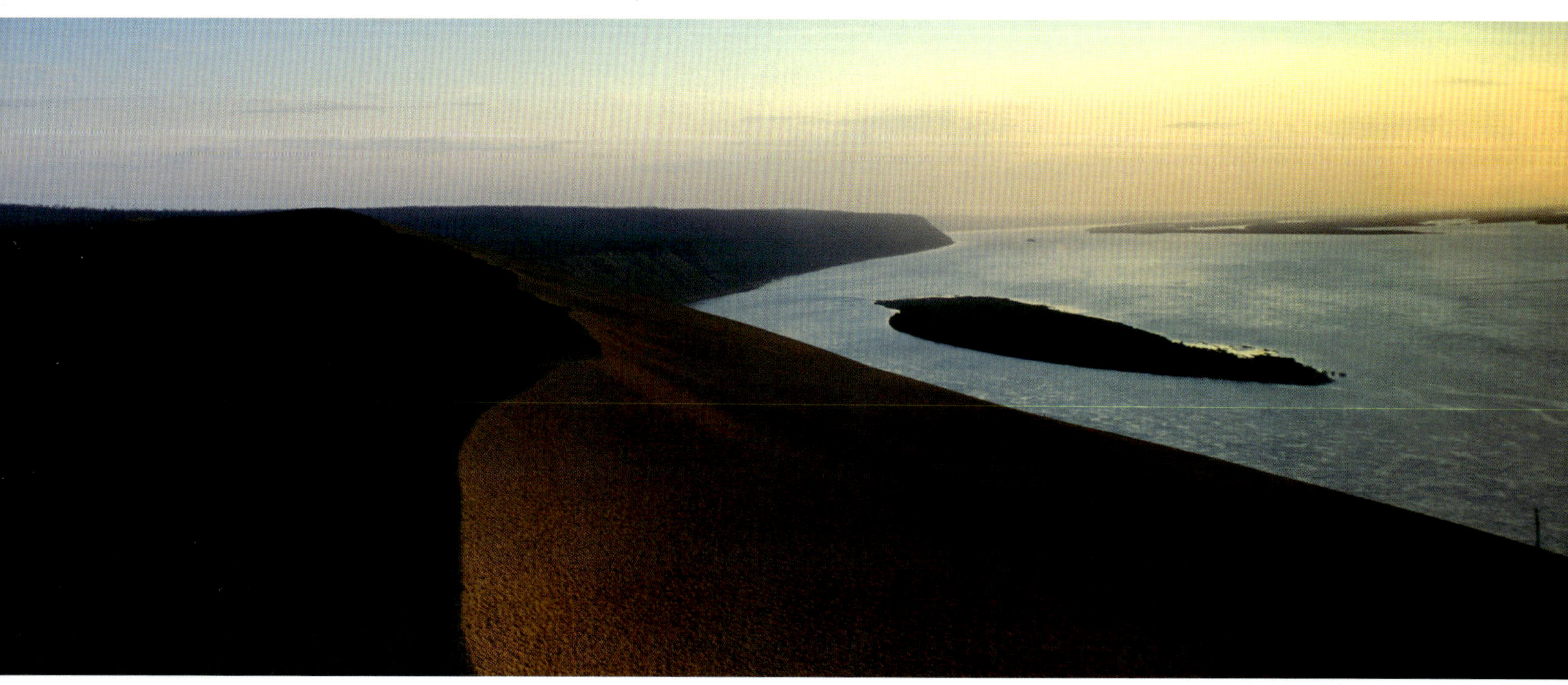

LENA PILLARS

Anyone going north by boat on the Lena River, about 300 km (186 miles) beyond Yakutsk in the Sakha Republic (formerly called Yakutia), will pass into a landscape with large numbers of up to 100-m- (328-ft-) tall columnar rocks. You can see the most varied shapes: straight columns, pillars in bundles, cliffs, towers, arches, as well as rocks with niches and caves. The parent rocks are calcium carbonate or lime-rich mud. The shapes developed through karst weathering, as in more southerly countries, combined with the so-called thermal or cryokarst, which is caused by thawing permafrost. The Lena rocks have survived without change since the Cambrian Period, 540 million years ago. They represent the most extensive reef built by multicellular animals at that time – comparable to today's Barrier Reef in Australia. Ten million ancient fossils are preserved in the rock.

The Sinjaja River is a tributary of the Lena (below). Here, as well as along the Lena River (right and bottom), you can admire bizarre rock columns on the banks.

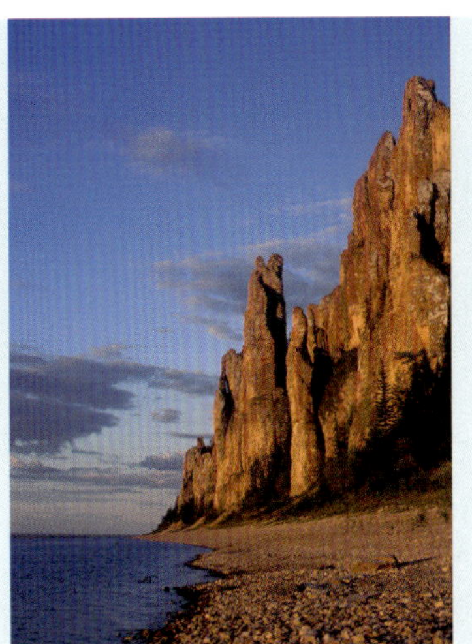

Date of inscription: 2012

At a length of 4,400 km (2,734 miles), the Siberian Lena is of the longest rivers in the world. In its middle reaches, the river flows for nearly 100 km (62 miles) through a bizarre landscape that has weathered into countless cliffs and stone towers.

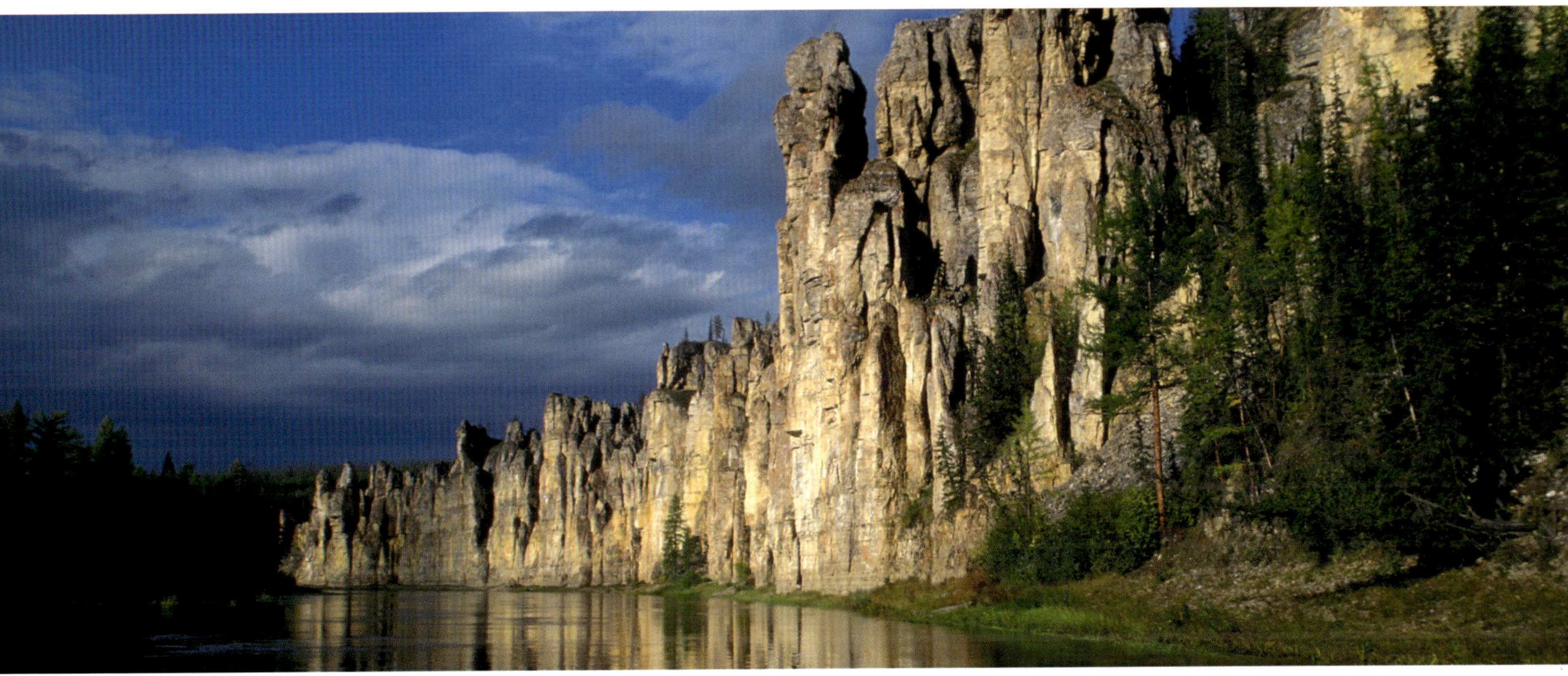

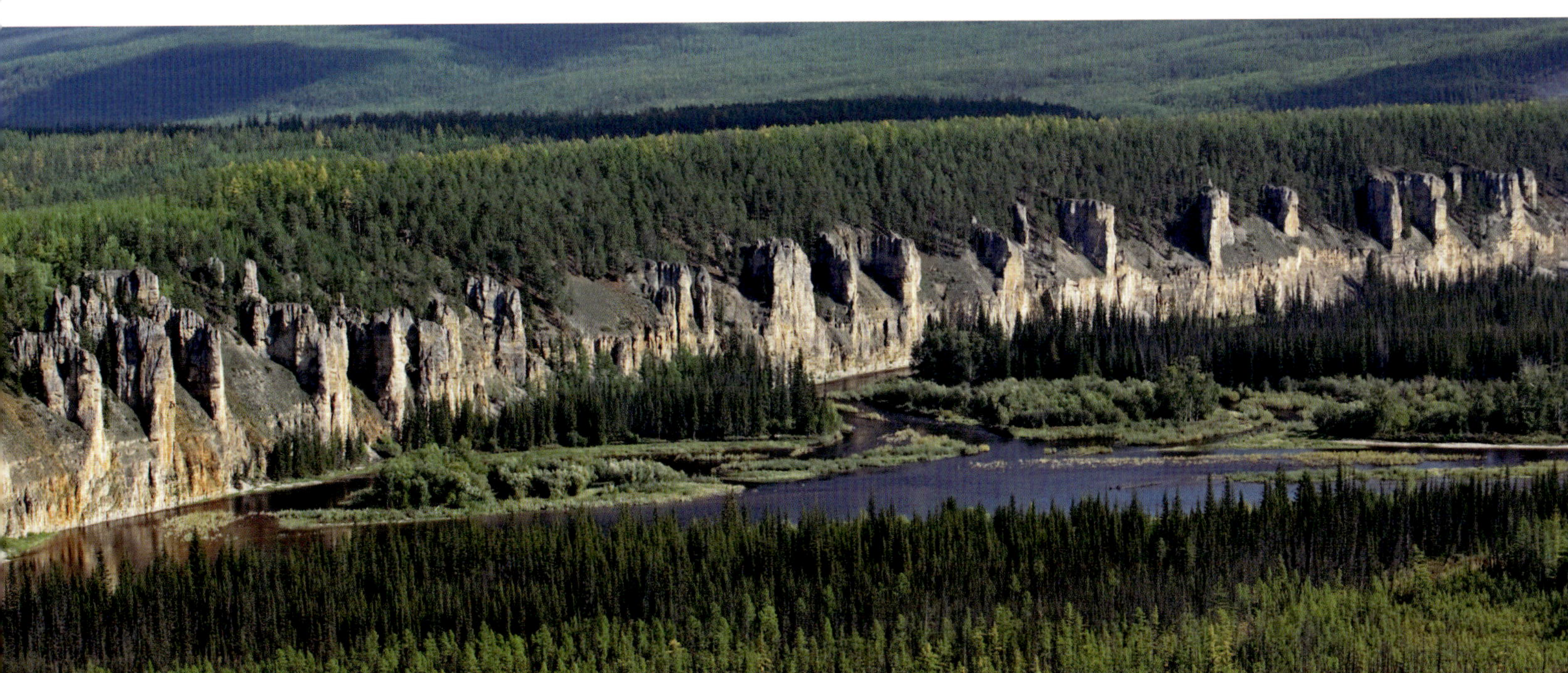

THE GOLDEN MOUNTAINS OF ALTAI

Date of inscription: 1998

The Altai mountains of central Asia lie at the borders of Russia, Kazakhstan, China, and Mongolia. Covering over 16,000 sq. km (6,200 sq. miles), the Altai World Natural Heritage Site falls within Russian territory.

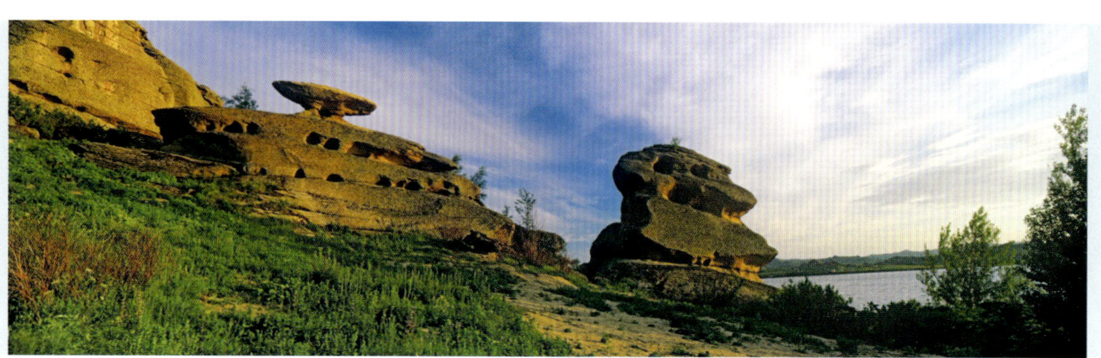

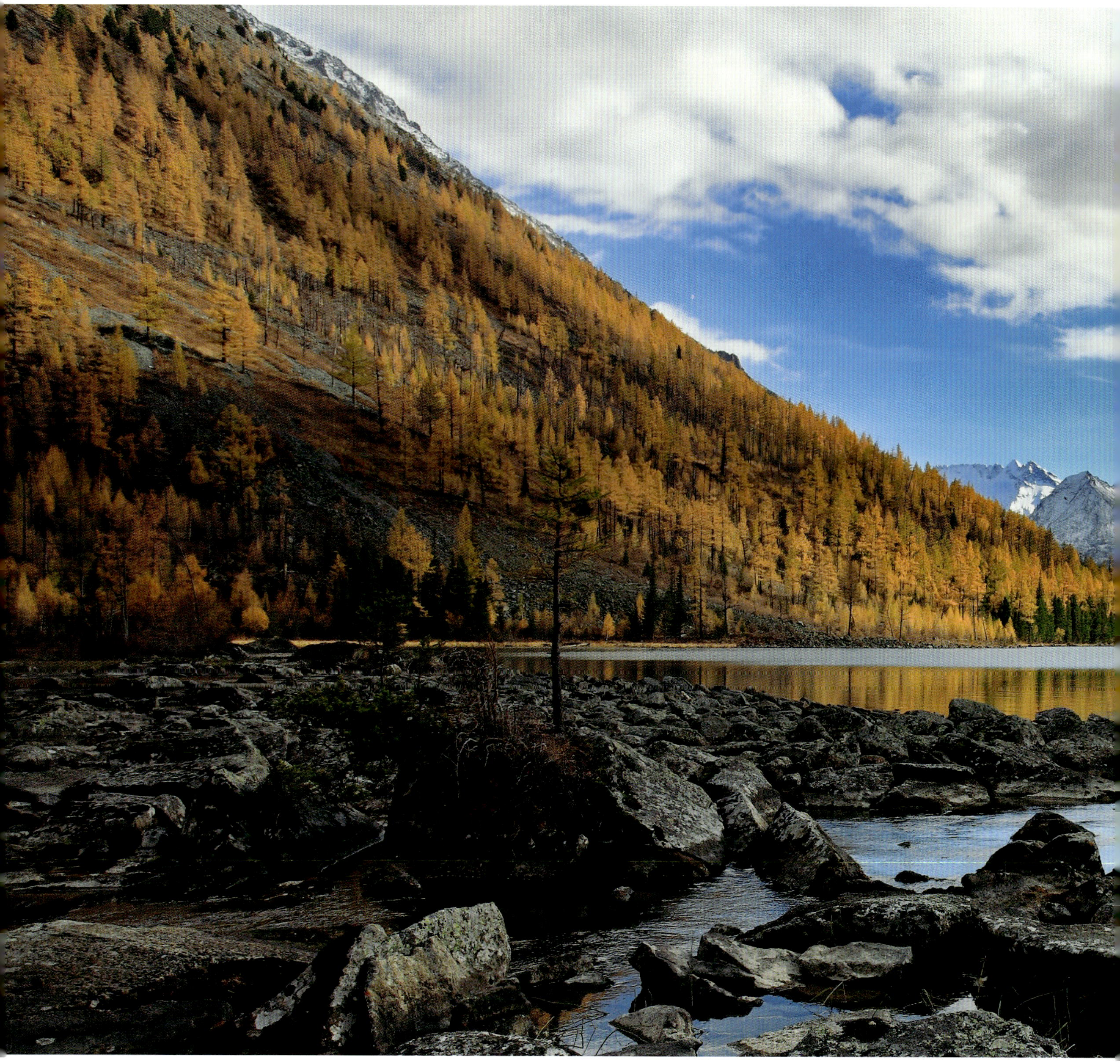

Russia's Altai mountains, in southern Siberia, form part of an Asian mountain range that also includes the Mongolian and Gobi Altai mountains. The World Natural Heritage Site in the Russian Republic of Altai is comprised of three distinct regions, namely the Altai reserve and buffer zone around the 80-km (50-mile) long Lake Teletskoye, the Katunsky reserve and buffer zone around Mount Belukha, and the Ukok Quiet Zone. From the steppe to its alpine areas, the Altai boasts the most complete sequence of vegetation zones in the whole of central Siberia. The variety of plant life is enormous. Over 2,000 genera have been identified, 212 of which are endemic. The area's animal population, meanwhile, is typical of its Siberian forest environment. There are over 70 different types of mammal, 300 types of bird, 11 types of reptile and amphibian, and more than 20 types of fish. Some of the mammals as well as many of the birds are included on the IUCN's Red List of Threatened Species, notably the golden eagle, the imperial eagle, and the snow leopard.

Lake Middle Moultinskoe (large picture), surrounded by larches and pines, provides a typical scenery of the Altai Mountain uplands. The 4,506-m (14,783-foot) high peak of Mount Belukha is the focal point of the impressive Altai mountain landscape. The mountain summits are reflected in clear mountain lakes like Lake Ak-Kem (left).

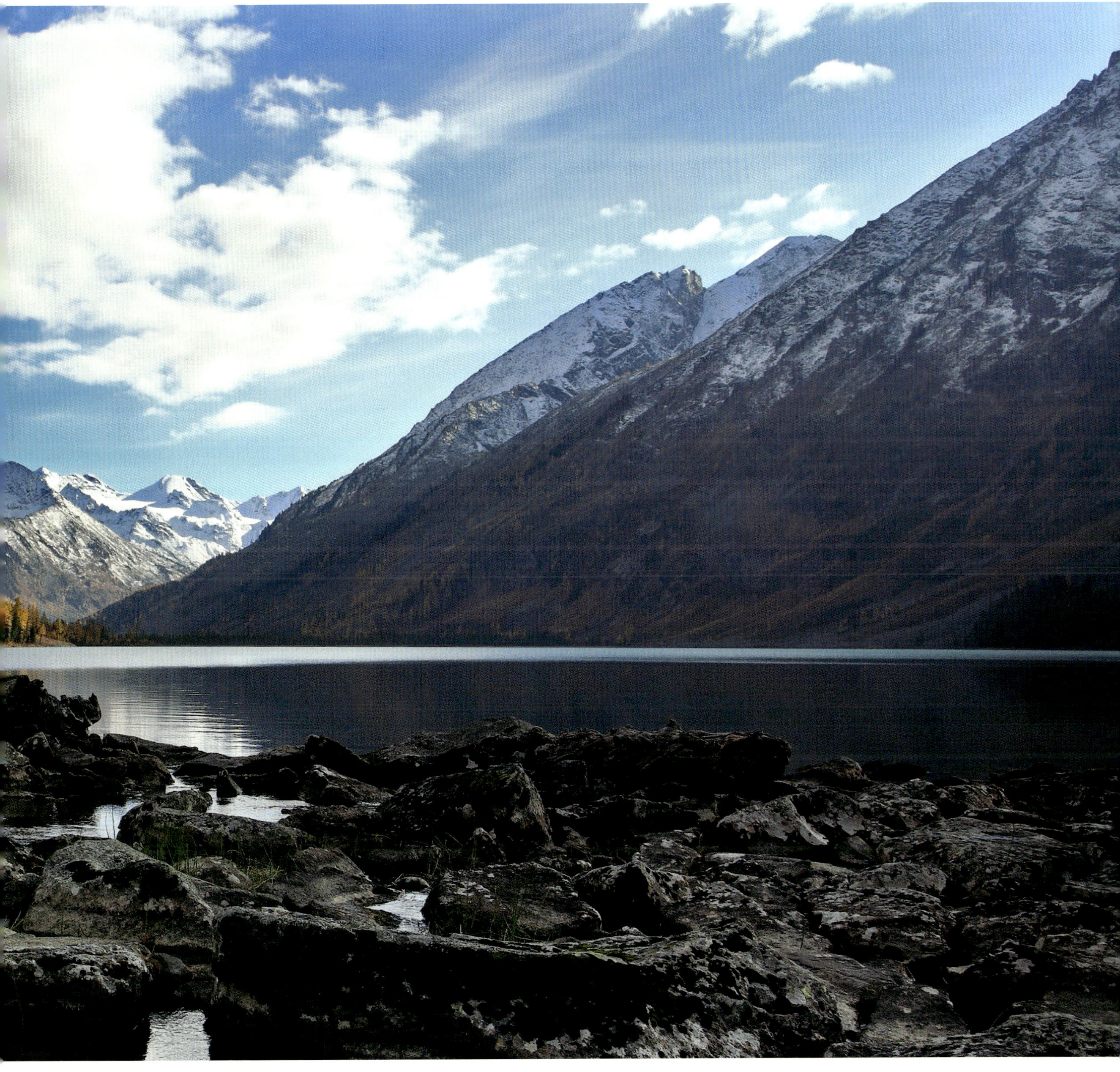

LAKE BAIKAL

Date of inscription: 1996

Lake Baikal is possibly the world's foremost lake. It is not only the deepest freshwater lake in the world with the greatest volume of water, but – dating back 25 million years – it is also the oldest.

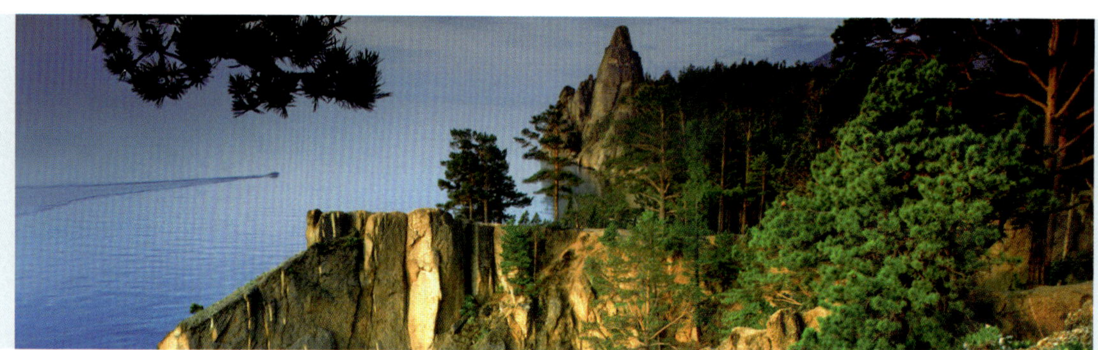

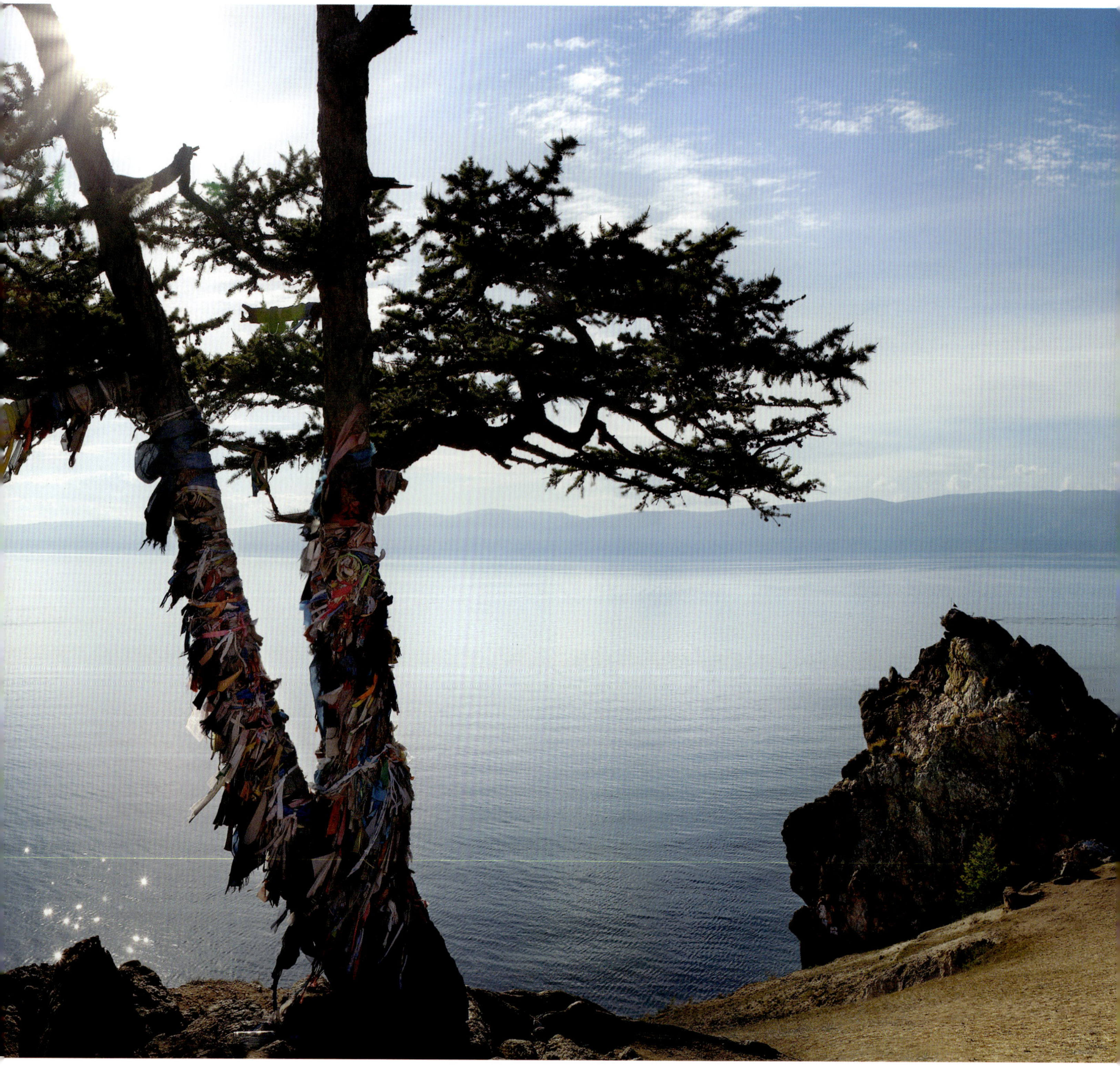

Lake Baikal is nearly 650 km (400 miles) long and, on average, just under 50 km (30 miles) wide. It is situated in southern Siberia, not far from the city of Irkutsk. Geologically, this is a highly active area, and the scene of frequent earthquakes. The mineral springs along the banks of the lake have led to the establishment of numerous spa resorts. In the Buryat language, Lake Baikal means "rich lake," and the lake and its surroundings are indeed home to a great diversity of plant and animal life. Over 1,200 animal species have been identified in the water alone, and most of these – like the Baikal seal or the live-bearing golomyanka fish – are endemic. Some 600 plant species grow on the water's surface and banks.

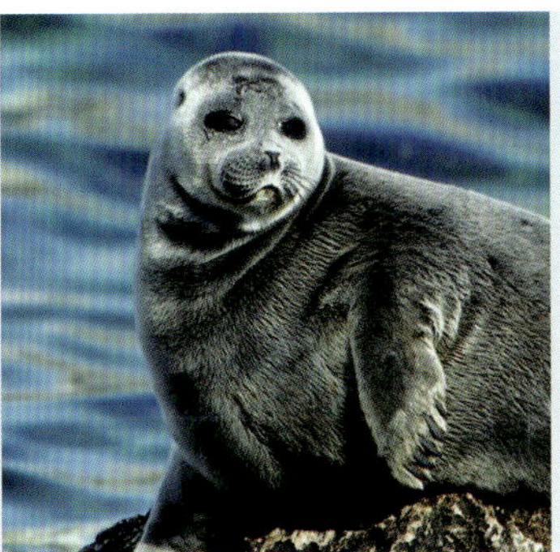

Olkhon is the largest island on the western side of Lake Baikal (large picture). The Baikal seal or nerpa (left) lives in fresh water. Places like Peschanaya Bay (far left) – »sandy bay« – are scenes of unspoilt peacefulness.

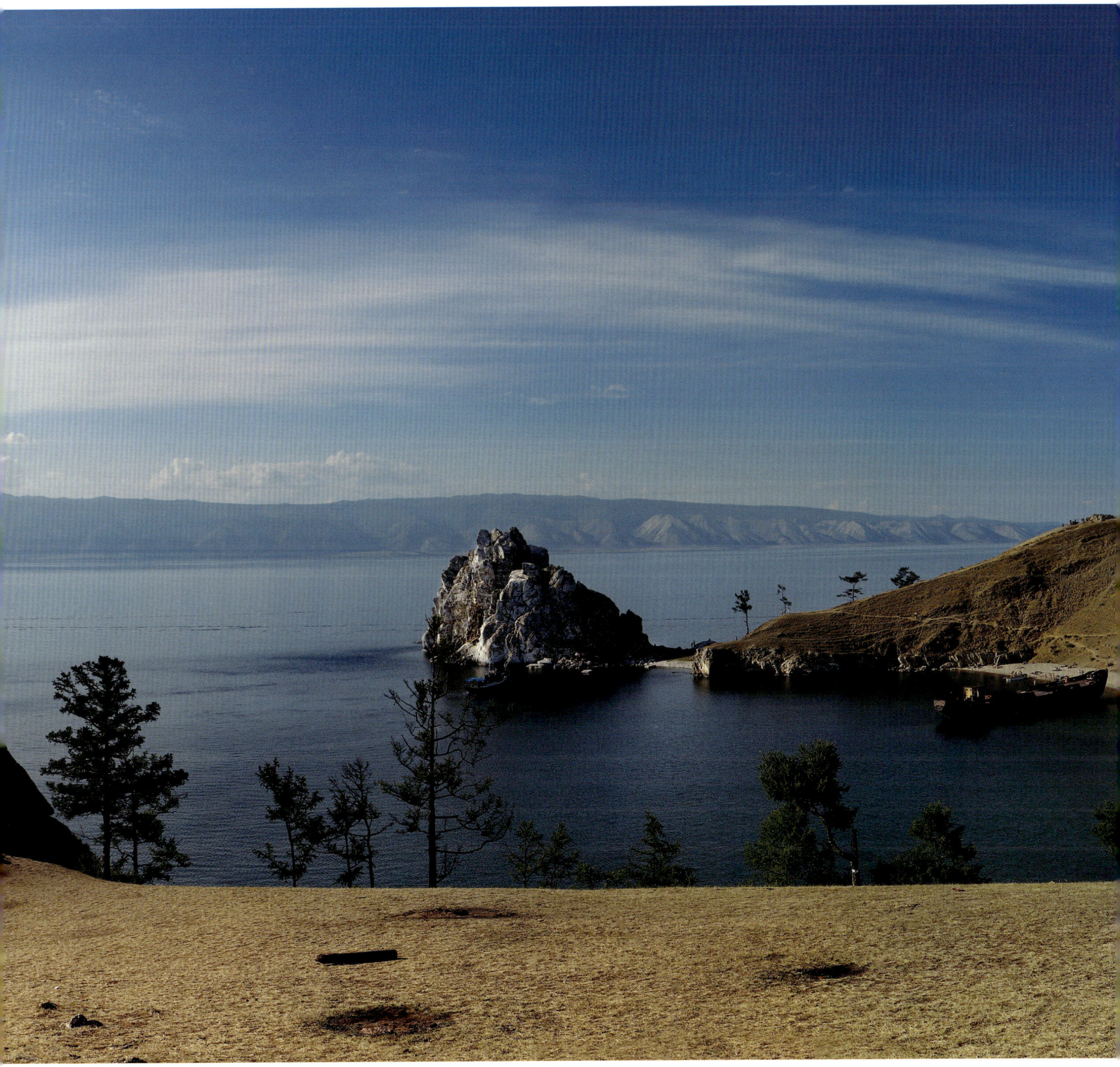

CENTRAL SIKHOTE-ALIN

Date of inscription: 2001

The Sikhote-Alin mountains protected area is the scene of a unique confluence of temperate and subtropical zones. Here, species of flora and fauna that usually belong to quite opposing ecosystems are found side by side.

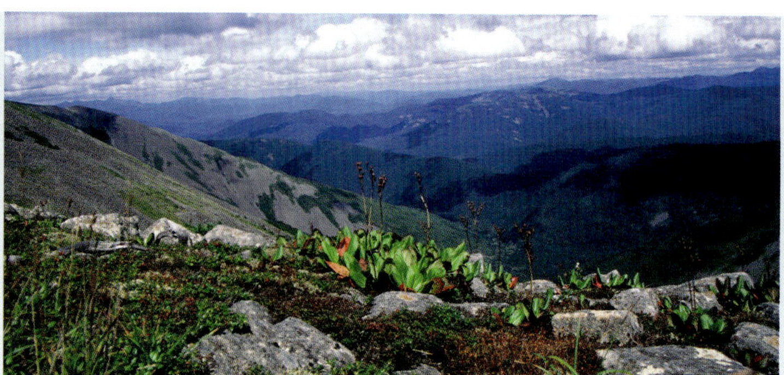

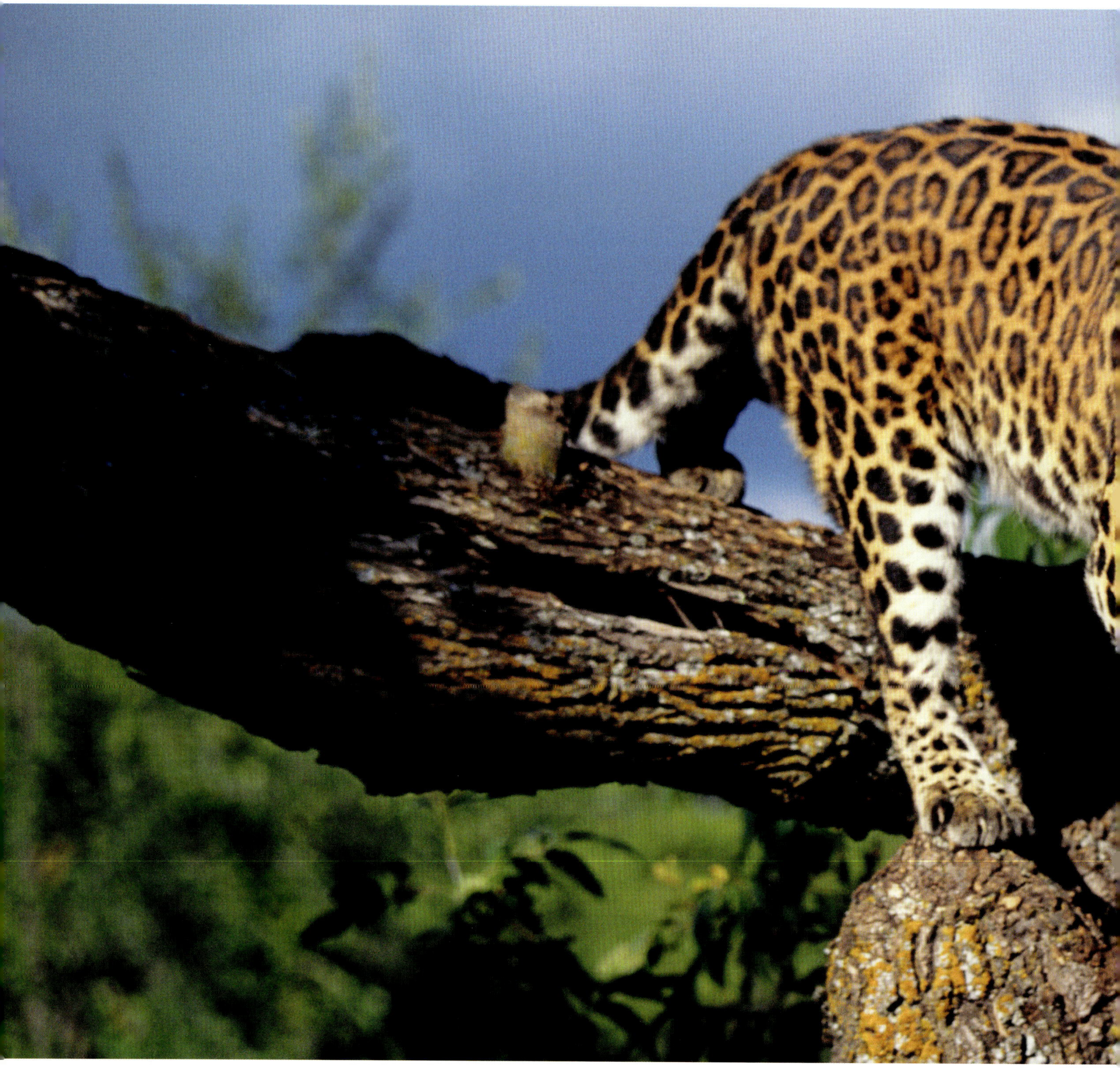

Covering approximately 15,000 sq. km (5,800 sq. miles), the central Sikhote-Alin heritage site comprises three nature and animal reserves in the mountainous regions of the Russian far east, as well as the mountain range along the coast of the Sea of Japan. It was first declared a biosphere reserve in 1979, and is notable for its mixed population of Siberian, Manchurian, and south-east Asian animal species. Here, brown bears live side by side with Asiatic black bears, endangered Amur (Siberian) tigers, and Amur leopards (whose population has now dwindled to very small numbers indeed). Over a hundred of the area's animal and plant species are included on the IUCN's Red List at either national or international level.

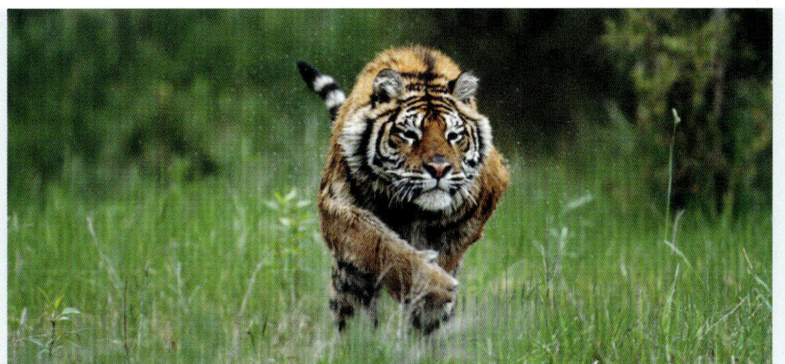

Dense forests are the predominant feature of the mountain landscape. Taiga and extensive wetlands dominate the more northerly regions, but they give way to subtropical deciduous forests in the south. Numerous endangered animals live here, not least of which is the Amur tiger (left) and the Amur leopard (below).

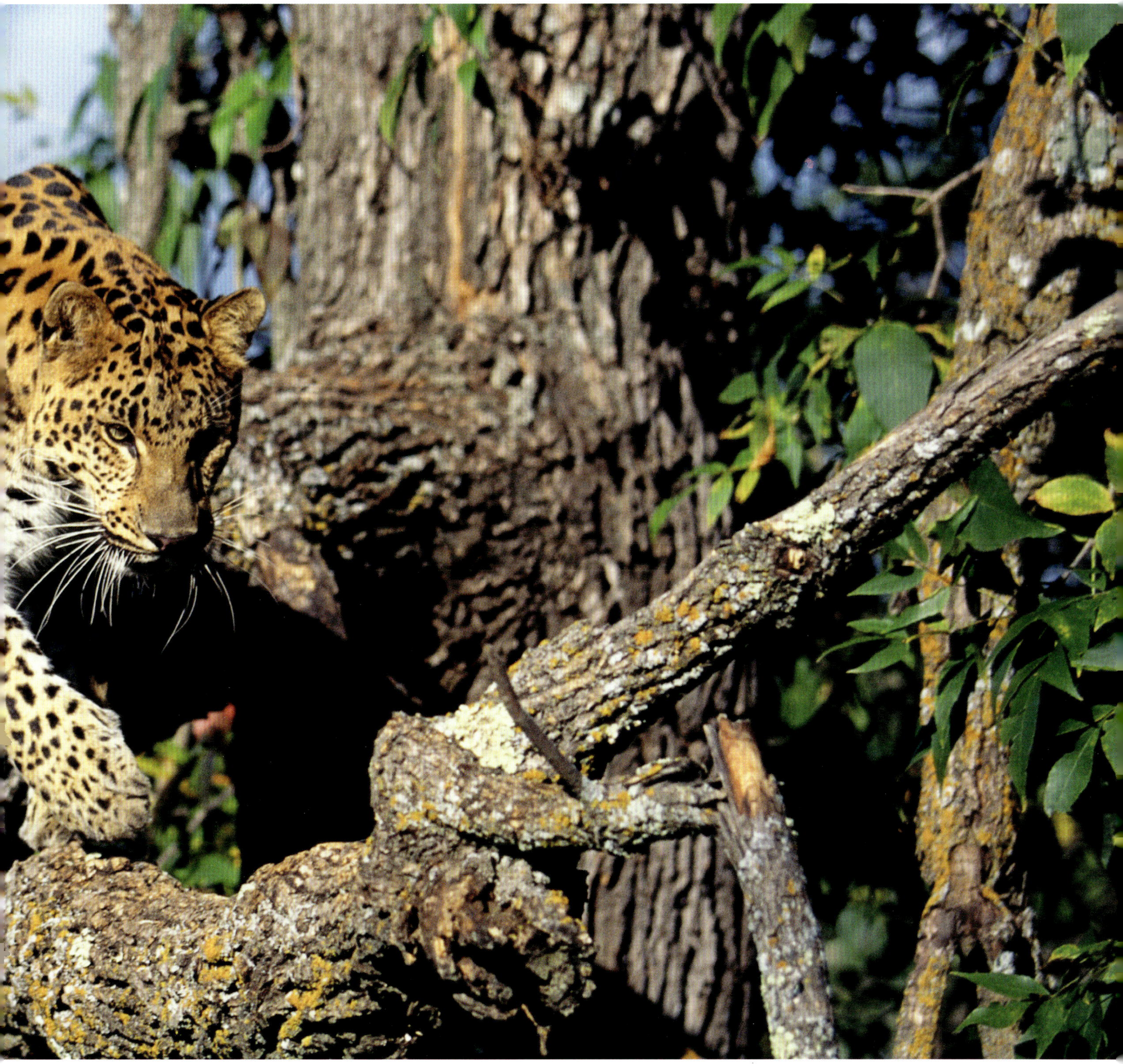

WRANGEL ISLAND RESERVE

Date of inscription: 2004

The mountains of Wrangel Island lie at the north-east extremity of Russia. Considering the island's northern latitude, the diversity of plant and animal life found here is quite extraordinary.

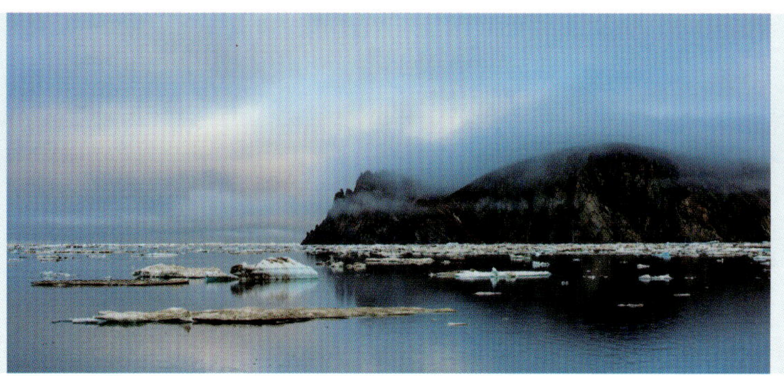

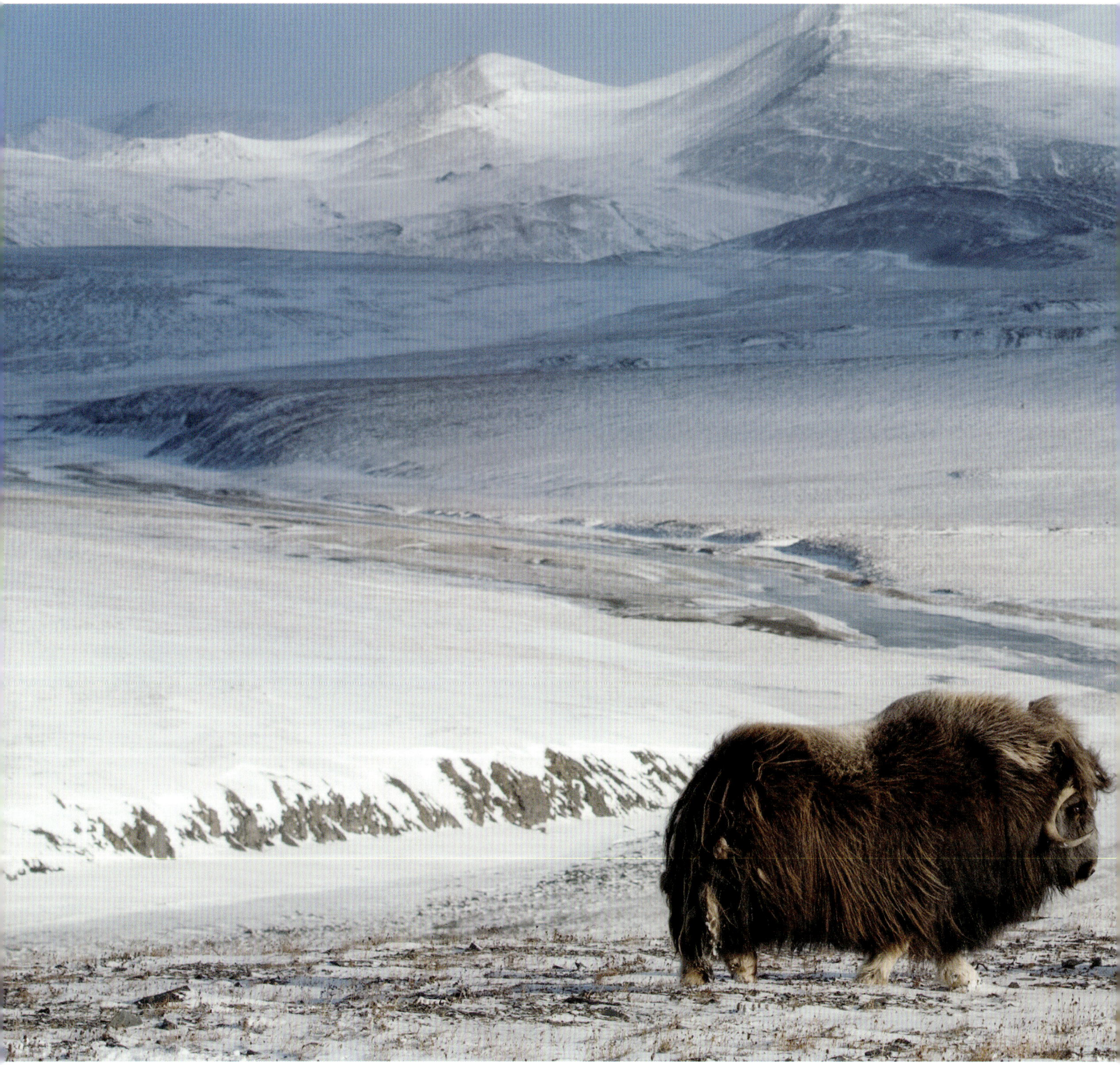

Wrangel Island is located far north of the Arctic Circle, on the western side of the Chukchi Sea. Named after the Russian admiral and Siberian explorer Ferdinand von Wrangel, the island covers an area of around 7,500 sq. km (2,900 sq. miles). It is rich in geological features and boasts a great diversity of natural habitats, each of which has its own microclimate. Thanks to its mountainous terrain, Wrangel was never fully glaciated during the ice age, and it is this fact that explains the survival of plants and animals here that have died out elsewhere.

In fact, there are over 400 species and subspecies of vascular plants on Wrangel Island – double the number found in any other similarly sized tundra area. Of these, 23 are endemic – the product of recent hybridization. The island is home to the world's largest population of Pacific walrus – numbering up to 100,000 animals – and also boasts the world's densest concentration of polar bear dens. Two further notable animals are the musk oxen grazing on the tundra landscape, and the grey whales migrating from Mexico, for whom this is a plentiful feeding ground. Some 100 species of migratory bird breed on the island, among them the snow goose. Wrangel Island's lemmings, meanwhile, are notable for behavior patterns that differ markedly from those of other Arctic lemming populations. Like the lemmings, the island's reindeer have also adapted to the local environment.

Musk oxen (large image) are not native to Wrangel Island, but are descended from animals released into the wild here. The musk oxen are ideally equipped for the harsh weather conditions. Their coat consists of different hair types that protect the body in layers. Ice floes drift on the water offshore from the coastal section known as Cape Waring (left).

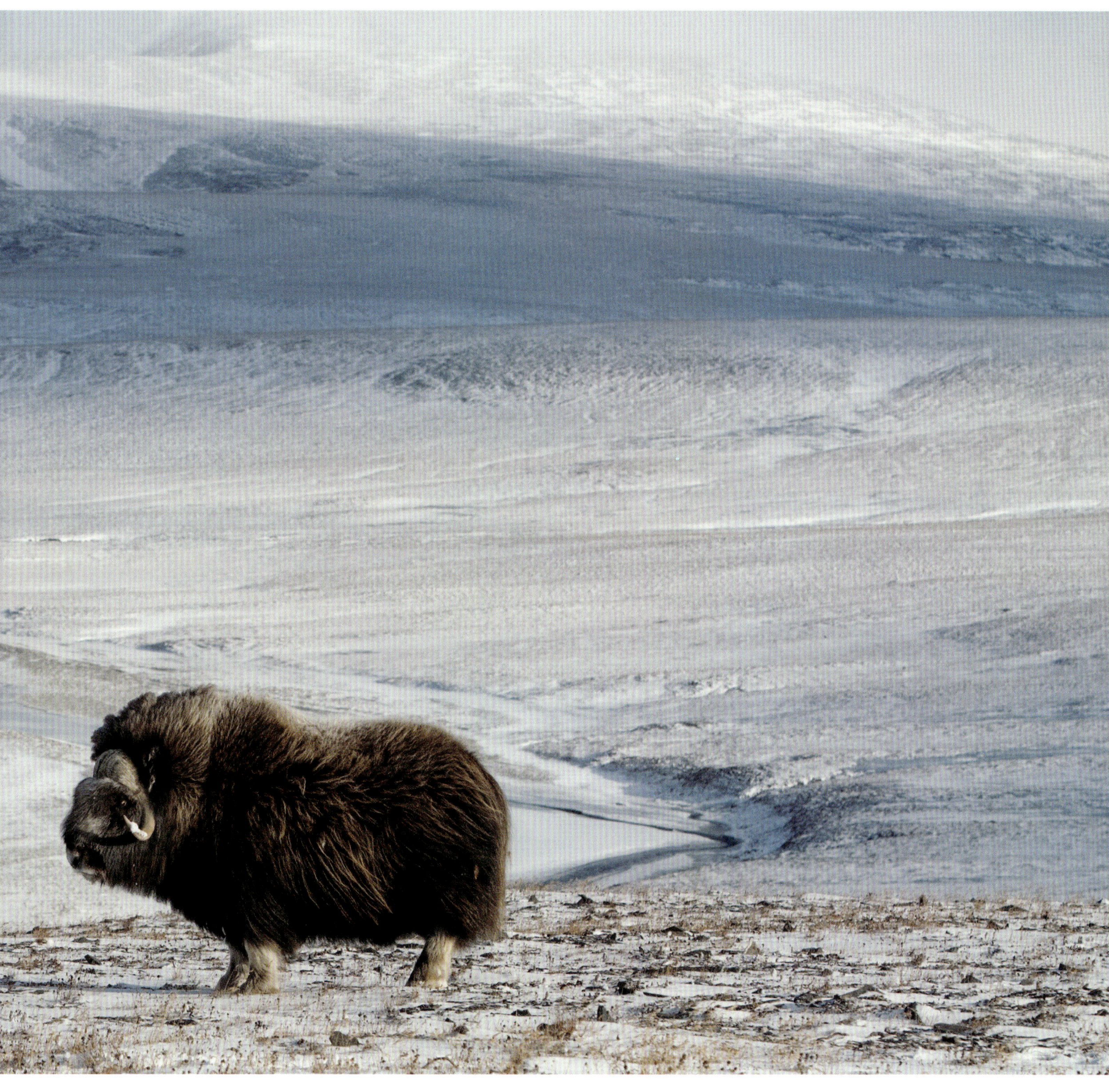

THE VOLCANOES OF KAMCHATKA

Date of inscription: 1996
Extended: 2001

The Kamchatka peninsula spans 350,000 sq. km of Russia's far east. There are 28 active volcanoes in the southern part of the peninsula. Since its inscription, the natural heritage site has been extended to include Kluchevskoy Nature Park.

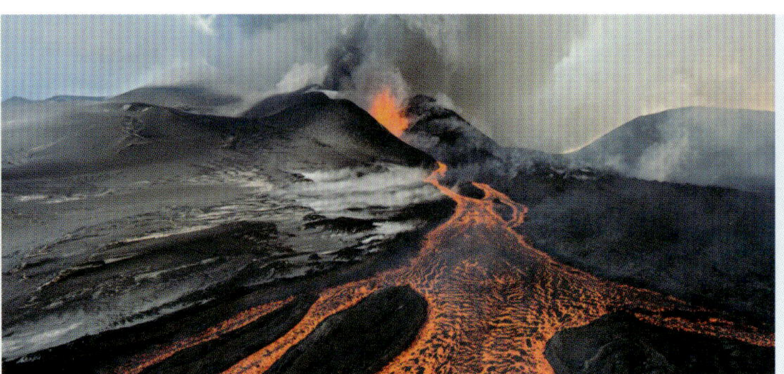

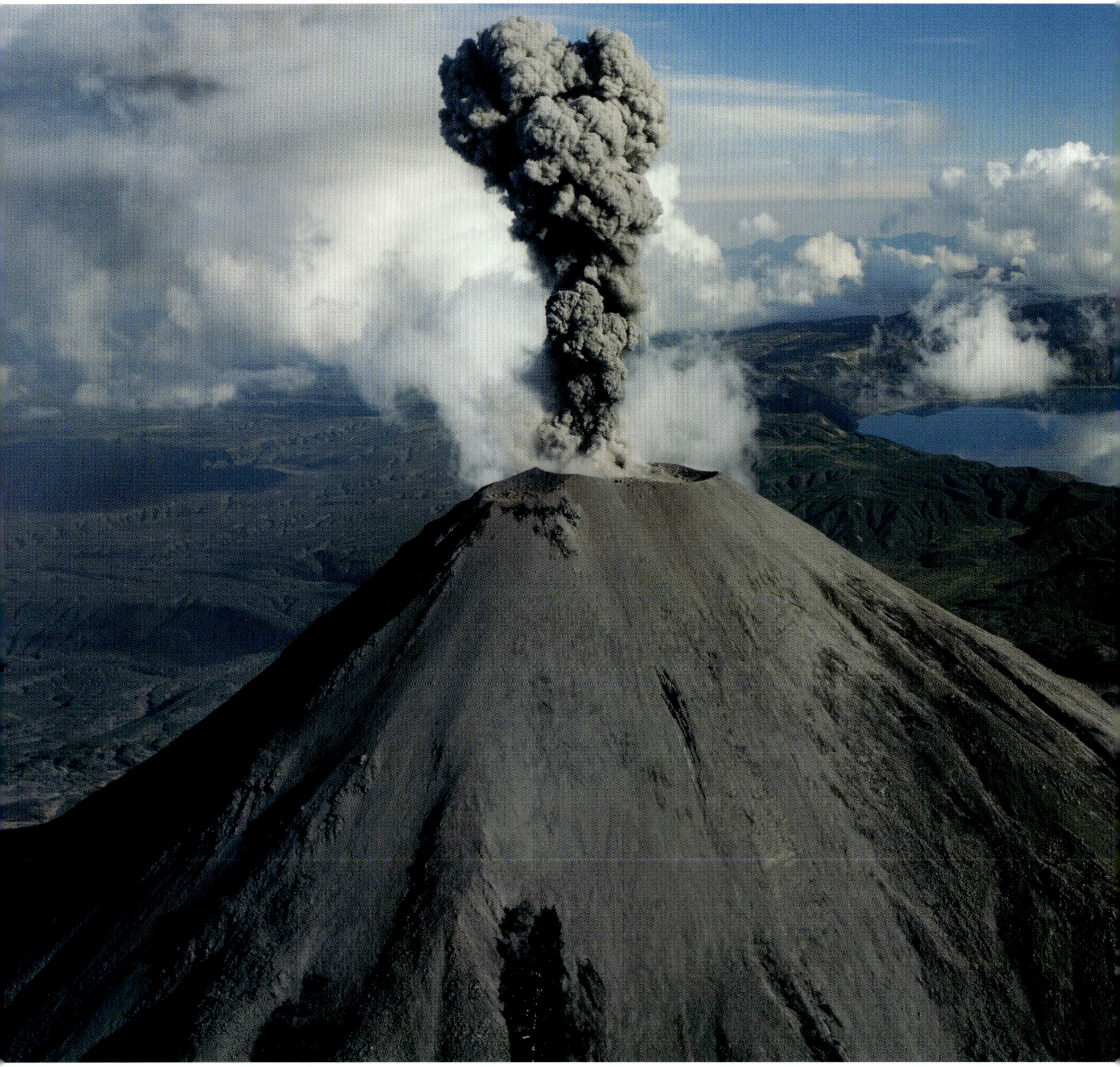

The peninsula is 1,200 km (746 miles) long and 480 km (298 miles) wide at its widest point. It lies between the Sea of Okhotsk to the west, and the Pacific and Bering Sea to the east. Two parallel chains of mountains run along the peninsula, with the Kamchatka river valley taking up most of the space in between. Reaching heights of 2,000 m (6,562 feet), the western or central

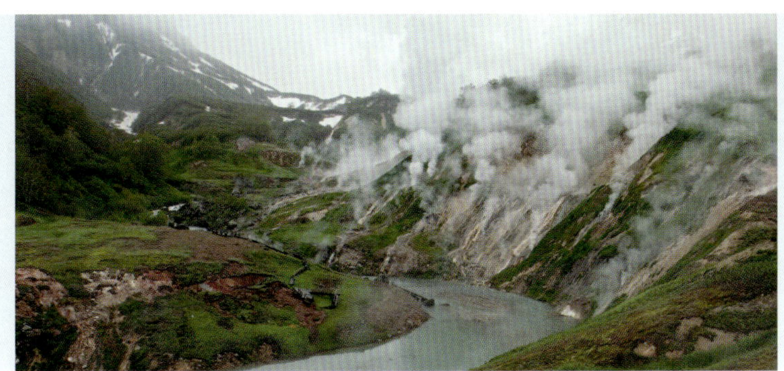

chain is dominated by extinct volcanoes. The eastern chain merges with the volcanic plateaus with their active volcanoes. In contrast to the marshes of the west coast, the landscape of the east coast is characterized by steep cliffs and deciduous forests cover the lower regions. The world heritage site boasts many primeval, endemic plants, while Kluchevskoy Nature Park is home to large populations of sea lions and brown bears. The peninsula is also the location of the world's largest variety of salmonoid fish.

Many of Kamchatka's volcanoes – like the Karymsky (large image), Kljutschewskoi or Tolbatschik (first and second image below and left above) – are still active. Third image below: meandering Vyvenka river.

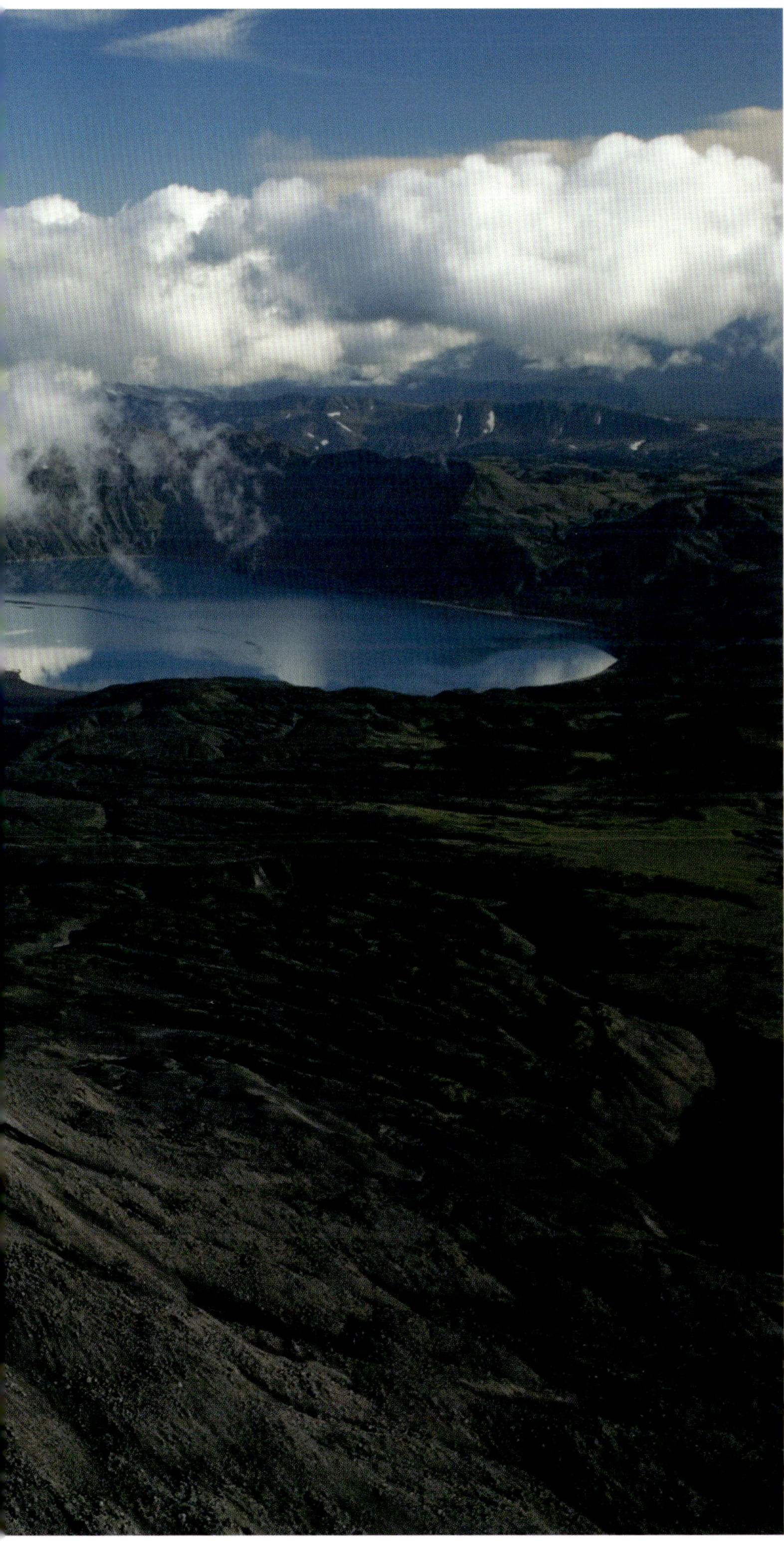

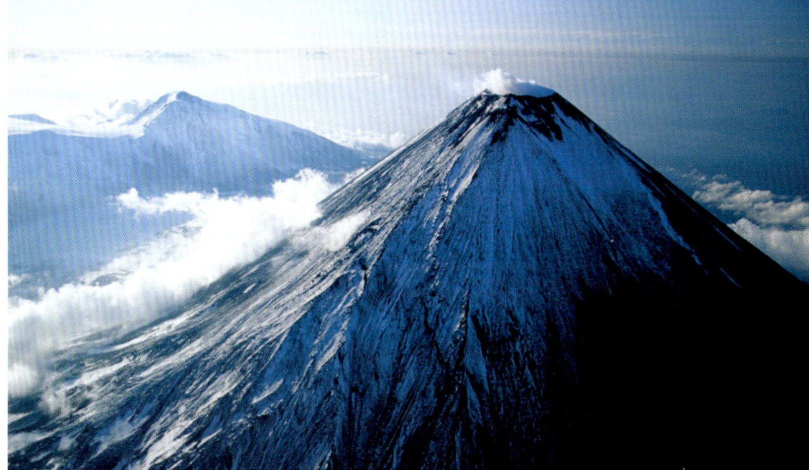

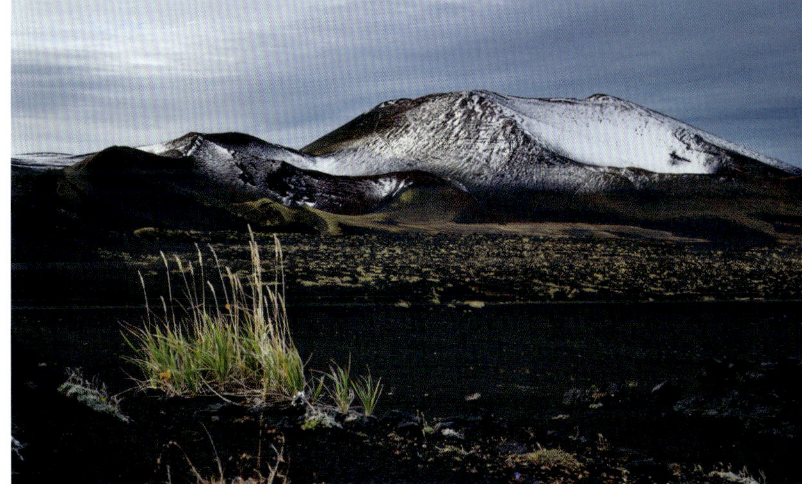

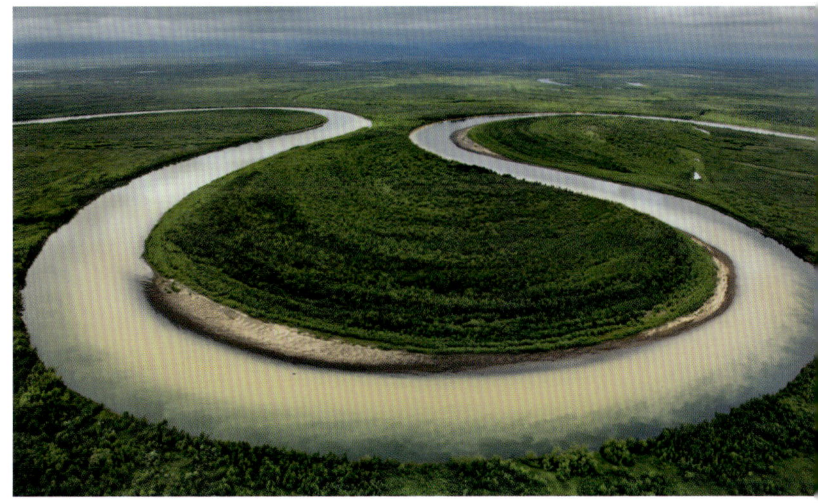

THE ANCIENT CITY OF HIERAPOLIS-PAMUKKALE

Date of inscription: 1988

Alongside its famous calc-sinter terraces, the World Heritage Site of Pamukkale (the former Hierapolis) also boasts numerous baths, temples, and other monuments dating back to the Hellenistic and Roman periods.

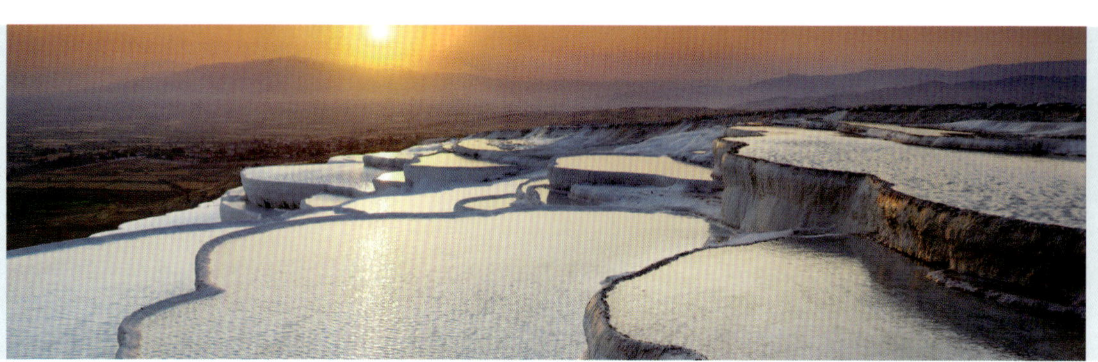

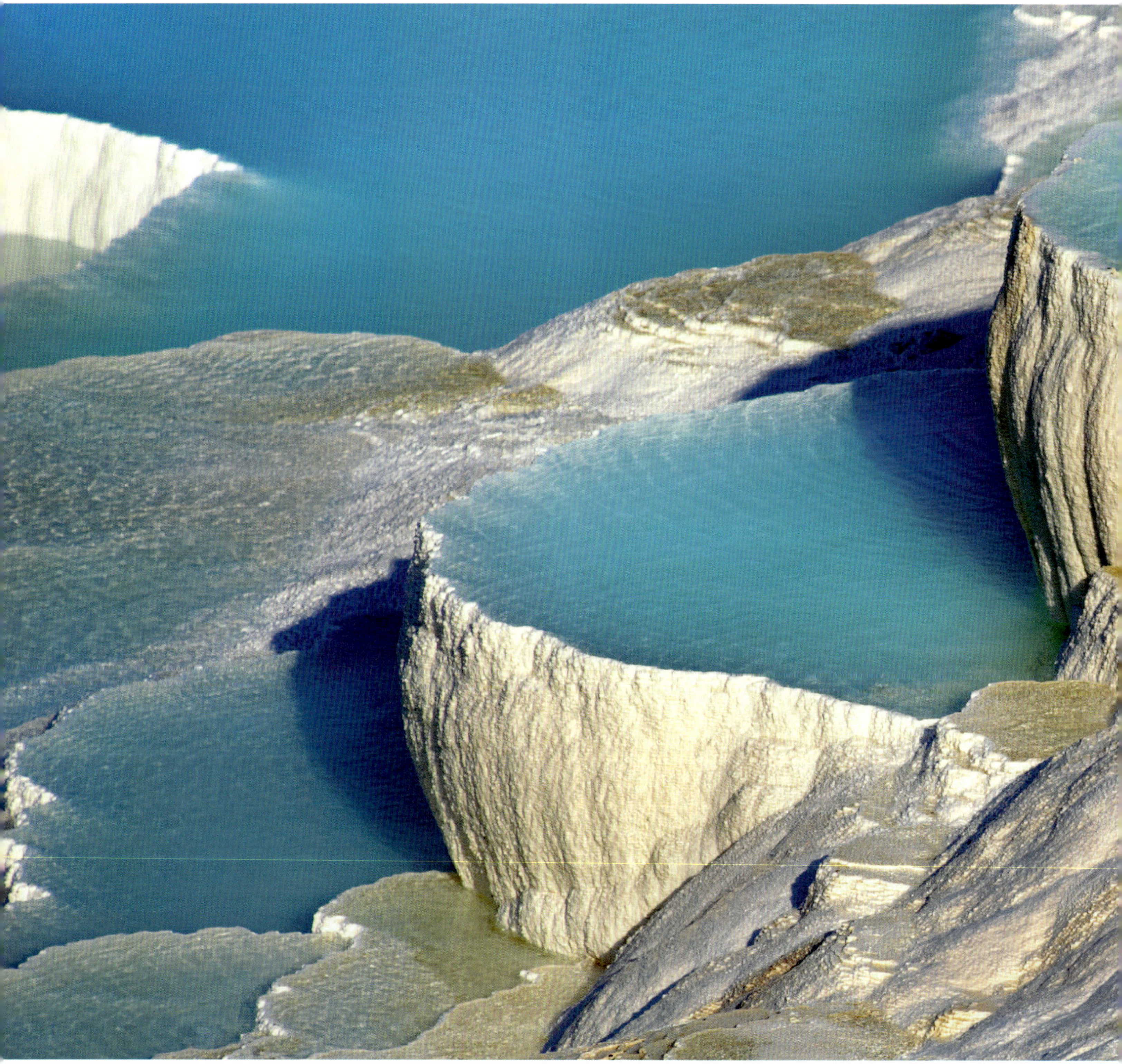

The area around the hot springs of Pamukkale was first settled in early times, becoming part of the Roman province of Asia in the 2nd century BC. The city of Hierapolis itself was built in 190 BC by order of King Eumenes II of Pergamon. Though essentially envisaged as a fortification, Hierapolis had its own baths right from the start. Residential buildings, temples, some early Christian churches, and other structures all sprang up around the baths, and the remains of these buildings can still be seen today.

The last of Pamukkale's ancient buildings date from the 4th century. Alongside the ruins, the area is also the scene of an extraordinary natural spectacle. About 100 m (330 feet) up Mount Çökelez, the hot springs emerge from a ledge protruding out of the rock face and flow down into the valley below. Over time, deposits of the mineral-rich water (sinter) formed petrified waterfalls, forests of limestone stalactites, and terraced basins. The overall effect is really quite otherworldly.

It's easy to understand why these fantastic natural terraces would attract numerous visitors, but the onslaught of tourists almost robbed the phenomenon of its existence. Since 1996, bathing has therefore been strictly forbidden here, and there are efforts to re-naturalize many of the areas that were destroyed.

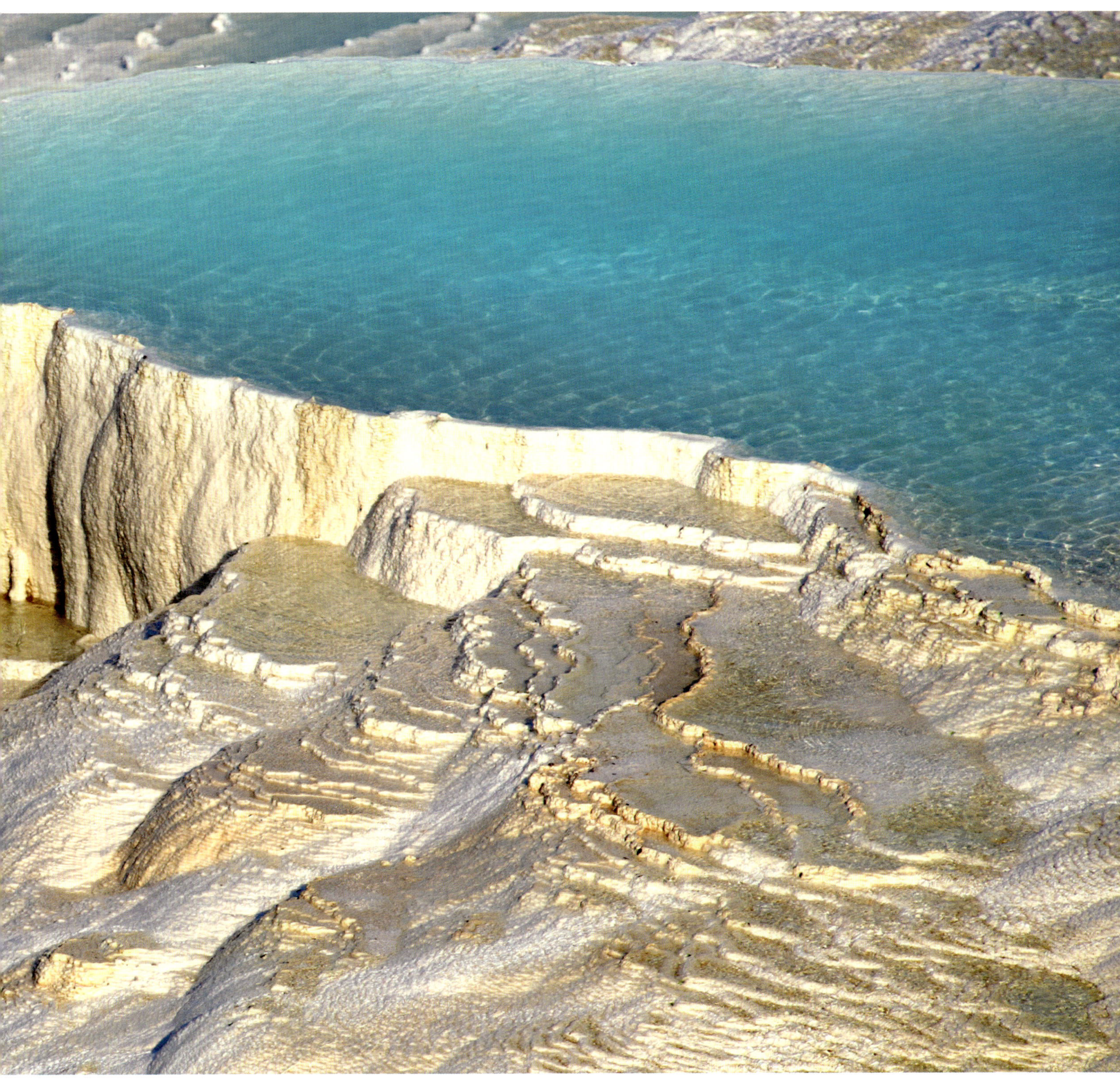

GÖREME NATIONAL PARK AND THE ROCK SITES OF CAPPADOCIA

Date of inscription: 1985

With its steep cliff faces and pyramid-like tuff formations, the Göreme valley, Cappadocia, is a truly fantastic landscape. Hundreds of chapels dating back to the Byzantine period are hewn into the rock. They are decorated with wall paintings from the period.

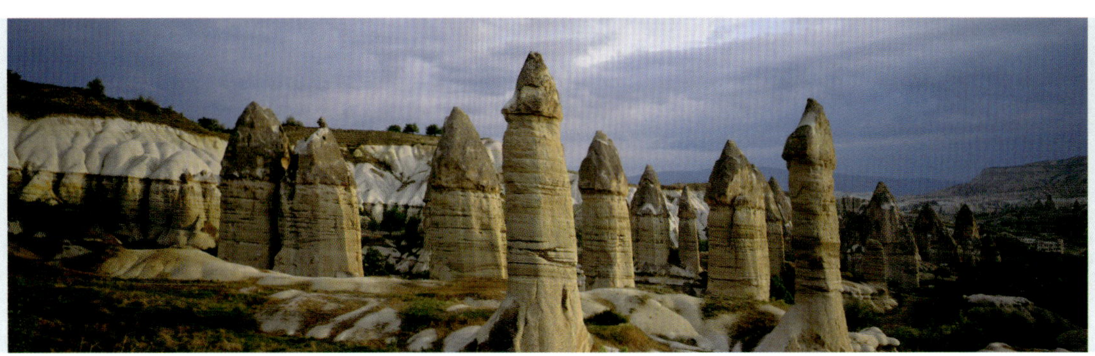

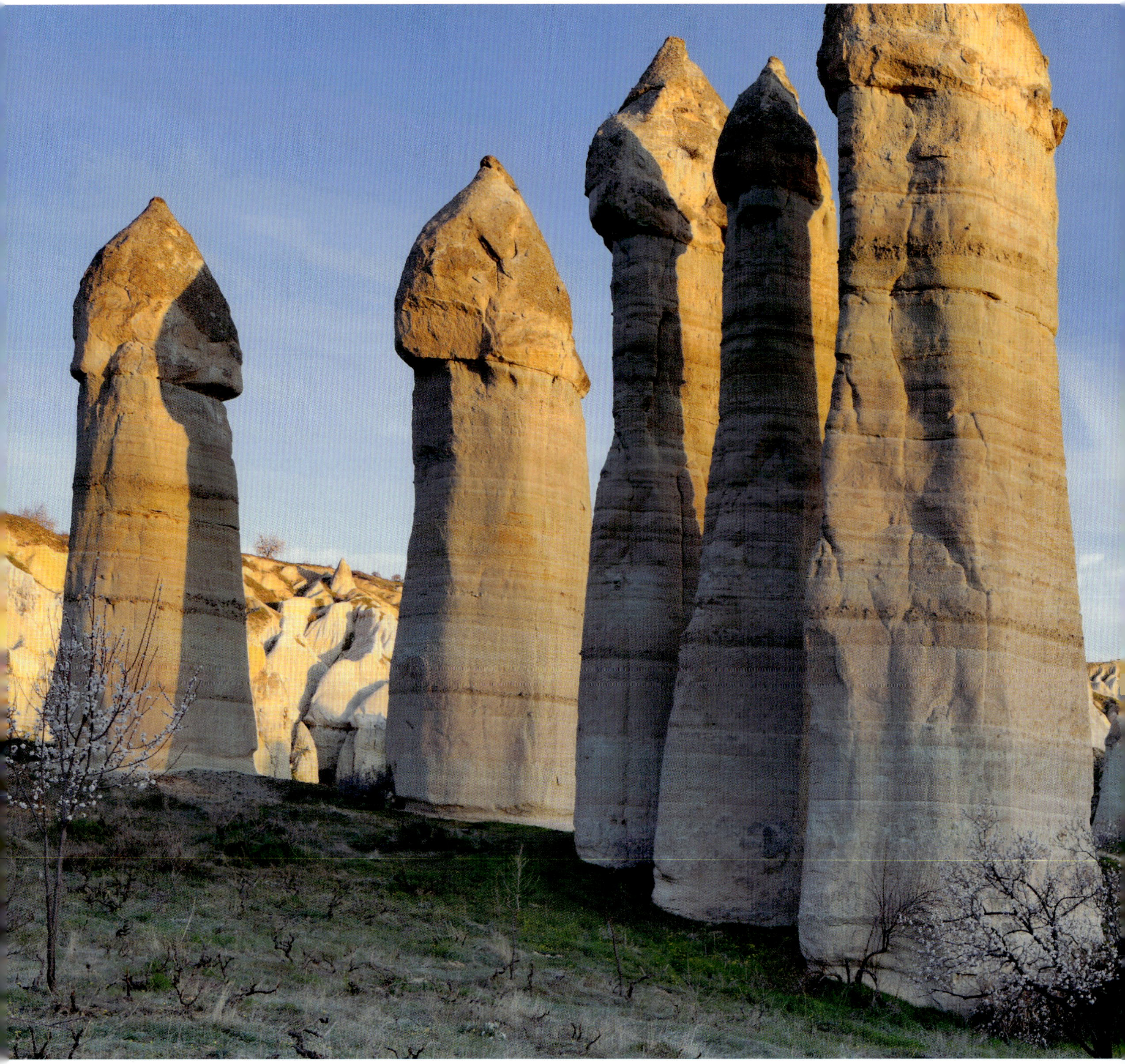

The tuff formations of Nevsehir Province (Cappadocia) were created on top of the existing rocks as a result of volcanic activity, and shaped into their current forms by varying degrees of erosion. Some have become stone pillars, while others resemble mushrooms and pyramids. Together, the rocks form a quite incredible landscape. The Christian population of the Byzantine provinces of Asia Minor once sought refuge from Arab persecution here, building domestic accommodation, monks' cells, and chapels into the soft tuff. From the 6th century, complete cave villages and underground cities became established in the Göreme valley and surrounding area. They were at their most vibrant in the 7th century, when several hundred thousand people are believed to have been living in this subterranean sanctuary.

The World Heritage Site encompasses both the historic rocks and the cave buildings. These include numerous monasteries and churches, whose construction draws upon several Byzantine styles of the period. The first figurative motifs in the church paintings date from the 9th century.

The Cappadocian landscape is characterized by its weird and wonderful tuff formations, into which numerous cave dwellings and churches were built. These rocky pillars (small image, left) are known as "fairy chimneys," and are sheltered by their "caps," which are made of harder stone.

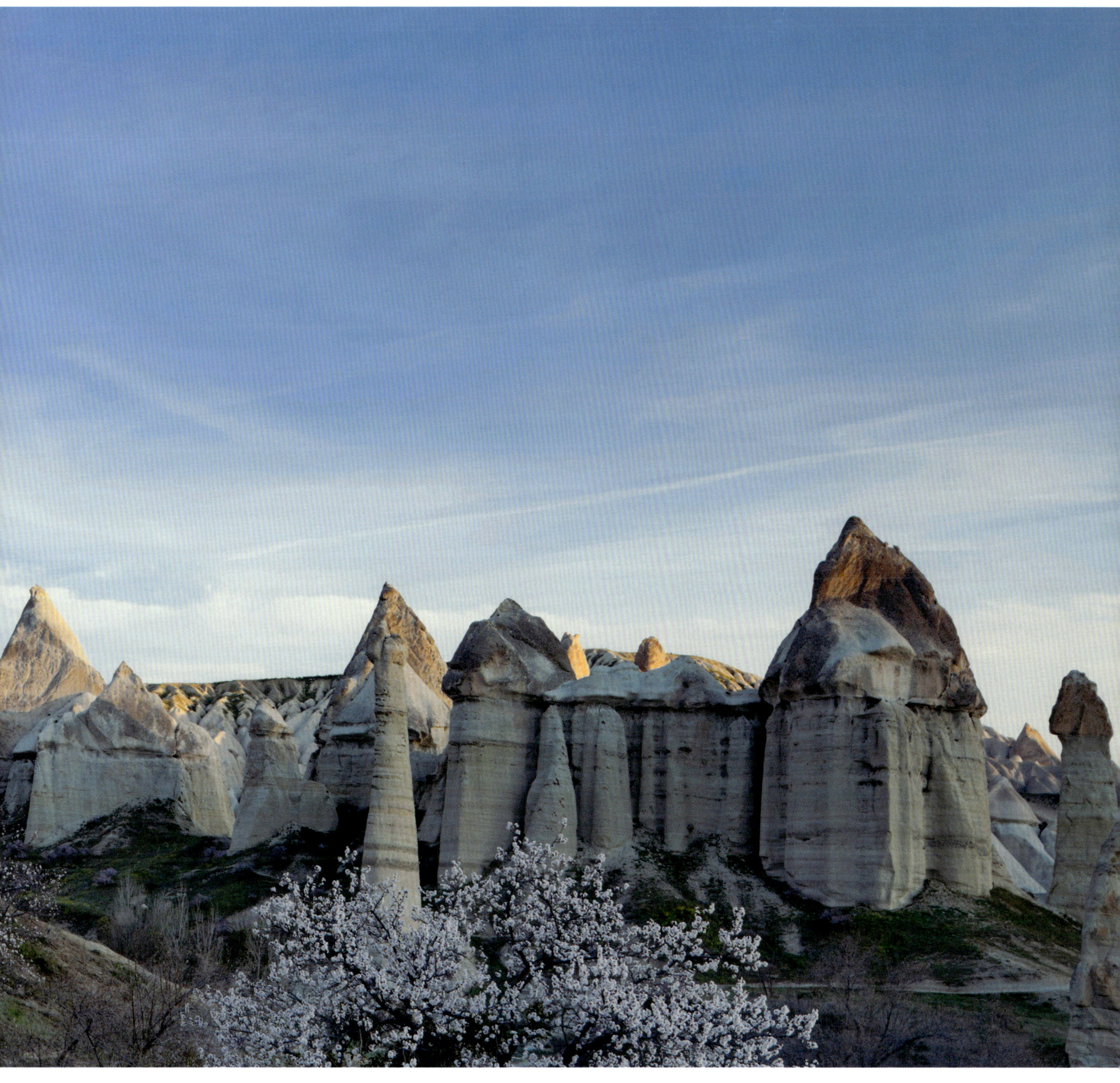

WADI RUM PROTECTED AREA

Date of inscription: 2011

Wadi Rum is the largest dry valley on the Arabian Peninsula, covering an area of about 740 sq km. Traces of human settlement dating back up to 12,000 years – including tens of thousands of rock carvings – make the valley a World Natural as well as Cultural Heritage site.

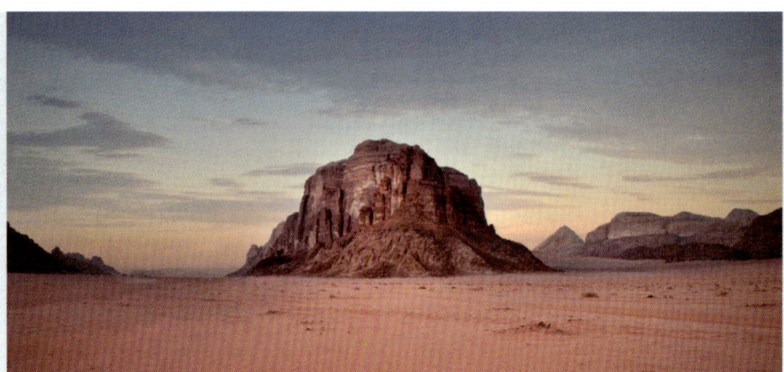

Wadi Rum, located on a sandstone plateau in southern Jordan on the border with Saudi Arabia, was formed about 30 million years as a result of a geological movement, during which a large geological fault tore open huge canyons, isolating individual mountains. Due to erosion over the course of millions of years, a spectacular desert landscape developed featuring narrow

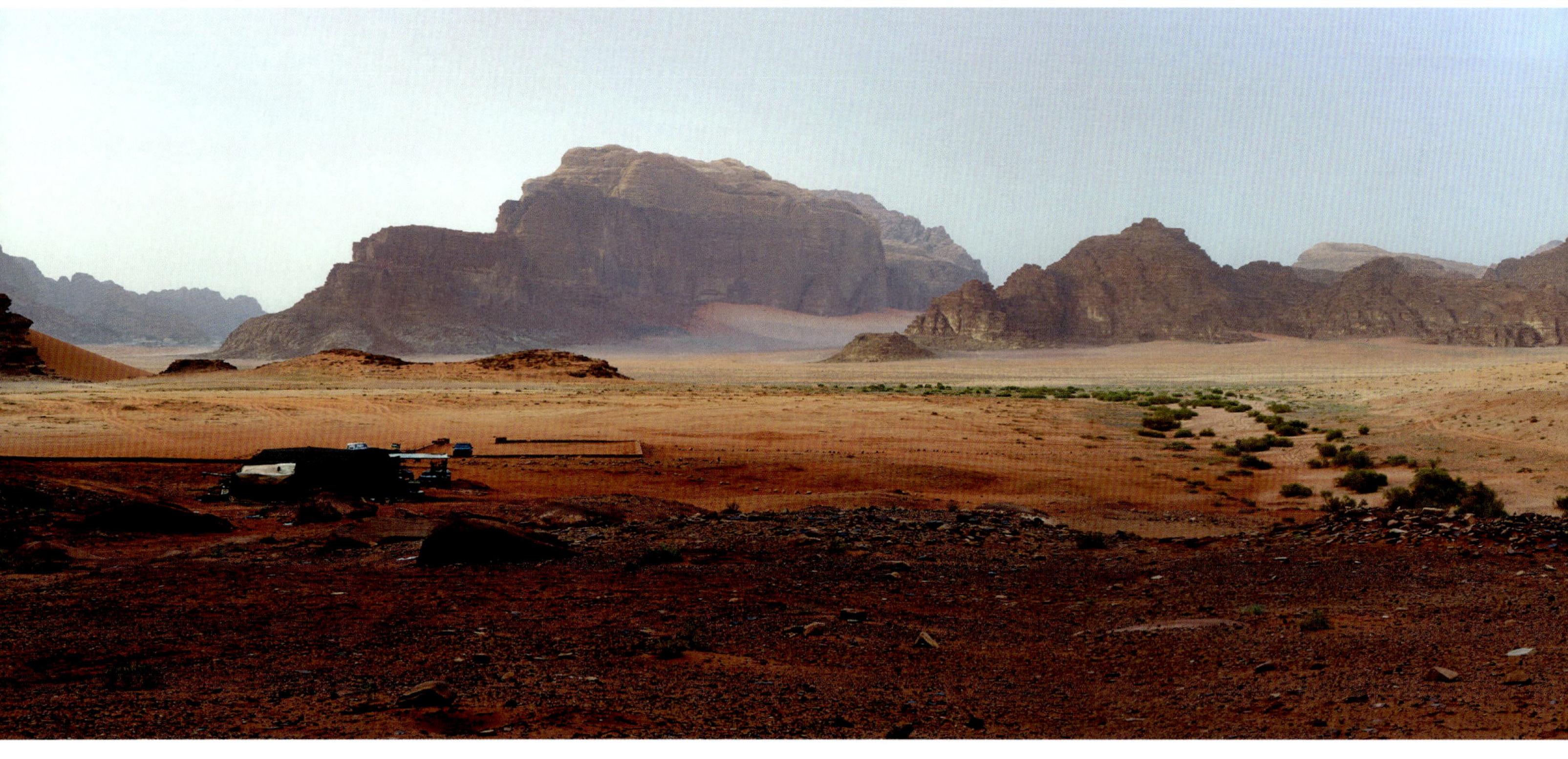

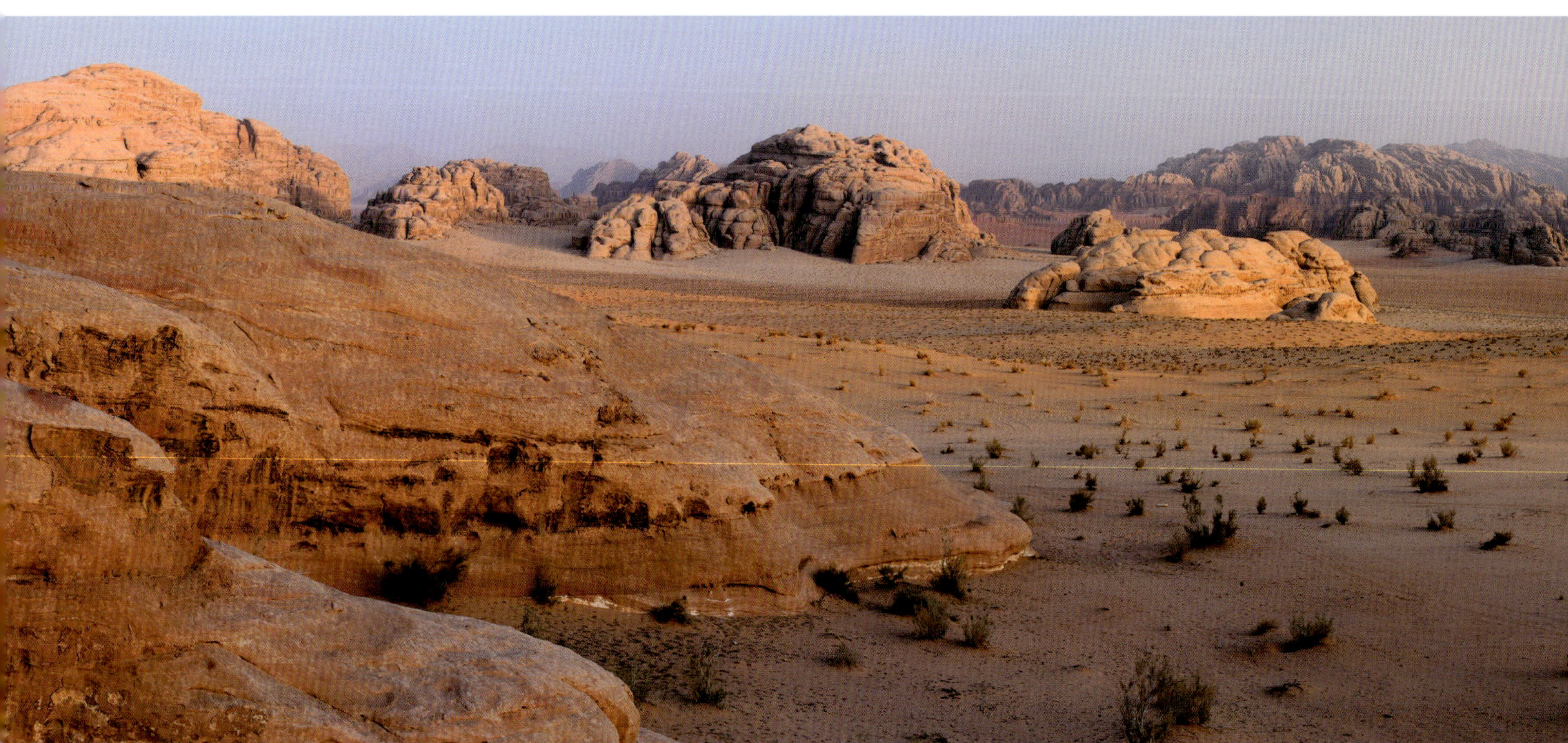

gorges, bizarre rock formations and many caves. The mountains around the Wadi Rum are composed of granite and sandstone. The darker granite forms the base and the reddish sandstone the peaks of the elevations. This is also the explanation for the many springs in the narrow sections of the desert valley: The water of the winter rainfall permeates the porous sandstone, encounters impenetrable granite and flows down the slope, where the springs often rise dozens of meters (yards) above the valley floor. These springs, in turn, explain the early settlement of this valley, probably as early as the Neolithic period (from 10,000 to 6,000 bc). Wadi Rum became famous mainly through the narratives of "Lawrence of Arabia" who in his opulent book, The Seven Pillars of Wisdom, writes: "...and then, towering gradually till their parallel parapets must have been a thousand feet above us, ran forward in an avenue for miles ... Our little caravan grew self-conscious, and fell dead quiet, afraid and ashamed to flaunt its smallness in the presence of the stupendous hills."

A magnificent scenery to inspire not only writers and artists. The sculpted rocks of the Wadi Rum stretch out barren, distant and at first glance unapproachable. Nevertheless, humans have settled here since time immemorial.

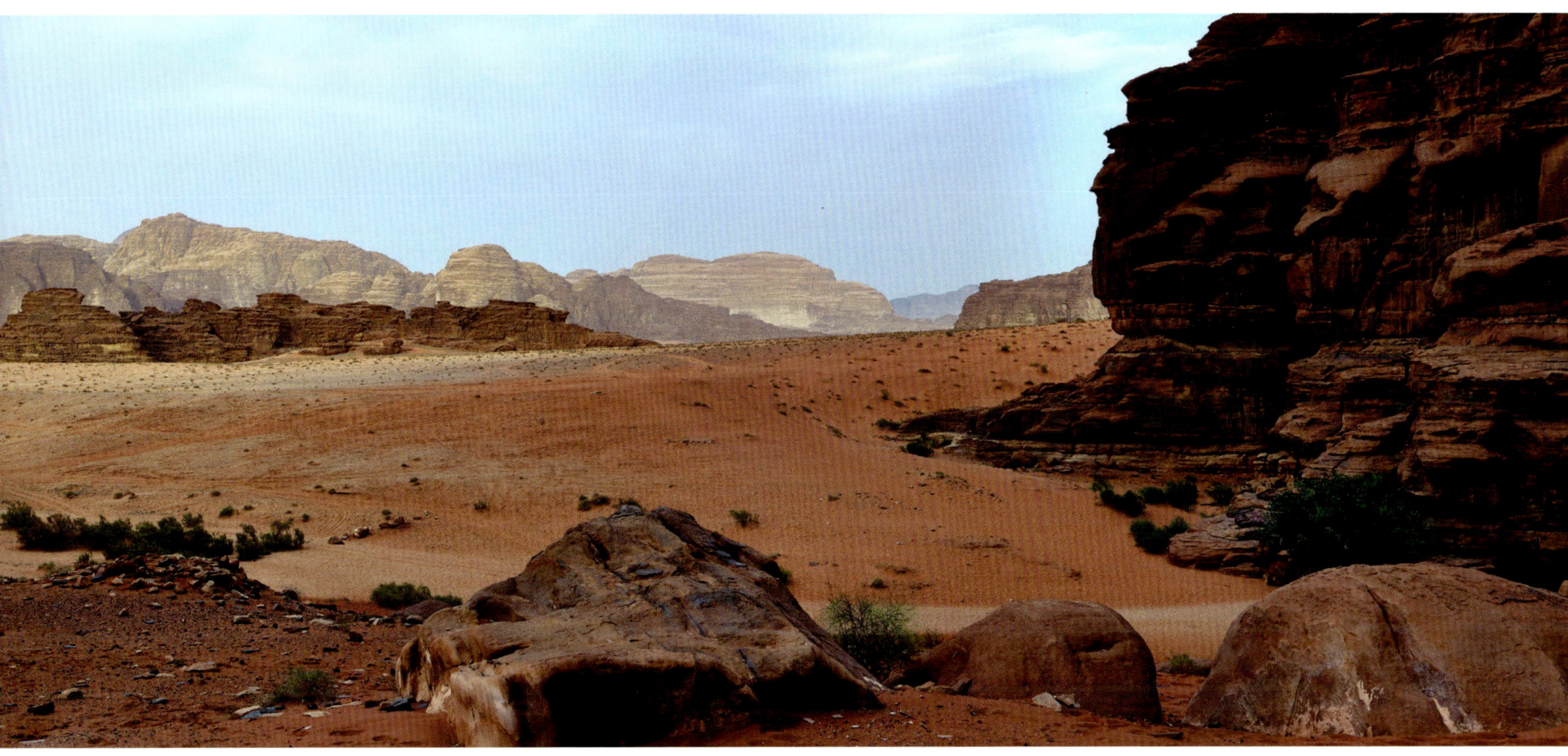

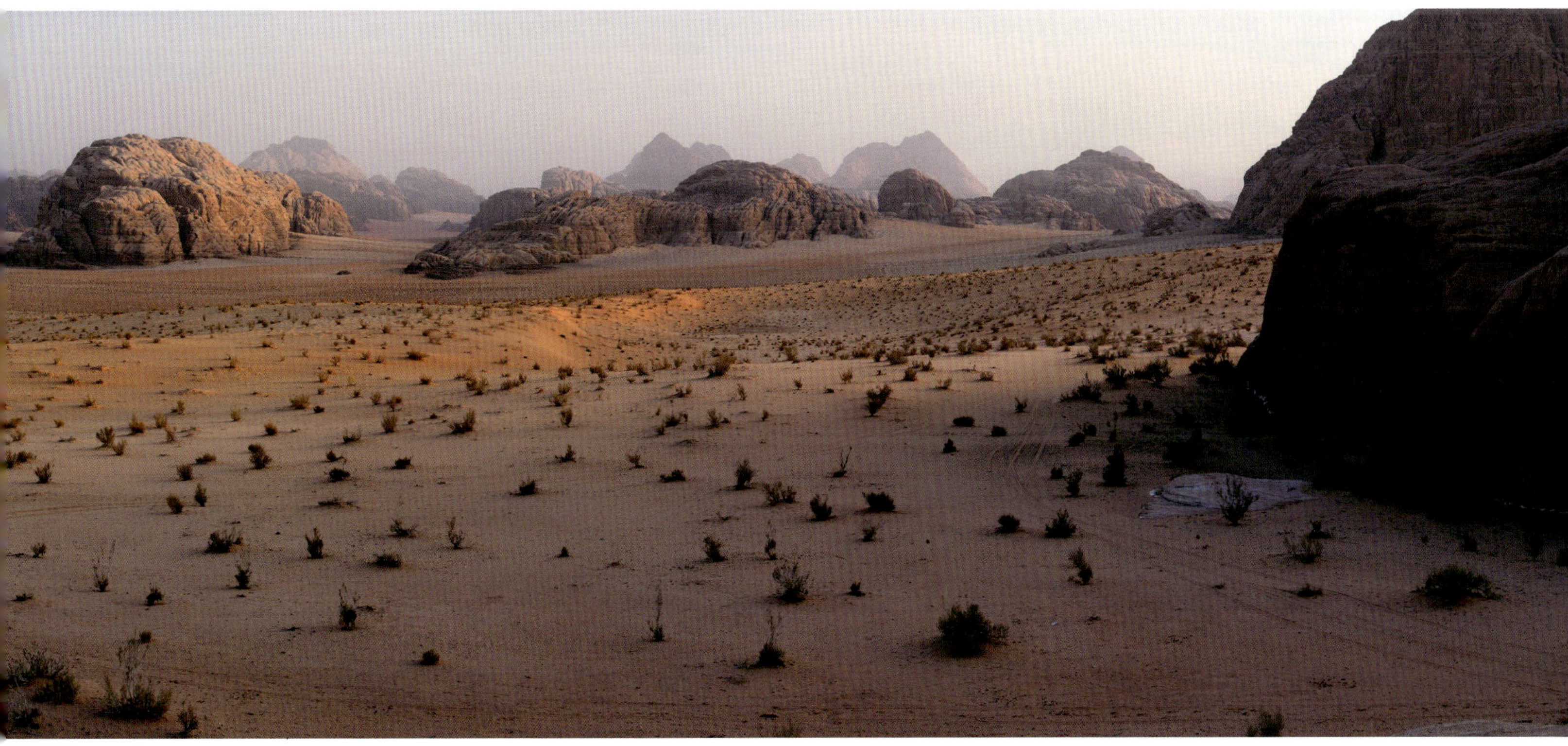

OUADI QADISHA AND THE FOREST OF THE CEDARS OF GOD

Date of inscription: 1998 *

Ouadi Qadisha, "the Holy Valley", with its rock monasteries, is an important site of early Christendom. Nearby is the most famous forest in the country. Its majestic cedars are considered the symbol of the Lebanon.

*** protected by UNESCO as a Cultural Heritage site**

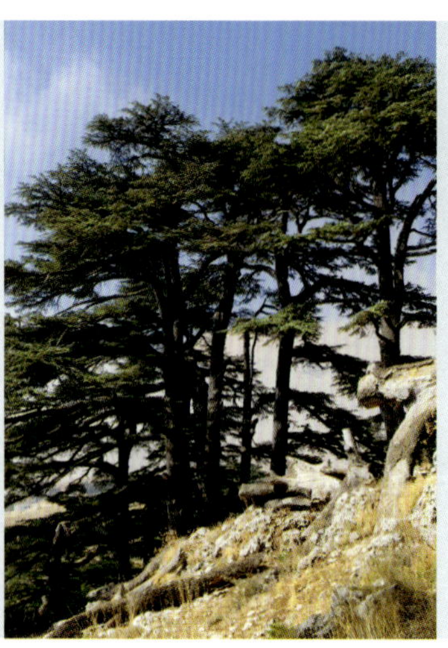

Roughly 120 km (74 miles) from the capital of Beirut begins the elongated Ouadi Qadisha, "the Holy Valley". In the first centuries of Christendom, monks built rock churches and monasteries, such as that of Qannoubine, in this remote landscape. Along the old road from Bcharré are the Qadisha Caves with their impressive dripstone formations. In spring, a waterfall splashes out of the cave. Not far away is a forest of cedars known as Horsh Arz el-Rab, "Forest of the Cedars of God". In the shadow of the country's highest mountain, the 3,088-m- (10,131-foot-) high Qurnat as Sawda', at an altitude of 1,950 m (6,397 foot) above sea level, grow around 400 mighty cedars. Allegedly, some of these trees are more than 1,500 years old, dating from the time when King Salomon had his palace and temple in Jerusalem built from cedarwood. The timber was once a sought-after export article.

The great significance of the beautiful, old cedar trees in the mountains of the Lebanon is also reflected in the national flag, which features the image of a cedar tree.

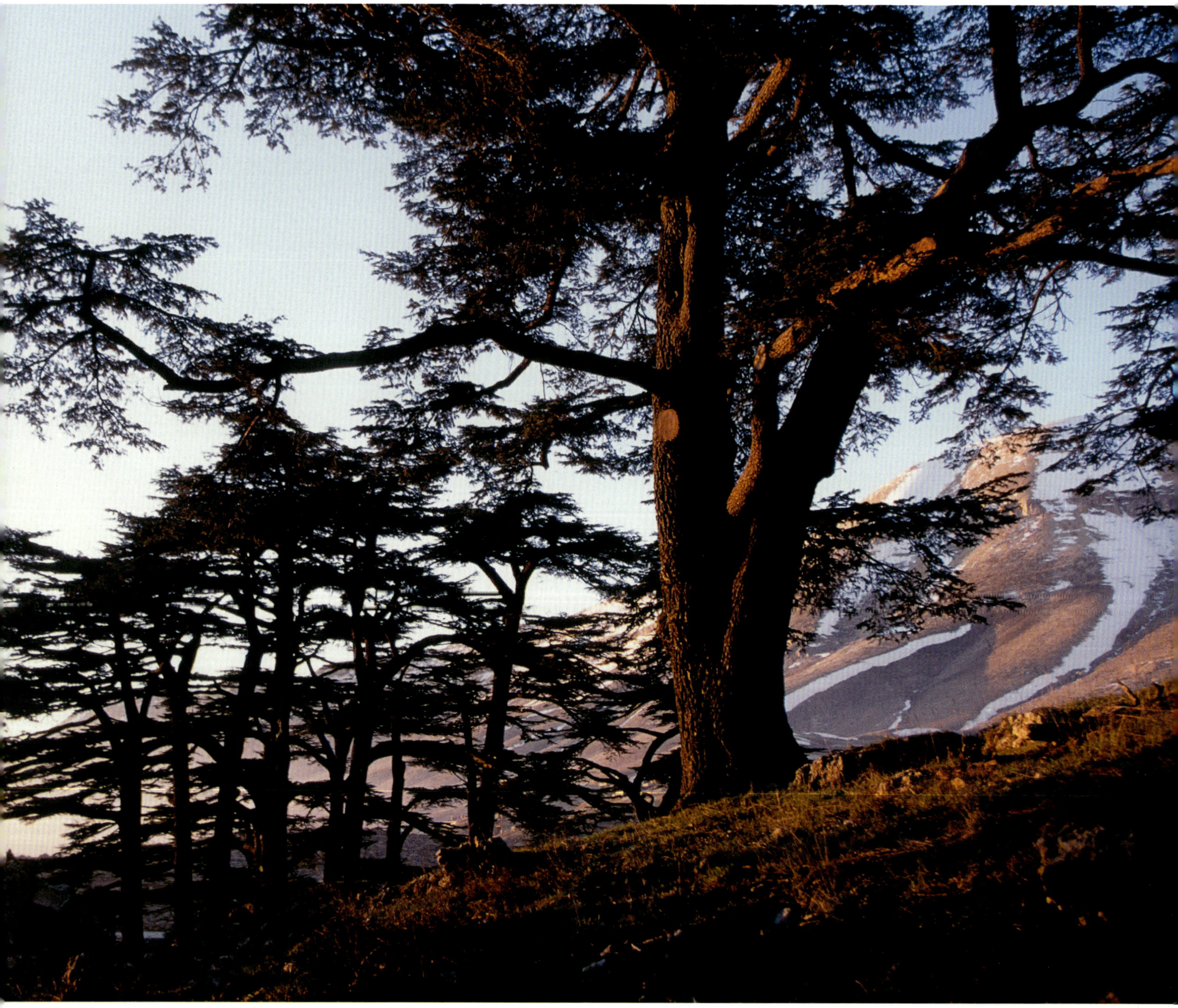

THE SOCOTRA ARCHIPELAGO

The abundance of incense ingredients, myrrh, and aloe, combined with its strategic position at the exit to the Gulf of Aden has made Socotra a destination for seafarers since the time of the Egyptian pharaohs. Nonetheless, the islands remained largely unknown to Europeans into the late 19th century, and scientific study on Socotra only began as Yemen opened up politically in the 1990s. Socotra, the main island in the archipelago, has an area of 3,626 sq. km (1,400 sq. miles) and rises to 1,503 m (4,931 feet) above sea level. Geologically, it is a continuation of the Horn of Africa, but since there has been no land connection for some 15 million years, the isolation of its location has allowed unique plant and animal life to evolve; there are no mammals at all, and 90% of the island's reptiles are endemic.

Dracaena cinnabari (below), the dragon tree,which is endemic to Socotra exudes a natural resin once known as "dragon's blood." The desert rose, Adenium obesum socotranum, is also endemic (right).

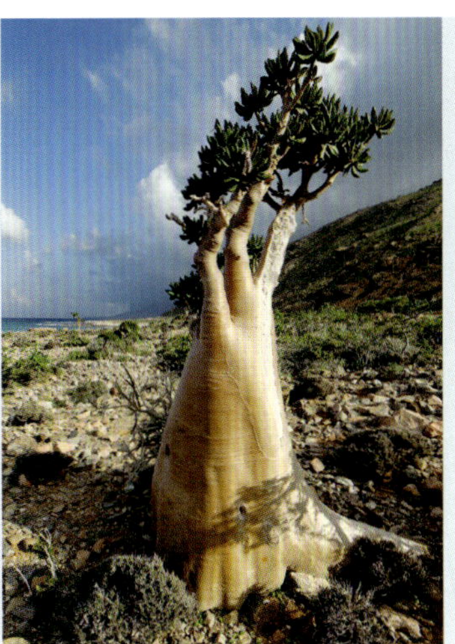

Date of inscription: 2008

The 250-km (155-mile) long Socotra Archipelago, with its four main islands of Socotra, Abd al-Kuri, Samha, and Darsa, lies just off the Horn of Africa. The islands' importance resides in their great biological diversity and numerous endemic species of plants and animals.

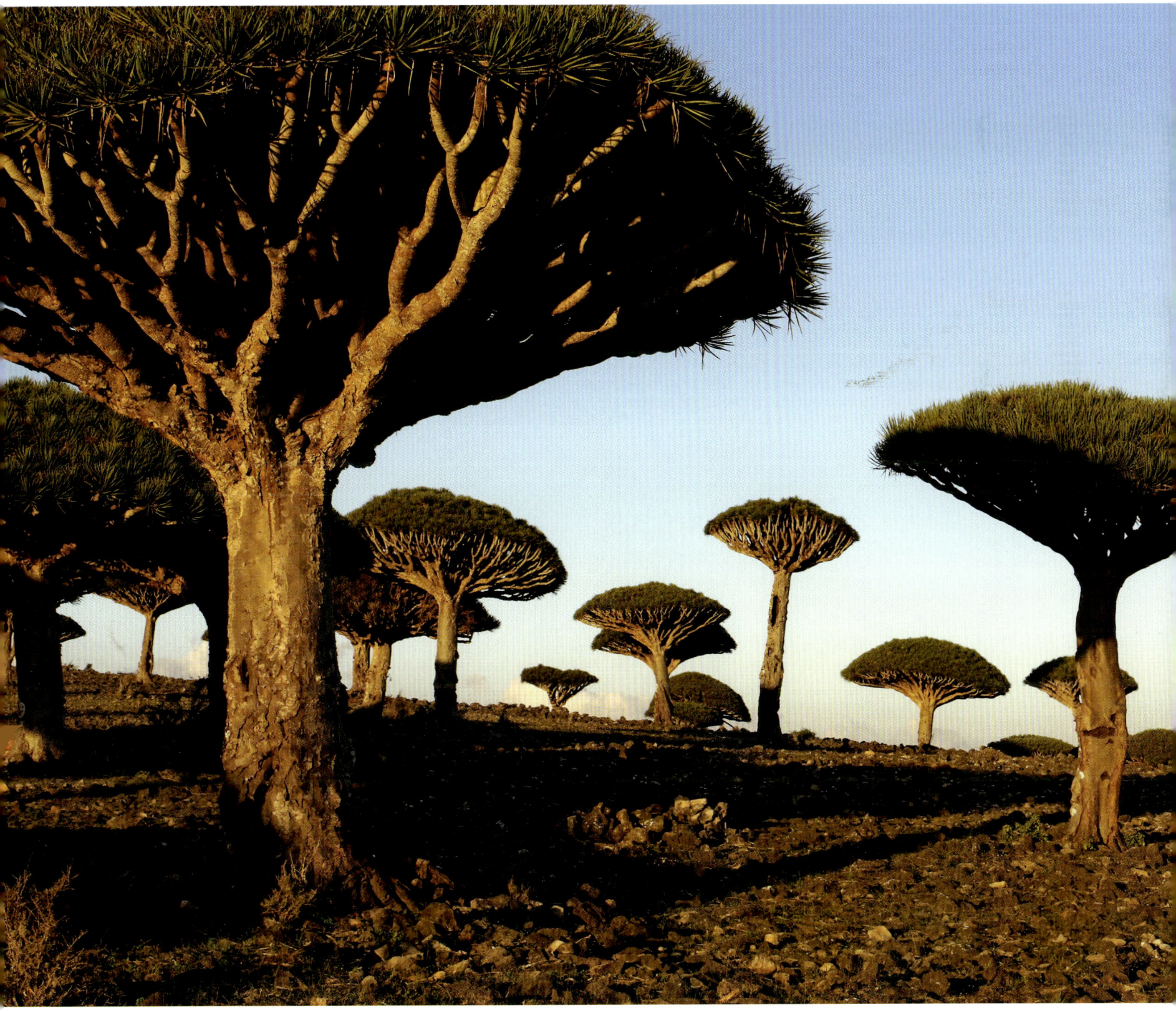

SARYARKA: STEPPE AND LAKES OF NORTHERN KAZAKHSTAN

Date of inscription: 2008

The World Heritage Site includes the State Nature Reserves of Naurzum and Korgalzhyn, with a combined total area of 4,500 sq. km (1,700 sq. miles), as well as a large area of central Asian steppe.

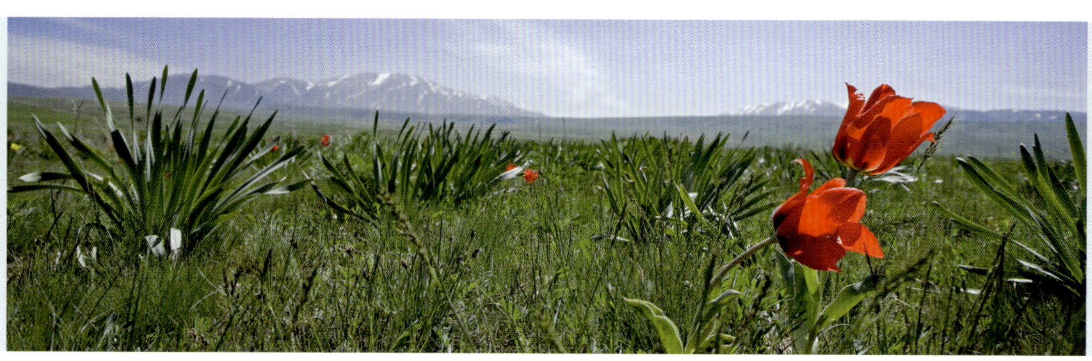

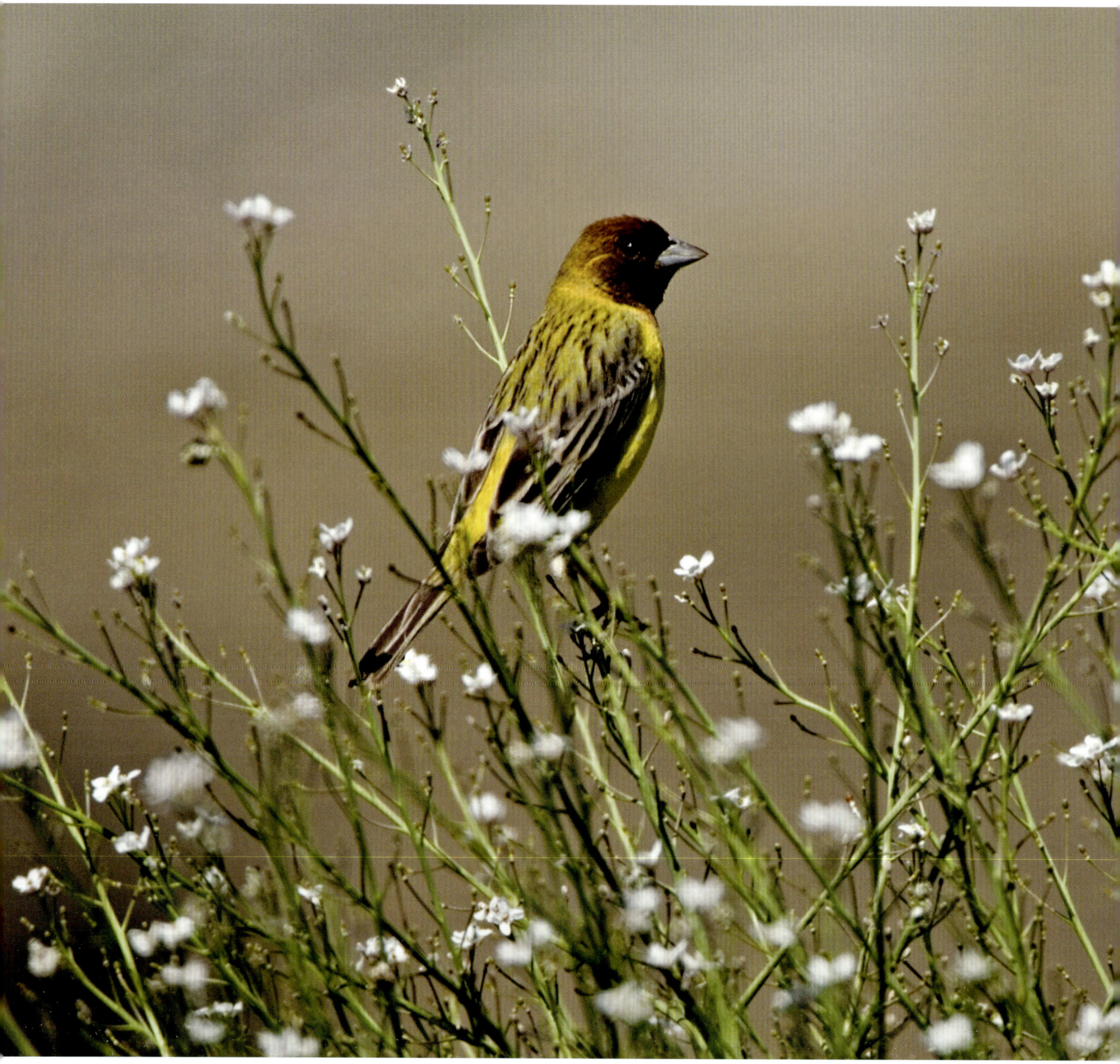

The Kazakh Uplands (Saryarka) are located in the eastern and central areas of Kazakhstan, mostly at an elevation of 300 to 500 m (990 to 1,640 feet), although the land can rise to about 1,000 m (3,280 feet) in the east. The Aksoran is the highest peak in the region at 1,565 m (5,135 feet). The landscape to the north is characterized by grass steppe, and to the south by stony semi-arid desert. The wetlands of Naurzum and Korgalzhyn are important staging-posts for migratory birds travelling from Africa, Europe, and South Asia to their breeding grounds in Western and Eastern Siberia. Many of these birds are endangered species or are very rare, such as the Siberian crane, the Dalmatian pelican, and Pallas' sea eagle. The wetlands' seasonal hydrological, chemical, and biological processes, brought about as climatic conditions alternate between wet and dry, are of great interest to scientists. The steppe areas of the World Heritage Site are home to more than half the country's native species of steppe plants, and even the rare saiga antelope has found a refuge here.

The wide expanses of the Kazakh grass steppes are a refuge for numerous bird species, including some that are endangered. Large picture: black-headed bunting; picture series from the top: Blyth's reed warbler, bearded reedling, bimaculated lark. Wild tulips (left) are splashes of colour in the grass.

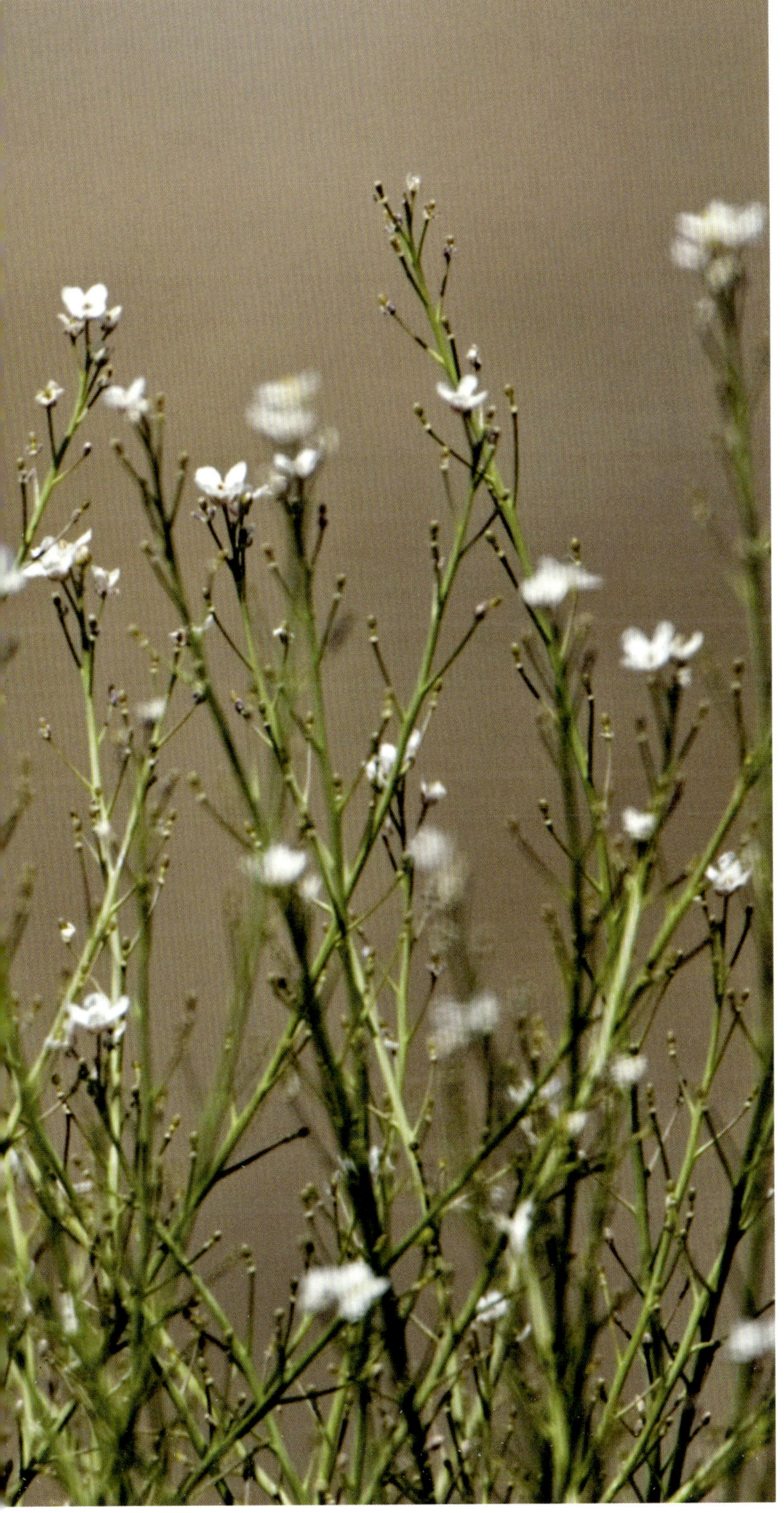

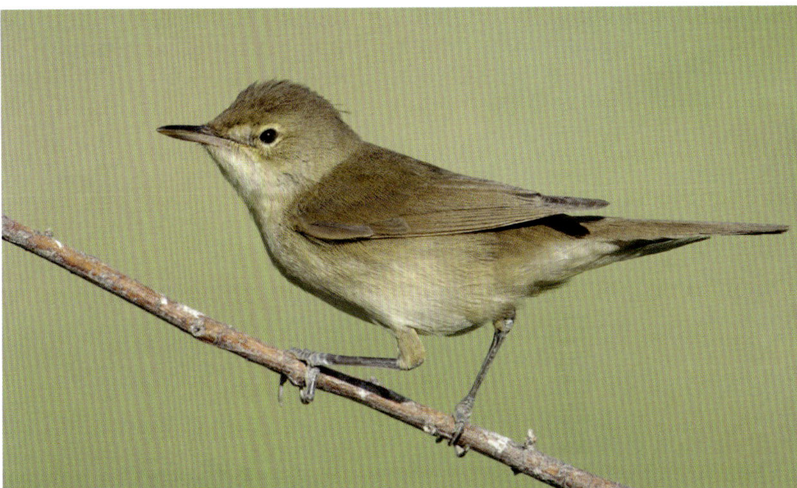

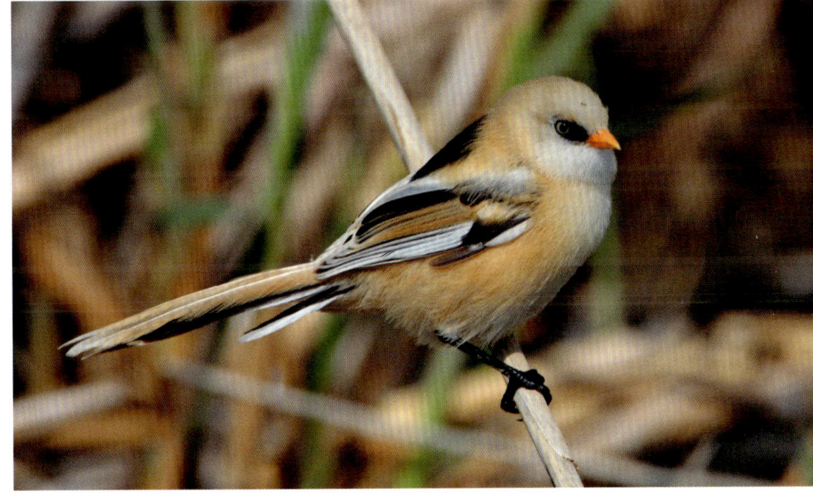

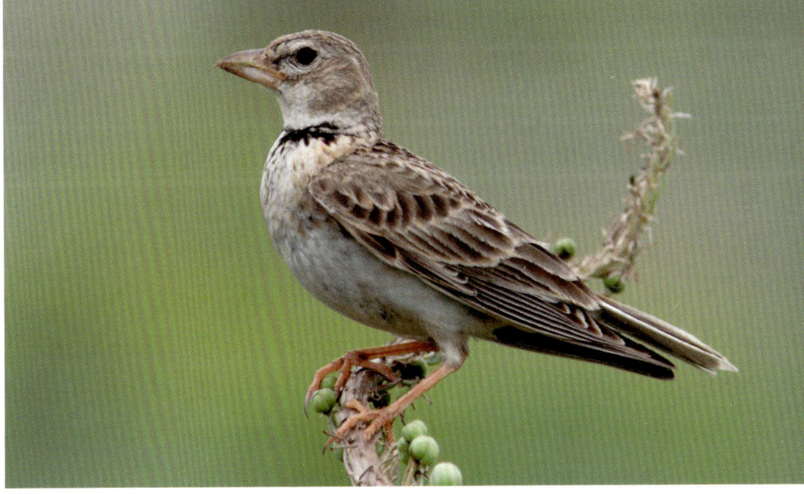

GREAT HIMALAYAN NATIONAL PARK

Date of inscription: 2014

The Himalayan region is not only one of the most popular mountaineering areas in the world; the landscape also offers a protected habitat to over 30 species of mammals and over 180 species of birds.

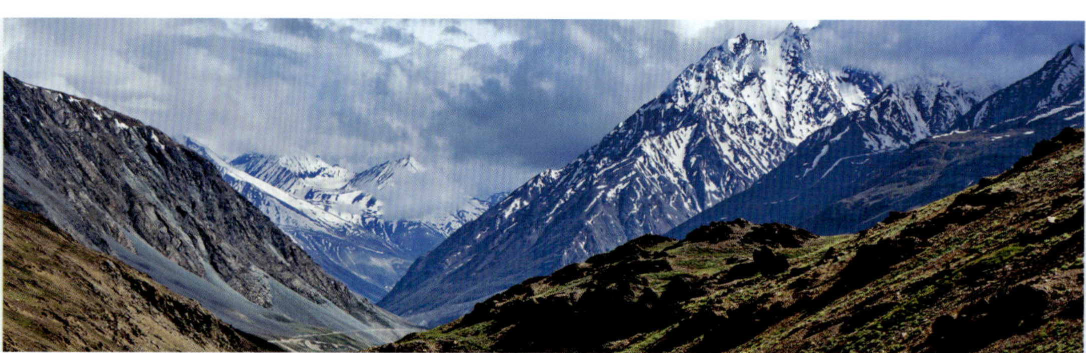

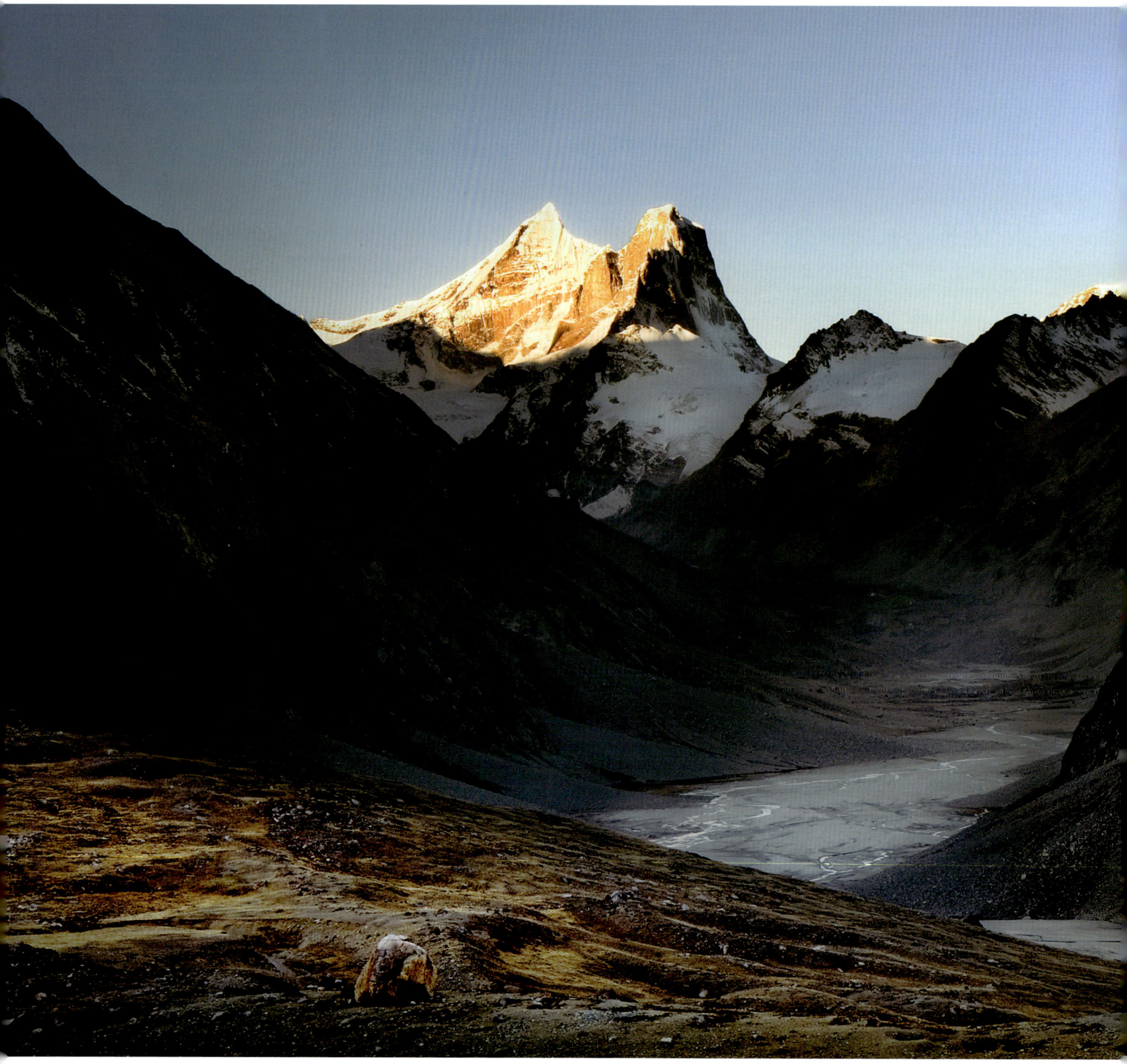

Originally founded in 1984 and officially declared a nature reserve in 1999, the national park is located in the North Indian state of Himachal Pradesh and is of outstanding importance for the conservation of biodiversity in the region. In addition, the study of the former and of the current glaciation allows important insights for the assessment of the future impact of global warming. The area inscribed as a World Heritage site covers 905 sq km on (349 sq miles) of an amazingly diverse landscape scenery, featuring high mountain peaks, blooming mountain meadows and romantic river valleys with 25 different forest types. The melt water collected in the upper regions is of enormous importance for the people living downstream. Among the many endangered species for which the National Park provides protection are the largest single population of the western horned tragopan (Tragopan melanocephalus) as well as the densest population of the Himalayan musk deer. The endangered snow leopard also has an important habitat here.

The reserve covers almost all types of habitat in the western Himalayas, from the subtropical lowlands right up to the highest mountain regions. Huge gorges traverse the massif (below). Left: the barren Spiti mountain valley.

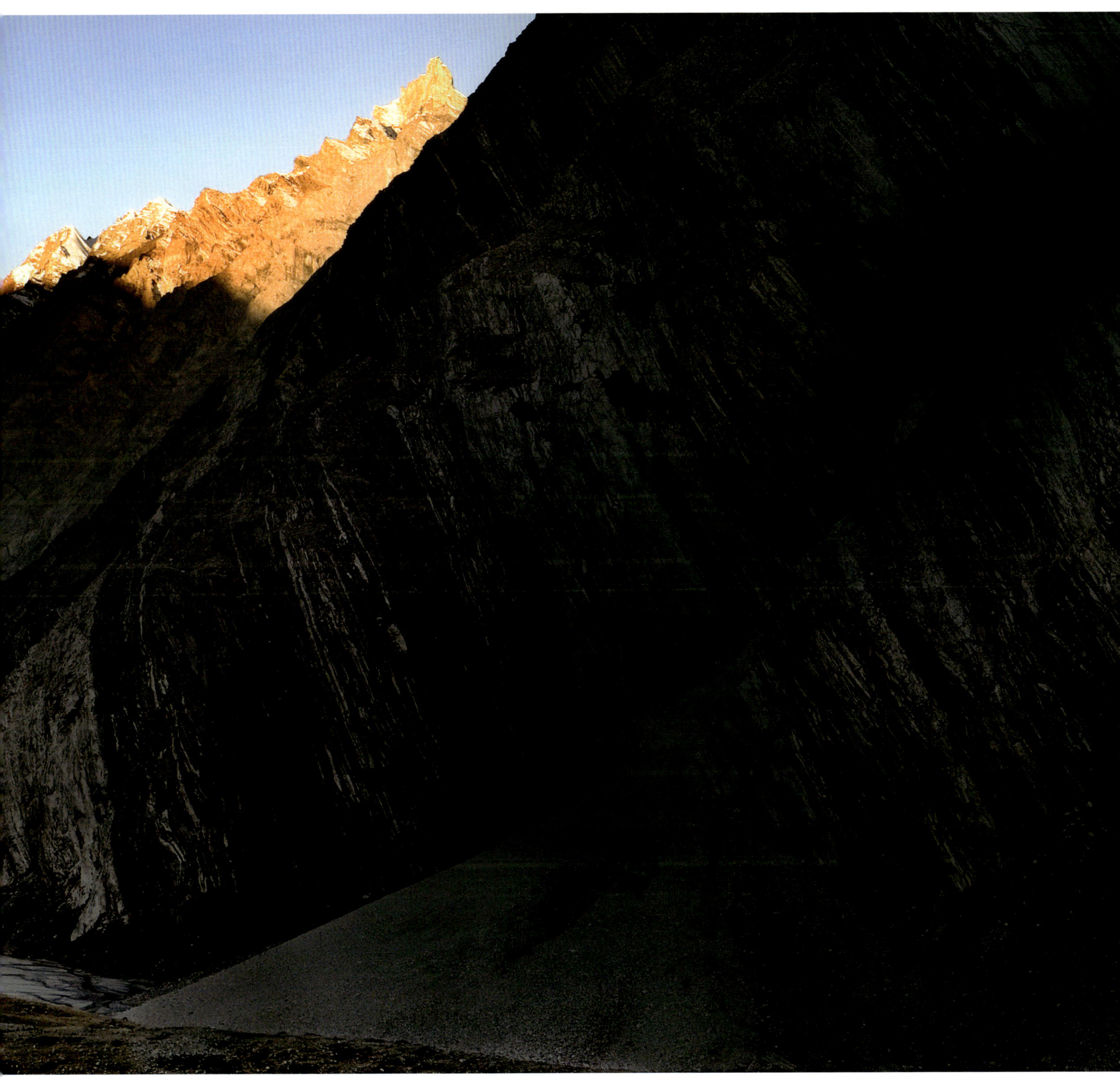

NANDA DEVI AND VALLEY OF FLOWERS NATIONAL PARKS

Date of inscription: 1988
Extended: 2005

Reaching an altitude of 7,816 m (25,643 feet), the Nanda Devi mountain lies on the border of Nepal and China. The surrounding area is an important sanctuary for numerous endangered plants and animals.

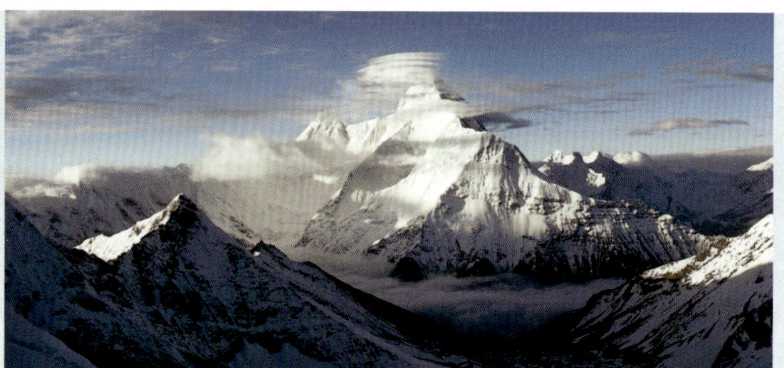

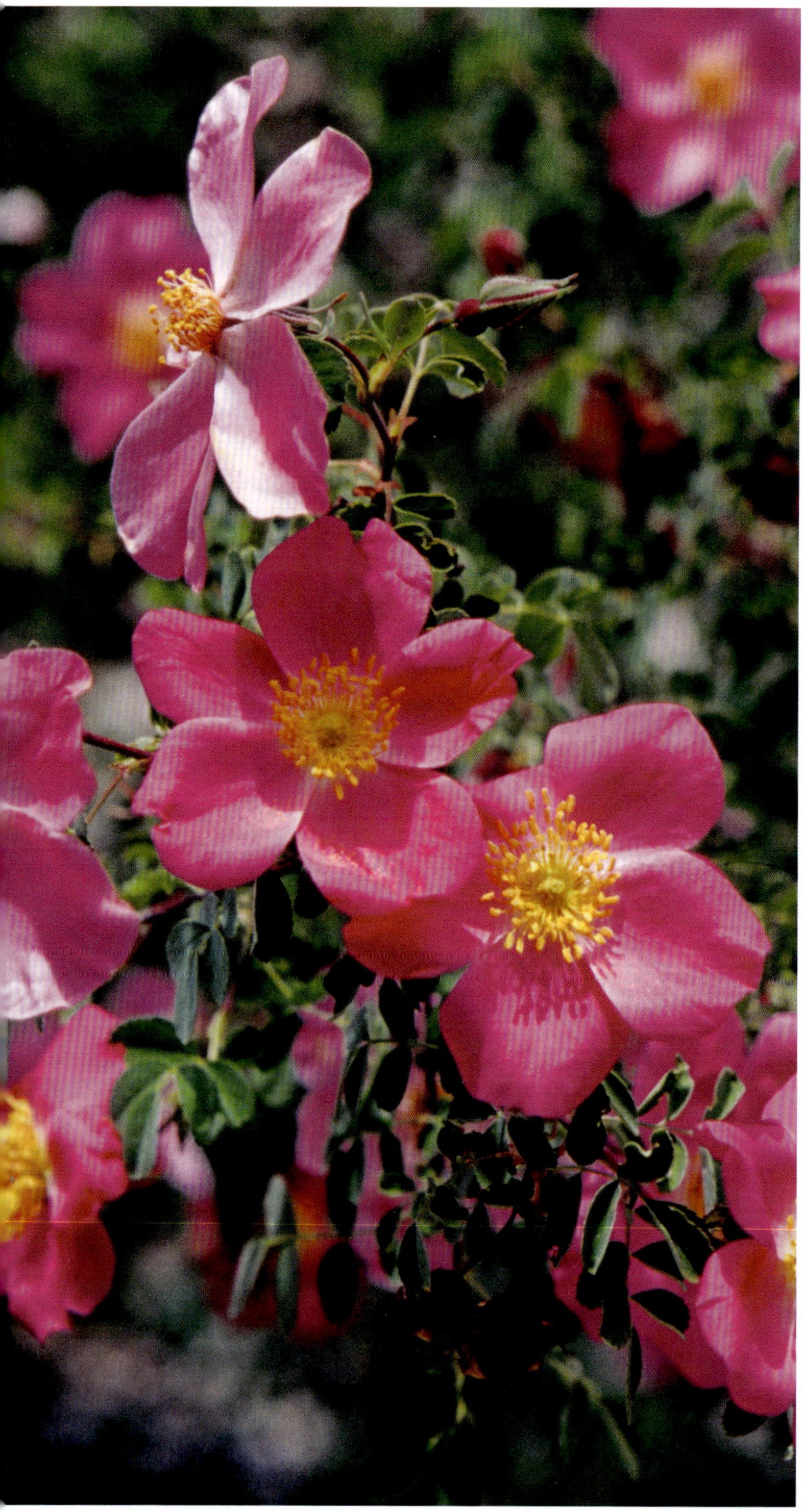

These days, no part of the world is beyond the reach of mass tourism, and – despite being almost inaccessible – the mountains around Nanda Devi are no exception. Even deep in the Himalayas, protected areas have played an important part in the preservation of the natural environment. Established in 1980, the national park around India's second highest mountain is home to

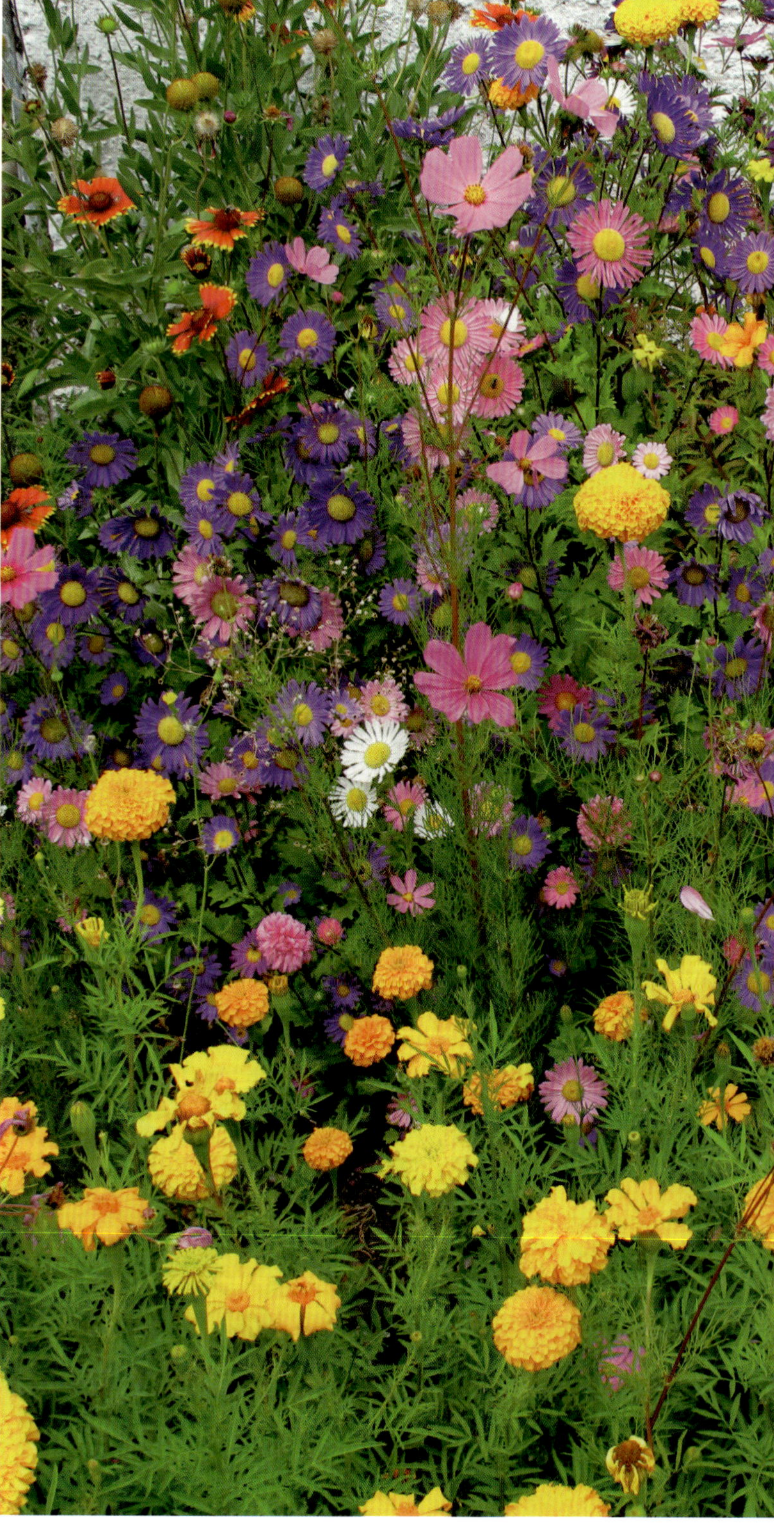

snow leopards, musk deer, and large herds of blue sheep (bharal) and goat antelope (goral). The Valley of Flowers National Park lies alongside Nanda Devi. It is famed for its meadows and endemic species of wild flower, notably the Himalayan maple (Acer caesium), the blue poppy (Meconopsis aculeate), and a type of saussurea (Saussurea atkinsoni). The landscape of the valley is multifaceted. Though only a short distance from the inhospitable environment of the Upper Himalayas, the valley is home to several rare animals, such as the Asiatic black bear.

Both the valley and Mount Nanda Devi – whose name means "goddess of joy" – play significant roles in Hindu mythology.

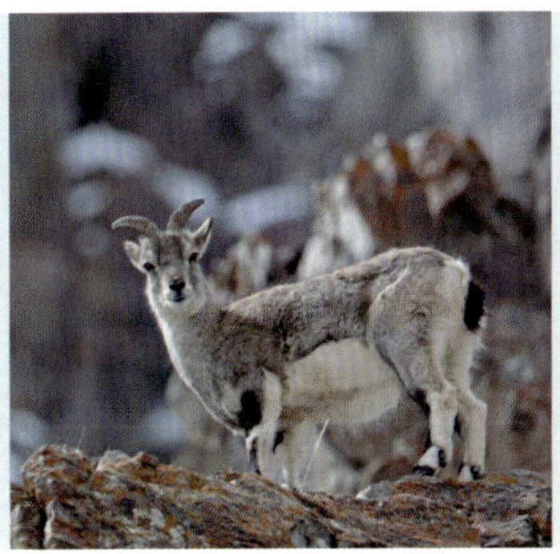

At a height of 7,434 m, the eastern summit of Nanda Devi is shrouded in cloud (far left), but on the lower slopes many different species of flowers thrive, including varieties of poppy, geranium and dog rose (far left, below). The Nanda Devi National Park provides a safe home for blue sheep (left) whose fur sometimes shines in a bluish grey.

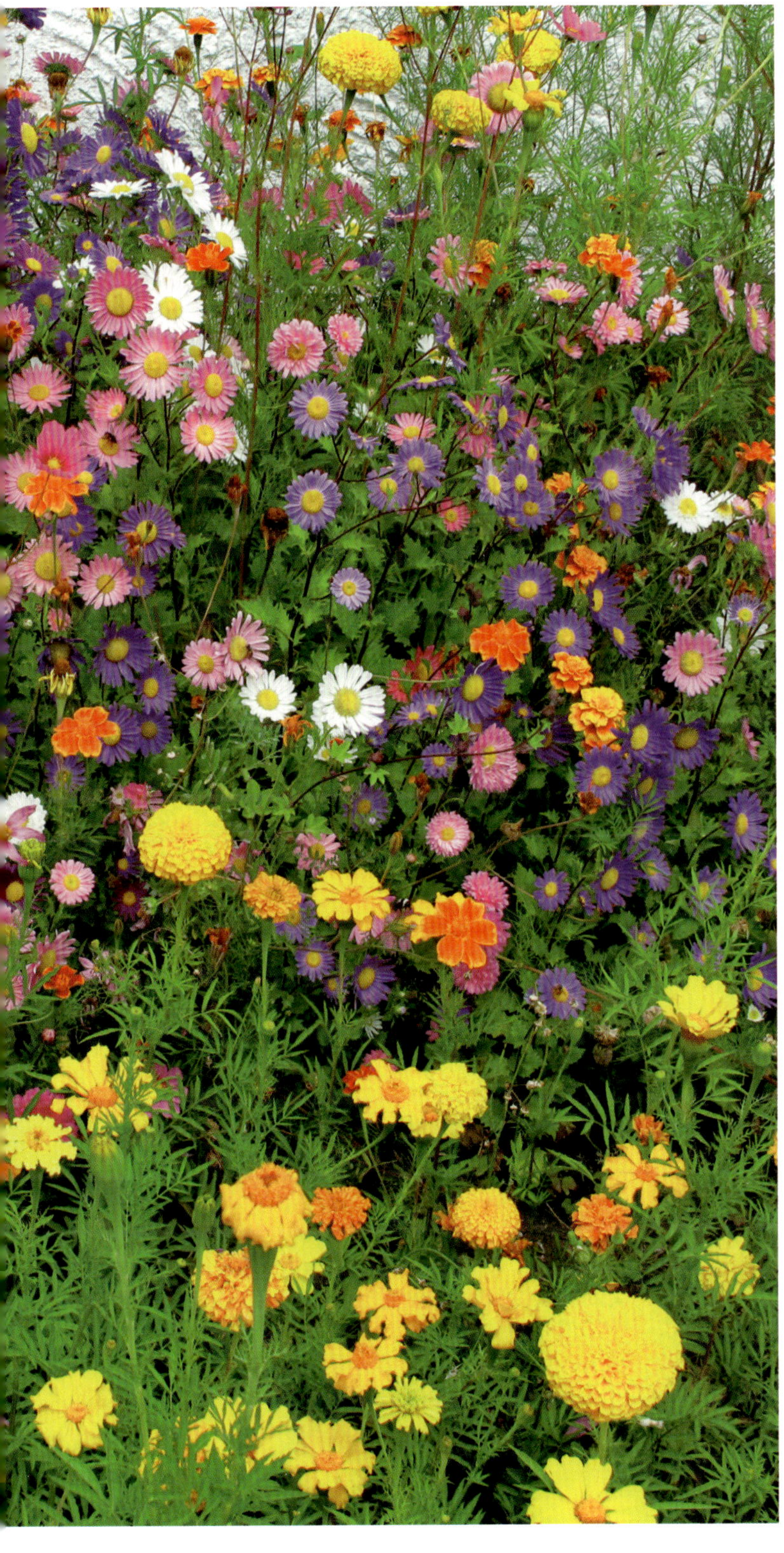

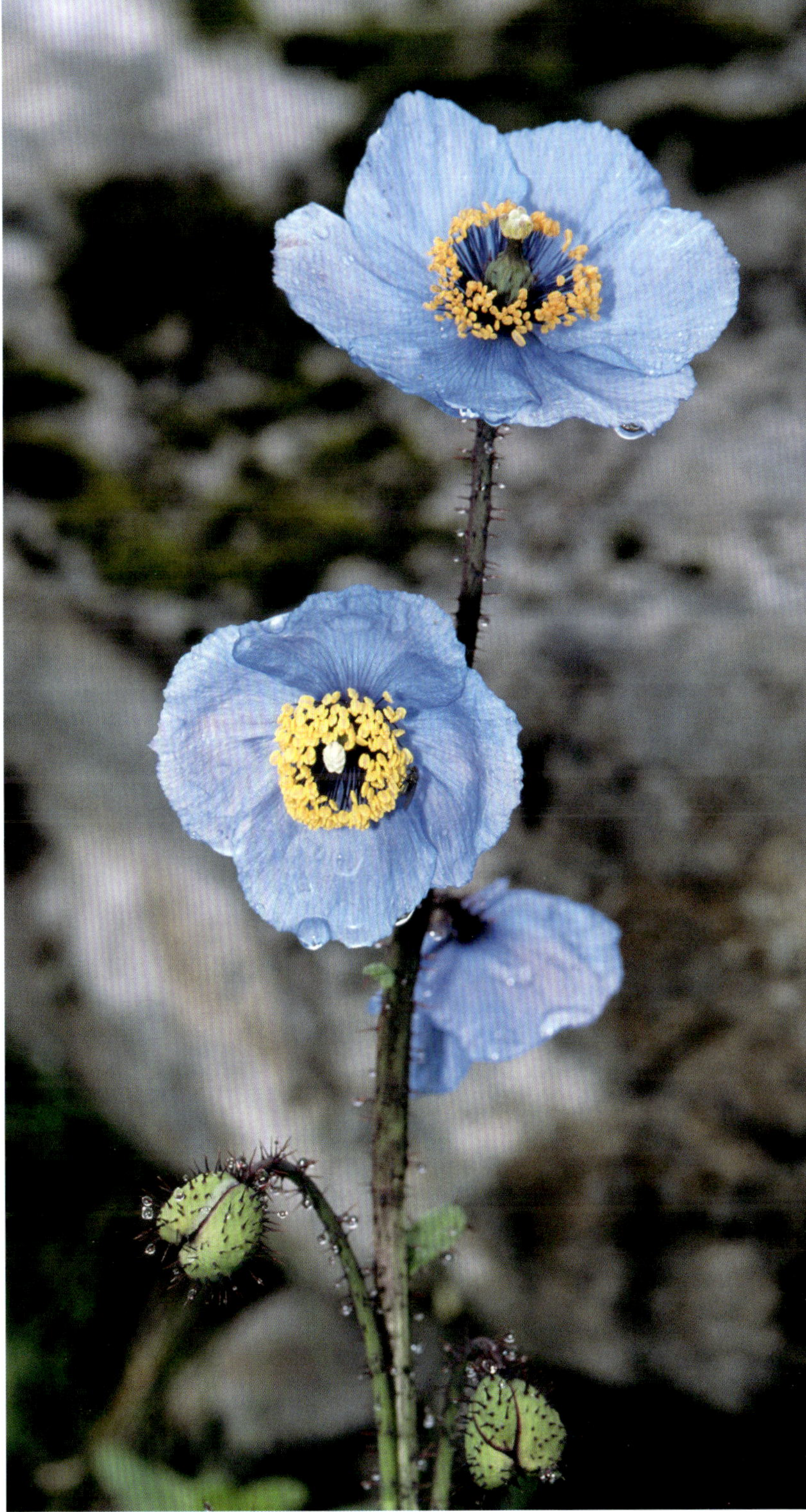

NANDA DEVI AND VALLEY OF FLOWERS NATIONAL PARKS

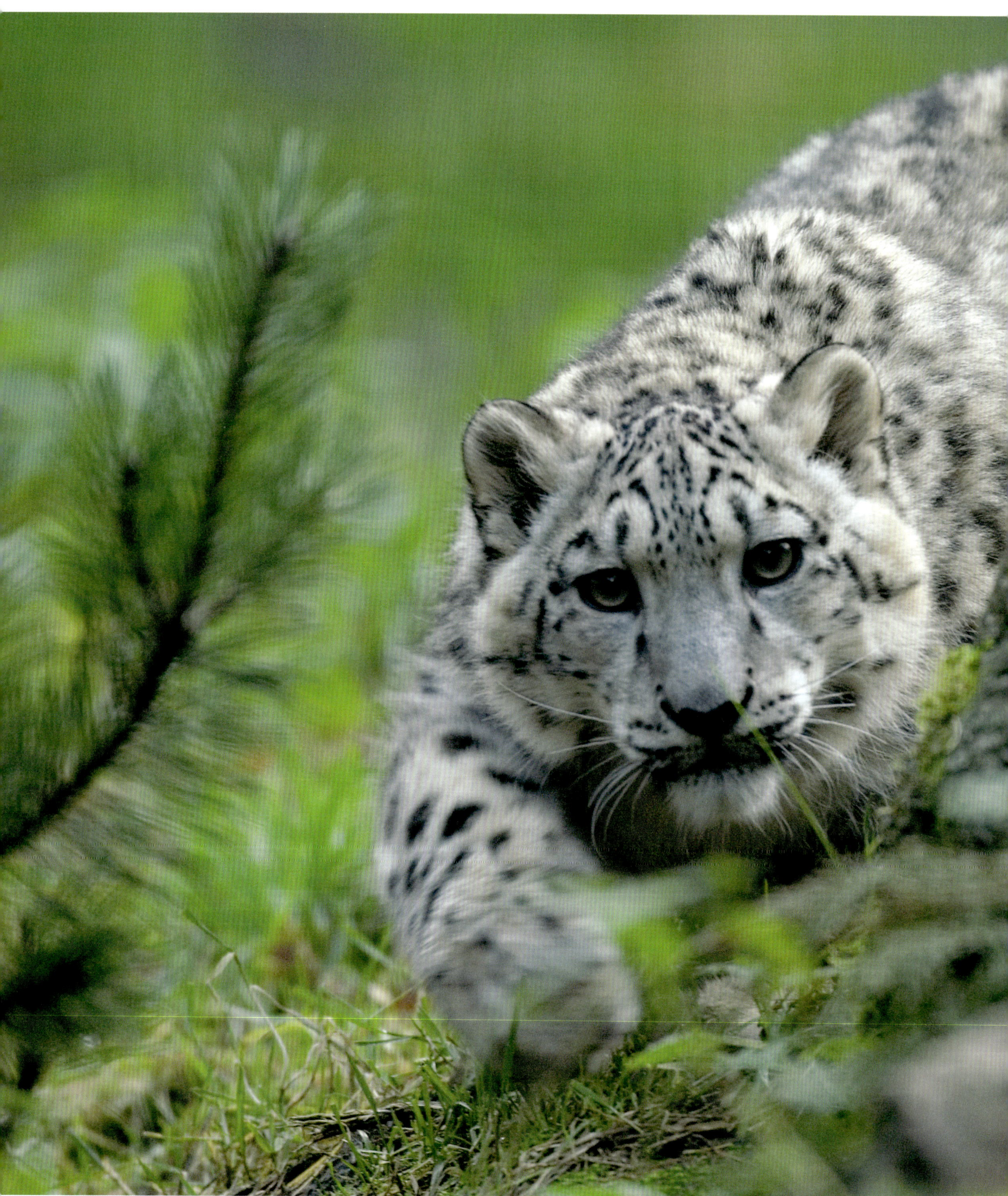

The exceptionally beautiful pattern of its coat almost became the snow leopard's undoing, because it was coveted for its fur. As a result, reserves were established to protect the beautiful big cats. In winter, the leopard grows an additional layer of warming, grey fur (below). Himalayan blue sheep feature on his menu, among others.

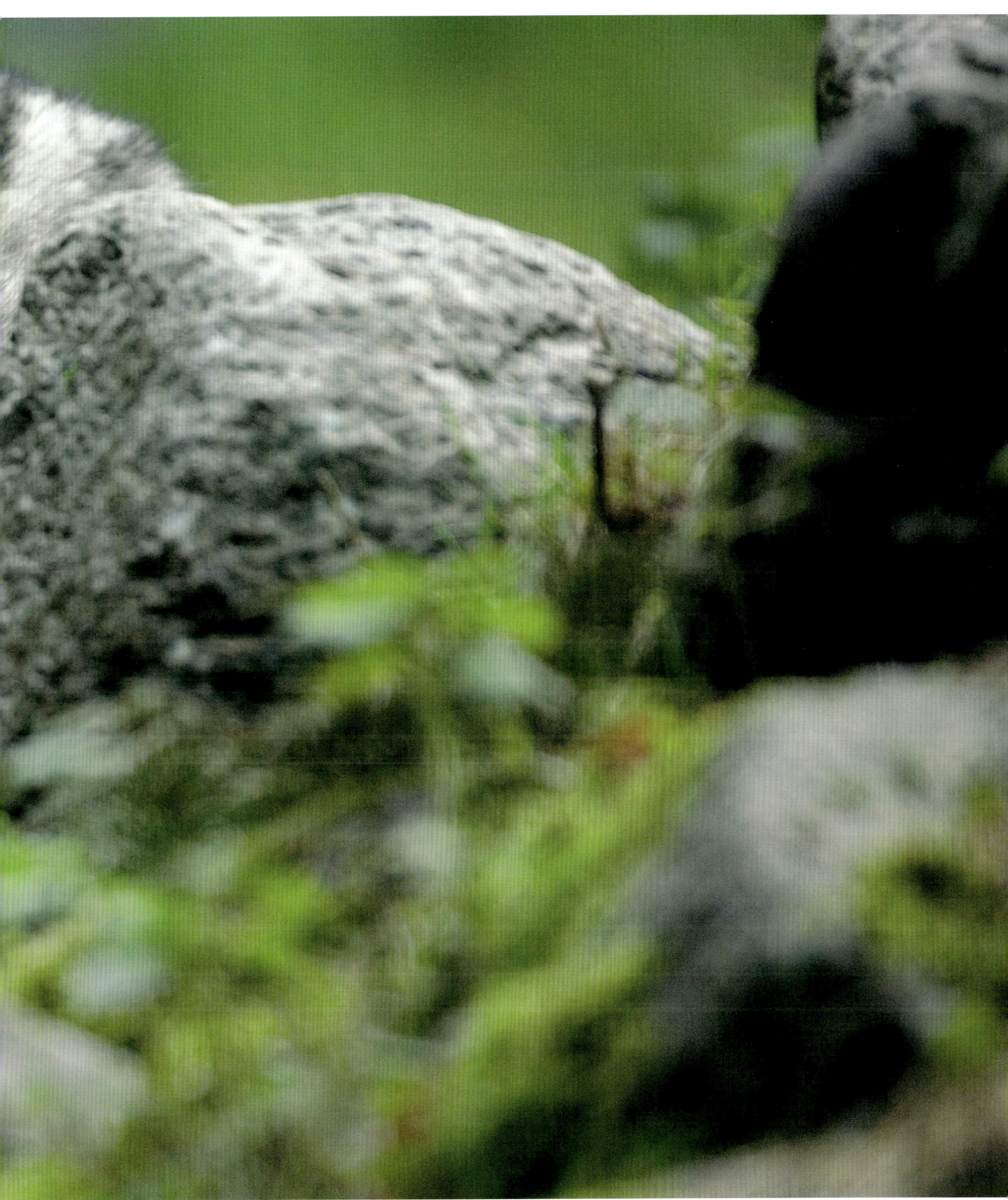

KEOLADEO NATIONAL PARK

Date of inscription: 1985

Set in the marshes of Rajasthan, Keoladeo is an ornithological paradise. The bird population is at its highest after the monsoon, when the local waterfowl are joined by large numbers of migratory birds – some of them rare species.

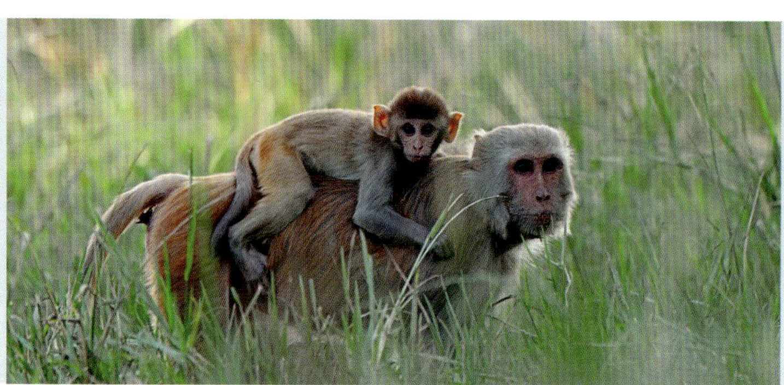

The national park's wetland landscape is man-made. It was formerly the hunting ground of the maharajas of Bharatpur, and the marshy natural depression provided plentiful bounty for duck hunters. In fact, a single day's hunting frequently yielded several thousand birds.

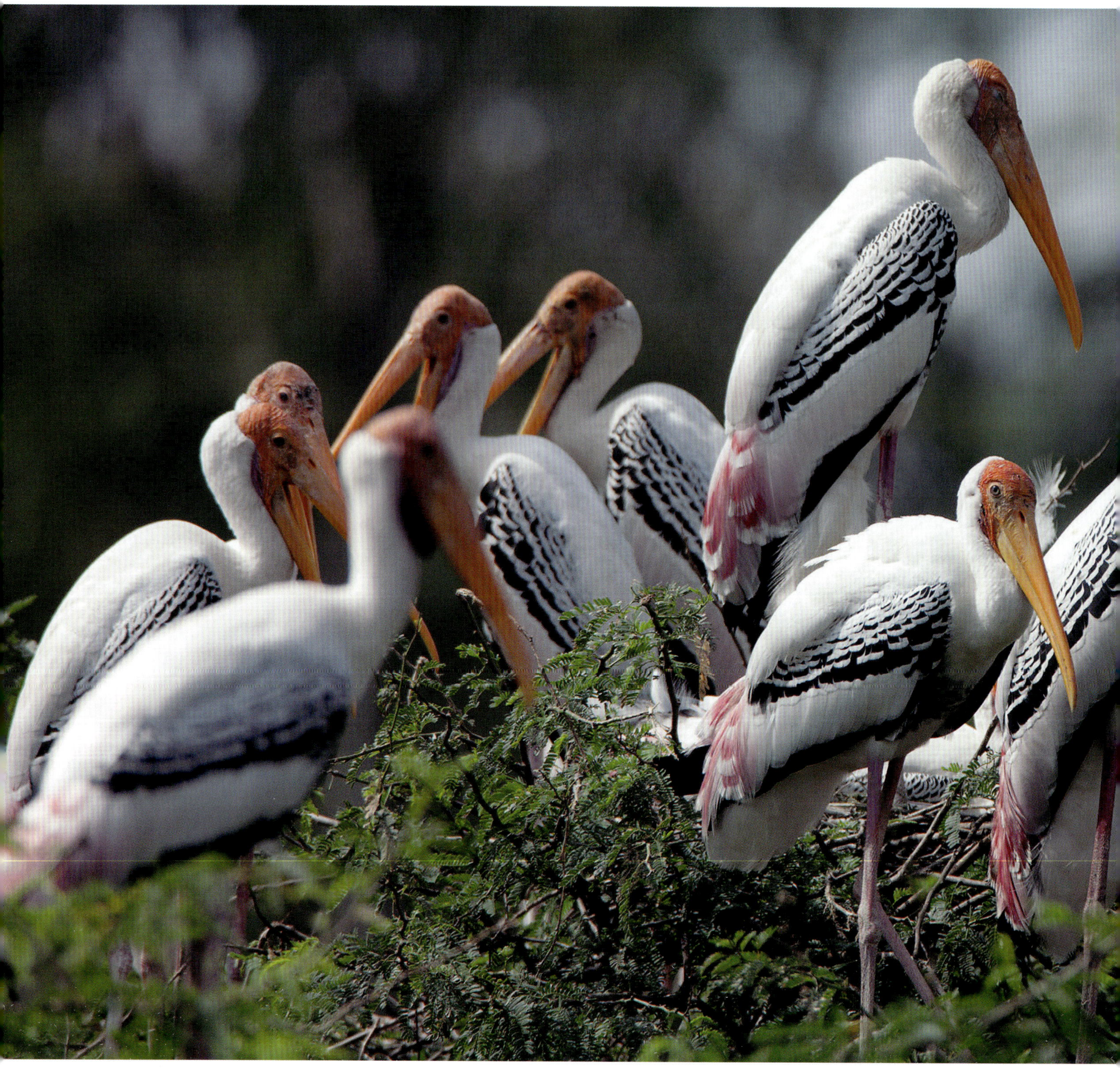

In the 19th century, the maharajas expanded the hunting waters through the construction of artificial canals and dams. In the middle of an otherwise extremely dry terrain, the maharajas had created what would later become a popular breeding ground for birds.

Today, the protected area is a permanent home to some 120 species of bird, including one of the world's largest heron colonies. In winter, around 240 different species of migratory birds also settle here, among them the rare Siberian crane (or snow crane) and the falcated duck. The Siberian crane has always been one of the park's biggest attractions. Back in 1976, more than a hundred Siberian cranes spent the winter here, but the bird is now feared to have become extinct.

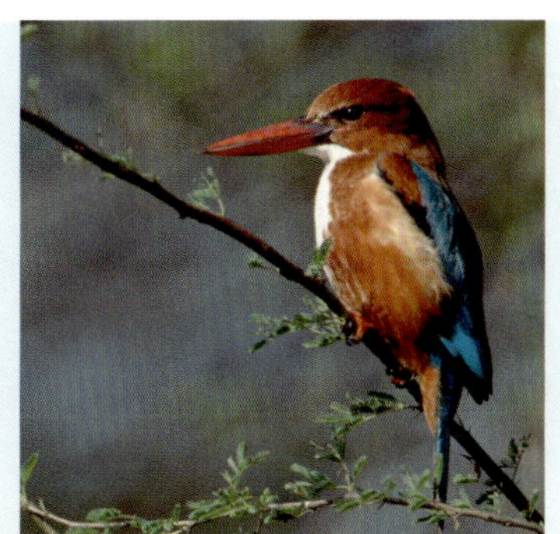

The artificial wetlands of Keoladeo National Park cover an area of less than 30 sq. km (12 sq. miles). Despite its small size, the park is a sanctuary for many endangered animals. These include painted storks (large picture), kingfishers with their pretty plumage (left), eagle-owls, sparrowhawks, nilgau antelopes, sarus cranes (from the top) and rhesus macaques (far left).

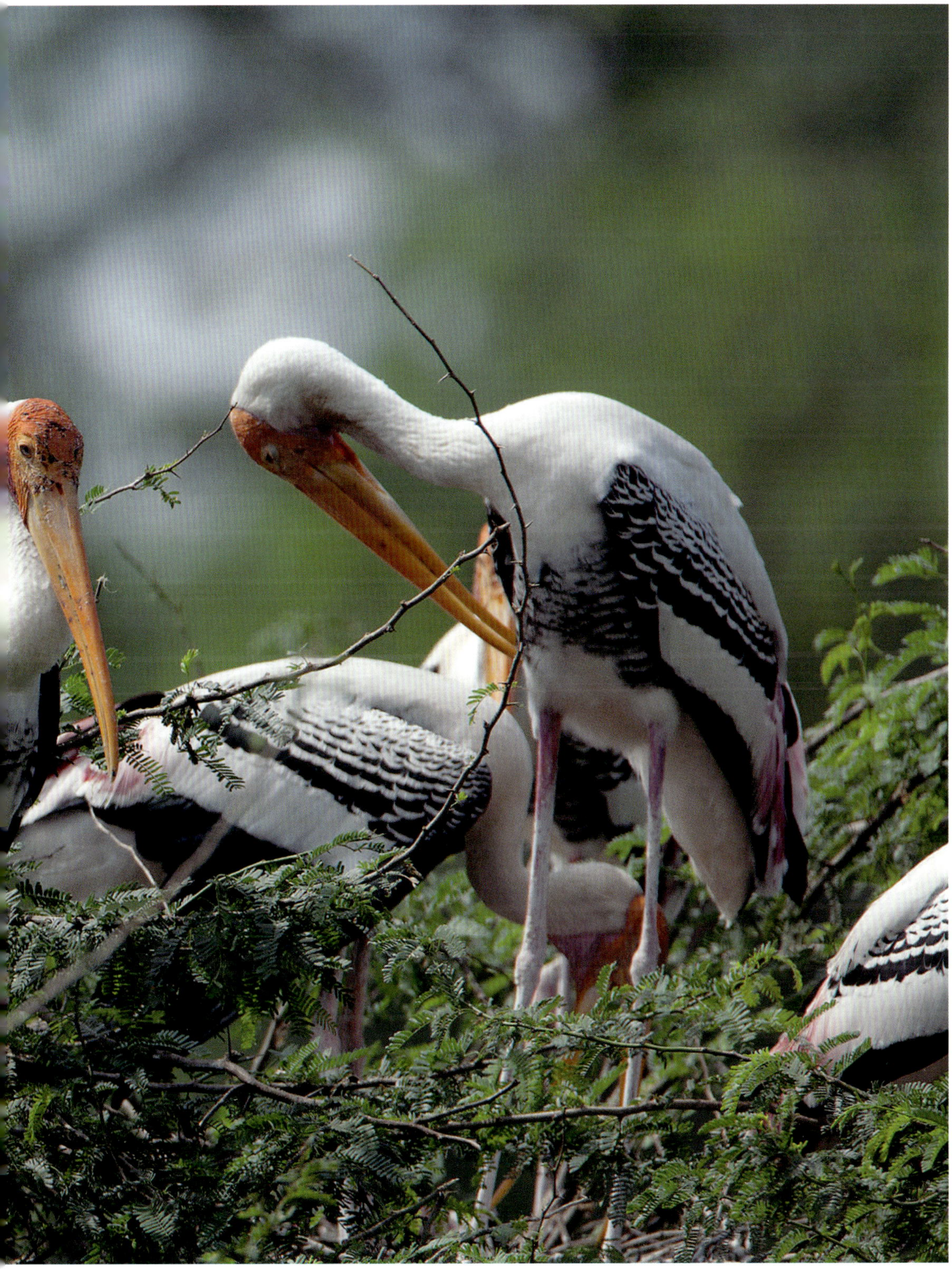

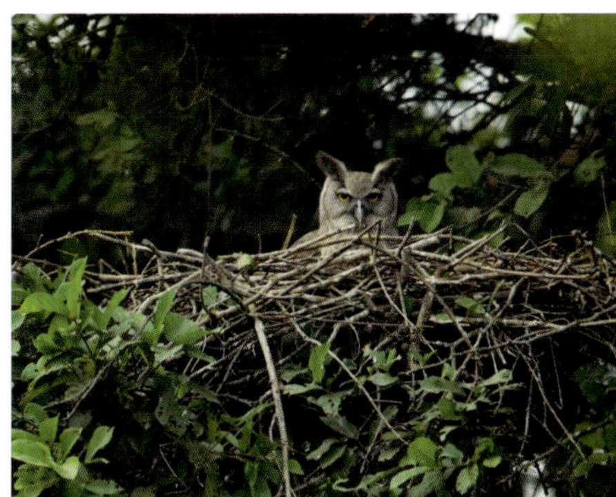

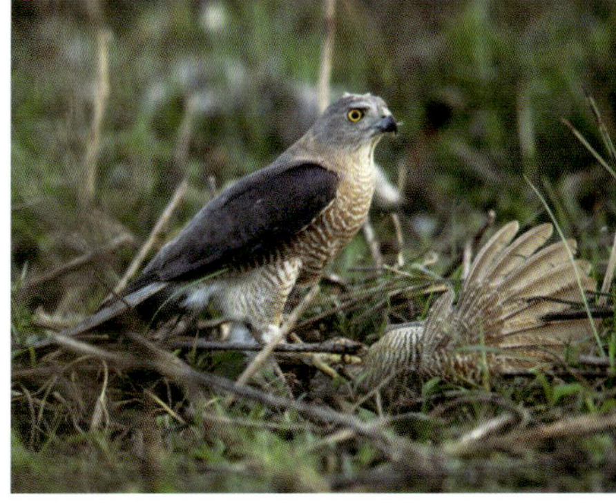

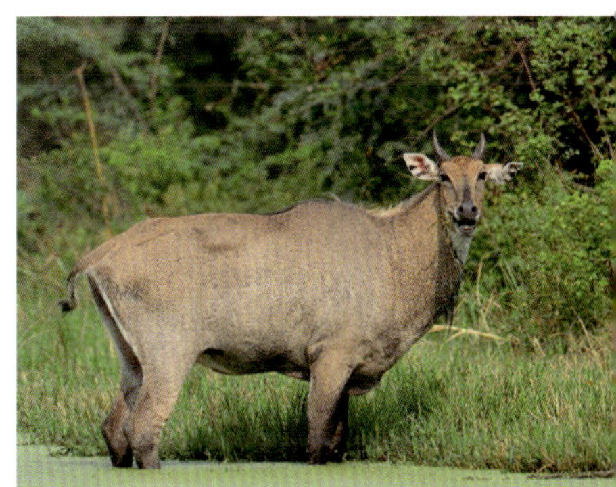

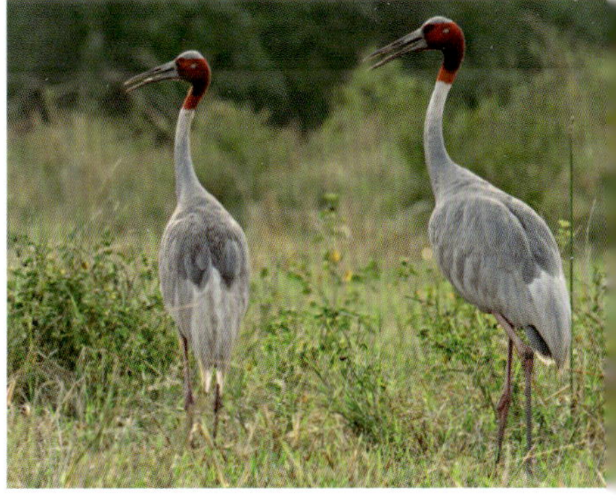

MANAS WILDLIFE SANCTUARY

Date of inscription: 1985

Most famous for its tigers and many elephants, this wildlife sanctuary lies at the feet of the Himalayas in Assam, not far from the border with Bhutan. The port takes its name from the fast-flowing Manas river.

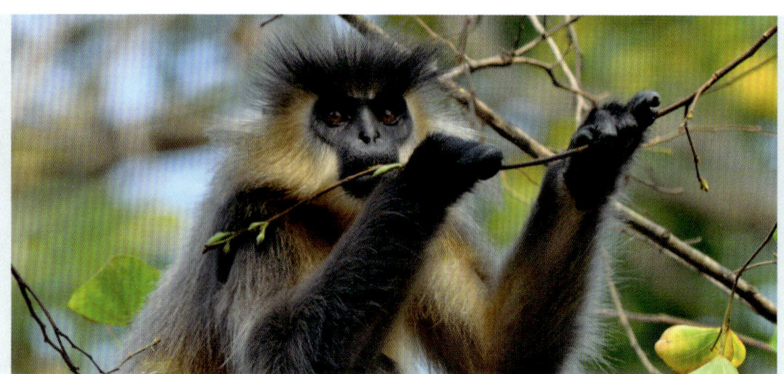

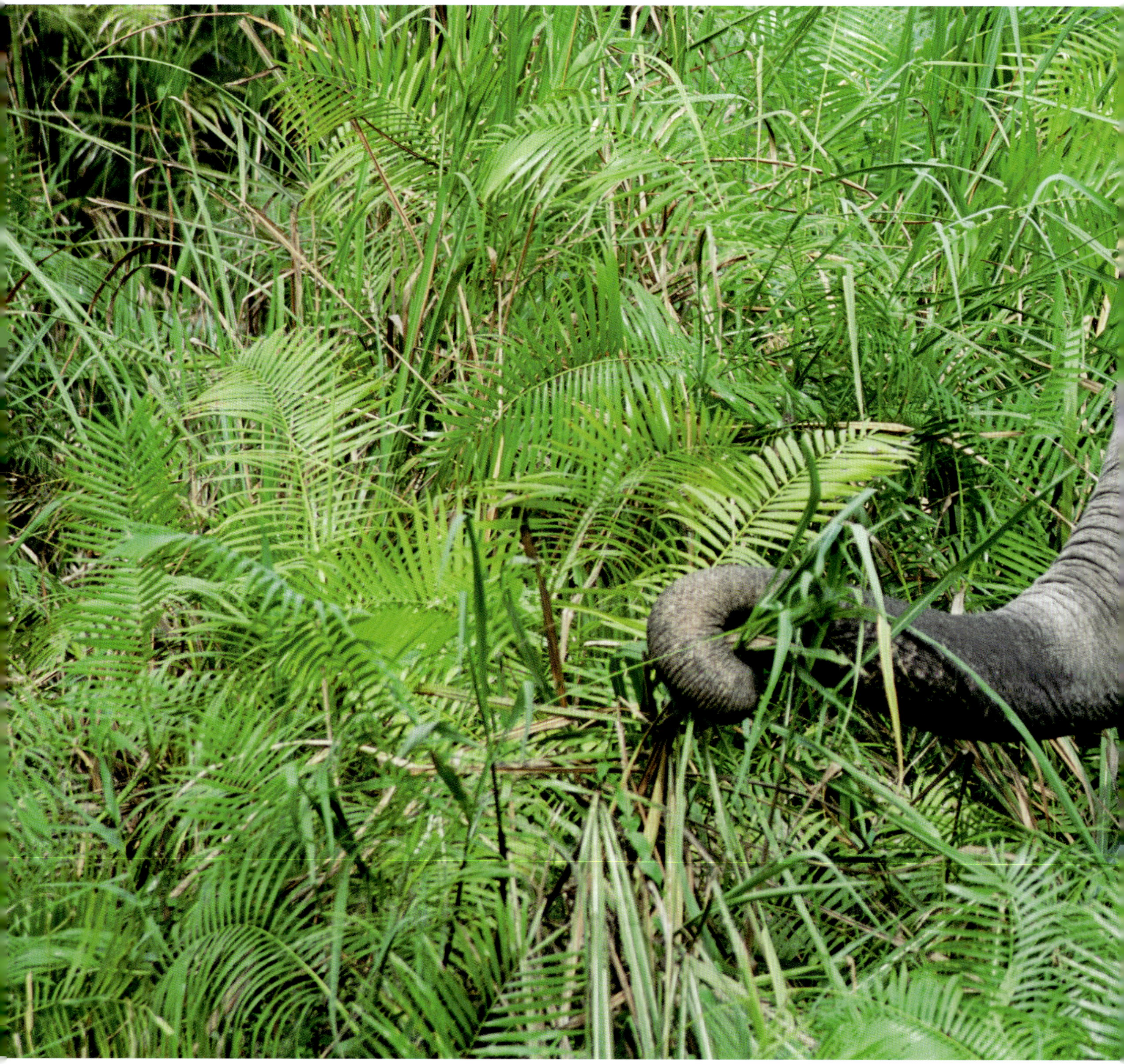

The core of the Manas reserve was declared a wildlife sanctuary in 1928. In 1992, however, the area was decimated by civil insurgency that saw the local elephant population fall from some 2,000 animals to just a few dozen. Thanks to rehabilitation efforts, elephant numbers were back up to 700 by 2006, and the sanctuary's population of Bengal tigers had also risen to around 60. The rare one-horned rhino, on the other hand, had completely disappeared from the area. It began to be reintroduced in 2006, when animals from other parks were released here. Grasslands constitute about 60 percent of the sanctuary's terrain, and are home to – among other animals – wild buffalo and pygmy hogs. Until spotted in Manas, the latter was thought to have become extinct. Barasingha (swamp deer), leopard cats, and pangolins are some of Manas's other animal inhabitants. The grassy savannahs, woodlands, and rivers that characterize the Manas landscape are also home to numerous species of bird, notably the Asian blue quail, drongo, and Indian eagle owl.

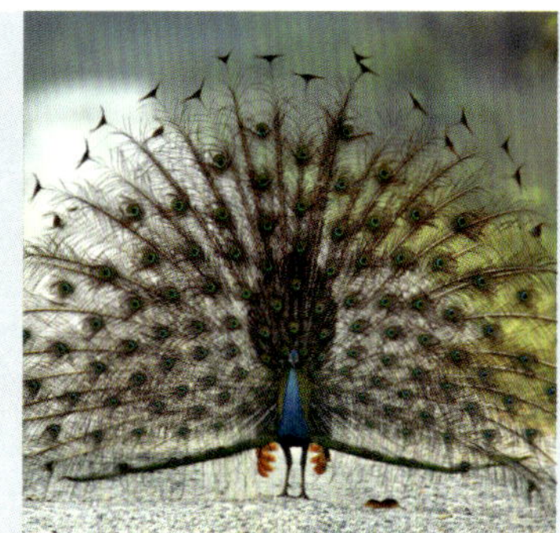

Langurs belong to the Colbinae monkeys. The Manas wildlife sanctuary is home to both the golden langur and capped langur (small image, far left). The area also boasts an important and growing population of Indian elephants (large image). Peacocks (left) may now be spread throughout the world, yet originally they come from India.

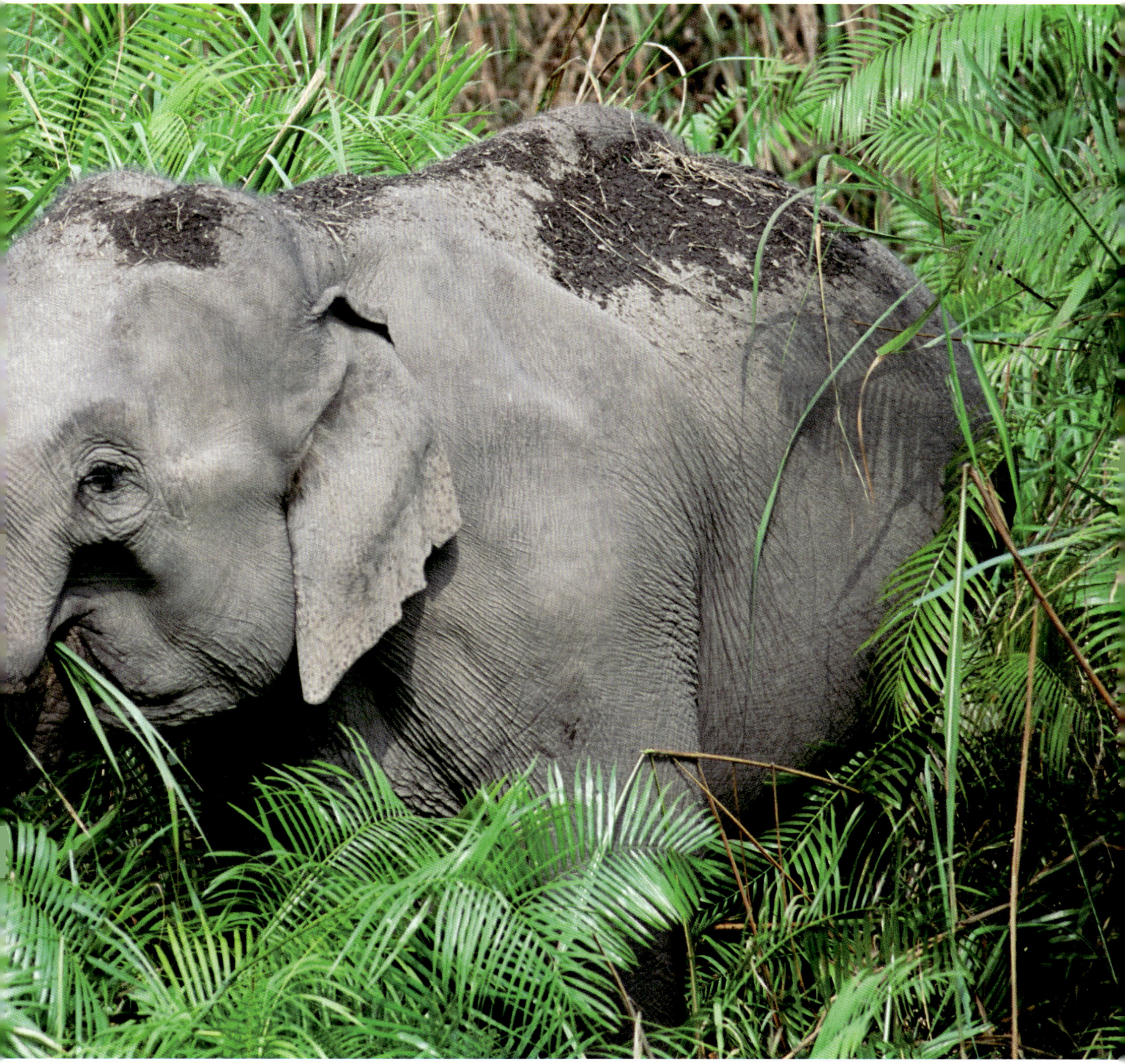

KAZIRANGA NATIONAL PARK

Date of inscription: 1985

Set over 430 sq. km in the heart of Assam, Kaziranga National Park is one of the region's last examples of an area untouched by human intervention. Rare animals found here include the world's largest population of the endangered one-horned rhinoceros.

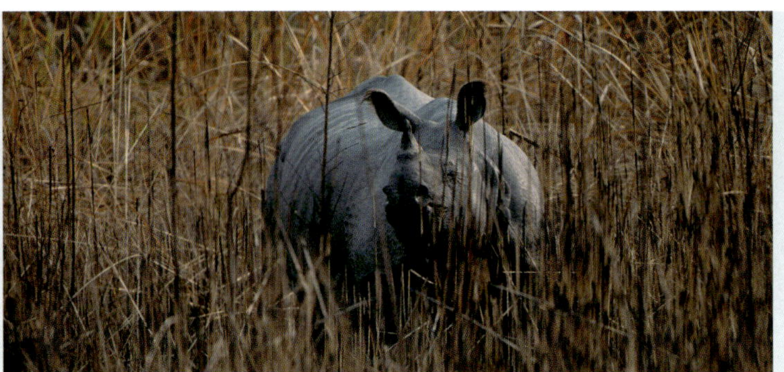

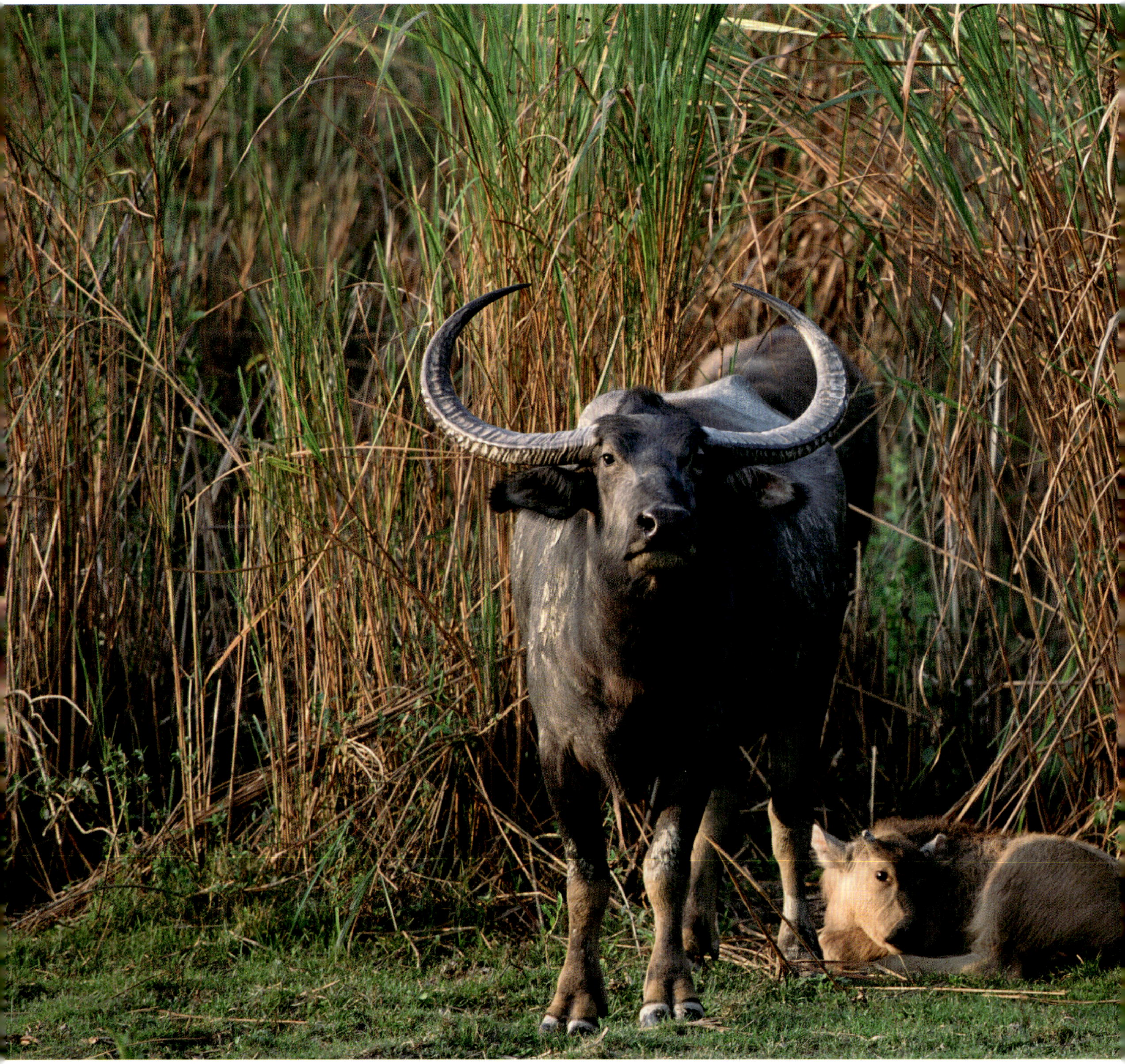

Conditions in Kaziranga National Park are closely linked to the heady fluctuations of the Brahmaputra river. During the monsoon season in July/August, two thirds of the park is regularly under water, forcing its animals to retreat to higher ground both within and outside the park. Local conservationists have traditionally focused their attention on the fate of the one-horned rhino. At the beginning of the 20th century, the animal's population was already depleted enough to require prohibition of the issuing of hunting warrants. The region was declared a nature reserve in 1908, becoming a wildlife sanctuary in 1950, and a national park in 1974. Today, the number of one-horned rhino here is estimated to be around 1,500, and some of the park's animals were recently moved to the nearby Manas wildlife sanctuary to boost the rhino population there as well. But rhinos are not the only animals here. The park boasts good numbers of elephants and buffalo, and several species of deer. There are also gibbons, tigers, wild boar, and rare birds like the bearded bustard and grey pelican, as well as Asian black bears and sloth bears.

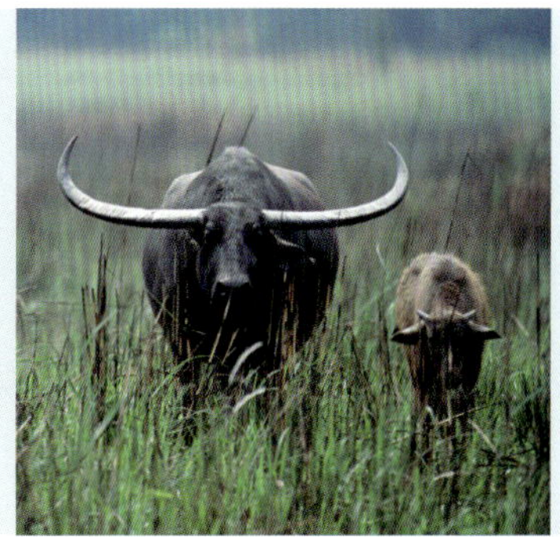

Kaziranga National Park, Assam, is truly a natural paradise. Traversing the grasslands, the park's one-horned rhinos (Rhinoceros unicornis) are its main attraction (far left, below). Only adult water buffalo (large picture and left) have the typical long horns. Barasingha, or swamp deer (below) are an Indian deer species.

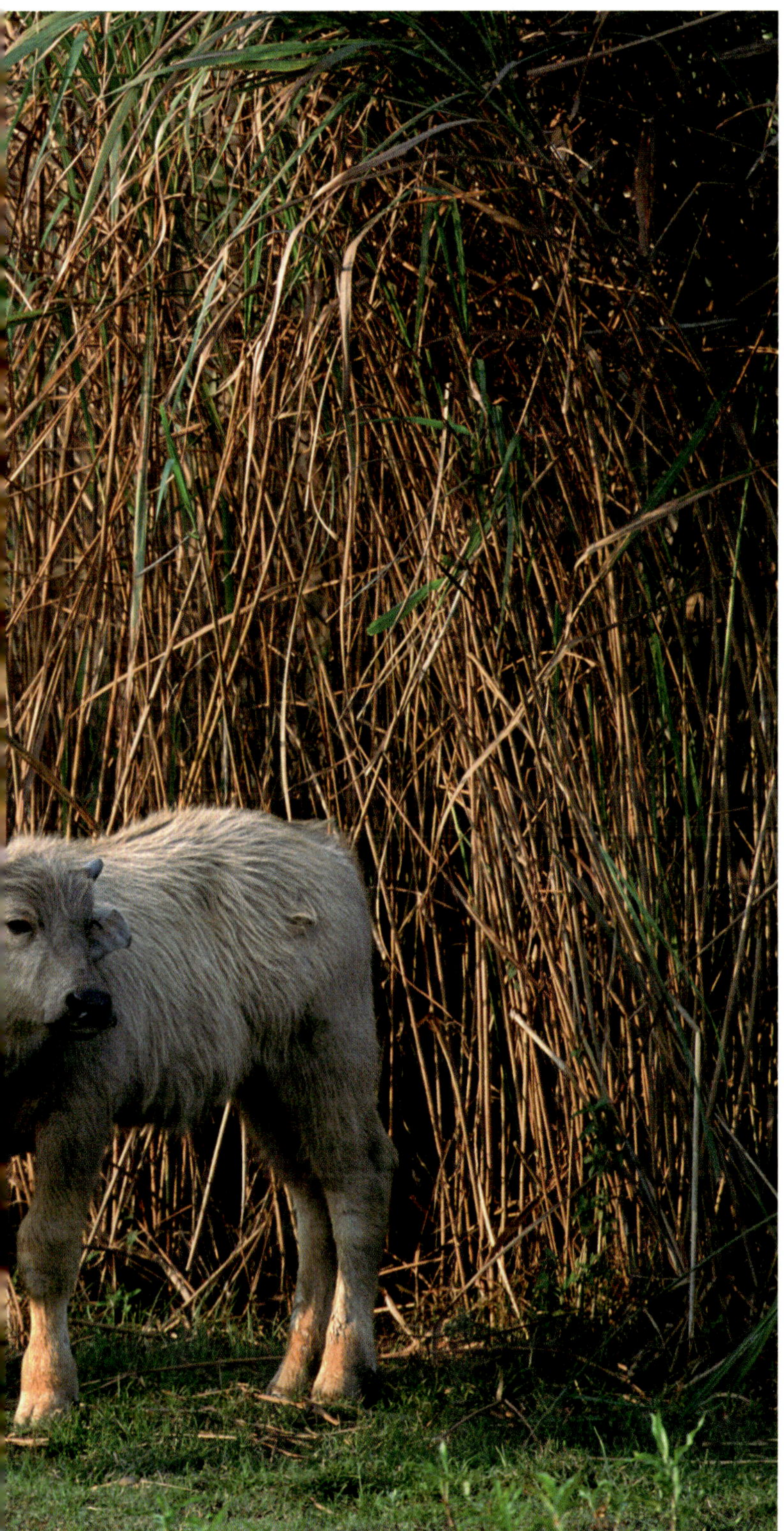

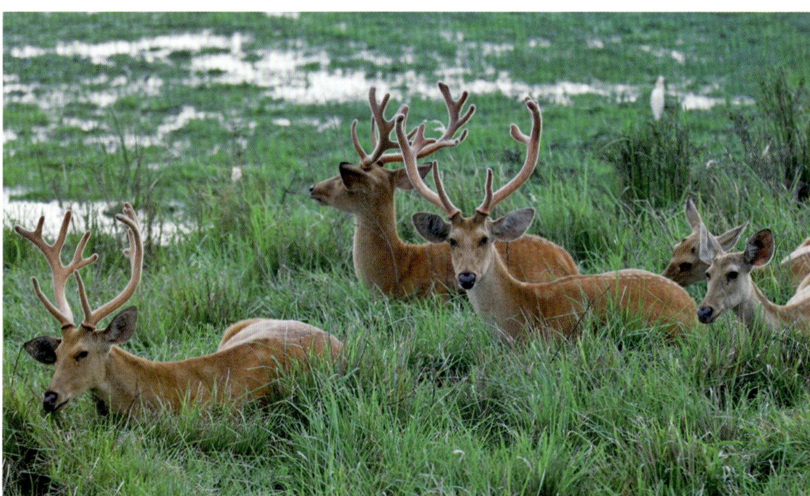

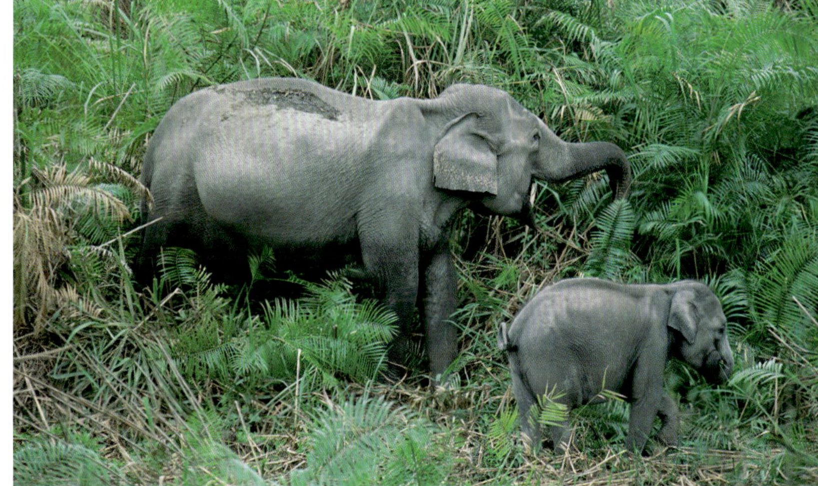

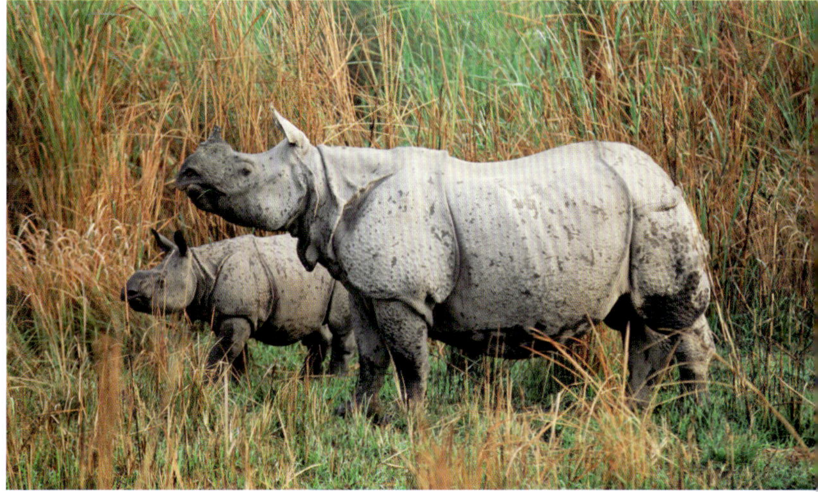

WESTERN GHATS

Date of inscription: 2012

The elongated mountains of the Western Ghats, or Sahyadri, in western India are one of the eight areas in the world with the greatest biodiversity, although on average they attain a height of only 900 m. The Ghats act as a barrier for the monsoon winds.

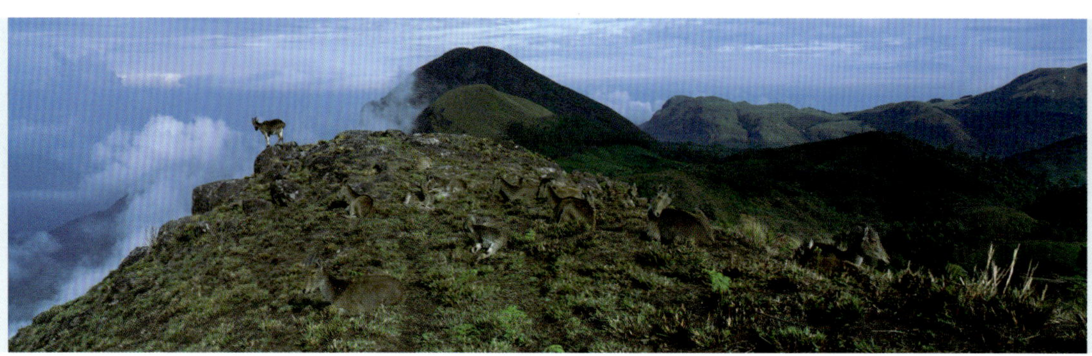

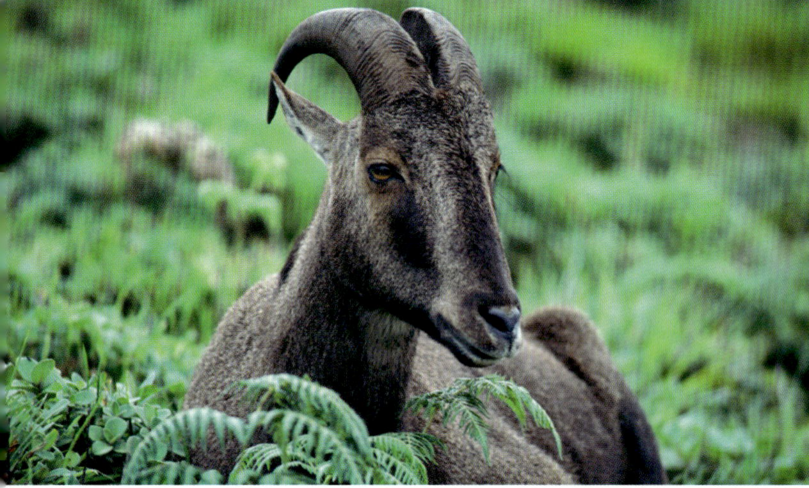

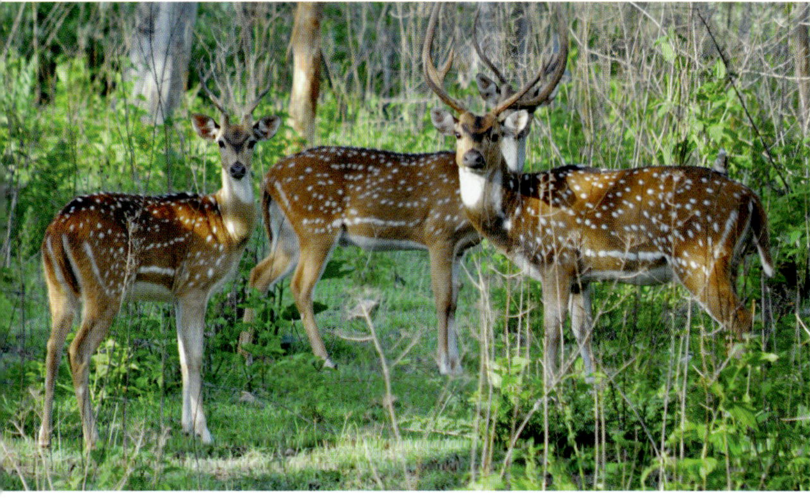

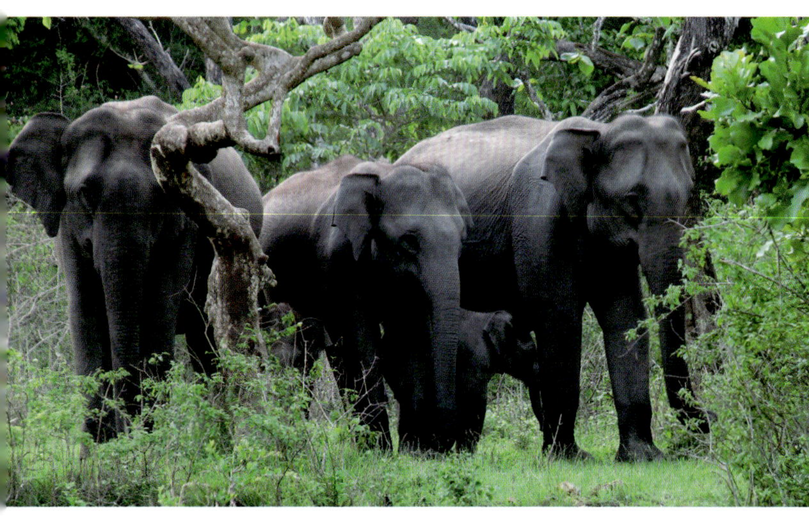

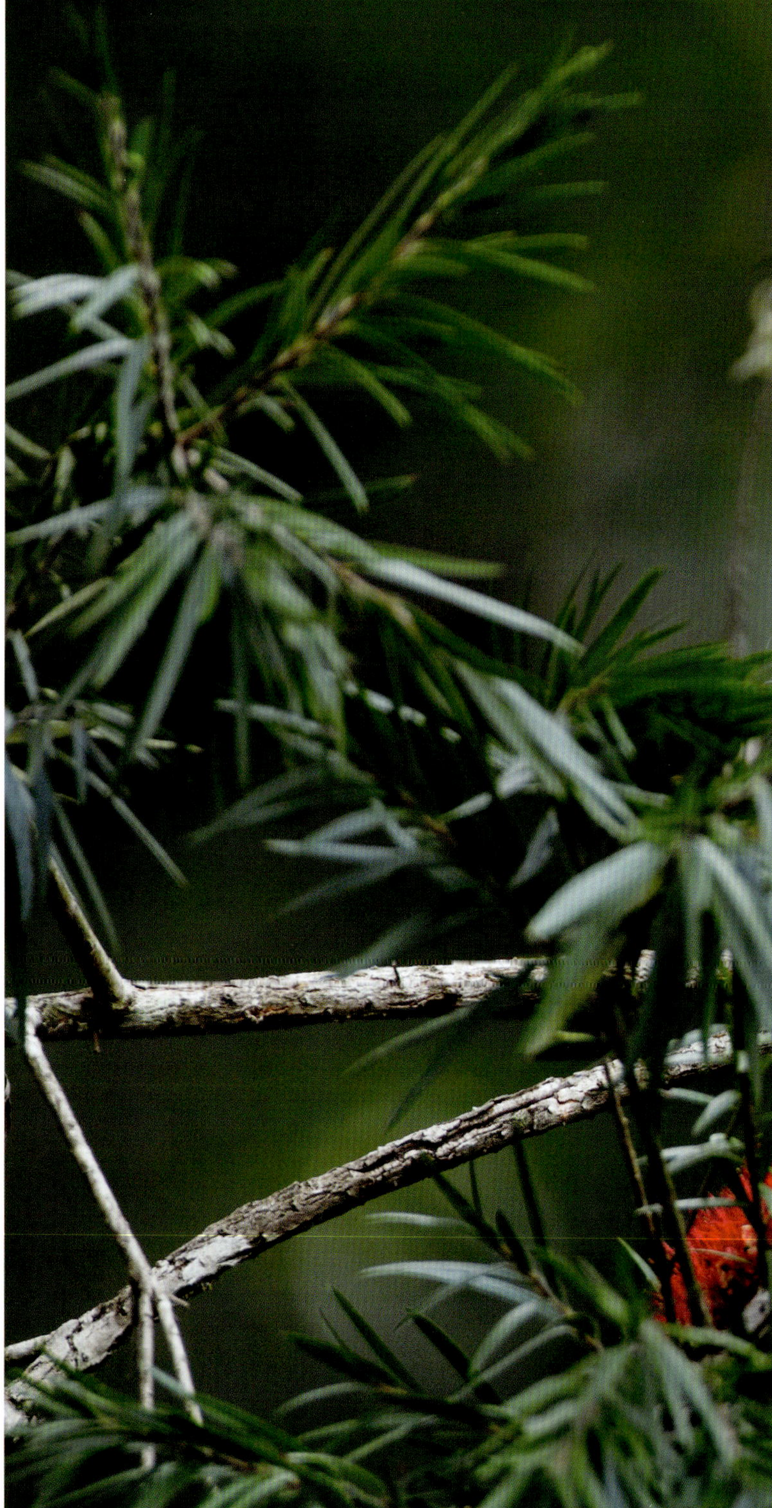

Parallel to the west coast of India extends an approximately 1,600-km- (994-mile-) long mountain chain: the Western Ghats. They receive a substantial rainfall, especially during the monsoon season from June to September, up to 6,000 mm per year. Thus, tropical evergreen and deciduous rainforests grow on the side facing the monsoon winds. But as humans have inhabited the mountains since time immemorial, only about one-fifth of the original forest cover remains, and the predominant ecosystem is made up of forest relics embedded in grasslands (known as "shola prairie"). The area of the Western Ghats is extremely rich in species, and the degree of endemic species is perhaps even worthy of a record. Of the 4,000 to 5,000 flowering plants, more than 30 per cent are likely to be endemic. The genus Impatiens, for example, is represented by 86 species, of which 76 only occur in the West Ghats. Seven larger areas were inscribed as a World Heritage site, largely coinciding with already existing national parks, game reserves and forest reserves.

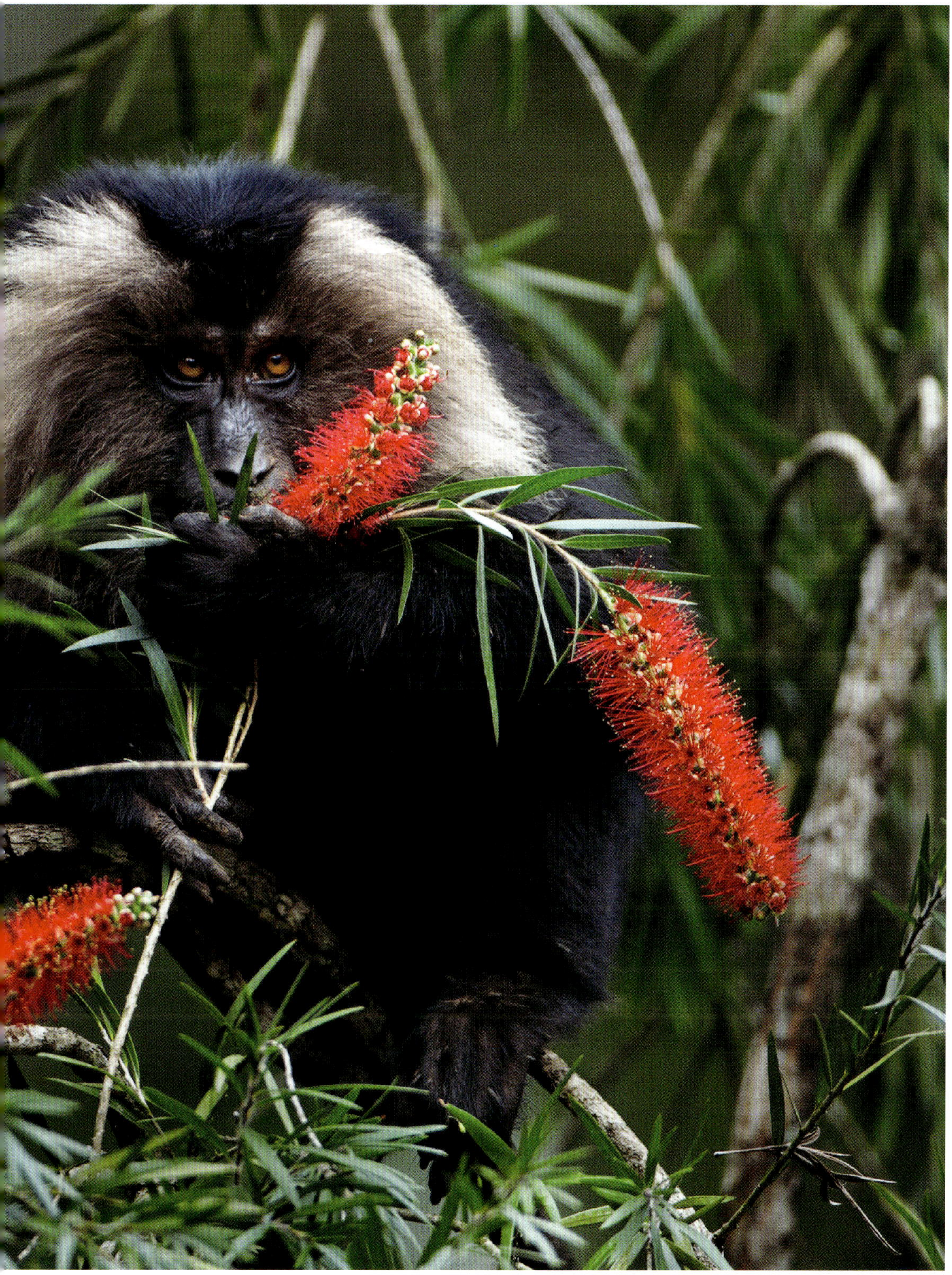

The World Heritage-listed Eravikulam National Park is home to the Nilgiri Tahr (top left), a goat-like ungulate. Chitals, elephants, grey langurs, peacocks and Indian bonnet macaques are also at home here (from centre left to bottom right). Large picture: A lion-tailed macaque.

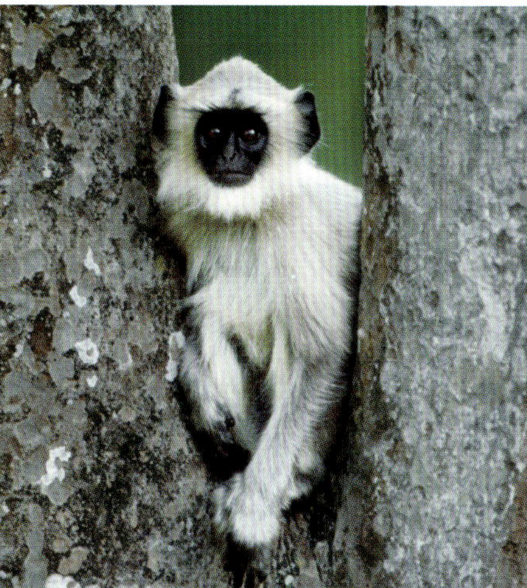

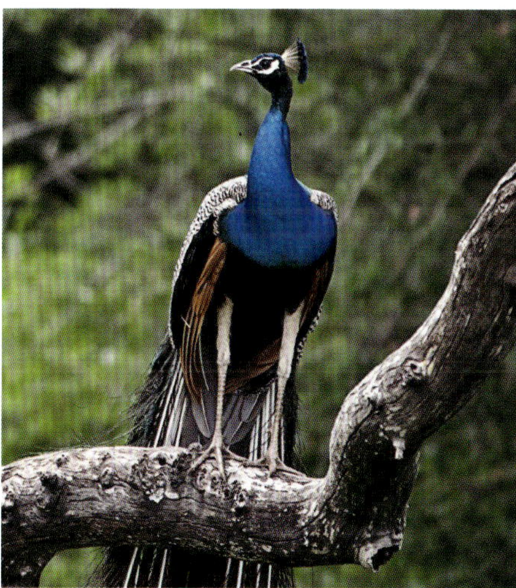

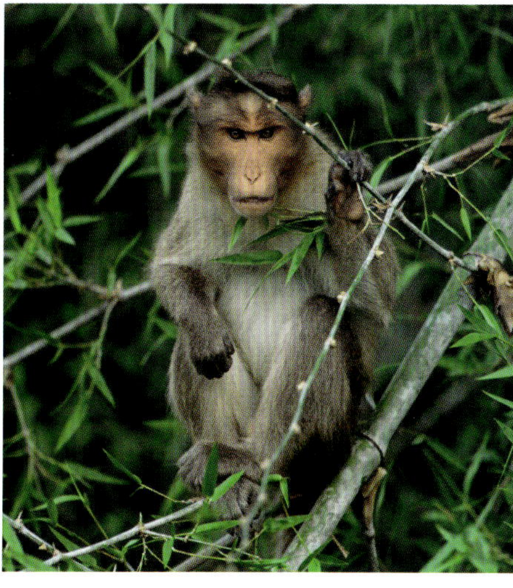

SUNDARBANS NATIONAL PARK

Date of inscription: 1987

The Sundarbans, the world's largest mangrove forests, lie in the delta of the Ganges, Brahmaputra, and Meghna rivers in the Bay of Bengal. These unique wetlands are shared between India and Bangladesh, and an area of each country has been declared a World Heritage Site.

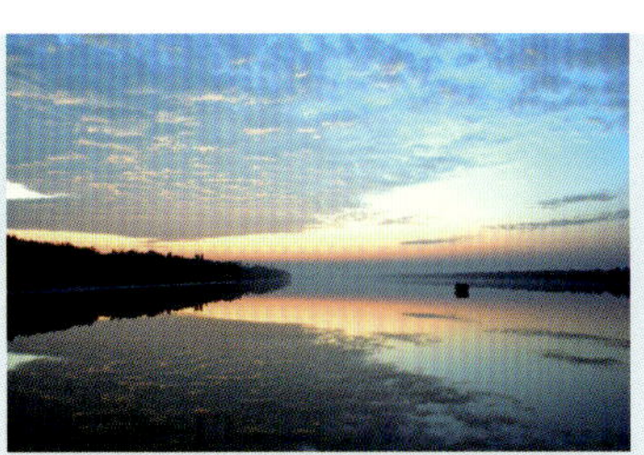

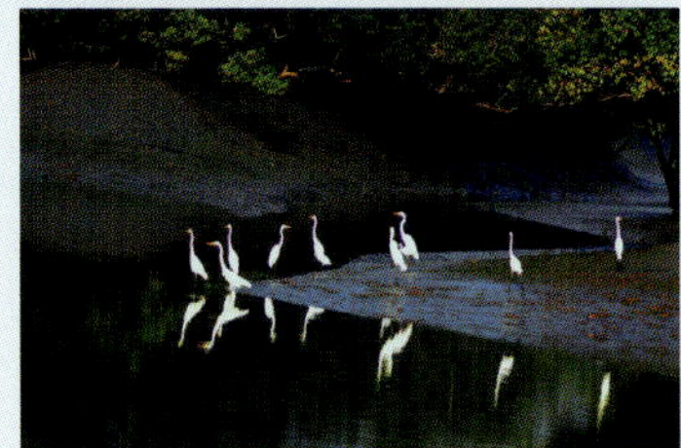

The Sundarbans are a highly complex system of rivers, channels, and marshlands. There is a 7.5 m (25 feet) difference between low and high tide, and the boundaries between land and water are constantly shifting. The Indian part of the Sundarbans covers more than half of the entire 10,000 sq. km (3,900 sq. mile) wetland area. Sundarbans National Park – the actual World Heritage Site – covers some 1,300 sq. km (500 sq. miles).

Fresh and saltwater zones come together here. The local ecosystem is characterized not only by its mangrove forests, but also by its rich fauna. Dolphins, otters, pythons, turtles, water monitors, crocodiles, storks, herons, cormorants, and curlews are all found here, not to mention chital and Barasingha deer, rhesus macaques, wild boar, and Bengal tigers.

The satellite image (below) shows the eastern part of the delta, including the Sundarbans. The dark green areas are the mangrove forests, while the light haze in the Bay of Bengal is caused by suspended sediment from the river tributaries. Herons line the bank (left).

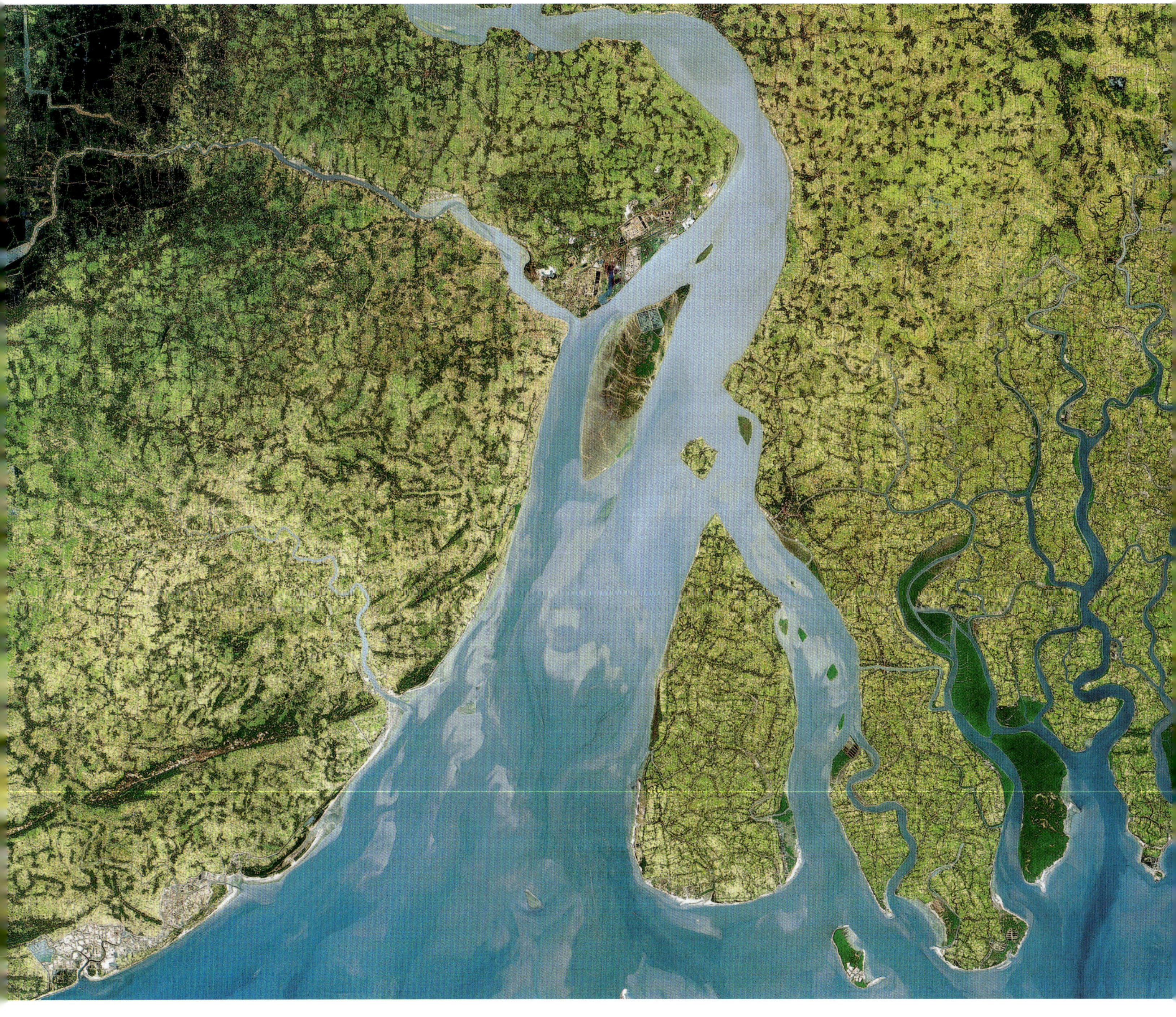

THE SUNDARBANS MANGROVE FORESTS

The Sundarbans are two separate World Heritage Sites. Around a quarter of the Bangladeshi Sundarbans are protected. The Sundarbans West Wildlife Sanctuary adjoins the Indian World Heritage Site directly and lies east of the river Raimangal. The South and East Sanctuaries complete the Bangladeshi World Heritage Site. Heavy rainfall and frequent flooding have created a transition zone of brackish and freshwater areas. Salt water dominates the western side of the site, meaning that the eastern part boasts the greater diversity of plant and animal life. There are 27 types of mangrove, around 50 different mammals, 300 bird species, and 50 types of reptile. The Bengal tiger is the area's most spectacular animal, and over 350 of the animals live here – the world's largest single concentration. The Sundarbans also form a kind of natural barrier that protects inland areas from tropical storms.

Mangroves, the salt-tolerant evergreen plants of tropical coastal marshes, use their stilt roots to anchor themselves in the soft mud and form aerial roots. Deer (right) come to drink.

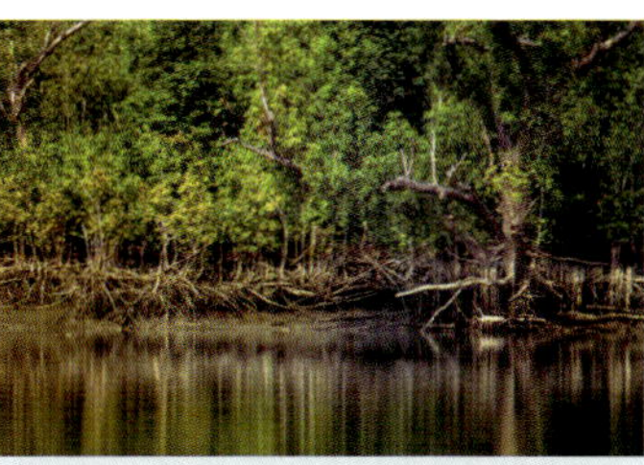

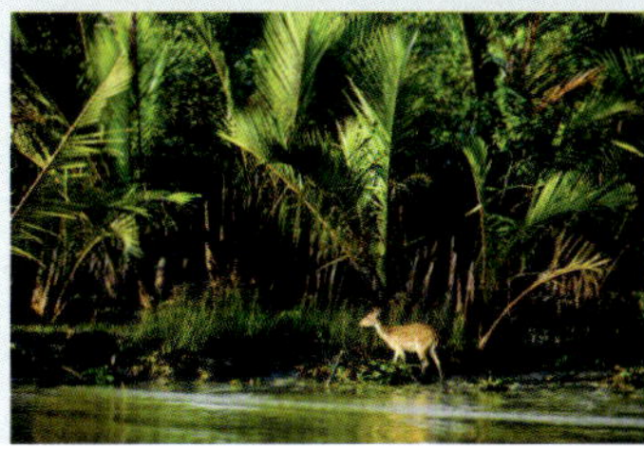

Date of inscription: 1997

Covering over 1,300 sq. km (500 sq. miles), the Sundarban Wildlife Sanctuaries comprise three separate protected areas that together form the World Heritage Site within the Bangladeshi part of the Sundarbans.

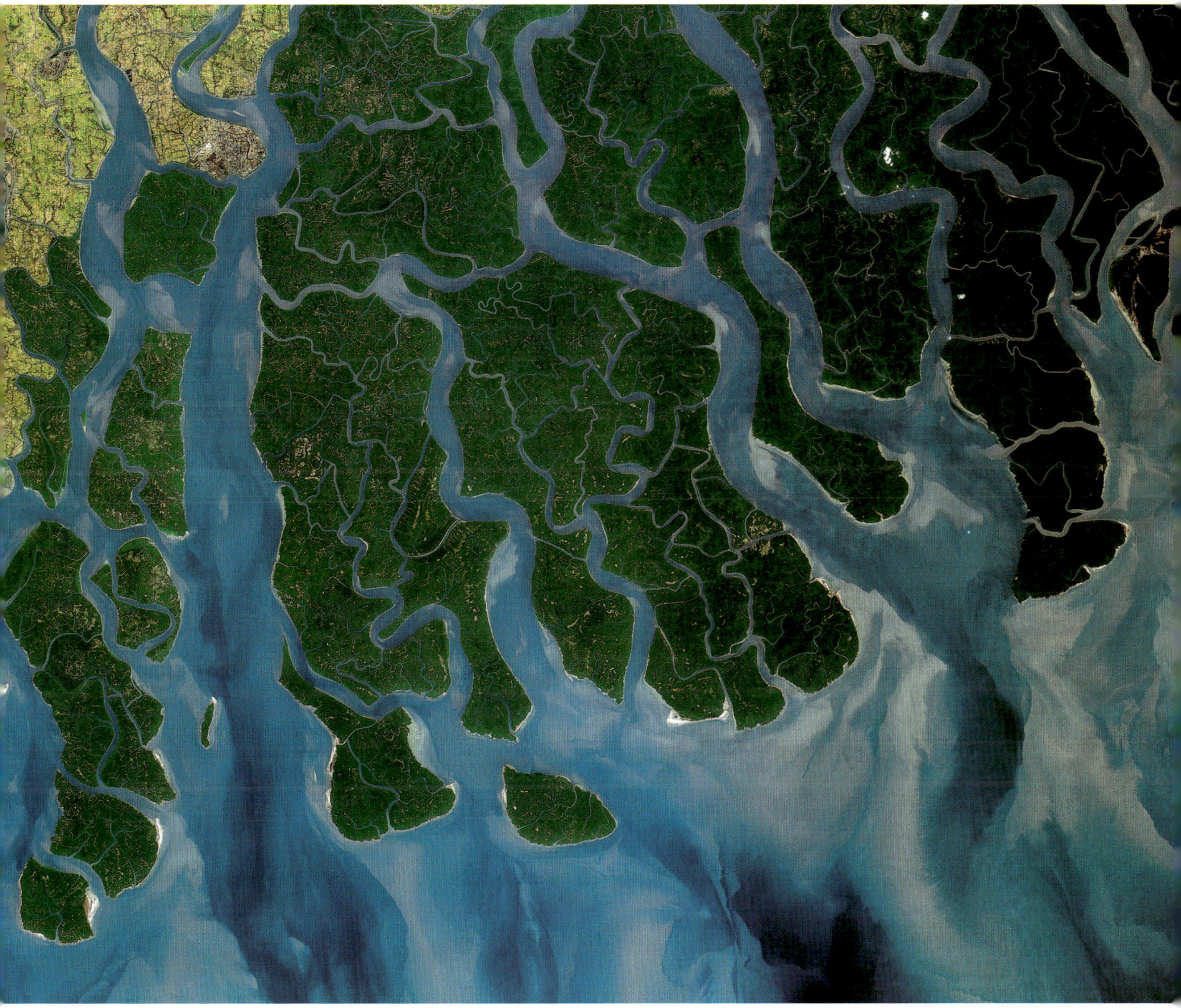

CENTRAL HIGHLANDS OF SRI LANKA

Date of inscription: 2010

Three protected areas in the Central Highlands of Sri Lanka are considered "hot spots" of biodiversity in the country. In the smallest of these, plants and animals can be seen here that are not found anywhere else on Earth.

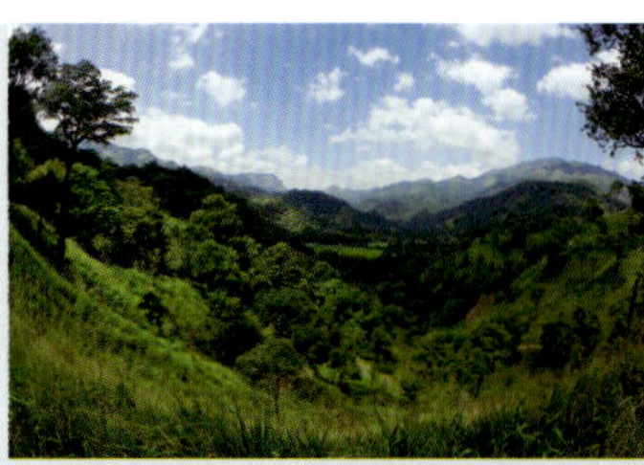

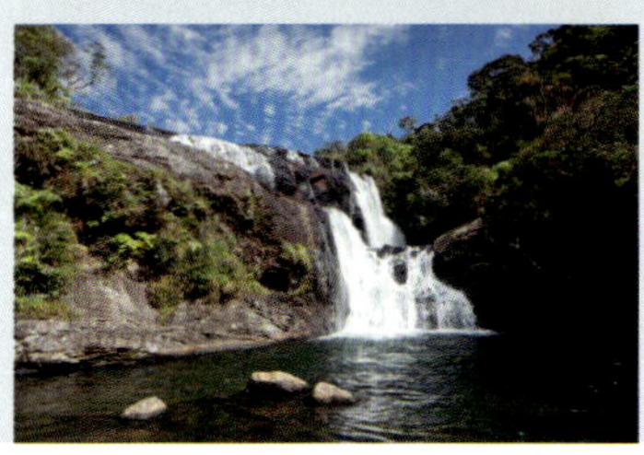

The Central Highlands of Sri Lanka include three regions that are of major importance to the country's biodiversity: the Peak Wilderness Sanctuary, the Horton Plains National Park and the Knuckles Conservation Forest. Grasslands, tropical rainforests and mountain forests dominate in the landscape, which extends up to 2,500 m above sea level. Numerous plant and animal species are found only here. Thus, 87 bird and 24 mammal species live in the Horton Plains Park. The largest animal is the sambar, the third largest deer on Earth after moose and wapiti. "World's End" is a famous, over 1,050-m high steep slope, from where you can see as far as the ocean. The Knuckles Conservation Forest covers all climate zones of the country. Although the forest area accounts for less than half a per cent of the total area of Sri Lanka, the greatest biodiversity is found here.

In addition to the river otters (large picture), numerous birds live in the highlands, many of them endemic, clockwise: Bonelli's eagle, Sri Lanka white-eye, Ceylon bush warbler and bee-eater.

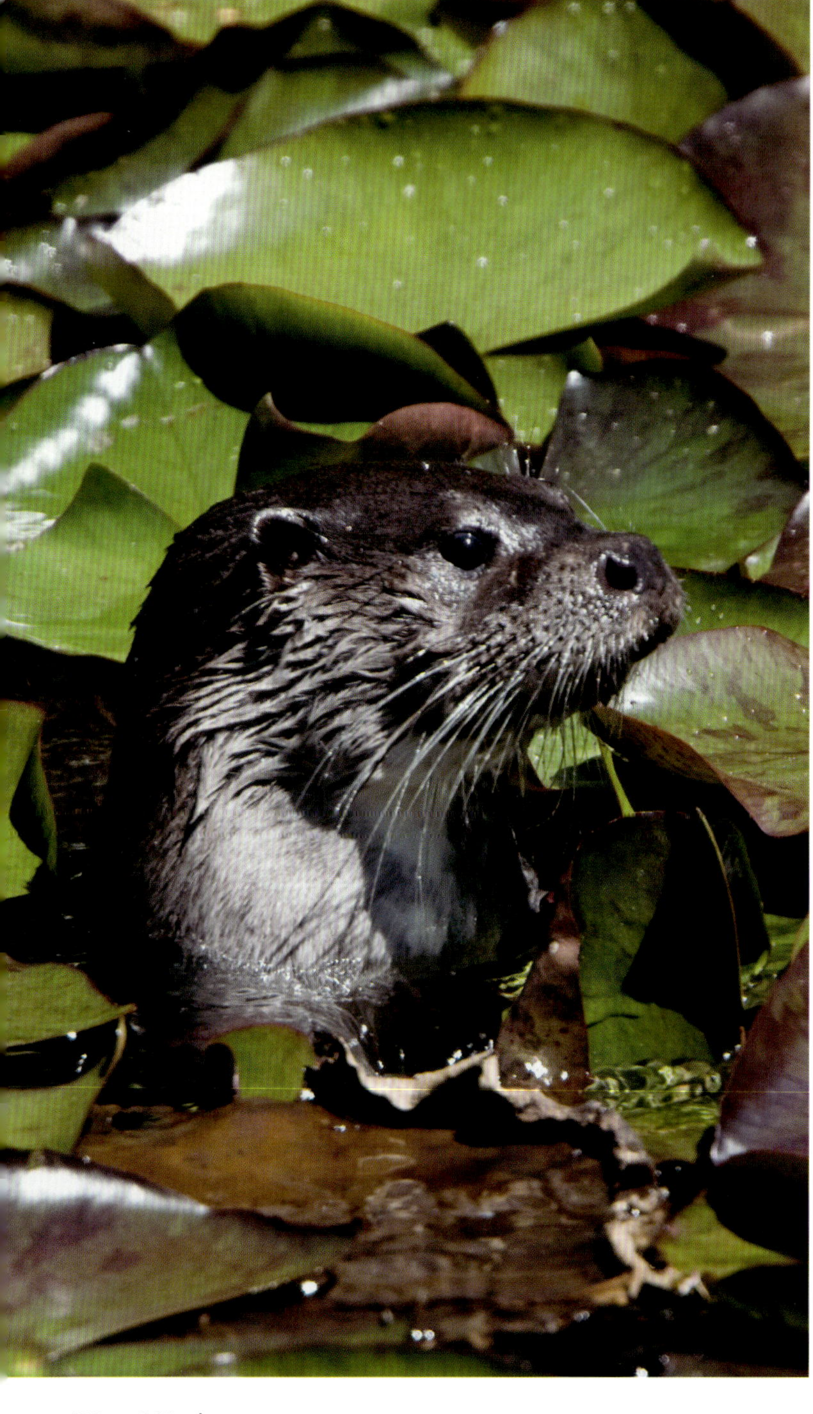

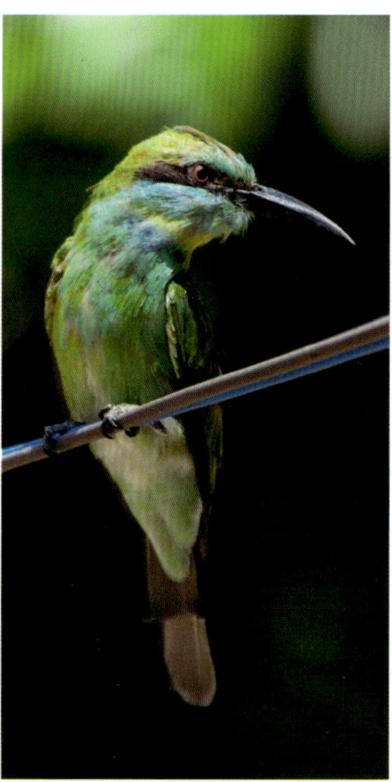

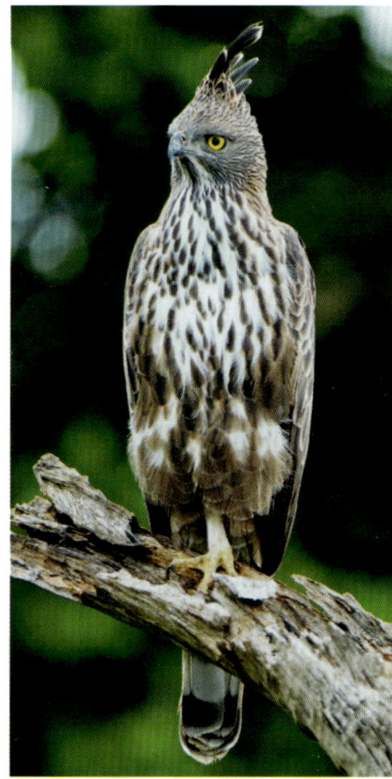

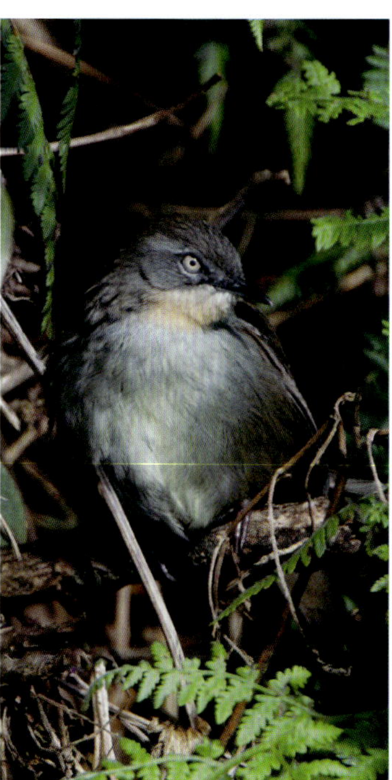

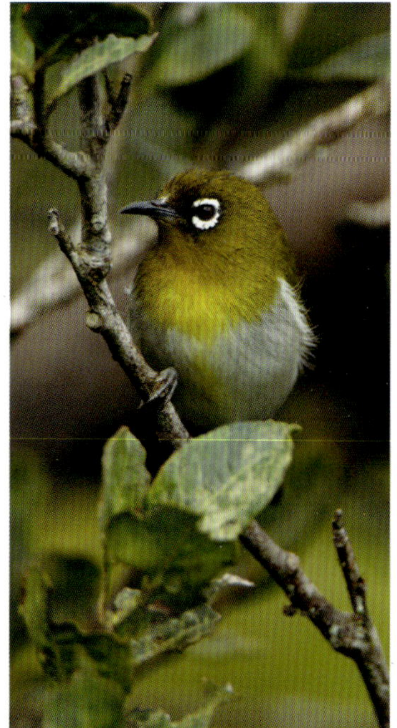

SINHARAJA FOREST RESERVE

Located in south-west Sri Lanka, the Sinharaja reserve is the island's last remaining area of primary rainforest. Sinharaja's name means "Lion King." The government declared the 85 sq. km area between Ratnapura and Matara a biosphere reserve to protect it from excessive logging. The very first nature reserve here in fact dates back to 1875. There is a long history of human exploitation of the tropical rainforests for economic gain – they provided material for house building, all manner of medicines and exotic spices. The rapid growth of the local population, however, means that this complicated ecosystem cannot survive any further large-scale human intervention unscathed. New laws have therefore been introduced to forbid all types of exploitation other than the collection of kittul fibers from the leaf sheath of the fishtail palm tree (Caryota urens).

The most beautiful and exotic animals hide behind and underneath the leaves of the trees, clockwise below right: the adaptable agama lizard, plum-headed parakeet, toque macaque and the cute Layard's palm squirrel.

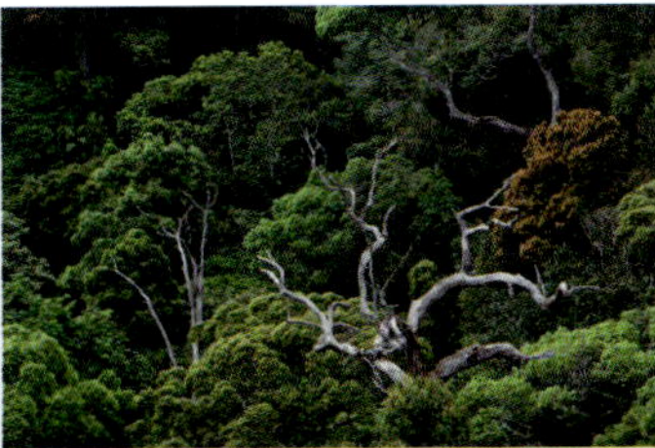

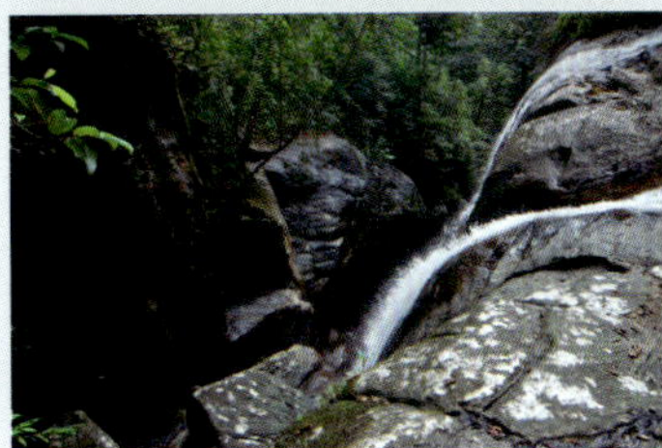

Date of inscription: 1988

At around 500–1,100 m (1,600–3,600 feet) above sea level, this hilly reserve is dominated by tropical rainforest. The protected area is rich in orchids and endemic species.

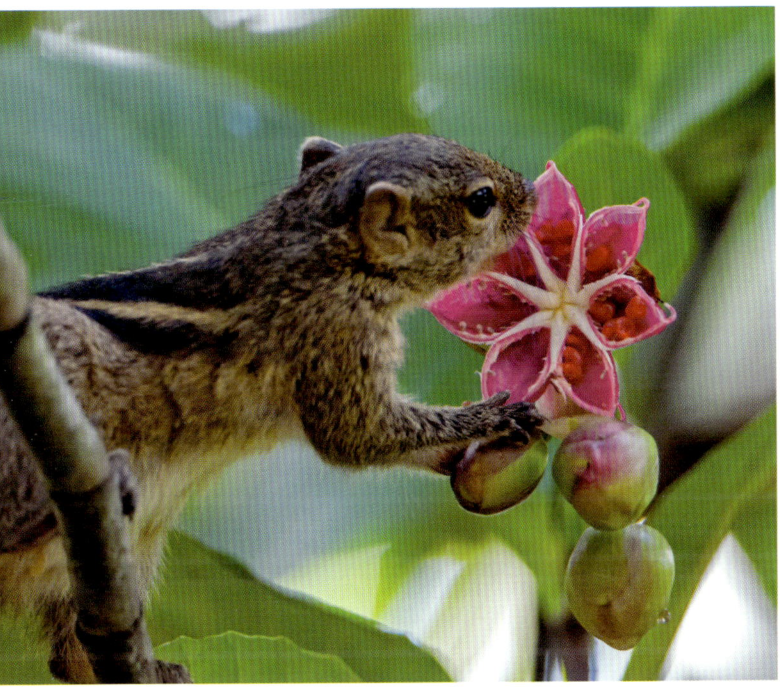

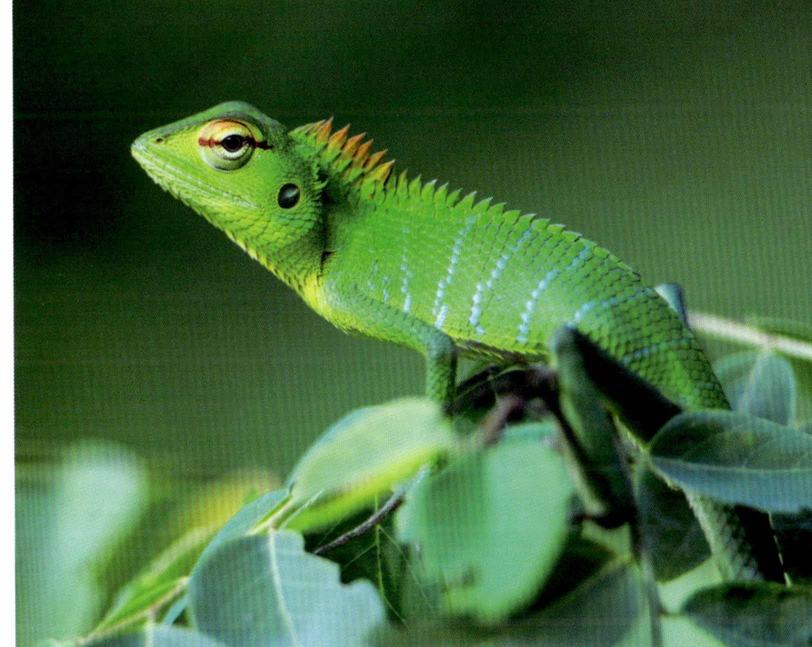

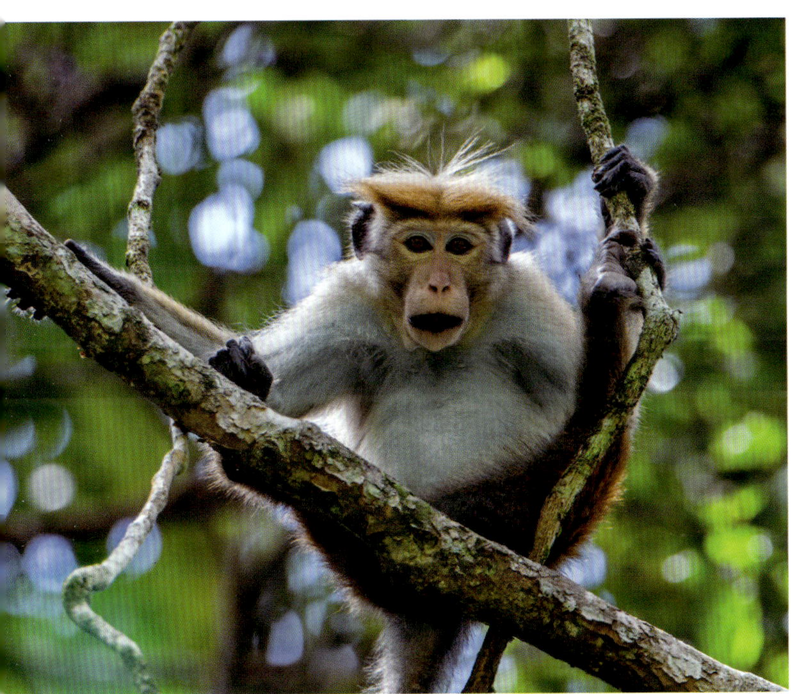

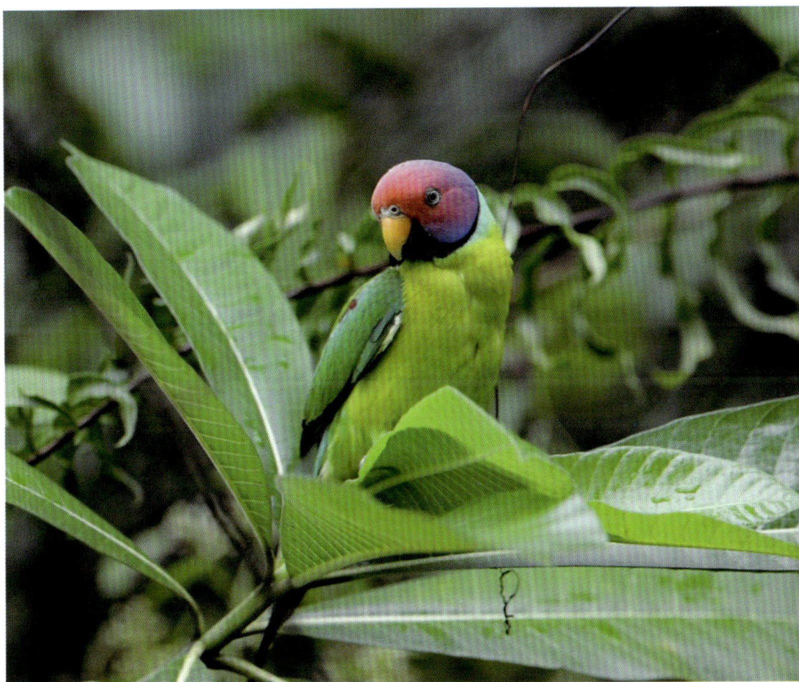

UVS NUUR BASIN

Date of inscription: 2003

This transnational World Heritage Site encompasses 12 protected areas in north-west Mongolia and the Russian republic of Tuva.

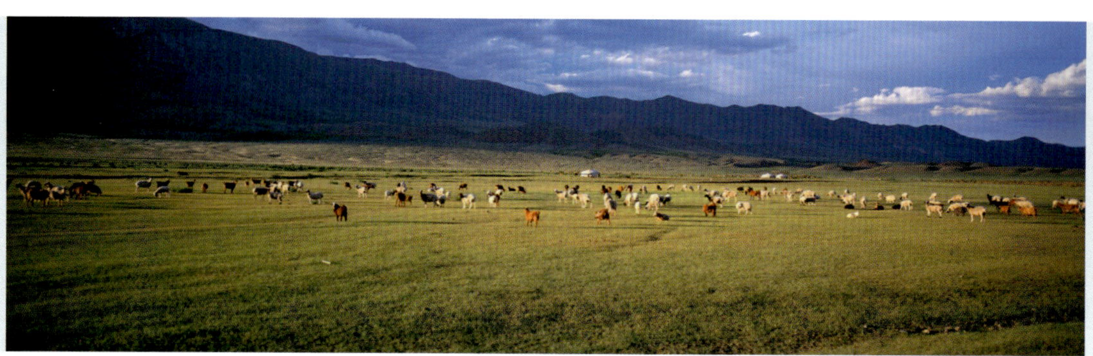

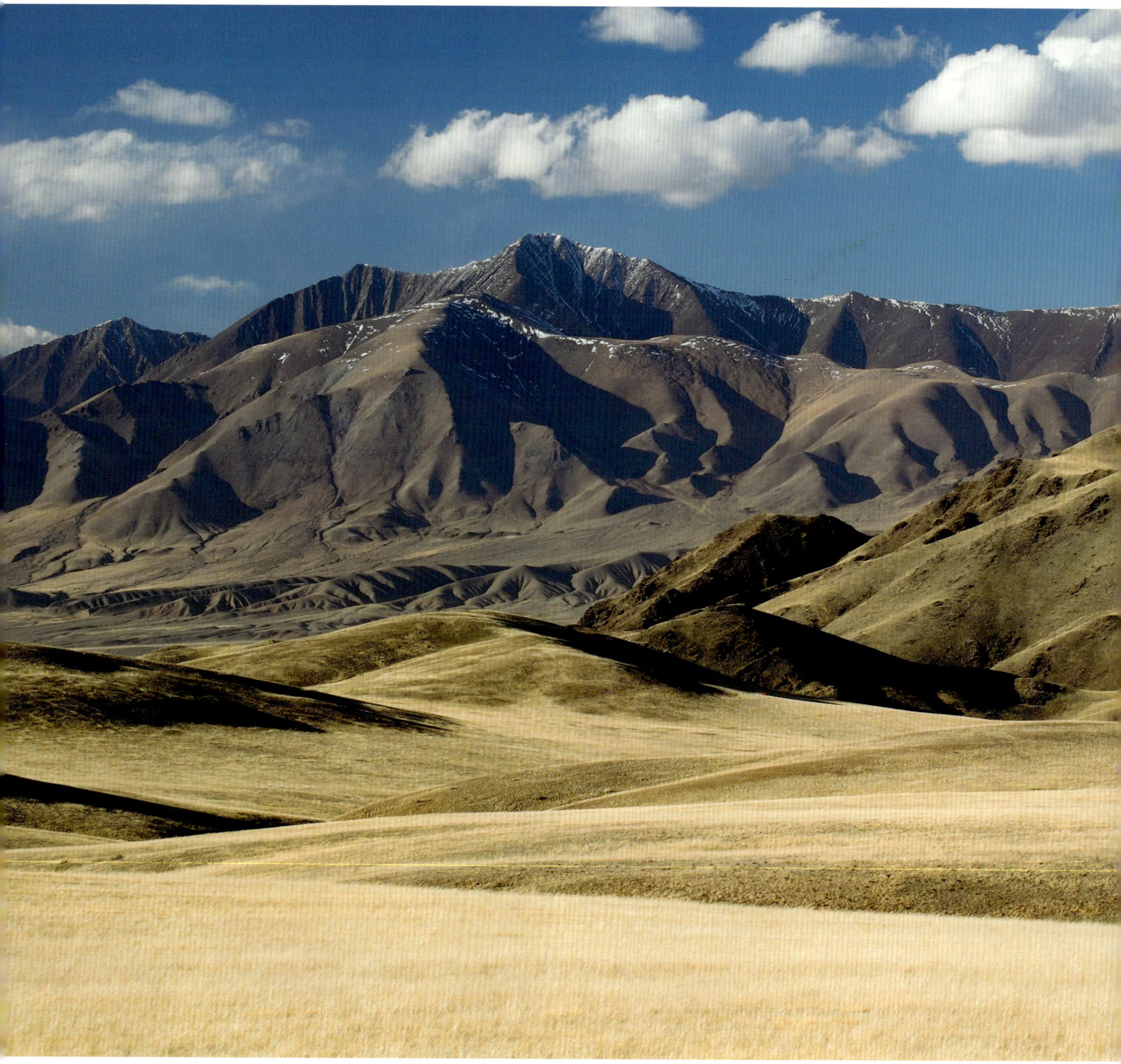

The Uvs Nuur basin is a 10,000 sq. km endorheic basin. Surrounded by mountains, the basin takes its name from the saline lake at its bottom. The region is notable for its wide range of ecosystems, representing all of central Asia's landscape and vegetation zones. The area is considered to be one of the largest intact watersheds in Central Asia, within it are located 40,000 archaeological sites. For thousands of years, nomads have roamed the grasslands here, living in yurts. Today, the stability of the region's ecology makes the Uvs Nuur basin a good place to measure global warming. Its various ecosystems are home to a wide variety of endemic plants and invertebrates. Some of the most common vertebrates, meanwhile, are jerboas, squirrels, dwarf hamsters, and marmots. The mountainous western regions of the site are particularly important as a refuge for endangered species such as the Siberian ibex, marbled polecat, argali, snow leopard, Mongolian gerbil, and polar cat. Both the saline Uvs Nuur lake and the freshwater Tere Khol lake are home to numbers of seabirds and seals, and in summer the two lakes provide a resting place for migratory birds. It provides a safe refuge for many endangered species.

Nomads and their animals roam the Uvs Nuur basin. They live in yurts (below). Cattle and goats (far left) graze in the seemingly endless expanses of the Uvs Nuur Basin, while yaks roam the mountain slopes (below centre).

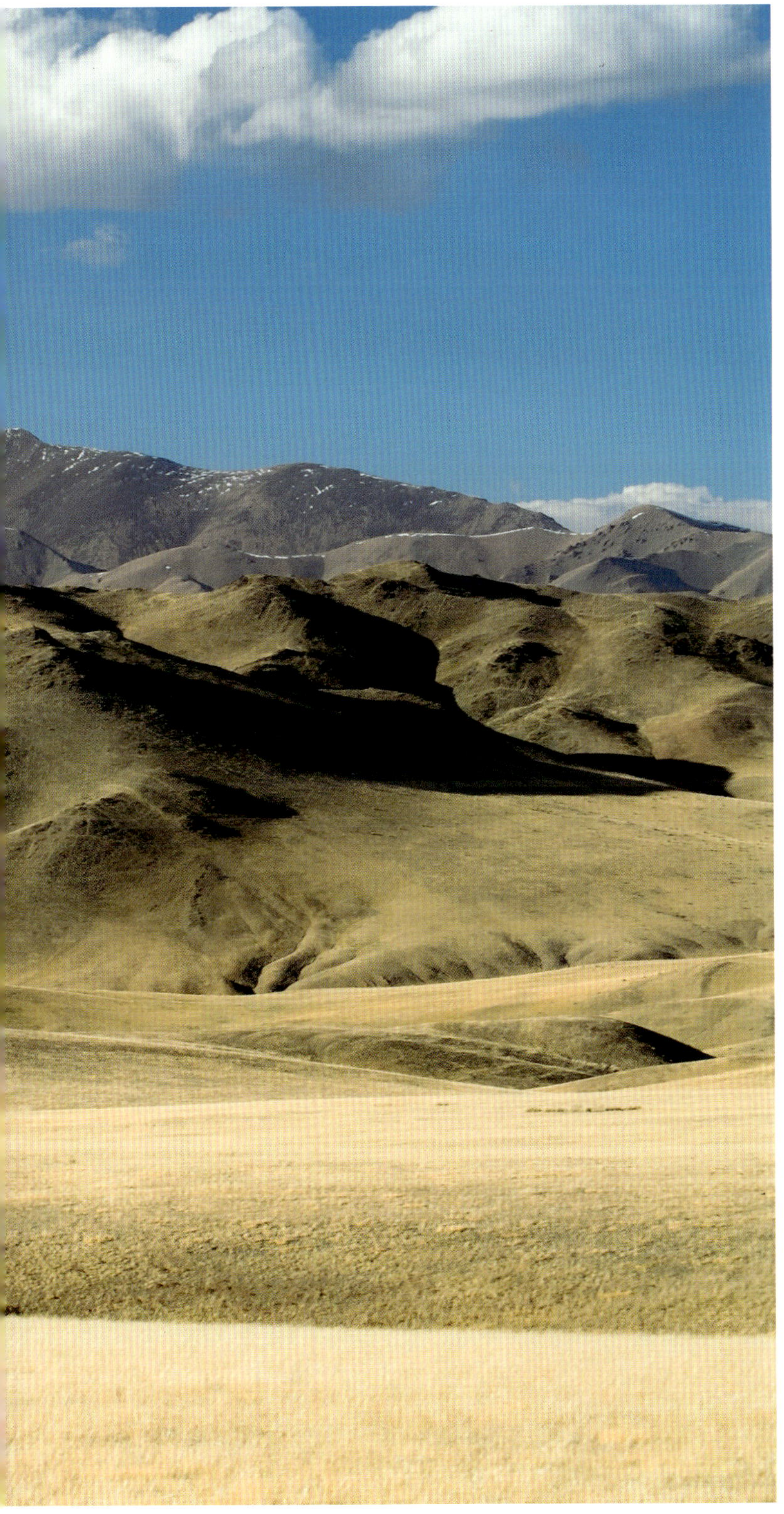

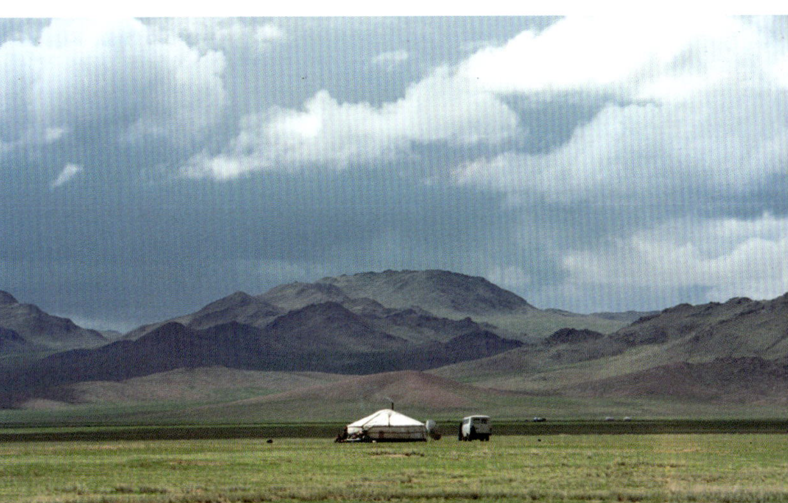

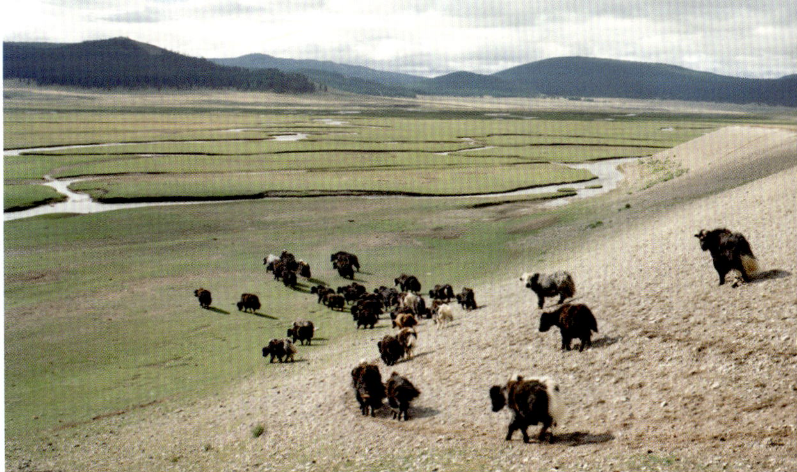

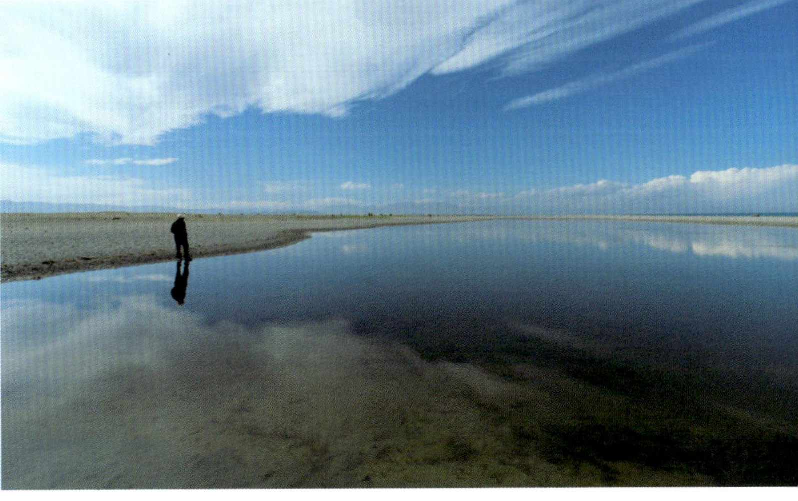

TIANSHAN MOUNTAINS IN XINJIANG

Date of inscription: 2013

The Tianshan mountain range extends over nearly 2,500 km (1,550 miles) from Tajikistan well into China. The World Natural Heritage site comprises four areas in Xinjiang Province, covering a total area of about 6,000 sq. km (2,320 sq. miles).

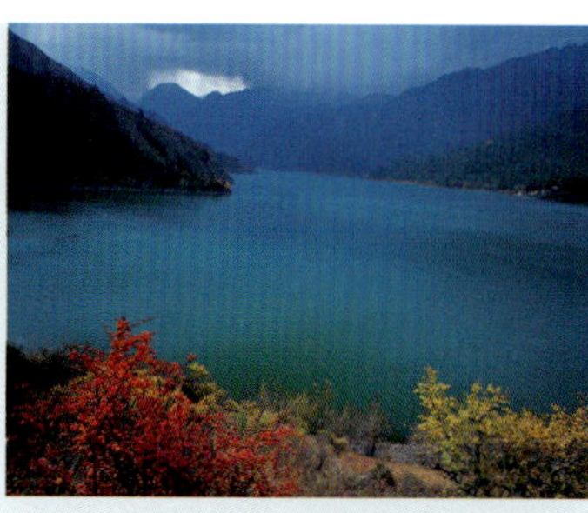

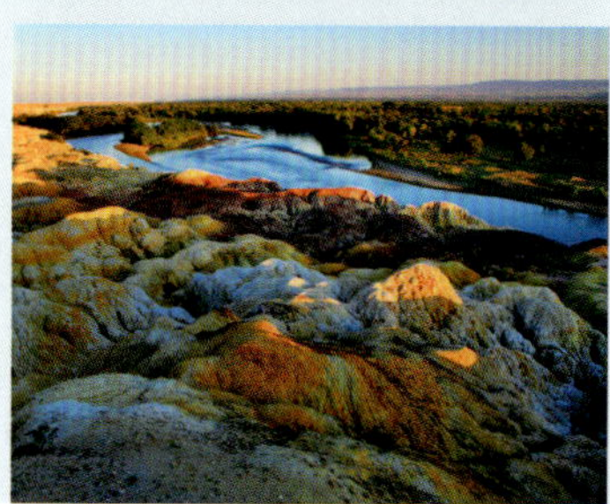

The World Natural Heritage site begins in the west with the Jengish Chokusu (Tomur Feng, 7,443 m/24,419 foot), followed by the Kalajun-Kuerdening and Bayinbuluke. The Bogda chain with the peak of the same name (5,445 m/ 17,864 foot) forms the limit in the east. Part of the Taklamakan Desert in the Tarim Basin is also part of the site. High mountains and glaciers, lush meadows and forests, clear rivers and lakes, wide valleys and narrow canyons characterize this region of great natural beauty. It stands in sharp contract to the desert-like environment to the south as well as to the north of the mountains.
Widely varied habitats are thus created, between hot and cold, dry and humid, lush and monotonous. The landforms and ecosystems have existed unchanged since the Pliocene – fauna and flora had sufficient time to adapt to the ecological diversity. The protected mountain retreat is especially important for some endangered animals like the snow leopard, but also for wildlife that is not at risk, such as the Tianshan bear, ibisbill, lynx and eagle owl.

China has its very own "grand canyon" in the north of the mighty Tianshan Mountains: the Kuitun Grand Canyon (large picture). Visitors probably feel close to the angels when they gaze at the Heaven Pool (top left).

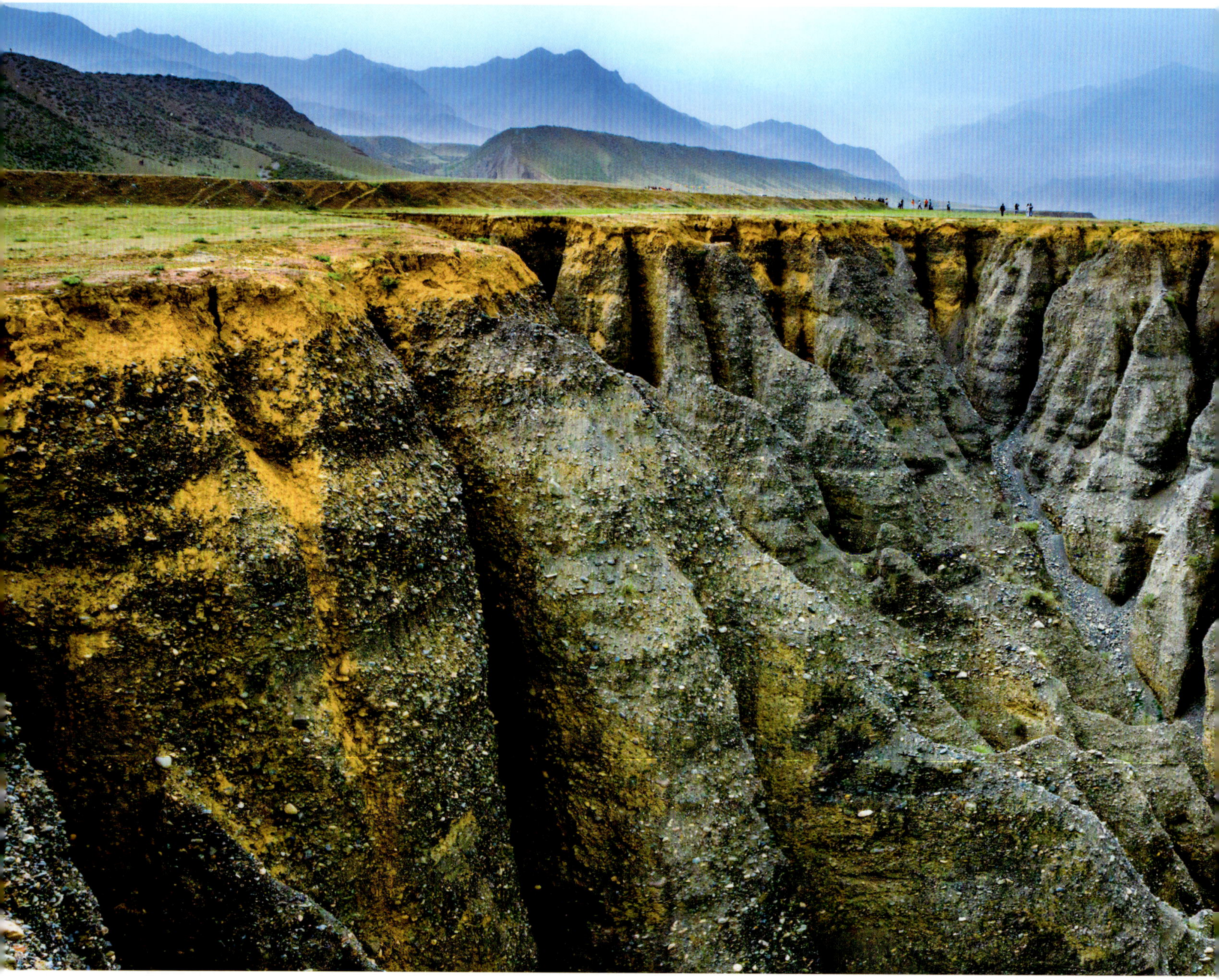

MOUNT TAISHAN

The Taishan massif is the highest mountainous region for 1,000 km (620 miles), and its streams and sheer mountain faces are truly magnificent. As the rock massif faces the sunrise, it was believed to preside over life and death. The first Chinese emperor, Qin Shi Huangdi, ascended the mountain as part of his first tour of the newly unified empire. Before him, Confucius pronounced Taishan a place that allowed man to see how small the world really was. Many more famous figures followed Confucius up Taishan, leaving more than a thousand stone inscriptions. Nearly a hundred temples once lined the path to the mountain summit, and 22 survive today. Nature worship dates back through over 2,500 years of Chinese history, and it was here that this tradition was most splendidly expressed. In fact, the ritual ceremony performed here is so elaborate and politically significant that it has only taken place four times since the beginning of the common era. The penultimate occasion was in 725, when Emperor Xuanzong visited the site. The event is commemorated by a 13-m (43- foot) high gilded inscription in the rock.

The mystical meaning of the mountain is easiest to feel and understand at sunrise (right). Thus nature becomes one with culture.

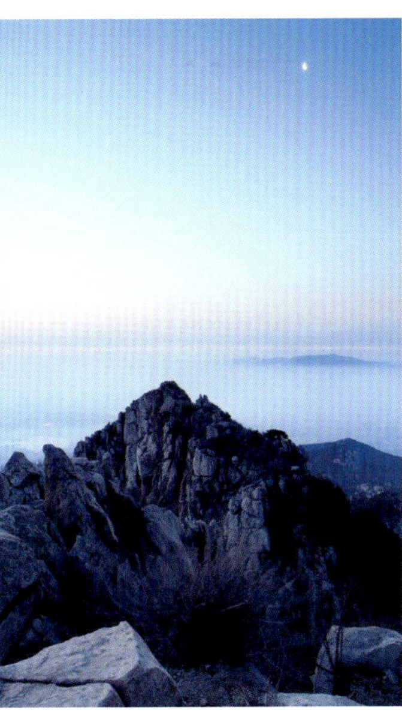

Date of inscription: 1987

This sacred mountain lies north of the city of Tai'an in China's Shandong province, and is 1,545 m (5,069 feet) high. In Chinese mythology, the mountain is associated with heavenly powers, and the tradition of Chinese emperors making sacrifices to the mountain goes back to the 2nd century BC.

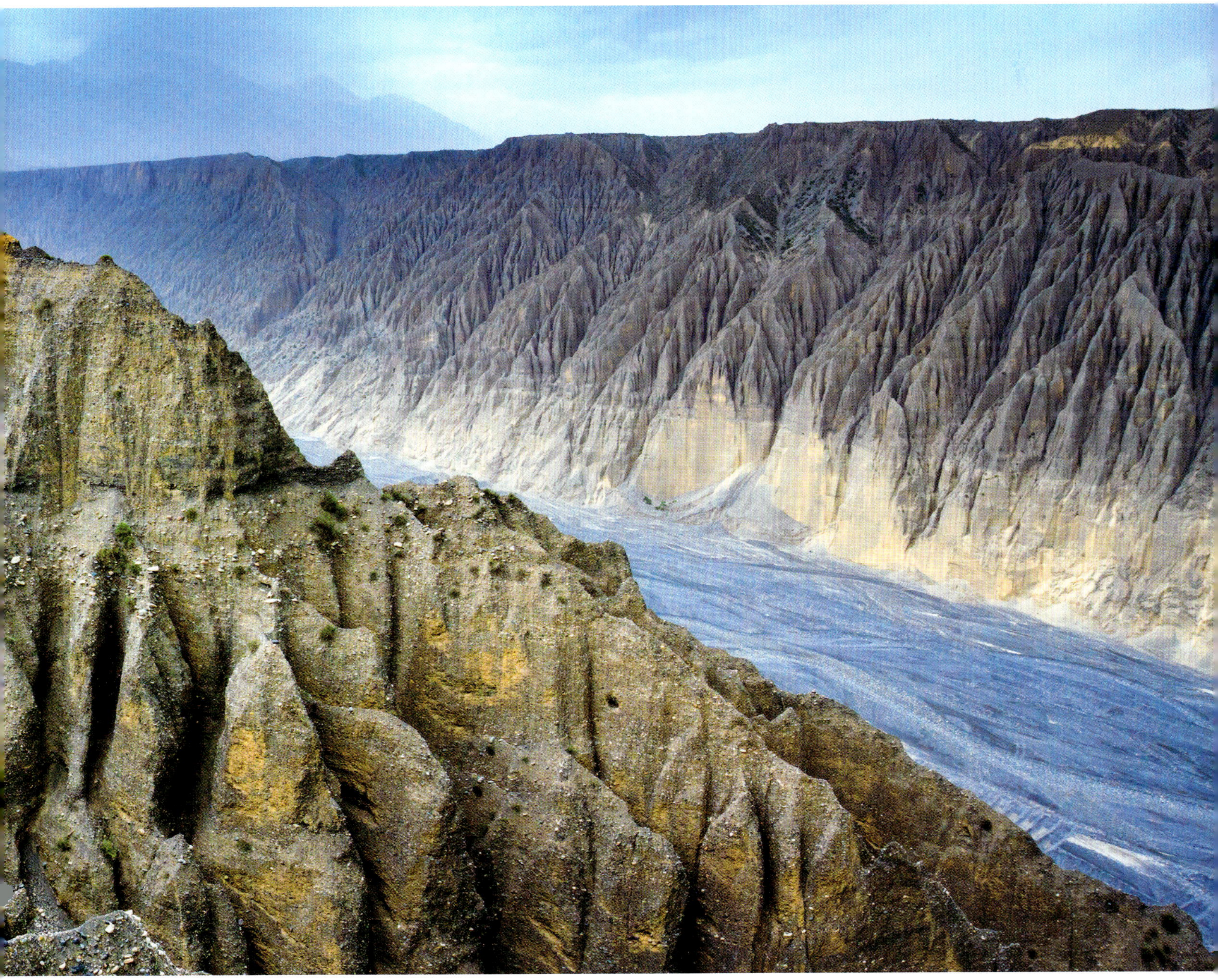

LUSHAN NATIONAL PARK

Date of inscription: 1996 *

In this magical mountain landscape north of the Yangtze River in Jiangxi Province – the name "Lushan" designates an individual mountain as well as a mountain range –, natural beauty forms a rare harmony with temples, monasteries and memories of historical personalities.

*** protected by UNESCO as a Cultural Heritage site**

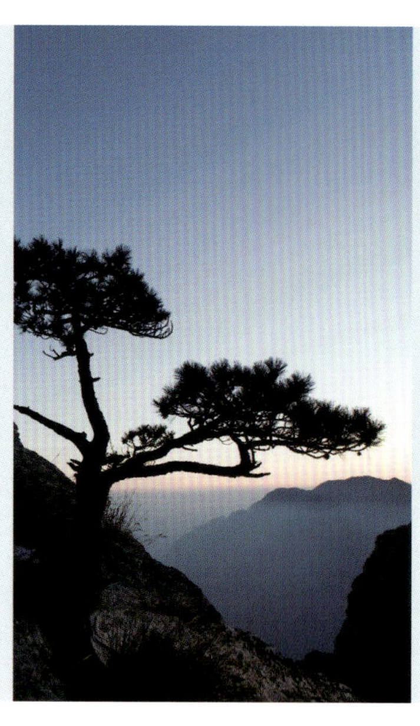

Few mountains have been praised in song as often as the Lushan. Almost all major Chinese poets have honoured it with a visit, leaving behind their inscriptions, and so did prominent philosophers, painters, monks and politicians. For Taoists and Buddhists, the "mountain of the supernatural being" was a favourite place of pilgrimage. With its lakes and waterfalls, forests and rocks it is also an ideal summer holiday retreat. Often shrouded in fog, the mountain influenced Chinese landscape aesthetics early on as much as the Huangshan later. In the 12th century, Zhu Xi (1130–1200), who created the synthesis of neo-Confucian philosophy, taught in the Bailudong Academy on the Lushan. Among the many temple monasteries at the foot of the 1,400-m- (4,595-foot-) high mountain range is the Donglin Monastery, the centre of the Buddhist Jingtu School founded in 384 by the monk Huiyuan. The nomination as a protected area by UNESCO was based on the combination of Chinese culture with this beautiful landscape.

The breathtaking beauty of the Lushan Mountains with their temples, pagodas and Chinese architectural works high above the Yangtze River inspired not only the poets but also made the region the birthplace of Chinese landscape painting.

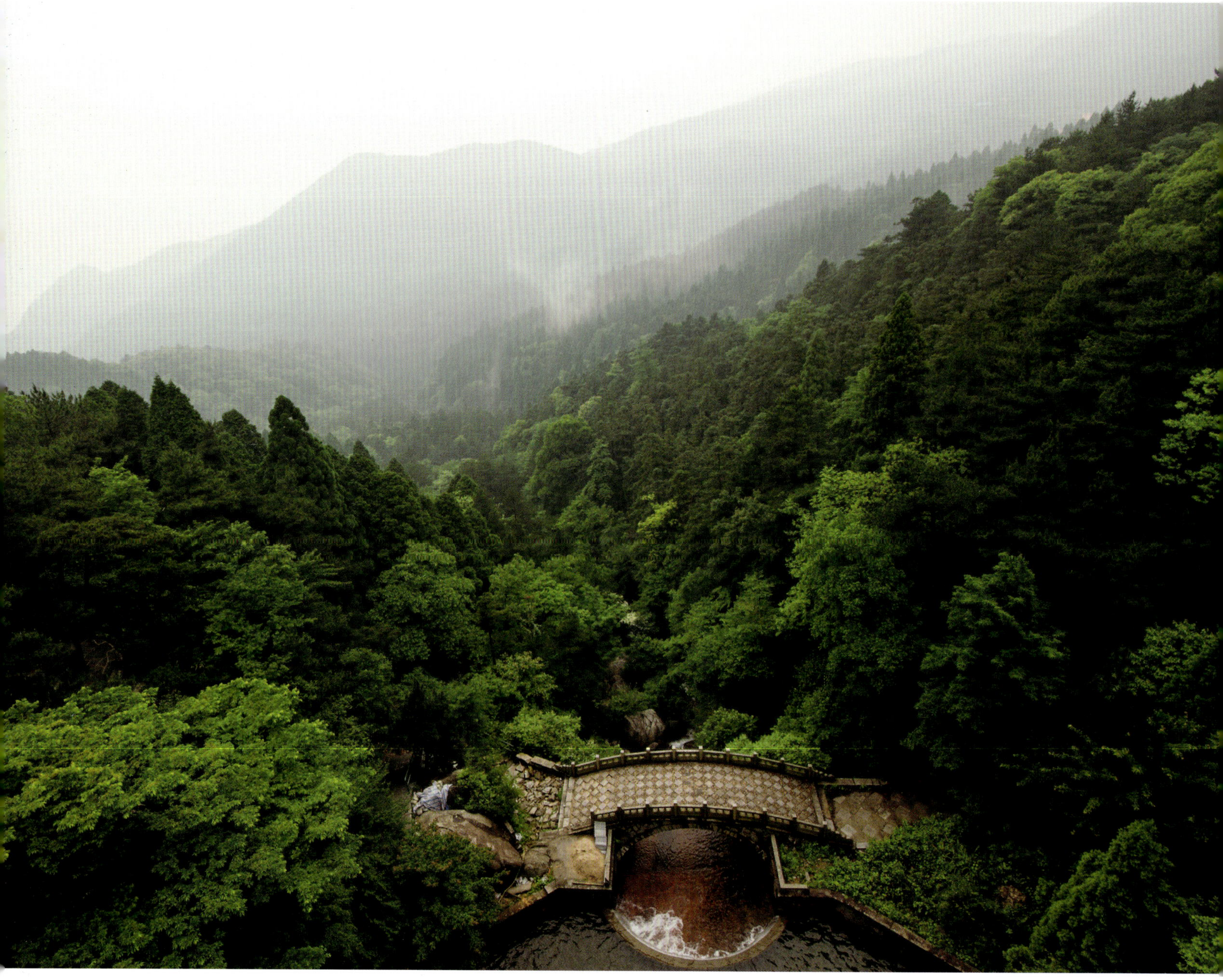

MOUNT WUYI

A subtropical forest habitat has survived in China at the highest point of the Wuyi mountains in the far northwest of Fujian province. Almost 2,500 higher plant species and around 5,000 types of insects as well as 475 kinds of vertebrates have been found here. For all of these, the Wuyishan represents an important refuge in densely populated China. Because the average altitude in the Wuyishan is only 350 m above sea level, temperatures are relatively mild here even in winter. The nature reserve is of biological importance, but the highly impressive landscape also has a charm of its own. This is due in particular to the 36 steep rocky peaks towering into the sky on both sides of the Jiuquxi, or Nine Bend river, which rises in the west of the region. This stretch can be explored by boat, with curious landscape features to admire along the way. For example, there is a high, shell-shaped grotto, from the top of which spring water flows down. In another place there is a vertical crack in the rock at the end of a tunnel-shaped cave, only half a meter wide and around 100 m in length, which reveals a strip of gossamer sky.

Literary figures and scholars once used the remote mountain country of Wuyi as a retreat. Idyllic rivers and streams cross the landscape.

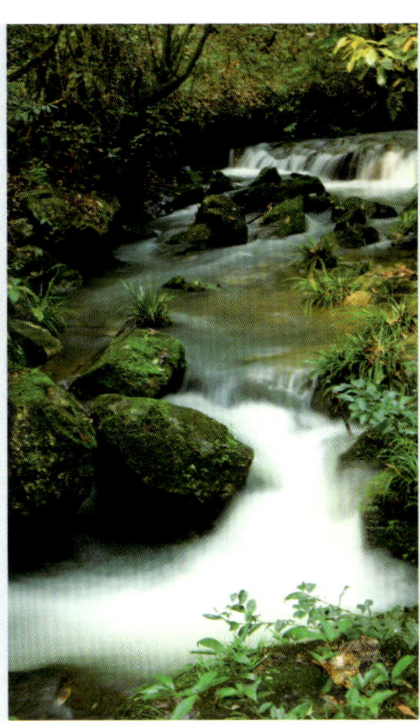

Year of inscription: 1999

The ancient, subtropical forest, with its rich flora and fauna, is a paradise for rare animals and plants, but its steep rocks and crystal-clear rivers also give it a special beauty.

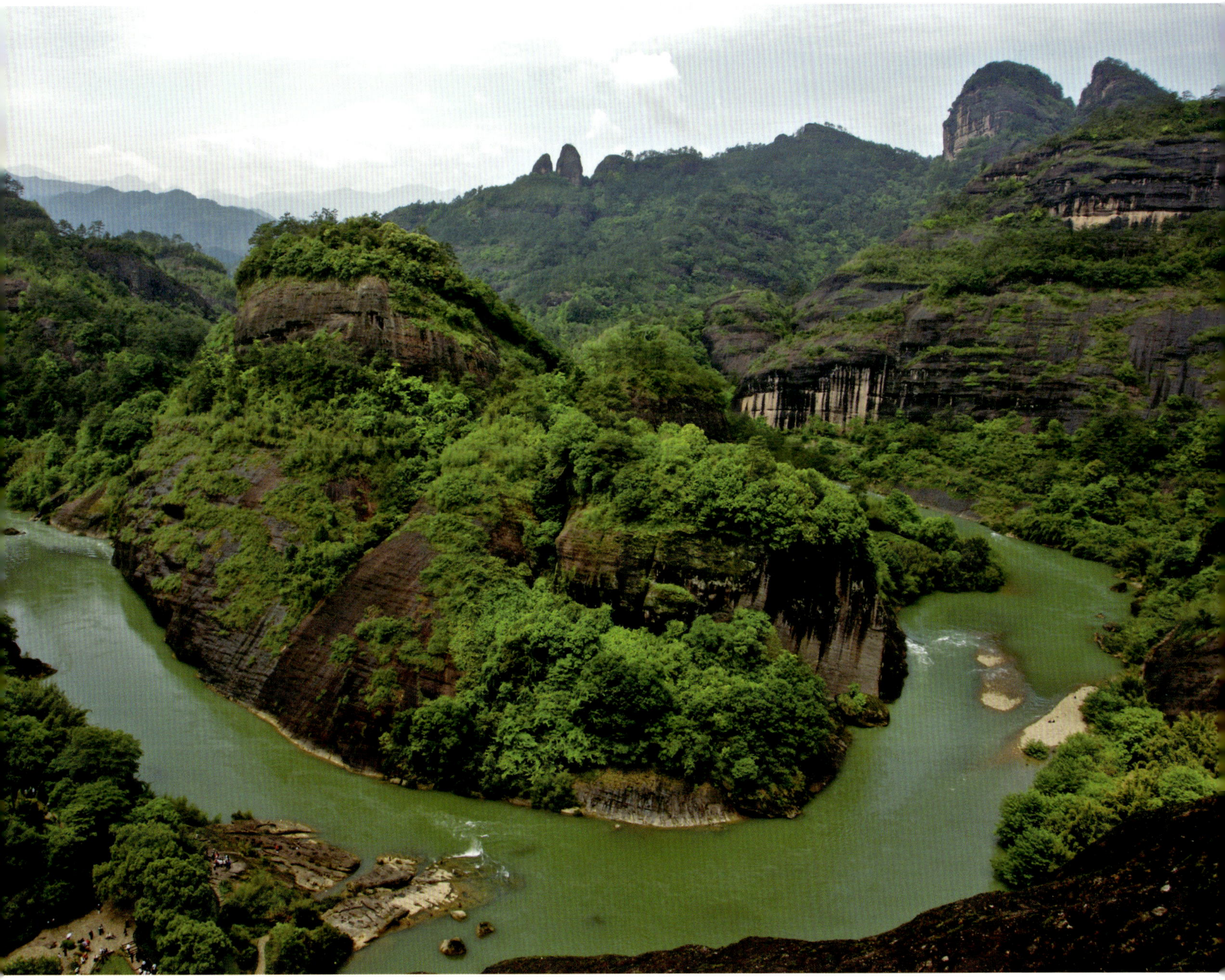

HUANGSHAN MOUNTAINS

Date of inscription: 1990

In the south of the People's Republic of China is the city of Huangshan, whose administrative area includes the famous Huangshan mountains. Here, rocks appear to float in a sea of clouds, as if nature had conjured up a fantasy landscape.

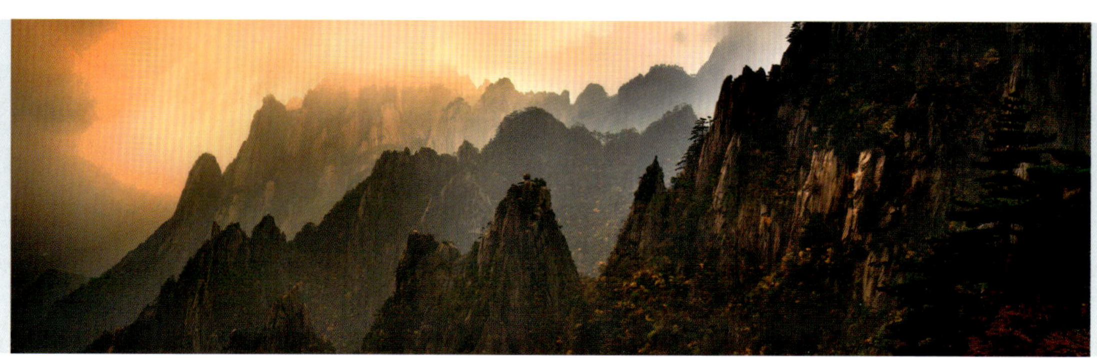

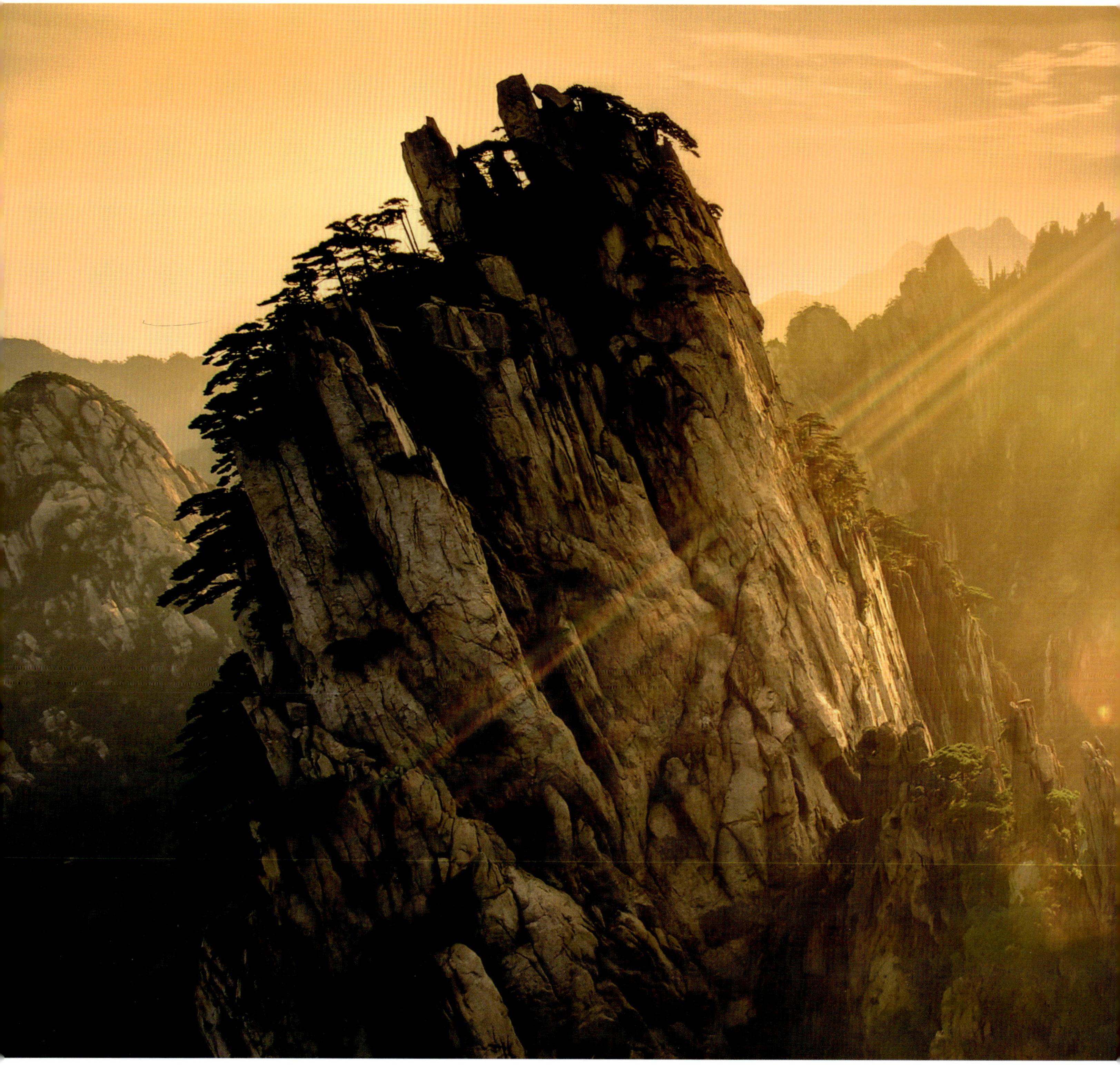

»There is no mountain as beautiful as Huangshan mountain«, the famous Ming dynasty geographer Xu Xiake (1587-1641) allegedly said. He is also known for his travel reports. And his fascination can still be very well understood: Although it covers only around 150 sq. km (90 miles) of Anhui province, there are no fewer than 77 peaks between 1,000 m (3,300 feet) and 1,850 m (6,000 feet) high tightly packed into the mountainous region of Huangshan (Yellow Mountain). On around 250 days of the year mist drifts through the deep valleys in such thick patches that, seen from above, the landscape looks like a sea on which the peaks are floating. Over the centuries numerous pavilions have been built from which people can gaze on the mountain scenery, which corresponds almost exactly to the Chinese ideal of a perfect landscape. The beauty of Huangshan, which strongly influenced China's classical academic culture, is perfected by the ancient pine trees that grow here.

The Huangshan massif is also known as the Yellow Mountains. In the spectacular sunsets, when sky and mountains are bathed in a golden yellow light, you'll understand why.

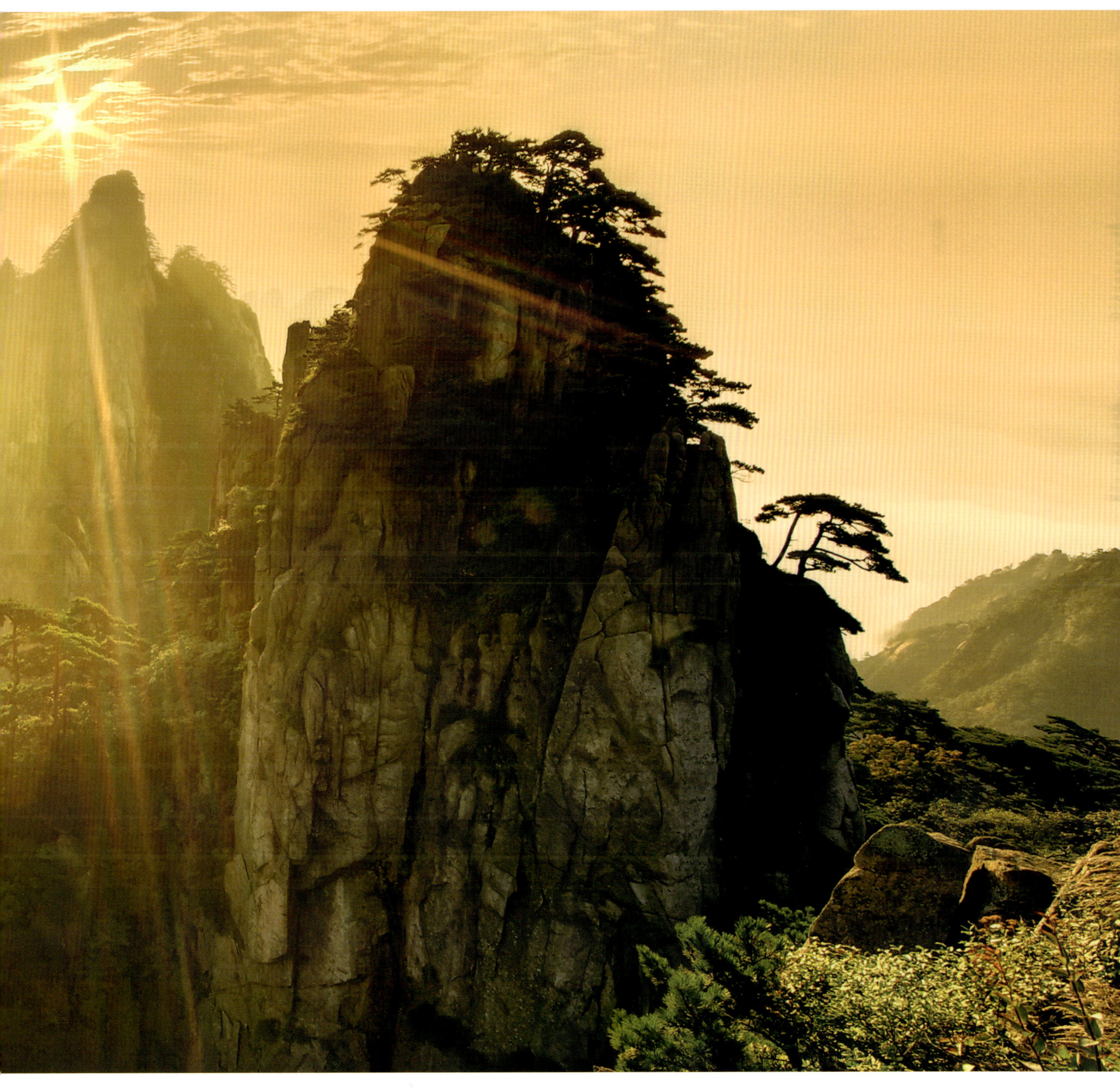

WULINGYUAN SCENIC AREA

Date of inscription: 1992

More than 3,000 overgrown quartz sandstone towers are crammed into the two parts of the nature reserve. The highest natural bridge in the world is also to be found here.

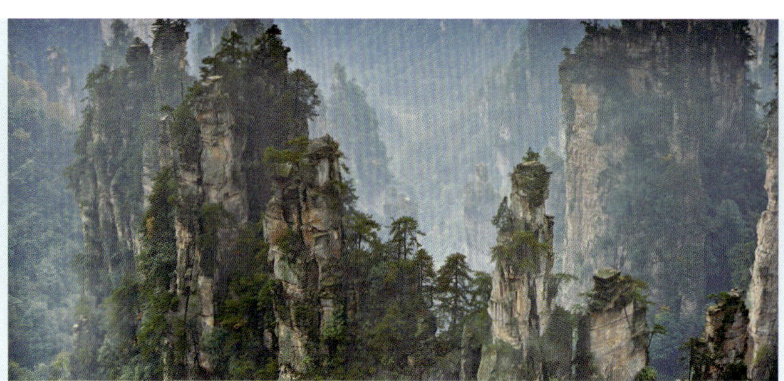

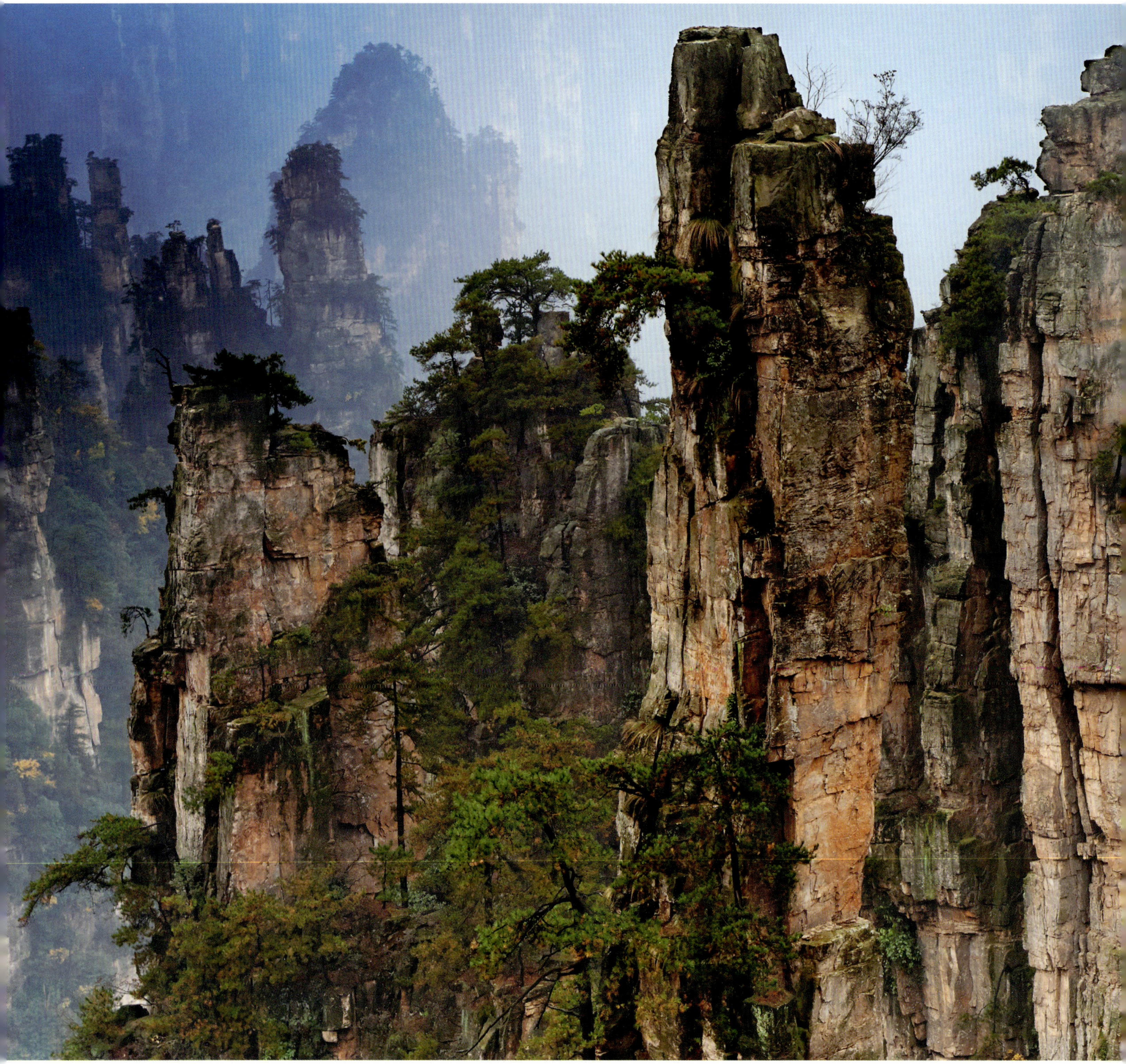

The peaks, which are spread across the two areas of Zhangjiajie and Tianzishan and along the Jinbianxi river bank, were formed by the forces of erosion from a layer of sediment 500 m (1,600 feet) thick. The valleys between the peaks are so narrow that it is impossible to farm there, which is why this region in Hunan province in the south-east of China remains unpopulated to this day. Almost all the distinctive rocks are now named after flowers. The whole area is densely overgrown with water courses running through it, and around 3,000 types of plants have been found here.

The special attractions in this park include two natural bridges. One of these, 26 m (85 feet) long, stretches across about 100 m (330 feet) above the valley floor; the other is a spectacular 40 m (130 feet) long, swinging about 350 m (1,150 feet) above the valley. There are also numerous underground wonders to admire, for example the incredible stalagmite forest in a 12,000 sq. m (40,000 sq. foot) cavern in nearby Huanglong Dong, Yellow Dragon Cave.

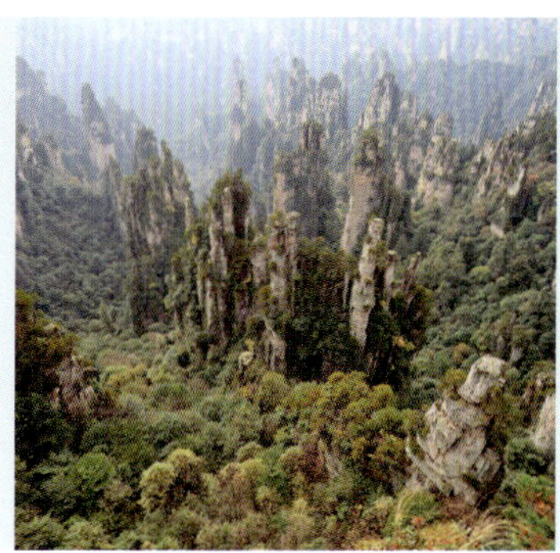

This untouched landscape is the ideal motif of Chinese artists and painters, whenever they wish to represent their country. A magical forest of stone, it seems to have escaped from a fairy tale.

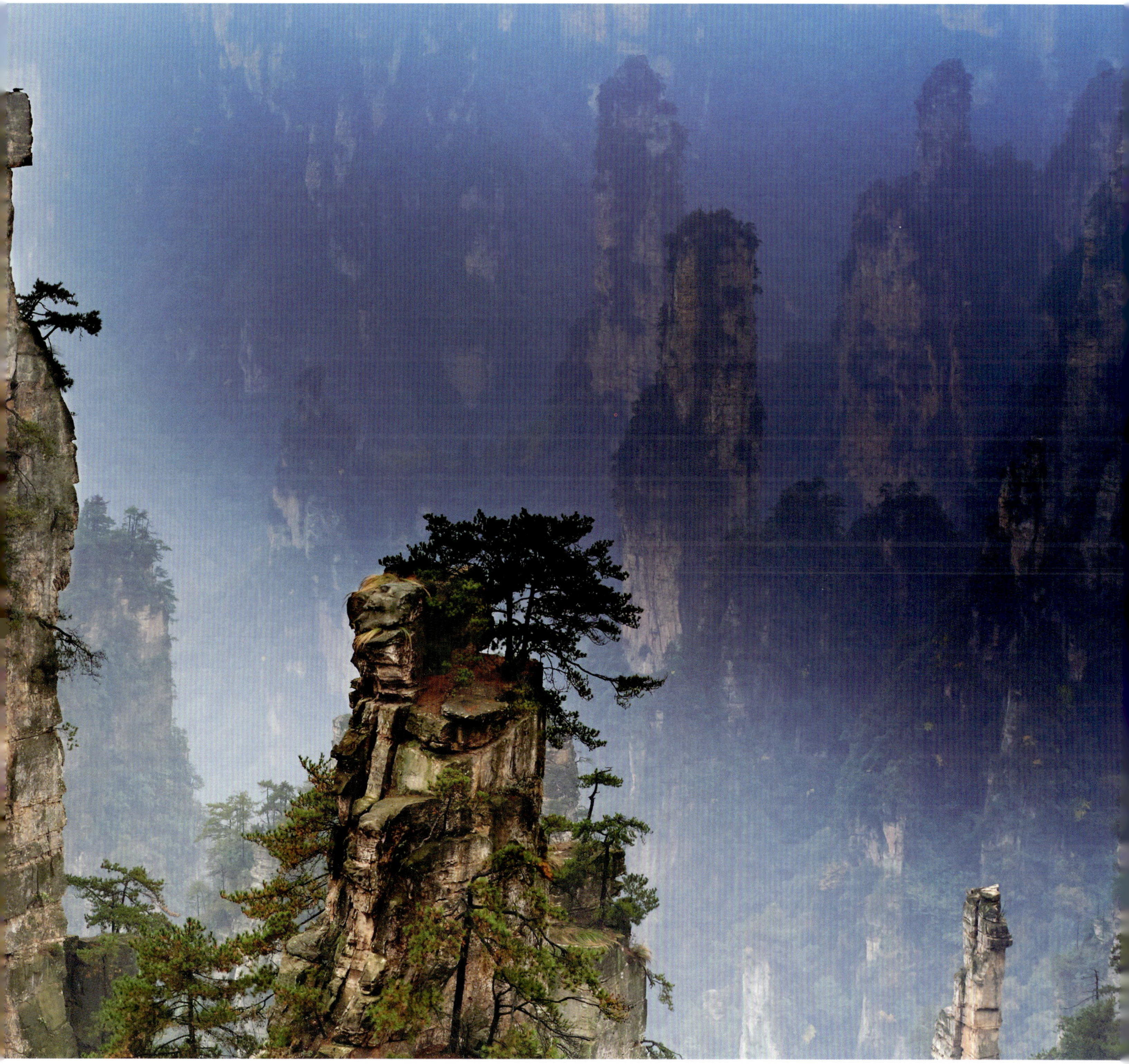

JIUZHAIGOU VALLEY SCENIC AREA

Date of inscription: 1992

A unique abundance of natural wonders is found here in three high valleys in the north-west of the Sichuan province, with brightly hued pools, torrential cataracts, rare animals, and lush vegetation.

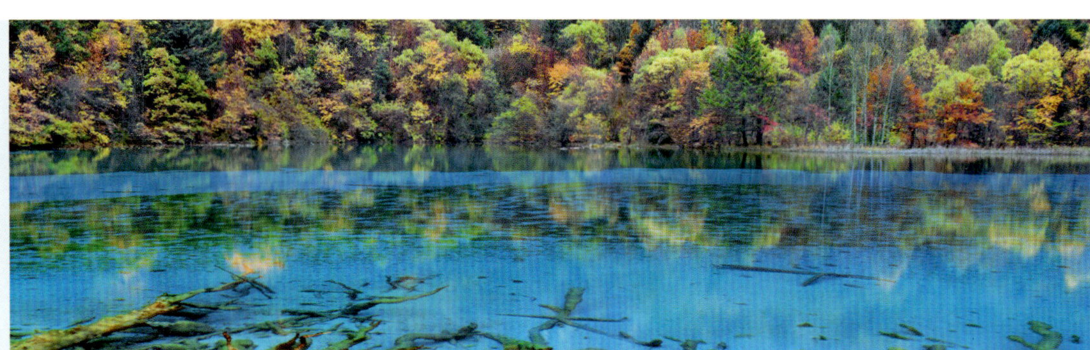

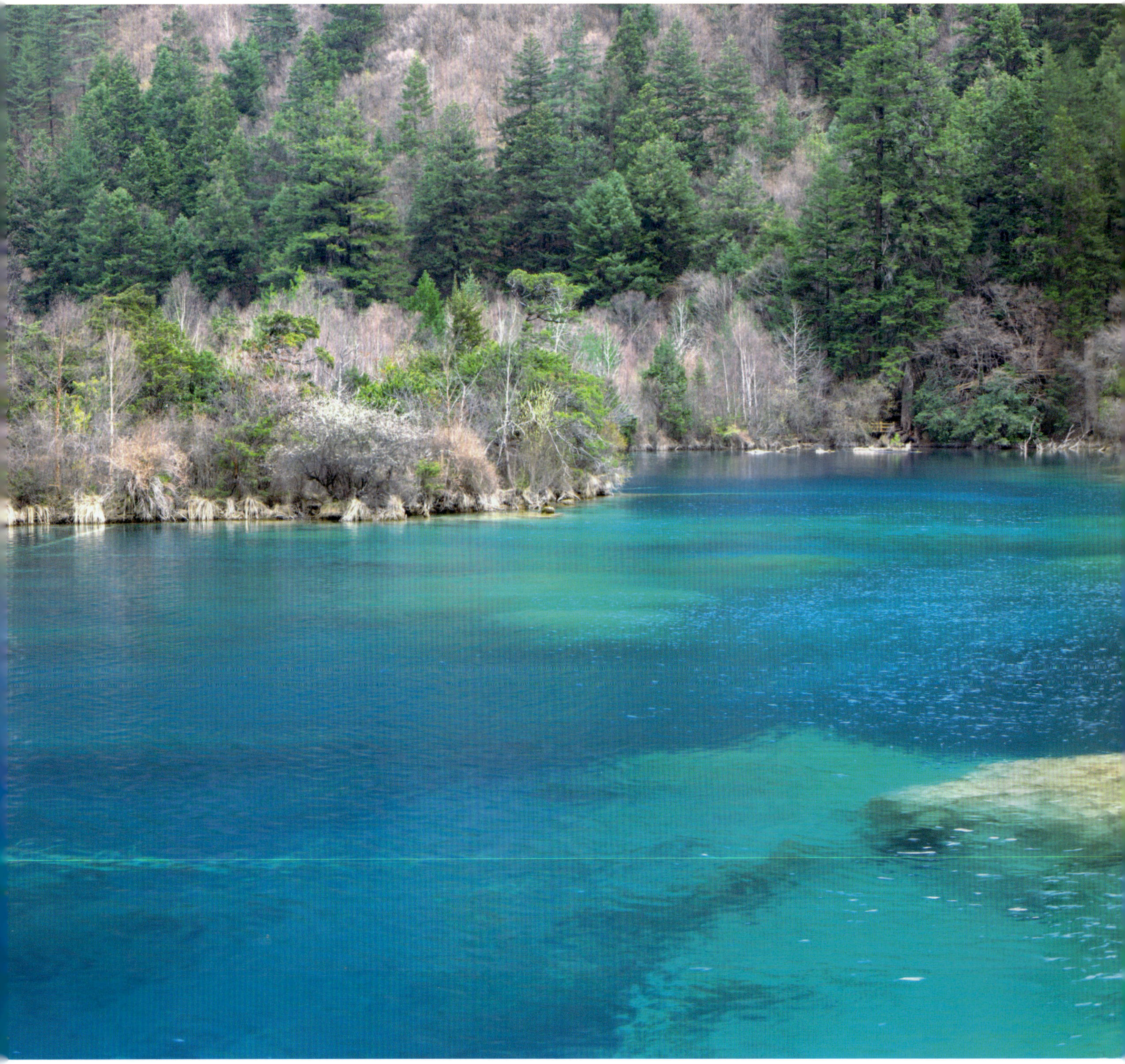

Three densely forested valleys rise up from a height of 2,000 m (6,500 feet) to form a Y-shape, towered over by snow-covered peaks up to 4,700 m (15,500 feet) high. The karstic subsoil enriches trickling water with calcium salt, which re-emerges in the form of large sinter terraces. Cataracts gush over tree-covered tufa embankments, with the largest waterfall plunging down almost 80 m (260 feet). Several lakes gleam in a variety of hues, from yellow and bright green through to blue.

With its secluded side valleys, Jiuzhaigou is also a refuge for some rare plant and animal species, for example giant pandas and golden hair monkeys, together with numerous species of birds.

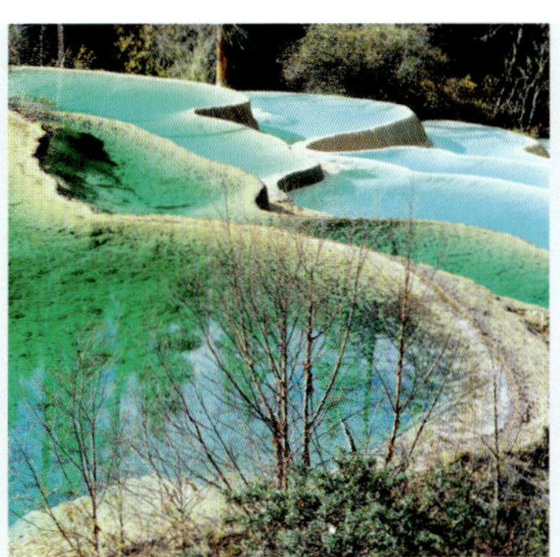

Waterfalls flow out of the lakes and plunge into more water basins, in turn forming new lakes. And Nature dips deeply into its paint pots, with the help of algae: Peacock Lake (far left) and Fairy Pond (left).

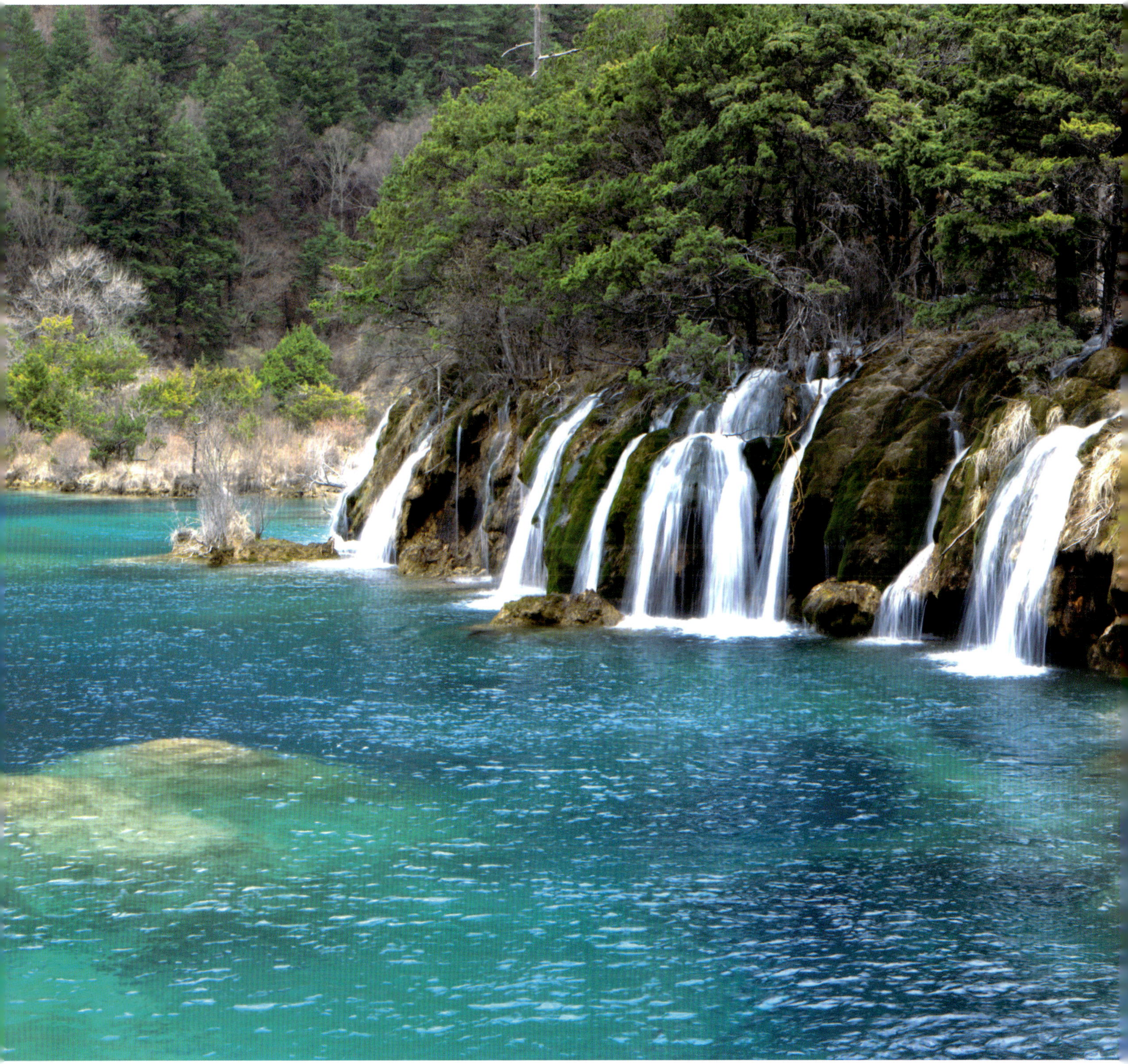

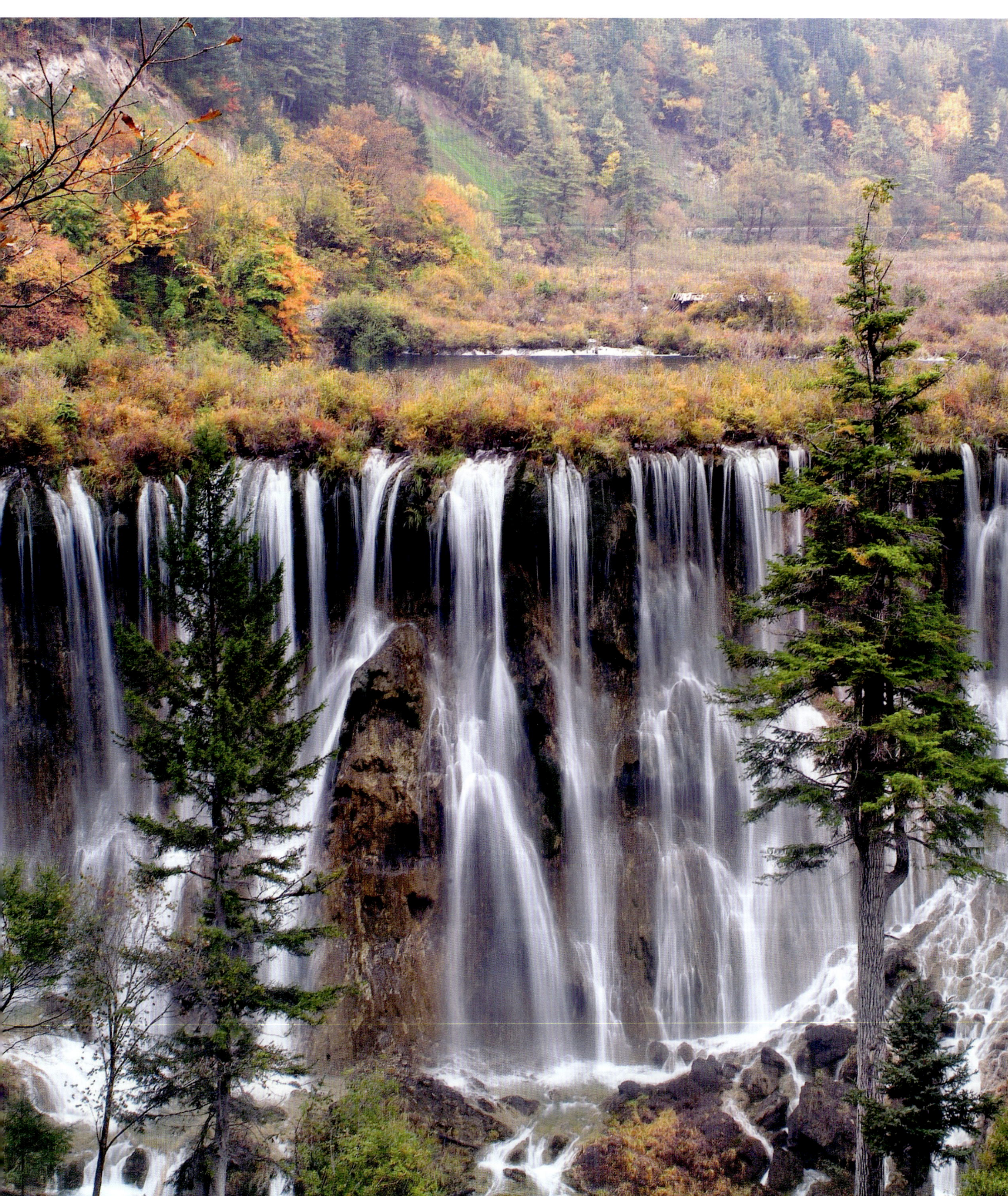

The best time to travel to the Jiuzhaigou Valley is perhaps the autumn, when in addition to the iridescent lakes, the red and yellow foliage of the deciduous trees illuminates the slopes.

Some waterfalls weave a vast network with their numerous courses. The watery landscape offers a home to pandas and other animals.

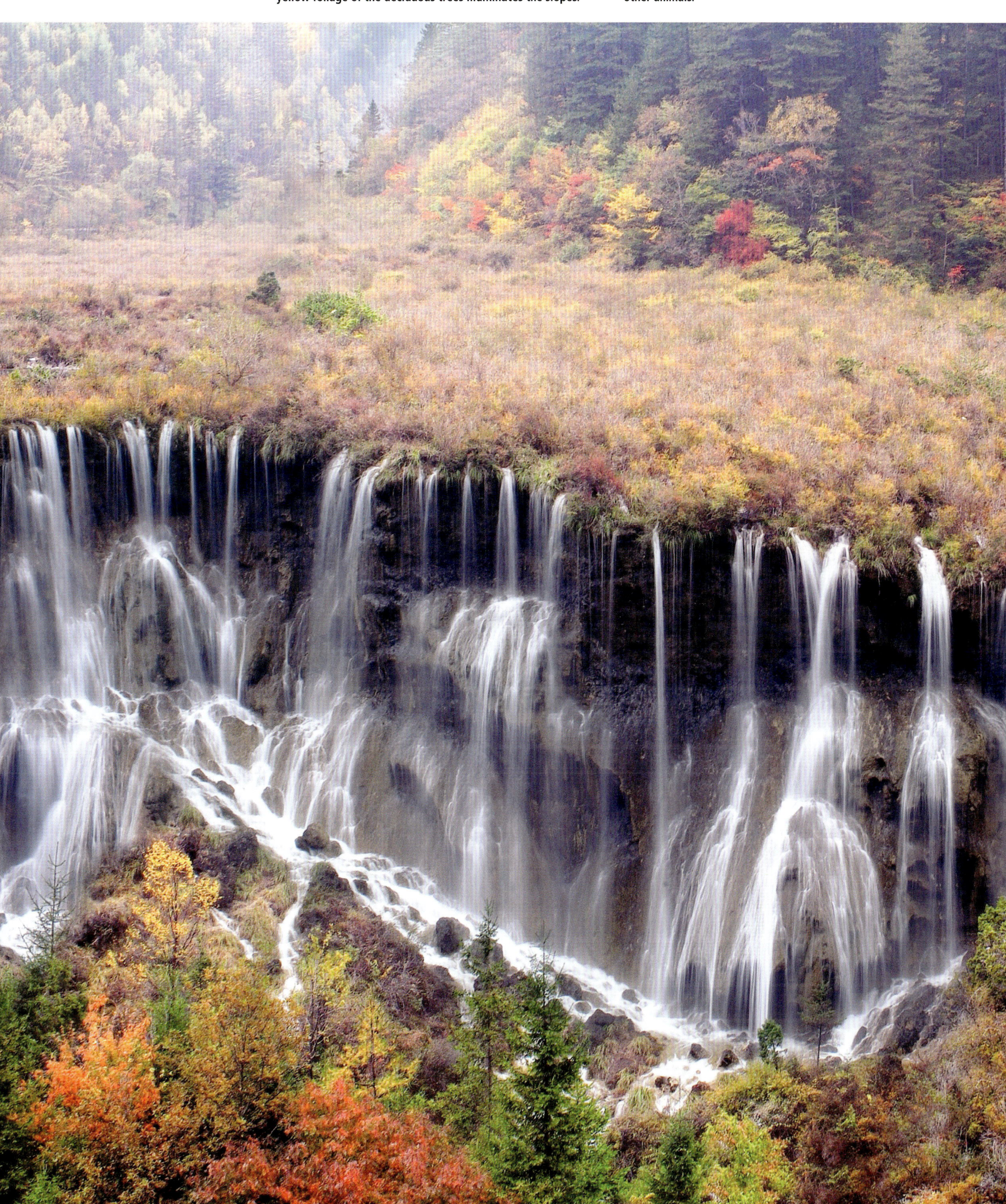

HUANGLONG SCENIC AREA

Date of inscription: 1992

As well as an impressive mountainous and glaciated landscape, visitors to the Huanglong Scenic and Historic Interest Area will also see a succession of sinter terraces almost 4 km (2.5 miles) long, stretching through a high, forested valley.

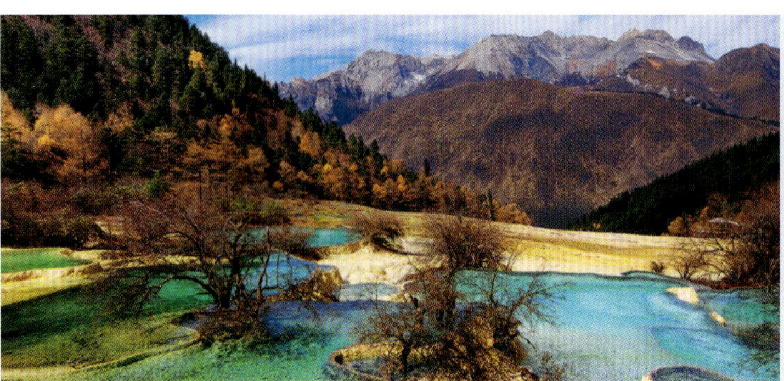

The former glaciated valley is in the autonomous region of Ngawa in Sichuan province, and rises from around 3,000 m (9,800 feet) above sea level to the high snow-capped mountain Xuebaoding, 5,588 m (18,300 feet) high. It is also known as the refuge of the giant panda.

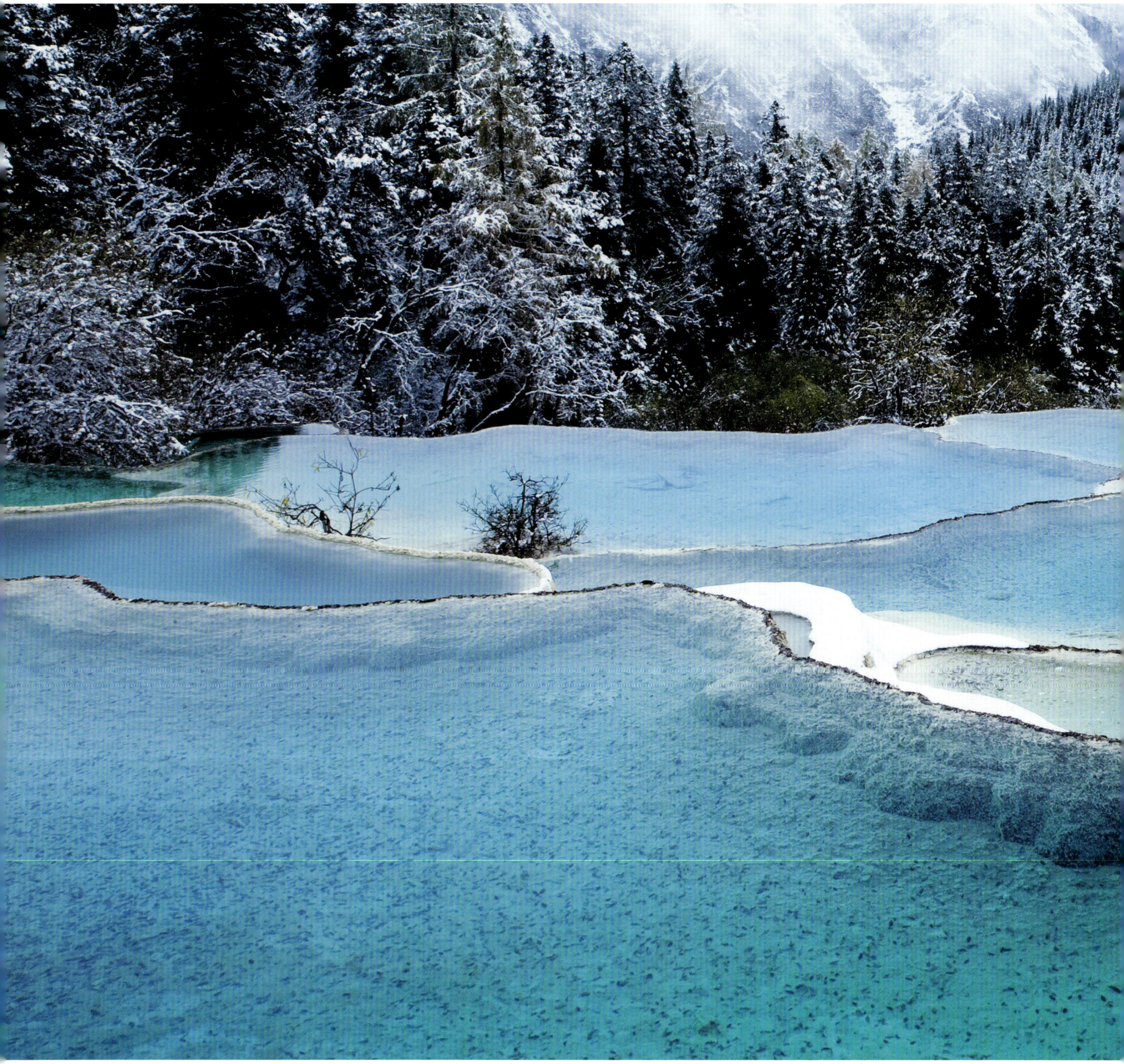

Yellow sinter terraces have formed here at the bottom of a thickly forested side valley. The water in the basins shimmers in many and varied hues due to the algae and bacteria living in it. Adjoining basins are consequently of very different shades which, along with the reflections of the foliage, sky and clouds, results in a fascinating play of colors. There are also small trees growing in some of the pools.

The main attraction of the nature reserve is a steeply sloping travertine area around 2.5 km (1.5 miles) long and 100 m (33 feet) wide, which is covered by a runnel only a few centimeters deep. This phenomenon is associated with a yellow dragon (Huanglong in Chinese) and is how the World Heritage Site gets its name.

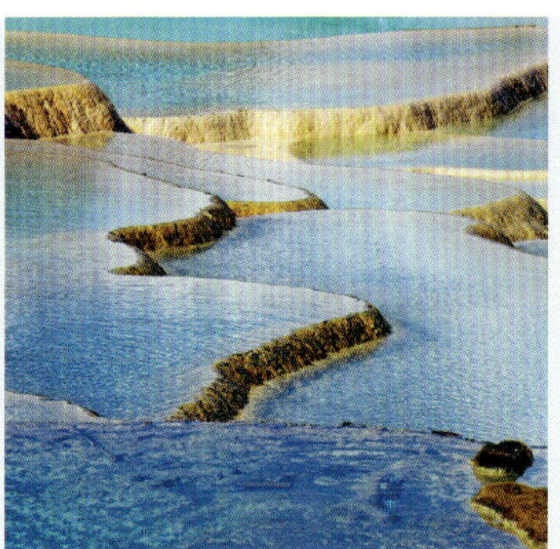

The terrace-like pools in the Huanglong valley formed during the ice age when the whole region still lay under a glacier. Due to its high mineral content, the glacial water eroded the soft limestone rocks, creating basins and hollows in which water has gathered. This water pours from one basin to another creating numerous stunning waterfalls.

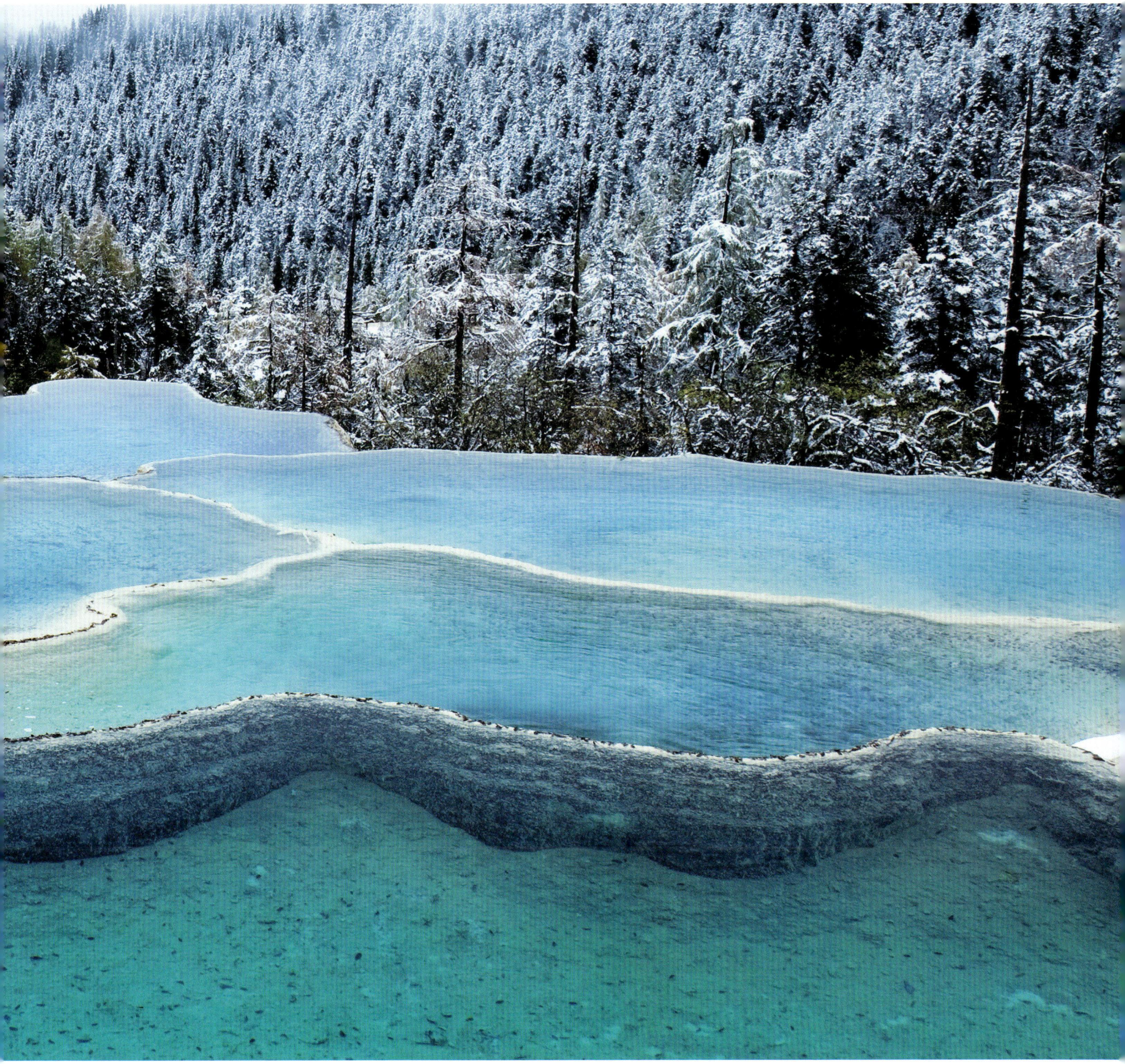

THE SICHUAN GIANT PANDA SANCTUARIES

Date of inscription: 2006

Around 900 animals live in the Sichuan panda reserves, including 30 percent of the world's remaining wild giant pandas. The area is also one of the richest in the world in terms of flora, outside the tropics.

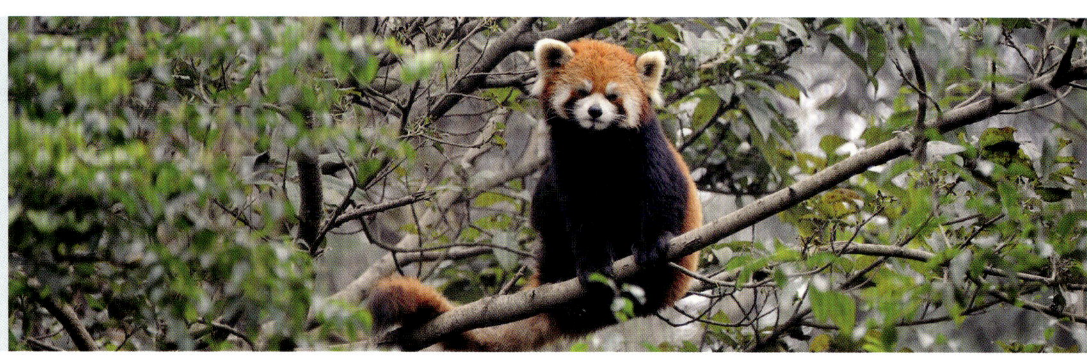

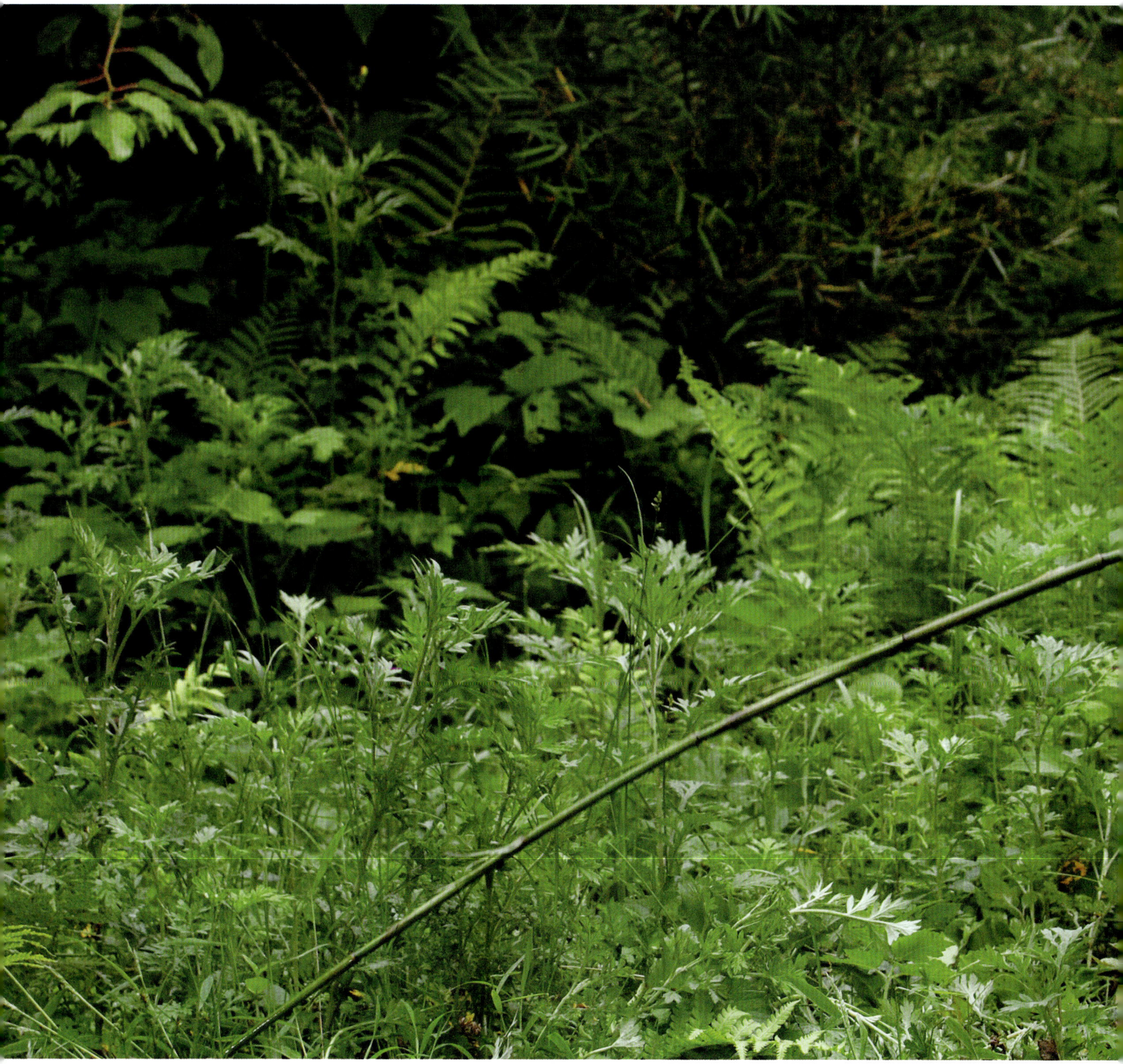

The Sichuan Giant Panda Sanctuary in south-central China is situated in the Qionglai and Jiajin mountains. As well as seven nature reserves, it comprises nine "scenic parks" that are also open to visitors. The nature reserve is home to almost a third of all wild giant pandas and so is the most important conservation and breeding area for this endangered species. five to six thousand types of flowering plants, belonging to more than 1,000 genera, also grow here, with around a fifth of the genera only found in China.
The area is also a veritable treasure trove for the medicinal plants used in traditional Chinese medicine. One reason for the abundance of plants is the enormous diversity in the landscape – the difference in altitude between the lowest and highest point is around 5,700 m (18,700 feet).
So far 543 vertebrates have been seen in this region, including 109 mammals, which constitutes around a fifth of all Chinese species. Endangered species found here include the snow leopard, the red panda, and the clouded leopard.

Bamboo is one of the plants typical of southern China, and forms the basic diet of the giant panda (large image) and the red panda (left). However, contrary to popular belief, bamboo is not their only food source; they also like to feed on roots and plants.

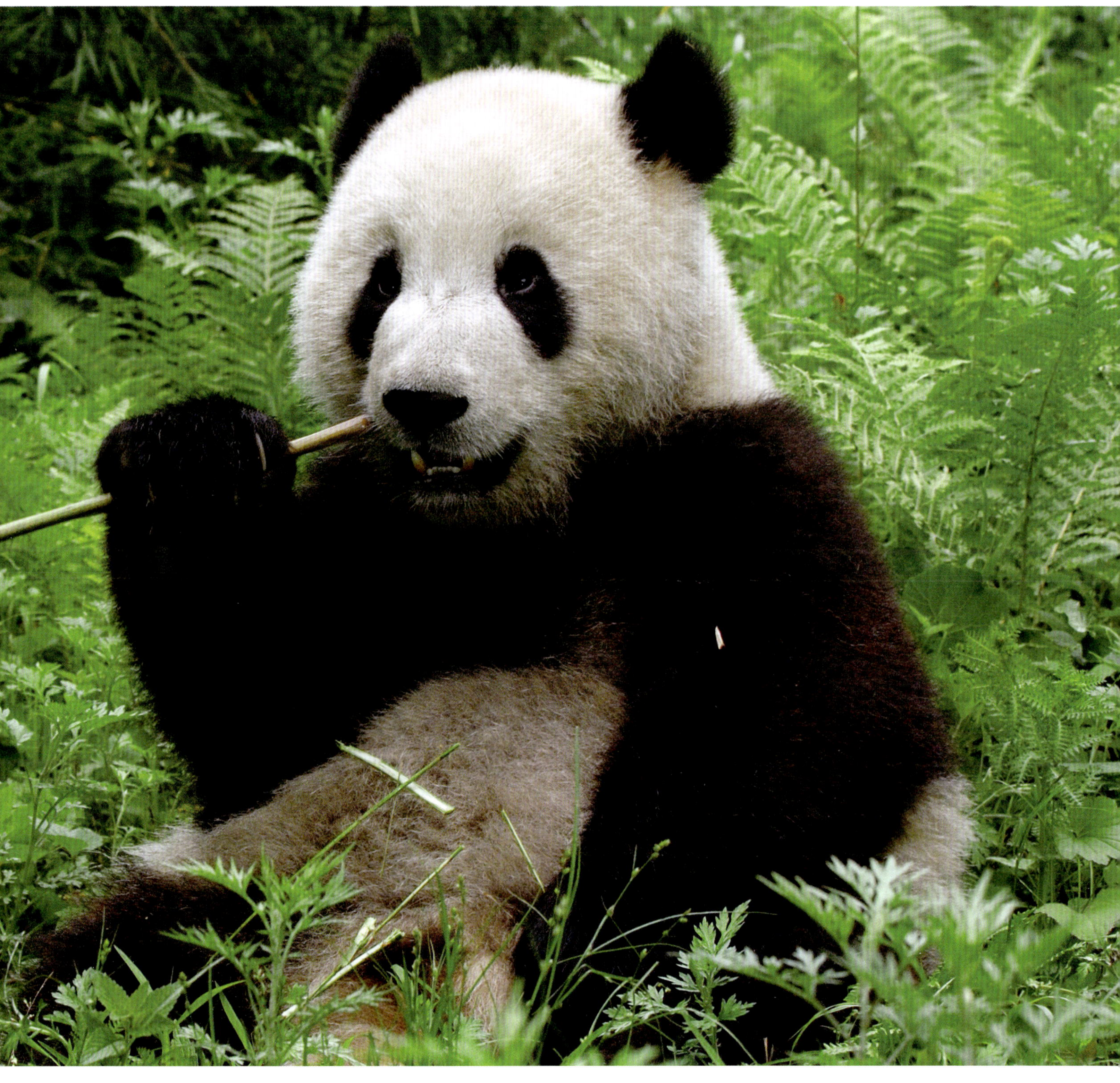

MOUNT EMEI SCENIC AREA

Date of inscription: 1996

The largest of the four sacred mountains of Chinese Buddhism goes back to the 2nd century. The largest Buddha figure in the world is also on the World Heritage list.

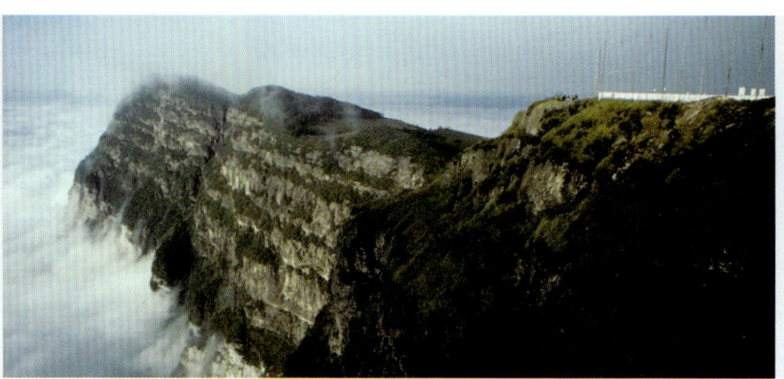

Precipitous rocks, deep crevices, mountain streams, waterfalls, steep, towering peaks, dense forests with trees sometimes over 1,000 years old: the sacred Mount Emei ("Delicate Eyebrow Mountain"), which is over 3,000 m (9,800 feet) high, has always been the perfect setting for anyone wishing to turn their back on the world. Mount Emei, on the south-western edge of the

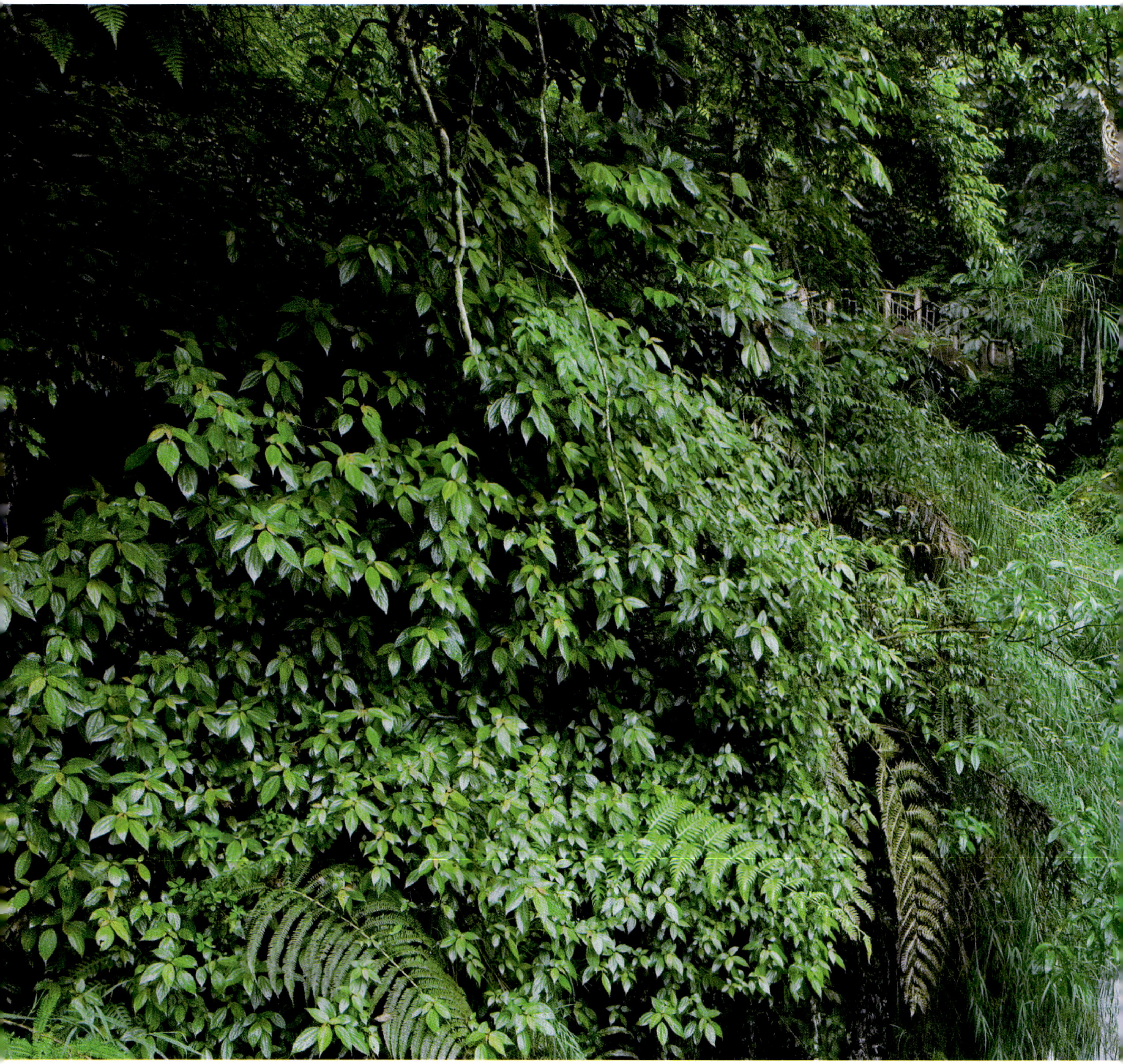

Red Basin in Sichuan, has been a sanctuary valued by hermits since the Eastern Han period (AD 25–220), and the first Buddhist temples and Chinese monasteries were built here soon after that. According to legend, Samantabhadra, bodhisattva of the Law and patron saint of the mountain, is said to have taught in this place. There is a statue over 8 m (26 feet) high in remembrance of him in a mountain temple. There are now more than 200 monasteries and hermitages here and the stream of pilgrims has continued to grow. Many of the sanctuaries fell victim to the Cultural Revolution, but among the 20 that survived, nestled against the rocks or built on peaks and ridges, are many that go back as far as the Sui period (AD 581–618). The buildings that remain today are predominantly from the 17th century.

The attractions for pilgrims in the region include the 71-m (233-foot) sitting Buddha statue in Leshan, 35 km (22 miles) away at the confluence of the Minjiang, Dadu, and Qingyi rivers. It was sculpted from a single rock face in the 8th century by Buddhist monks

Qingyin-Ge, the Pavilion of Clear Sound (below), stands at 710 m (2,330 feet) above sea level, on the path to the summit of Mount Emei. The name of the sacred Mount Emei (left) means "Delicate Eyebrow Mountain." On the Golden Summit, 3,077 m (10,000 feet) up, stands a temple inhabited by monks.

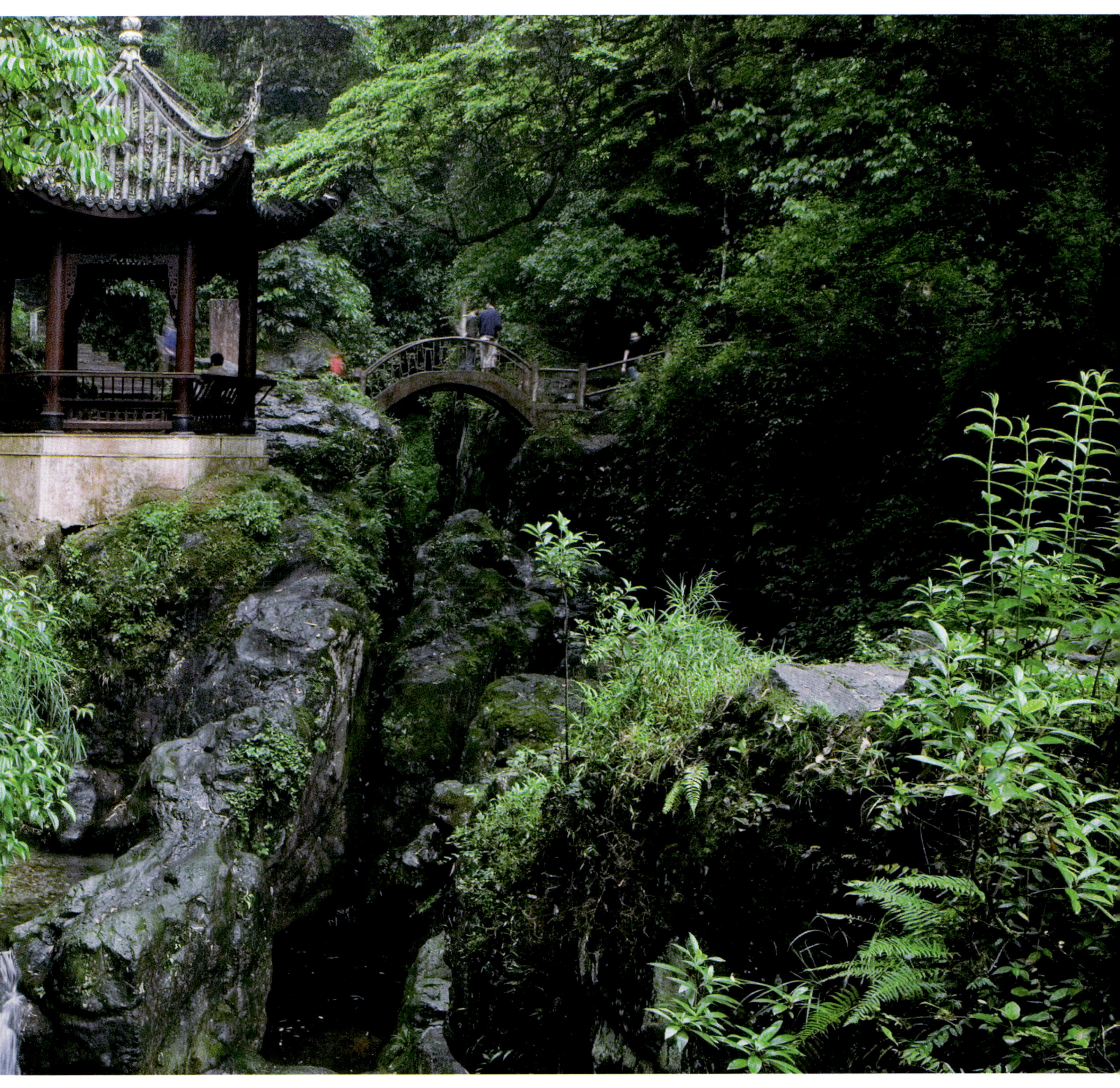

THREE PARALLEL RIVERS

Date of inscription: 2003

In Yunnan, three rivers, the Yangtze, Mekong, and Salween, run largely parallel to each other for a distance of around 170 km. Almost all northern hemisphere types of landscape and ecosystems can be found in this area, as well as immense biodiversity.

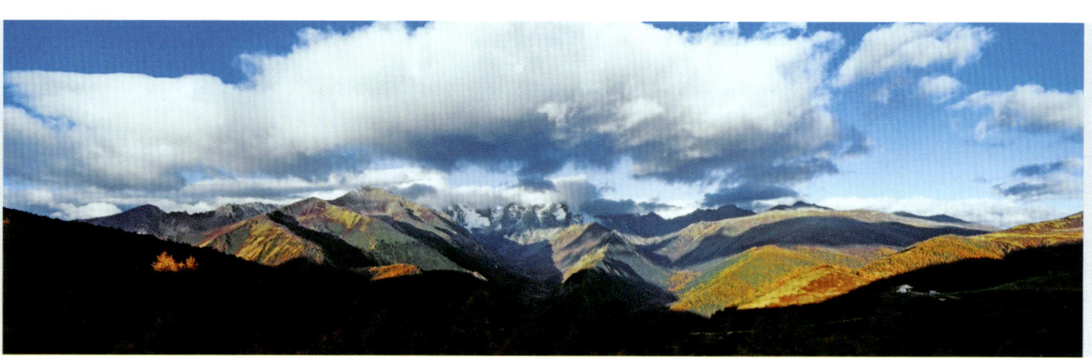

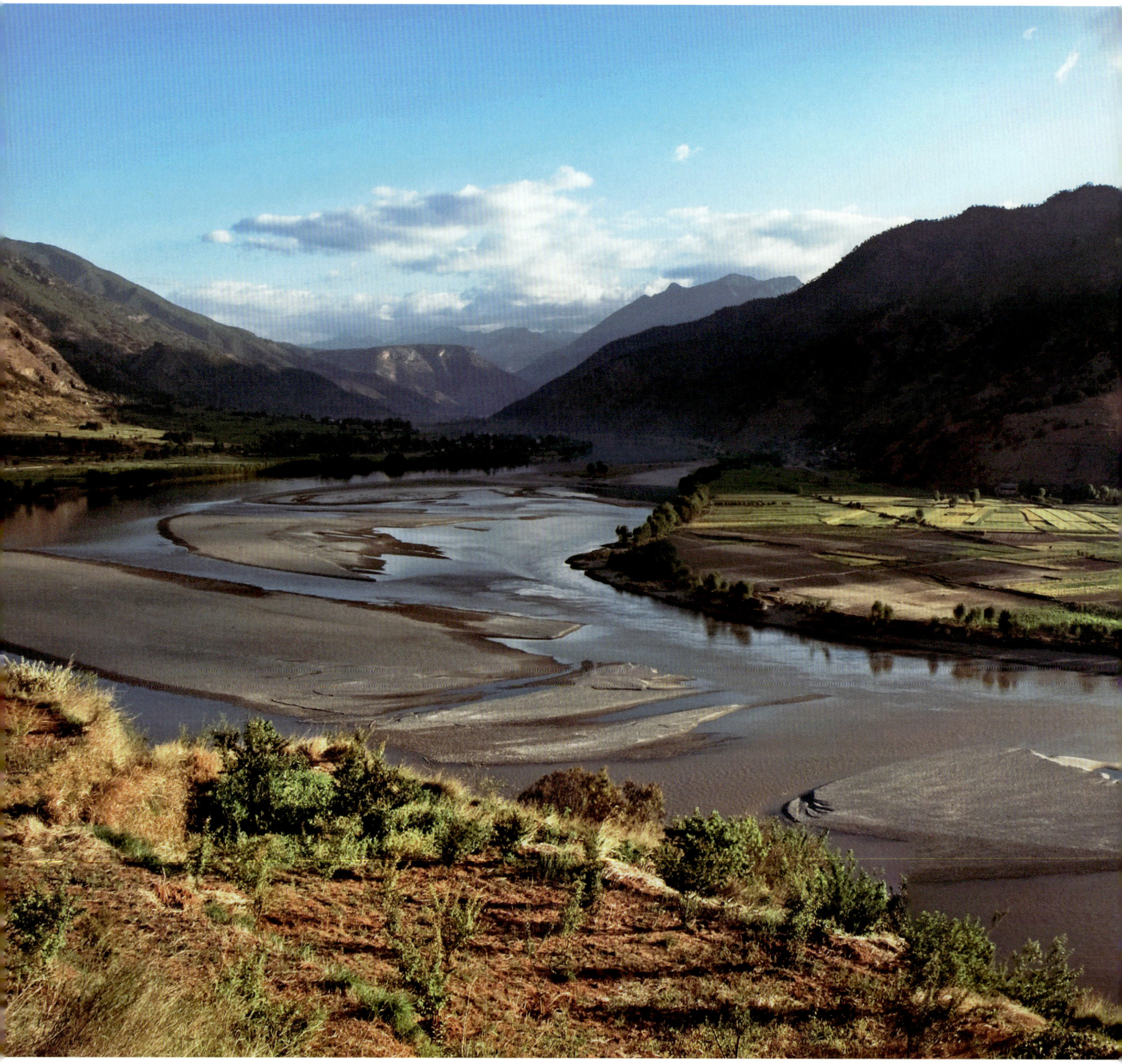

From a geological standpoint, the area known as Sanjiang Bingliu is exceptionally diverse. In places the three rivers form extremely steep gorges, up to 3,000 m deep. They are surrounded by 118 mountains over 5,000 m high, the highest being the Kawagebo at 6,740 m, with the Mingyongqia glacier that stretches up to 2,700 m. This steepness is linked to recent geological history, as about 50 million years ago the Indian and Eurasian plates collided, pushing up the Himalayan mountains we know today. The Three Parallel Rivers National Park lies in the biogeographical convergence zone between the Palearctic and Oriental regions and therefore has features of both the temperate and tropical zones.

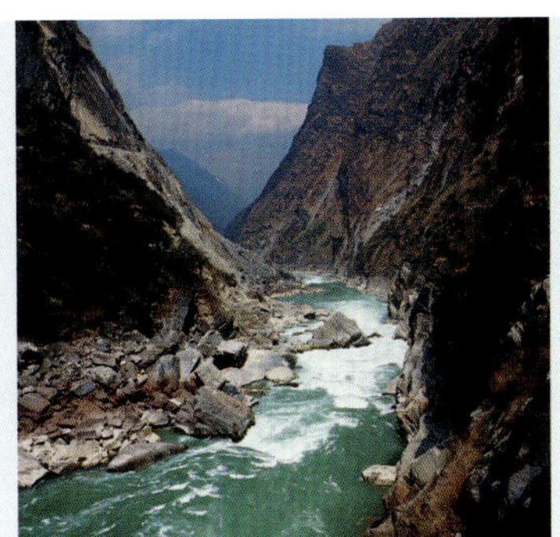

The Yangtze (below) has carved a spectacular gorge 15 km (9 miles) long out of the stone of the Yunnan mountains. Known as the Tiger Leaping Gorge (left), it is considered one of the deepest canyons in the world (left). The mountains of Baima Snow Mountains (far left) extend in the south-west of Yunnan Province.

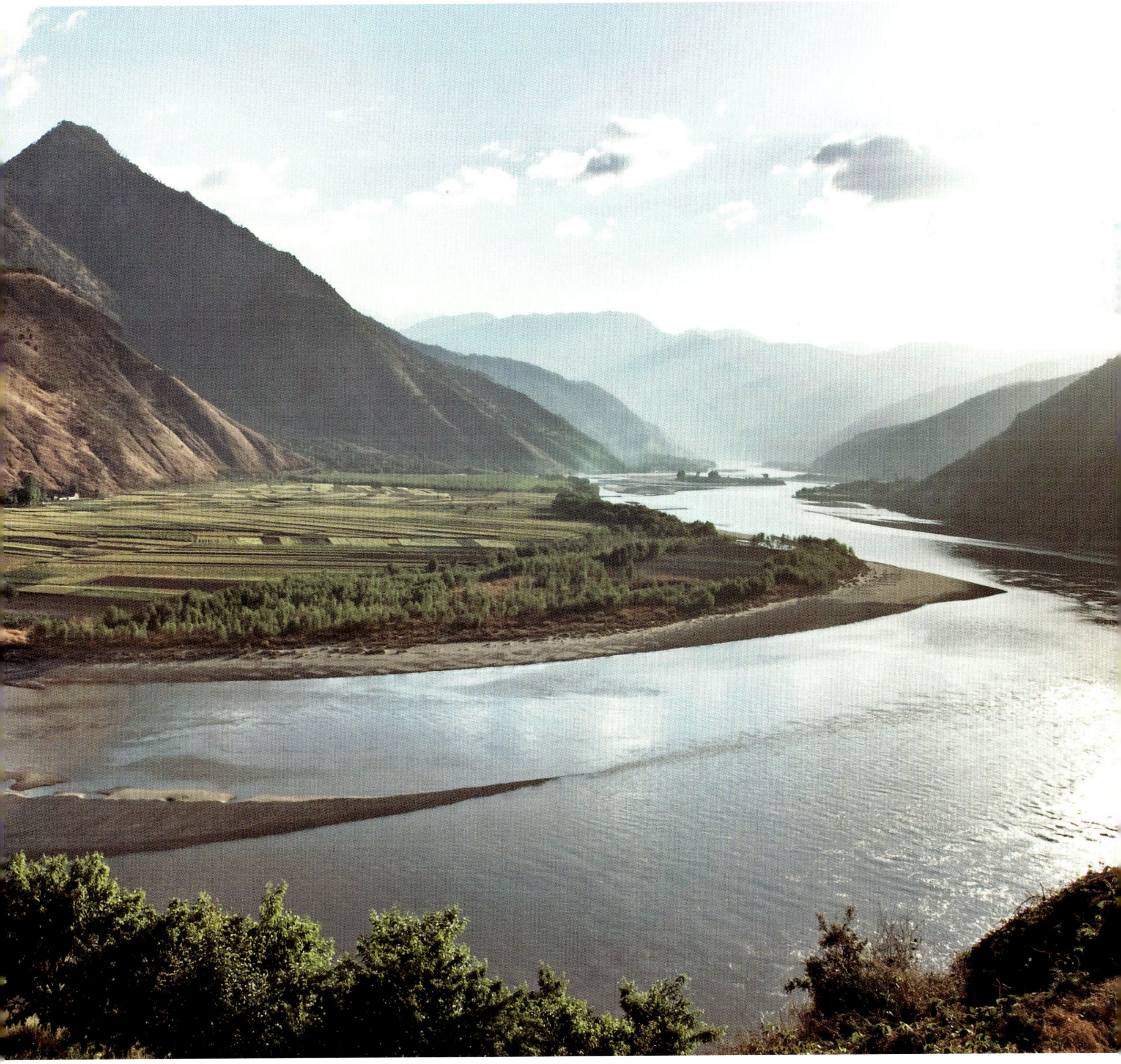

SOUTH CHINA KARST

Date of inscription: 2007
Extended: 2014

The region around Guilin with its bizarre limestone peaks is often regarded as the quintessential Chinese scenery. Together, these formations make up one of the largest contiguous karst topographies.

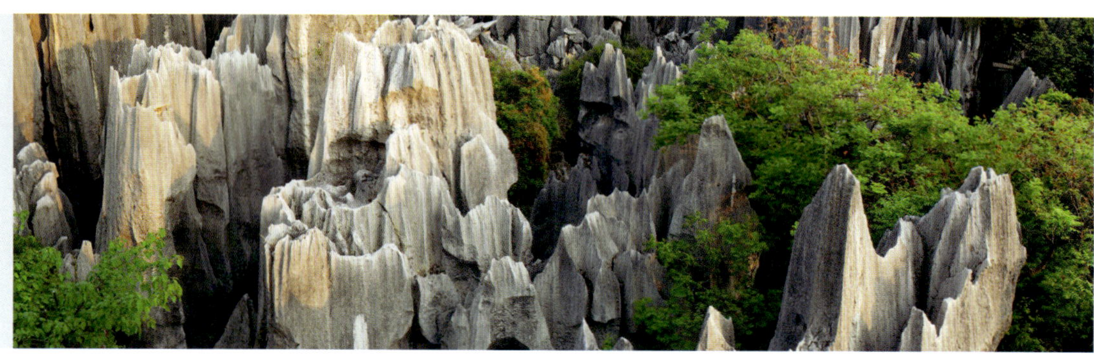

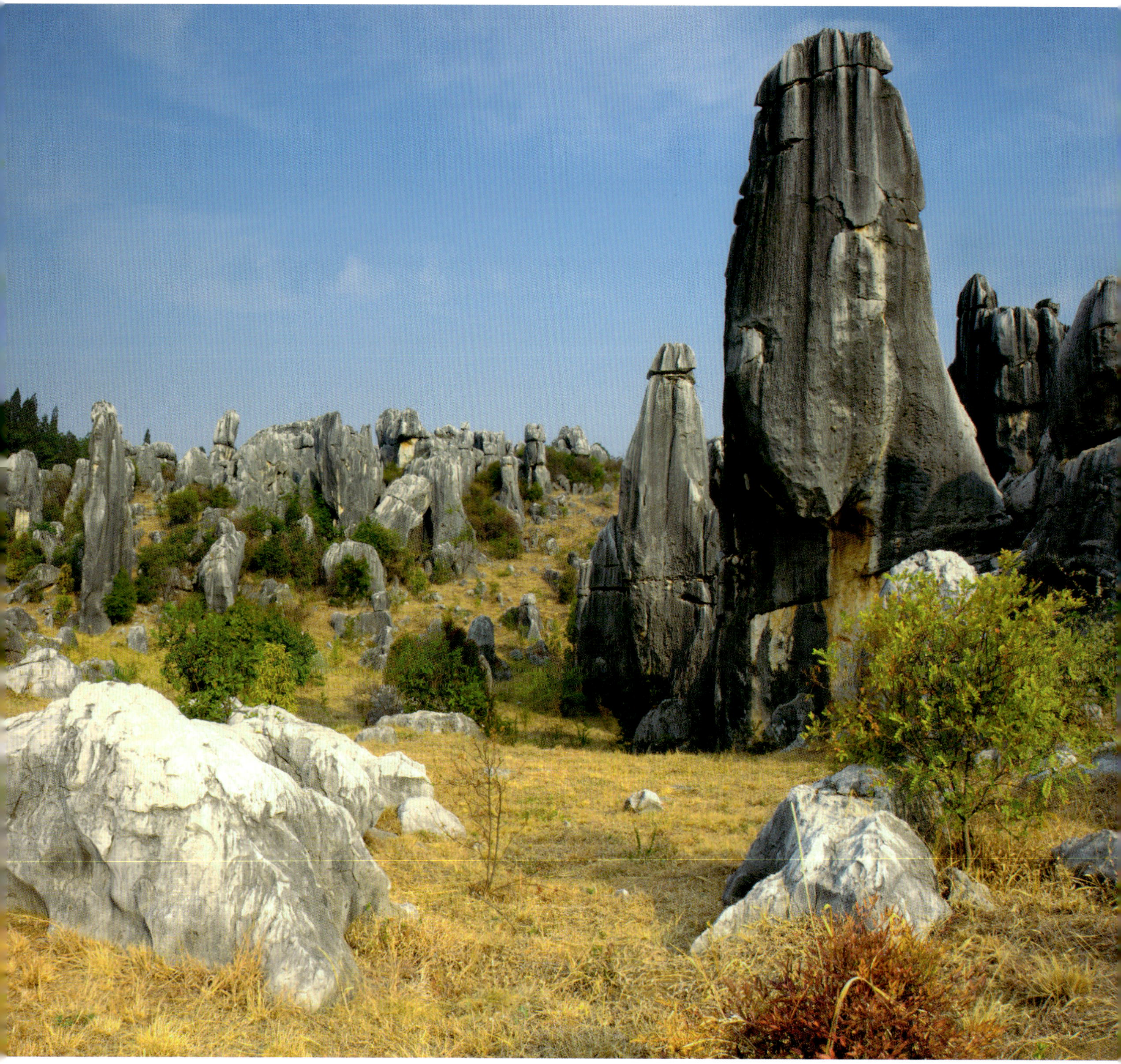

In tropical South China, remarkably weathered rocks known as karst were created by carbonic acid reactions. Here, intensive weathering has produced some fantastic shapes – including cone karst, tower karst and stone forests. The World Heritage site comprises several areas, covering in total around 1,186 sq km (458 sq miles) and featuring appropriately named formations in Shilin near Kunming, Libo near Guiyang and Wulong near Chongqing. The Shilin Karst in Yunnan consists of stone forests with deep, sharp fissures. The Libo Karst of Guizhou illustrates especially well the transition from cone to tower karst. In the Wulong Karst in Chongqing, dolines (sinkholes) dominate, with deep gorges, caves and bridge-like structures. In the caves it is particularly evident that carbonic acid weathering may also have the opposite effect, depositing dissolved lime in stalactites and sinter terraces. Newly added to the World Heritage site were the Jinfo Mountain karst in Chongqing, Shibing's karst landform in Guizhou province and the Guilin and Huangjiang of the Guangxi Zhuang autonomous region.

Around 270 million years ago, the Shilin Karst ("stone forest"), a karst mountain landscape, was formed from a shallow sea near the present city of Kunming. The rock formations often resemble animals or humans and have names like "birds feeding their young", or "phoenix preening itself".

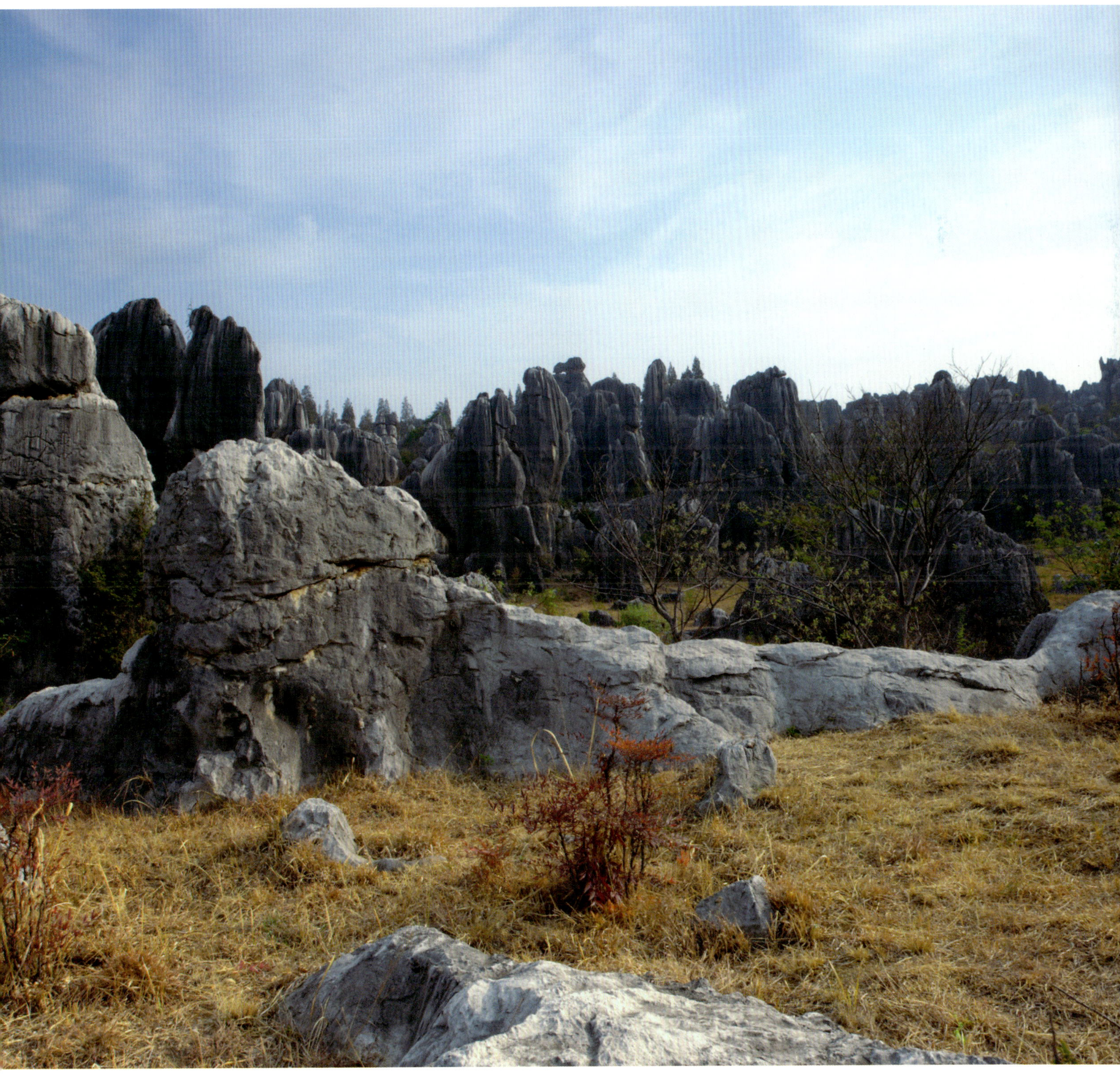

SOUTH CHINA KARST II

Extended: 2014

Karst landscapes had first been declared a World Heritage site in the year 2007, and at its meeting in Doha in 2014 the UNESCO Committee decided on a major extension. This increased the protected area by a further 500 sq. km (200 sq. miles).

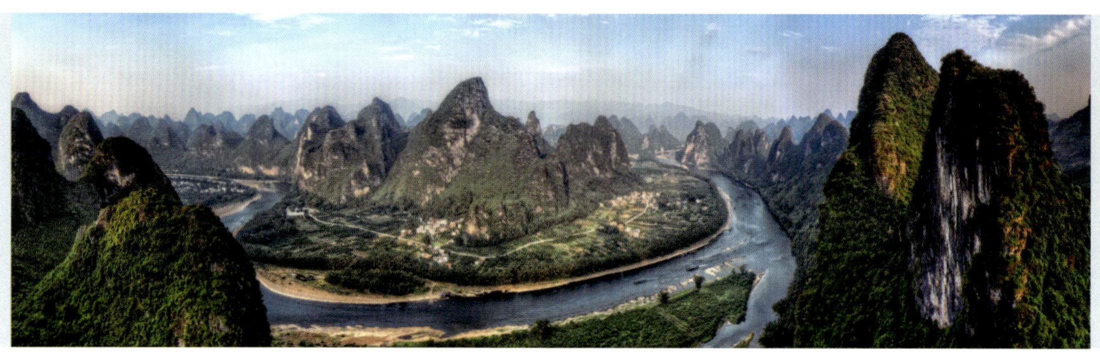

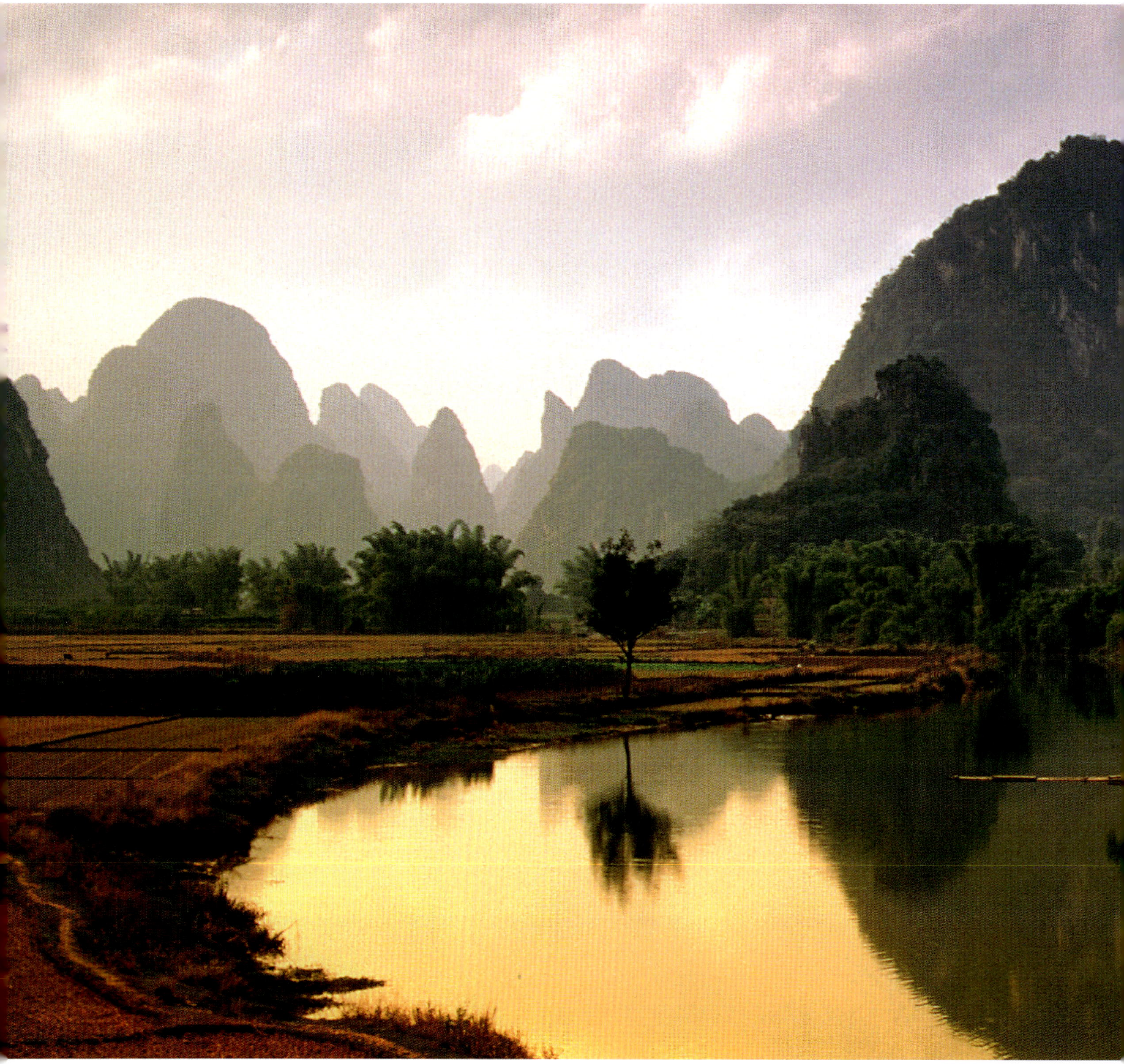

Newly added were Mount Jinfo in Chongqing, the Shibing Karst component in Guizhou and the karst landscape of Guilin and Huangjiang in the Guangxi Zhuang Autonomous Region. The total area of the karst landscapes, which comprise twelve zones in the provinces of Guizhou, Guangxi, Yunnan and Chongqing Municipality, is now 1,762 sq. km (680 sq. miles). Its origin dates back to an era of the Earth's history when the entire area was still below sea level. Over time, ocean sediments formed a mile-thick layer of lime. When the Indian subcontinent collided with the south of Asia, the Himalayas were pushed upwards, and at the same time the landmass in the south of present-day China was also lifted. The former seabed turned into dry land and the limestone deposits began to weather. Then time and erosion got to work again, and over millions of years, wind and water created the most varied shapes of rock formations – today's karst landscapes.

Large picture: The almost unreal karst landscape in Guilin has a dignified backdrop at dusk. Karstification is a process progressing in geological time dimensions. Far left: Xianggong Hill in Guilin.

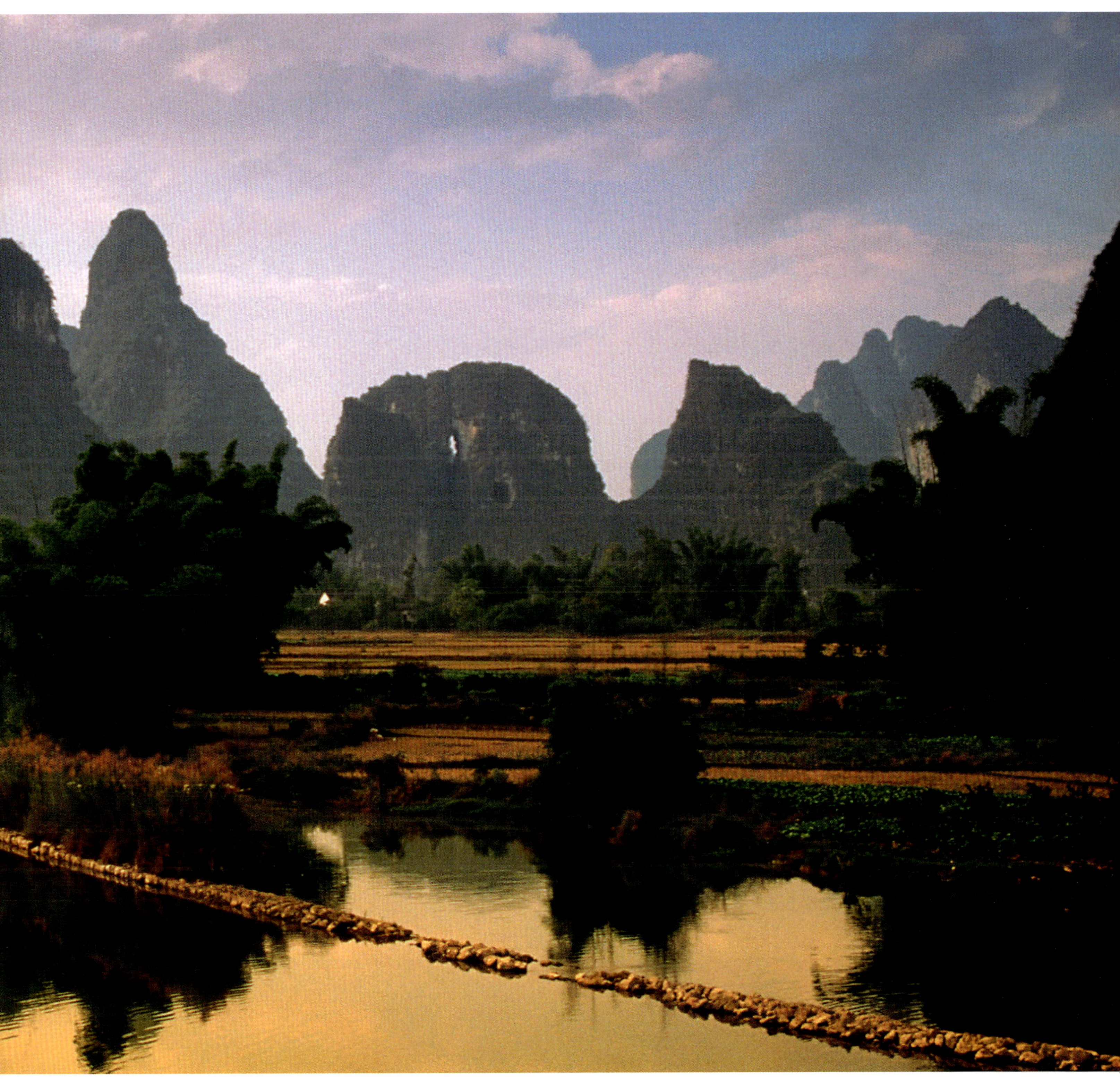

DANXIA SCENIC AREA

Date of inscription: 2010

All Danxia landscapes feature the same special rock formations, caused by wind and weather. In addition, the landscapes offer a habitat for unique plant and animal species.

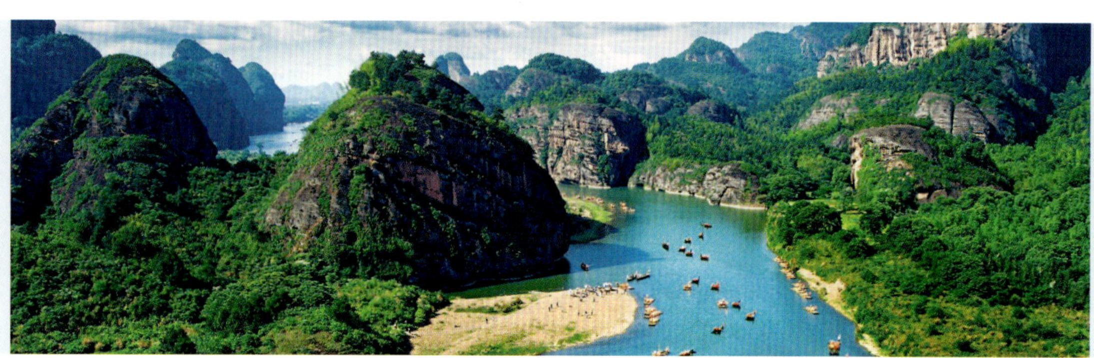

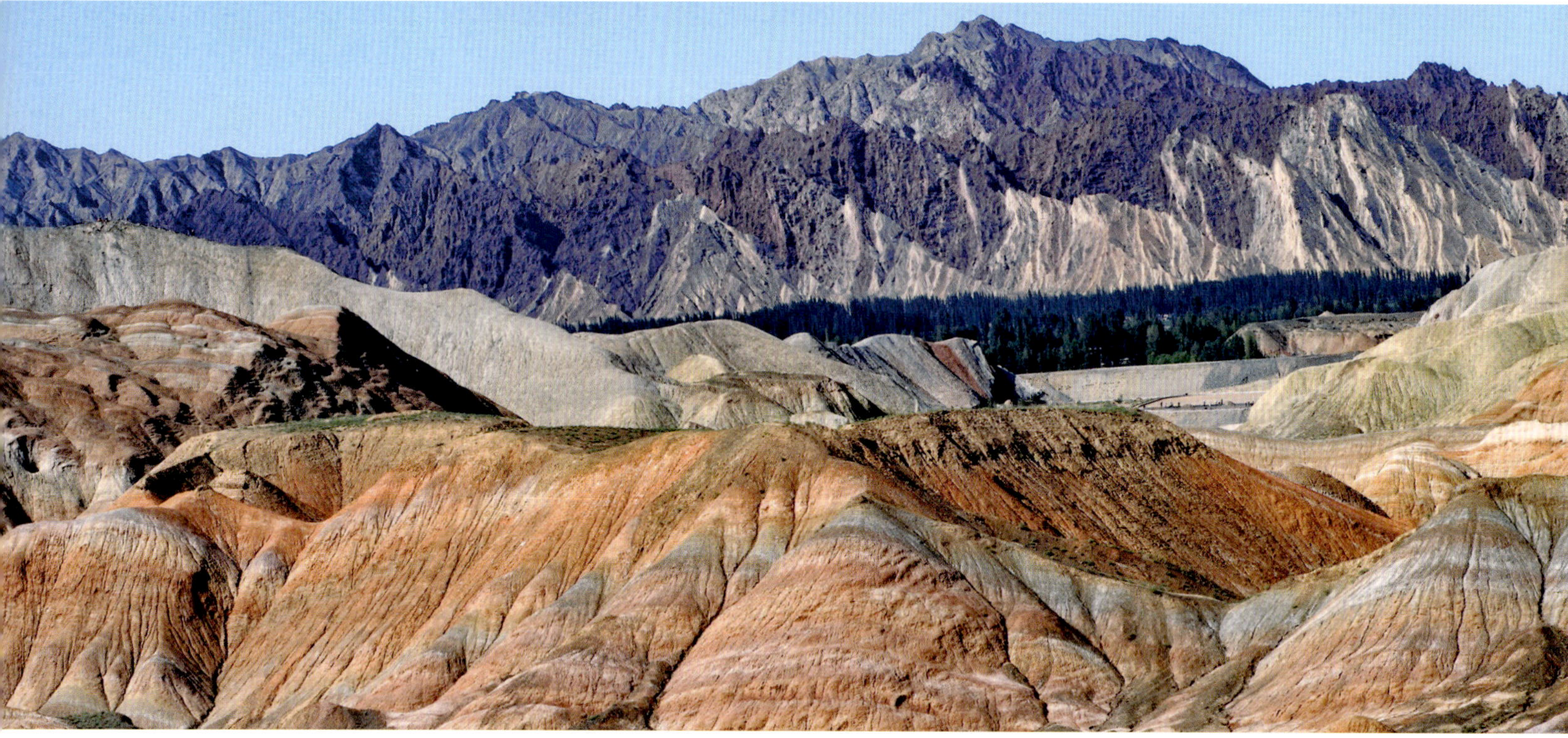

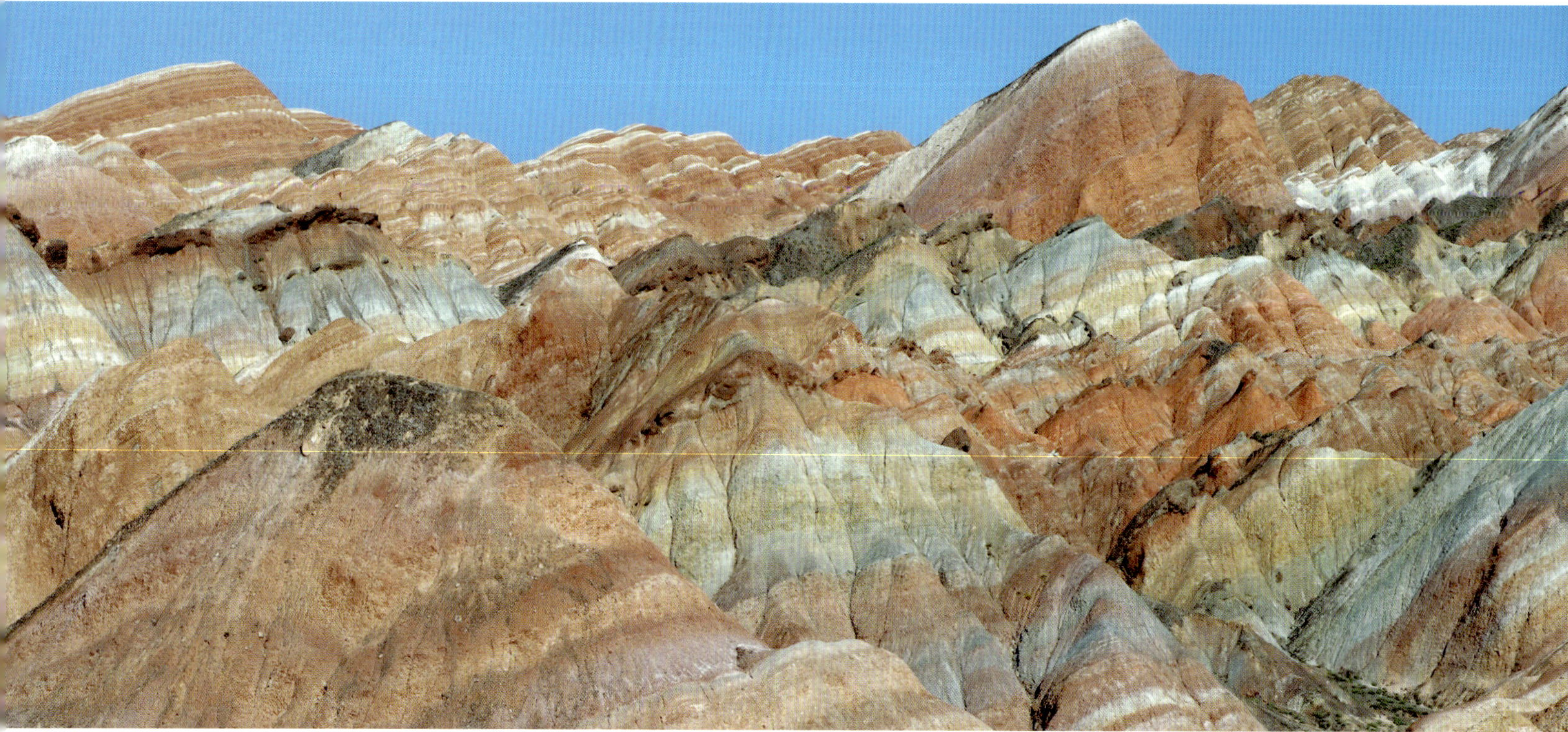

The name "Danxia" designates a specific landform in the subtropical area of south-western China. It is characterized by red sandstone which has been shaped into steep slopes, columns and figures. This may have happened because of weathering on the one hand and through the lifting of the rock on the other. The at times bizarre collection of rock shapes is complemented by narrow valleys, steep ravines and narrow waterfalls. A subtropical evergreen forest thrives in these seemingly enchanted landscapes, which are home to numerous endangered animal and plant species. A total of six of these landscapes have been declared a World Natural Heritage site: Mountain Lang-shan and Mountain Wanfoshan in Hunan Province, Taining and Guanzhoushan in Fujijan Province, Longhushan and Guifeng in Jiangxi Province, Chishui in Guizhou Province, Fangyan Jianglangshan in Zhejiang Province and finally Danxiashan in Guangdong Province.

The landscape types named after the Danxia Mountains (Danxiashan) in China are characterized by pillar, tower or slab-like structures into which the reddish sandstone has eroded. Pictured far left are the spectacular rock formations of Longhushan in Jiangxi Province. Below: The mountains striped in shades of red also belong to the Danxia Group.

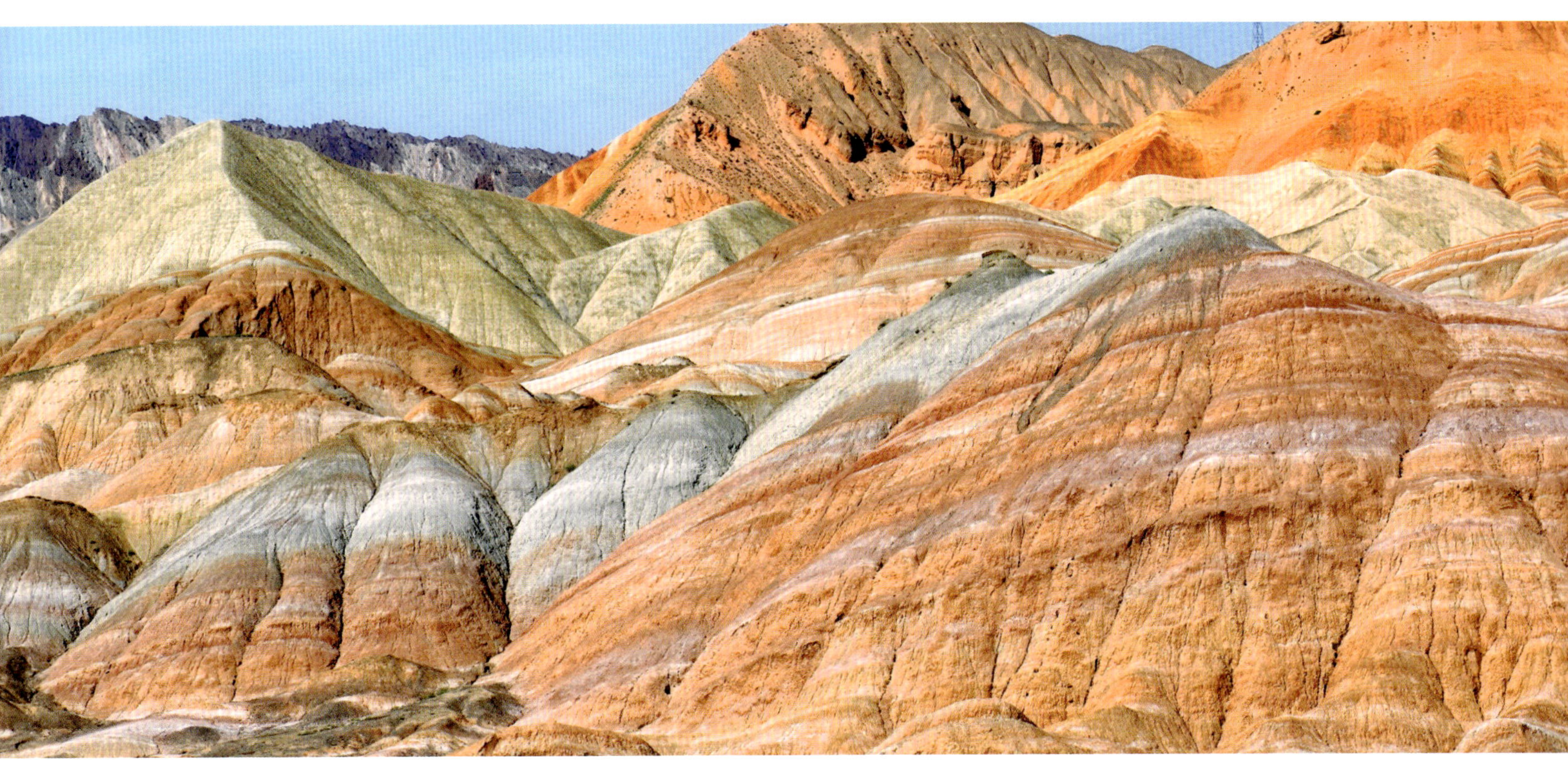

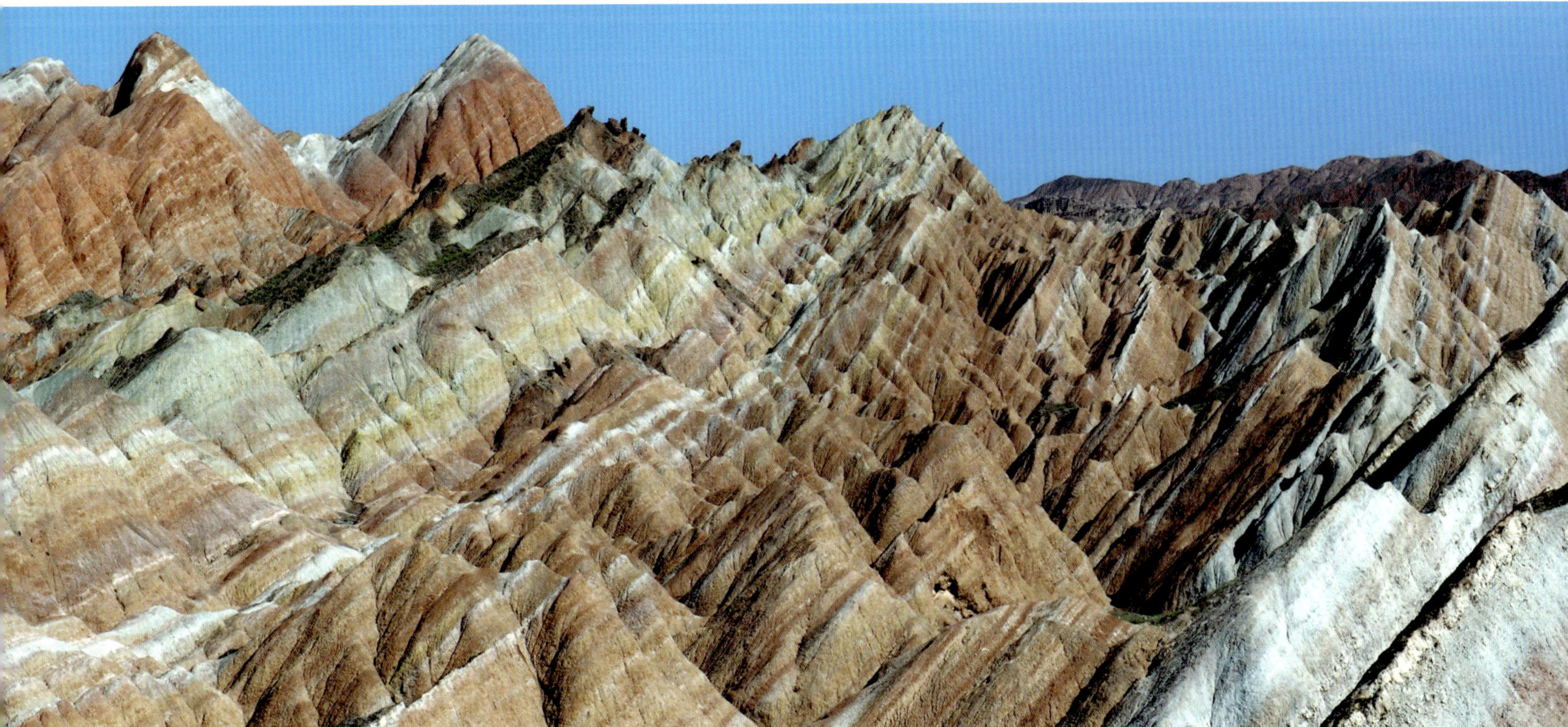

MOUNT SANQINGSHAN NATIONAL PARK

Date of inscription: 2008

Characterized by lush forests, countless waterfalls, and fantastically shaped rock formations, Mount Sanqingshan National Park in south-east China is a fascinating landscape of extraordinary beauty.

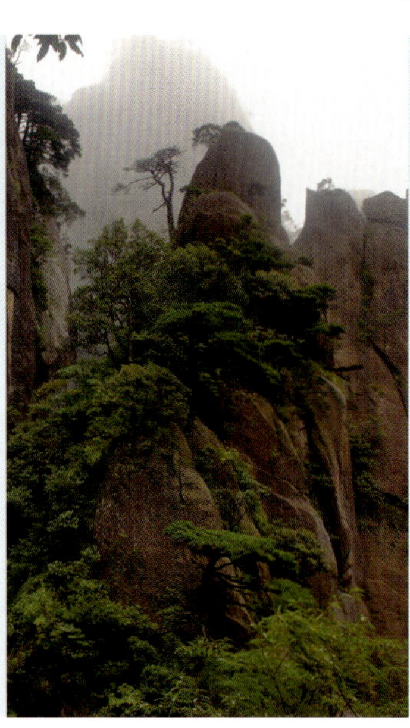

Mount Sanqingshan National Park in the Chinese province of Jiangxi is at the western end of the Huyaiyu mountain chain and was declared a national monument in 1988. The protected area of 230 sq. km is at an elevation between 1,000 and 1,800 m above sea level, although the highest peak is Huyaiyu, at 1817 m. These differences in altitude mean that the national park includes areas of subtropical and maritime climates, with rainforest and evergreen regions covering an area of some 145 sq. km. The lush forests are home to more than 300 animal and 1,000 plant species. Between the peaks and the canyons there are numerous lakes, springs, and waterfalls of heights up to 60 m. The unique granite formations of the Huyaiyu chain are one of the main attractions: many of the 48 peaks and 89 pillars are reminiscent of human figures or animals. Banks of cloud and mist increase the effect, creating a constantly changing landscape with fascinating light effects, such as the so-called "white rainbow." The great age of the mountain chain, up to 1.6 billion years, has made research of the area of great interest to geologists.

Mountain peaks of various heights with sharp, craggy edges, which trees nevertheless recklessly cling to, are typical of the Mount Sanqingshan National Park.

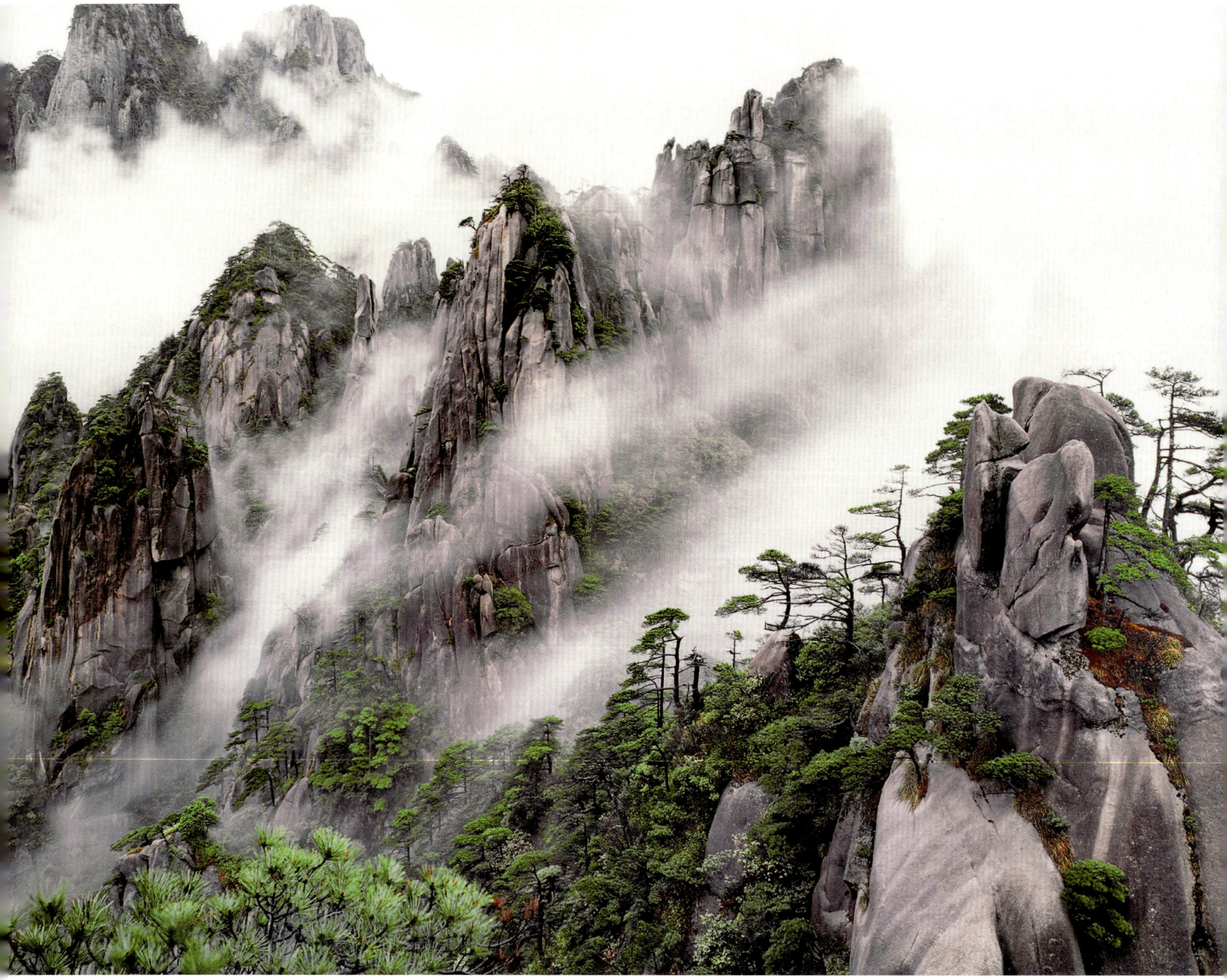

CHENGJIANG FOSSIL SITE

In Chengjiang, scientists have so far found the fossil remains of 196 different species. They are not isolated finds, but an entire wildlife community – a habitat that has been preserved in its entirety and which permits far-reaching investigations into the ecological conditions of that time. The fossil site, which is characterized by a particularly excellent preservation of the finds, was discovered as late as 1984. The fossils are between 520 and 525 million years old and come from the "moment" in the Earth's history that became known as the Cambrian explosion of species or radiation. Within at most ten million years, representatives appeared of almost all sea-dwelling animal phyla known today. In addition to plants and animals, which can be clearly assigned, forms whose kinship is still unclear also lived in Chengjiang. The mysterious Yunnanozoon, for example, recalls a lancelet. And trilobites are also among the extinct arthropods that were once at home in the oceans.

An archaeologist at the fossil site in Chengjiang cleans one of the relics that has been excellently preserved in both its hard and soft parts (right).

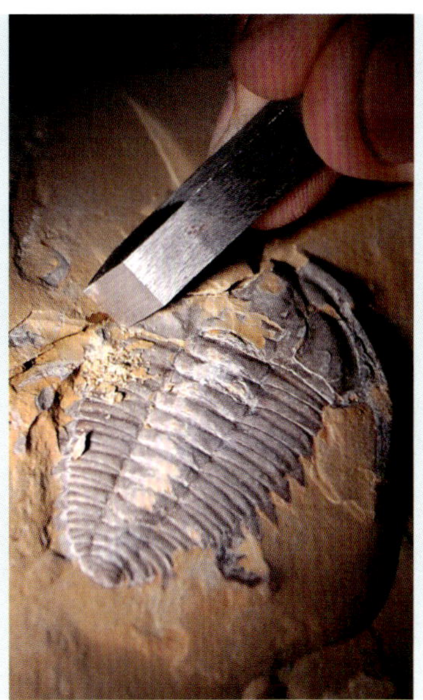

Date of inscription: 2012

The hilly reserve in Yunnan Province, covering approximately 500 ha (1,235 acres) southeast of the capital Kunming, seems initially unremarkable. Well-preserved fossils from the Cambrian can only be encountered when studying several layers of soil.

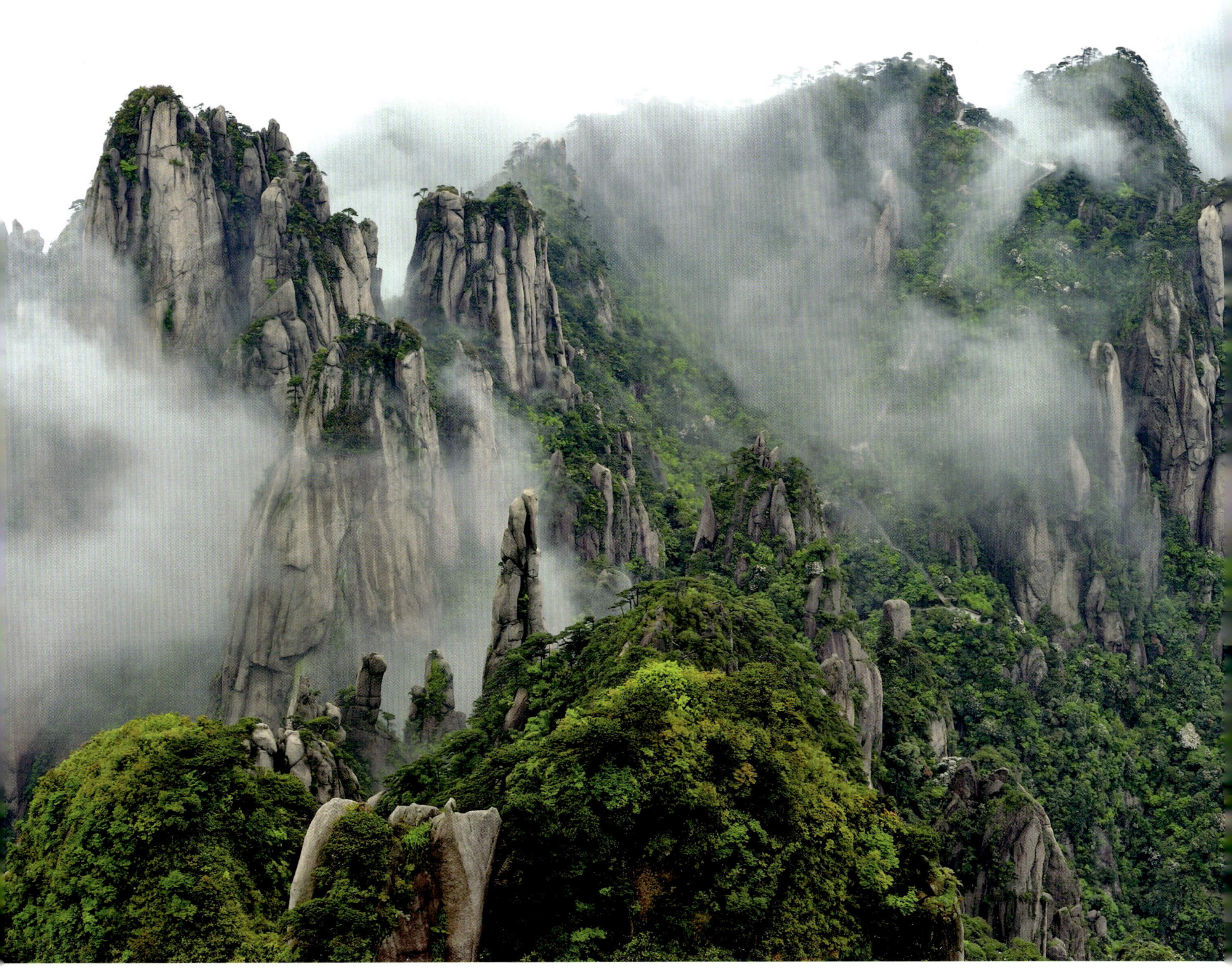

SAGARMATHA NATIONAL PARK

Date of inscription: 1979

The mountains around Everest are not only a popular destination for trekkers, but also a showcase of the fascinating flora and fauna of the eastern Himalayas.

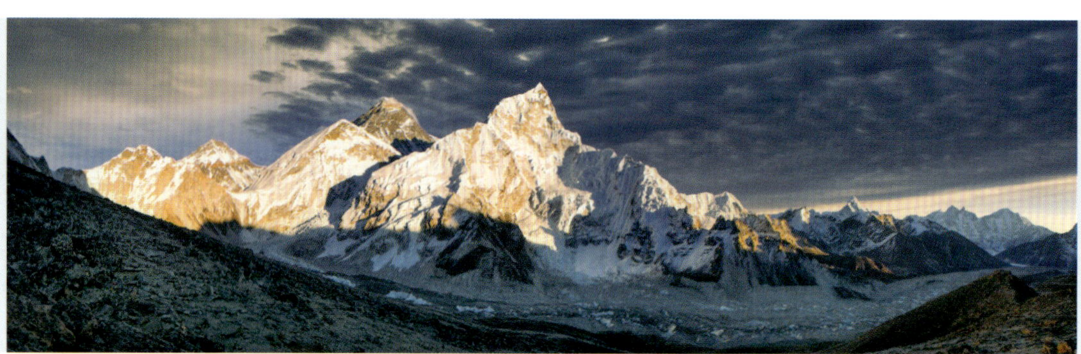

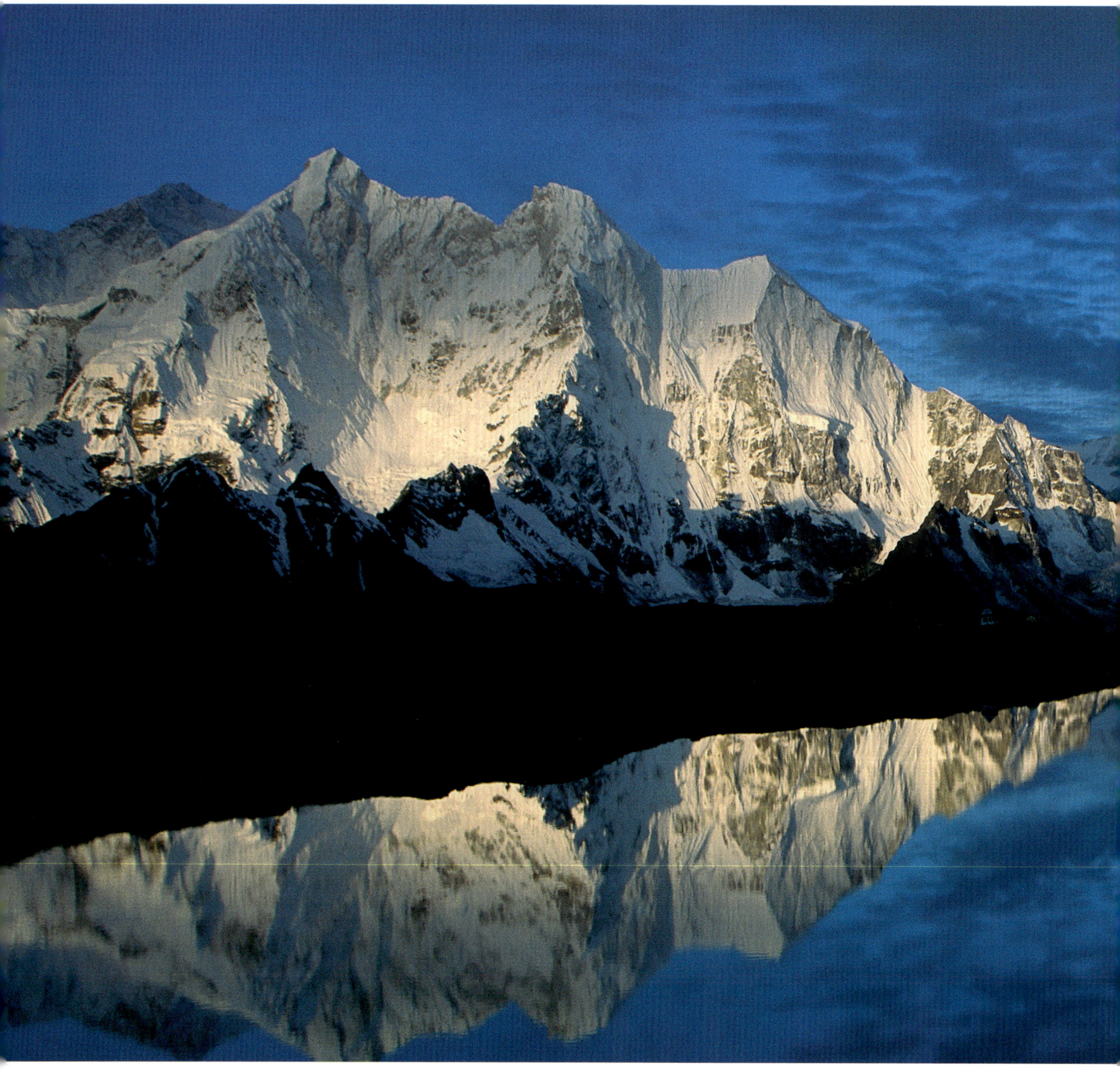

The popularity of trekking created real environmental problems for the Himalayas, and thus the site was declared a national park. The Nepalese call the world's highest mountain Sagarmatha, or "head of the sky," while the Tibetan name, Chomolungma, means "goddess mother of the world." Like Everest, Mounts Lhotse and Cho Oyu also rise above 8,000 m, and with further peaks reaching altitudes as high as 7,000 m, this is the highest mountainous region in the world. Mount Nuptse stands out for its 3,000-m high south face, while at 20 km the Ngozumpa glacier is the longest glacier in Nepal. Only extremely undemanding soil funghi can survive at higher altitudes, but in the lower regions mountain plants like edelweiss, Himalayan lilies, and other shrubs all flourish. The deciduous and coniferous forests are found at up to 4,000 m. Around 30 different mammal species live within the park: the Himalayan tahr, the musk deer, the snow leopard, the Himalayan fox, Himalayan weasel, Himalayan black bear, wolf, and small panda, while majestic predatory birds like the golden eagle, bearded vulture, and griffon vulture are kings of the skies. The yeti, however, is probably best consigned to the realm of fantasy.

The gigantic Mount Everest rose when the Indian subcontinent collided with the Eurasian tectonic plate around 50 million years ago. The tectonic movement is still in progress, and the mountain continues to grow by around 3 cm (1.2 inches) each year.

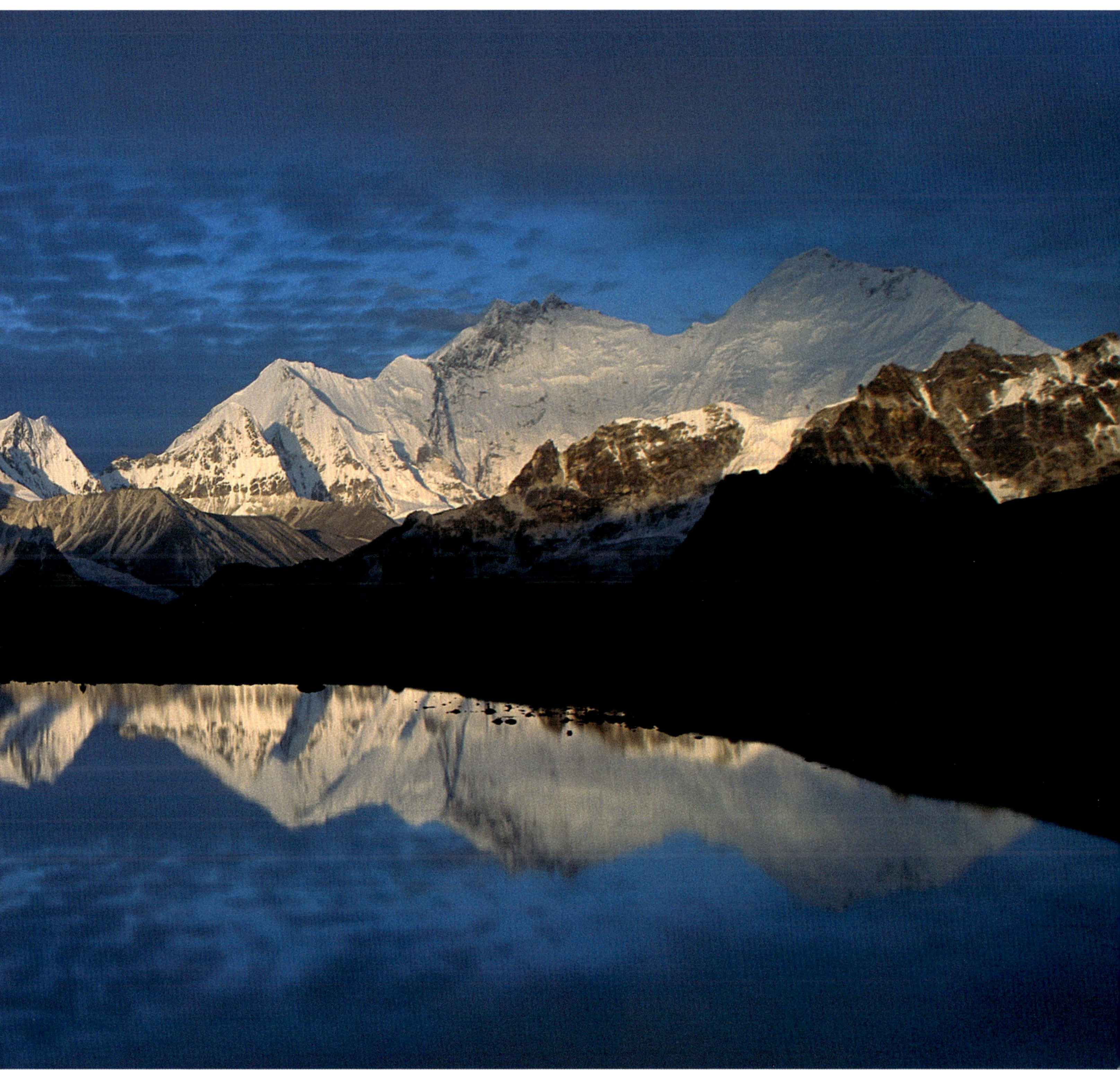

CHITWAN NATIONAL PARK

Date of inscription: 1984

Nepal's oldest national park is dominated by sal forests and extensive areas of elephant grass. It is home to one-horned rhinoceroses and many other endangered animals.

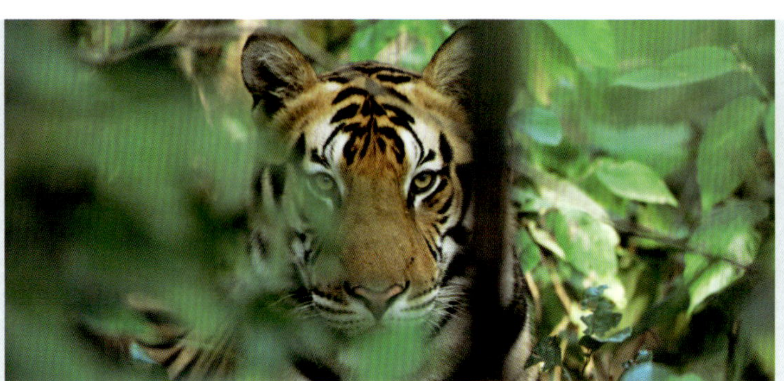

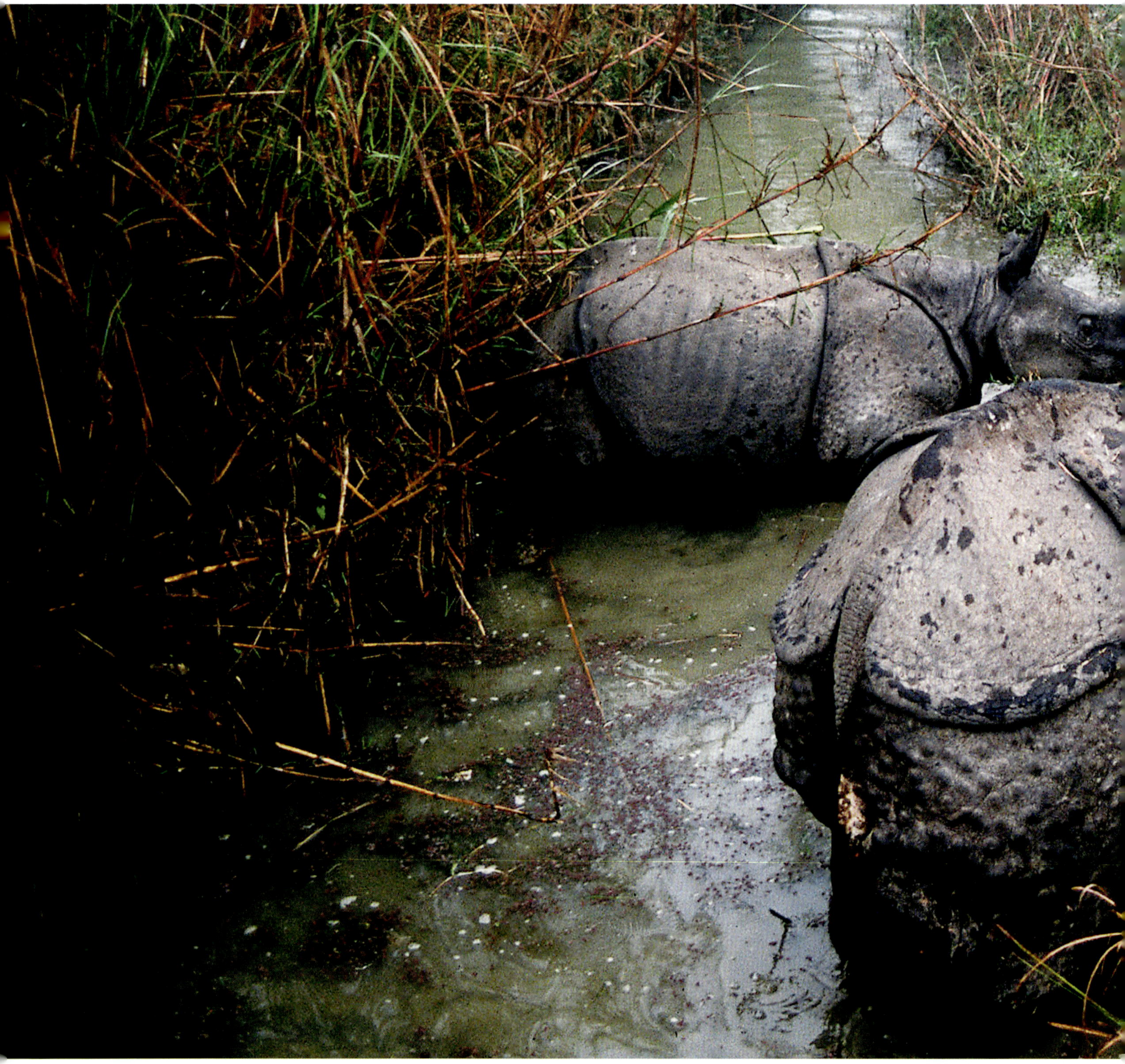

Chitwan National Park lies in southernmost Nepal. Visitors are sure to come across at least one of the roughly 400 resident one-horned rhinos; adults can eat 200 kg (441 pounds) of grass and drink 100 litres (26 gallons) of water a day. Around 200 leopards and 80 tigers also prowl the park's tall elephant grass, and although their protected status has failed to save them from the poachers, the once decimated population of these three species has nonetheless quadrupled in recent times. The origins of the park go back to the land that was designated as a protected area by King Mahendra in 1962, in order to help save the one- horned rhino. This reserve was then made a national park in 1973. Some of its most common wildlife includes sambar and chital deer, four-horned antelopes, wild boar, sloth bear, wild bison (gaur), and rhesus macaques while langur monkeys swing through the treetops. At dusk, mongoose and honey badgers are out hunting, and at night the howl of the golden jackal resonates through the darkness. Mugger crocodiles and gharials – famous for their striking, elon-gated jaws – doze away the days in the park's rivers. They measure up to 7 m (23 feet), but do not present a threat to man. The Bengal monitor, another of the park's resident species, is found in the more open areas. Chitwan National Park is also an idyllic home for over 400 species of bird, among them the sarus crane, kingfisher, great hornbill, and the cormorant.

There are still several hundred one-horned rhinoceroses living within the boundaries of Chitwan National Park (large image). Few visitors to Chitwan National Park are lucky enough to get a glimpse of the Bengal tiger (small image). This rare, endangered, and extremely shy animal is most active at night.

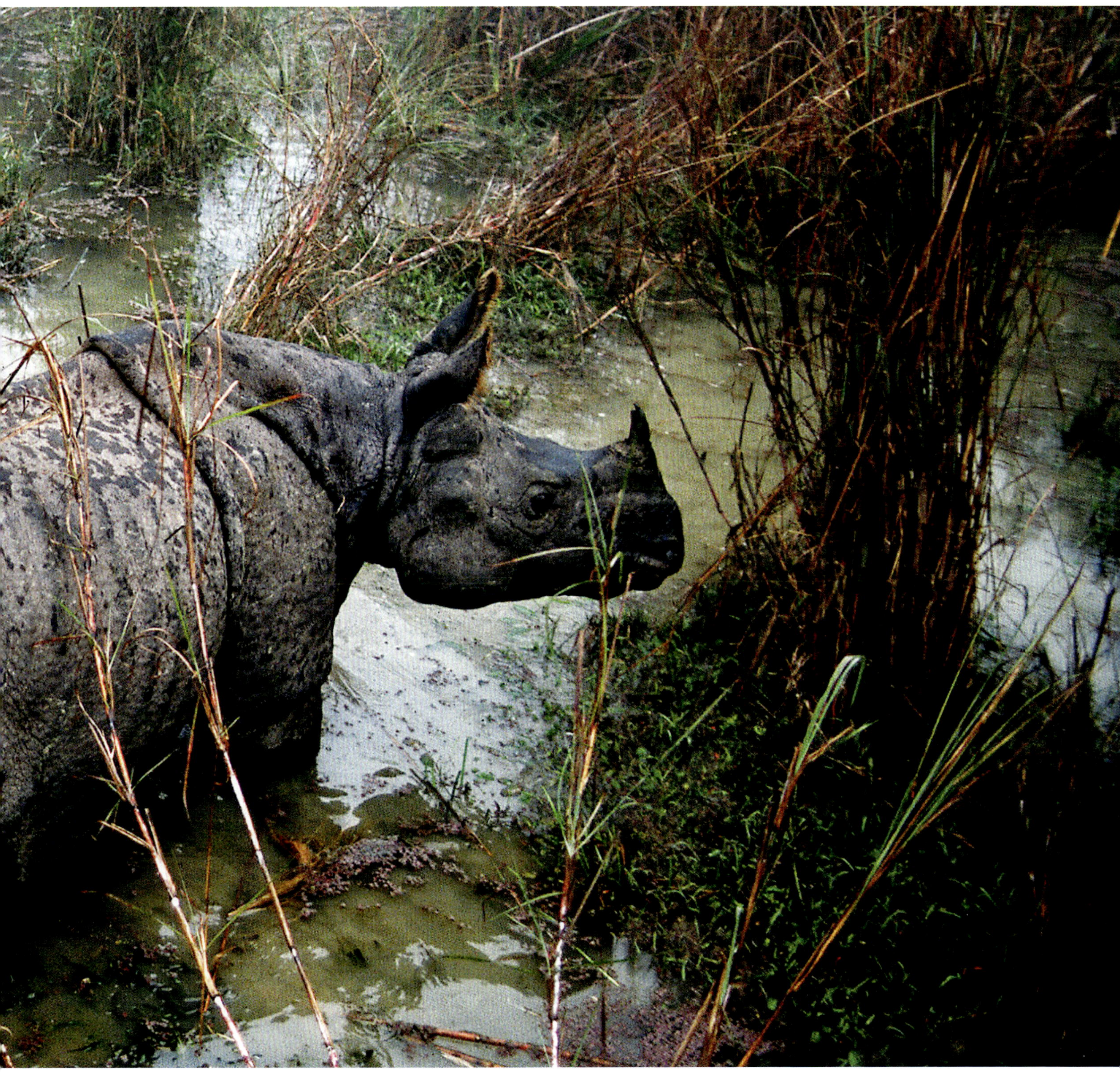

JEJU VOLCANIC ISLAND AND LAVA TUBES

Date of inscription: 2007

Three sites and landscapes on the South Korean island of Jeju make up the Natural Heritage Site. Important phenomena concerning the geological development of the island are in evidence.

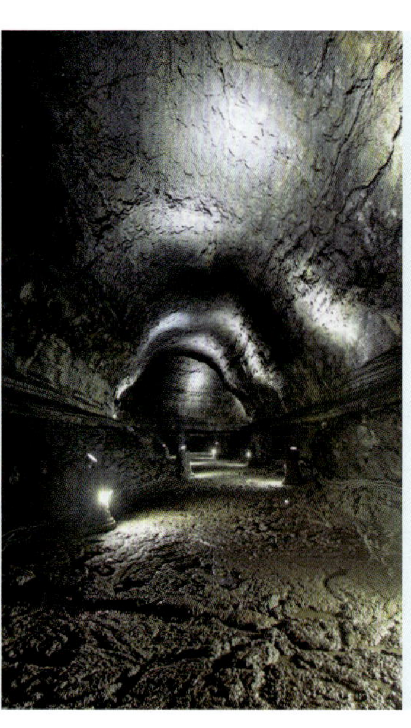

The island of Jeju, off the south coast of Korea, is an undersea shield volcano on a continental plate. It was formed over a hot spot – a "weak point" in the earth's crust – that was dissolved from the interior of the earth outward by rising magma. The conservation area around Mount Hallasan, the highest mountain in South Korea at 1,950 m, makes up the largest part of the Natural Heritage Site, which covers a total of 1,890 sq. km; the surrounding region ranges in height from 800 m to 1,300 m and includes a crater with a 1.6 hectare lake, a trachyte dome, waterfalls, and basalt columns. The vegetation, with many endogenous plants, ranges from temperate deciduous oak forests to subalpine evergreen conifer forests. The geomunoreum, part of the World Heritage Site, comprises five lava tunnels formed when the top layer of liquid lava cooled. This finally solidified to create a roof over an area in which hot lava continued to flow. When the lava stopped flowing, a hollow mould was left. The 182-m high tuff cone Songsan Ilchulbong, at the eastern end of Jeju, was formed by a volcanic eruption on the shallow seabed. Erosion by wind and water exposed the sediment layers.

The lava tubes (in the image to the left Manjanggul Cave) formed 100,000 to 300,000 years ago. Hallasan, the highest summit on Jeju, is an extinct volcano.

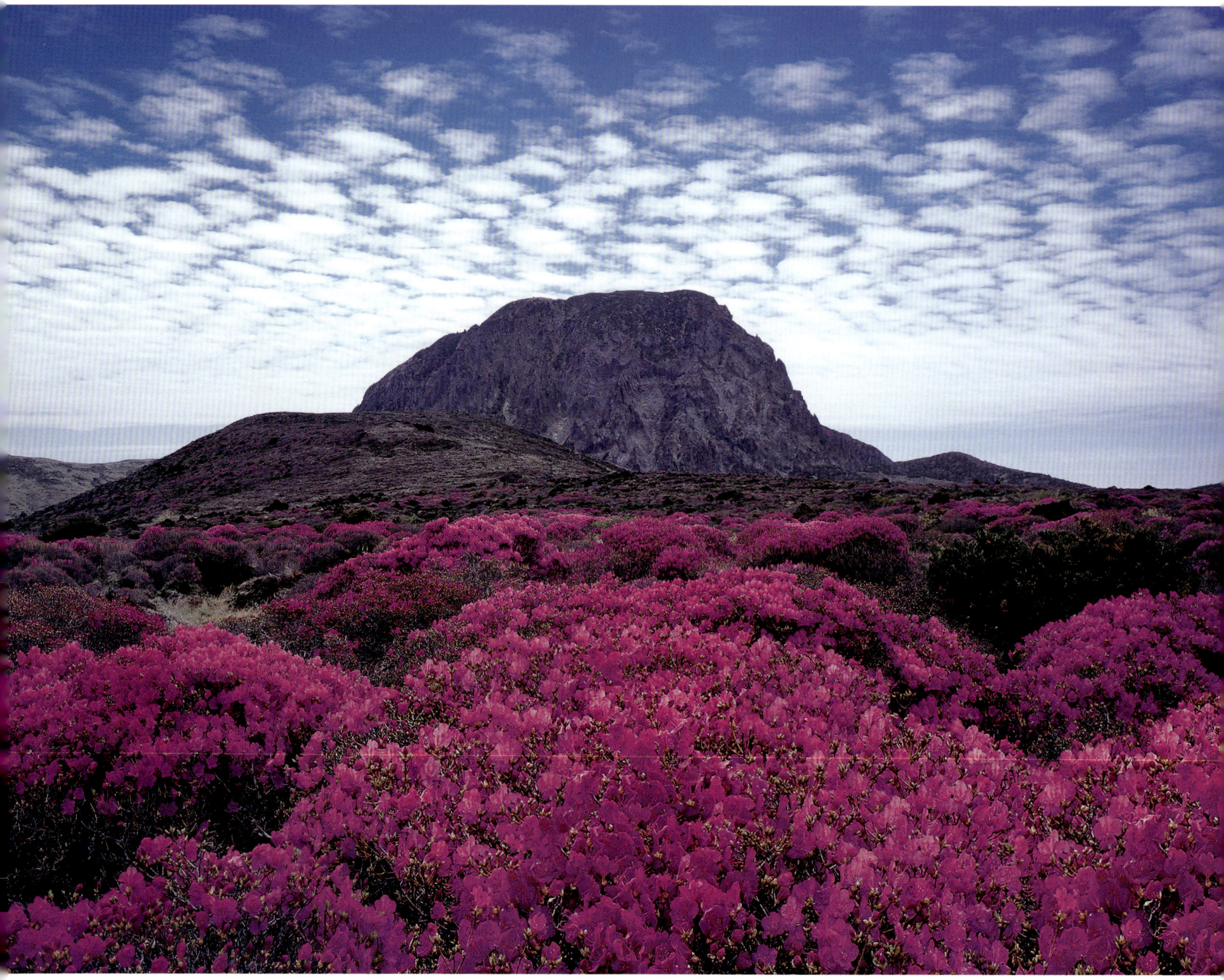

SHIRETOKO

Cold winds blowing across from Siberia cause the sea to freeze just off the coast of Shiretoko in the north-east of Hokkaido, the lowest latitude in the northern hemisphere to experience seasonal ice. Beneath the layer of ice, large quantities of phytoplankton grow, the start of a long food chain. They are the staple diet of krill and other tiny aquatic animals, which nourish crustaceans and small fish. These in turn are consumed by larger fish, marine mammals such as seals and sealions, and sea eagles. Large numbers of salmon and trout swim up the rivers to spawn inland. They provide food for the Hokkaido brown bears as well as for the endangered Blakiston's fish owl and Steller's sea eagle. One of the reasons for the enormous productivity of the marine ecosystem is the different salt content in the layers of water, which scarcely ever mix because no large rivers flow into the Sea of Okhotsk. A total of 223 types of fish, including ten types of salmon, and 28 sea mammals have been recorded off the coast of Shiretoko. The yellow-brown Steller's sealion, which is almost hairless apart from its opulent mane, needs special protection.

The Mount Rausu stratovolcano (large picture) rises behind a colourful wildflower meadow. Sika deer and giant eagle (right) inhabit the heights.

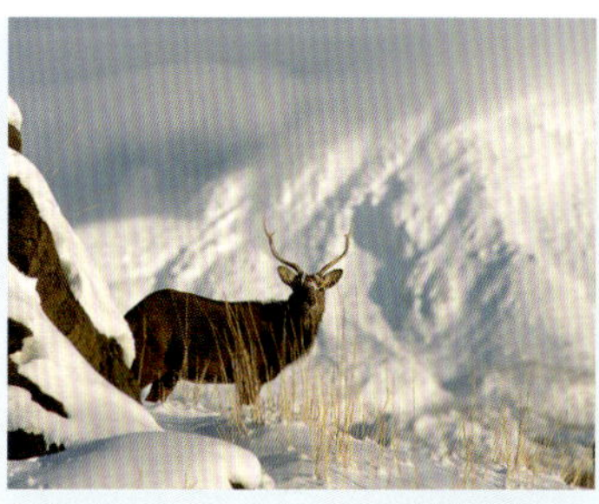

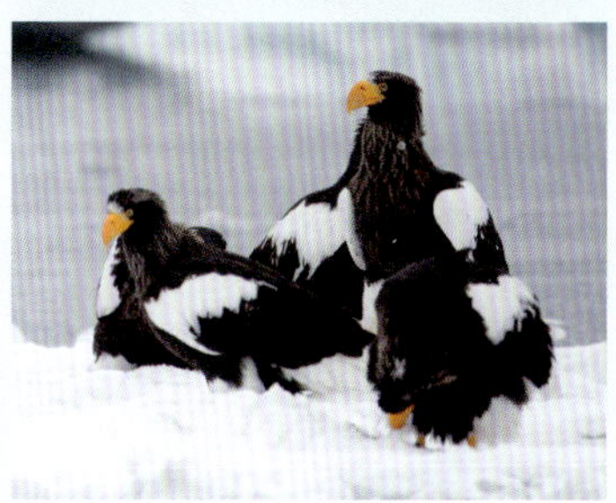

Date of inscription: 2005

Due to the distinctive climatic features, the ecosystems on the Shiretoko peninsula and in the surrounding sea are exceptionally rich in nutrients and contain a great many species.

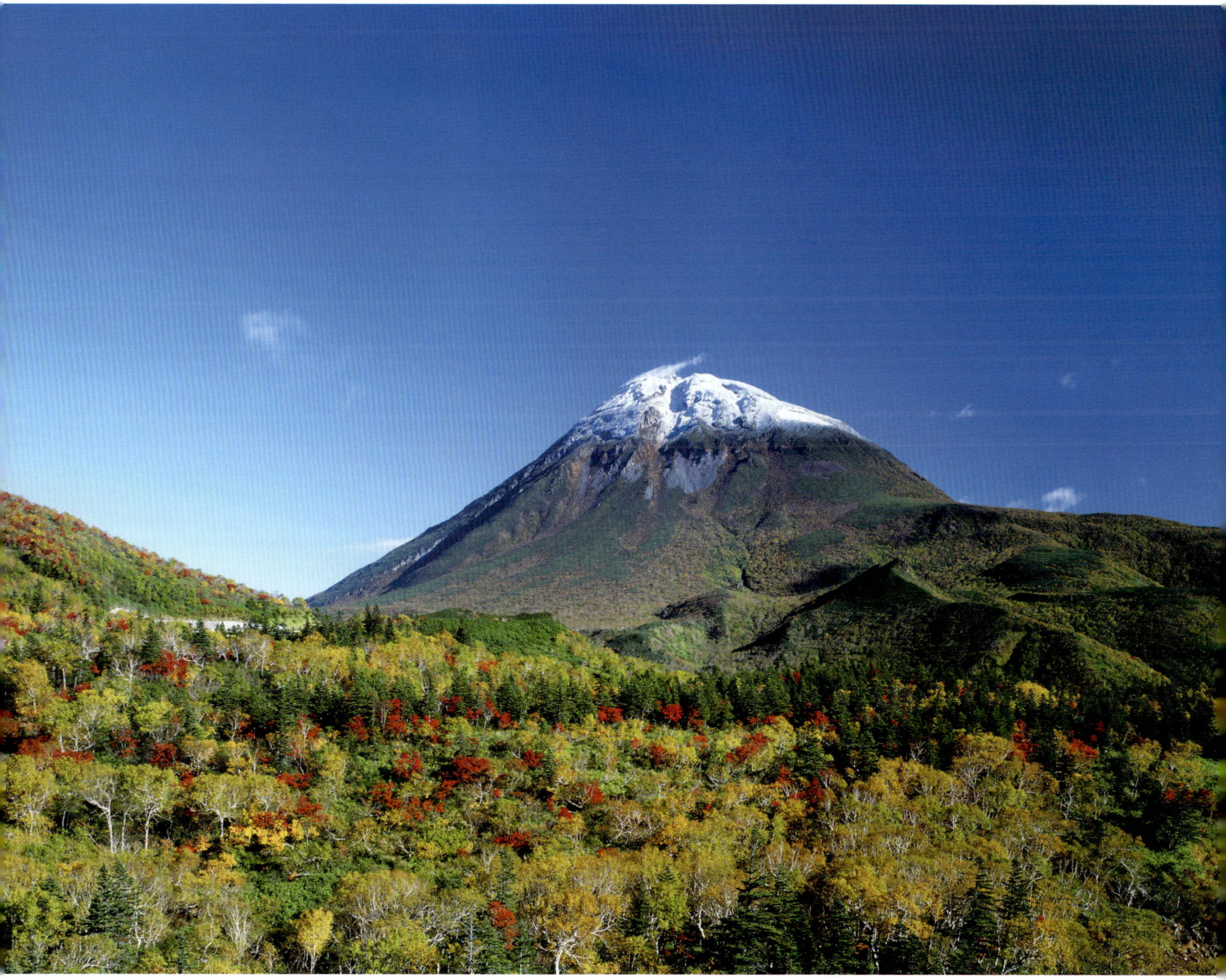

SHIRAKAMI-SANCHI BEECH FOREST

Date of inscription: 1993

One of the last ancient Siebold's beech forests in East Asia is symbolic of the preservation of the natural habitat in densely populated Japan. The Shirakami-Sanchi World Heritage Site comprises around 170 sq. km (105 sq. miles).

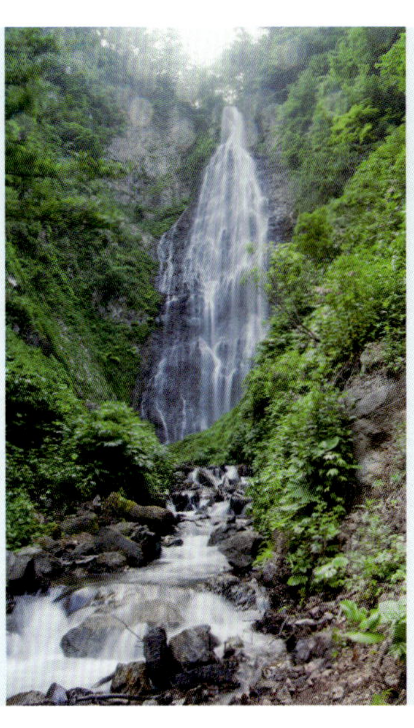

Ancient forests once covered almost all of Japan, with Siebold's beech the predominant type of tree. Most forests were severely decimated by felling, but after protracted discussions in the 1980s, the trees that had been spared in the north of the island of Honshu were protected by law, with the core zone of the Shirakami-Sanchi comprising around 100 sq. km (38 sq. miles). The largest primeval beech forest in East Asia is an important sanctuary for the most northerly monkey population in the world, as well as Asiatic black bears, the Japanese serow, which belongs to the goat family, and 87 types of bird, including the black woodpecker, which is on the IUCN's Red List of Threatened Species. Over 500 types of flora also grow in the Shirakami-Sanchi forest, including rare orchids. The mountainous landscape, up to an altitude of 1,240 m (4,000 feet), in which 15 rivers have their source, has very few paths and herb gatherers have lost their way in this region on at least one occasion. By contrast the part of the ancient forest that is a World Heritage Site is almost untouched by man.

The beech forests (below) are today no longer freely accessible – the fear of further deterioration is too great. But visitors can obtain an access permit for the waterfalls (left).

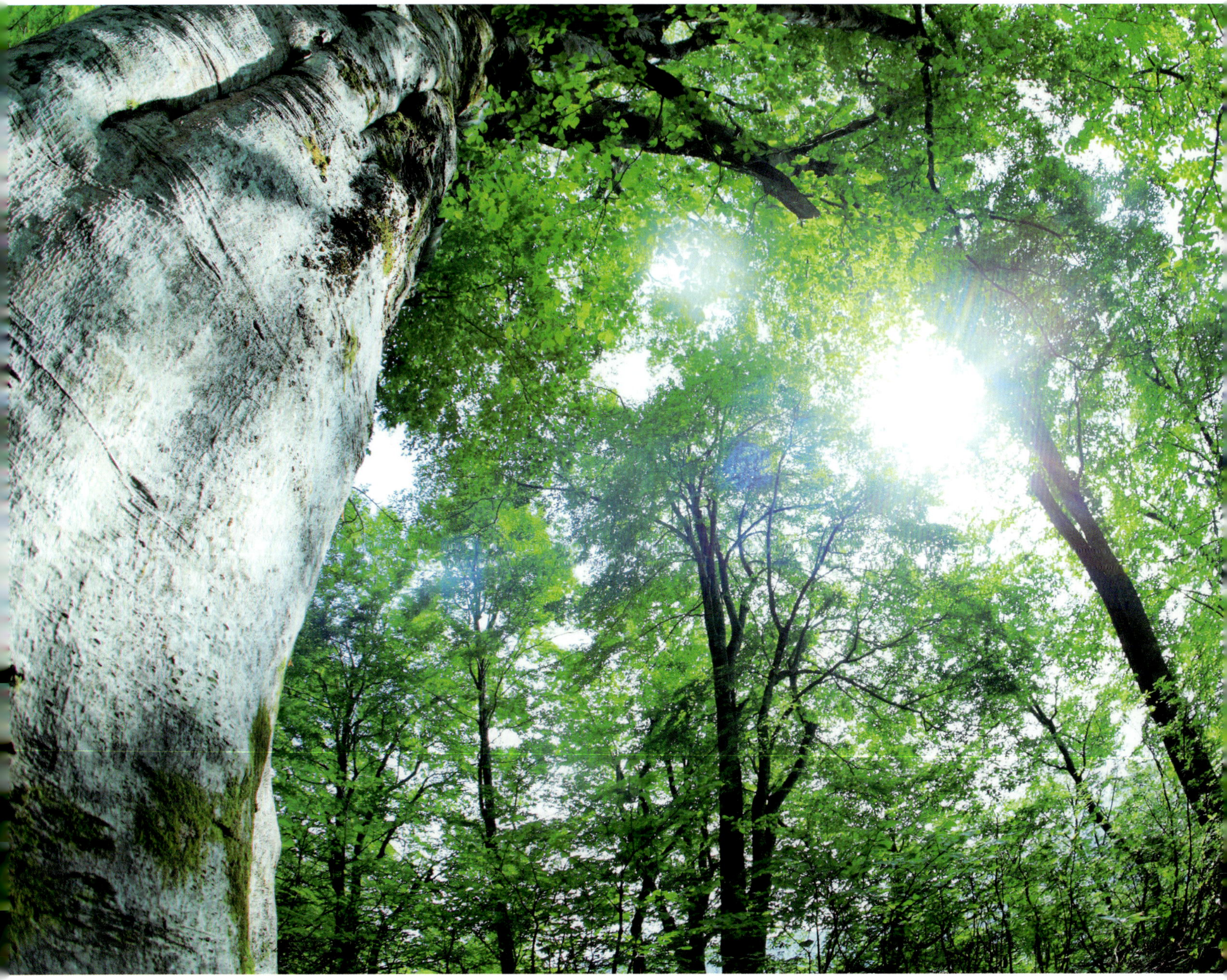

YAKUSHIMA CEDAR FOREST

This island of granite lies 60 km (37 miles) off the southern point of Kyushu Island and rises to 1,935 m (6,350 feet) above sea level. An annual rainfall of up to 10,000 mm (390 inches), together with different climatic zones, ranging from the subtropical coastal region to the alpine mountain regions, have enabled about 1,900 plant species to flourish. The central, temperate zone is home to a unique primeval forest containing ancient Japanese cedars and sickle pines (Cryptomeria japonica). This pine tree, distantly related to the Cedar of Lebanon, is a member of the Cypress family; it grows to heights of 40 m (130 feet) and its timber was traditionally used in Japanese buildings. The timber trade played an important part in the Yakushima economy right up until the 1960s. At that point, one third of the island was declared a national park, mainly due to the large number of impressive giant trees, the most famous of which is the Jomon Cedar, first discovered in 1966. Its trunk has a diameter of 16 m (52 feet) at chest height, and it is reckoned to be about three thousand years old.

The Senpiro Waterfall is one of the most beautiful sights on Yakushima. However, the impression varies depending on weather conditions and time of year. If a rain front draws near, which hides the sun, small rainbows can play across the water.

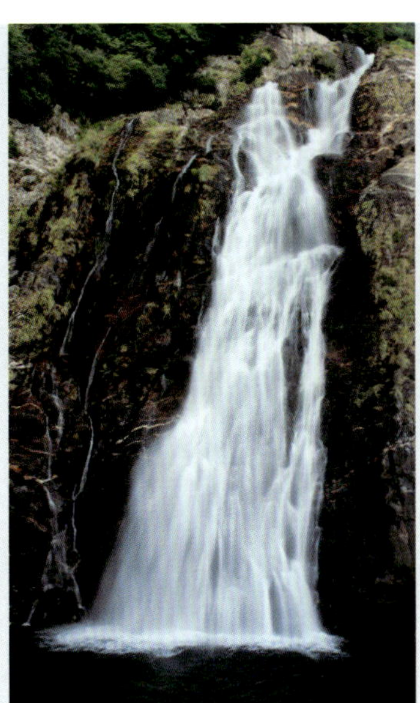

Date of inscription: 1993

Japanese cedars up to 3,000 years old are the most precious botanical specimens in the evergreen primeval forest on Yakushima Island. They are the reason that the interior of the island has been designated a World Heritage Site.

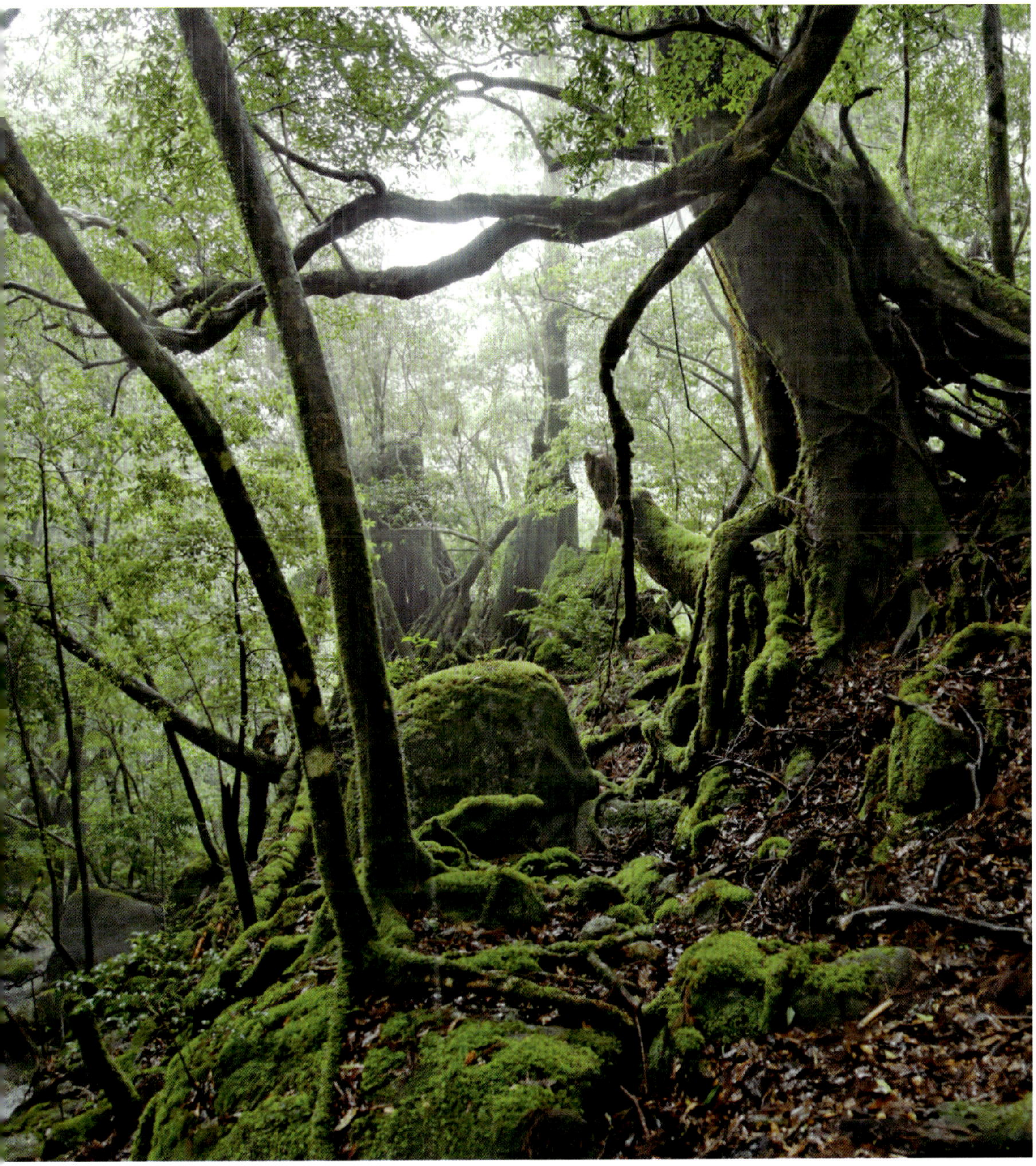

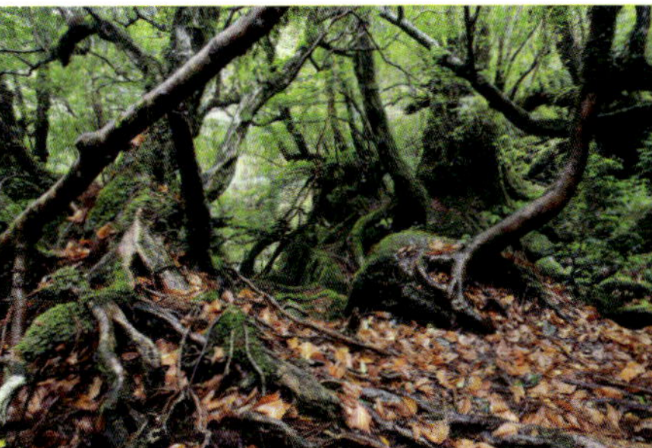

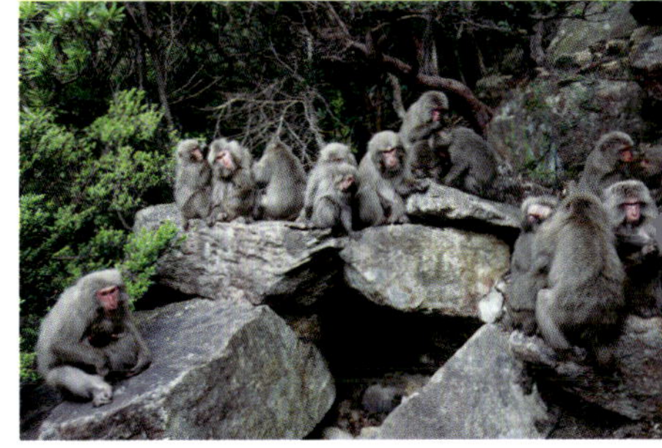

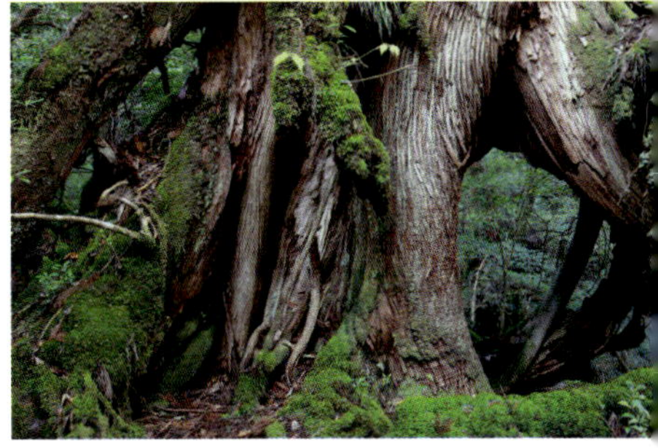

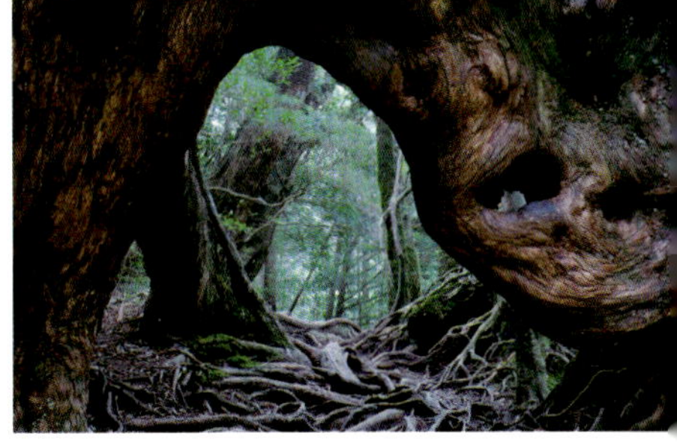

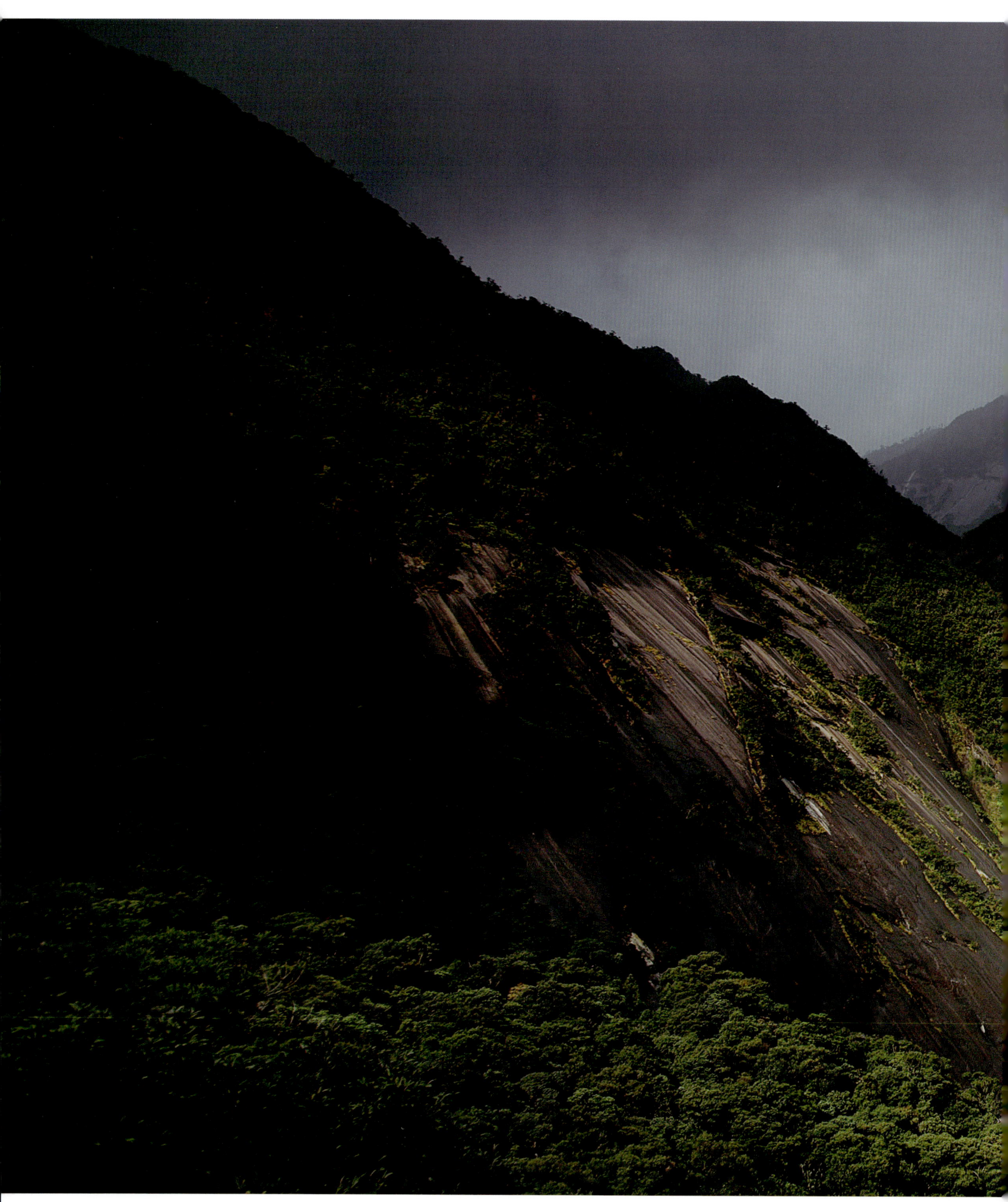

The Senpiro Waterfall is one of the most beautiful sights on Yakushima. However, the impression varies depending on weather conditions and time of year. If a rain front draws near, which hides the sun, small rainbows can play across the water. After a prolonged rainfall, the water masses carried by the falls are gigantic.

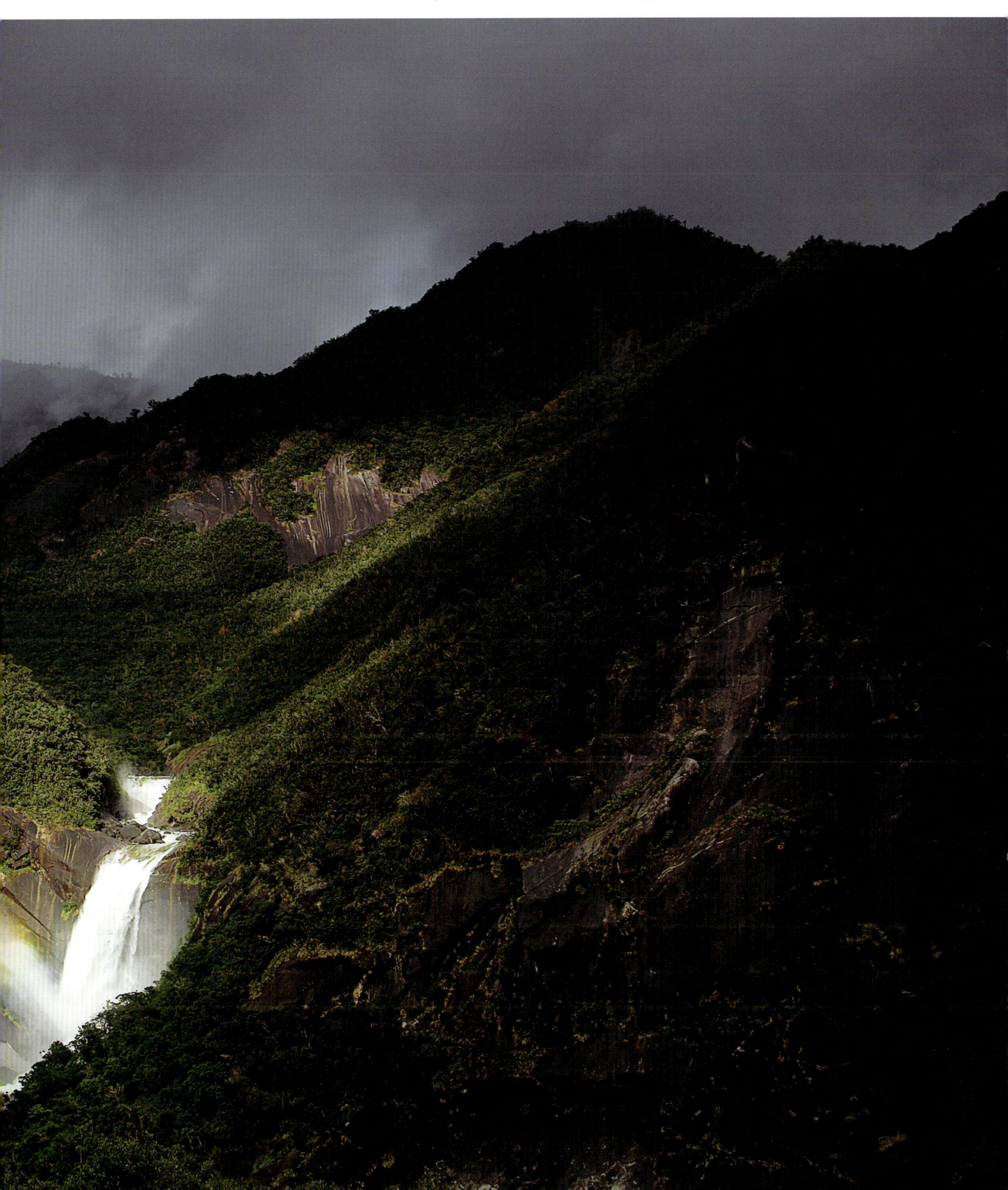

OGASAWARA ISLANDS

Date of inscription: 2011

Because of their isolation, the Ogasawara Islands, located in the western Pacific, some 1,000 km (621 miles) south-east of the main Japanese island of Honshu, have until today remained a seemingly archaic retreat of nature, a "showcase of evolution".

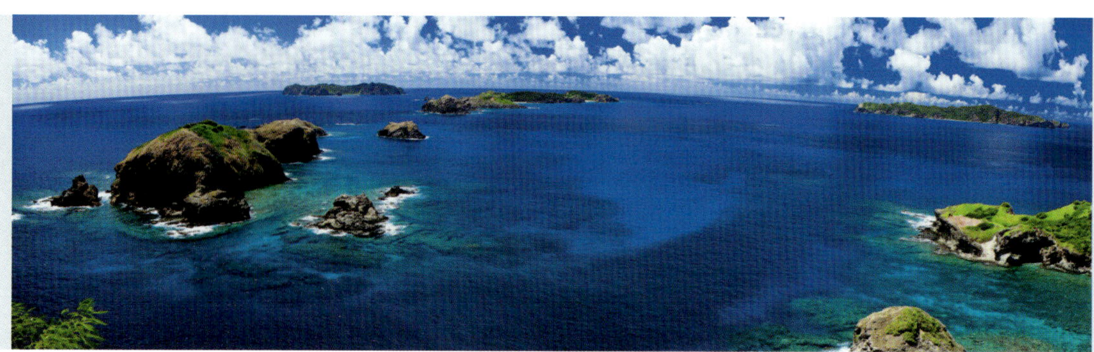

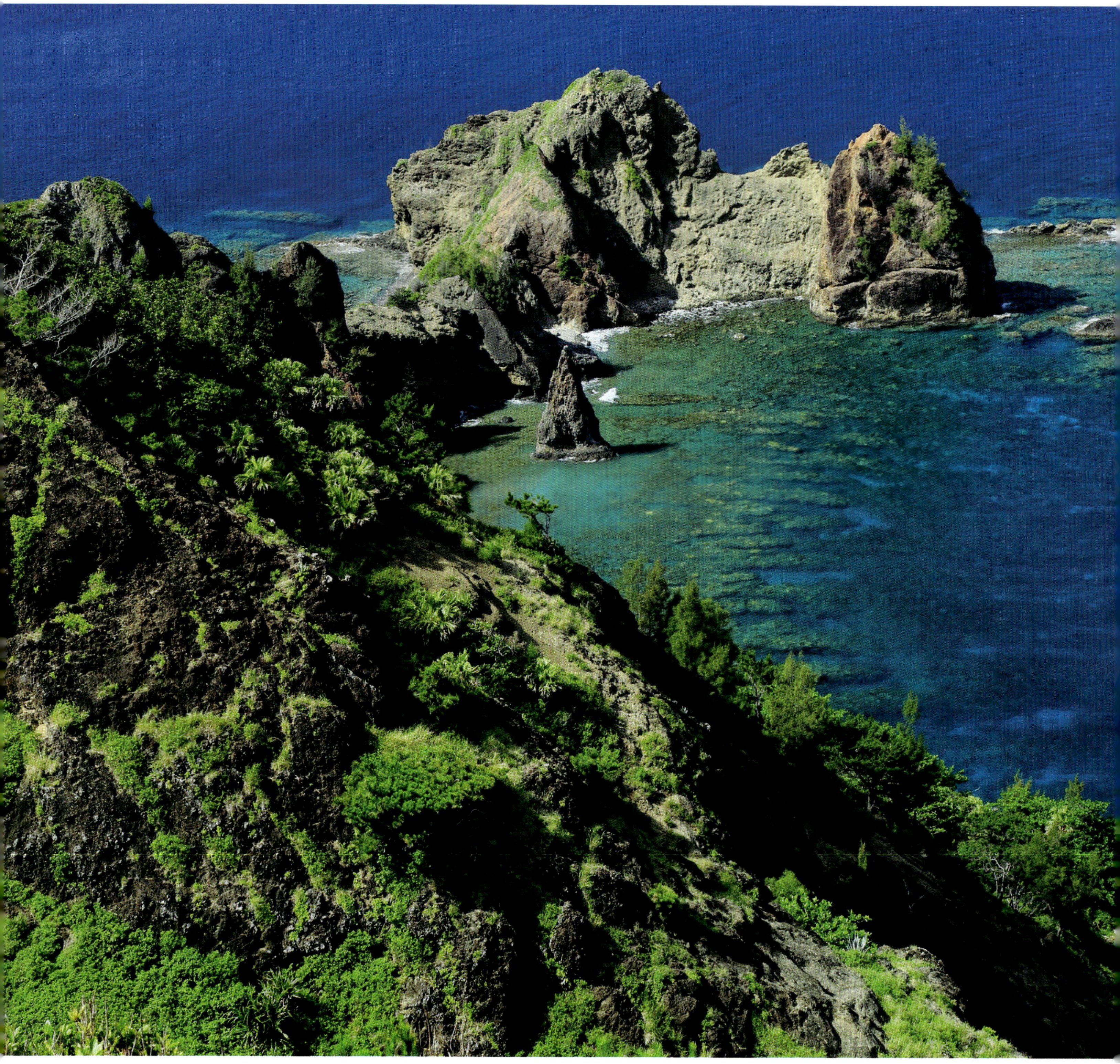

Extending from north to south over a distance of 400 km (249 miles) and covering a total area of 79.4 sq km (30.7 sq miles), only two of the more than 30 islands, Chichijima and Hahajima, are populated; in addition, around 400 U.S. soldiers are stationed on Iwo Jima. The archipelago is the result of around 48 million years of tectonic shifts and volcanic activity. The subtropical climate and frequent mists on some of the islands favour the growth of rare epiphytes: also known as "air plants", these grow on top of other plants without depriving them of nutrients and without having contact with the ground (instead they store water in organs specially developed for the purpose). More than 400 endemic plant species have been documented; in addition, the islands boast nearly 200 endangered bird, 1,400 insect and many rare lizard species. A quarter of snakes occurring on the islands are endemic, as is the only land mammal living here, the Bonin flying fox.

Since 1876, the islands have belonged to Japan. From 1951 until 1968 they were under U.S. administration, and in 1972 they became a protected national park. Sperm whales, humpback whales and bottlenose dolphins frolic in the water (from the top).

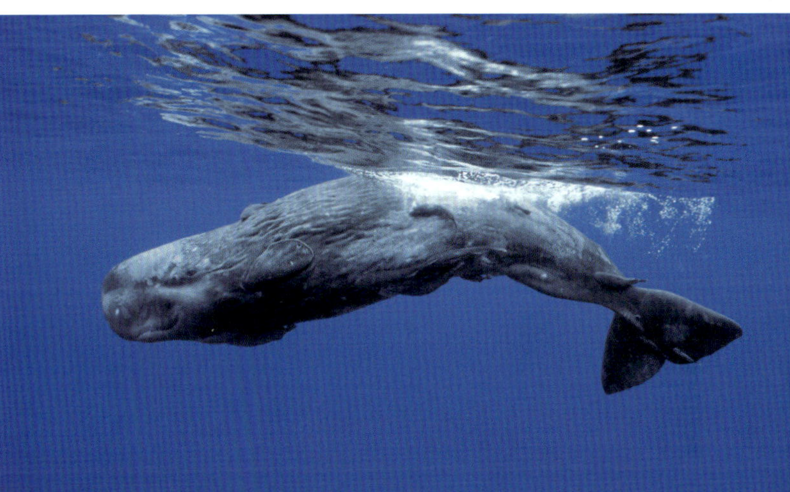

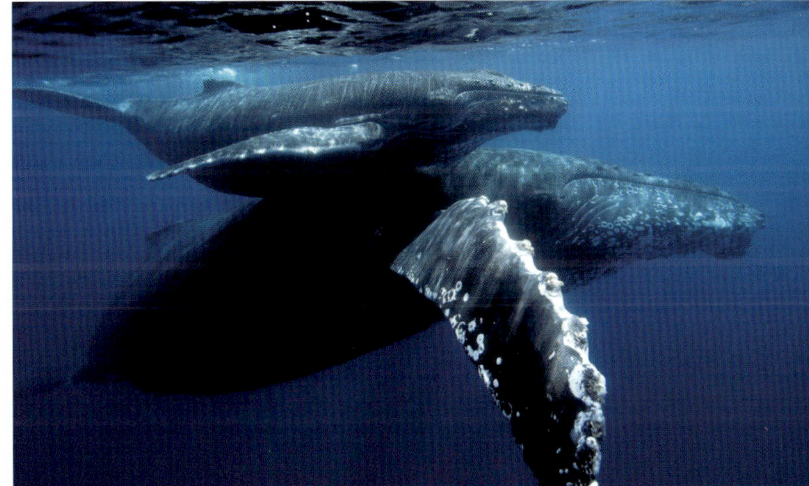

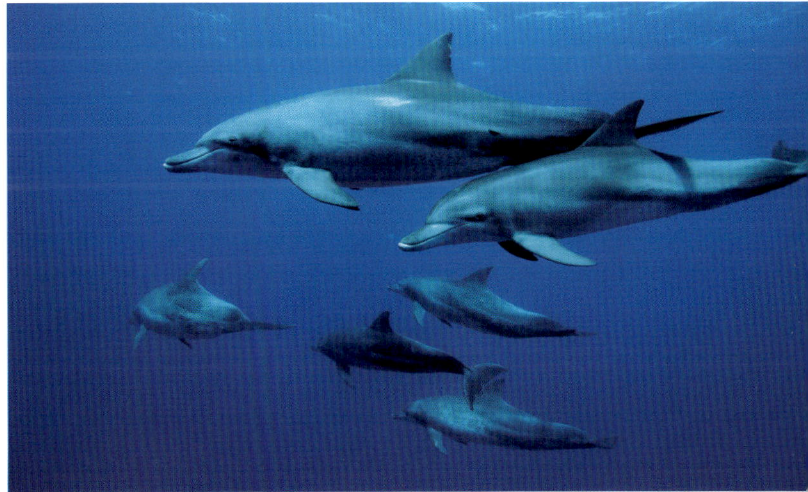

THUNG YAI AND HUAI KHA KHAENG WILDLIFE SANCTUARIES

Date of inscription: 1991

Taken together, these forest sanctuaries, Thung Yai and Huai Kha Khaeng, in western Thailand, cover an area of 6,100 sq. km (2,350 sq. miles) and constitute one of south-east Asia's largest wildlife reserves.

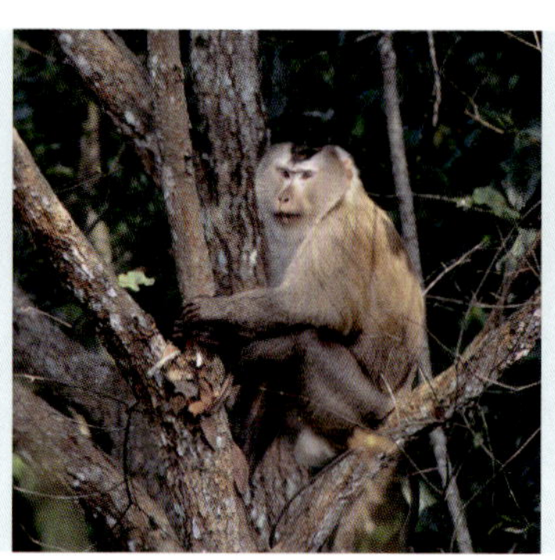

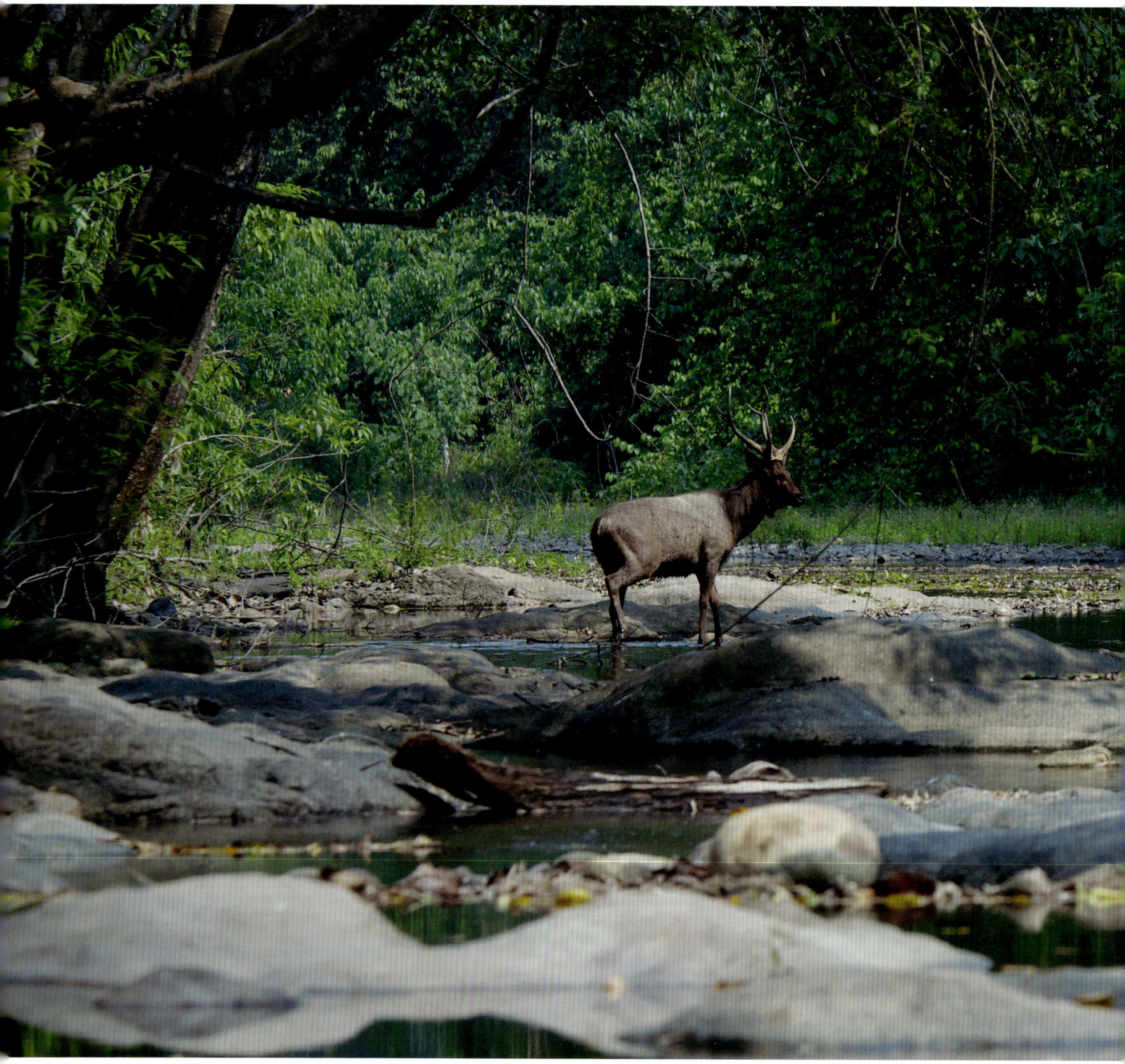

In the mountainous country along the Burmese border, where rivers and streams rush down slopes that vary in height from 250 m to 1,800 m, savanna-type highlands (Thung Yai) alternate with dense forests that consist primarily of bamboo, though tropical trees such as teak also grow here. Indeed, there is scarcely any plant species native to the south-east Asian mainland that does not grow here. The region is also home to about 120 species of mammals, 400 bird species, more than 100 types of river fish, almost 50 amphibian species, and about 100 types of reptiles. These protected areas were deliberately not registered as national parks, since this would have required opening them to the public, as is the case with the national parks to the south and east of the Sri Nakharin dam. Special permission is needed to visit Thung Yai and Huai Kha Khaeng. As a result, large mammals such as tigers, leopards, clouded leopards, elephants, bears, and tapirs are able to live almost undisturbed by humans, though under the watchful supervision of the keepers. It is, however, permitted to log tropical timber within a prescribed area.

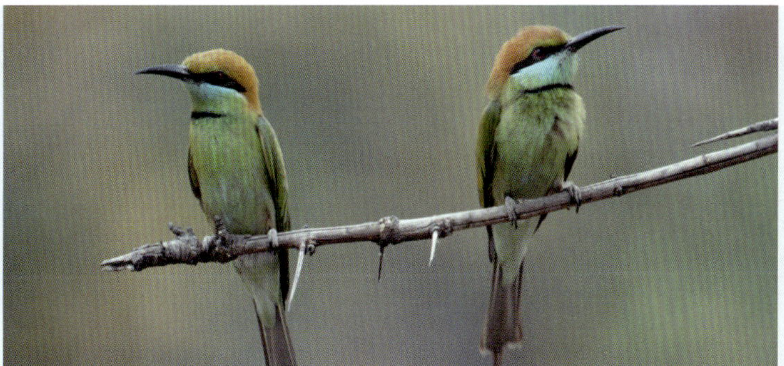

The northern pig-tailed macaques (far left) were named for their slightly curled tail. Another inhabitant from southern Asia, a typical forest dweller, is the sambar deer. Left: the beautiful green bee-eater.

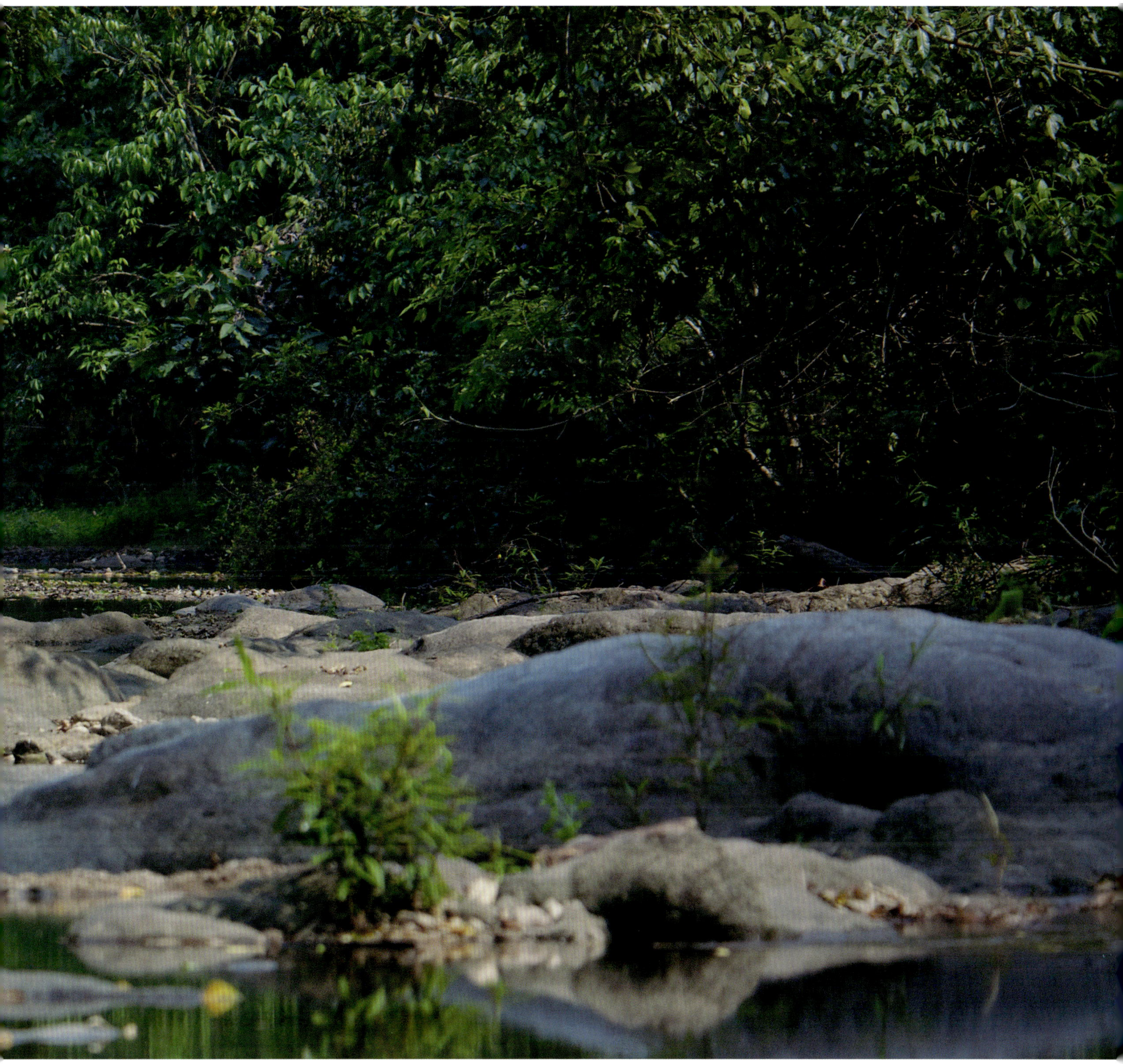

DONG PHAYAYEN–KHAO YAI FOREST AREA

Date of inscription: 2005

The huge tropical forest of Dong Phayayen–Khao Yai covers more than 6,000 sq. km (2,300 sq. miles) and constitutes an ecologically valuable refuge for endangered mammals, birds, and reptiles.

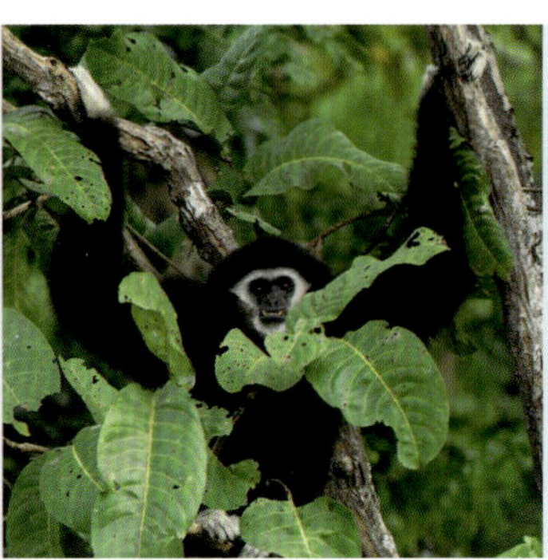

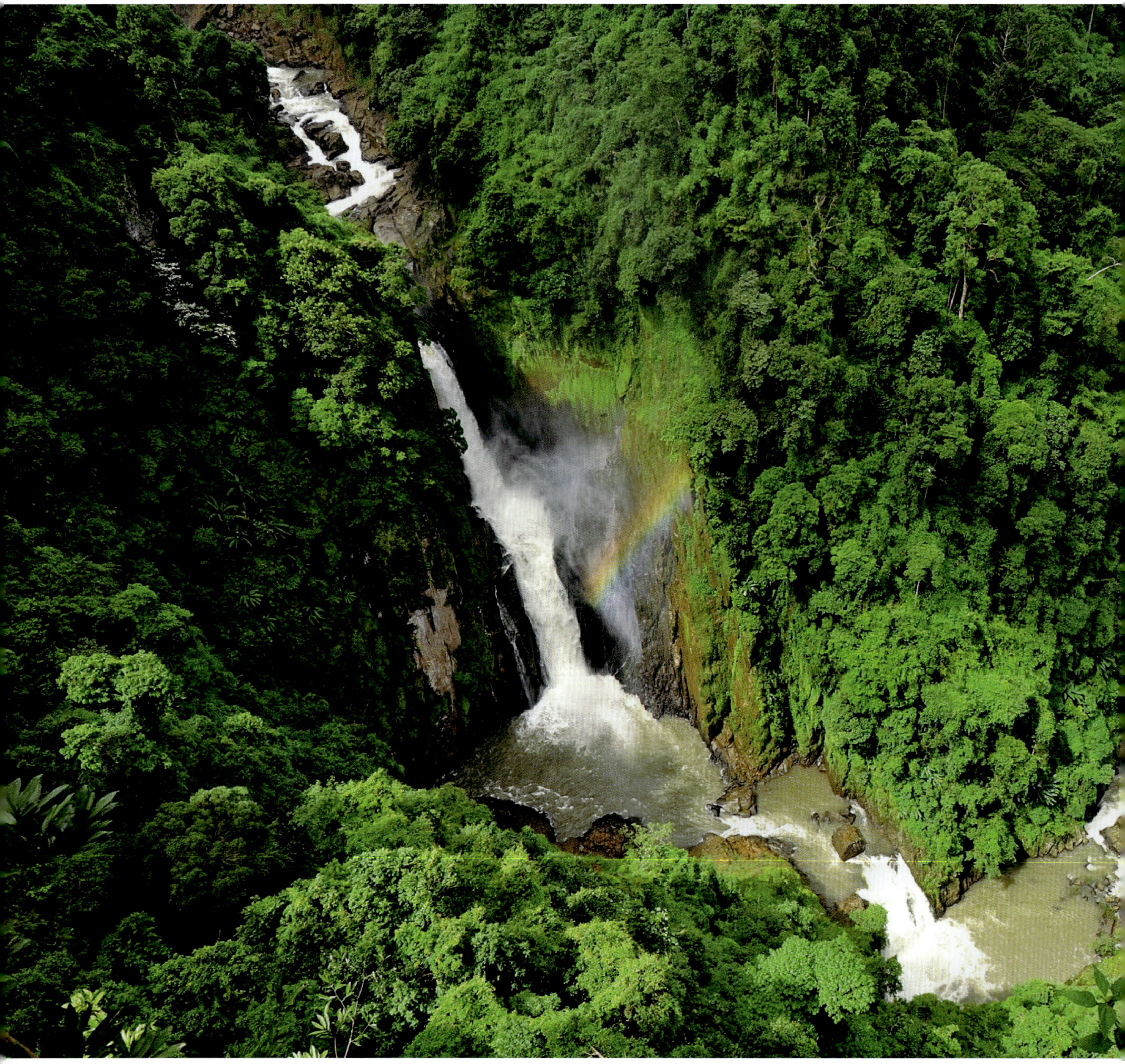

This forest area lies in the rough hill and mountain landscape that rises 100 to 1,350 m (330 to 4,430 feet) above sea level, and extends from the southern part of the Khorat plateau to the Cambodian border. It comprises the four national parks, Khao Yai, Thap Lan, Pang Sida, and Ta Phraya, and the Dong Yai Wildlife Reserve. There are several vegetation zones, ranging from rainforest to bush and grassland, in which 800 animal species flourish. The average annual rainfall varies between 3,000 mm (120 inches) in the west (the Khao Yai National Park) and 1,000 mm (40 inches) in the east (Ta Phraya National Park). Most of the rainfall comes during the monsoon season, which lasts from May to October. During the long dry season that starts in November, the evergreen forests remain sufficiently damp, but the mixed deciduous forest further to the east tends to dry out. There are extensive bamboo forests in Pang Sida.

In the Dong Phayayen–Khao Yai region there are almost 400 types of birds, including endangered species such as copper doves, maroon orioles, green peafowl, and the masked fin-foot. Among the world's most endangered mammals are the Indian elephant – Khao Yai has the largest herd, with 200 elephants – and various wild cat species. These include Bengal cats, clouded leopards, tigers and their relations, marbled cats (which, although related to tigers, are no bigger than domestic cats), and Asiatic gold cats, the latter being practically extinct everywhere else due to the destruction of the rainforest. This forest area is also a refuge for bear macaques and capped gibbons, as well as Malaysian bears, Asian wild dogs, and large spotted civets. In addition, there are wild cattle species such as the banteng, serow, and gaur, and the hairy-nosed otter, as well as more than 2,000 reptile and amphibian species.

The animals in the forests all have a unique feature – they are particularly fast or big or extraordinarily beautiful: gibbons (below, top) or white-handed gibbons (left); gaur, one of the largest bovines (below, centre) and pretty-as-a-picture clouded leopard (below, bottom). Large picture: Hewnarok Waterfall.

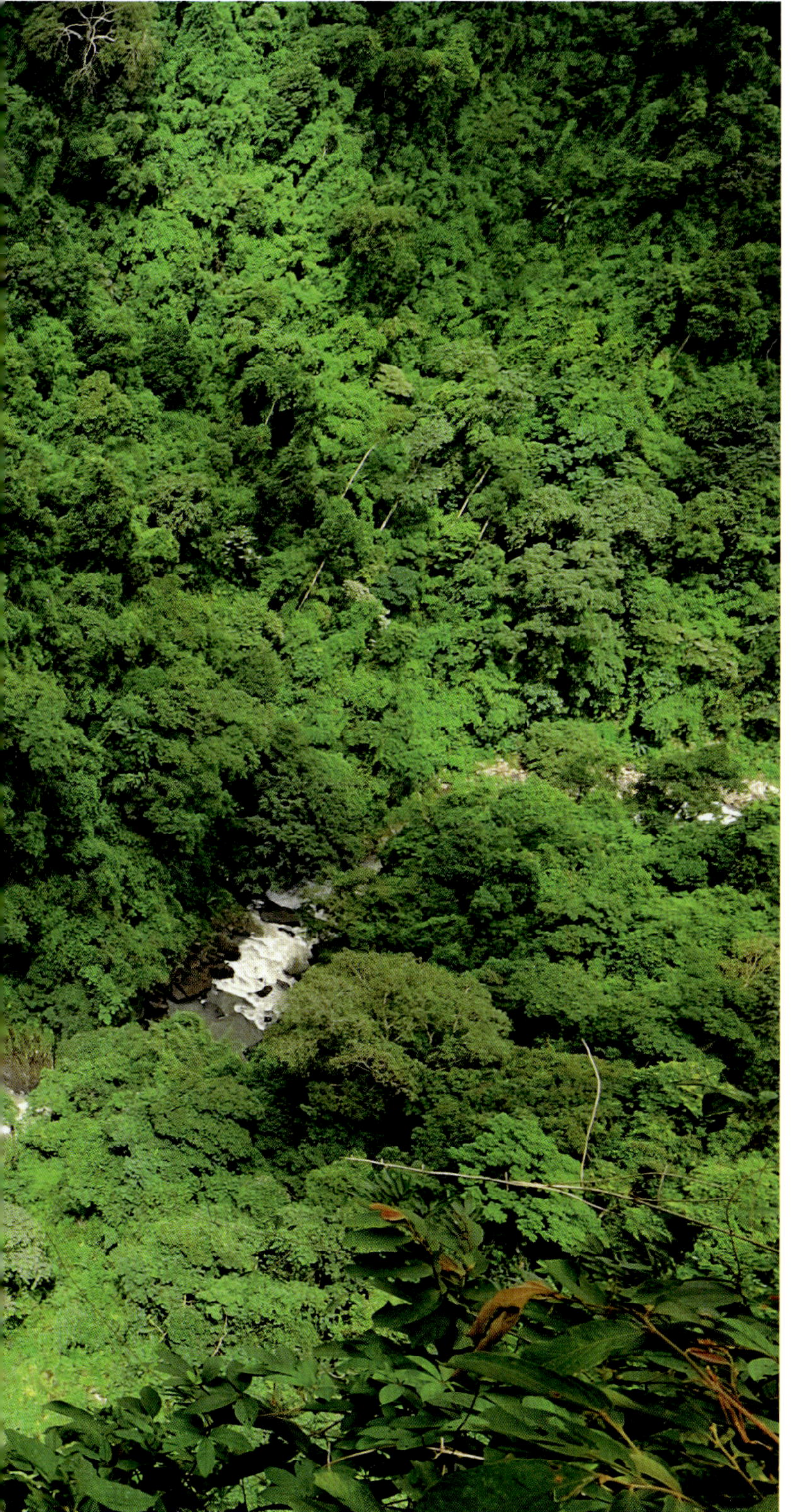

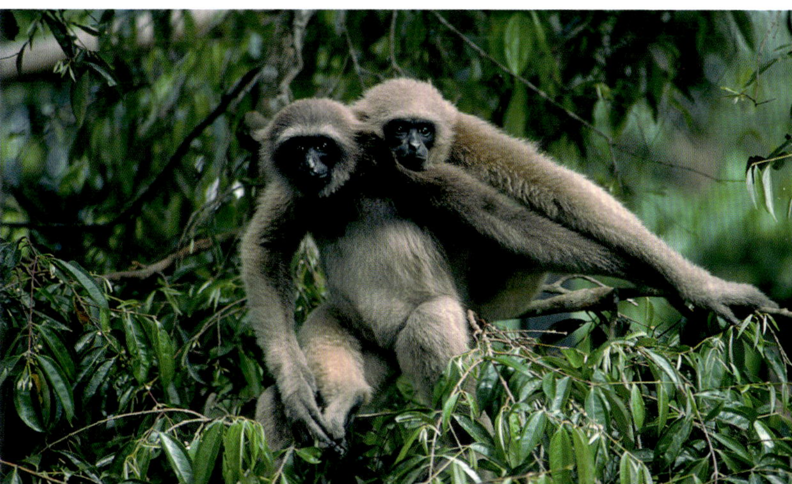

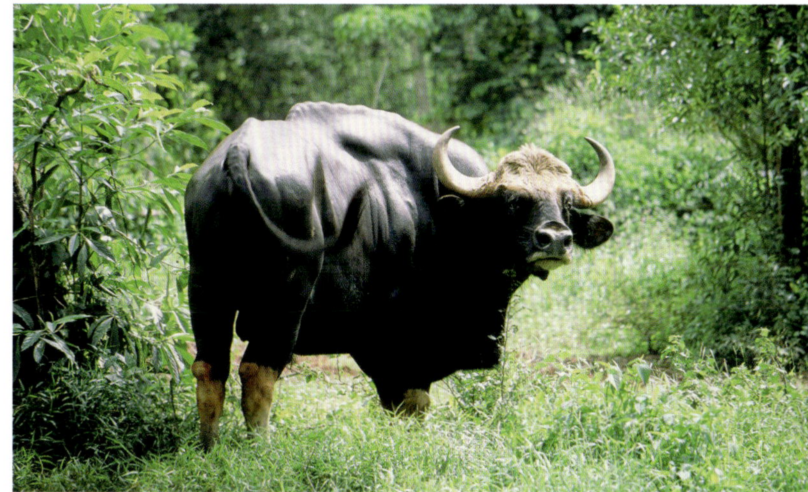

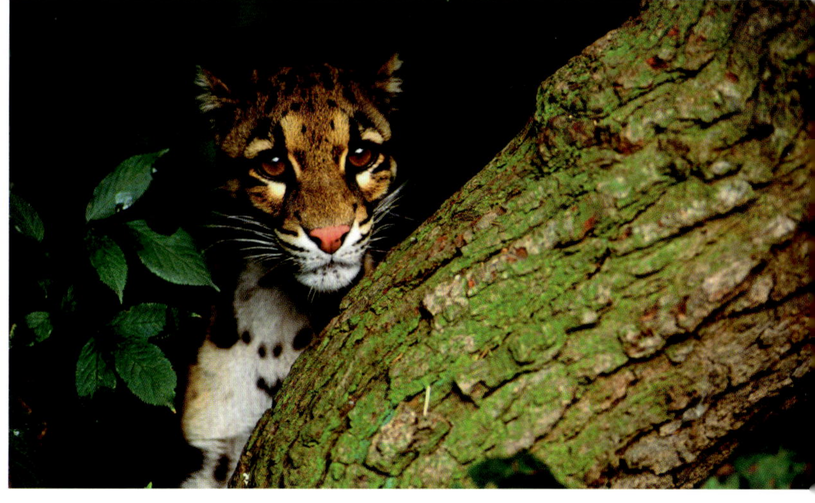

TRANGAN LANDSCAPE COMPLEX

Date of inscription: 2014

Located south of Hanoi in the Red River Delta (Song Hong), Trang An is a karst landscape with numerous caves, where archaeological traces bear testimony to almost 30,000 years old human activity. The complex is a World Natural and Cultural Heritage site.

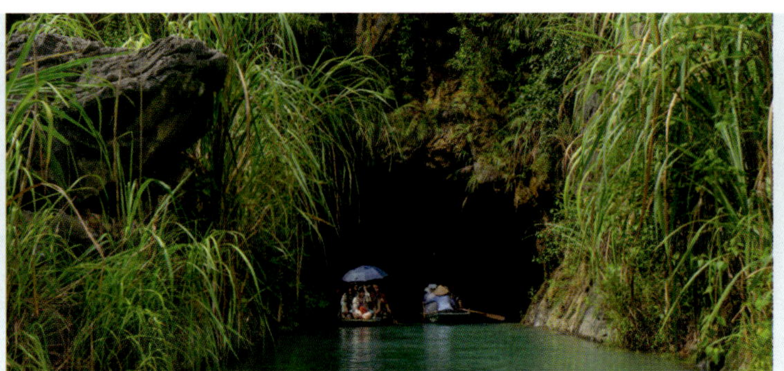

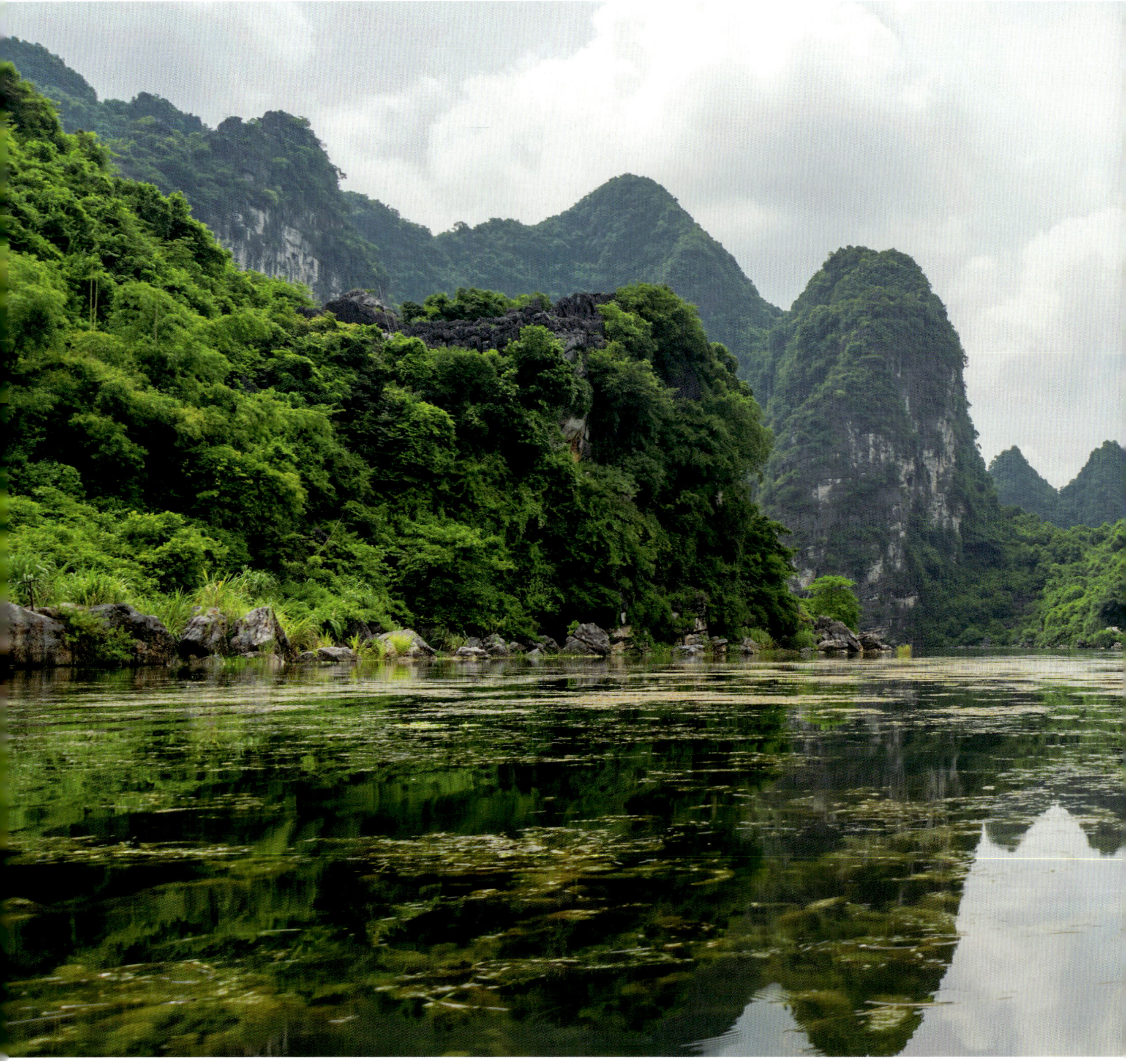

The first of now nine Vietnamese World Heritage sites, the landscape complex of Trang An is listed as both a natural and a cultural heritage site. The protected area covers just 72 sq km (28 sq miles) in Ninh Binh Province, whose capital city of the same name, located about 90 km (56 miles) south-east of Hanoi, is a good starting point for exploring the region. Its biggest attractions are the up to 200-m- (656-ft-) tall karst rocks, numerous caves and grottos in the dry Halong Bay, in Tam Coc ("three caves") and in Hoa Lu. The latter is also the name of a royal city (10th/11th centuries), which is also a World Heritage site; however, only the foundations of the palace remain.

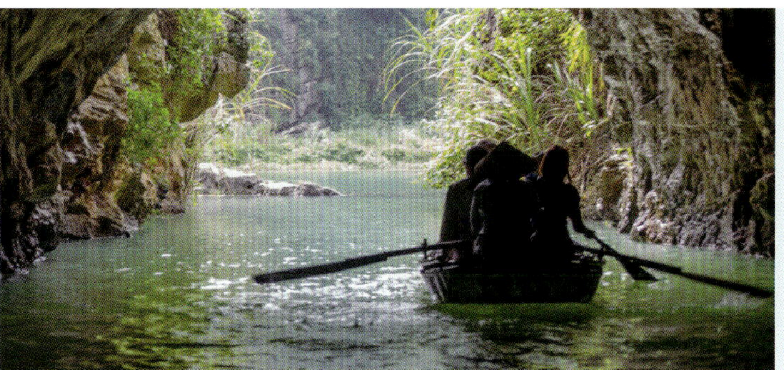

Ideally, you should explore the spectacular karst landscape from the water, on one of the two- to three-hour boat tours offered in Nihn Binh, which take you through some very narrow caves in shallow barges.

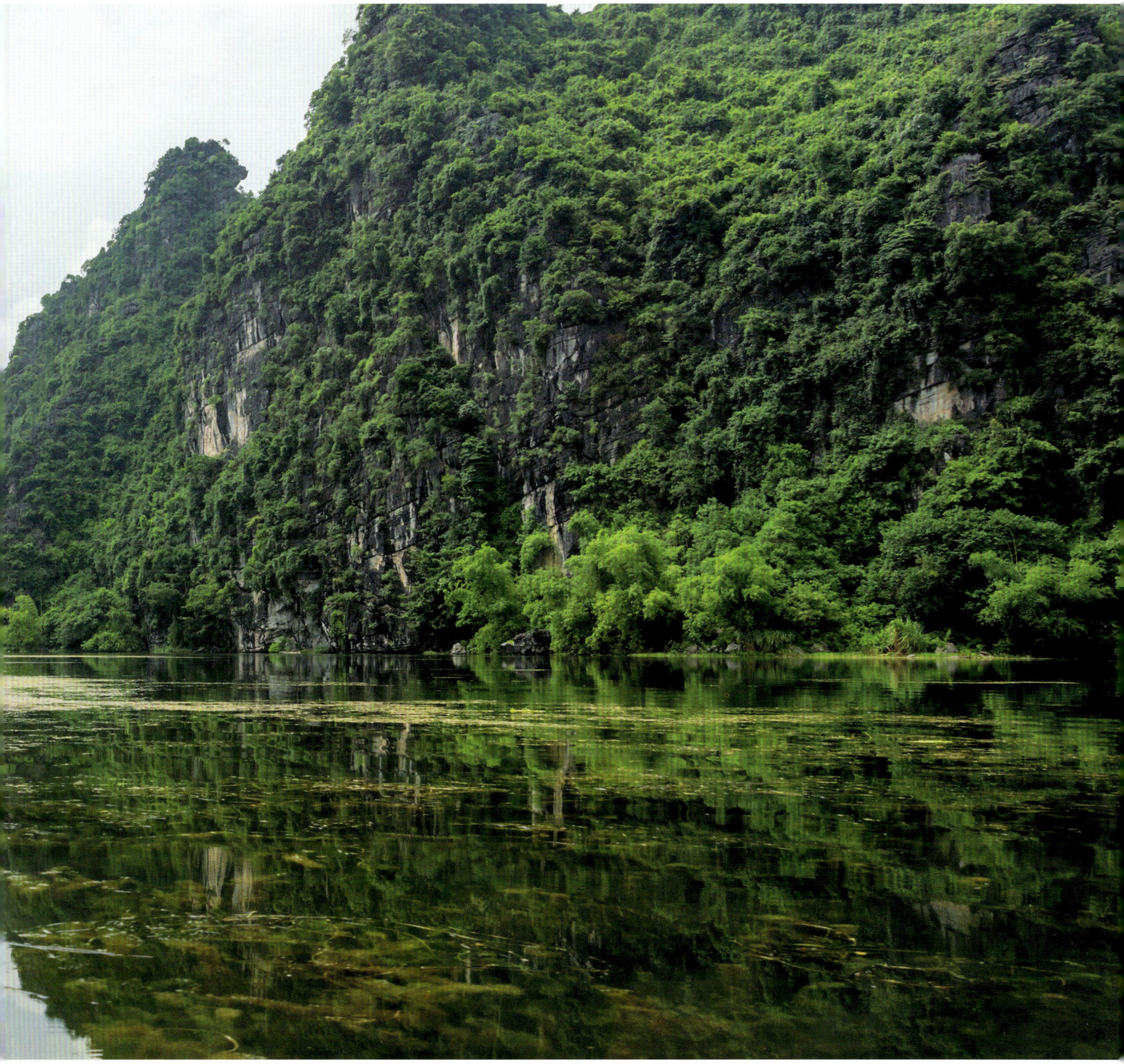

HALONG BAY

Date of inscription: 1994
Extended 2000

Situated in the Gulf of Tonkin in North Vietnam, this island landscape with its bizarre shapes contains about 2,000 limestone islets and cliffs. Wind, weather, and time have conspired to create this dramatic natural artwork.

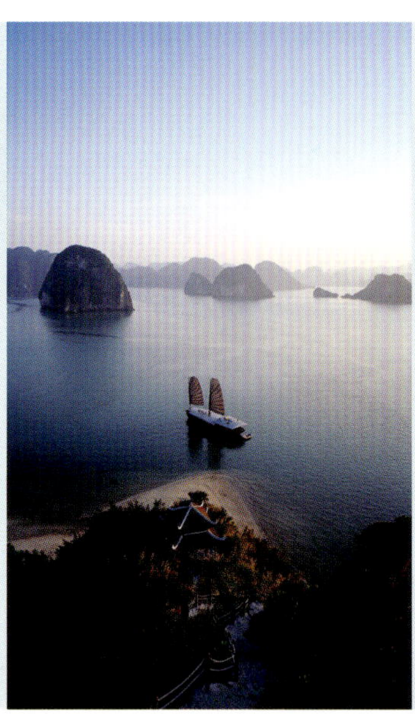

Halong bay contains dense clusters of limestone karsts that rise out of the water, achieving heights of up to 100 m (330 feet), and are reminiscent of Chinese landscape paintings. The cliffs and mountains present an extraordinary variety of shapes: the range extends from broad-based pyramids to high overarching "elephant backs" and slim needles.

The inhabitants regard this island landscape as the result of mythical events rather than as a natural phenomenon. A dragon (Ha Long, hence the name) is supposed to have fallen from the mountains, or out of the sky, and to have created this natural wonder when he destroyed an invading army with great blows from his mighty tail – or maybe he was simply giving vent to his rage at being disturbed? The channels and gorges thus created were flooded with water when the dragon dived into the sea. The geological facts are rather less dramatic: after the last ice age, the thick limestone layer along this part of the coast sank and was covered with water. These bizarre forms are the result of erosion.

Dong Thien Cung (large picture) is a fantastic stalactite cave, in translation it means something like "cave of the heavenly palace". The bay can be explored by boat (left).

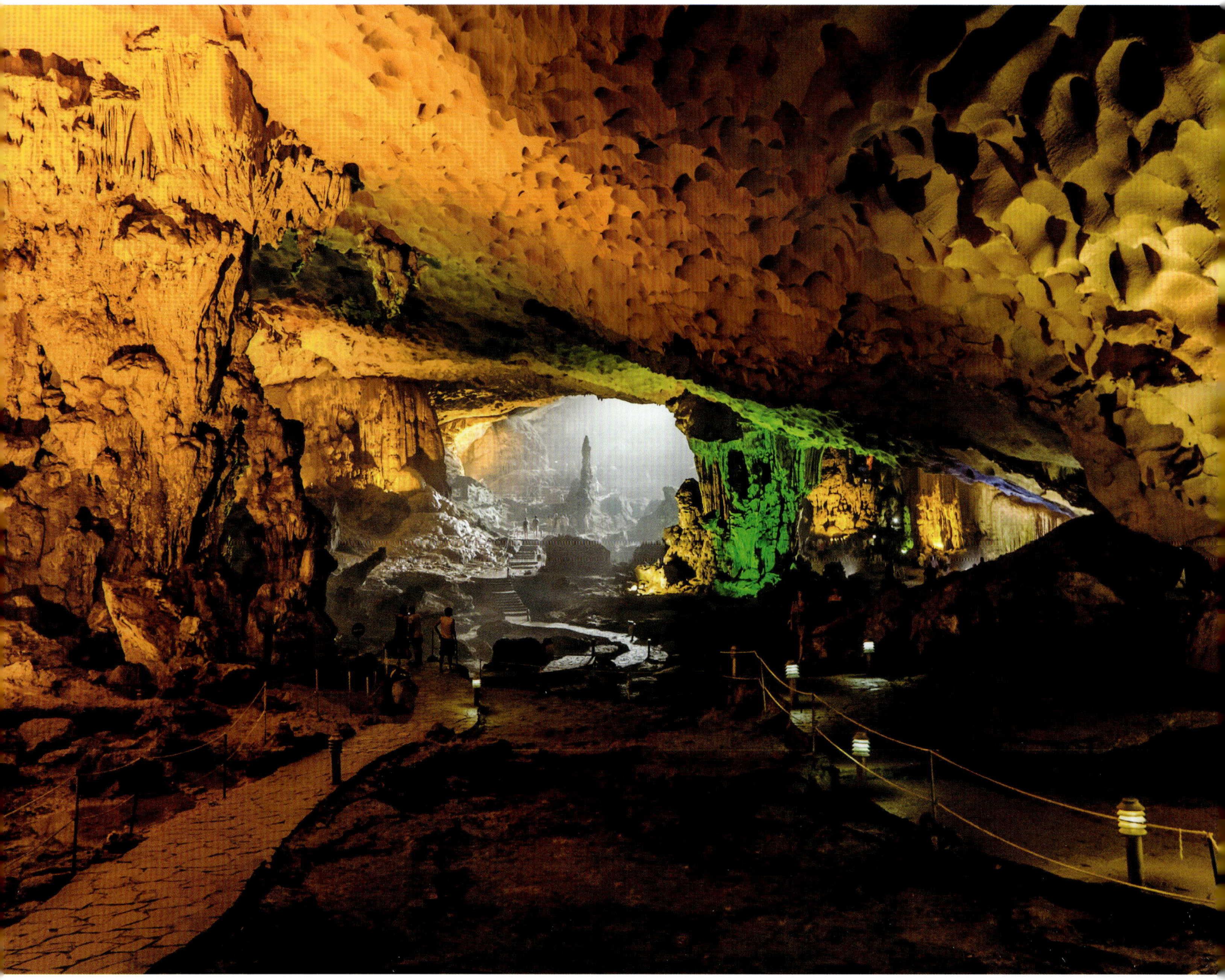

PHONG NHA-KE BANG NATIONAL PARK

Phong Nha Cave has given its name to this nature reserve in the Minh Hoa province of north-central Vietnam, which is largely covered in tropical rainforest; it is, after all, the country's largest and most beautiful cave. The name means "Cave of the Teeth," a reference to the numerous stalactite and stalagmite formations inside it. The Cham people, who ruled central Vietnam in the first century, erected Buddhist shrines in some of these caves, and remnants of these can still be seen today. Thecaverns are especially illuminating with regard to geomorphology, revealing more than 400 million years of the earth's history. The latest research has established that there are 14 endemic species of flora in the national park. In addition, nearly 400 animal species enjoy a protected existence here. Among the 113 different kinds of mammals are many threatened species, especially monkeys. As late as the 1990s, the Vu Quang ox or saola (Pseudoryx nghetinhensis), was discovered, as was the giant muntjac (Megamuntiacus vuquangensis), a species belonging to the deer family that only lives in the jungle in south and south-east Asia.

The main habitat of the Hatinh langurs (right) focuses on central Vietnam. The moss frog is a clever camouflage artist (below).

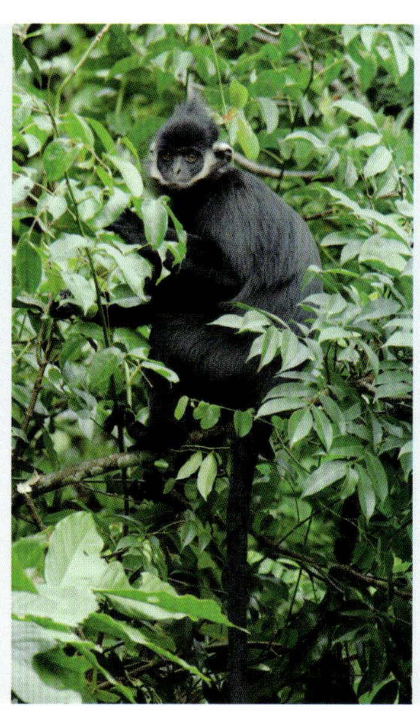

Date of inscription: 2003
Extended: 2015

The central feature of the national park is a tropical karst region, which exhibits very varied geological features, and is the oldest such region in Asia. It contains a multitude of caves and underground rivers, extending over a distance of 65 km (40 miles). Due to the biological progress made in the development of flora and fauna, the national park was extended in 2015 and nominated for a second time.

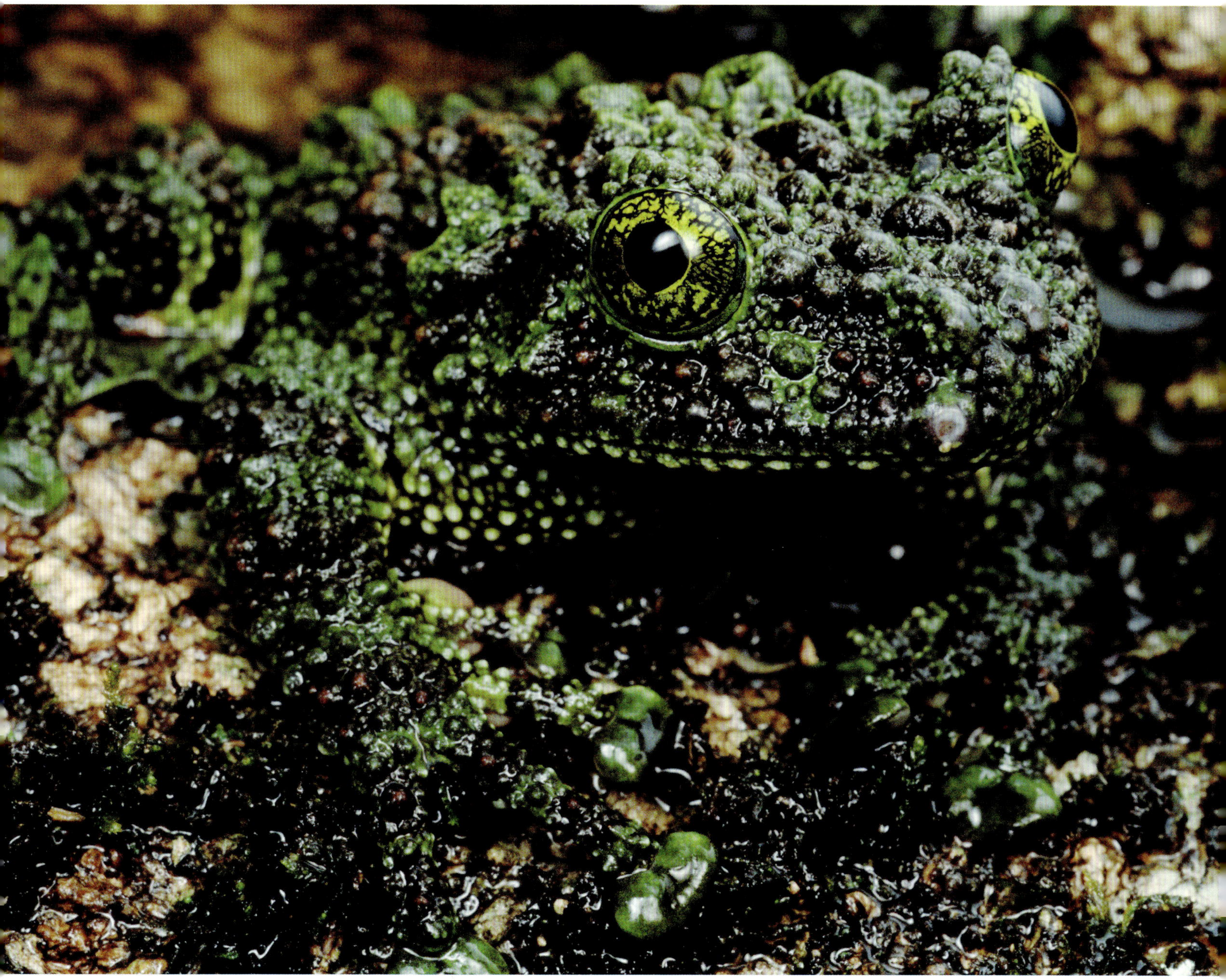

MOUNT HAMIGUITAN

Date of inscription: 2014

Located in one of the most remote parts of the Philippines, this reserve is of major importance as a refuge for endangered and rare species, such as the critically endangered Philippine eagle.

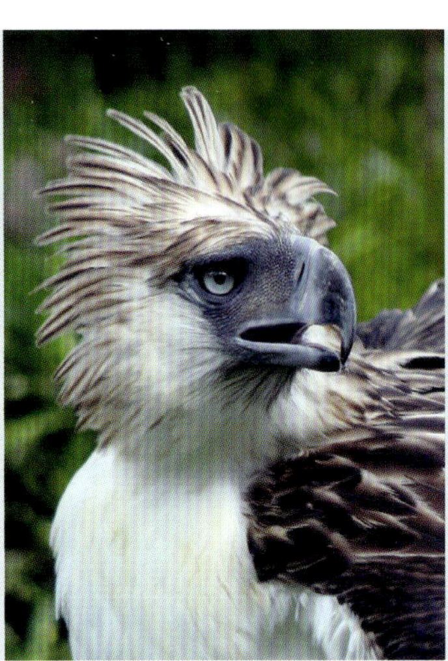

The 1,620-m (5,315-ft-) high Mount Hamiguitan dominates the Davao Oriental province on the island of Mindanao. The surrounding mountains form a watershed between the Gulf of Davao and the Philippine Sea, a marginal sea of the Pacific Ocean. Now a World Natural Heritage site, the around 160 sq km (62 sq miles) area owes its great biological diversity (biodiversity) to its geographical isolation. Thus, a largely endemic flora and fauna were able to evolve in the area, first designated a wildlife reserve in July 2004. The hillsides of Hamiguitan are famous for their tropical dwarf tree forest, in part over 100 years old, and for rare species of carnivorous pitcher plants, to be found only in the highlands of Mindanao. Scientists suspect that the area is home to a number of other, hitherto undiscovered endemic species.

The Philippine eagle is a powerful bird of prey with a high, narrow beak and a crest, which he can raise. The preservation of forests is important for the bird's survival.

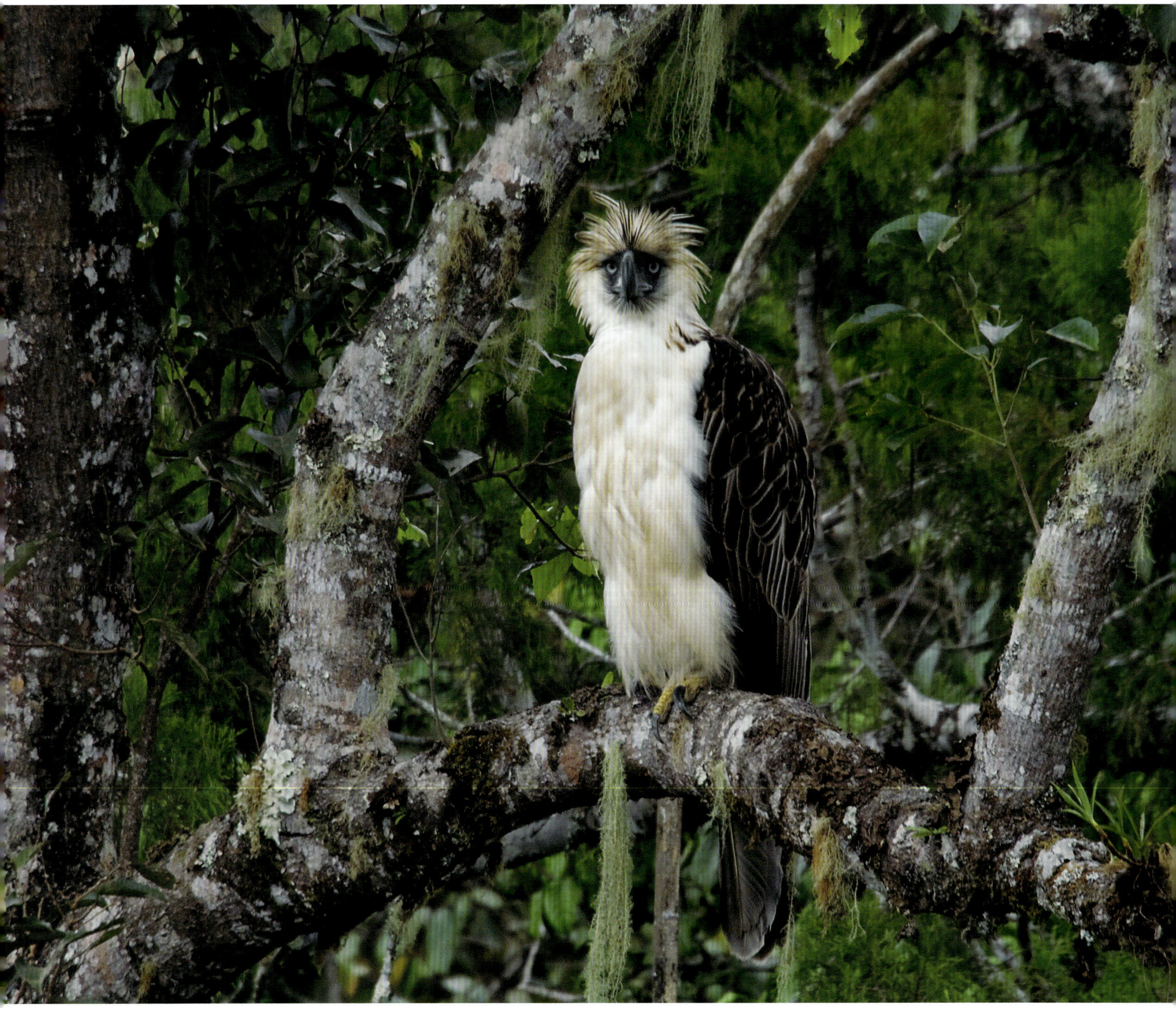

PUERTO PRINCESA SUBTERRANEAN RIVER NATIONAL PARK

This national park is situated about 80 km (50 miles) to the north-west of Puerto Princesa, the capital of the island of Palawan. Its most impressive features are the limestone formations in the St Paul mountain range. Mount St Paul rises to a height of 1,027 m (3,369 feet) and is the highest peak in a chain of rounded limestone mountains that runs from north to south.

The main geological attraction here is an underground river, which flows for a distance of about 8 km (5 miles) – more than 4 km (2.5 miles) are navigable – and in the process has hollowed out a sequence of enormous caves. These caverns can rise to heights of 60 m (200 feet) and they are filled with huge, strangely shaped stalagmites and stalactites, which also feature in the smaller caves. This cave-system terminates in a large grotto, where daylight can enter.

The underground river rises about 2 km south-west of Mount St Paul, and then, having followed an almost entirely subterranean route, emerges into the light of day in St Paul's Bay. Visitors can visit the caves on boats..

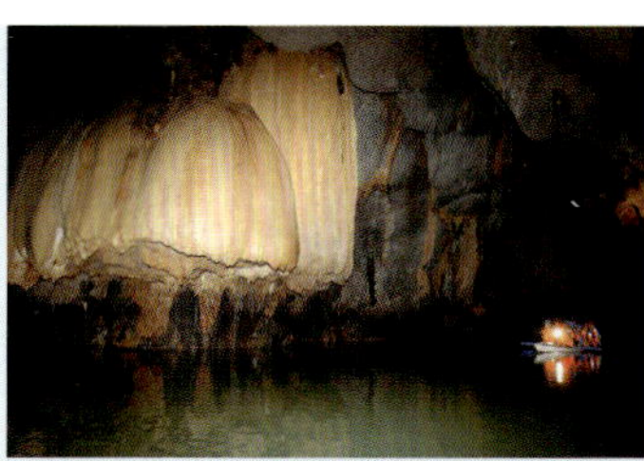

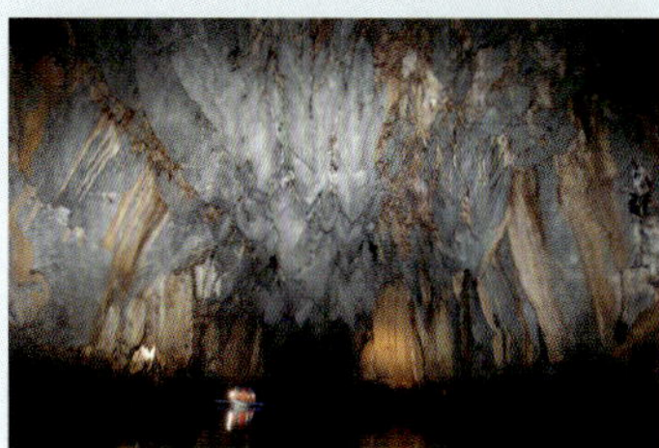

Date of inscription: 1999

The main attraction of this national park with its tropical karst landscape is the navigable subterranean river, the longest in the world.

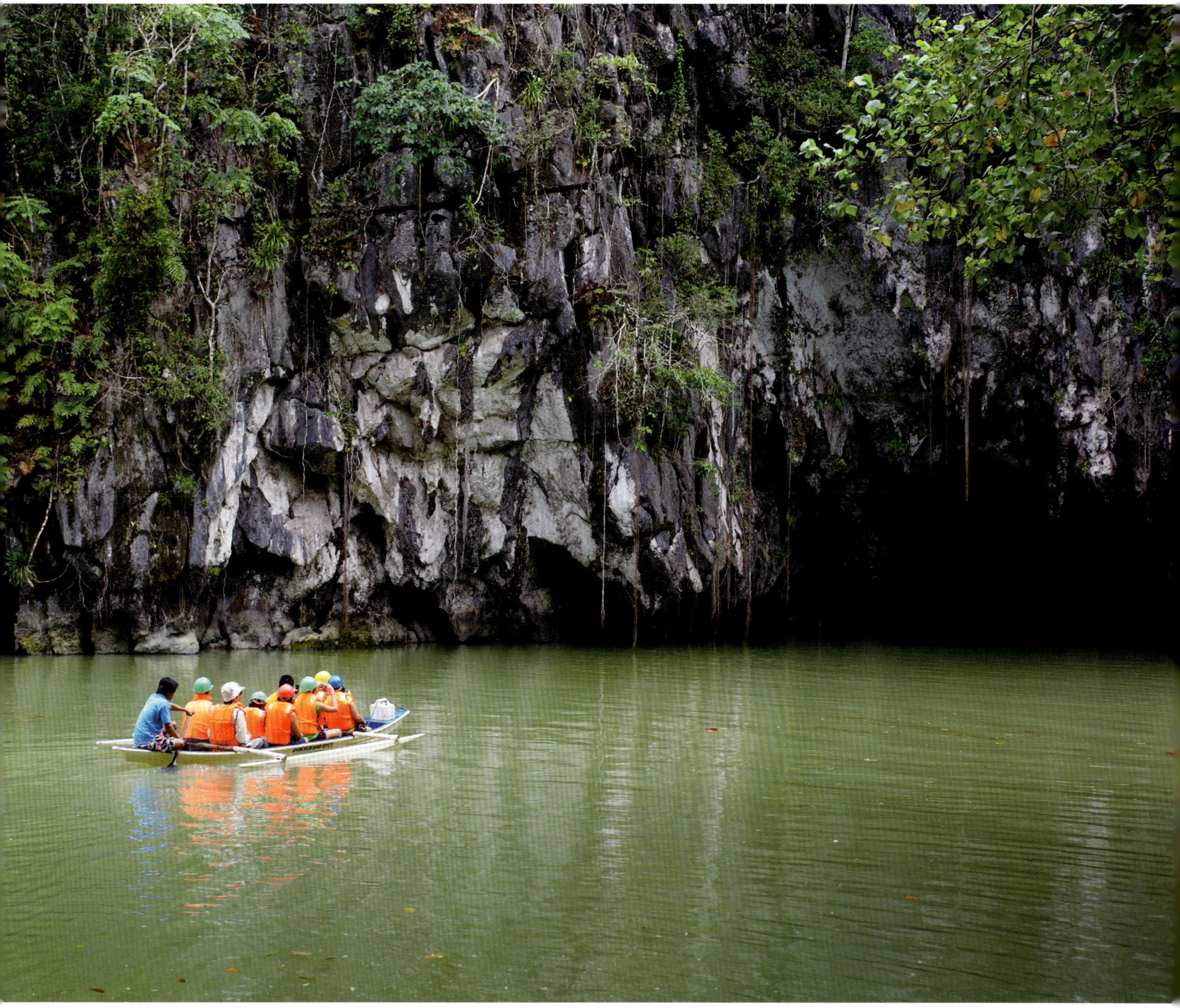

TUBBATAHA REEF MARINE PARK

Date of inscription: 1993
Extension: 2009

This maritime national park in the middle of the Sulu Sea consists of two ring-shaped atolls, which are famous for their extensive coral reefs and fascinating underwater world.

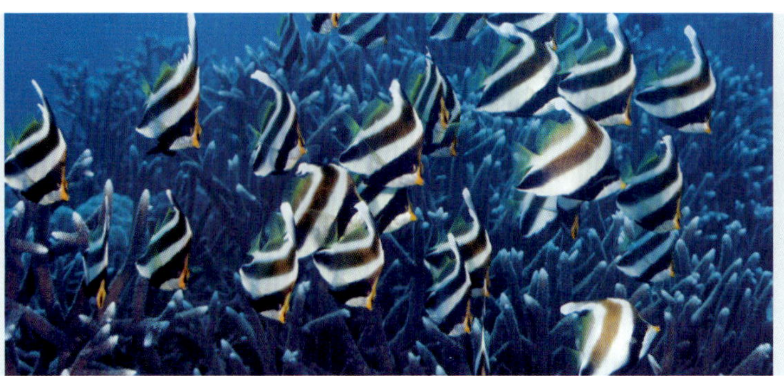

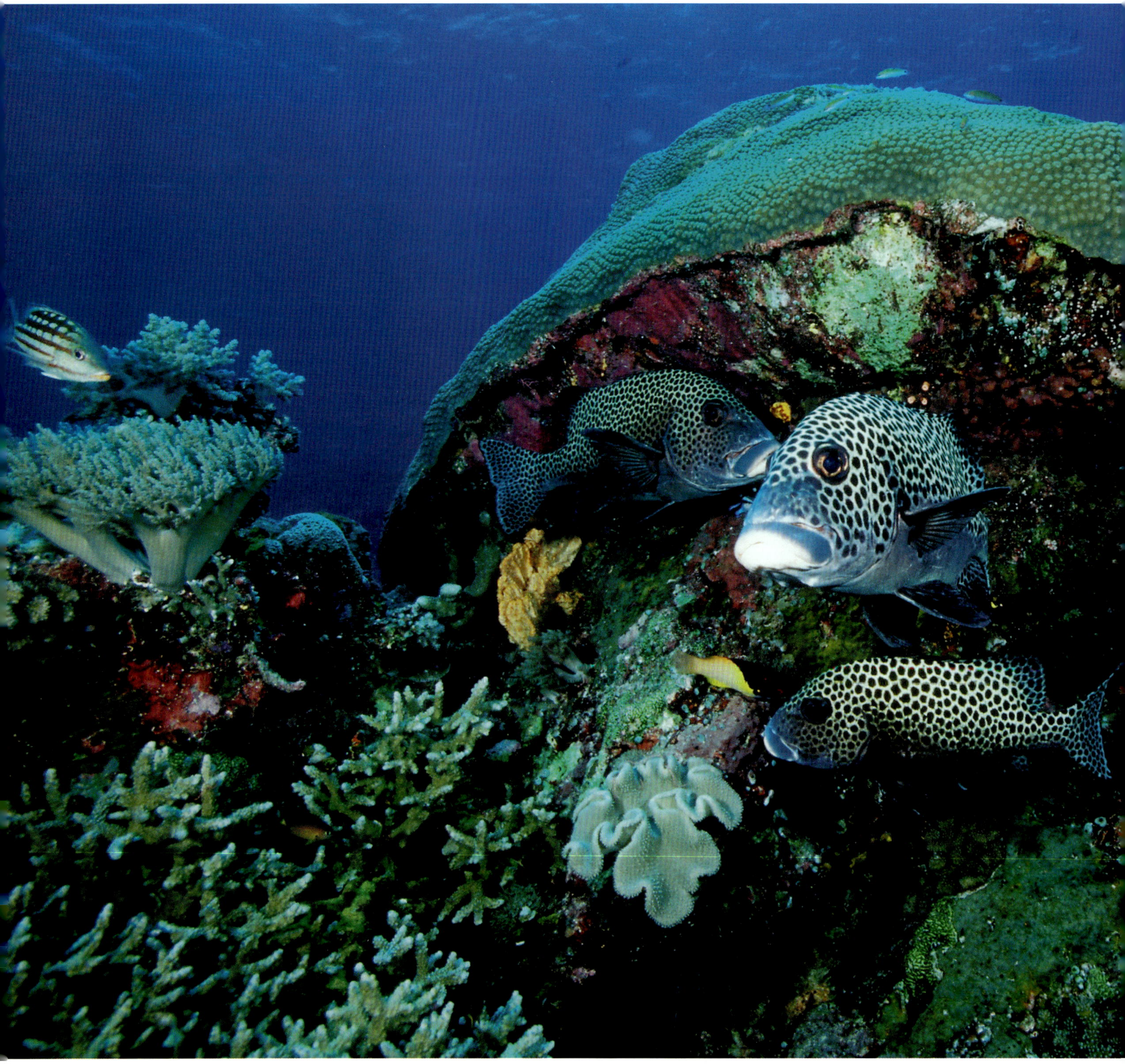

About 180 km from the south coast of Palawan Island lie two small atolls, which represent the central point of this marine park. These atolls are very hard to reach; they stand only 1 m above sea level, and thus offer an almost undisturbed habitat for a great number of creatures. For instance, they are home to the now rare hawksbill and green turtles, as well as all kinds of swallows and boobies, and numerous corals – there are more than 40 kinds. The larger northern reef is also known as "Bird Island," and forms an oval approximately 16 km long and 4.5 km wide, surrounding a lagoon of coral sand, and thus providing an ideally sheltered nesting site for birds. The southern atoll is the smaller of the two, and they are separated by 8 km of sea.

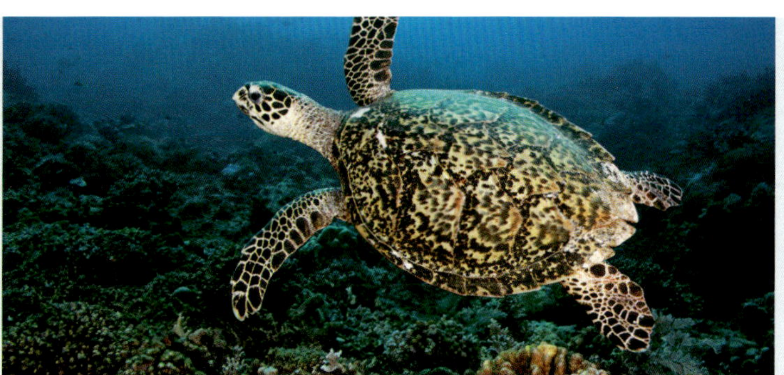

With about 380 species of fish of at least 40 genera, this park contains an even more diverse underwater world.

A kaleidoscope of fascinating underwater creatures awaits divers in the marine park: butterflyfishes (far left), harlequin sweetlips (large picture), hawksbill sea turtle (left), squirrelfish, goatfish and triggerfish (picture series from the top).

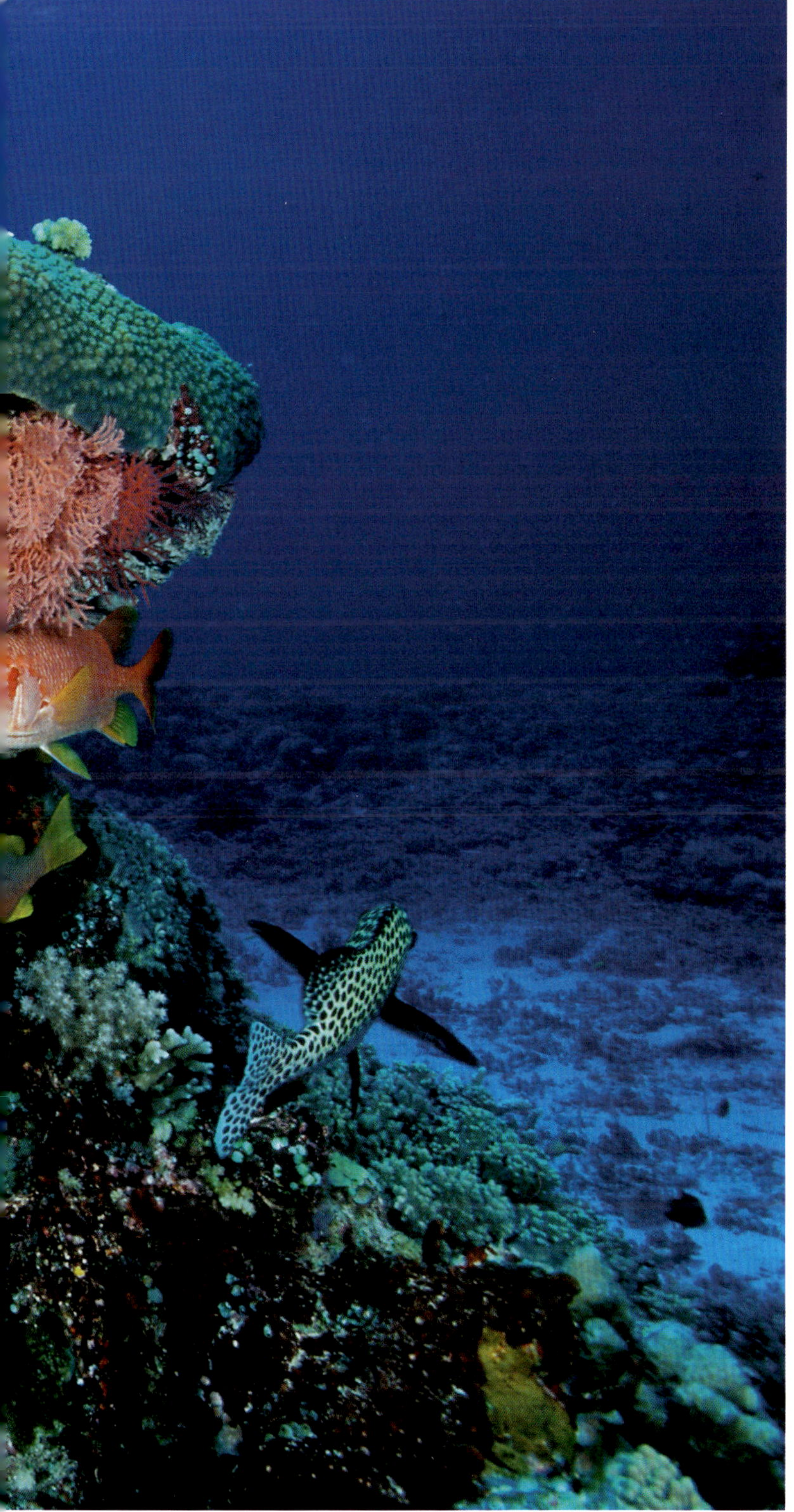

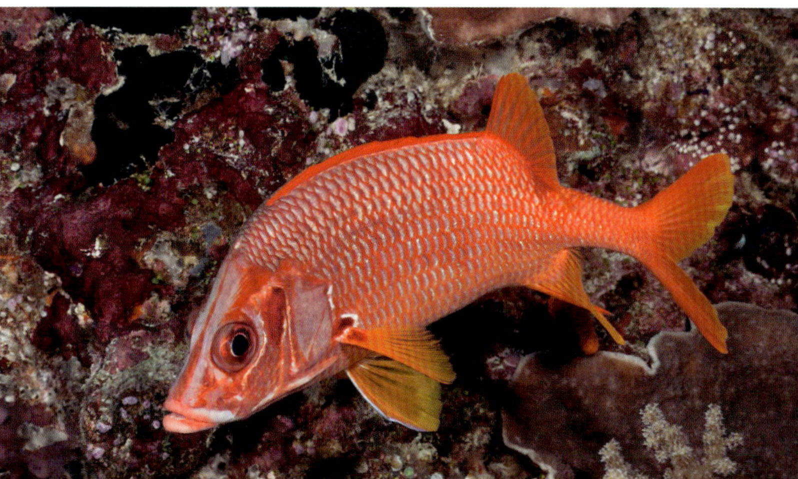

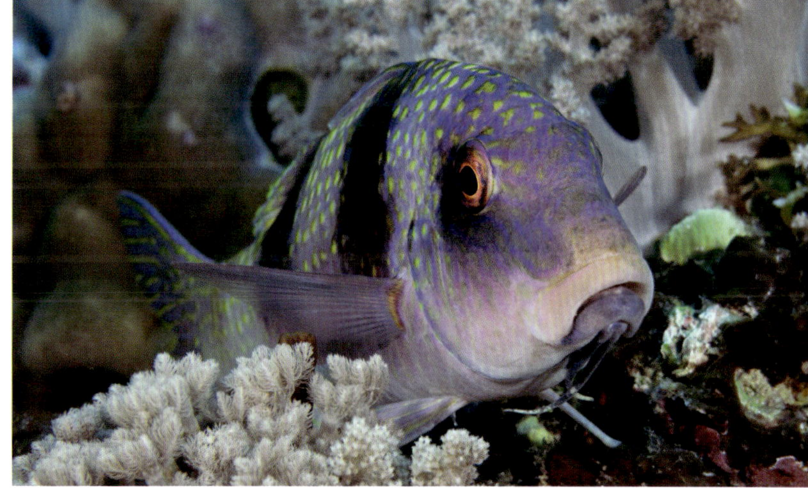

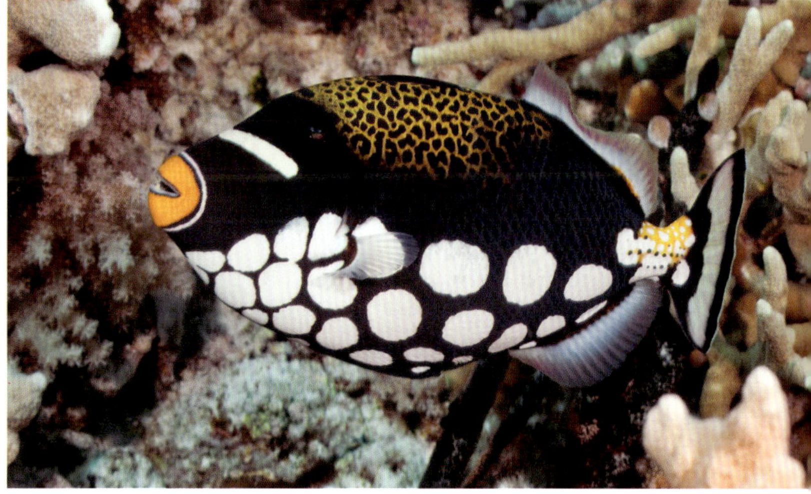

KINABALU NATIONAL PARK

Date of inscription: 2000

Kinabalu National Park is in the Malaysian province of Sabah, at the northern end of the island of Borneo. It is particularly famous for its very ancient flora and its mountain, which is the highest in south-east Asia.

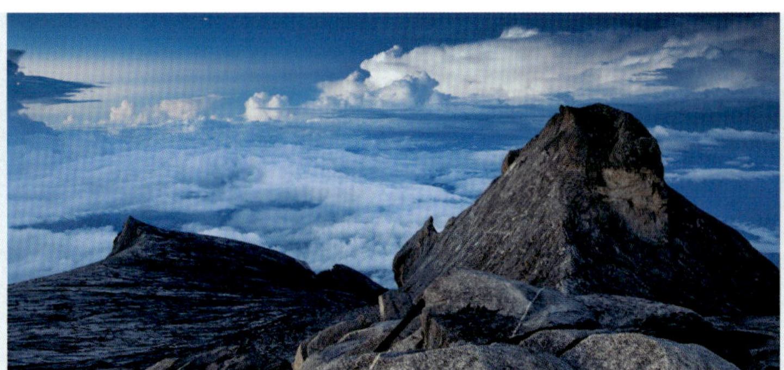

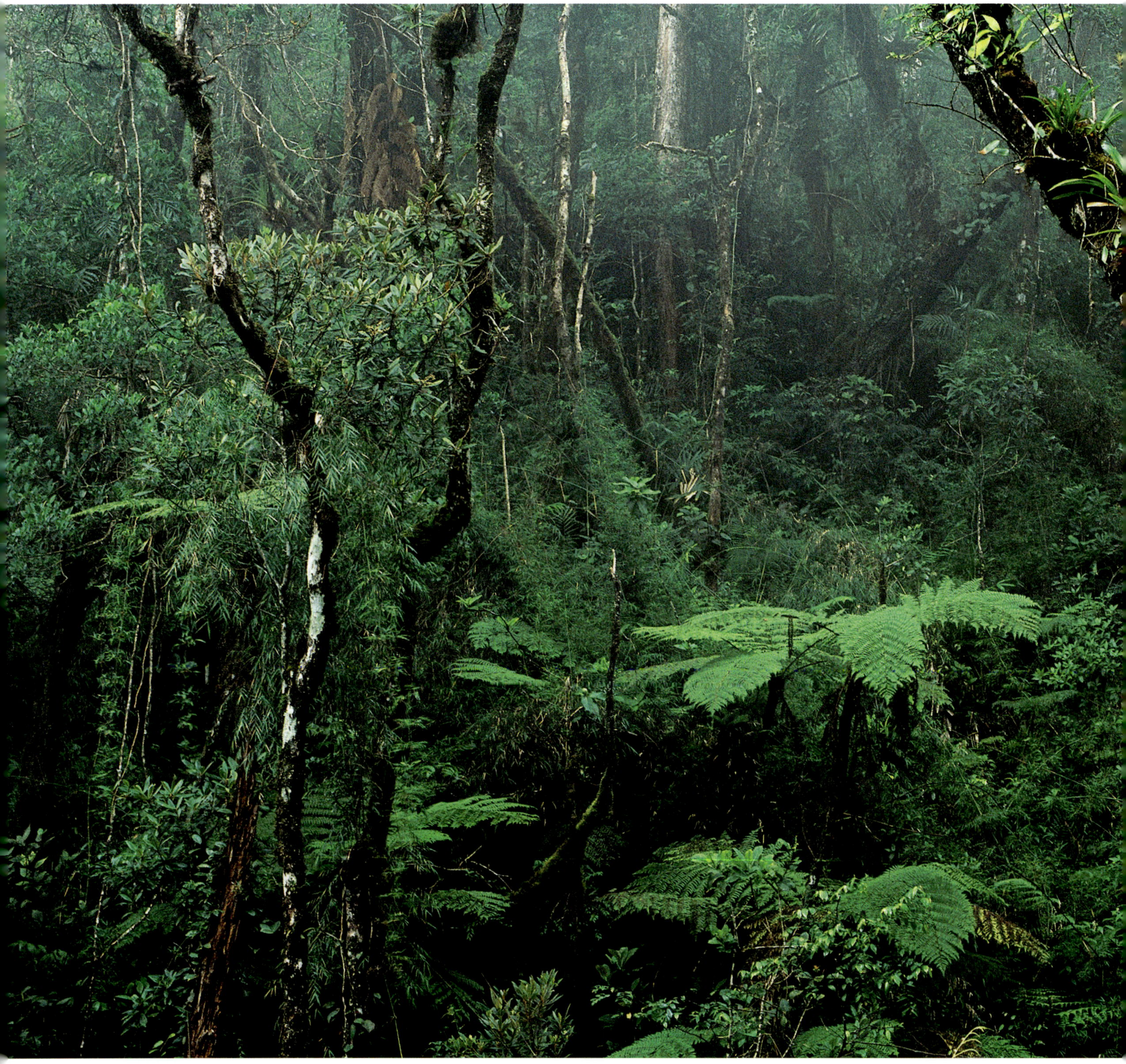

Mount Kinabalu forms an impressive focal point for this park – it is 4,095 m (13,435 feet) high, and is the highest mountain between the Himalayas and New Guinea. This site features a great variety of flora, ranging over very different zones, starting with the topmost alpine region. In the lowest area, the tropical rainforest contains more than 1,200 wild orchid species and many rhododendrons. The flowers vary in hue from the deepest red to pale pinks and whites. Further up, in the highlands, the mountain forests feature 40 different types of oak, their branches draped in mosses and ferns, which then give way to pine woods. Closest to the summit lies an alpine region of meadows and shrubs, along with other forms of dwarf vegetation.

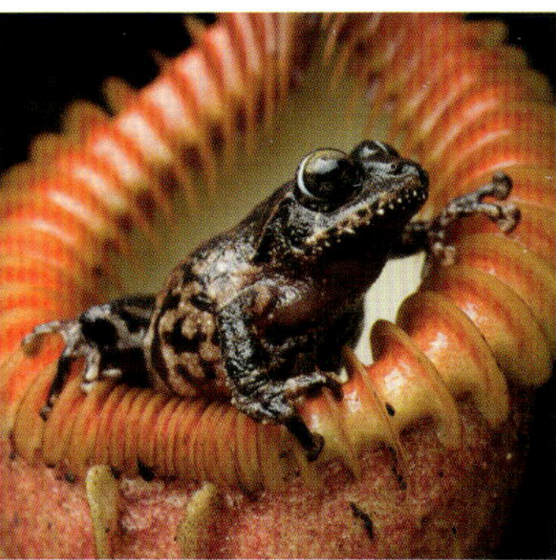

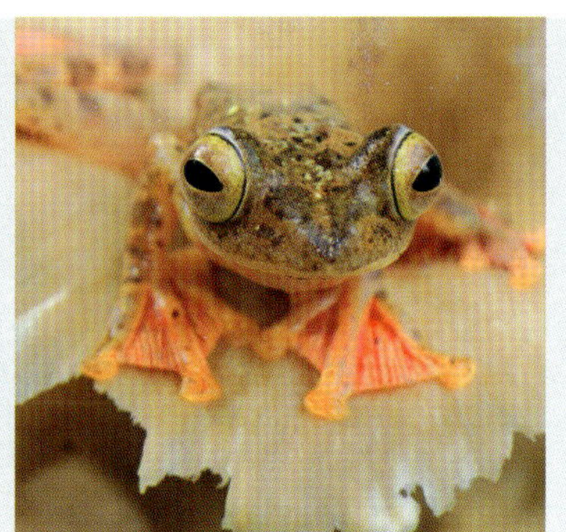

The jagged peak of Mount Kinabalu (far left) in Borneo looms over the Kinabalu National Park, and offers a fascinating panorama of the surrounding mountains and lowlying country, with their varied habitats. Lush rainforest (large picture) grows to an altitude of 7,000 m (22,965 foot). Here live tree frogs (left) and grow magnificent rhododendrons and orchids (picture series).

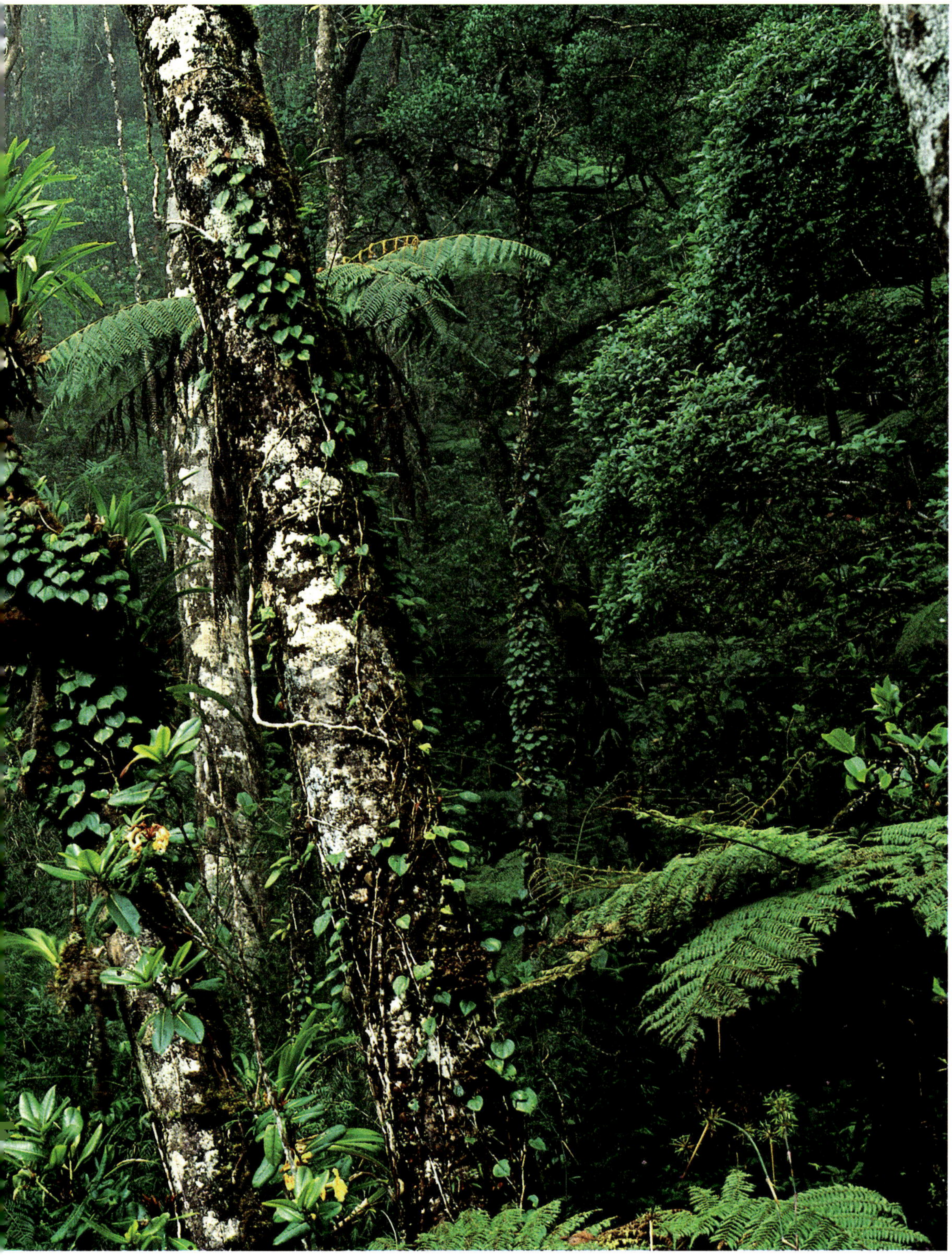

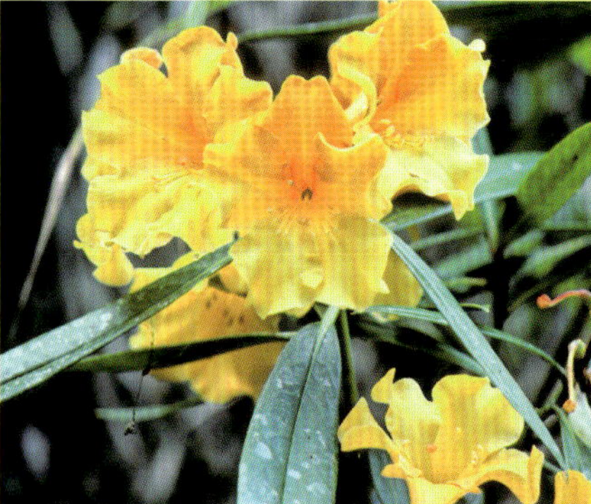

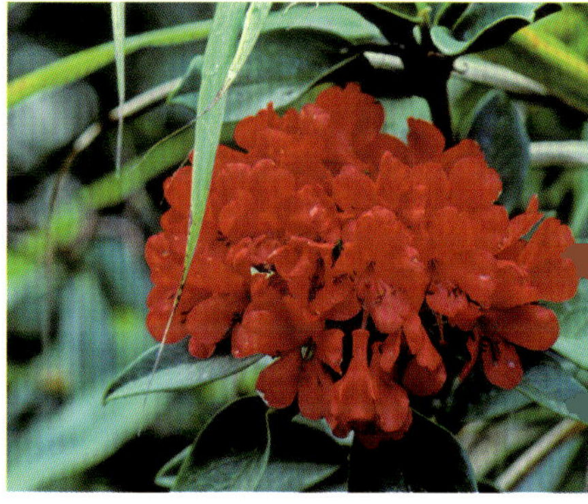

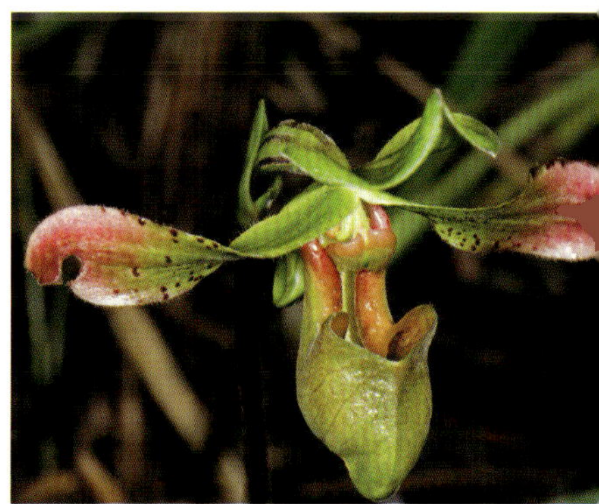

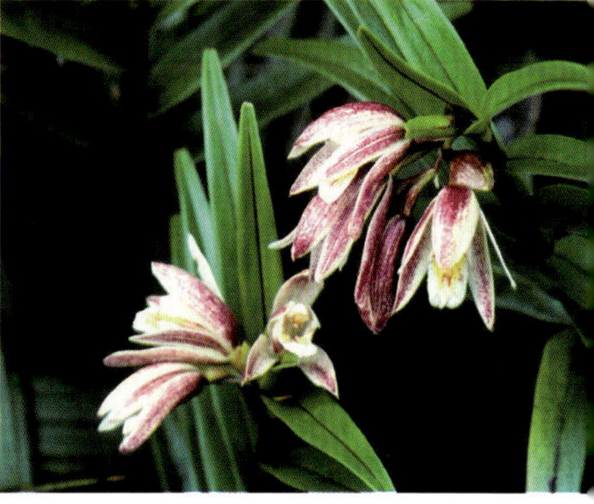

GUNUNG MULU NATIONAL PARK

Date of inscription: 2000

The world's largest complex of caves can be found in the spectacular mountains of the Gunung Mulu National Park in the Malaysian province of Sarawak in Borneo.

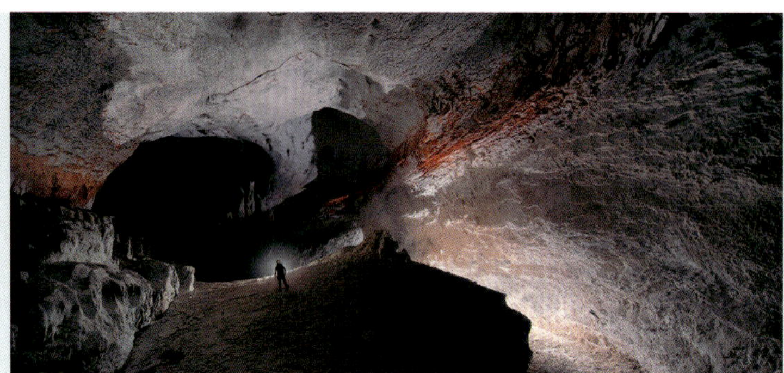

This cavernous landscape first began to emerge some thirty million years ago. Back then, a layer of volcanic rock that had been ground into sand and sediment was covered by the sea. Over millions of years, corals and other marine creatures formed limestone deposits on top of it.
Changes in sea level forced the land to warp, so that mountains such as Gun-

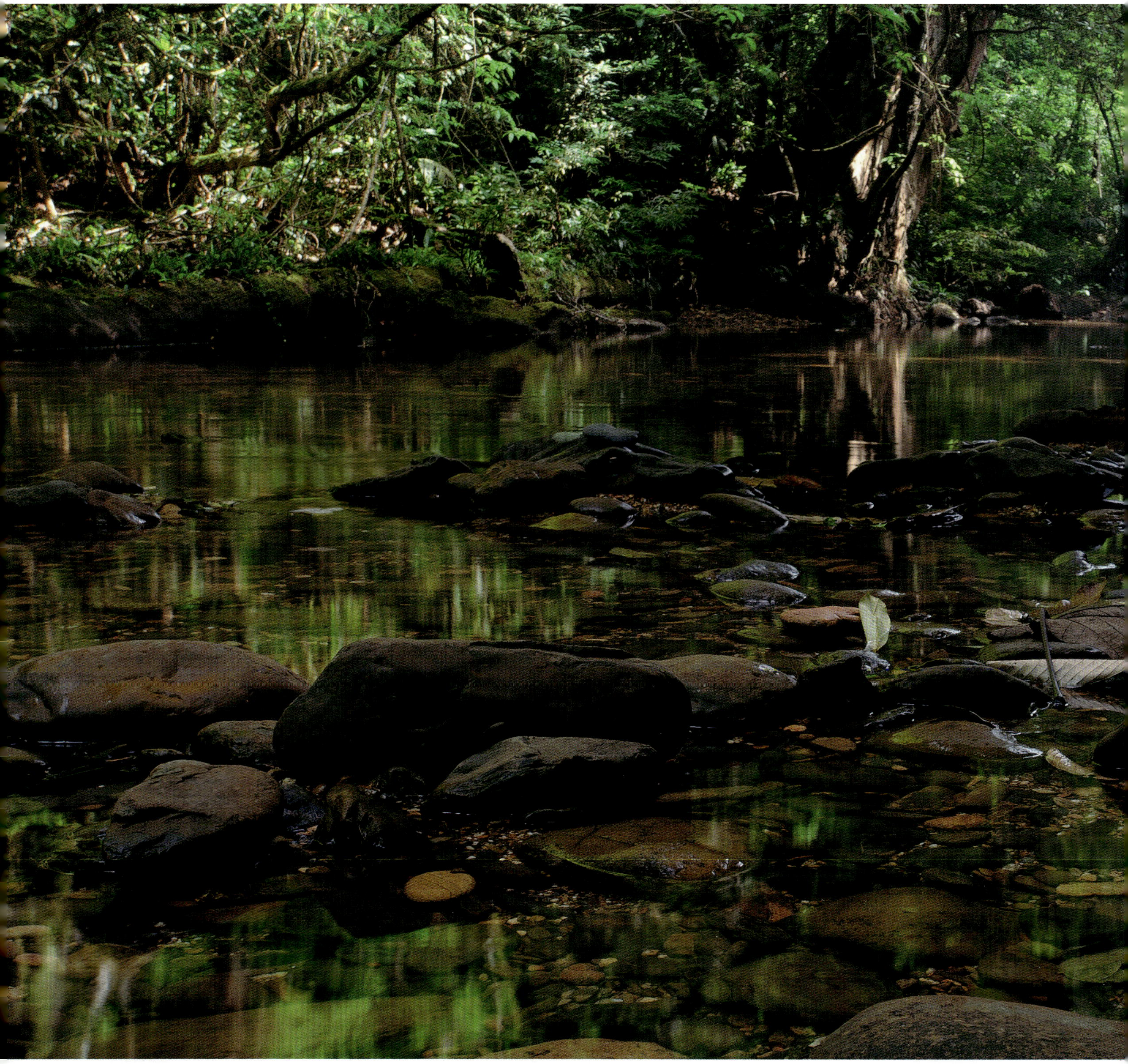

ung Api (1,750 m; 5,741 feet), consisting of extremely pure limestone, rose up next to the sandstone. The latter can be found on the highest peak, Gunung Mulu (2,377 m; 7,799 feet), after which the park is named. Over millions of years, rivers tore through this huge system of caves, which are inhabited by numerous bats and insect species, and hollowed them out.

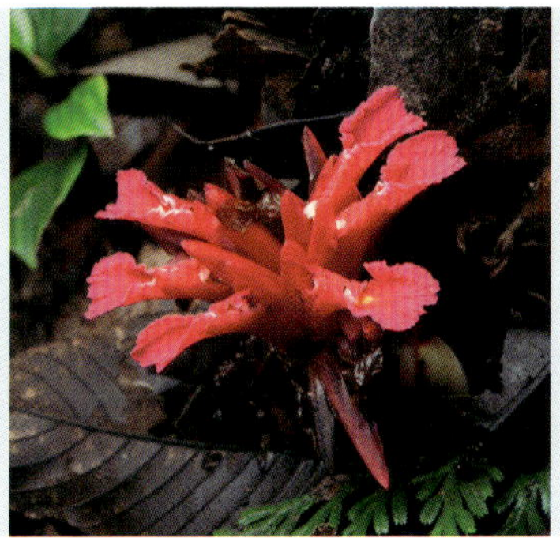

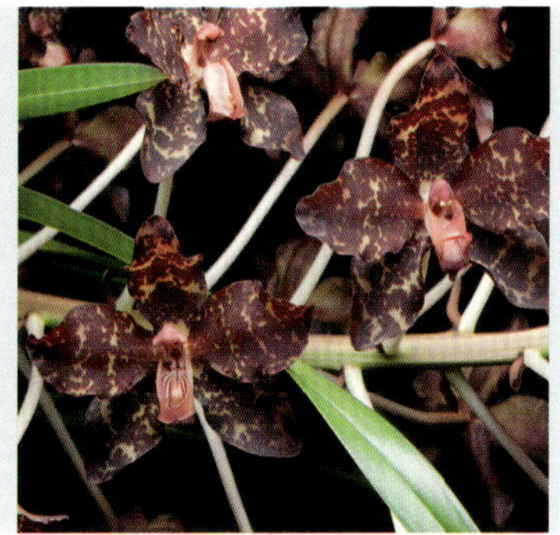

Gunung Mulu National Park fascinates above and below ground. Far left: the gigantic cave system. Picture series from the top: The red-tailed green ratsnake bites quickly, but is not poisonous; a Sunda pangolin; a treeshrew and a South American horned frog. Ginger-like plants and orchids (left) line the banks.

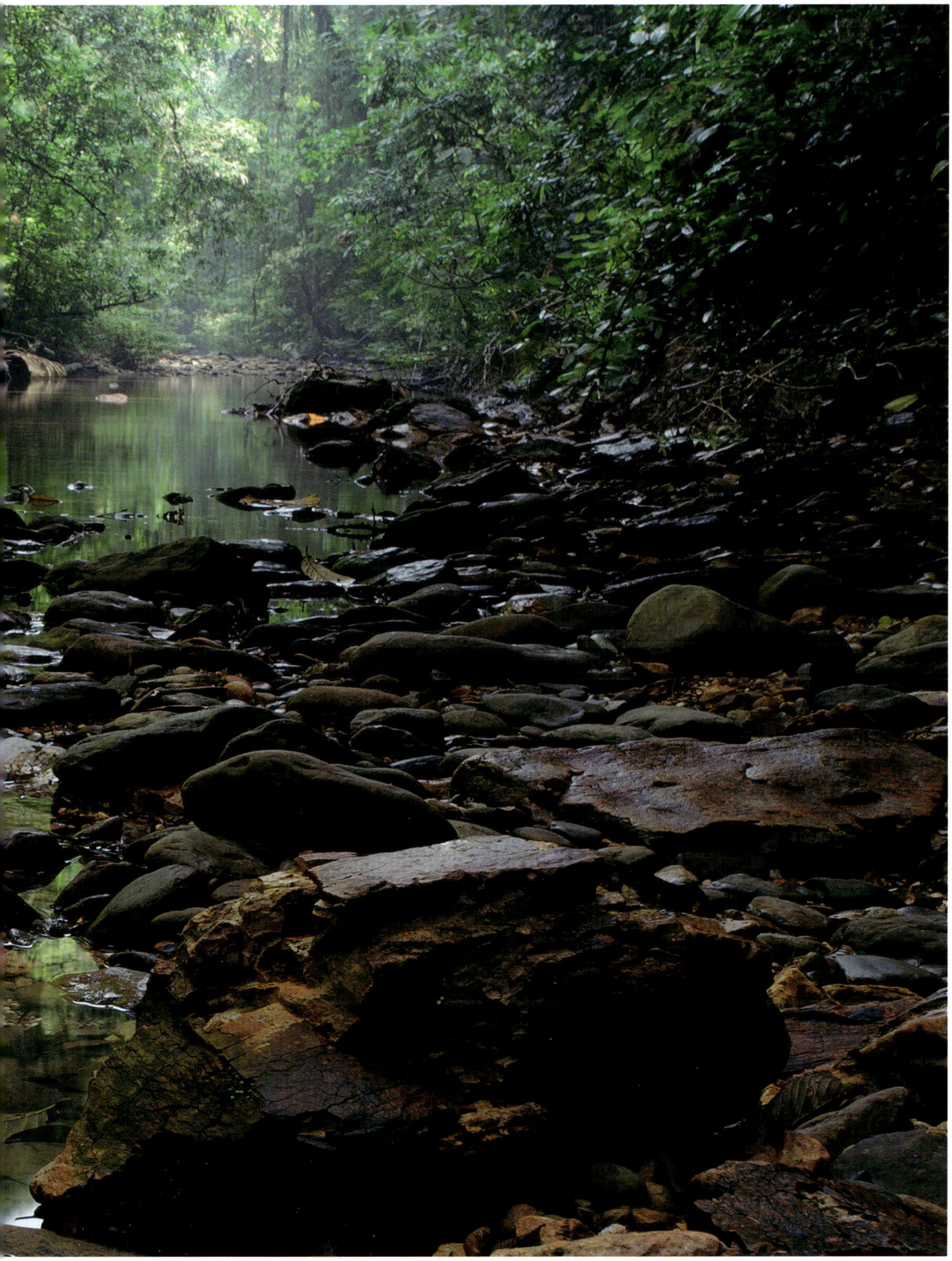

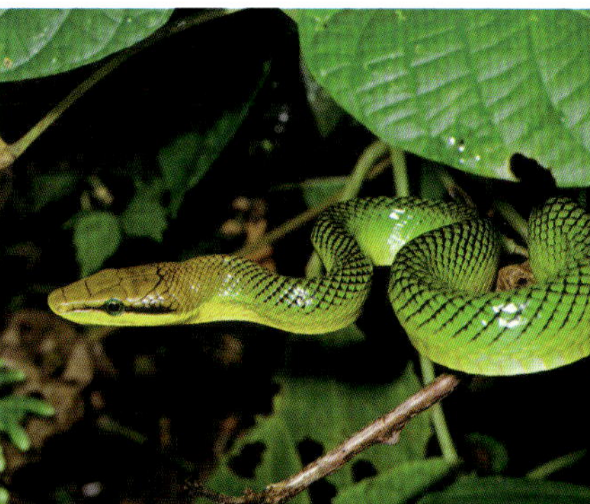

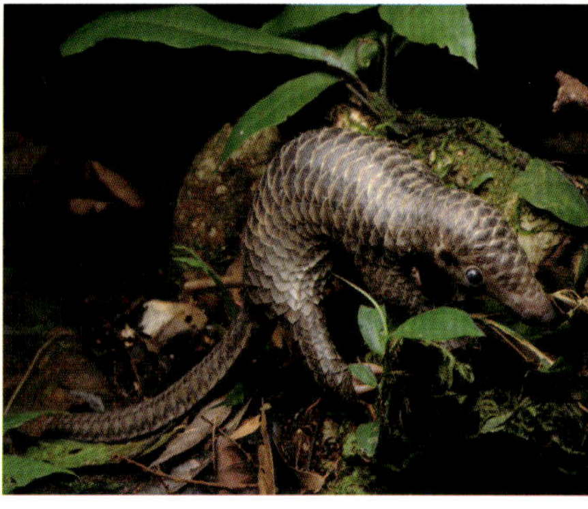

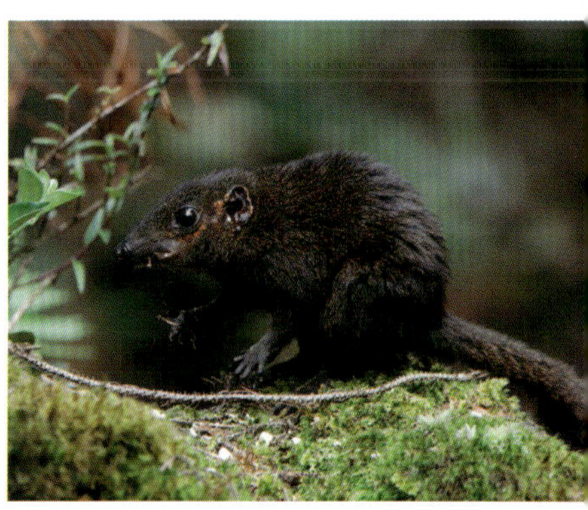

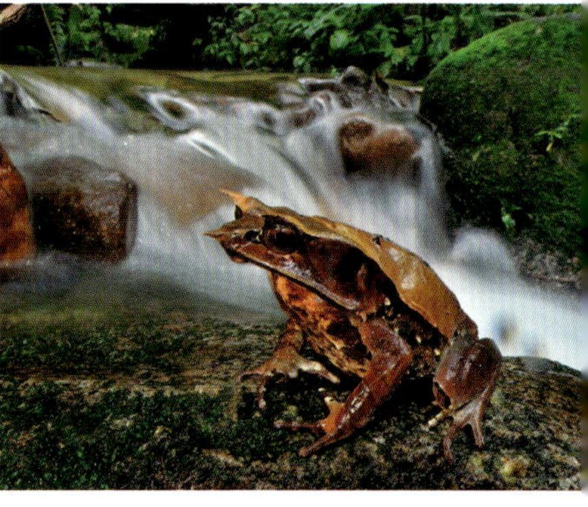

THE TROPICAL RAINFOREST OF SUMATRA

Date of inscription: 2004

Three national parks have been combined here to form one World Natural Heritage Site, and they protect one of the world's last large continuous rainforest sectors.

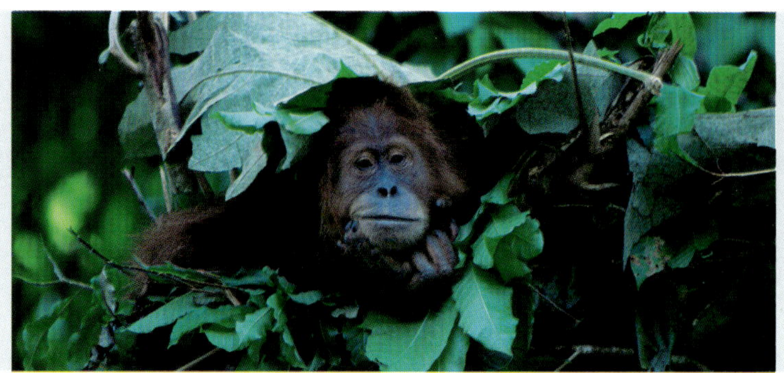

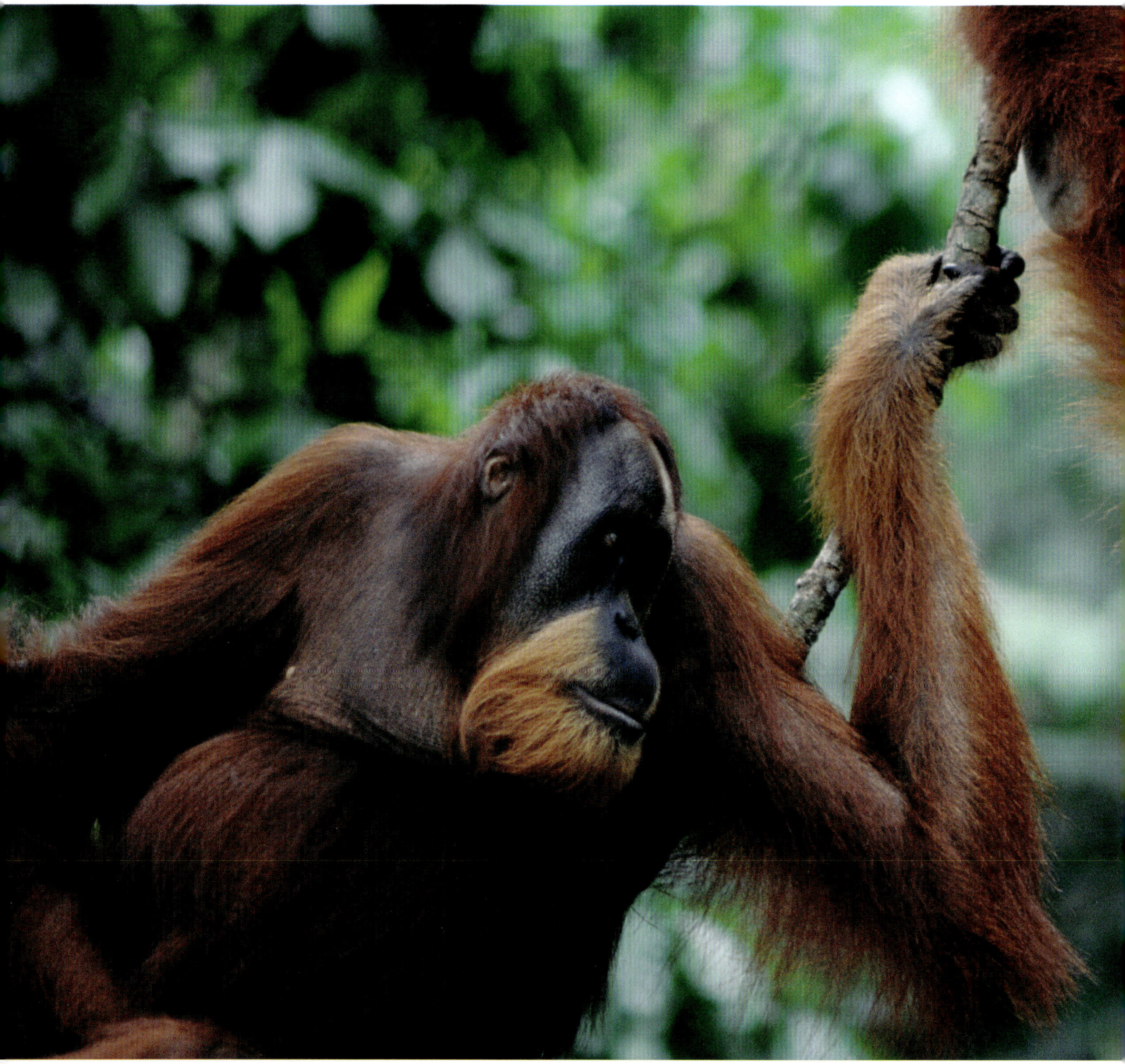

This World Natural Heritage Site includes the Gunung Leuser National Park in the north and Kerinci Seblat in the central part, as well as Bukit Barisan Selatan, which lies further to the south of Sumatra. Around 10,000 plant species flourish in this area, including 17 endemic plant types. More than 50 percent of the plant types present in Sumatra can be found beneath the flowering canopy. Among the most famous are the largest flowers in the world (Rafflesia arnoldii) and the flowers with the tallest blooms, the Titan arum (Amorphophallus titanum). The variety of fauna is just as great, and only part of it has been classified scientifically. To date, 580 bird species have been identified, of which 21 are endemic. The most spectacular animals to be found here are the orang utan, tiger, rhinoceros, elephant, serow, tapir, and cloud leopard.

This high level of biodiversity corresponds to a wide range of geological formations and habitats. In addition to the tropical rainforest, there are high and beautiful mountains, with forests, lakes, volcanoes, fumaroles, waterfalls, caves, and wetlands.

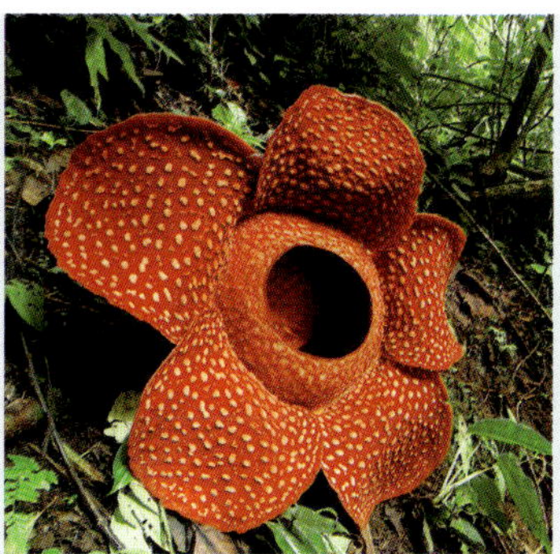

The diameter of the giant Rafflesia bloom (left) can measure up to 1 m (3 foot). Orang-utan is the Indonesian word for "man of the forest" (far left and below). Their habitat is much reduced and is today confined to Borneo and Sumatra. In a family, the female is the main caregiver for the young.

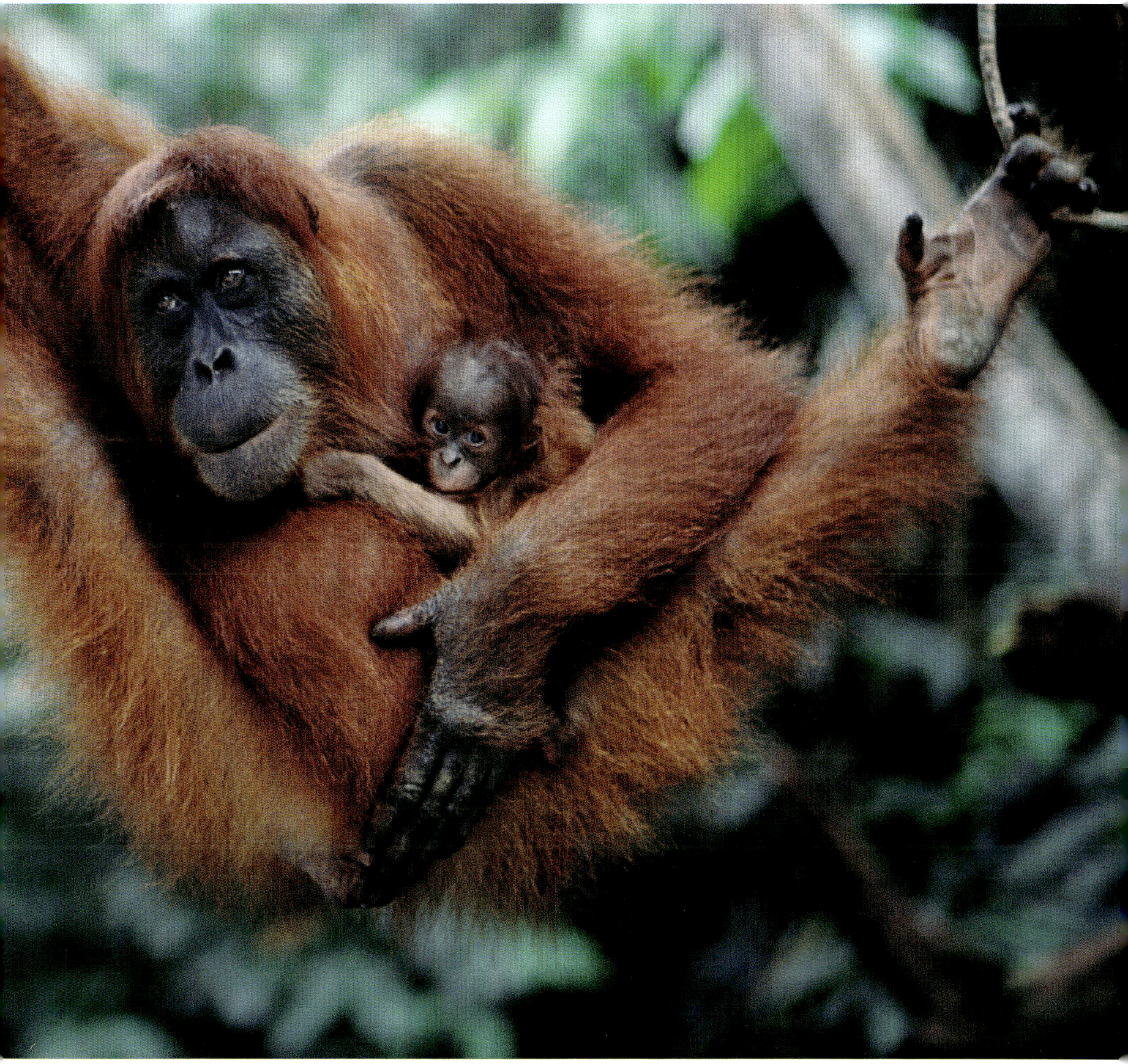

KOMODO NATIONAL PARK

Date of inscription: 1991

The Komodo dragon is found in the wild only here, and enjoys ideal conditions for hunting wild pigs and deer in the rainforest and savannah of its protected area in the national park.

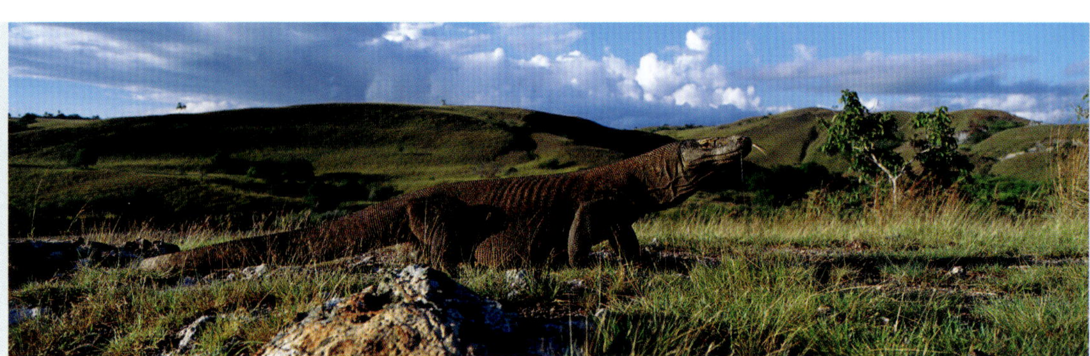

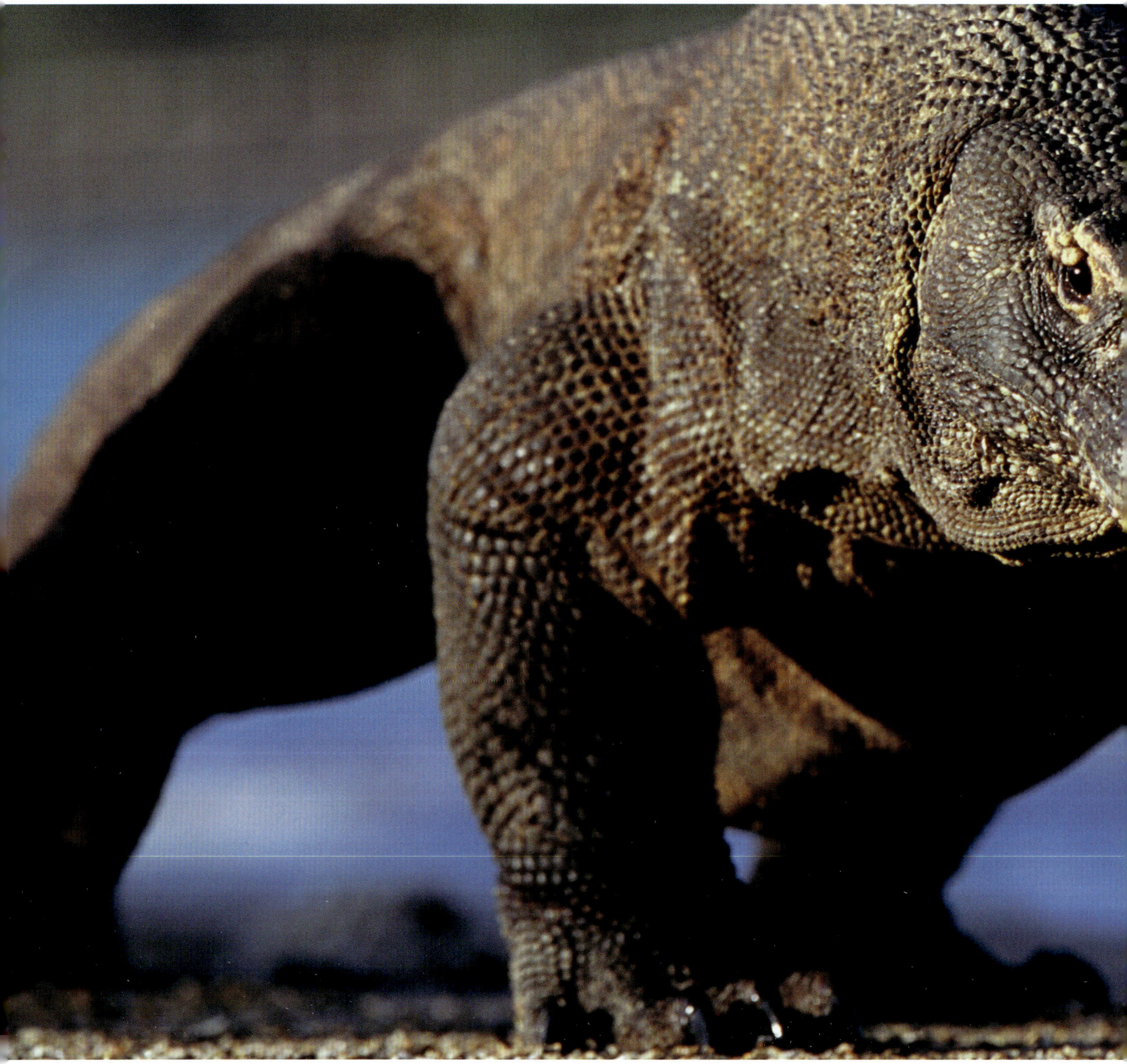

The national park is not limited to the island of Komodo, which measures only 35 km by 25 km (22 miles by15 miles) and is part of the Lesser Sunda island chain. It also encompasses the smaller neighboring islands of Padar, Rinca, and Gili Montang, and the west coast of Flores. The abundant vegetation is divided between tropical monsoon rainforest, grassland, and savannah, and in many places there are mangrove forests. The main attraction is the Komodo dragon (Varanus komodoensis), the world's largest species of lizard. This diurnal ground-dweller lives on mammals such as wild pigs, deer, larger birds, vipers, and tortoises.

The park authorities estimate the total population of these approximately 3-m (9-foot) long "dragons" at around 6,000; on the island itself there seem to be at most 3,000 specimens, or perhaps considerably fewer. These can be viewed by tourists accompanied by park wardens. Artificial feeding has reduced many of the giant lizards to lethargy; however, their dangerousness should not be underestimated.

The Komodo dragon uses its long, deeply forked tongue to waft the faintest of scents onto an olfactory organ seated in its palate. It can detect carrion at a distance of 5 km (3 miles).

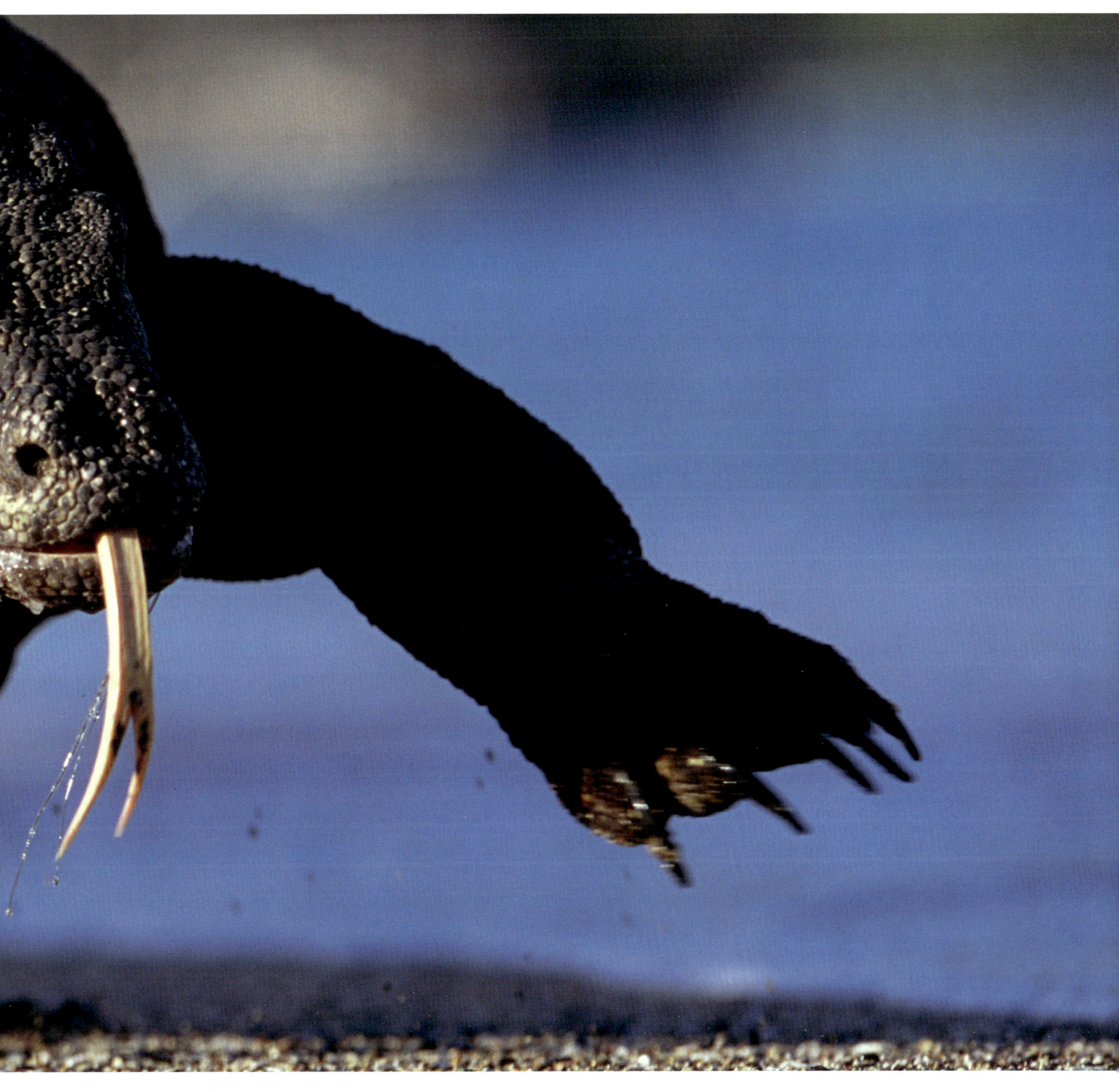

UJUNG-KULON NATIONAL PARK

Date of inscription: 1991

Ujung-Kulon was Indonesia's first national park. Its importance resides above all in these last remnants of lowland rainforest and the small population of very rare Javan rhinoceroses.

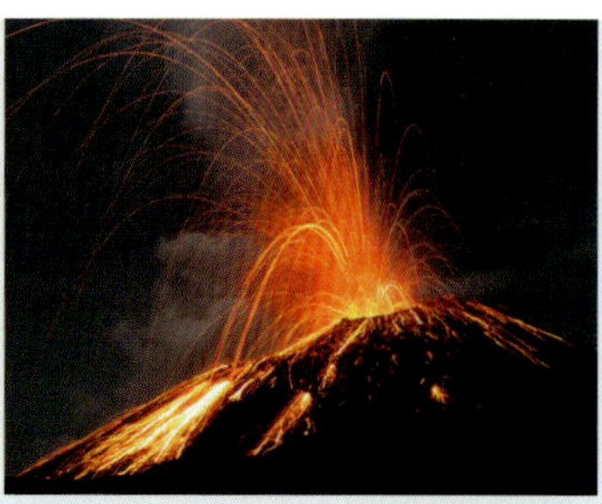

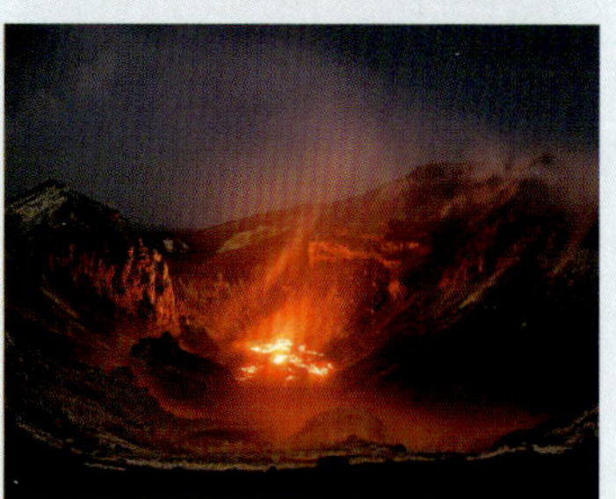

Java is the smallest, but most important, of the Greater Sunda islands in the Malay archipelago. The national park comprises the Ujung-Kulon peninsula in south-west Java and the islands of Krakatau, Panaitan, and Peucang in the Sunda Strait. It encloses Javan lowland rainforest, coastal coral reefs, and the flora and fauna on the volcanic island of Anak Krakatau. The most endangered species in the rain forest is the Javan rhinoceros, a nocturnal loner who feeds mainly on leafs, fruit, shoots and branches. At one point, poaching had reduced the population to 25, but this now seems to have risen back to 60 animals. Still, the Javan rhinoceros – sporting like its relative, the great one-horned rhinoceros, only one horn – remains one of the rarest large mammals on our planet.
The timid Javan banteng, a species of wild cattle, is represented more numerously in the national park, along with deer, apes, leopards, saltwater crocodiles, and hornbills.

Krakatoa (left) is located between the islands of Java and Sumatra. The explosive eruptions of the volcano in the year 1883 had deadly consequences for land and climate. Today, it is still considered highly active.

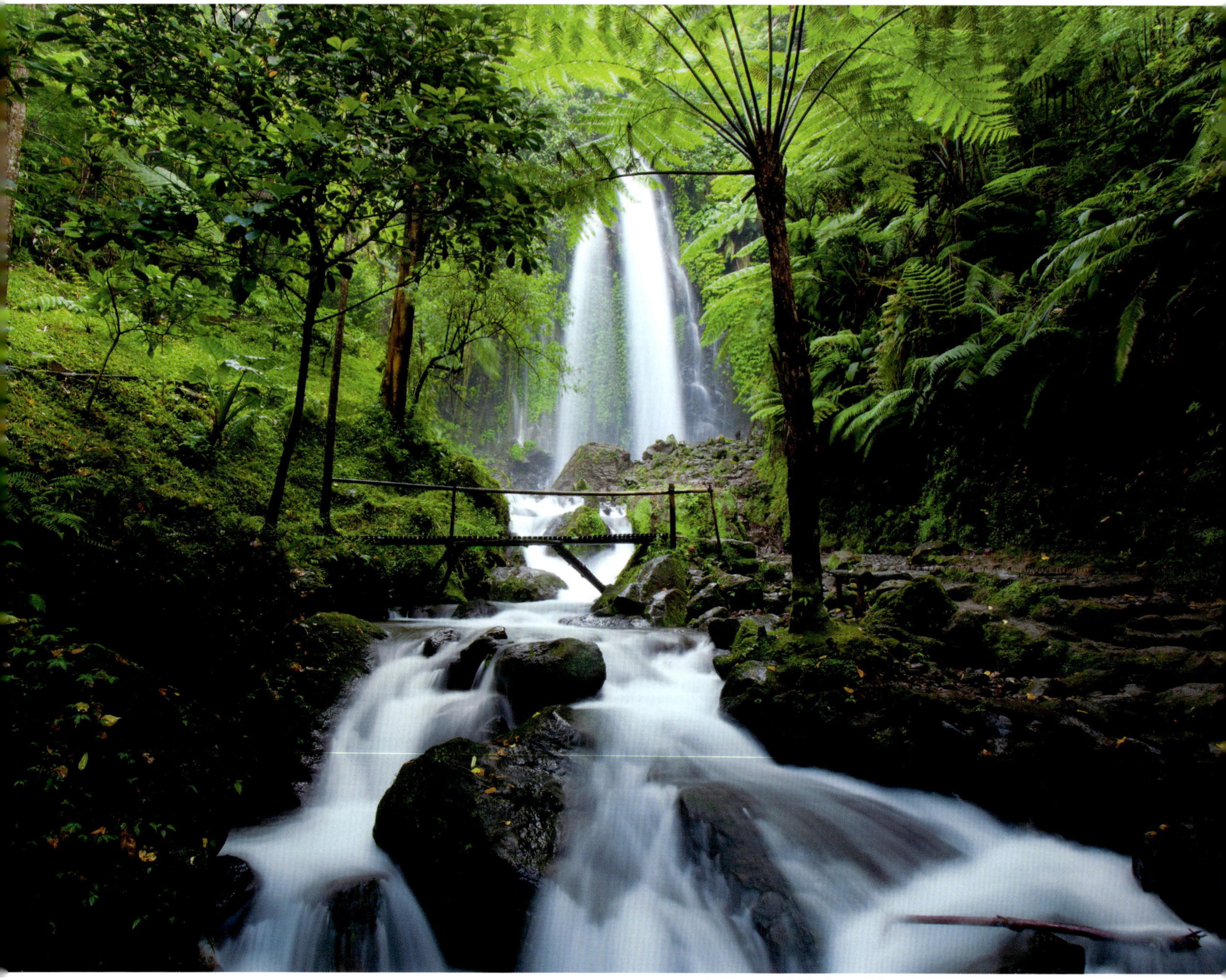

LORENTZ NATIONAL PARK

This unique national park boasts a complex geological structure and a variety of species. The area can be roughly divided into swampy lowlands and a higher region of mountains. The central mountainous region arose – and still do – through two converging continental plates The glaciated summits reach a height of about 5,000 m. The lowlands are a swampy plain with largely undisturbed forests and countless watercourses. The lowland vegetation consists of simple plant cultures on the beach, and more complex ecosystems in the evergreen mixed forest inland. The most varied flora in New Guinea is to be found further inland, at an altitude of 600–1,500 m. Unbroken forest ranges up to an altitude of 4,100 m. Above the tree line only low bushes, grasses, mosses, and lichens can survive. Many of the bird species found here are endemic, including the various brilliantly hued birds of paradise. Several species of marsupials, tree kangaroos, and monotremes like the echidna are only otherwise found in continental Australia. Around 150 varieties of amphibians and reptiles remain largely unresearched.

A cartilage-like barb on the inside of the fruit bats' (right) leg joint enables them to relax in their head-down position. The diamond python (below) moves in a different way.

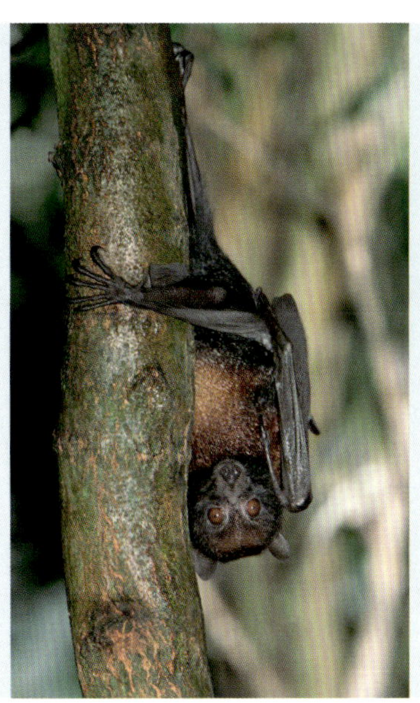

Date of inscription: 1999

South-East Asia's largest nature reserve in Irian Jaya, the Indonesian part of New Guinea, combines the most diverse scenery with a variety of flora and fauna.

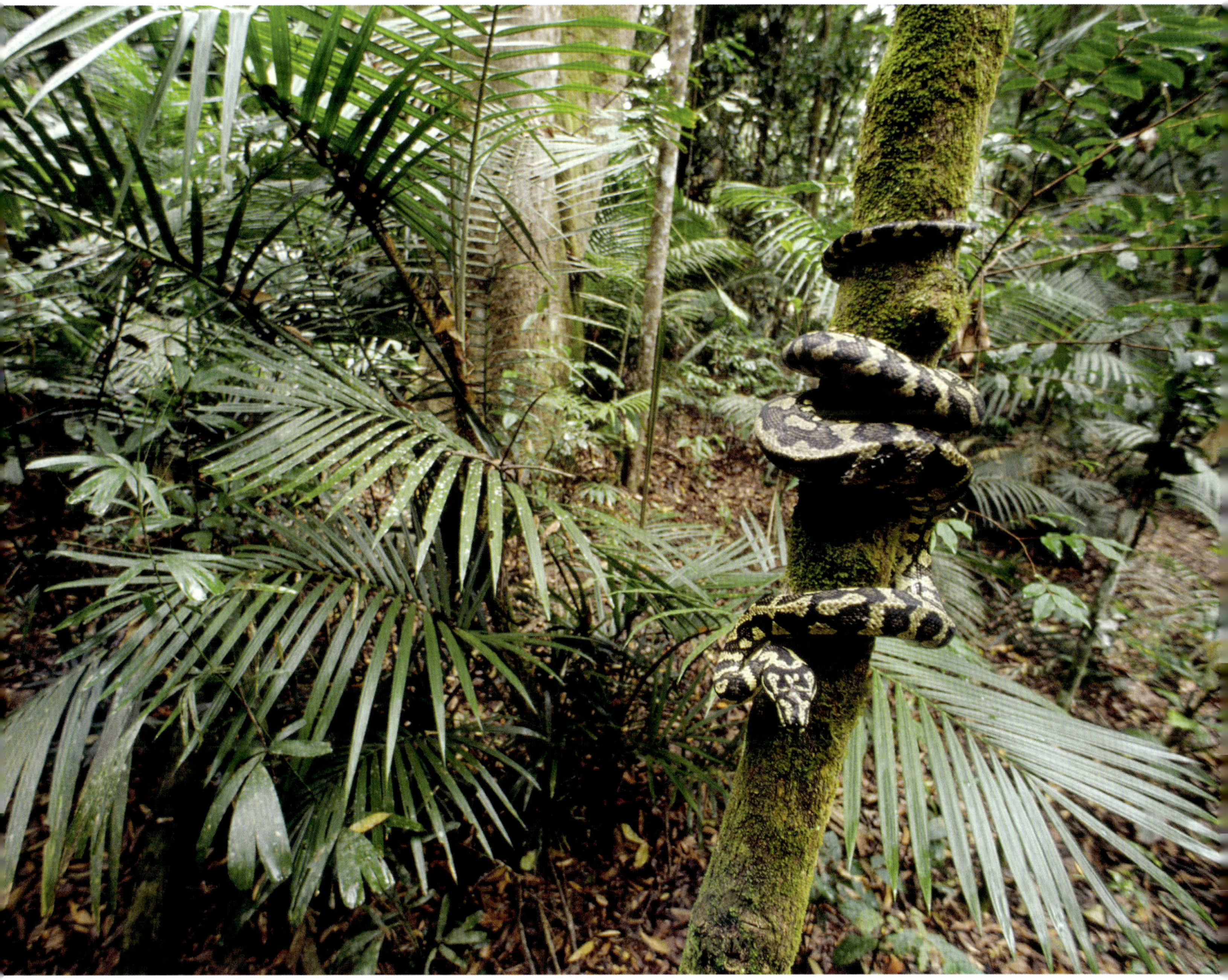

Erosion has created bizarre reliefs and stone sculptures in the Mungo National Park, which forms part of the Willandra Lakes Region (large picture), a lunar landscape in the most beautiful sunshine shades. The perentie lizard (right) is one of the largest representatives of the monitor lizards living in Australia. It can reach a length of up to 2 m (6 feet) and has a netlike body pattern.

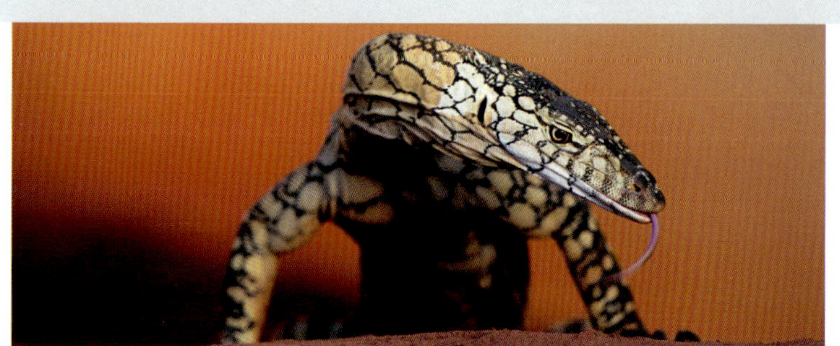

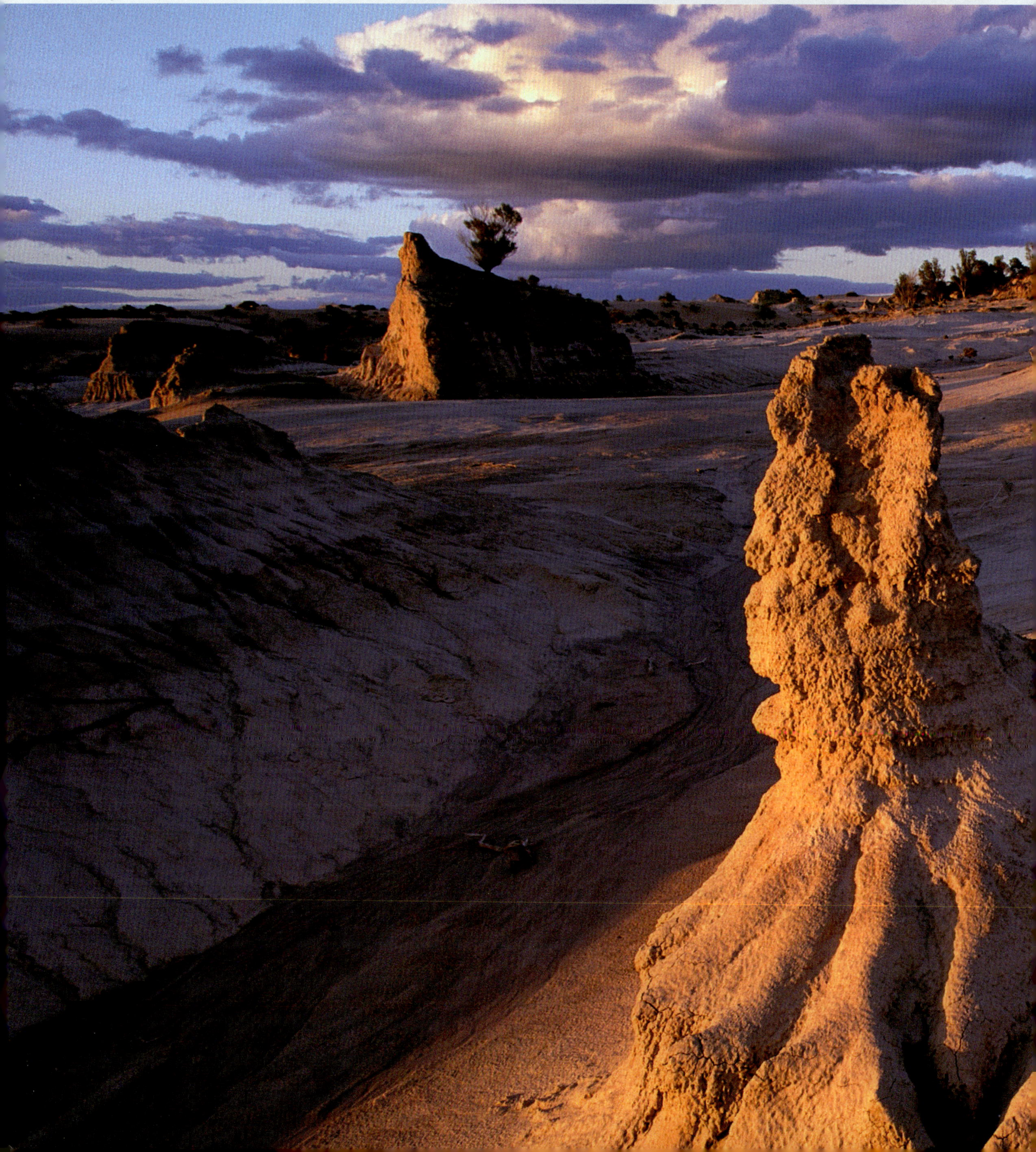

AUSTRALIA & OCEANIA

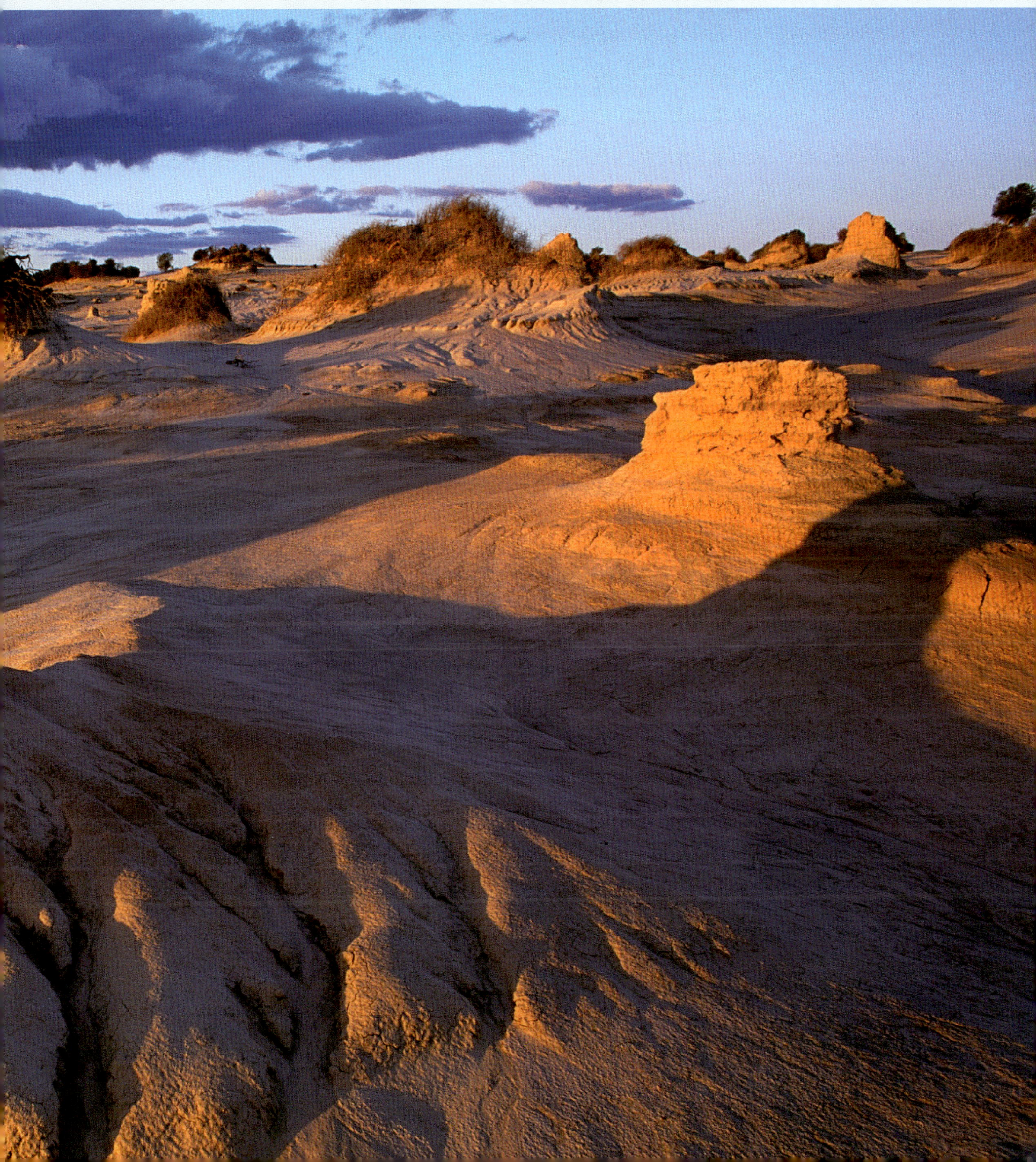

KAKADU NATIONAL PARK

Date of inscription 1981
Extended: 1987, 1992

Kakadu National Park boasts not only diverse scenery but also impressive Aboriginal rock paintings.

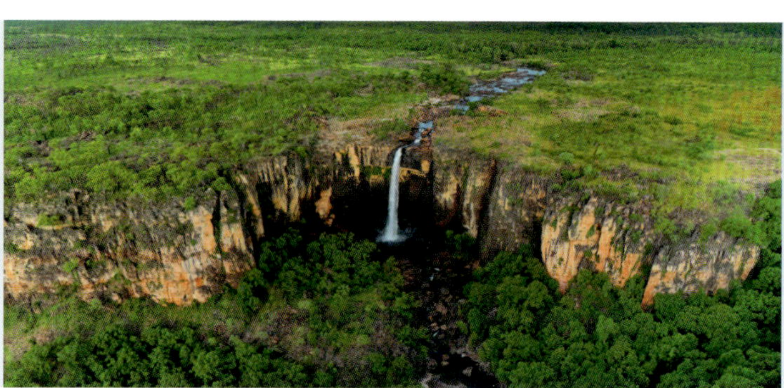

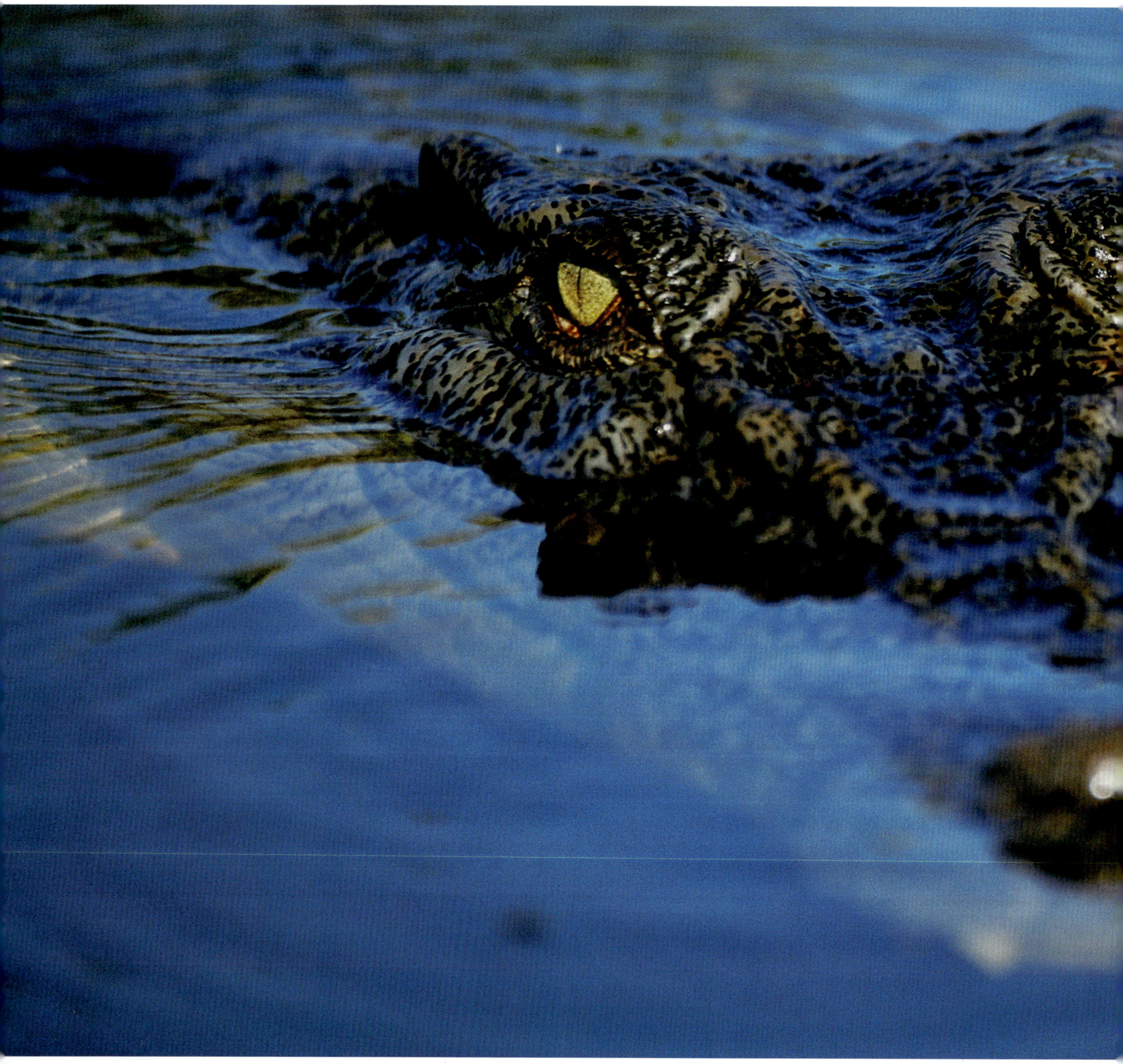

Kakadu National Park, now expanded to its current area of 20,000 sq. km (7,700 sq. miles), lies 250 km (155 miles) east of Darwin and encloses five distinct kinds of landscape. In the tidal river estuaries, mangroves have established root systems in the silt, protecting the hinterland from the destructive effects of wave action. In the rainy season, the coastal areas transform themselves into a bright carpet of lotus flowers, water lilies, and floating ferns. Rare waterfowl, such as the brolga, the Jesus bird, the white-faced heron, the great Indian stork, and the snake bird are native to here, as is the saltwater crocodile, the largest living reptile.

The adjoining hills, with their wide variety of open tropical forest, savannah, and grassy plains vegetation, form the greater part of the park and offer a refuge for endangered species, such as dingoes and wallabies. Several of the rarer kangaroo species live on the sandstone plateaus of Arnhem Land and on the Arnhem escarpment, a 500-km (310-mile) long cliff crossing the park from the south-west to the north-east. The park, which is jointly managed by its traditional Aboriginal owners and the Australian Government, became internationally famous in the middle of the 20th century, when excavations uncovered Stone Age tools that were at least 3,000 years old. Numerous rock paintings reveal details of the hunting habits, myths, and customs of the Aboriginal tribes who lived here.

The saltwater crocodile, at up to 6 m (20 feet) in length, is one of the most aggressive of the Crocodylidae (large image).Other things you may come across in the Kakadu National Park are snakes such as the black-headed python, frilled-neck lizards, wallabies and little egrets (picture series, from the top), plus no end of beautifully shaped waterfalls (left).

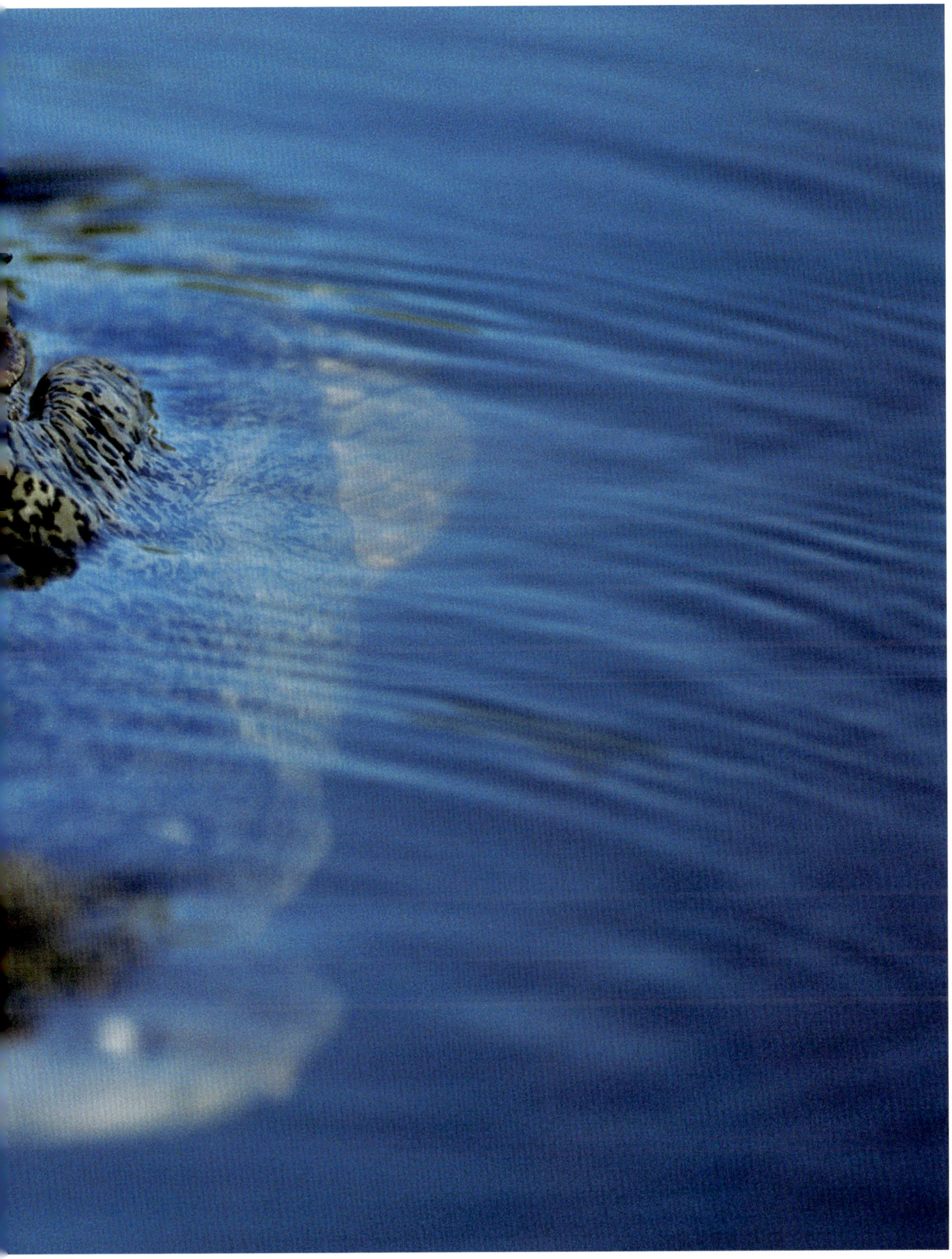

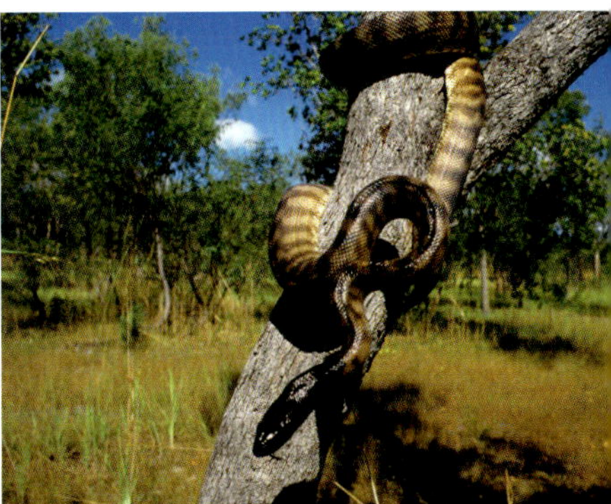

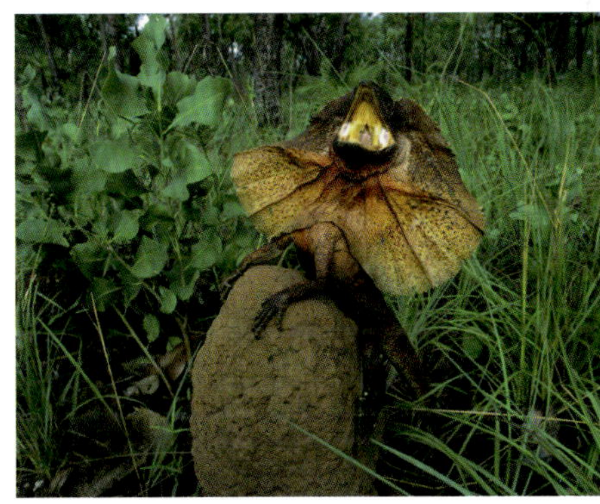

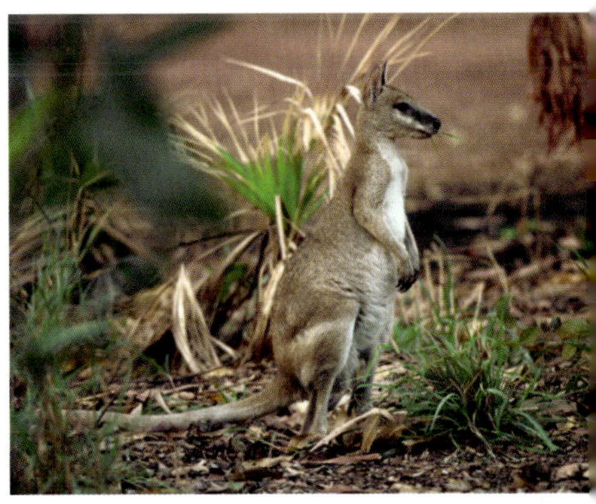

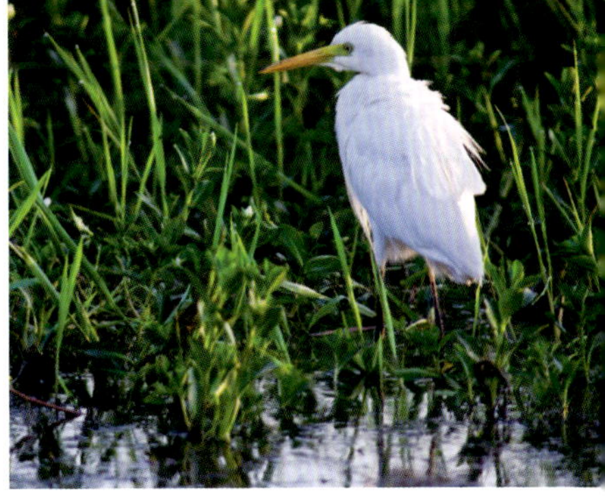

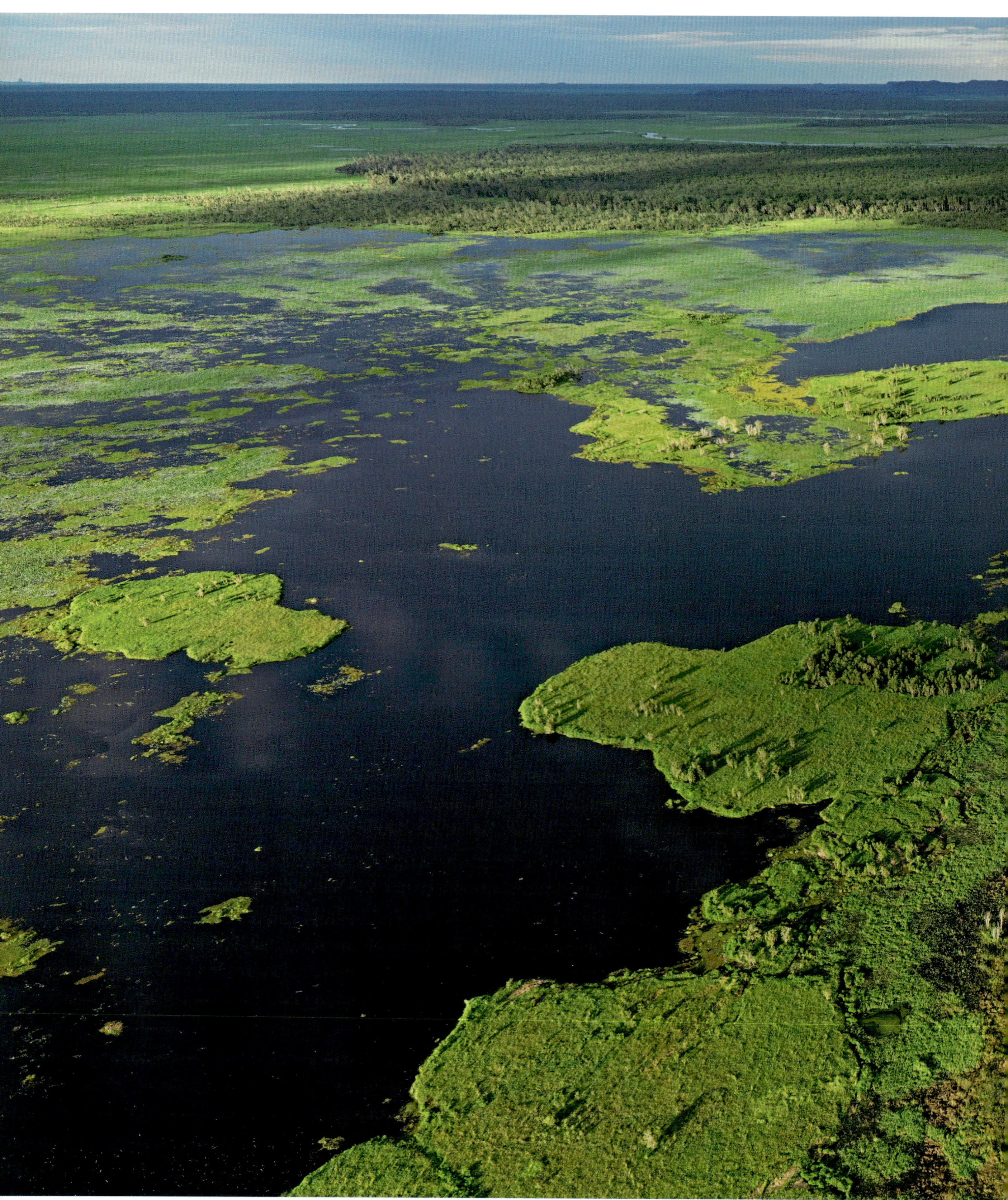

The park is a large, luminously green universe of primeval forest and mangroves, savannahs and sandstone plateaus, eucalyptus woods, countless waterfalls and thousands of thousands of watering holes. The view from above shows the endless, lush green of the wetlands, a magnificent carpet of plants that provide a home for numerous animals.

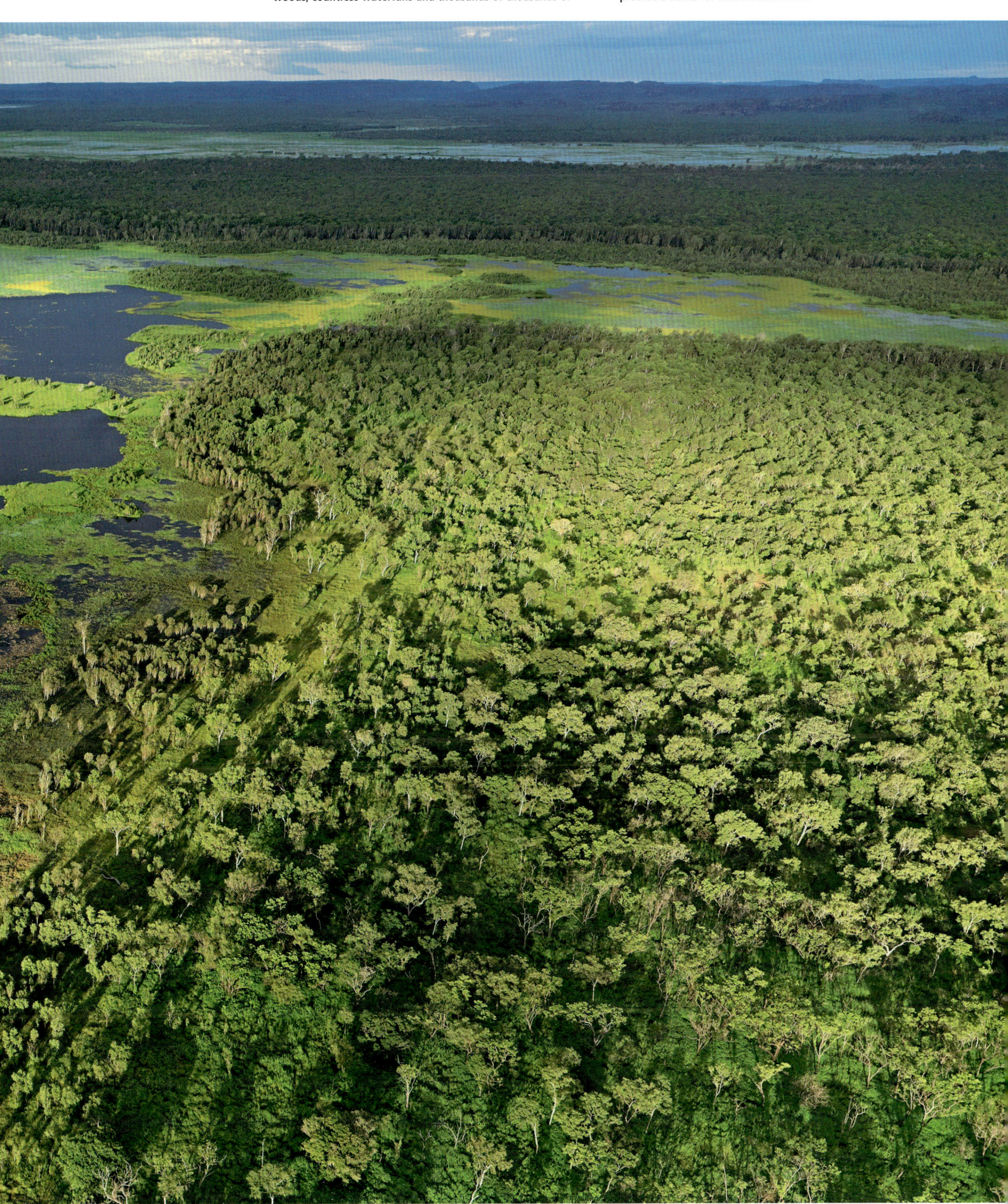

PURNULULU NATIONAL PARK

Date if inscription 2003

Purnululu National Park in the northern part of Western Australia is distinguished by extraordinary, dome-shaped rock formations, caused by the weathering of sandstone. "Purnululu" means sandstone in the language of the indigenous Kija Aborigines.

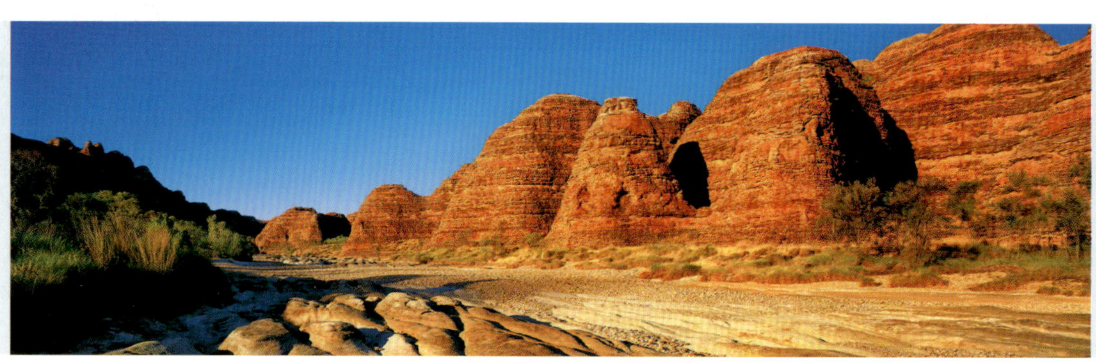

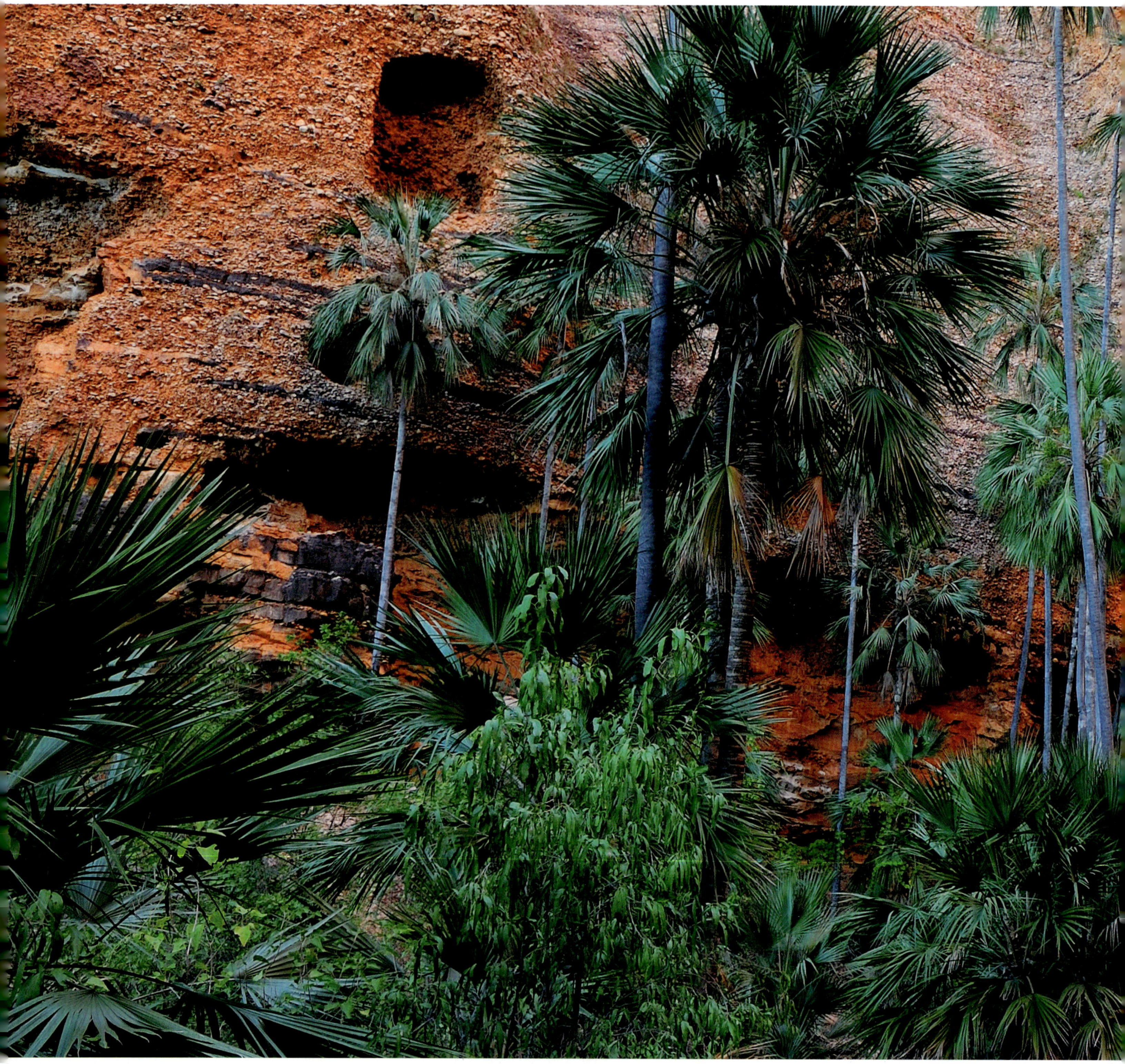

In the heart of the Purnululu National Park is the Bungle Bungle mountain range, rising to 578 m (1,896 feet) above sea level. The mountains are composed of Devonian quartz sandstone and are approximately 370 million years old. In the last 20 million years, horizontally striped, beehive-shaped rock formations have arisen through the effects of water erosion. The stripes are characteristic of softer, porous rock, on which cyanobacteria are able to grow, darkening the surface. The harder, interposed strata are orange, betraying the presence of iron and manganese. These tones change in the course of the seasons and are especially stiking after rain. Between the domed rocks lie gullies, with streams and pools fringed with large Australian fan palms (Livistona australis). Aborigines have inhabited the Purnululu area for millennia, leaving behind numerous rock paintings and burial sites. There are approximately 130 bird species, including the European bee-eater and bright budgerigars, the most striking creatures in the park.

The most popular ambassadors of the nature park are the dolphins in Monkey Mia. The bay is also home to requiem and whale sharks (left, from the top). A satellite picture shows the maritime nature paradise from above (large picture).

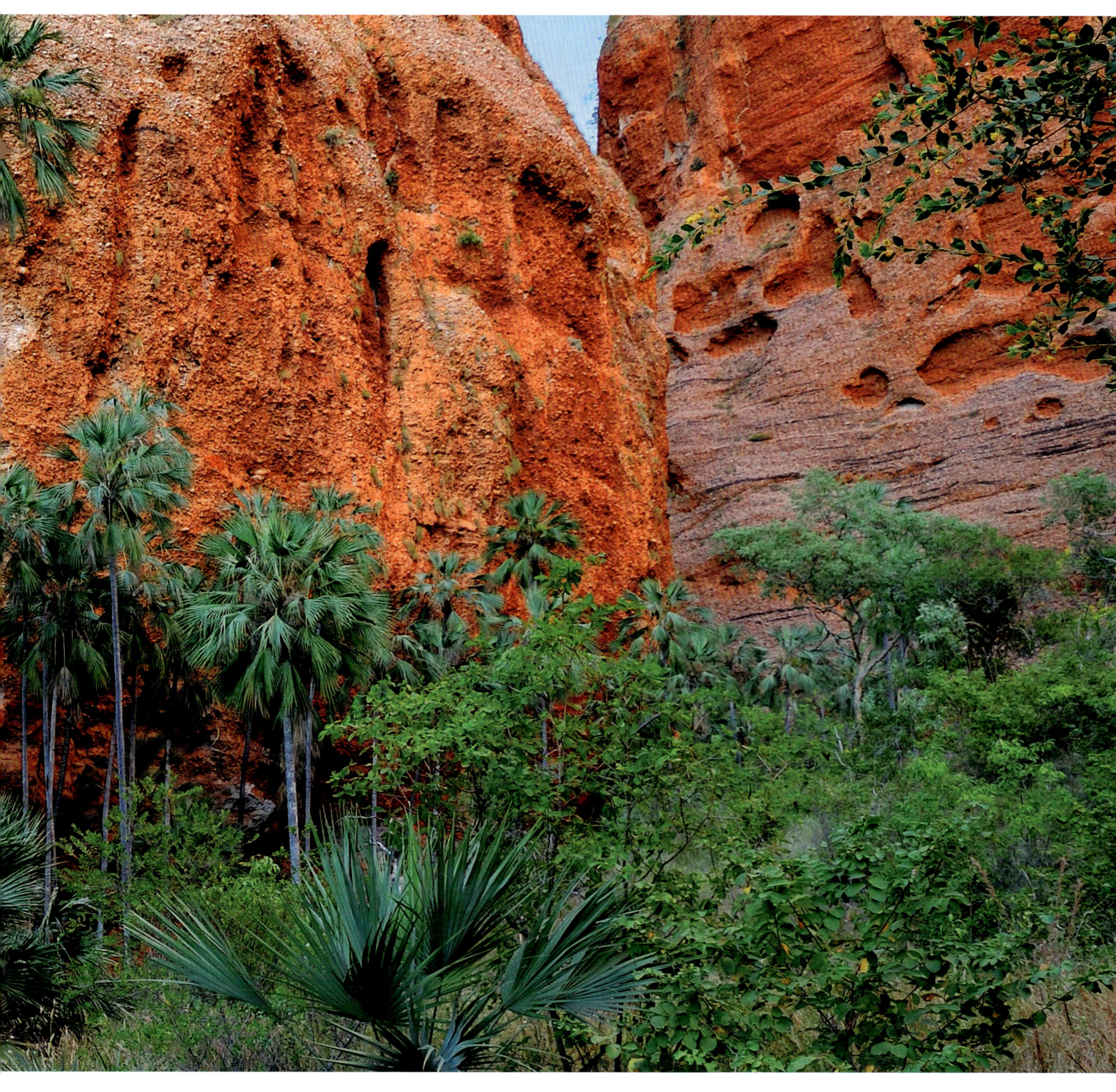

NINGALOO COAST

Date of inscription: 2011

A marine park in the north-west of Australia, Ningaloo is a fascinating coastline featuring an amazing wealth of animal species.

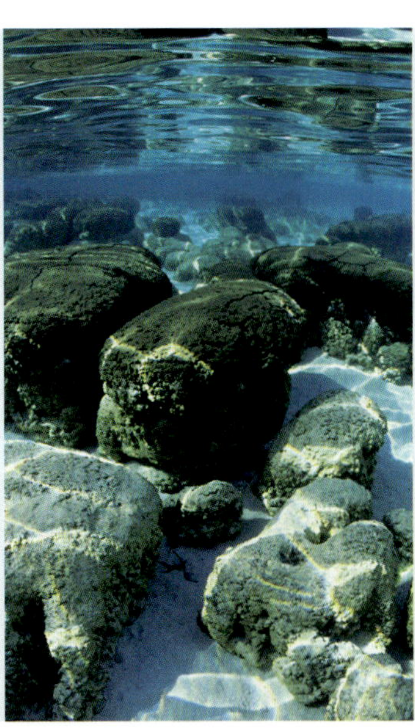

Stromatolites (right), formed of layered limestone, are thought to be the oldest fossils in the world; they have existed for some 3.5 billion years. Large picture: a picturesque sunset

The Ningaloo marine park, covering approximately 6,000 sq km (2,317 sq miles), is located at the remote northern tip of Australia's west coast. Its coral reef is one of the world's largest near-shore reefs, in many places only 100 m (328 ft) off the coastline, protecting a 300-km- (186-mile-) long coastal stretch. The coast itself boasts impressive limestone formations, which are traversed by underground streams. Many caves provide nesting sites for birds and protection for rare reptiles. Colourful clownfish, poisonous lionfish and predatory moray eels are among the 500 species of fish that live among the more than 300 species of coral in the reef. The most exciting reef inhabitants are green turtles which lay their eggs on the coast here, shy reef sharks and up to 6-m- (20-ft-) long tiger and hammerhead sharks, stingrays and manta rays, dolphins and dugongs, which graze in the large sea grass beds. About a week after the full moon in late March or early April all the corals in the reef spawn simultaneously, releasing millions of bright pink eggs and sperm parcels, which form a floating spawning carpet on the water surface. The three-day spectacle also announces the arrival of the whale sharks. Towards the end of June or the beginning of July, the humpback whales arrive to take their place.

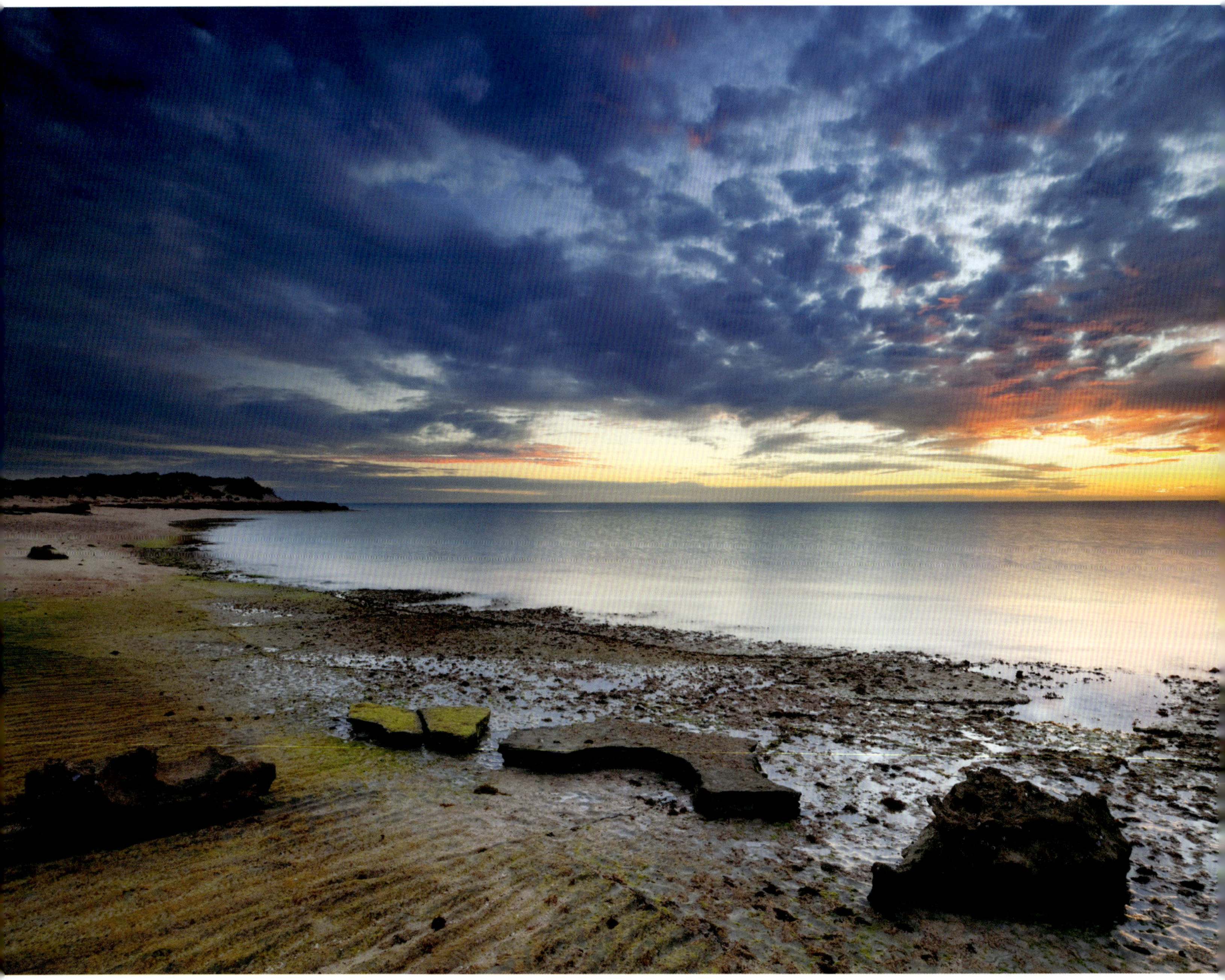

SHARK BAY

The Shark Bay Marine Park, a coastal area of abrupt cliffs, lagoons, and sand dunes located about 800 km (500 miles) from Perth, is the habitat of many endangered aquatic and land-dwelling animals. The nearly 5,000 sq. km (1,900 sq. miles) of seagrass meadow, among the richest in species variety in the world, are particularly impressive. These meadows serve above all as a refuge for small fish, crustaceans, and larger crabs. They also foster the formation of stromatolites (layered algal accretionary structures). In the shallow, brackish waters of the lagoons these tiny organisms, in existence for 3.5 million years, form cabbage-shaped, chalky clumps, sometimes breaking the water's surface at low tide. In summer in Shark Bay, you can see humpback whales mating, marine turtles laying eggs, and dugongs raising their young. These sea mammals, once thought extinct, exist here in a population of about 10,000, one of the world's largest. The islands and cliffs are the preserve of several rare seabirds. Australasian gannets, fish and sea eagles, and pied cormorants hunt for fish in the abundant waters. The coastal islands and the area around Cape Peron are the habitat of the Shark Bay mouse, which was once found throughout the greater part of Australia.

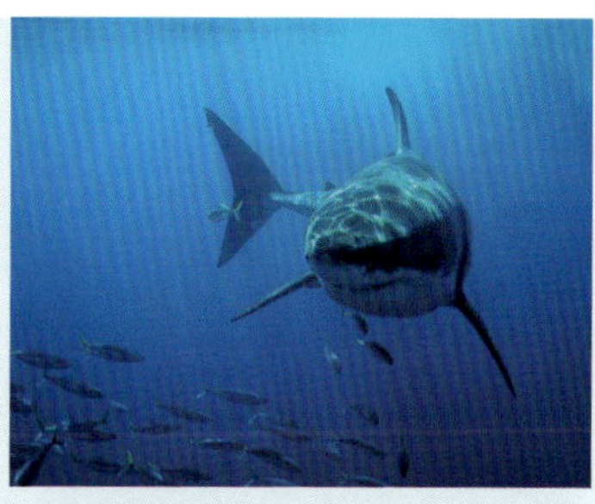

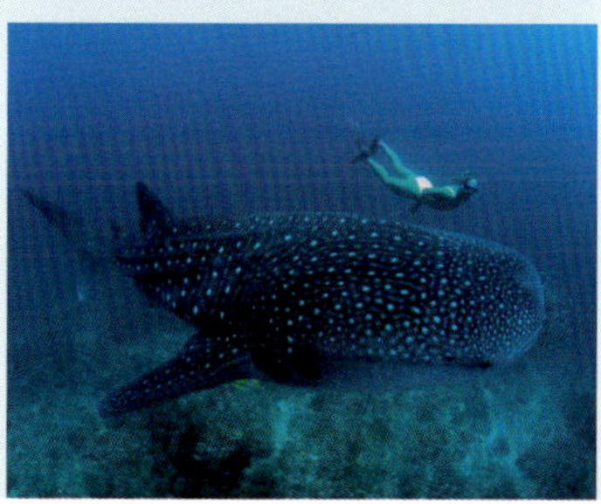

Date of inscription: 1991

The distinguishing features of this protected area are the varied species of the seagrass meadows, the stromatolite colonies, and the world's largest dugong population.

The most popular ambassadors of the nature park are the dolphins in Monkey Mia. The bay is also home to requiem and whale sharks (left, from the top). A satellite picture shows the maritime nature paradise from above (large picture).

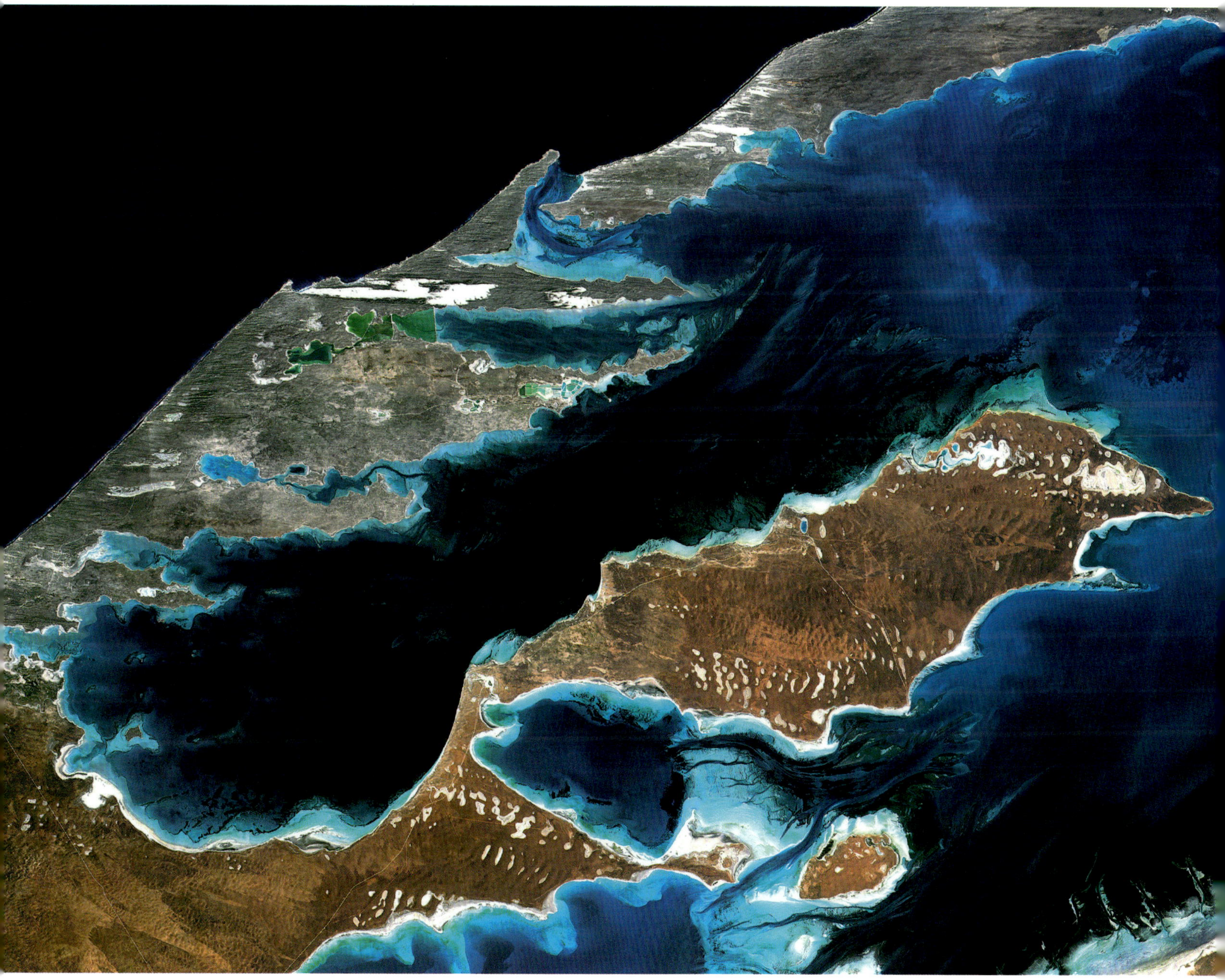

ULURU – KATA TJUTA NATIONAL PARK

Date of inscription: 1987
Extended: 1994

The spectacular geological formations of Uluru and Kata Tjuta jut out like mountainous islands in the middle of the fifth continent. They reflect varying shades of red, depending on the time of day.

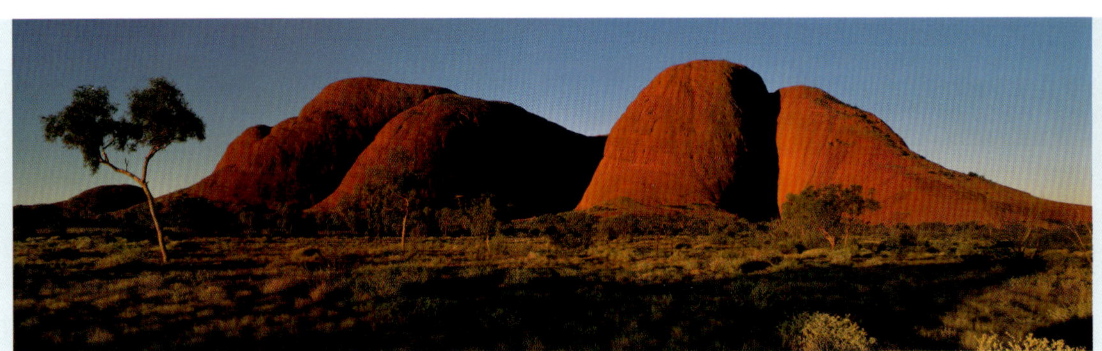

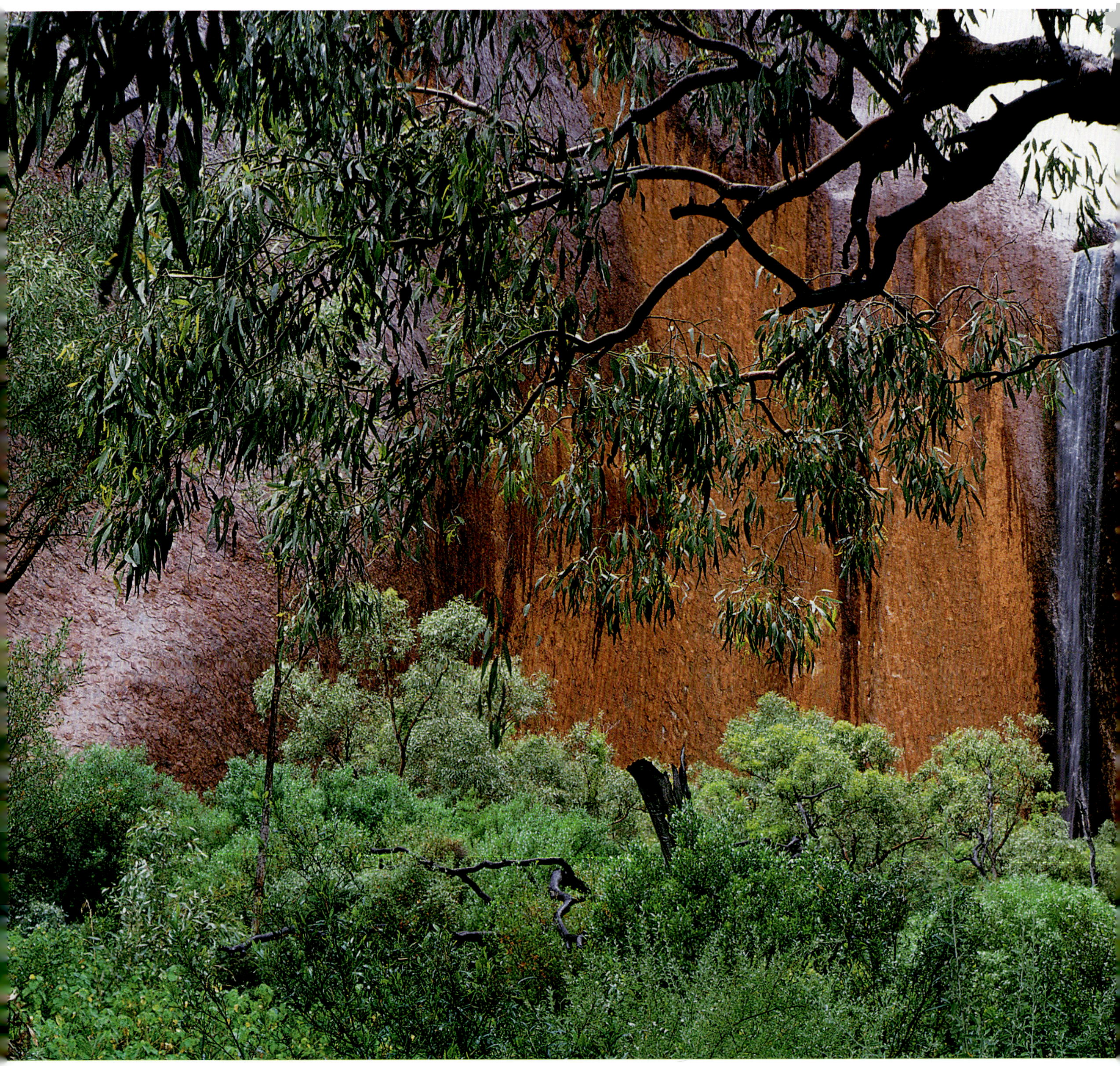

In the middle of an expanse of barren, dry savannah south-east of Alice Springs lies the "red heart of Australia," the Uluru–Kata Tjuta National Park. The immense rocky monolith, Uluru ("shady place," once called Ayers Rock), and the 36 summits of Kata Tjuta ("many heads," once called The Olgas), are the best-known natural wonders of Australia.

The history of their formation, beginning 570 million years ago, is closely linked with that of the formation of continental Australia. In contrast to the surrounding rock formations, the monoliths' resistant stone weathered only slowly, and thus today they tower over the plain as mighty, petrified testaments to earth's prehistory. Uluru is a mythical place for Aborigines, with rock paintings and sacred sites. It was a meeting place for their ancestors when they created the land and every living thing, during their wandering in the Dreamtime. There are also rock paintings at Kata Tjuta. Despite the dry, inhospitable climate, the Anangu Aborigines have lived here for millennia.

While Uluru rises like an isolated island with a circumference of about 10 km (6 miles), Kata Tjuta is formed of 36 smaller rounded peaks. This area's inscription as a World Heritage Site is also explicitly related to the mythological importance of the rock formations for the Aborigines.

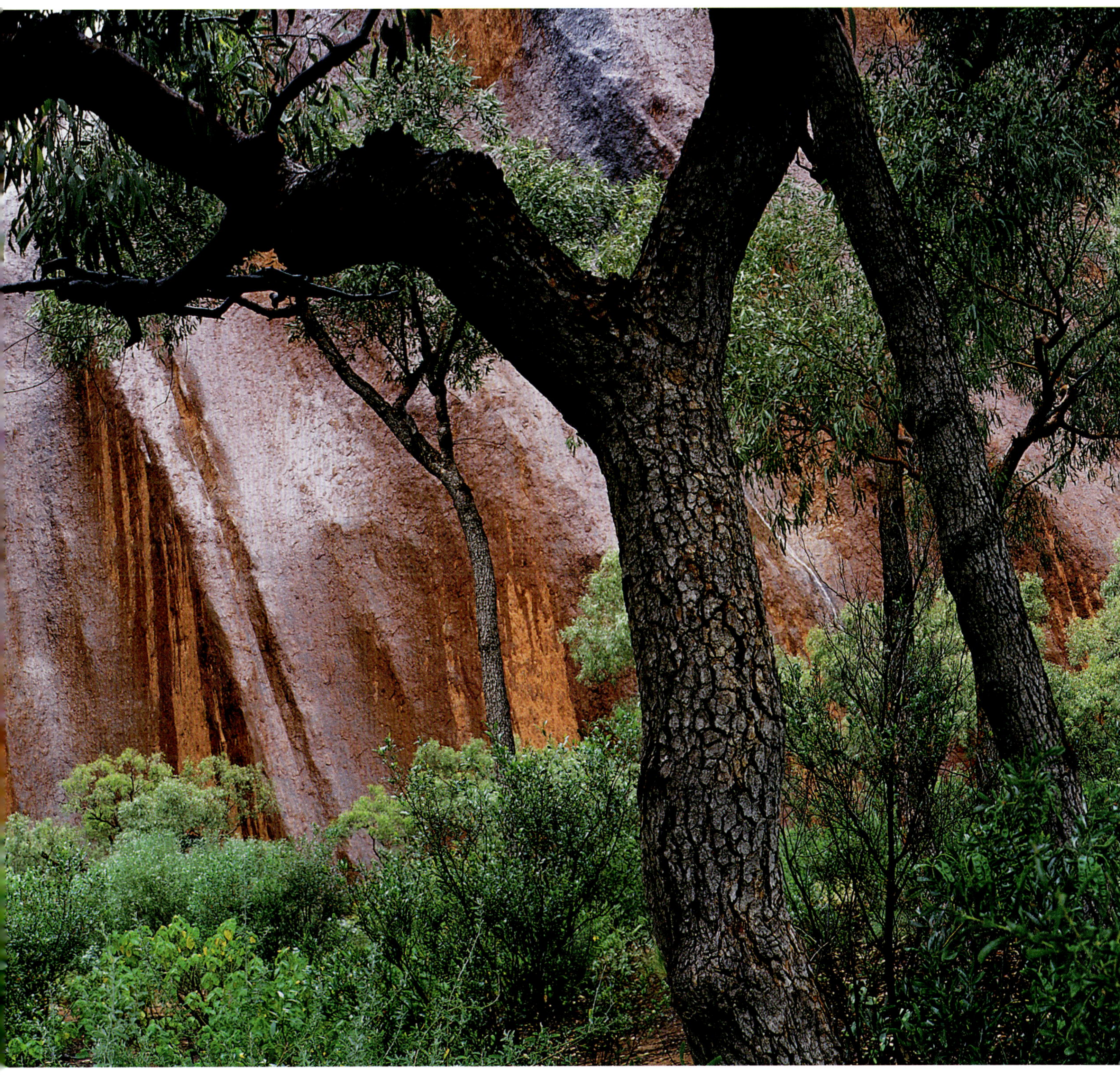

QUEENSLAND'S WET TROPICS

Date of inscription: 1988

The approximately 450-km (280-mile) long littoral is one of the most extensive and varied rainforest areas in the state. This World Heritage Site of some 9,000 sq. km (3,400 sq. miles) encloses about 20 national parks and other protected areas.

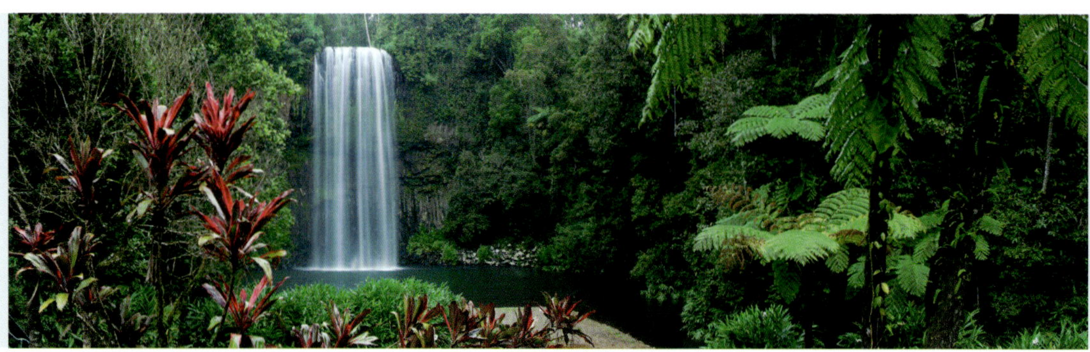

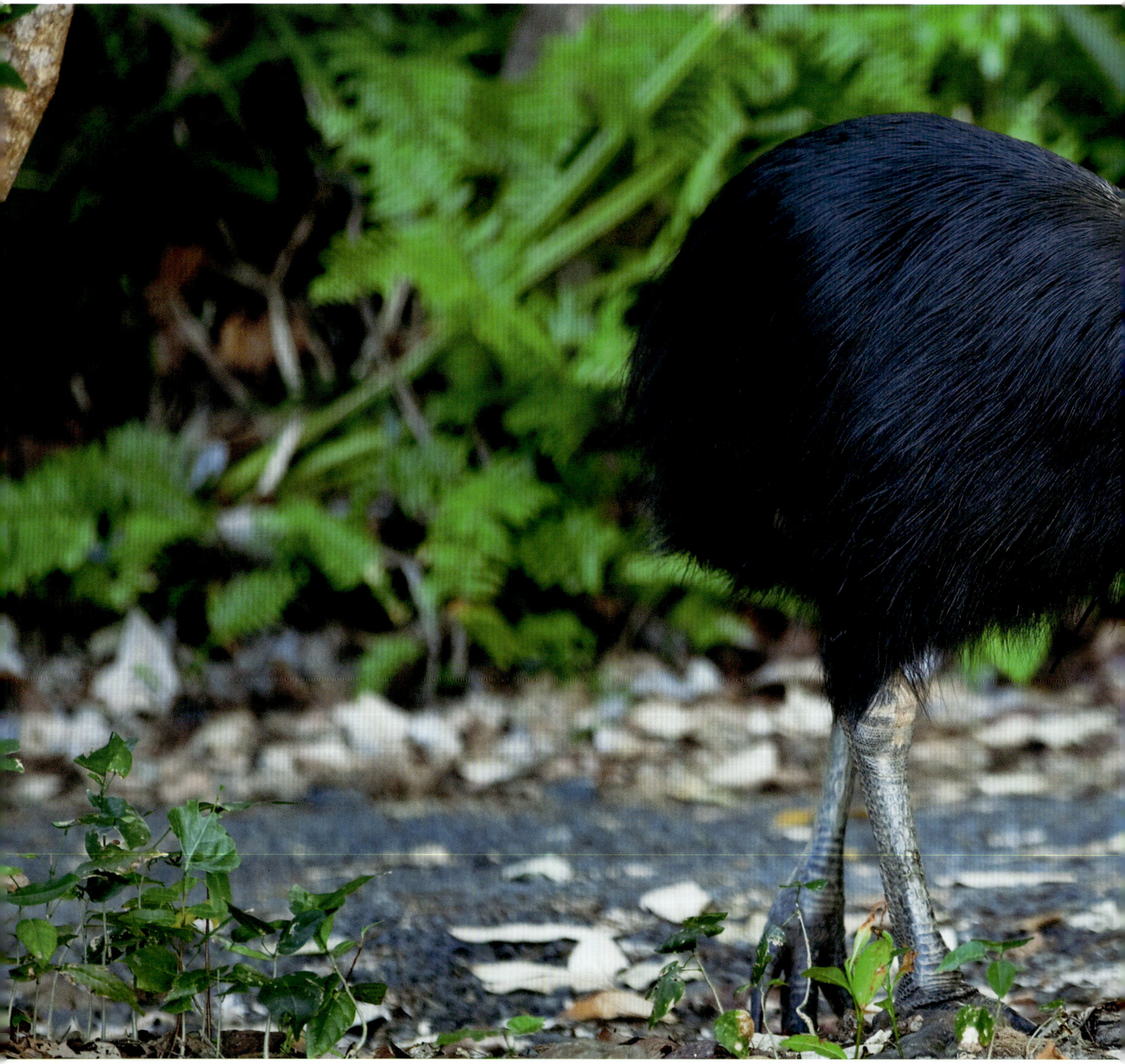

Until deforestation began in the late 1700s, tropical rainforest completely covered the Australian continent. Today, it covers only parts of the Great Dividing Range mountains, the dip slope of the Great Escarpment, and a section of the Queensland coast, where, in contrast to other areas of Australia, the tropical climate has remained stable over millions of years. A varied animal and plant biotope was thus able to develop undisturbed. More than 800 species of tree form a forest in various "layers." Beneath the almost impenetrable canopy of the giant trees, up to 50 m (164 feet) in height, grow more than 350 species of the various higher plants, especially ferns, orchids, moss, and lichen. The animal kingdom is also richly abundant. The Wet Tropics National Park boasts the greatest variety of fauna on the continent. Approximately a third of all Australian marsupials and reptiles and two-thirds of all bat and butterfly species are indigenous to this relatively small area, which occupies only a tiny fraction of the whole continent. Typical inhabitants include the sugar glider, the saltwater crocodile and the stockwhip bird.

The area, crossed by several rivers, is a biotope for the most diverse species. The protected area also includes the Milla Milla Falls in the Atherton Tableland, part of the national park (left). The exotic southern cassowary lives in the park's woodlands (large picture).

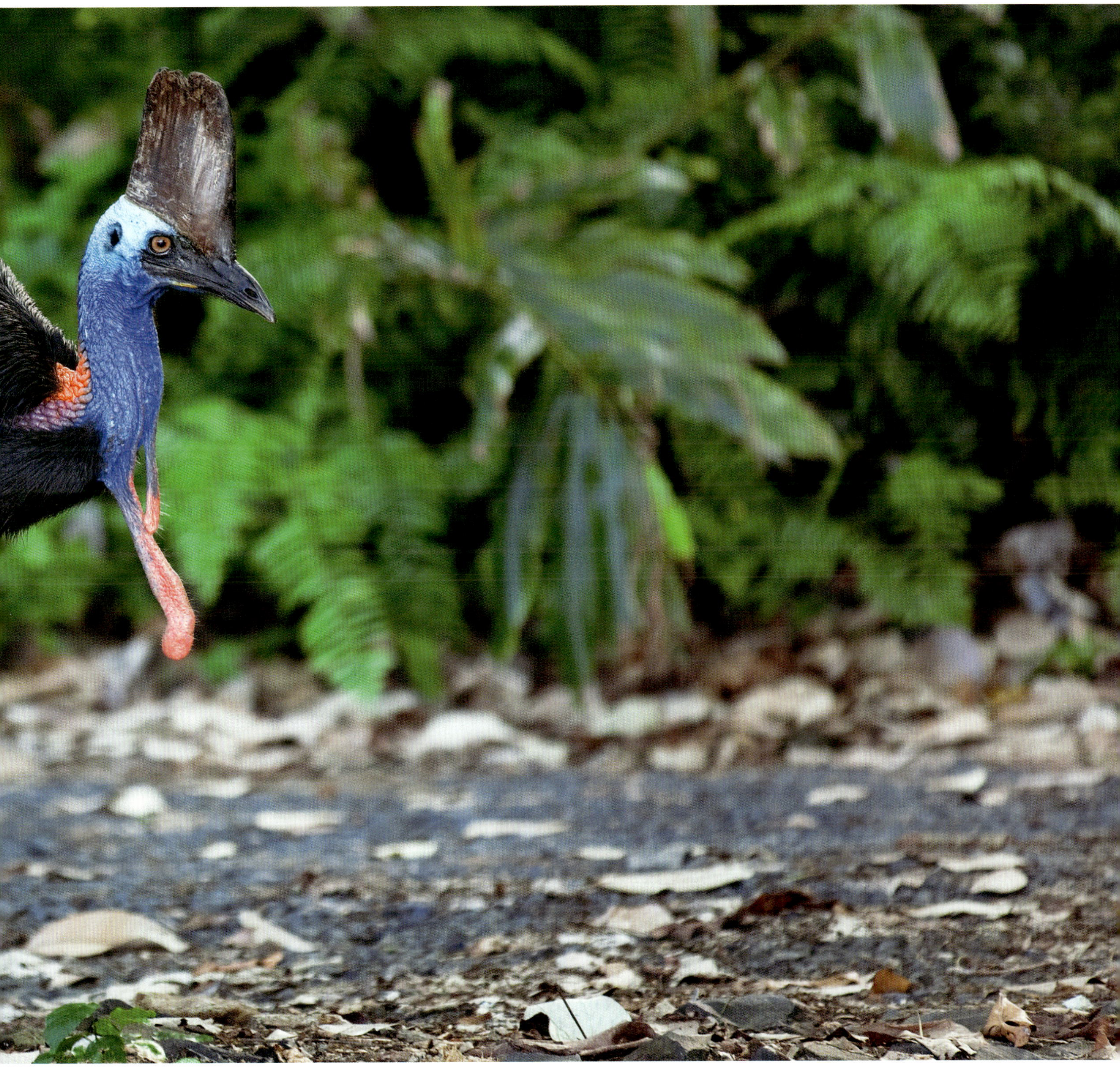

QUEENSLAND'S WET TROPICS: ATHERTON TABLELANDS

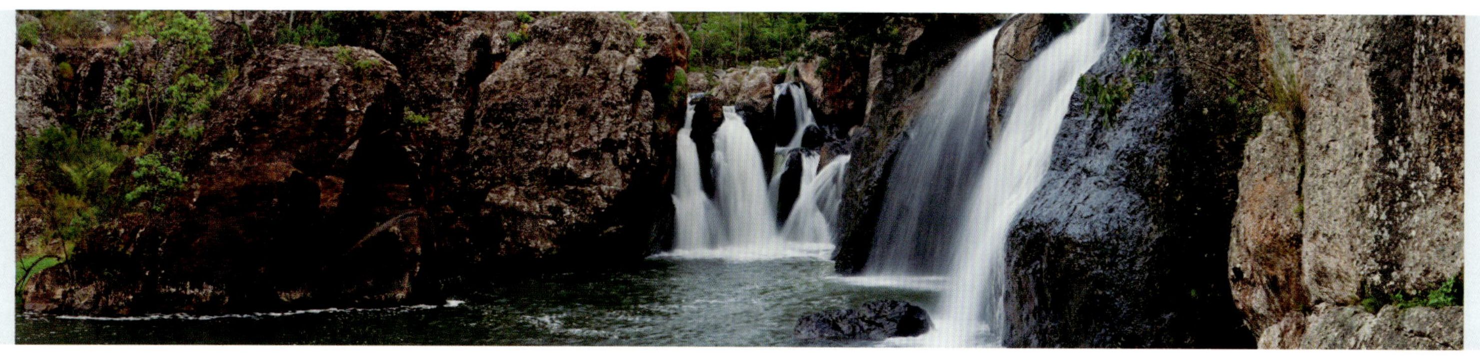

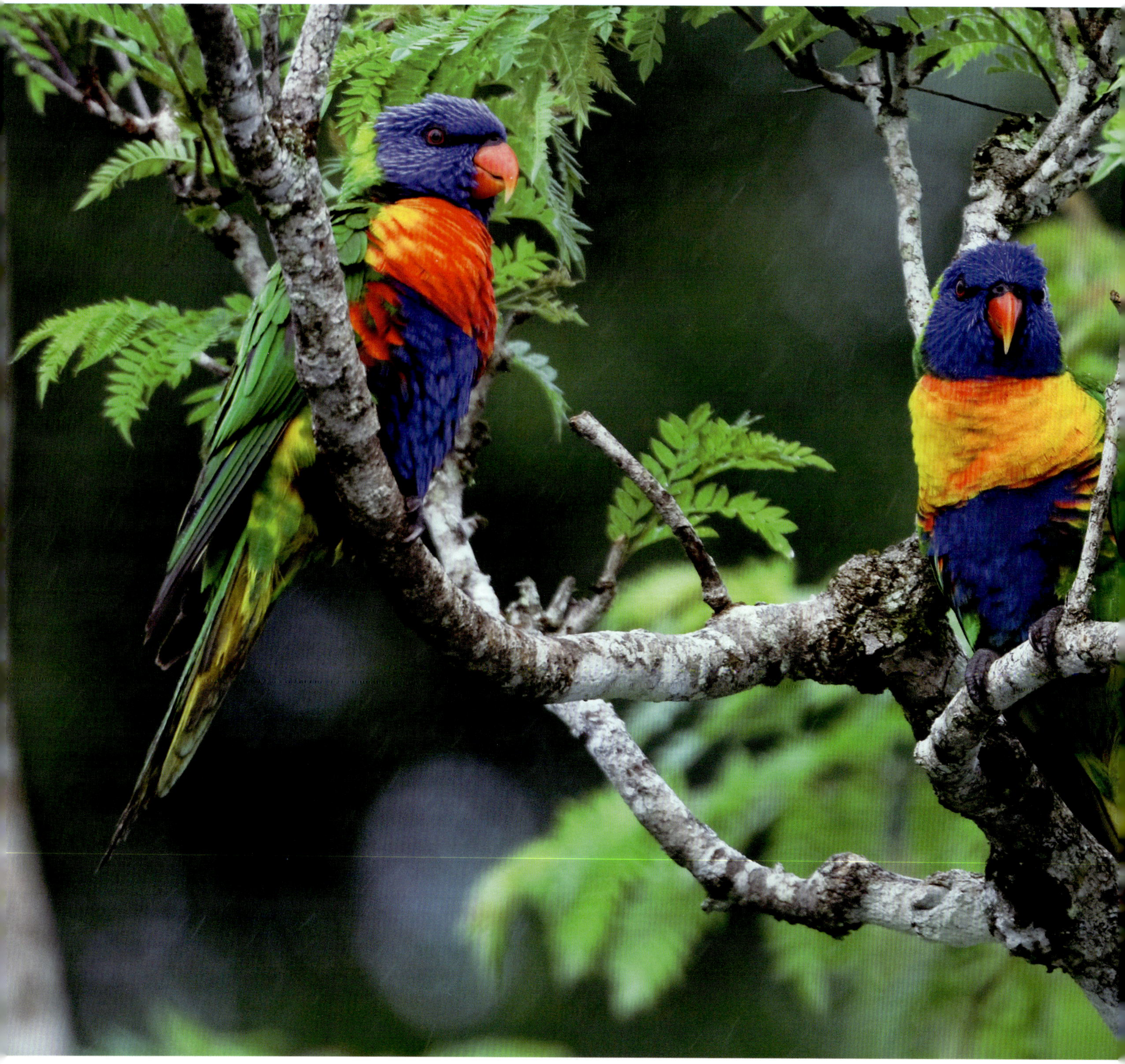

The Atherton Tablelands form a part of the Great Dividing Range, which extends along the Australian east coast. Only 100 years ago, the uplands, rising between 600 and 1,100 m (1,970 and 3,610 feet) in the coastal hinterland between Innisfail and Cairns, were an impenetrable jungle. From 1884 to 1891, pioneers cut the first railway track into the rocky mountainscape, using pickaxe and shovel, so that the zinc from the mines and the timber from the rainforests could be transported to the settlements along the coast. Today, the railway journey along the 34-km (21-mile) stretch from Cairns to Kuranda is one of the classic excursions in the Atherton Tableland. The Kuranda Scenic Railway puffs up the mountains through 15 tunnels and across 40 bridges, arriving at Kuranda 90 minutes later. Today, there are many small businesses selling bric-a-brac and junk, kitsch and crafts at the "Original Kuranda Markets", the "Rainforest Market" and the "Kuranda Heritage Market".

The best of them all, the rainbow lorikeet (large picture) shines in all the most beautiful colours of the rainbow, in good company with the golden bowerbird, Australian king parrot and honeyeater (1st, 2nd and 4th picture from the top). The Victoria's riflebird can afford to appear in elegant black (3rd picture from the top). Left: the Little Millstream Falls.

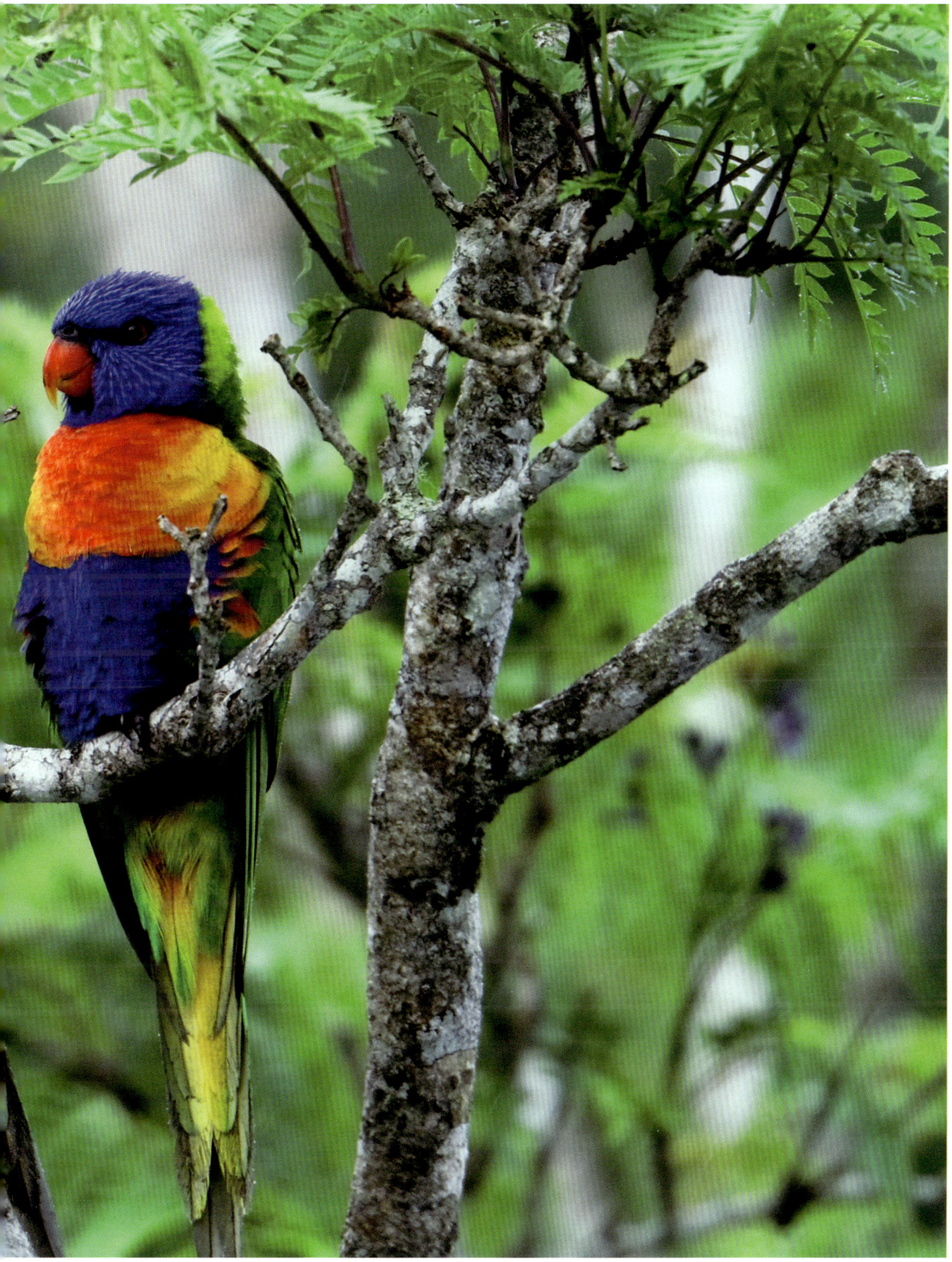

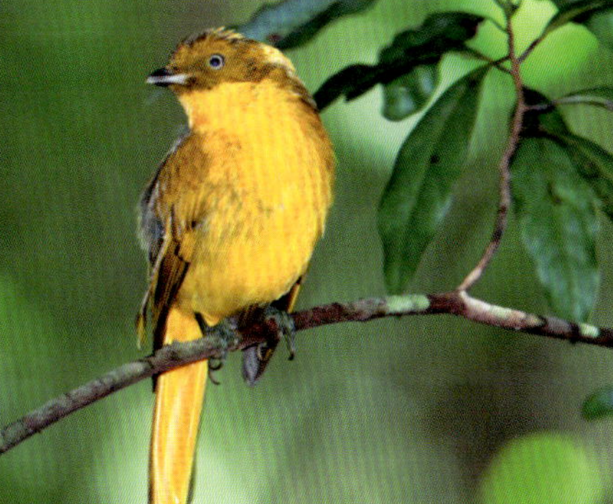

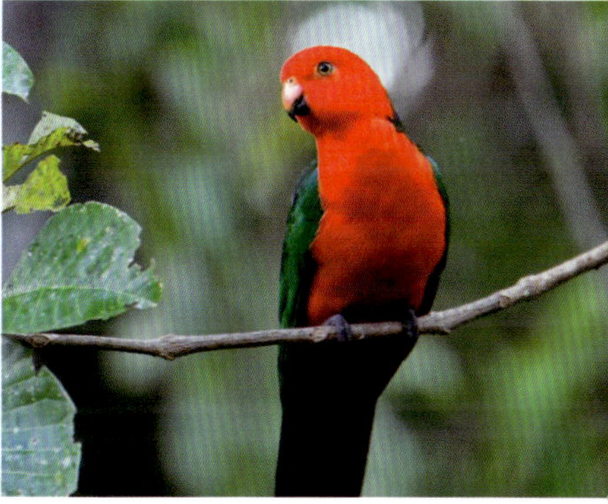

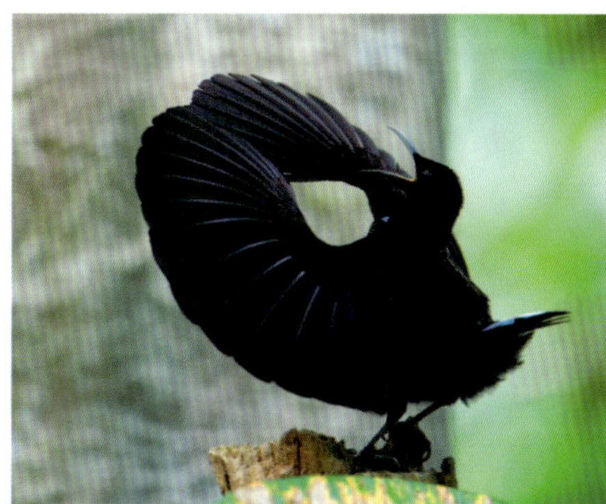

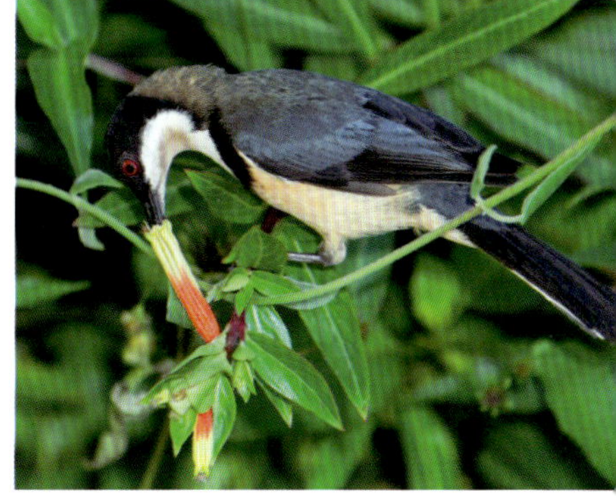

QUEENSLAND'S WET TROPICS: DAINTREE NATIONAL PARK

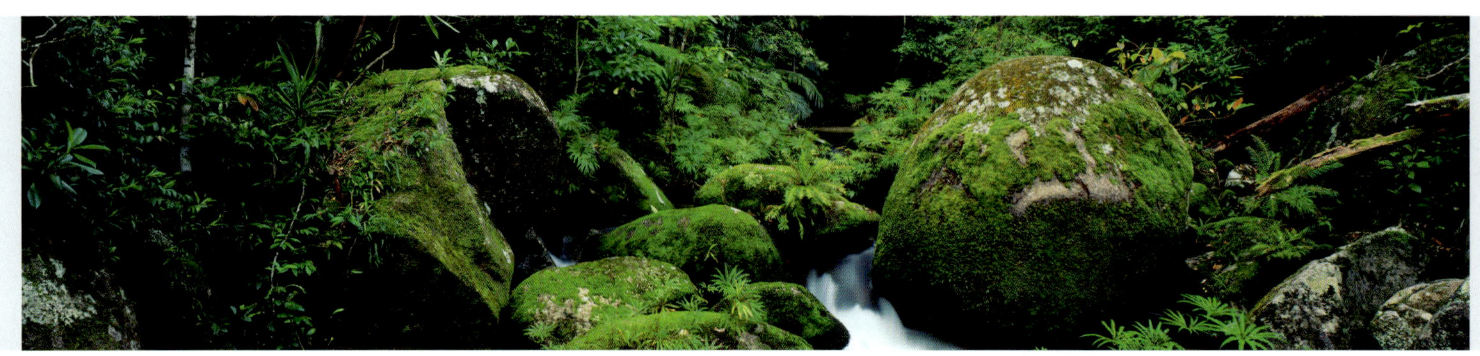

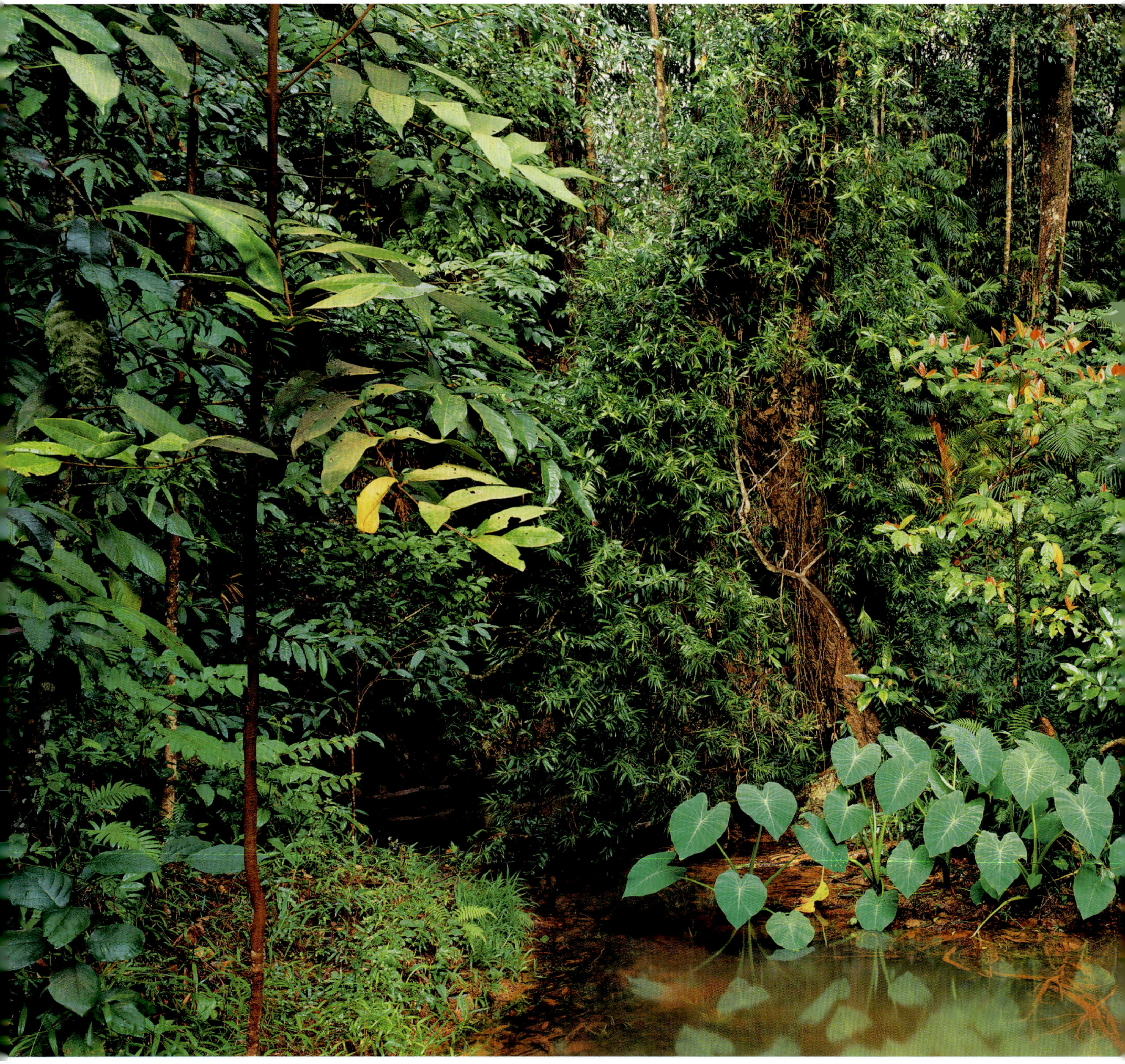

Australians love horror stories that can spread fear and panic among gullible people. One of them goes like this: Crocodiles are clever chaps and they specifically target white trainers – because they've learned that these always contain tourists who often come too close to the water's edge. This is one of the favourite stories told at Daintree National Park in Queensland, where there are actual signs warning you of the crocodiles' great appetite.

However, this should not detain you from visiting the park, which is a miracle of creation: the oldest tropical rainforest on Earth, covering only 0.01 per cent of Australia's land mass, but harbouring 30 per cent of all the mammal species on the continent. The oldest flowering plants in the world are at home here; the park resembles an archive of time.

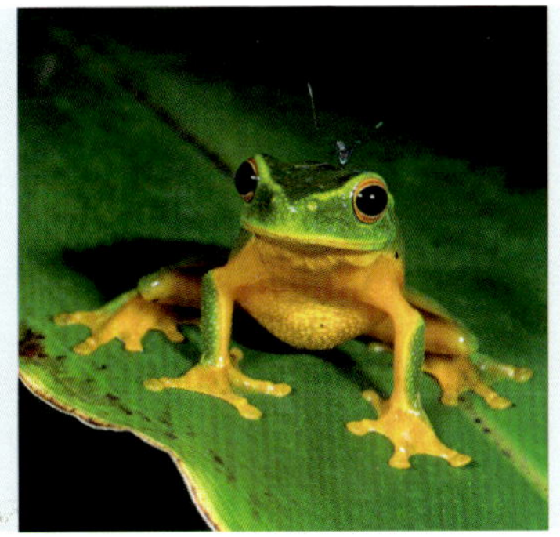

The inhabitants of the forest show themselves from their best side: the Boyd's forest dragon, a bat hanging upside down, a scrub python (from the top) and the cute dainty green tree frog (left).

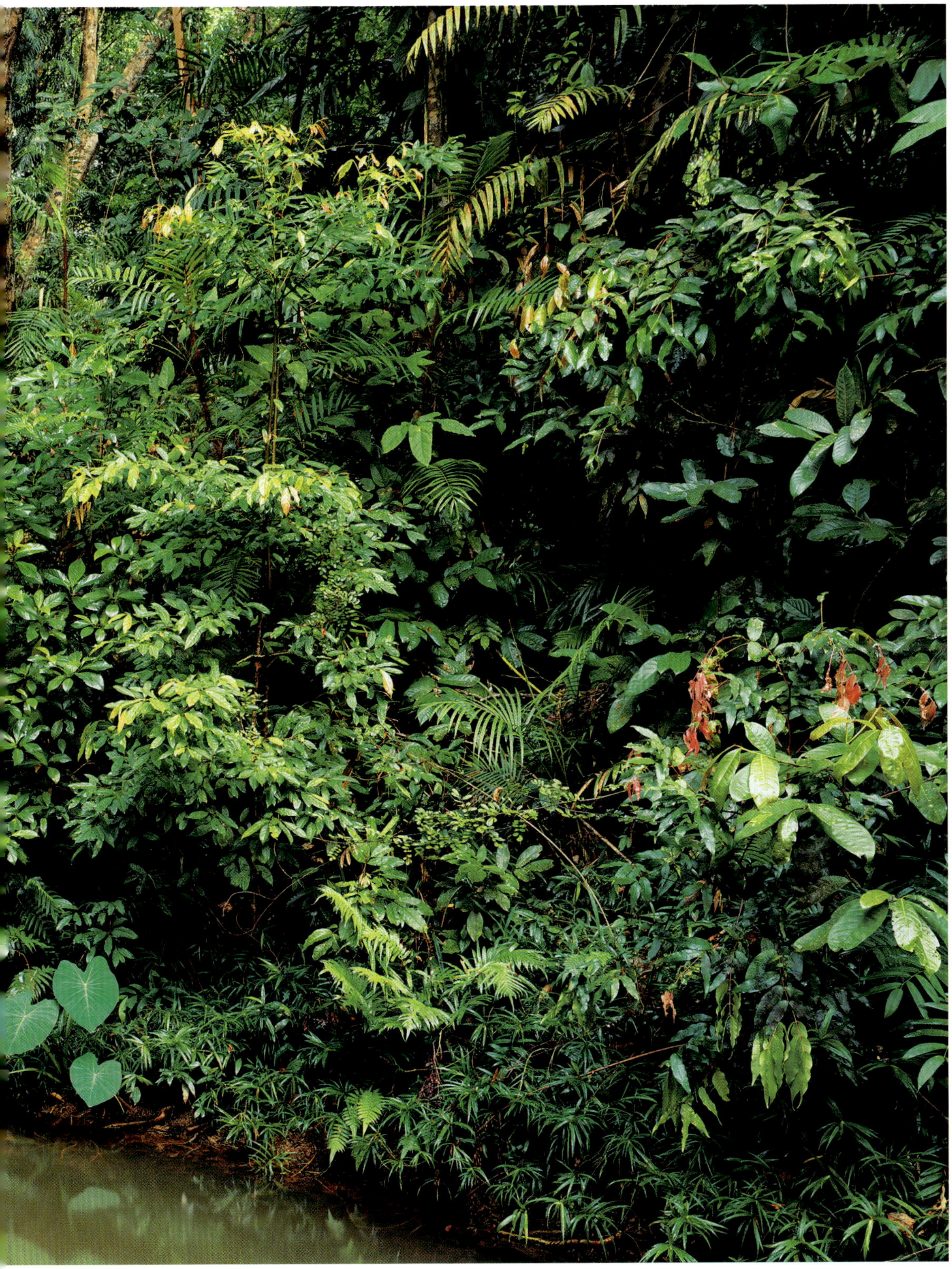

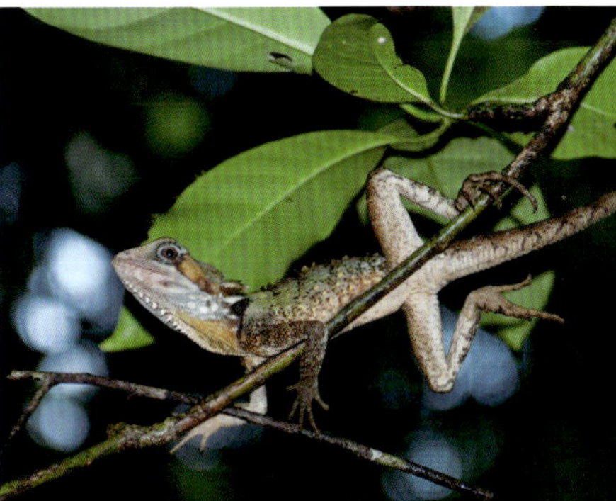

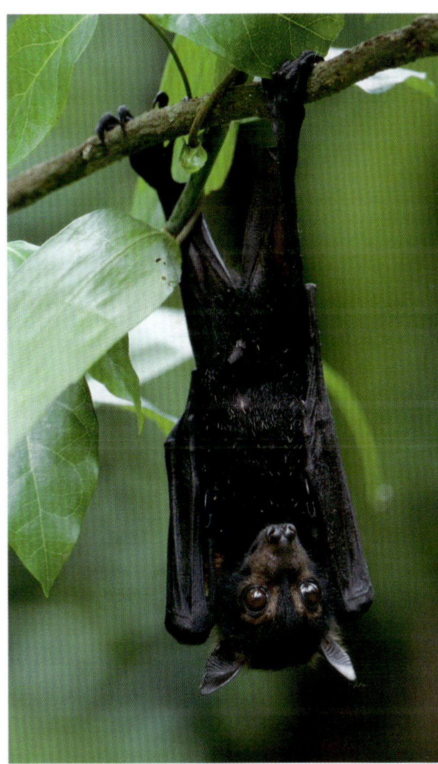

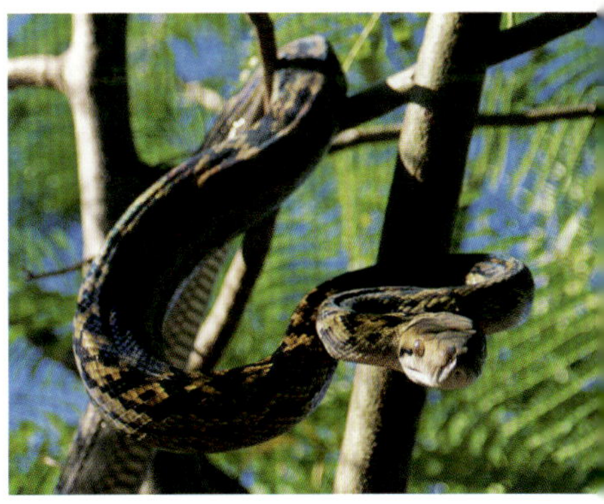

THE GONDWANA RAINFOREST OF AUSTRALIA

Date of inscription: 1986
Extended:1994

The World Heritage Site once known as "Rainforests of the East Coast" was renamed "Gondwana Rainforest of Australia" in 2007 and encloses 15 national parks and conservation areas in Queensland and New South Wales.

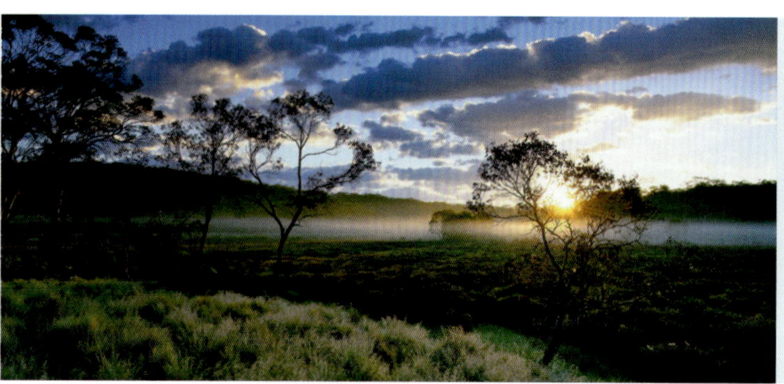

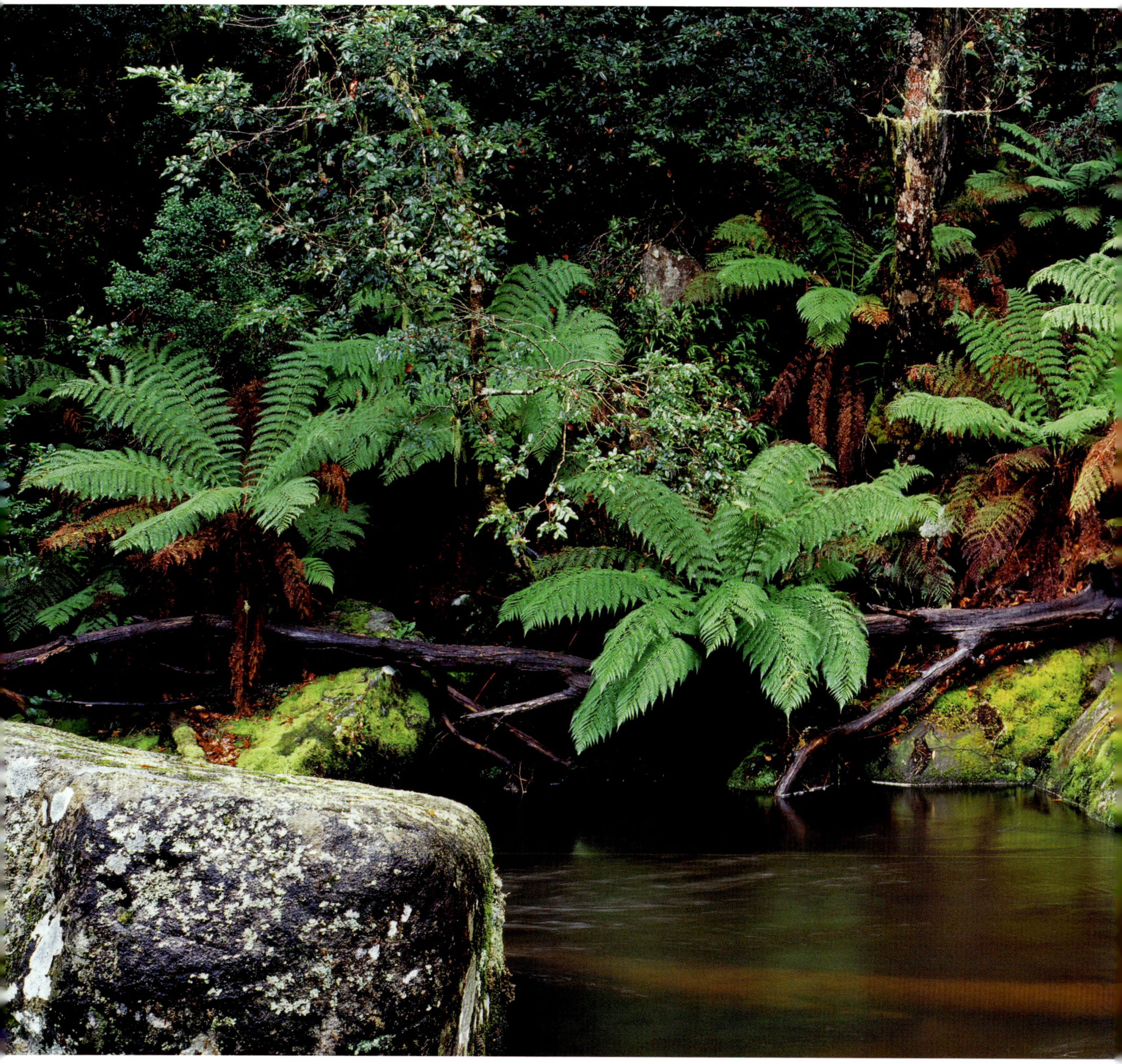

All the following UNESCO-protected regions are in the transitional zone between a damp, tropical climate and a warm, temperate zone, with the result that a huge variety of vegetation has been able to evolve within a relatively small area. Southern beeches grow alongside temperate forest in the south, while on the high plateaus, expanses of rain moor are host to red toons and species of eucalyptus. Subtropical rainforest, with banyan fig trees, orchids, and ferns, predominates further north, on the volcanic plateaus. Subalpine forest with eucalyptus trees is encountered at altitudes of up to 1,500 m (4,900 feet). The national parks of Border Ranges, Mount Warning, Night Cap, Washpool, Gibraltar Range, New England, Dorrigo, Werrikimbe and Barrington Tops were inscribed as World Heritage Sites in 1986. Springbrook, Lamington, Mount Chinghee, Main Range, and parts of Mounts Mistake and Barney National Parks were added in 1994. Barrington Tops and the Border Ranges are famed for their enormous wealth of bird life. Satin bowerbirds, rainbow lorikeets, king parrots, and kookaburras are seen here relatively frequently, although the rare Albert's lyrebird is less common. The Heritage Site's new name harks back to the supercontinent of the southern hemisphere, Gondwana, which in the middle geological period (Mesozoic) fragmented into the continents we know today.

The Barrington Tops National Park (below left and below) is characterized by temperate rainforest on the valley floor. An amazing variety of species can be found in the marshy areas of the national park (left).

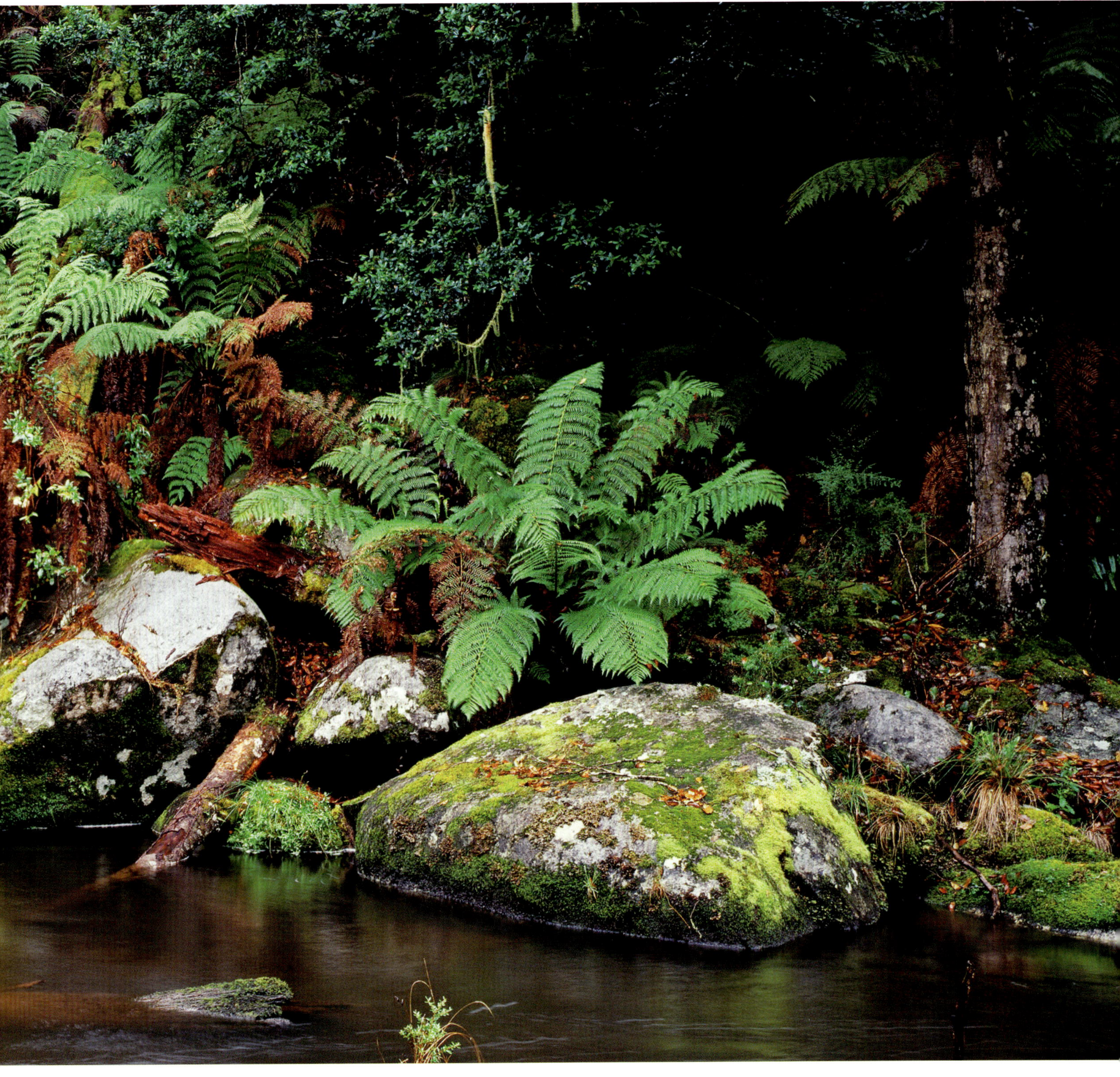

GREATER BLUE MOUNTAINS

Date of inscription: 2000

At the gates of Sydney there is an expanse of primeval landscape which even today has been only partly explored. The Blue Mountains arose about a million years ago in the Pliocene era and belong to the Great Dividing Range chain.

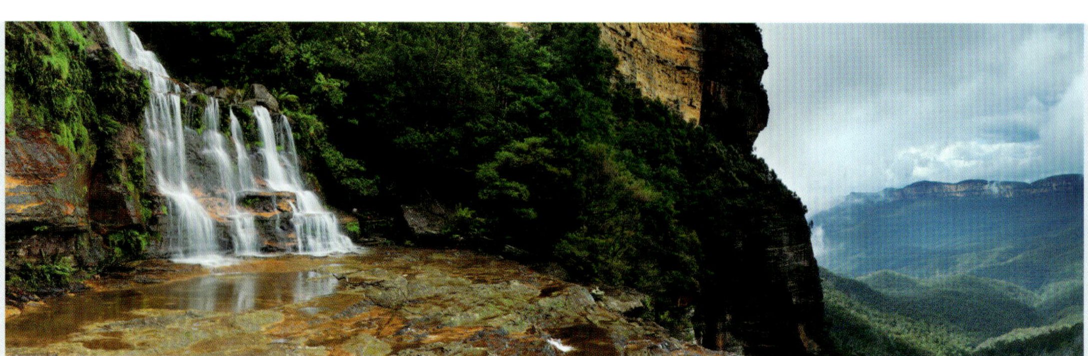

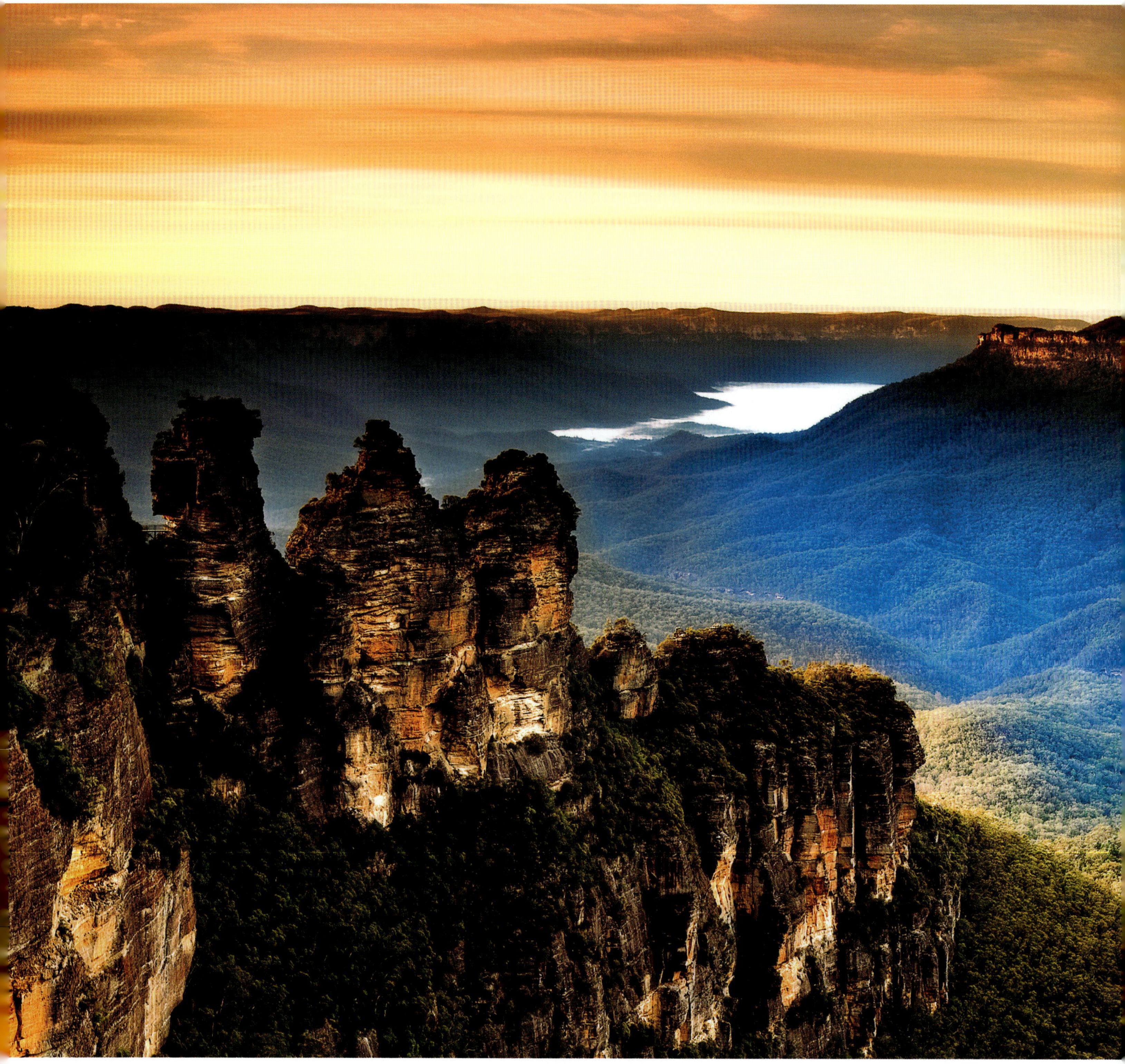

The charming landscape of the Blue Mountains is a living laboratory of jagged sandstone formations, caves, and complex ecosystems. Although they are not very high, between 600 and 1,000 m (1,970 and 3,280 feet), the mountains are steep, with many valleys and canyons still untouched by humans. There is an unprecedented wealth of eucalyptus species and rare and endangered plants. Around 150 indigenous plants and trees flourish in the thick forest, including the Wollemi pine, discovered only in 1994. This is regarded as a living fossil, with roots reaching back at least 90 million years. Cave paintings and rock drawings attest to early Aboriginal settlement.

The Blue Mountains are a globally unique example of dynamic interaction between extreme climatic conditions, adapted eucalyptus species, poorly nutritious soils, and fire. Their name is derived from an optical illusion – the eucalyptus forests appear blue in the vapour haze of the oils exuded by the trees.

The most famous rock formation in the Blue Mountains is the "Three Sisters," which rises some 300 m (990 feet) above the Jamieson valley (below).The Greater Blue Mountains are fascinating, with impressive gullies and waterfalls (left).

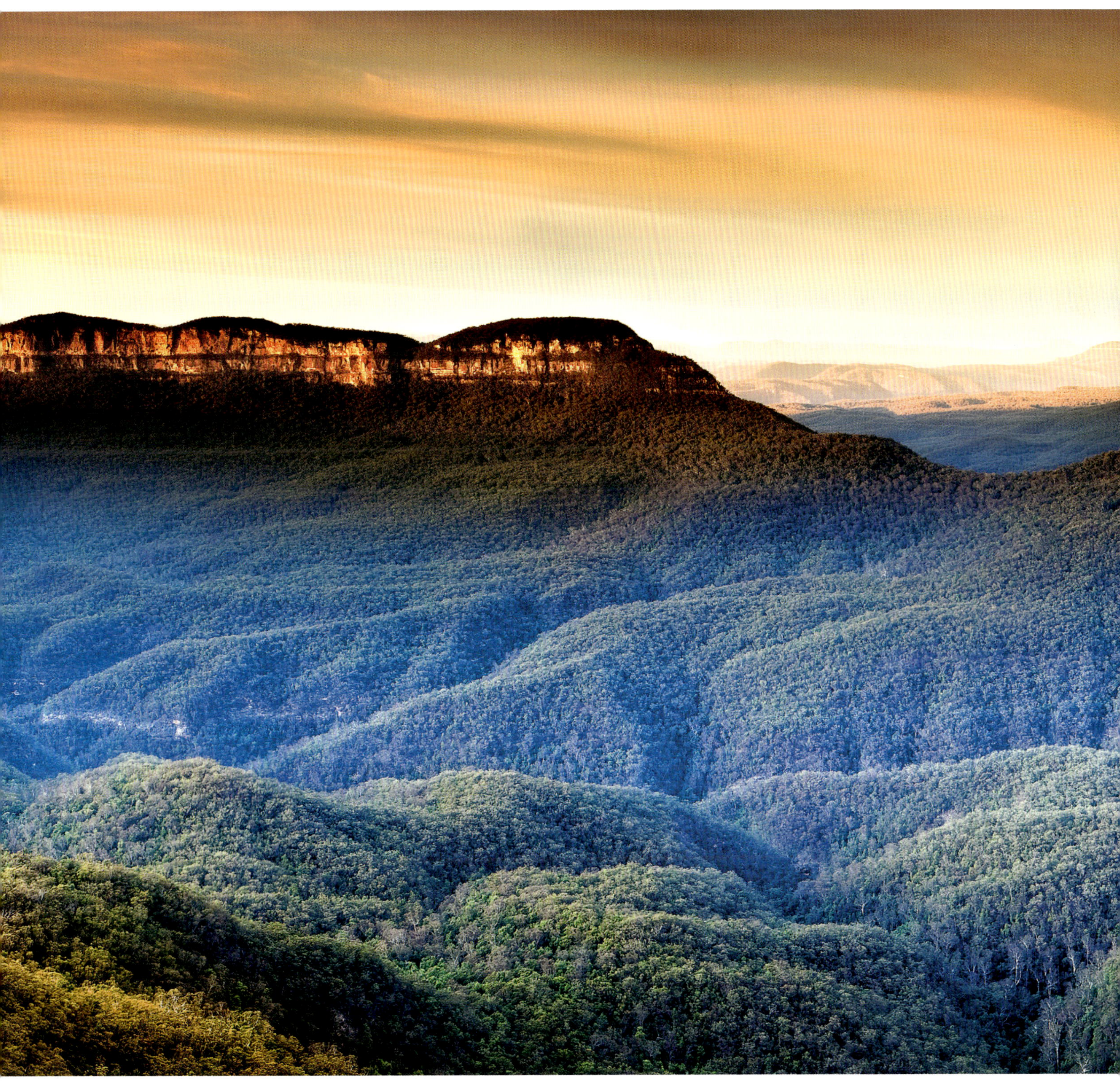

FRASER ISLAND

Date of inscription: 1992

The world's largest sand island, still partially covered with primeval lowland rainforest, provides a habitat for rare birds and frogs.

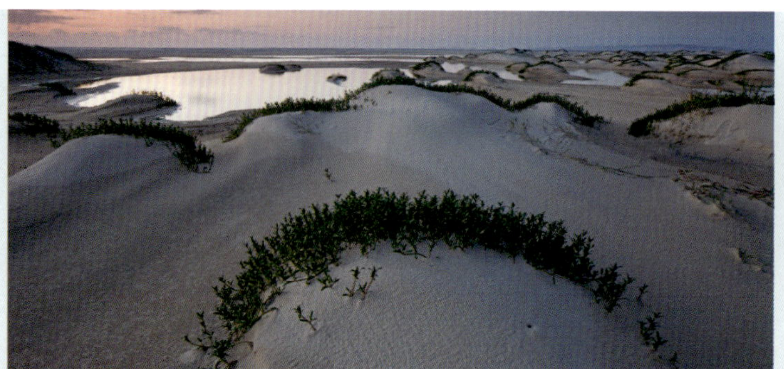

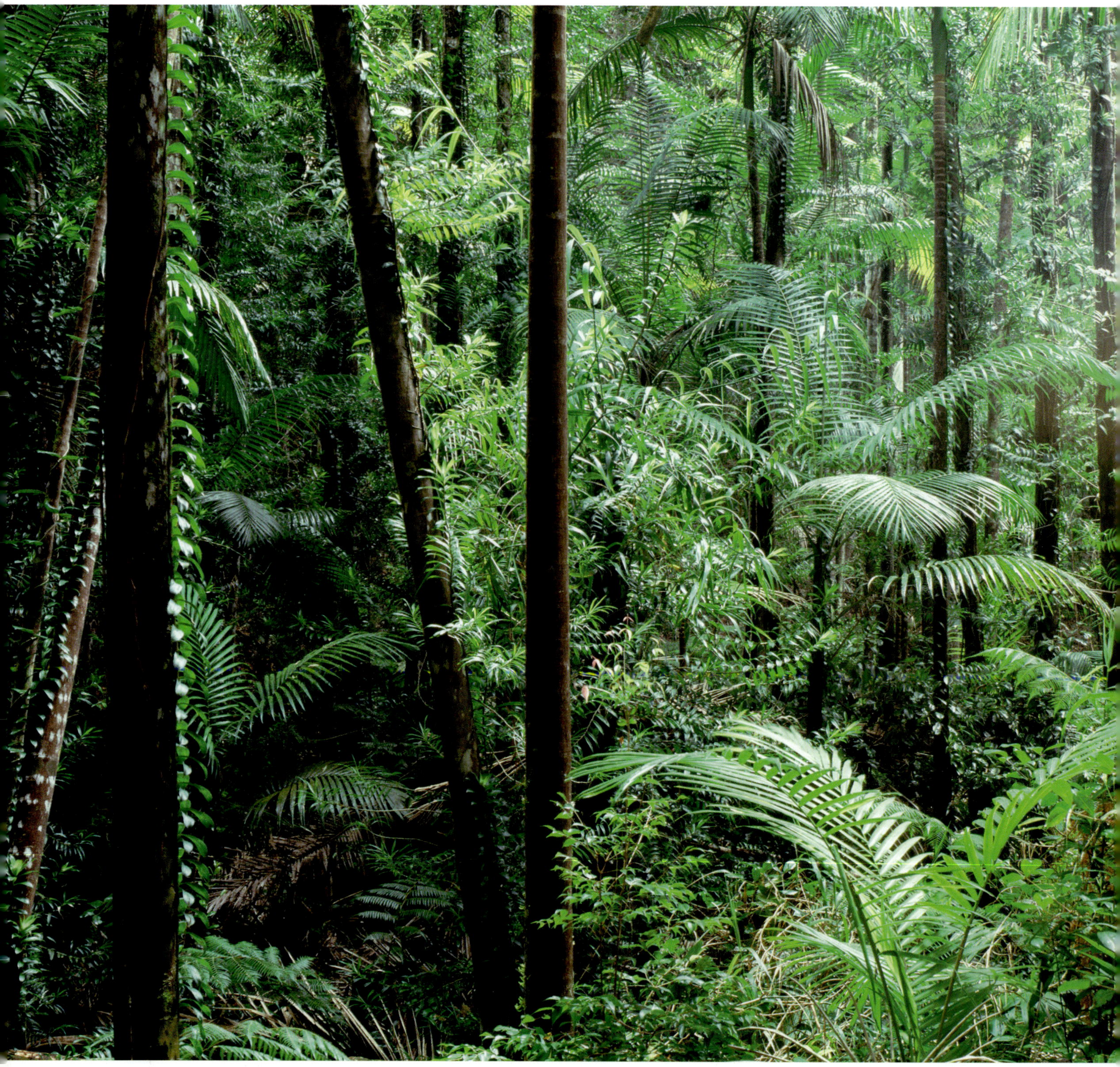

The surface of this 120-km (75-mile) long island, located at the southern end of the Great Barrier Reef, has been on the move for 140,000 years. The crescent dunes, which reach a height of up to 250 m (820 feet), migrate up to 3 m (10 feet) to the north-east every year, driven by the constant south-westerly winds. No sooner had the island been discovered in 1836 than the settlers began the exploitation of the tropical rainforest and its variety of species. The Queensland kauri, the bunya-bunya tree, the tallow and blackbutt eucalyptus, and the 70-m (230-foot) high satinay tree were regularly felled. Today, only small areas of the island's interior are covered in rainforest. The remaining landscape is diverse and offers a refuge for over 240 species of bird. The mangrove honey-eater lives in the mangroves on the coast, while the ground parrot is found on coastal heaths. The red-green king parrot hunts for nectar in tropical forests, and the stubble quail is indigenous exclusively to damp areas of moor. Many migratory birds stop here.

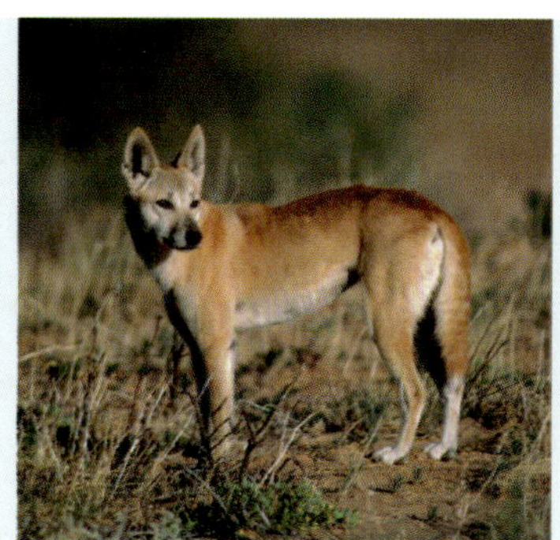

In the southern half of Fraser Island, the plant world has painted green garlands into the barren coastal landscape (far left). The dingoes that live here (left) are used to humans. The island's interior is a dense rainforest (below).

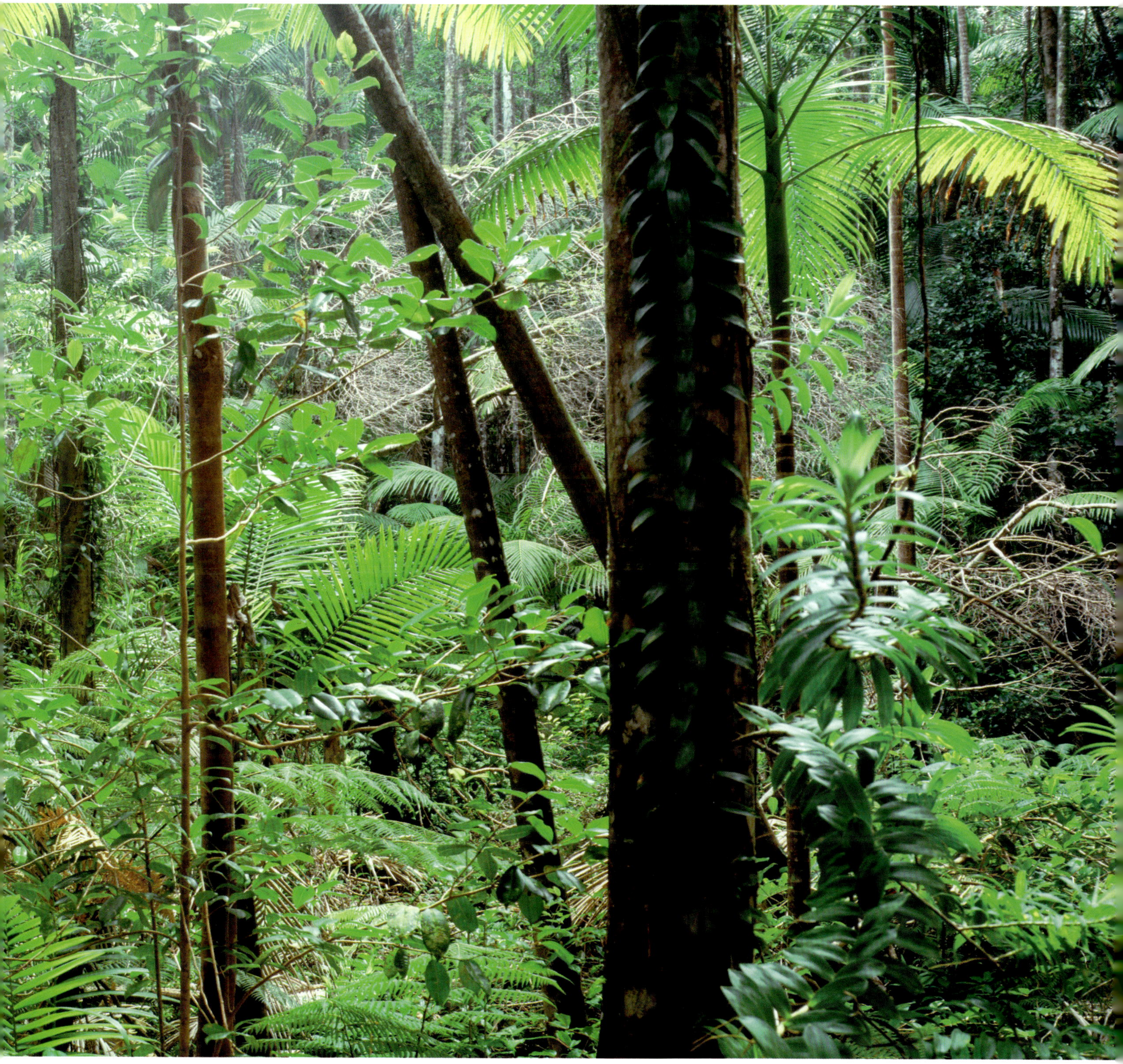

GREAT BARRIER REEF

Date of inscription: 1981

The Great Barrier Reef follows the north-eastern coast of Australia from the 10th to the 24th parallel south. Coral polyps, in their singular underwater world, have been building this largest of natural "edifices" for 8,000 years.

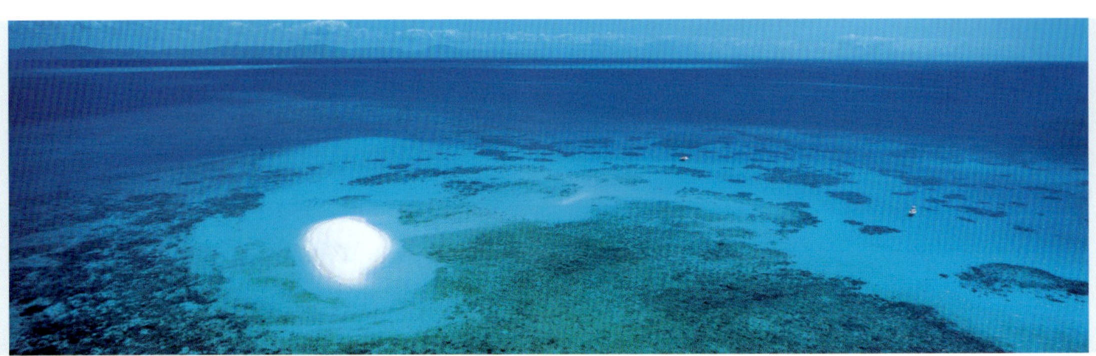

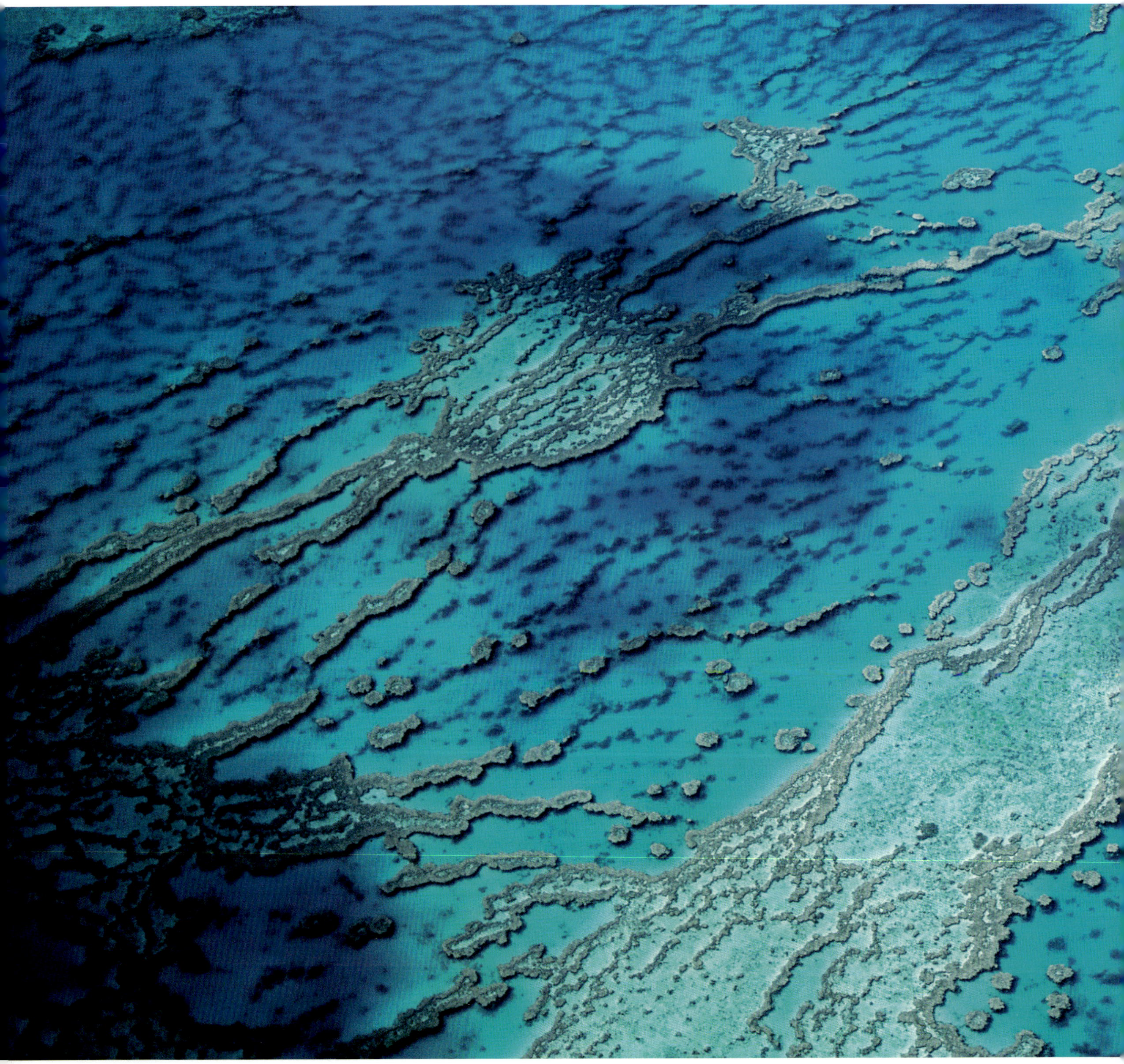

The reef, which is composed of about 2,500 individual reefs and 500 coral islands, follows 2,000 km (1,250 miles) of the coastline of continental Australia at a distance of 15 to 200 km (9 to 124 miles). It was "constructed" by coral polyps, working symbiotically with cyanobacteria. Able to swim from birth, the polyp larvae hatch in the spring and settle on the reef, near the water's surface. They develop a skeletal structure and form a colony with others of their kind. After a while they die off and their coral skeletons are ground to a fine sand. The algae then "bake" the sand into an additional layer of the reef, upon which new polyp larvae can settle, and thus the reefs and islands have grown over millennia. Among the 1,500 species of fish that live in the waters surrounding the reefs are the brilliant and exotic coral trout, the golden damselfish, the parrotfish, and the stingray. Hundreds and thousands of varieties of birds, corals, and molluscs live here. Bird species include pelicans, frigate birds, noddies, and a number of terns including sooty, roseate, and crested.

The longest living coral reef in the world reaches from the Tropic of Capricorn to the estuary of the Fly river (New Guinea). The reef is the habitat of multi-hued flora and fauna (below). This small Coral Cay (left) is situated close to the coast of Cairns.

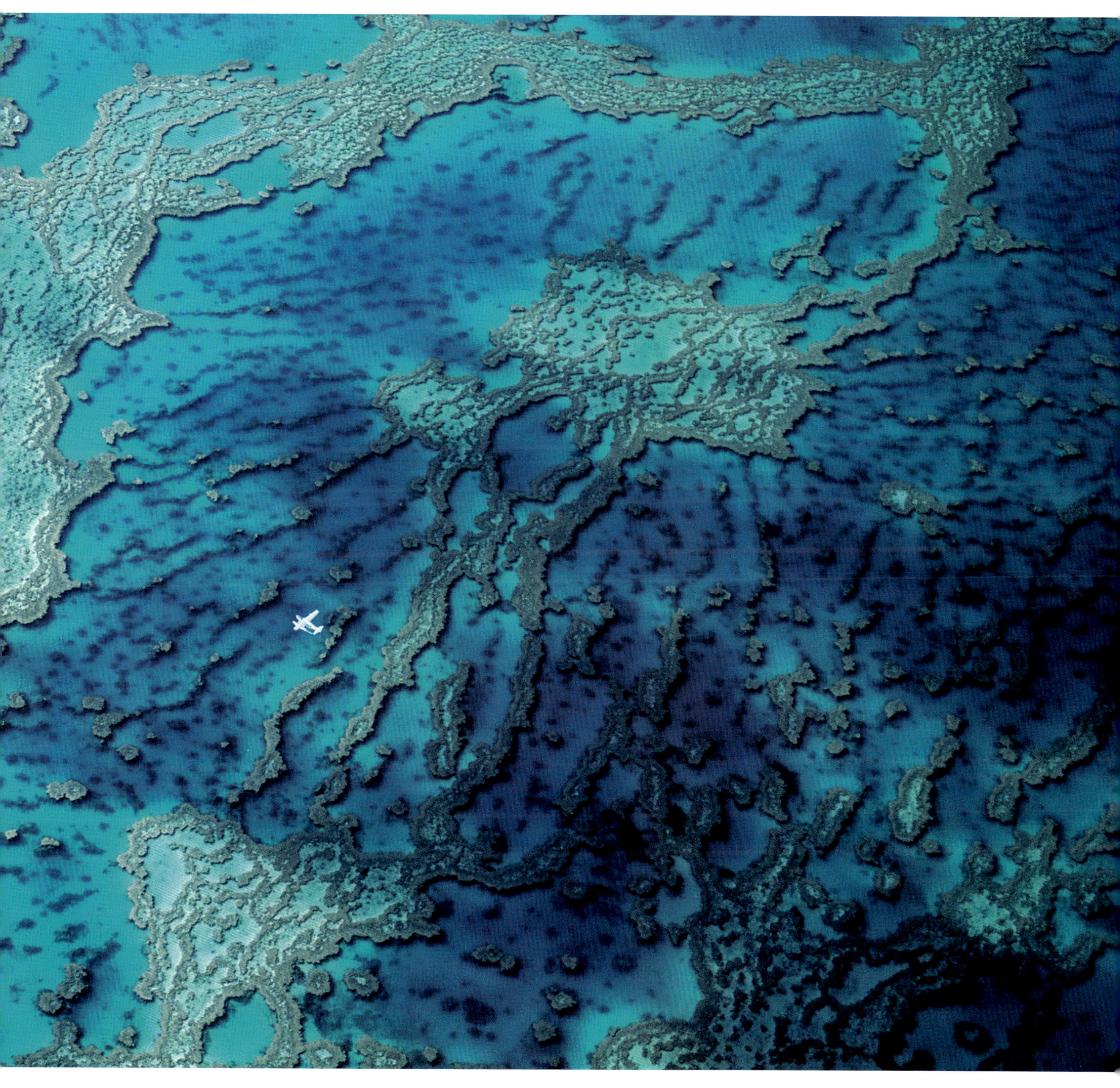

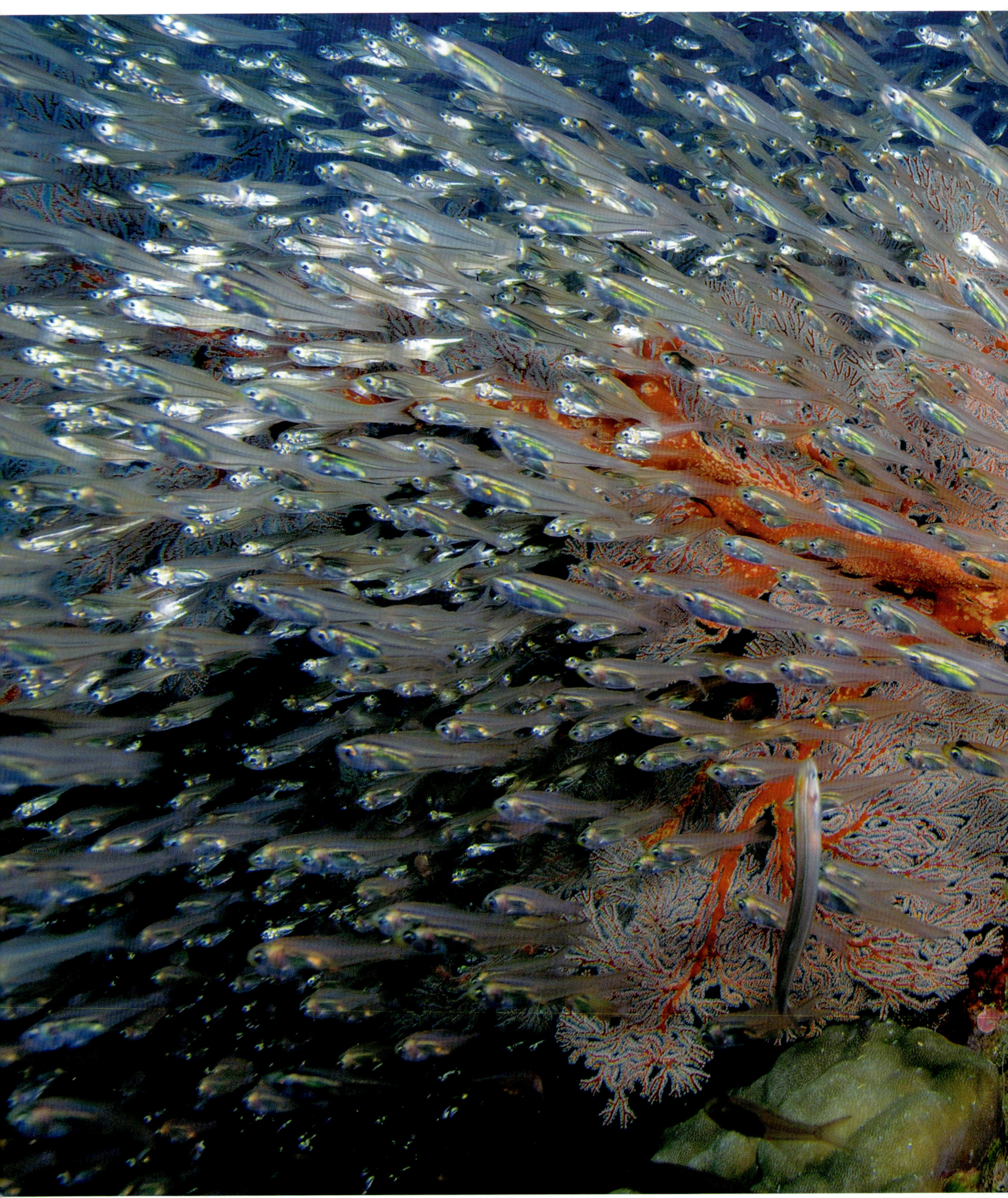

Like an explosion of colours, brightly shimmering shoals of fish shoot along the ocean floor with the waves. Around the world, an estimated 4,000 fish species live in the reefs. In the Great Barrier Reef alone, 1,625 species of fish have been recorded, making it the most diverse habitat on Earth. It is an underwater paradise.

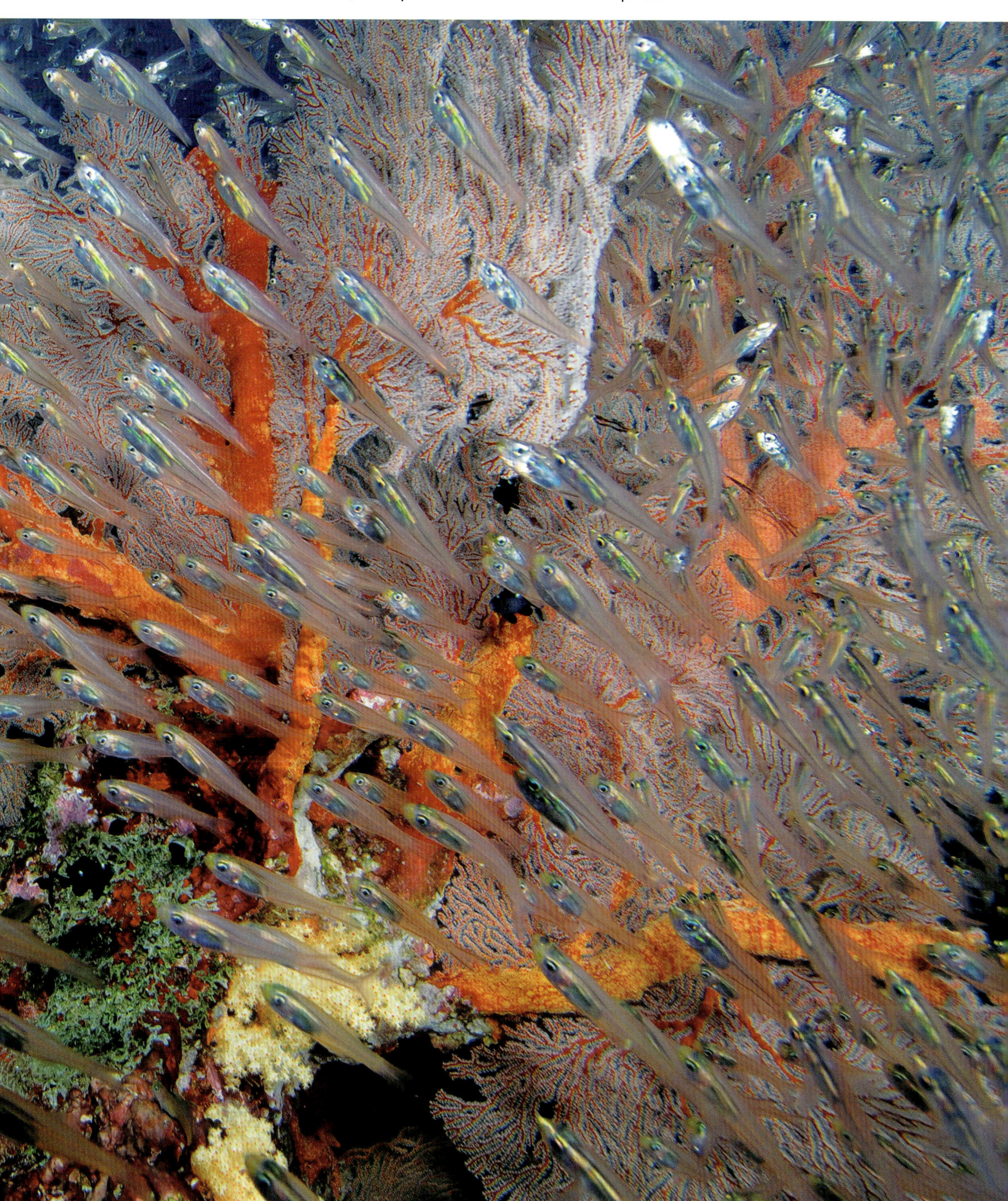

WILLANDRA LAKES REGION

Date of inscription: 1981

The Willandra Lakes Region in the south-western part of New South Wales, which dried out very rapidly about 15,000 years ago, is equally as interesting for geologists as for paleoanthropologists. On the banks of the former lakes can be found traces of settlements that are 40,000 years old, as well as fossilized human remains.

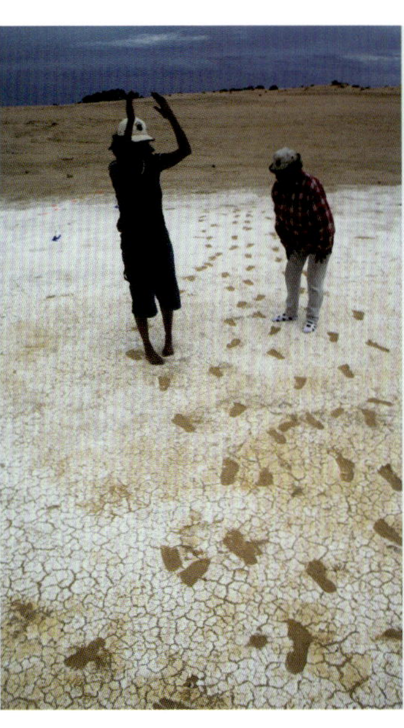

In 1968, exciting prehistoric remains were found in a lunette dune known as the "Walls of China," situated on what 24,000 years ago had been the shores of Lake Mungo in the Willandra Lakes Region. Next to 18,000-year-old tools were found human skeletons, approximately 35,000 to 45,000 years old – the oldest traces of Homo sapiens sapiens, modern humans, ever found in Australia. A further scientific sensation came to light during the examination of a 30,000-year-old camp fire. Proof was found in the remains that, in the course of 2,500 years, the earth's magnetic field had shifted by 120 degrees to the south-east. Rare animals, such as the emu, Australia's largest flightless bird at up to 1.75 m (6 feet) tall, have retreated to the grassland of the Willandra Lakes Region. Thousands of parrots and budgerigars populate the waterholes and prehistoric-looking monitors – one of the largest lizard species in the world – warm themselves in the midday sun.

The Mungo National Park (below) makes up part of the Willandra Lakes Region's 2,400 sq. km (950 sq. miles). Human footprints, thousands of years old, have been found in the area's clay soil (left).

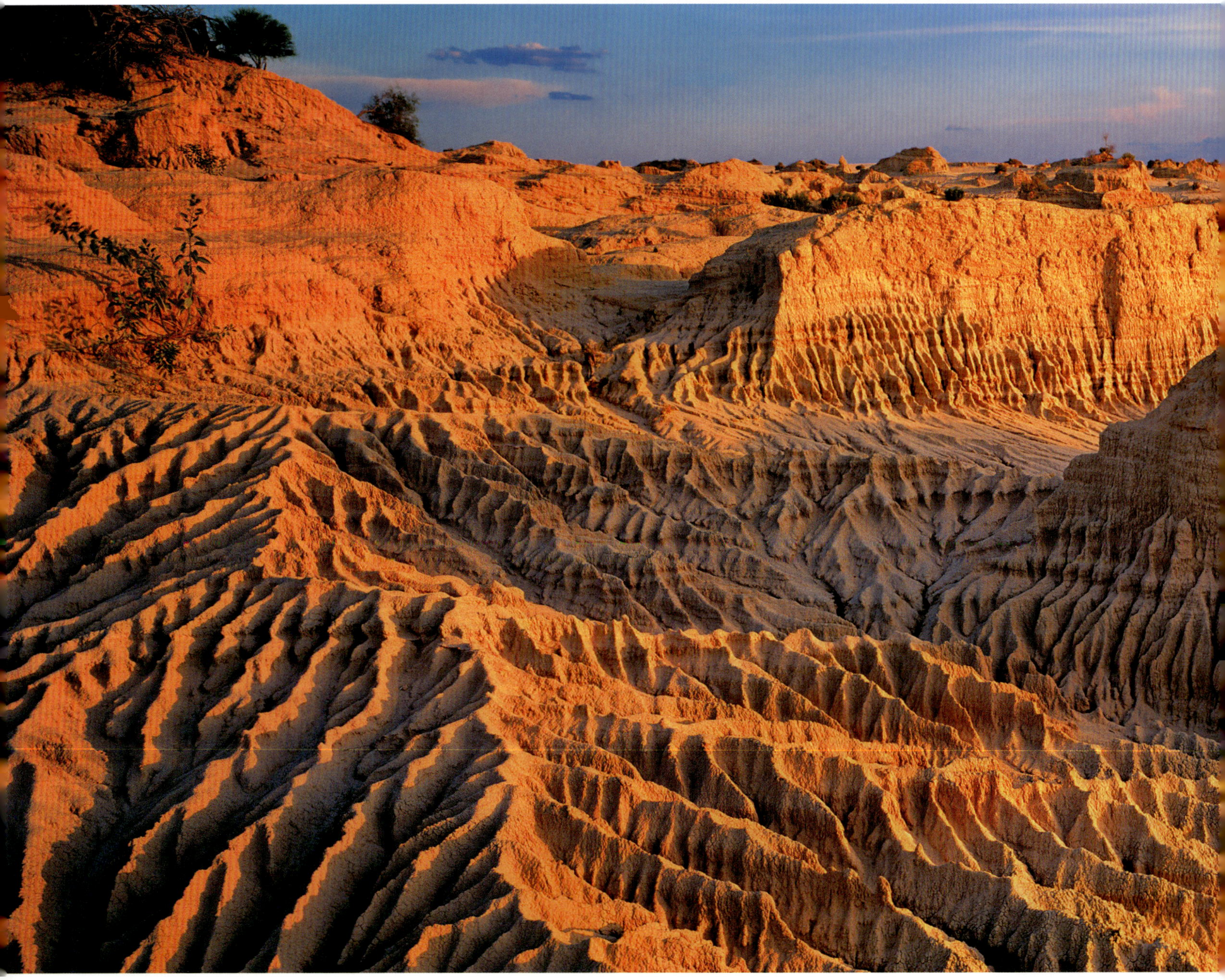

RIVERSLEIGH AND NARACOORTE

Painstaking work in Victoria karst cave at Naracoorte has allowed the excavation, collection, and reconstruction of the skeletons of lungfish, reptiles, monotremes, marsupials, and mammals. Amongst the finds are echidnas and platypuses, the so-called 'missing links' in the development of mammals from reptiles.

The reconstruction of the skeletons of extinct species such as the marsupial lion, with its prehensile paws, and the 3-m (10-foot) tall giant short-faced kangaroo has answered many questions about mammal development.

Finds at Riversleigh's fossil sites, located in Boodjamulla (Lawn Hill) National Park, have contributed much to our understanding of continental drift, which started about 45 to 50 million years ago. Bones from 100 species have been found from a time when Australia was still a part of the Gondwana supercontinent, as well as proof of the migration of south-east Asian species across the land bridge which existed at that time.

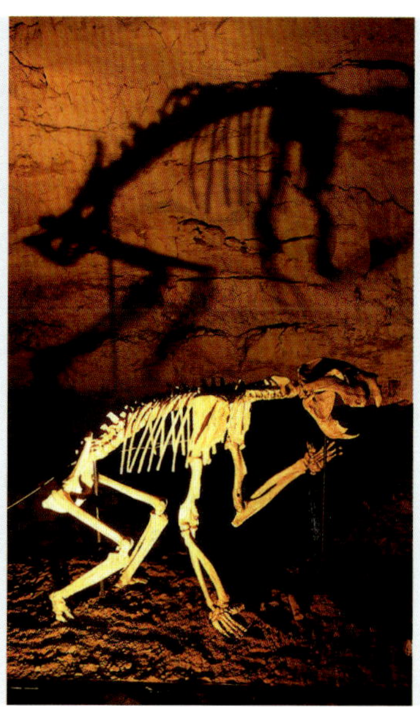

Victoria Cave, near Naracoorte, is a prehistoric treasure trove. Excavations of bones have permitted the reconstruction of the extinct marsupial lion, Thylacoleo carnifex (right).

Date of inscription: 1994

Riversleigh in north-western Queensland and Naracoorte in south-eastern South Australia are among the most spectacular and important fossil sites on earth.

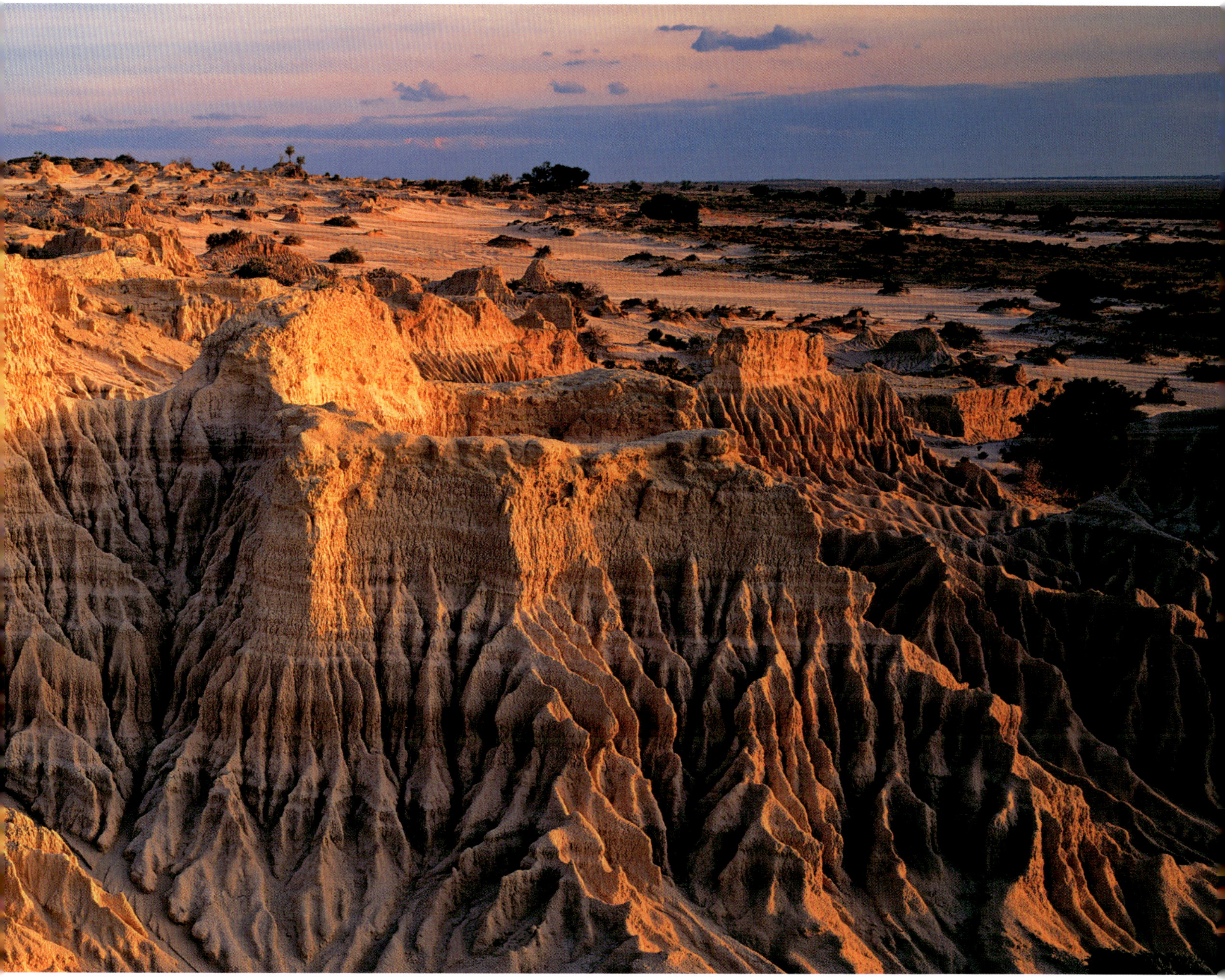

THE TASMANIAN WILDERNESS

Date of inscription: 1982
Extended: 1989

The national parks of Western Tasmania, with their temperate rainforests and singular fauna, are considered one of the world's last untouched ecosystems.

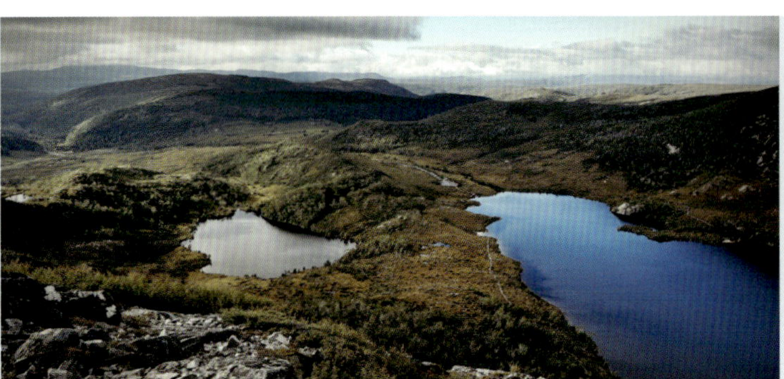

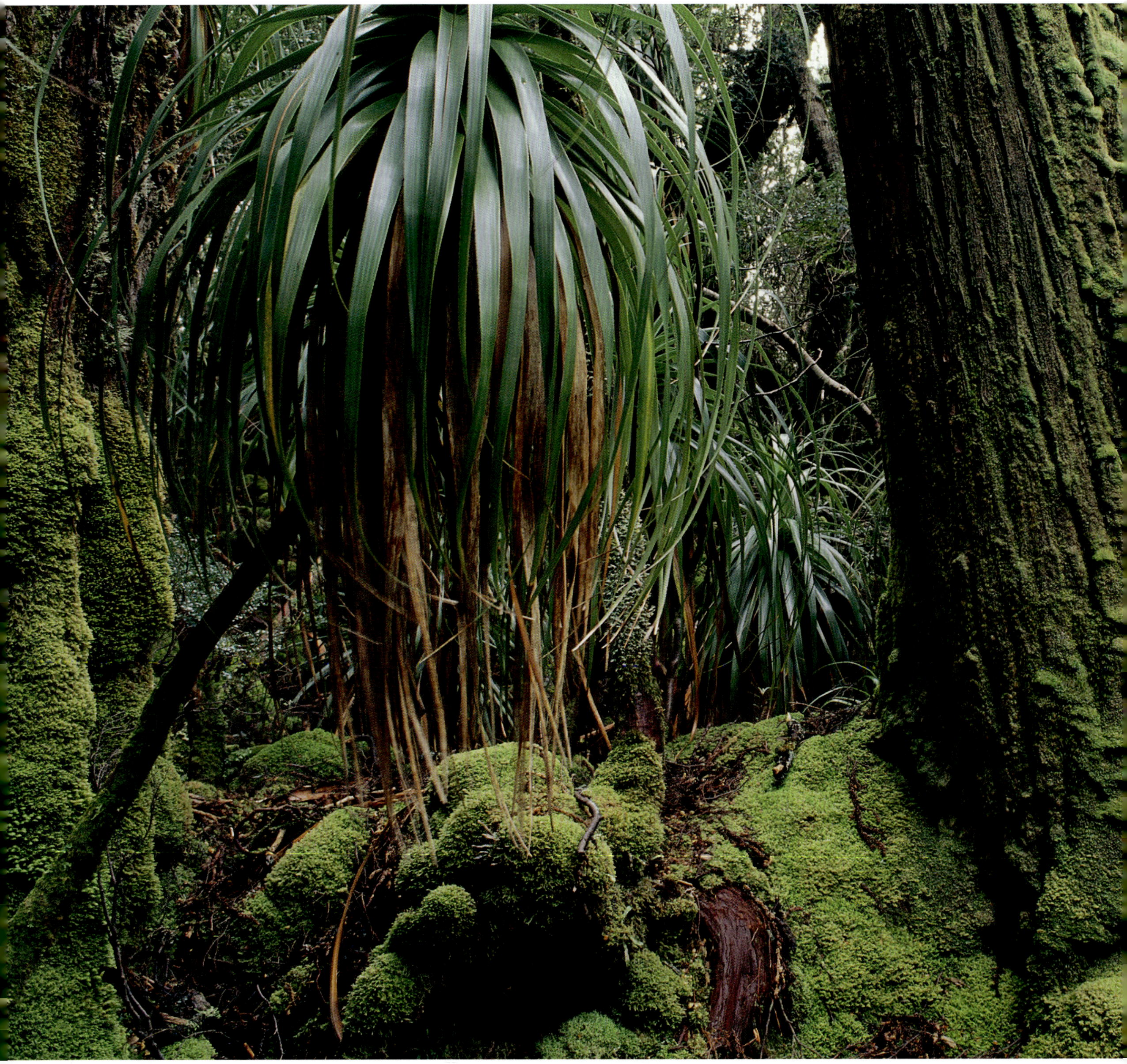

This World Heritage Site, which is located between Cradle Mountain and Tasmania's south-western cape, is composed of five national parks – Lake St Clair, Franklin–Lower Gordon Wild rivers, South-West, Walls of Jerusalem, and Hartz mountains – and several other conservation areas. Deep gullies, steep summits, eroded plains, raging waterfalls, and trough-like lakes are typical of this glaciated landscape. At greater altitudes, there are expanses of moor and heath, and, nearer sea-level, stretches of bogland. Although the temperate rainforest has been much reduced by intensive logging, there are still traces of these great mixed forests, composed of numerous subantarctic and Australian tree species. A singular animal world, including numerous unique species, is at large in this diverse landscape. The nature reserves are home to 27 mammal, 150 bird, 11 reptile, six amphibian, and 15 freshwater fish species. The endangered orange-bellied parrot, the Tasmanian wedge-tailed eagle, the Tasmanian devil, and the Pedra Branca lizard occur only in Tasmania.

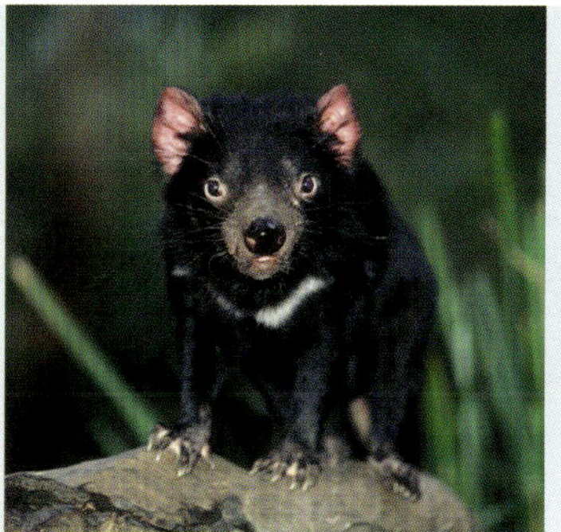

Picture series from the top: The New Holland honeyeater lives on nectar and insects; red-necked wallaby, spotted-tail quoll and tawny frogmouth. The Tasmanian devil is found only in Tasmania (left). Far left: From Marion's Lookout you can enjoy great views of Lake Dove.

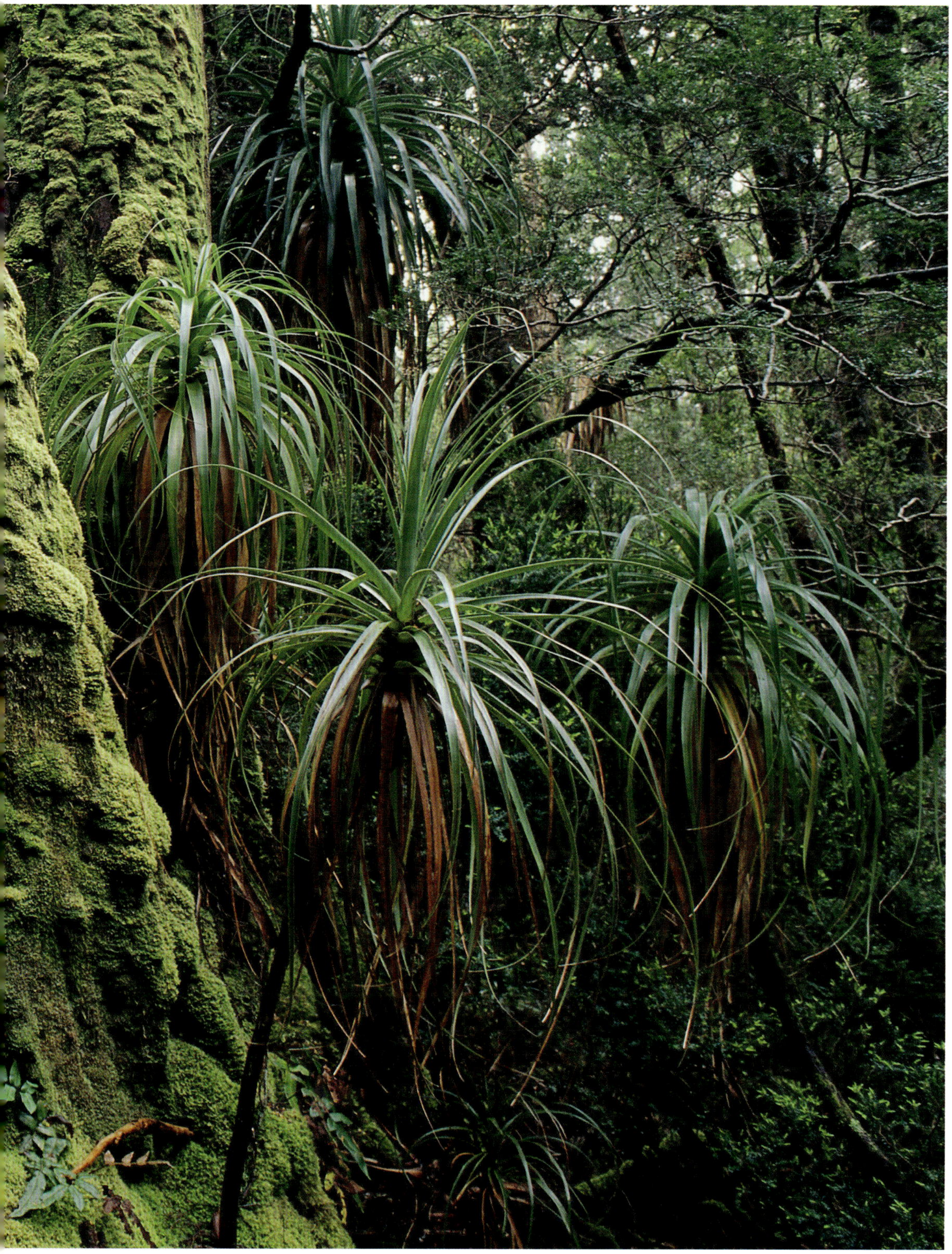

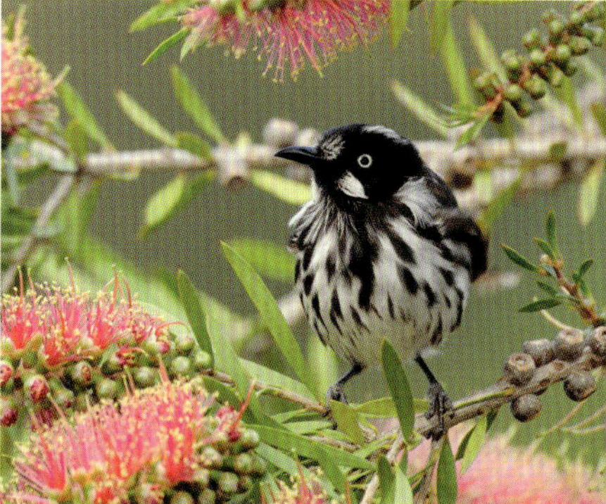

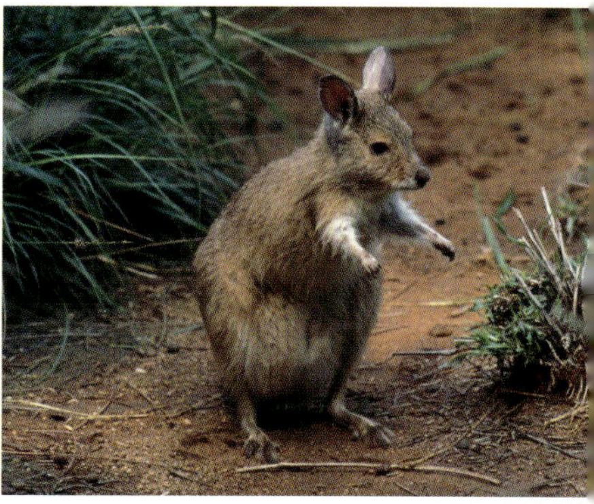

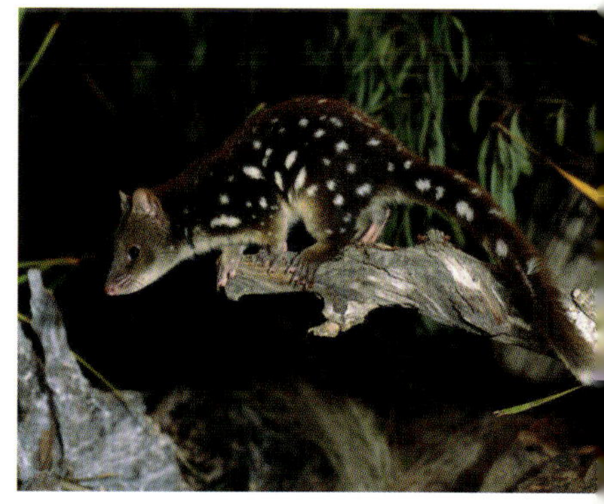

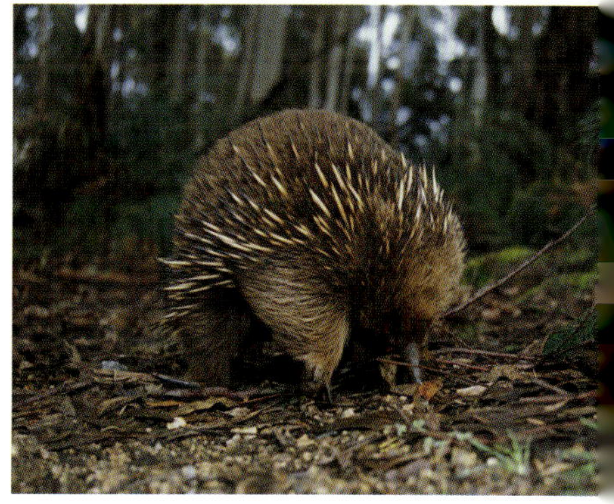

LORD HOWE ISLANDS

Date of inscription: 1982

Lying 600 km (370 miles) from Port Macquarie, the island group owes its World Heritage status to its spectacular topography and its flora and fauna, much of which is unique.

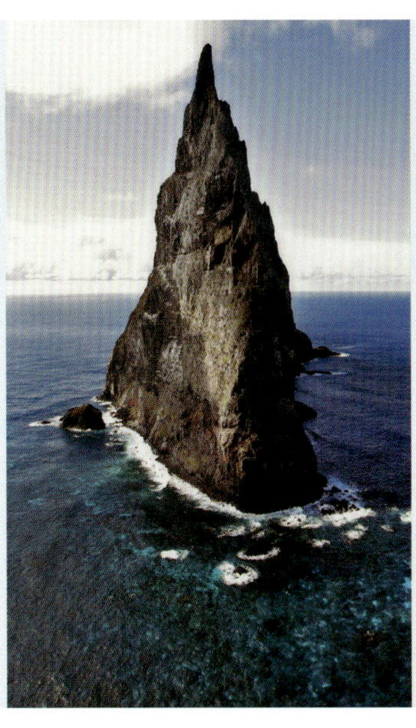

About seven million years ago a giant, 2,000-m (6,600-foot) high shield volcano erupted in the Tasmanian Sea off the east coast of continental Australia. As a result of the erosive power of rain, wind, and wave action, the only remnants of this colossus today are the 28 islands that form the Lord Howe island group. Because of its isolated geographical location, a quite distinct biotope has developed here. Sheltering some 220 species of plants, of which roughly a third are unique to the area, dense cloud forest has become the habitat of many endangered bird species, including the wedge-tailed shearwater, the Kermadec petrel (which nests on the steep cliffs), the oddly hued, white-bellied storm petrel, and the flightless Lord Howe woodhen. Off the southwest coast of the Lord Howe islands, stone coral and calcified red algae form a fantastic reef. In the waters between the spurs of reef live numerous exotic fish, such as the coral trout, the parrotfish, and the sablefish.

A mighty rock island and the remains of a shield volcano, Ball's Pyramid (left) rises more than 500 m (1,640 feet) above the water. The Kim's Lookout vantage point provides a superb view across North Bay (large picture).

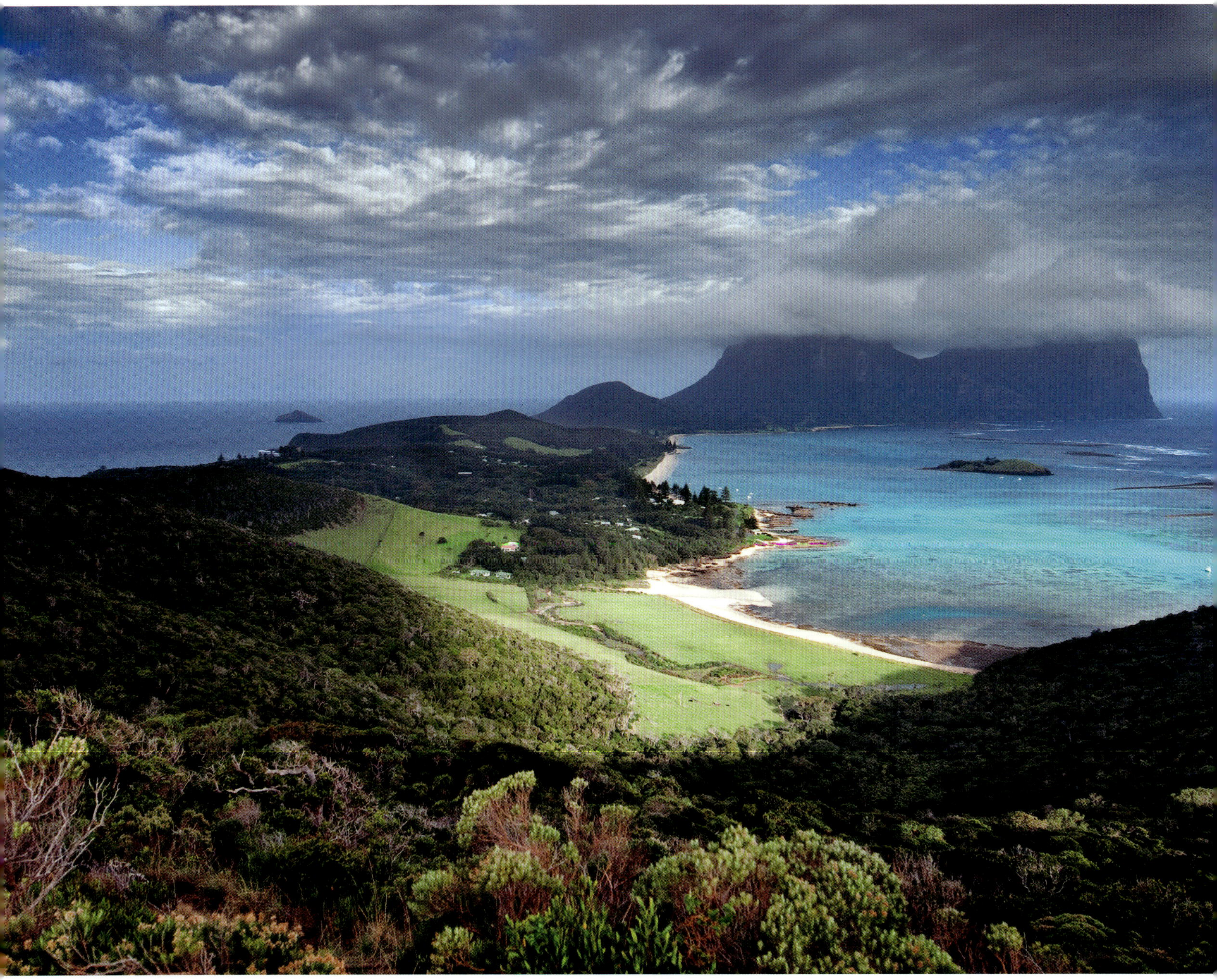

MACQUARIE ISLAND

Macquarie Island is only 35 km (22 miles) long and about 5 km (3 miles) across, and lies approximately 1,500 km (930 miles) south-east of Tasmania and 1,300 km (800 miles) north of the Antarctic. It is a paradise for elephant seals, and fur seals, as well as numerous bird species. King and emperor penguins congregate in giant mating colonies in the winter and spring, and stormbirds and some species of albatross nest here too. The only sign of human habitation is a research station. Macquarie Island, situated in a subduction zone, is of the greatest geological interest, as it is the only place on earth exposing rock formations from the earth's crust that would otherwise lie deep beneath the surface.

The island was named after Lachlan Macquarie, the British Governor of New South Wales from 1810 until 1821 – after it had been accidentally discovered in July 1810 by the Australian Frederick Hasselborough, who was searching for seal-hunting grounds. Initially under the administration of New South Wales, the island is today a part of Tasmania.

Elephant seals (below) and various species of penguin, such as the royal penguin (right) are ubiquitous on Macquarie Island in the South Pacific.

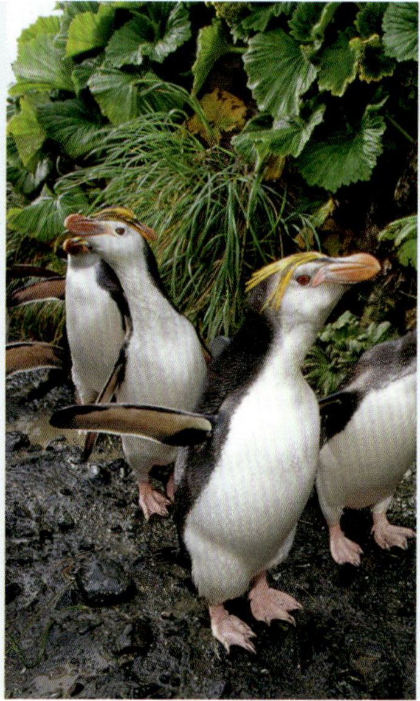

Date of inscription: 1997

This small subantarctic island, home to a range of fauna, is the highest point of the Macquarie Ridge, formed underwater by the convergence of the Indo-Australian and Pacific continental plates.

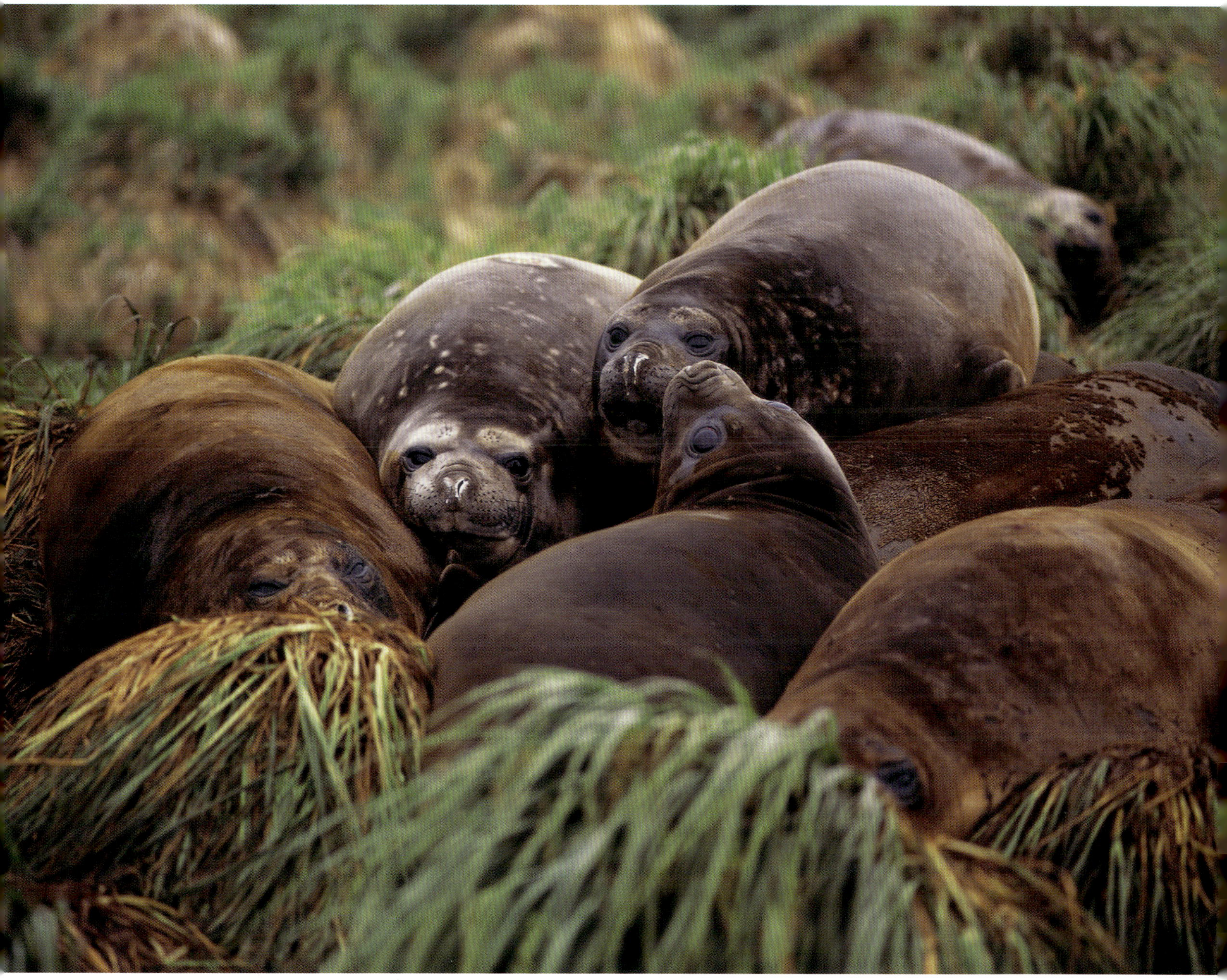

HEARD AND MCDONALD ISLANDS

Date of inscription: 1997

These, the only subantarctic islands displaying volcanic activity, provide great insight into the dynamic processes of the earth's interior. Their ecosystems remain largely unaffected by outside influences.

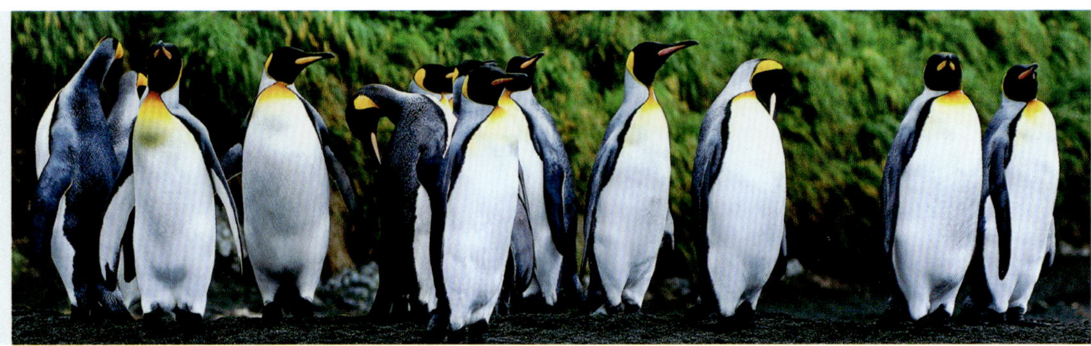

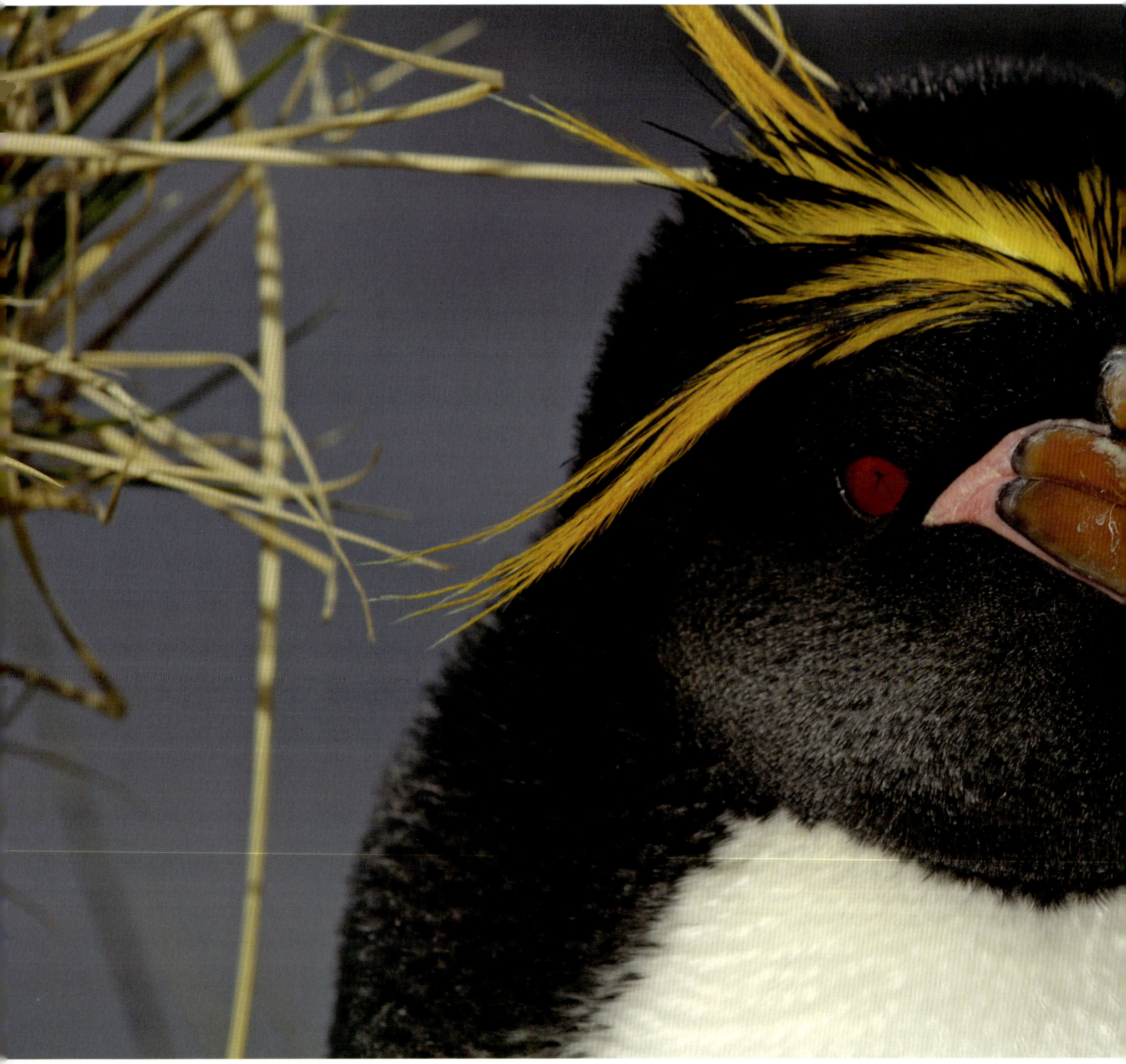

The islands lie some 4,000 km (2,500 miles) south-east of Perth and about 1,500 km (930 miles) north of the Antarctic continent. Mawson Peak ("Big Ben"), 2,745 m (9,000 feet) high and Australia's highest mountain, is an active volcano on Heard Island. Since 1992, McDonald has also suffered volcanic eruptions. Glaciers and ice sheets cover about 80 percent of the islands' surface and the inhospitable climate permits only sparse vegetation, grasses, and algae. To date, 42 varieties of moss have been recorded but the taxonomy of many of the lower plants, algae, and mosses has yet to be determined. The islands have been spared unwelcome "immigrants" such as cats and rats so the penguins, sea mammals, and seabirds are undisturbed.

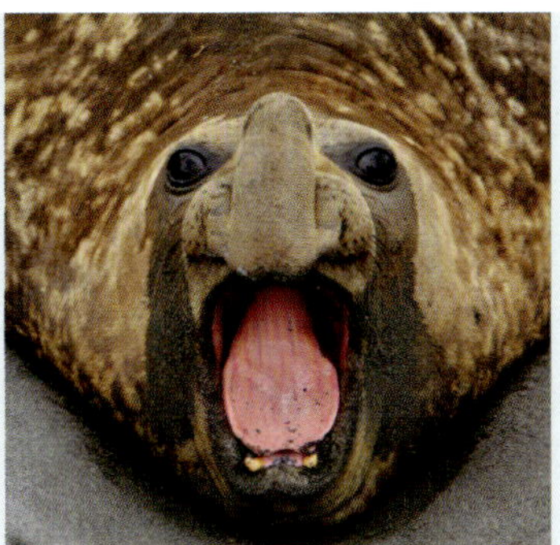

Thousands of sea birds use the Heard and McDonald Islands in spring as breeding grounds, including the king penguins (far left) and the royal penguins (large picture). The corpulent bulls of the southern elephant seals (left) each have some 15 females in their harems.

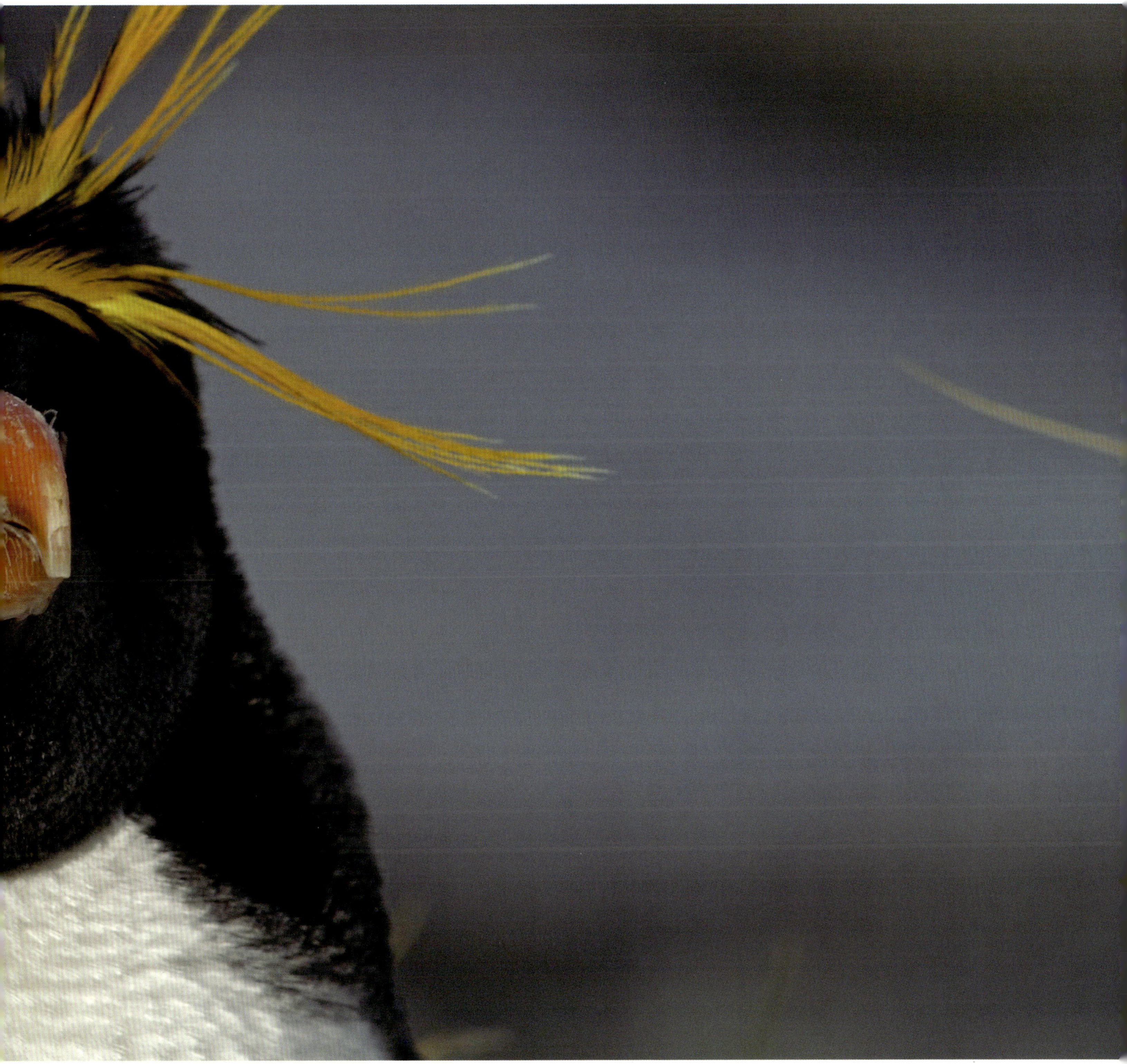

TONGARIRO NATIONAL PARK

Date of inscription: 1990
Extended: 1993

New Zealand's oldest national park (established in 1887), in the middle of North Island, can be traced back to a gift from the Maori to the New Zealand government. Its 750 sq. km (300 sq. miles) enclose three active volcano systems.

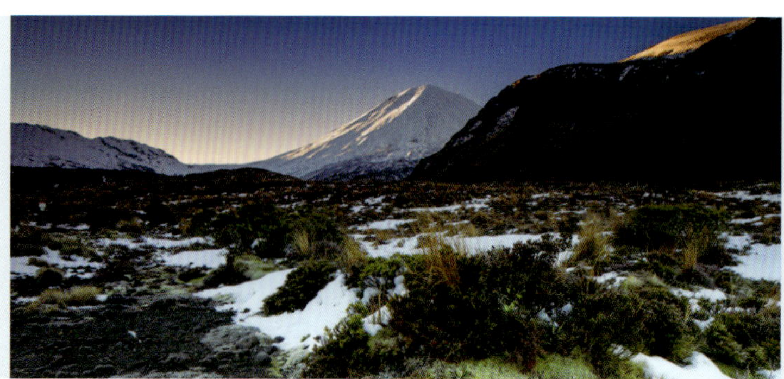

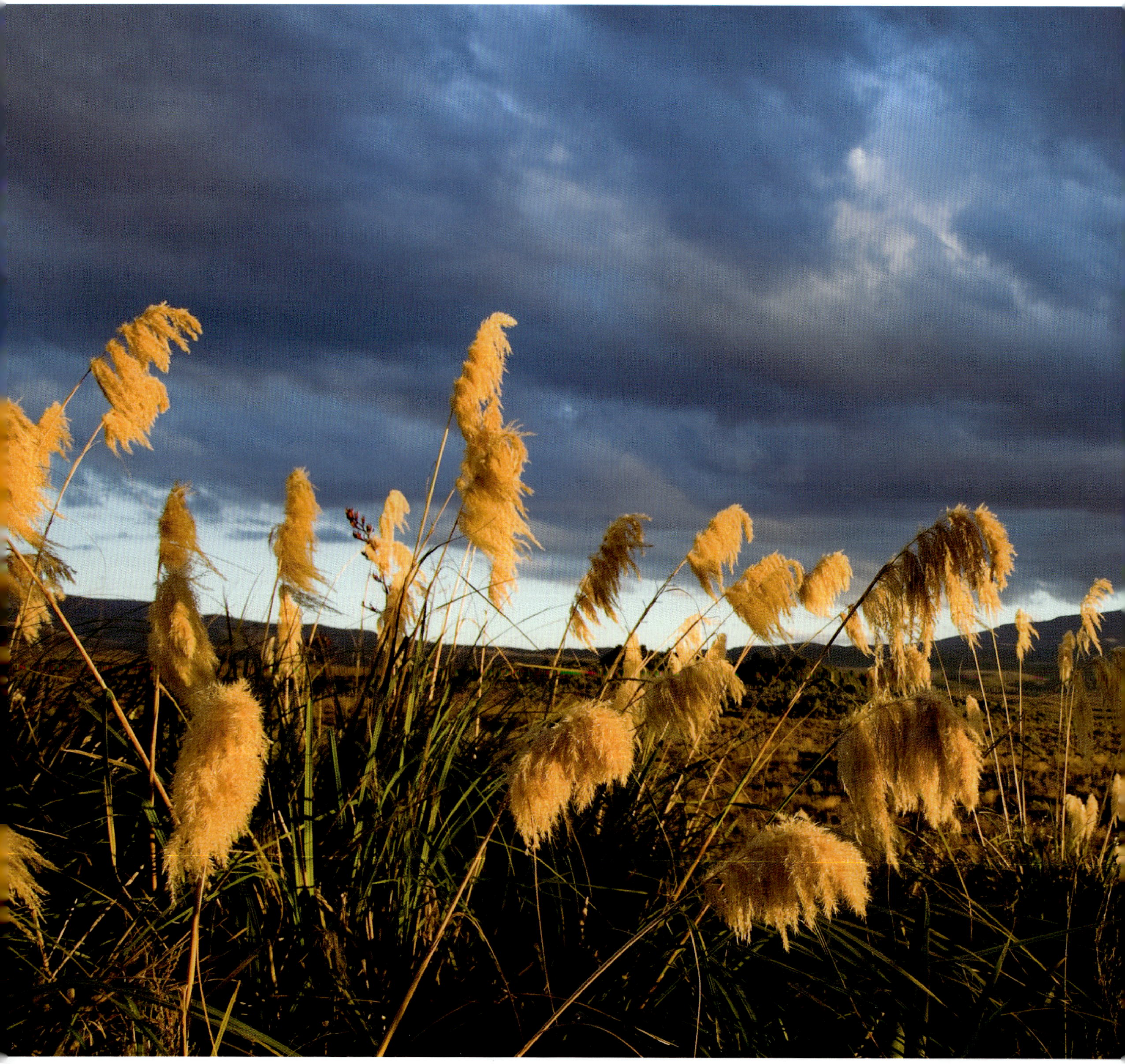

The history of this volcanic landscape began about two million years ago, when the Indo-Australian and Pacific continental plates converged. Because of the plates' resistance, a large amount of frictional energy was released which melted the surrounding rocks. Hot magma resulted, and strong volcanic activity began above the plates' friction points. The eruptions of the three active volcanoes, Tongariro, Ngauruhoe, and Ruapehu, are evidence of this continuing geological process, leading to the creation of the mightiest lava plateau in the world. The vegetation is extremely diverse. Rimu, matai, and miro trees grow in the lowland rainforest, adjacent to which is the Inaka bushland with its tussock grass. At higher altitudes, mushrooms, lichen, and mosses flourish on the desolate ash and lava plain. Particularly notable among the animal life are the birds: there are more than 50 species, including rare indigenous birds such as the North Island brown kiwi and the Maori falcon.

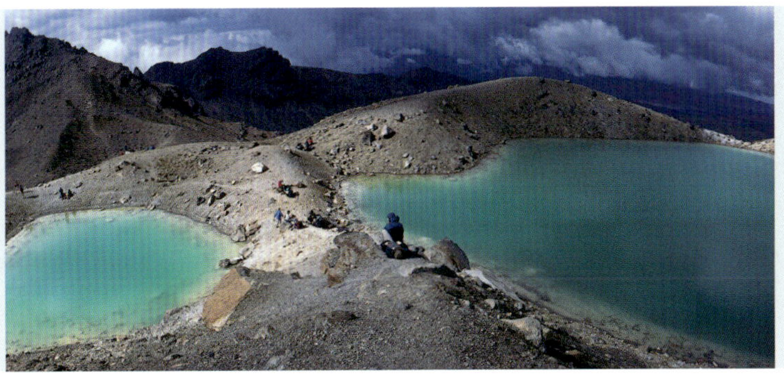

Emerald Lake (left) is a veritable gem, featuring turquoise green water. Below: at the foot of Mount Ruapehu.

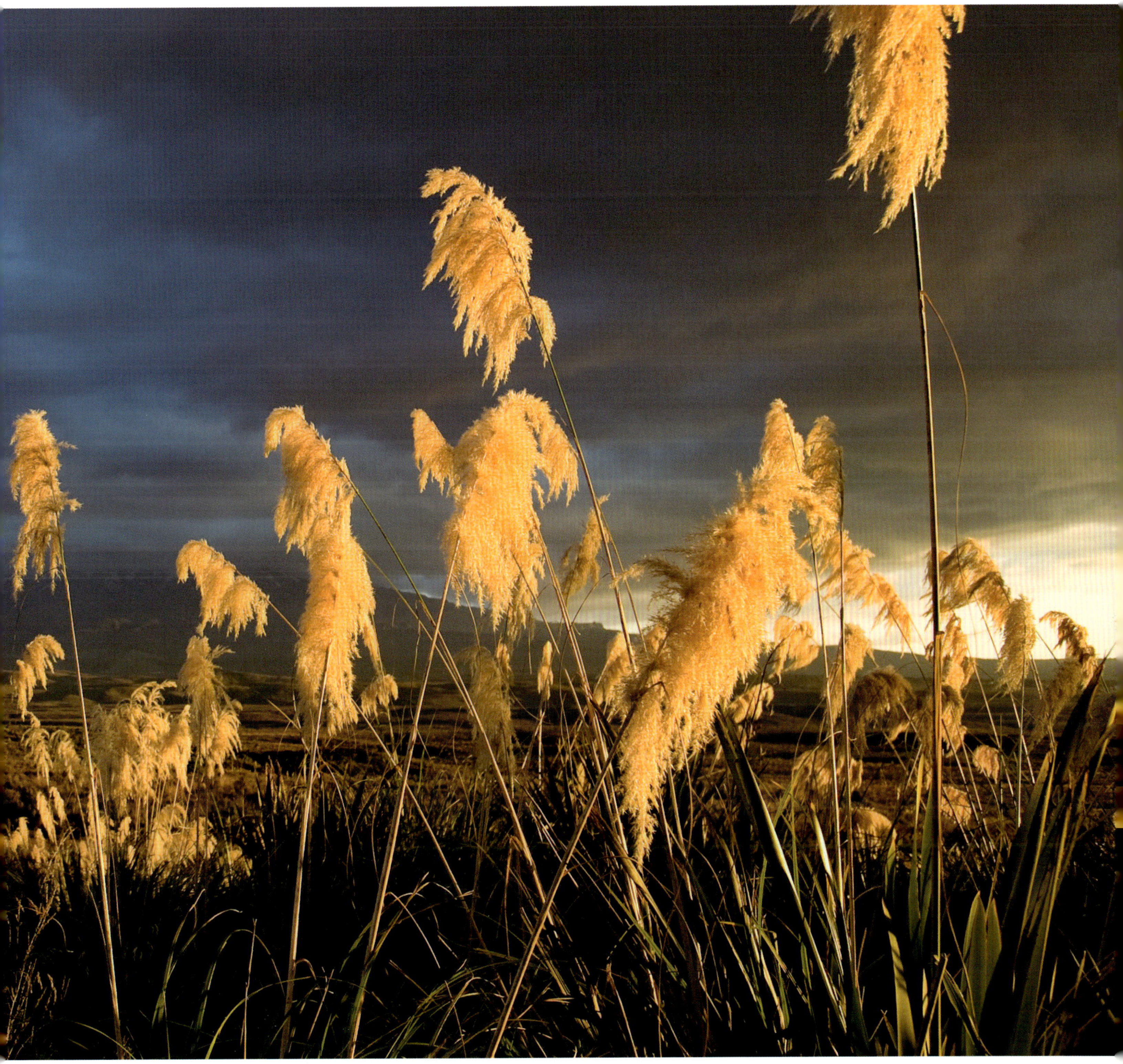

TE WAHIPOUNAMU – SOUTH-WEST NEW ZEALAND

Date of inscription: 1990

On the south-western coast of New Zealand's South Island, four national parks boast impressive mountainscapes and numerous ancient species of animal and plants.

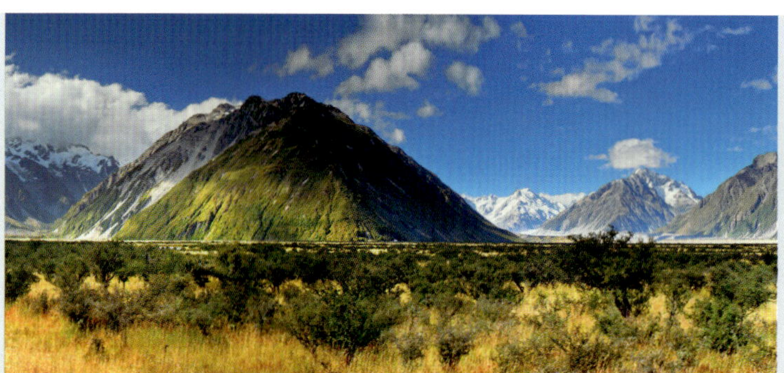

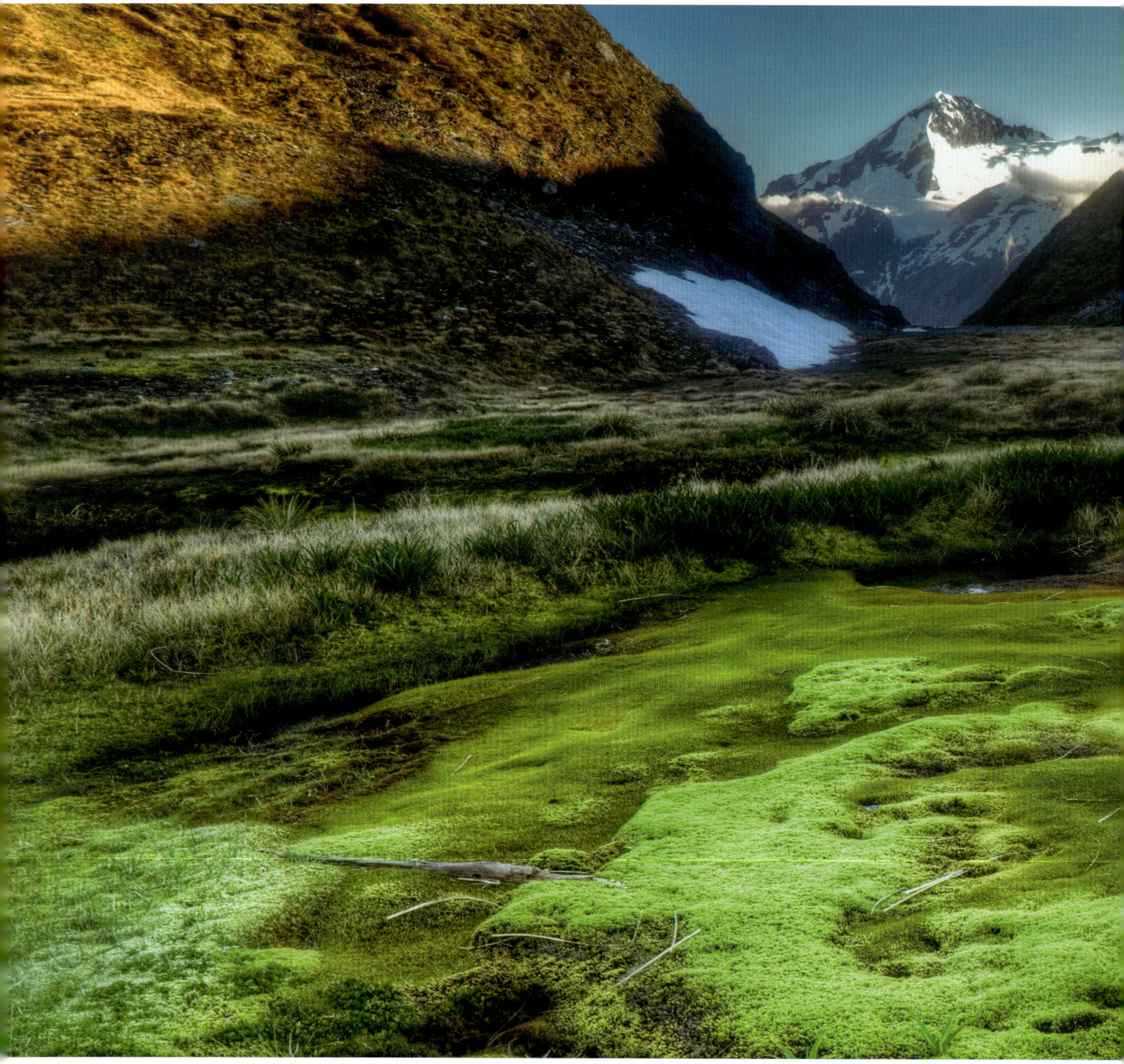

At about 26,000 sq. km (4,100 sq. miles), Te Wahipounamu (Maori: "place of jade") is one of the largest conservation areas in the world, and includes Westland, Mount Aspiring, Mount Cook, and Fjordland National Parks. Spread over large parts of the south-western coast of New Zealand, Fjordland is the largest of the four conservation areas and owes its name to its coastal fjords, underwater valleys up to 400 m (1,320 feet) deep. Annually, up to 10,000 mm (394 inches) of precipitation fall on this glaciated landscape, ideal conditions for subtropical rainforest to flourish. There are many species of plants and animals still in existence here which, millions of years ago, were indigenous to Gondwana, the southern hemisphere's former supercontinent. Trees here are often overgrown with carpets of lichen and creepers. Innumerable varieties of fern flourish in the undergrowth. Unique bird life lives in the seemingly impenetrable foliage. Dolphins and eared seals swim alongside the indigenous Fjordland penguin in the crystal-clear waters of the fjords. Mount Cook, at 3,754 m (12,310 feet) the highest mountain in New Zealand, rises amid the Southern Alps. The highest points of the mountainscape, especially Mount Tasman at 3,498 m (11,470 feet), are dominated by glaciers. The two picturesque lakes lying at the foot of Mount Cook, Tekapo and Pukaki, teem with fish. In early spring, the shores of the lake bloom with unexpected beauty. The Westland and Mount Aspiring National Parks are equally fantastical, glaciated landscapes; the long protrusions of the Fox and Franz-Josef glaciers in Westland National Park stretch down through trough-like valleys almost to the coast.

A path across moss-covered hills takes you to the summit in Mount Aspiring National Park (large picture). Left: a view of Mount Cook from Tasman Valley.

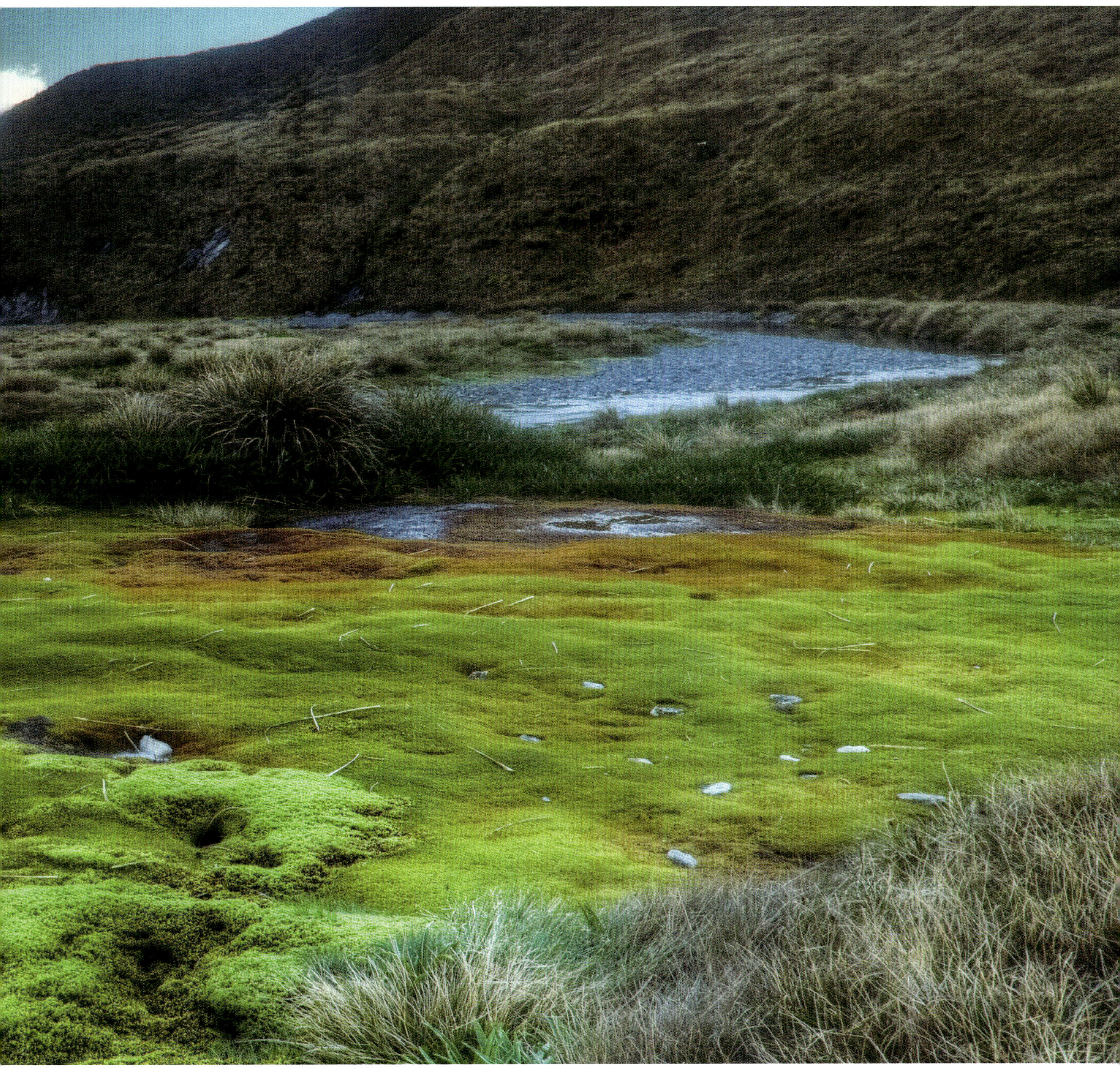

TE WAHIPOUNAMU –THE SOUTH-WEST OF NEW ZEALAND: MOUNT COOK NATIONAL PARK

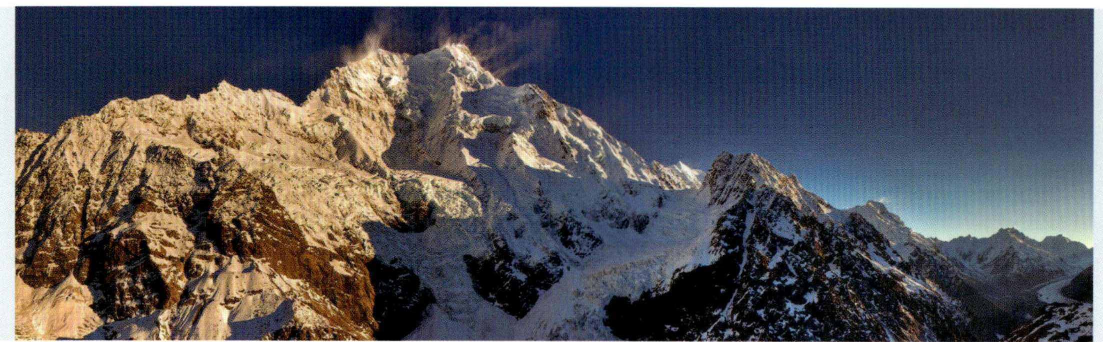

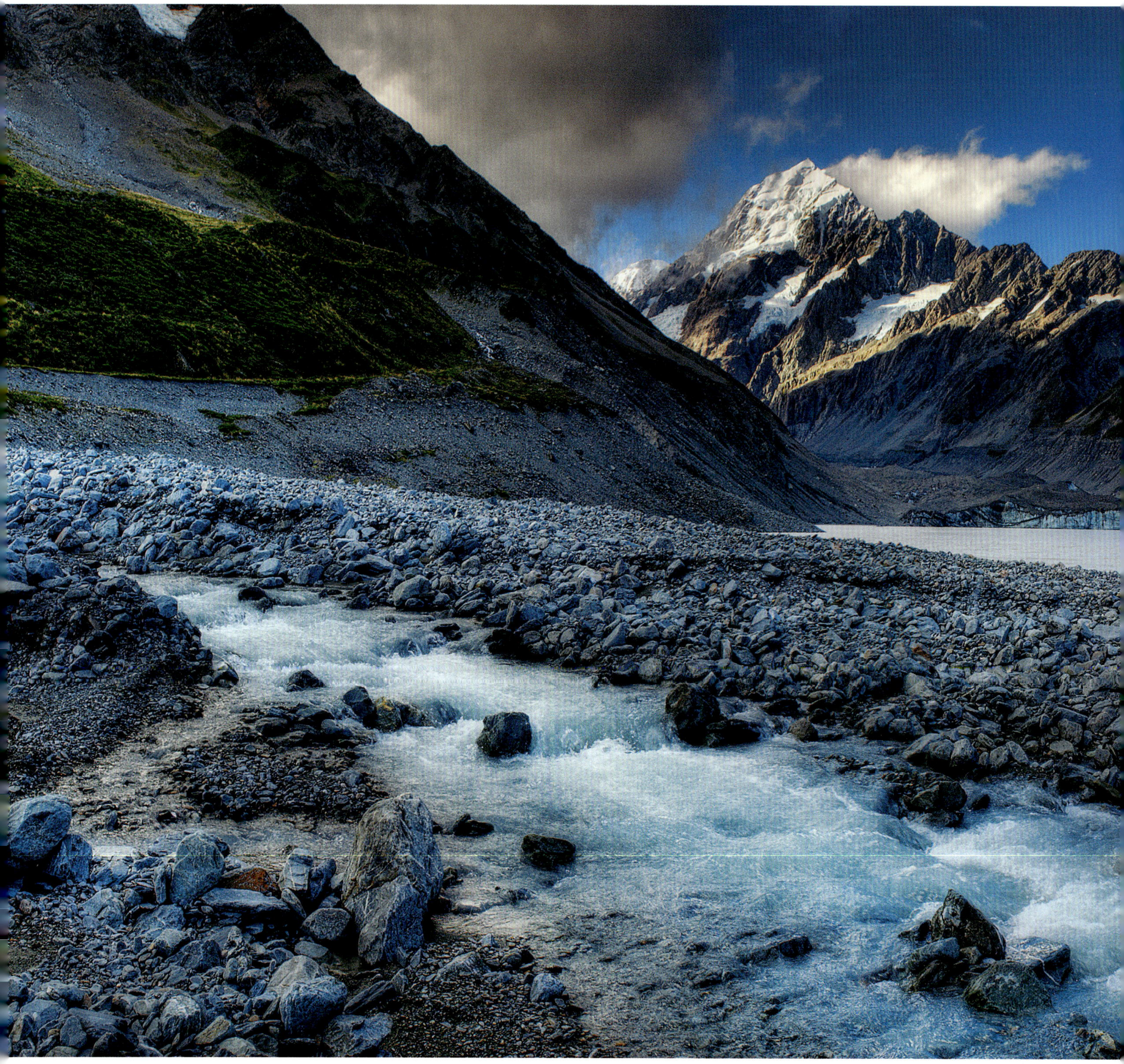

Within a small area, Mount Cook National Park comprises 140 mountains of more than 2,000 m (6,560 feet) height and five of the largest glaciers in New Zealand. A gravel track to Mount Cook Village on Lake Pukaki forks towards the Tasman Glacier, the largest ice field. If you wish to visit the astonishing ice caves, you should ideally book a guided tour once you are there because the walk is burdensome without a guide. Considerably easier are ten short walks, well signposted and starting from Mount Cook Village. Here you'll also find a luxury hotel from whose terrace you will have a superb view of the mountain world. Among the animal attractions of this national park are, besides the cheeky kea, also rare species of falcons and owls. Star among the plants is the Mount Cook lily, a delicate, white buttercup that is often regarded as the symbol of New Zealand.

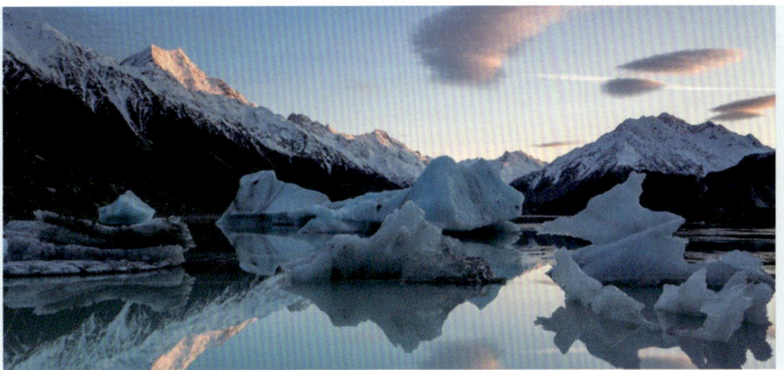

The different moods at Mount Cook are evident from magnificent pictures. Far left: a storm on the summit; left: sunset at the Tasman Glacier. Below: a glacial stream finds its path through the countryside.

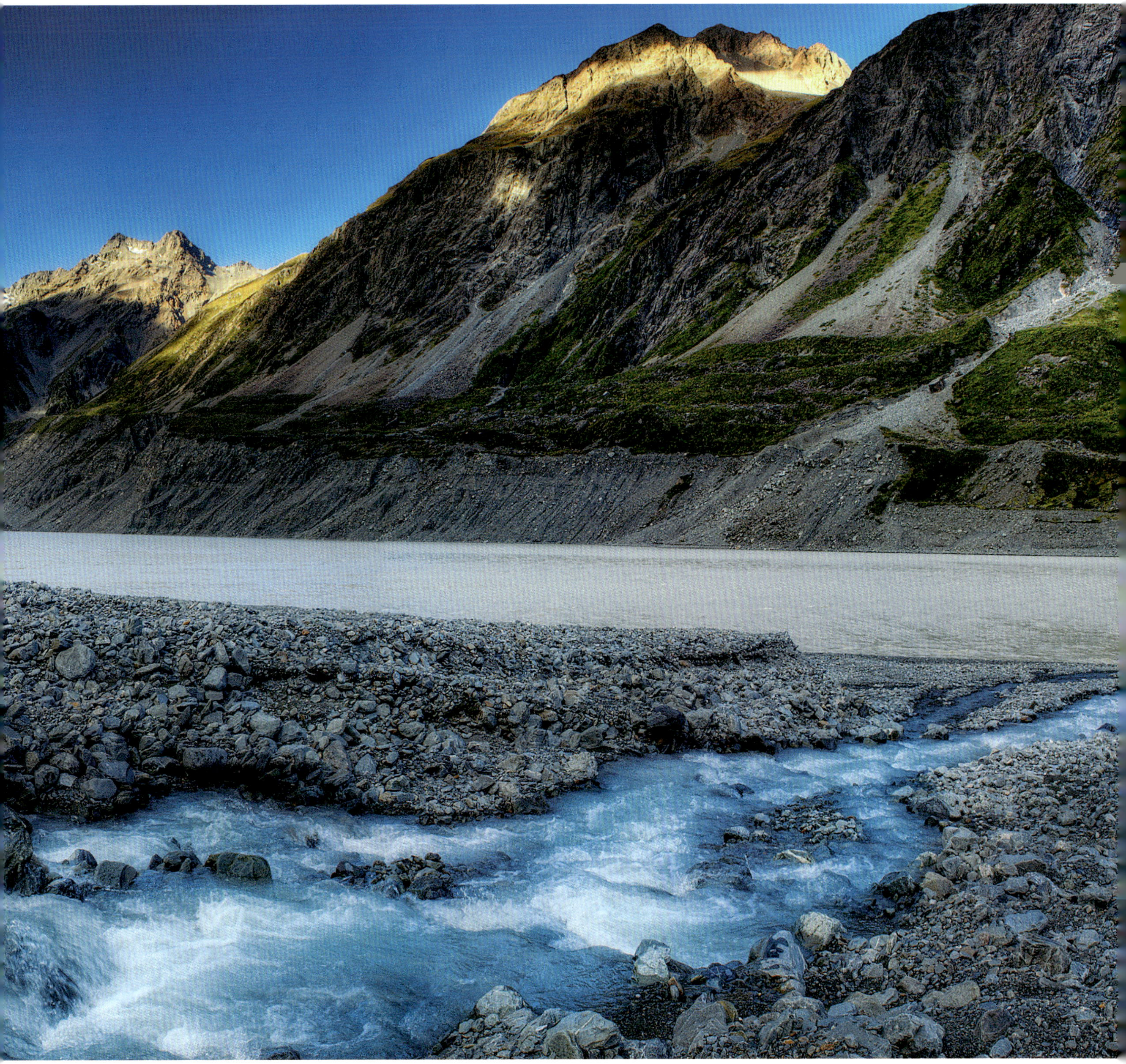

TE WAIIIPOUNAMU – THE SOUTH-WEST OF NEW ZEALAND:WESTLAND NATIONAL PARK

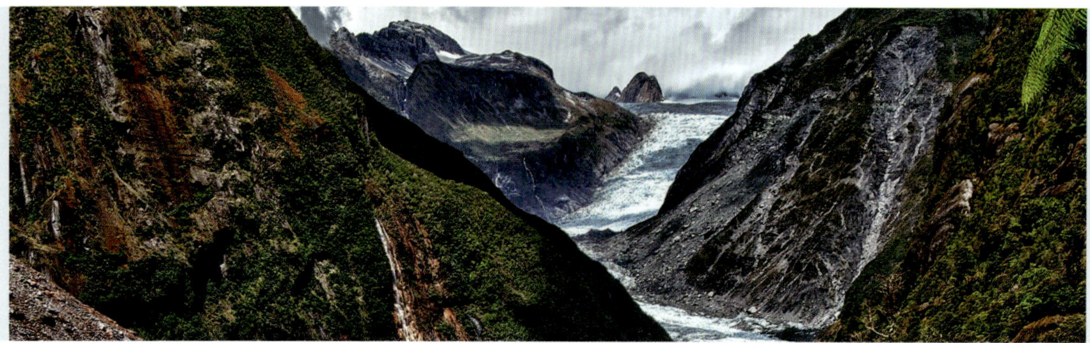

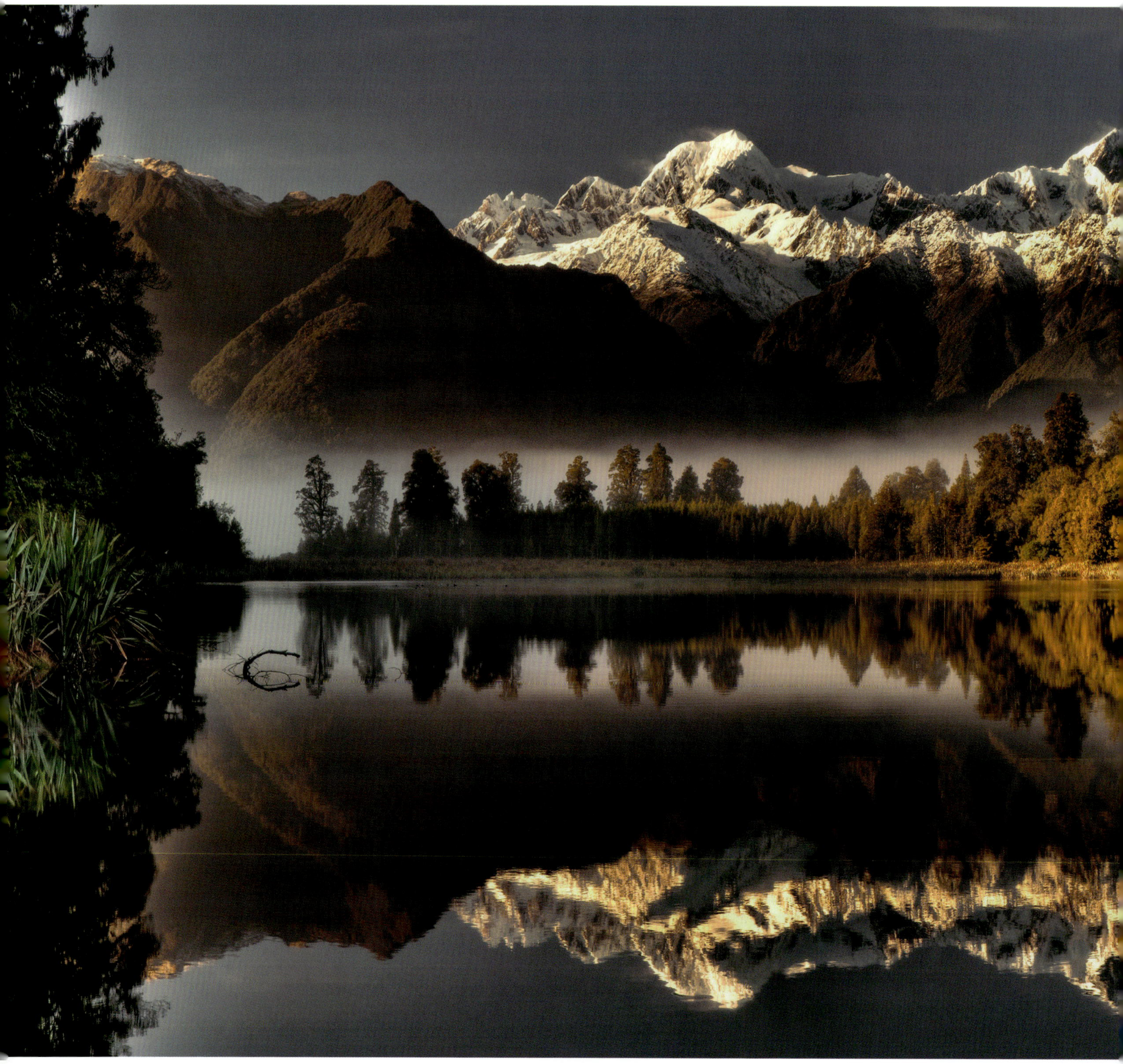

The last light of a long summer's day plays around the summits of Mount Cook and Mount Tasman, New Zealand's highest mountains; the glaciated summits are mirrored in the fairy-like, tranquil lake: The view from the western side of Lake Matheson back to the Southern Alps is famous and emblematic of the Westland National Park's beauty. Mount Cook and Fiordland, together with the Mount Aspiring National Park, form the UNESCO World Natural Heritage site known as Te Wahipounamu (Maori: "the place of greenstone"). Two glacier tongues, Franz Josef and Fox, flow through the deep green rainforest down to 300 m (984 feet) above sea level, with New Zealand's highest mountains as a backdrop. The Franz Josef Glacier was christened by the geologist Julius von Haast after the Austrian emperor; Fox was the name of an earlier New Zealand's prime minister.

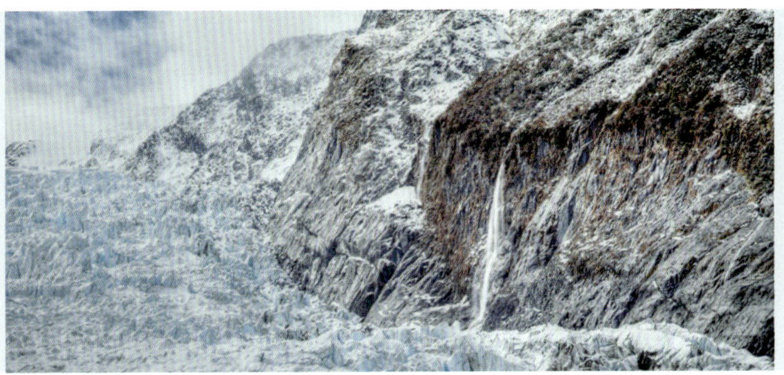

A vast mountain panorama in duplicate (large picture): Lake Matheson reflects the summits of Mount Tasman and Mount Cook. Glaciers and waterfalls characterize the superb scenery (top).

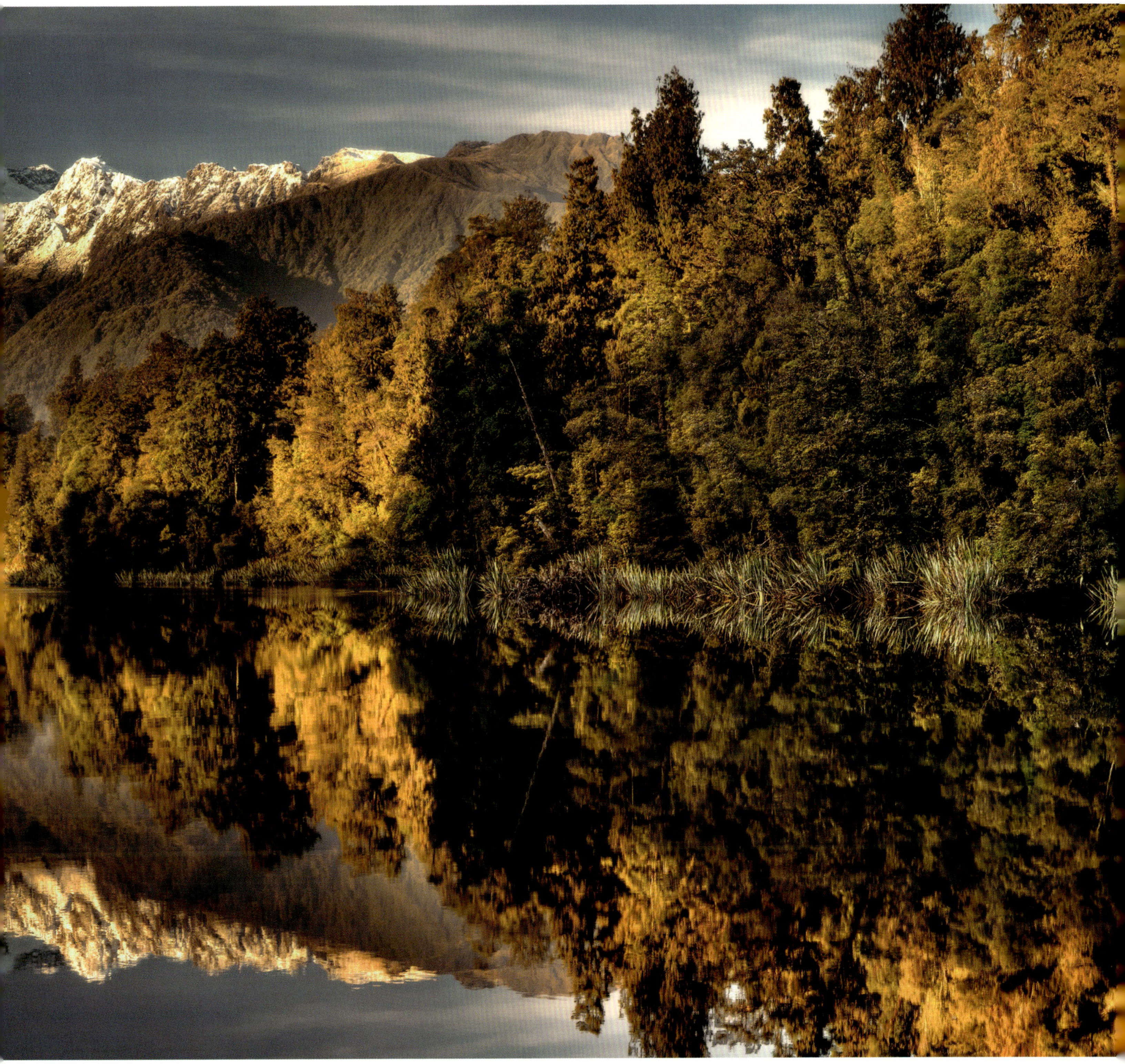

TE WAHIPOUNAMU – THE SOUTH-WEST OF NEW ZEALAND: FIORDLAND NATIONAL PARK

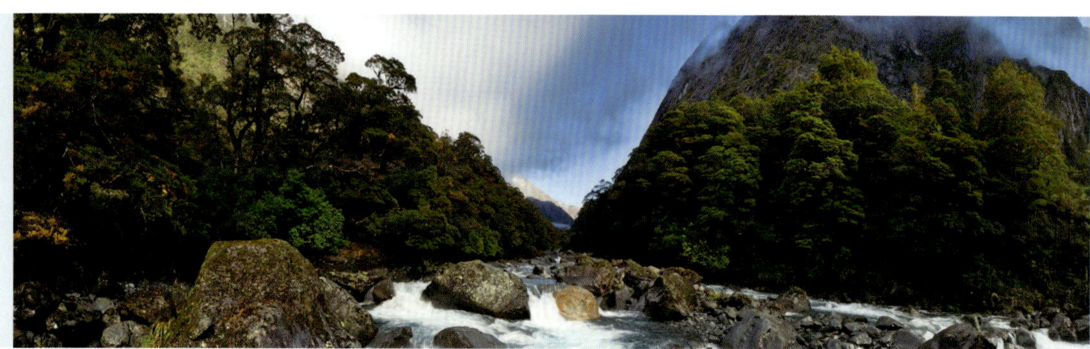

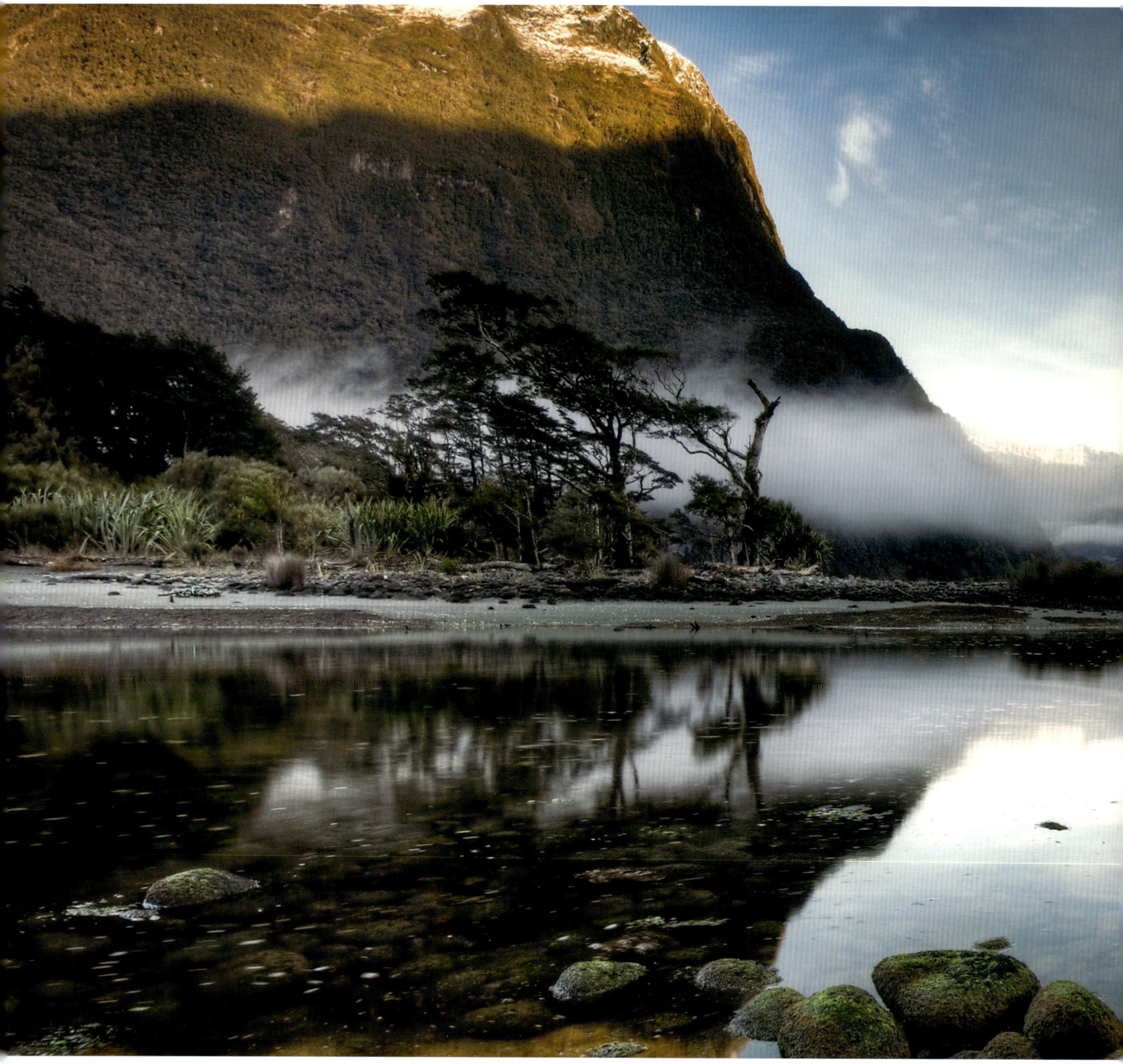

New Zealand's largest national park, covering 12,520 sq. km (4,834 sq. miles), is probably also the most beautiful in the country: Snow-covered mountains form the backdrop, and in front of these are extensive beech forests with century-old, moss-covered tree giants. Crystal-clear rivers and still lakes fill wide valleys which were shaped by glaciers on their retreat. Here you will find around 700 endemic plants and rare fauna. Lined up along the west coast are majestic fjords. Only one of these, Milford Sound, is accessible by road. The area is one of the most popular trekking areas in the world. The only downside to that pleasure are the irritating black sandflies. According to a Maori legend, they were created by the goddess of death who wished to put hikers off the perfect beauty of the landscape.

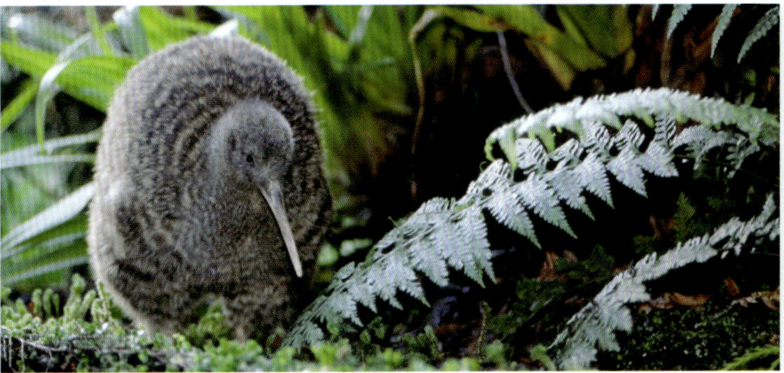

Majestic and unmistakeable, Mitre Peak dominates the Milford Sound with its white "bishop's hat" (large picture). Hollyford River (far left) burbles through the valleys. Kiwis (left) are at home here.

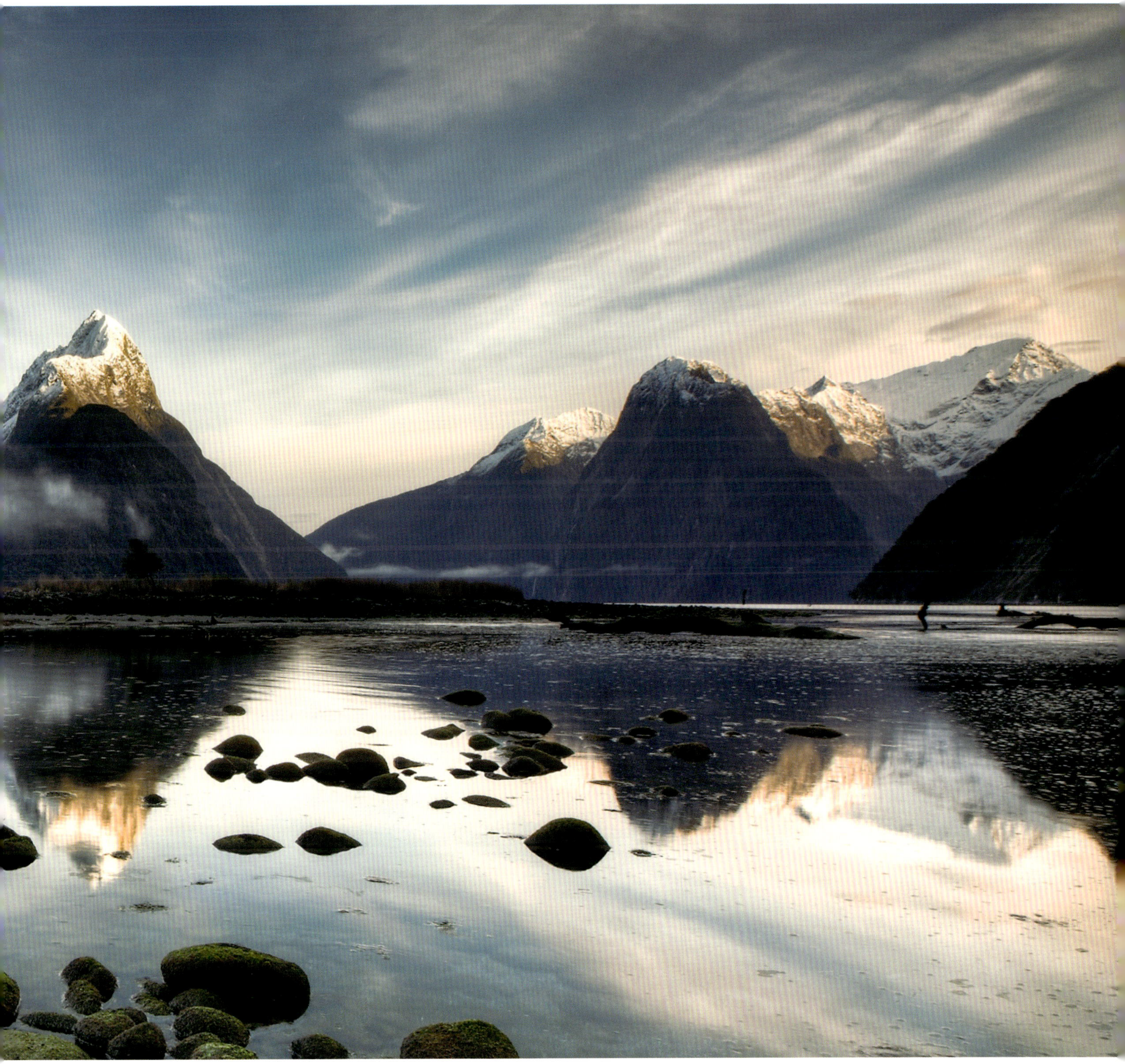

NEW ZEALAND'S SUBANTARCTIC ISLANDS

Date of inscription: 1998

These five island chains in the South Pacific represent a singular ecosystem. A diverse – and often unique – biotope has developed at the confluence of the Antarctic and subtropical ocean currents.

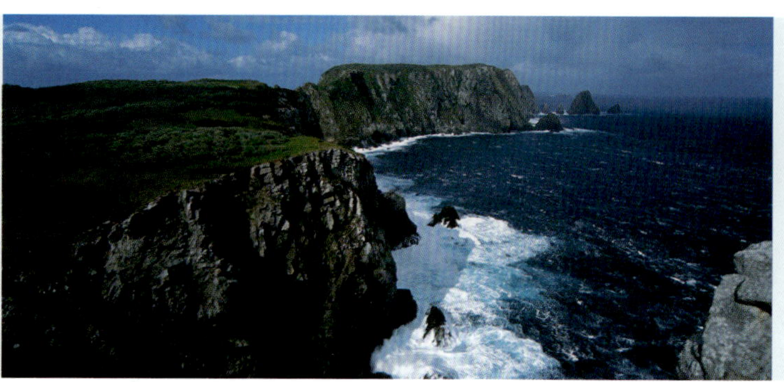

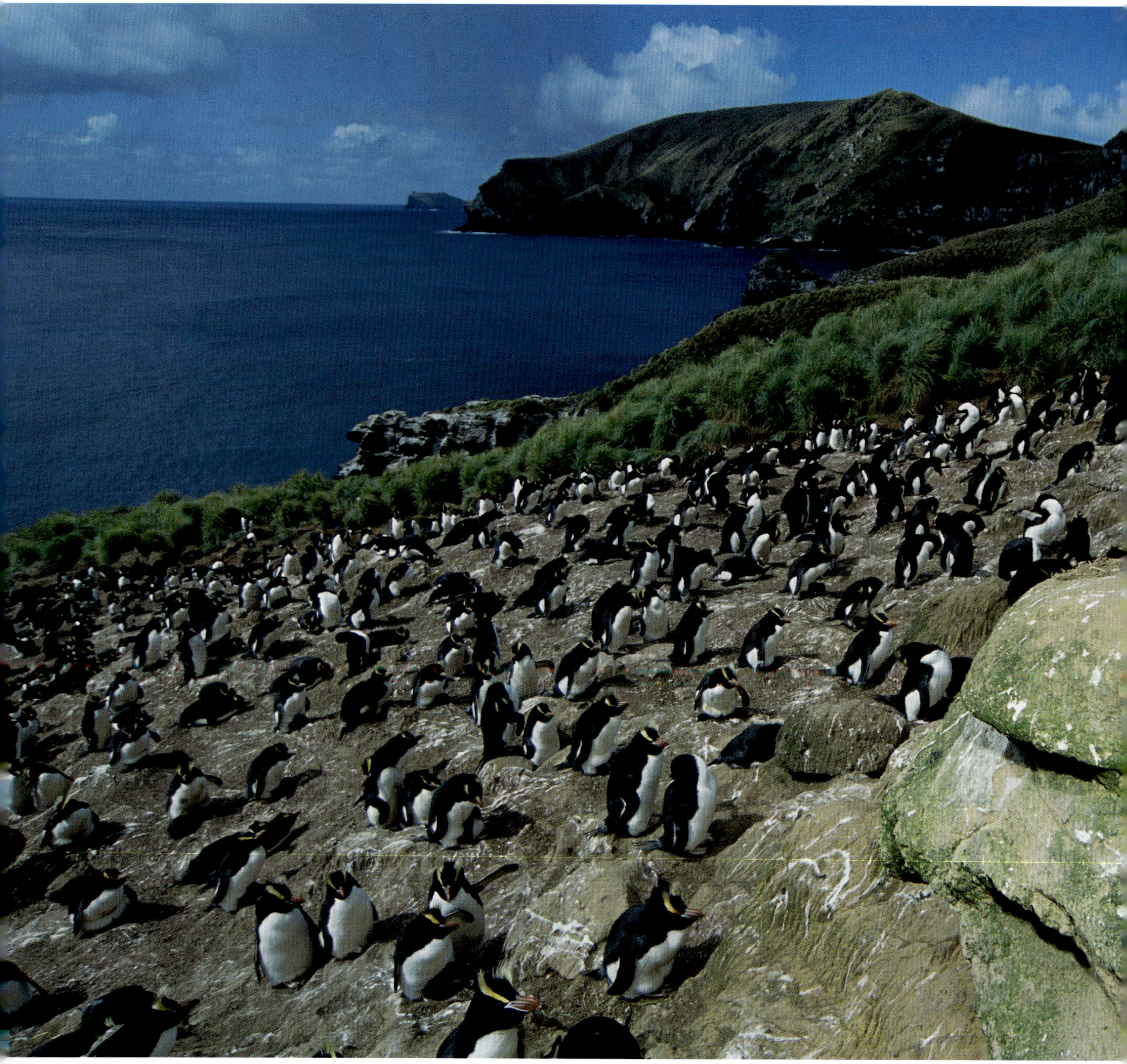

The uninhabited Auckland, Campbell, Antipodes, Snares, and Bounty island groups lie south and east of the New Zealand coast. With the exception of the low cliffs of the Bounty Islands, they are carpeted with moorland. The deep fjords of the Campbell and Auckland Islands show signs of a prolonged period of glaciation. With the exception of the Bounty Islands, these island groups have the richest wealth of flora of all the subantarctic islands. Of more than 250 species, 35 are endemic and 30 considered very rare. The world's southernmost forests are to be found on the Auckland Islands, with great numbers of tree ferns.

Among 120 recorded varieties of bird are 40 different seabirds, of which five nest only here. Of 24 species of albatross, 10 are unique to the islands, including the southern royal albatross. Also unique are two of the four species of penguin.

In addition, the islands afford a refuge to the rare New Zealand sealion and large colonies of New Zealand fur seals. Several species of insects, snails, and spiders are also found only here.

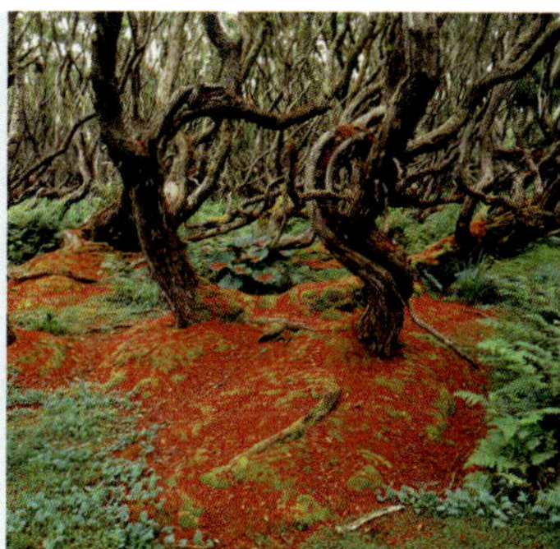

Erect-crested penguins (large picture) and Snares penguins (bottom) belong to the genus of crested penguins. Southern royal albatross and New Zealand sea lions (picture series) also cavort here. The fallen blossom of the Rata trees forms a red carpet (left). Far left: spectacular cliffs.

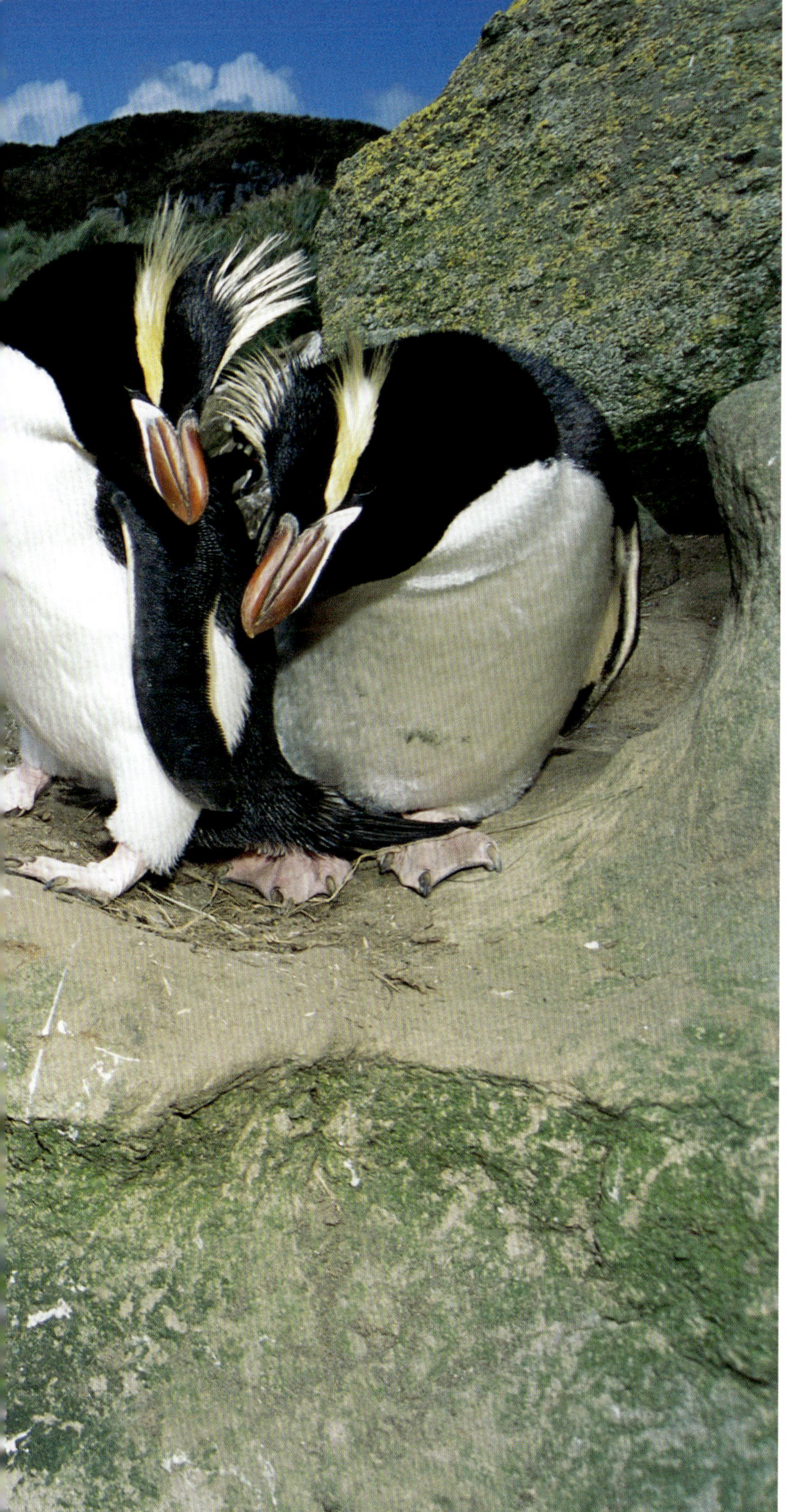

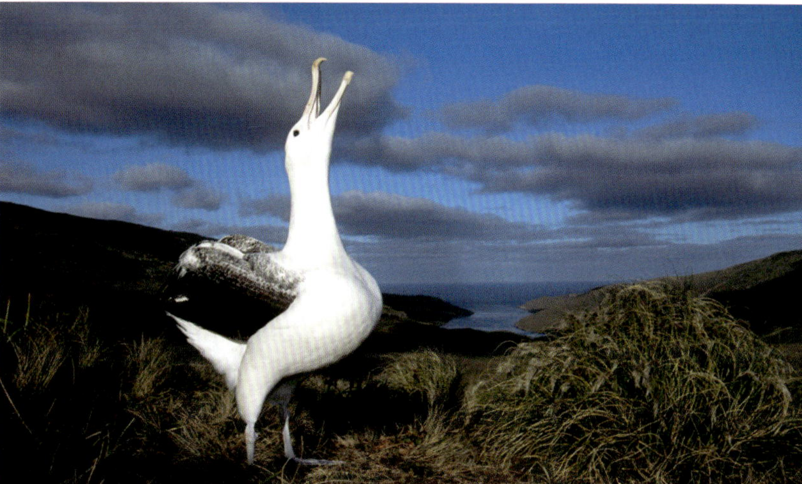

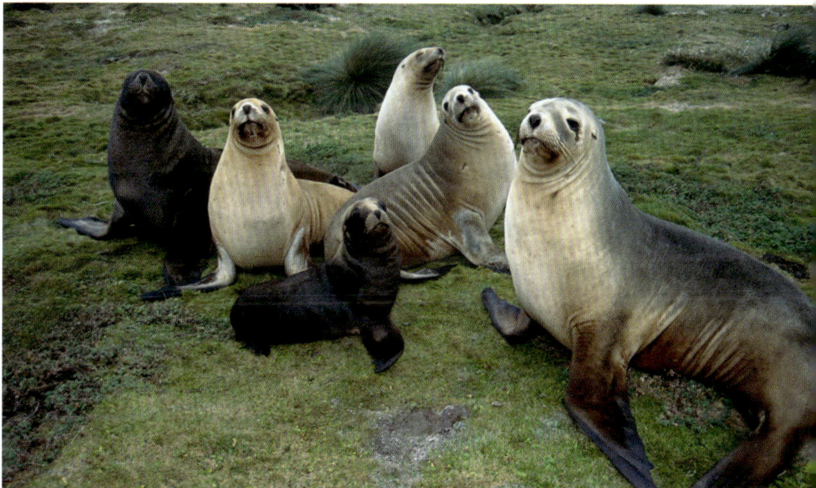

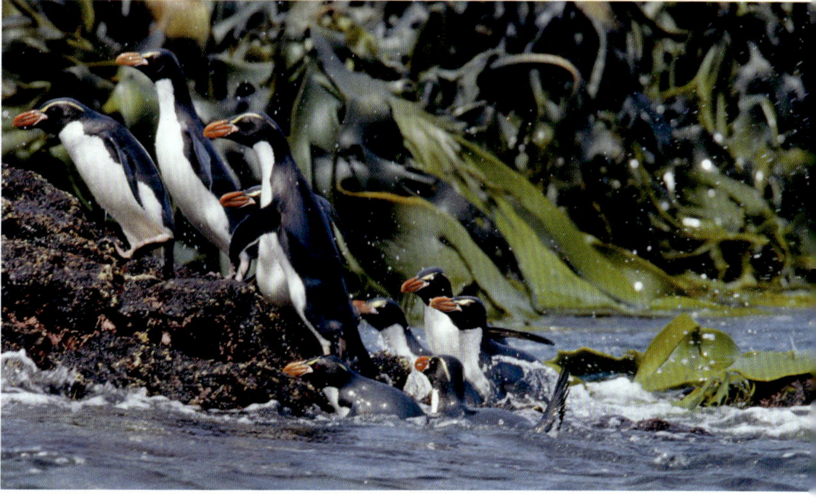

SOUTHERN LAGOON OF THE ROCK ISLANDS (CHELBACHEB ISLANDS)

Date of inscription: 2012

This UNESCO Heritage site boasts an extraordinary variety of habitats, an as yet largely unspoiled marine environment and numerous karstified islands featuring a great variety of species and evidence of the first immigrants, which is why it is both a Natural and a Cultural Heritage site.

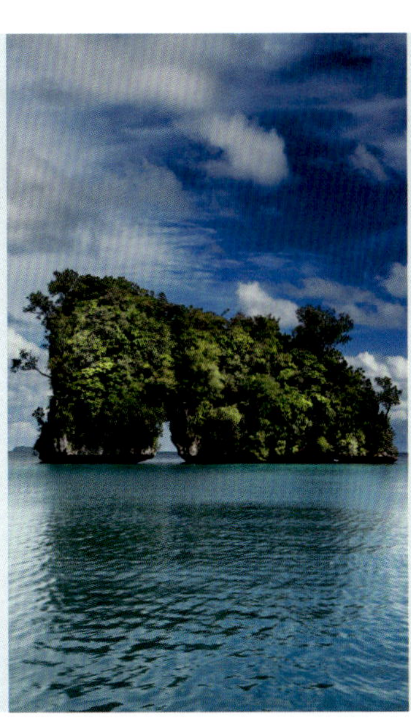

The Southern Lagoon of Palau, covering an area of more than 1,000 sq. km (386 sq. miles), comprises 445 uninhabited limestone islands. Weathering and karstification have caused many of these to take on bizarre shapes. The islands are covered by virginal forests, home to a very rich terrestrial fauna and flora, including many birds such as the emblematic Micronesian scrubfowl. A megapode, it incubates its eggs by burying them in fermenting compost heaps. The marine habitats display an impressive variety. They are home to, for example, the dugong, a total of 1,350 fish species – including 13 types of shark – and 385 coral species. An interesting peculiarity are the marine lakes, separated from the ocean by land barriers: Since they receive their waters through gaps from the ocean, they also rise and fall with the ocean's tides. Some of the lakes are famous for their great populations of jellyfish of the genus Mastigias, with each lake featuring its own species. Archaeological evidence of the islands' first settlement 3,000 years ago right up to the first contact with the Europeans in the 18th century was also found in the Southern Lagoon.

The green, forested Rock Islands lie like jewels in the turquoise ocean (large picture). Natural rock formations divide the watercourses (left).

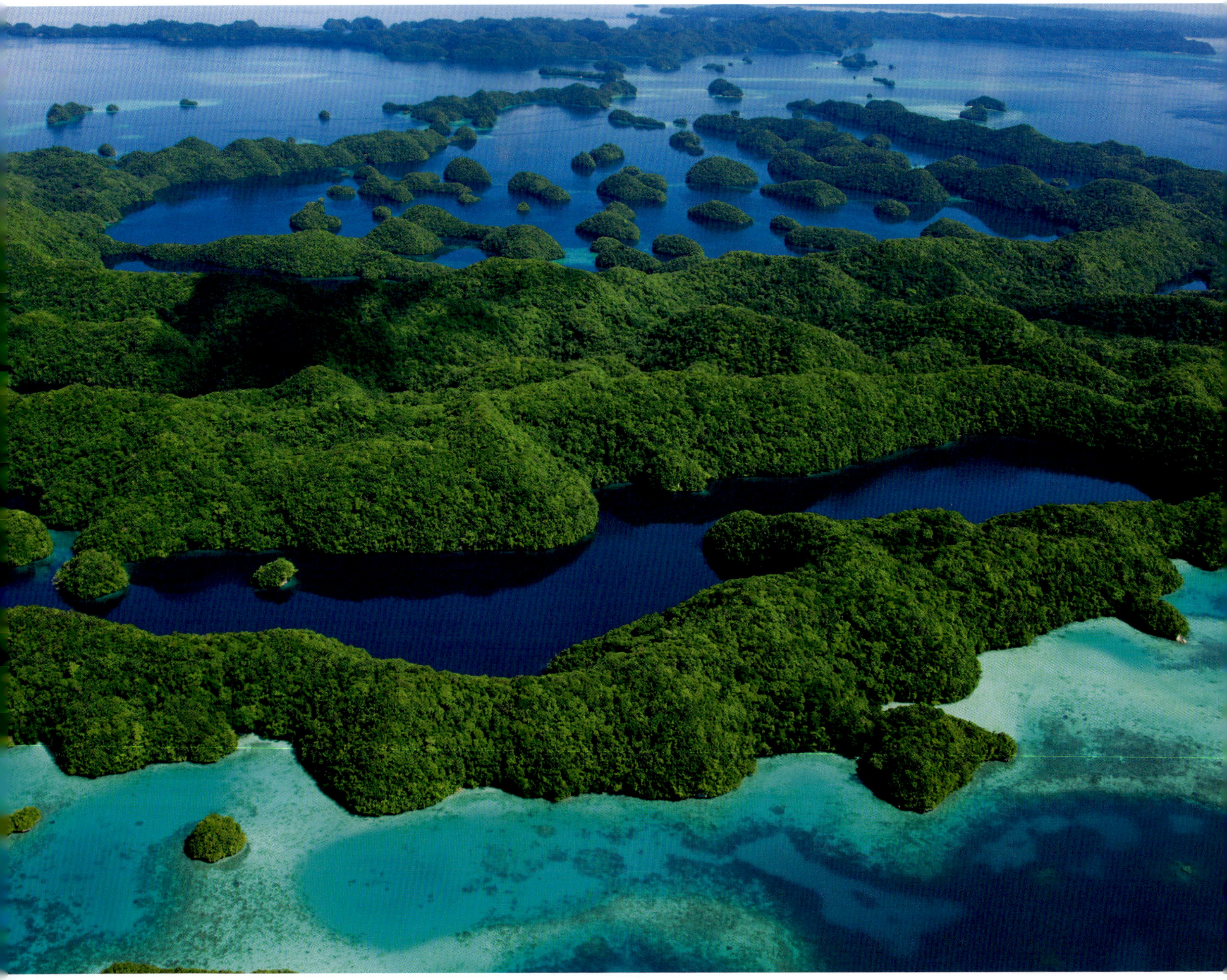

EAST RENNELL

Rennell Island is the southernmost of the Solomon island chain, and East Rennell occupies the southern third of the island. The conservation area, which rises to 1,000 m (3,280 feet), totals about 370 sq. km (143 sq. miles), including an area of ocean up to 3 nautical miles from the coast. The climate is typical of the tropics, with an annual average of 4,000 mm (158 inches) of precipitation. Lake Tegano, once a lagoon in the atoll, takes up 18 percent of the island's surface area. At 150 sq. km (60 sq. miles), this saltwater lake, with its jagged limestone islands, is the largest in the Pacific islands.
Because of its geographical seclusion, unique flora and fauna have evolved on East Rennell, unaffected either by human interference or the "immigration" of species like rats or land snakes. The primary forests offer a habitat for many rare plants, including various orchids and screw pine trees. The Rennell flying fox, one of the 11 species of bat found here, is unique to the island. A good 40 bird species nest on the island, including four endemic species and nine endemic sub-species.

The underwater world around the atoll is home to some strange inhabitants: the red-spotted blenny (large picture) and the decoratively patterned partner shrimp (right).

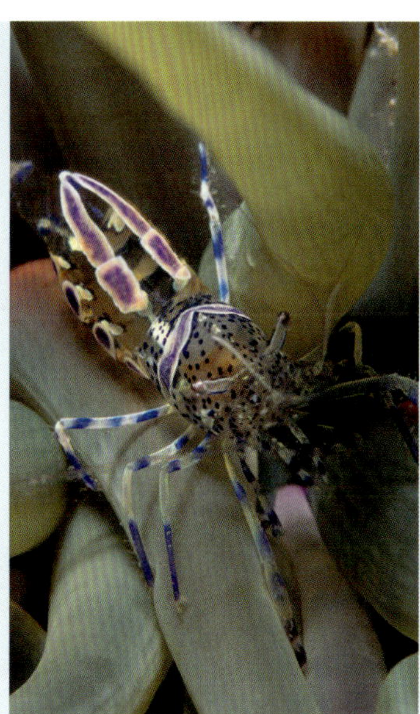

Date of inscription: 1998

Rennell is the world's largest dry coral atoll, and the southernmost third of the island, including Lake Tegano, is a World Heritage Site.

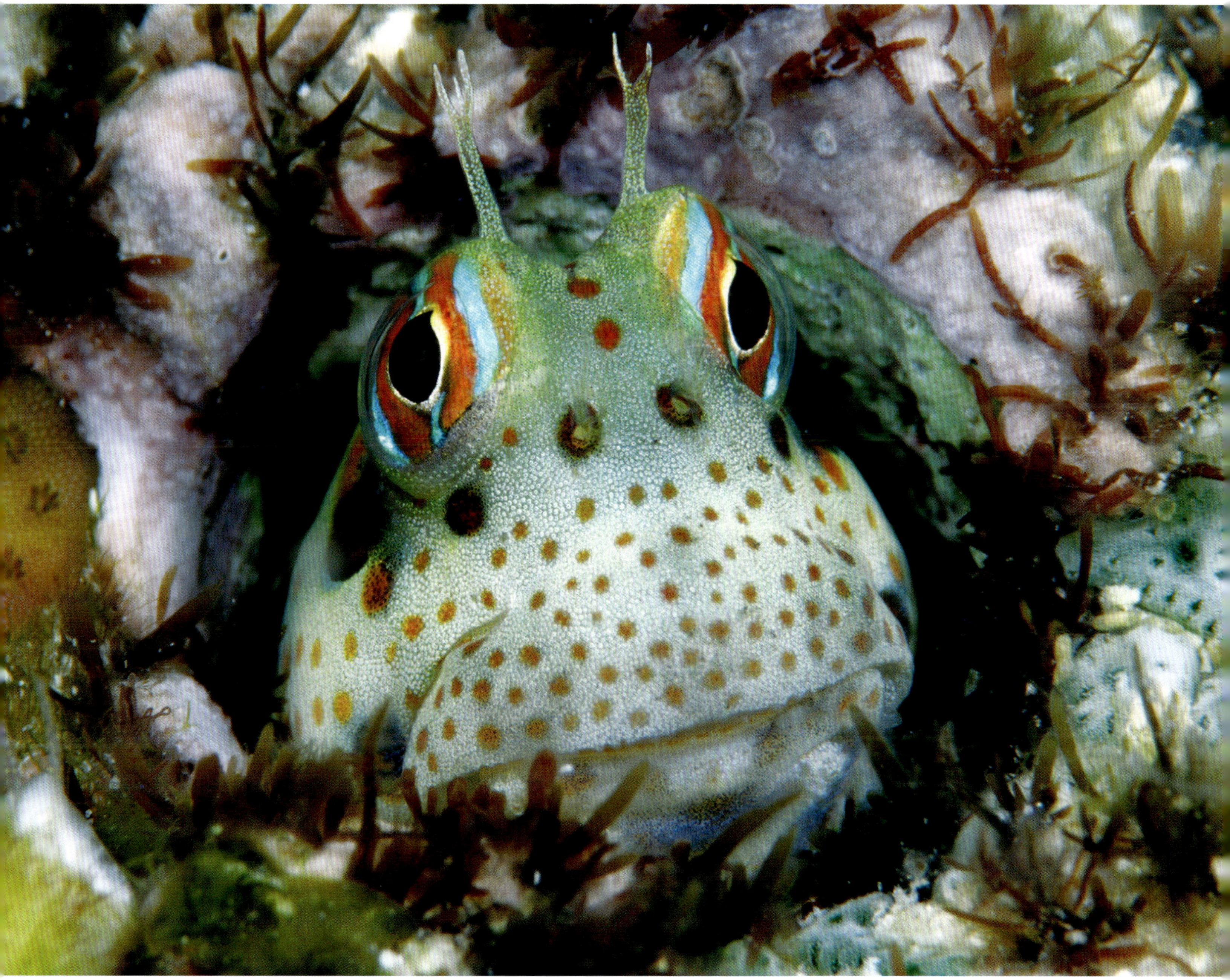

PHOENIX ISLANDS PROTECTED AREA

Date of inscription: 2010

The virtually untouched nature of the region around the Phoenix Islands is one of the largest intact coral ecosystems in the world.

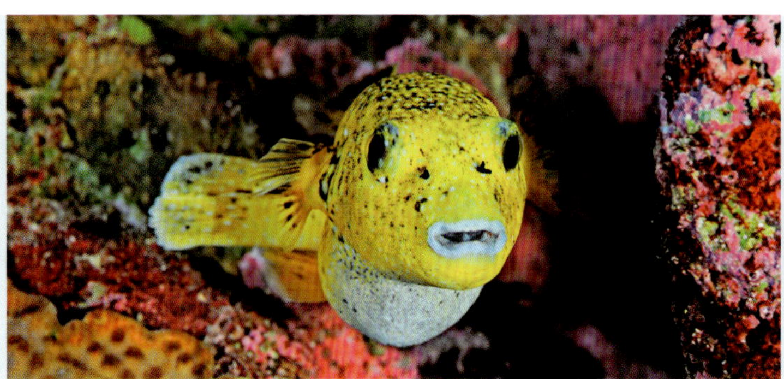

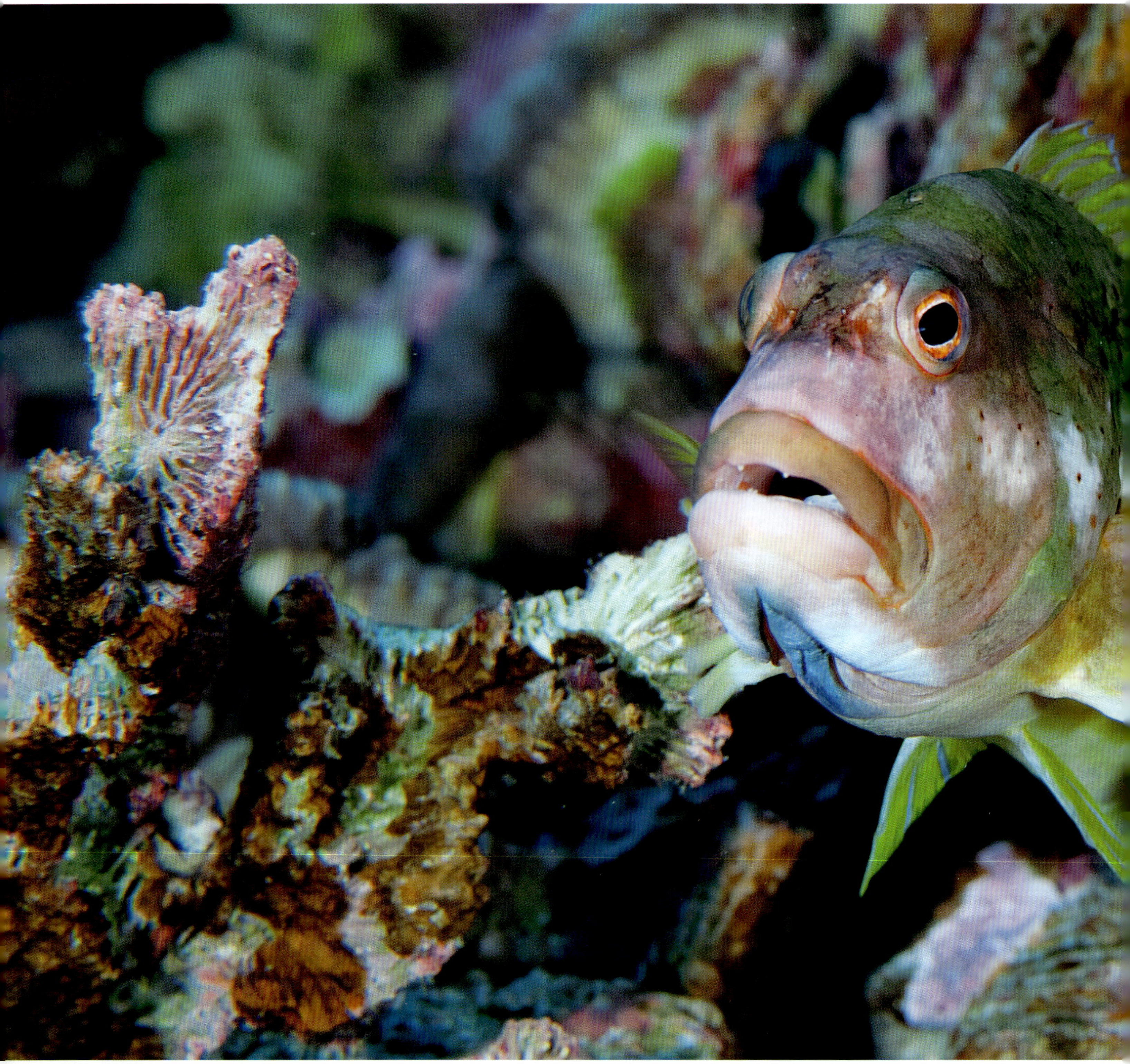

With a surface area covering more than 400,000 sq km (154,440 sq miles), the marine reserve of the Phoenix Islands is larger than Japan. Worldwide there is no marine reserve larger than that of the the natural paradise located between Hawaii and the Fiji islands, and belonging to the Pacific island nation of Kiribati. The Phoenix Islands comprise a total of eight atolls, which together have only 28 sq km (11 sq miles) of land area. There are also two reefs that remain constantly below the waterline. The average water depth is 4,000 m (13,123 ft), reaching a maximum depth of 6,147 m (20,167 ft). Scattered about this huge ocean area are probably more than 30 undersea peaks, of which 14 are known. A unique feature is the islands' diversity of habitats: In the reserve alone there are 200 coral and 500 fish species. Eighteen species of marine mammals live here, and 44 species of birds have erred into the endless expanses of the Pacific Ocean. The islands represent an important stopover point during their migrations.

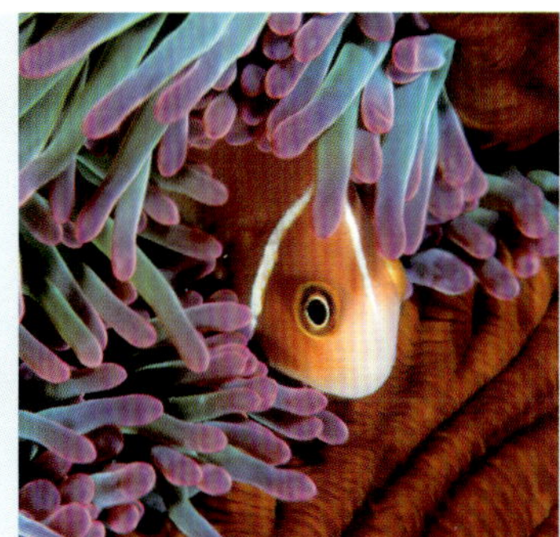

Anemones and corals are a good hiding place, not only for the anemone fish (left). The guineafowl puffer (far left) and the hawkfish (large picture) also make use the colourful underwater world with their camouflage, adapting themselves perfectly in colour.

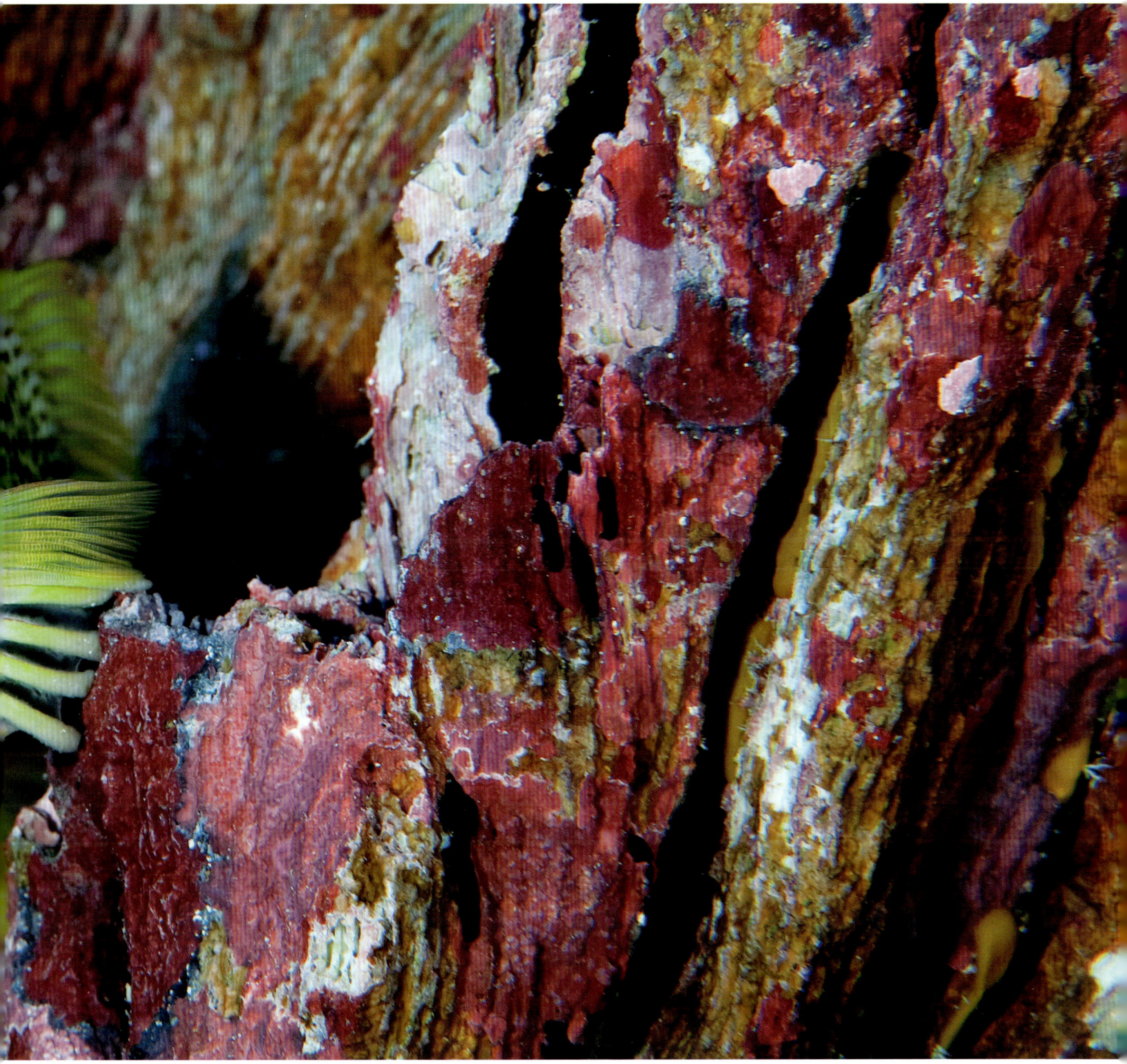

In 2013, a large part of the Namib Desert on the west coast of Africa was inscribed as a UNESCO Natural Heritage site. One of the oldest deserts in the world, it is also one of the most barren anywhere.

Nevertheless, some animals defy the adverse living conditions, for example gemsboks (right), from the genus of oryx antelopes. There may not be a drop of rain for decades.

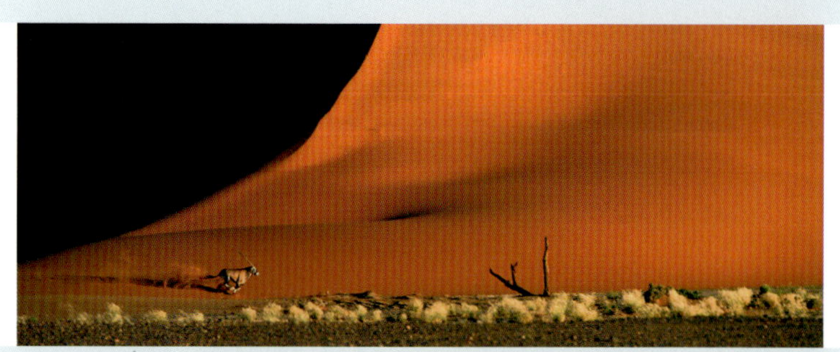

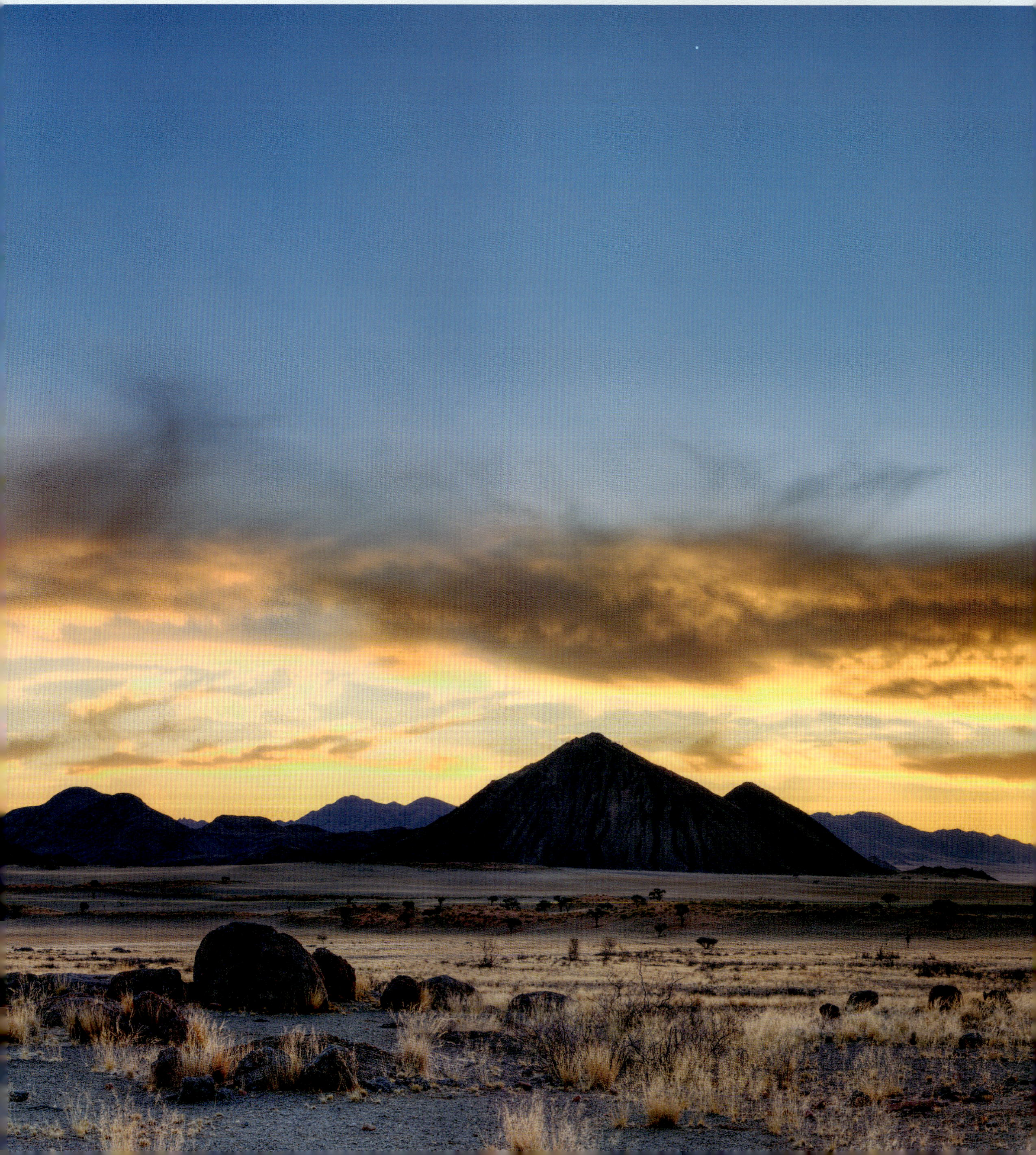

AFRICA

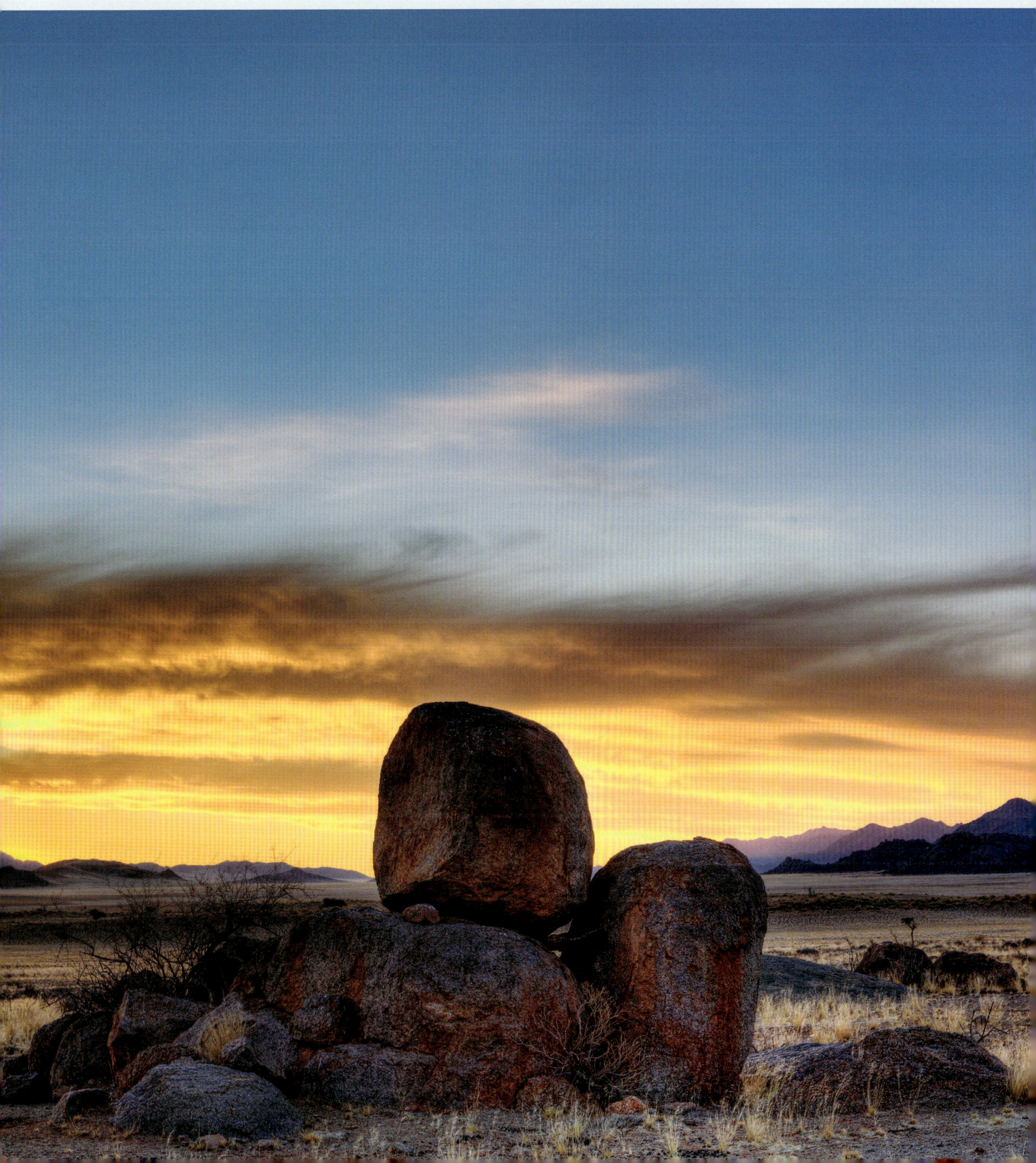

TASSILI N'AJJER

Date of inscription: 1982

Many prehistoric rock paintings have been preserved in the jagged terrain of the Hoggar mountains – invaluable documents of the earliest period of human development. This desert region, characterized by bizarre rock formations, is home to rare animals and plants.

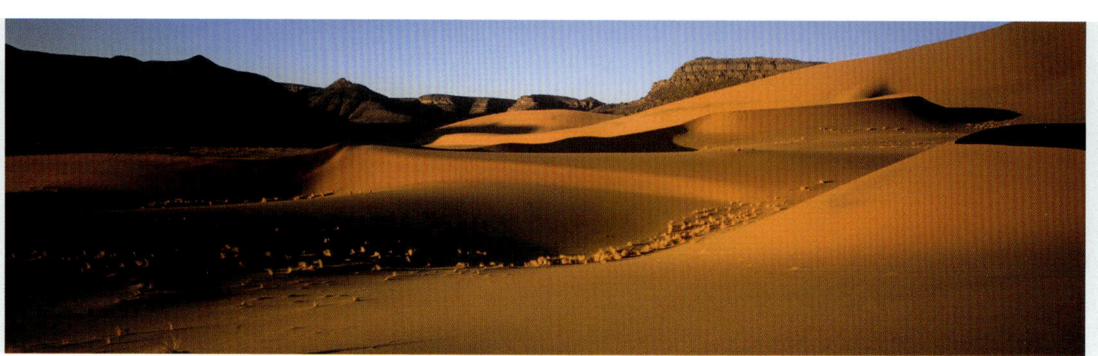

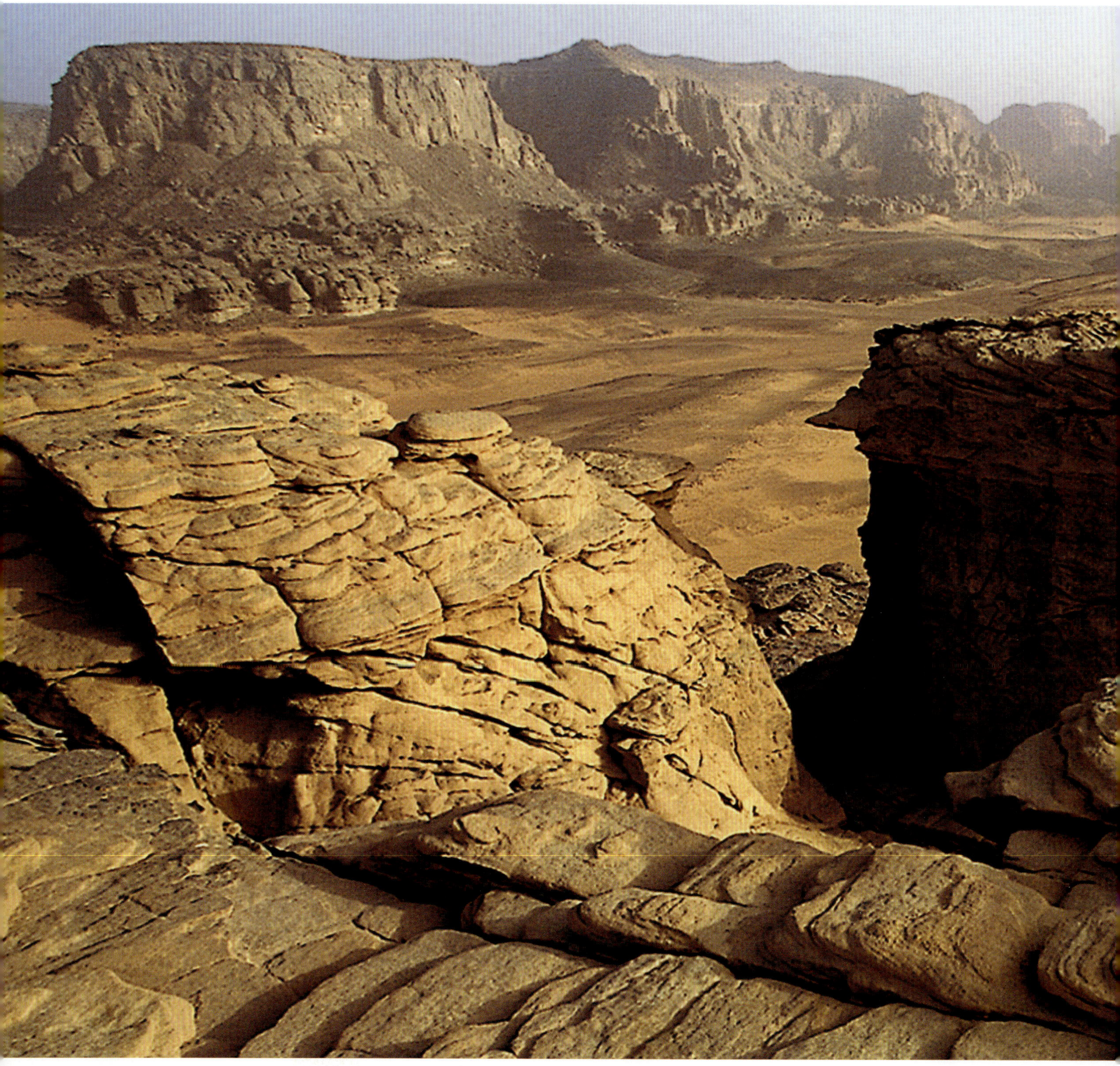

The Tassili N'Ajjer mountain plateau ("plateau of the rivers") covers an area roughly the size of England in one of the least hospitable areas of the Sahara, near the Libyan and Niger borders. In 1933, numerous cave paintings were discovered in this magnificent rocky landscape.

More than 15,000 cave drawings and engravings have been documented so far. The designs date back to various periods, the earliest to 6000 bc. They document decisive stages in human cultural development from a time when today's desert still enjoyed a damp, tropical climate. The rock paintings, protected from the ravages of the elements in ravines and caves, depict hunters and herds of elephants, giraffes, and buffaloes. Domestication also seems to have been practiced, as herdsmen are shown grazing their animals on the savannah. Camels appear in the later paintings. The indigenous Saharan cypress and the Saharan myrtle are typical of the vegetation, and among the indigenous animals are the endangered Barbary sheep, the dorcas gazelle, the caracal lynx, and the sand cat.

The mountain chain resembles a moonscape; its appearance is due to erosion. Rocks jut out of the sand like giant stalagmites, but plant life can nonetheless flourish, thanks to the water-retentive properties of sandstone.

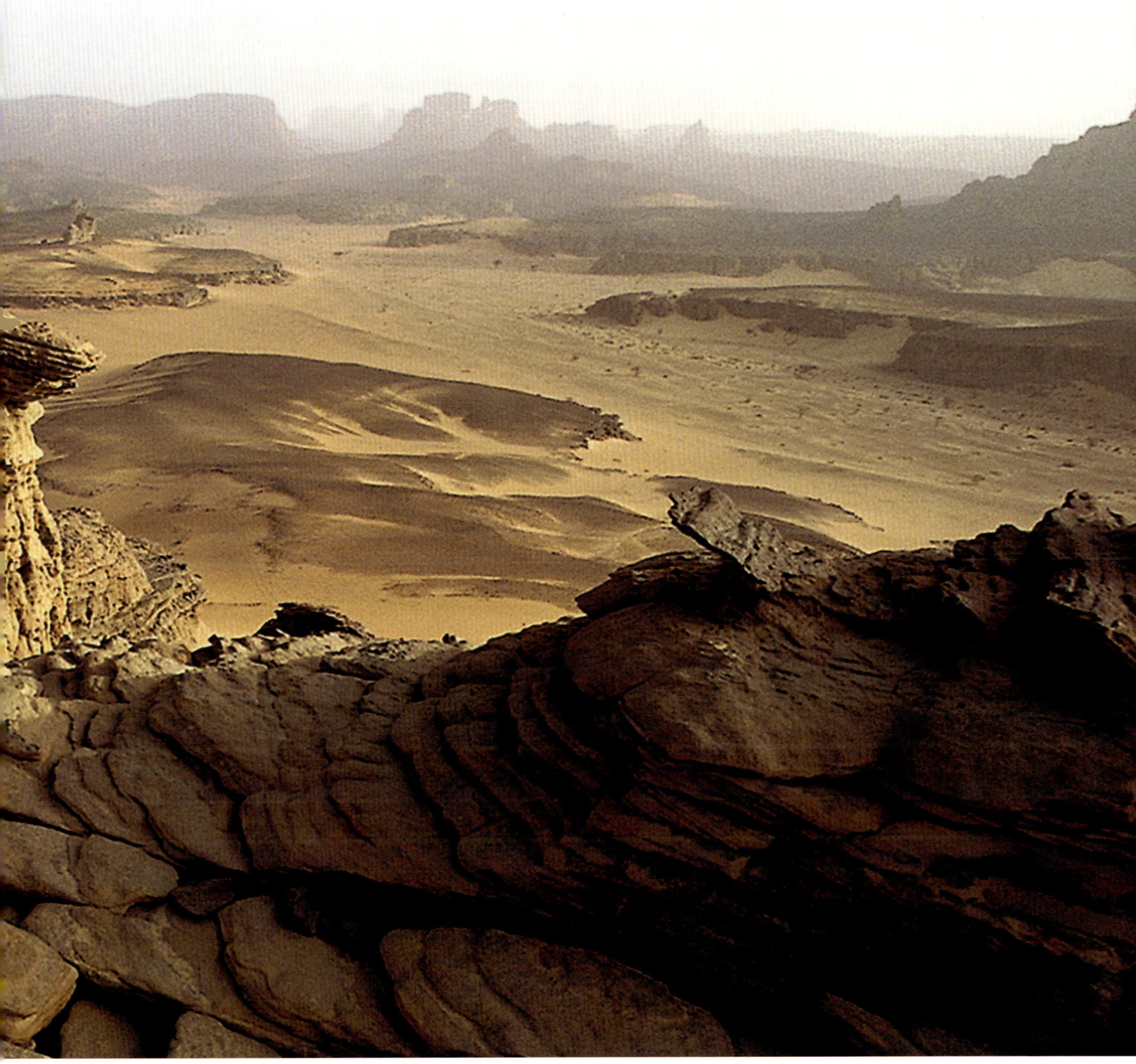

ICHKEUL NATIONAL PARK

Date of inscription: 1980

At 100 sq. km (39 sq. miles), the national park encloses both Lake Ichkeul and its tributaries and the 511-m (1,680-foot) high Djebel Ichkeul massif.
It is one of north Africa's most important wetlands and a habitat for numerous bird species, water buffaloes, and bog plants.

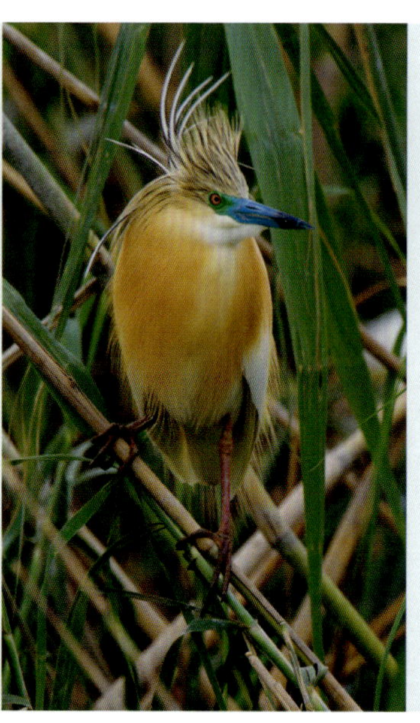

At a distance of 25 km (16 miles) southwest of Bizerta, and connected to the Bizerta Lagoon by the Oued Tinja, the region immediately surrounding the 100 sq. km (39 sq. miles) of Ichkeul Lake, with its teeming fish life, is fed by streams from the Mogod mountains. The lake has both fresh and salt water, the salt content increasing in the dry summer months and decreasing with heavy rainfall.
Various species of rushes, irises, swamp lilies, reeds, and water lilies grow in the fertile oases. The conservation area is also a refuge for Tunisia's largest mammal, the water buffalo, weighing up to 1,200 kg (2,900 lb), as well as almost 200 species of bird, of which the majority are waterfowl, such as ducks and coots. In the winter, it is home to hundreds and thousands of migratory birds from Europe. Nowhere else in north Africa are there so many gray geese. Fossil deposits of hominids, primates, and extinct giant mammals are also found in the area.

The dense vegetation on the shores of Lake Ichkeul teems with life. Among the inhabitants are the squacco heron (left) and the African sacred ibis (large picture), which was once venerated as a deity in Ancient Egypt.

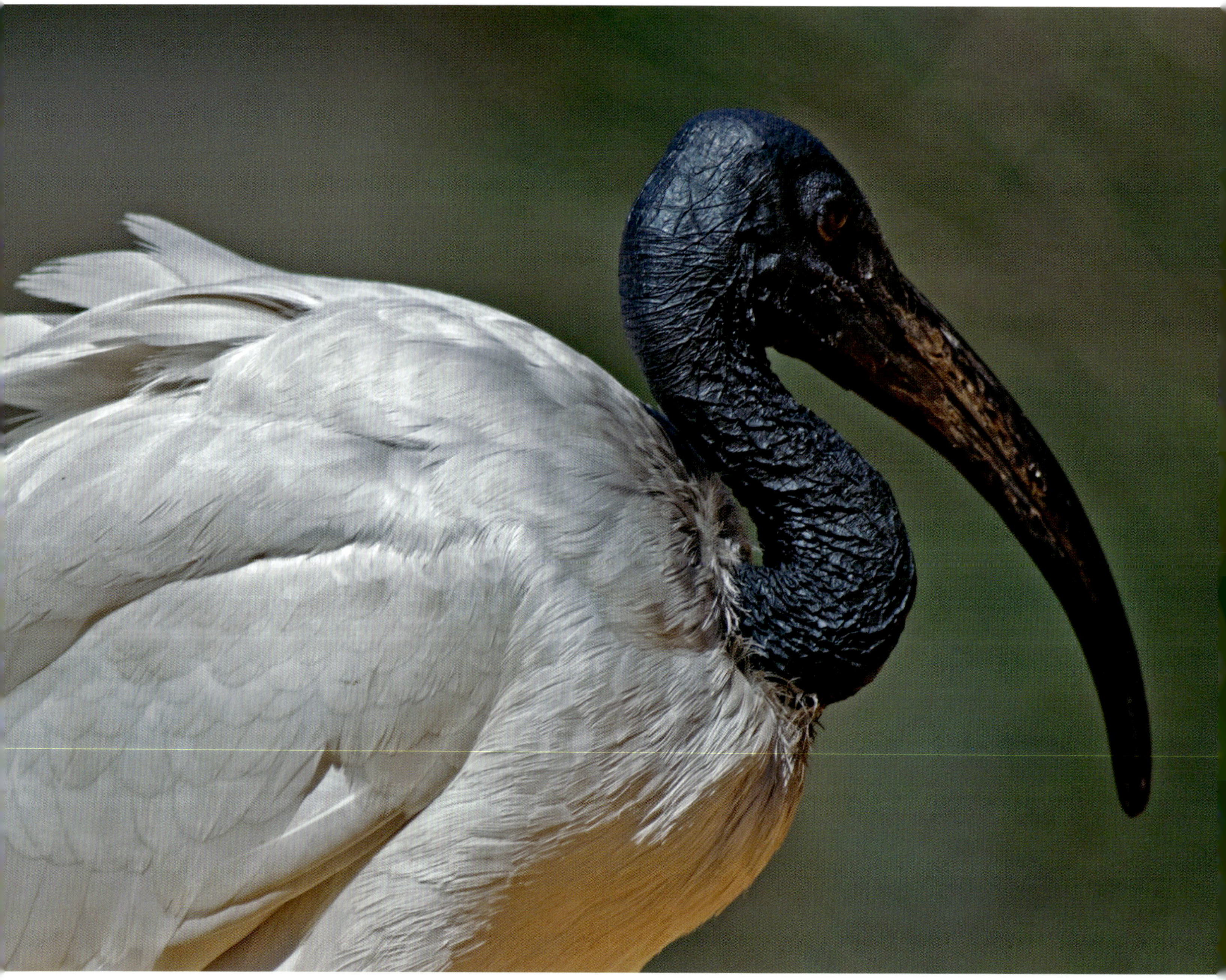

WADI AL-HITAN

Wadi Al-Hitan lies 250 km (155 miles) west of Cairo, in an extraordinary landscape of cushion-shaped rock formations caused by wind erosion. However, the main attractions in this dry valley are 380 well-preserved whale fossils. Sixty million years ago, the earliest ancestors of the whale were land-dwellers, although they lived close to the lake shore. The Mesonychids are most closely related to modern ungulates, but were carnivorous and resembled the common otter. From these developed the life-forms whose remains were found in the valley. Zeuglodon isis lived from 45 to 38 million years ago, was more than 20 m (66 feet) long, hunted in the water and probably only returned to land to reproduce. By this stage its back legs had already atrophied and, instead of forelimbs, it had five-fingered fins. The fossilized remains of the whales are preserved in sandstone, slate, marl, and limestone. The rock strata were laid down at the bottom of the prehistoric Tethys Ocean, which once stretched south beyond the modern Mediterranean coast. The oldest strata in the whales' valley are about 40 million years old and contain numerous whale and manatee skeletons, shark's teeth, turtles, and crocodiles. Fossilized whales are also to be found in younger strata.

Wadi Al-Hitan is an important fossil site. Numerous whale fossils lie embedded in the desert sand.

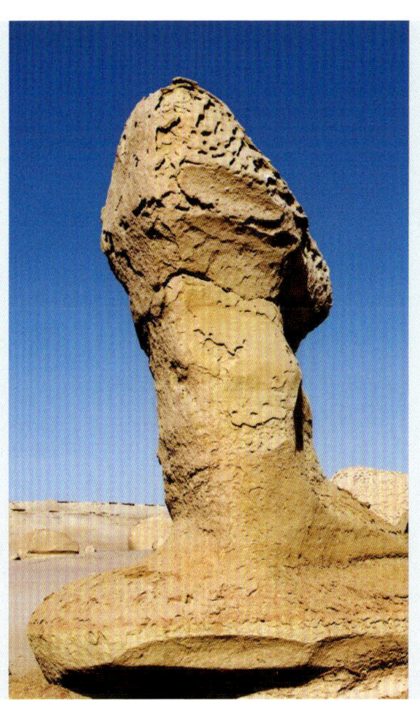

Fossilized precursors of modern whales, the Archaeoceti, have been found in Wadi Al-Hitan ("valley of the whales").

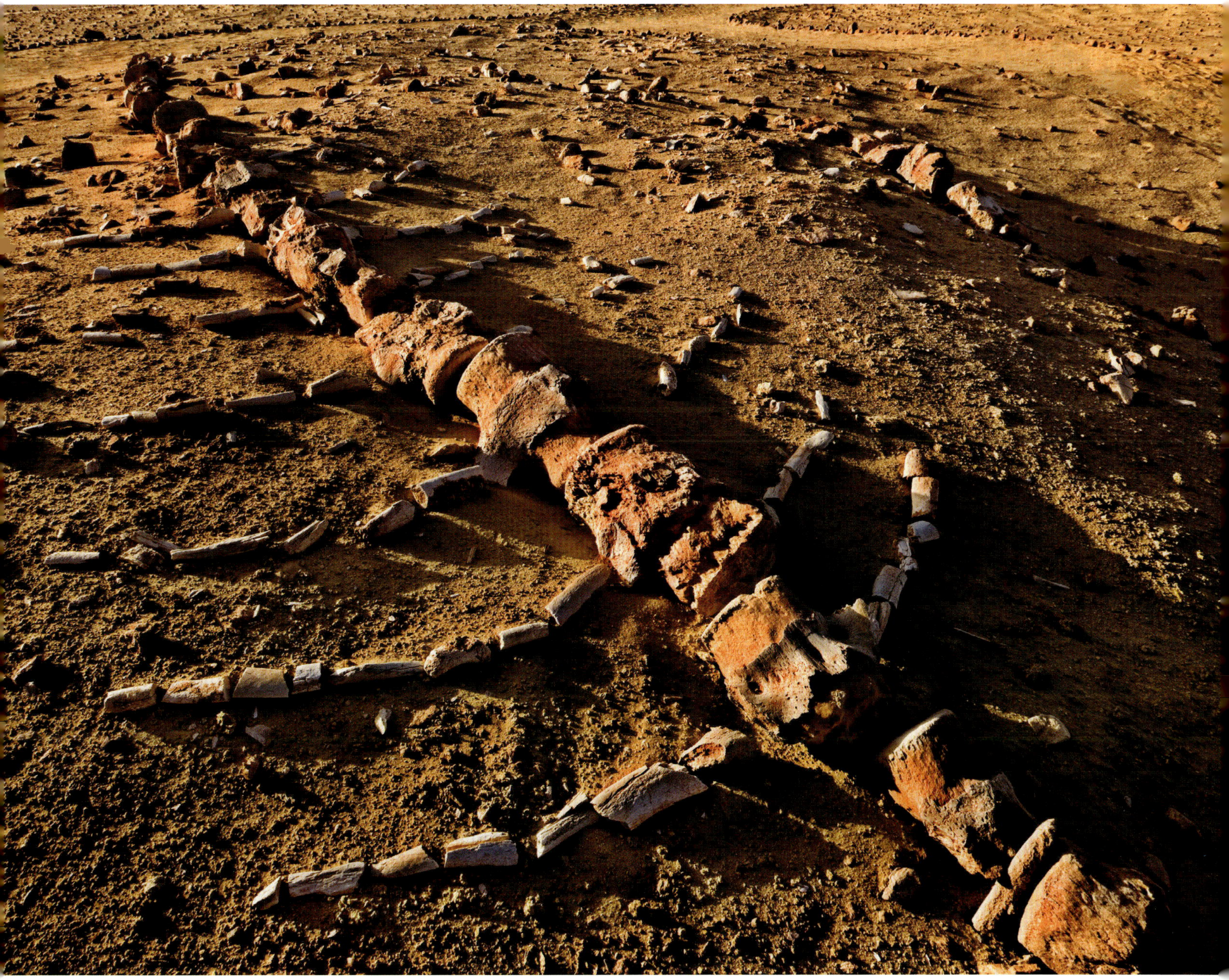

BANC D'ARGUIN NATIONAL PARK

Date of inscription: 1989

With a total area of around 12,000 sq. km (4,700 sq. miles), of which half is marine, this bird sanctuary on Mauritania's Atlantic coast is one of the largest breeding grounds in west Africa. Many migratory birds from Europe and Asia spend the winter here.

Located halfway between Nouakchott and Nouadhibou in the transition zone between the Atlantic and the Sahara, this national park consists of stretches of coastline frequented mainly by seabirds. They populate mangrove swamps, coastal sand dunes, open water, and the small, sandy islands grouped off the coast around the main island of Tidra. Around 100 species regularly nest and winter here. The number of breeding pairs fluctuates between 25,000 and 40,000.

Among the other residents of the shores and coastal waters, which teem with fish, are flamingos, pelicans, herons, spoonbills, and cormorants, as well as assorted species of sea turtle and dolphin.

Located where the Sahara and the Atlantic converge, Banc d'Arguin National Park represents a unique transition zone from sand dunes and sandbanks to silt and mudflats, reefs, peninsulas, and islands.

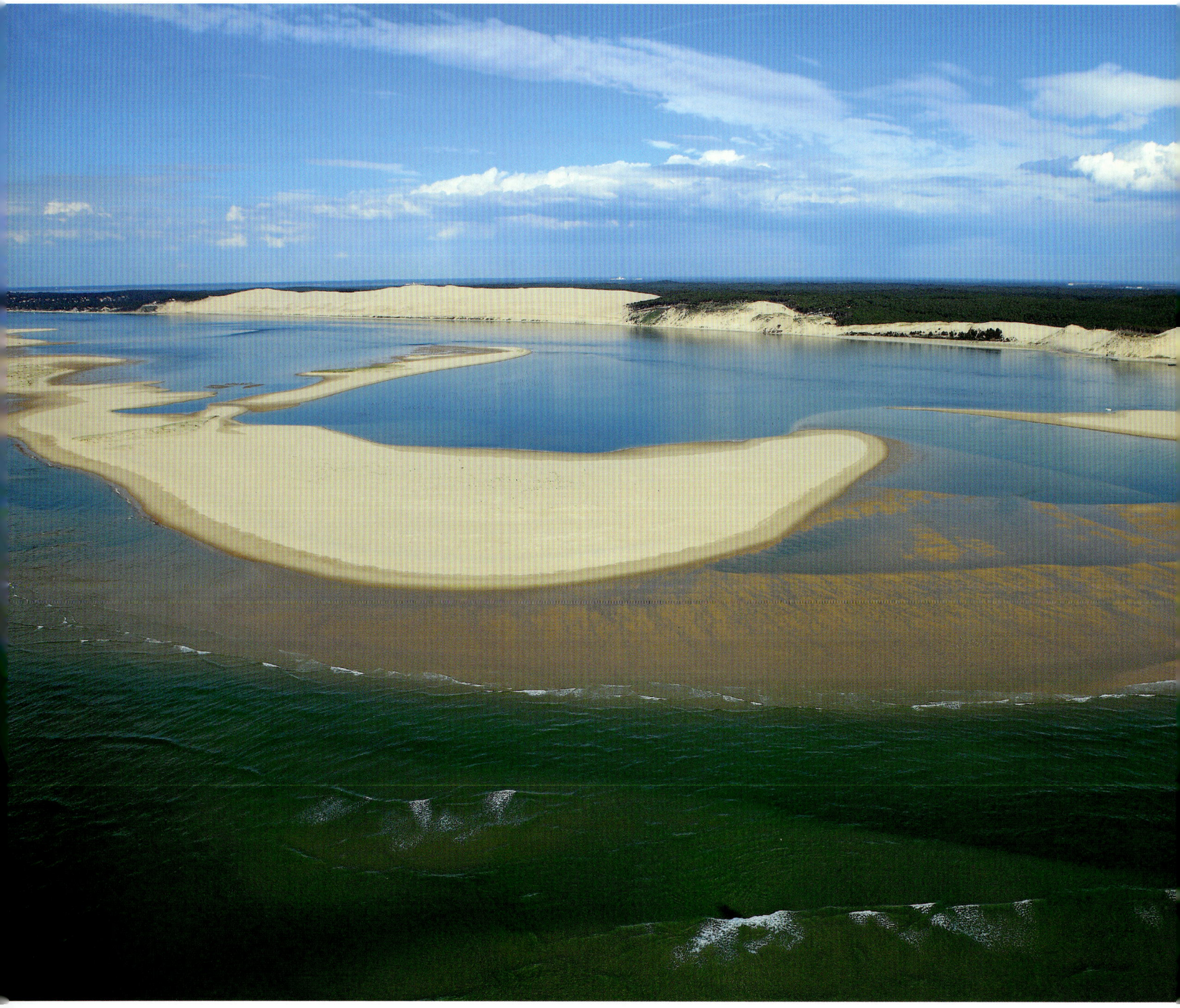

THE BANDIAGARA ESCARPMENT – LAND OF THE DOGON

This World Heritage Site includes both the dip and scarp slopes of the Bandiagara escarpment and the plain below it, as well as 250 Dogon villages and the surrounding Songo community. In the worldview of the Dogon, all elements of the universe are closely interlinked in a dense concatenation of symbolic relationships. The architecture of their dwellings, temples, and communal buildings is thus determined by religious and mythological considerations. A house façade, a village, a garden, a field, or a shroud can all display similar patterns. The village is laid out in an anthropomorphic form received from their mythical ancestors, and the architecture of the mud huts reflects the duality of man and woman. Men and women each have separate granaries, in which millet, their main subsistence crop, is stored, along with their jewelry. The most spectacular Dogon villages are situated on steep cliffs, with squared-off mud huts

The mud huts of the Dogon cling to the cliffs of the Bandiagara escarpment like bird's nests. Many can only be reached by ladder. Even graveyards are built here.

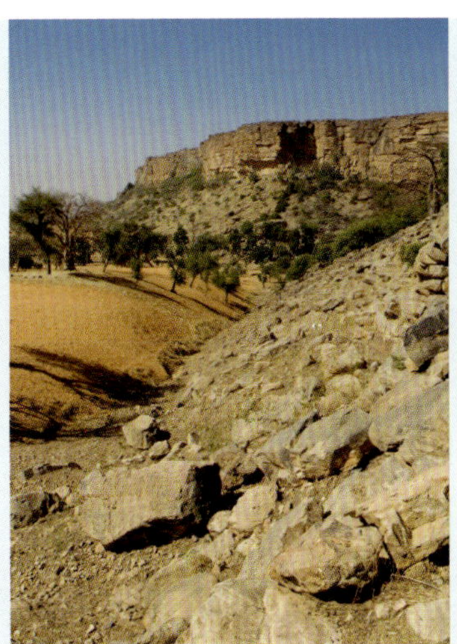

Date of inscription: 1989

A 150-km (93-mile) long escarpment lies east of Mopti. It is the home territory of the Dogon, famed for their mud huts and masks.

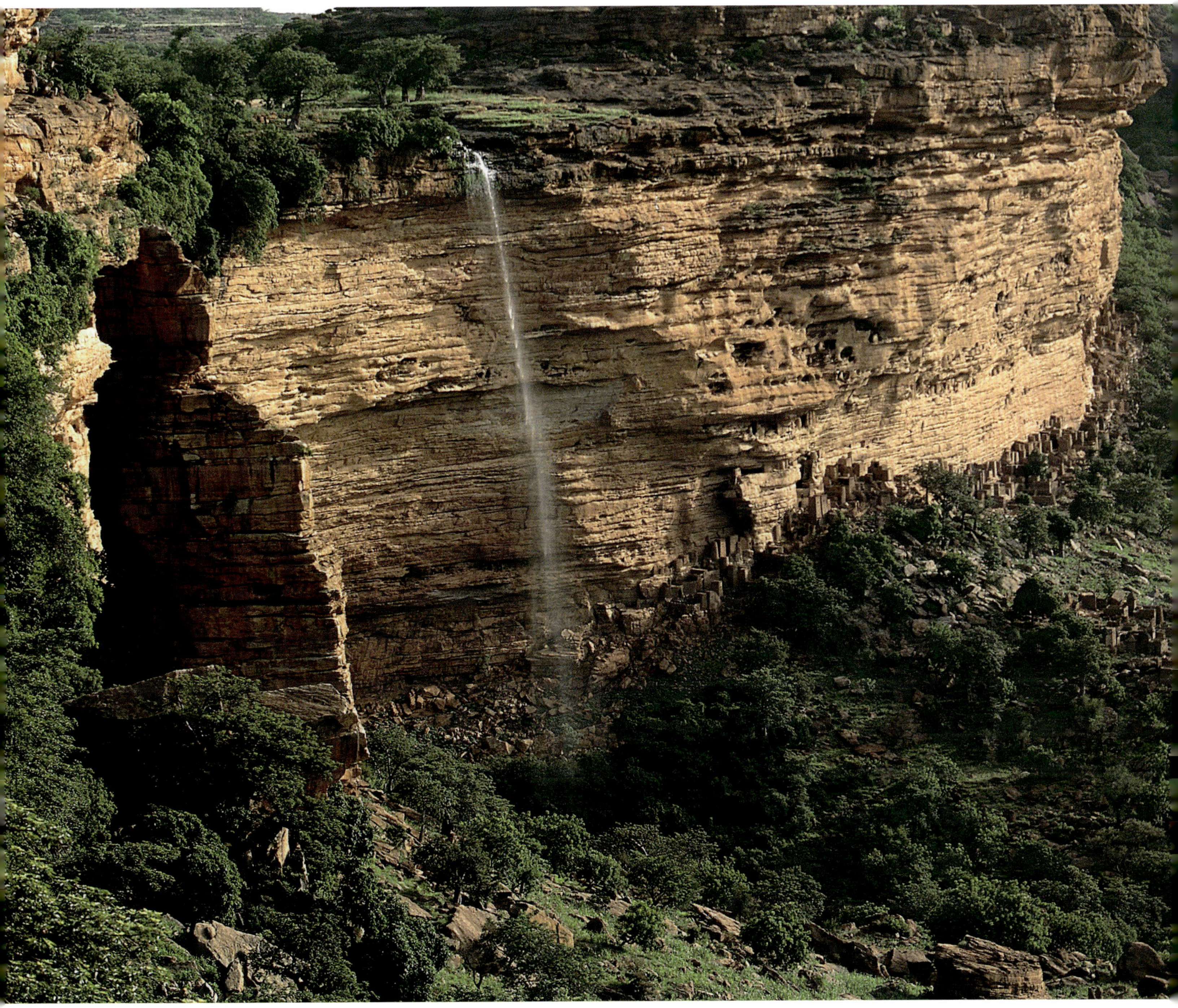

AÏR AND TÉNÉRÉ NATURE PARKS

Date of inscription: 1991

The Aïr massif and the Ténéré desert offer fantastical scenery, typical Sahara and Sahel flora and fauna, and unique prehistoric rock art.

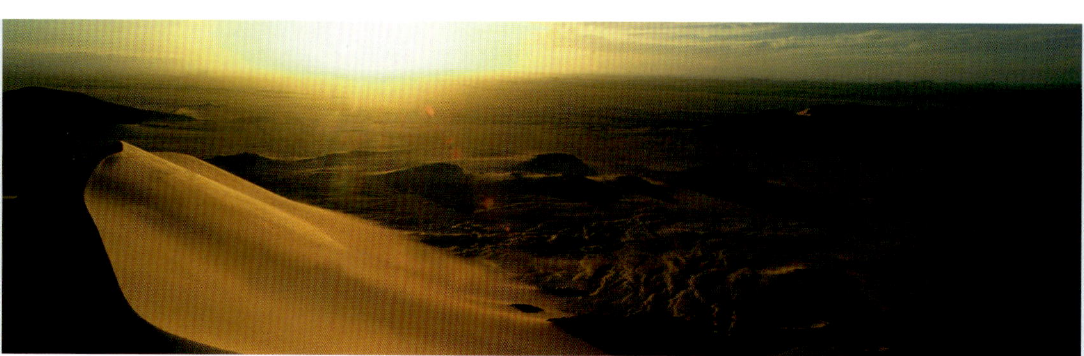

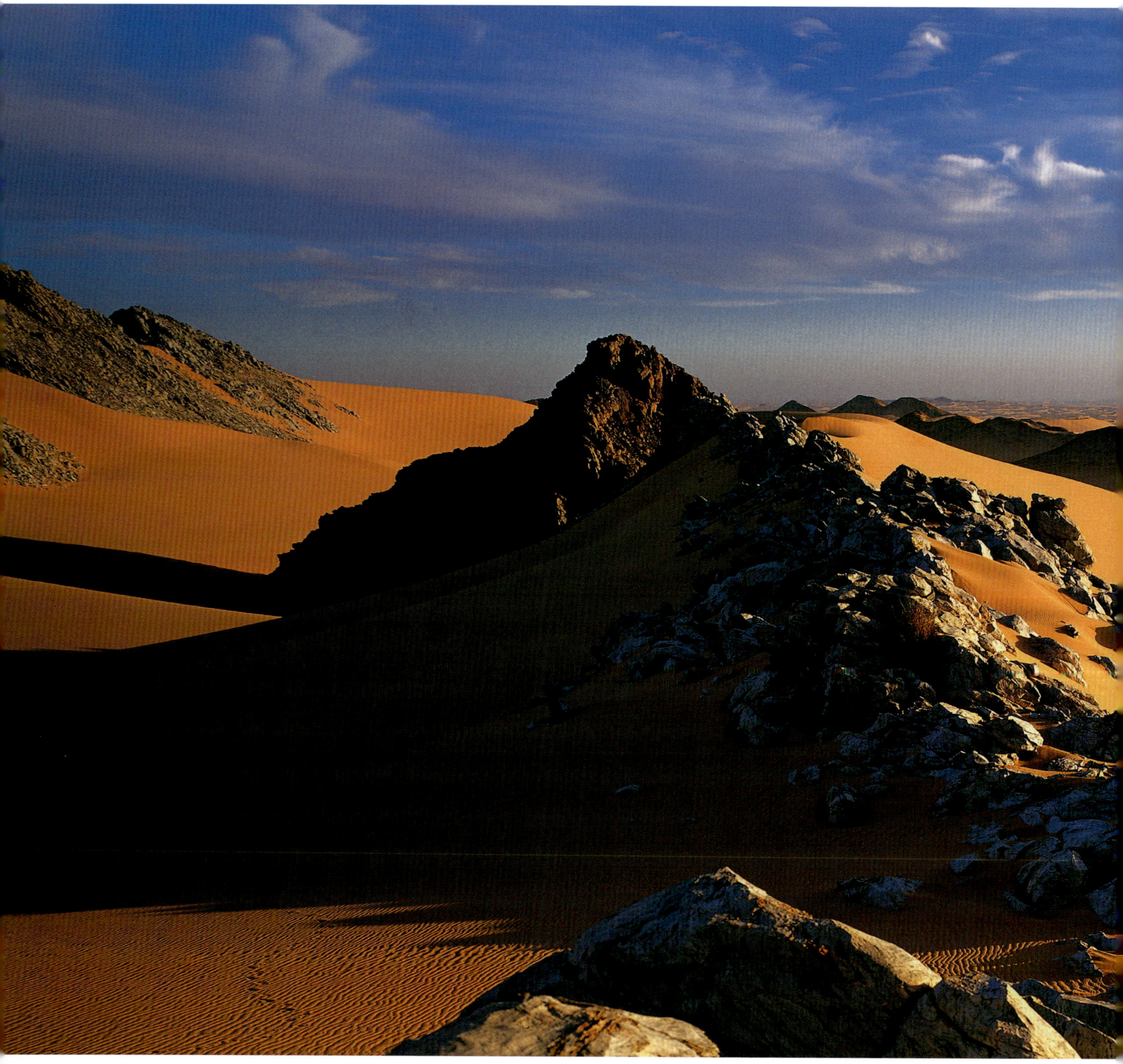

Africa's largest nature reserve covers some 80,000 sq. km (31,000 sq. miles). The Aïr massif in north-western Niger runs for 400 km (250 miles) from north to south. It is a crystalline peneplain of volcanic origin, 700 m (2,300 feet) high in the middle, with a series of steep intrusion peaks separated by sand-filled valleys (koris), culminating in Mont Gréboun, the highest point at 2,310 m (7,580 feet). Adjacent and to the east, the Ténéré desert gradually develops from plains of gravel and sand into a sea of dunes at its center. Often, no rain falls here for years at a time and there are vast variations in temperature.

On the damper south-western slopes of the Aïr lie grass prairies. Palms and acacia shrubs flourish in the koris, which retain groundwater, and olive trees and cypresses find a hold in the mountains. Aïr mouflon, wild asses, and desert foxes also live here. Prehistoric humans created great rock art in the northern part of the mountain range. The oldest paintings and engravings, from the neolithic period of cattle domestication, suggest a period of damper savannah climate.

Some of the most impressive scenery in the nature reserve is to be seen in the transition zone between Aïr and Ténéré, where rock formations and desert converge, providing a fascinating contrast.

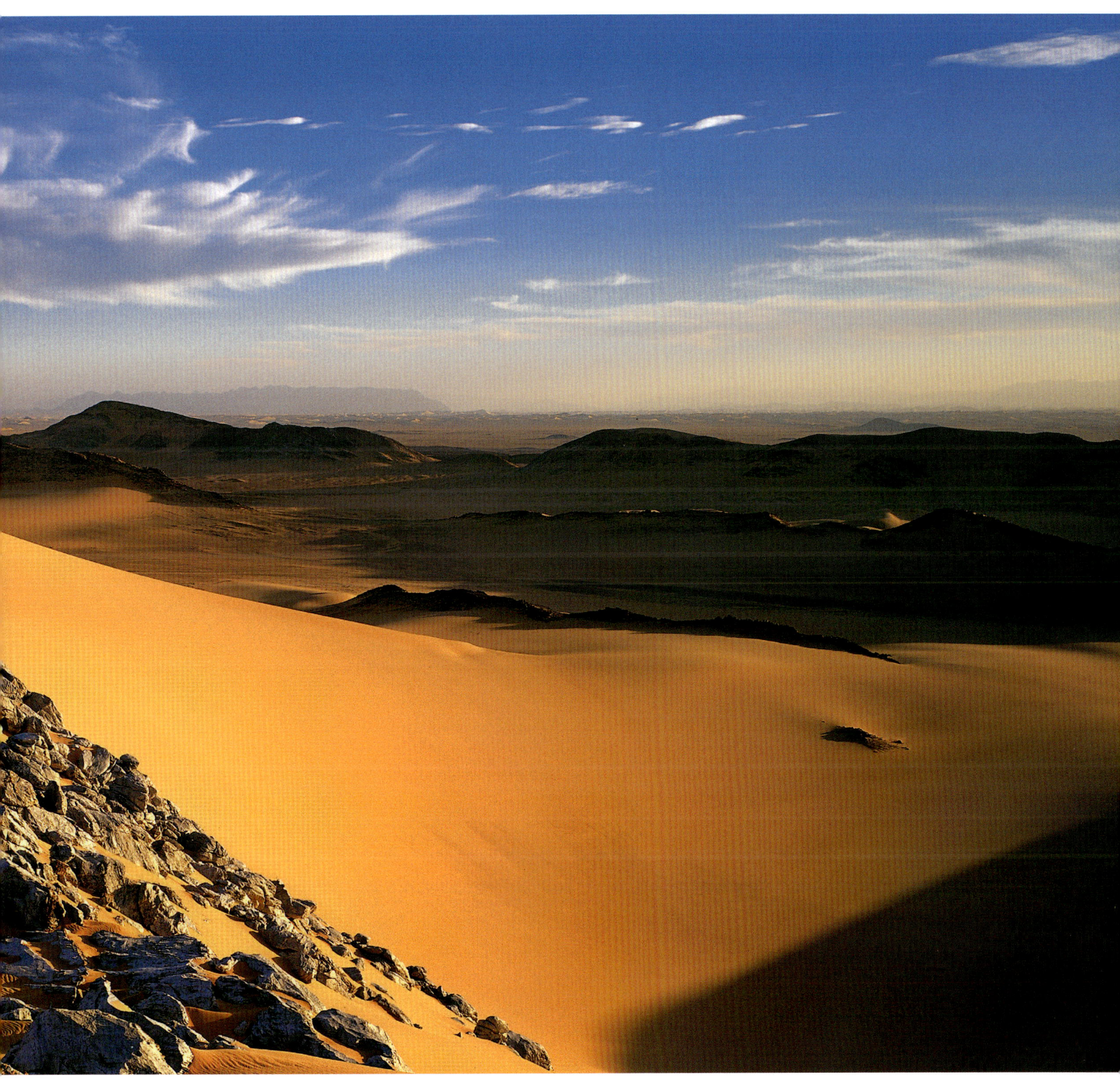

»W« NATIONAL PARK

Date of inscription: 1996

This cross-border nature reserve, the largest in west Africa, takes its name from the meandering of the Niger river at its northern edge, which forms a "W" shape.

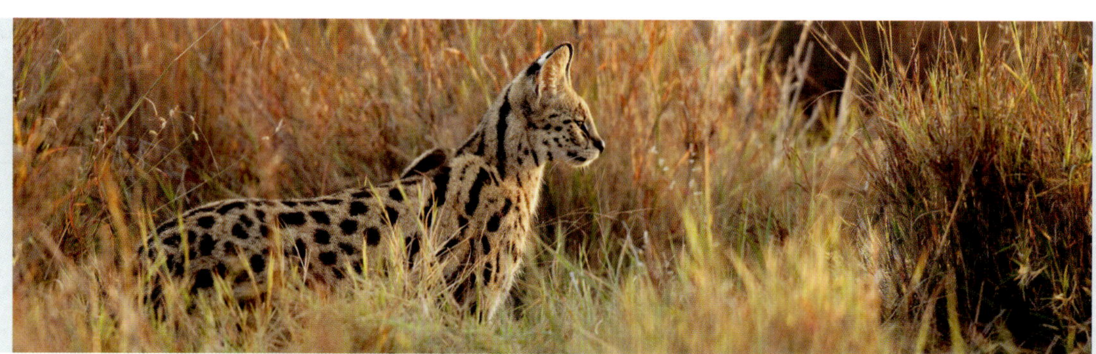

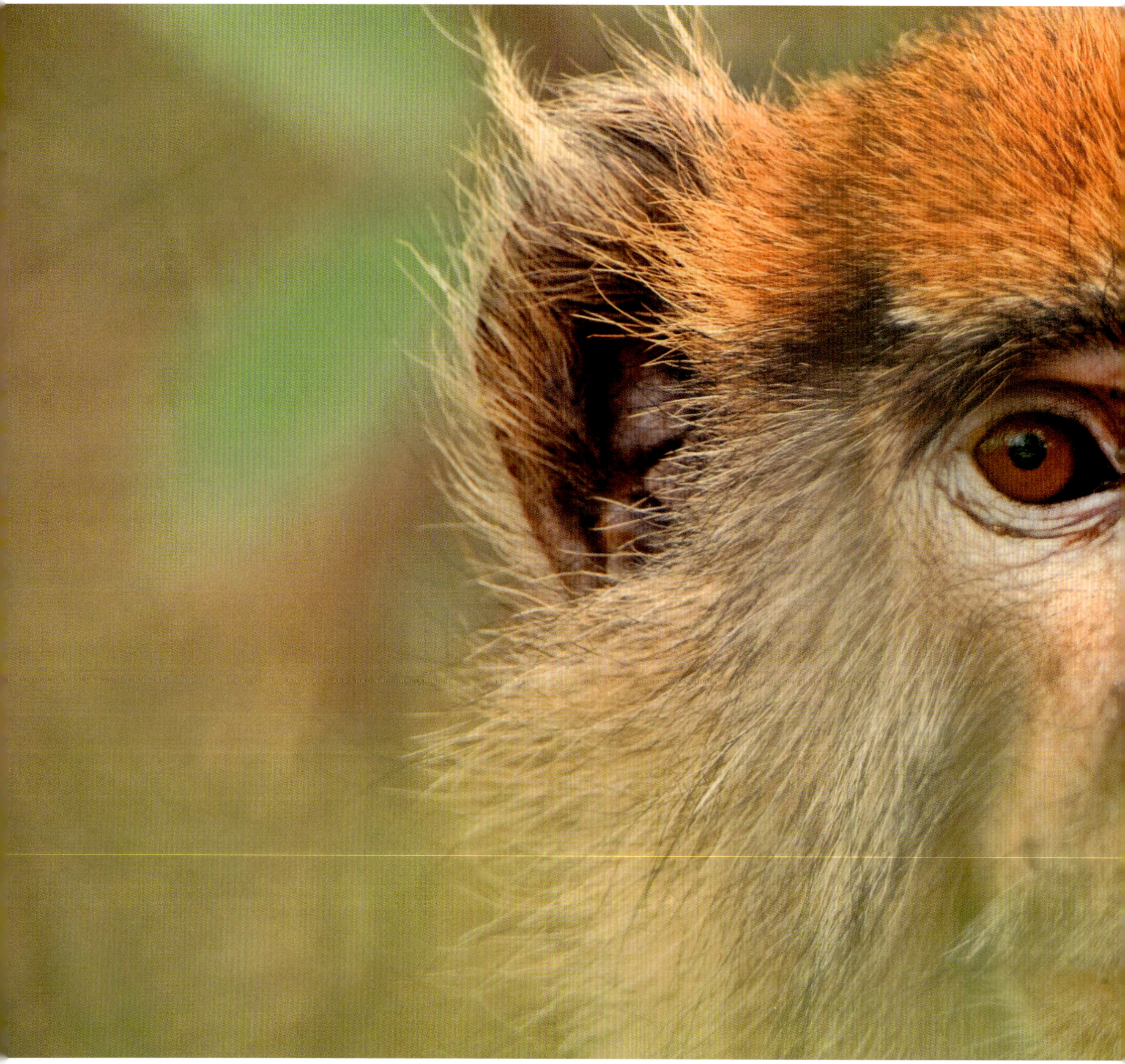

About 150 km (93 miles) south of Niamey in the border area between Niger, Burkina Faso, and Benin is the entrance to this national park, which extends to more than 10,000 sq. km (3,900 sq. miles), of which a section of approximately 2,200 sq. km (845 sq. miles) in Niger is recognized as a World Heritage Site. The park is on the right bank of the river Niger in a transition zone consisting of both Sudanese savannah and wooded areas with gallery forest, in the Sudan-Guinea zone. At the eastern border of the park, near the Niger, the Mékrou river has cut a deep ravine into the sandstone. In the rainy season, the river is transformed into raging rapids and, in the dry season, water lilies grow in the rock pools that remain. Green monkeys and baboons live in the luxuriant vegetation on the banks of the Mékrou and other tributaries of the Niger. Hippos, Cape buffaloes, and large herds of elephants inhabit the dry savannah and gallery forest beside the rivers and streams. Among some 70 mammal and 450 bird species in the park are lions, cheetahs, hyenas, jackals, antelopes, warthogs, ibises, storks, and herons.

The patas monkeys (large picture) are members of the family of vervet monkeys. Characteristic of these primates are primarily their red coats and their speed. Unlike their peers, they live mostly on the ground, not in trees. Left: the rare serval, a wild cat.

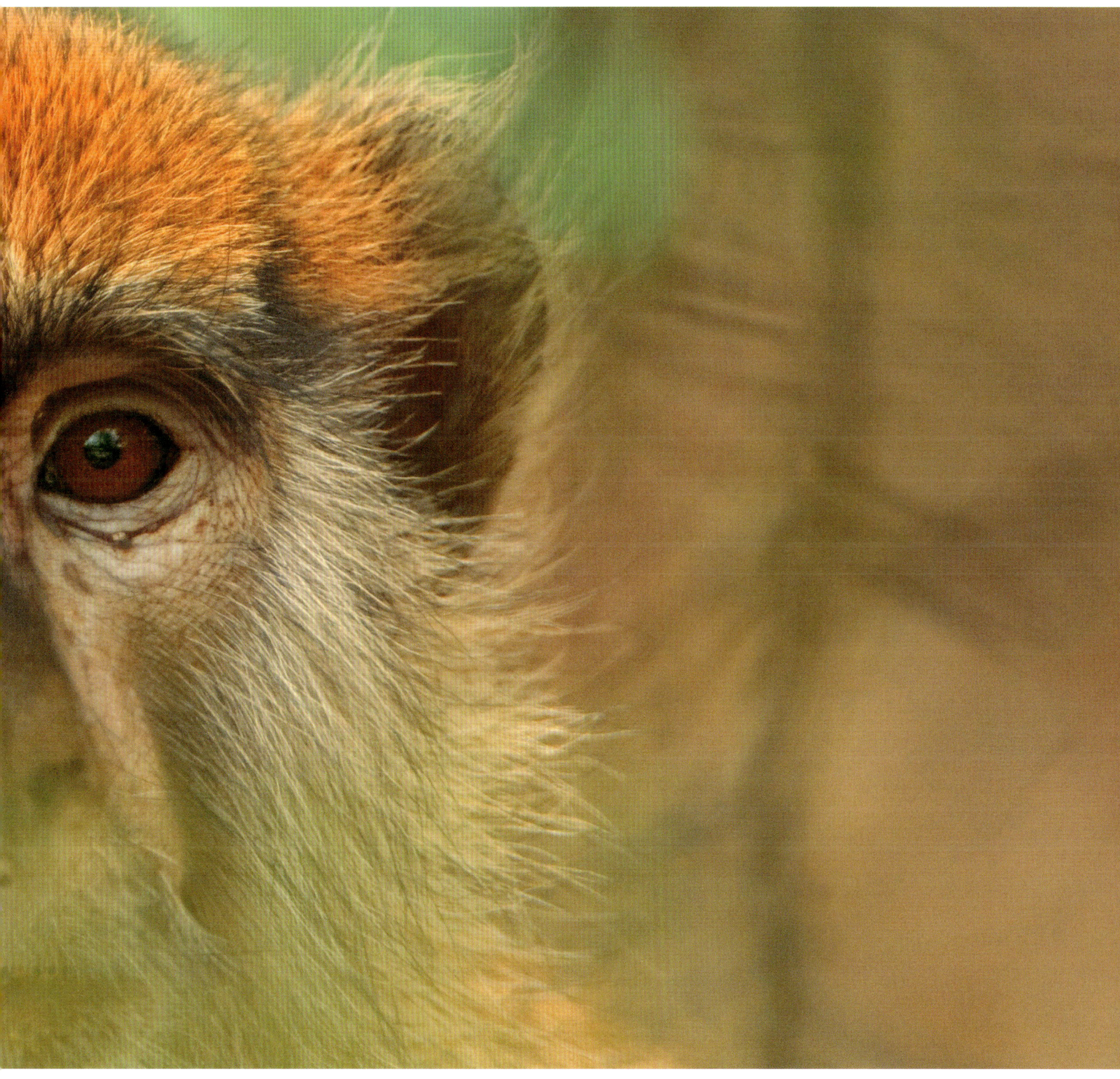

LAKES OF OUNIANGA

Date of inscription: 2012

In a hyperarid Sahara region, which receives only two millimetres of rain per year on average, surrounded by sandstone mountains and dunes, lies a chain of blue, green and red lakes that draw their water from underground.

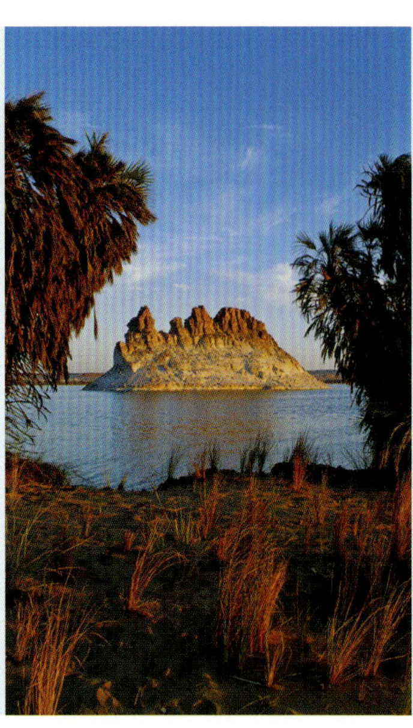

The World Natural Heritage site consists of two groups, situated about 40 km (25 miles) apart, with a total of 18 lakes. The largest lake in the Kebir group has a very high soda content and is virtually lifeless. In the other three lakes live algae of the Spirulina genus. The 14 Ounianga Serir lakes are covered to about 50 per cent by a buoyant reed carpet of the Eragrostis genus. This restricts the evaporation of water in the Sahara sun. Nevertheless, it loses some 7 m (23 ft) per year through evaporation.

The lake replenishes itself with fossil groundwater, which accumulated during the wet phases of the Holocene, between 11,000 and 2,700 years ago. The water of some lakes is of drinking water quality and is used for irrigation. The lakes attract numerous waterfowl and waders, and several species of fish live in the waters. Lake Teli of Ounianga Serir is the largest; it has an area of 400 ha (988 acres) and measures less than 10 m (33 ft) deep.

The lakes are divided into the Ounianga Serir and Ounianga Kebir groups. Serir is Arabic for "small", kebir means "large". For the smaller lakes, the reed cover is an efficient protection from evaporation.

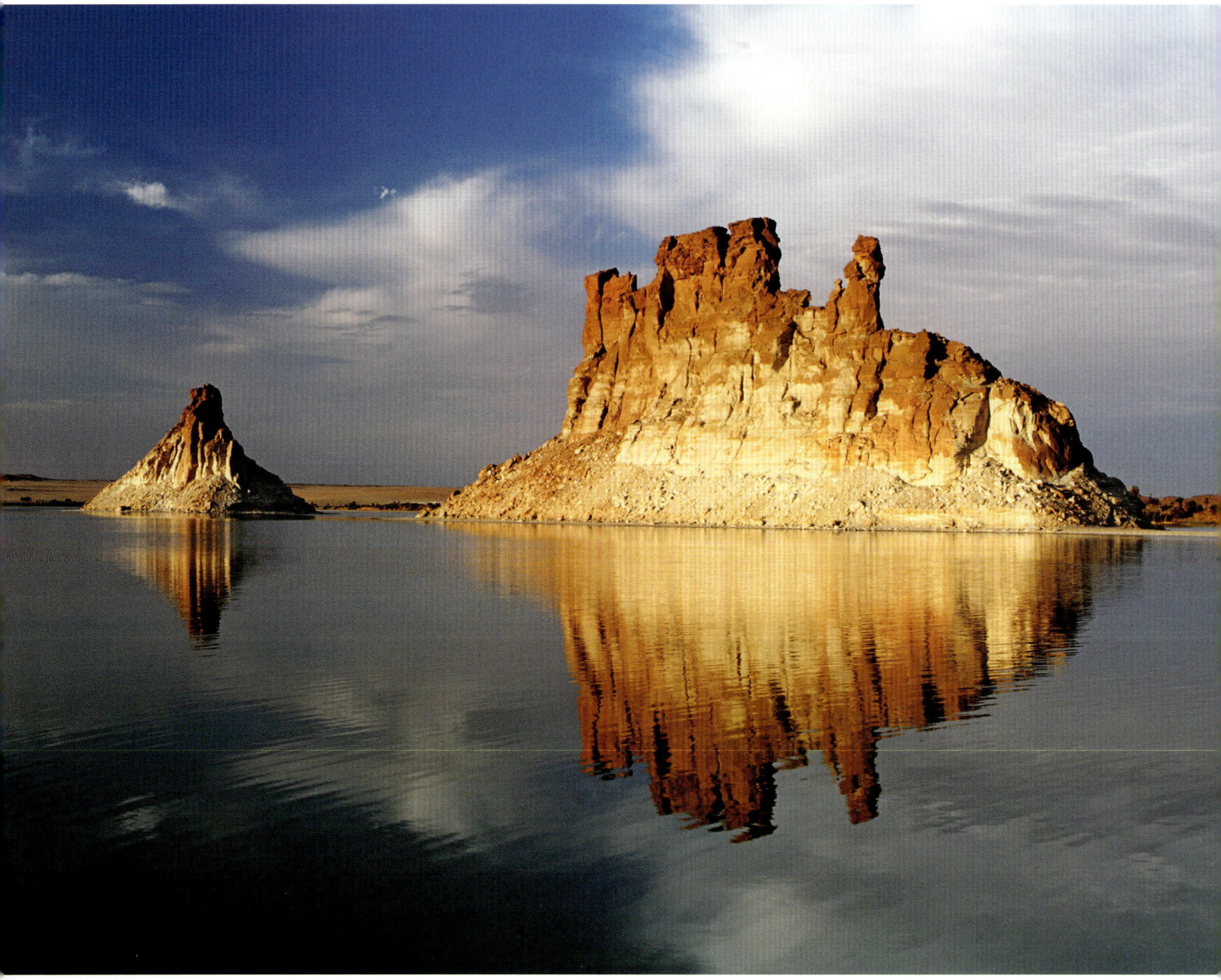

DJOUDJ BIRD SANCTUARY

Situated about 60 km (38 miles) north-east of St Louis on the Mauritanian border, this bird sanctuary is one of the largest in the world, covering an area of 160 sq. km (60 sq. miles). It is home not only to many resident, but also to numerous migratory birds from Europe and Asia, depending on the time of year. After an exhausting transit of the Sahara, up to three million migrants take up their winter home near these richly stocked waters.When the back-waters of the delta evaporate away in the dry season, the birds are attracted to the few remaining water source – the Gorom, which never dries out, and the bays of Lake Djoudj. Around 1.5 million waterfowl and waders populate the expanses of this unique paradise for birds, including flamingoes, cormorants, cranes, spoonbills, herons, storks, black-tailed godwits, white-faced whistling ducks, spotted redshanks, Arabian bustards, aquatic warblers, and other rare species. West Africa's largest pelican colony, with a population of over 1,000, is a particular attraction for visitors. The conservation area not only houses feathered inhabitants, however – turtles, crocodiles, warthogs, jackals, and gazelles can also be found here.

There are birds wherever you look in Djoudj National Park: cormorants, white-faced whistling ducks and pelicans.

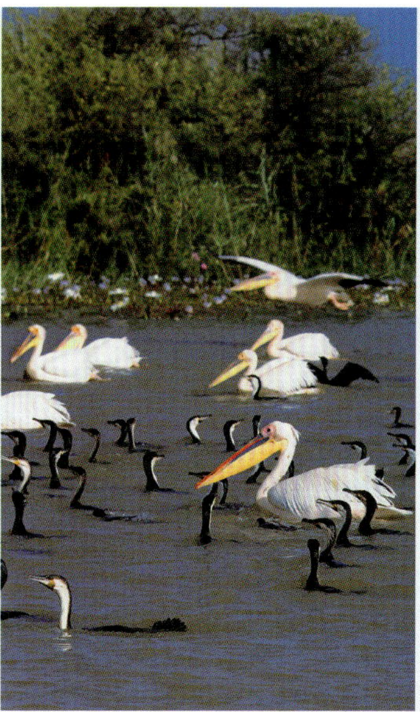

Date of inscription: 1981

In the old delta area of the river Senegal, between the Gorom tributary and the main river, can be found a bird population that is unparalleled elsewhere in West Africa.

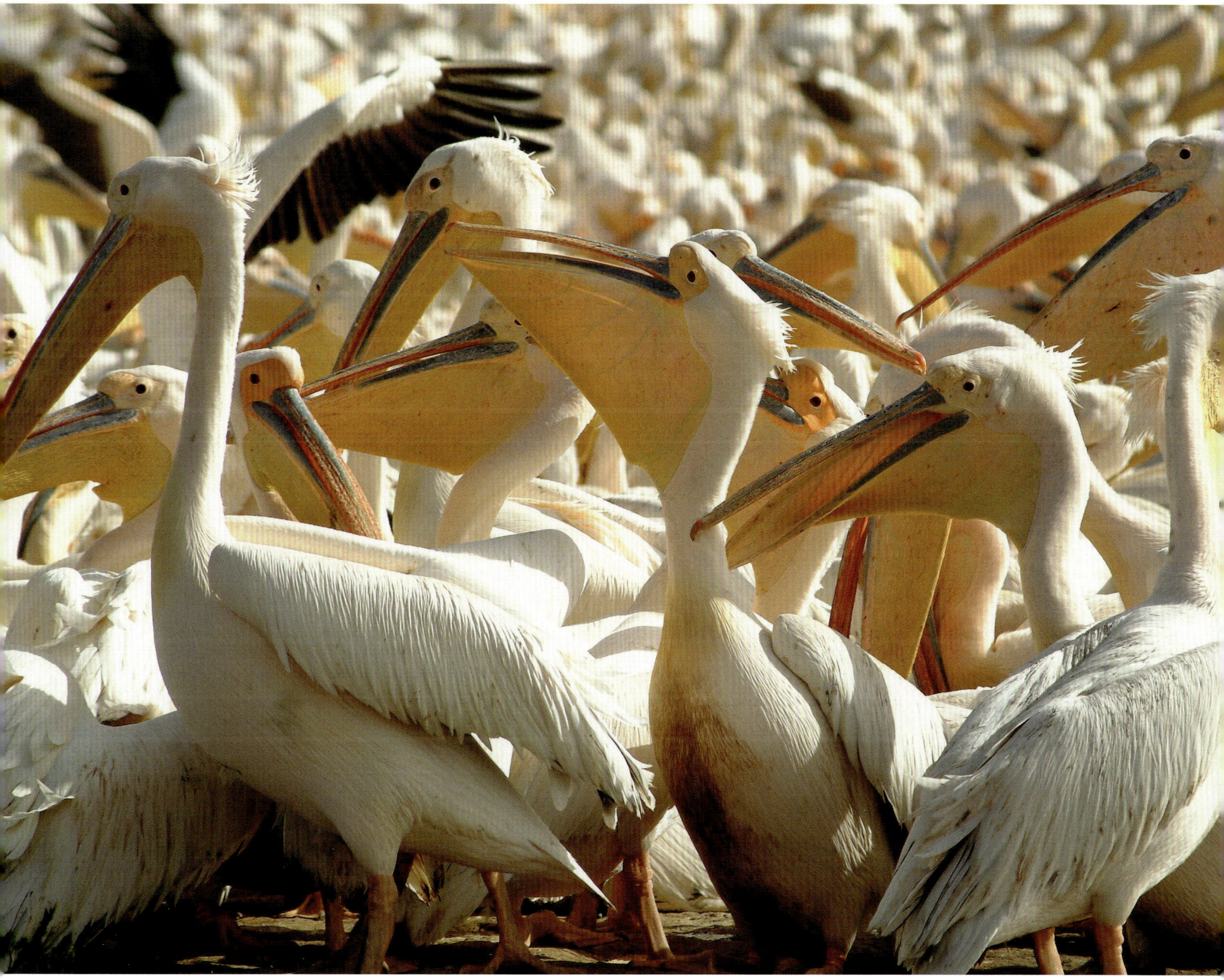

NIOKOLO-KOBA NATIONAL PARK

Date of inscription: 1981

One of the largest nature reserves in west Africa, the region offers a last refuge for savannah animals such as lions and antelopes, whose ranges once stretched as far as the coast.

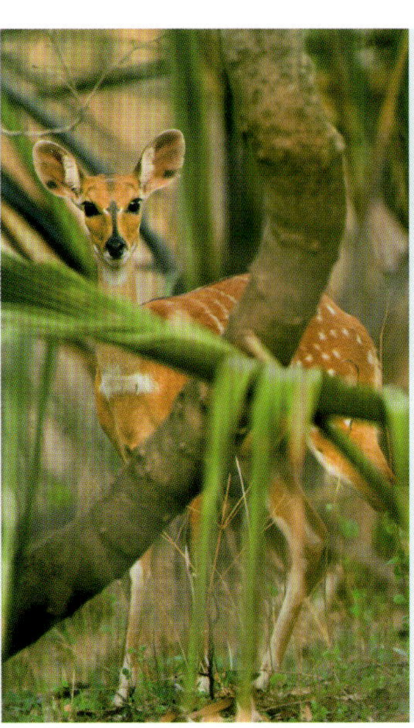

The greater proportion of this national park's 10,000 sq. km (3,900 sq. miles) in south-east Senegal lies in the transition zone between dry savannah and Guinea's wetland forest. It is bordered to the south by the upper reaches of the Gambia river and territory belonging to Guinea, and to the north it runs out into dry savannah in eastern Senegal. The three great rivers of the Gambia system, the Gambia river itself, the Koulountou to the west and the Niololo-Koba to the east, drain the area in endless meanders with a low river drop. During the rainy season, wide expanses of the park turn into marsh and mud. Along the rivers and streams, wooded savannah develops into the luxuriant vegetation of gallery forest, with around 200 species of trees and shrubs. This diverse biosphere affords a home to numerous animals. Around 80 mammal species live here, including the hippopotsmus, an admittedly tiny population of elephants, giraffes, Cape buffaloes, gazelles, giant elands, leopards, cheetahs, jackals, hyenas, African wild dogs, chimpanzees, baboons, hyraxes, and mongooses.

Nikolo Koba National Park has the ideal living conditions for bushbucks (left), because this antelope species needs dense bush and waterholes to survive. Chimpanzees (large picture) swing from branch to branch.

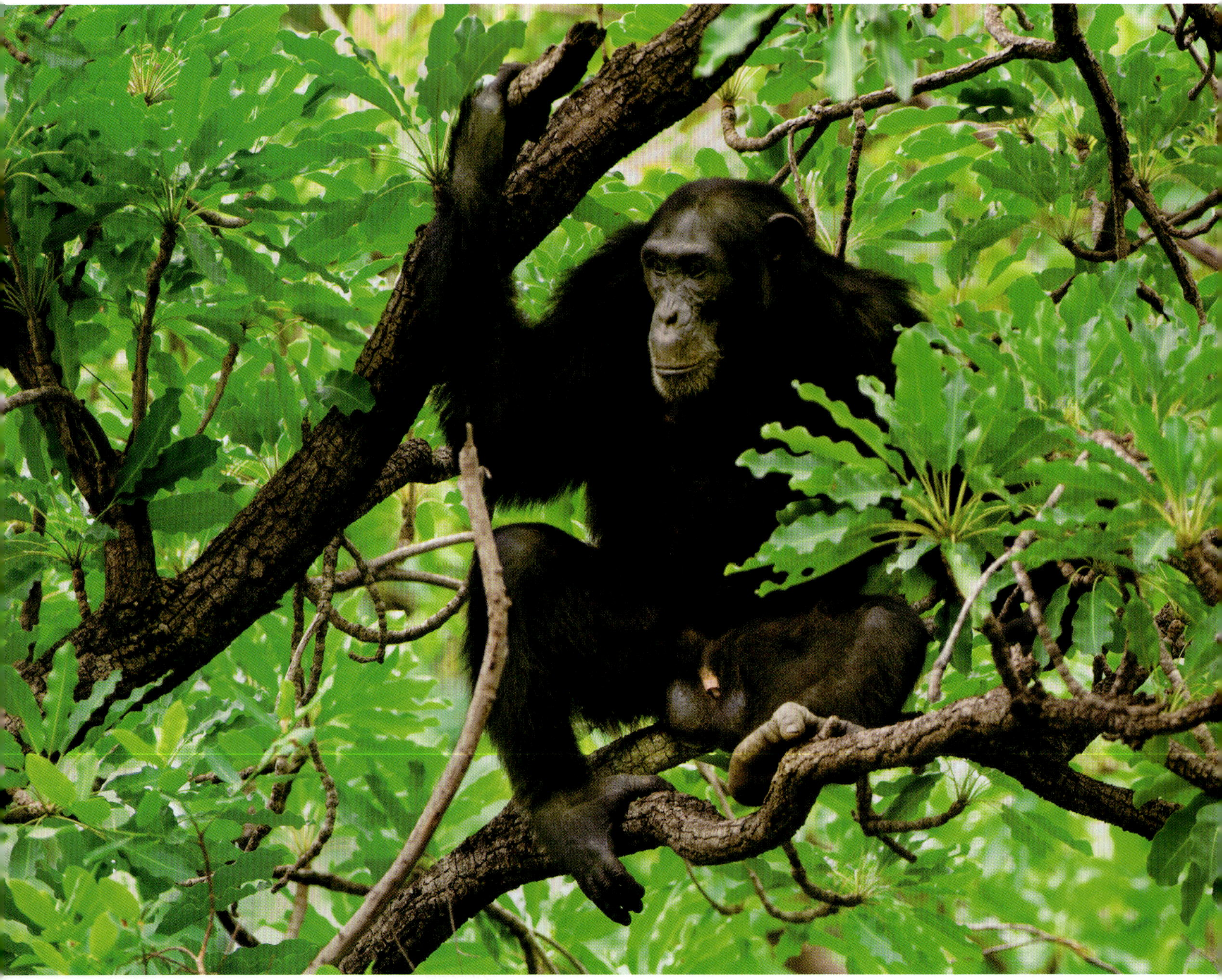

MOUNT NIMBA STRICT NATURE RESERVE

Straddling the borders of the Ivory Coast and Guinea, Mount Richard-Molard in the Nimba massif is, at 1,752 m (5,748 feet), the highest point of both countries and the central point of this conservation area of about 180 sq. km (70 sq. miles). It features an almost unbroken forest canopy: on the lower slopes, deciduous trees predominate, above 1,000 m (3,300 feet) there is montane forest, and the summit area is characterized by mountain savannah. Around 40 plant and 200 animal species are indigenous to the reserve, among them elephants, buffaloes, antelopes, lions, hyenas, guenons, and chimpanzees. Pygmy hippos and dwarf crocodiles are found in the wetlands. Vultures, snakes, and rare amphibians, such as the Mount Nimba viviparous toad (Nectophrynoides occidentalis), are also encountered here. This World Heritage Site, threatened due to iron ore mining and civil war refugees from the Ivory Coast hunting in the nature reserve, has been inscribed on the UNESCO Red List since 1992.

The mandrill (large picture), a relative of the vervet monkeys, presents itself in war paint. At the water's edge you'll also find marsh crocodiles (right, top) and lizards on the hunt for insects, including the odd praying mantis (right, bottom).

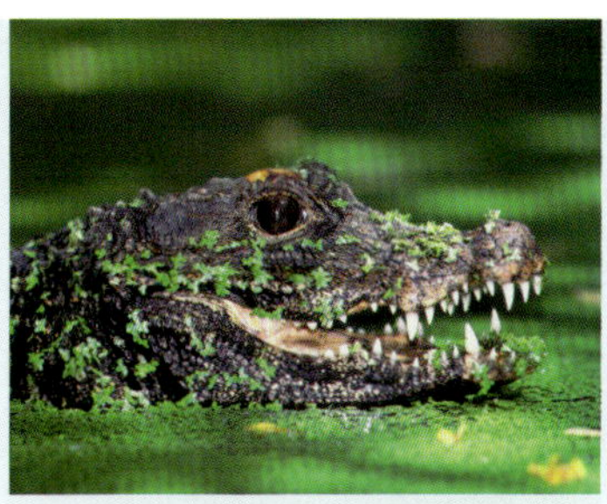

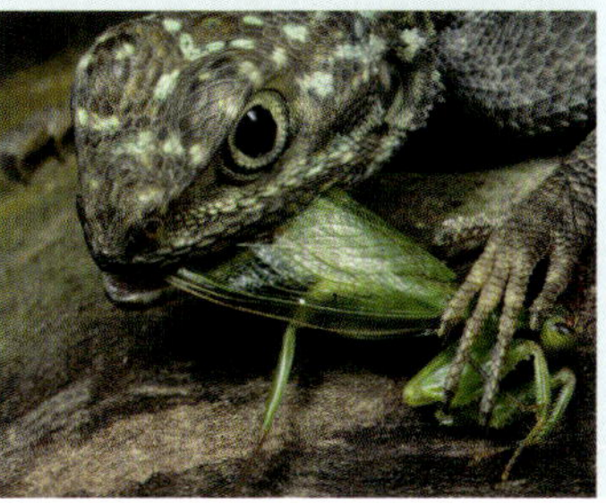

Date of inscription: 1981
Extended: 1982

The reserve, at the meeting-point of the Liberian, Guinean, and Ivory Coast borders, is a transnational World Heritage Site, shared between the two last-named countries.

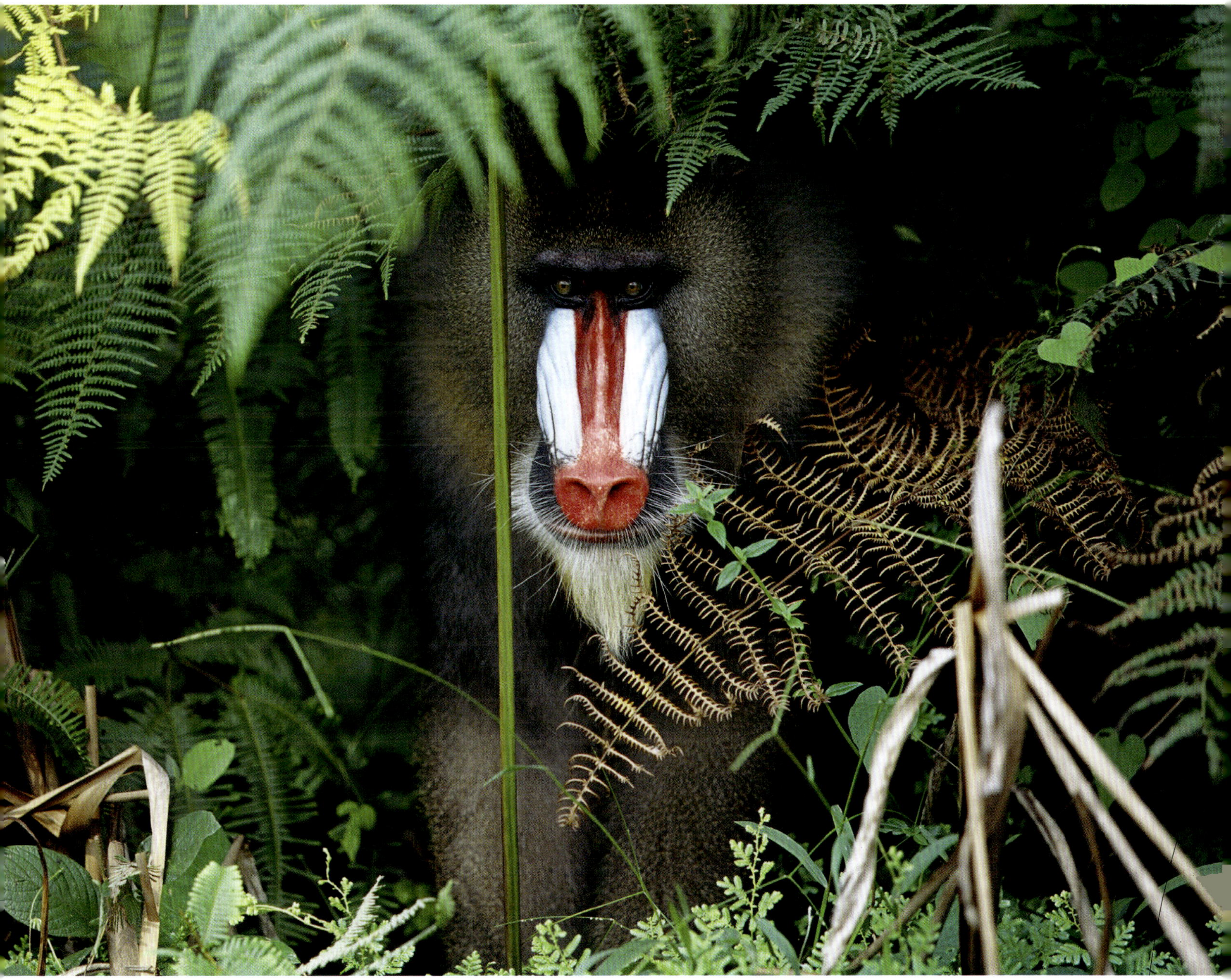

COMOÉ NATIONAL PARK

Date of inscription: 1983

Composed of a variety of habitats, the largest and most diverse game reserve in the Ivory Coast is located in the north-east of the country, in the transition zone between savannah and rainforest.

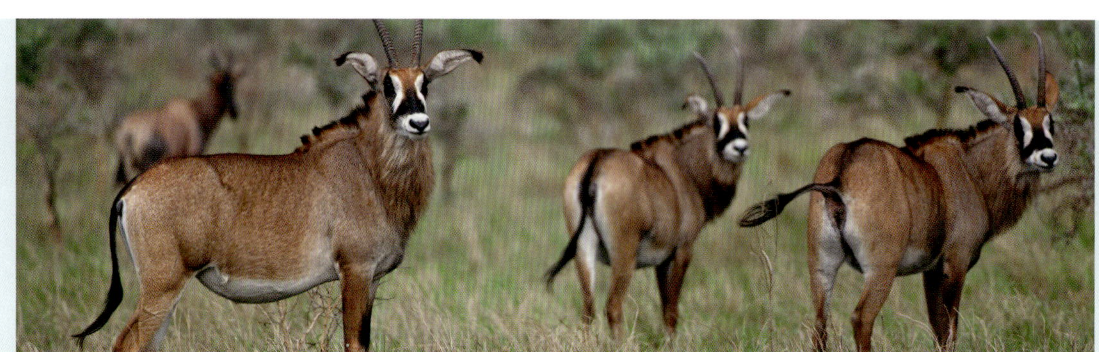

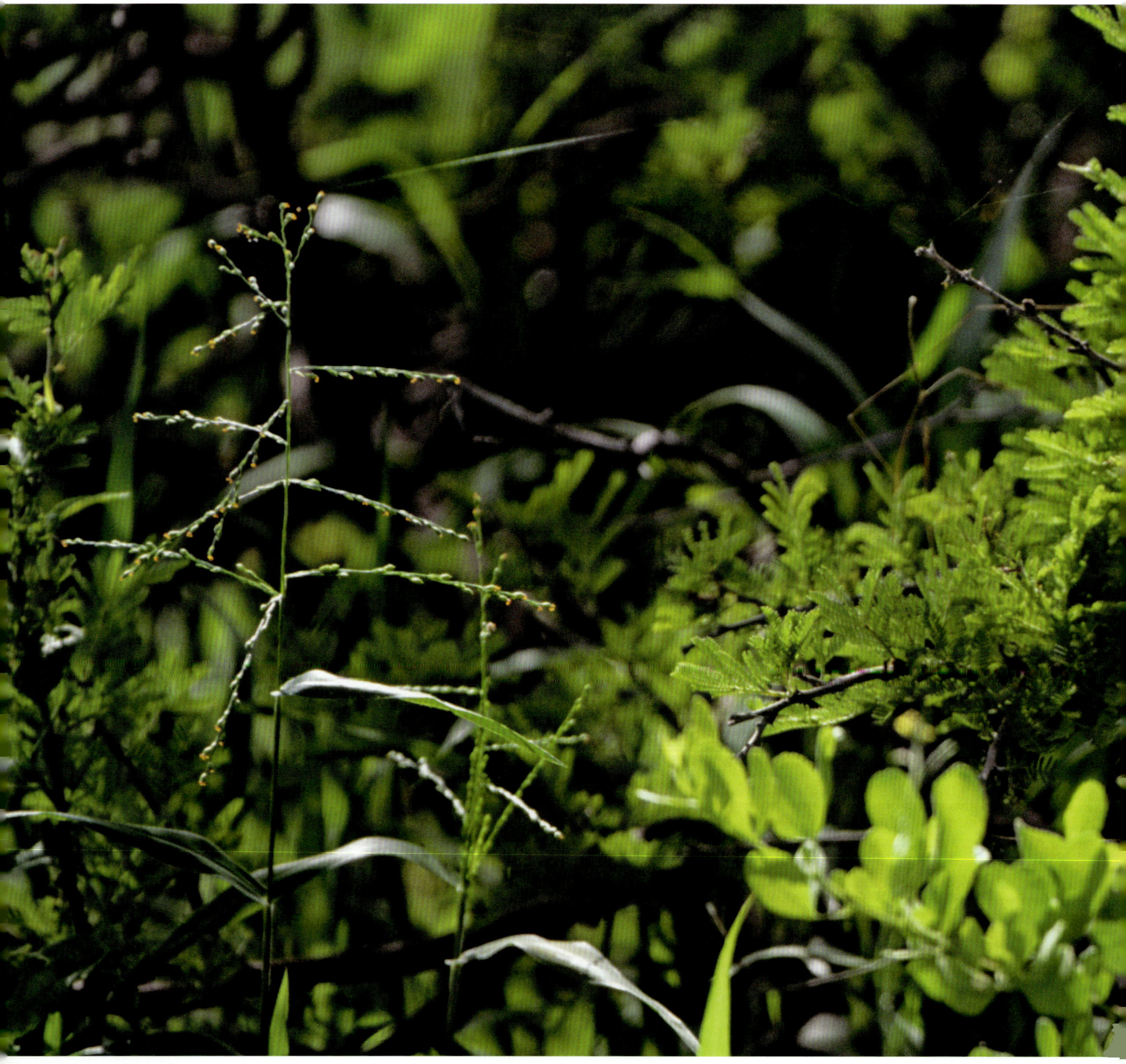

The park owes its name to the Comoé, a river between 100 and 200 m (350 and 700 feet) wide which flows from north to south for 230 km (148 miles) through the park's 11,500 sq. km (4,500 sq. miles). The river is shrouded in dense gallery forest and continues to flow even in the dry season.

Hippopotamuses, crocodiles, and numerous bird species live in close proximity to the water. The savannah is home to Cape buffaloes, warthogs, and 11 species of ape and antelopes. The forests in the southern part of the park are the preserve of elephants; while predators such as lions, leo-pards, and hyenas also patrol here, their numbers are few. Also at home in the national park are three different species of endangered crocodiles. Because of poaching and overgrazing, however, this reserve is under threat and was placed on the Red List of World Heritage in Danger.

Roan antelopes (left) are recognizable by their black and white facial patterning and their backward-curved horns, worn by both males and females. Large picture: the leopard, perhaps the most graceful of the big cats.

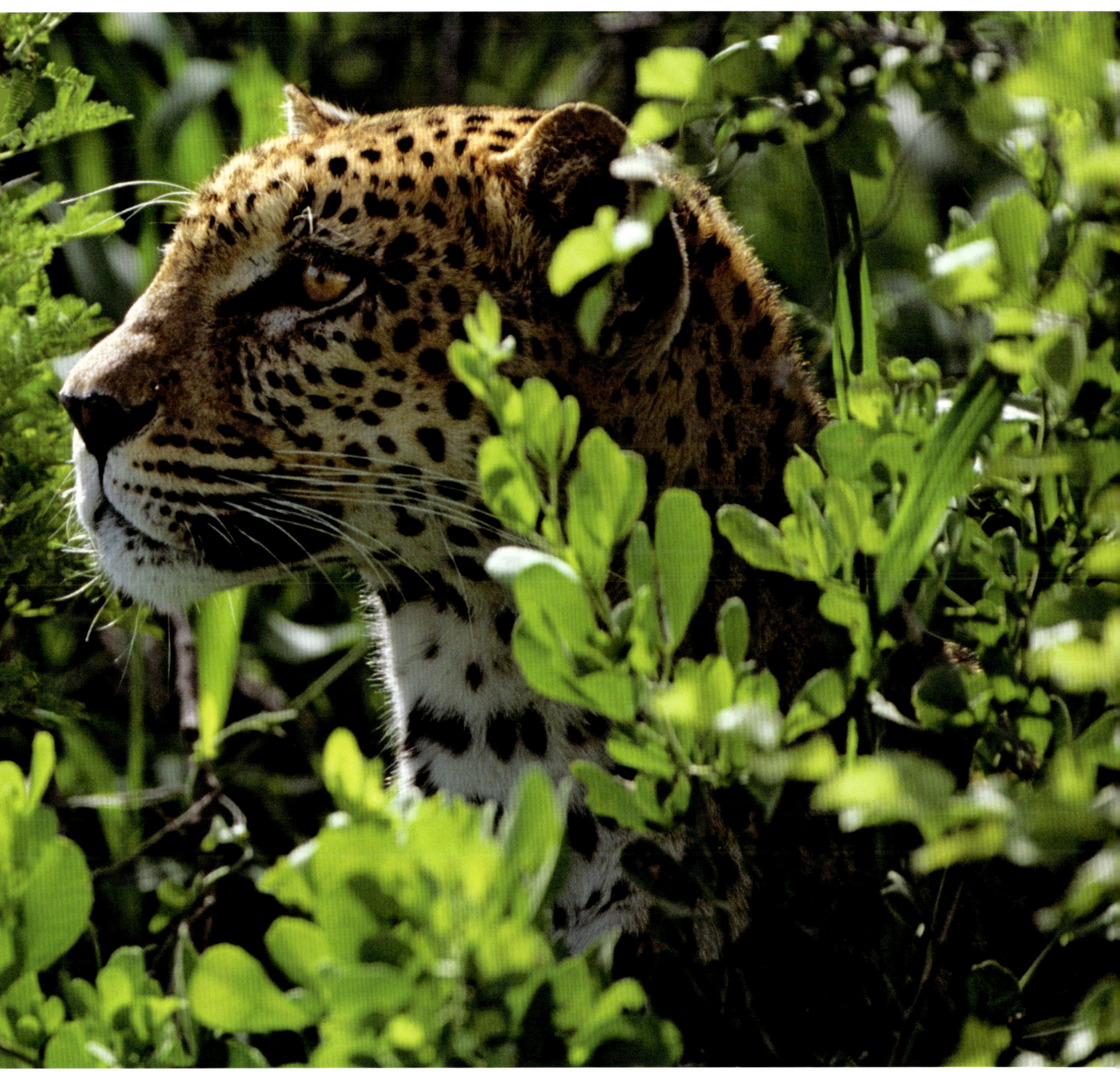

NATIONALPARK TAÏ

Date of inscription: 1982

The nature reserve encloses the greater part of Africa's remaining tropical rainforest, which once stretched across Ghana, the Ivory Coast, Liberia, and Sierra Leone.

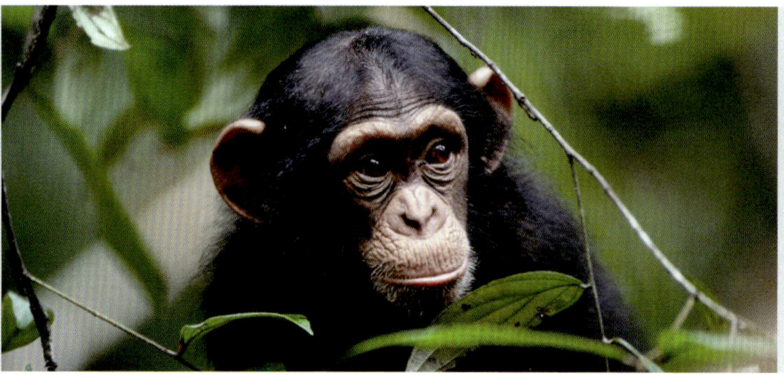

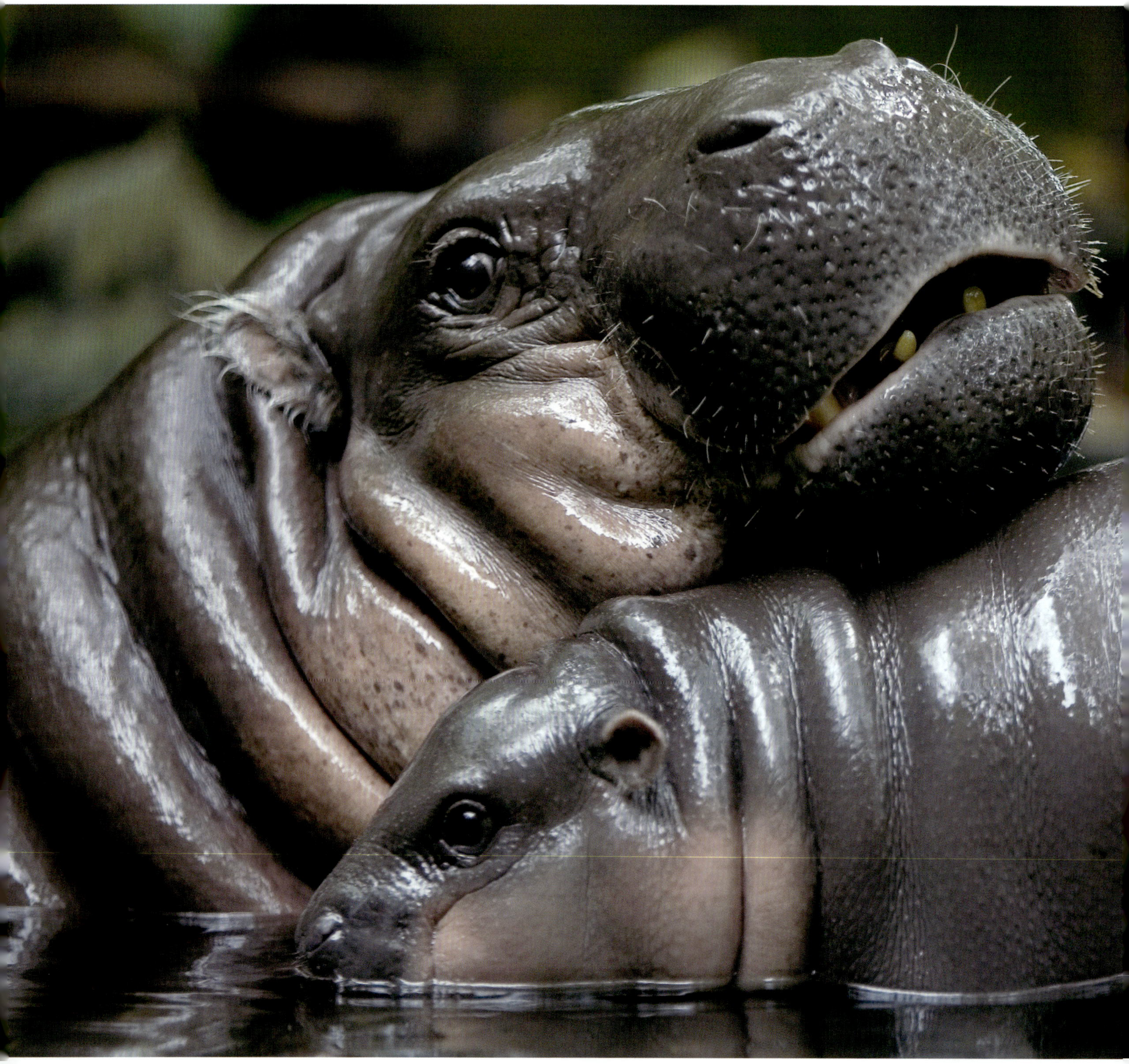

The dense, tropical vegetation covering the 3,300 sq. km (1,320 sq. miles) of this reserve in the south-western region of the Ivory Coast is characterized by numerous indigenous species and primeval forest, whose canopy of foliage and lianas up to 50 m (164 feet) high barely allows light to penetrate. Two kinds of forest are distinguished here, according to their undergrowth and the composition of the forest floor: to the north and south-east, poorly nourished Diospyros manii forest predominates, while in the south-west there is the damper soil of Diospyros-spp. forest. Characteristic of the Taï National Park's luxuriant primary forest, with its 1,300 plant species, are lianas, tree trunks tumbled across streams, mangroves with stilt and buttress roots, and tree ferns. Elephants, pygmy hippopotamuses, leopards, antelopes, and buffaloes live here, along with many varieties of bird and ten species of ape, including chimpanzees.

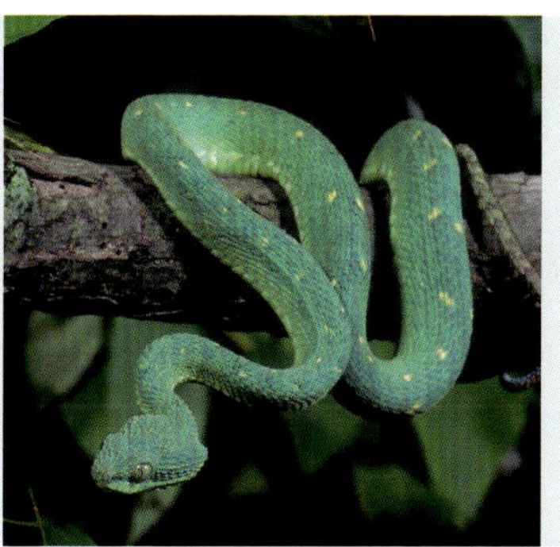

The tropical rainforest is also a habitat for numerous reptiles and mammals, such as the green bush viper (left), the Ivory Coast Running Frog (below), chimpanzees (far left) and hippopotamuses (large image).

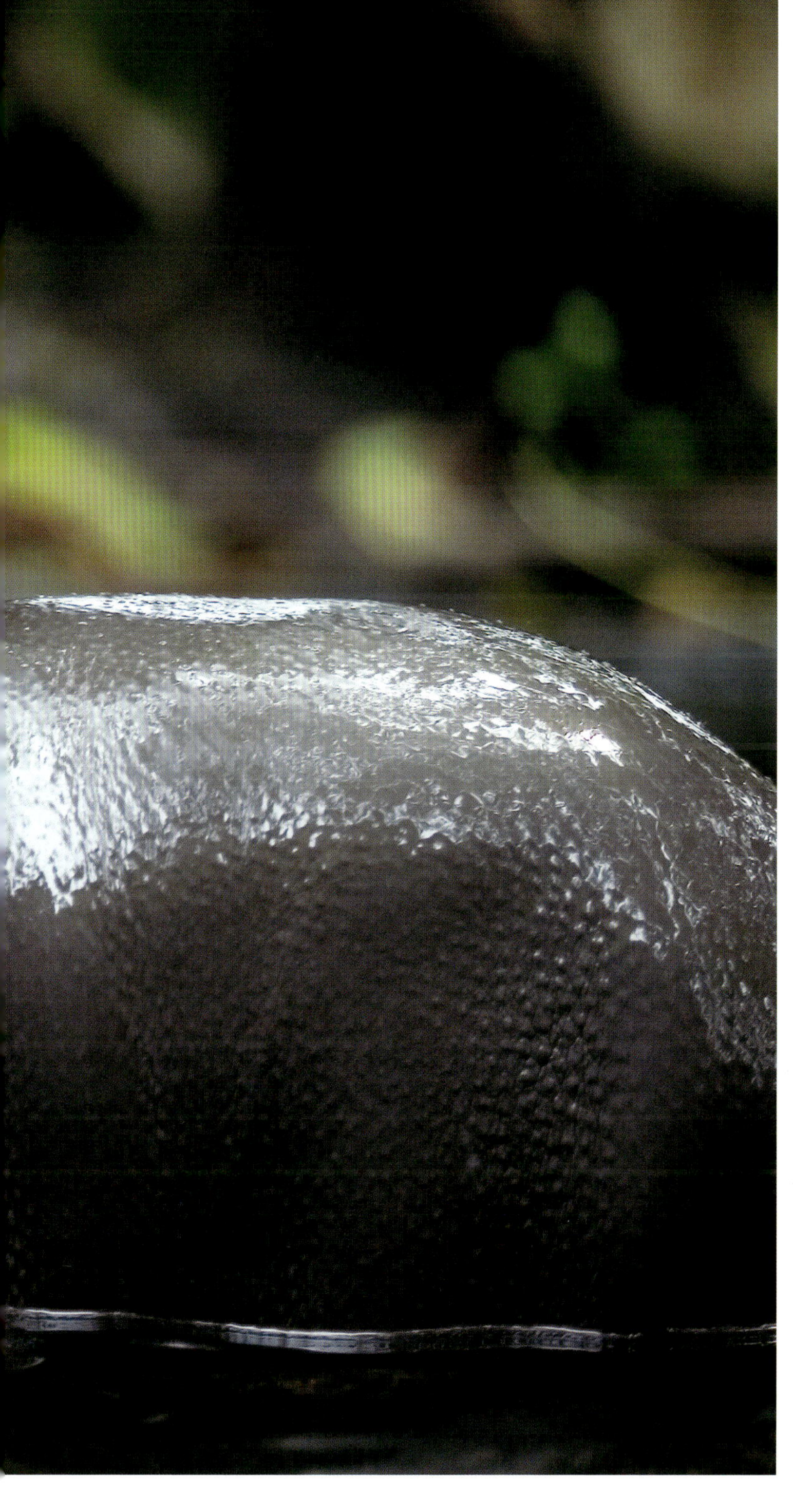

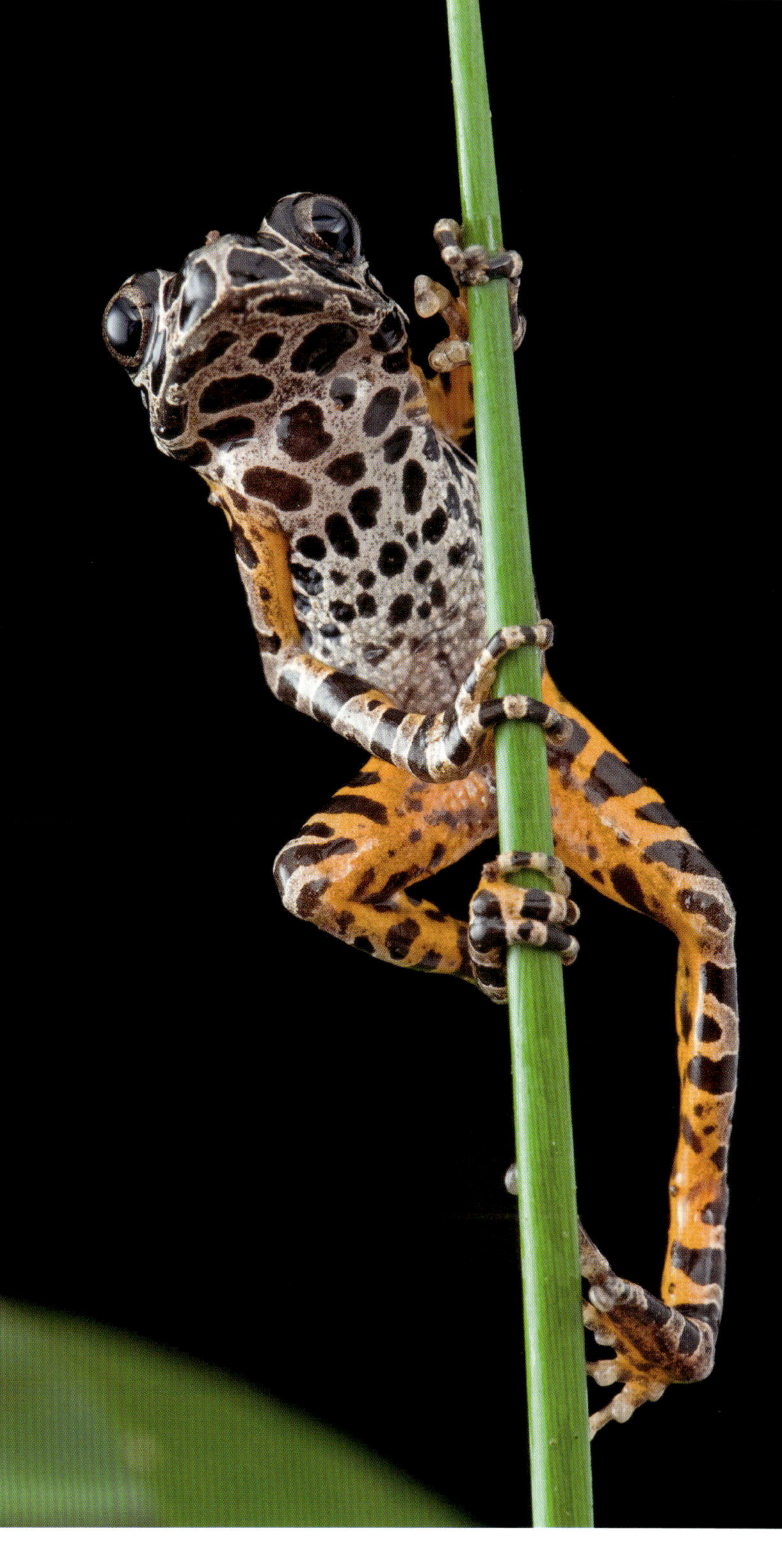

ECOSYSTEM AND RELICT CULTURAL LANDSCAPE OF LOPÉ-OKANDA

Date of inscription: 2007

Lopé-Okanda in Gabon embodies an unusual interaction of dense tropical rainforest and drier derived savannah. Archaeological sites from the neolithic and Iron Age are evidence that the region has been a cultural area since prehistoric times.

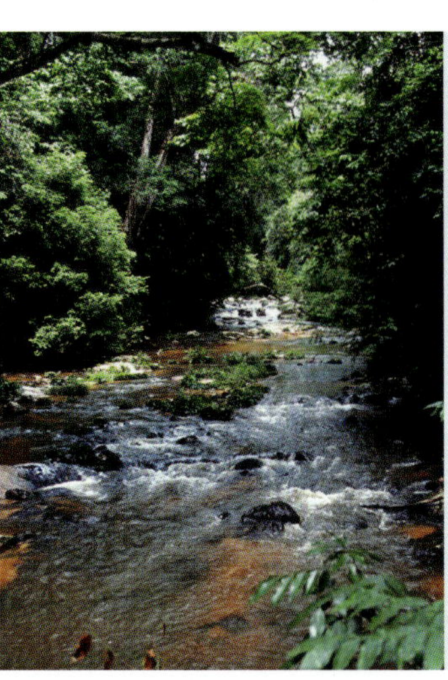

The central arm of the Ogooué river is to be found directly beneath the equator, in the north of the central African rainforests. Savannah and gallery forest alternate here across an area of about 1,000 sq. km (390 sq. miles). This open landscape is not just naturally formed; it is also the result of human intervention since the Stone Age, especially through the starting of bushfires. This permitted the ancestors of west African tribes to penetrate into the interior of the northern Congo. In the last 2,000 years, Bantu tribes from sub-Saharan areas in particular have taken this route. The river valley and its surrounding hills form a significant archaeological site. Round blocks of stone are adorned with rock art of the greatest importance, depicting humans with iron tools such as throwing knives. The close community of forest and savannah ecosystems has had a positive influence on biodiversity. Around 1,550 flowering plant species, 400 birds, and 50 mammals, have been identified.

Two juvenile mandrills, baboon-like primates, peek out of the dense leaf cover.

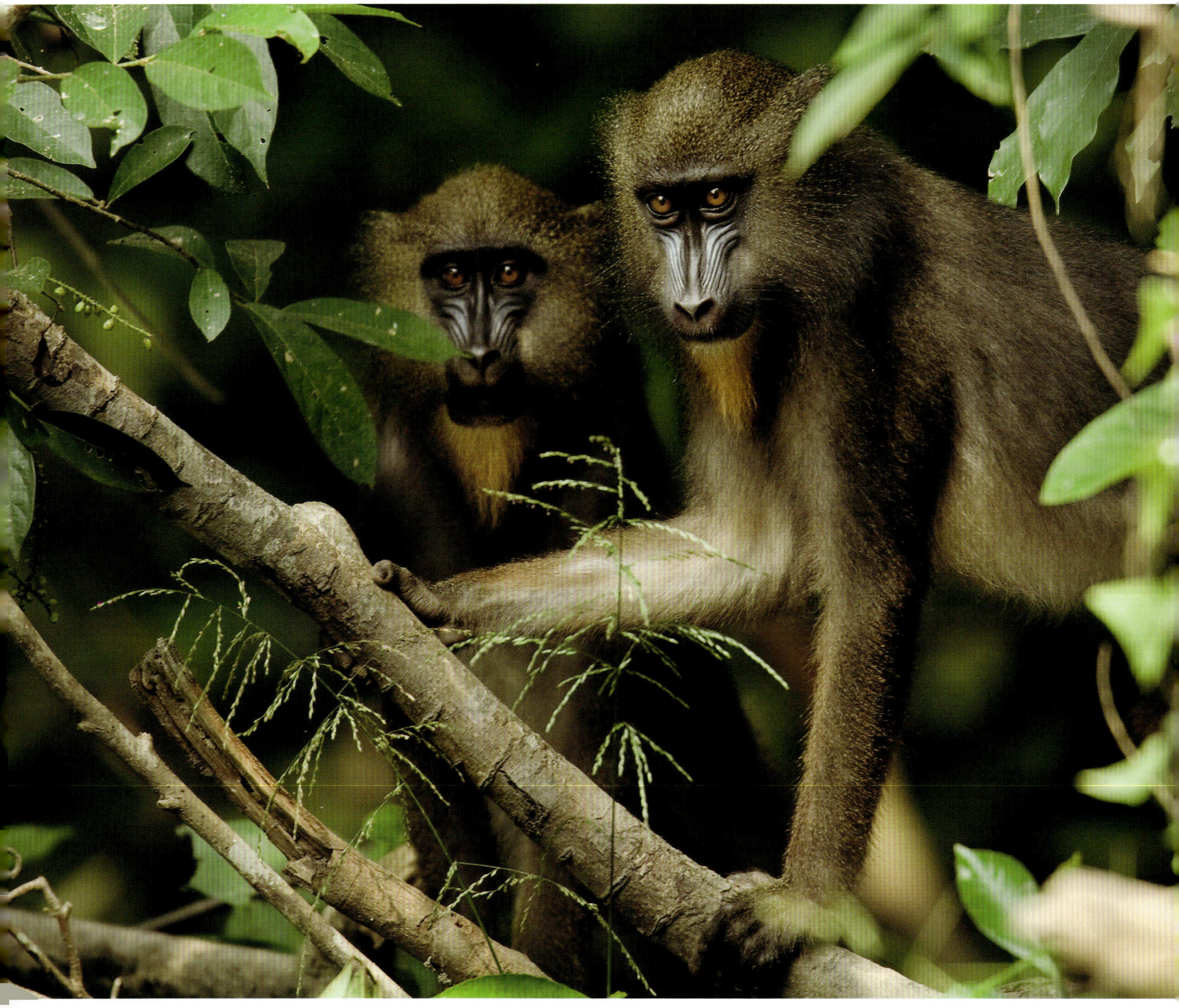

DJA FAUNAL RESERVE

The Dja Faunal Reserve's 5,000 sq. km (1,900 sq. miles) lie in a natural bend in the upper reaches of the Dja river. The region is not readily accessible, and thus one of the world's largest continuous areas of rainforest has been preserved here, with its concomitant biodiversity. The forest, which is composed of about 50 different tree species, provides a habitat for an immense variety of animals, including more than 100 mammals. The reserve is especially prized for its population of great apes (gorillas and chimpanzees) and the extremely rare African forest elephant. However, the area, inhabited only by a few pygmies, is threatened by bush fires and poachers have many of the animals in their sights.

The sitatunga are a type of antelope that occur only in areas where water is nearby. They are also known as marshbucks (large picture). Right: the nocturnal potto.

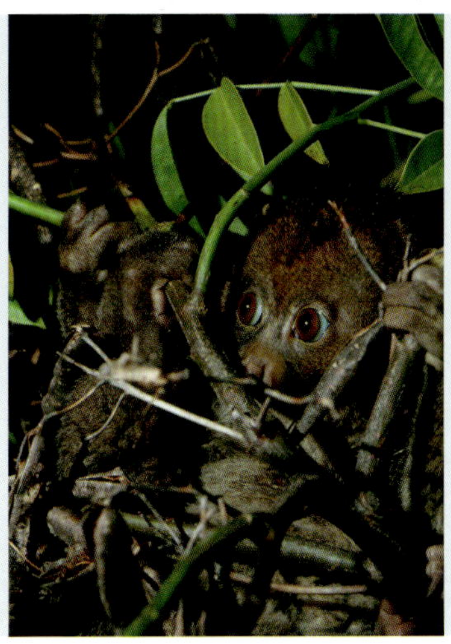

Date of inscription: 1987

The Dja Faunal Reserve, almost entirely enclosed by the Dja river in south-east Cameroon, is distinguished by an exceptionally diverse animal population, including many primates.

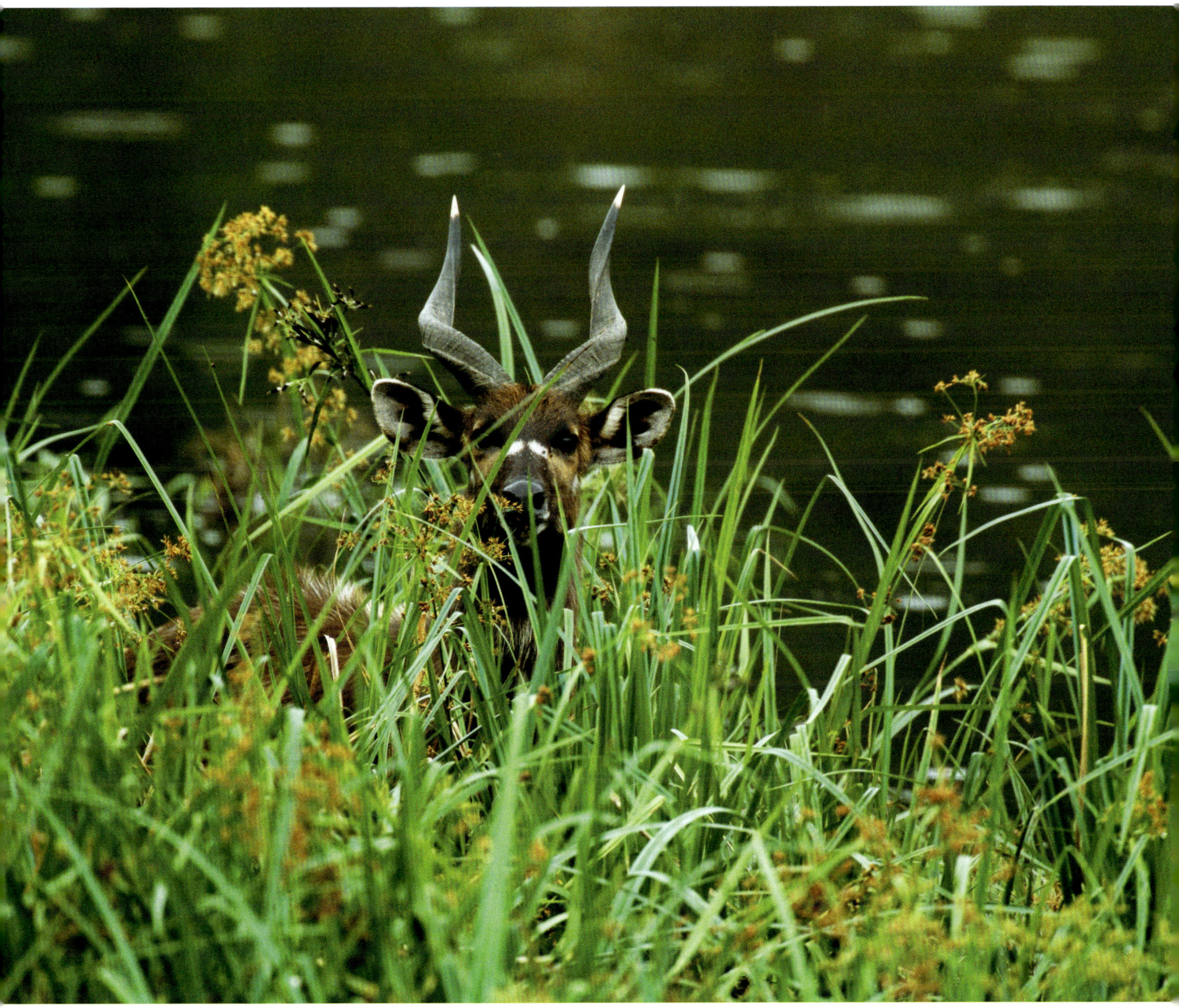

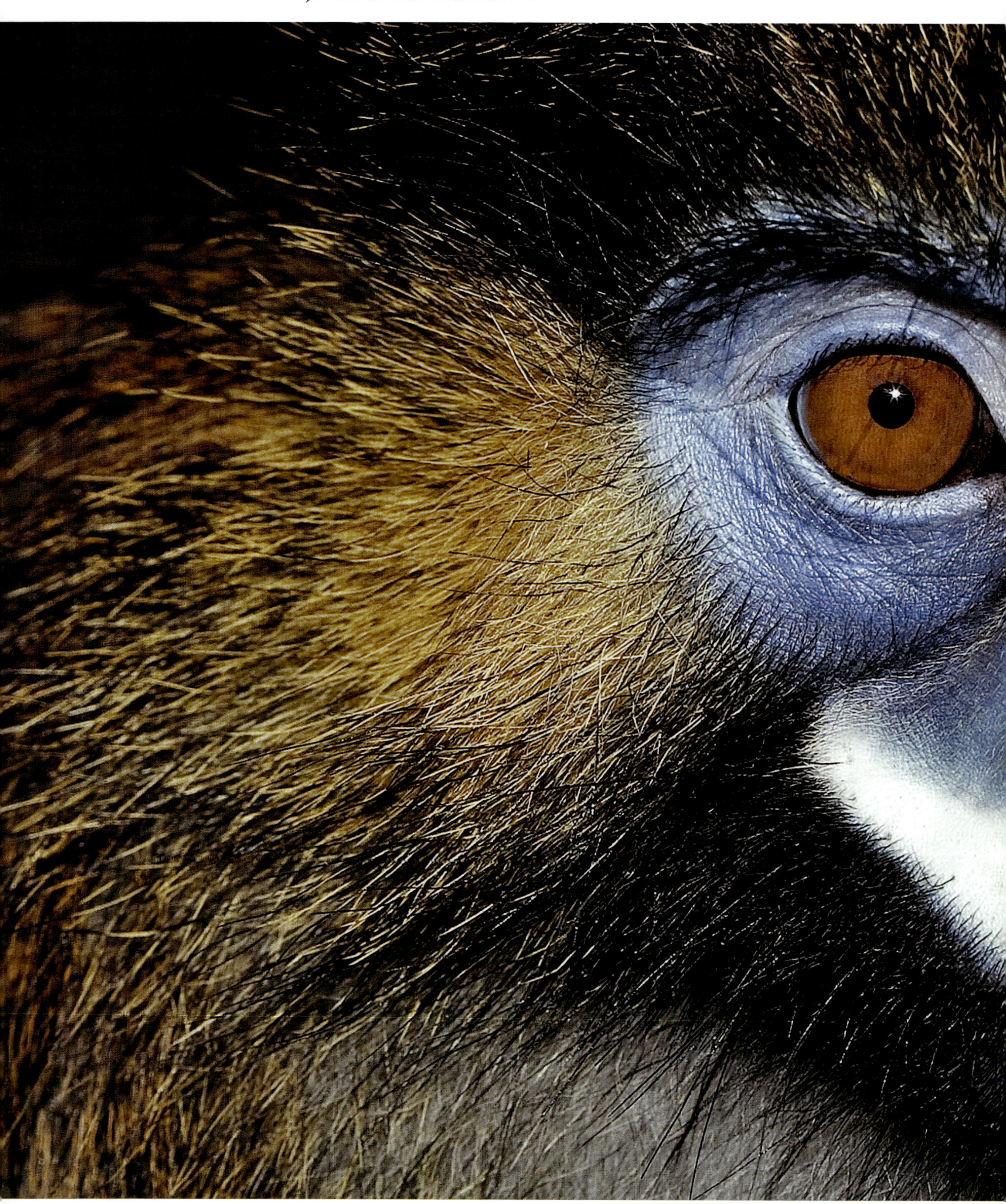

The distinctive facial pattern of the blue mouth vervet monkey is unique, as if Nature had demanded a clear visual trait to distinguish it from the many other primates. The blue eyes and the white-coloured upper lip framed by yellow whiskers are its characteristic features. Its area of population is Cameroon, the Congo and Angola.

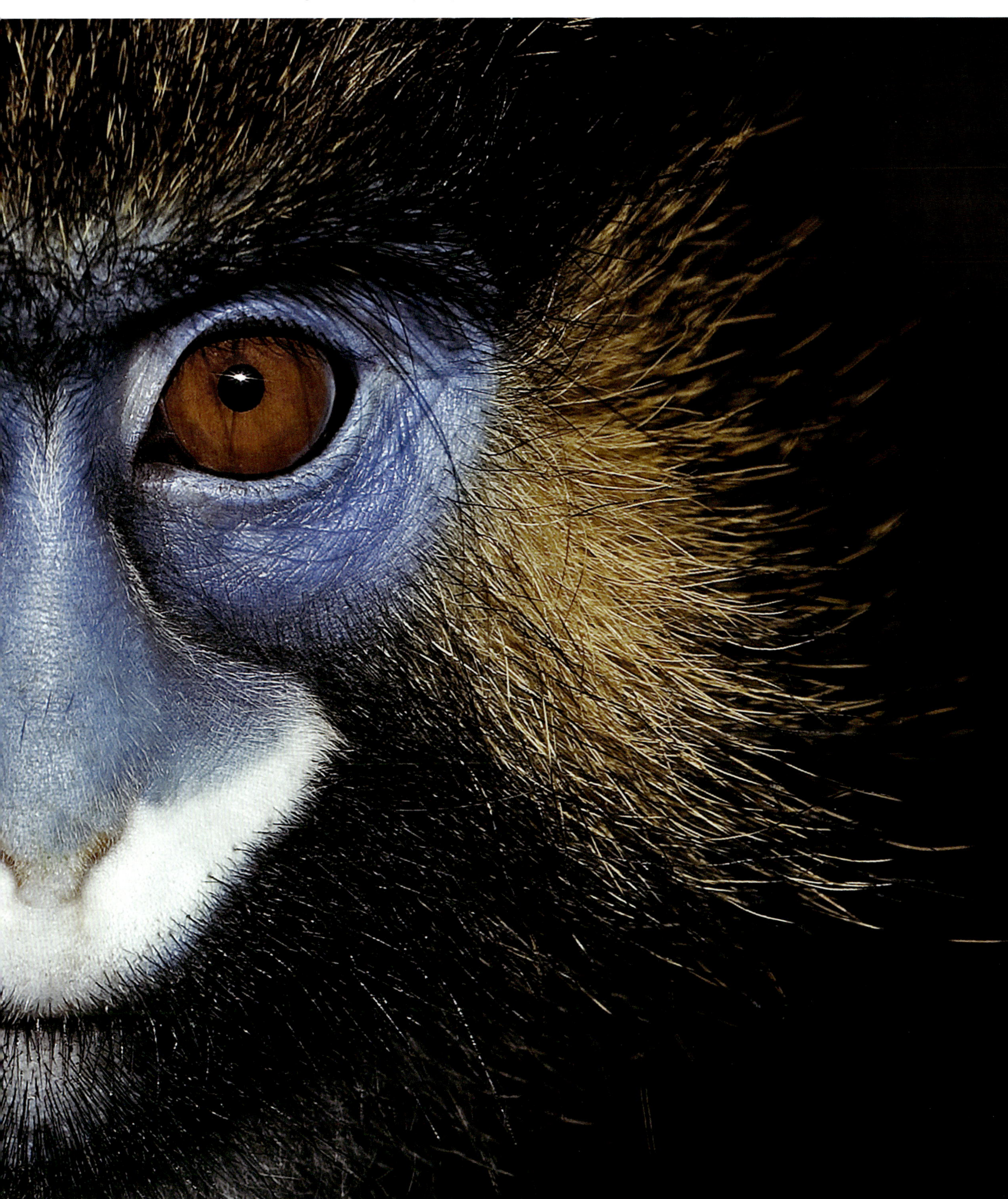

SANGHA TRINATIONAL PARK

Date of inscription: 2012

The national parks of three countries meet in the north-west of the Congo Basin. These now constitute a single natural heritage site, covering an area of 7,500 sq km (2,896 sq miles) and named after the main river, the Sangha.

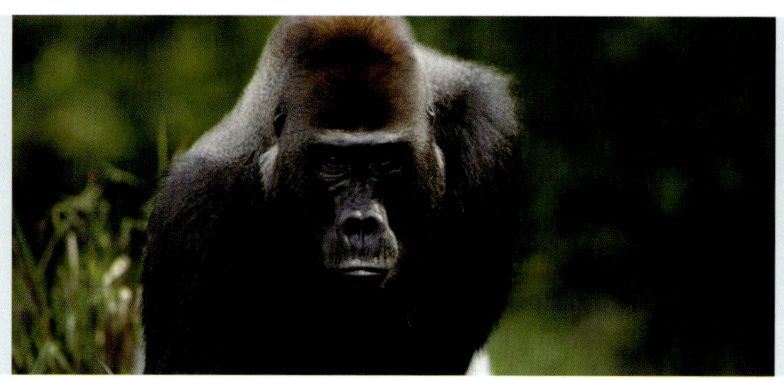

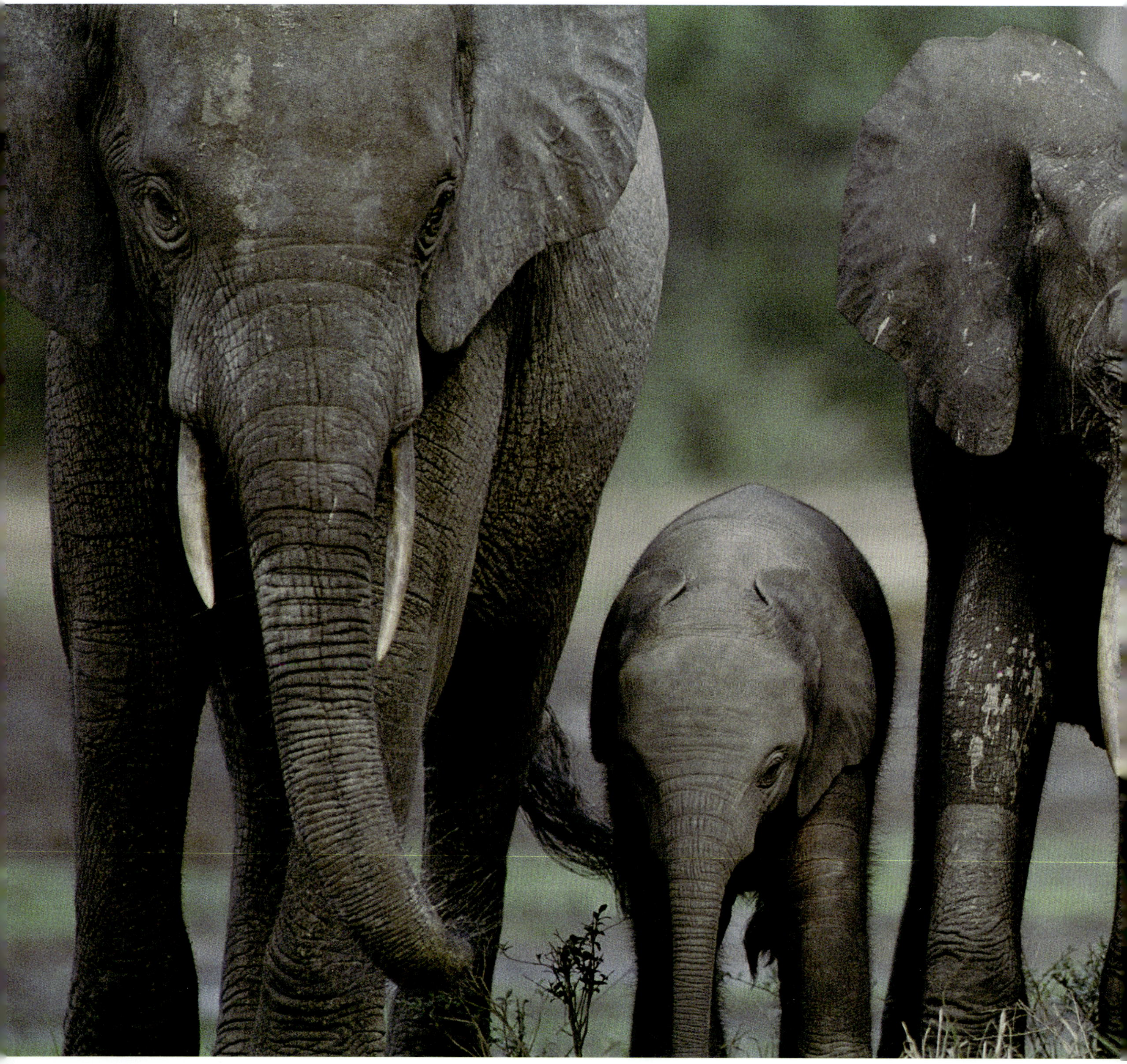

The national parks are the Lobéké National Park in Cameroon, the Nouabalé-Ndoki National Park in Congo and the Dzanga-Ndoki National Park in the Central African Republic. The human impact on land and nature here is still very low here. Although about one-third of the forest was selectively cleared in the second half of the 20th century, the area was then left to regenerate again naturally. Thus, the region is today covered by a magnificent tropical lowland rainforest, albeit with numerous clearings which however contribute significantly to the biodiversity, both in animals and in plants.

The Sangha River flows through the region from north to south, then empties itself into the Congo. In the river live Nile crocodiles and goliath tigerfish. The so-called "Hydrocynus goliath", also known as goliath tigerfish, giant tigerfish or mbenga, is a freshwater fish. It may reach a length of well over 1 m (3 ft) and features an impressive set of closely intermeshing, pointed and protruding teeth. However, it still falls prey to passionate anglers. The Sangha Trinational Park is of major importance as home to populations of forest elephants, chimpanzees and lowland gorillas that are still largely undisturbed by humans. Because of its remoteness, the park is free from the dreaded Ebola virus that infects primates.

The western lowland gorillas live in these regions. A splendid specimen of a silverback makes sure that no one gets too close to his territory (left). Large picture: a family African forest elephants.

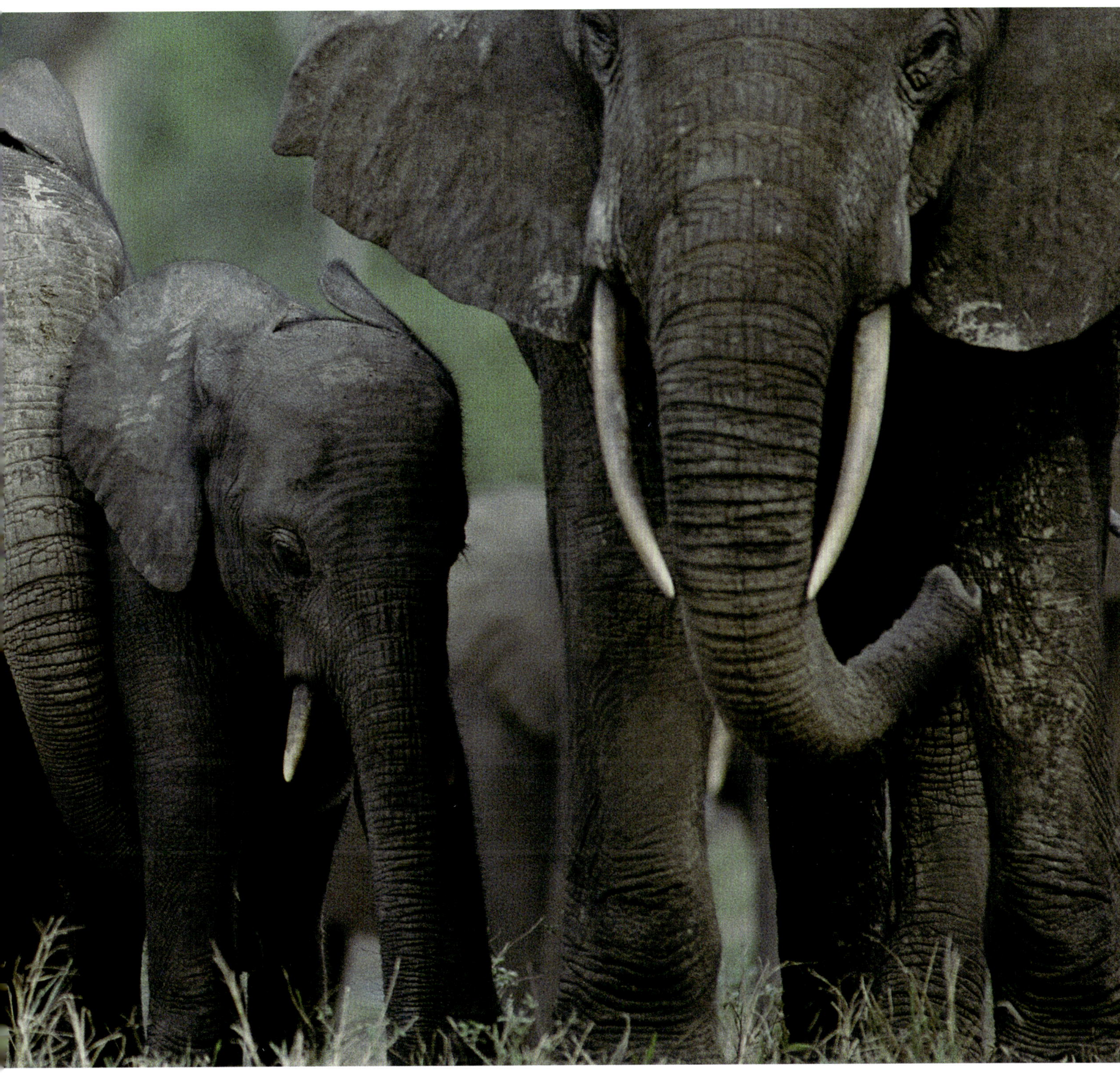

SANGHA TRINATIONAL: LOBÉKÉ NATIONAL PARK

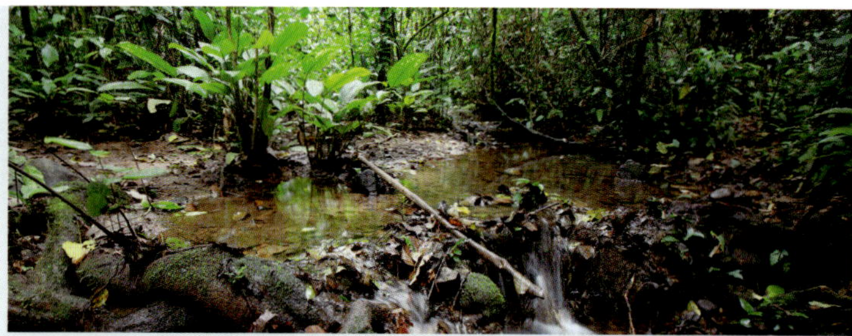

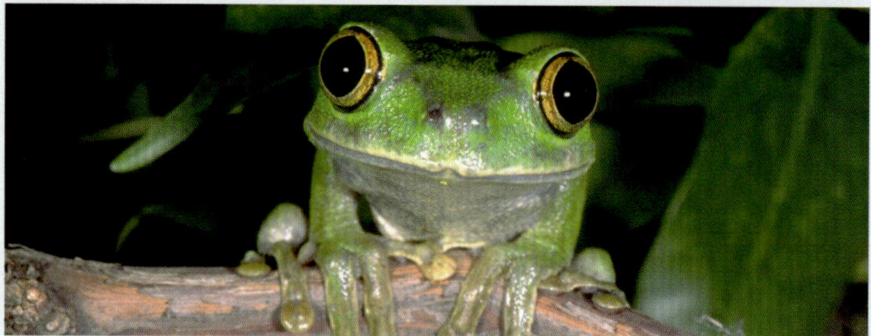

Nearly 4,500 Years ago, the Egyptian pharaoh Pepi sent an expedition into the heart of Africa, to an unknown land where he expected miracles. And he was not disappointed. For his people brought back with them to the Nile a strange man, who was not much bigger than a child, but undoubtedly an adult. The ancient Egyptians called their prisoner "the child of the divine dance". In ancient Greece, the term pygmy, from the Greek word for "fist", was to become established for the diminutive peoples of Central Africa. And the most amazing thing is that today almost 200,000 pygmy peoples still live in the inaccessible forests in the interior of the continent, for example in the Lobéké National Park in the south-east of Cameroon. They are hunter-gatherers and share the wilderness with an equally astonishing diversity of animals and plants, so that Lobéké is considered one of the most important national parks between the Sahara and the Cape of Good Hope. Almost 300 bird species are found here, as well as more than 300 tree species plus gorillas, chimpanzees, African forest elephants, giant forest hogs – and, well, "pygmies", the peoples of the forest.

A swarm of African grey parrots has gathered on a palm tree (large picture). They can be recognized from their typical red tail feathers. Left: big eye tree frog.

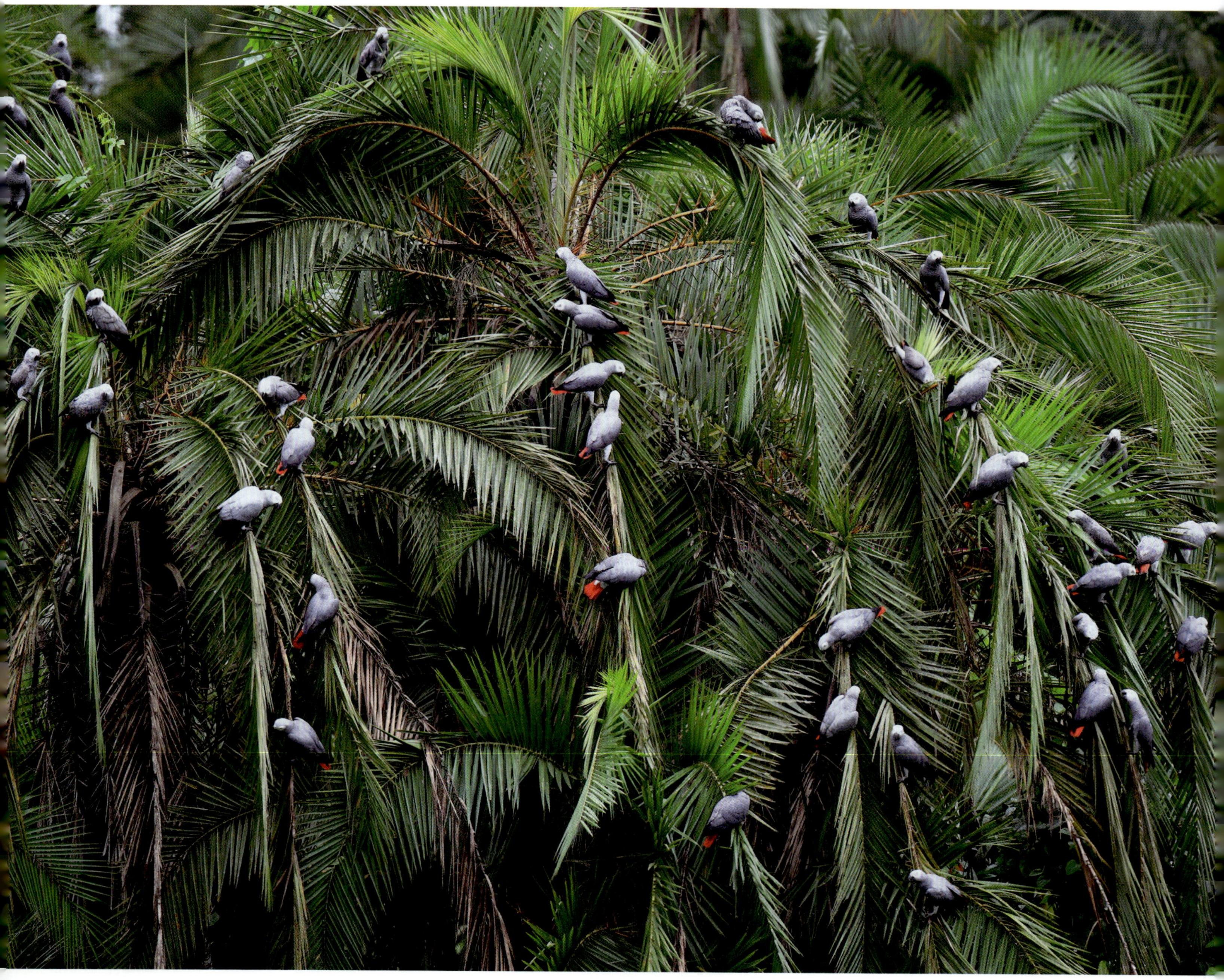

SANGHA TRINATIONAL: DZANGA NDOKI NATIONAL PARK

Africa is no longer untouched and virginal, not even at its innermost heart. Not even where it is at its wildest and most inaccessible are the animals still on their own, able to live their lives in peace. The Dzanga-Ndoki Reserve, located in the extreme south-west of the Central African Republic, on the borders with Cameroon and the Congo, is at the very heart of Africa. The place teems with forest elephants and leopards, buffaloes and bongos, chimpanzees and red river hogs, bushbucks and especially lowland gorillas. The chances of seeing one of these colossal animals are better here than anywhere else. The statistical average is one and a half animals per square kilometre. Yet, unfortunately, they share the Dzanga-Ndoki, which has been protected as a national park since 1990, with far too many illegal loggers, who slash deep wounds into the forest, reducing the habitat of the wild animals ever more; and they also share it with unscrupulous diamond hunters who in their greed tear open and exploit the ground, then leave it seriously damaged. That, probably, is the tragedy of Africa.

Bongos, a type of antelope, gather at the waterholes, together with forest elephants (right, top) and forest buffaloes (right, bottom). Large picture: western lowland gorilla.

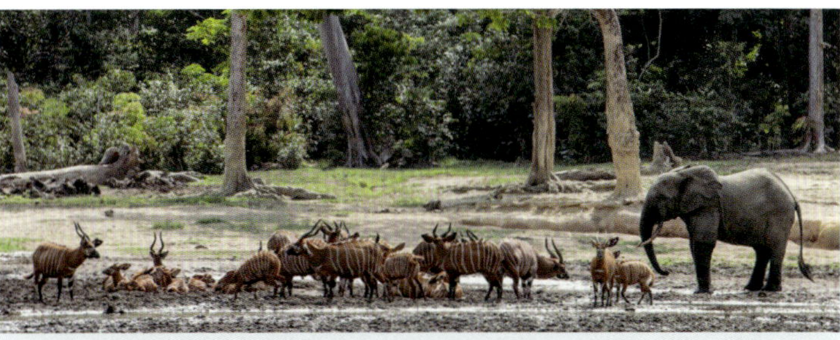

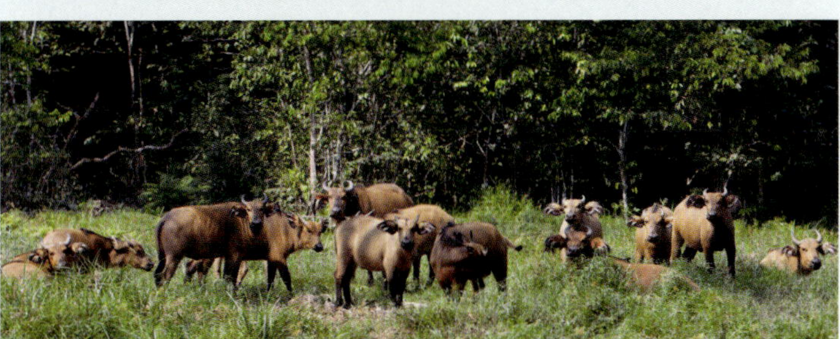

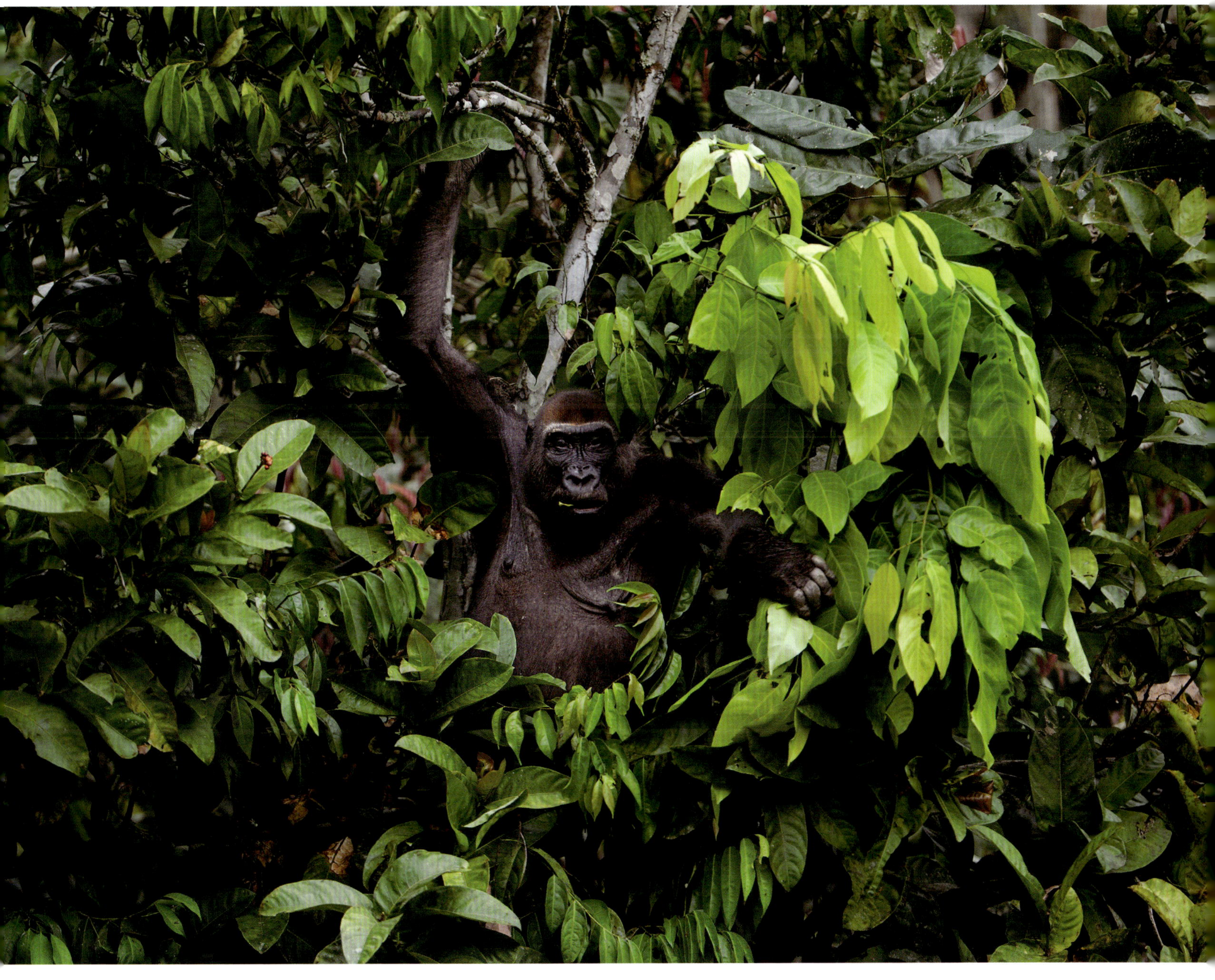

SANGHA TRINATIONAL: NOUABALÉ NDOKI NATIONAL PARK

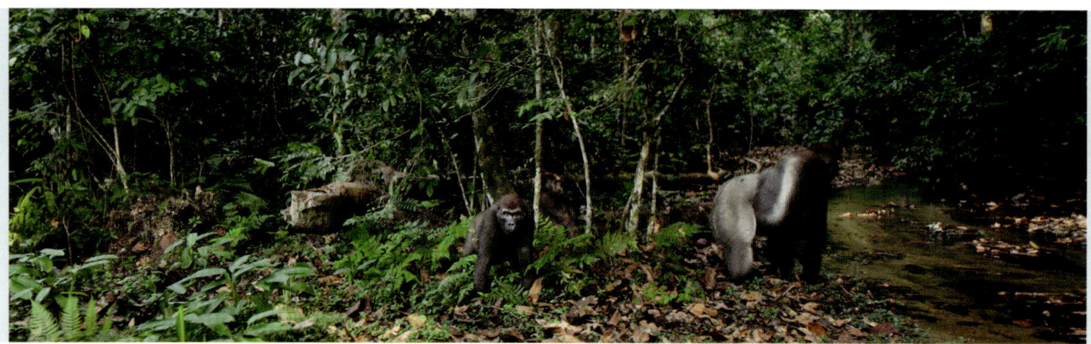

The humanity of the great apes is the strongest and most astonishing impression when you meet them in the wild. Even the gorillas, the largest of all primates, leave no doubt that genetically they are our closest relatives.
The likelihood of encountering them is particularly high in the Nouabalé Ndoki National Park in northern Congo, because this reserve is considered the

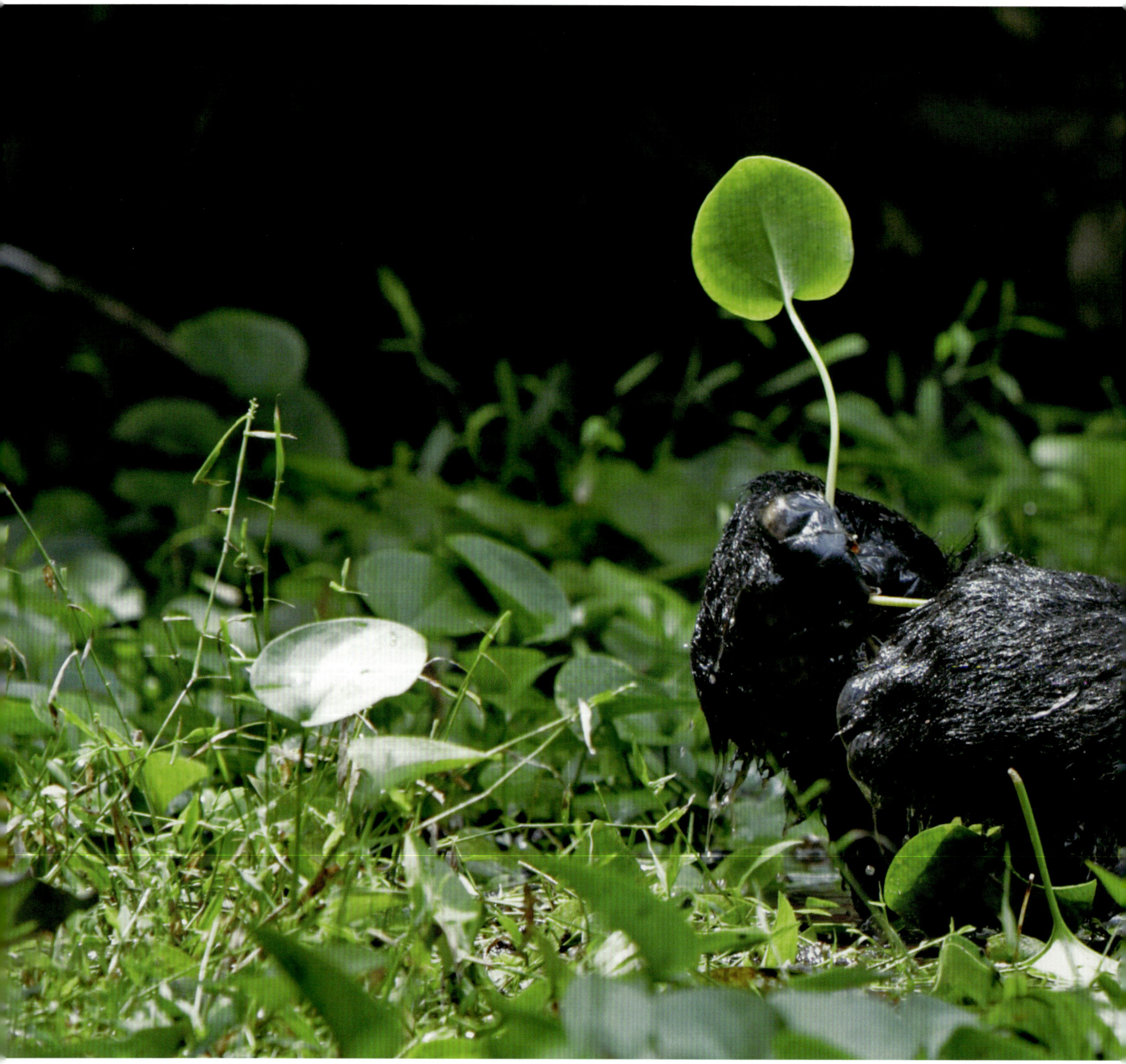

region with the highest density of wildlife in Africa. Hardly any other animal dares approach the mighty gorillas, these colossuses weighing up to 200 kg (440 lbs) and standing as tall as a man, whose arm span may be almost 3 m (10 feet).

Although they are herbivores, they can make short shrift of their enemies with their fearsome canines. It is hard to believe, however, that they might ever make use of these formidable weapons, especially when you watch a gorilla family where the young peacefully cuddle each other and the older males take care of their offspring with a touching patience, quite like model grandads.

The national park is also home to many chimpanzees, black-and-white colobus monkeys, moustached guenons, leopards and forest buffaloes.

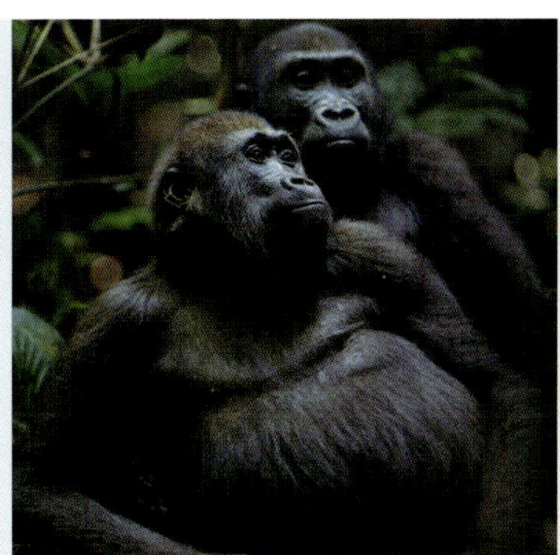

This is what leisure time looks like for gorillas: A silverback takes a swamp bath while chewing on herbs and grasses (large picture). The young western lowland gorillas love playing (left).

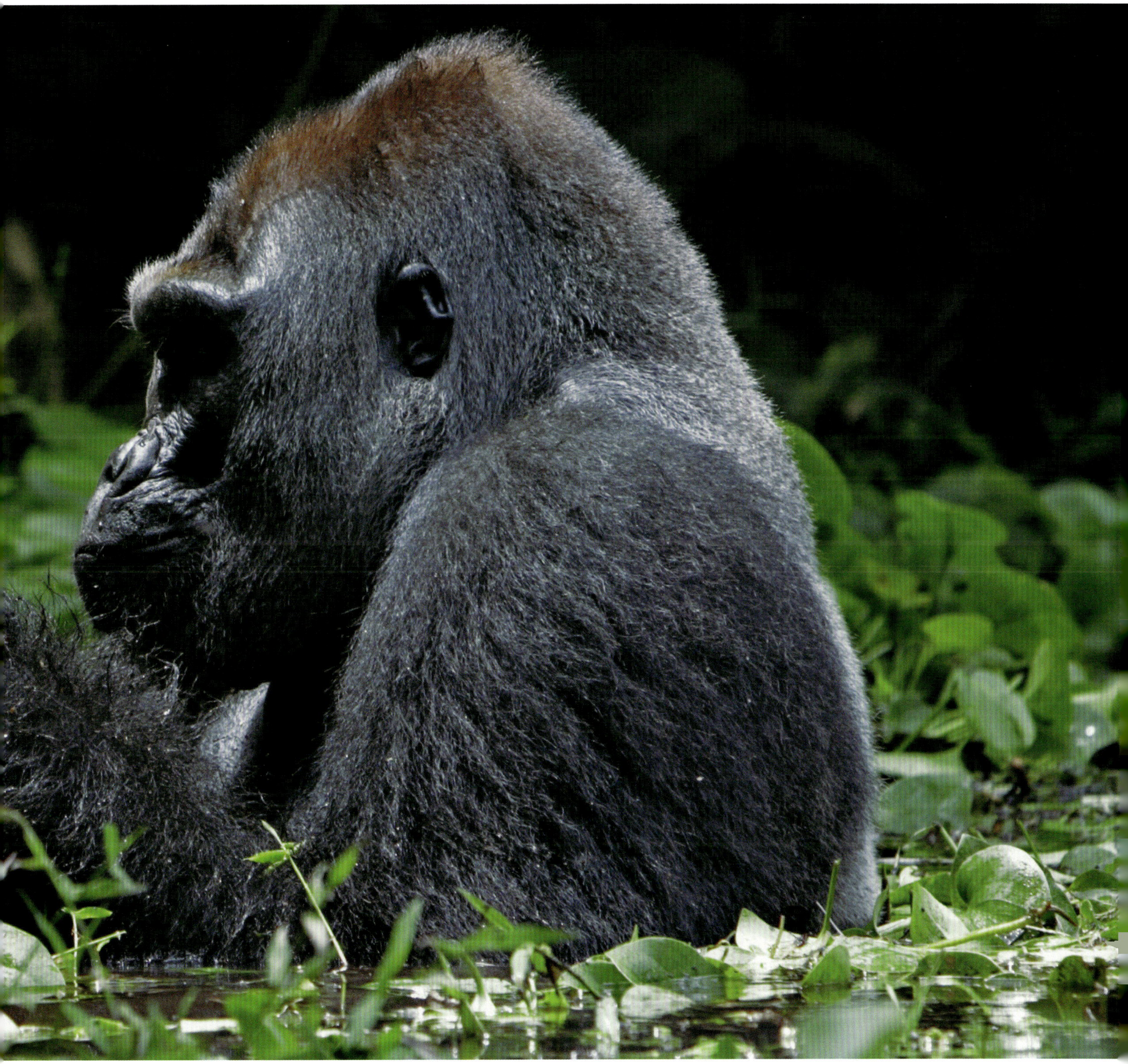

MANOVO-GOUNDA ST FLORIS NATIONAL PARK

Date of inscription: 1988

The importance of this reserve in the Central African Republic resides in its wealth of plants and animals, especially its waterfowl and megafauna.

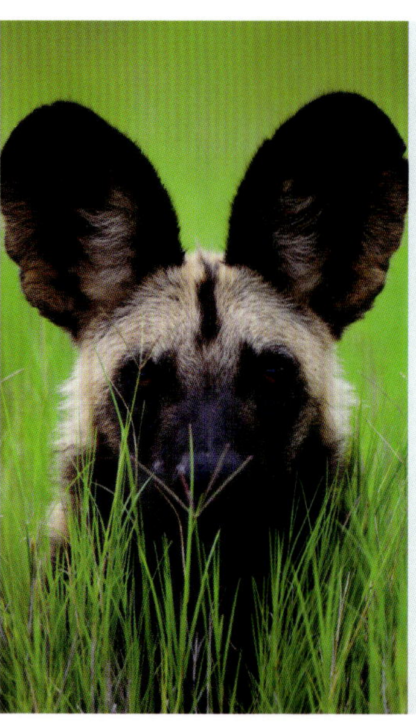

Part of this area in the far north of the Central African Republic was declared a national park as early as 1933, and it can be divided into three zones of vegetation: the grassy plains of the north, which flood in the rainy season; the gentle hills of the savannah in the transition zone; and jagged sandstone mountains to the south.

On the northern plain, various species of waterfowl – including marabou storks and white pelicans – share about 2,000 sq. km (770 sq. miles) of the park with lions, leopards, cheetahs, wild dogs, buffalo, red-fronted gazelles, giraffe, hippos, and numerous primate species, among others. The forest elephant and the almost extinct black rhinoceros are in particular need of protection. In the past, these rare species have fallen victim to unscrupulous poachers; in the 1990s illegal hunters reduced the total wildlife population by 80 percent (as well as murdering several park rangers). A further danger is the continuing misuse of the reserve as pasture for domesticated animals.

The African wild dog (left) resembles a hyena in its looks. Its coat is patterned in various shades of brown. In the males of the African buffaloes (large picture), the horns are turned in above their heads.

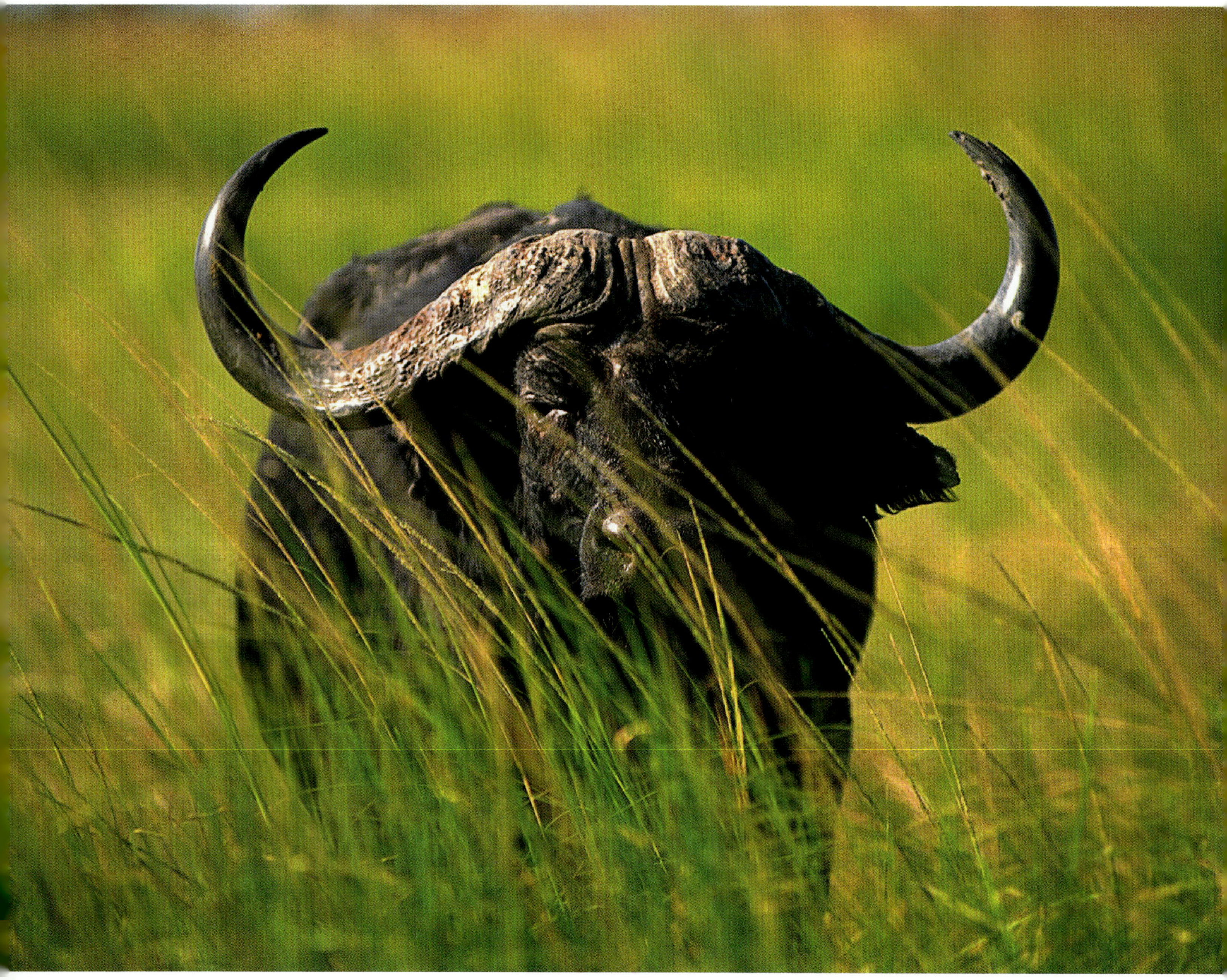

GARAMBA NATIONAL PARK

From broad savannah and grassland to forest and marshy lowlands: the Garamba National Park, located on the river of the same name, provides an extraordinarily diverse range of habitats. This 5,000 sq. km (1,900 sq. mile) area was declared a national park as early as 1938. More than 40 species of mammals live in the barely accessible conservation area, among them elephants and hippos. The park was in fact specifically established for the protection of giraffes and the northern subspecies of square-lipped rhinoceros, commonly known as the white rhinoceros, which, though larger than the black rhino, is harmless. The last specimens living in the wild are found only in the Garamba National Park. The already tiny population has further declined in recent years as a result of war and poaching, and it is feared that this species will die out in the wild. One of the problems facing conservationists in the Congo is that of finance: the greater part of the necessary funds can only be raised through tourism, and this is weakened by the country's unstable political situation.

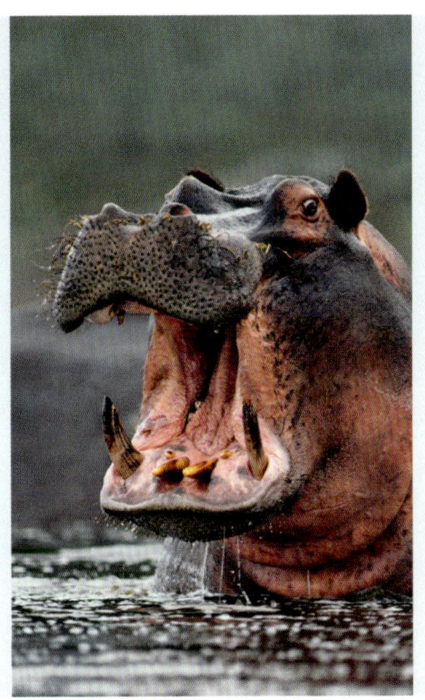

Hippos also cavort in the rivers and lakes. Although the animals seem peaceable and complacent, in a fight they can inflict serious injuries on other animals with their enormous canine teeth.

Date of inscription: 1980

Garamba National Park, lying on the Sudanese border in the far north-east of the Democratic Republic of Congo, is home to several large mammals, including the rare northern white rhinoceros.

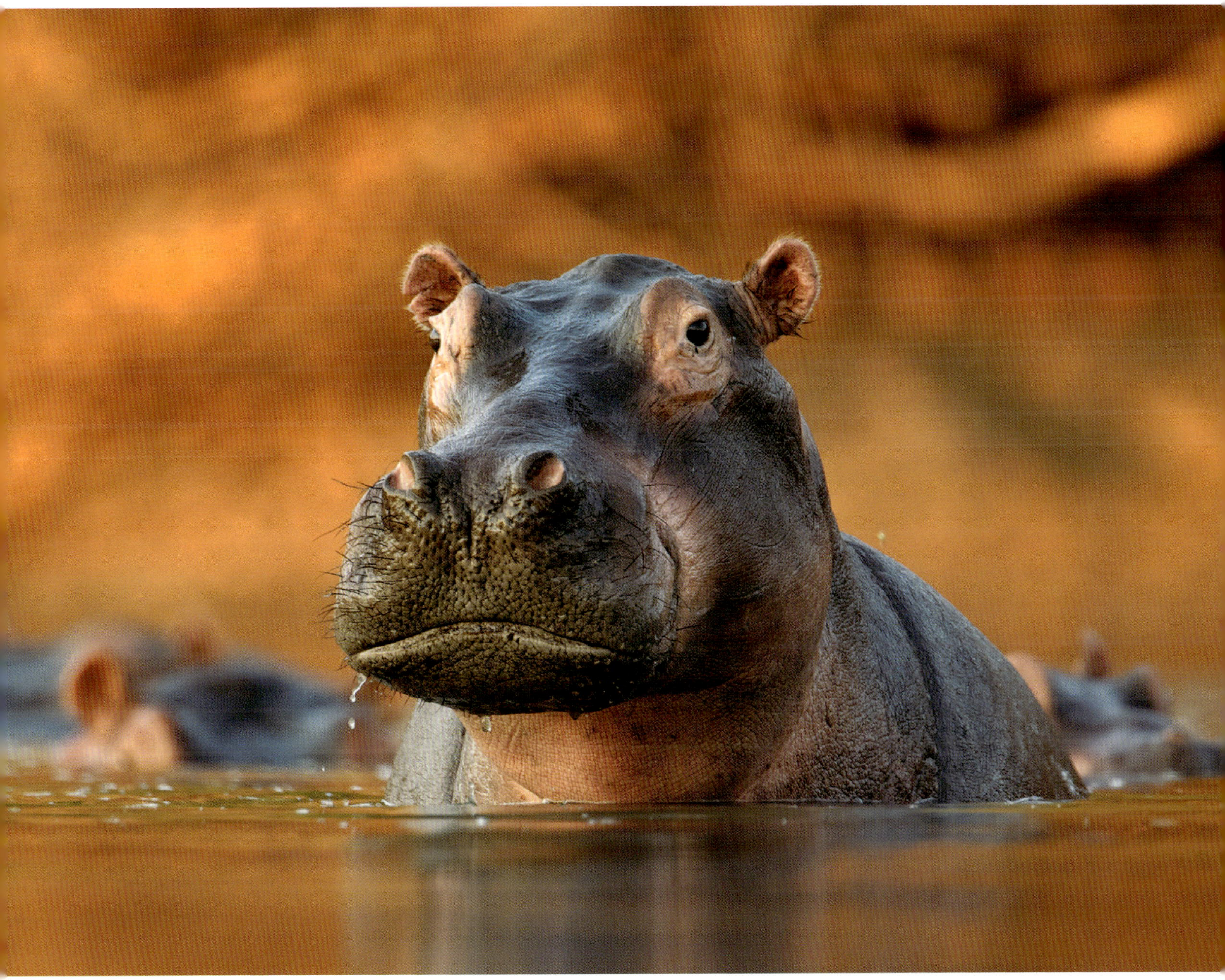

THE OKAPI WILDLIFE RESERVE

Date of inscription: 1996

This reserve, covering 14,000 sq. km (5,400 sq. miles) in the north-east of the Democratic Republic of Congo, is famed for the okapi after which it is named. This ungulate has been known to science for little more than a century.

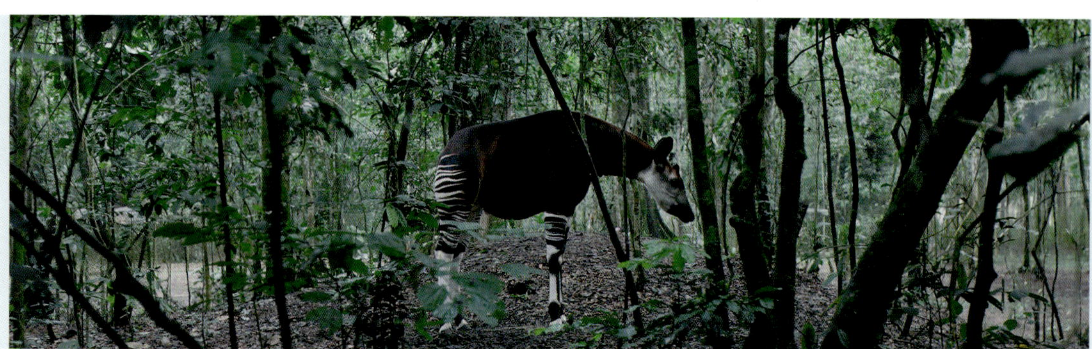

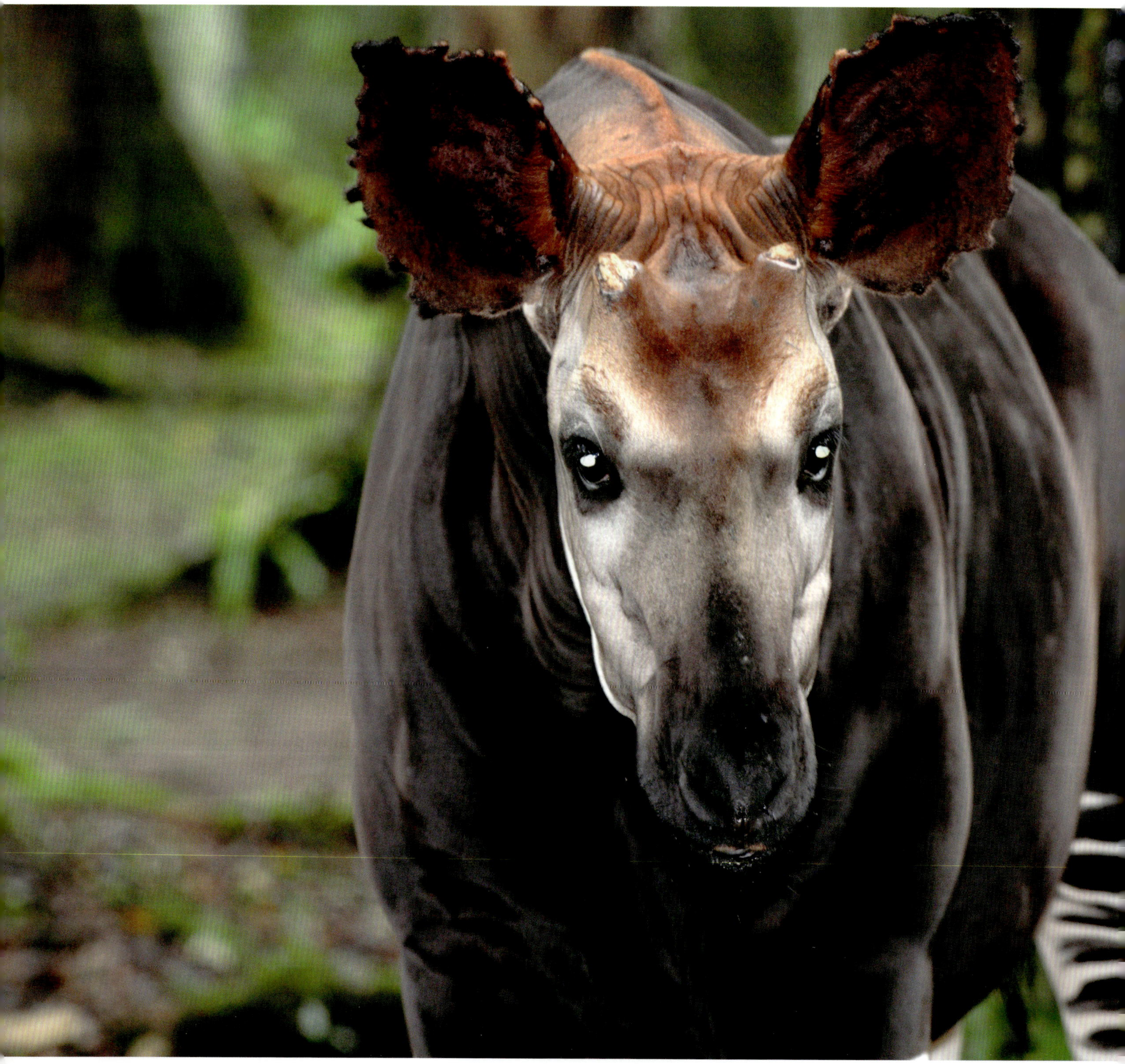

The Okapi Wildlife Reserve was officially declared a conservation area in 1992. It covers about a fifth of the Ituri rainforest in the Congo basin, one of the largest drainage basins in continental Africa. The reserve offers charming scenery, including the impressive waterfalls on the Ituri and Epulu rivers. The reserve was, however, initially established for the okapi, which was first recorded by Sir Henry Morton Stanley in 1890. He had never seen the animal and knew it only from descriptions by the local Batwa tribe, picturing it as vaguely similar to an ass. On the evidence of skeletal remains, the British Governor, Sir Harry Johnston (who was responsible for the species' scientific name, Okapia johnstoni), categorized the animal, which had initially been considered a member of the Equus (horse) family, among the giraffes. Living specimens were not sighted by Europeans until the early 20th century. It is thought that about 30,000 specimens still live in the wild, of which some 5,000 are to be found in the Okapi Wildlife Reserve.

The okapi is now also known as the short-necked or forest giraffe. In contrast to its long-necked cousin, which prefers the savannah, it lives exclusively in the rainforest, where it eats twigs, leaves, and tree shoots. The zebra stripes on its legs and rear almost give the impression that it is composed of several animals.

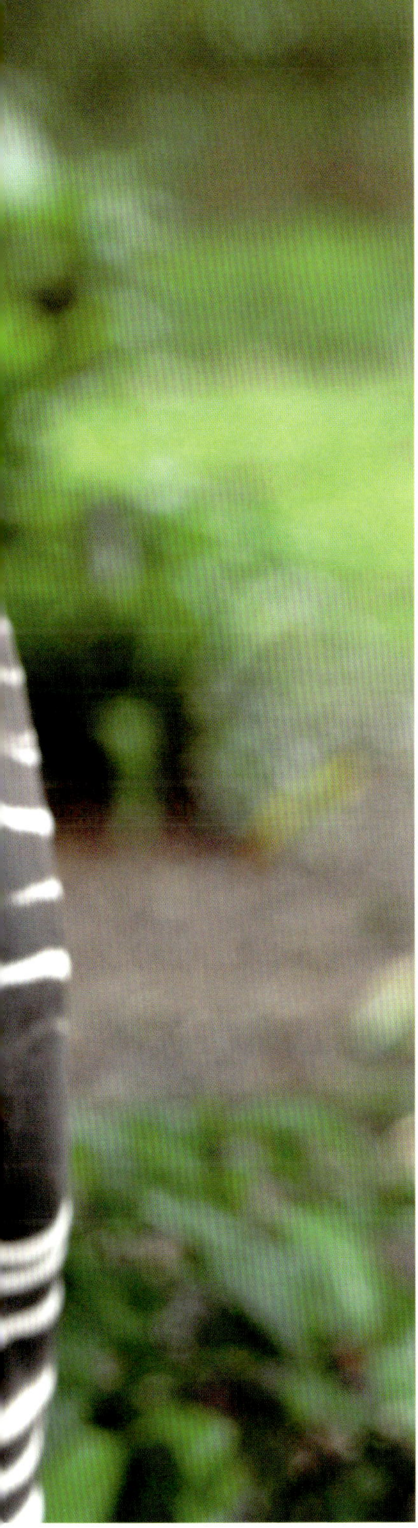

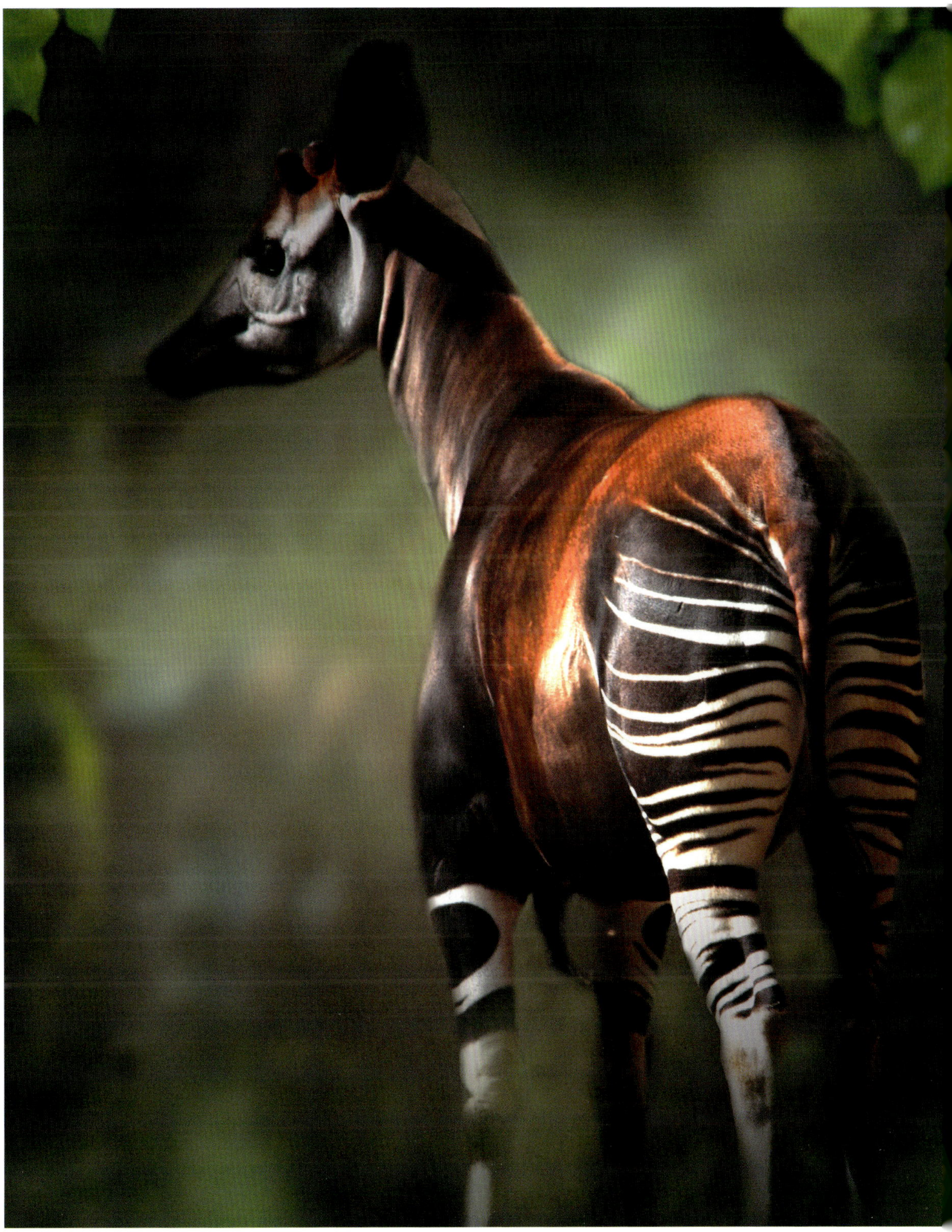

SALONGA NATIONAL PARK

Date of inscription: 1984

The national park flanking the Salonga, an eastern tributary of the Congo river in the middle of the Democratic Republic of the Congo, holds one of the largest continuous areas of rainforest in central Africa.

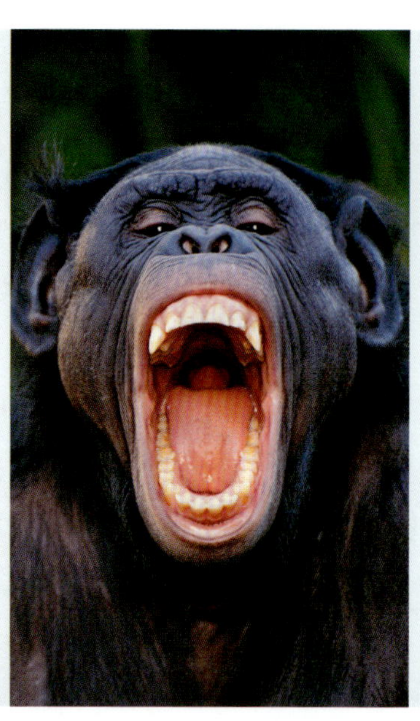

Salonga was inscribed as a national park in 1970. At 36,000 sq. km (13,900 sq. miles), it is the second-largest national rainforest park in the world. Together with Maiko National Park, the Salongo area, which consists of two equal sections separated by a corridor of human settlement 50 km (31 miles) wide, was placed under protection in order to preserve representative parts of central African rainforest. Large portions of ecologically vital rainforest in the country had already either fallen victim to forest fires or been consumed by ever-expanding agriculturalization.

The national park is accessible only by water and is thus a refuge for many species, including okapi, bongo antelopes, aquatic genets, Congo peafowl, and the African slender-snouted crocodile. The forest elephant of the central African rainforest is also to be found here. Probably the best-known inhabitant of the Salonga, however, is the pygmy chimpanzee, also known as the bonobo (Pan paniscus), a great ape and a close relative of the chimpanzee, found in the wild only in conservation areas south of the Congo.

Bonobos are probably the most famous animal inhabitants of the Salonga National Park in teh central Congo Basin.

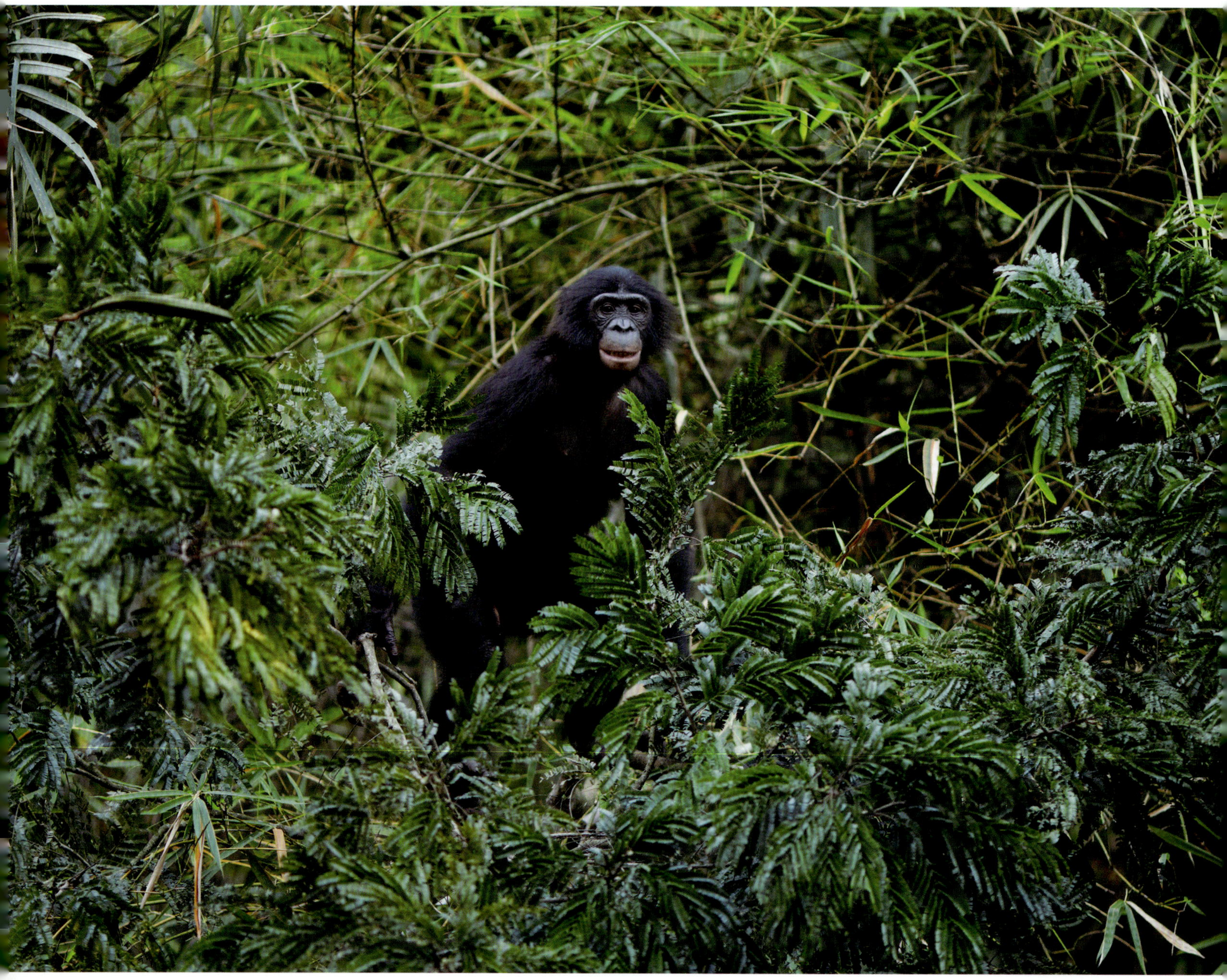

KAHUZI–BIEGA NATIONAL PARK

Just like Viruga, Kahuzi–Biega National Park, situated 100 km (62 miles) west of Lake Kivu, was also established for the protection of gorillas, although for eastern lowland gorillas rather than mountain gorillas. These imposing members of the great ape family live in small troops at an altitude of between 2,100 and 4,000 m (6,900 and 13,200 feet). The vegetarian "gentle giants" can live for up to 40 years. Older males have silver-gray markings on their backs. They intimidate rivals by rearing up with a roar and beating their chests. The gorillas, which are diurnal, forage for their diet of leaves until sundown, and then sleep at night in improvised nests made of branches and leaves. The 6,000 sq. km (2,300 sq. miles) of the conservation area, in the shadow of the two extinct volcanoes of Kahuzi and Biega, shelter two further primate species, one of which is the common chimpanzee, our closest relative. Their natural enemy, the leopard, is also found here in the conservation area, along with elephants, buffaloes, and numerous other species.

The total world population of eastern lowland gorillas (below) has declined to only a few thousand, of which the majority live in the Kahuzi–Biega National Park. They are typically forest-dwellers, as are the mountain gorillas (rigt).

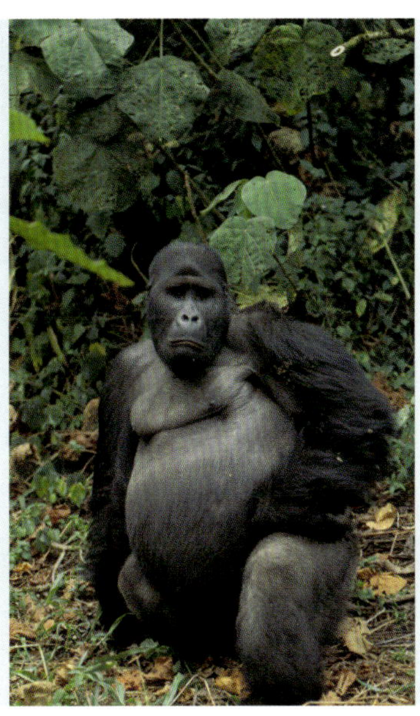

Date of inscription: 1980

One of the last few remaining groups of eastern lowland gorillas, close relatives of the mountain gorilla, live in the forests of this conservation area in the eastern Democratic Republic of Congo.

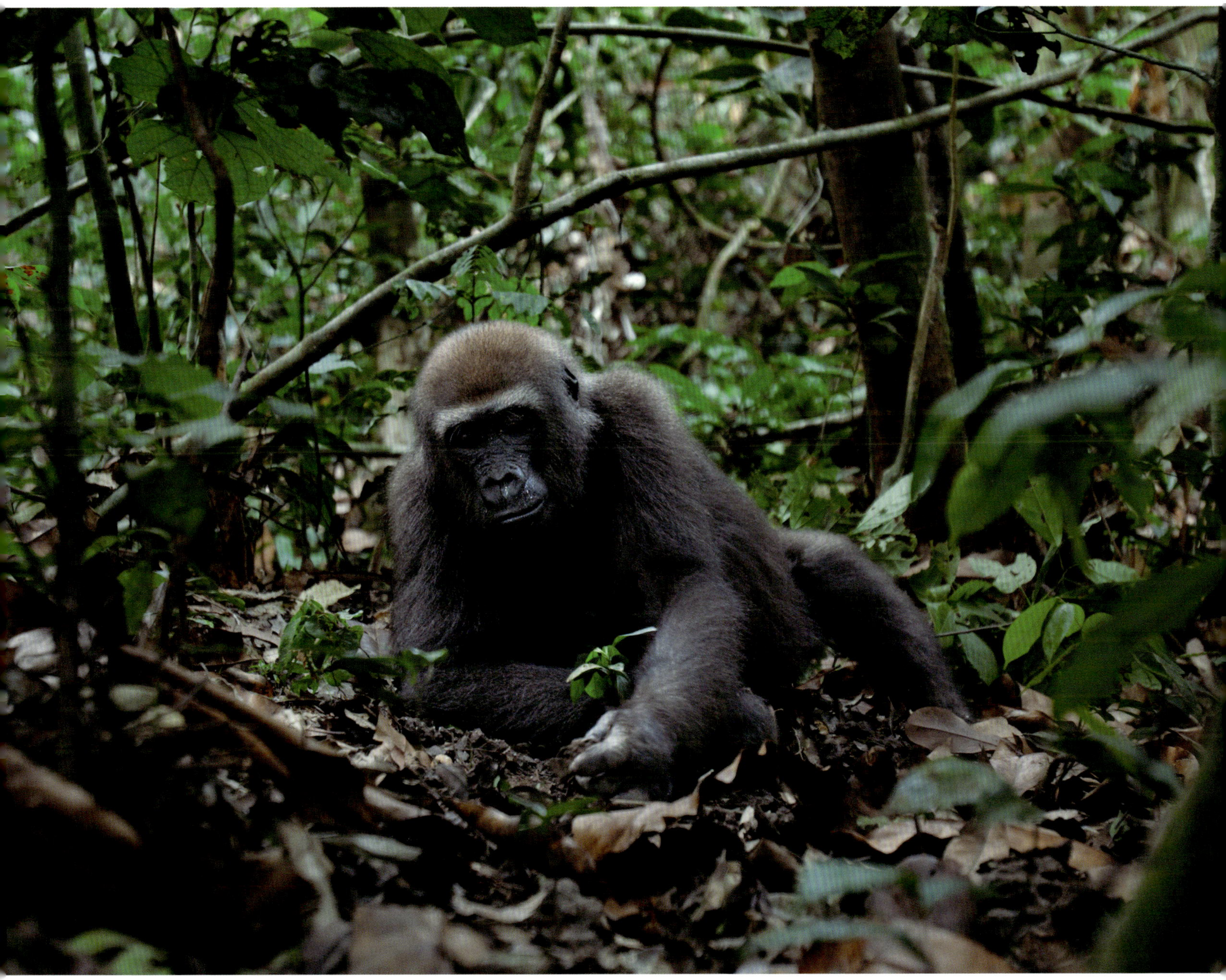

VIRUNGA NATIONAL PARK

Date of inscription: 1979

In western public consciousness, Virunga National Park is virtually synonymous with its most famous animal inhabitants, the mountain gorillas; nonetheless, its varied scenery provides a habitat for many other species.

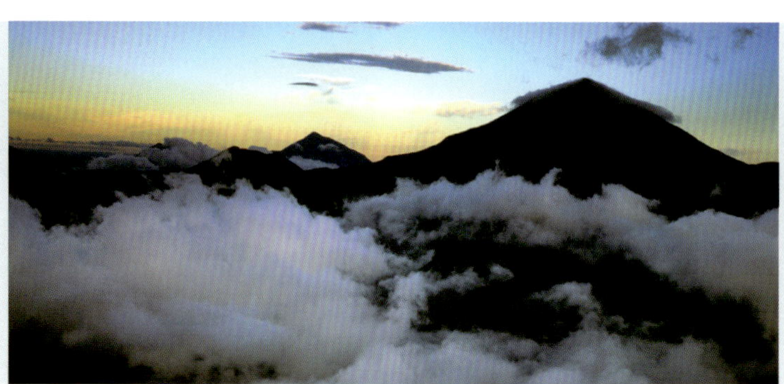

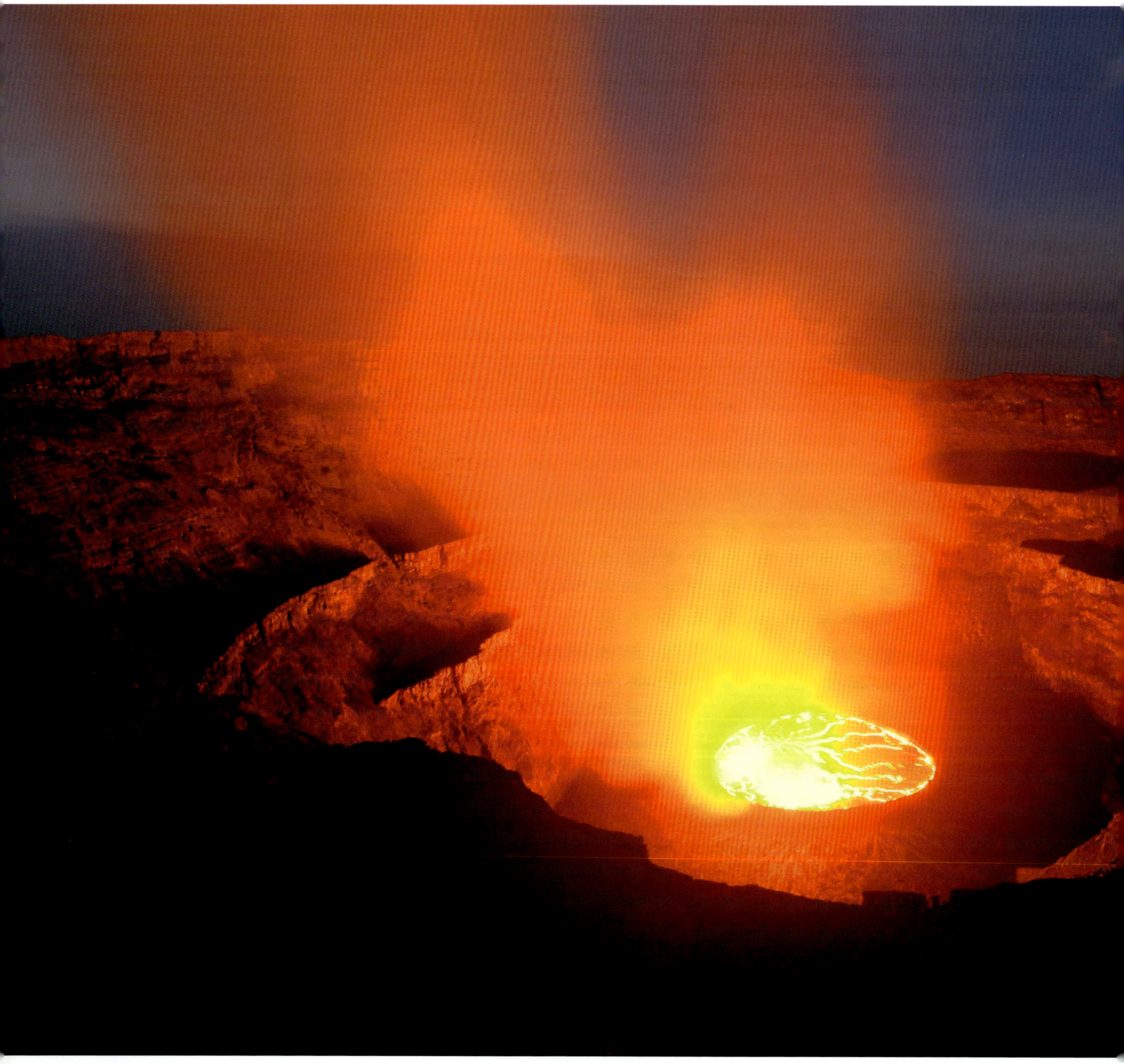

Virunga National Park covers some 8,000 sq. km (3,000 sq. miles) of the Great Rift Valley north and south of Lake Edward – also known as Lake Rutanzige – in the north-east of the Democratic Republic of Congo, on the Ugandan and Rwandan borders. It is part of the area established in 1925 as Albert National Park, the first African national park. In the course of time, the greater part of the park has been agriculturalized. Virunga National Park offers an unparalleled diversity of biospheres: swamps, steppes, savannah, lava plains, rainforest, snowfields on the Rwenzori mountains, which reach 5,109 m (16,760 feet), even volcanoes, both extinct and active.

The fauna is correspondingly varied: around 200 mammal species populate the national park, including elephants, hippos, lions, leopards, okapis, and several antelope and primate species. Migratory birds from Siberia and Europe spend the winter here.

The mountain gorilla, threatened with extinction, has found one of its last refuges here in the Virunga mountains. The American zoologist Dian Fossey began her extended study here in 1967, initially on the Congolese, and then on the Rwandan side of the border. Of today's estimated total population of 700 specimens, about half of these great apes live in Virunga. The Democratic Republic of Congo, Uganda and Rwanda conduct special patrols to preserve these close relatives of humans from extinction.

The eight volcanoes of the Virunga chain are located between Lake Kivu and Lake Edward. Nyiragongo (large image) and Nyamuragira, the two most active, with 30 eruptions recorded since 1882, lie within the borders of the park. The iridescent coat of the golden monkey (below) gave scientists the idea for this appropriate name.

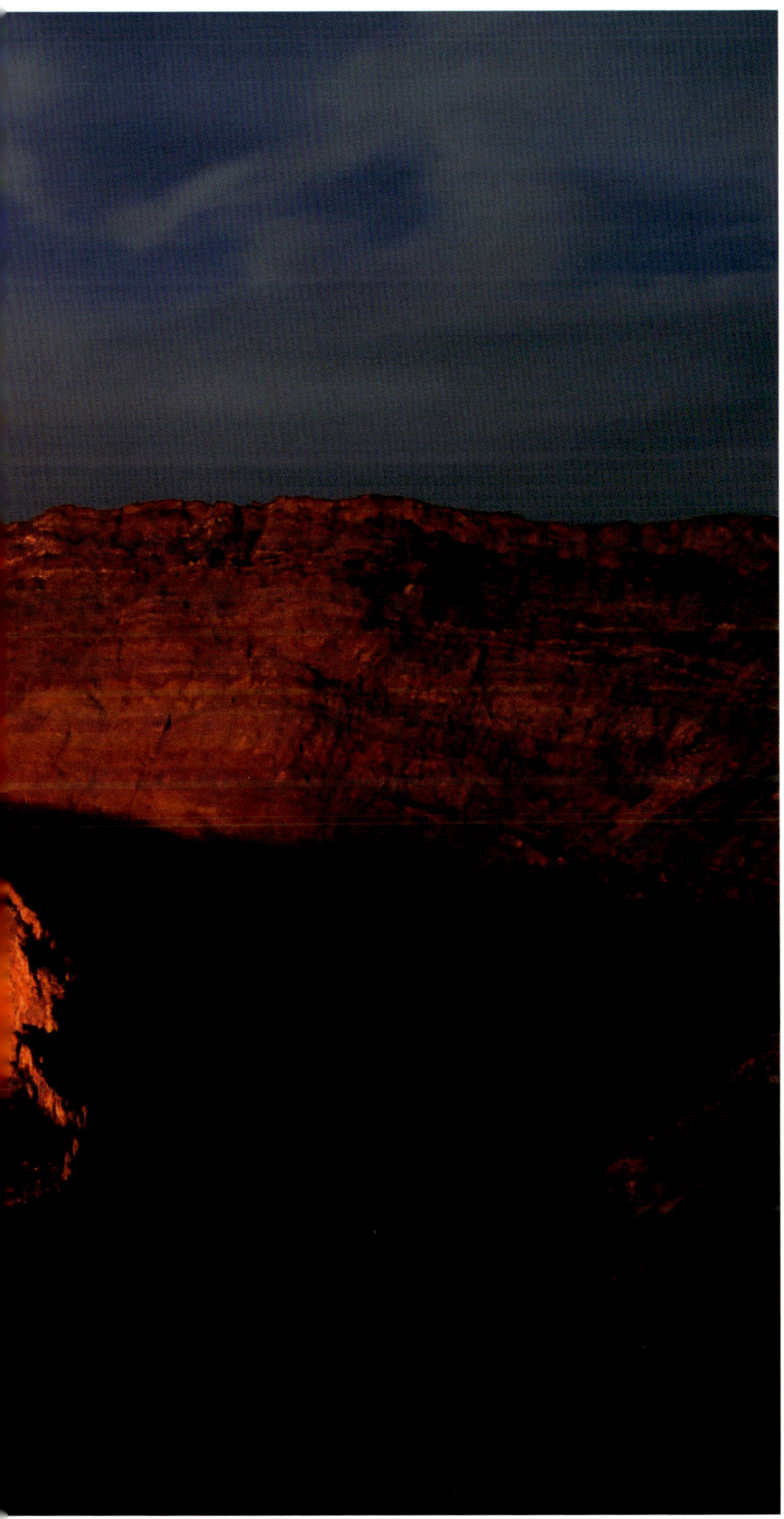

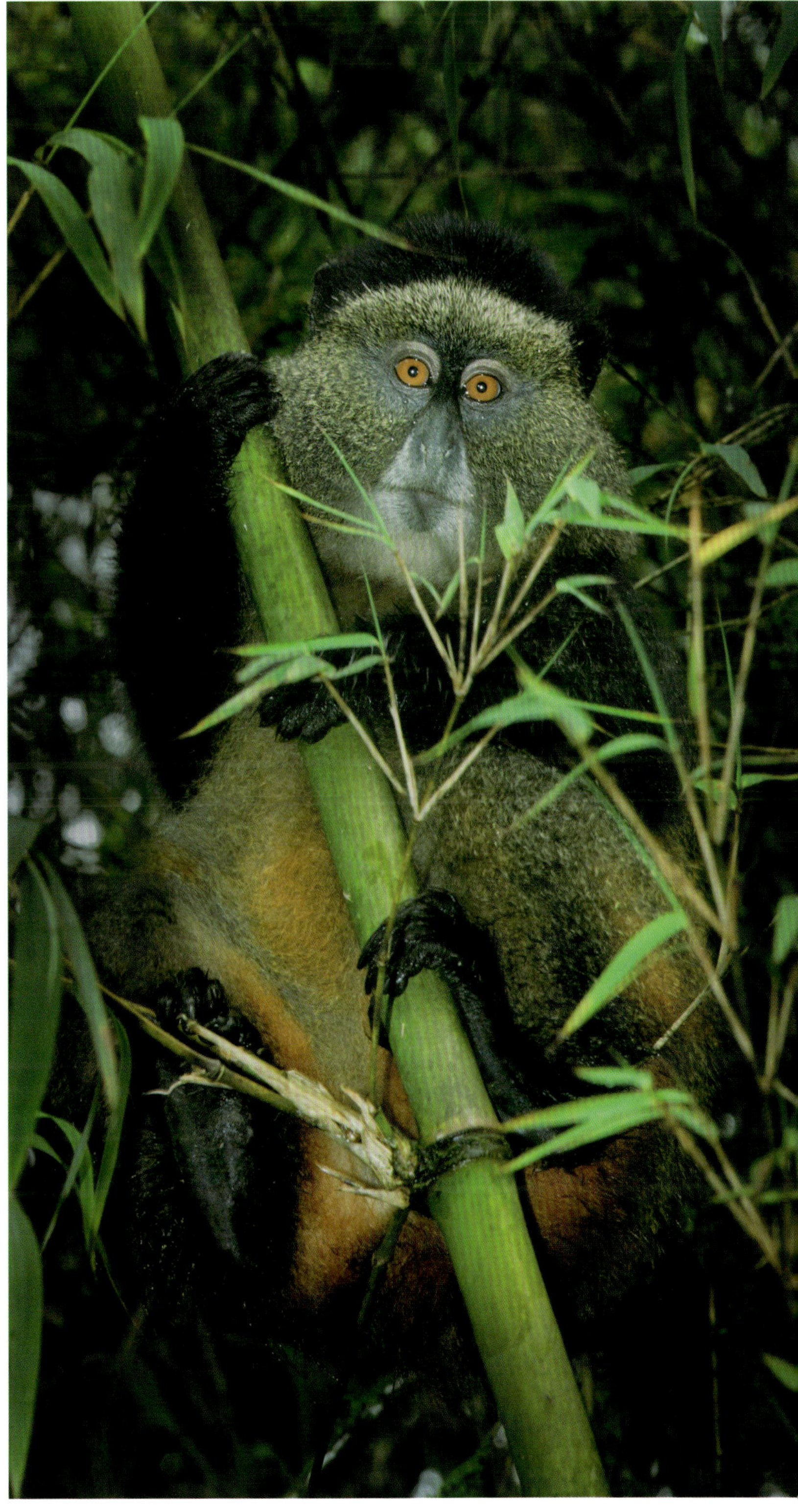

SIMIEN NATIONAL PARK

Date of inscription: 1978

The park, located 100 km (62 miles) north of Gondar in northern Ethiopia, includes an area of mountain plateau, characterized by abrupt precipices and raging rivers.

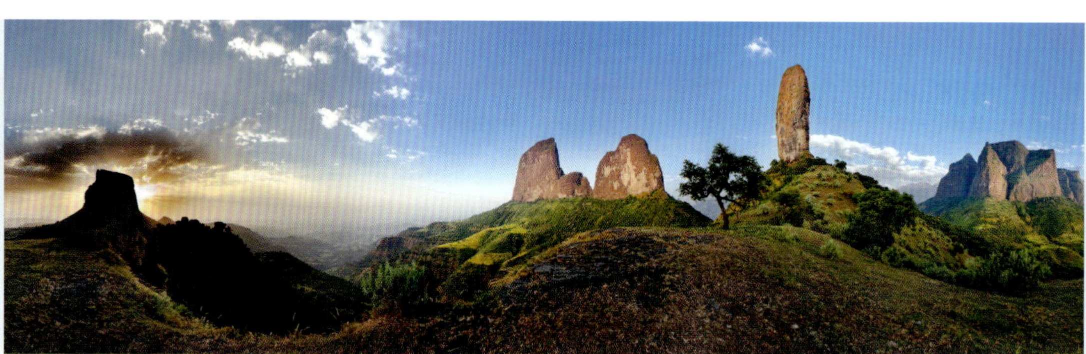

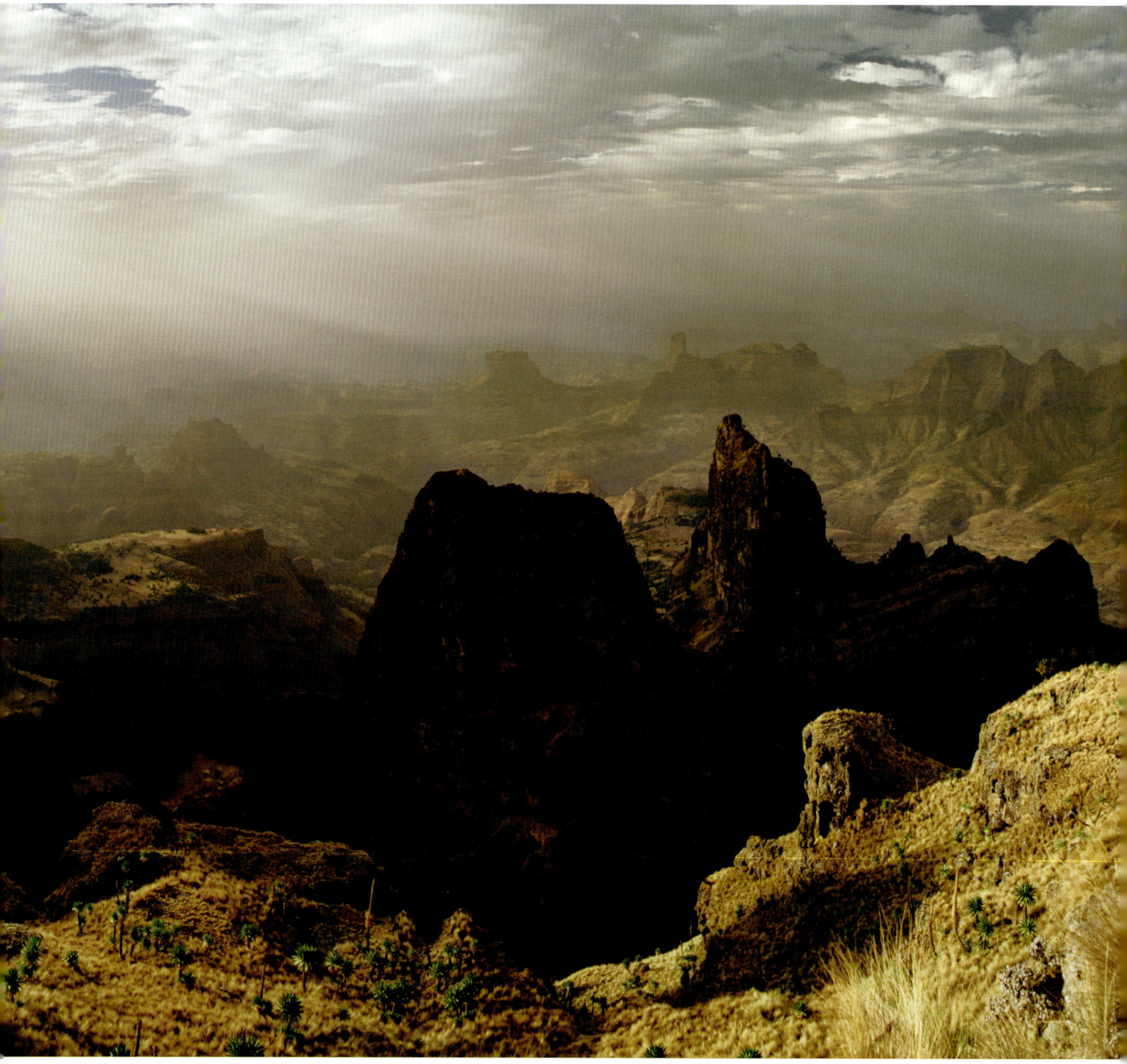

In the Simien massif, constant erosion has created some of the world's most striking scenery, with mountain peaks up to 4,500 m (14,800 feet) high, basalt valleys, roaring rivers banked by jagged rocks and cliffs, and ravines of depths of up to 1,500 m (5,000 feet). Standing over all of this is Ras Dashen, at 4,620 m (15,160 feet) the fourth-highest mountain in Africa.

The national park, named after the mountain plateau, provides a habitat for several extremely rare species, among them the gelada baboon, the Simien red fox, and the Walia ibex. When in 1996 the population of foxes and ibexes fell beneath the critical level of 20 and 250 specimens respectively, the park was inscribed in the UNESCO Red List. The ever-encroaching settlement of the Simien National Park represents a particularly acute threat to the wild animal population.

Simien National Park impresses with its high mountain plateaus. The gelada, identifiable by the red patch on its chest (top), the Ethiopian ibex and the rare Ethiopian wolf (middle and bottom) also live in the park.

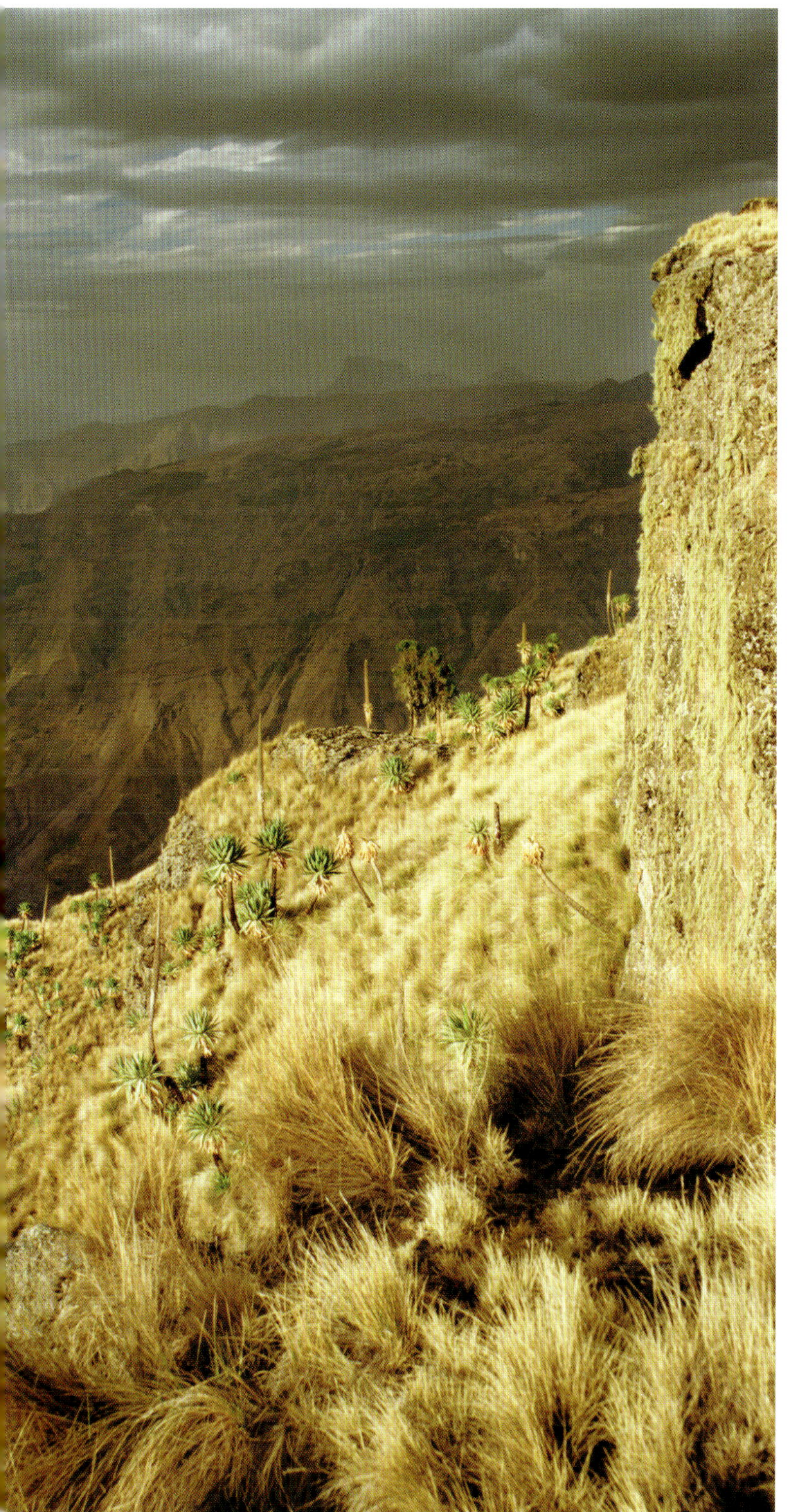

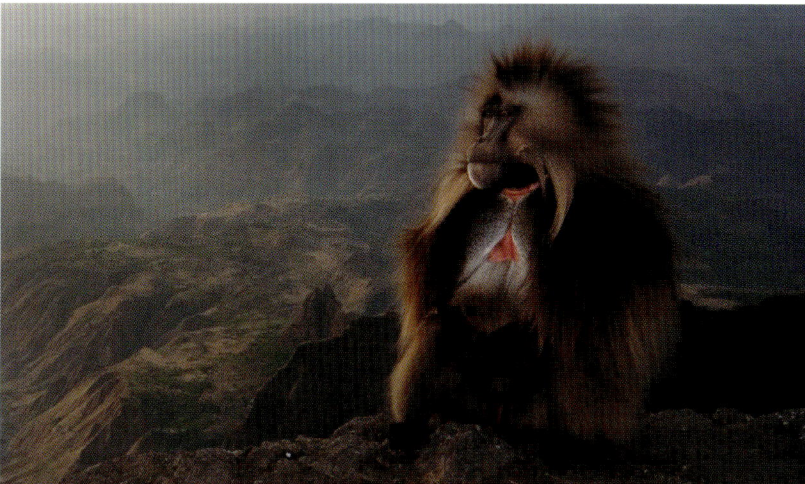

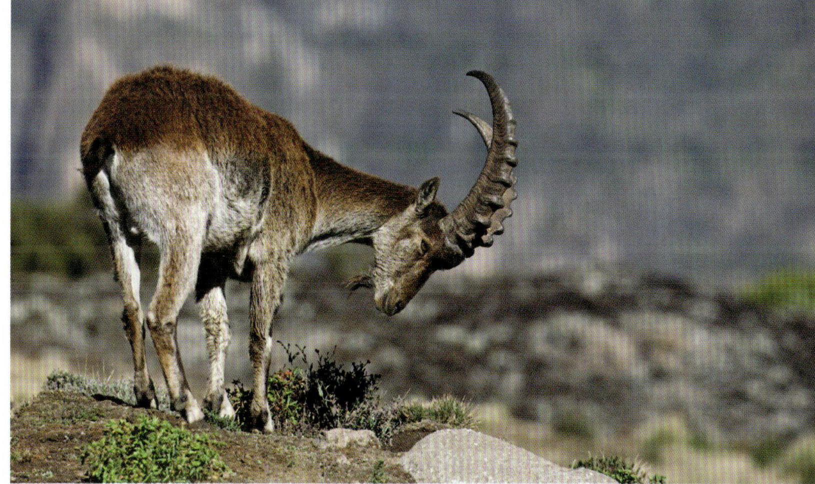

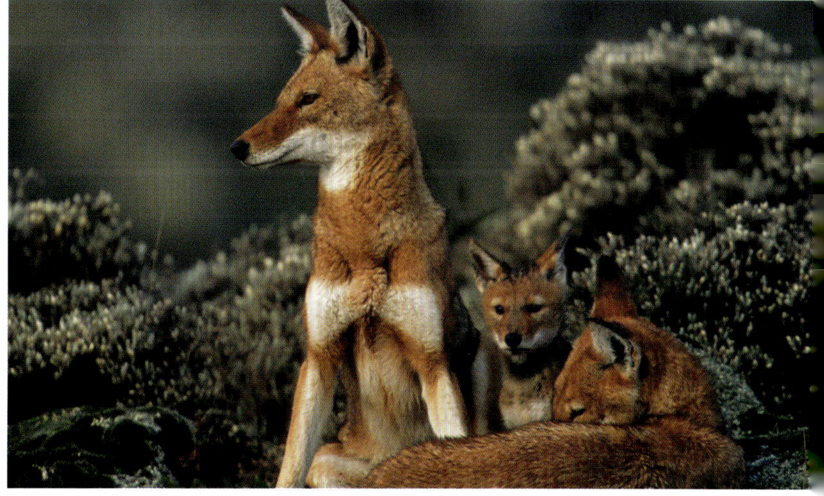

BWINDI IMPENETRABLE NATIONAL PARK

Date of inscription: 1994

Bwindi, in the extreme south-west of Uganda, is known both for the diversity of its trees and ferns and for its rare species of butterflies and birds. The montane forest is also one of the last refuges of the rare mountain gorilla.

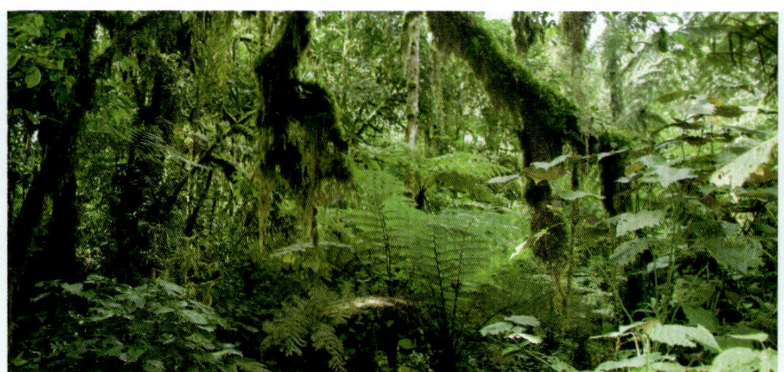

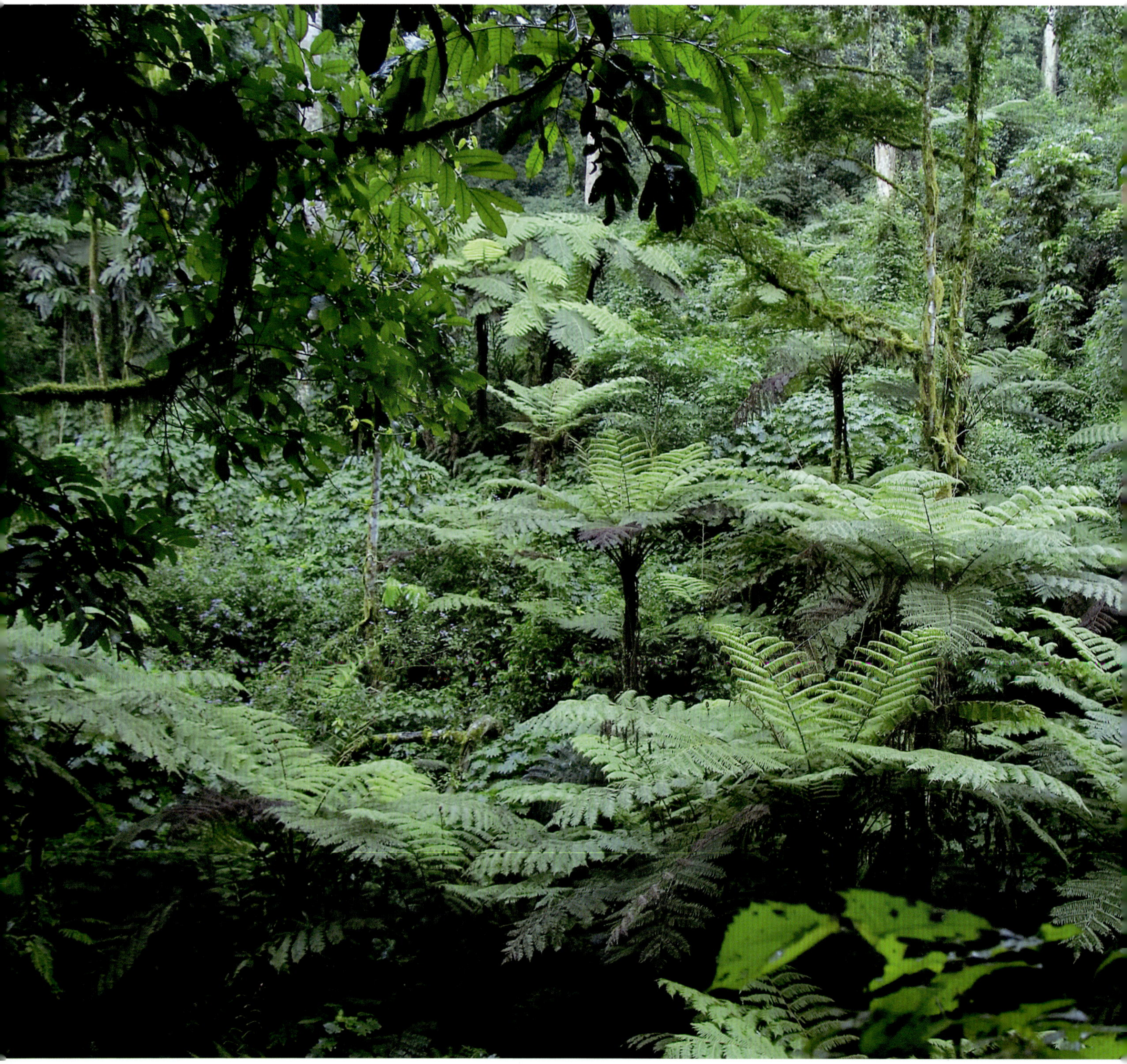

The barely accessible Bwindi National Park (Bwindi means "impenetrable") lies in a transition zone between the steppes and the mountains, and is distinguished by a unique variety of flora and fauna. There are more than 100 indigenous varieties of fern, and the national park's montane forest is composed of no less than 160 tree species. After the last ice age, the flora here was able to develop largely undisturbed. The forests of the Bwindi National Park are among the oldest and least disturbed in Africa. Woodland birds make up about two-thirds of the 300 avian species so far recorded, and there are about 200 varieties of butterfly.

However, the reserve is most famous for its mountain gorillas. On its upper slopes, in docile family groups led by a silverback, around 300 specimens survive, forming about half the total world population of this endangered species. A guided tour allows the close observation of mountain gorillas. Elephants, antelopes, chimpanzees and red colobus monkeys also live here.

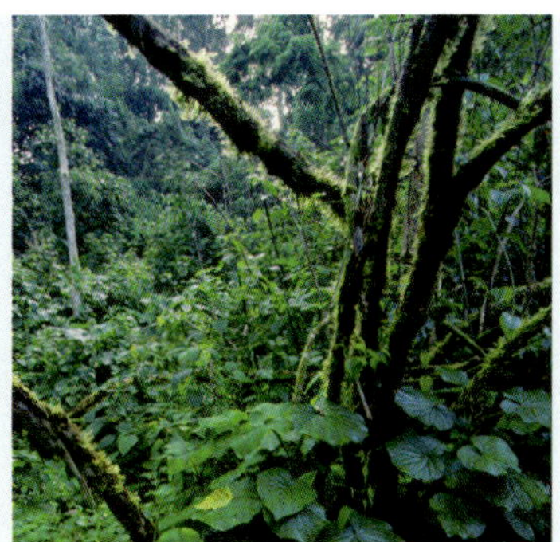

Covering 330 sq. km (130 sq. miles) and incorporating both mountain and lowland rainforest, Bwindi National Park is located on the edge of the Western Rift Valley in south-west Uganda. Many plants in the primary forest have evolved only since the last ice age.

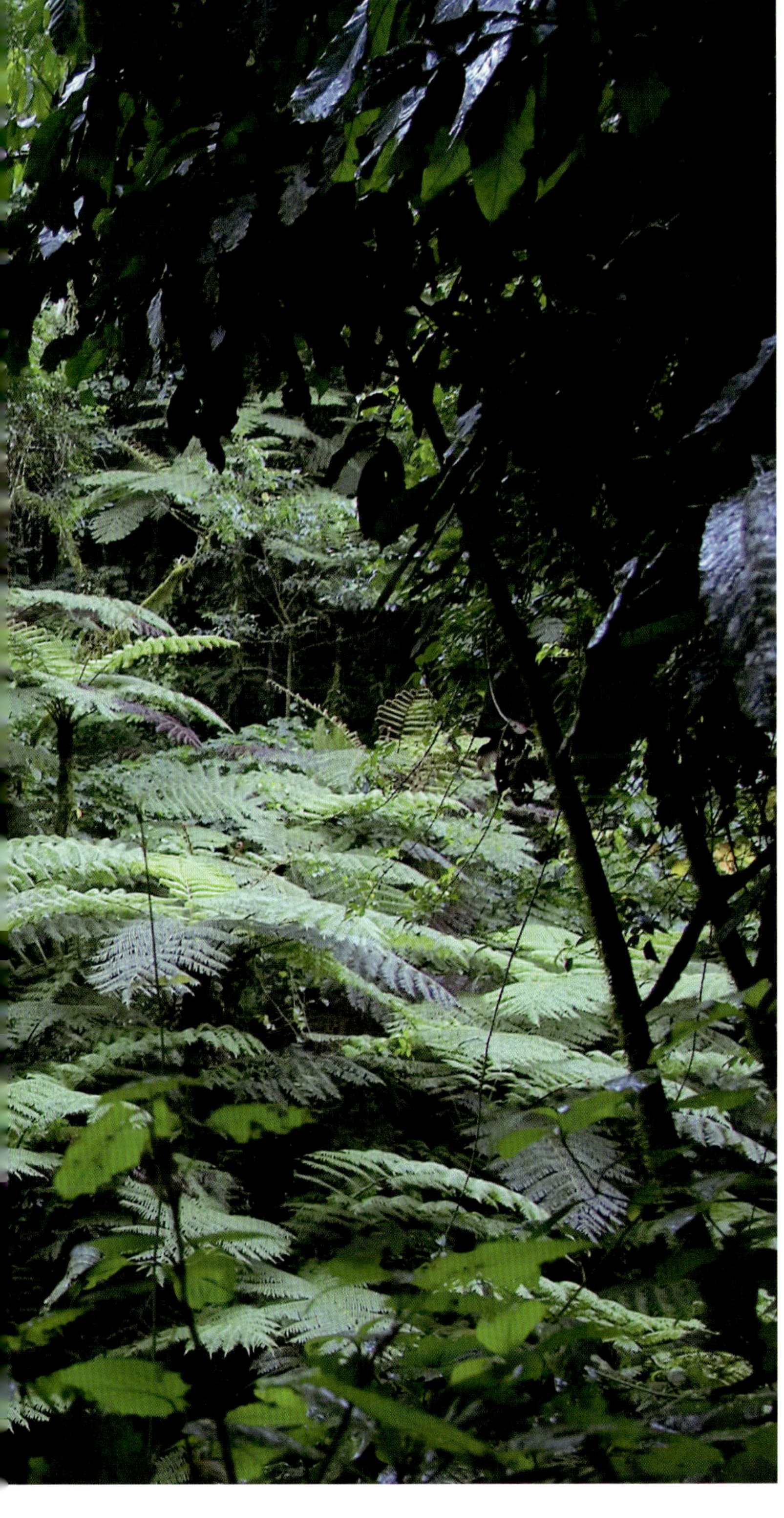

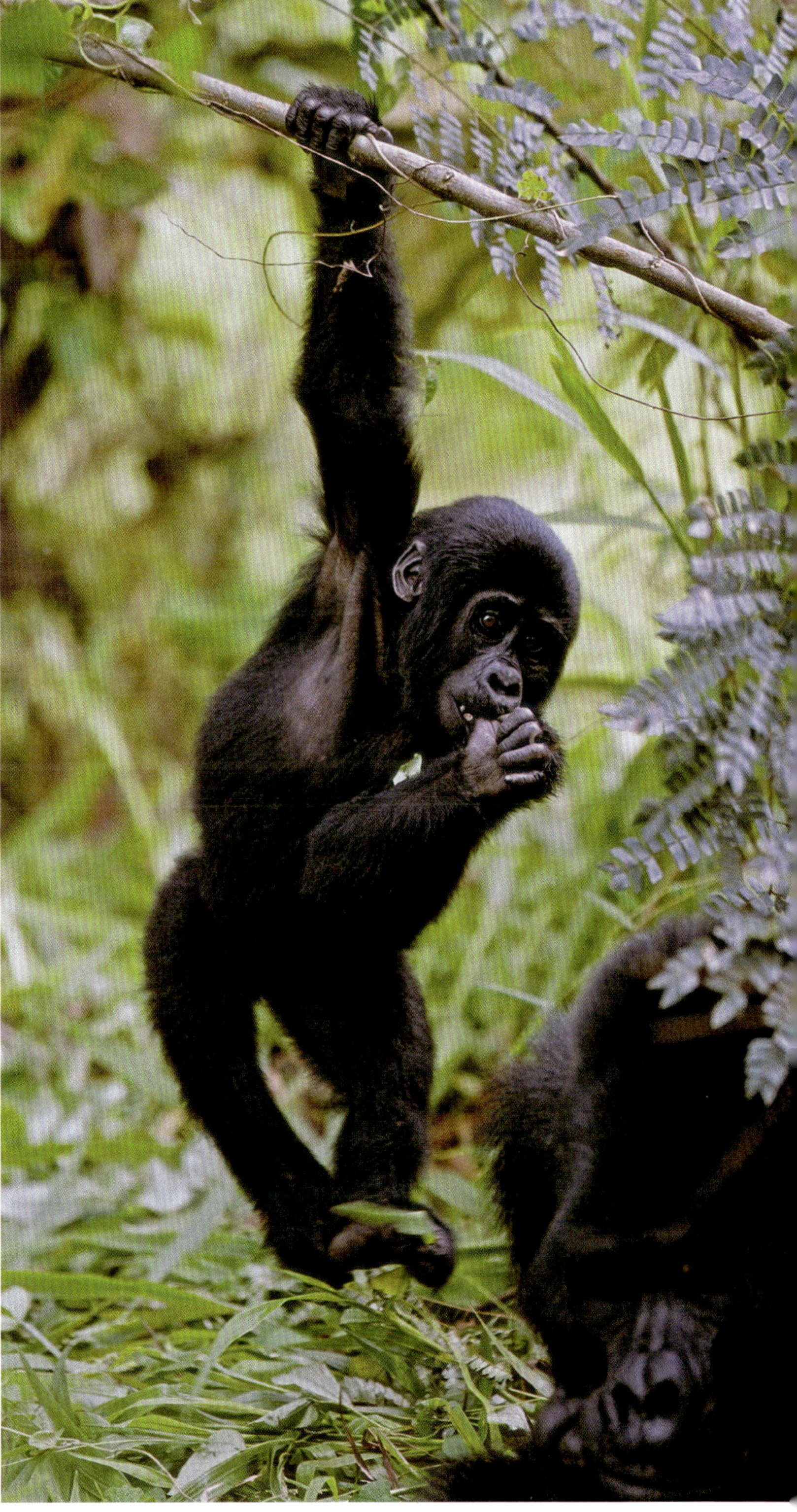

RWENZORI MOUNTAINS NATIONAL PARK

Date of inscription: 1994

The montane forest and marshlands of the Rwenzori area are a habitat for many endangered species and for plants of extraordinary size.

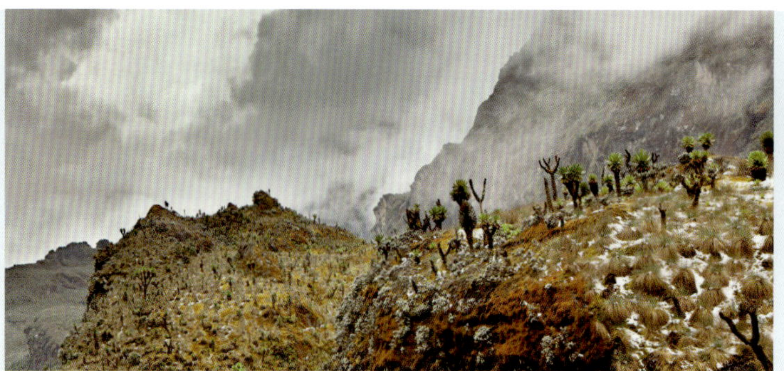

The Rwenzori mountains lie between Lakes Albert and Edward on the border between Uganda and the Democratic Republic of Congo. The mountain chain, formed by tectonic activity, is about 120 km (74 miles) long and 50 km (31 miles) wide, and its highest elevation, at 5,109 m (16,760 feet), is the Margherita summit of Mount Stanley. The national park encloses an area of about

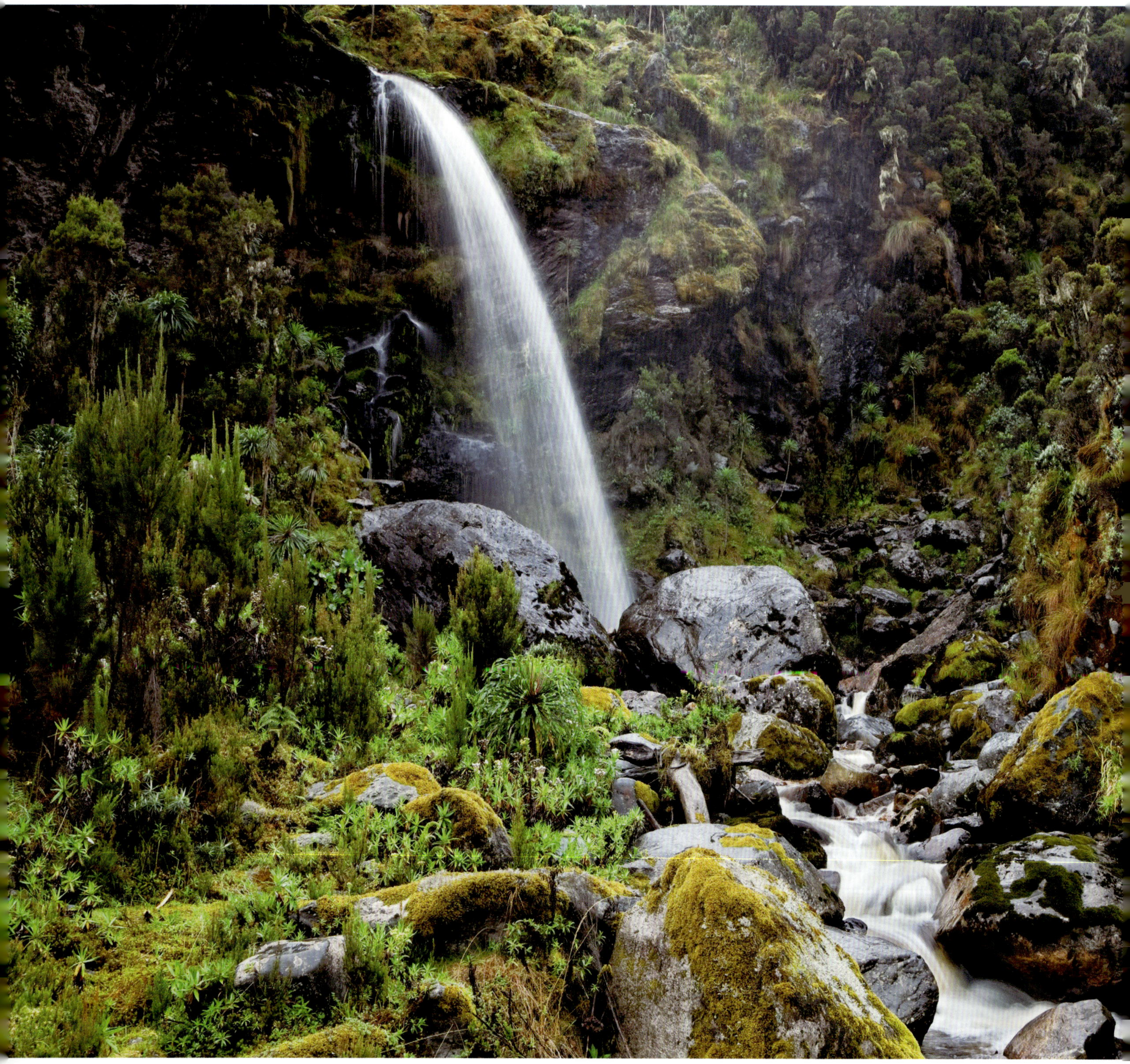

1,000 sq. km (390 sq. miles) in the extreme south-west of Uganda. Along with the glaciers, lakes, and waterfalls of its higher reaches, the Rwenzori has marshland in its valleys and foothills, where tall undergrowth like papyrus provide protection for elephants. Vast numbers of gazelles, antelopes, and buffaloes find food in the wealth of grasses in the craters. Stands of bamboo grow at altitudes of about 2,000 m (6,600 feet). This is a habitat for leopards, and also for rock hyraxes, which find shelter in the many fissures in the rocks. The tropical montane forest on the upper reaches, almost continually shrouded in mist, hides a world of plants of unusual proportions – lobelias (picture below), whose growth normally stops at 30 cm (12 inches), here reach a height of 6 m (20 feet). When protected from the elements, some fern species grow to a height of 10 m (33 feet), and some types of heather can grow as big as trees. This immense plant growth is attributable to a combination of mineral-rich soils, stable temperatures, high humidity, and the strong ultraviolet light on the upper slopes.

A treasure chest of life – the Ruwenzori National Park offers protection to many animals and plants. Right picture series, from the top: blue or diademed monkey, giant forest hog, southern tree hyrax.

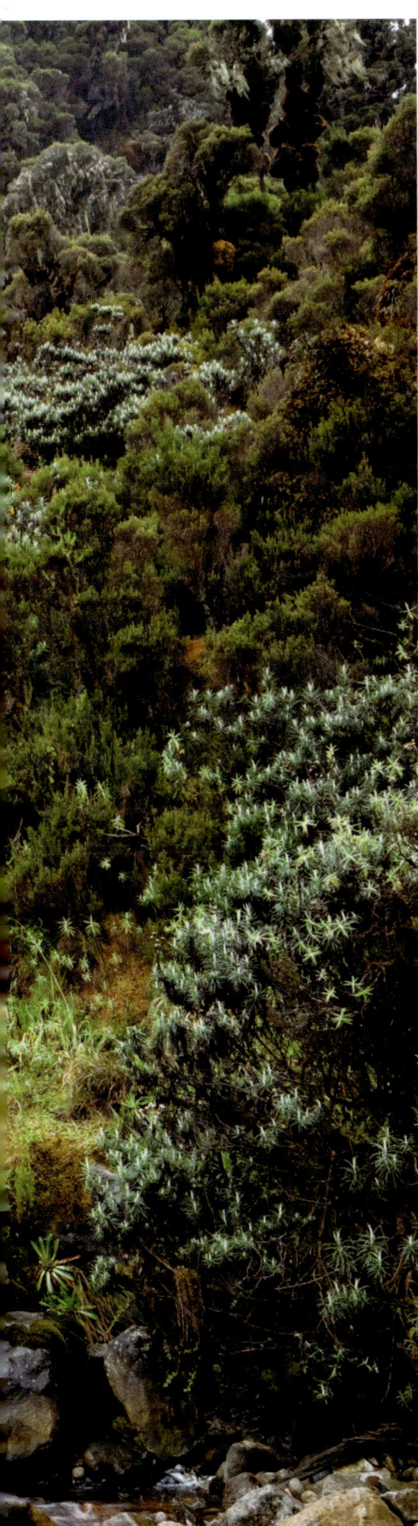

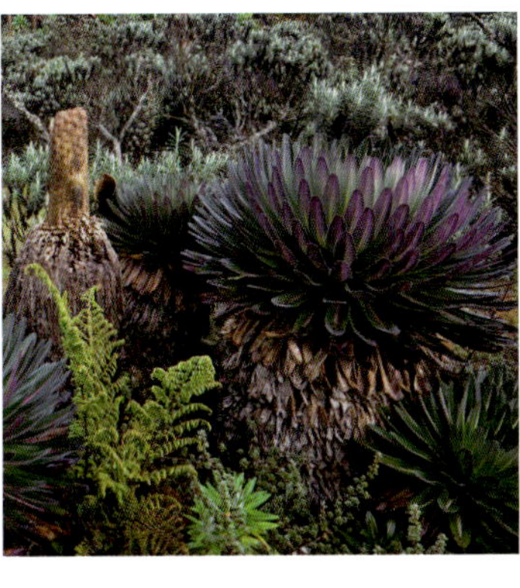

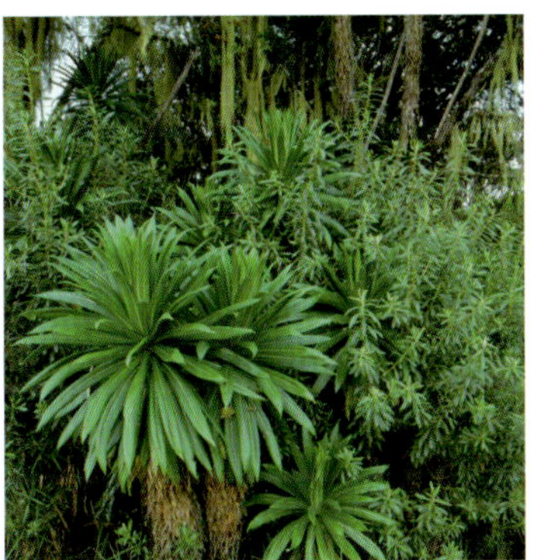

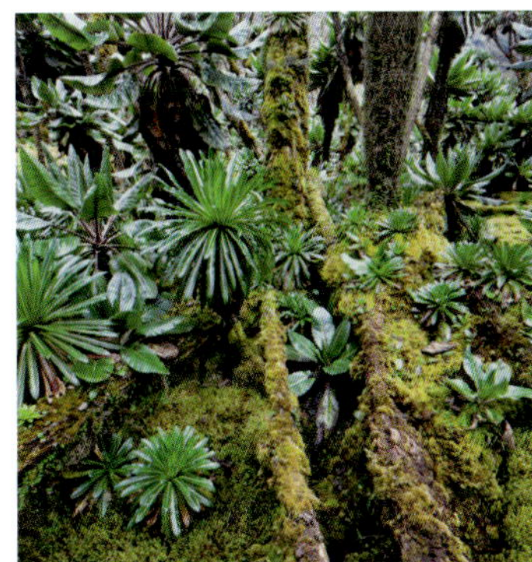

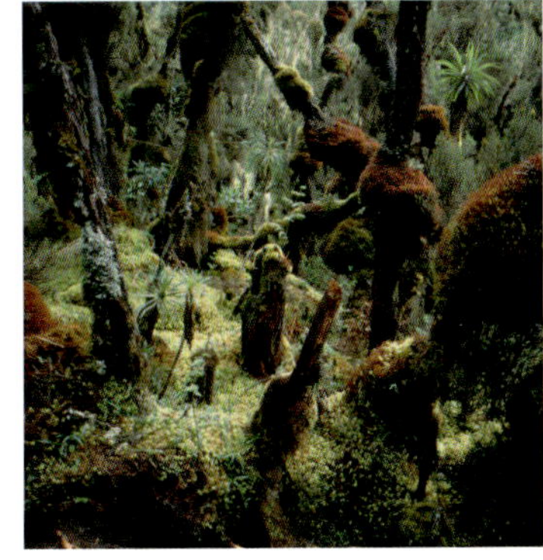

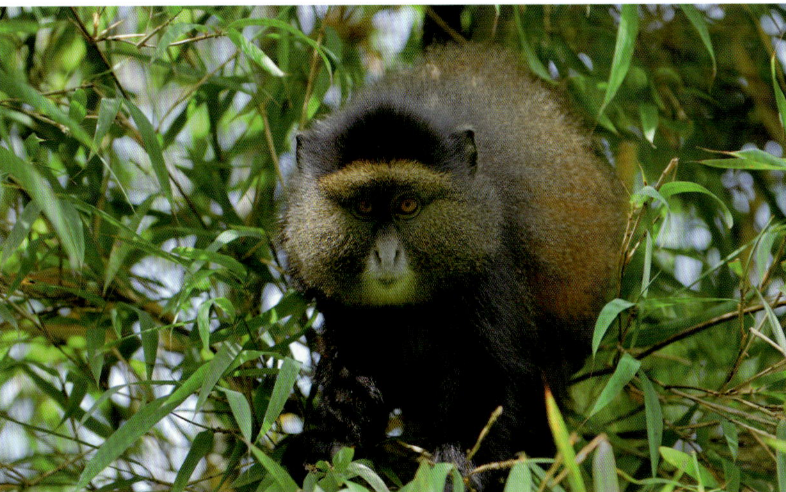

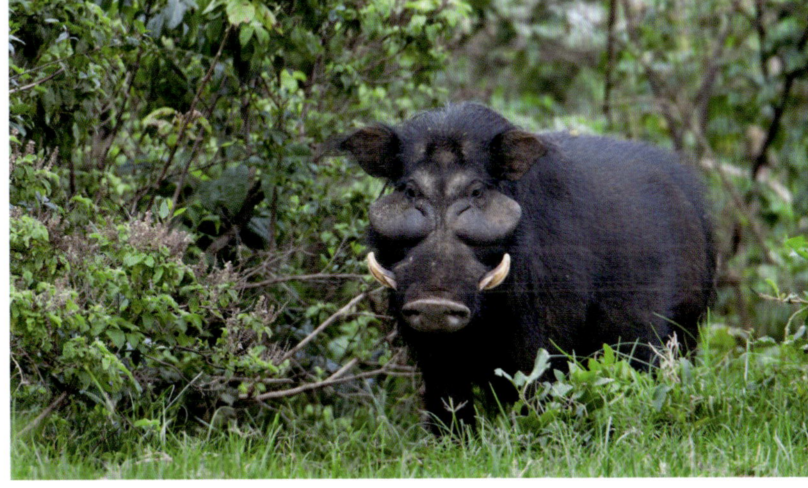

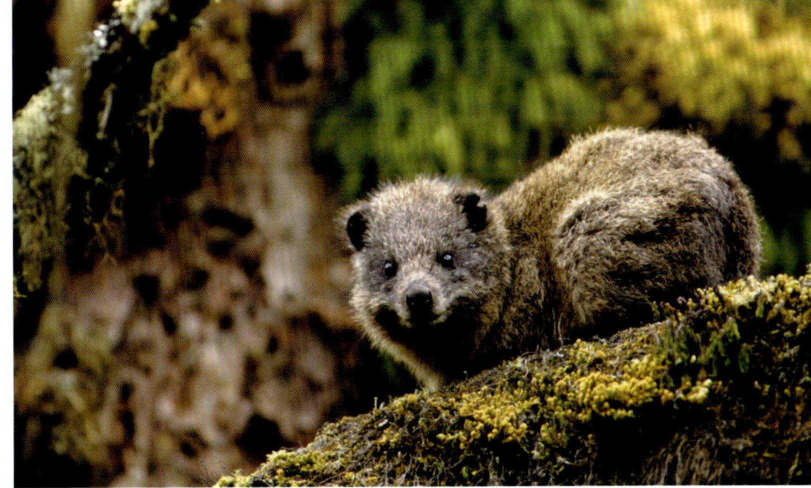

LAKE TURKANA NATIONAL PARK, SIBILOI ISLAND AND SOUTH ISLAND

Date of inscription: 1997
Extended: 2001

This World Heritage Site, internationally known for its diverse fauna, is composed of three national parks, from north to south: Sibiloi, Central Island, and South Island.

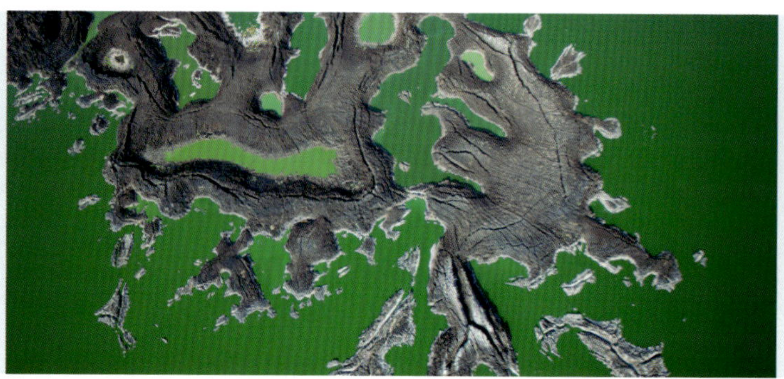

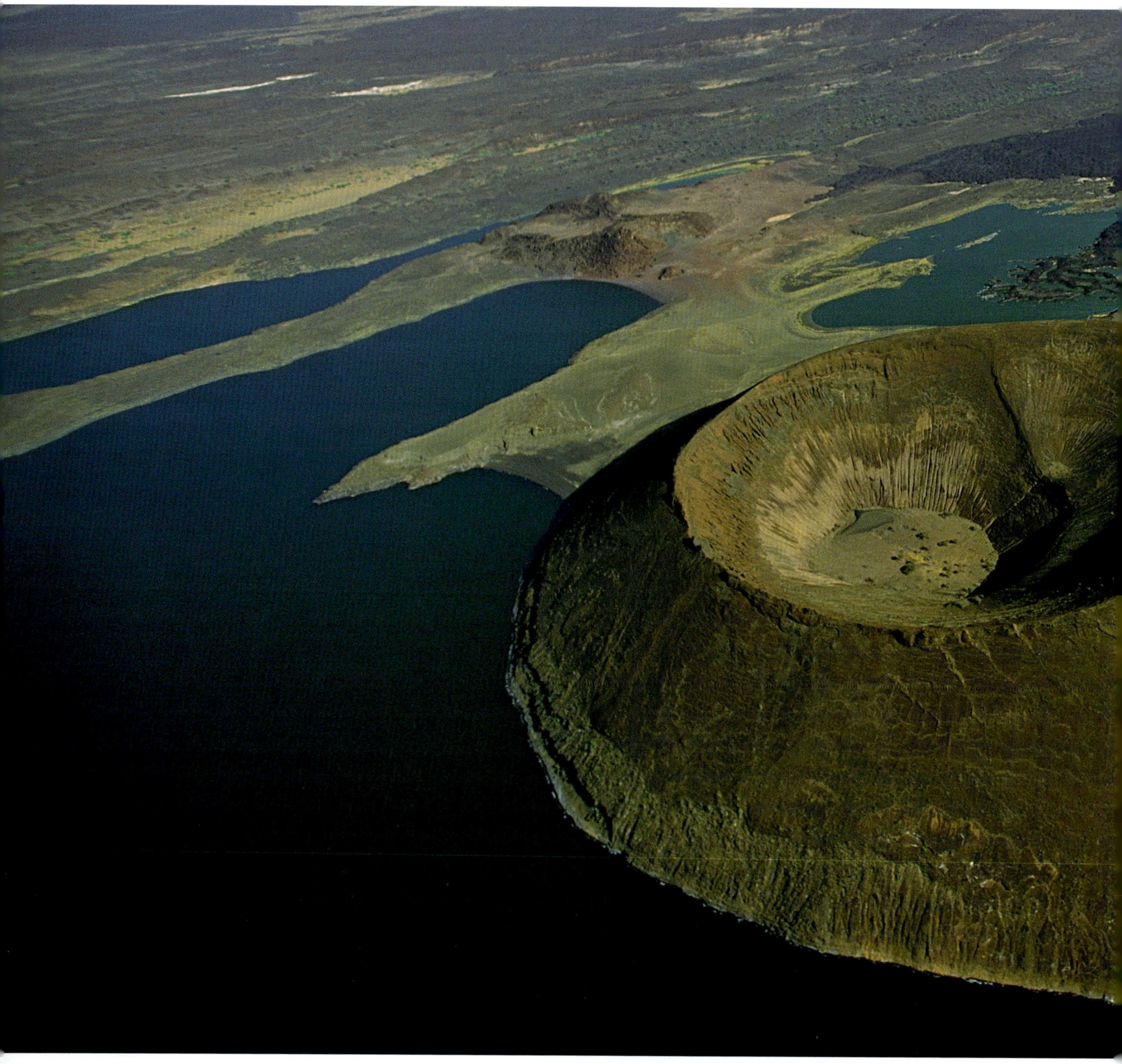

In the desert-like dry steppes of the far north-west of Kenya, near the border with Sudan and Ethiopia, lies Lake Turkana, an endorheic lake with a high salt content. The Sibiloi National Park (1,500 sq. km, 580 sq. miles), lying along its eastern shore, is a habitat for lions, zebras, antelopes, and gazelles. It is, however, much better known as a breeding ground and stopover point for all kinds of birds: wading birds, flamingos, pelicans, seagulls, and other migratory birds. In the middle of the lake lie the 5 sq. km (2 sq. miles) of bare volcanic rock that make up Central Island, on which numerous species of waterfowl have made their nests, and which provides a refuge for a reasonably large colony of Nile crocodiles. South Island, which is located 100 km (62 miles) further to the south of Central Island, has very similar fauna, and even hippos can be seen here. At Koobi Fora, a promontory of the national park jutting out into the lake, significant palaeontological finds of Australopithecus, Homo habilis, Homo erectus, and Homo sapiens have been found.

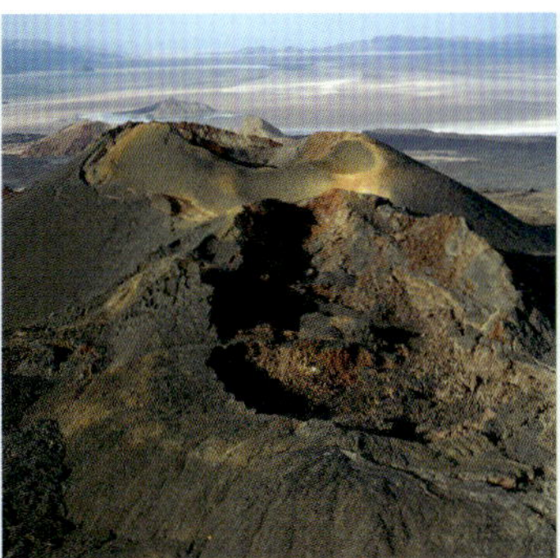

Far left: Lake Turkana is Kenya's largest body of water. The lake is situated in a highly active volcanic area (left: Andrews; below: Nabuyatom)

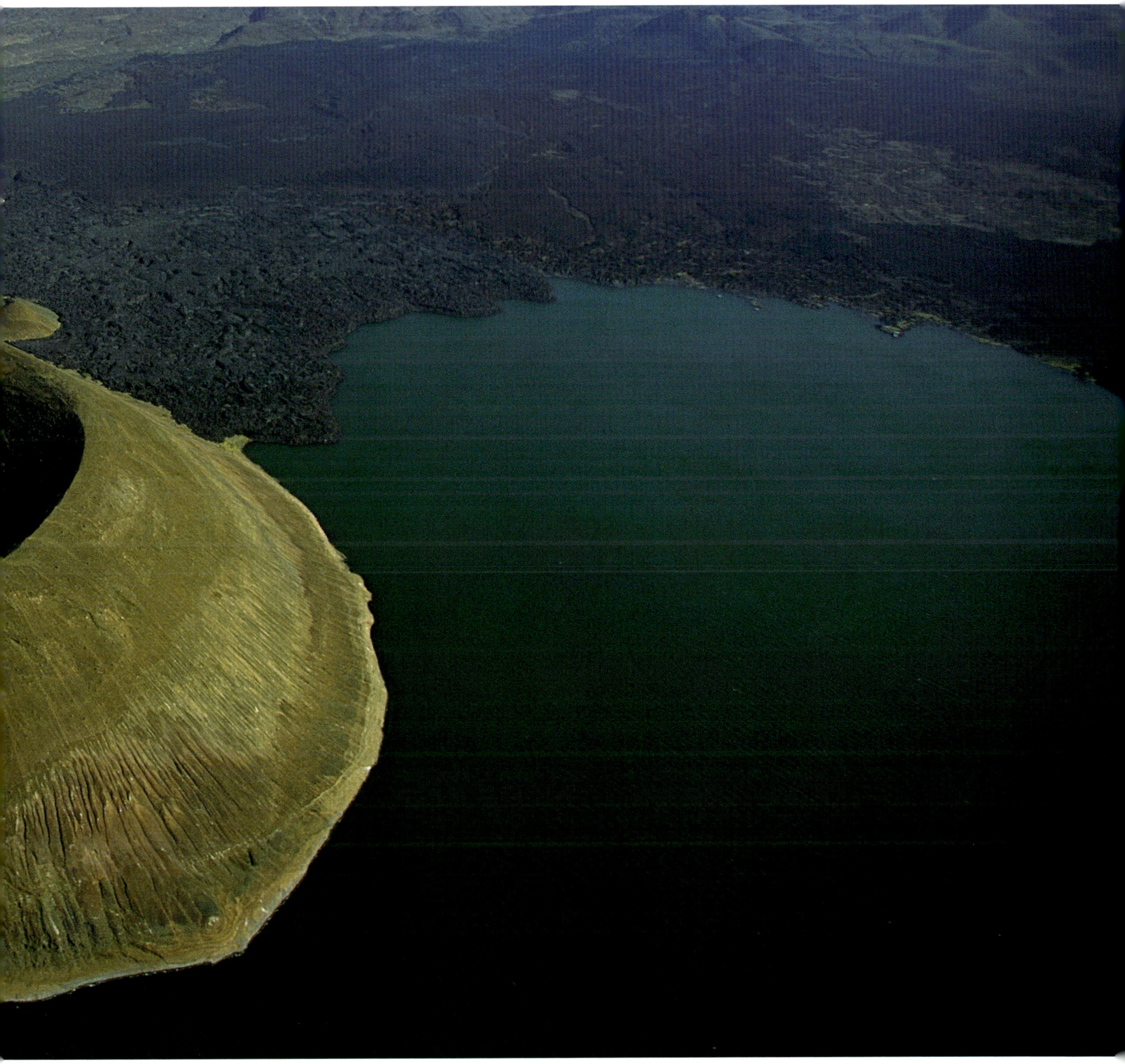

MOUNT KENYA NATIONAL PARK

Date of inscription: 1997
Extended: 2013

The slopes of 5,199-m (17,057-foot) high Mount Kenya are characterized by a succession of highly diverse zones of vegetation and forestation.

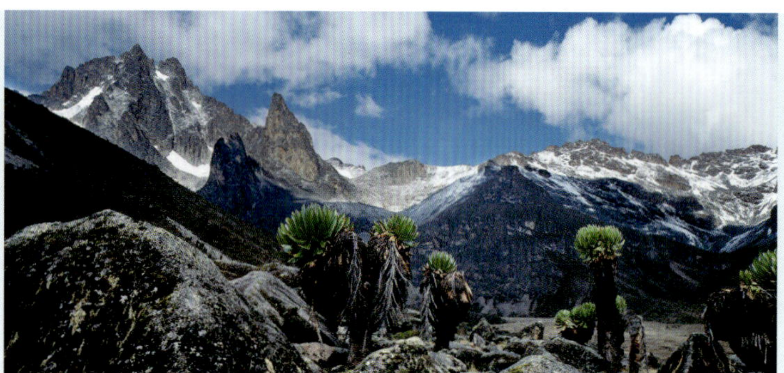

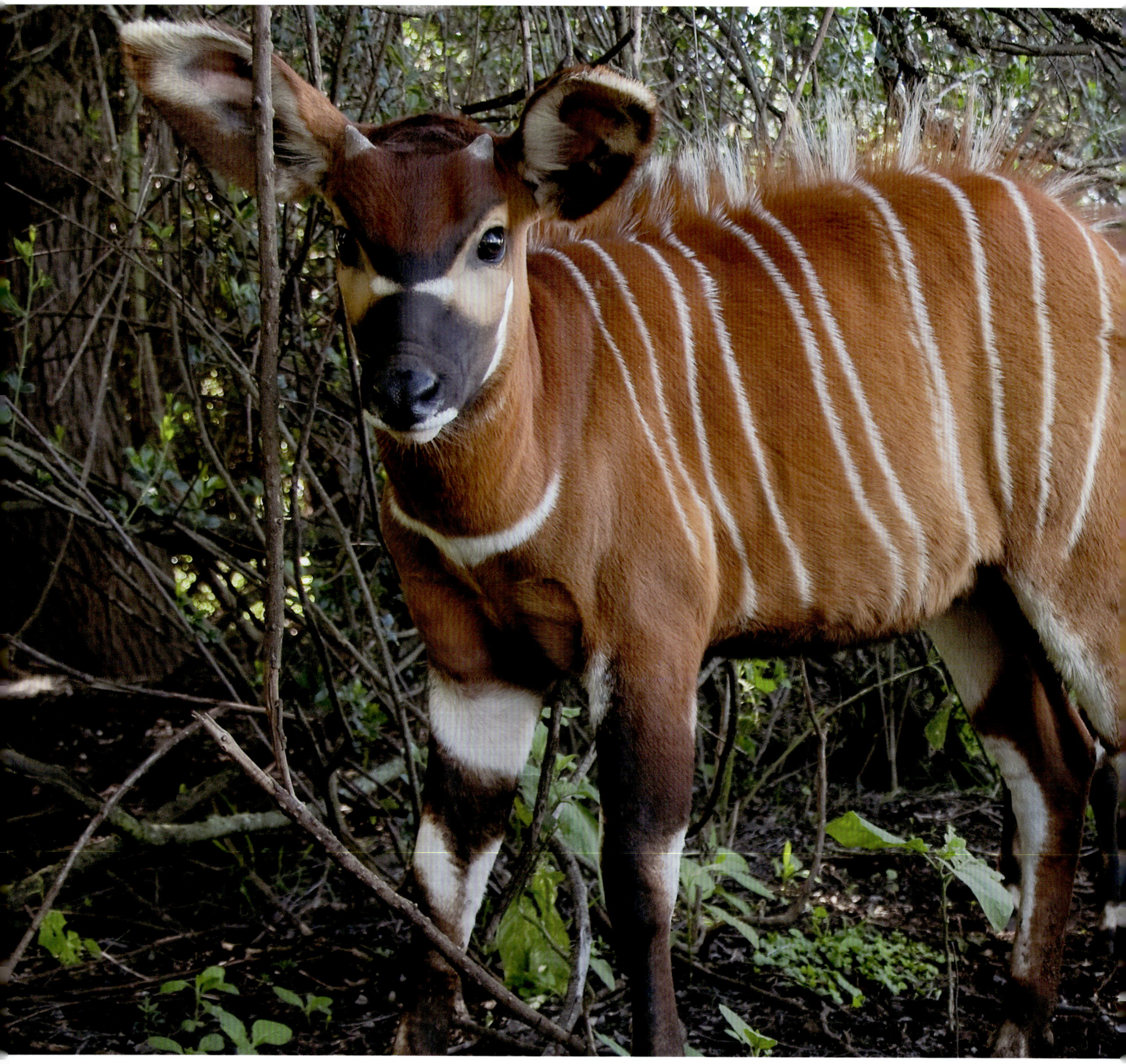

At 5,199 m (17,057 feet) above sea level, the impressive massif and twin summits of Mount Kenya make up the highest mountain peak in the country. Its slopes are covered in meadow and forest to an altitude of some 2,000 m (6,600 feet), at which point the moist deciduous forest is replaced by evergreen cloud forest. Beyond this forest, a zone of dense bamboo growth continues to an altitude of some 2,500 m (8,200 feet). Above 3,500 m (11,500 feet) there is open grassland which merges into moorland on the higher slopes. Predominately ericaceous berries and shrubs grow in this area of heathland; of particular note is the tree heath, which can grow to a height of around 10 m (33 feet). Giant lobelias and various species of groundsel, which can reach a height of 5 m (17 feet), grow in the alpine zone, where the actual borders of the national park zone begin. Although these two plants display many similarities in form, they are not related. Above all this lies the Afro-alpine zone covering the summits, with several cirque glaciers in the extinct volcano. The animal life in Africa's most diverse national park is usually found in the nutrition-rich regions of bamboo and forest: elephants, rhinos, cape buffaloes and antelopes are all found here, along with rare species such as bush and rock hyrax.

Around 150 varieties of birds are distributed throughout the various vegetation zones.

Starlings and sparrows are found worldwide, but some subspecies occur exclusively in Central Africa. From the top: violet-backed starling, malachite sunbird (picture series, 2nd and 4th picture), chestnut sparrow. Large picture: bongos are a type of antelope.

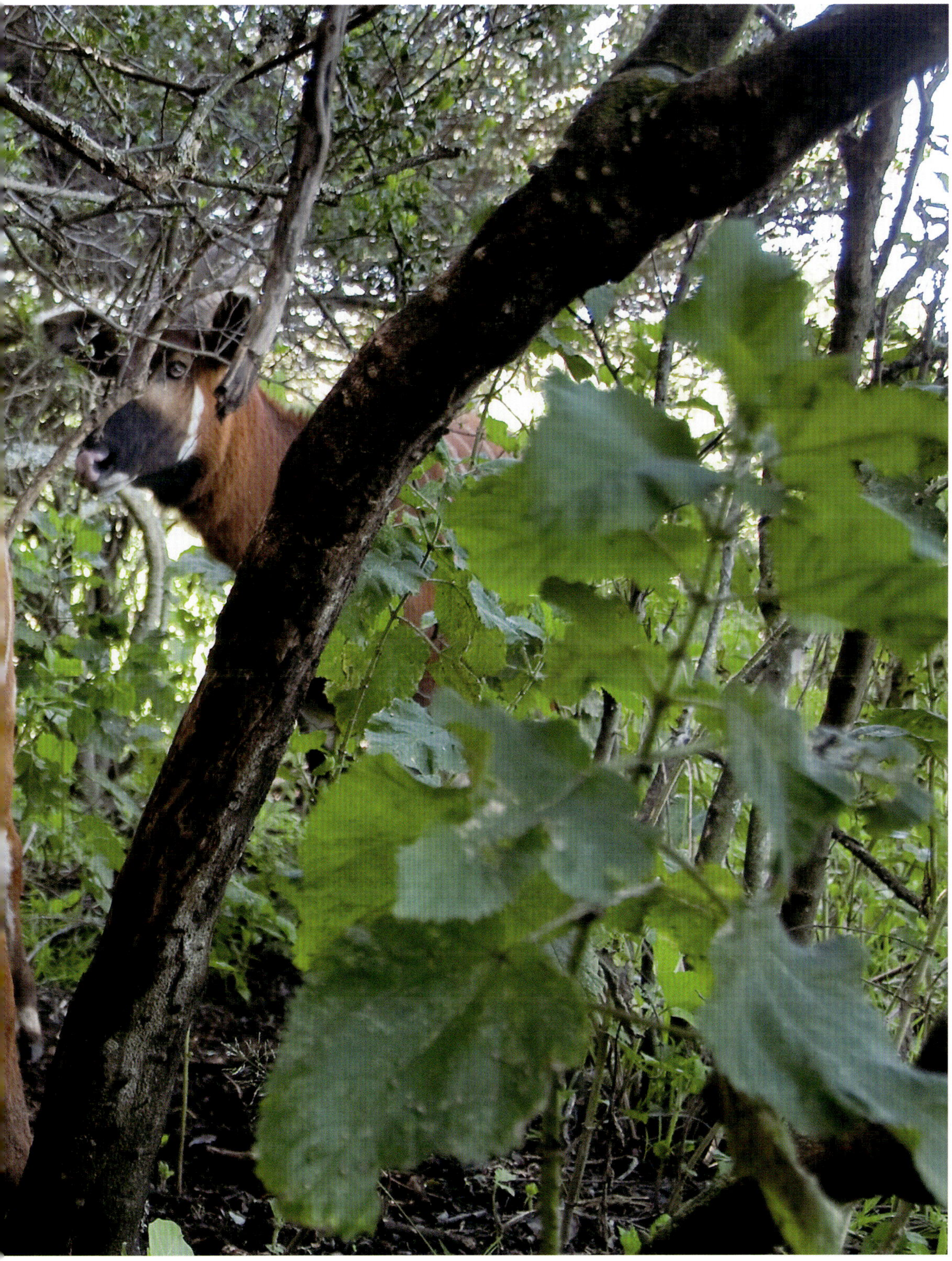

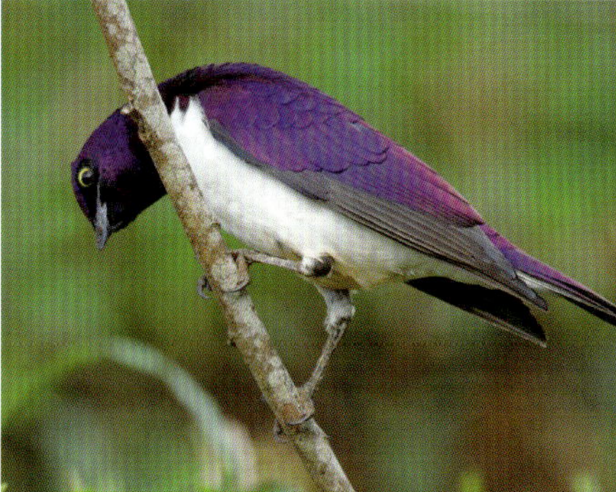

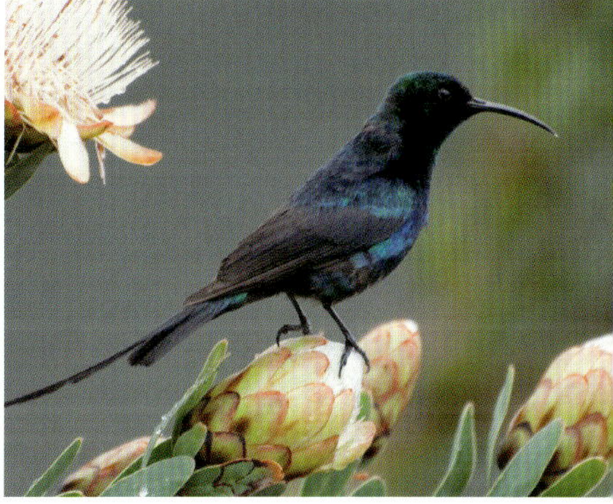

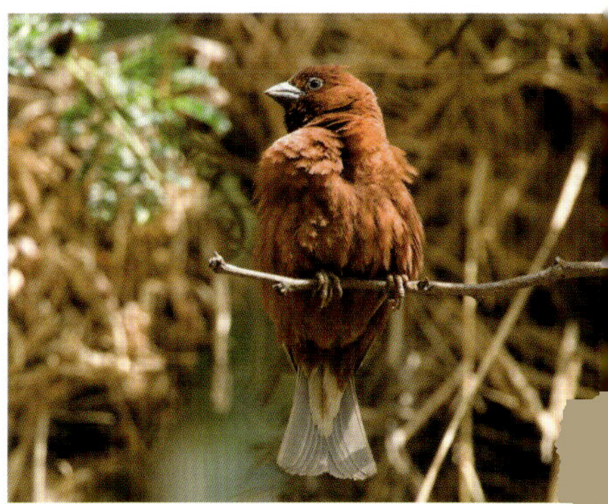

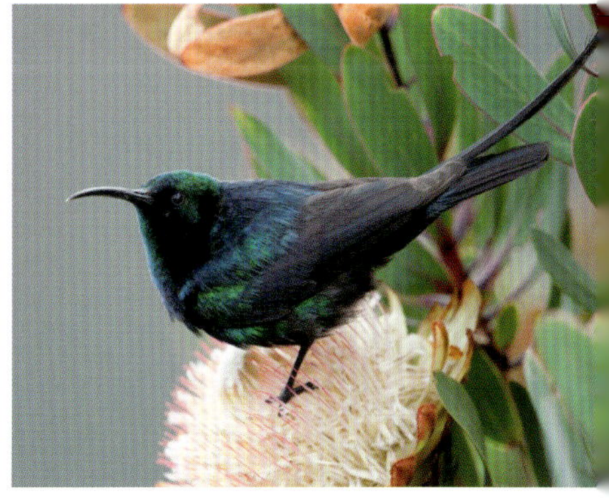

LAKES OF GREAT RIFT VALLEYS

Date of inscription: 2011

Kenya's alkaline or soda lakes form an important refuge for endangered species of birds and rare mammals.

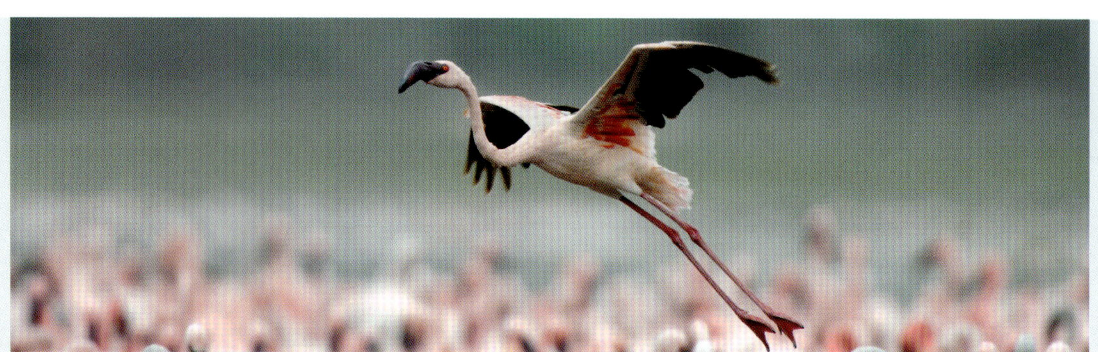

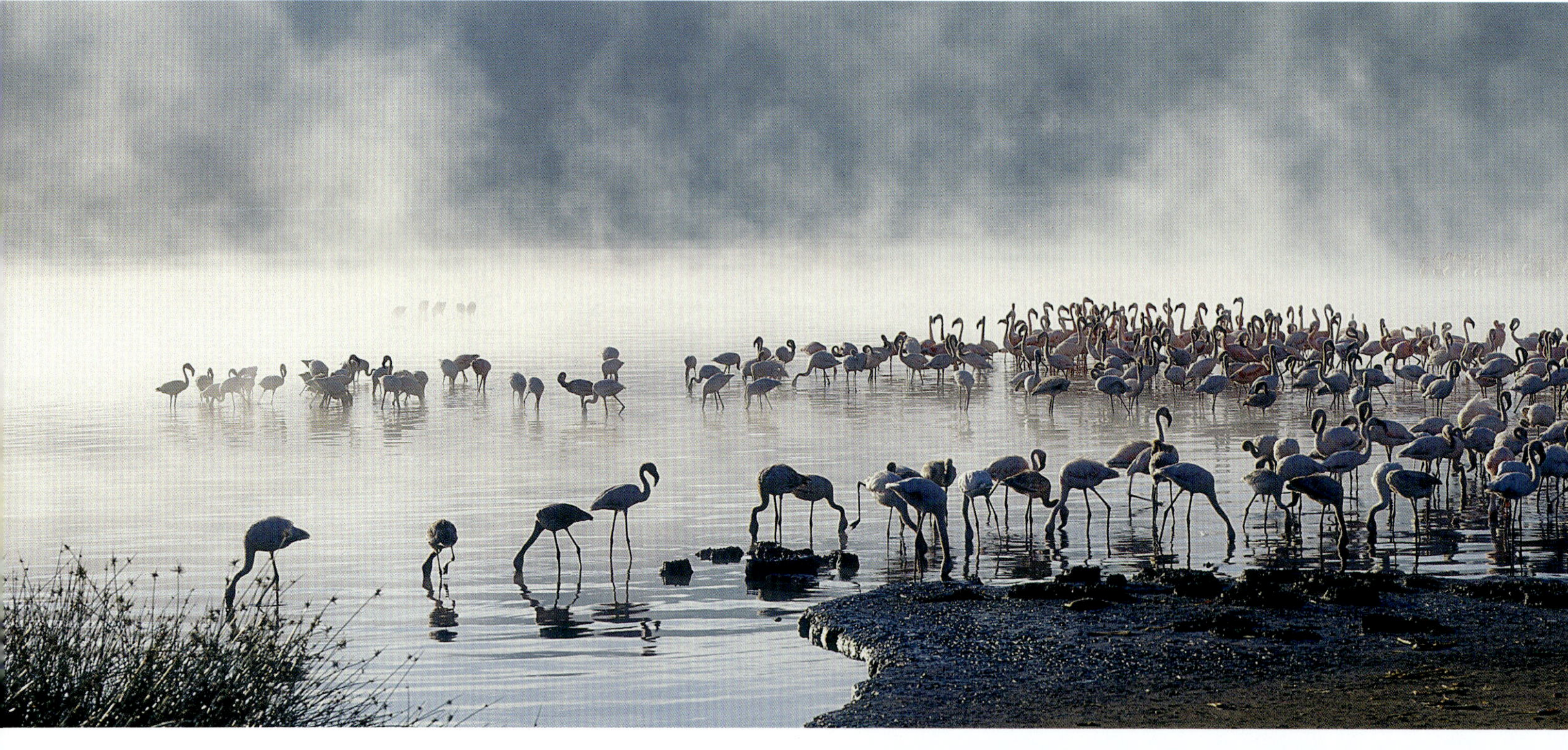

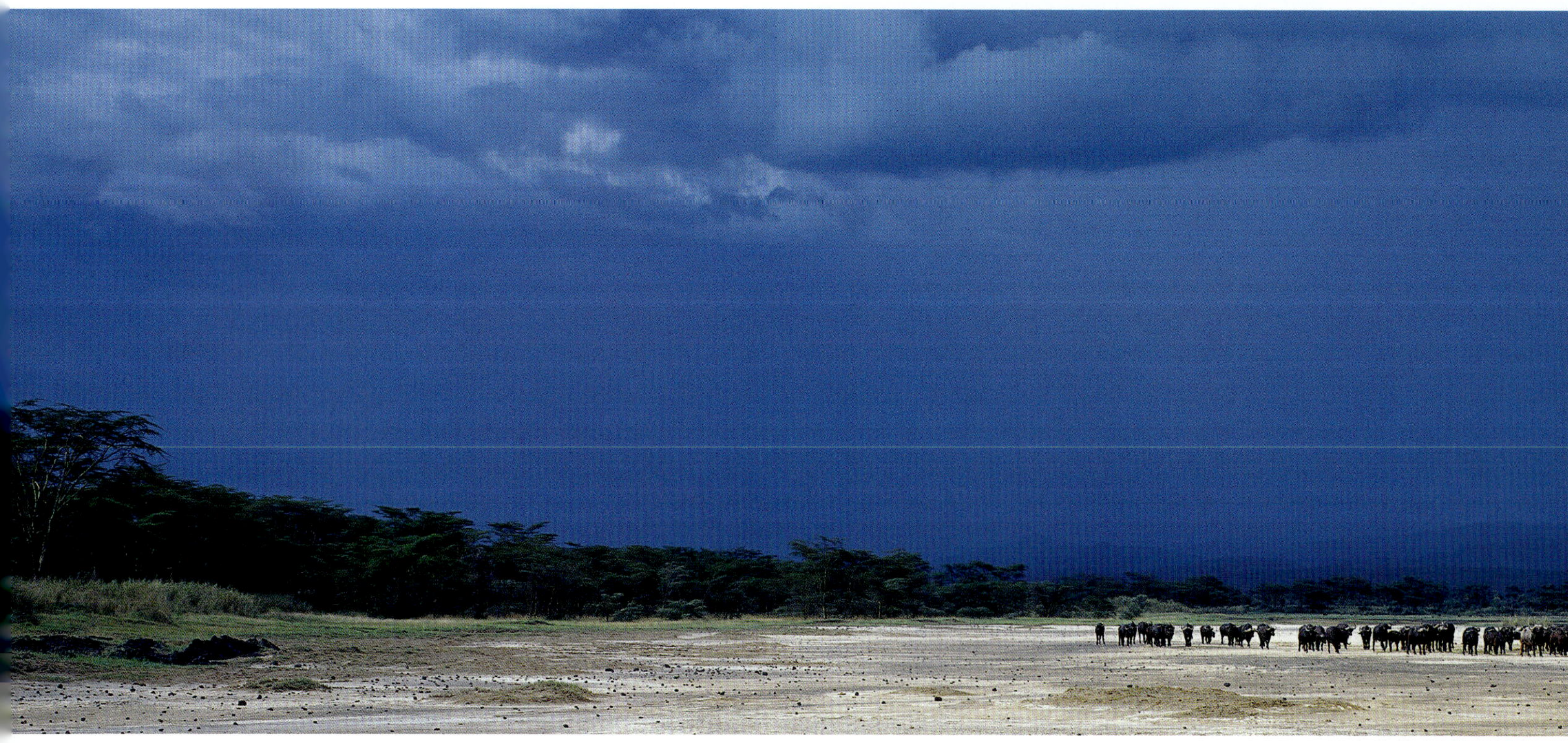

The lakes of the Great Rift Valley in the Rift Valley Province of south-western Kenya – Lake Bogoria, Lake Elementaita and Lake Nakuru, which was declared a National Park in 1968 – are shallow waters containing soda. The chain of lakes, a World Heritage site covering around 320 sq km (124 sq miles), is of major importance as a habitat for numerous species of animals. In almost no other region around the world do so many different species of birds live in so small a habitat. So far, more than 450 species have been counted on the waters, including 13 endangered species. Another unique feature are the huge flocks of pink and lesser flamingos, each comprising several million birds. Nearly 75 per cent of the world population of lesser flamingos are at home on the lakes. The flamingos feed on small crustaceans and cyanobacteria (blue-green algae), which thrive in the shallow alkaline waters. Moreover, countless pink pelicans fish in Lakes Nakuru and Elementaita for tilapia. More than a hundred species of migratory birds, including many from Central Europe, use the lakes as wintering grounds or as a resting place on their long journeys to their summering or wintering areas.

Hot springs and geysers characterize Lake Bogoria (large picture top), which is famous for its flamingo colonies. Bottom: buffalo in the gathering storm.

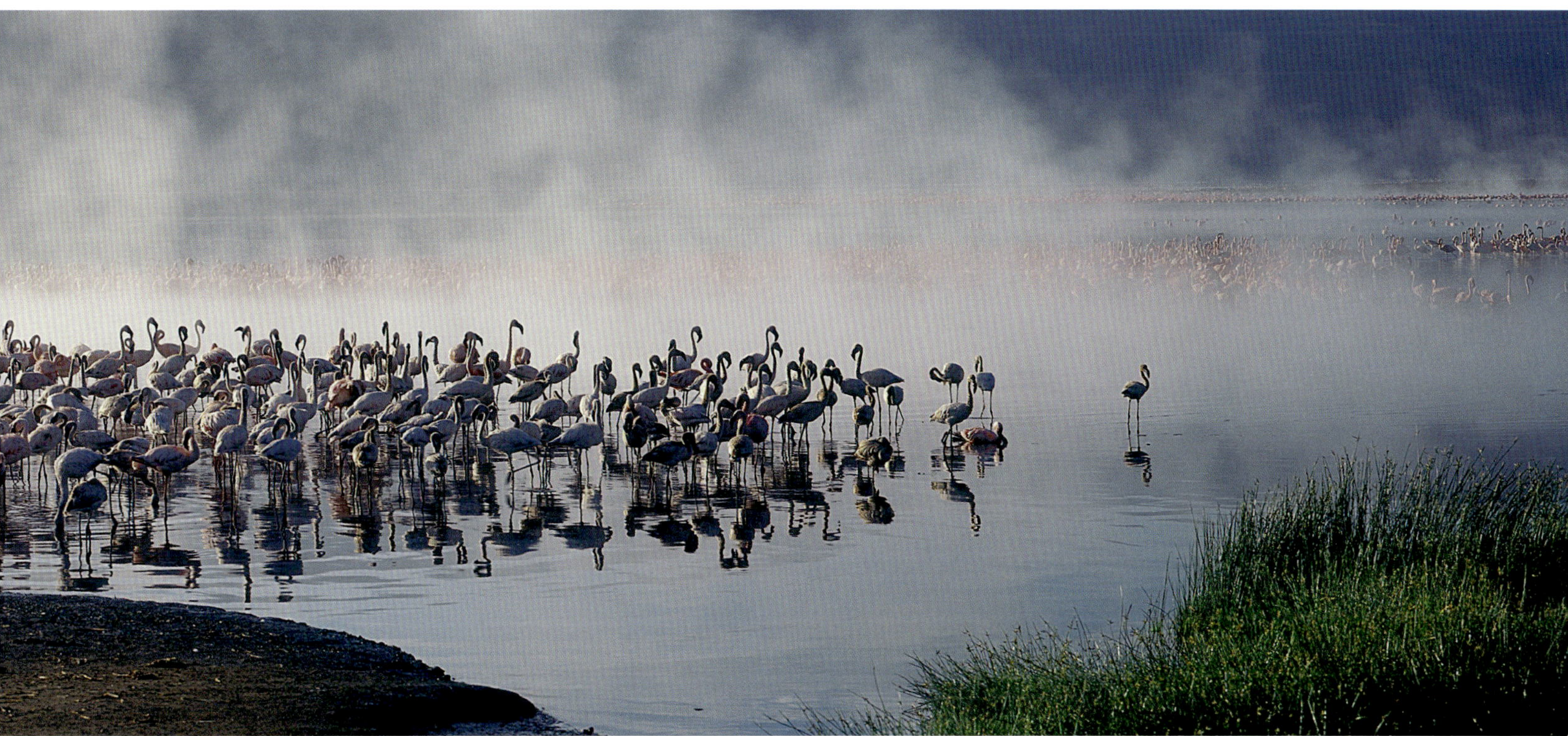

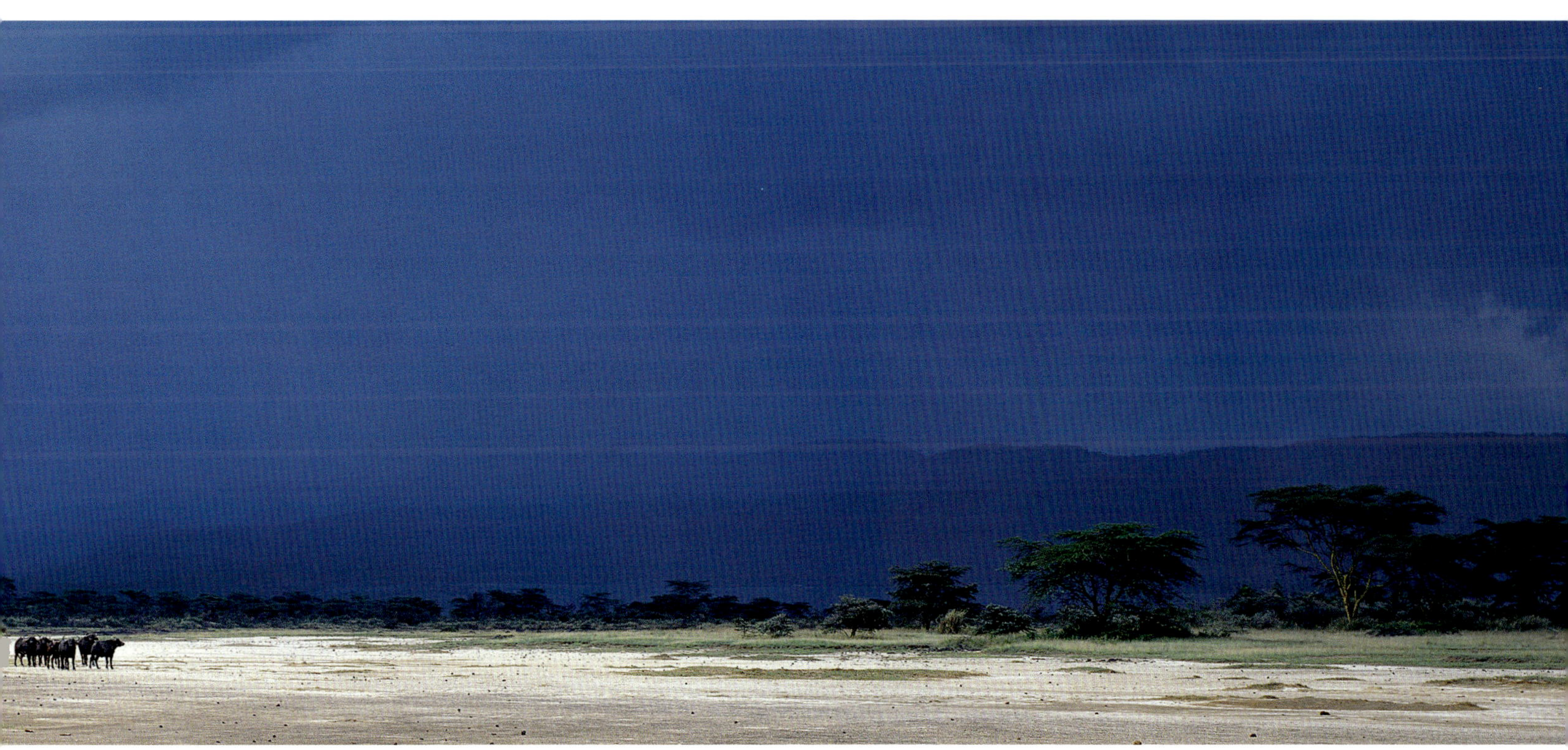

SERENGETI NATIONAL PARK

Date of inscription: 1981

The Serengeti is a giant area of savannah, east of Lake Victoria, stretching from north-west Tanzania into neighbouring Kenya. Approximately 15,000 sq. km (5,800 sq. miles) of Tanzanian territory was turned over to the national park.

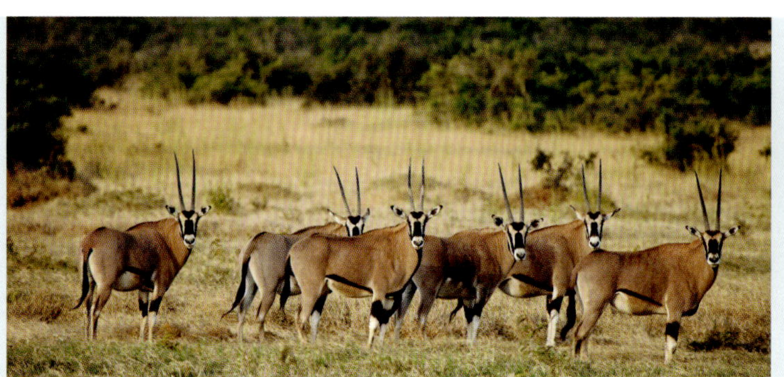

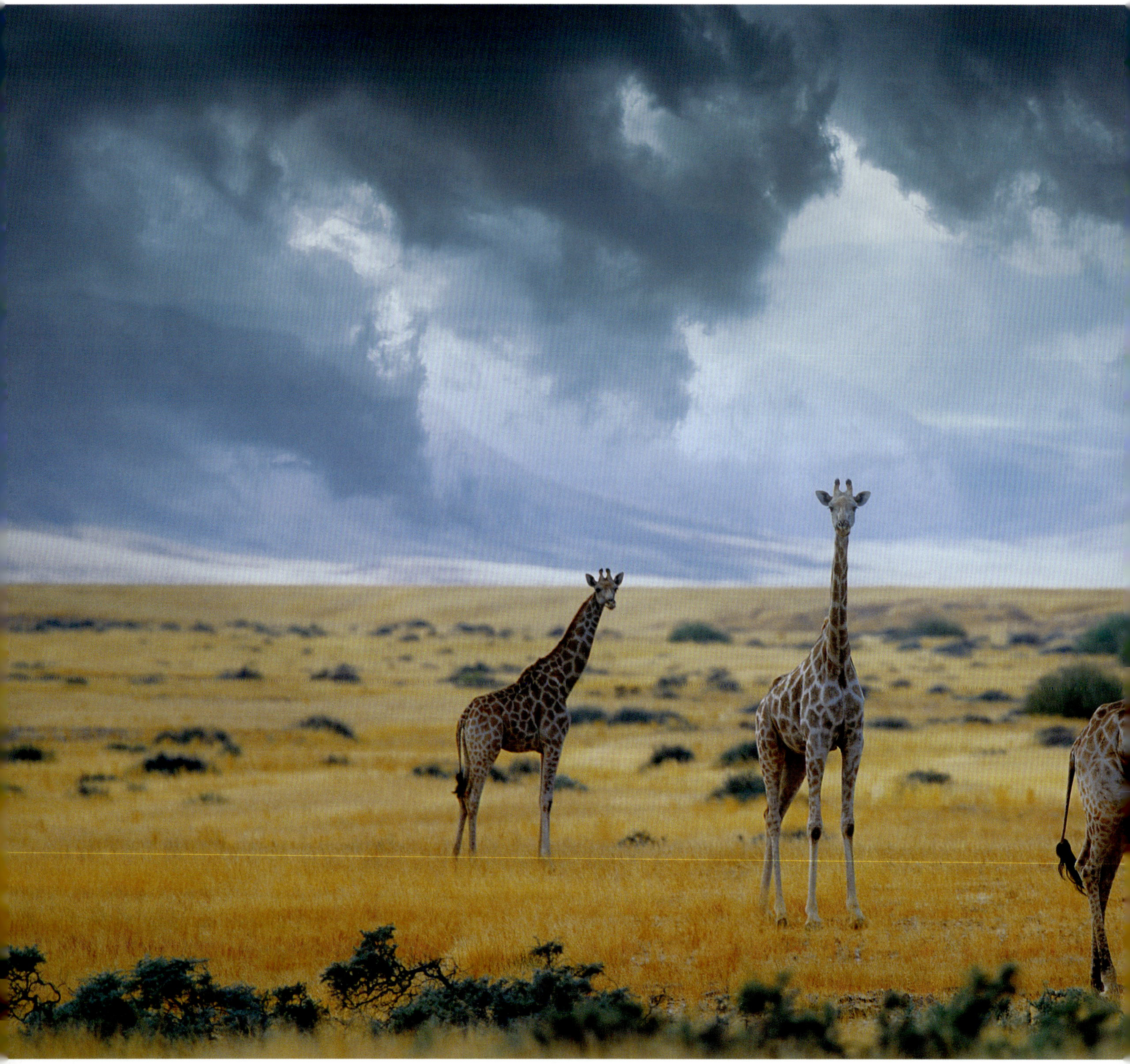

The scene is every year of extensive migration: mighty herds of more than two million Boehm's zebra, white-bearded wildebeest, and Thomson's gazelle roam the grassland and savannah of the Serengeti in search of food and water, often covering distances of up to 1,500 km (930 miles). Overcoming great hardship, these animals always follow the same routes, which are governed by the alternation of the dry and rainy seasons. Their natural enemies are hot on their trail: lions, leopards, cheetahs, and hyenas. Hardly anything else on earth portrays the struggle for life – eat or be eaten – on such an imposing scale as this mass animal migration on the Serengeti. This area, among the world's richest in terms of animal life, is also home to giraffes, Cape buffaloes, topi and kongoni antelopes, elands, hippos, rhinos, hyenas, African wild dogs, patas monkeys, aardwolfs, crocodiles, emus, and elephants. These last are not indigenous, but were introduced in 1957. Over the millennia, a biosphere for very diverse species has developed. All this changed with the arrival of Europeans at the end of the 19th century. Big game hunters dealt the animal world a blow from which it may never fully recover. The Serengeti was placed under partial protection as early as 1921 and under full protection in 1929. The national park was inscribed in 1951.

The elegantly patterned oryx antelopes (left), giraffes (large picture), cheetahs and zebras (below) are all at home in the vast plains of the Serengeti. When a storm approaches, the quiet scenery changes dramatically.

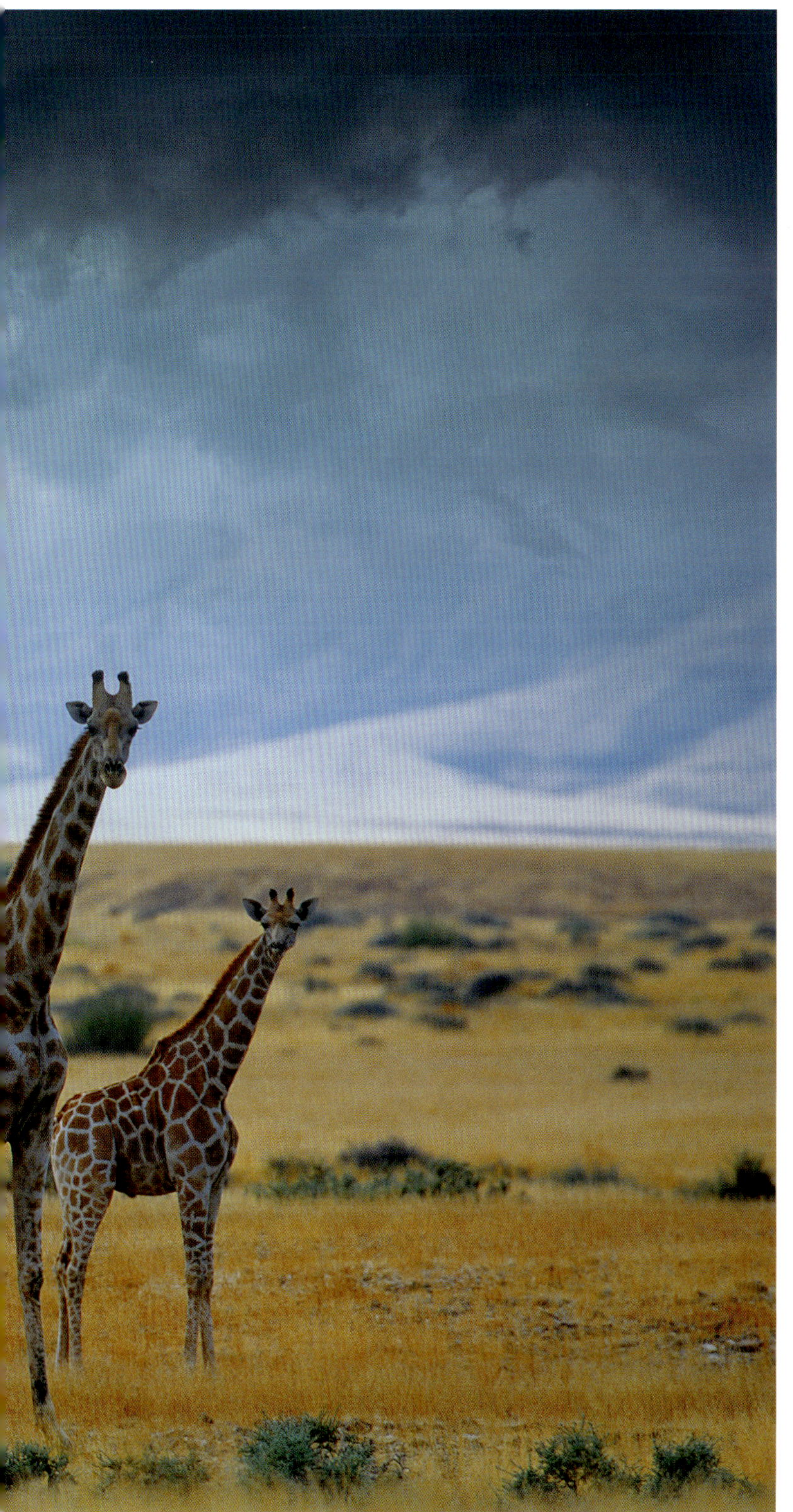

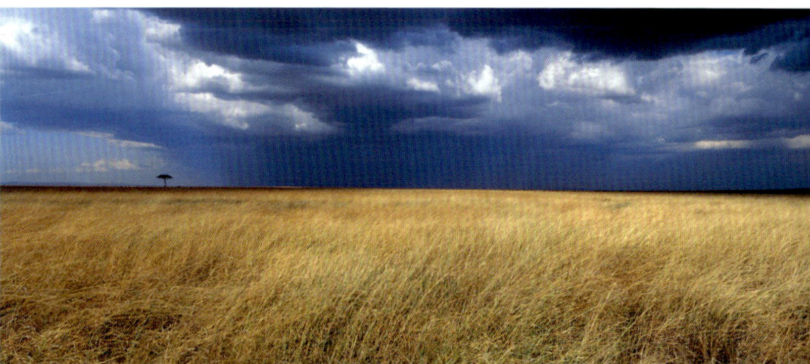

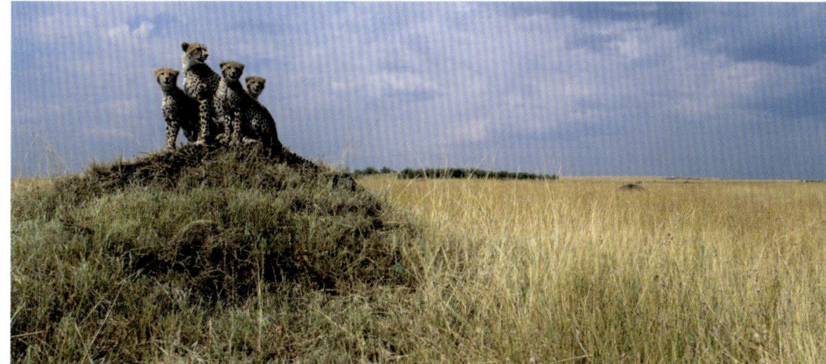

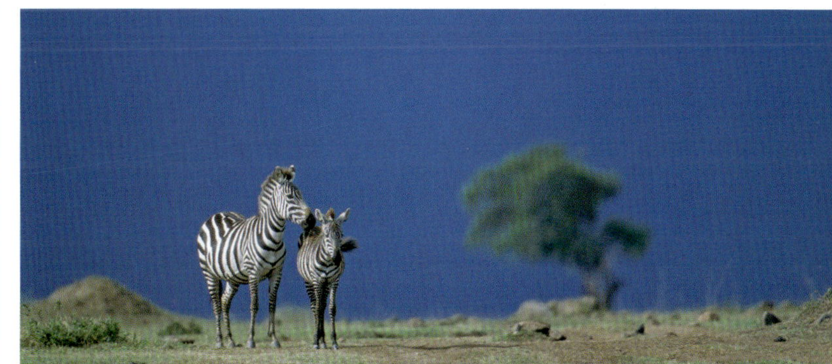

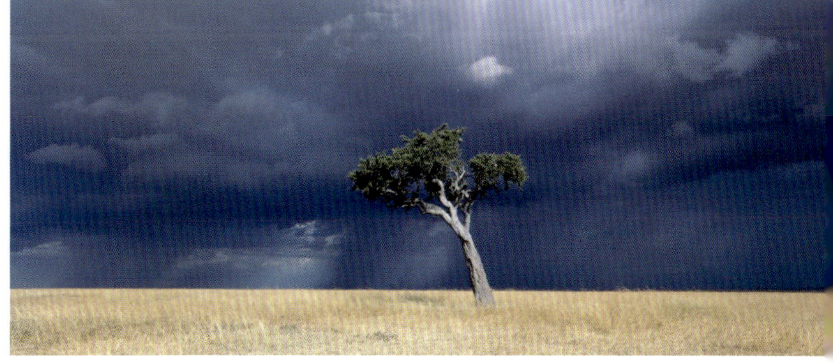

NGORONGORO CONSERVATION AREA

Date of inscription: 1979
Extended: 2010

The conservation area covers 8,000 sq. km (3,000 sq. miles) of the floor of the Ngorongoro crater in north Tanzania. Its imposing scenery is roamed by thousands of wild species.

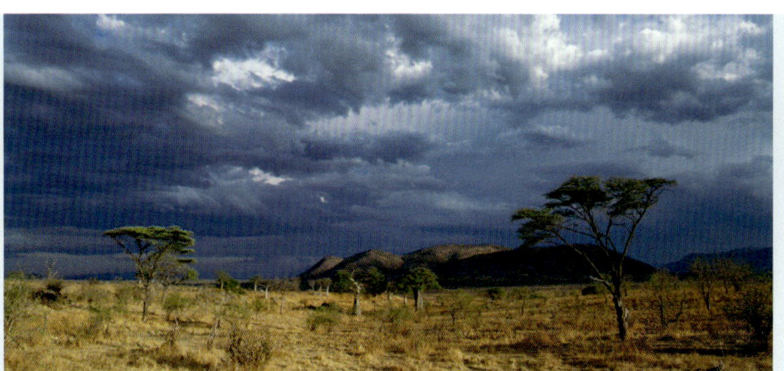

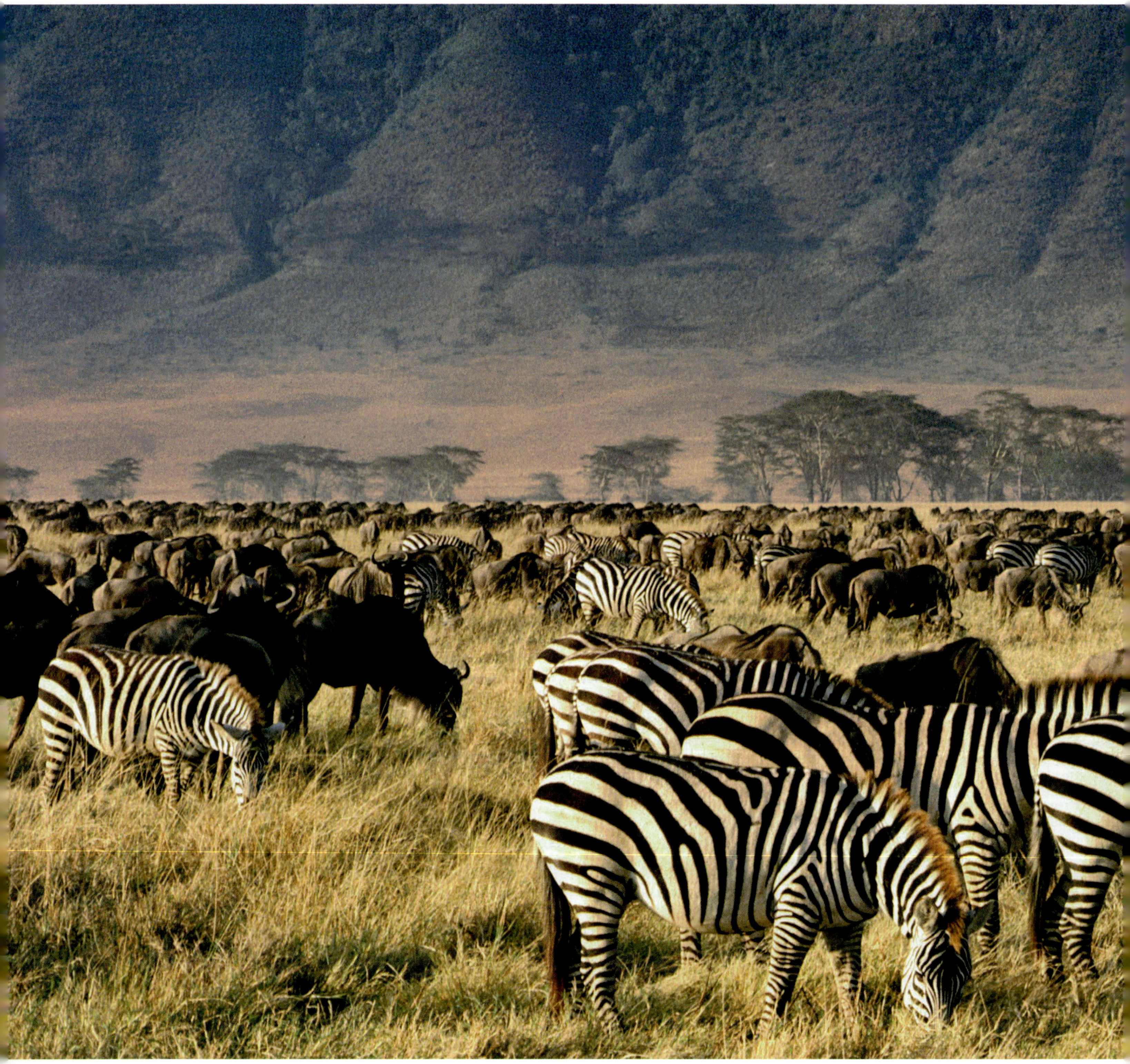

The Ngorongoro crater area was for a long time part of the Serengeti National Park, only becoming an independent conservation area in 1974. The newly established park included the Empakaai crater with its freshwater lake, as well as the active volcano, Oldonyo, Olduvai Gorge, and the Laetoli site, where fossilized remains of early ancestors of Homo habilis (early ancestors of Homo sapiens sapiens) have been found. Between the savannah and steppes of the giant Ngorongoro crater, a habitat for numerous species of wildlife, lie areas of marsh and acacia forests. The crater floor, which is largely covered in grassland, serves as pasture for the Masai's herds, and has become massively overgrazed due to the extent of this tribe's traditional pastoralism.

The indigenous wildlife of the Ngorongoro area consists principally of wildebeest, gazelles, eland, waterbucks, and zebras. Elephants, hippos, black rhinos, lions, hyenas, and leopards complete this cross-section of Africa's wealth of fauna.

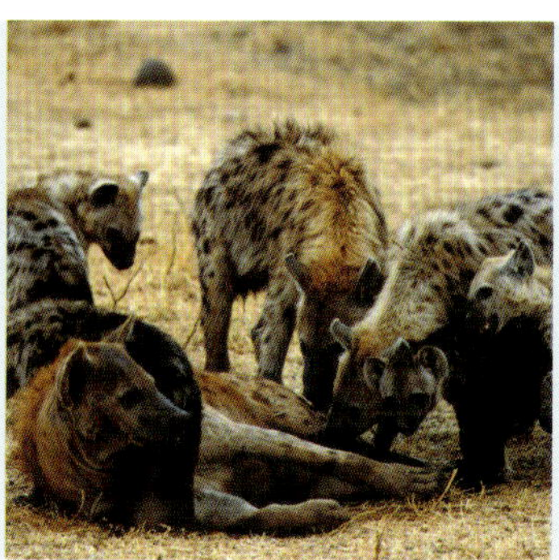

Thousands of wildebeest and zebras graze on the expansive grass plains of the Ngorongoro crater (large image). This pack of hyenas is among the 25,000 wild creatures in the crater (left).

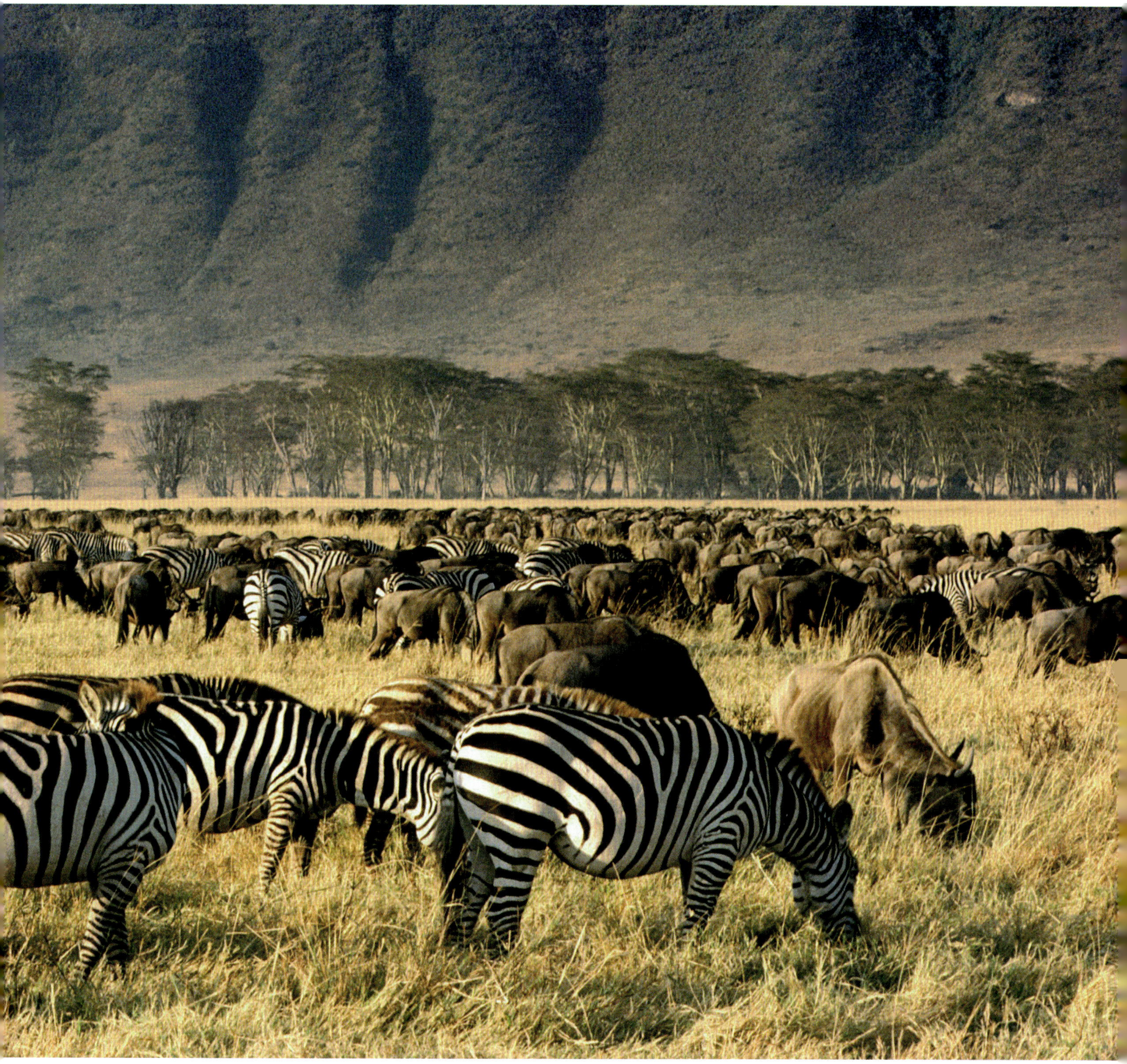

KILIMANJARO NATIONAL PARK

Date of inscription: 1987

In north Tanzania, on the Kenyan border, the savannah is startlingly interrupted by the volcanic massif of Kilimanjaro. Approximately 750 sq. km (295 sq. miles) of the upper slopes of the mountain were enclosed as a national park to protect its unique montane forest.

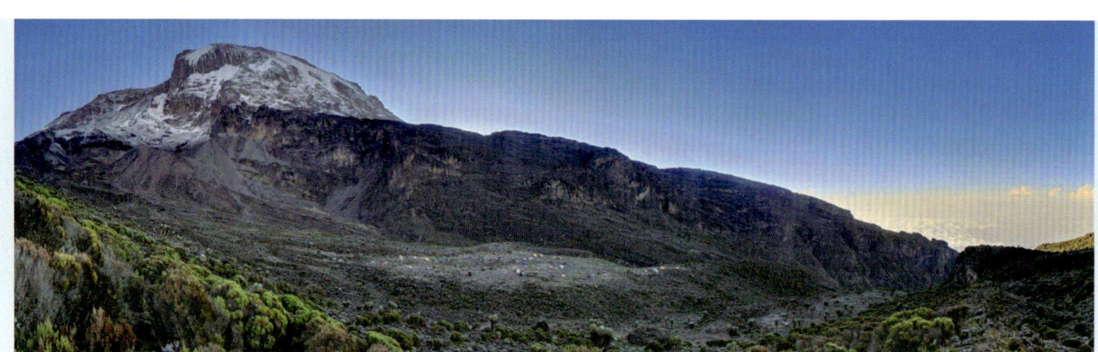

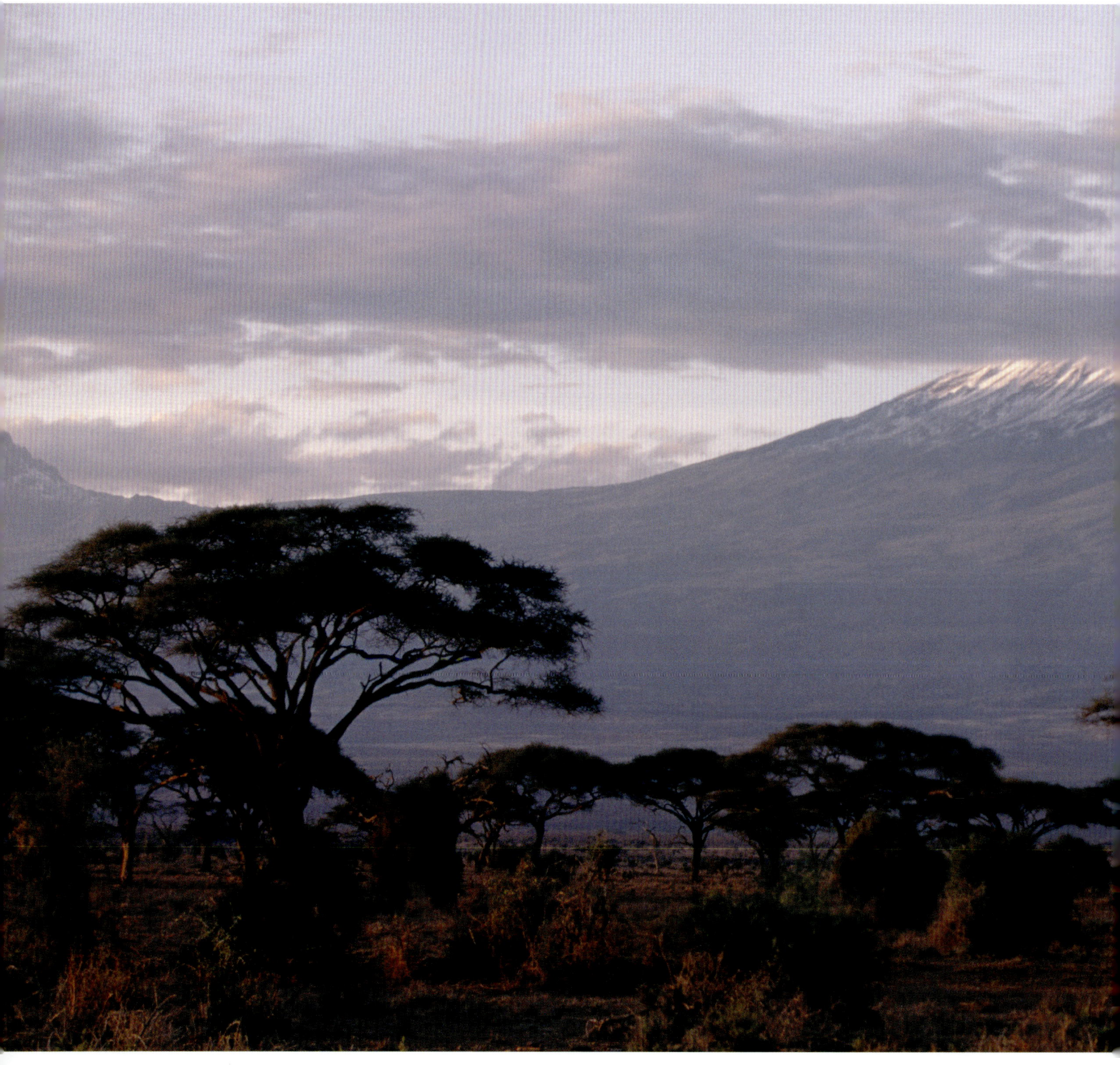

Kilimanjaro is composed of three main volcanic cones and numerous smaller summits of volcanic origin. To the west lies the 4,000-m (13,200-foot) high Shira; in the middle is Kibo, at 5,895 m (19,340 feet) the highest point in Africa; and to the east lies Mawenzi, the smallest at 5,270 m (17,290 feet). The other crests form a chain running south-east to north-west. Although not far from the equator, Kilimanjaro's peaks are always covered in snow.

This massif in the middle of the savannah enjoys extremely diverse climatic areas and zones of vegetation. Above the savannah there is a region of cultivated land, once covered in a forest savannah, which is now found only on the northern slopes. This zone merges into a deciduous montane forest which rises to 3,000 m (9,900 feet). This is followed by expansive grassy uplands, and these in turn are replaced by the cold desert of the summit region. The national park is home to many animal species, including some that are endangered, including gazelles, rhinos, Cape buffaloes, elephants, and leopards.

A mountain route goes from the Barranco Camp via a steep rise to the Great Barranco Wall (left), also known as Breakfast Wall, at an altitude of 4,300 m (14,110 feet). From there you have a fantastic view of the Kibo. Large picture: Mount Kilimanjaro in a soft morning light.

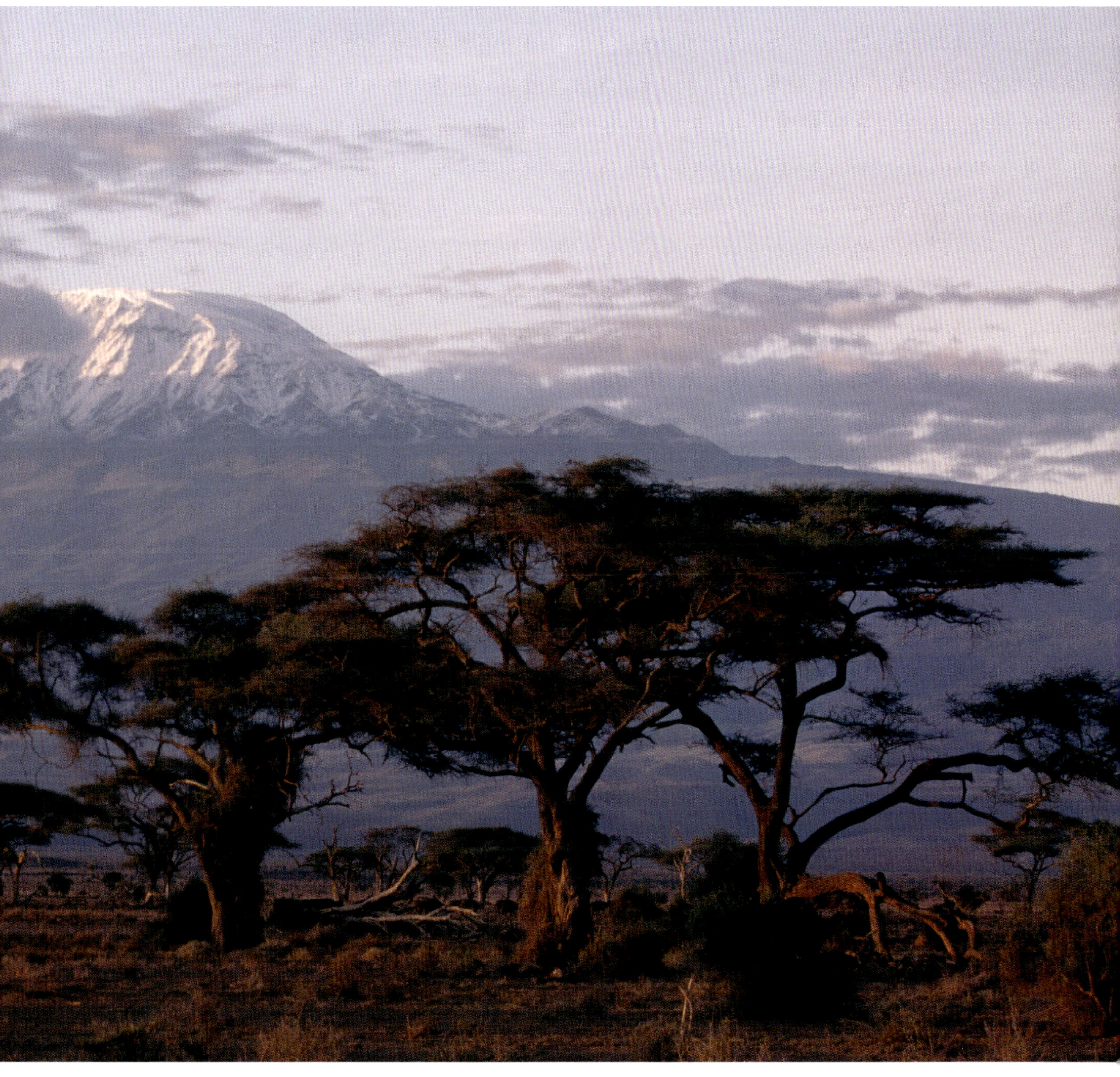

SELOUS GAME RESERVE

Date of inscription: 1982

In south-east Tanzania, Africa's largest game reserve is home to about a million animals, including, among many others, representatives of the "big five" – elephant, rhino, buffalo, lion, and leopard.

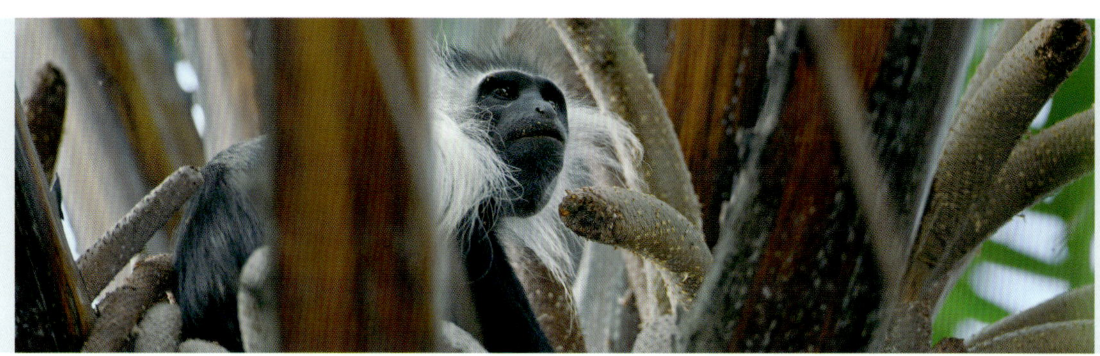

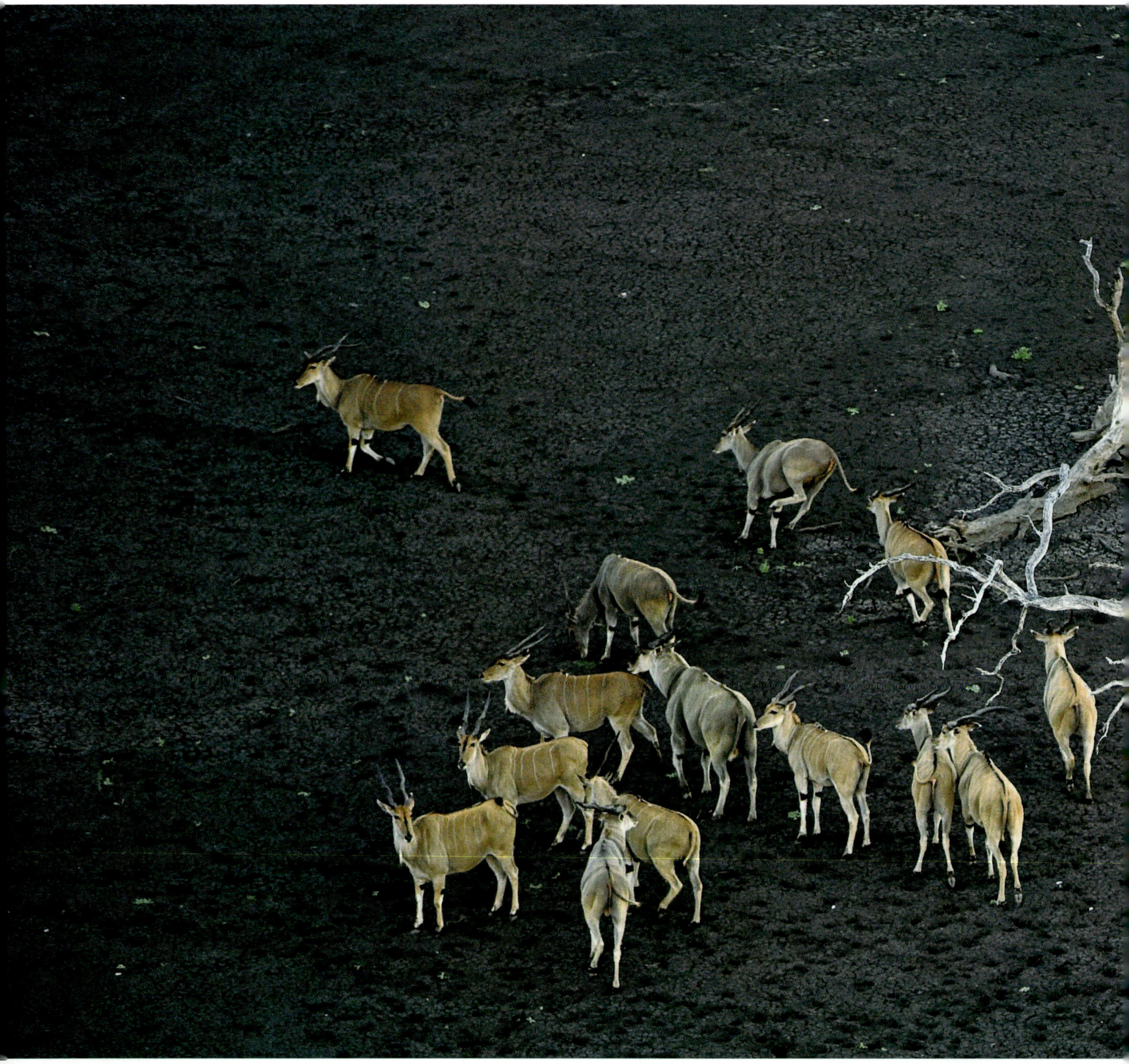

The Rufiji river, one of the largest in east Africa, and its many tributaries flow through the Selous Game Reserve, whose 50,000 sq. km (19,400 sq. miles) were declared a conservation area at the beginning of the 20th century. Approximately 200 km (124 miles) from Dar es Salaam, the area is largely avoided by humans because of the presence of tsetse flies, and thus provides a largely undisturbed habitat for a variety of wildlife. More than 150,000 wildebeest, 100,000 elephants, 150,000 buffaloes, 50,000 antelopes and zebras respectively, and approximately 20,000 hippos have been recorded. The world's largest crocodile population also lives here, and the various vegetation zones of the reserve are host to a considerable number of big cats, including cheetahs, leopards, and lions, as well as numerous giraffes.

These zones encompass steppes, savannah, lightly forested grassland, and the thick undergrowth of the gallery forest on the banks of the Rufiji and its sources, the Luwegu and the Kilombero. Miombo forest dominates the landscape.

Numerous herds of animals can be found near the many watering holes. Large picture: Eland antelopes congregate on the shores of Lake Nzerakera. Angola colobus also live here (left).

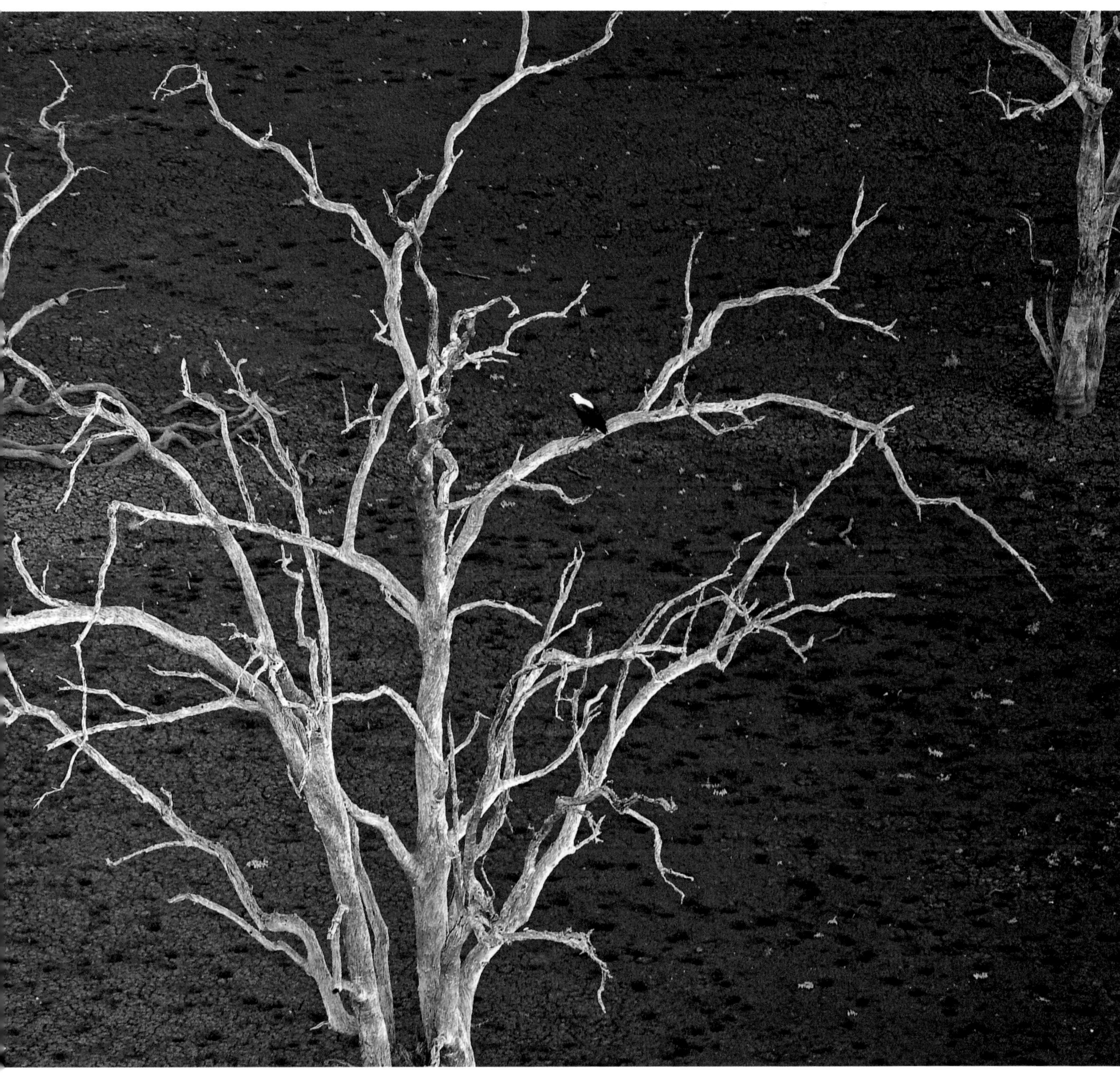

VICTORIA FALLS (MOSI-OA-TUNYA)

Date of inscription: 1989

The Victoria Falls are among the most spectacular in the world; the waters of the Zambezi plummet from a series of basalt cliffs into a chasm over 100 m (330 feet) deep.

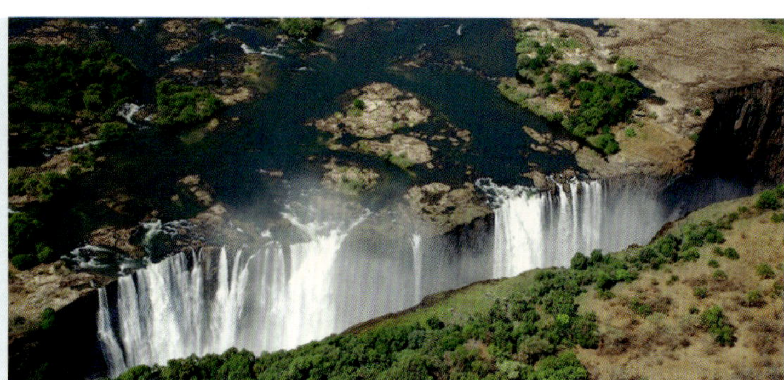

The first intimation of the presence of the gigantic Victoria Falls is visible at a distance of about 20 km (13 miles), in the form of a cloud of spray rising 300 m (990 feet) into the air. With a deafening roar, the Zambezi, the natural border between Zambia and Zimbabwe, plunges 100 m (330 feet) into the depths, making this a truly international World Heritage Site.

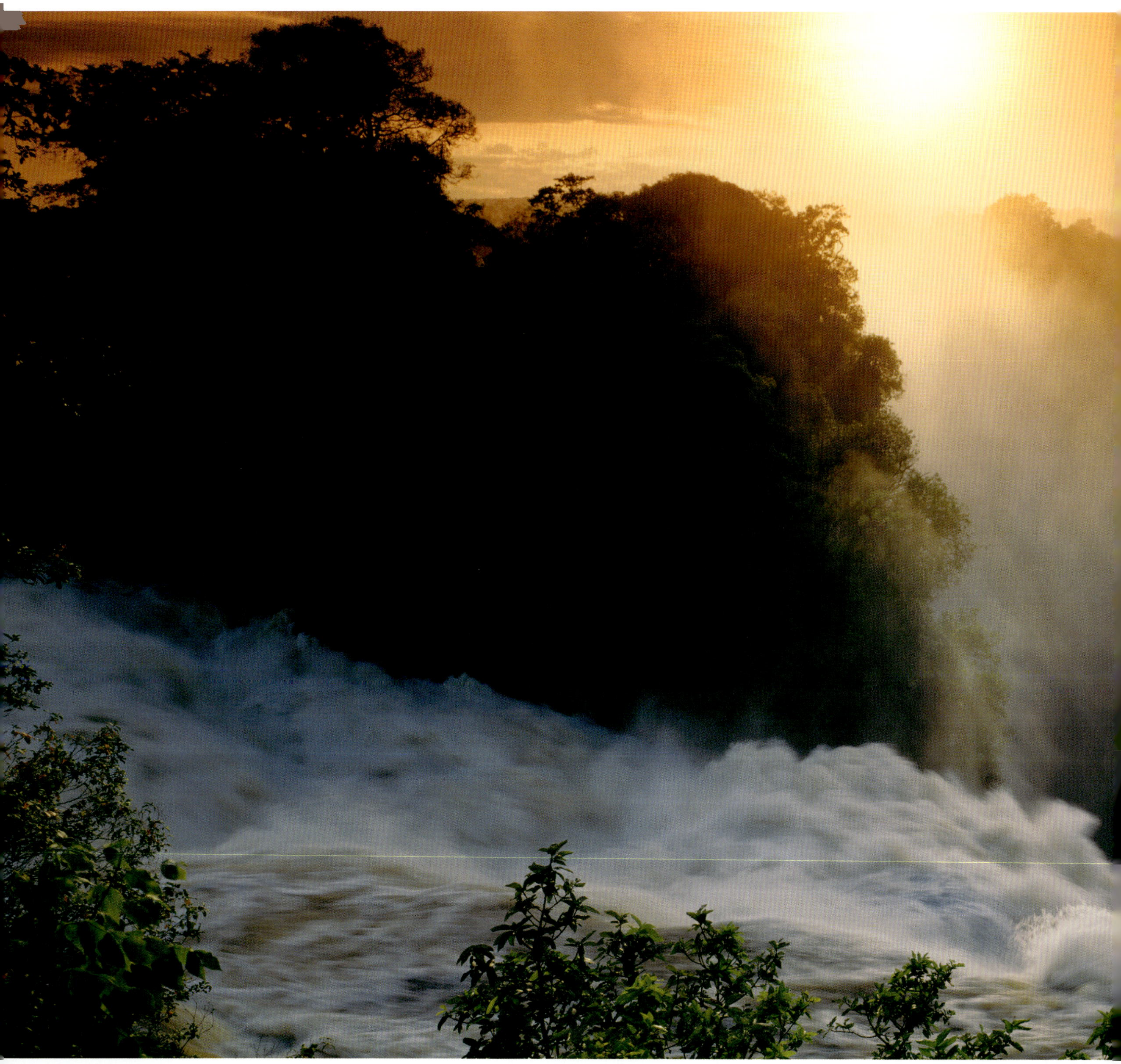

This natural spectacle is echoed in the indigenous name for the five falls: Mosi-oa-tunya, meaning "the smoke that thunders." At high water in March and April the falls become a continuous curtain of water, almost 2 km (1.5 miles) wide, depositing 10,000 cu. m (353,000 cu. feet) of water per second into the gorge. During the rest of the year's dry season, the individual falls, of which the Rainbow Falls are the highest, separate out again. The area surrounding the falls is home to some 30 mammal, 65 reptile, and 21 amphibian species.

David Livingstone, the British scientist and missionary, was the first European to discover the Victoria Falls (1855), naming them after the reigning queen of England.

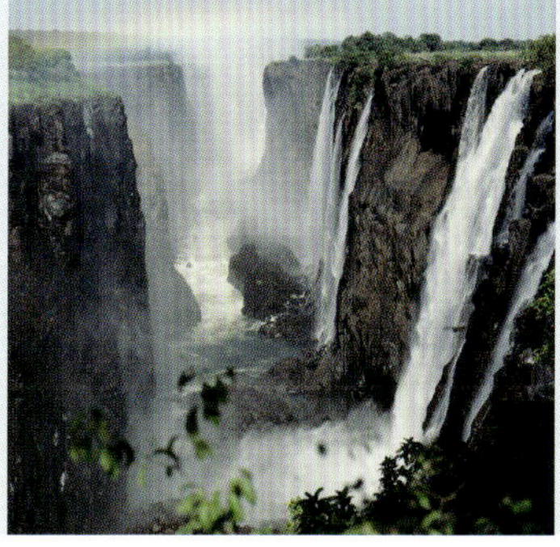

The deep gorge into which the Zambezi drops at the Victoria Falls was cut by the river itself during the course of millions of years (below and left). Even today the water continues to erode the stone and the Victoria Falls are "moving."

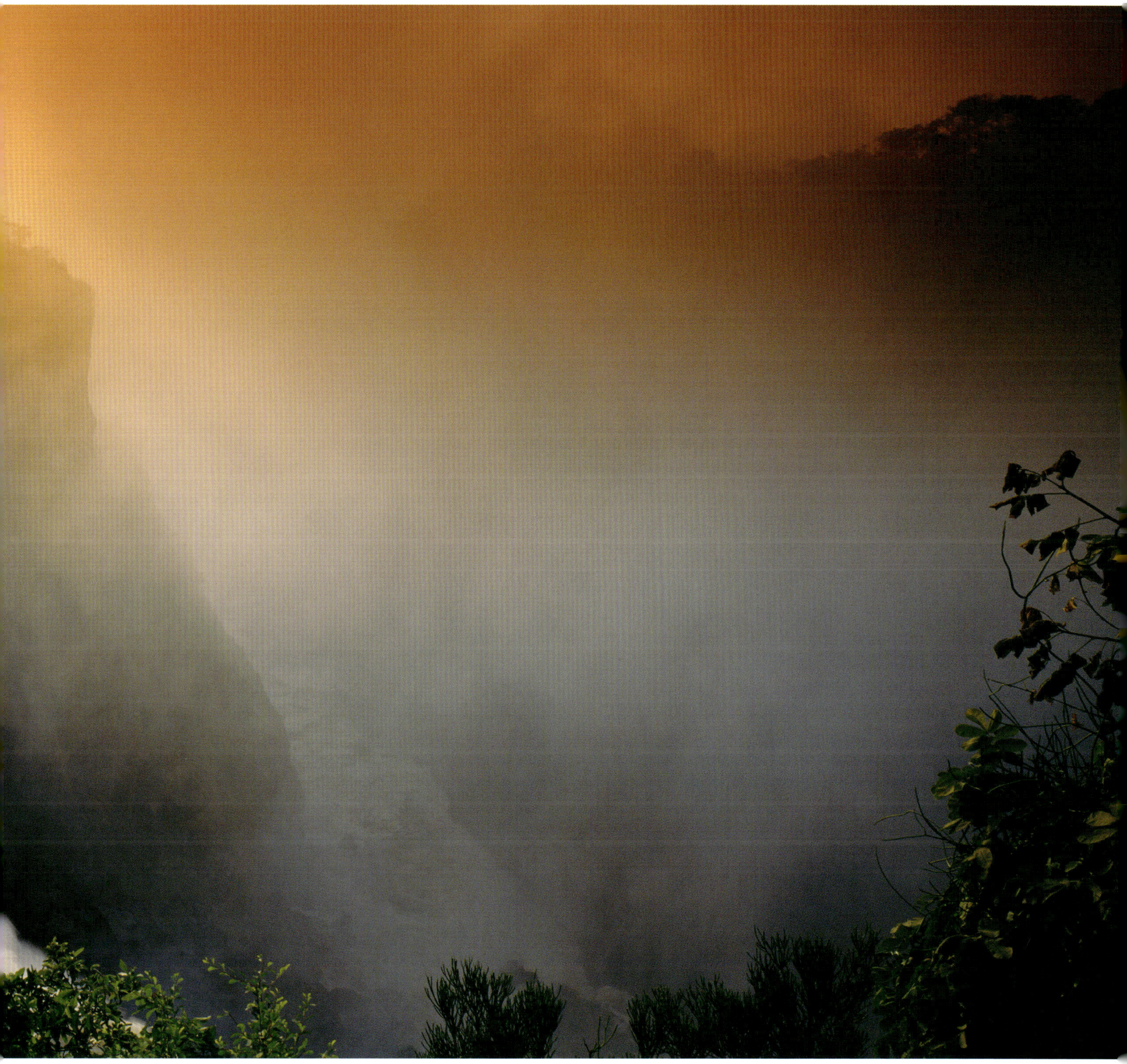

MANA POOLS NATIONAL PARK

Date of inscription: 1984

Situated on the southern banks of the Zambezi river, this national park, and its associated safari areas of Sapi and Chewori, is a paradise for animals.

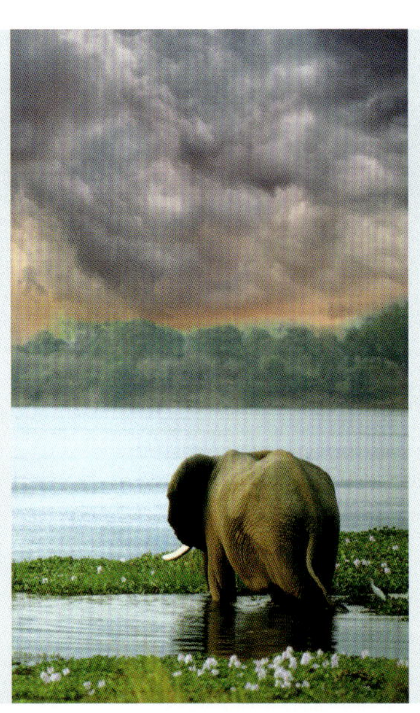

Mana Pools was inscribed as a national park in 1963, and a year later the neighboring safari ranges of Sapi and Chewore were also placed under protection. Situated at the meeting-place of the Zimbabwean, Zambian, and Mozambican borders, these three areas together cover an area of about 7,000 sq. km (2,600 sq. miles), of which Chewore makes up about half. The Zambezi river forms the park's natural border to the north. The river regularly floods the grasslands and forests of the conservation area, and "Mana Pools" refers to the four permanent pools thus created. This fertile landscape is home to a variety of animals. About 400 bird species live in the forests, thousands of elephants roam the plains, and herds of buffalo and zebra offer rich prey for predators such as leopards and cheetahs. The Chewori Safari Area has recently become home to one of the largest populations of the giant white rhinoceros. Hippos and a large number of the otherwise endangered Nile crocodile roam the peaceful waters and banks of the Zambezi.

The yellow-billed stork (large picture) is a species of stork. During the rainy season, when the Zambezi and its tributaries burst their banks, many animals, including elephants, take full advantage of the freely available waters (left).

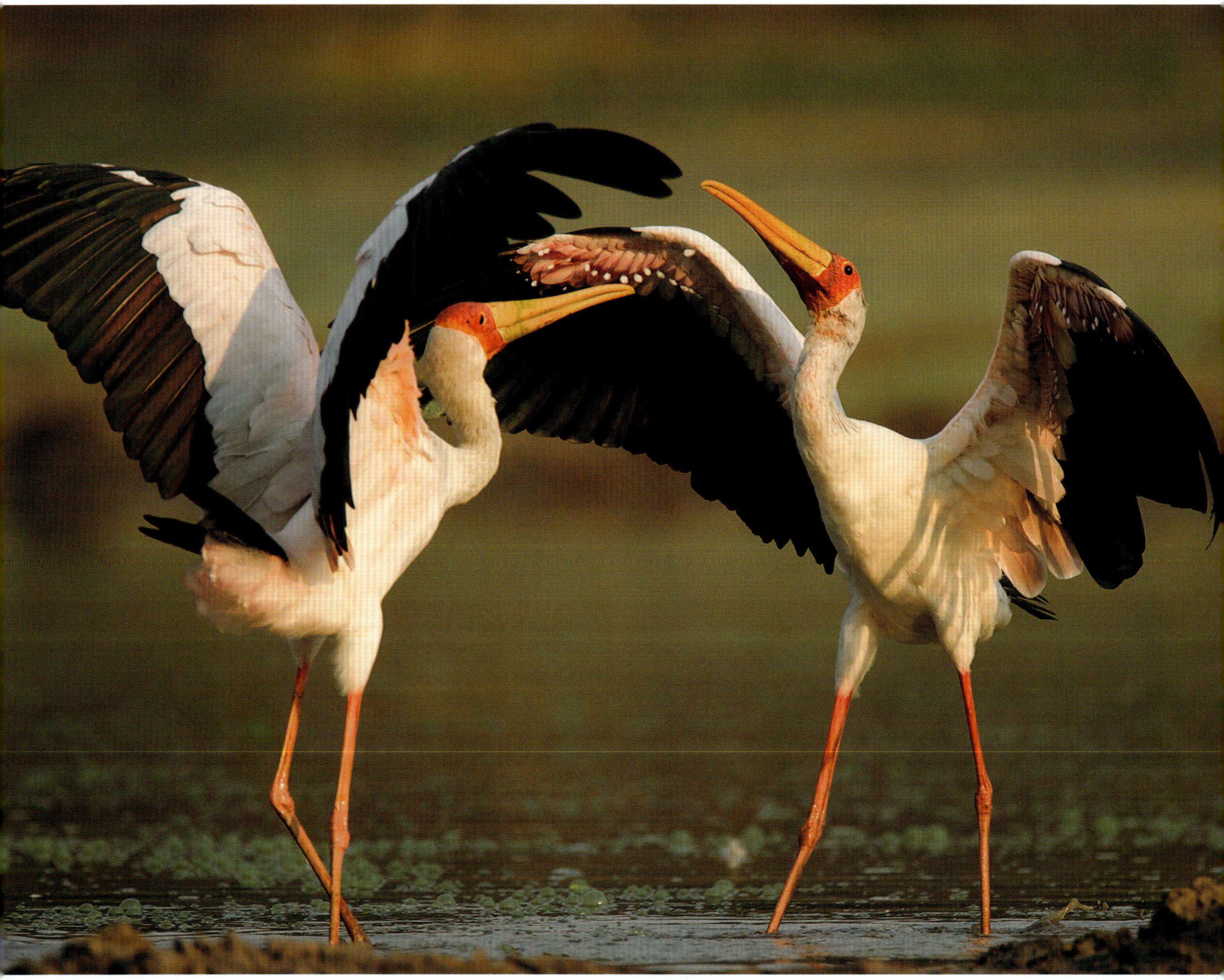

LAKE MALAWI NATIONAL PARK

As early as 1616, the Portuguese explorer, Gaspar Boccaro, had reported the existence of a great body of water in south-east Africa, and in 1859 the British missionary, David Livingstone, reached the shores of what he called Lake Nyasa, now known as Lake Malawi. The lake is fed by 14 tributary rivers. The largest are the Ruhuhu and its only headstream, the Shire, a tributary of the Zambezi, which crosses the south of Malawi. Today, three states – Tanzania, Mozambique, and Malawi – border the lake, which is 500 km (310 miles) long and 50 km (31 miles) wide. This unique national park was established in 1980 at the southern end of the lake, on Malawian territory. Its 100 sq. km (39 sq. miles) include the Cape Maclear peninsula, three separate sections of shoreline, 12 islands, and part of the lake nearest the shore. In the clear waters of the lake, more than 200 species of fish have developed, of which 80 percent are endemic. The reason for this concentration of unique species is the natural barrier to the species of the Zambezi formed by the Kablega Falls.

Offshore from the Cape Maclear peninsula lies Mumbo Island, which is covered with fig and carob trees (right). Cichlids In the lake shimmer in the most beautiful colors (picture series). Large picture: a night heron on the hunt.

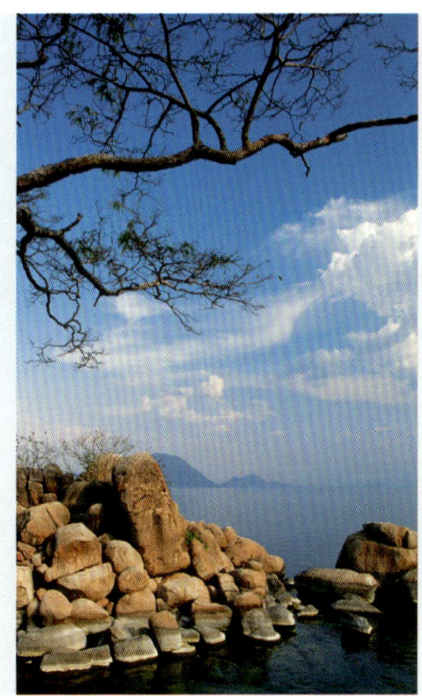

Date of inscription: 1984

Situated at the southern end of the third-largest lake in Africa, the first national park exclusively devoted to the conservation of fish is home to several hundred species of cichlid, of which the majority are indigenous.

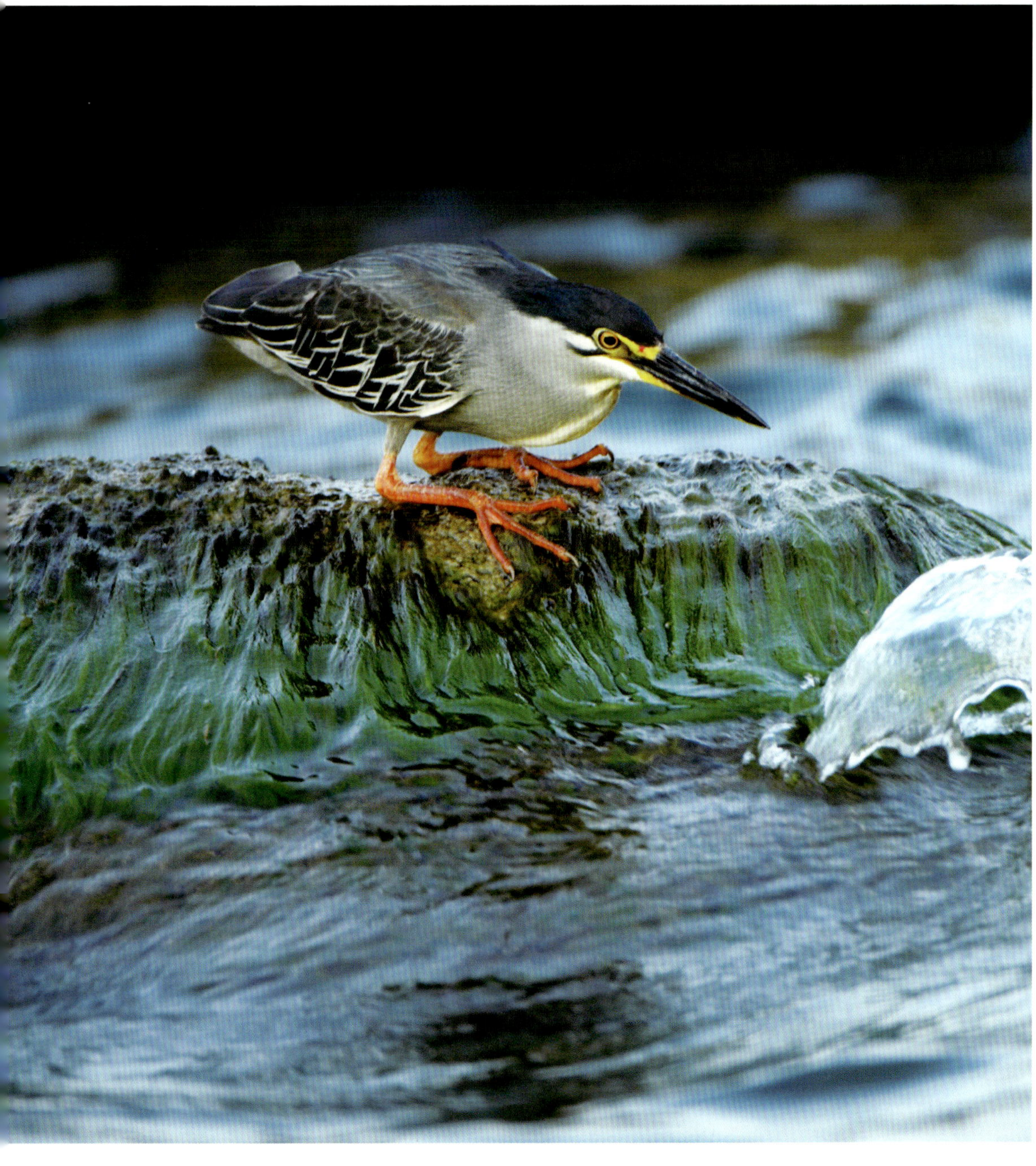

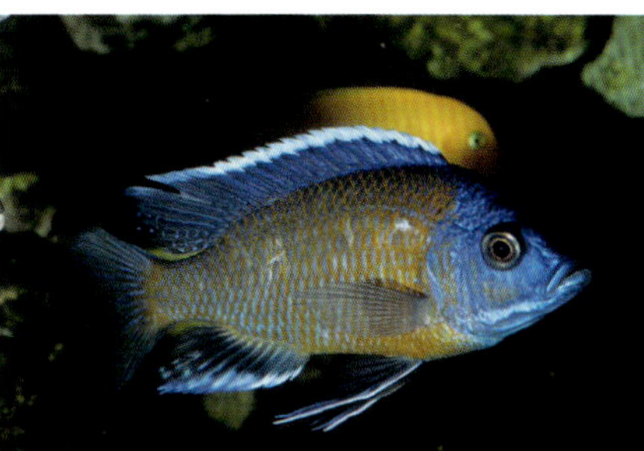

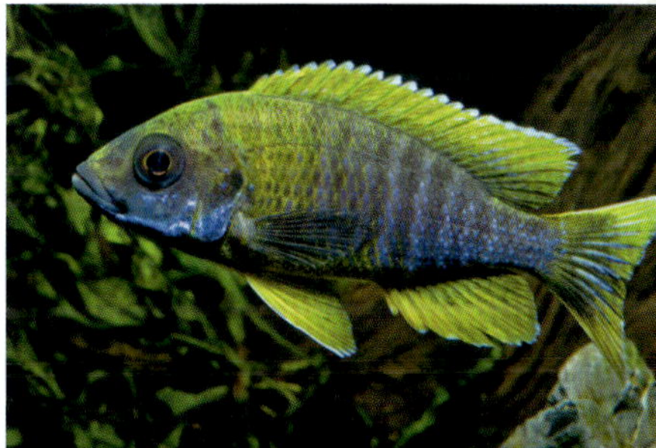

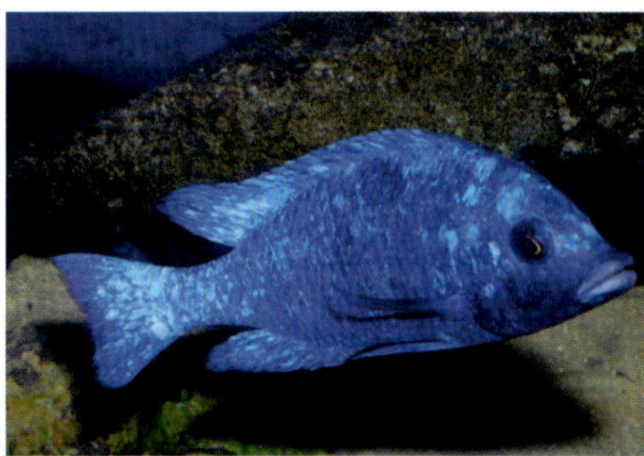

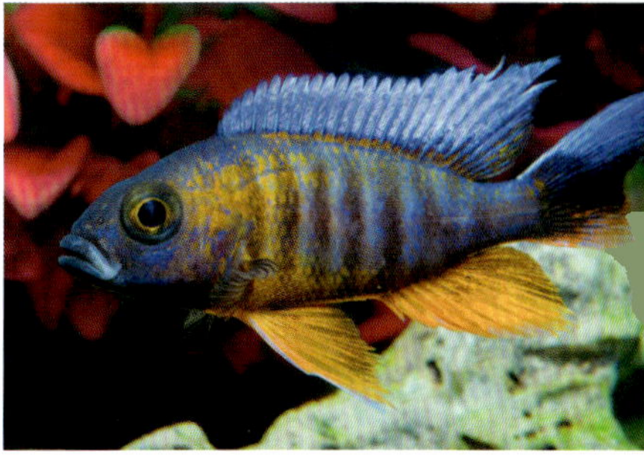

NAMIB DESERT

Date of inscription: 2013

At about 80 million years, the Namib is the oldest desert in the world and one of the most inhospitable regions on the planet. During the day the temperature is about 50°C (122°F), but at night it drops below freezing at times.

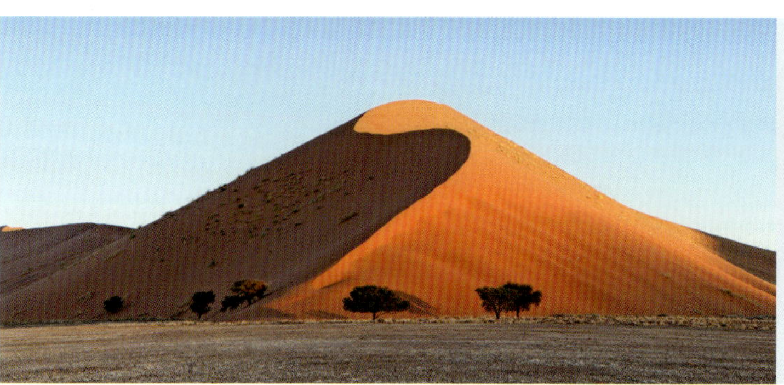

The Namib Desert stretches for 2,000 km (1,243 miles) from southern Angola to northern South Africa. The protected core area, covering around 40,000 sq km (15,444 sq miles), is located in the state of Namibia. It consists of two dune systems: The older one is largely consolidated ("petrified"). On top of this exists a second, much younger system of shifting sand dunes. In the

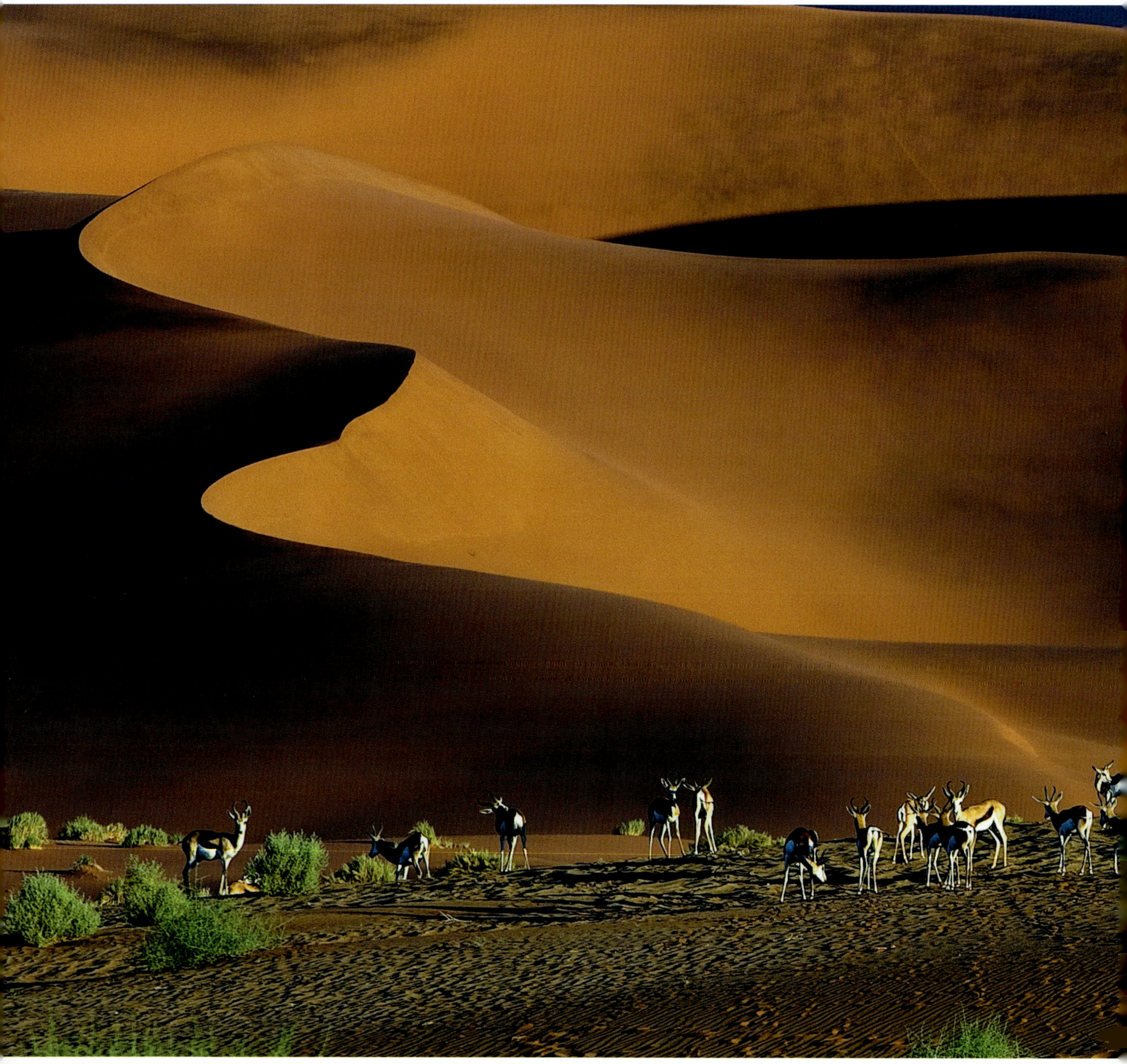

Namib, it may not rain for years; the extreme aridness of the desert is caused by the cold Atlantic Benguela Current, which causes frequent fog but hardly any rainfall. Nevertheless, the desert is home to a surprisingly rich flora and fauna. Some black beetles have become famous: Standing on the dunes, they raise themselves at an angle into the ocean fog. The fog condenses as droplets on their exoskeleton, and the water runs down into their mouths.

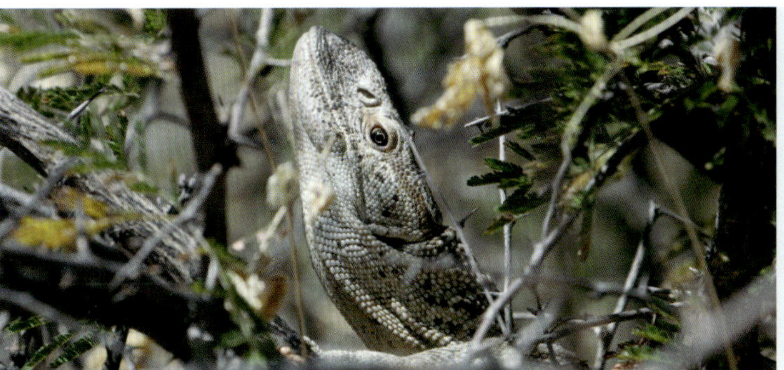

Monitor lizards (left) and springbok (large picture) are among the survivalists in the Namib Desert. The Sossusvlei salt pan is surrounded by the seemingly endless sand dunes of the Namib.

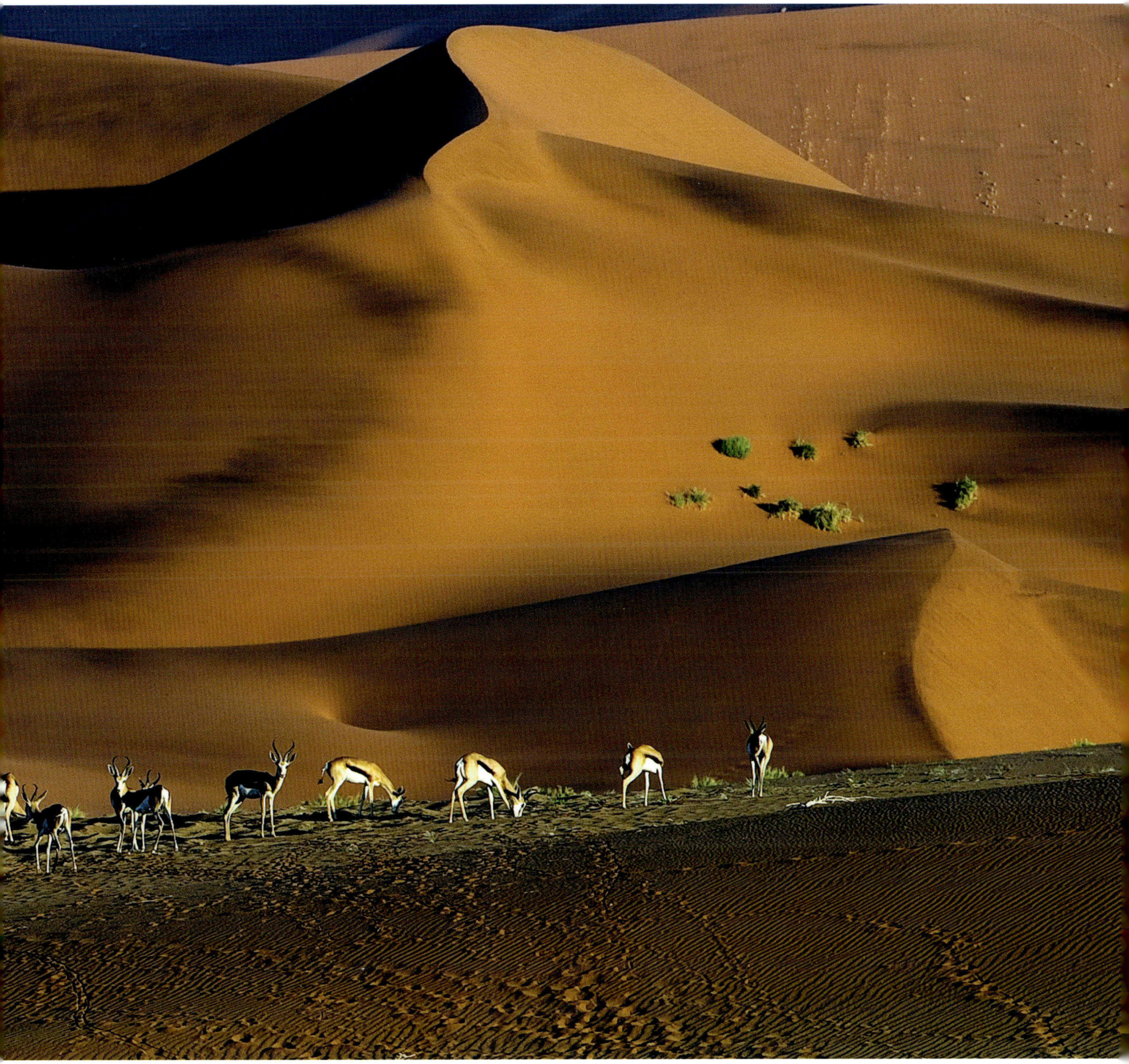

OKAVANGO DELTA

Date of inscription: 2014

The Okavango Delta is a unique natural area in the Kalahari. A large wetland, it provides an ideal haven for wildlife here and in more distant surroundings during the dry season.

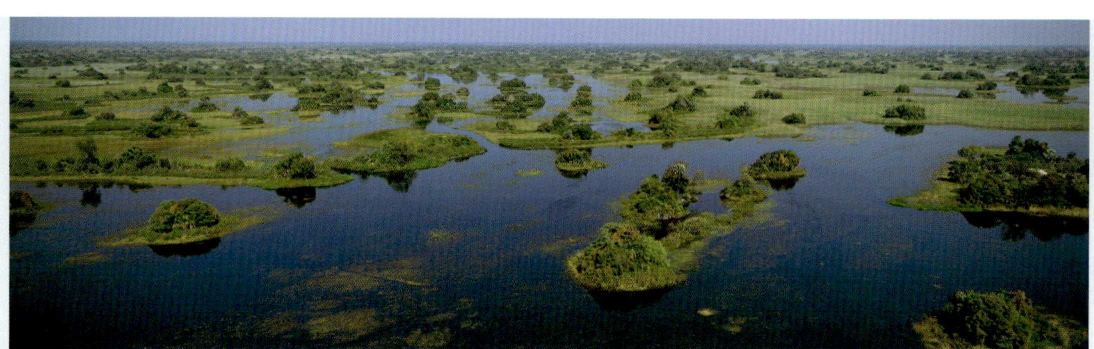

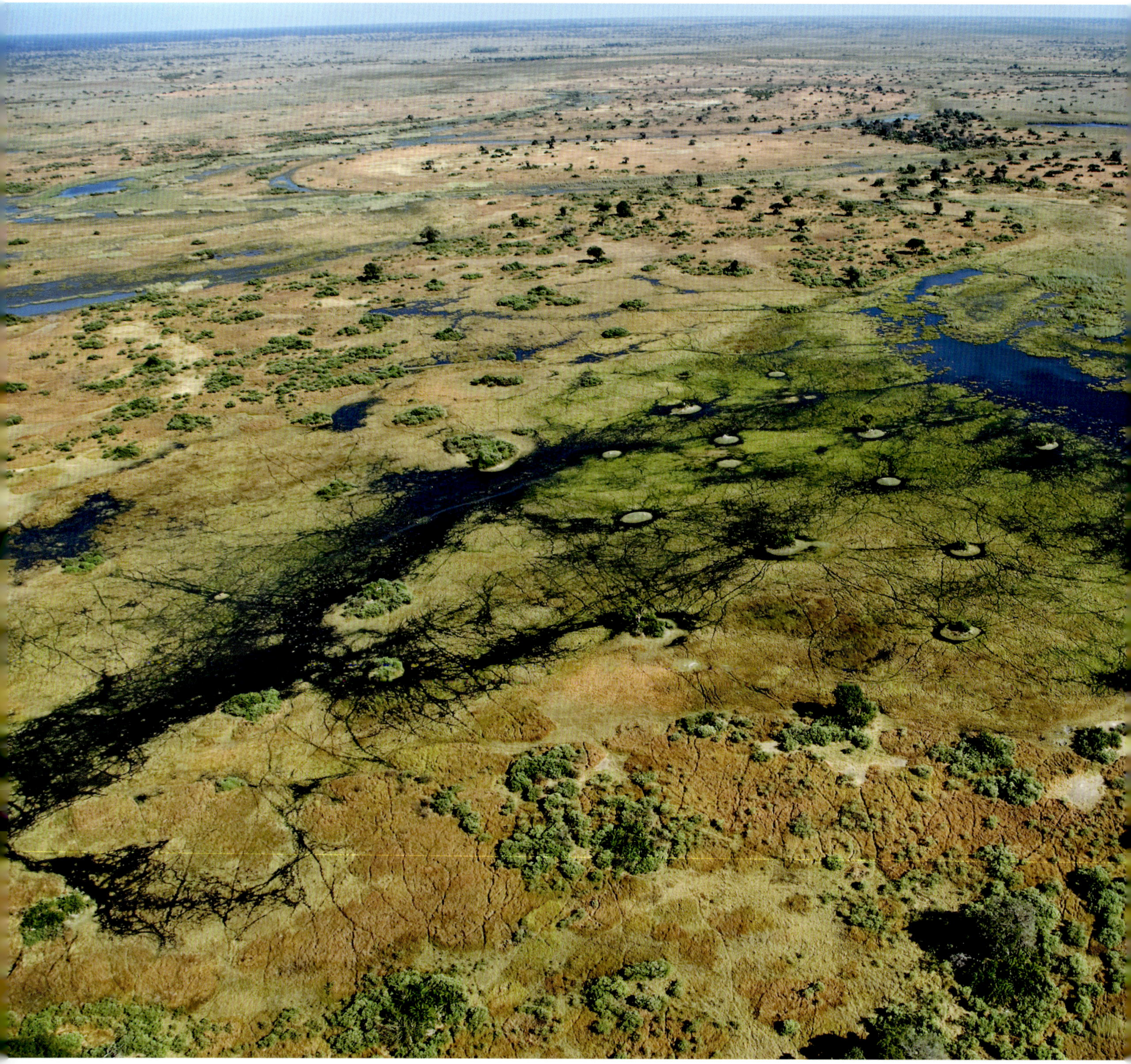

The Okavango Delta is fed by the river of the same name, which has its source in the Angolan highlands. After having traversed Namibia and northern Botswana, it evaporates and drains away in an approximately 16,000 sq km (6,178 sq miles) large inland delta. When the waters reach the Okavango Delta after the rainy season in June, the largely flat landscape, which is dotted by only a few peaks, is flooded. In the process, the high ground is transformed into islands, and the red sands of the Kalahari into a lush green paradise. The river and the marshland that owes its existence to these floods, feed vast herds of zebra, wildebeest, buffalo, antelopes and elephants, pursued by lions, leopards, cheetahs and other predators. Crocodiles and hippos live in the water channels. About 480 species of birds have been counted in this area, as well as 71 fish, 33 amphibian, 64 reptile and 122 mammal species. The delta is a key area for the survival of the world's largest population of elephants, counting around 130,000 animals. In addition, it is home to an amazingly diverse flora.

Given the abundance of precious drinking water in the otherwise semi-arid environment of the Kalahari, it's no wonder that archaeological finds indicate the area was already inhabited by humans more than 100,000 years ago. For white rhinos, giraffes and lions (from the top), the delta is an equally important habitat.

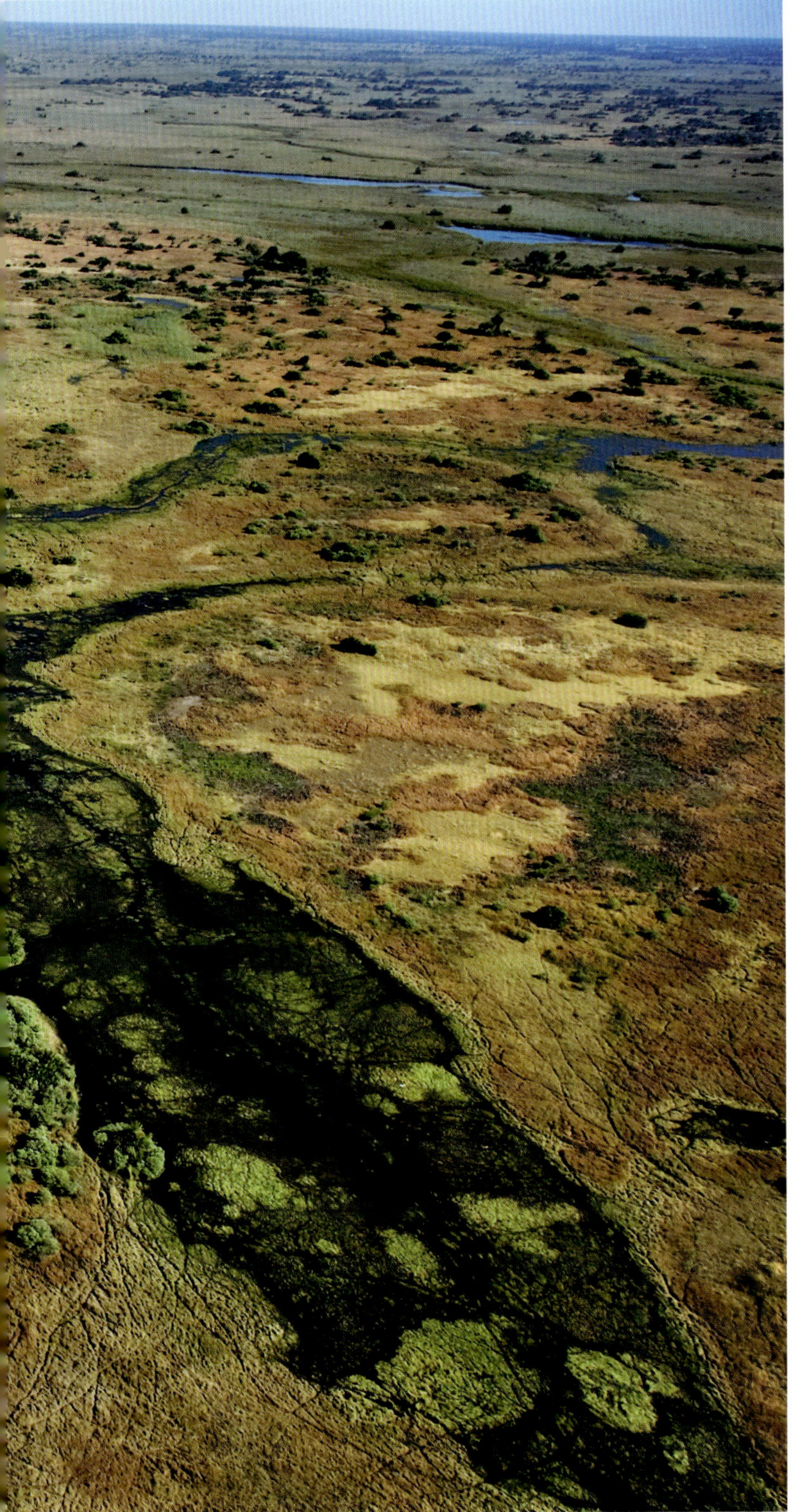

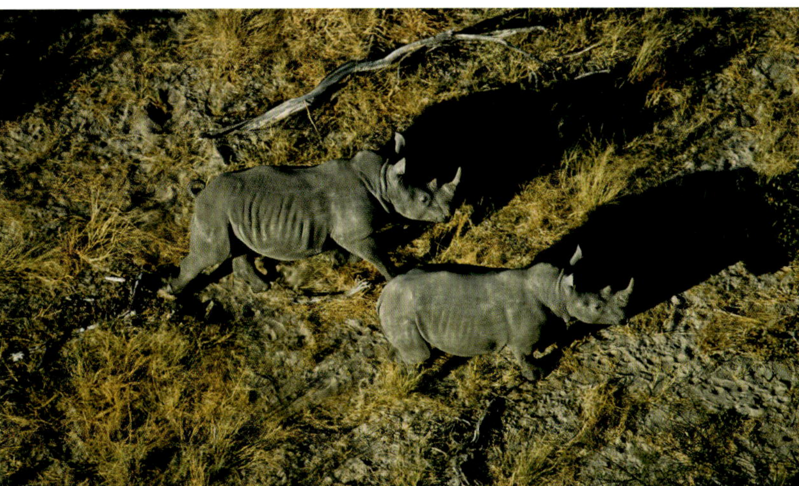

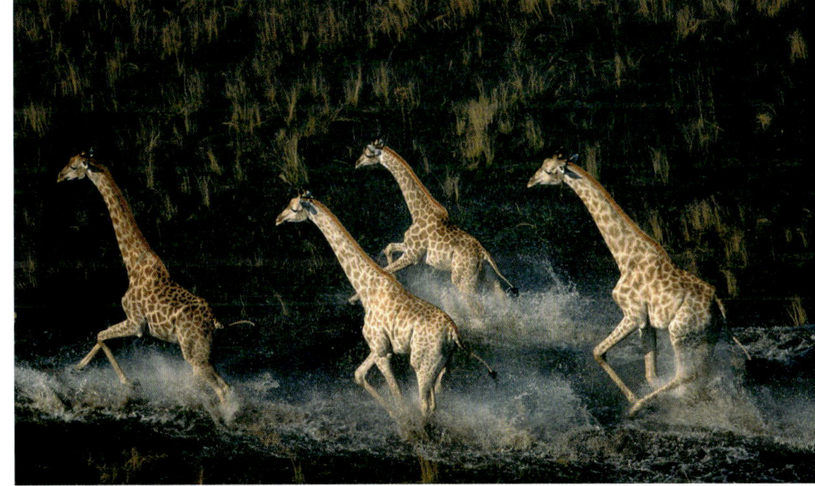

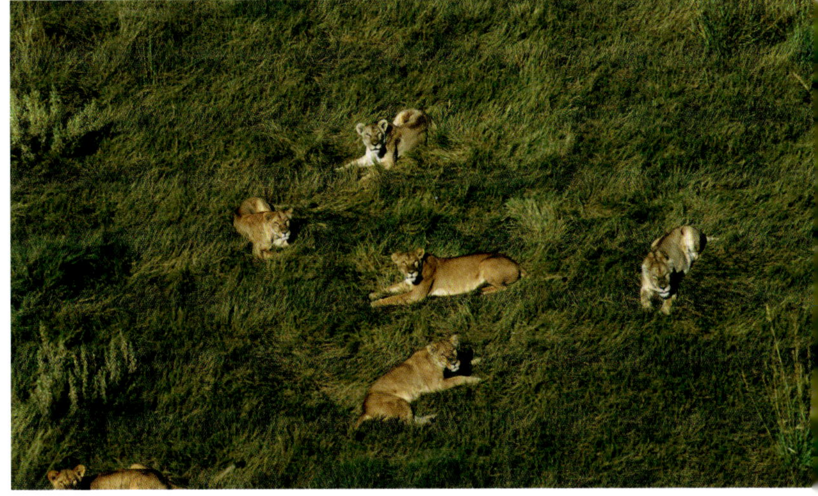

VREDEFORT DOME

Date of inscription: 2005

The Vredefort meteorite crater, 120 km (75 miles) south-west of Johannesburg, is now considered the largest and oldest of its kind. It is thought to be a little over two billion years old and has a diameter of 190 km (118 miles).

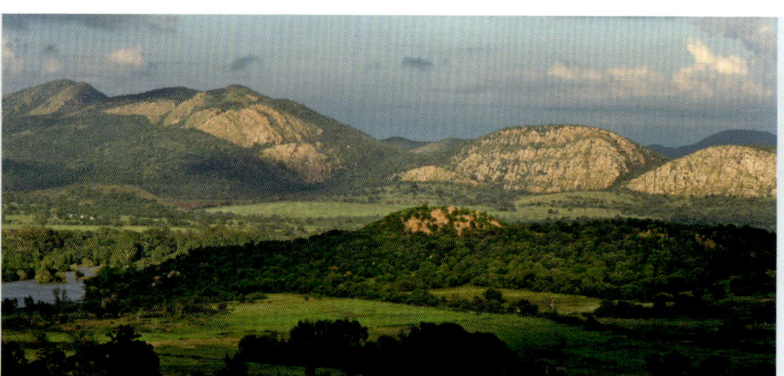

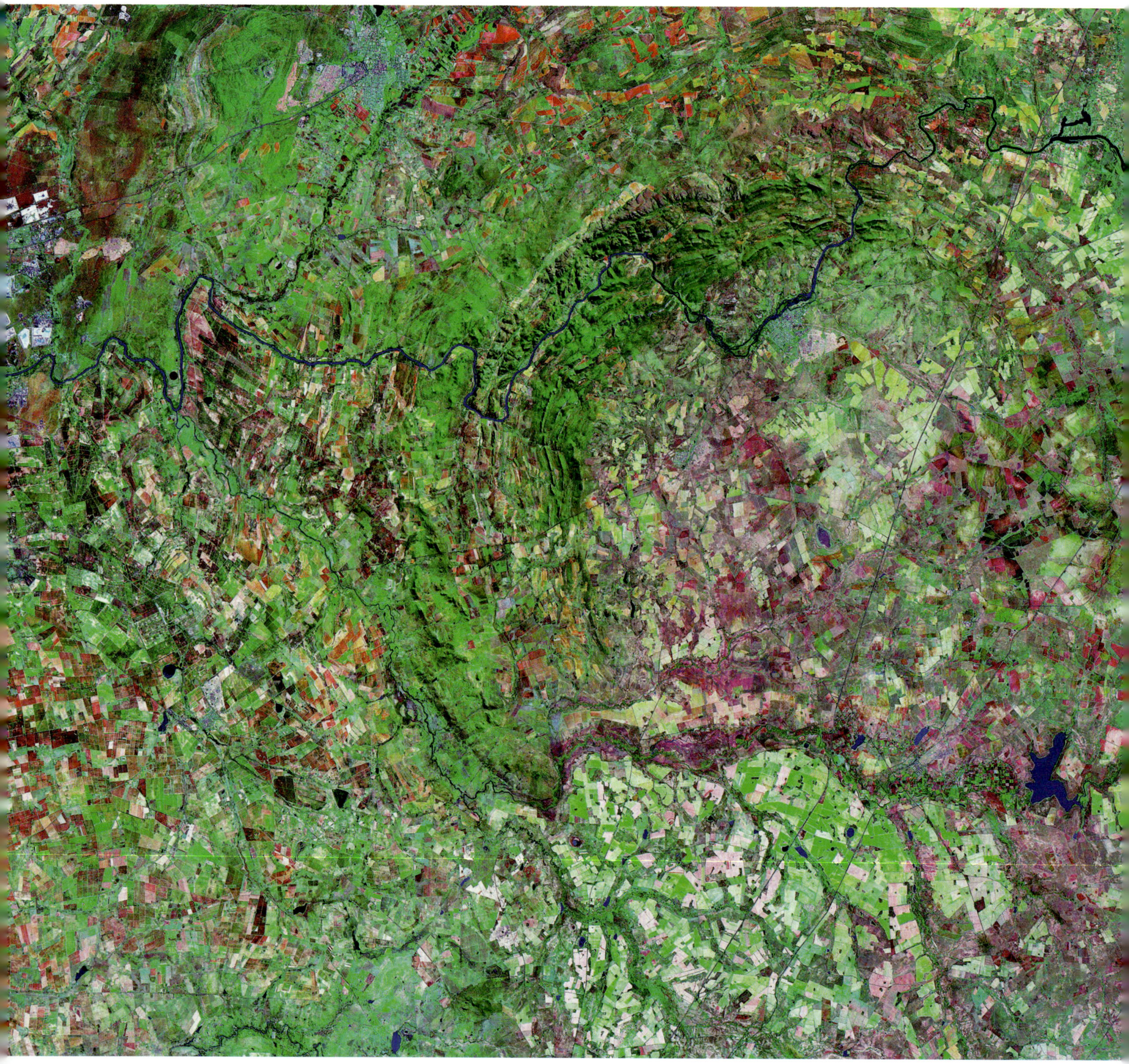

The greatest natural catastrophes in world history have been asteroid impacts. They are now considered to have exerted an influence on evolution, and it is possible that the dinosaurs died out due to the effects of a meteorite strike. The exact make-up of the mass of rock that thundered down on South Africa is difficult to determine today, but it is possible it was an asteroid, with a diameter of about 12 km (7.5 miles) and a speed through space of about 20 km (13 miles) per second, or perhaps a smaller comet core, moving at a still higher speed. When a meteorite hits the earth, its energy is converted into heat in fractions of a second, leading to a powerful explosion and resulting in a crater. Material thrown up by the impact falls to form the crater wall. The impact energy causes changes in the minerals beneath; for example, shock pressure transforms quartz into the stishovite and coesite also found in the Vredefort Dome. So-called "shatter cones" have also been found. Stone broken into angular fragments at impact which then reform is known as "breccia." Among scientists, the Vredefort crater is known in particular for a specific kind of breccia named pseudotachylite. Horn stone, which usually only occurs in strata deep underground, can also be brought to the earth's surface by the impact.

The semi-circular structure of the Vredefort meteorite crater can be clearly seen from the air (large image). Left: The Vredefort Dome refers to the convex hump formed in the middle of the crater by the impact.

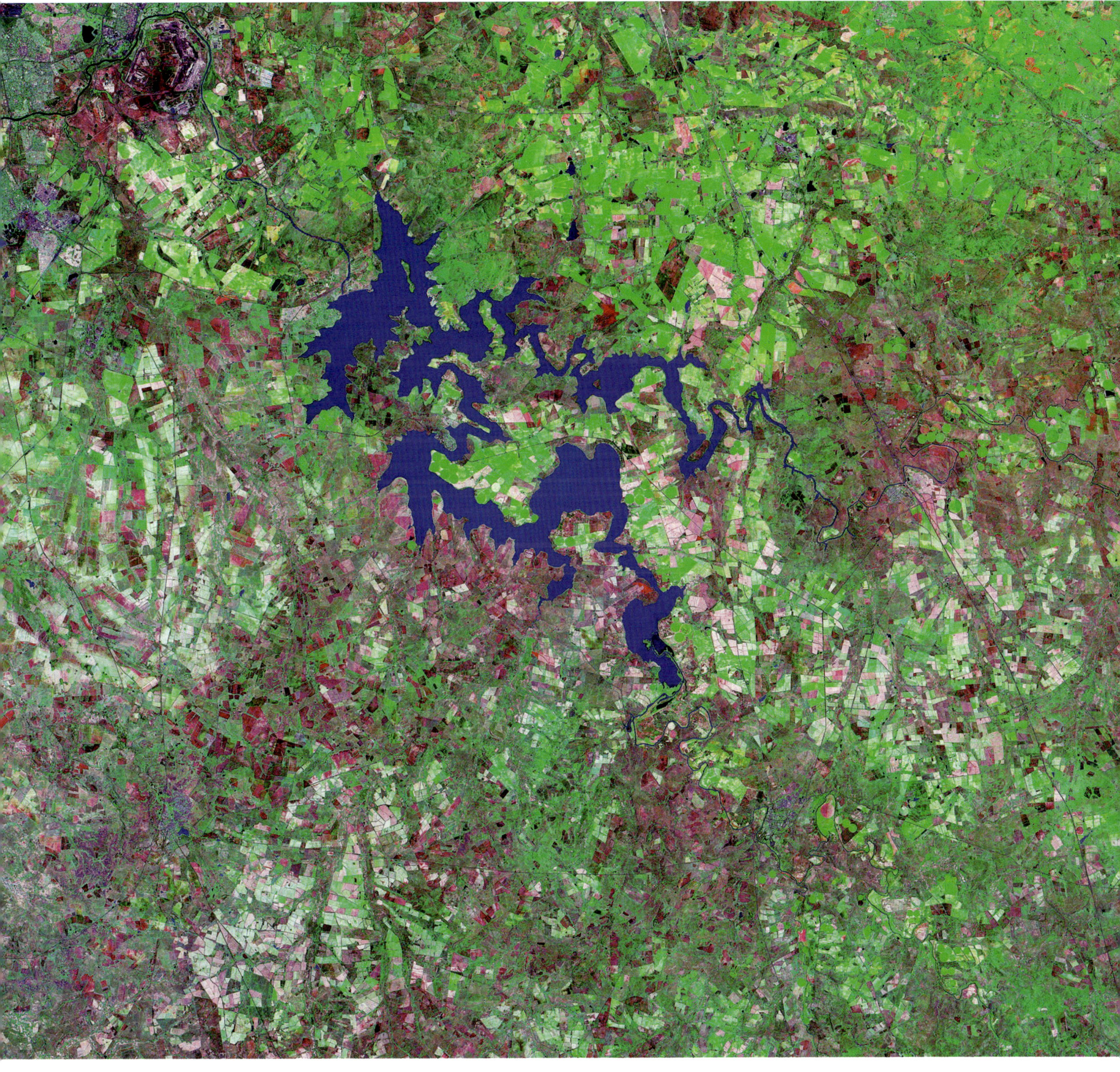

MALOTI / DRAKENSBERG NATIONAL PARK

Date of inscription: 2000
Extended: 2013
The South African Drakensberg Mountains have been inscribed as a World Natural and Cultural Heritage site since 2000. In 2013, the site was extended to include the Sehlabathebe National Park in Lesotho, which thus received its first entry in the UNESCO list.

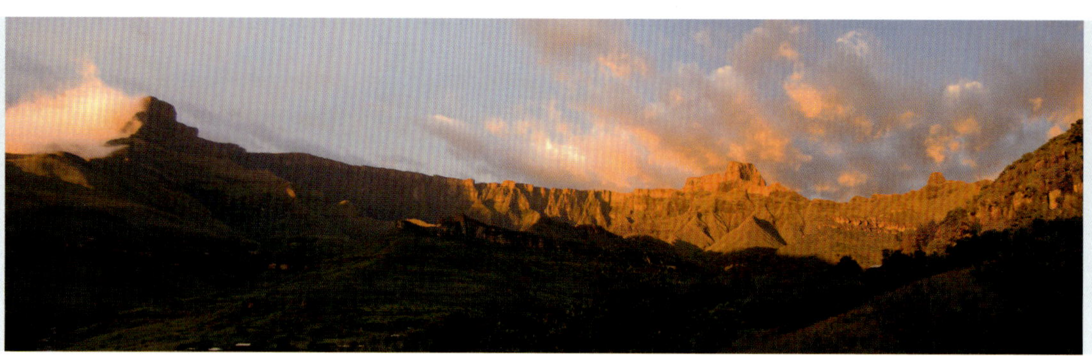

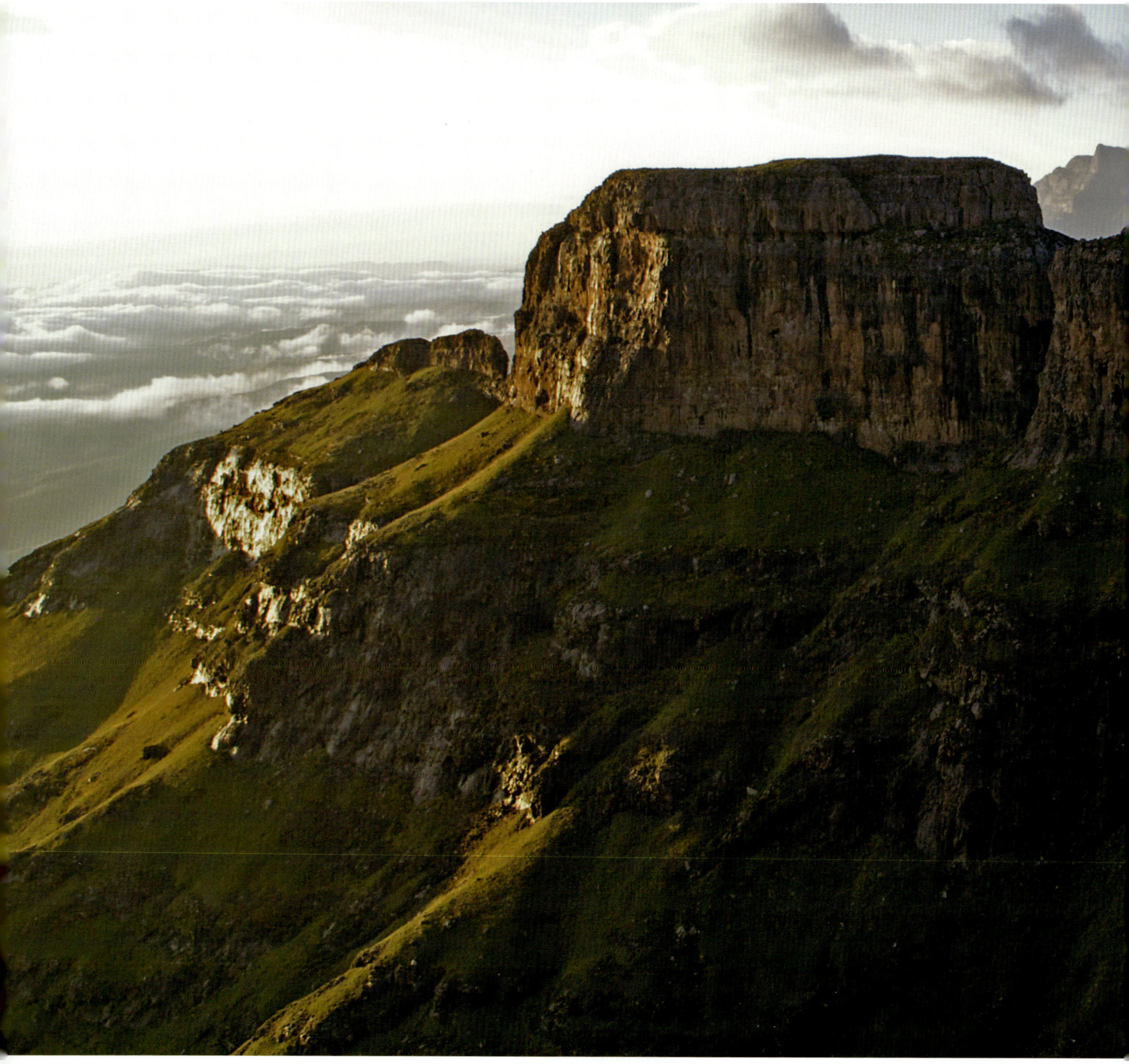

The Drakensberg Mountains are the highest mountain range in southern Africa. Their highest elevation (3,482m/ 11,424 feet) is located in Lesotho, where the range is known as Maloti Mountains. In the language of the Zulu, the massif is called uKahlamba, which roughly translates as "wall of raised spears", an allusion to the ruggedness of the landscape with its many canyons and pinnacles. Over a stretch of 12 km (7 miles), the South African Drakensberg Nature Park adjoins the Sehlabathebe National Park in Lesotho. In 2013 the parks were combined into the joint Maloti-Drakensberg Park World Heritage site. The Sehlabathebe National Park, covering 65 sq. km (25 sq. miles), consists mostly of savannah landscape with some sandstone formations. Some rivers in this park permanently carry water, and so the wetlands are very pronounced at all levels of altitude. Indeed, the Sehlabathebe water lily (Aponogeton ranunculiflorus), an endemic species, can be found in the sandstone pools. This flower is often described as the "jewel of Sehlabathebe". The fauna of the park is also very rich in species.

The rock curtains of the Drakensberg in South Africa pile up at sunset like an over-sized amphitheatre. Just like in the neighbouring Sehlabathebe National Park, plenty of research has been carried out here and San rock paintings have been identified.

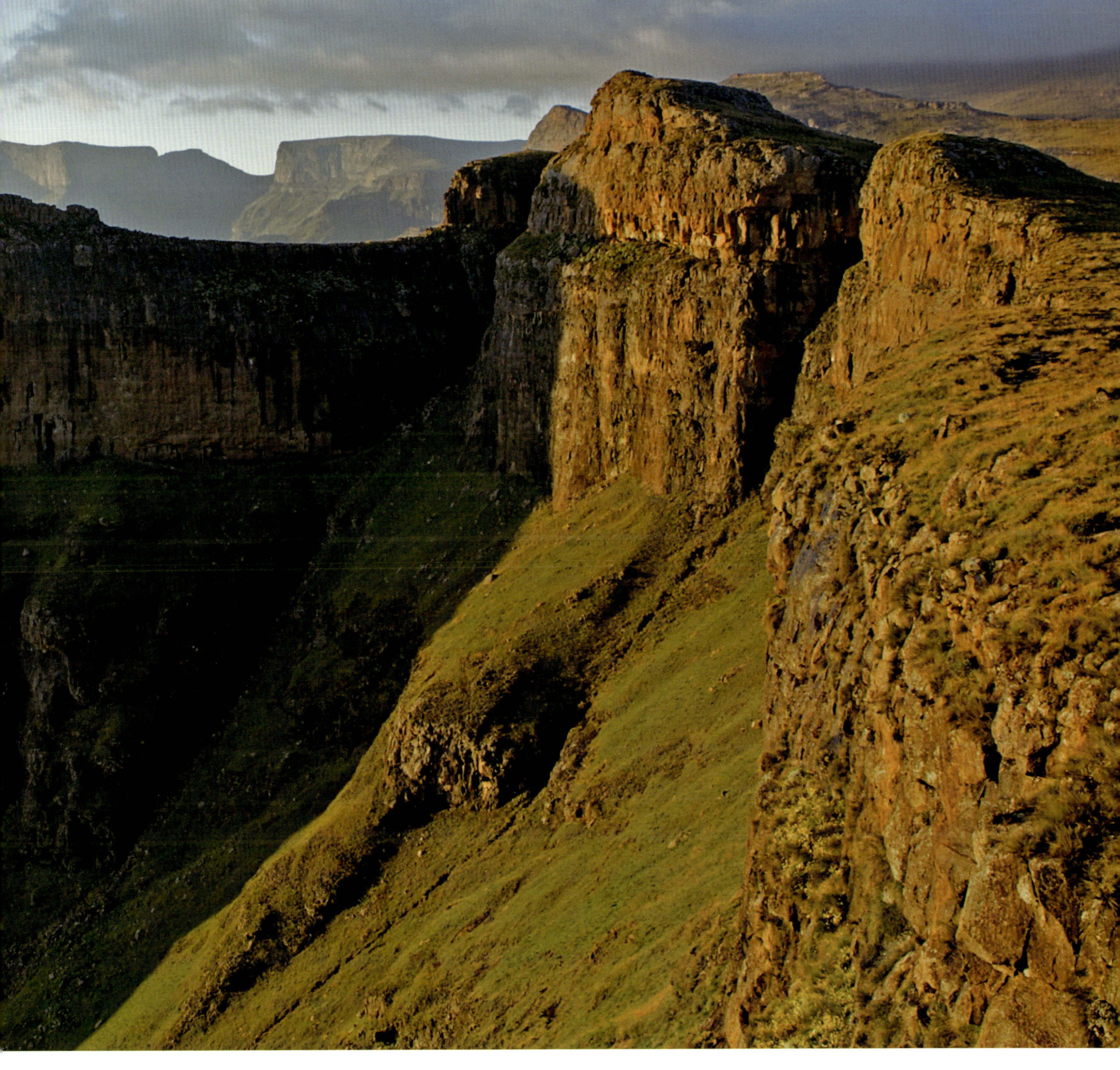

ISIMANGALISO WETLAND PARK

Date of inscription: 1999

This reserve on the north-eastern coast of South Africa is among the largest national parks in the world and has a striking diversity of habitats.

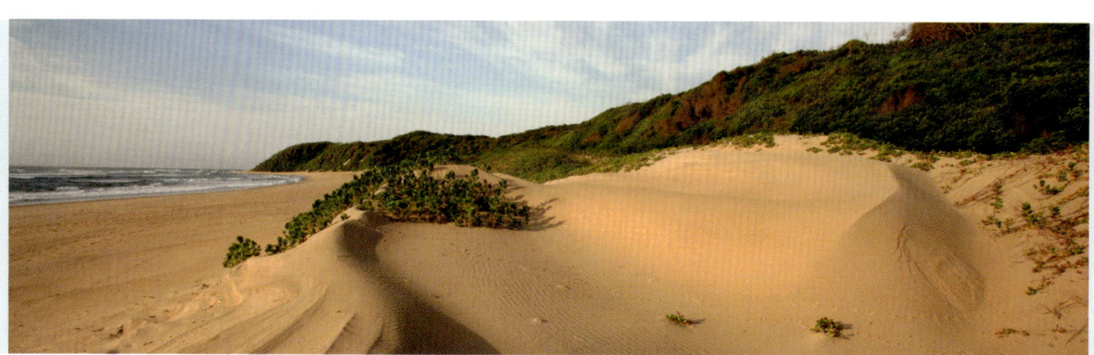

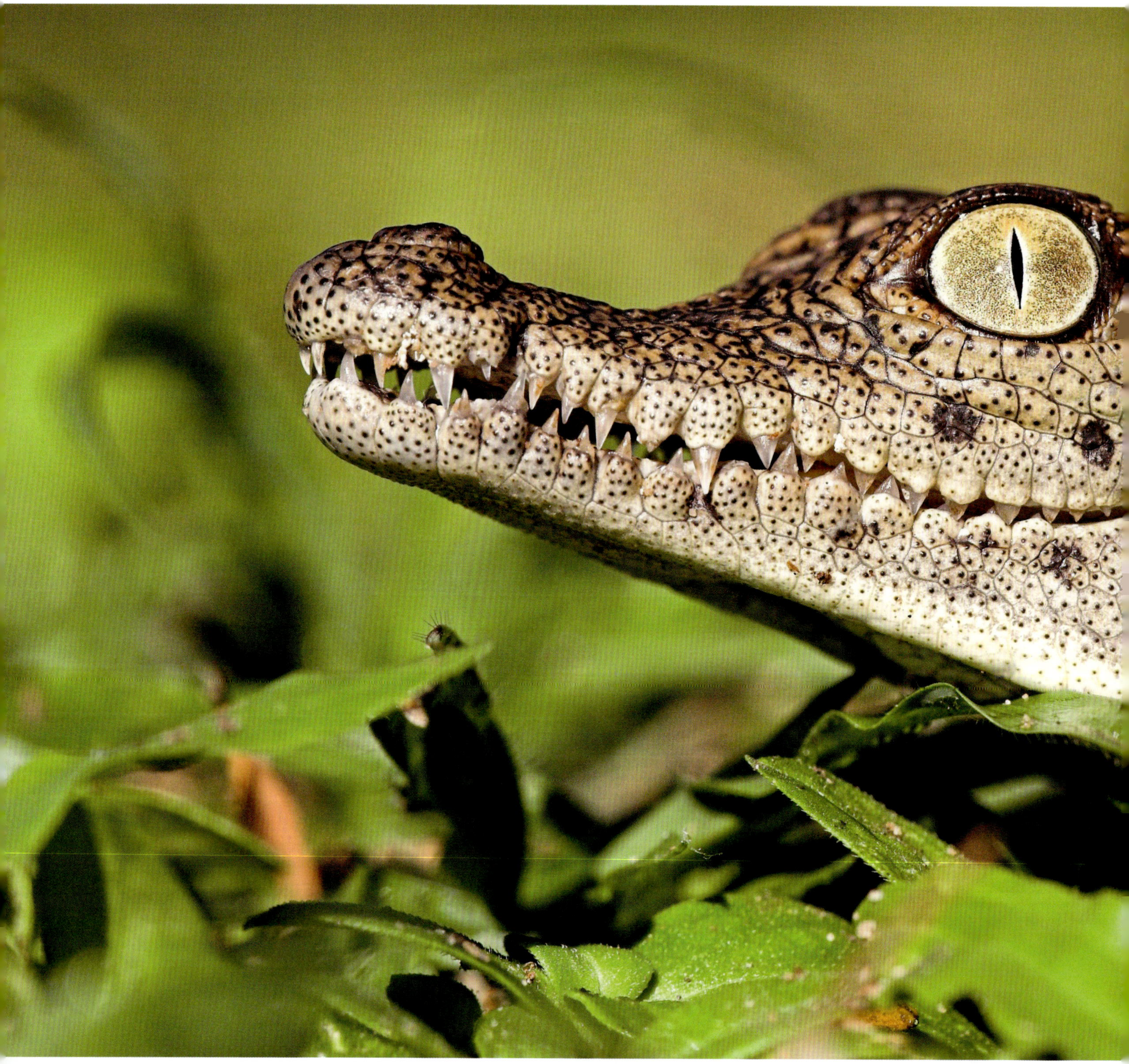

The 2,500 sq. km (950 sq. miles) of the iSimangaliso Wetland Park are distributed throughout large parts of Maputaland, in north-eastern South Africa, stretching as far as the Mozambican border. The conservation area includes some quite differing ecosystems: the aquatic flora and fauna of the Lake St Lucia Marine Reserve; Lake St Lucia's wetlands; the Mkuze swamps, Sodwana Bay, and Eastern Shores; Cape Vidal State Forests and the coral reefs that lie just offshore there; and the grasslands of the Lebombo mountains located in the hinterland. The world's largest crocodile population lives in this marshy area, along with large populations of hippos and more than 400 bird varieties, such as pelicans, spoonbills, and fish eagles. Numerous wildebeest roam the lake shore. Rare somango monkeys and other tree-dwellers live among the thickly forested dunes, and the sandy beaches around Cape Vidal are the territory of several species of sea turtle. Lying off the cape are extensive coral reefs, among the southernmost on earth. The wide grassland of the interior is a habitat for both the white and black species of rhinoceros.

Wooded dunes and beach areas characterize the park on the ocean side north of the St Lucia Lake (left). Crocodiles (large picture), vervet monkeys, kudus (a type of water antelope), the highly poisonous Gaboon viper and the Goliath heron (picture series, from the top) live in the swamps.

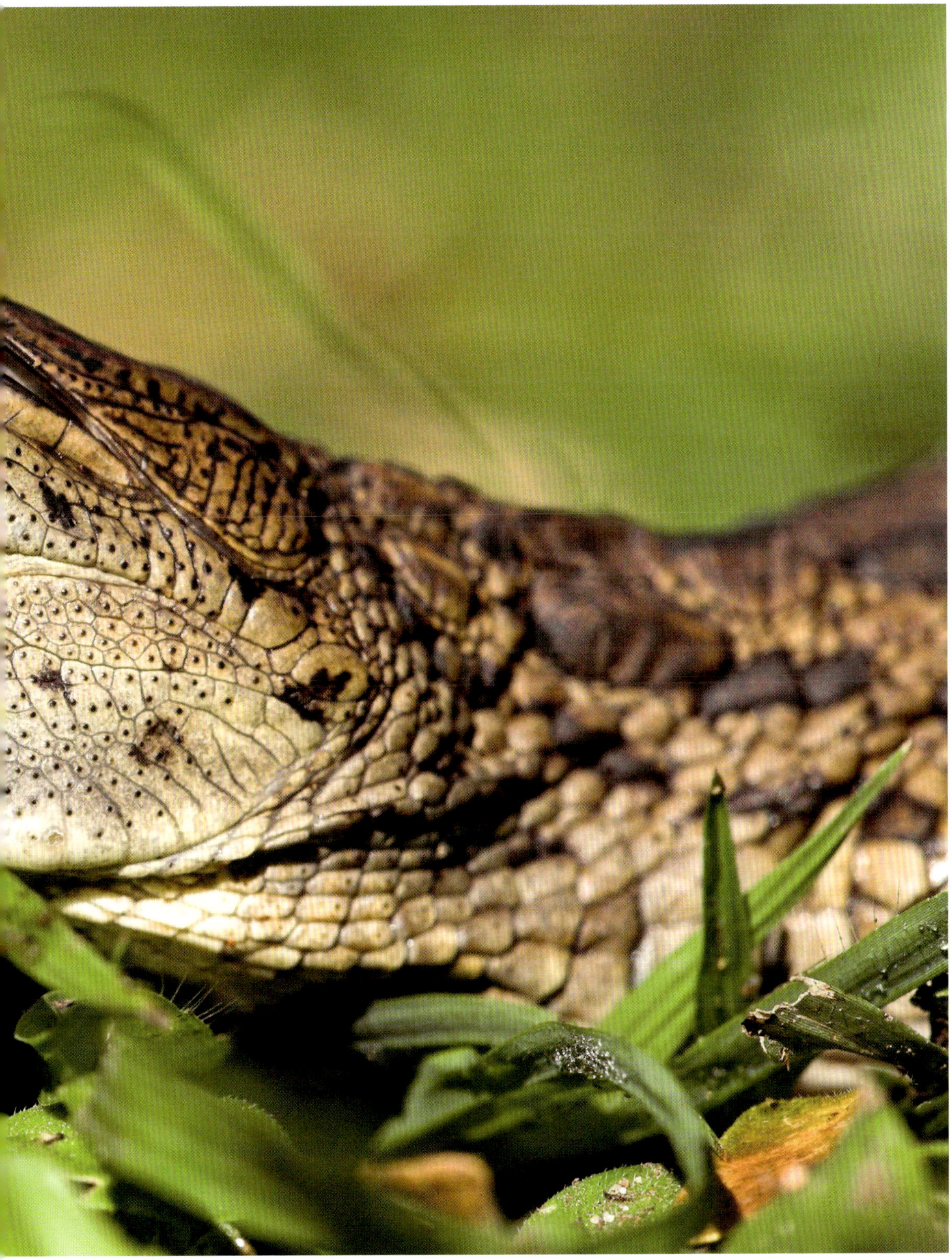

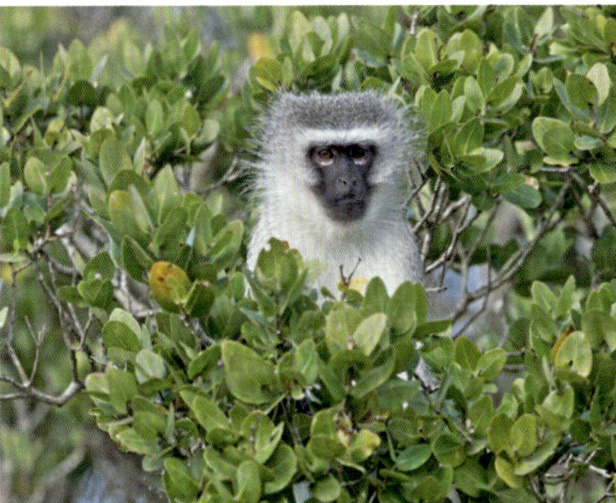

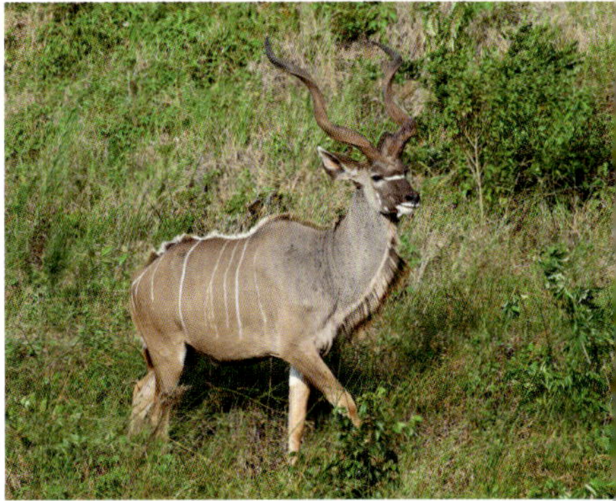

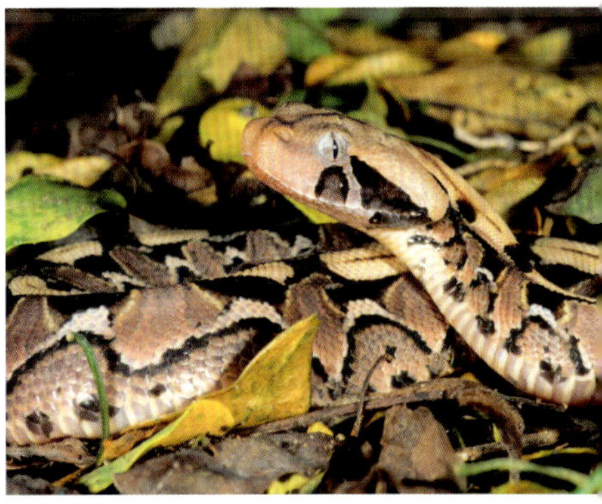

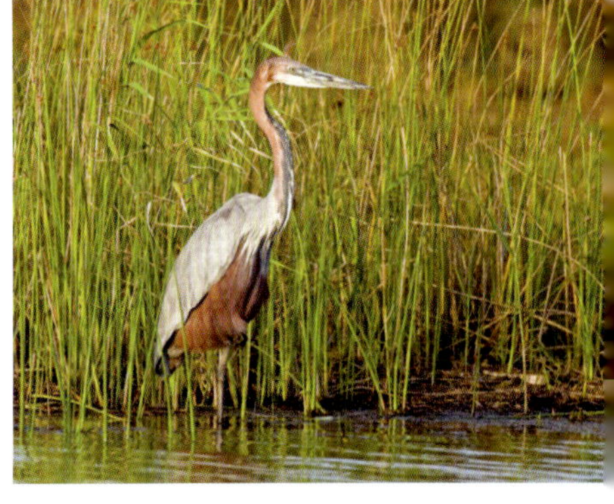

THE CAPE FLORAL REGION

Date of inscription: 2004
Extended: 2015

Relative to its area, the southern tip of Africa has the greatest number of plant species of any region on earth, more than any tropical rainforest. The extension increases the number of protected area from 8 to 13.

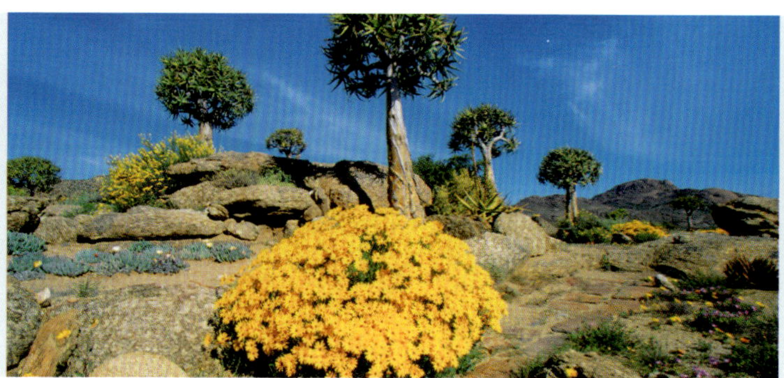

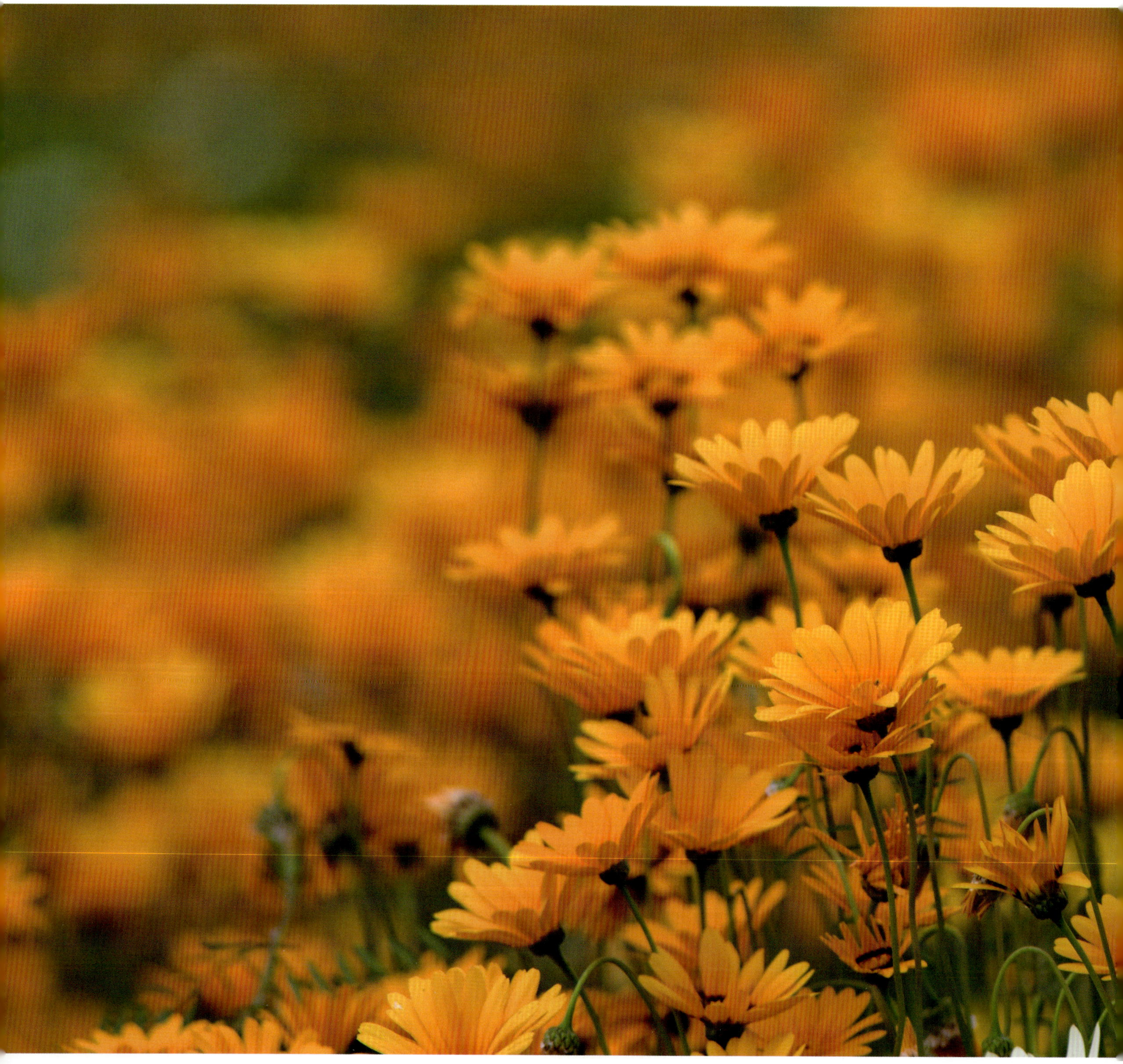

Botanists divide the earth into various floristic kingdoms. Each floristic kingdom, distinguished by a relatively uniform composition of plant species, is determined and defined by the species endemic to the region or subregion. Central Europe, for example, is part of the Holarctic kingdom, which includes all the temperate zones in the northern hemisphere. The smallest, most peculiar and also the most diverse region is the Cape Floral Region on the southern tip of Africa, where 6,000 flowering plants, of which a high percentage are endemic, grow in the closest proximity to one another. The thirteen reserves of the conservation area represent a section through the Cape Floral region. The extension brings the size of the World Heritage Site to 1,094,742 hectares. It is also home to 20 percent of all the plant varieties to be found on the continent, foremost among which are 450 species of Proteaceae and Ericaceae. Much of the region is covered in unique fynbos vegetation, a shrub that has adapted perfectly to the periodic bushfires. There are various refined strategies that promote seed dissemination and pollination by insects and the evolution of further species is in full swing. The theory of adaptive radiation, whereby one species diversifies into several within a short period of time, adapting to fill particular ecological niches, has permitted many fascinating insights into the evolution of flowering plants.

The African daisy (large image) and the yellow daisy, the fynbos and the protaceae (left) are just some of the plants typical of the southern tip of Africa, transforming the scenery into a sea of flowers.

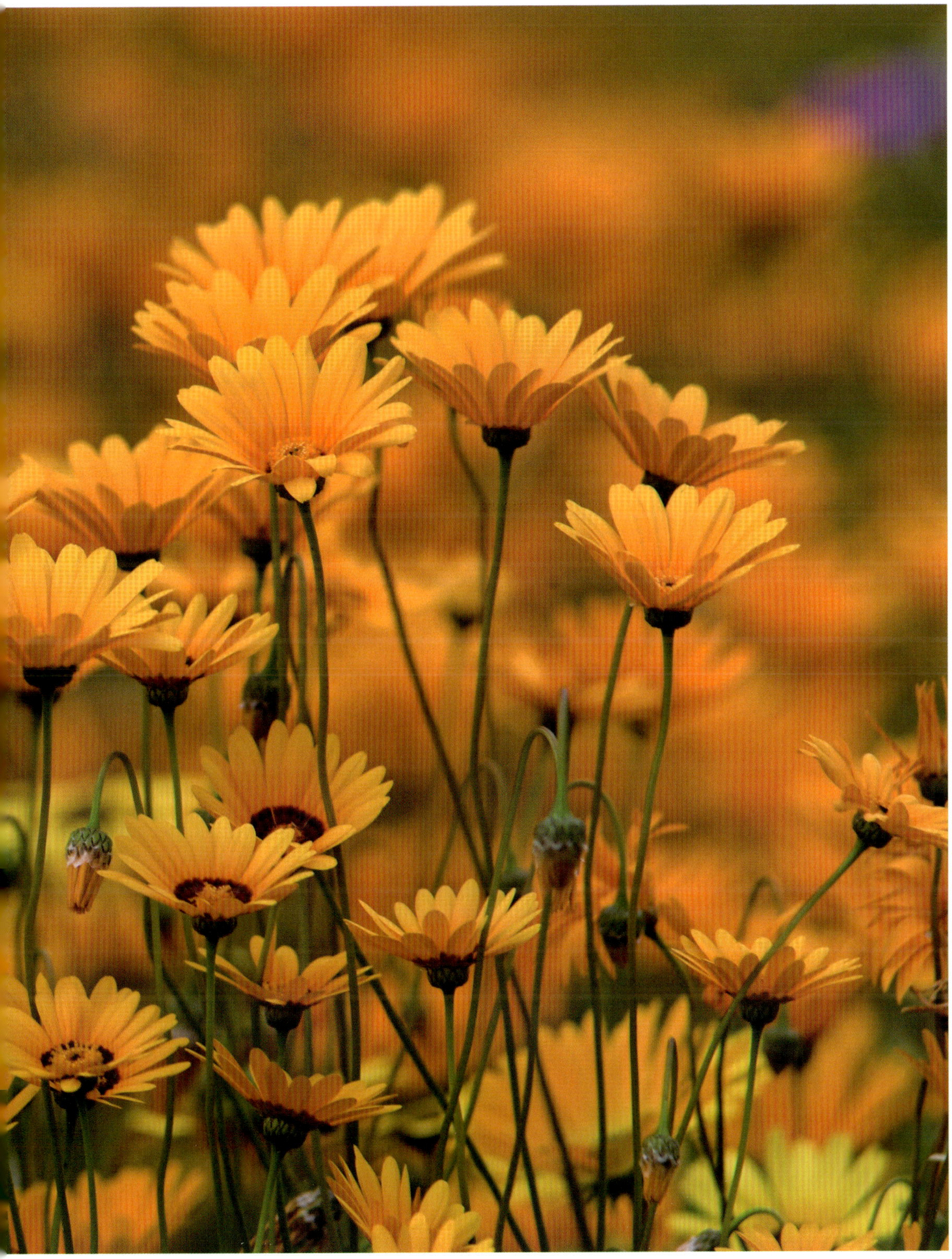

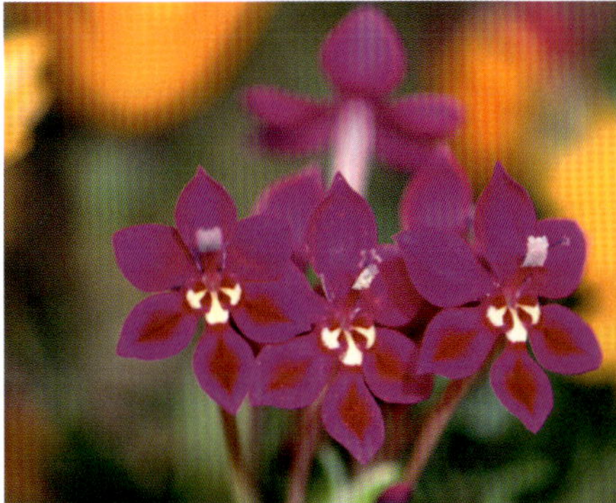

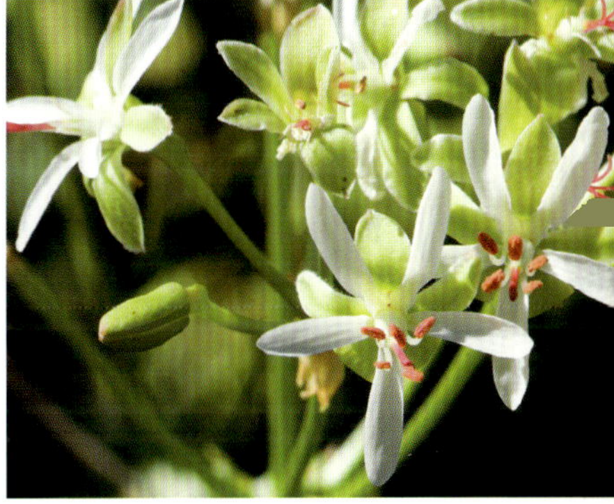

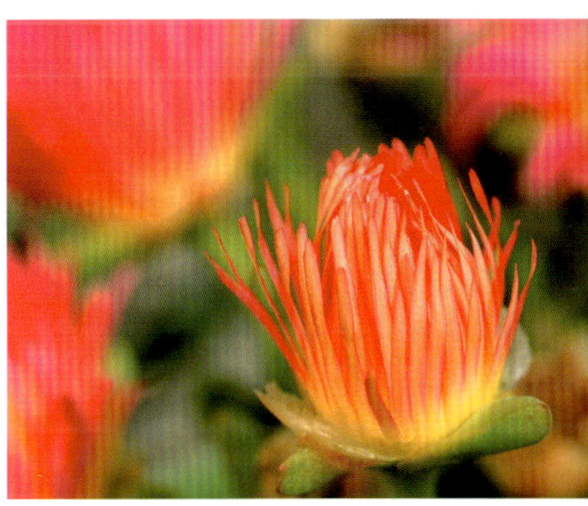

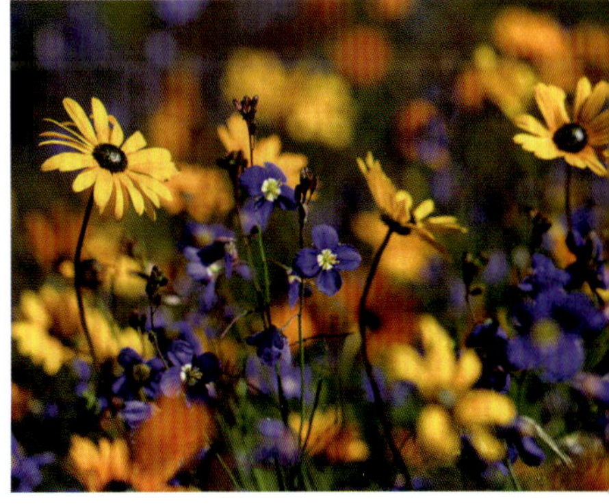

RAINFORESTS OF THE ATSINANANA

Date of inscription: 2007

Six separate national parks in the eastern part of Madagascar have been grouped together under the heading "Rainforests of the Atsinanana," and they play an important part in the preservation of the island's biological diversity.

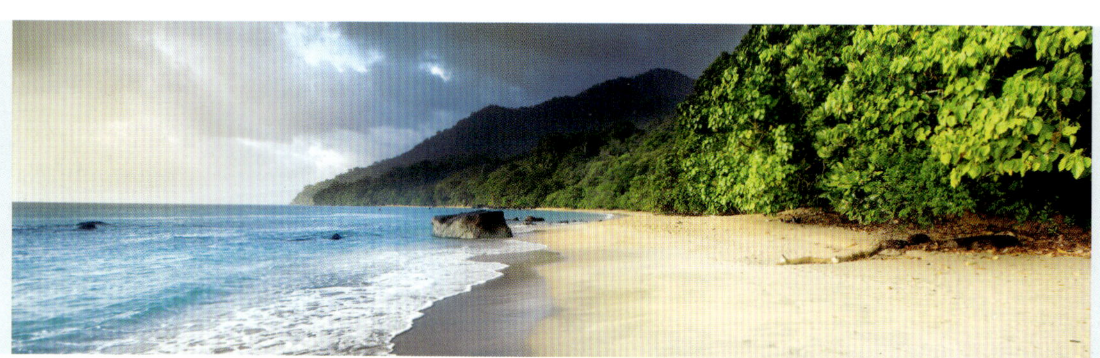

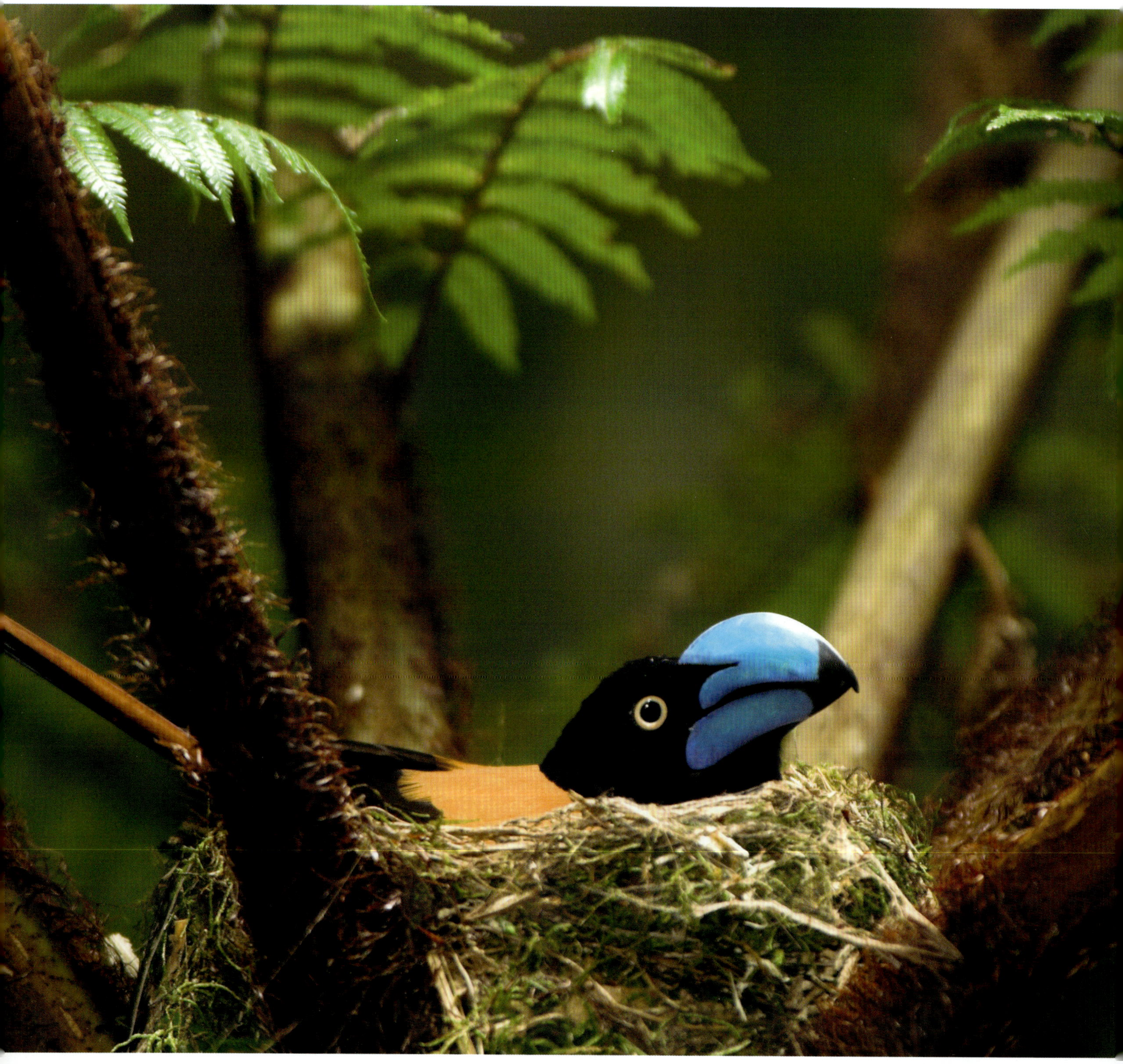

Madagascar has been separated from continental Africa for 60 million years. This extensive period of isolation has been responsible both for the evolution of new plant and animal varieties and for the preservation of many ancient species. Madagascar and its surrounding island group is thus home to around 12,000 endemic plant species.

The best-known animal species are the lemurs, of the family once known as prosimians, now called strepsirrhines. Only Australia, thirteen times the size, has more indigenous species than Madagascar. Forests, especially rainforests, are the cradle of species diversity; unfortunately, only 8.5 percent of the formerly rainforested area of Madagascar now remains. Now protected, the six areas of this World Heritage Site, covering a total area of about 5,000 sq. km (1,900 sq. miles), are (from north to south): Marojejy, Masoala, Zahamena, Ranomafana, Andringitra, and Andohahela National Parks. They are isolated from one another, although some of the parks are still interconnected by stretches of unprotected primary forest.

Fascinating camouflage artists live in the national parks, left picture series: panther chameleon (top) and Parson's chameleon (bottom). Right picture series: red ruffed lemur, aye-aye, mouse lemur. Large picture: A helmet vanga with its strikingly blue beak is seated in its nest. Males and females do not differ in appearance. Left: the Masoala National Park.

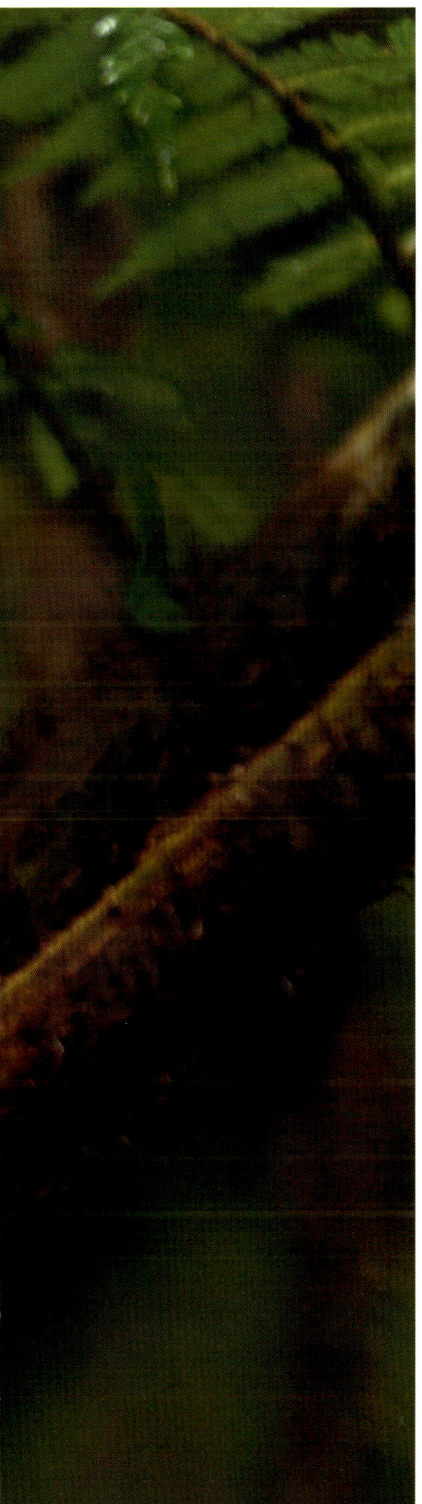

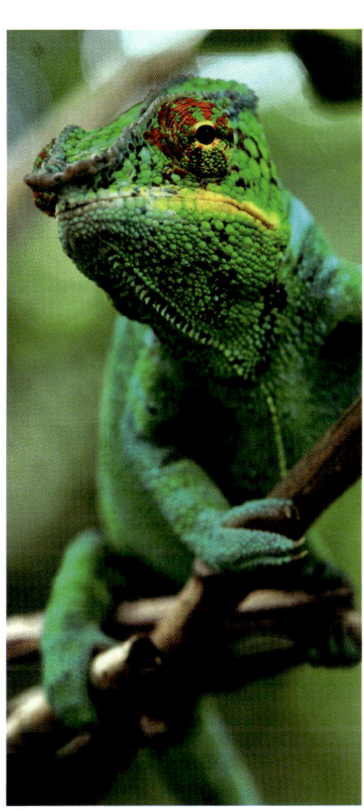

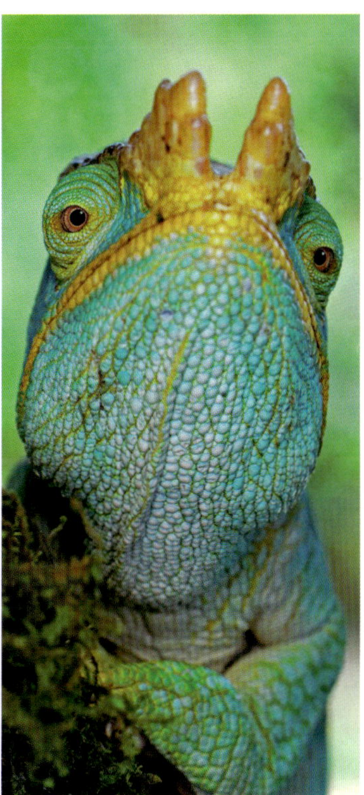

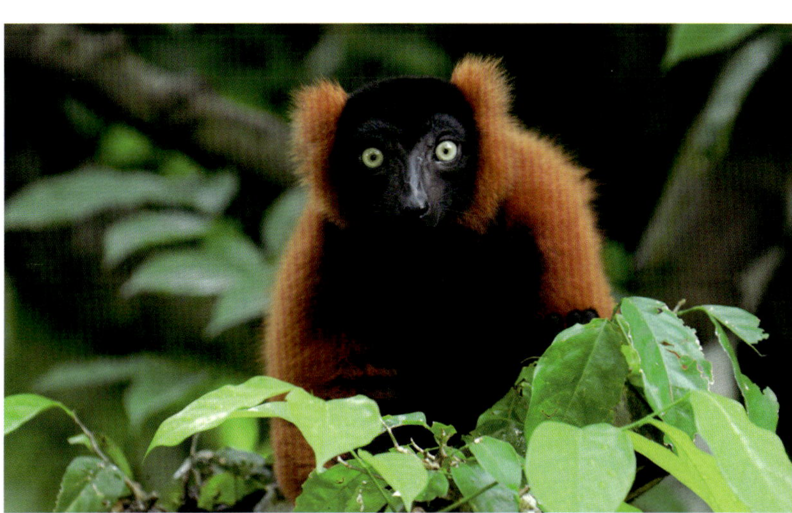

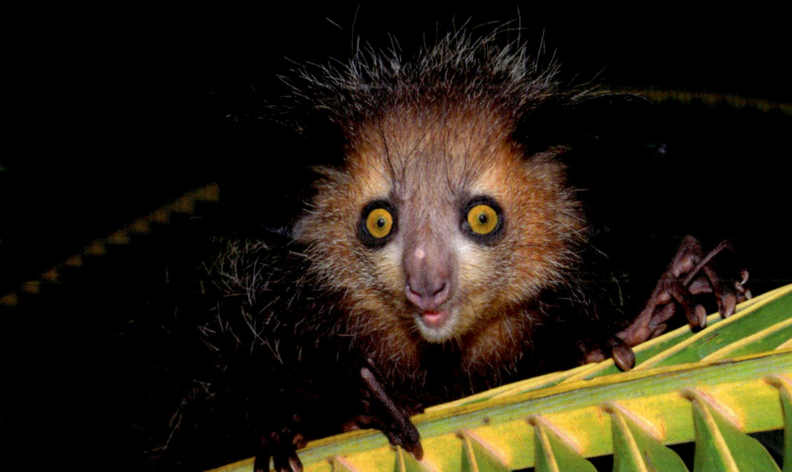

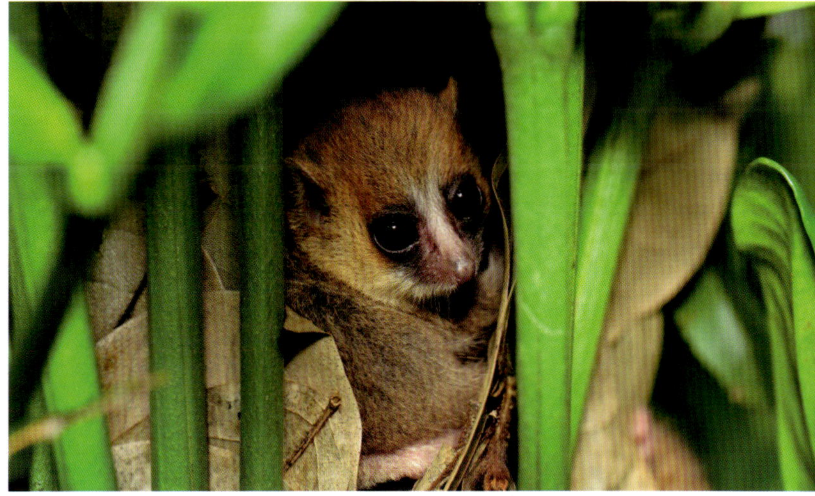

TSINGY DE BEMARAHA STRICT NATURE RESERVE

Date of inscription: 1990

Bizarre rock faces and undisturbed forests, lakes, and mangrove swamps are all components of this unique natural paradise, which is a home for many rare varieties of animals and plants.

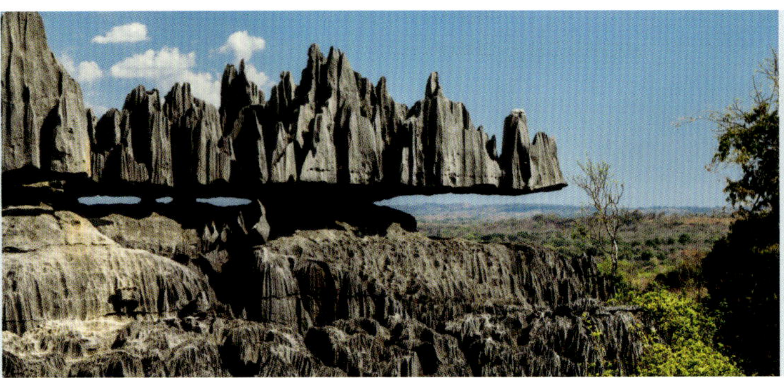

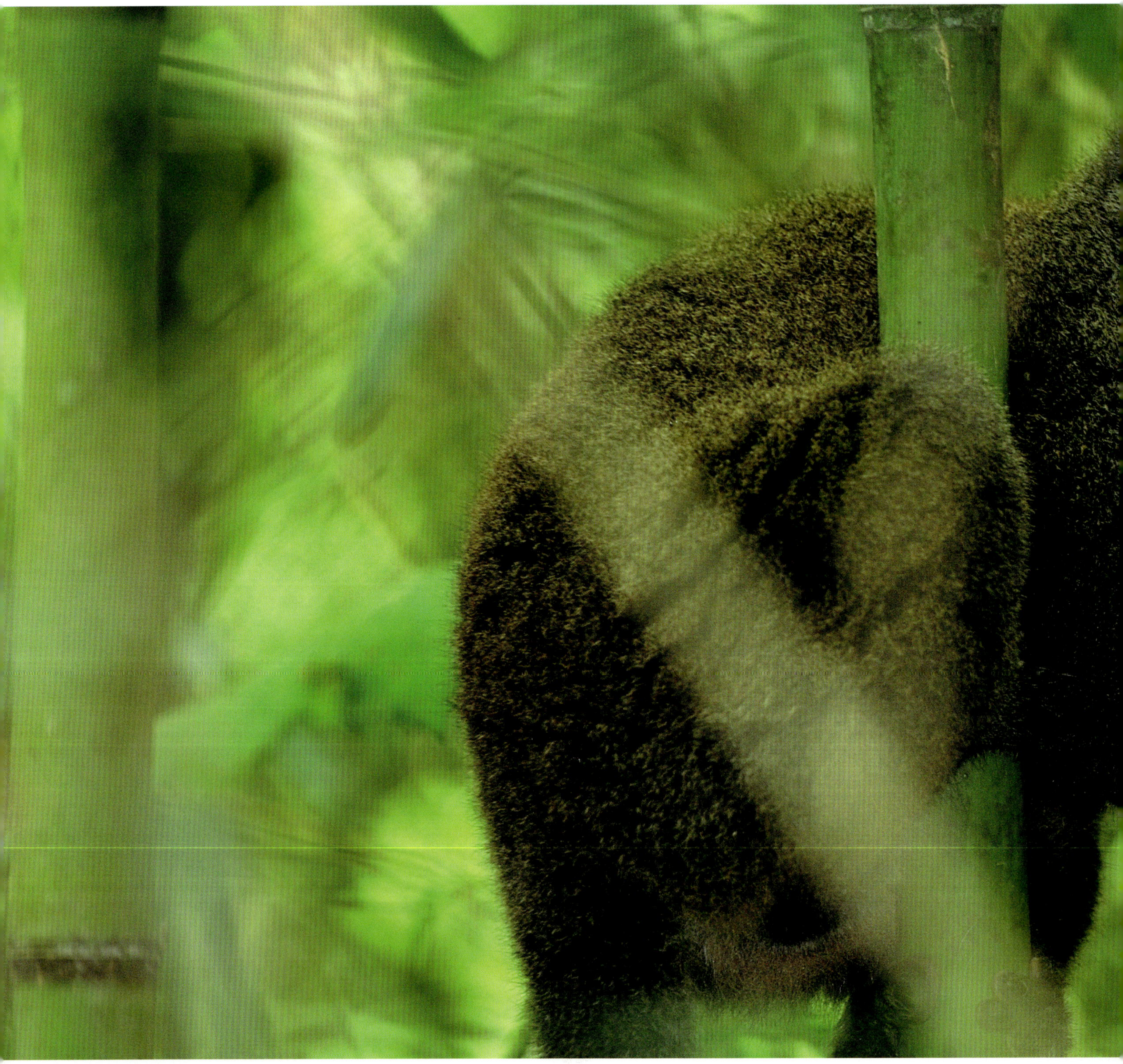

The imposing karst landscape of the Bemaraha plateau on the west coast of Madagascar lies at roughly the same latitude as the capital, Antananarivo. Its spectacular highlights include the Manambolo river canyon and the bizarre Tsingy, a "forest" created by limestone projections. The undisturbed rainforests, lakes, and mangrove swamps of the conservation area are home to innumerable species of orchid. The Bemaraha Strict Nature Reserve's 1,500 sq. km (580 sq. miles) are particularly important as the habitat of lemurs, which occur naturally almost exclusively on Madagascar. This prosimian species reached the island more than 40 million years ago and discovered ideal living conditions. Madagascar's extremely remote location has led to the evolution of around 40 different species of lemur, and the region is also home to numerous birds, bats, amphibians, and reptiles, including geckos and chameleons.

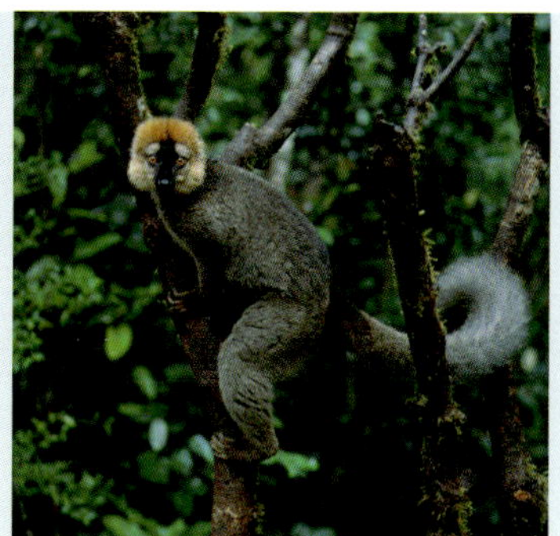

Lemurs of all colours and sizes: brown lemur (left), Coquerel's sifaka, ring-tailed mongoose, ring-tailed lemur (picture series, from the top) and the cute eastern lesser bamboo lemur (large picture). 4th picture from the top: The fossa is the enemy of all these primates and the largest predator of the island, because it feeds on primates and other mammals.

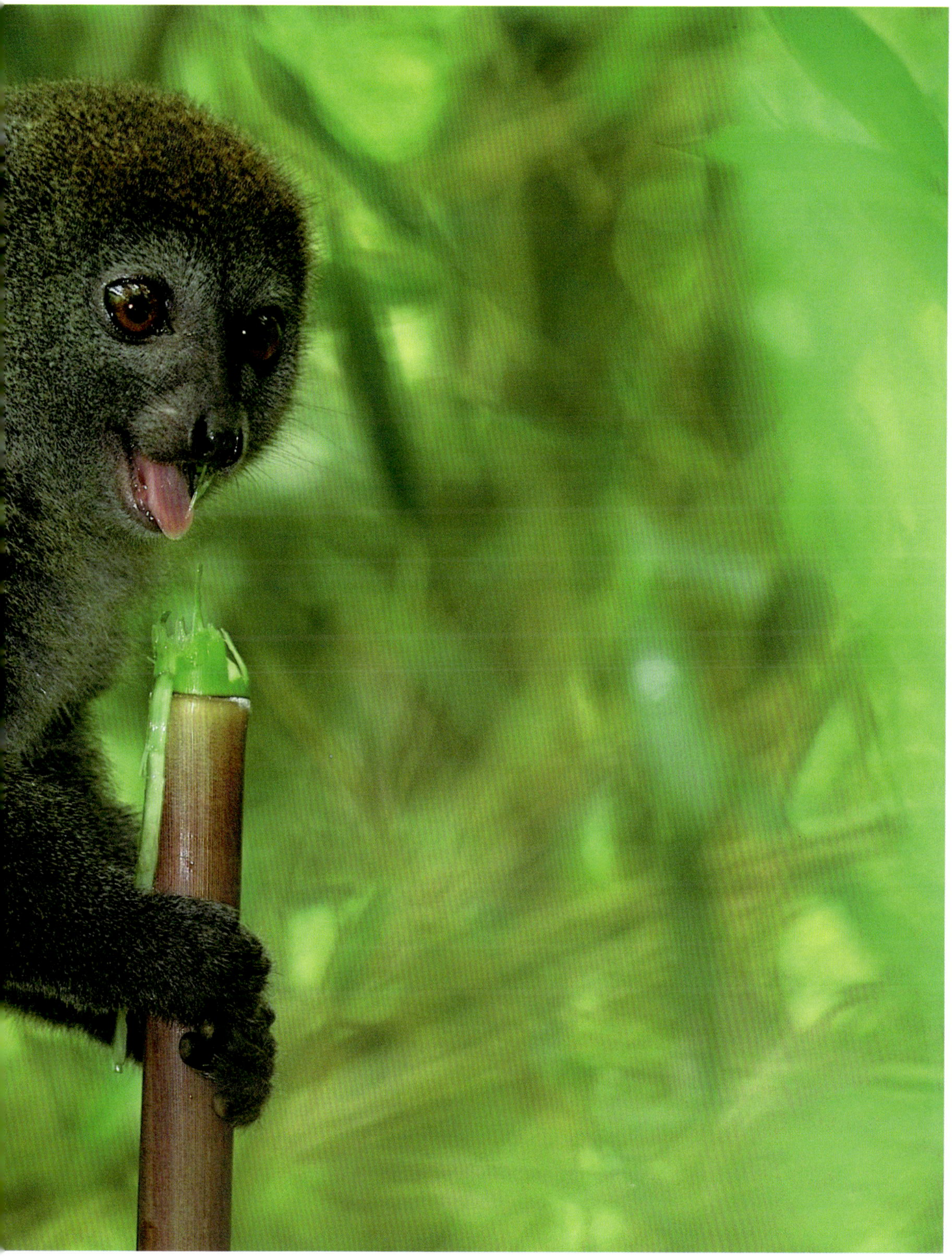

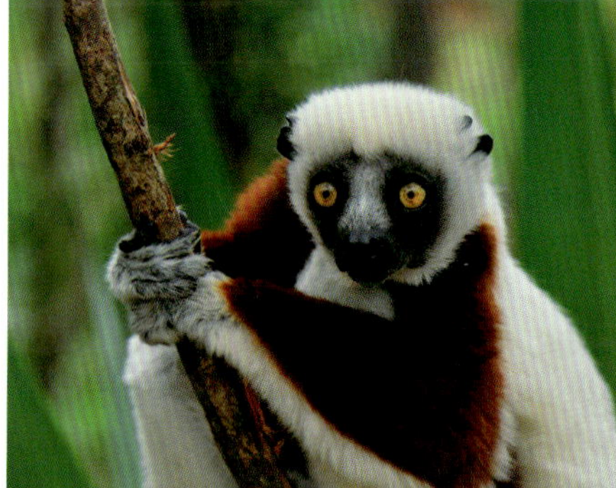

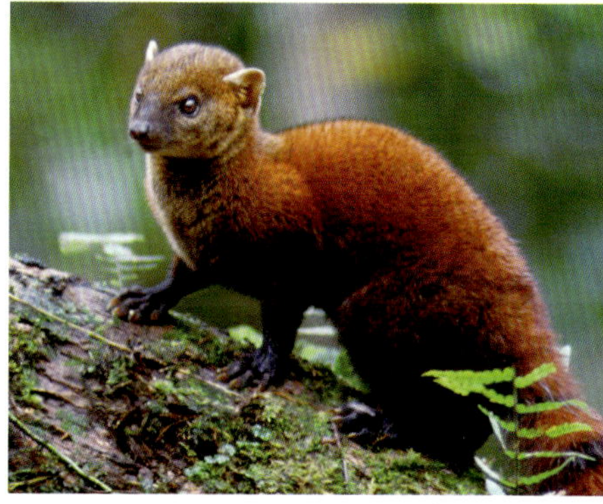

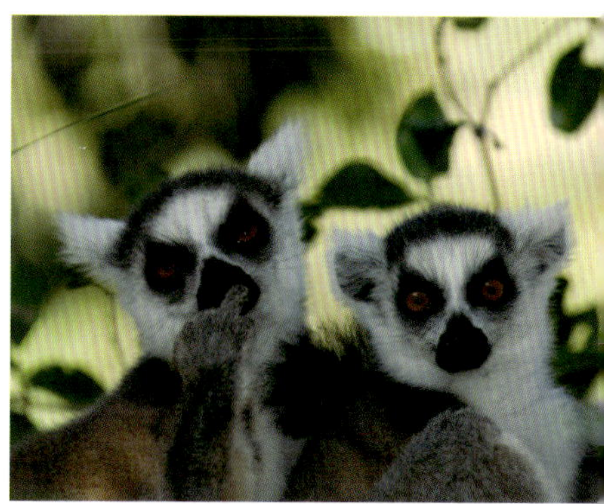

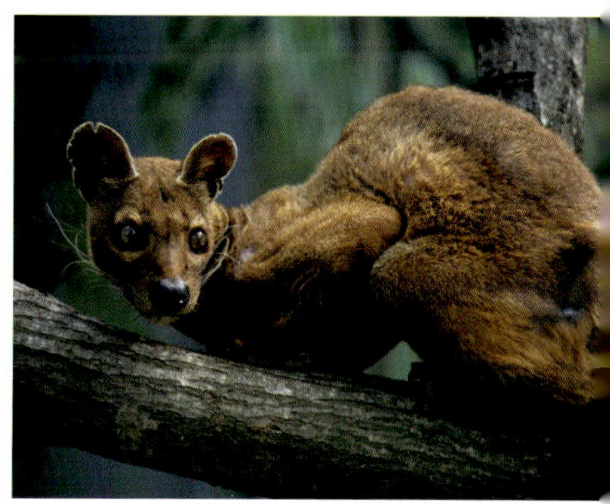

ALDABRA ATOLL

Date of inscription: 1982

Inaccessible to the general public, these four islands form the world's largest coral atoll. Over 150,000 giant tortoises are the chief attraction of this, the westernmost island chain of the Seychelles in the Indian Ocean.

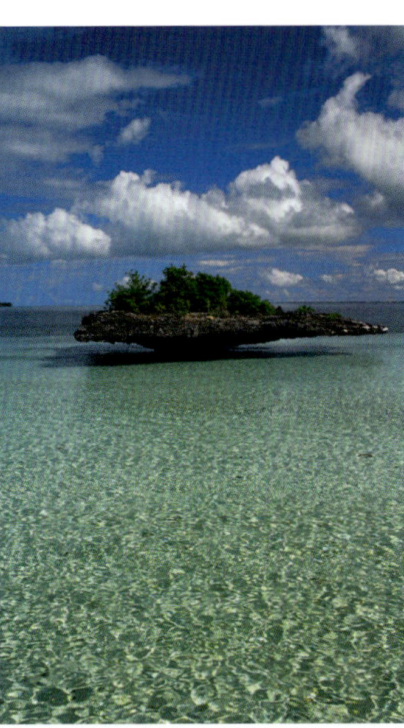

Surrounded by the turquoise waters of the Indian Ocean, the islands perfecttly correspond to our preconceived ideas of paradise islands. The four islands of the Aldabra Atoll – Picard, Polymnia, Malabar and Grande Terre – enclose a shallow lagoon and are surrounded in turn by a coral reef. Due to its remote location, a completely natural environment, untouched by human hand, has been allowed to develop here. The Aldabra Atoll, inscribed as a conservation area in 1976, is home to a diversity of flora and fauna astonishing for an oceanic island. It is a nesting place for numerous seabirds, but the atoll is best known for the population of Aldabra giant tortoises (Dipsochelys dussumieri), a species of Seychelles tortoise. These reptiles can achieve a weight of 250 kg (550 lb) and an age of 100 years. Green and hawksbill turtles are also found here.

Arab seafarers named the remote atoll of the Seychelles "al chadra," the green islands, when they discovered it many centuries ago. The majority of the giant tortoises live on Grande Terre, the main island of the atoll (below).
Left: Mushroom Atoll.

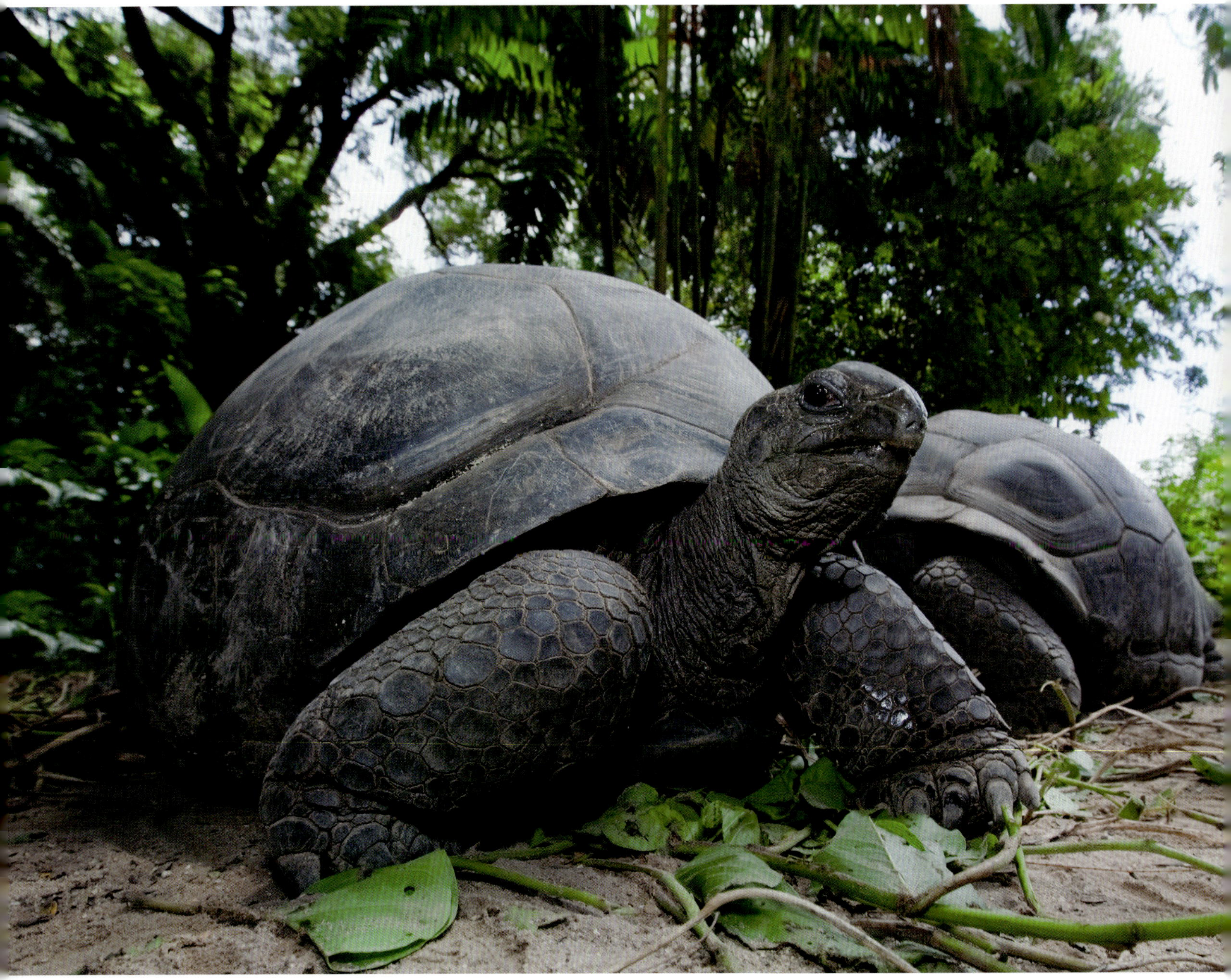

VALLÉE DE MAI NATURE RESERVE

Just north of Mahé, the main island, lies Praslin, the second-largest island in the Seychelles group. In 1966 the Vallée de Mai Nature Reserve was established within the Praslin National Park at the heart of this granite island. This conservation area of only 20 hectares (49 acres) ensures the preservation of the Seychelles palm (Lodoicea maldivica), a living remnant of prehistoric vegeta tion. Due to the long evolutionary isolation of the island group, many prehistoric plant species have been retained, although for a long time all that was known of these were the seeds of a plant known as coco de mer, which could weigh up to 18 kg (40 lb) and which the Portuguese circumnavigator Ferdinand Magellan assumed to be the fruit of a tree growing in the depths of the sea. The Vallée de Mai is also a habitat for a wealth of animal life: various species of chameleon and gecko and many bird varieties live here, including the endemic lesser Vasa parrot, the Seychelles cave swiftlet, and the Seychelles black bulbul, as well as hummingbirds.

The prehistoric forest and idyllic waterfalls of the Vallée de Mai remained untouched until 1930, ensuring the preservation of this ancient biosphere right). The Seychelles palm, whose seeds take six or seven years to ripen, is the symbol of this island republic.

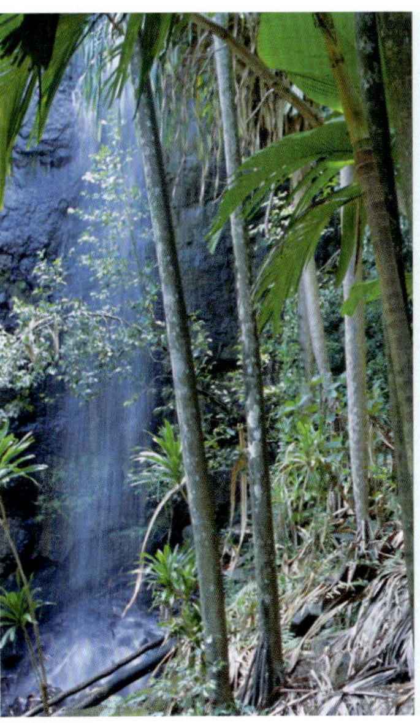

Date of inscription: 1983

The home of the Seychelles palm is a high valley at the heart of the island of Praslin. This tree has the largest seed in the plant kingdom and lives for several hundred years.

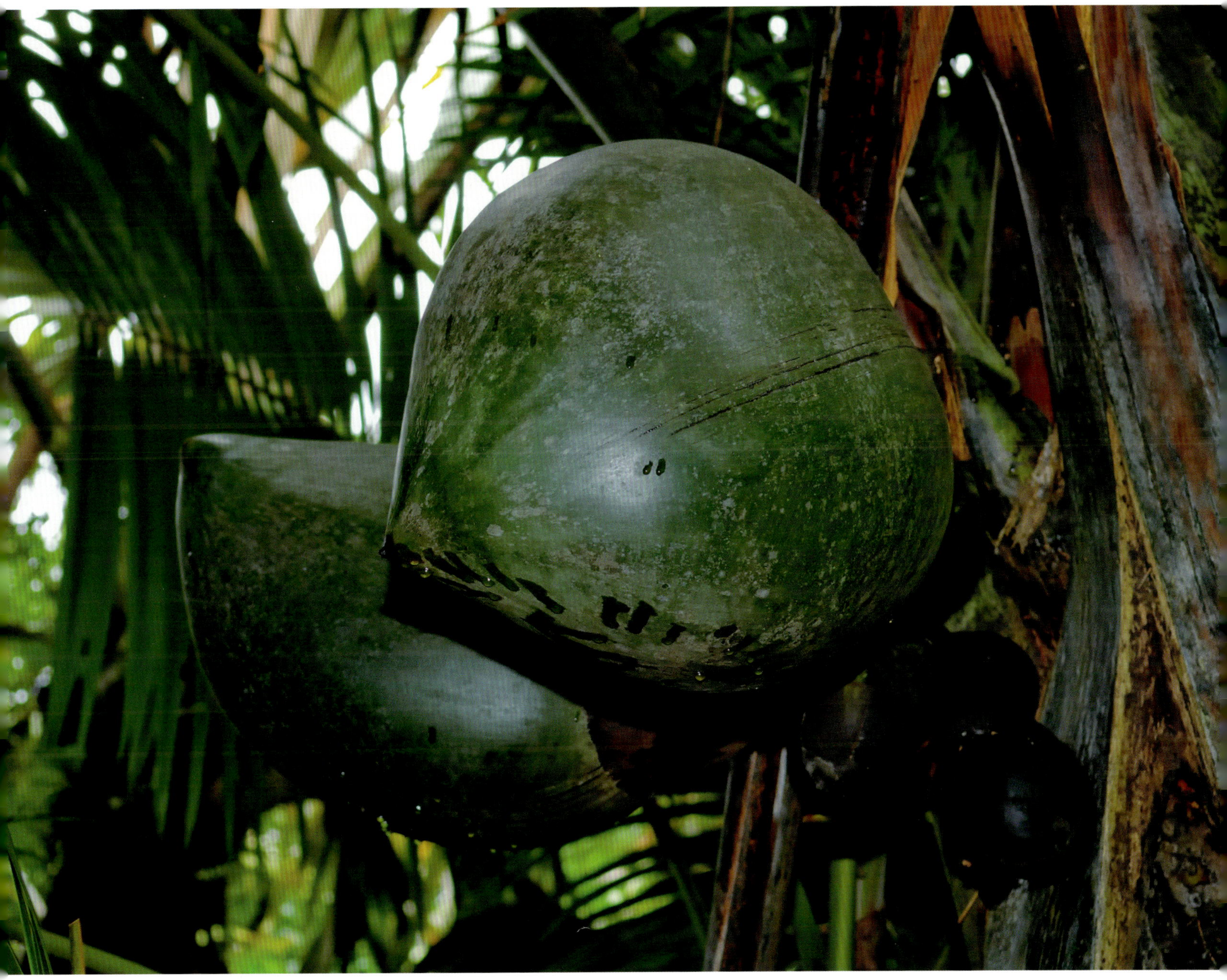

Gigantic stone steps lead into the deep gorges of the Grand Canyon, which became a UNESCO World Heritage site as early as 1979. The various layers, distinguished from one another by different shades of red, allow laypersons as well as scientists to read the history of the Earth like an open book. Sure-footed mountain goats are at home here, in Canada, Alaska and the Rocky Mountains.

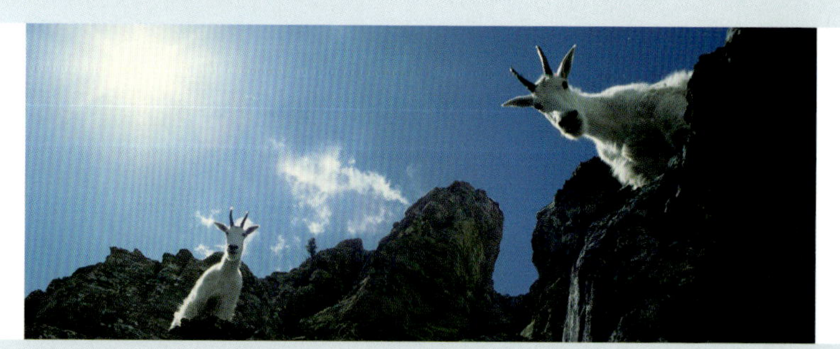

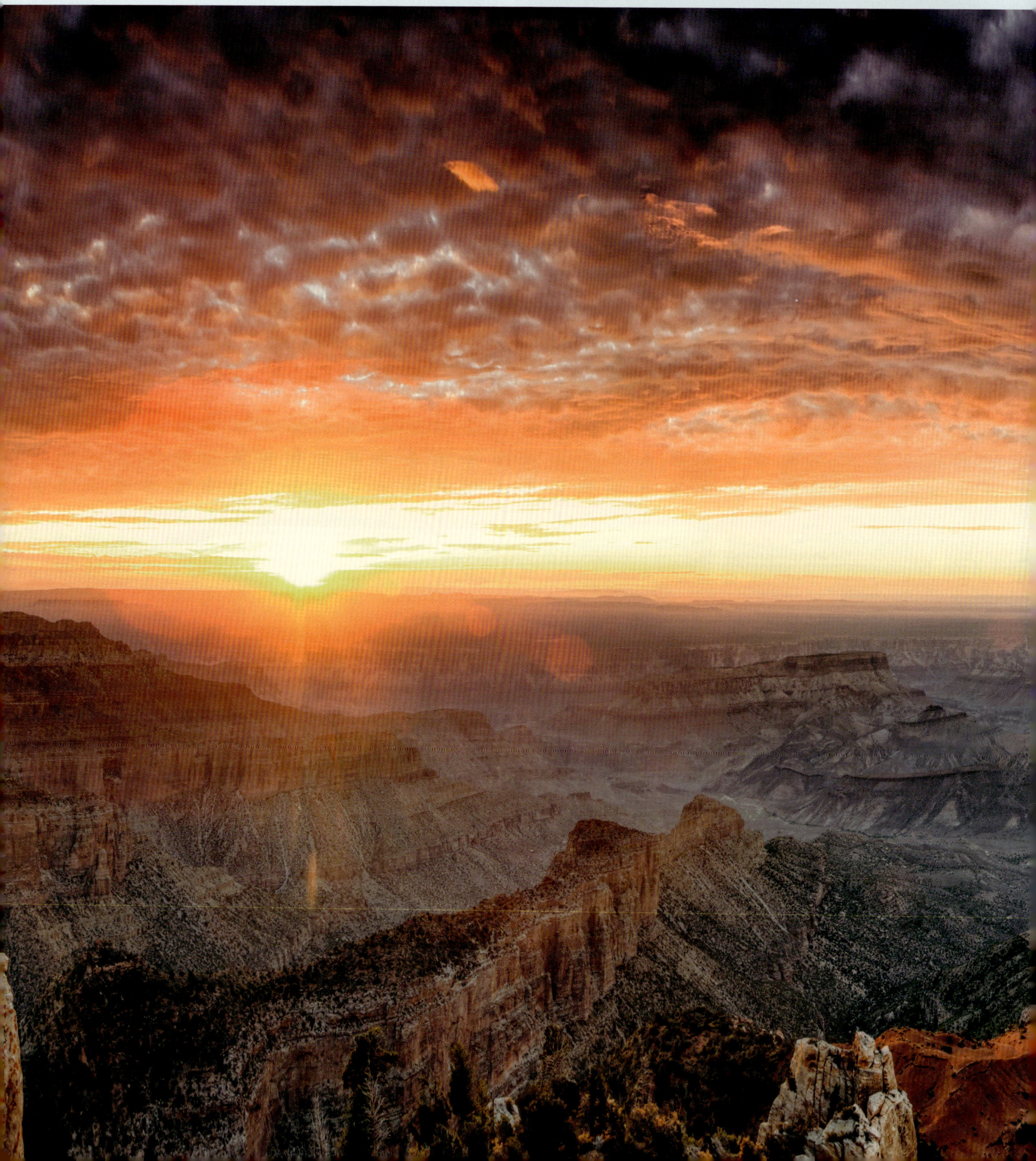

NORTH- AND CENTRAL AMERICA

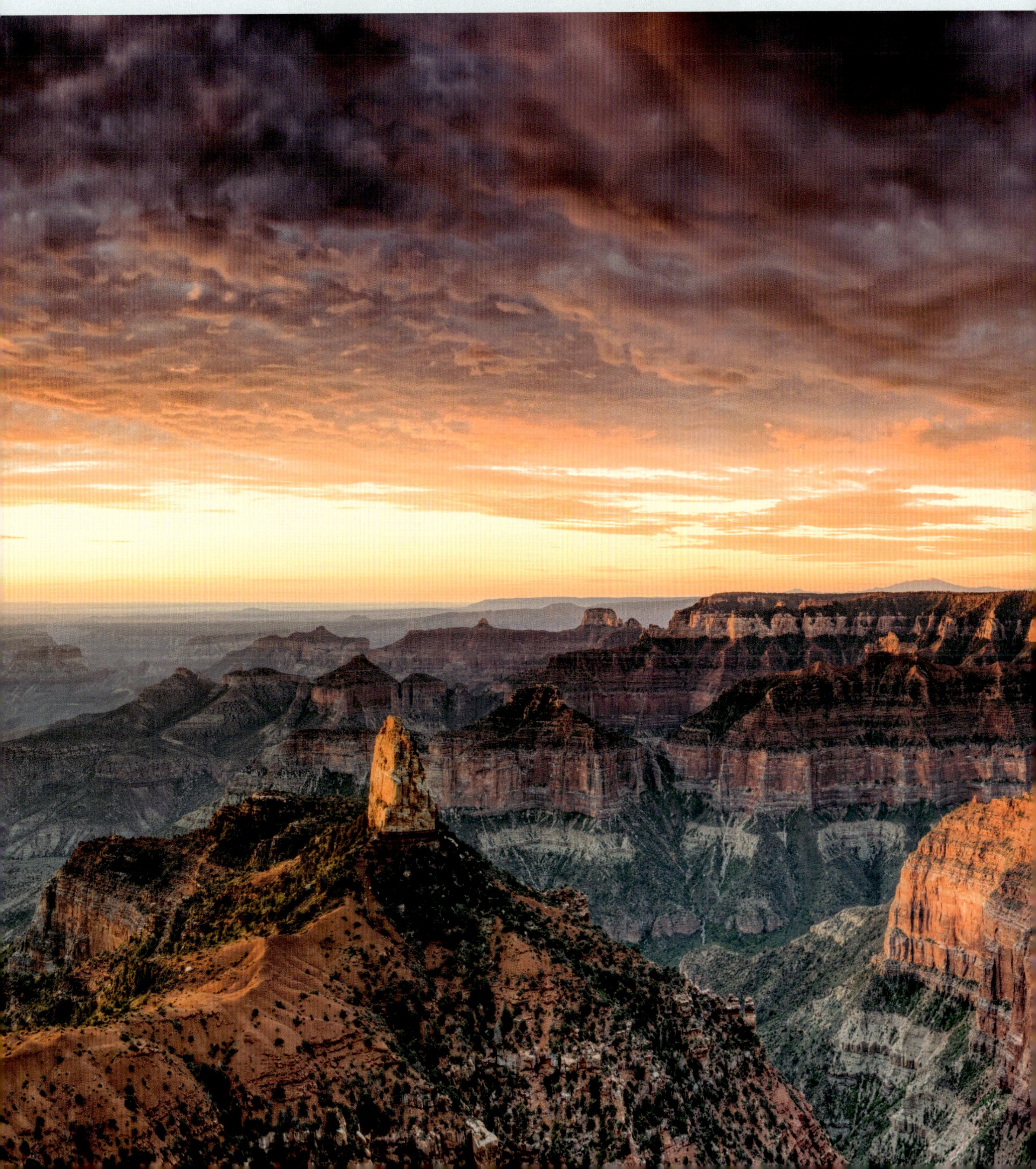

KLUANE / WRANGELL-ST. ELIAS / GLACIER BAY / TATSHENSHINI-ALSEK

Date of inscription: 1979
Extended: 1992 (Glacier Bay), 1994 (Tatshenshini-Alsek)

The International Biosphere Reserve is home to an astonishing range of fascinating flora and fauna.

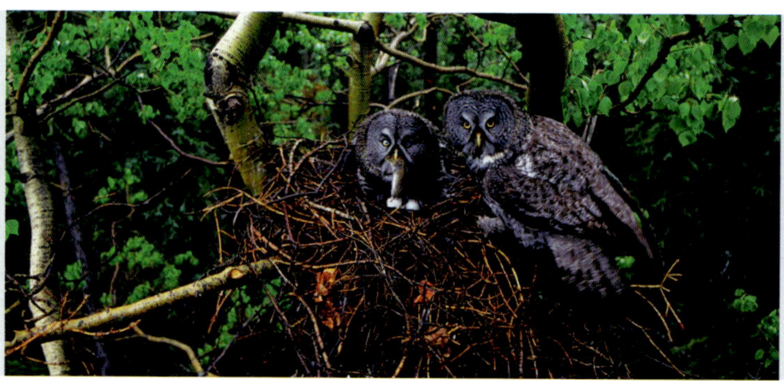

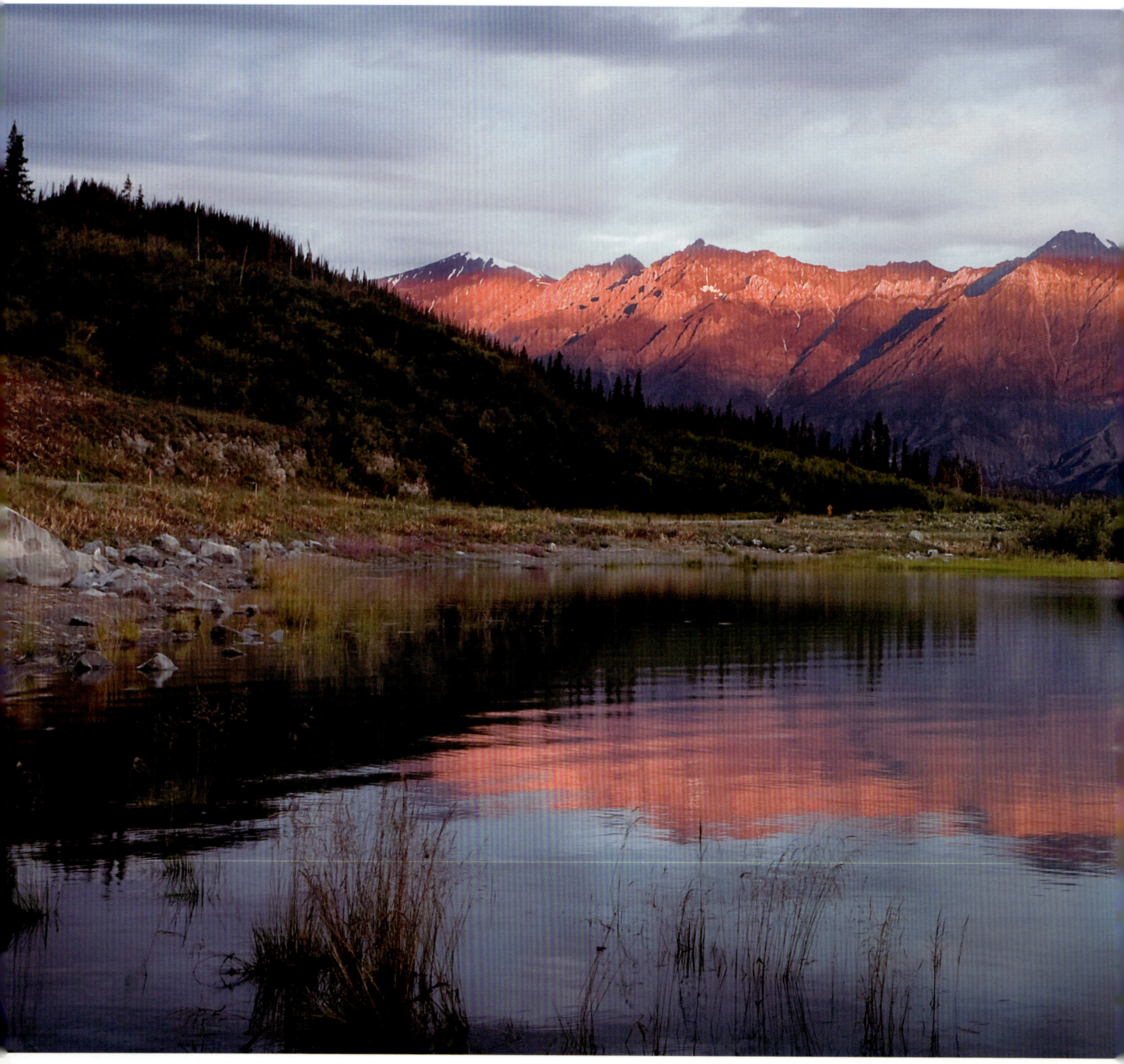

Two national parks on the Canadian side, Kluane (in the Yukon Territory) and Tatshenshini-Alsek (in British Columbia), and Wrangell–St Elias and Glacier Bay National Parks (both in Alaska) together form the first binational UNESCO World Heritage Site, and also constitute the largest dry land nature reserve in the world. Its scenery is characterized by giant ice fields, mighty glaciers, high mountains, waterfalls, roaring rivers, silent lakes, and expanses of tundra and forest.

In spite of a climate typified by long winters, the local flora is astonishingly varied. Large forested areas are to be found at elevations of up to 1,100 m (3,600 feet), made up of betula, berry bushes, and deciduous and evergreen tree species, including the impressive Sitka spruce, which can reach heights of up to 90 m (300 feet). Varieties of willow and mountain meadowgrasses are found at subalpine elevations of 1,100 to 1,600 m (3,600 to 5,200 feet). Heather, wild flowers, lichen, low bushes, and cripple birch are characteristic of the alpine tundra between 1,600 and 2,000 m (5,200 and 6,600 feet). The diversity of the animal life is also impressive, with black, brown, and grizzly bears roaming the rivers, which teem with fish. The rare Dall sheep and the mountain goat share a habitat on the upper slopes. The four national parks are home to 170 species of bird, as well as red deer, wolves, red foxes, lynxes, muskrats, Arctic hares, gophers, and chipmunks.

The Sheep Mountains (large picture) are reflected in the clear waters of Lake Kluane. Covering an area of 405 sq. km (156 sq. miles), it is the largest lake in the Yukon Territory. The distinctive pattern of facial feathers gave the great grey owl (left) its name.

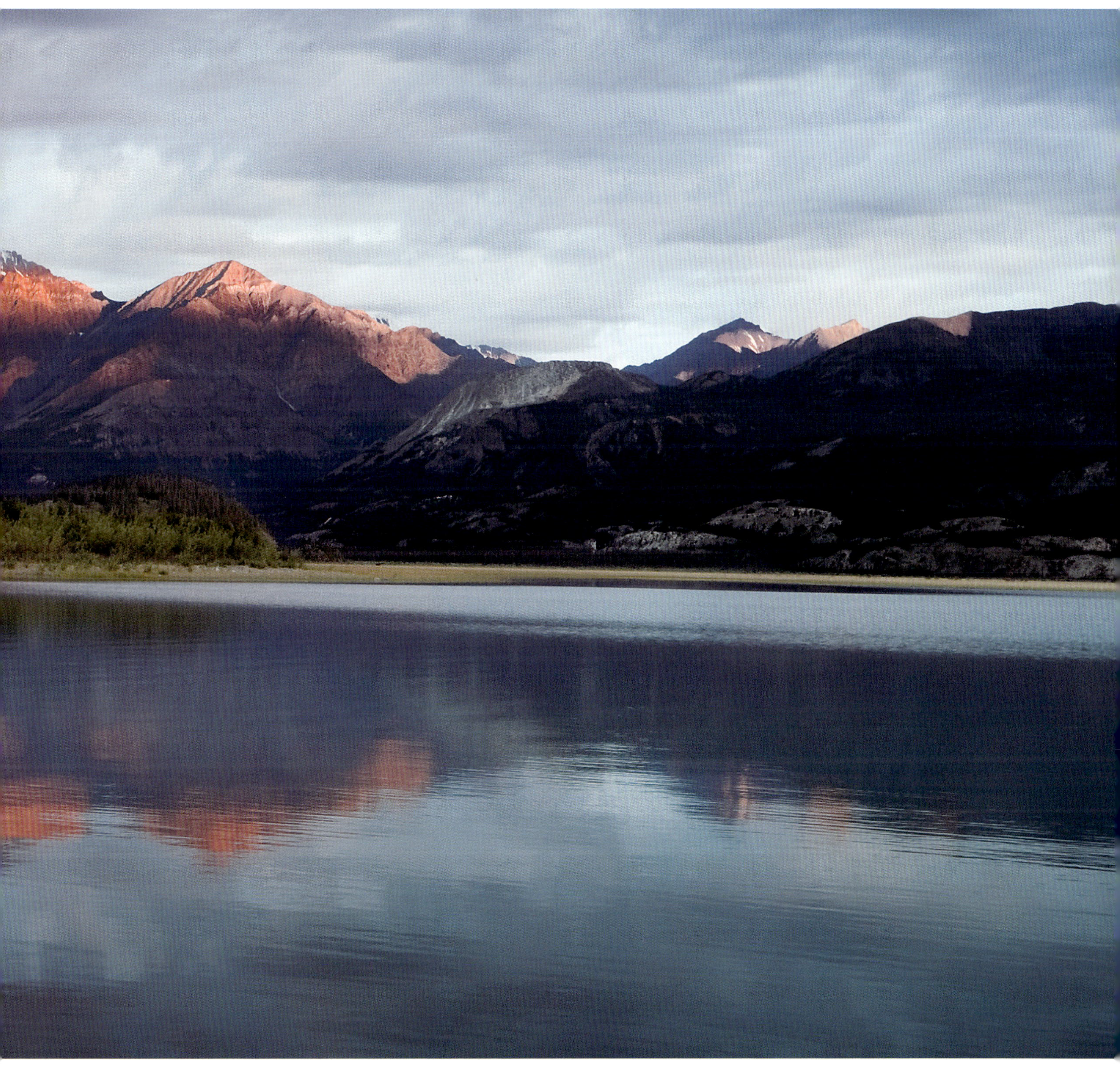

KLUANE NATIONAL PARK

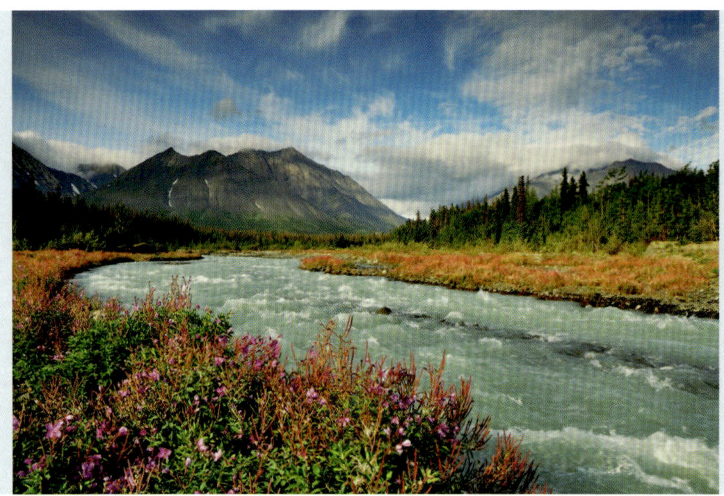

This romantic nature reserve lies in the south-west of the Yukon Territory, in the wilderness of the Northern Coast Mountains Natural Region. Part of its northern border is formed by the Alaska Highway.

At the heart of the park is a rugged mountain landscape with Mount Logan, at 5,959 m (19,550 feet) the highest mountain in Canada. Here are also the largest ice fields on Earth outside of Greenland and Antarctica. The mountains of the park belong to the mighty Wrangell–St. Elias chain, which ranges as far as Alaska in the Wrangell–St. Elias National Park. The Alsek River flows fizzing and foaming through its valleys and gorges, carrying along drifting icebergs and often framed by up to 4,500-m- (14,765-foot-) high peaks. The area is a paradise for nature lovers and hikers. A widely branched network of hiking tracks and routes makes the national park accessible.

Kathleen Lake is located in the farthest eastern corner of the Kluane National Park (large picture). Purple fireweed (left) grows on the banks of the Quill Creek.

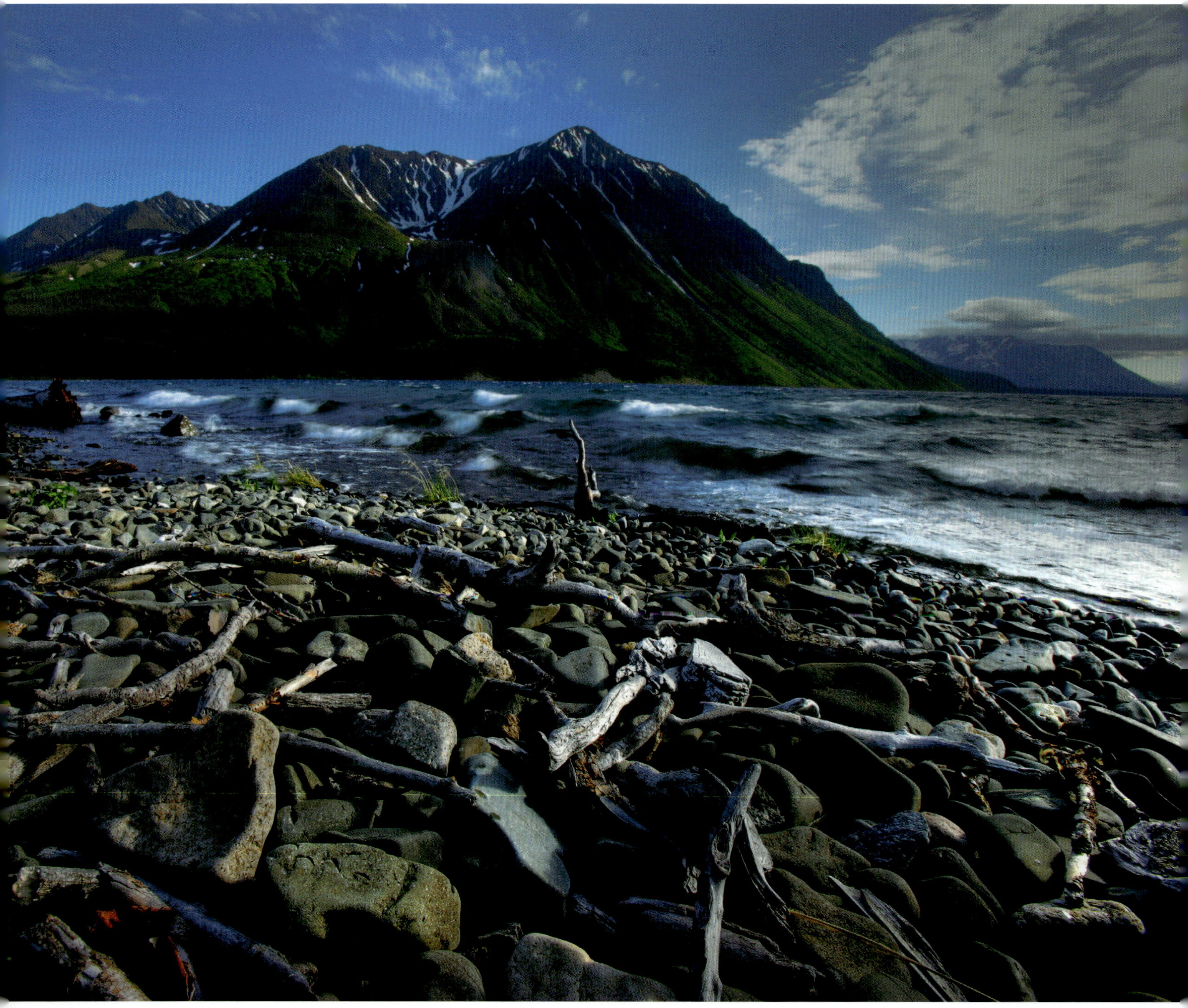

WRANGELL-ST. ELIAS NATIONAL PARK

This wilderness in southeast Alaska is second to none: Together with the Canadian Kluane National Park, which lies across the border in the Yukon Territory, Wrangell–St. Elias, the largest national park in the United States, has been a UNESCO World Natural Heritage site since 1980. It is also one of the most beautiful. It comprises a huge collection of high mountains, including Mount St. Elias – at 5,489 m (18,010 feet) the second highest mountain in the United States after Mount McKinley (6,194 m/ 20,321 feet). The more than 100 glaciers in this nature reserve make up the largest ice field south of the Arctic Circle. The landscape is marked by an adventurous mountain wilderness with impressive gorges and roaring rivers, with hardly any human presence.

The Alsek River pours itself into the Alsek Lake. The Elias Mountains rise from the shore (large picture). Right: The Hubbard Glacier is over 10 km (6 miles) wide at the front. At the terminus or toe, where the glacier merges with the sea, numerous seals frolic on the ice floes.

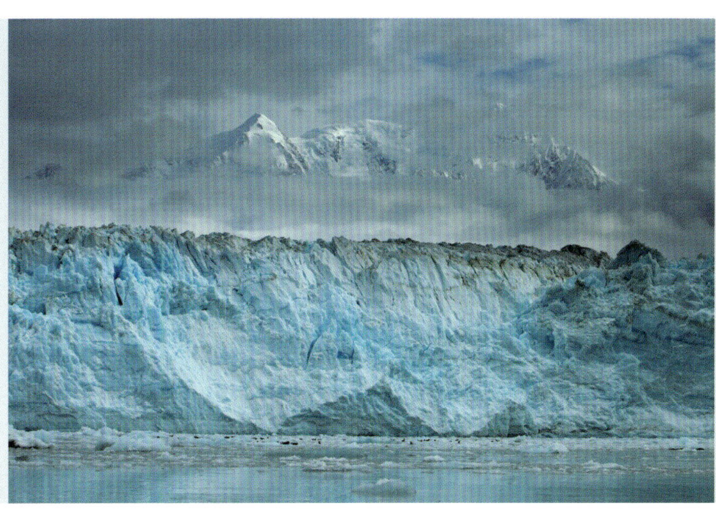

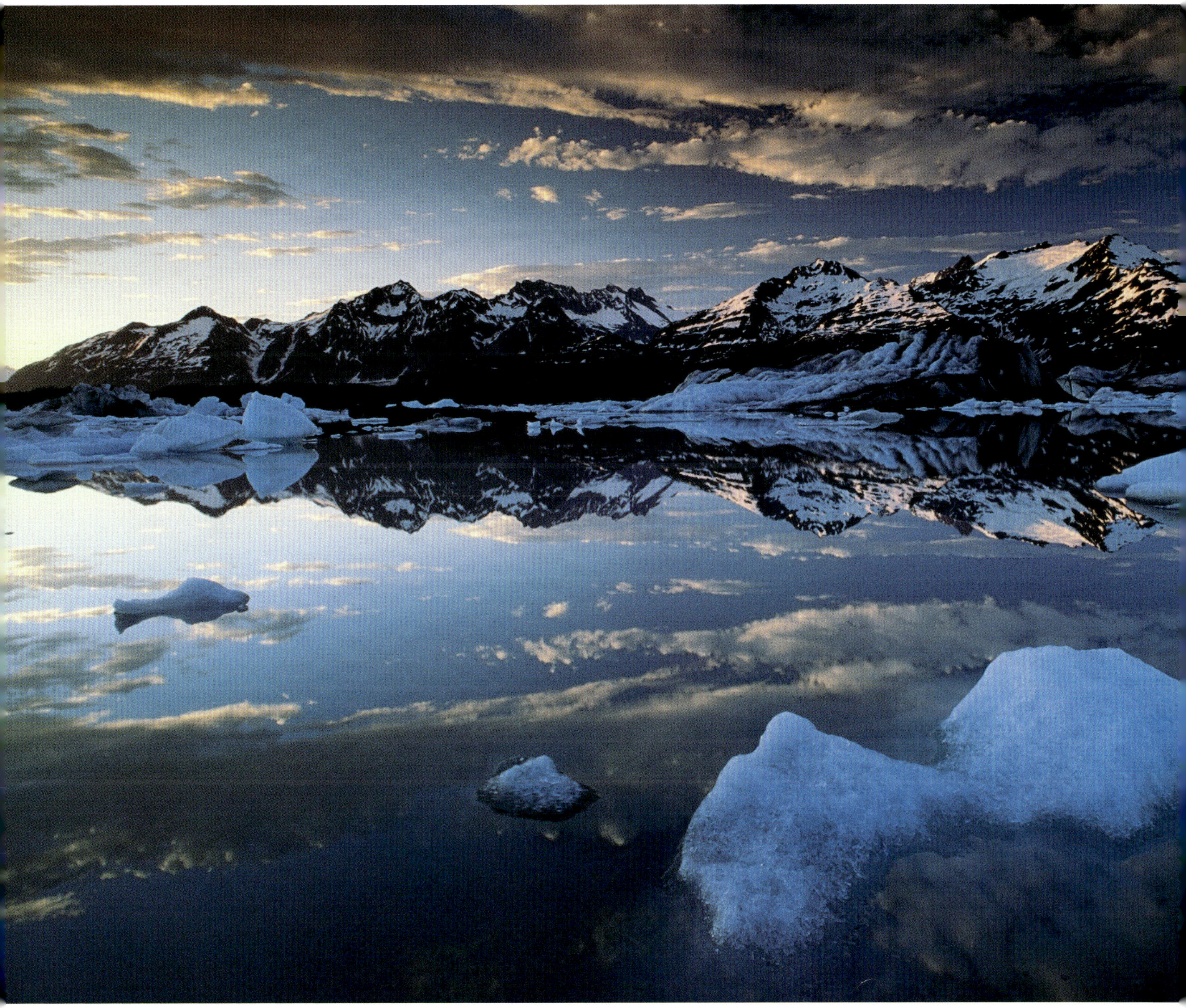

GLACIER BAY NATIONAL PARK

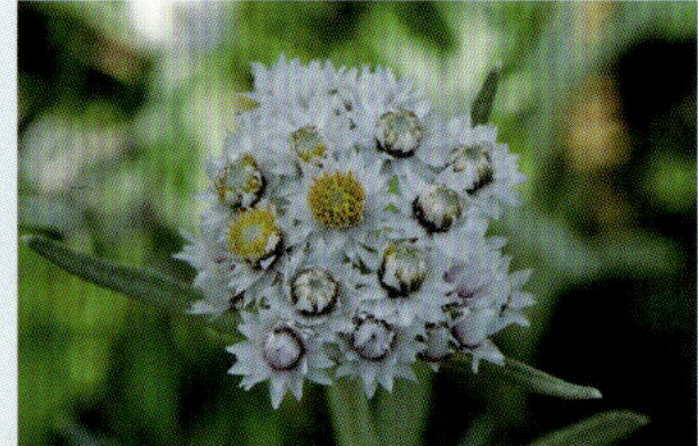

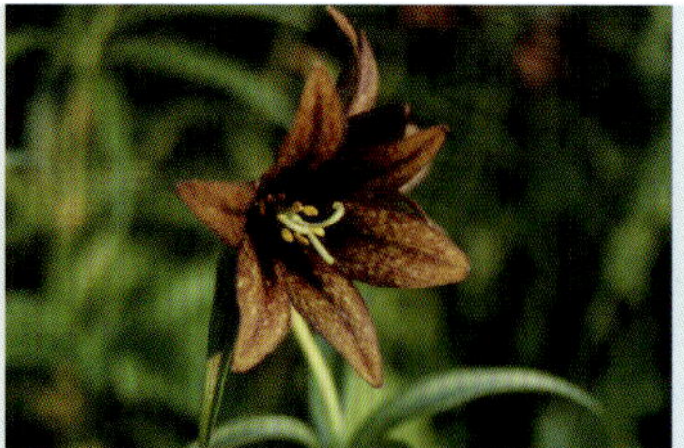

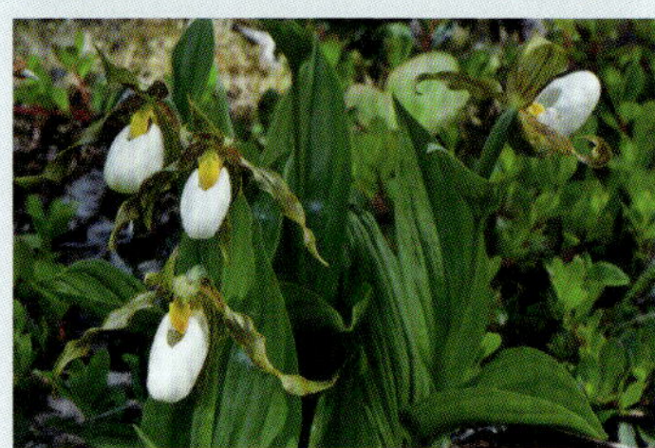

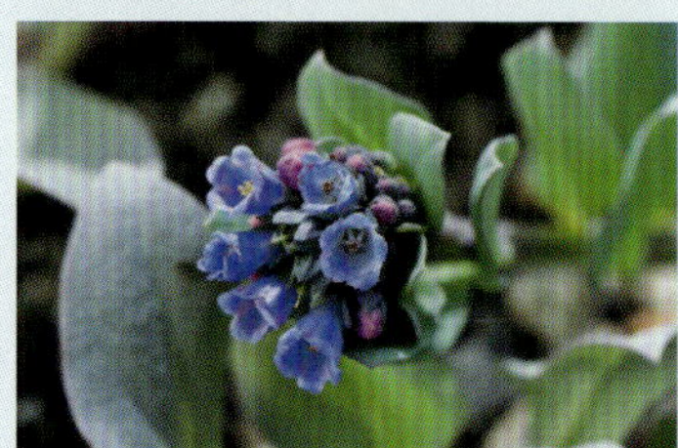

The Glacier Bay National Park, a cross-border World Heritage site, is a perfect example of how quickly change can happen in nature. Just under 250 years ago, you could hardly see anything of this bay – a massive wall of ice then closed the access to this unique glacial paradise. Within 100 years, the ice wall shifted inland by 70 km (44 miles). In October 1879, the conservationist John Muir wrote in his diary: "And here, too, one learns that the world, though made, is yet being made; that this is still the morning of creation; that mountains long conceived are now being born …". Seven glaciers reach down to the coast and calve into the sea. Glacier Bay was declared a national park in 1980. Still covered by about one-third with ice, a large section of the coast and the marine waters also form a part of the park.

The meadows are a sea of wildflowers; lupines dominate (large picture). Left, clockwise: chocolate lily, oyster plants like Virginia bluebells, mountain lady's slipper and pearly everlasting also known as "new snow".

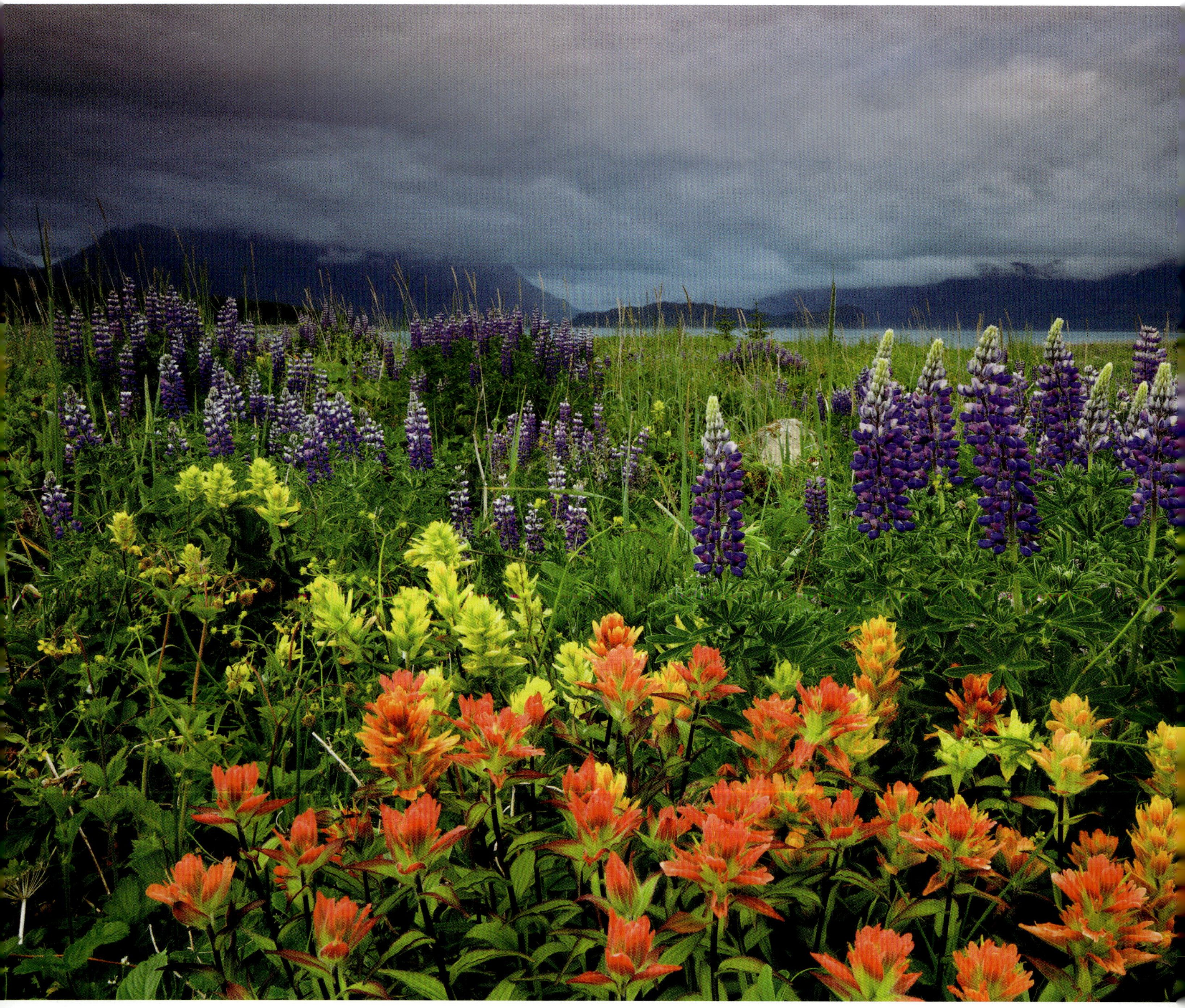

TATSHENSHINI-ALSEK PROVINCIAL PARK

In the extreme northwest of British Columbia, the two rivers Tatshenshini and Alsek form one of the greatest river systems on Earth. Up to 1.5 km (1 mile) wide, the Tatshenshini River meanders through a rugged mountain wilderness, in which the glaciers go right down to the river and push icebergs into the water. The Alsek River winds through equally dramatic scenery. Together with the three national parks – Kluane (Yukon Territory), Wrangell–St. Elias and Glacier Bay (both in Alaska), founded in 1993 –, the Tatshenshini-Alsek Park was the first bi-national UNESCO World Heritage site. It covers approximately 10,000 sq. km (3,860 sq. miles), making it the largest nature reserve on Earth on a mainland. Canadian and American conservation groups had campaigned for its establishment.

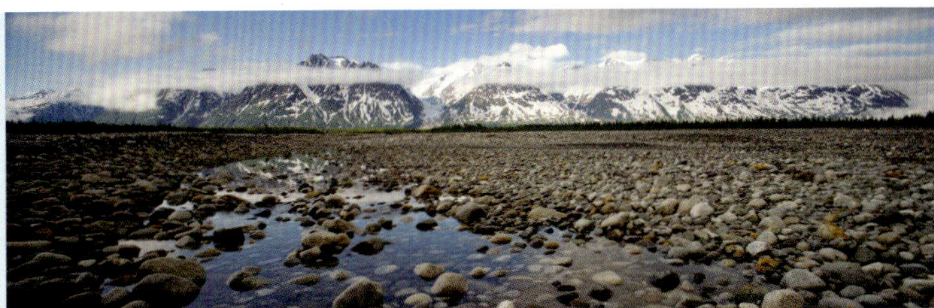

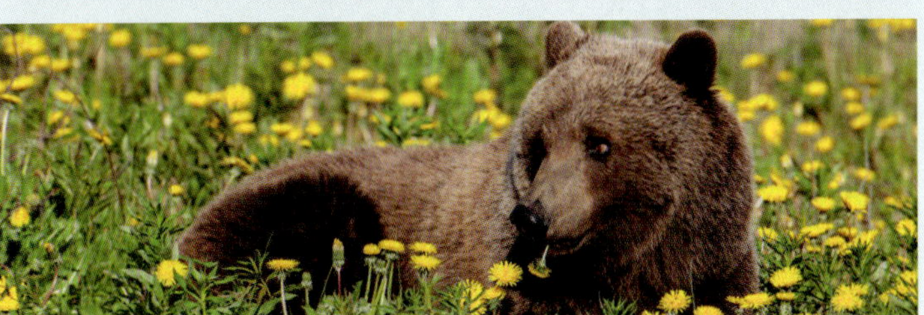

Even brown bears seem to experience something like spring fever as they peacefully chew on dandelion flowers (right bottom). In summer, fireweed flowers on the banks of the Alsek River (large picture). Right top: view of the Alsek River.

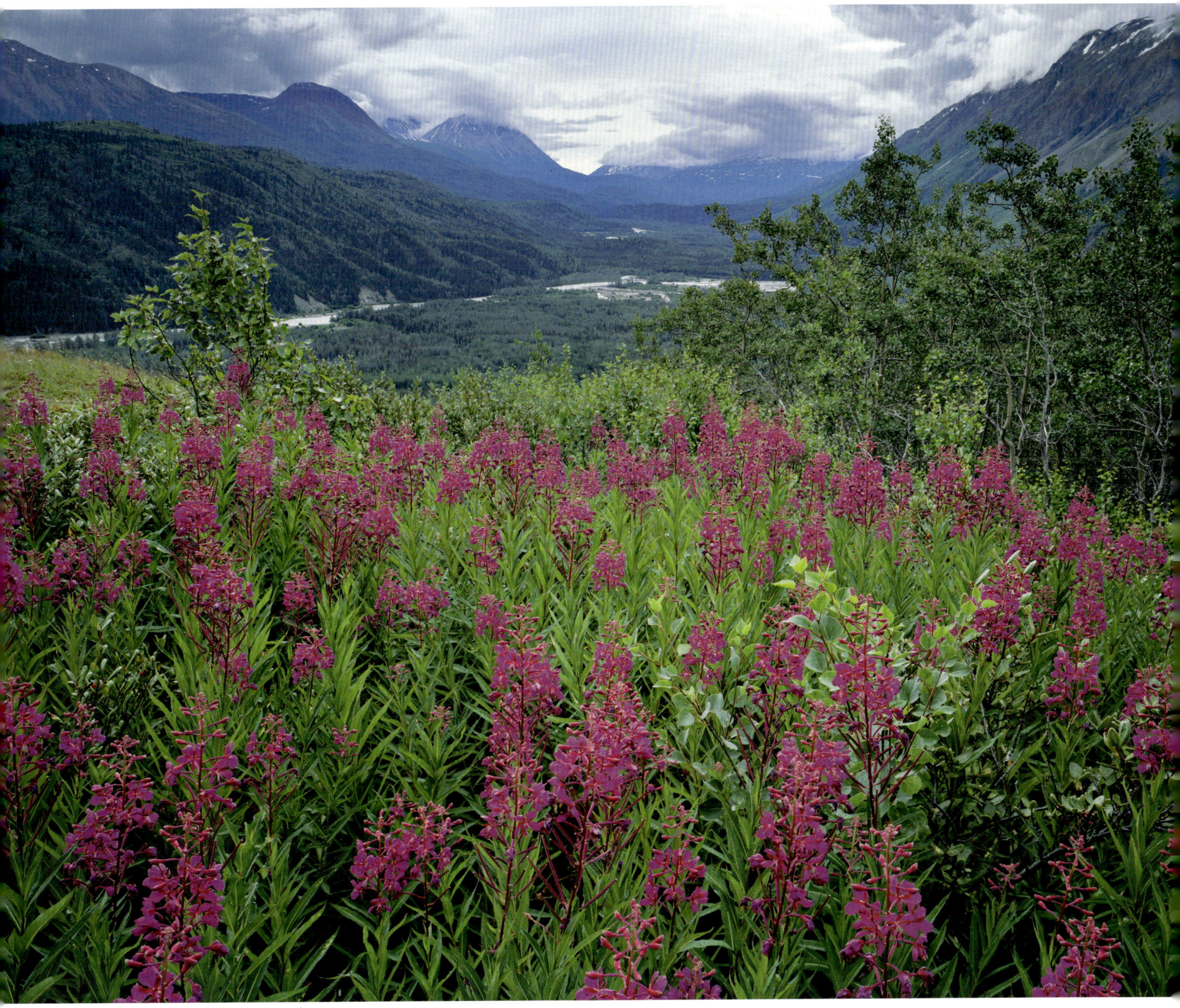

NAHANNI NATIONAL PARK

Date of instinction: 1978

The South Nahanni river – one of the world's wildest and most beautiful – gave this barely accessible national park its name.

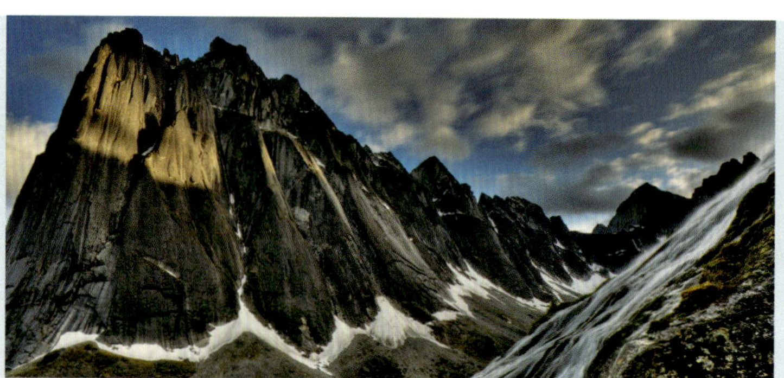

The source of the 540-km (335-mile) long South Nahanni river is to be found 1,600 m (5,240 feet) above sea level on Mount Christie in the Mackenzie mountains of Canada's Northwest Territories. The national park area, extending along both river banks as a relatively narrow strip, 320 km (200 miles) long, begins just south of Mount Wilson. The hot mineral springs of the area, such as

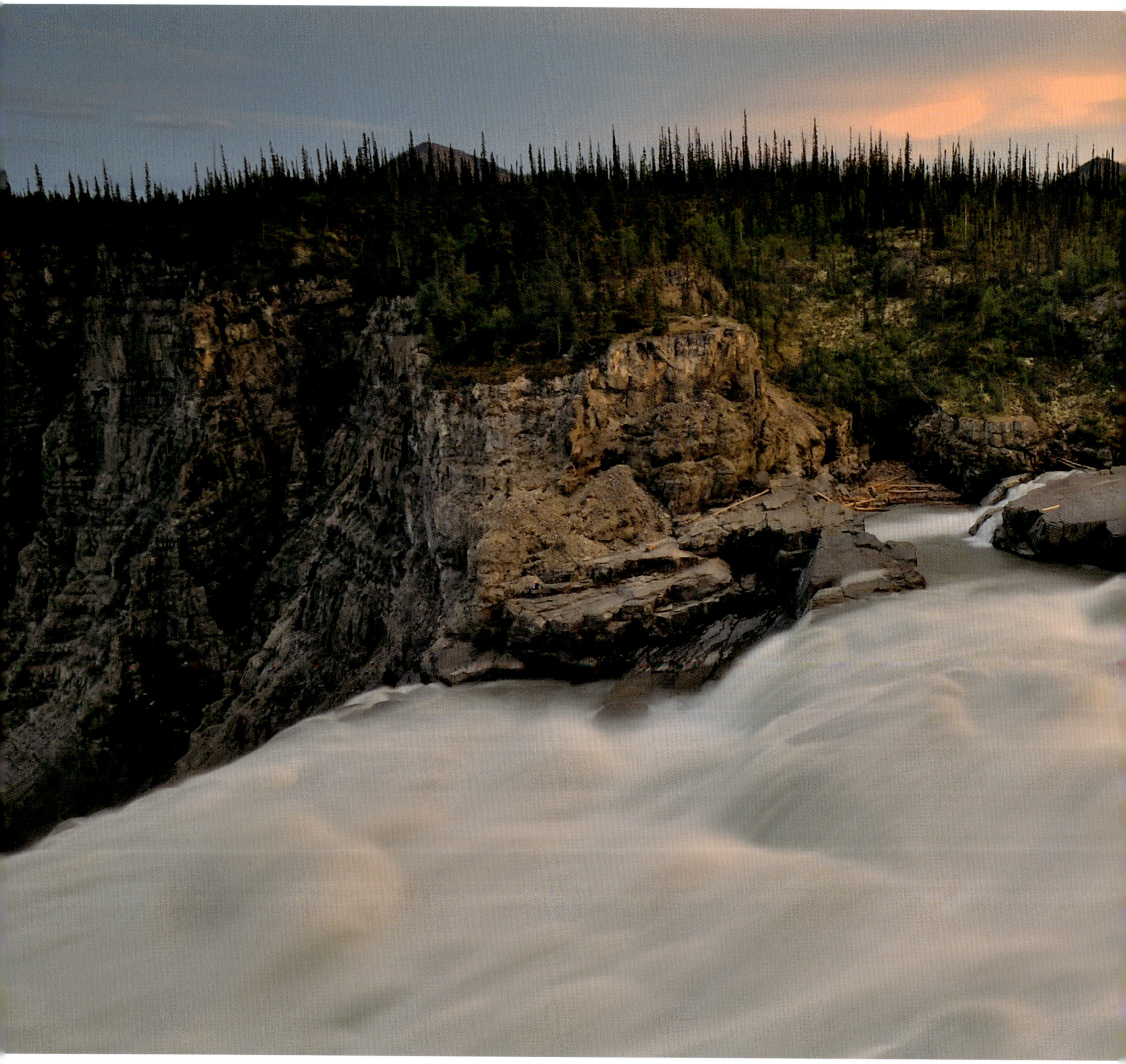

Rabbitkettle Hotsprings and others, ensure a mild environment and support types of vegetation unusual at such northerly latitudes. Numerous ferns, wild mint, rosebushes, parsnips, goldenrod, asters, and varieties of orchids are all to be found here. The river meanders for 120 km (75 miles) through tundra overgrown with grasses, lichen, and dwarf shrubs, on which live caribou – gigantic North American reindeer with shovel-like antlers. In its course, the river descends through numerous rapids, representing a considerable challenge for whitewater rafters.

With a drop of 90 m (295 feet), Virginia Falls is among the most impressive of the waterfalls, and the three main canyons are similarly breathtaking, their sheer walls rising to a height of 1,300 m (4,250 feet). Bizarre rock formations and caves are typical for this landscape. The South Nahanni river flows past peaks reaching heights of 2,700 m (8,300 feet) before it finally disperses into many distributaries not far from the national park's southern extreme.

Mount Harrison Smith is 1,597 m (5,240 feet) high; it's not by chance that the steep, vertical mountain range has the telling name Cirque of the Unclimbables (left). The thunderous Virginia Falls plunge into the depths (large picture).

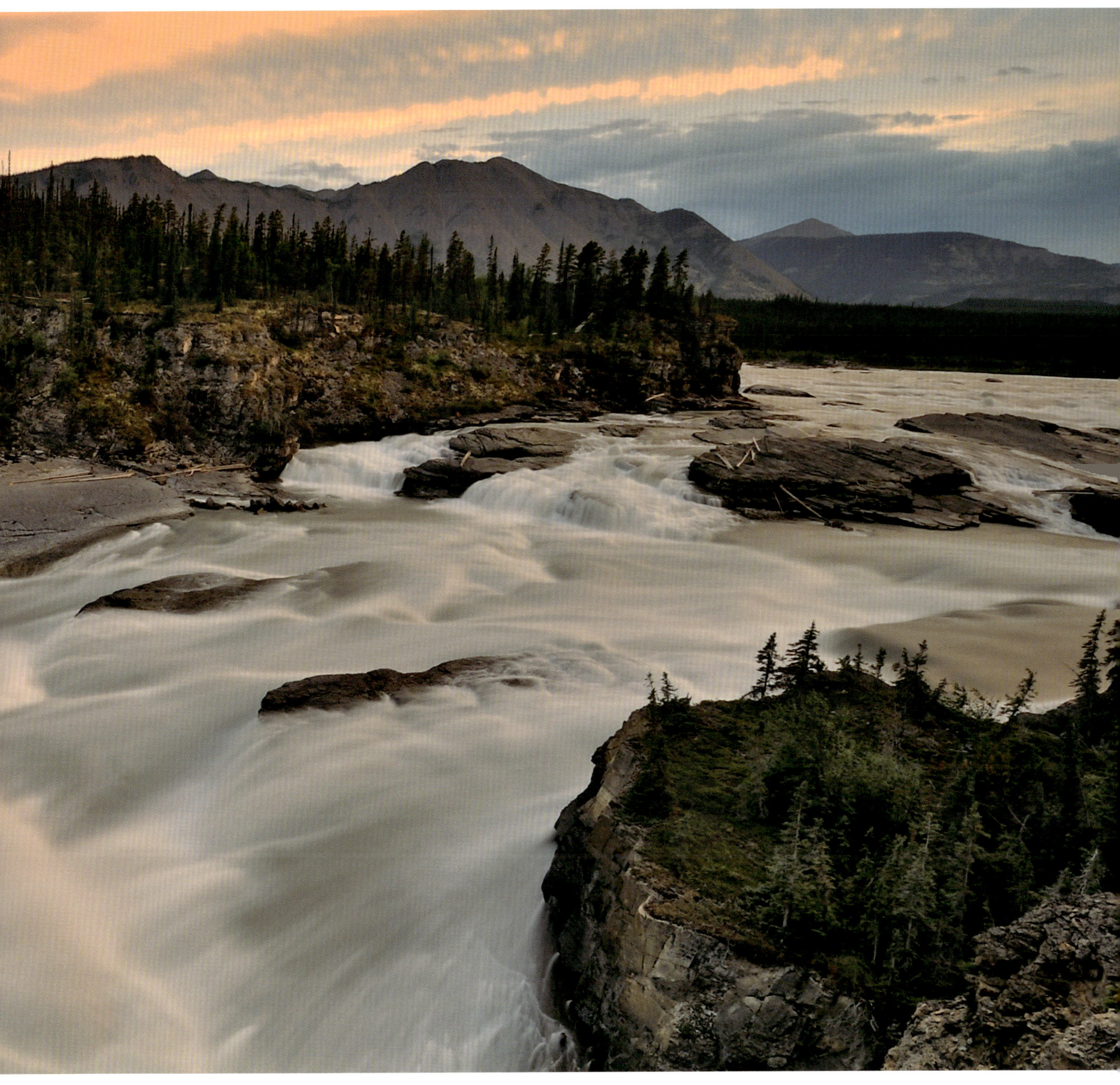

WOOD BUFFALO NATIONAL PARK

Date of inscription: 1983

Canada's largest nature reserve – an area of almost 45,000 sq. km (17,375 sq. miles), two-thirds of which are located in Alberta and one-third in the Northwest Territories – was established in 1922 to protect the last herds of wood buffalo.

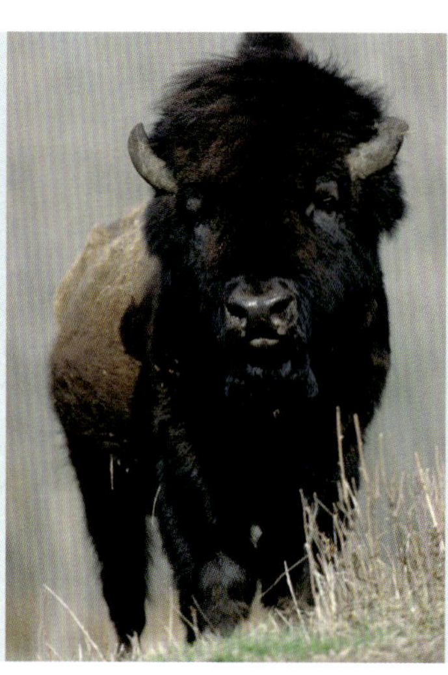

Two-thirds of the 44,807 sq. km (17,400 sq. miles) that constitute Canada's largest national park are situated in Alberta, the remainder lying in the Northwest Territories. The park was founded in 1922, both to protect the nesting places of the endangered whooping crane and to conserve the few remaining wood bison living here. The current total bison population, including both wood bison and the equally endangered prairie bison which has in many cases joined the herds, amounts to some 6,000 specimens, the world's largest group in the wild. The conservation area is divided into three habitats: a prairie upland cleared by forest fires; a barely drained plateau with meandering rivers, oxbow lakes, salt flats, marsh, and bog areas; and the Peace and Athabasca river delta, an enchanting world of reed meadows, marshland and shallow lakes. The park is thus a refuge for a variety of animals: moose, caribou, black bears, and gray wolves live here.

The mighty bison, with its powerful skull, grows to a length of 3 m (10 feet) and can weigh up to 1 metric ton (2,200 lb).

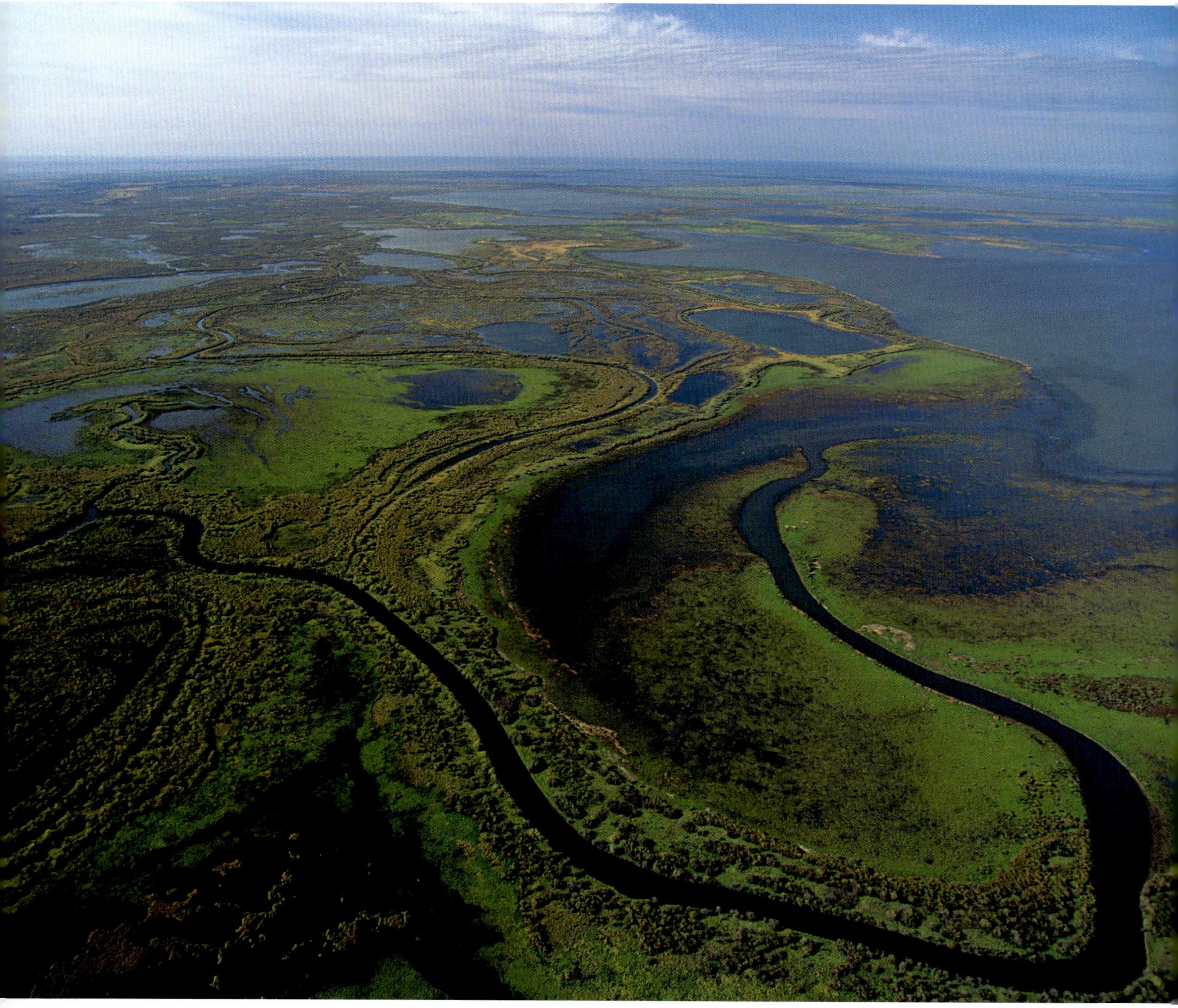

SGANG GWAAY (ANTHONY ISLAND)

When the last inhabitants of the small island of Ninstints, or S'Gang Gwaay, left in 1880, the Haida people already looked back on a thousand-year-old history. At that time, Europeans had decimated this tribe, which belonged to the Northwest Coastal People, through introduced diseases. Today the number of surviving Haida is estimated to be about 2,000. On the island, artfully designed, often several meters (feet) high, carved and painted totem poles testify to the history of this ancient people, who first came into contact with white people at the end of the 18th century. Specialized artisans created these posts in honour of important personalities. Their carvings depict scenes from everyday life, mythical creatures and important figures. The totem poles all had an opening to take the ashes of the deceased, and the tops of the poles were adorned with the token of each respective tribe.

Originally brightly painted, the colours on the totem poles in Ninstints have faded and almost entirely disappeared due to wind and weather, moss and plantlife.

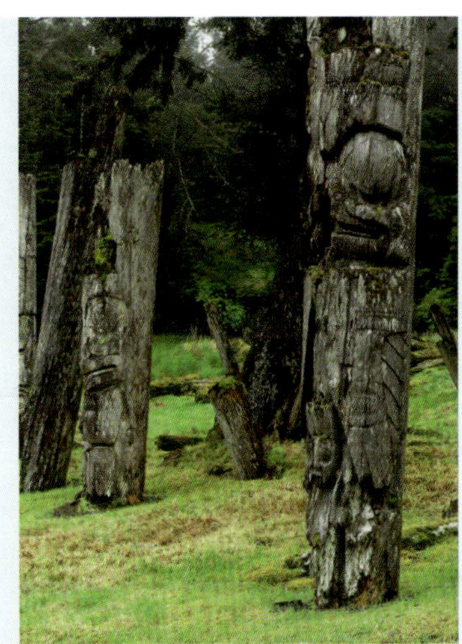

Date of inscription: 1981 *

In the village of Ninstints, located on SGang Gwaay (Anthony Island) south of the Queen Charlotte Islands (Haida Gwaii) in British Columbia, 32 totem poles and ten cedar wood houses testify to the millennia-old culture of the Haida people.

*** protected by UNESCO as a Cultural Heritage site.**

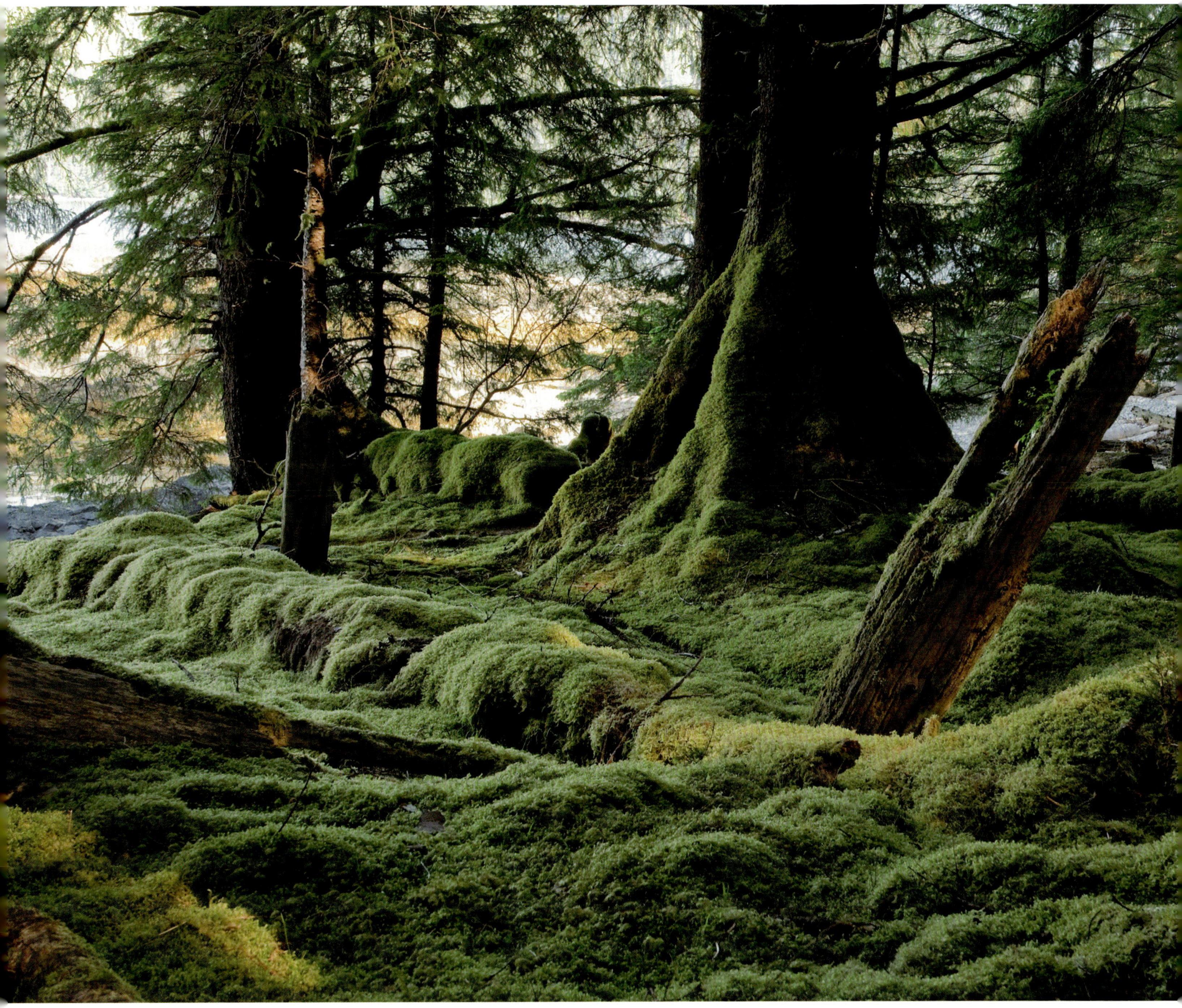

THE CANADIAN ROCKY MOUNTAINS

Date of inscription: 1984
Extended: 1990

This World Heritage Site of four National Parks (Banff, Jasper, Yoho, and Kootenay) has been expanded to include the Provincial Parks of Mount Robson, Mount Assiniboine, and Hamber to conserve the Canadian Rocky Mountains.

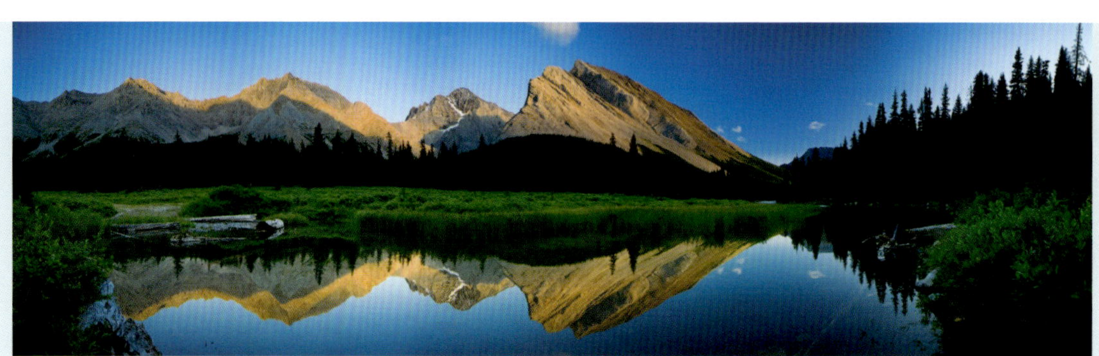

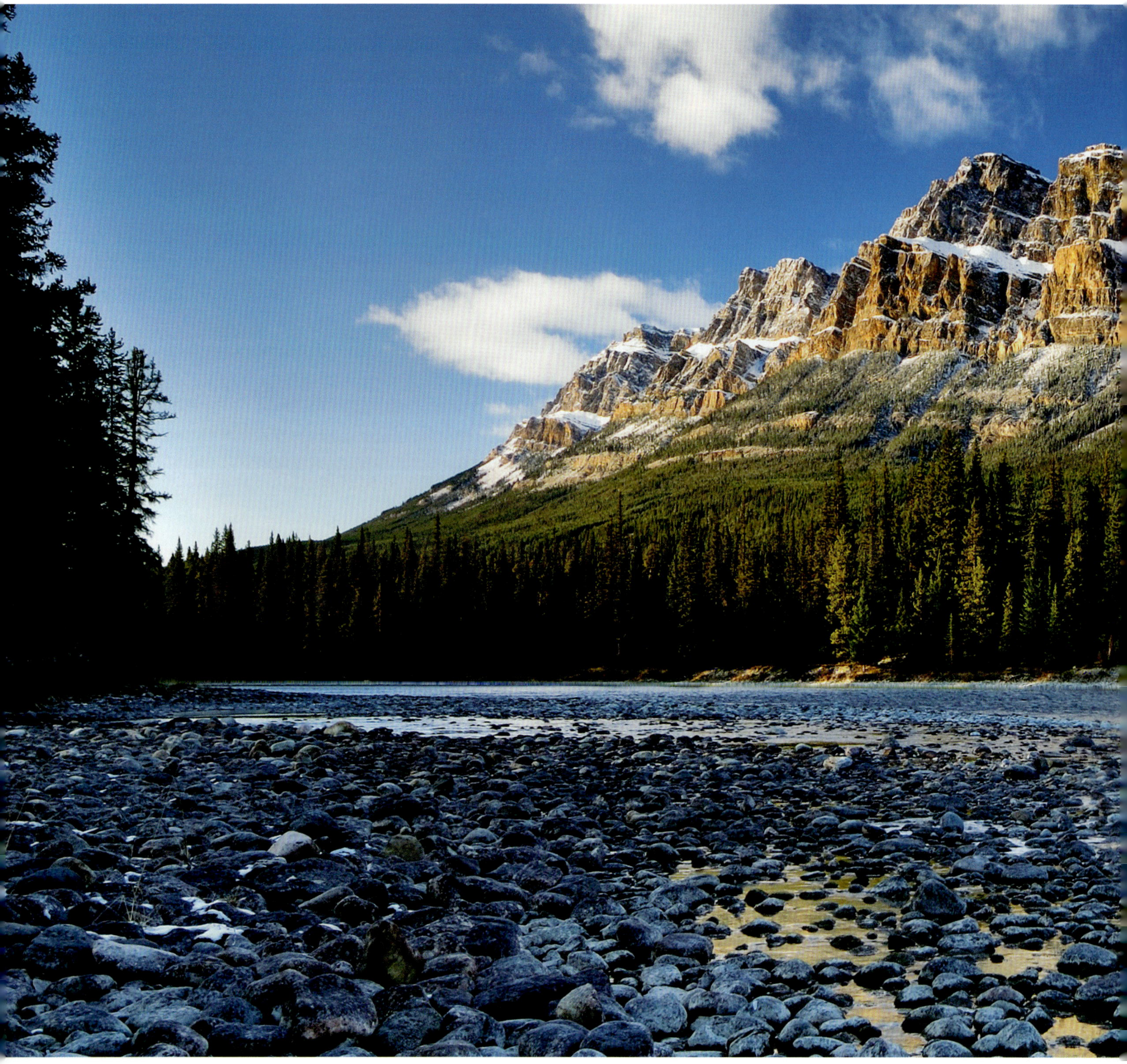

The Canadian Rockies are a 2,200-km (1,400-mile) long section of the American Cordillera, which runs down both halves of the continent from Alaska to Tierra del Fuego. The largest of the four national parks, Jasper, is also the most northerly, and boasts numerous peaks over 3,000 m (9,900 feet); Maligne Lake, which is over 20 km (13 miles) long; hot sulphur springs; and the largest continuous glacier field in the Rockies. Banff National Park, through which the Bow river flows, adjoins the park to the south and was founded as early as 1855. Picturesque Lake Louise lies at the foot of the 3,364-m (11,040-foot) high Mount Victoria glacier, and to the west lie the Kootenay and Yoho National Parks. The falls on the Yoho river are among the world's highest. Mount Robson and Mount Assiniboine Provincial Parks owe their names respectively to these two imposing peaks, each almost 4,000 m (13,200 feet) high. The Rocky Mountains parks, set amid glaciers, primary forest, and mountain torrents, are an undisturbed habitat for many species which have become rarer in recent times, including grizzly bears, moose, mountain goats, lynxes, wolves, beavers, and golden eagles.

A mountain range like a fairytale castle setting: The Bow River winds its way along the foot of Castle Mountain (large picture). From Elbow Lake you can enjoy a fantastic view of the surrounding peaks (left).

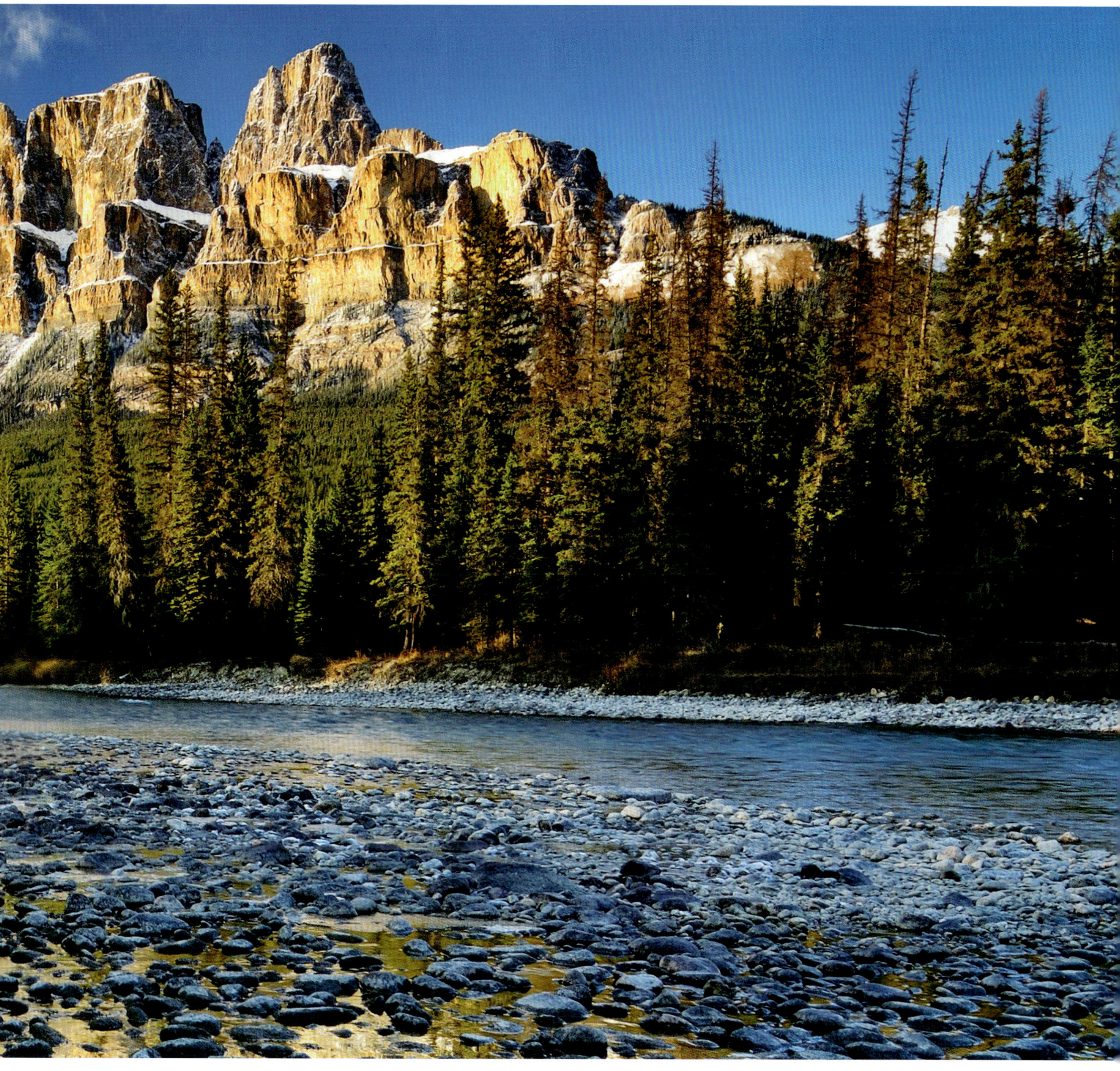

THE CANADIAN ROCKY MOUNTAINS: MOUNT ROBSON PROVINCIAL PARK

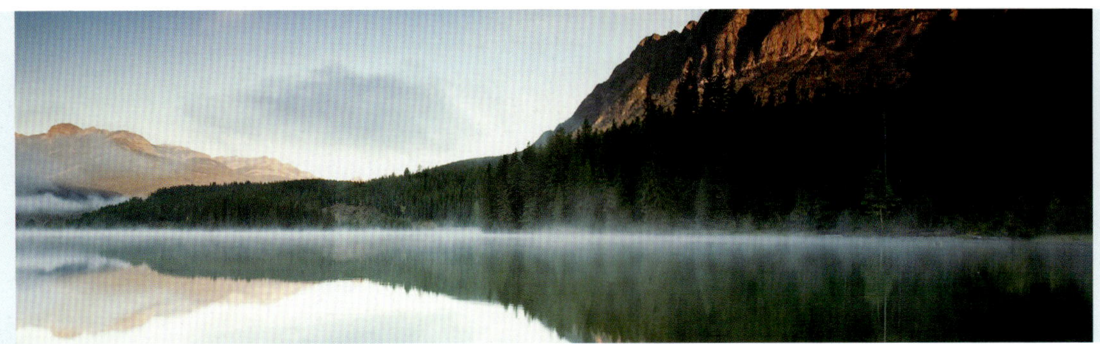

Mount Robson (3,954-m-/12,972-foot-) and Mount Fitzwilliam (2,911-m-/9,550-foot-) are the highest mountains in the park and in the Canadian Rocky Mountains. The First Nation tribes called Mount Robson Yuh-hai-has-hun (meaning "mountain of the spiral road"), an allusion to its upwardly spiralling rock layers, which resemble hairpin bends in a road. The white people called it

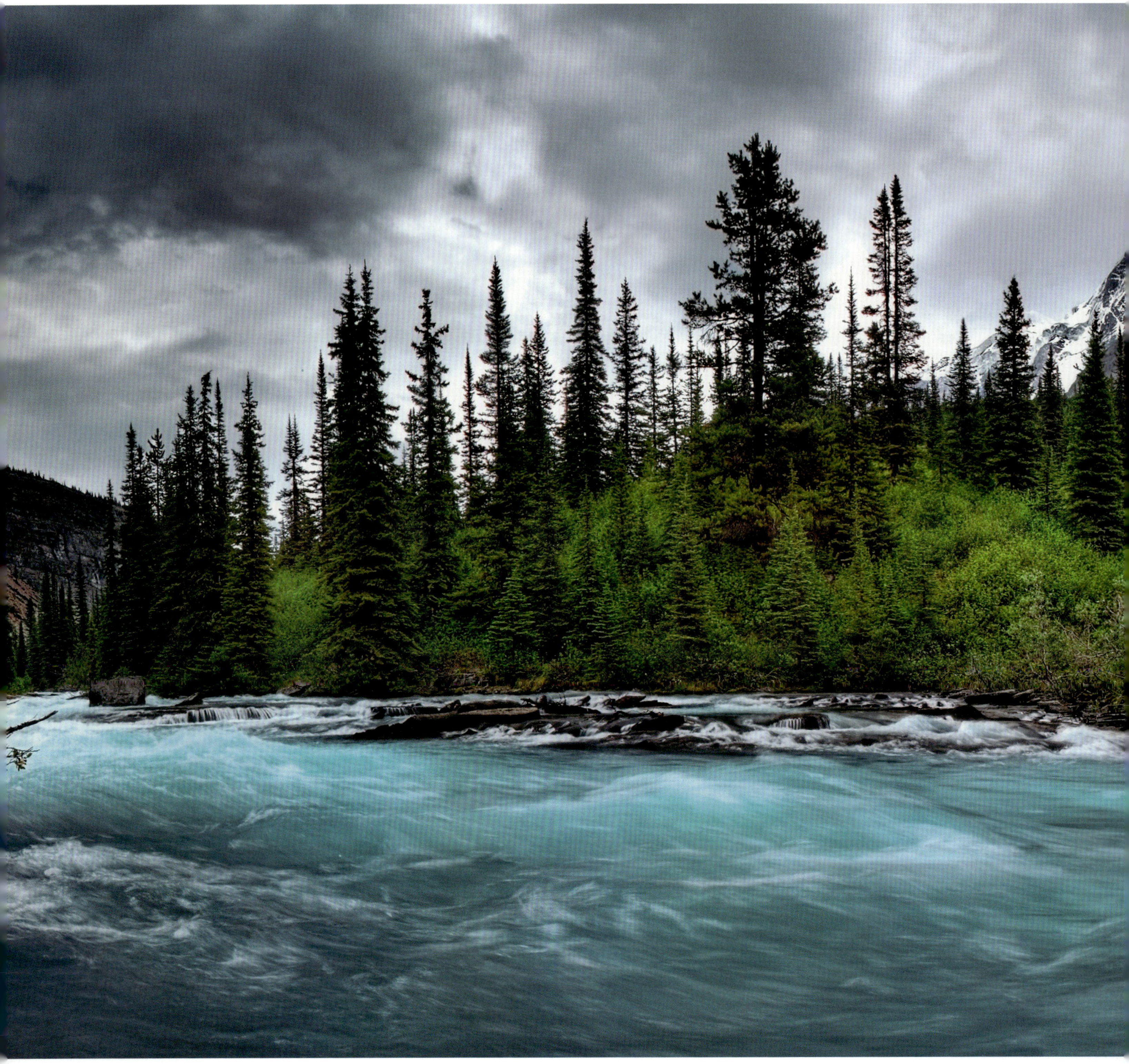

Mount Robson to honour John Robson, who was the province's prime minister from 1889 to 1892. In 1913, the government declared the area directly adjoining Jasper National Park in Alberta to the east the "Mount Robson Provincial Park". The park features fauna worth protecting, and in 1990 it was incorporated by UNESCO into the extended World Natural Heritage site known as as the Canadian Rocky Mountain Parks.

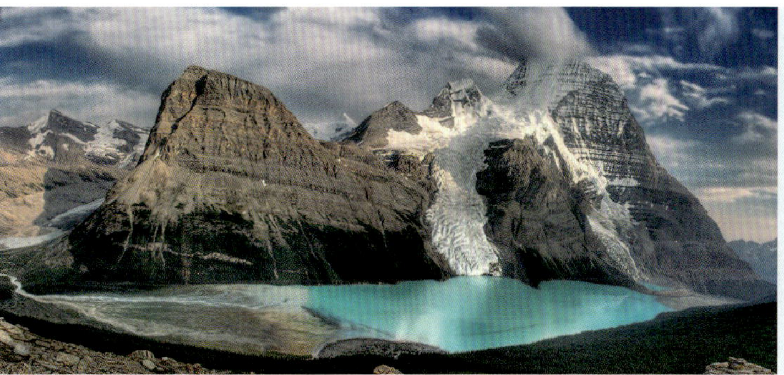

The mountain lake at the foot of Mount Robson sparkles in a deep turquoise (left). Yellowhead Lake and Yellowhead Mountain also belong to the Mount Robson Provincial Park (far left). The summit of Mount Robson rises majestically into the sky (large picture).

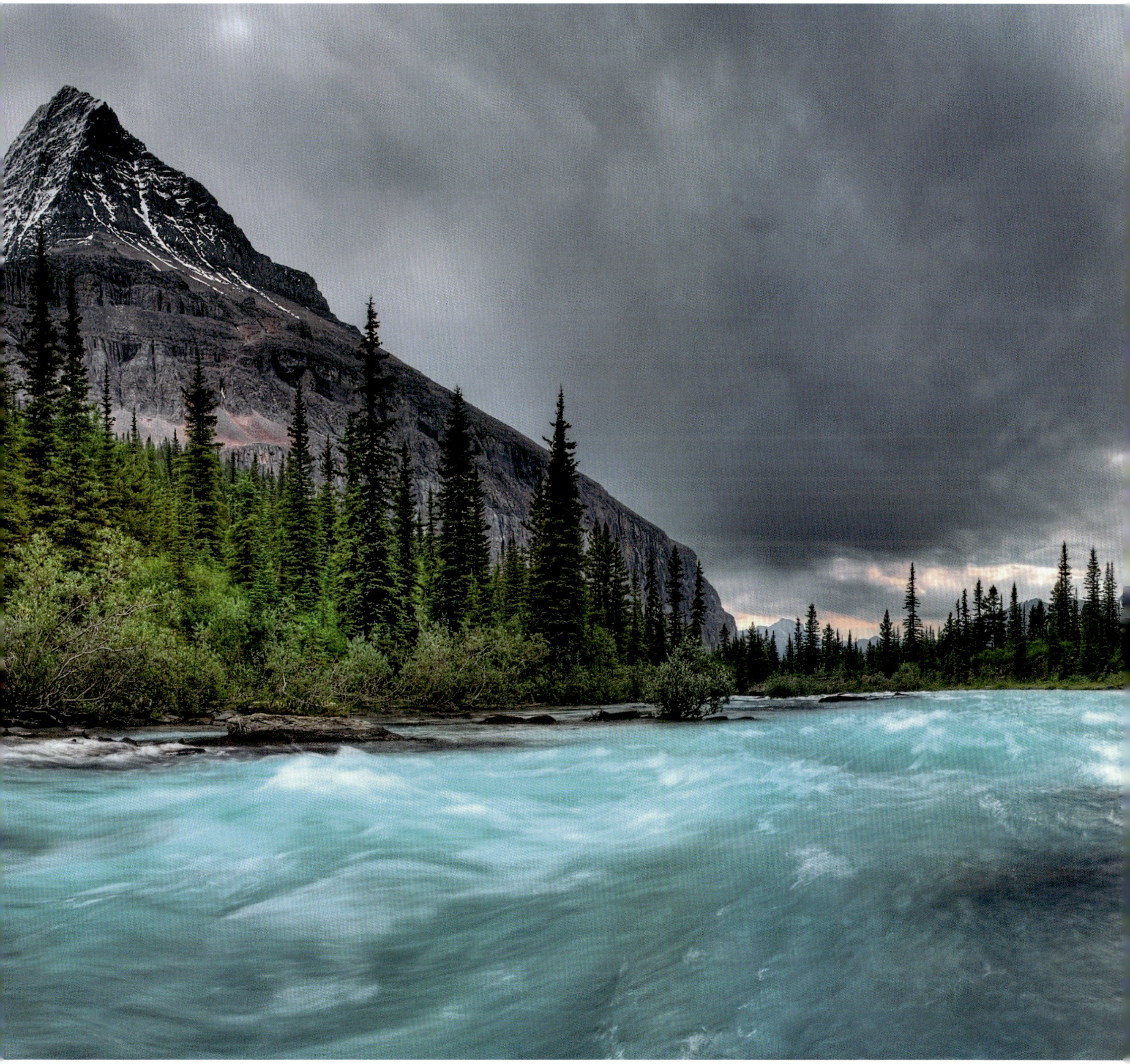

THE CANADIAN ROCKY MOUNTAINS: YOHO NATIONAL PARK

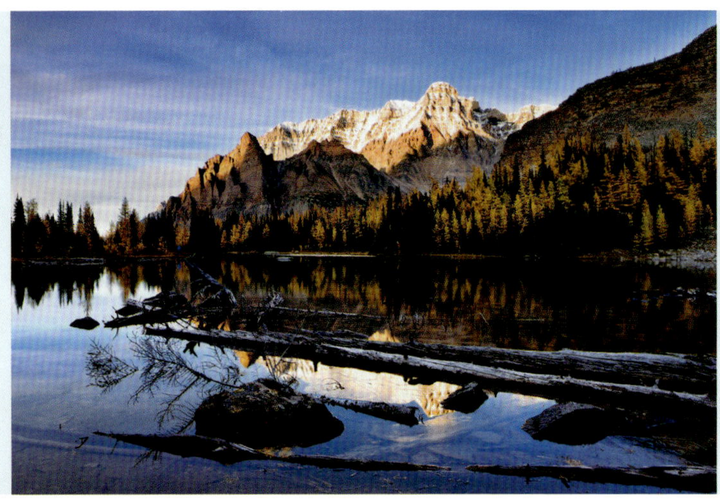

The four national parks –Yoho, Kootenay, Banff and Jasper – were established in order to preserve the unique natural landscape of the Canadian Rockies with their still largely unspoiled flora and fauna. In 1984 they were inscribed as a World Heritage site, and in 1990 the site was extended to include the Mount Robson, Mount Assiniboine and Hamber provincial parks. The mountains of the Yoho National Park are on the western slope of the Rocky Mountains. The landscape is shaped by glaciers, mountain forests and raging torrents, and offer a largely undisturbed habitat to many now rare animals. In addition to numerous other mammal and bird species, grizzly bears, moose, mountain goats, lynx, wolves, beavers and eagles can be observed. The Canadian Pacific Railway and the Trans-Canada Highway both run right through the park.

The Kicking Horse River flows through three waterfalls along its course; one of these is the Natural Bridge Fall (large picture). Left: Schaffer Lake, at the foot of Mount Huber at sunset.

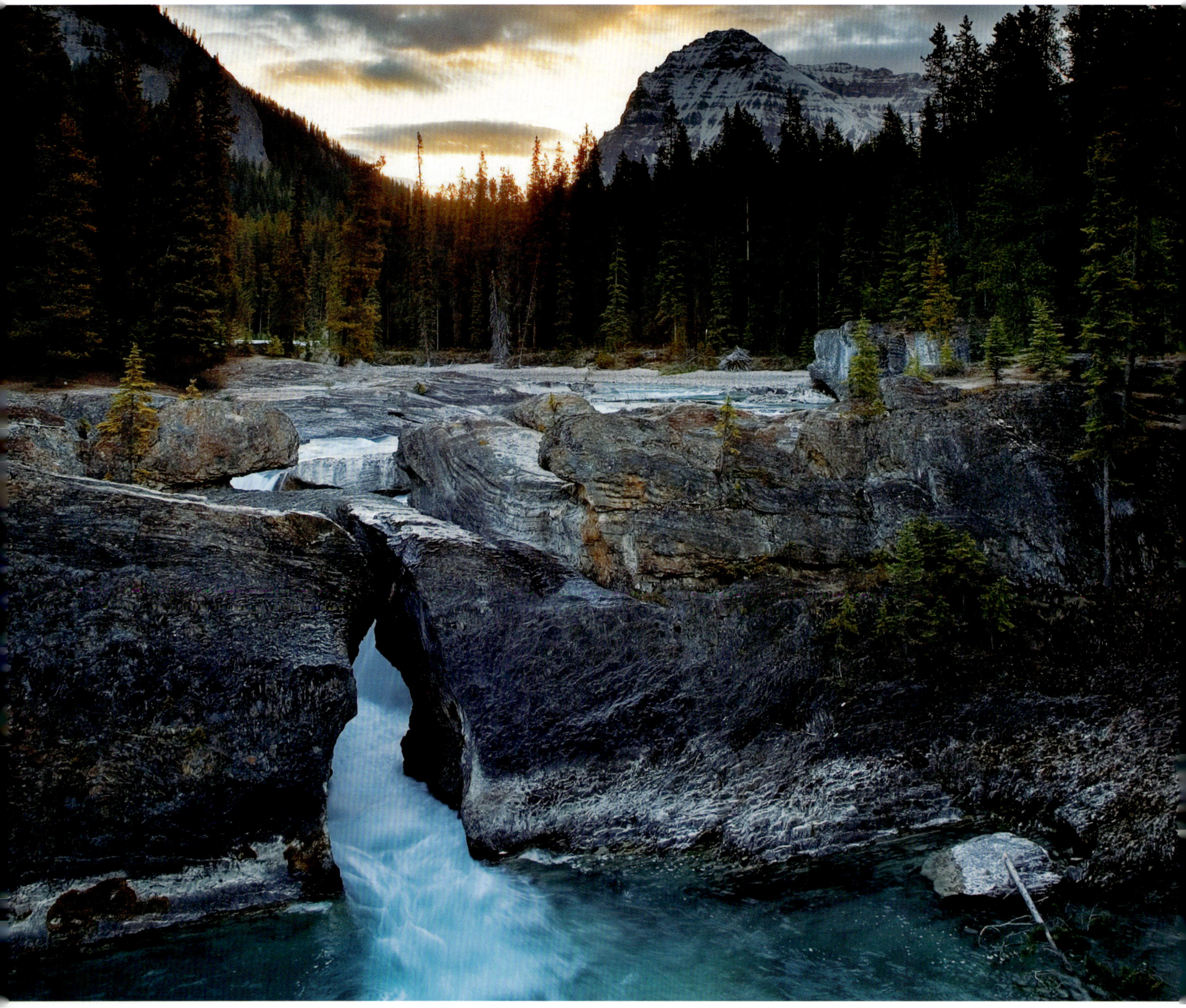

THE CANADIAN ROCKY MOUNTAINS: KOOTENAY NATIONAL PARK

The heart of the Kootenay National Park is formed by the valleys of the Kootenay River and the Vermilion River. From the 1,637-m- (5,370-foot-) high Vermilion Pass you can clearly see the Fireweed Trail, only 1 km (1,090 yards) in length, and how nature is able to regenerate itself, even after devastating fires. The area around the Stanley Glacier south of the pass is also known for its fossil finds. Worth seeing are the Marble Canyon, dug 37 m (121 feet) deep into the limestone; the "Paint Pots", with the clay that once served the indigenous people to make their body paint; and the slightly radioactive thermal springs in the spa town of Radium Hot Springs. The Native Americans believed in their curative effect. The park is home to elk, white-tailed deer, mule deer, wapiti and bighorn sheep, grizzly and black bears, coyotes, cougars, bobcats and mountain goats.

Following the Rockwall Trail, you will eventually reach the Tumbling Pass, which is covered with mountain larches (large picture). Wolves, too, are at home on the wooded plains of the Kootenay National Park (right).

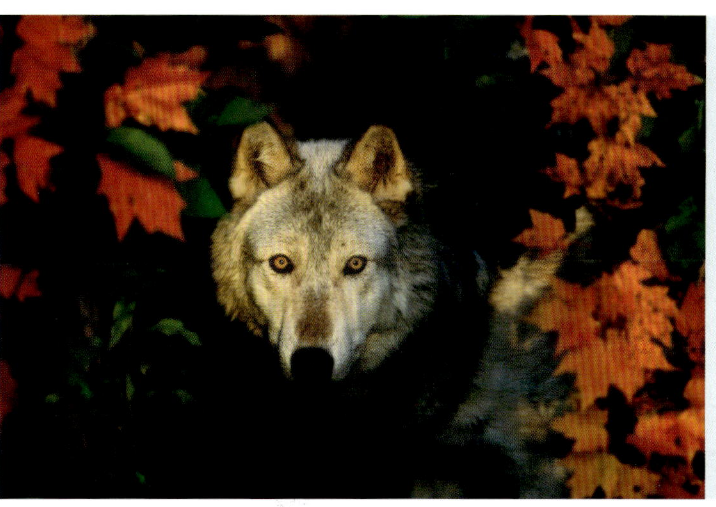

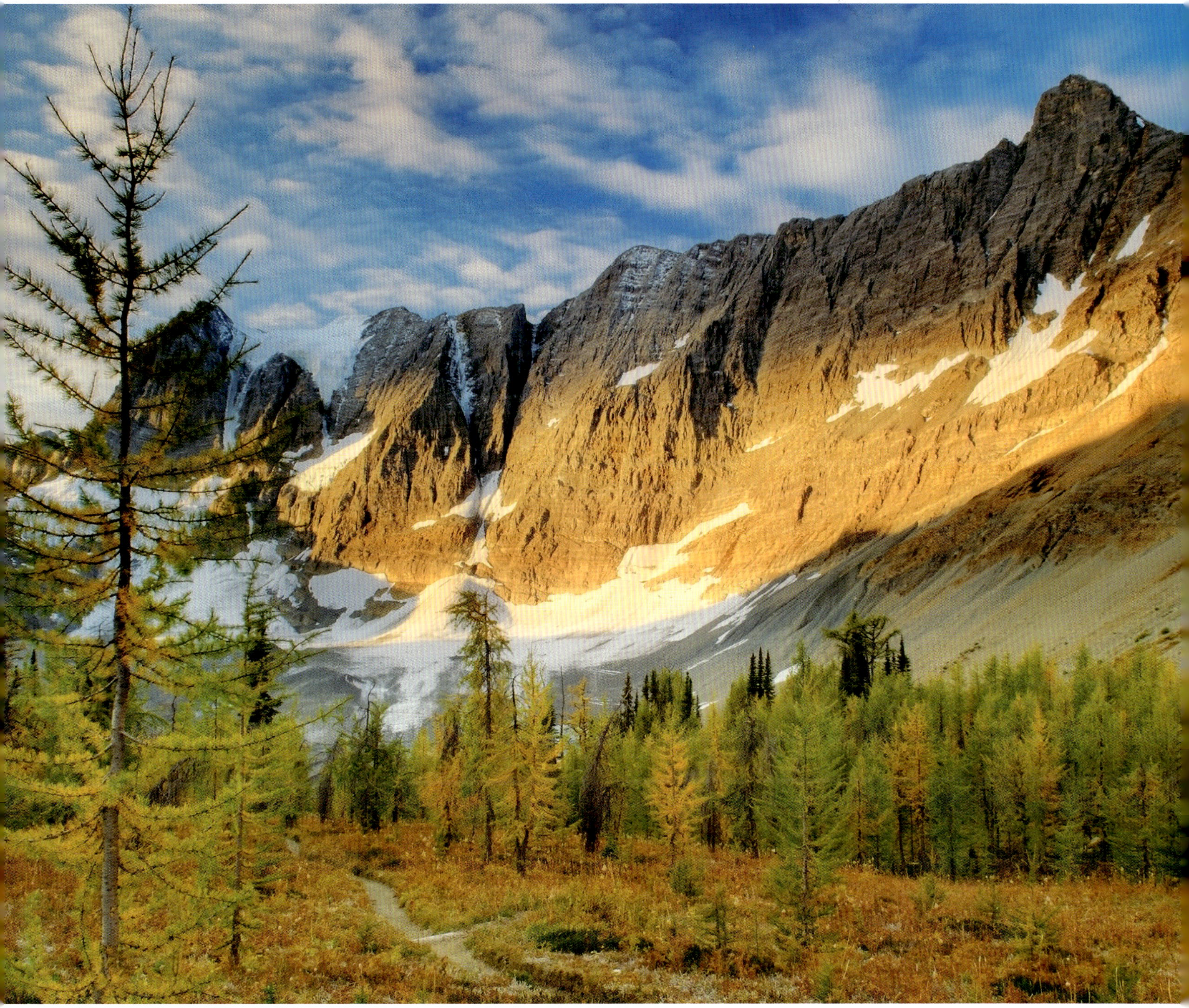

THE CANADIAN ROCKY MOUNTAINS: MOUNT ASSINIBOINE PROVINCIAL PARK

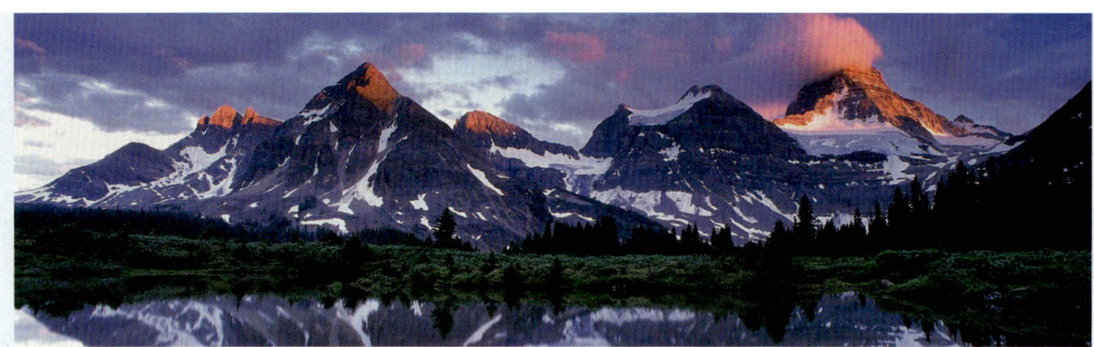

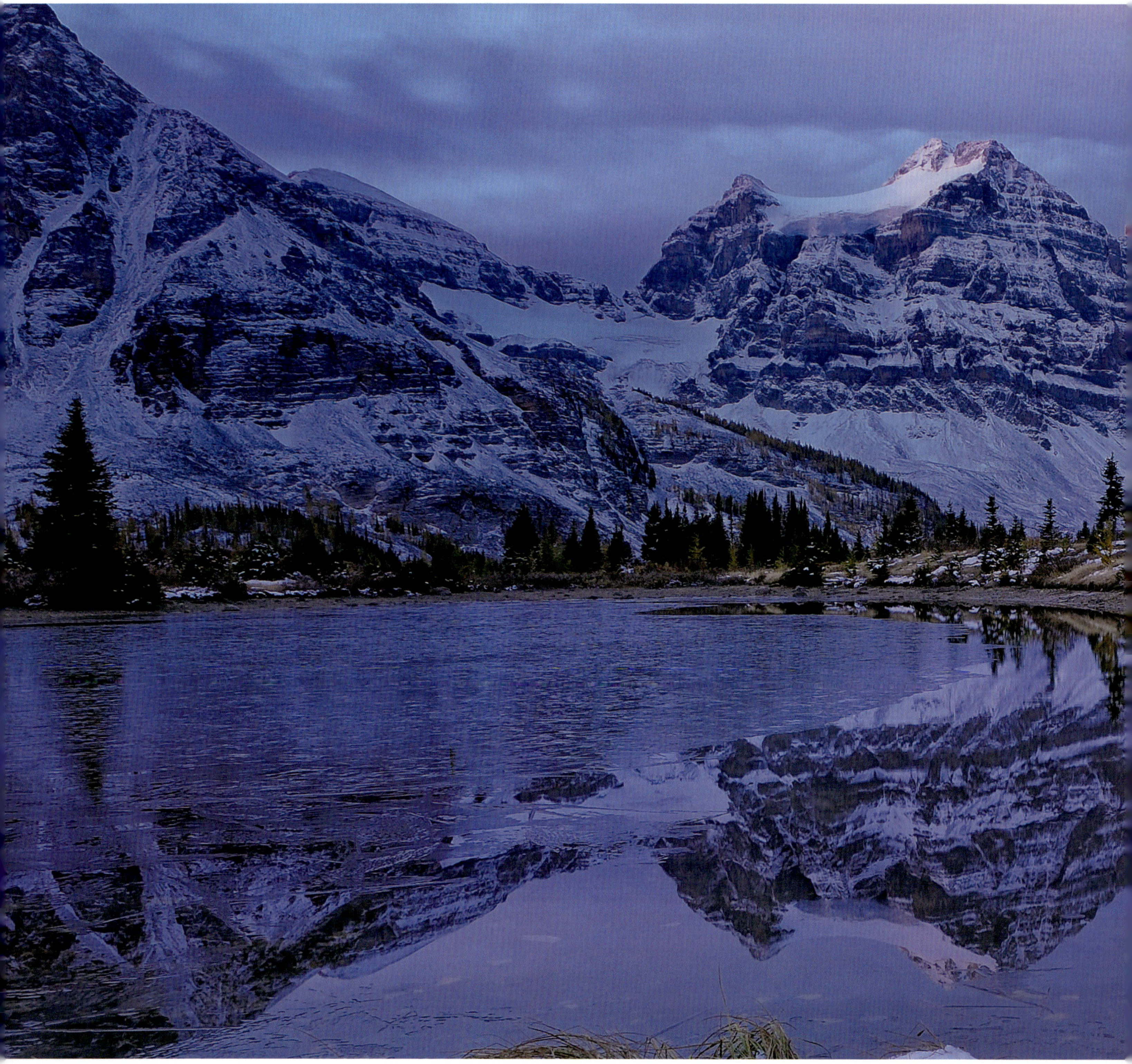

For some days, there was no entry in the diary of the French Jesuit Father Pierre-Jean de Smet, who travelled through Canada in the middle of the 19th century. He passed through terrain of extreme monotony, like the endless prairie. People say of these plains that if your dog runs away from home, you can still see it three days later. After this endless expanse of flat wastelands, one day the man of God reached a mountain in the Rockies, which compensated him for all this desolate tedium. He saw Mount Assiniboine, was impressed and wrote into his diary, comparing the mountain to the pyramids of ancient Egypt: "The monuments of Cheops and Chephren dwindle into nought before this gigantic architectural cliff of nature." Later, the magnificent but as yet nameless mountain was to be called after the Assiniboine Indians, because the clouds here reminded a pioneer of the smoke trails emerging from the tops of the Assiniboine tipis. Again and again, the bold and he audacious tried to scale the colossus, but failed, until eventually it was defeated by two Swiss men, perhaps because the mountain's shape reminded them of home.

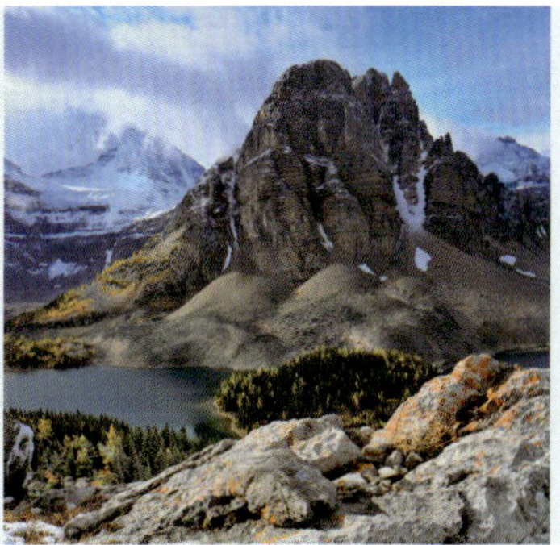

The pyramidal mountain peak of Mount Assiniboine is also known as the "Matterhorn of North America" (large picture). At sunset, the surrounding mountain peaks glow in the most beautiful shades of red (far left). Left: Sunburst Peak, with Sunburst Lake in the foreground.

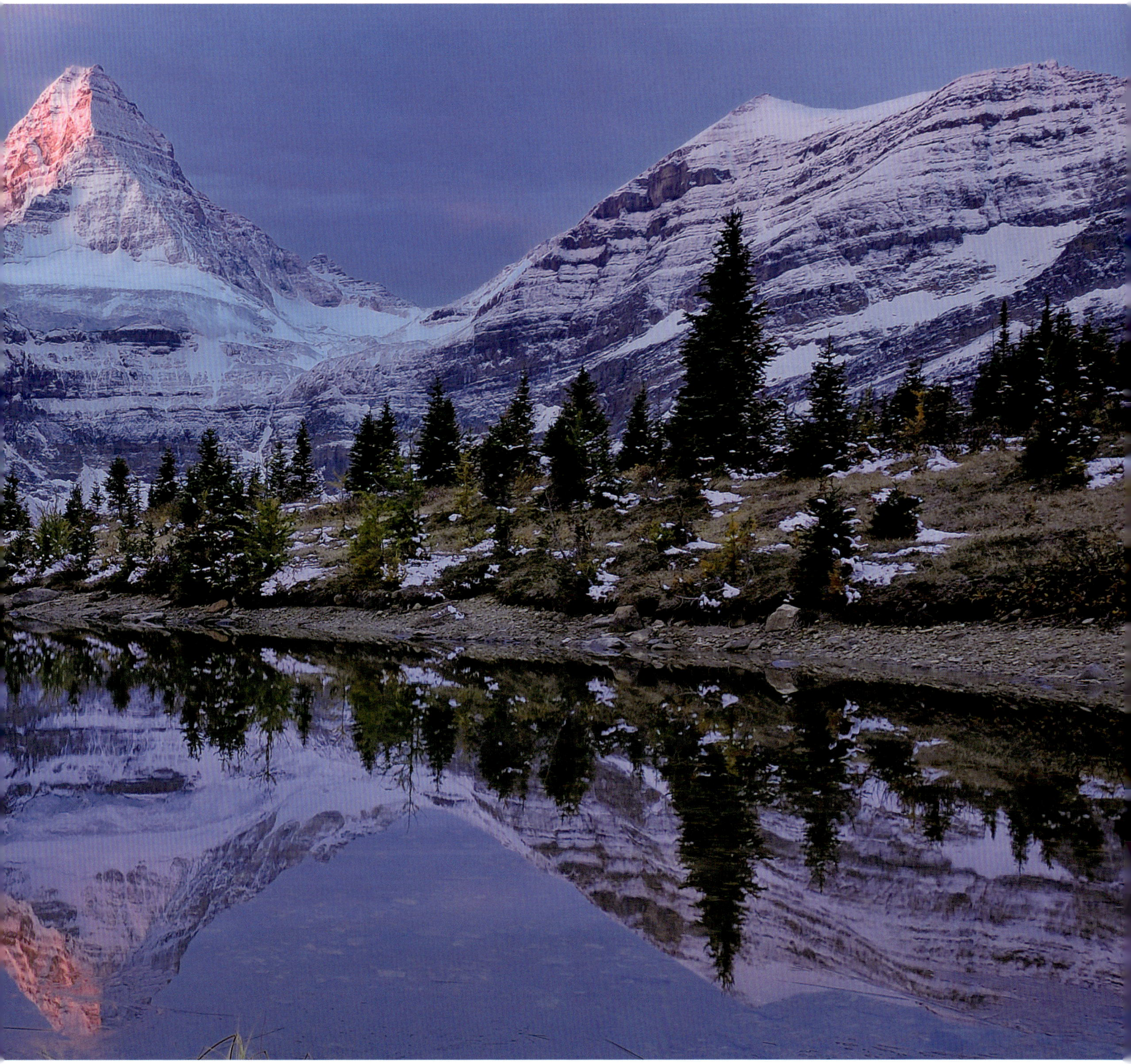

THE CANADIAN ROCKY MOUNTAINS: JASPER NATIONAL PARK

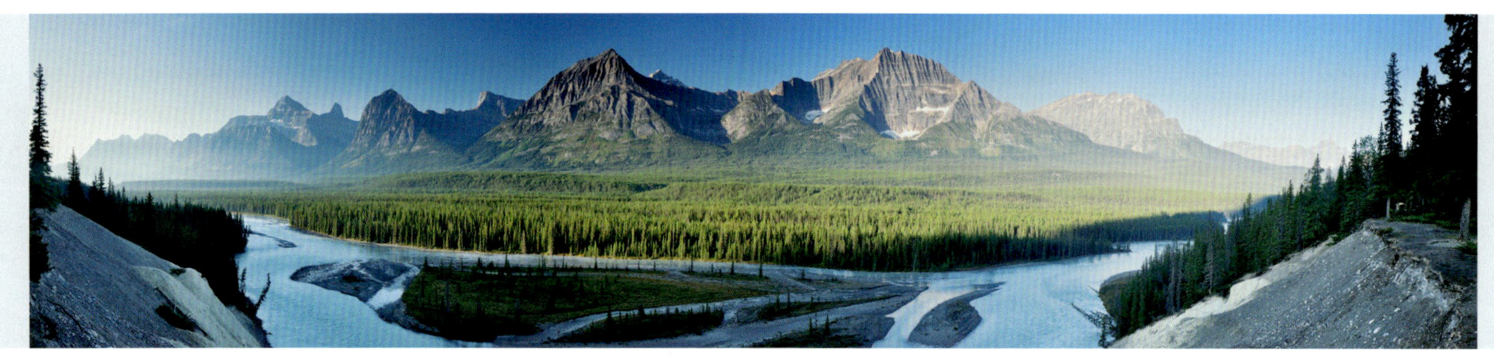

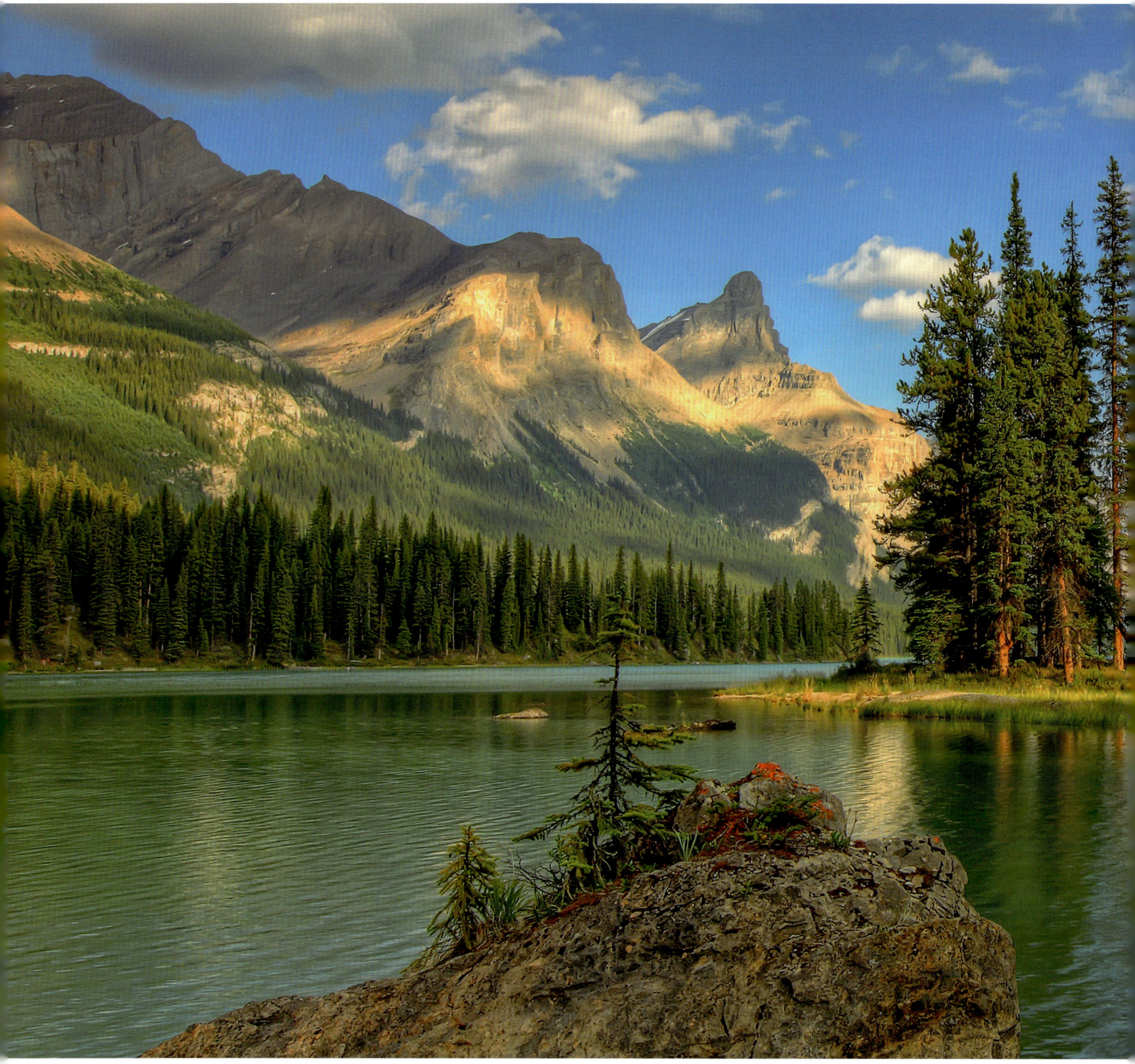

Picture-postcard Canada: Jasper National Park in the Rocky Mountains is one of the most popular tourist destinations on the North American continent. Within its boundaries are more than 800 lakes, most of which are fed by the surrounding glaciers. Lac Beauvert, a jade-green glacial lake, is located in the immediate vicinity of the town of Jasper. The Jasper Park Lodge, the former Grand Trunk Railroad's successful competitor to the Banff Springs Hotel in the nearby park, was built on the shores of the lake. Jasper is less crowded than Banff, and on the trails in the hinterland you can experience an impressive array of nature almost undisturbed. You can ascend the much-visited Whistler Mountain by cable car and enjoy breathtaking panoramic views from the top. Numerous trails take you into the lonely, incomparably beautiful wilderness, such as at Maligne Lake.

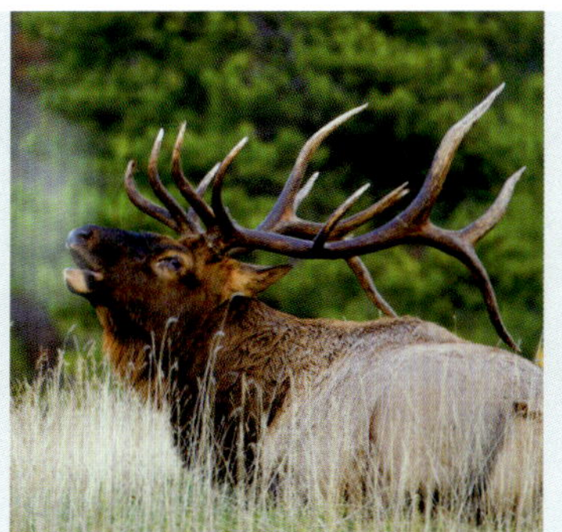

Picturesque Spirit Island in Maligne Lake (large picture), with the Rocky Mountains lining up as a backdrop behind. From Goat Lookout, you can enjoy superb views of the Athabasca Valley (far left). Left: a bull moose.

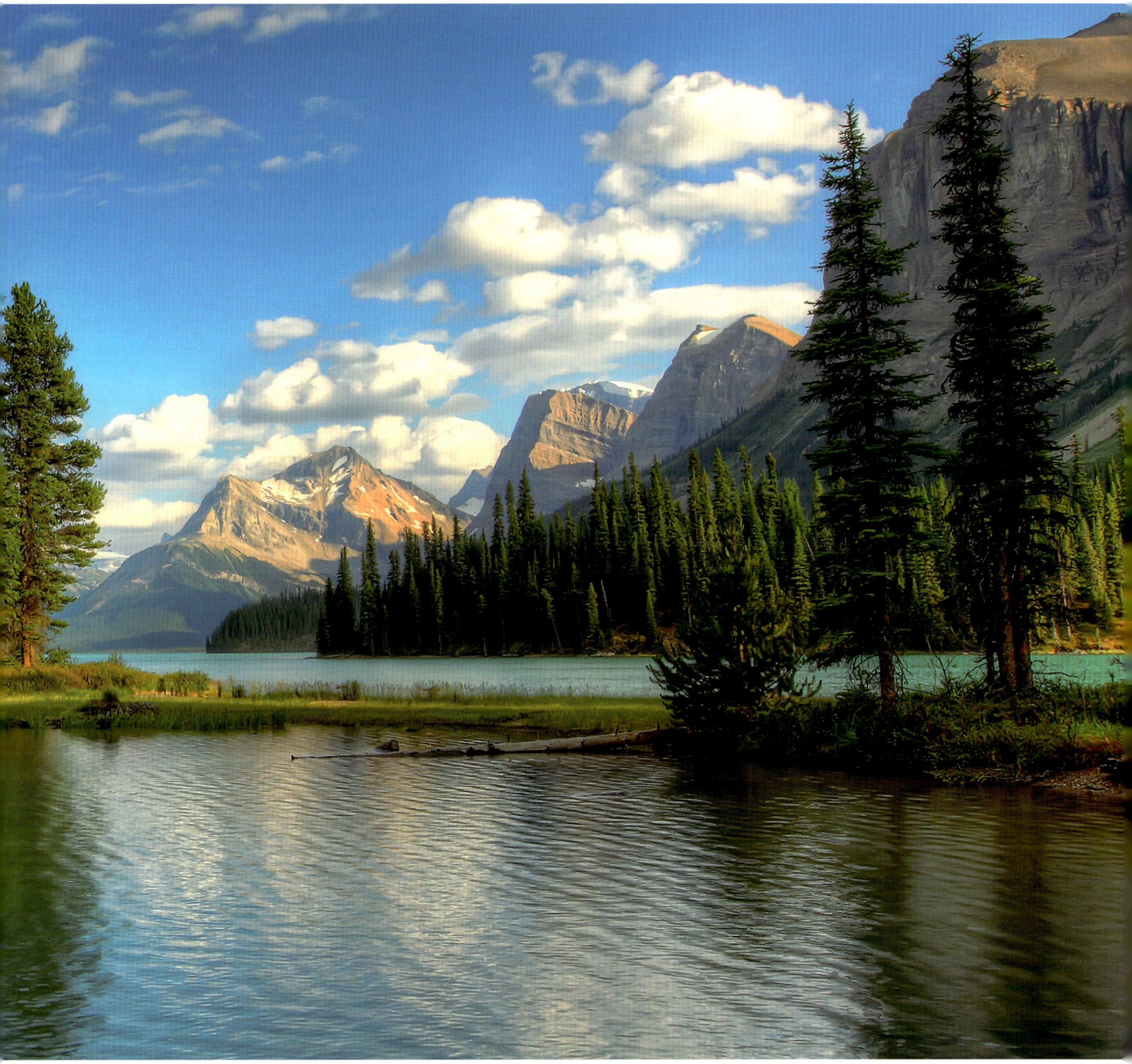

THE CANADIAN ROCKY MOUNTAINS: BANFF NATIONAL PARK

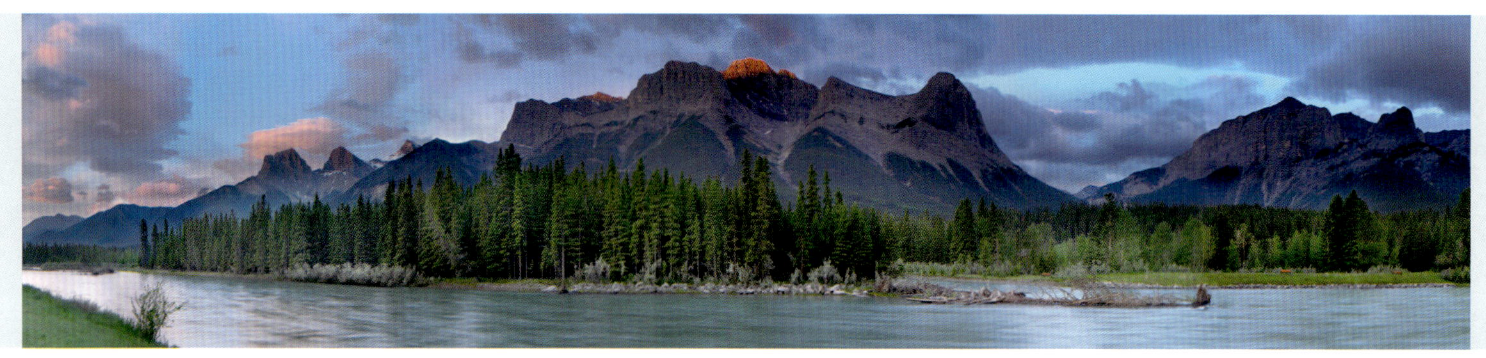

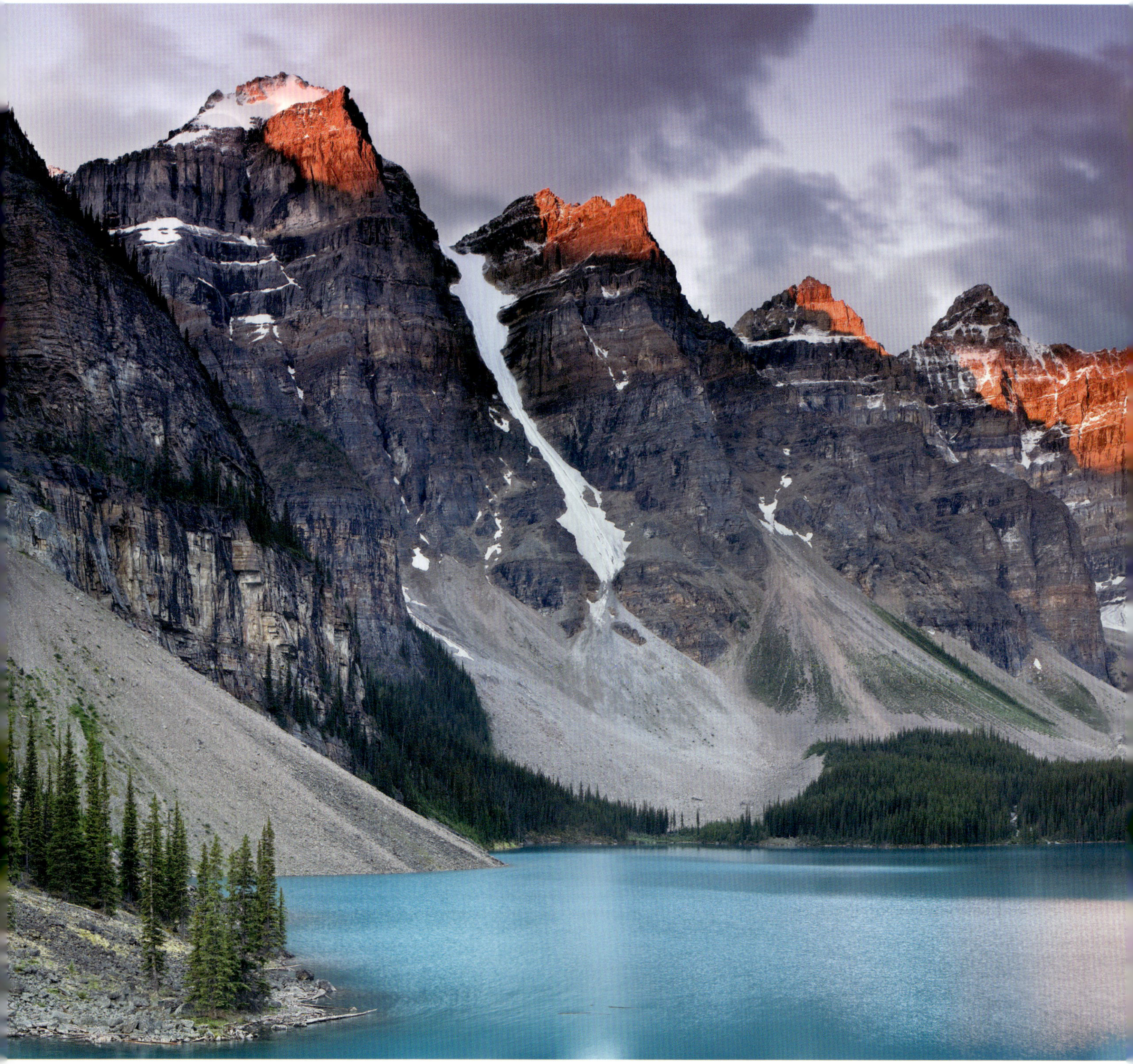

Sir William Cornelius Van Horne was one of those legendary men from the pioneering days of America, without whose strong will and inexhaustible energy the vast continent would not have been conquered so quickly. Van Horne saw to it virtually single-handedly that the first transcontinental railway in Canada was built in the late 19th century. No sooner was the last rail section laid, and he already pounced on the next task: the tourist development of the Rocky Mountains. "If we can't export the scenery, we'll import the tourists", was the motto of Van Horne, who had luxurious grand hotels built for wealthy customers along his railway line, especially in the middle of Banff in the Rocky Mountains. His plan worked. The Banff Springs Hotel in particular flourished, and it was soon frequented by legendary Hollywood stars like Ginger Rogers and Douglas Fairbanks, but also by royals like Queen Victoria and Prince Edward. The fame of the hotel may now be a bit faded, but Sir William Cornelius Van Horne is still surrounded by the aura of a national hero.

Moraine Lake lies in the Valley of the Ten Peaks like a turquoise-shimmering gemstone, probably one of the most striking sceneries in the Rocky Mountains. The mountain giants are all over 3,000 m (9,840 feet) high.

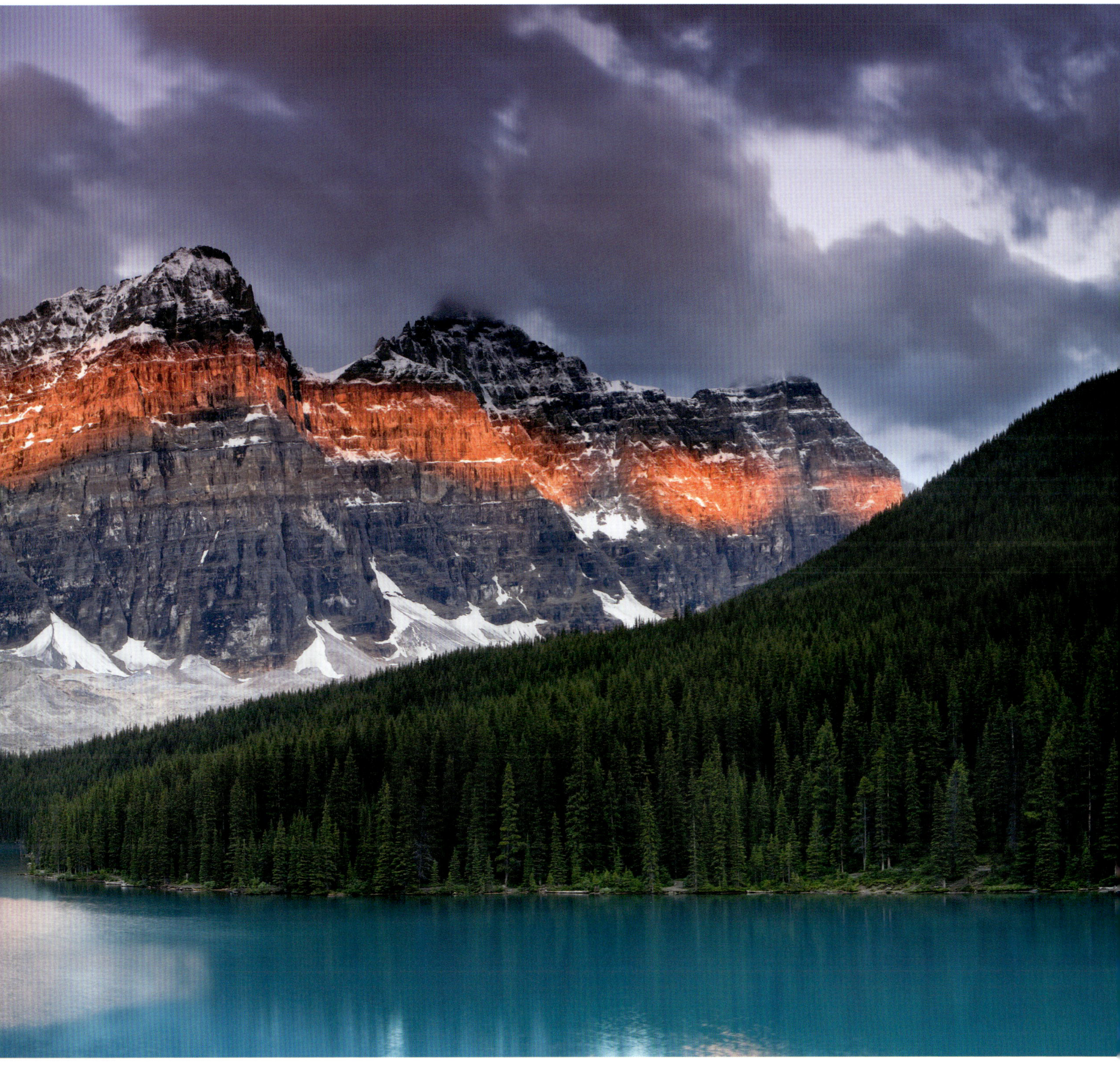

HEAD-SMASHED-IN BUFFALO JUMP

Date of inscription: 1981 *

A more than 10 m (33 feet) high sandstone wall in the Porcupine Hills in Alberta recalls a particular form of bison hunting as practiced by Native Americans.

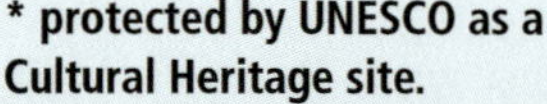

*** protected by UNESCO as a Cultural Heritage site.**

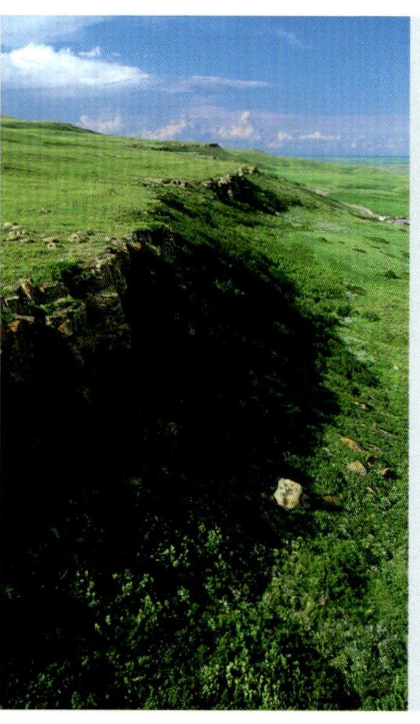

Entire herds of wild cattle were chased by lance-swinging hunters towards the precipice here, in the middle of gently undulating prairie. Stampeding, the animals did not realize the danger in time and fell, urged on by their likes from behind, head first into the abyss. There, the bison were carved up and meat that was not meant for immediate consumption was preserved by drying. The skins were processed for clothing and tents, the bones were used as raw material for weapons and tools in everyday life. While there were other such "buffalo jumps" elsewhere in North America, this one was the biggest and oldest of its kind. This method of hunting was common until the proliferation of guns; it is believed to have been practised here for the last time in 1850. The local finds provide important information for archaeologists about the lives of pre-Columbian civilizations after 3,600 BC. They include the traces of marked trails, a Native American camp and a burial mound with large numbers of bison skeletons.

At first glance this is simply a magnificent landscape in south-western Alberta, featuring green plateaus and canyons. However, for the indigenous people the steep slopes mainly represented a sophisticated technique for hunting and killing large numbers of the bison.

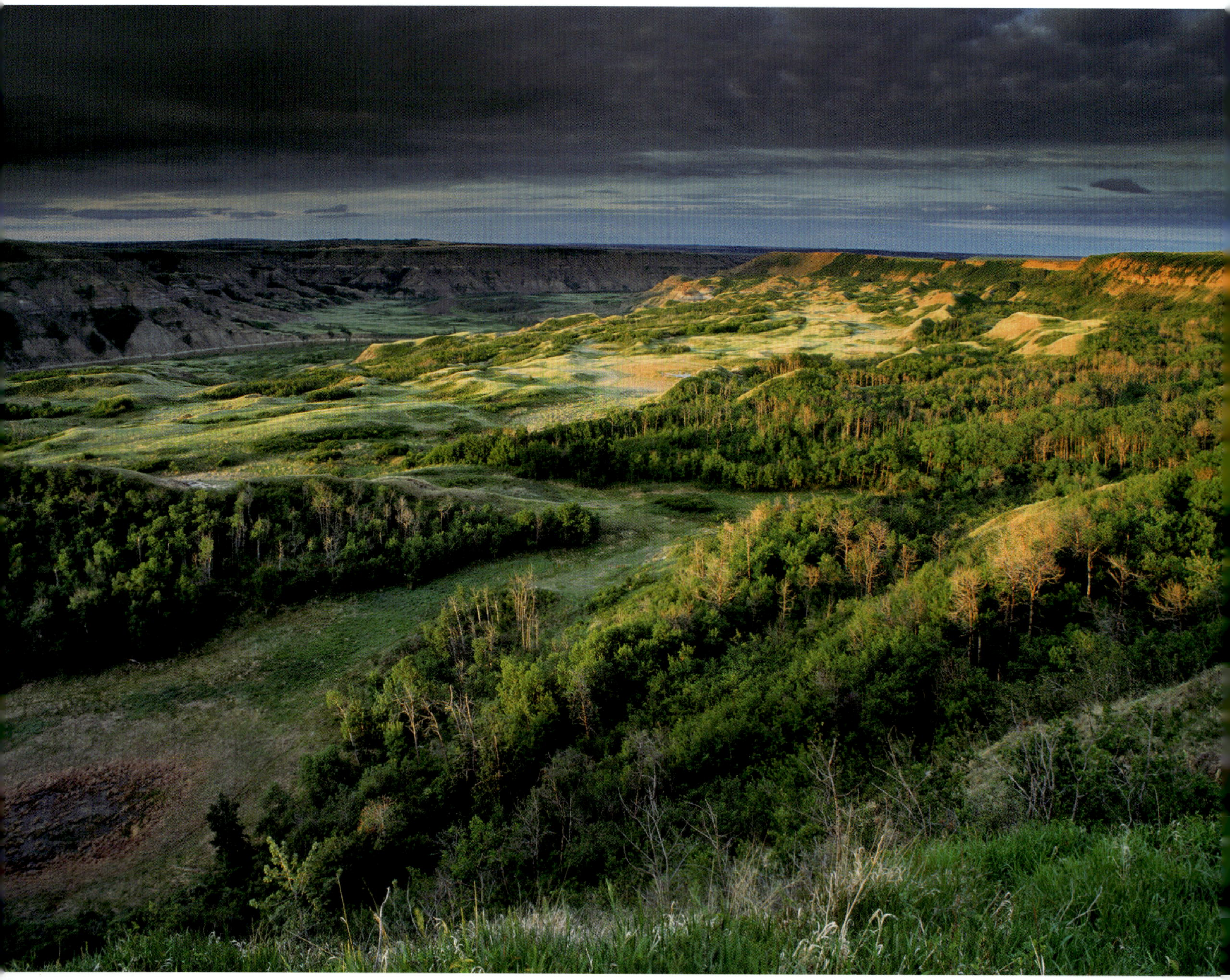

DINOSAUR PROVINCIAL PARK

During the Cretaceous period, approximately 65 million years ago, a variety of dinosaur species inhabited the North American continent. Some particularly well-developed Triceratops specimens could reach a height of around 15 m (50 feet), although these died out, along with the other dinosaur species, at the end of the Mesozoic period.

In no other region on earth have greater deposits of these giant lizards' remains been found. The numerous fossils, including those of turtles, fish, mammals, and amphibians, afford scientists a fascinating insight into the animal world of 200 million years ago, and these exciting finds can be viewed in a museum. This area has scenic charms as well: the Badlands are a barren zone of erosion in which the power of wind and weather has transformed the rocks into a landscape that looks almost alien. However, the river banks are thickly vegetated, in spite of the desert-like climate, and this provides an optimal habitat, not just for a few species of red deer but also for a variety of birds including curlews, Canada geese, and nighthawks.

The site of the world's most important dinosaur fossil finds lies in the loamy soil of the Canadian Badlands – a barren, eroded landscape formed by wind and weathering.

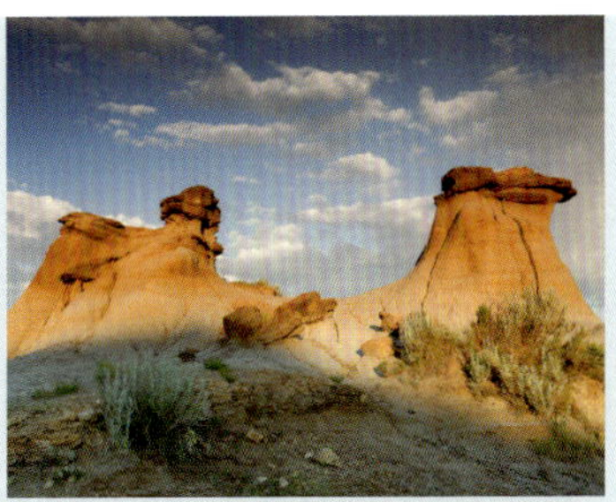

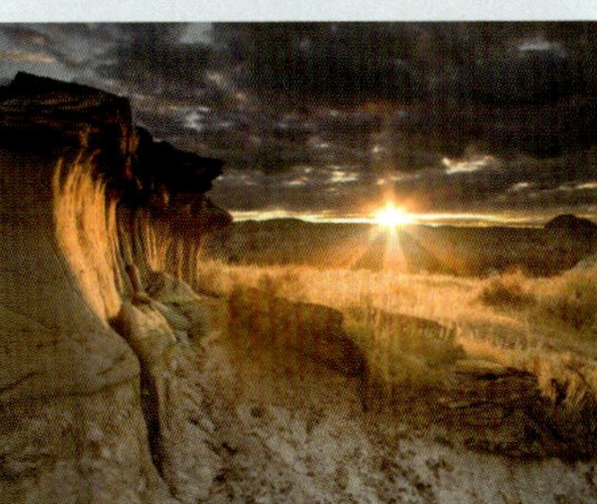

Date of inscription: 1979

Giant dinosaurs lived 65 million years ago in the Dinosaur Provincial Park, a bizarre landscape situated on the Red Deer river in modern-day Alberta.

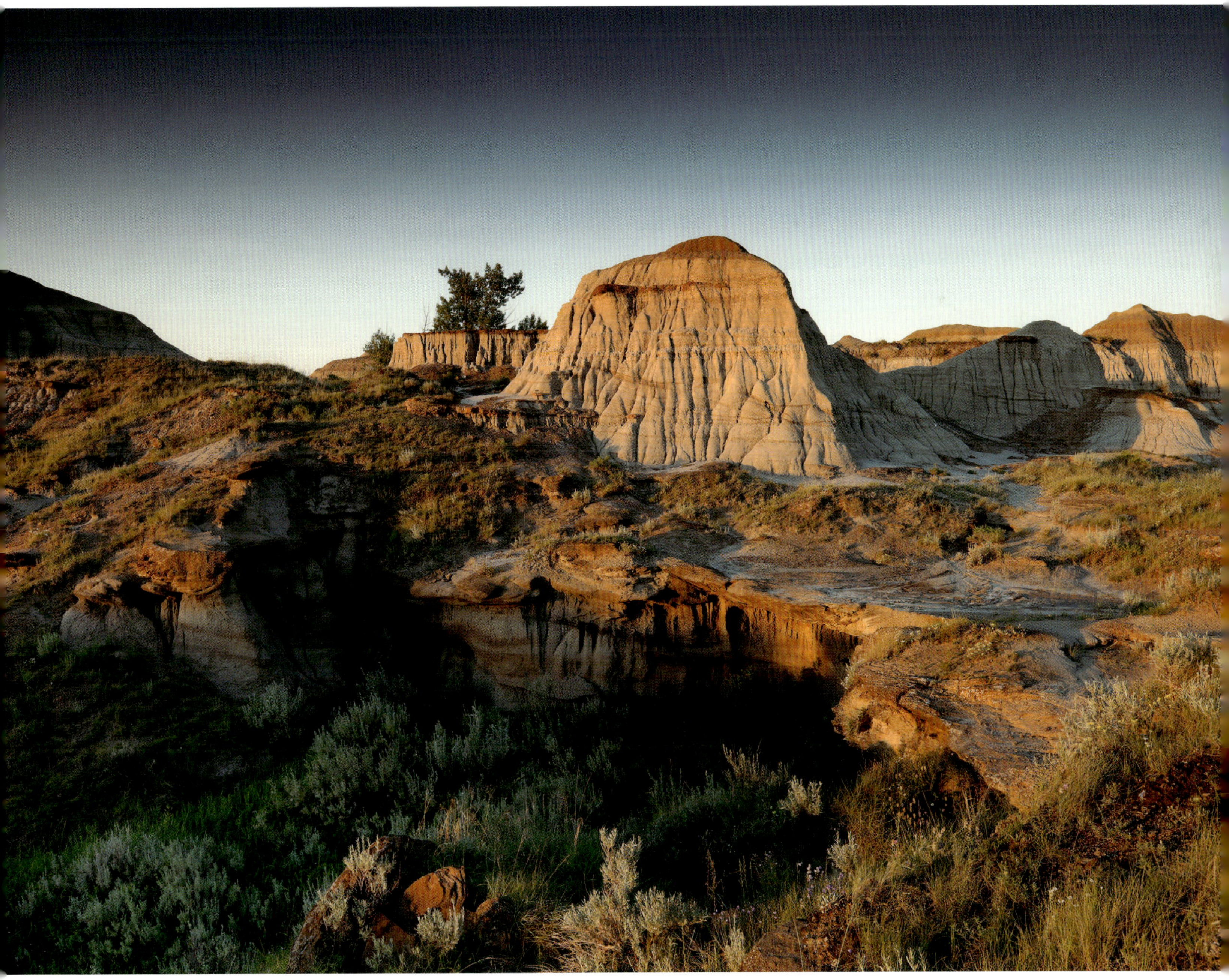

GROS MORNE NATIONAL PARK

Date of inscription: 1987

Over 4,500 years ago, the Dorset Eskimos settled in the varied landscape on the west coast of Newfoundland that was to become the site of the Gros Morne National Park – long before the Vikings became the first Europeans to land here.

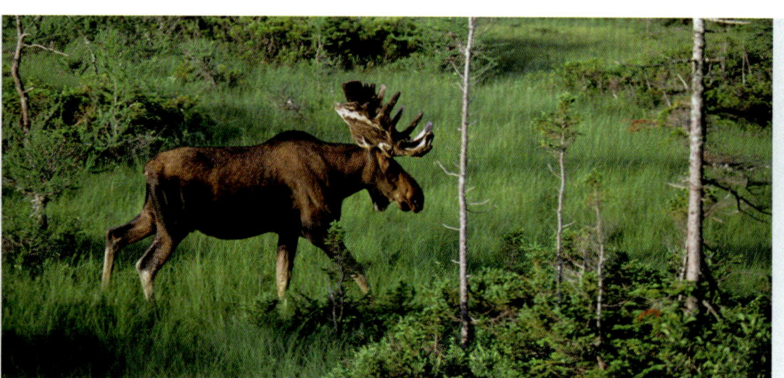

The national park takes its name from the 806-m (2,650-foot) high Gros Morne; adjoining this great hill there is also a 600-m (1,970-foot) high limestone plateau, setting the tone for the area with winding streams, paternoster lakes, and moraines. The subarctic climate has given rise to tundra vegetation which is found this far south nowhere else in the world.

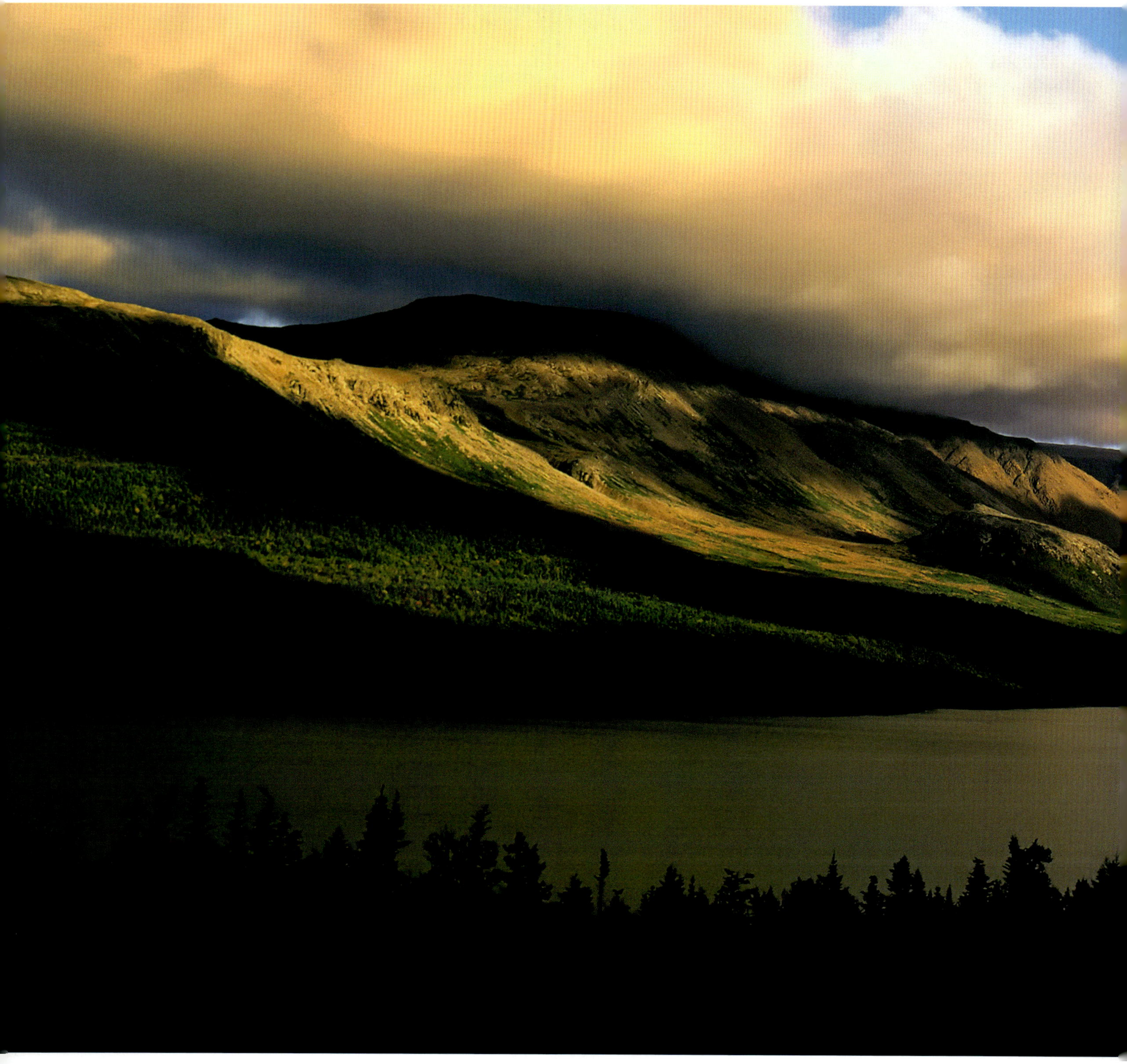

Caribou, grouse, Arctic hares, Arctic foxes, and lynxes are all to be found here. The Long Range mountains, whose rock formations have yielded valuable geological discoveries, are of particular interest to scientists. Gros Morne National Park's picturesque fjords were created in the last ice age. Western Brook Pond, an enclosed fjord lake with walls 600 m (1,970 feet) high, is an incredible natural spectacle. The coastal region is characterized by steep cliffs, moving dunes, and a great variety of wild birds, who derive as much benefit from the fish-rich waters as the seals. Archeological finds have shown that there were settlements on the site of the modern park as early as 2500 bc. The Dorset Eskimos were succeeded by the Beothuk Native Americans around ad 800, and these were given the name of "redskins " by Europeans because of their red-ochre body paint, with which they also painted their houses and possessions. There is much to suggest that this culture had contact with the Vikings, including some suspicion that so-called "blond Indians" were the result of intermarriage.

Gros Morne National Park is characterized by fjords cutting deep into the high plateau, stony coastlines, and beaches. The Trout River Pond (large picture) offers fabulous views. Bull moose (left) in Canada and Alaska are characterized by particularly large antlers.

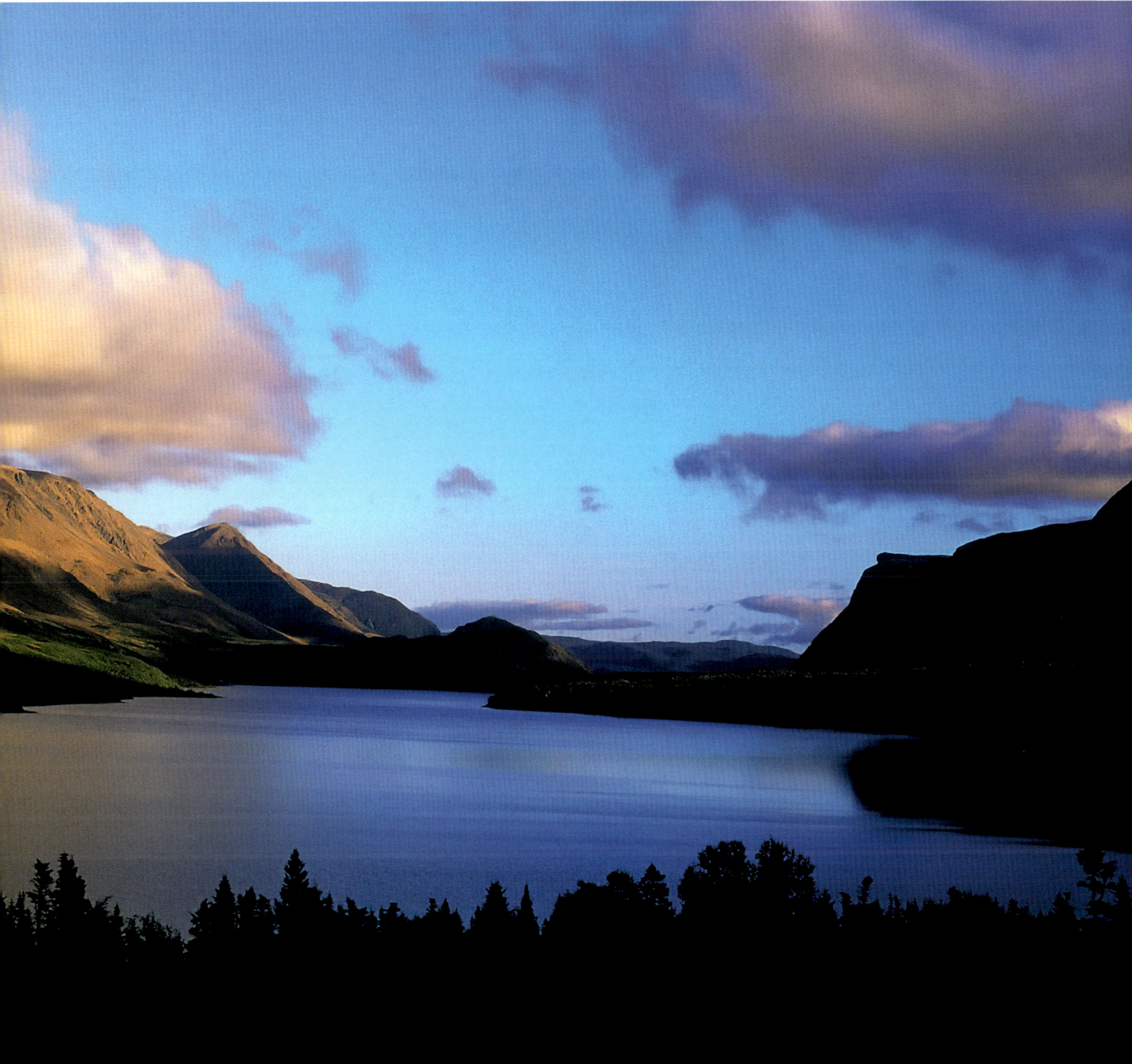

MIGUASHA NATIONAL PARK

Date of inscription: 1999

Miguasha National Park is the site of the most significant Devonian fossil finds in the world. Its most important fossils are the lobe-finned fish, precursors of the first four-legged vertebrates.

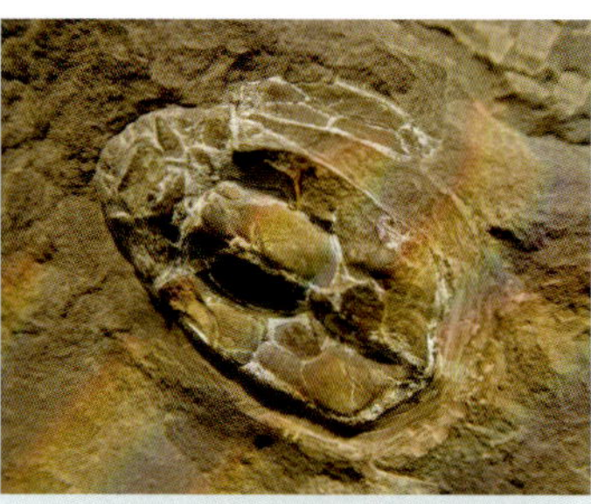

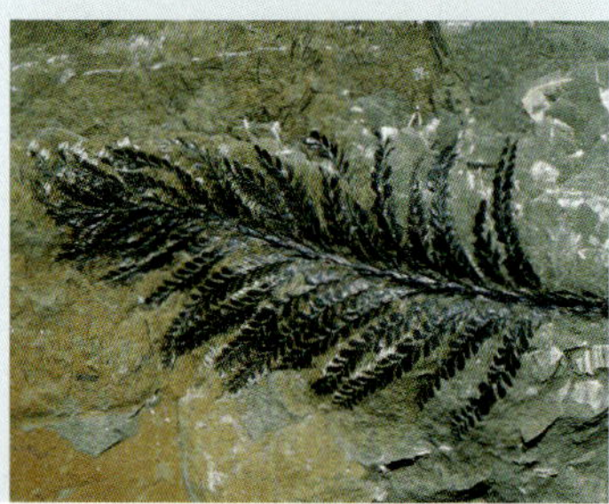

Fossilized remains of six of the eight fish species that lived during the Upper Devonian have been found in the rocks of the southern coast of the peninsula Gaspésie (large image; image above), including petrified plants such as ferns (right).

Great advances in the study of the Devonian geological period are largely due to discoveries made at this World Heritage Site, located on the south coast of the Gaspésie peninsula in the south-east of Canada's Québec province. The area was first studied in 1842 by German-Canadian doctor, physicist, and geologist Abraham Gesner, and is named for the color of its rock formations; in the language of the indigenous Native American Mic-Mac tribe, "miguasha" means "reddish." Scientific documentation of the objects found here began in the 1880s. In the ensuing years, great collections were shipped to museums in England and Scotland. In 1985, Miguasha, including the steep cliffs of the 350- million-year-old Escuminac rock formation, became a conservation park, and since then some 5,000 fossils have been identified, conserved, and recorded on computer: vertebrates, invertebrates, plants, and spores from the Devonian. One of the best-known finds is the "Prince of Miguasha," a fossilized Eusthenopteron – an extinct lobe-finned fish species that lived during the Upper Devonian, about 370 million years ago, and marks the turning point between fish and land-dwelling vertebrates. This species possessed gills, rudimentary lungs and a strong endoskeleton that probably allowed it to leave the water for short periods.

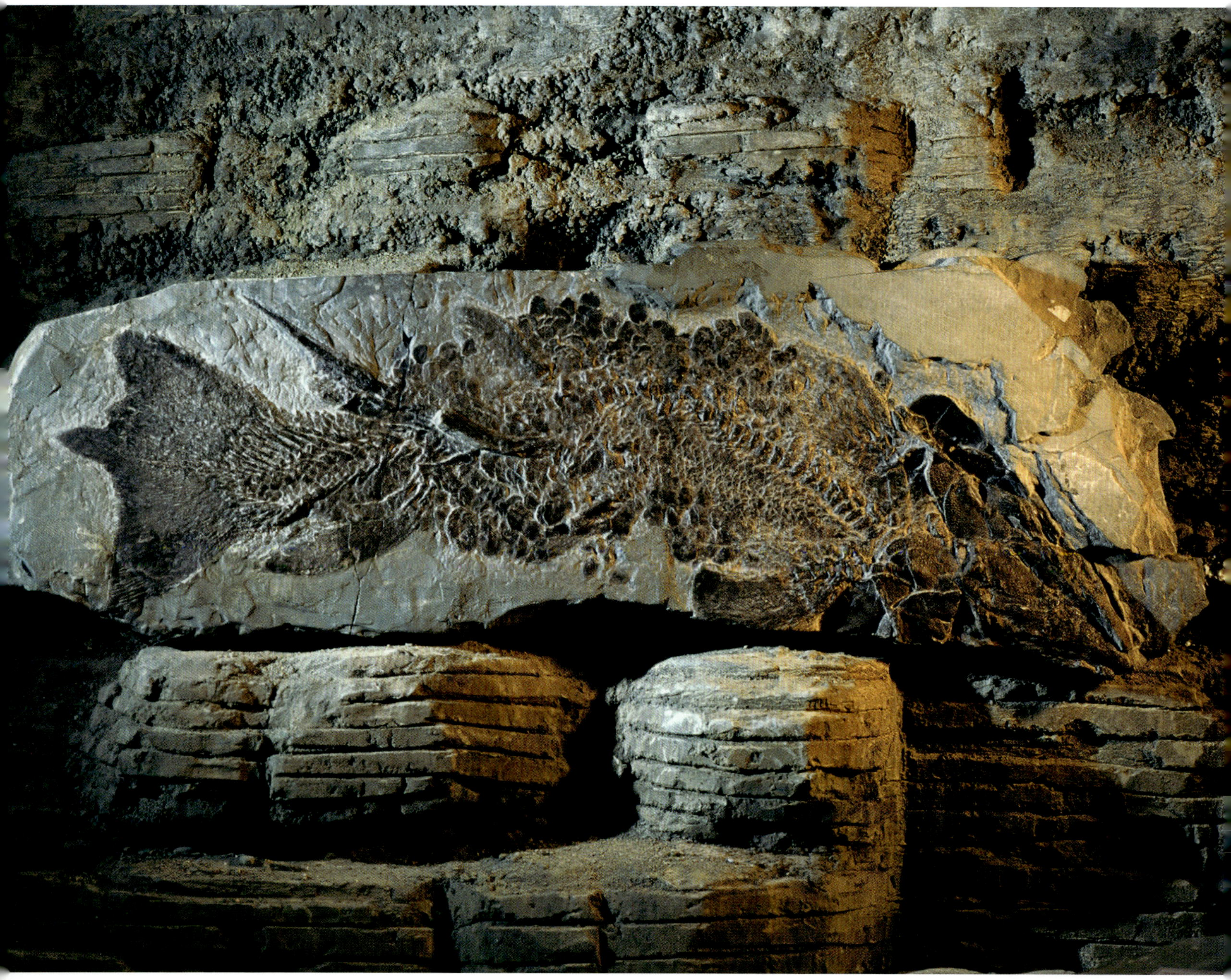

JOGGINS FOSSIL CLIFFS

Known as "the Galapagos of the Carboniferous" or „the coal age Galapagos" to scientists, the cliffs have been an important source of fossil finds since the middle of the 19th century. The Canadian geologist, Sir William Dawson, discovered the first fossilized specimens of Hylonomus here in 1851. This extinct reptile species, reaching some 20 cm (8 inches) in length, was one of the first creatures to adapt fully to life on land. The British naturalist, Charles Darwin, founder of modern theory of evolution, also used finds from Joggins in the development of his revolutionary scientific principles. The area of particular paleontological interest covers about seven square kilometers (two and a half square miles) along the coast of the Bay of Fundy in Nova Scotia, where there are fossilized tree stumps from a rainforest, reptile fossils, and specimens of the earliest amniotes (egg-laying vertebrates) from the Carboniferous period, 354 to 290 million years ago. The 15 km (9 miles) of cliffs, rocky platforms, and beaches have retained fossilized traces of three ecosystems: an estuary, a flood plain covered in rainforest, and a marshy plain with fresh water pools, which appears to have been prone to forest fires. In total, 96 genera and 148 species of fossil have been discovered.

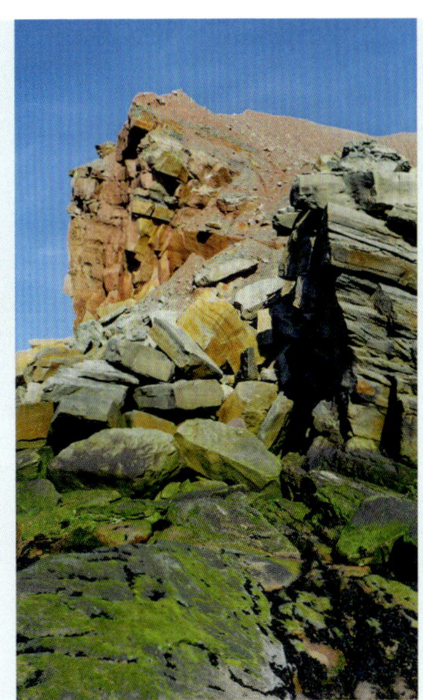

Date of inscription: 2008

Joggins Fossil Cliffs in the Canadian province of Nova Scotia are famous for their wealth of prehistoric material. The cliffs and their roughly 300 million-year-old fossils are considered the most significant source of finds from the Carboniferous period.

It is thanks to the erosion caused by one of the highest tidal ranges in the world – up to 15m (50feet) – that the fossilized tree stumps and reptiles were discovered on the Joggins Fossil Cliffs.

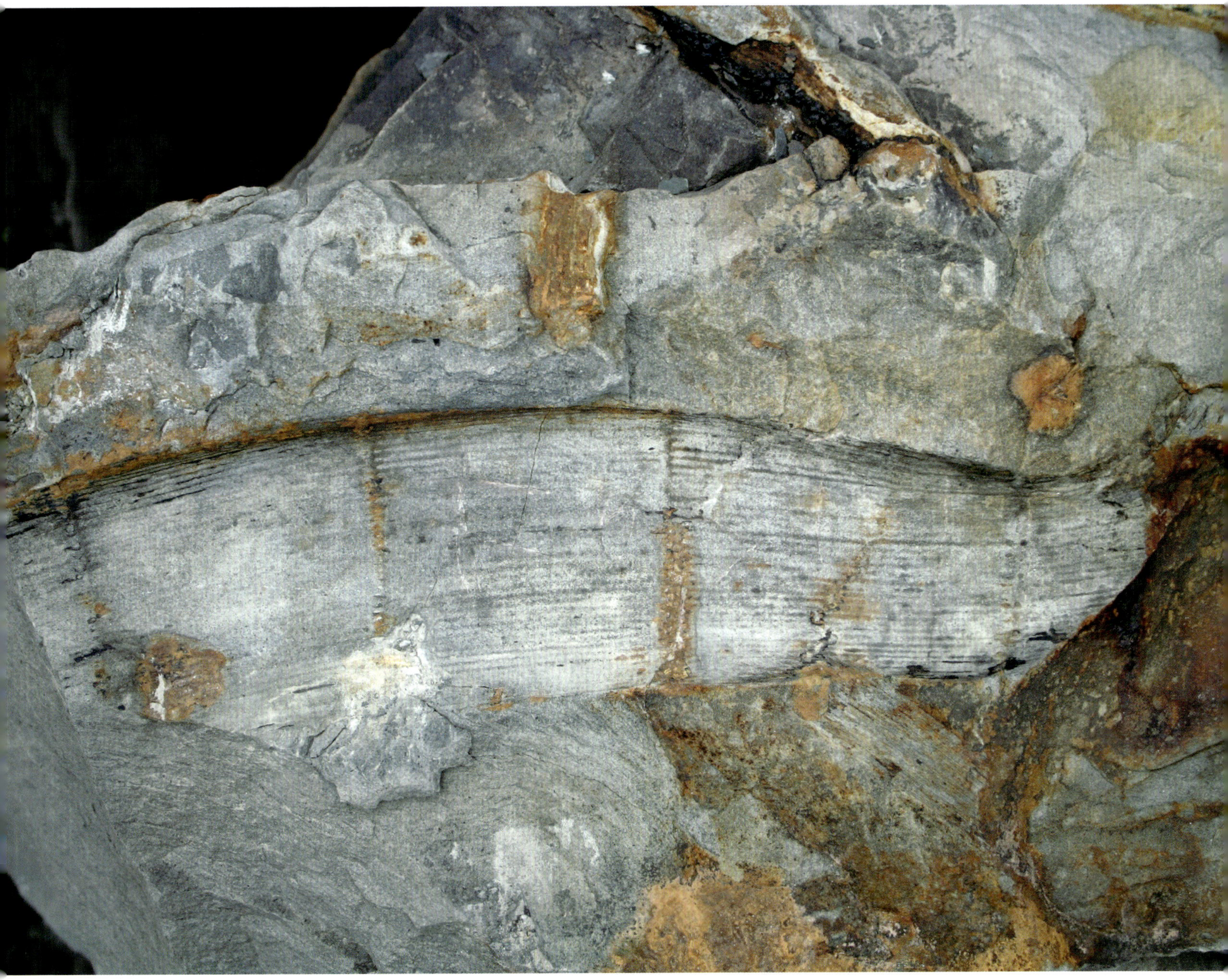

WATERTON GLACIER INTERNATIONAL PEACE PARK

Date of inscription: 1995

The United States' Glacier National Park and the Canadian Waterton Lakes National Park were united as the first "International Peace Park" in 1932.

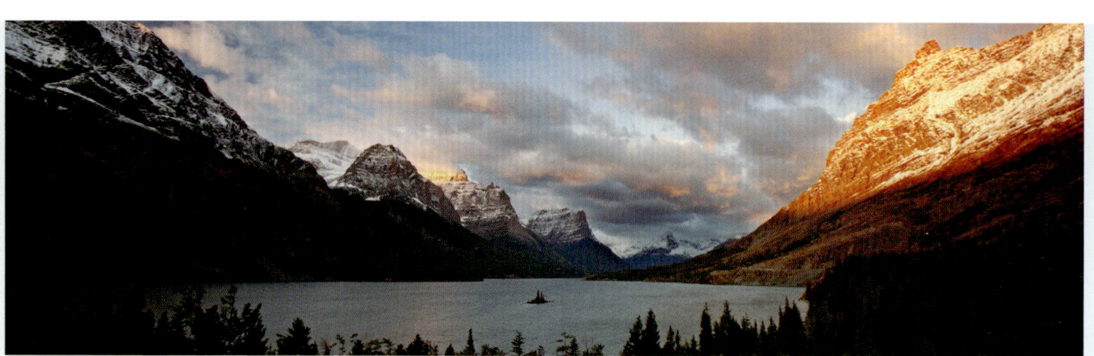

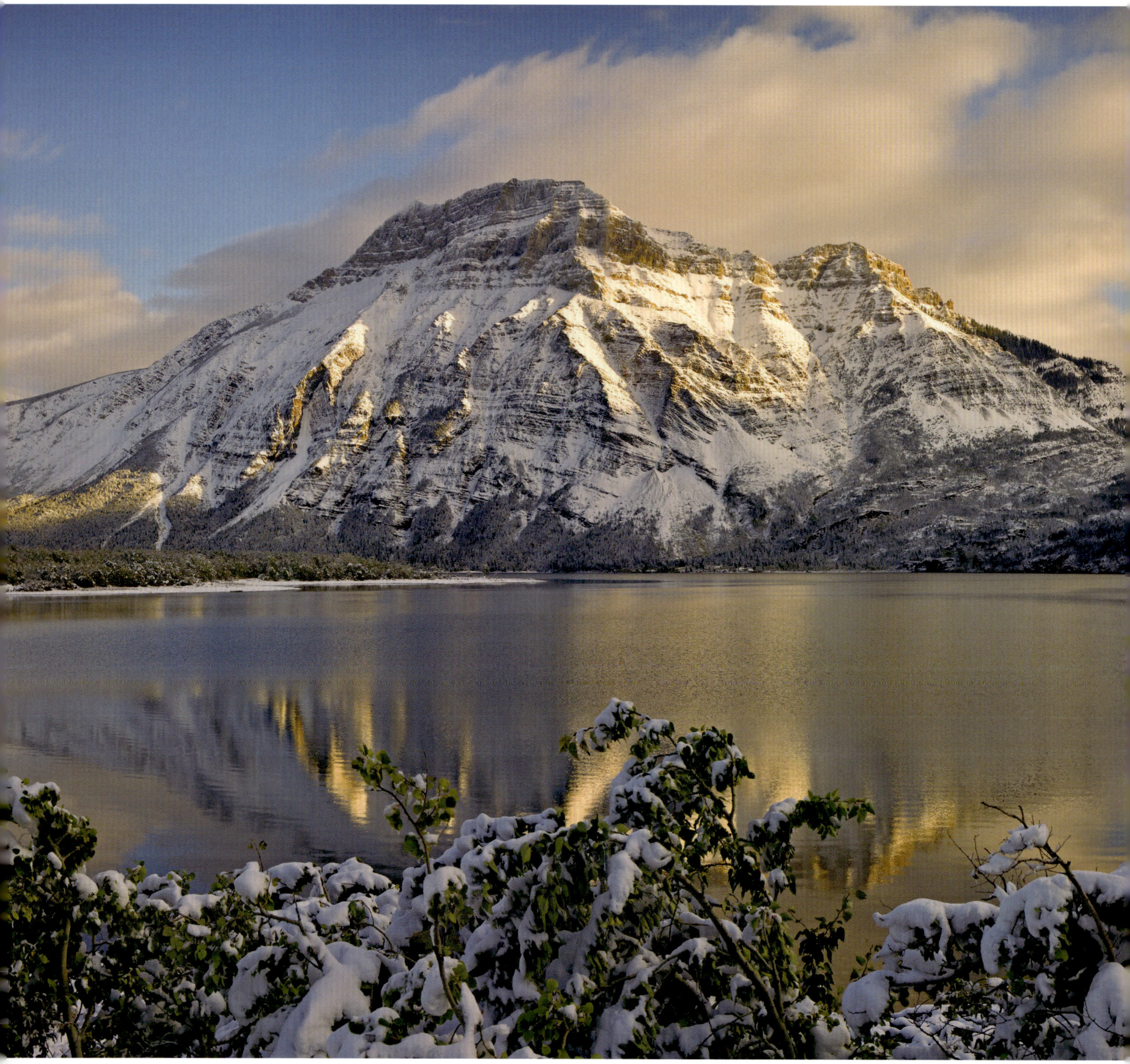

Waterton Glacier International Peace Park is a joint undertaking of the Rotary Clubs of Alberta (Canada) and Montana (USA). It was established on 30 June 1932 as a "sign of peace and goodwill between Canada, the USA, and a confederation of Blackfoot Indians." The peace park is situated on the Alberta–Montana border and comprises remote mountain valleys, windswept peaks, and fairy-tale scenery, with some 650 lakes and a wealth of flora and fauna. More than 1,200 varieties of plants and 60 mammal, 240 bird, and 20 fish species inhabit the alpine meadows, prairies, and taiga forest here.

More than 200 archeological excavation sites have yielded information about the living conditions of the park's primeval inhabitants, who were already present as far back as 8,000 years ago – long before the first European fur trappers turned up in the area at the beginning of the 18th century.

During the 19th century, prospectors, adventurers, and settlers forced the Native Americans out onto new territory on reservations.

The Middle Waterton Lake (large picture), together with the Upper and Lower Middleton Lakes, make up the Waterton Lakes National Park, which is located adjacent to the Glacier Park. The Saint Mary Lake (left) is the second largest in the Glacier National Park.

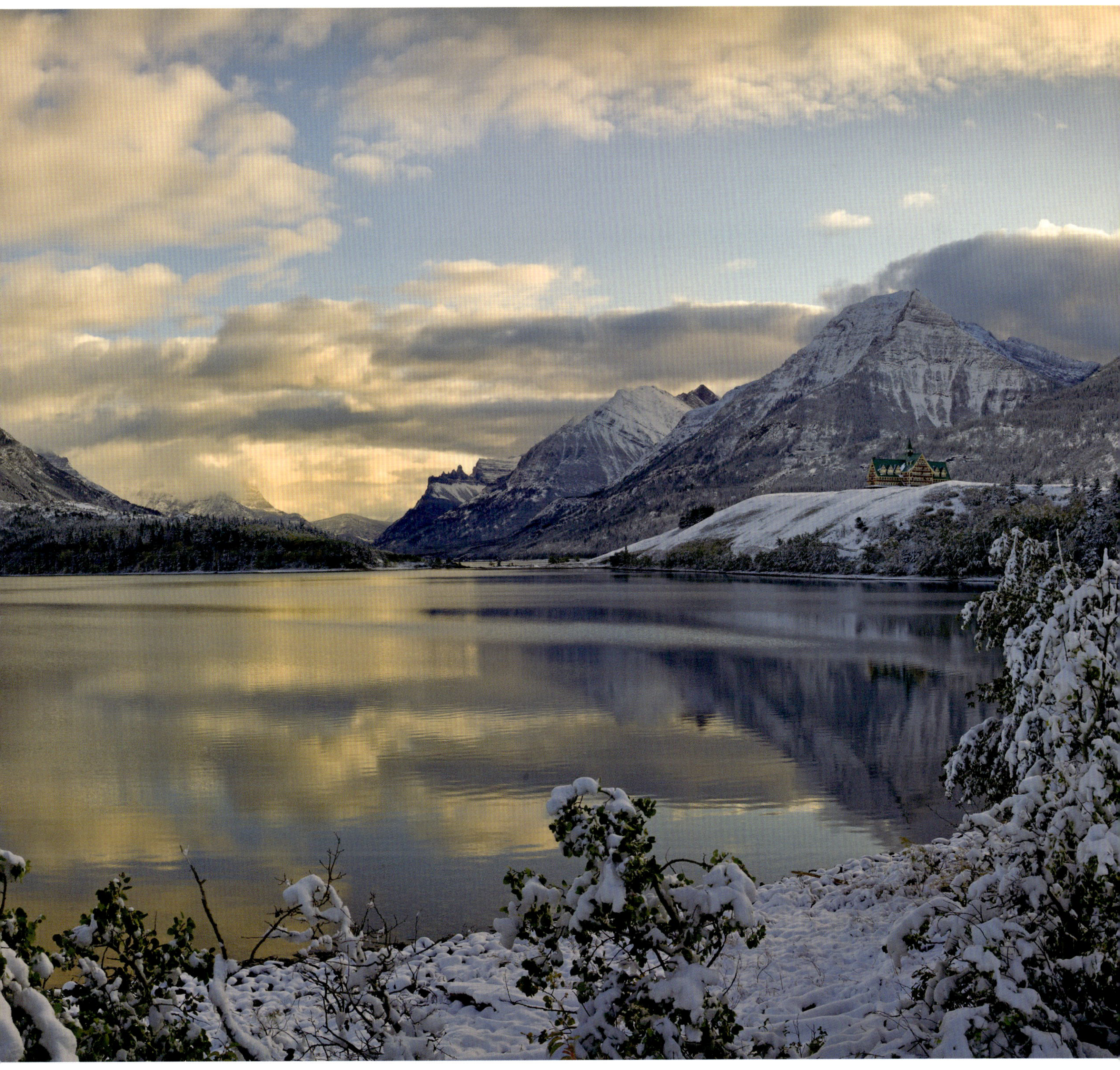

OLYMPIC NATIONAL PARK

Date of inscription: 1981

The most striking aspect of this national park situated in northwest Washington State is the temperate rainforest full of moss-covered trees.

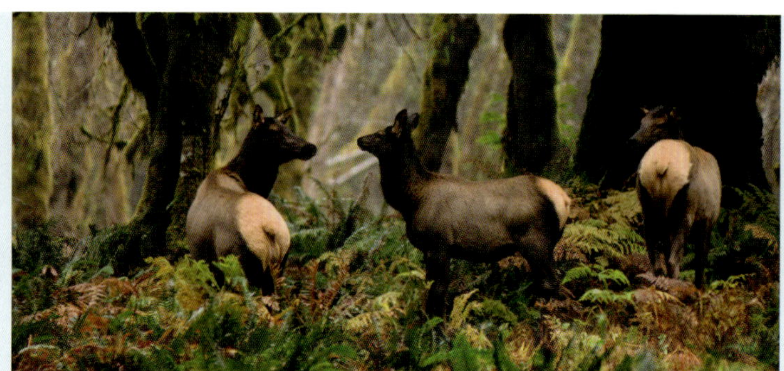

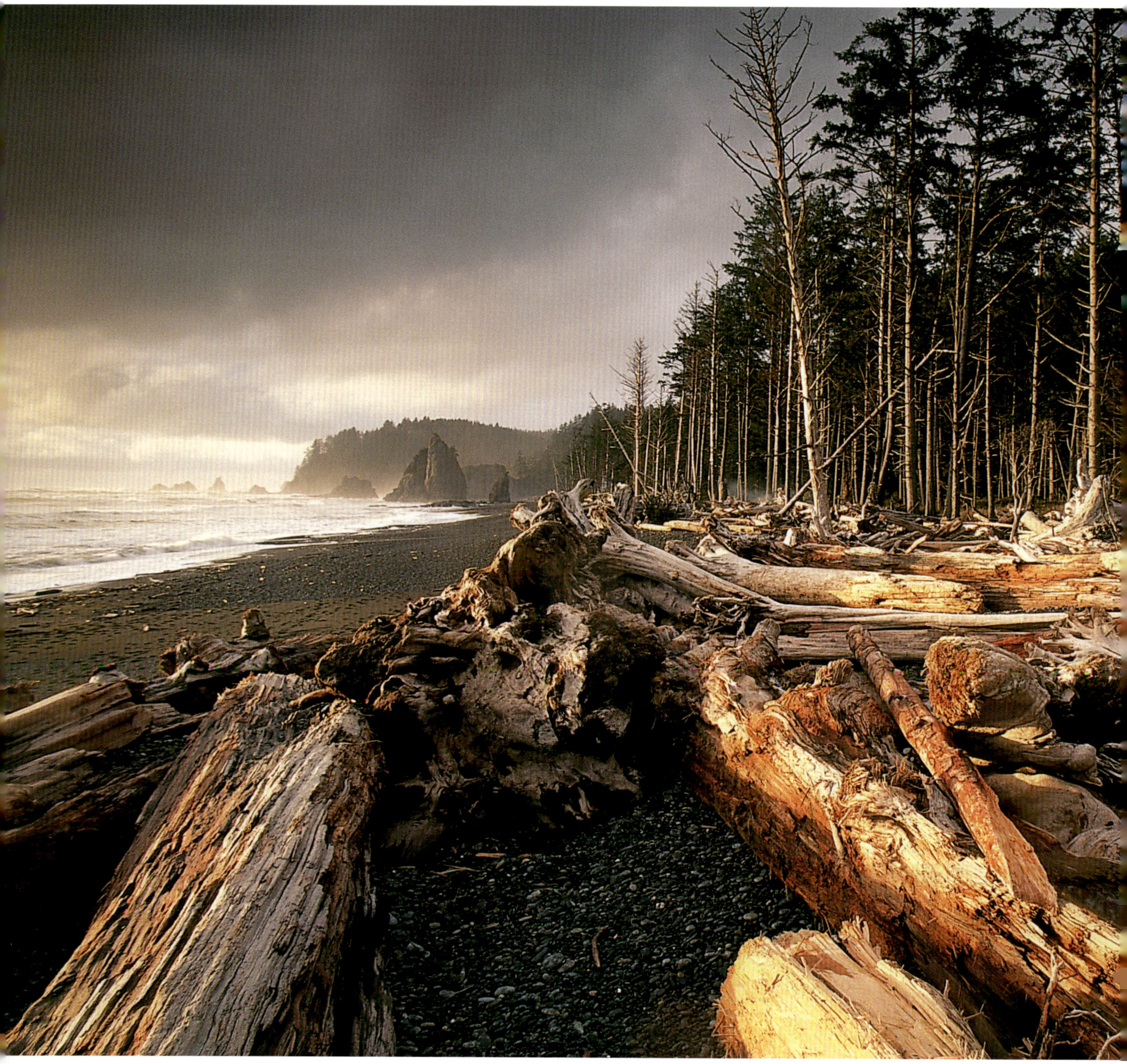

Olympic National Park, which covers the greater part of the Olympic peninsula to the west of Seattle, is surrounded by the Pacific Ocean to the west, the Strait of Juan de Fuca to the north, and Puget Sound to the east. Due to its geographic location, it has become a unique biosphere. Coniferous trees (firs, spruce, and cedar) the height of steeples grow in the damp primary forest. Their trunks routinely reach a circumference of 7 m (22 feet), but exceptional cases can be much larger; the record is held by "The Big Cedar Tree" which measures 20 m (66 feet) around. Thirteen plant species, mostly wild flowers, are endemic to the region, which is divided into three ecological zones. Douglas, hemlock and giant fir, Sitka spruce, bigleaf maple, and western red cedar make up a rainforest that is home to elks, pumas, black bears, and beavers.

The almost circular cluster of the Olympic mountains in the park's interior forms a glaciated landscape of exquisite beauty. Eleven river systems have their source here, offering an ideal biotope for fish alternating between salt and fresh water. The approximately 100-km (330-mile) long Pacific littoral is a perfect habitat for mussels, crabs, sea urchins, and starfish, as well as for the seabirds that eat them. Twice yearly, gray whales pass by on their journey to and from the warm-water lagoons of Mexico's Baja peninsula.

The Olympic peninsula was placed under protection as early as 1909, and inscribed as a national park in 1938. It boasts one of the world's few temperate rainforests. Driftwood accumulates on the Pacific coast and dolphins roam the seas (large image). Left: Roosevelt elks.

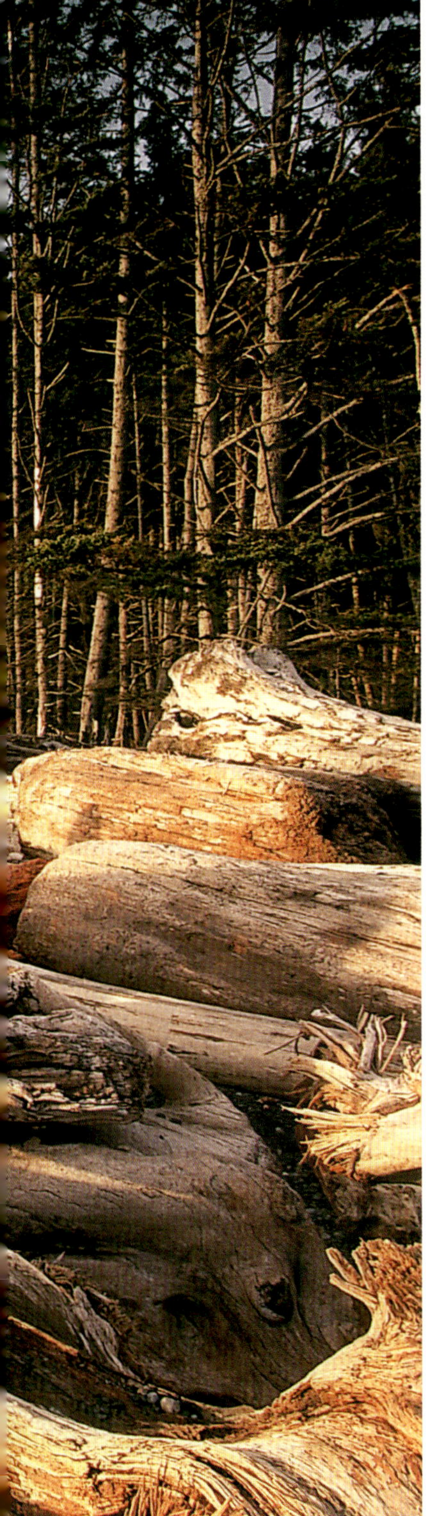

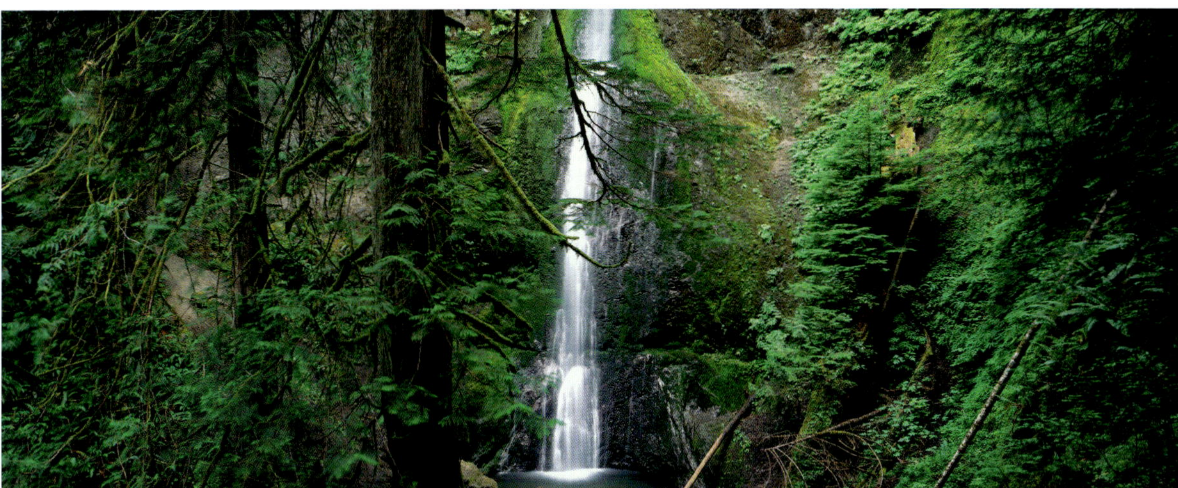

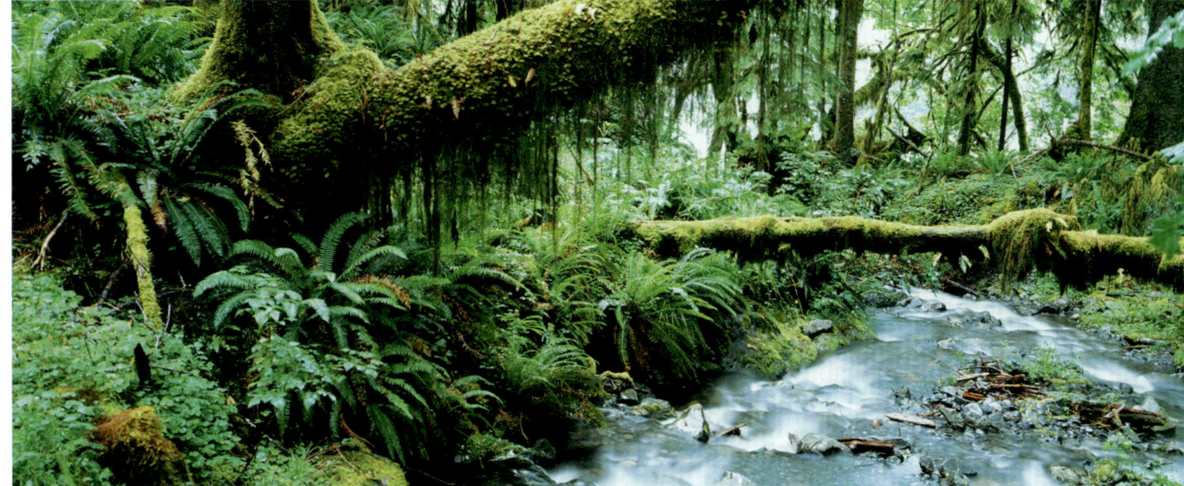

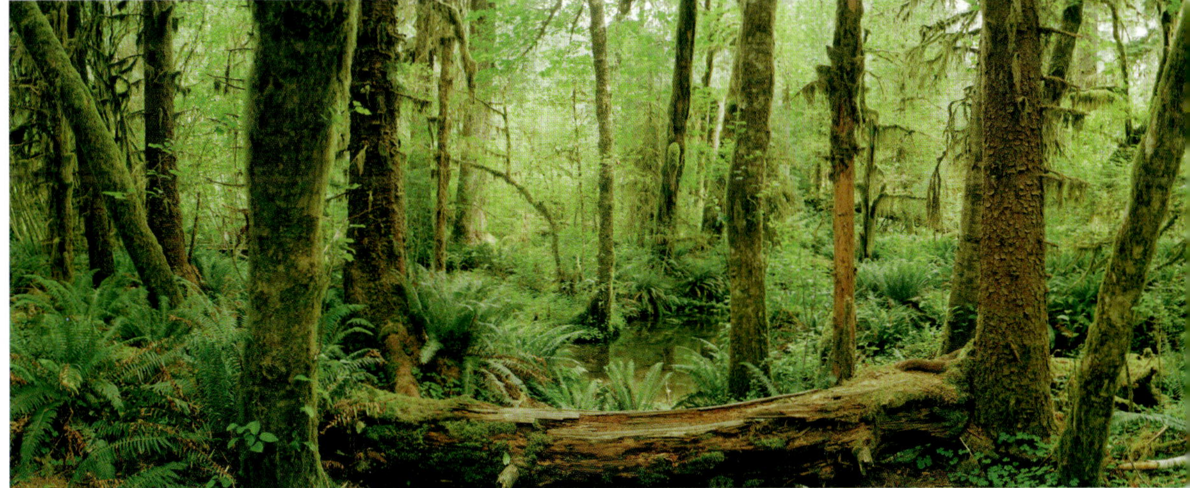

REDWOOD NATIONAL PARK

Date of inscription: 1980

The biggest plants in the world are the sequoias, called redwoods in English on account of their red bark. These giant trees give their name to this World Heritage Site lying on the Pacific coast of north California.

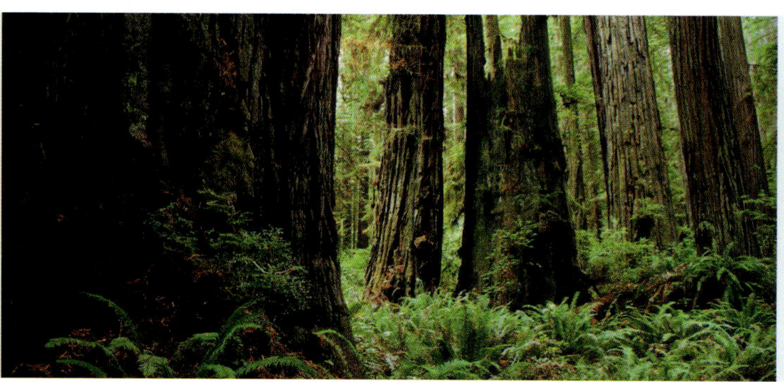

The coast redwood (Sequoia sempervirens), an evergreen conifer, was once widespread throughout North America. Today, there are only a few patches of these primeval giants remaining on the American West Coast. Several state parks were realized to protect these nearly 100-m tall trees. Three of these parks – Jedediah Smith, Del Norte Coast Redwoods, and Prairie Creek

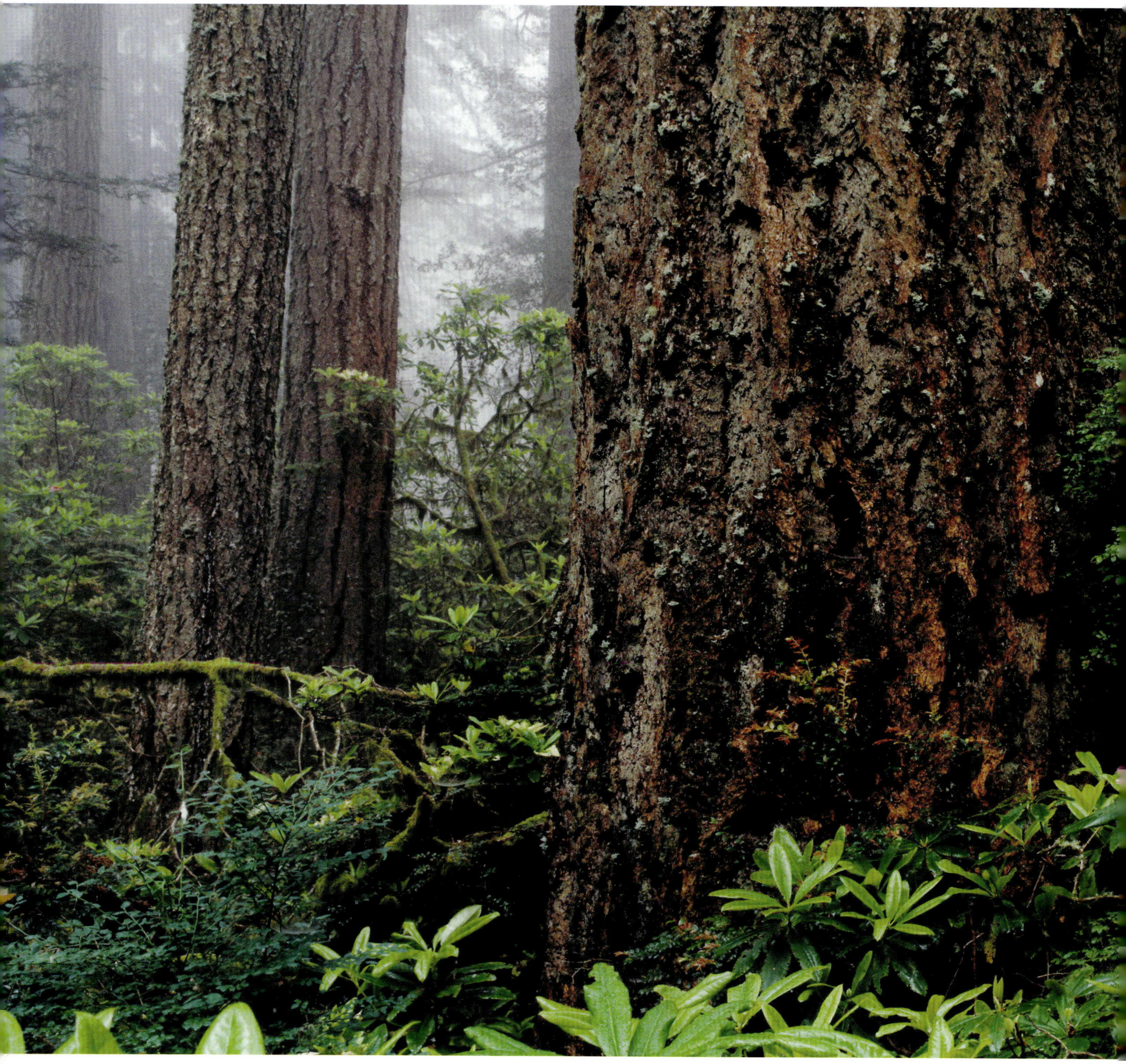

Redwoods – were combined in 1968 to form the Redwood National Park. About a third of the park's area (446 sq. km) consists of sequoia forest wherein the 111 m tall "Nugget Tree," the tallest known in the world, stands. The imposing trees regularly reach 500 to 700 years of age; some individuals grow to an age of 2,000. Other giant trees also grow at higher elevations, including Sitka spruce, Douglas and hemlock fir, bigleaf maple, and Californian laurel. Seals, sealions, and a wide variety of seabirds, including guillemots, marbled murrelets, brown pelicans, and double-crested cormorants also live on the Pacific coast, Pumas, skunks, Roosevelt elks, and white-tailed deer, gray foxes, black bears, otters, and beavers roam the mixed forests.

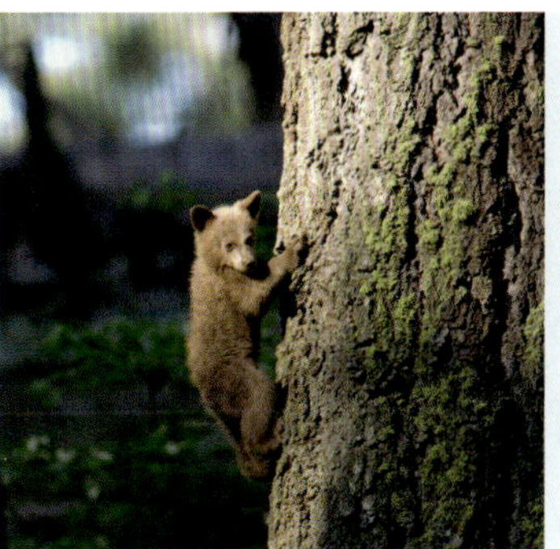

The redwoods were sacred to the Native Americans. They believed that these trees had a soul, and, before the establishment of the national park in 1968, they considered felling them a crime and an endangerment of native species; left: a young brown bear.

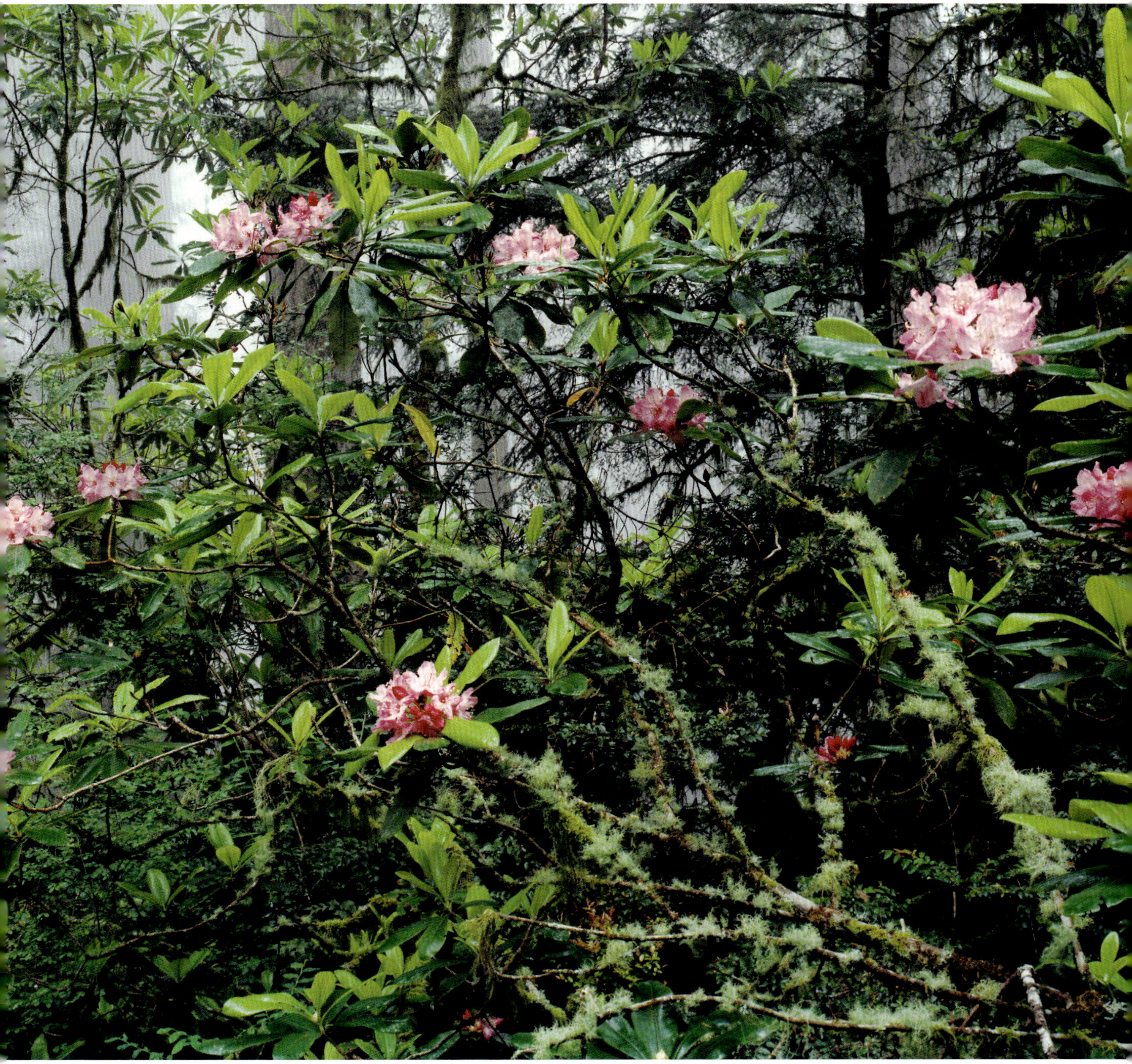

YOSEMITE NATIONAL PARK

Date of inscription: 1984

The mountainous scenery of this World Heritage Site in eastern California, encompassing expanses of coniferous forest and crystal-clear paternoster lakes, is one of the most impressive relics of the ice age.

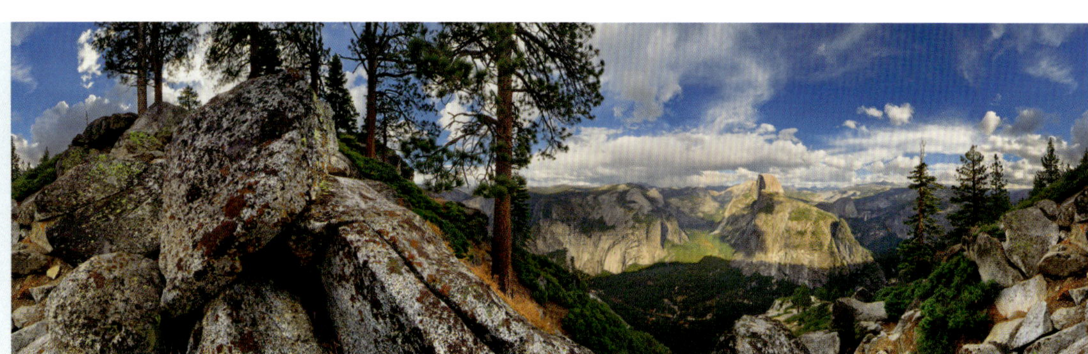

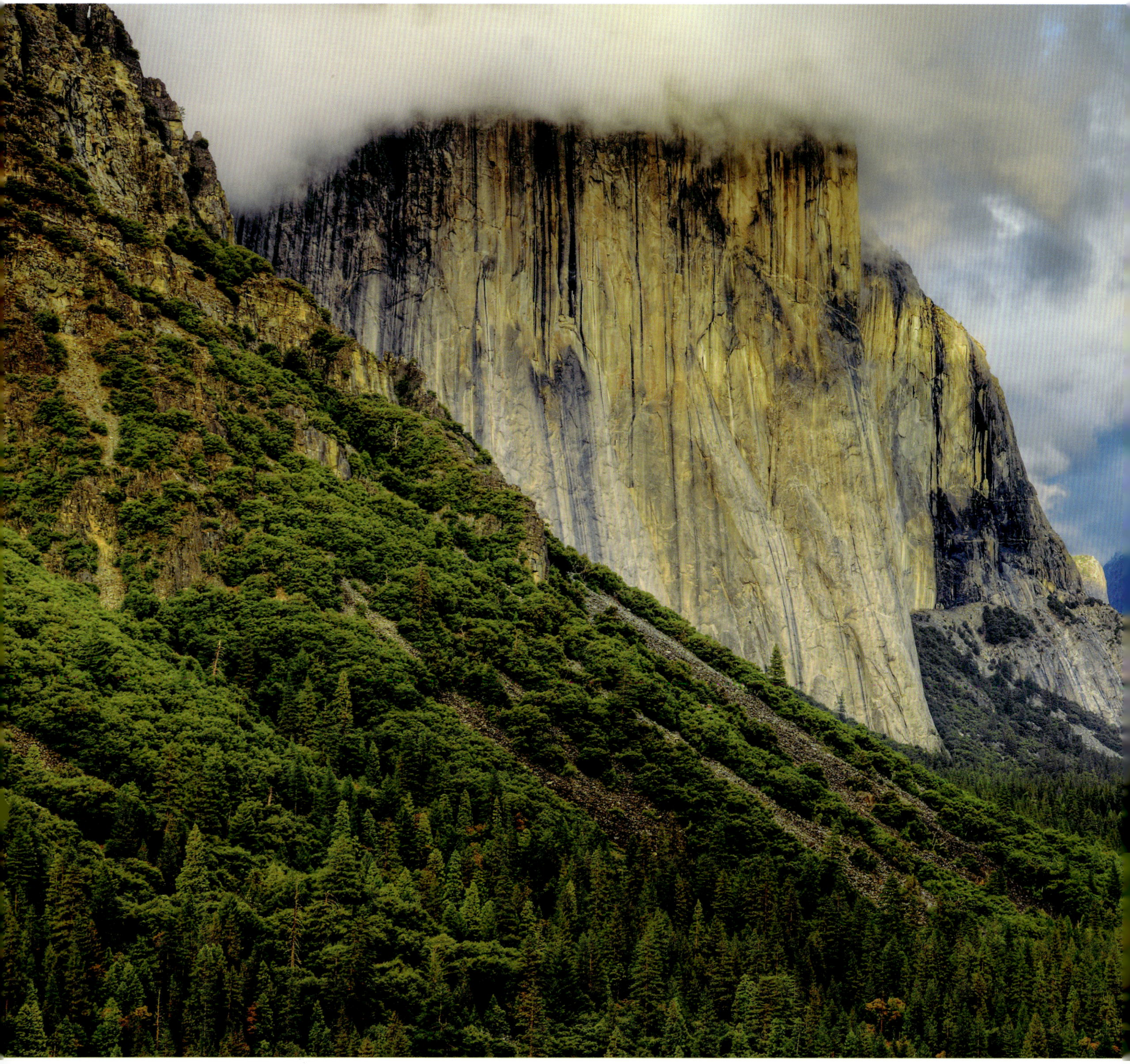

Yosemite National Park in the Sierra Nevada is among the most beautiful granite plateaus in the world. This landscape of U-shaped valleys, horn peaks, paternoster lakes, and waterfalls was carved out by ice-age glaciers. Many monolithic rocks jut out from the Merced river valley. The Half Dome, the park's symbol, almost 2,700 m (8,900 feet) high, is particularly impressive. There is a concentration of high waterfalls here that is found practically nowhere else on earth. At 740 m (2,440 feet) in height, the Yosemite Falls are the second largest in America, and there are yet still more imposing natural spectacles of this kind here.

There is a wide variety of vegetation: as many as 37 tree species have been recorded, including some 3,000-year- old giant sequoias. The mountain meadows conceal a great number of herbs and wild flowers. Although grizzly bears and wolves have died out here, there are still black bears, pumas, chipmunks, squirrels, fisher martens, black-tailed deer, pikas, wolverines, and many species of bird in the park.

The Yosemite National Park is distinguished not only by steep cliffs and challenging climbing routes; lakes and tranquil creeks also characterize the park. Thus, the Tuolumne Glacier, for example, created Tenaya Lake (large picture) when it calved. The name of the lake is that of the chief of a neighbouring tribe of Native Americans.

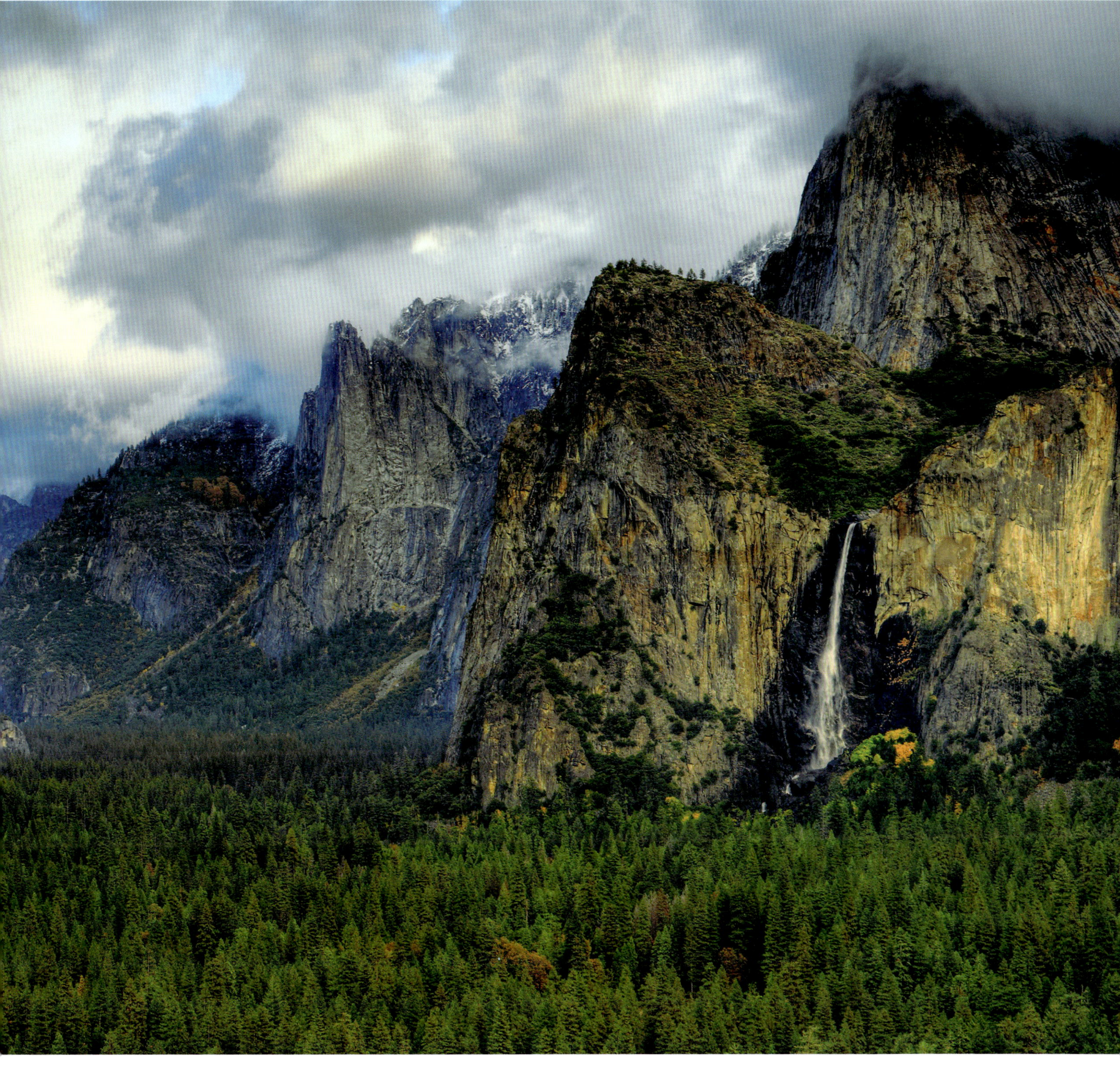

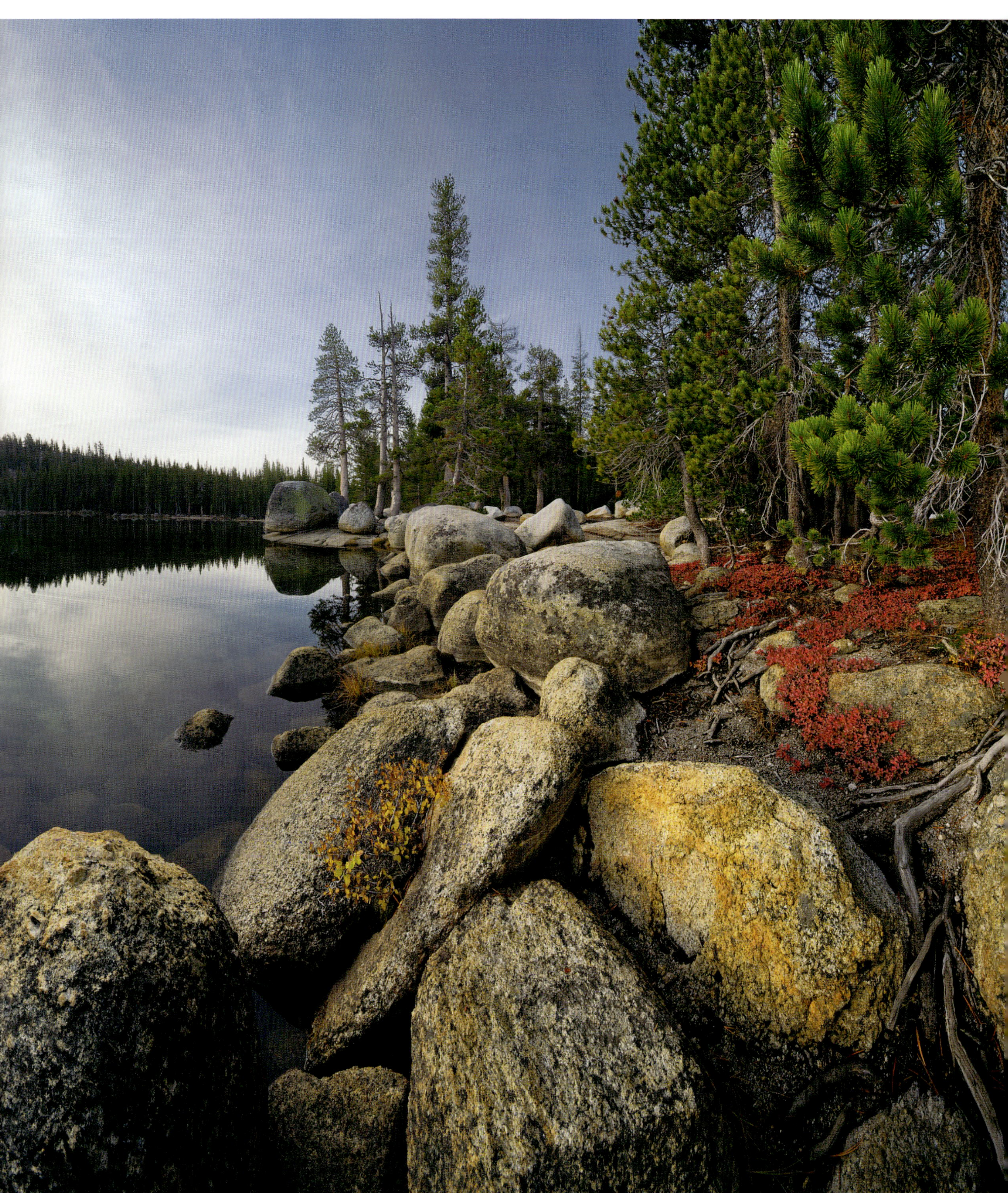

The Yosemite National Park is distinguished not only by steep cliffs and challenging climbing routes; lakes and tranquil creeks also characterize the park. Thus, the Tuolumne Glacier, for example, created Tenaya Lake (large picture) when it calved. The name of the lake is that of the chief of a neighbouring tribe of Native Americans.

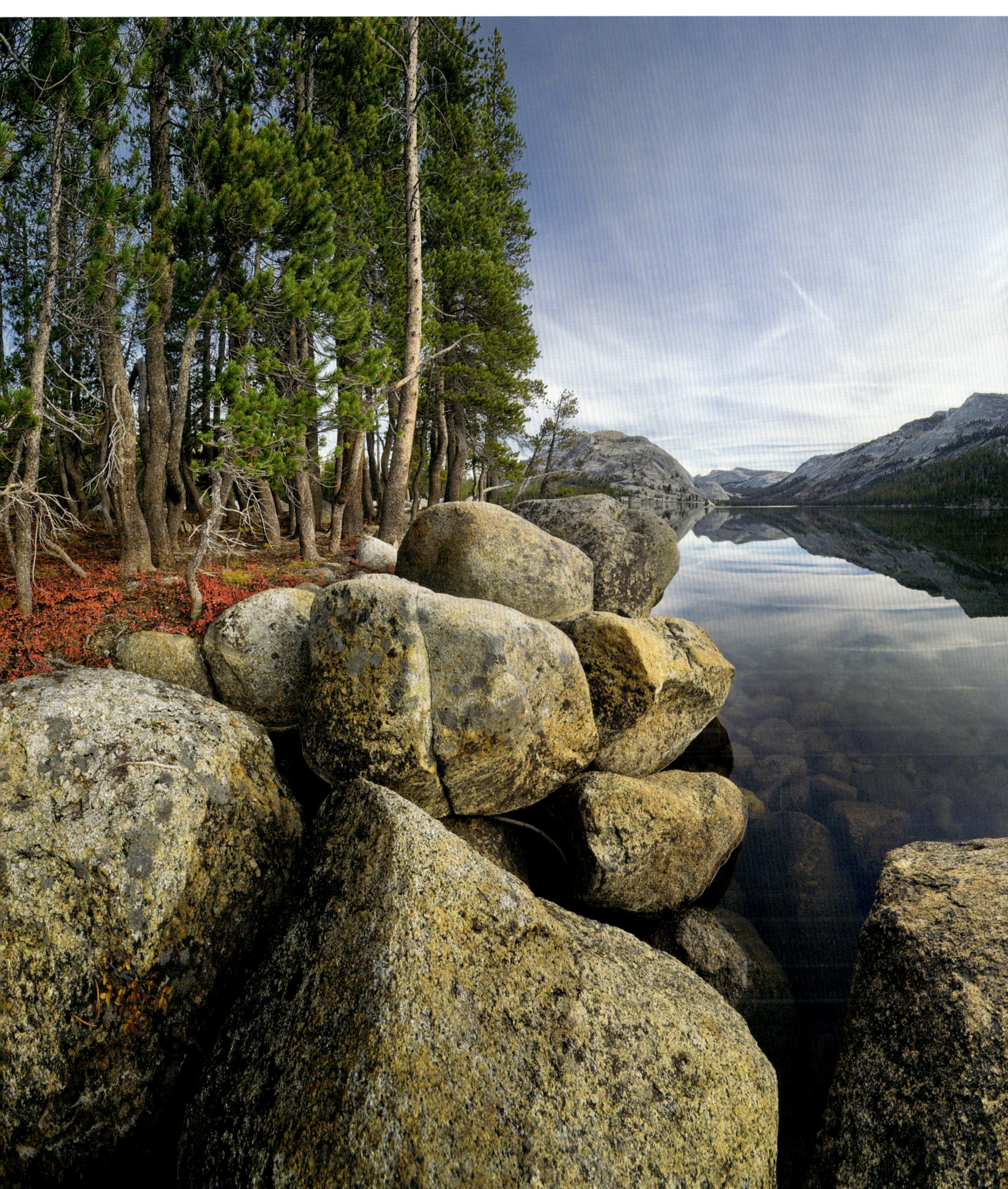

YELLOWSTONE NATIONAL PARK

Date of inscription: 1978

The world's oldest national park is a majestic wilderness of mountains, rivers, and lakes, as well as more than 3,000 geysers. Approximately 96 percent of its total area (around 9,000 sq. km, 3,500 sq. miles) lies in Wyoming, 3 percent in Montana and 1 percent in Idaho.

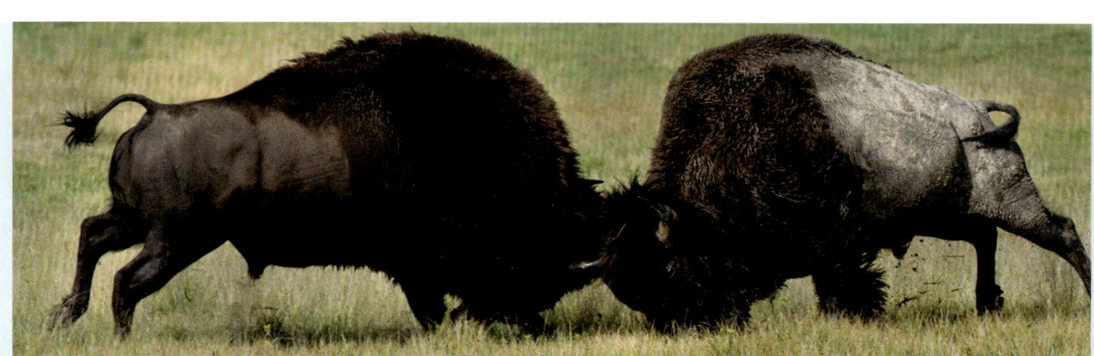

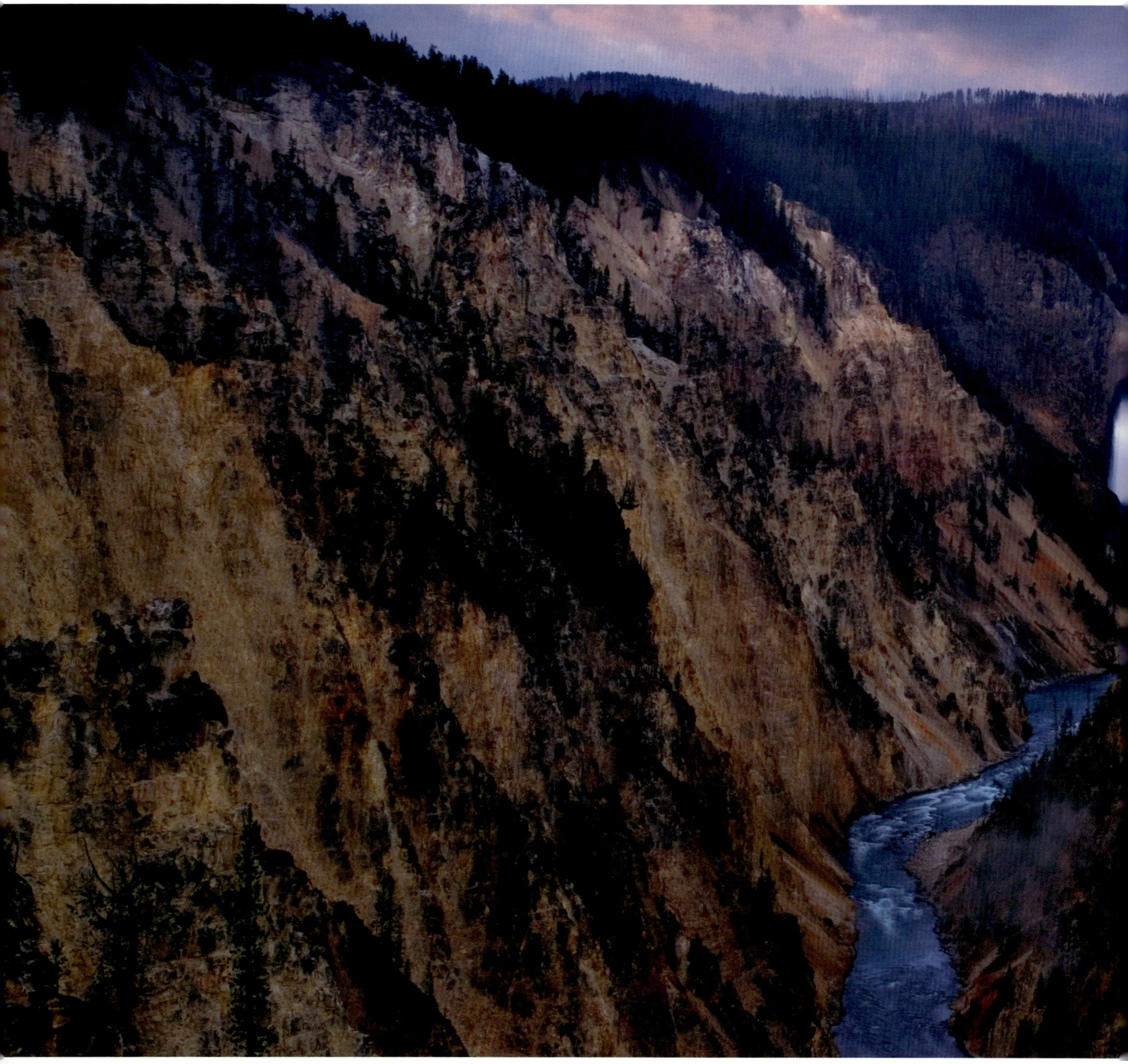

The heart of the national park is the 2,000-m (6,600-foot) high Yellowstone plateau, a rock feature surrounded by mountains reaching up to 4,000 m (13,200 feet) in height. The volcanic origin of this landscape is still visible today, and petrified forests bear witness to the streams of lava and ash rain which most recently flowed through this region 60,000 years ago. The earth has not yet come to rest, however, as is shown by the many hot springs, fumaroles, and geysers. Of these, Old Faithful is the most famous, shooting a fountain 60 m (200 feet) high into the air roughly every hour. Spring pools with multi-hued, boiling water, bursting mud bubbles, and hot steam shooting from rock fissures attest to the forces that are still at work beneath the earth's surface. This World Heritage Site, which was founded in 1872 and named after the yellow rock forming the banks of the Yellowstone river, is home to a variety of animals, with the grizzly bear as king, but also including wolves, bison, and elk, a North American stag with great antlers.

The Yellowstone River cuts its way through deep gorges and rock faces, and in between drops into the depths in mighty waterfalls such as the Lower Yellowstone Fall (large picture). Left: bison defending their terrain.

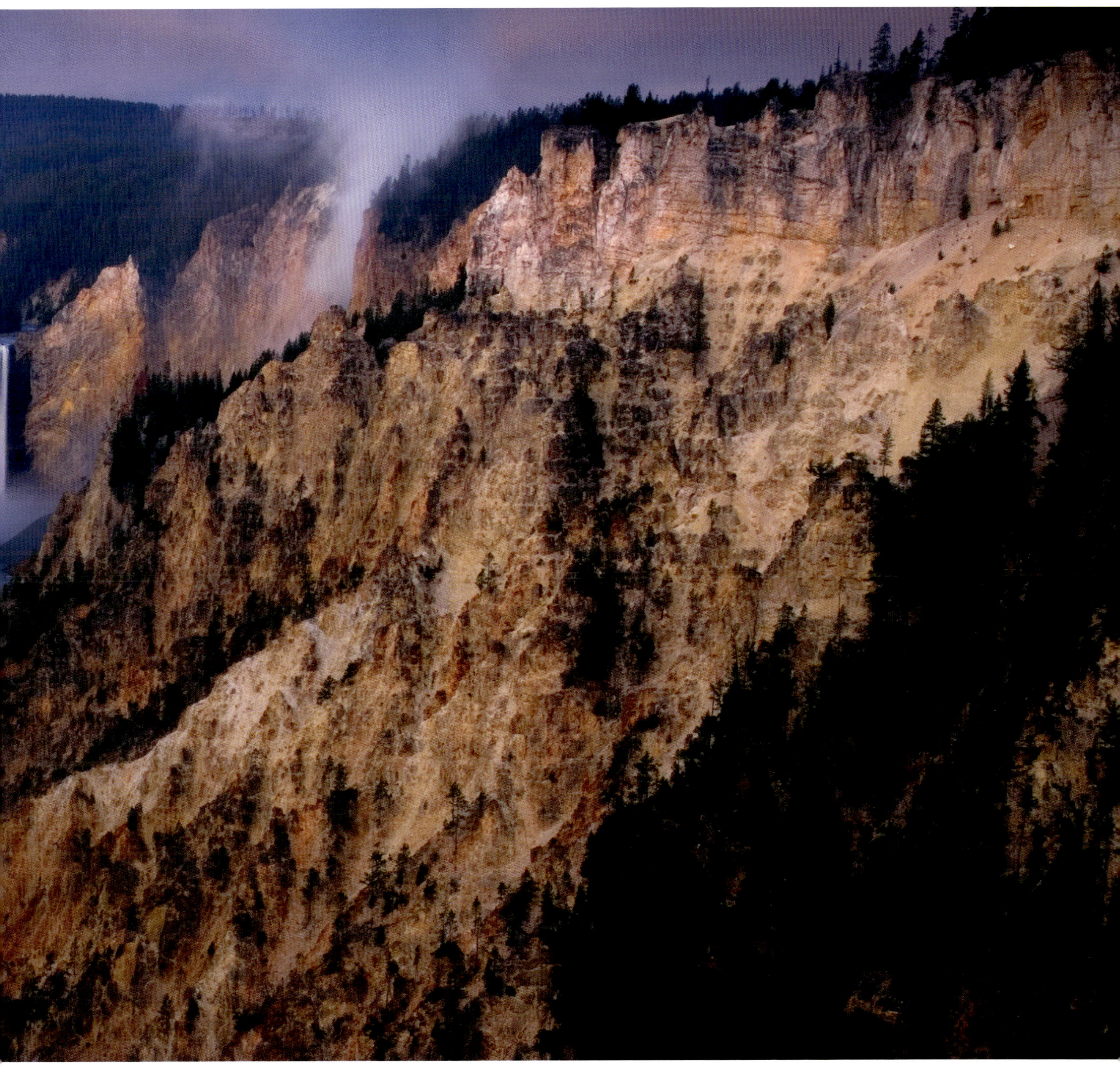

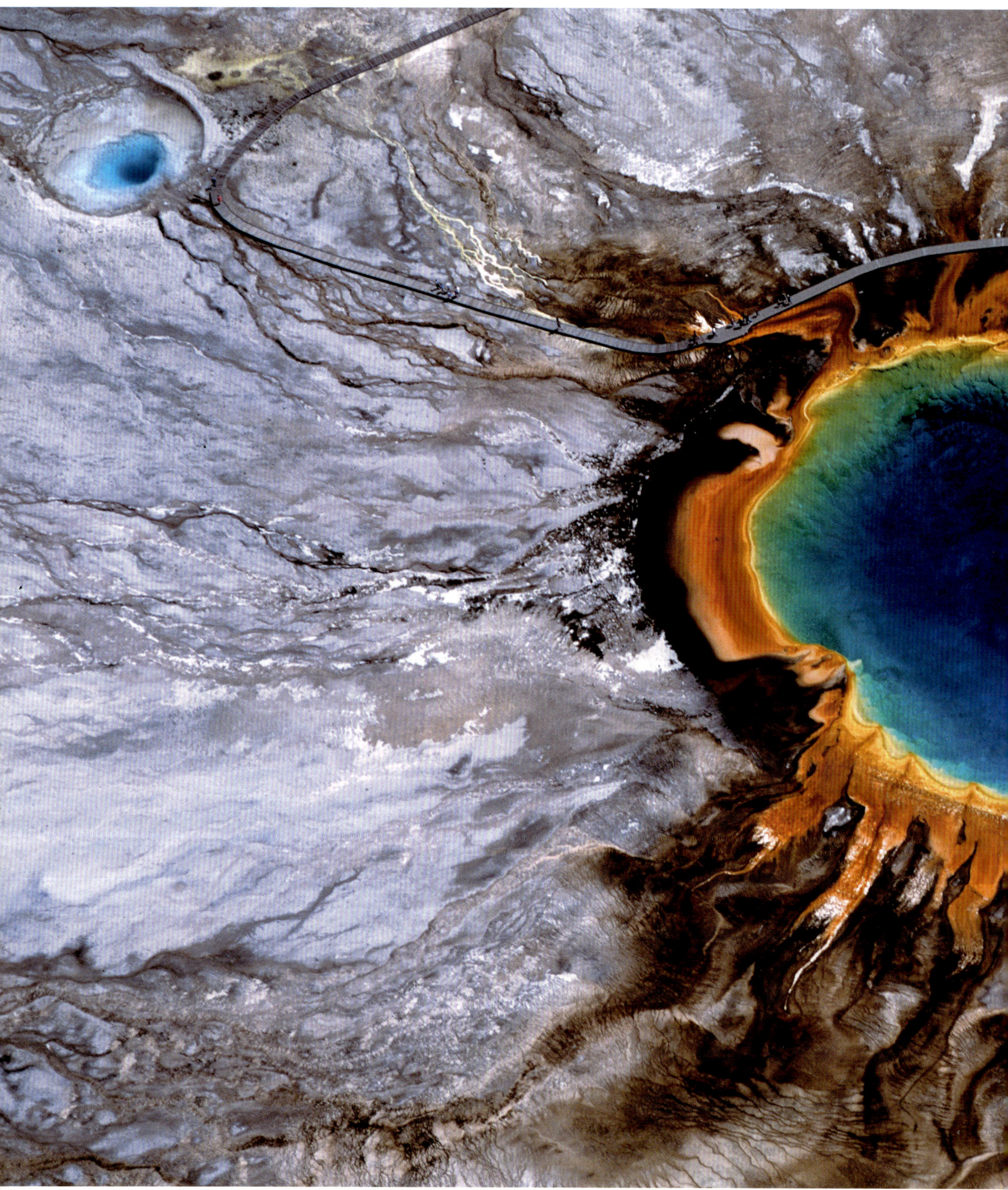

A spectacular aerial view shows a natural wonder that, at first glance, resembles a giant flaming eye. This is the Grand Prismatic Spring, an oversized hot spring in the west of Yellowstone National Park. Microorganisms live along the water's edges, painting its shores yellow and red; only the inner, hot water is clear and blue.

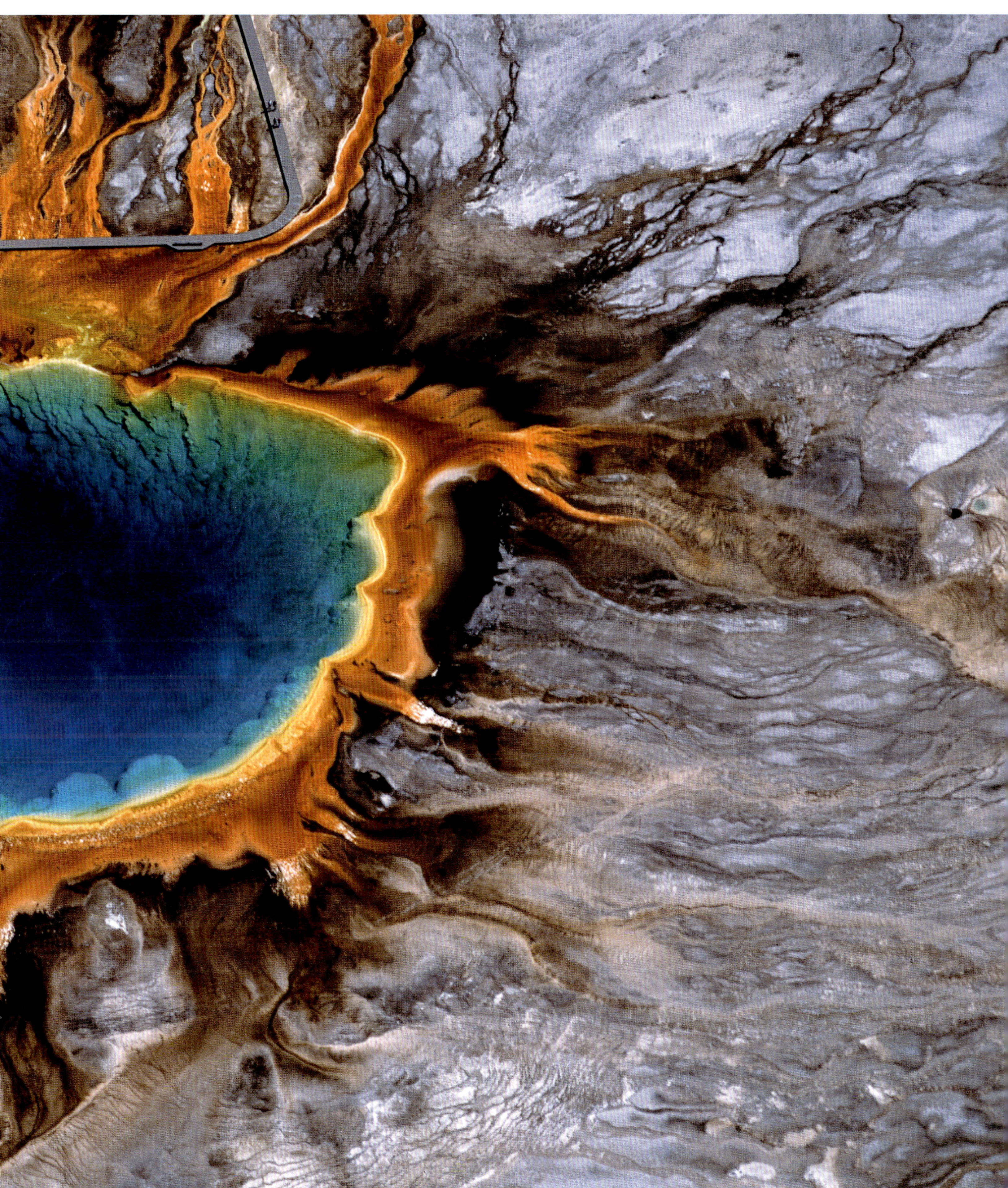

GRAND CANYON NATIONAL PARK

Date of inscription: 1979

This gigantic rocky panorama, cut into the stone by the Colorado river over millions of years, affords an impressive glimpse of the earth's geological history. The Grand Canyon in north-western Arizona is probably the most spectacular chasm in the world.

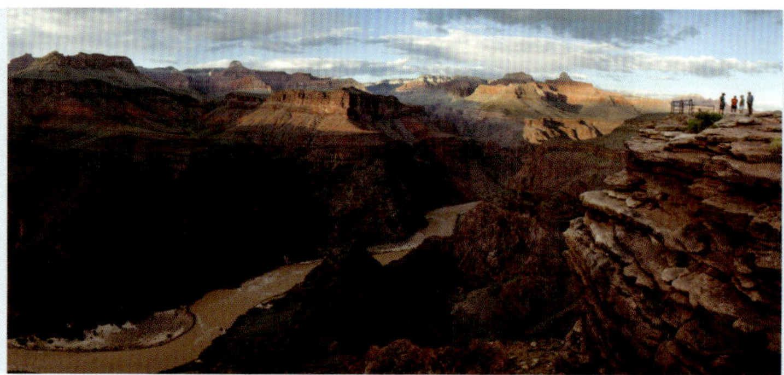

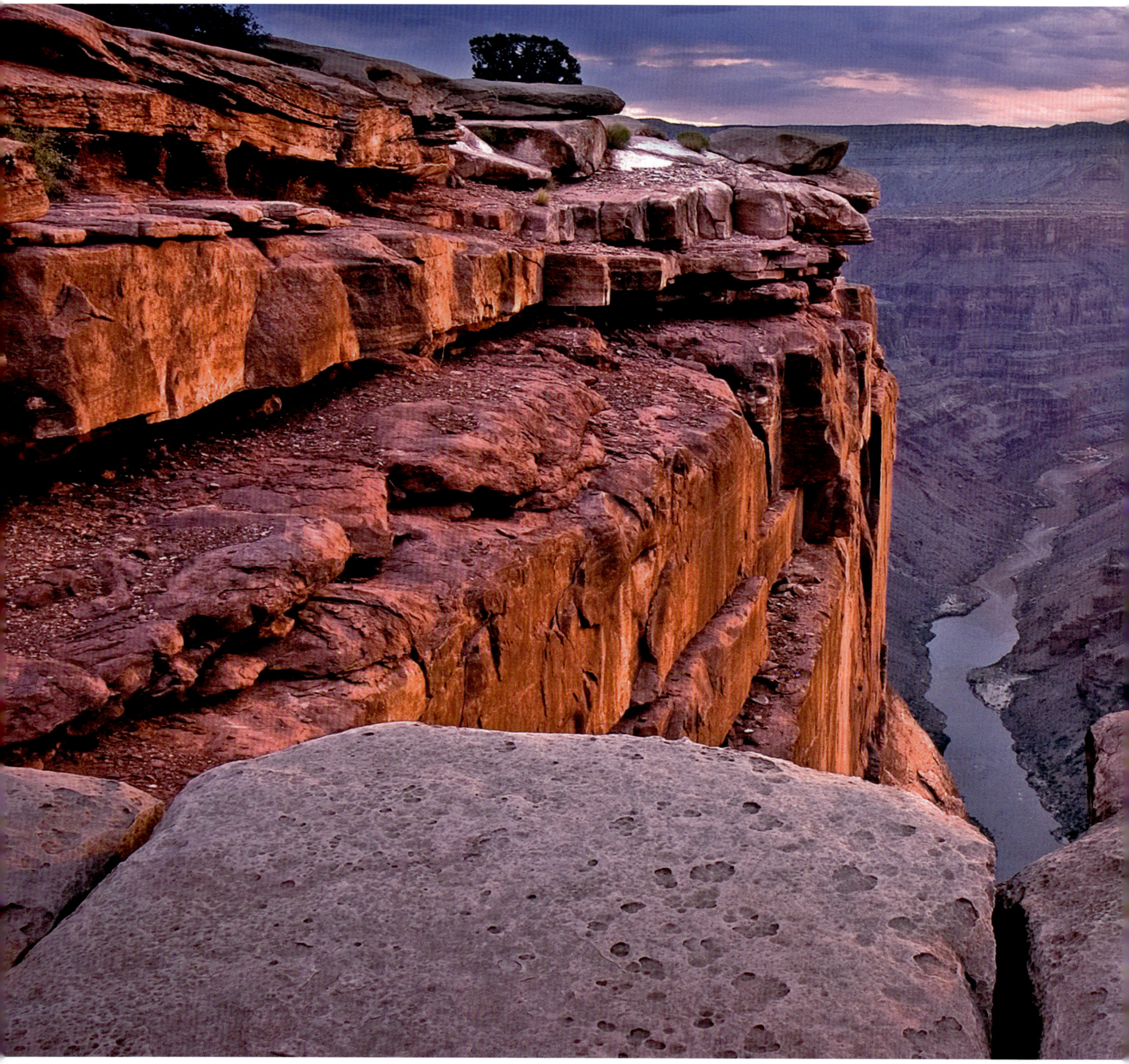

Although Garcia López de Cárdenas, a Spaniard, was the first European to glimpse the magnificent panorama of the Grand Canyon in 1540, the area was not properly mapped until the middle of the 19th century. The Grand Canyon's geohistory is still scientifically disputed. It is conjectured that the river began seeking a way across the rocky plateau about six million years ago, and this led in the course of time to the development of this unique chasm, called by the naturalist John Muir "the greatest of God's earthly places." Wind and weathering also contributed to the bizarre formations on the rocky walls. The sequence of strata in the walls is easily discernible and clearly documents the different periods of the earth's geological history; fossils found here afford an insight into life in prehistoric times. Only the hardiest of plants and animals are able to survive the temperatures of up to 50o C in the canyon, and these include various cactuses, thornbushes, rattlesnakes, black widows, and scorpions. Because of the extreme conditions, the river is a habitat for very few species of fish, but iguanas, toads, and frogs live on the banks. In some locations, even beavers and otters survive. Only the forests on the northern and southern edges offer a viable habitat for a large variety of flora and fauna. Numerous finds attest to a history of human settlement in the Grand Canyon going back some 4,000 years. The most impressive are the thousand-year-old rock dwellings of the Anasazi.

Plateau Point (left), located at the far end of the Tonto Plateau, offers great views and insight into the canyon, without you having to descend all the way down to the Colorado River. Large picture: view from Toroweap Overlook on the North Rim.

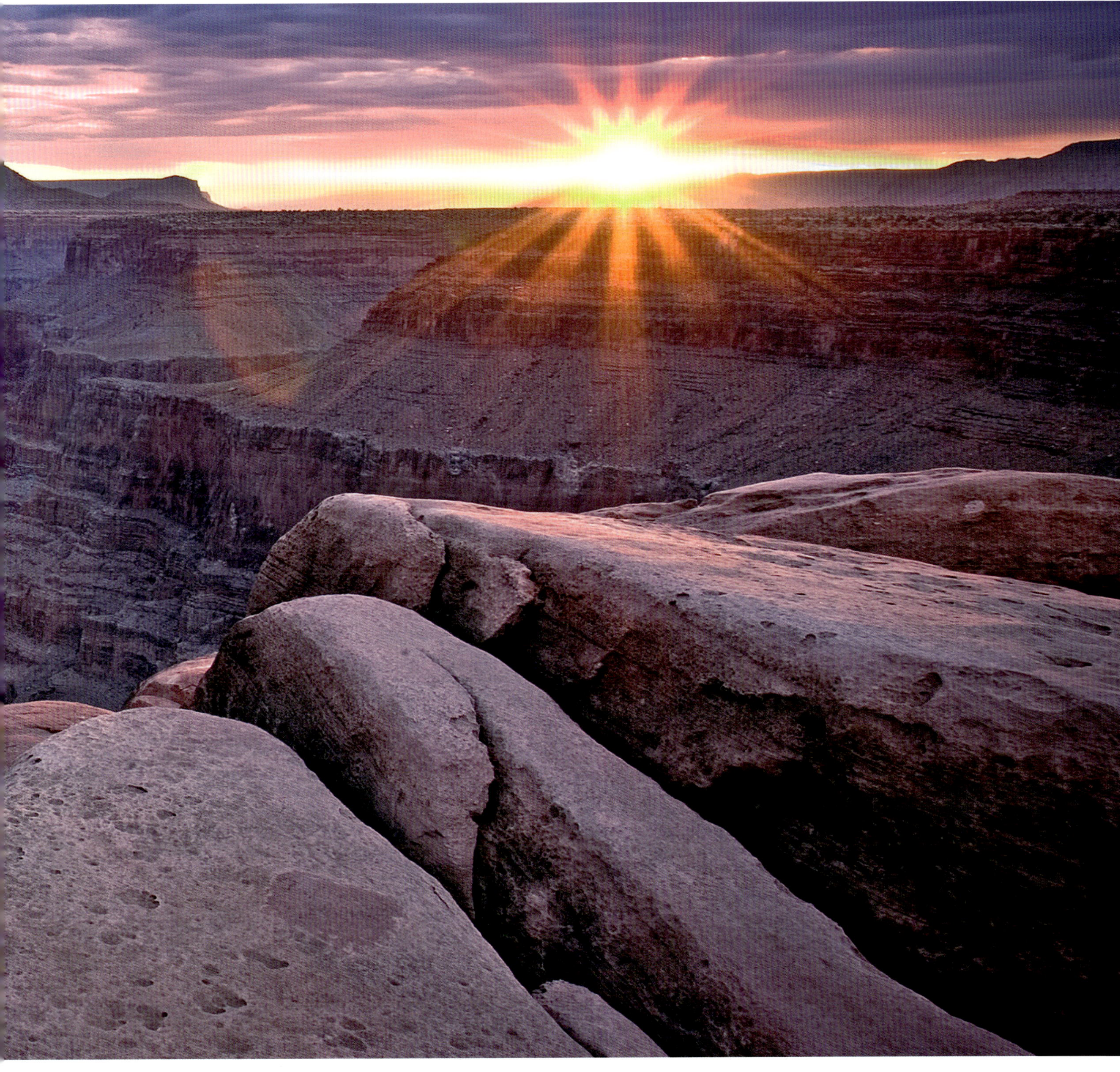

MESA VERDE NATIONAL PARK

Date of inscription: 1978 *

These rock dwellings, created in south-western Colorado between the 6th and 12th centuries, are unique with regard to their number and condition.

* protected by UNESCO as a Cultural Heritage site.

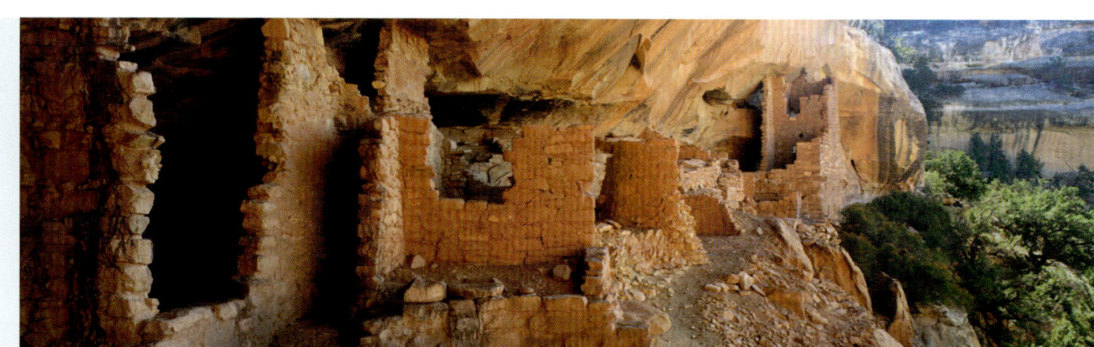

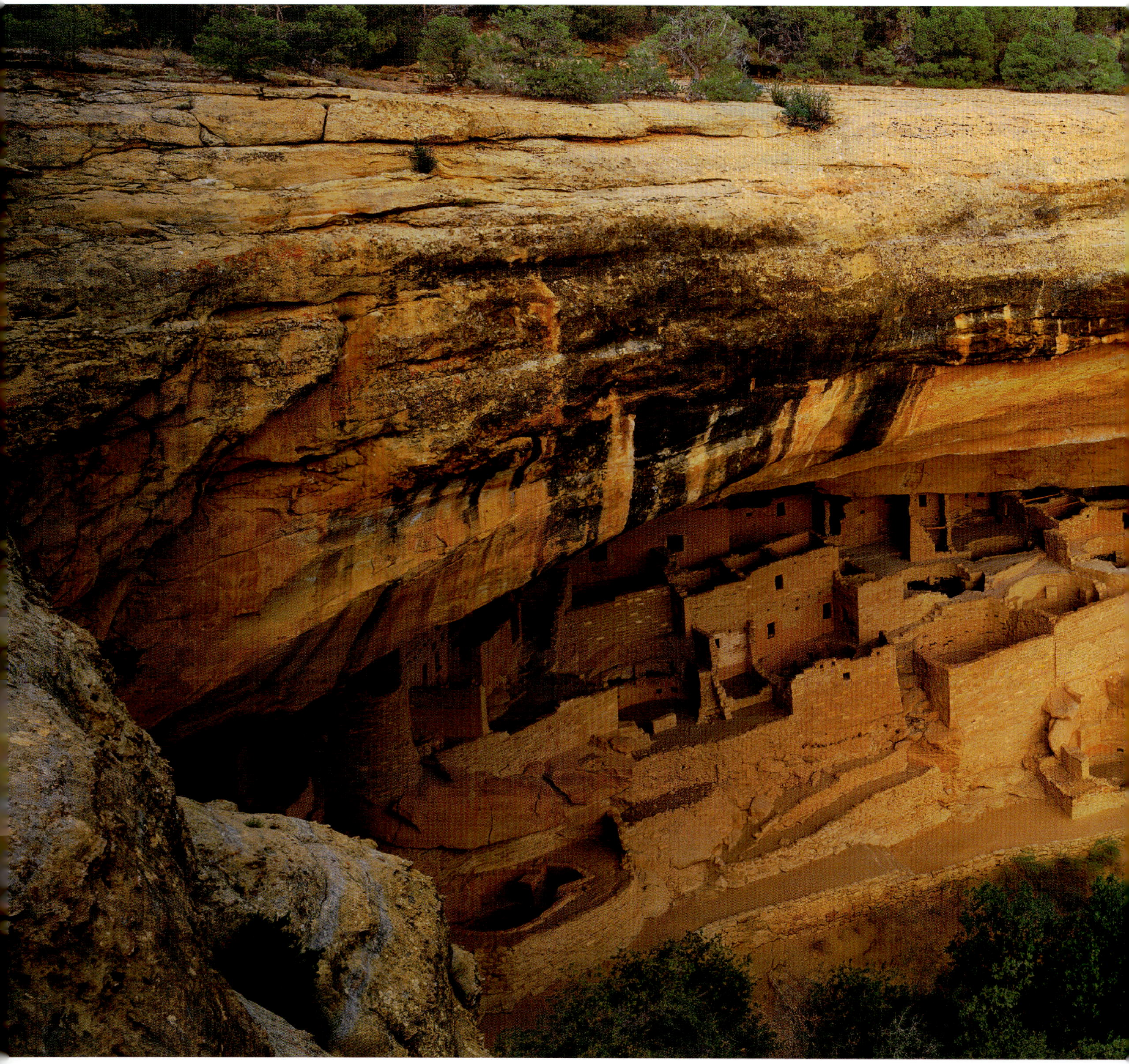

The oldest and best-preserved ruins of the Anasazi are found on the elongated, approximately 2,600-m-(8,530-foot-) high table mountain of Mesa Verde ("green table"), whose terrain was designated as a national park as early as 1906. In the local gorges and rock niches, archaeologists have identified and restored entire villages. Many houses were built into the rocks, sometimes in extreme positions, suggesting that the Ancestral Pueblo people were trying to protect themselves against their enemies. Of the total of approximately 4,600 ruins in the national park, many have been preserved in a very good condition. Best-known are the four-story Cliff Palace, whose 220 rooms and 23 kivas offered space for more than 200 residents; the Long House in Rock Canyon with its 181 rooms and 15 kivas; and the Spruce Tree House, built for about 110 people, with 114 rooms and eight kivas. The complex was first discovered by white men in the winter of 1888, when two cowboys on the lookout for stray cattle suddenly found themselves in front of the walls of Cliff Palace.

The rock houses of the Anasazi are visible proof of the Ancestral Puebloans' ability to build stable homes in an inhospitable wilderness. The people have long disappeared from the history books – but for them, nature and landscape remained the paramount principles.

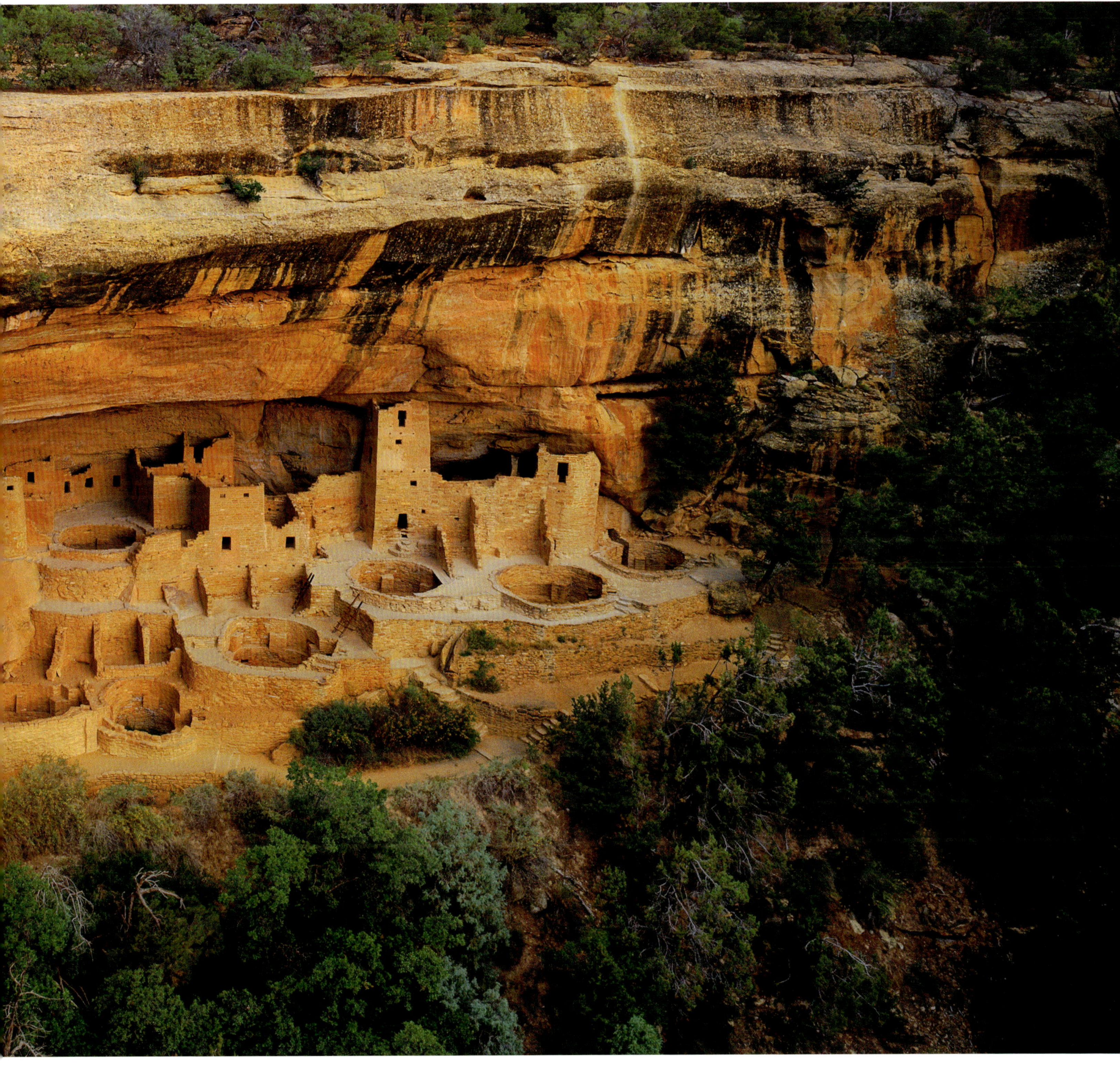

CARLSBAD CAVERNS NATIONAL PARK

Date of inscription: 1995

Near the small town of Carlsbad, in south-east New Mexico, there is a complicated labyrinth of bizarre limestone caves, which fascinates scientists and tourists alike.

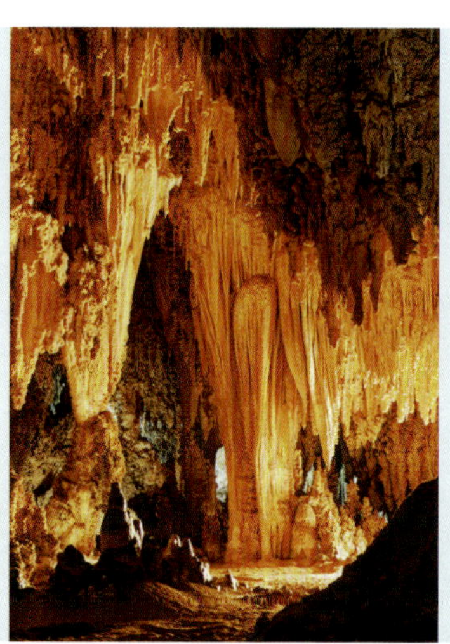

At first glance, the desert and forest scenery surrounding the Guadalupe mountains might be a disappointment, but the actual charms of the Carlsbad Caverns National Park's 200 sq. km (75 sq. miles) are hidden in the mountains, in an extensive cave system. Millions of years ago, the effects of water and sulphides began hollowing out a subterranean reef dating back to the Permian era, creating giant cracks, fissures, and chambers – the modern-day Carlsbad caverns. More than 80 caves have been discovered so far, of which the Lechuguilla Cave is both the deepest (477 m, 1,600 feet) and the longest (133 km, 83 miles). Hundreds and thousands of bats sleep in the Bat Cave, and rock art dating back to before Columbus has been found. The New Cave is also a fascinating spectacle of stalagmites and stalactites. There are still many natural wonders remaining to be discovered in this fantastical, fairy-tale cave world.

The bizarre world of the Carlsbad caverns and its stalagmites and stalactites is still being created. Its development began 250 million years ago.

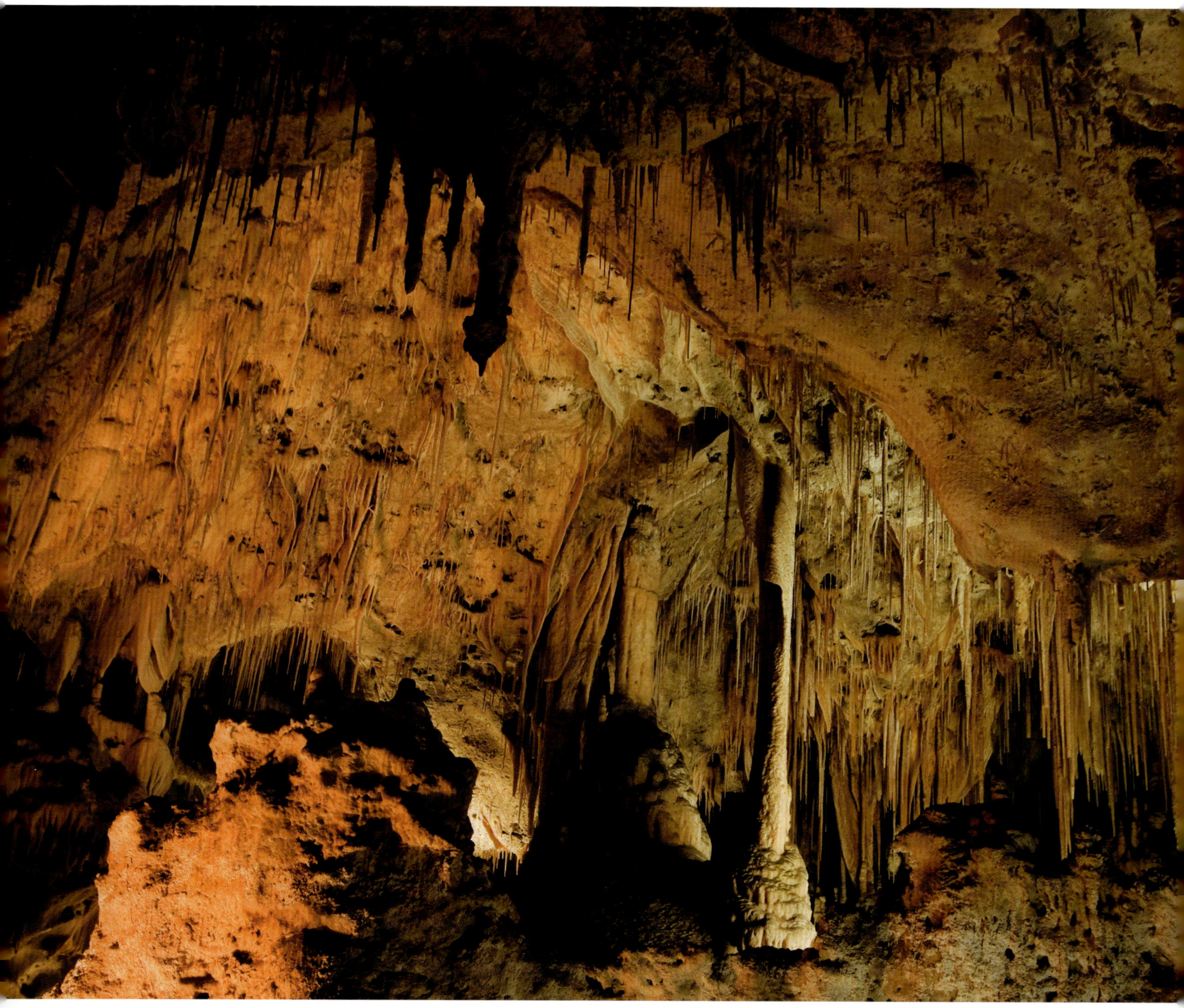

MAMMOTH CAVE NATIONAL PARK

In the karst scenery on the banks of the Green river in Kentucky, intertwining tunnels that would take days to walk through lead the visitor into a world of bizarre limestone formations, formed from the porous rock over millions of years by constantly dripping water. The giant chambers, with their impressive stalagmites and stalactites, were formed from crystallized layers of calcium carbonate over 300 million years, starting in the Carboniferous period. Water permeated through a porous stratum of sandstone into a layer of limestone lying beneath. Chemical processes created hollow spaces, which dried out as the water table dropped. Water with a high mineral content then dripped down through the cave, forming columns of calcite deposits. These enormous caves are a habitat for such extraordinary creatures as the blind cave fish, the Kentucky cave crab, and the cave cricket. Various salamander and frog species also live here, and the caves are an important refuge for several endangered species of bat.

A spotlight reveals the dimensions of the underground scenery.

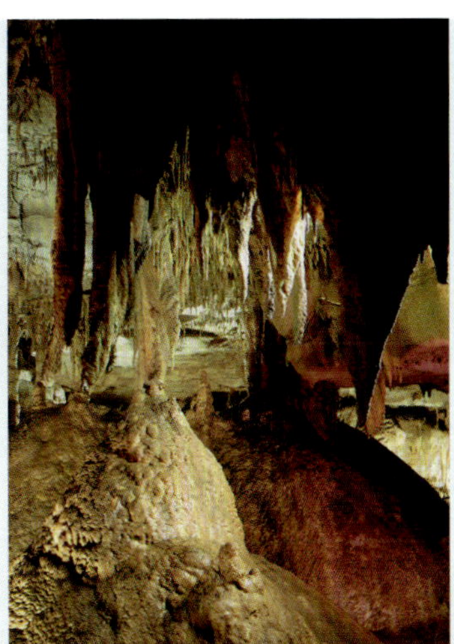

Date of inscription: 1981

The Mammoth Cave is the world's largest and most convoluted cave system and its tunnels are a habitat for more than 200 species.

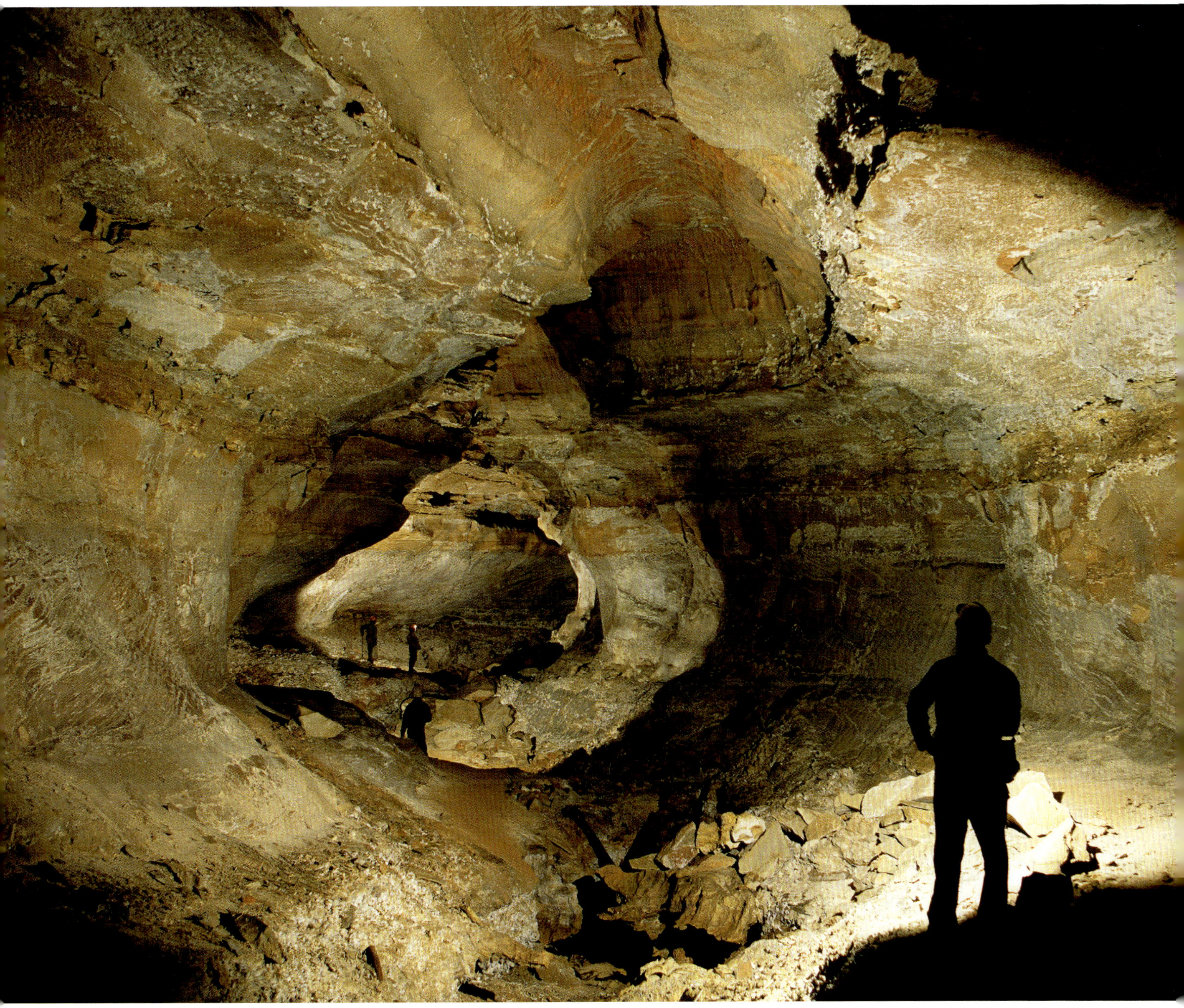

GREAT SMOKY MOUNTAINS NATIONAL PARK

Date of inscription: 1983

Thanks to the establishment of this breathtakingly beautiful national park, a primeval forest landscape with an incomparably varied biotope has been preserved in the southern Appalachians of North Carolina and Tennessee.

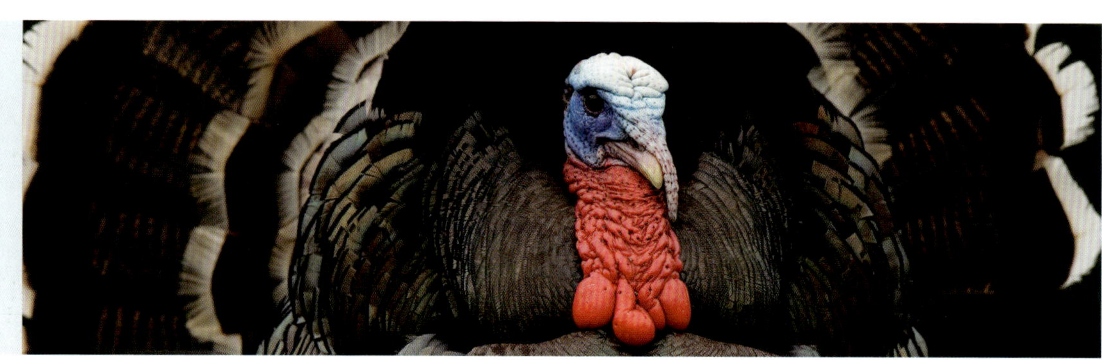

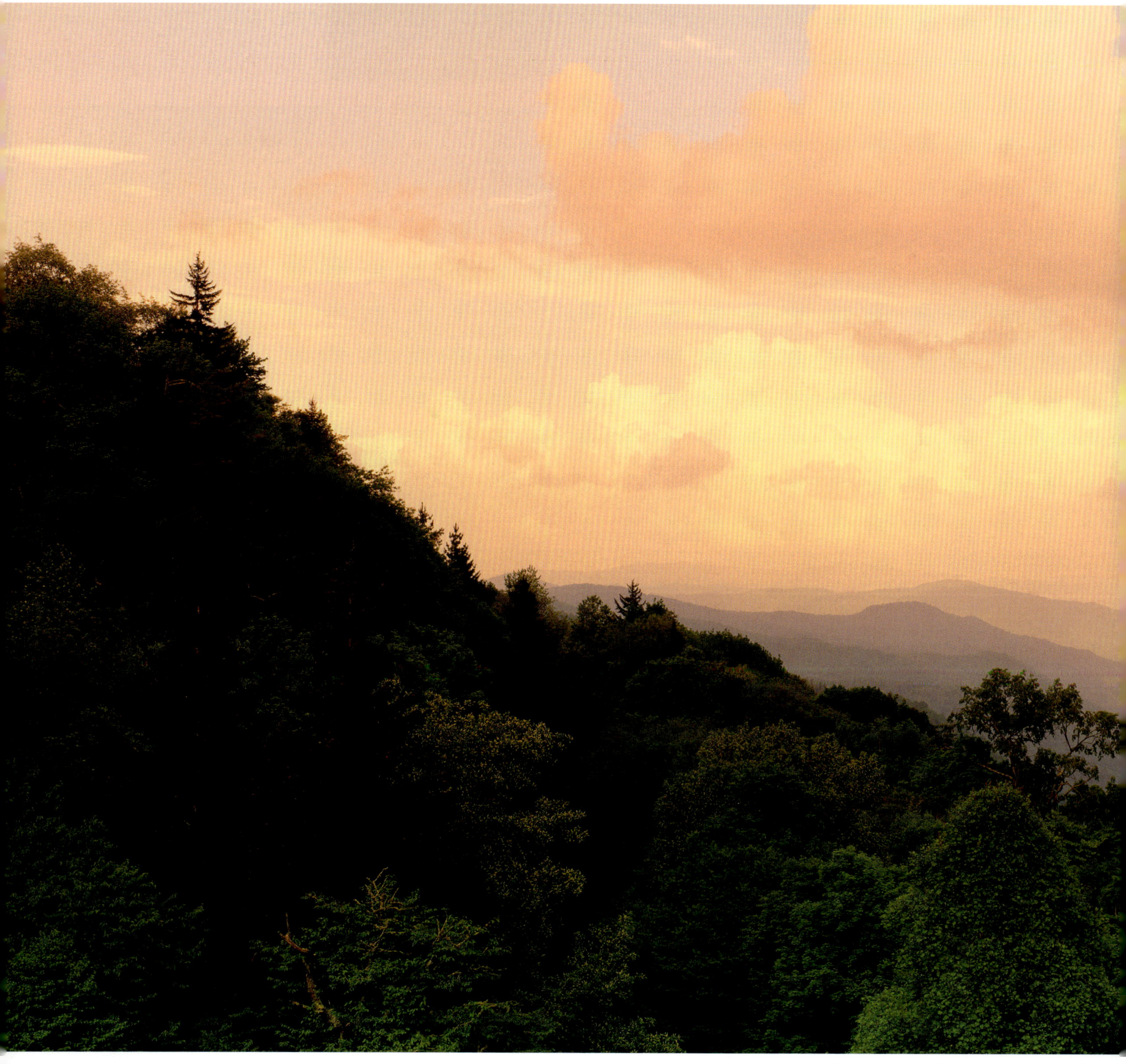

This national park is best known for the mist that frequently shrouds the mountains; it looks like smoke, hence the name. The high humidity is a result of luxuriant vegetation and high precipitation. The area, which was inscribed as a national park as early as 1934, has 16 peaks of a height greater than 1,800 m (5,950 feet) and mountain streams and rivers with a total length of 3,000 km (1,850 miles), as well as numerous waterfalls. Some 130 species of deciduous and coniferous trees are to be found in the primary forest that makes up a third of the total area, along with a wealth of shrubs, lichens, mosses, and fungi. The animal life is similarly diverse: black bears, white-tailed deer, and many species of birds and reptiles all live here.

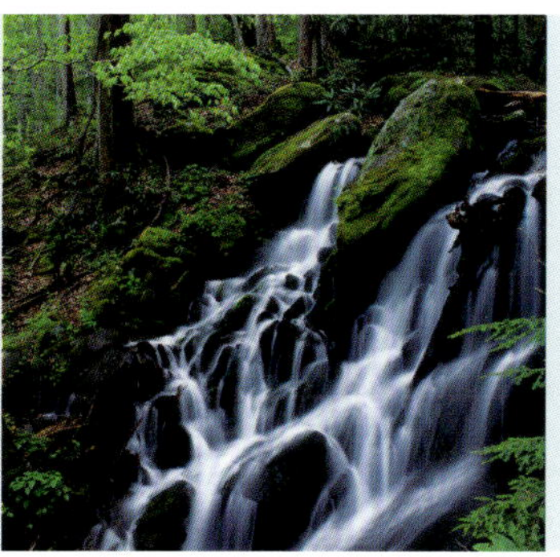

The Great Smoky Mountains are among the world's oldest mountain ranges. The eponymous national park contains some of the most beautiful deciduous forests to be found in America (large image), numerous waterfalls (left), and among the diverse fauna, wild turkey also can be found (far left).

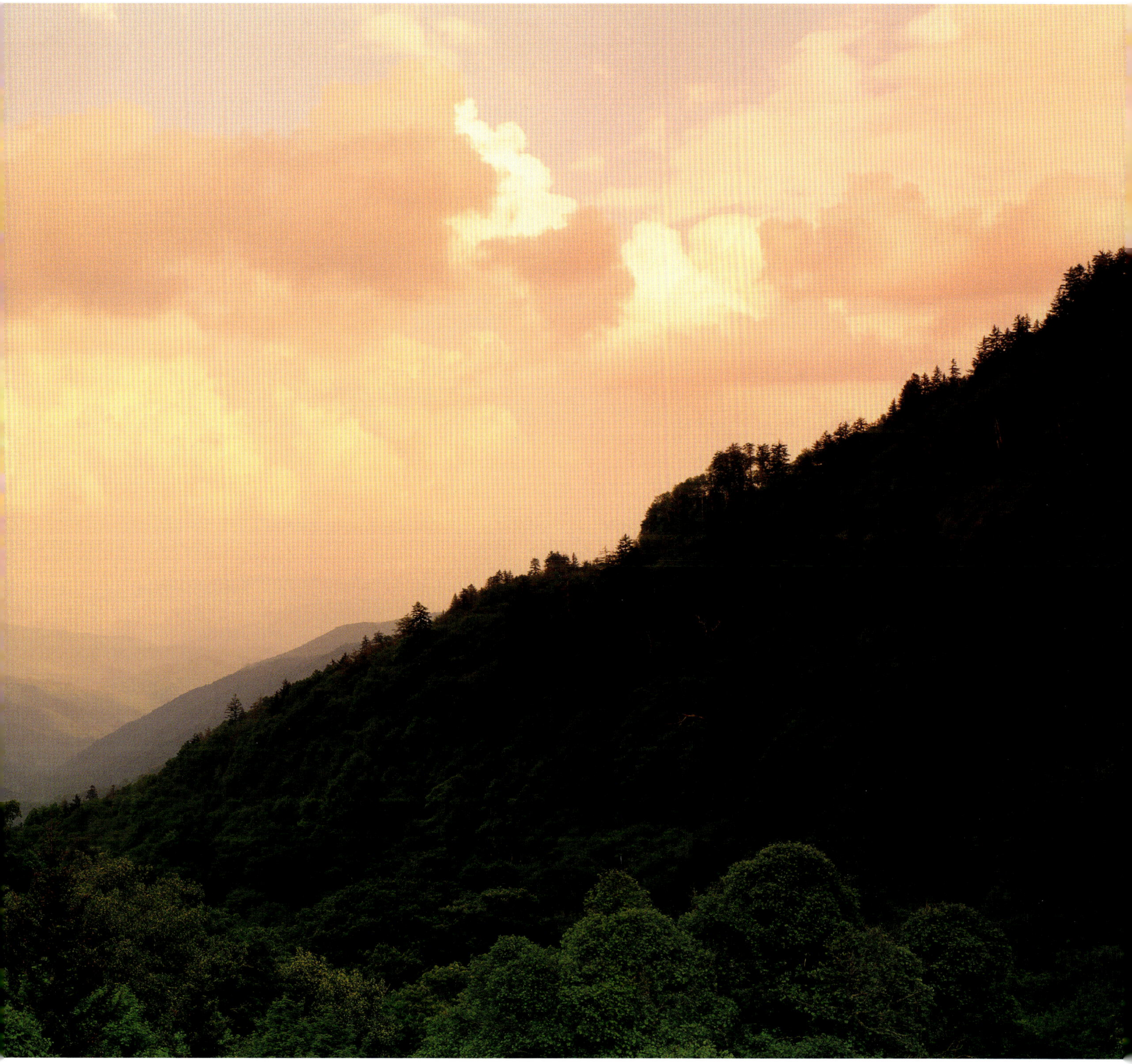

EVERGLADES NATIONAL PARK

Date of inscription: 1979

Here in the south of Florida, mangrove forests and marshland, overgrown with seagrasses, form a unique ecosystem, providing a habitat for a fascinating variety of life.

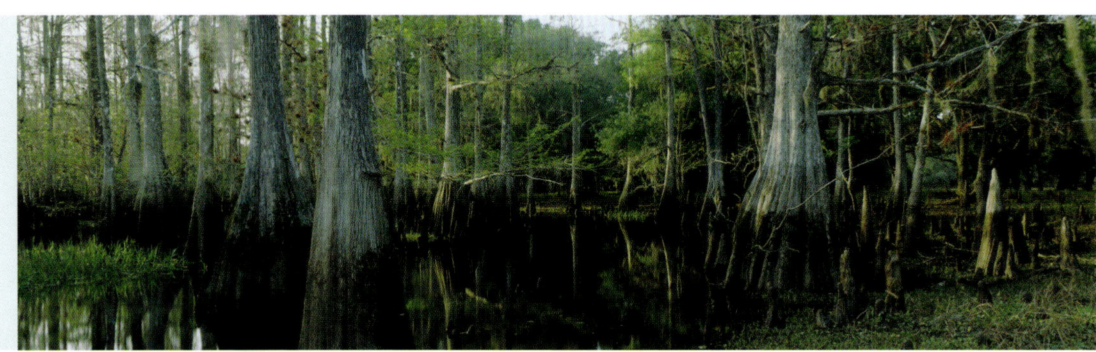

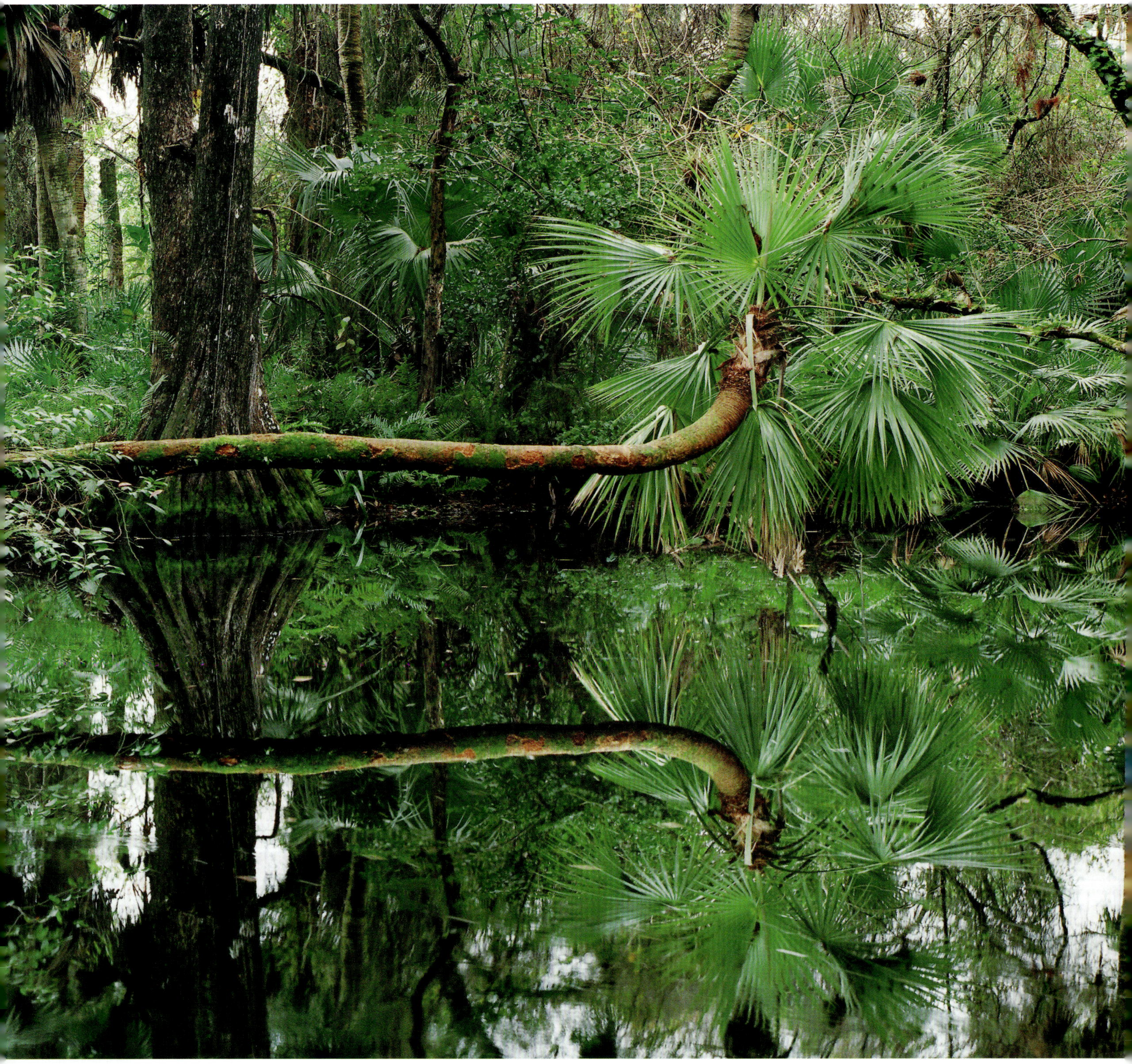

Low elevation and a lack of natural drainage in this region led to the trapping of its high precipitation, and thus to the formation of areas of marshland. The Everglades' complex ecosystem is nonetheless coming under ever greater threat through increasing agriculturalization, rapacious overfishing, and the considerable drinking water requirements of neighboring cities. Despite intensive efforts, this unique habitat for animals and plants is becoming increasingly endangered. In just the last fifty years, 90 percent of the bird and 80 percent of the fish species in the Everglades have been wiped out. The endless savannah of reeds is interrupted by so-called "hammocks," stands of cypresses, pines, and mahogany on little islands. Towards the coast, mangrove forests provide an ideal habitat for microorganisms, amphibians, snails, and fish; the abundance of these is particularly appreciated by the many species of heron, which include the great blue heron and the green-backed heron. In total, the Everglades are home to around 1,000 plant species and 700 animal species.

The Loxahatchee River crosses the Everglades (large picture); many excursion boats use it as a route for explorations. In between dead trees and dense mangroves live river otters, alligators and herons (from the top). Left: Fisheating Creek.

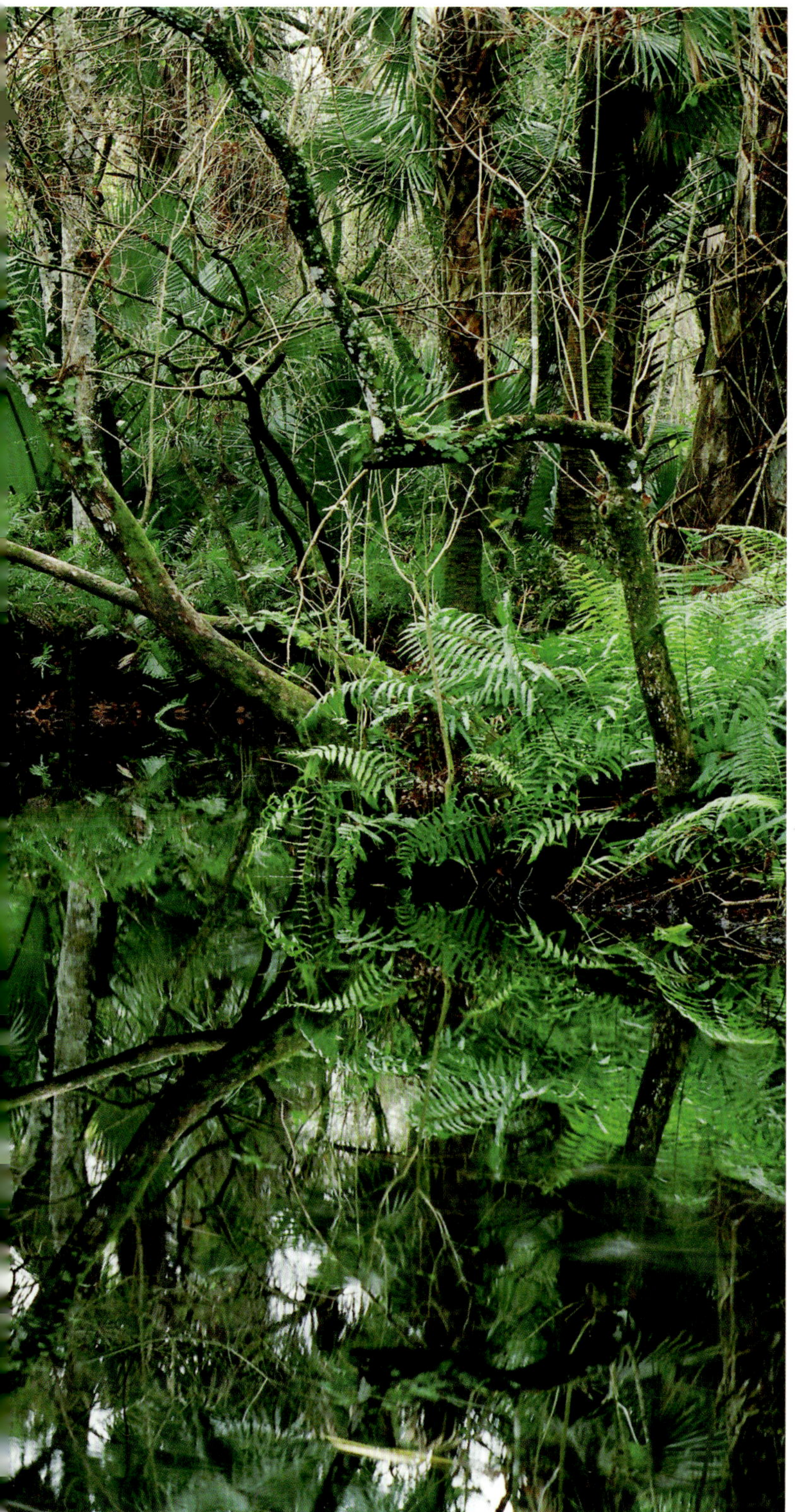

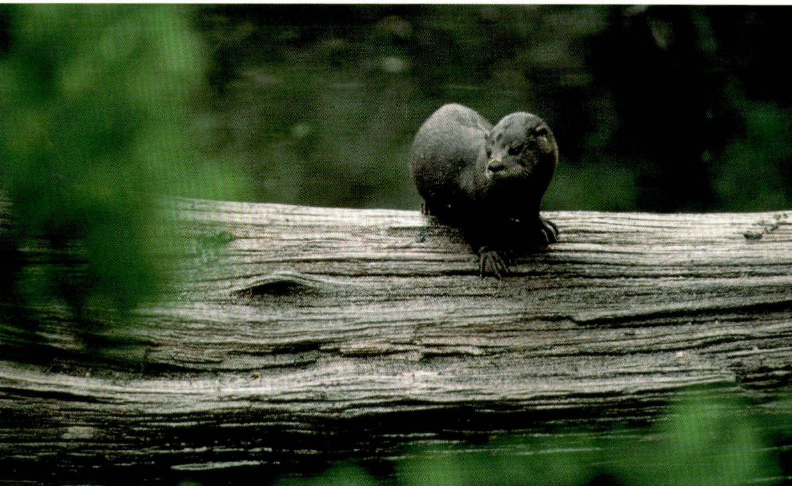

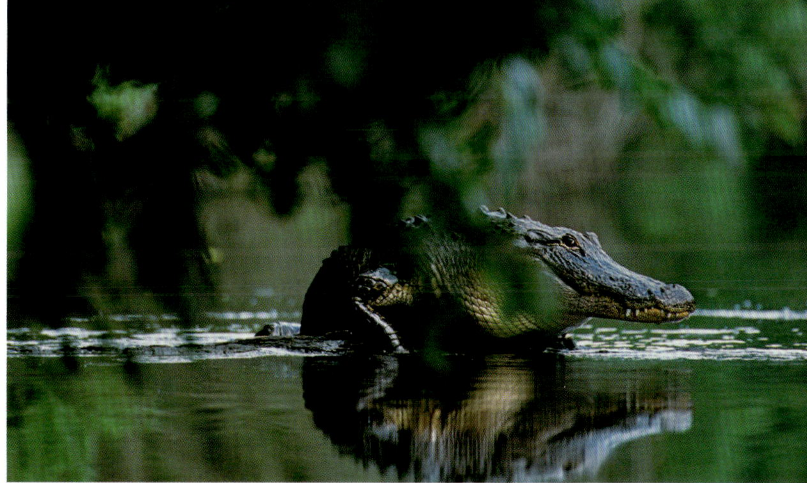

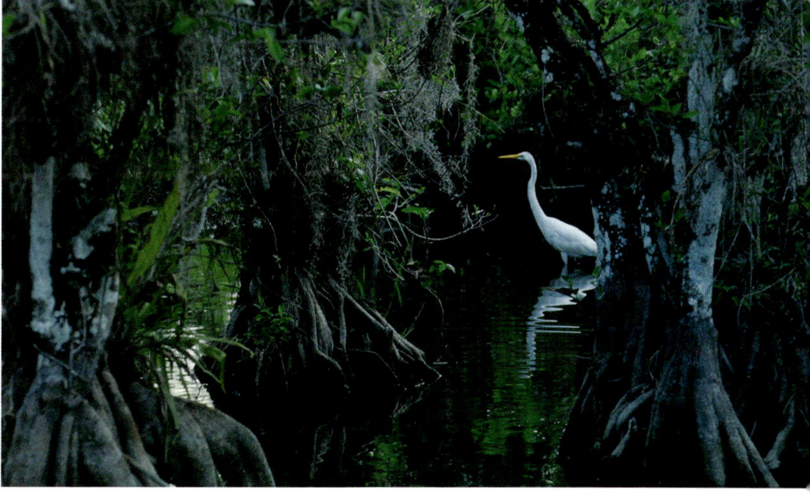

HAWAII VOLCANOES NATIONAL PARK

Date of inscription: 1987

Nowhere else on earth can volcanism be better observed than on Hawaii's "Big Island." Two of the most active volcanoes on earth are part of the Hawaii Volcanoes National Park, and to this day lava is still forcing its way out of the depths of the earth to the surface.

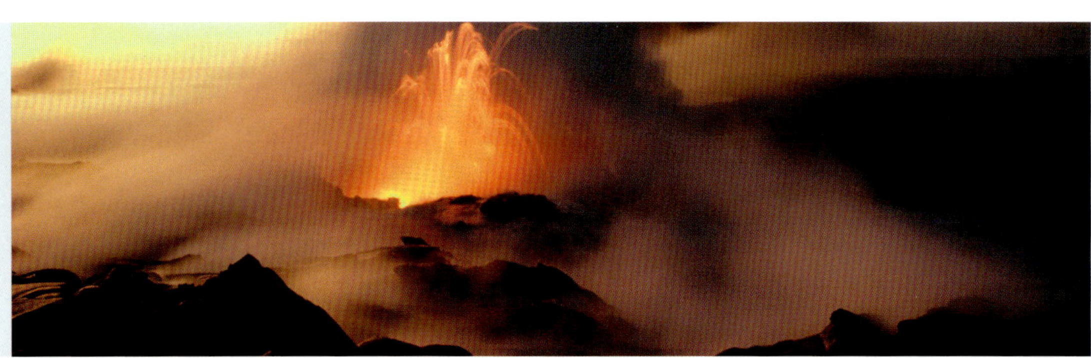

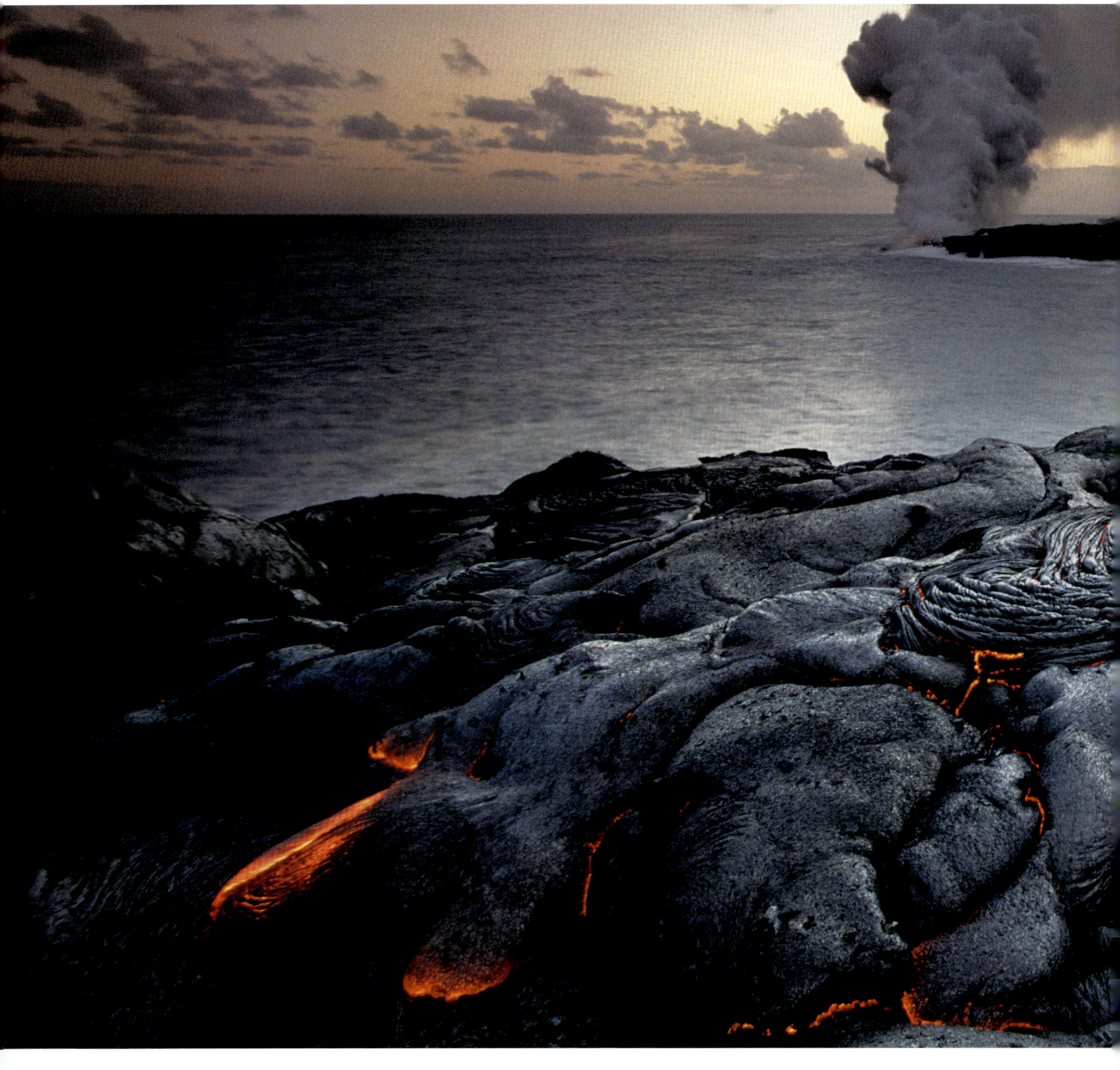

The landscape of the main island's south-eastern coast is forever being recreated by the eruptions of the volcanoes of Mauna Loa (4,170 m, 13,680 feet) and Kilauea (1,250 m, 4,100 feet). At relatively short intervals, these two active volcanoes eject quantities of red-hot lava, which flows down to the sea where it cools in clouds of steam, increasing the area of the island by 81 hectares (200 acres) in just the last thirty years. Local religion explained the eruptions as manifestations of the moods of the fire goddess, Pele. For geologists, the eruptions are not just an impressive natural spectacle, but also the object of intensive study. Over the years, Mauna Loa has been created from layer upon layer of cooled lava. The slopes of the more active Kilauea afford an insight into the various forms taken by volcanic vegetation.

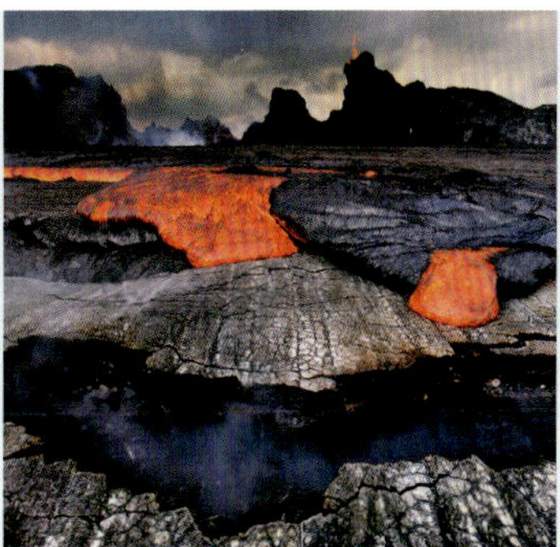

Kilauea, spitting molten lava into the ocean (far left left). According to local lore, when the lava flows, Pele, the Hawaiian fire goddess, is angry. As the viscous lava flows cooled, bizarre rock formations were created.

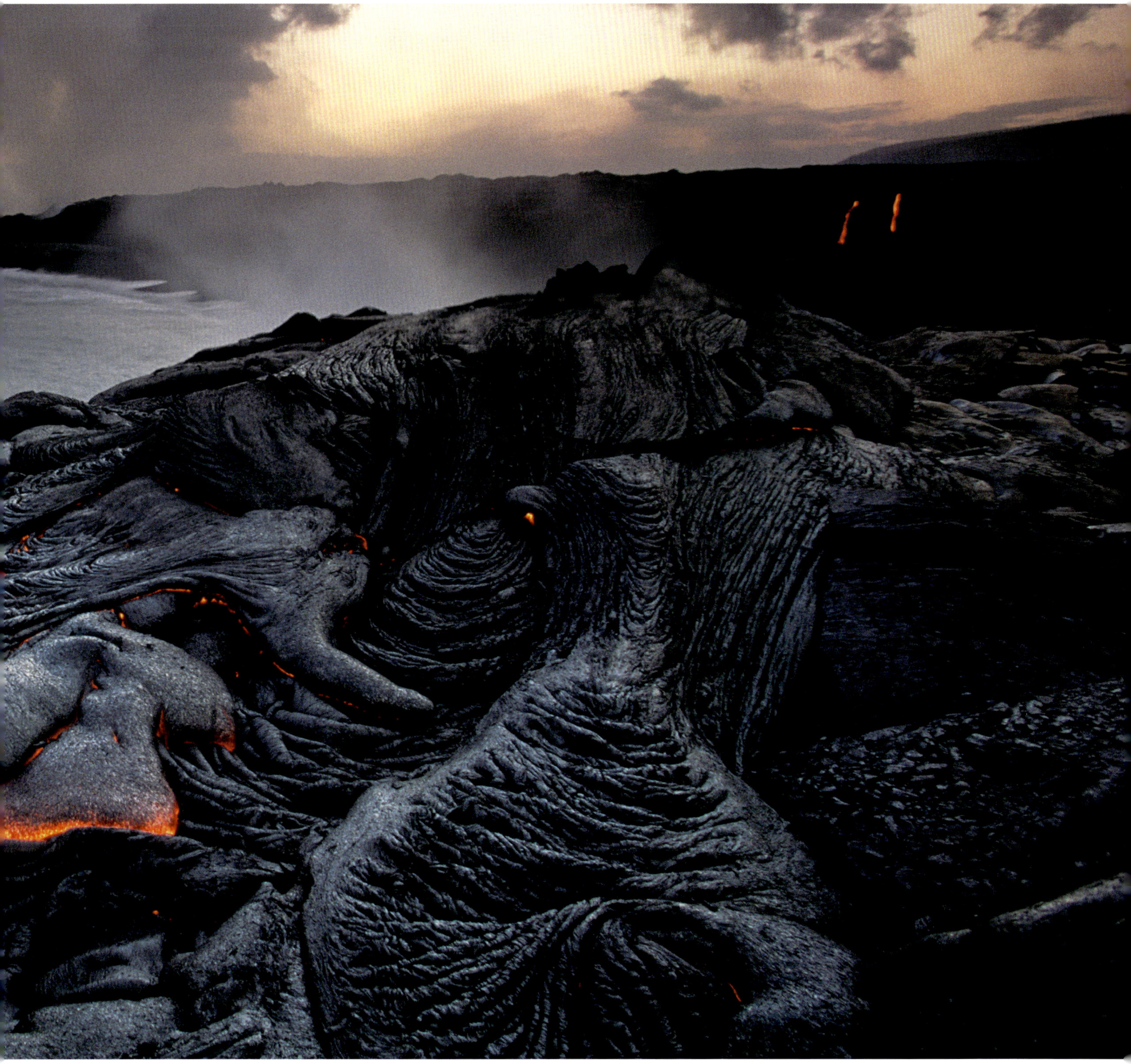

PAPAHĀNAUMOKUĀKEA MARINE NATIONAL MONUMENT

Date of inscription: 2010

The marine reserve is of outstanding importance for the ecology as well as for the spirituality of the native people of Hawaii. The area thus belongs to both the natural and the cultural heritage lists.

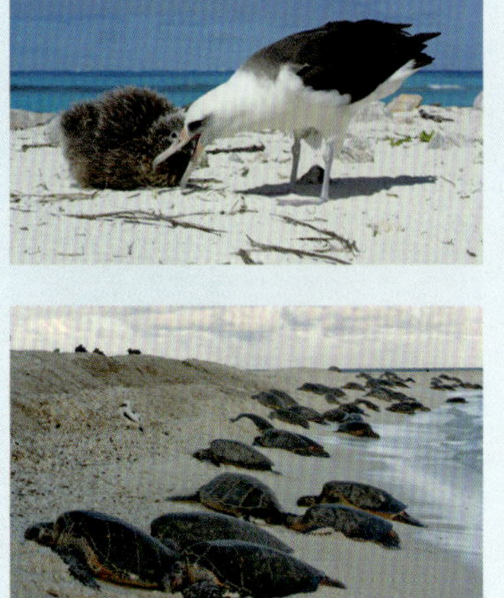

The Papahānaumokuākea reserve, located north-west of Hawaii, extends over almost 362,000 sq. km (139,770 sq. miles) – an area slightly larger than that of Germany. The protection zone includes, aside from the open sea, a number of islands, which rise only slightly above the water's surface, as well as atolls and their lagoons, and coral reefs. Some 7,000 animal and plant species live in Papahānaumokuākea, and of these some are endemic and many are endangered. Some islands have a special significance for the culture of the Polynesian population. Thus, Papahānaumokuākea is, according to the traditional religious beliefs of the local population, the cradle of life and the place to which the spirits return after death. In addition, traces of historical human settlement were discovered on the islands of Nihoa and Makumanamana, dating from the time before the arrival of the first Europe.

Left top: A Laysan albatross feeds its young; left bottom: green sea turtles always come back to their birthplace to lay their eggs.

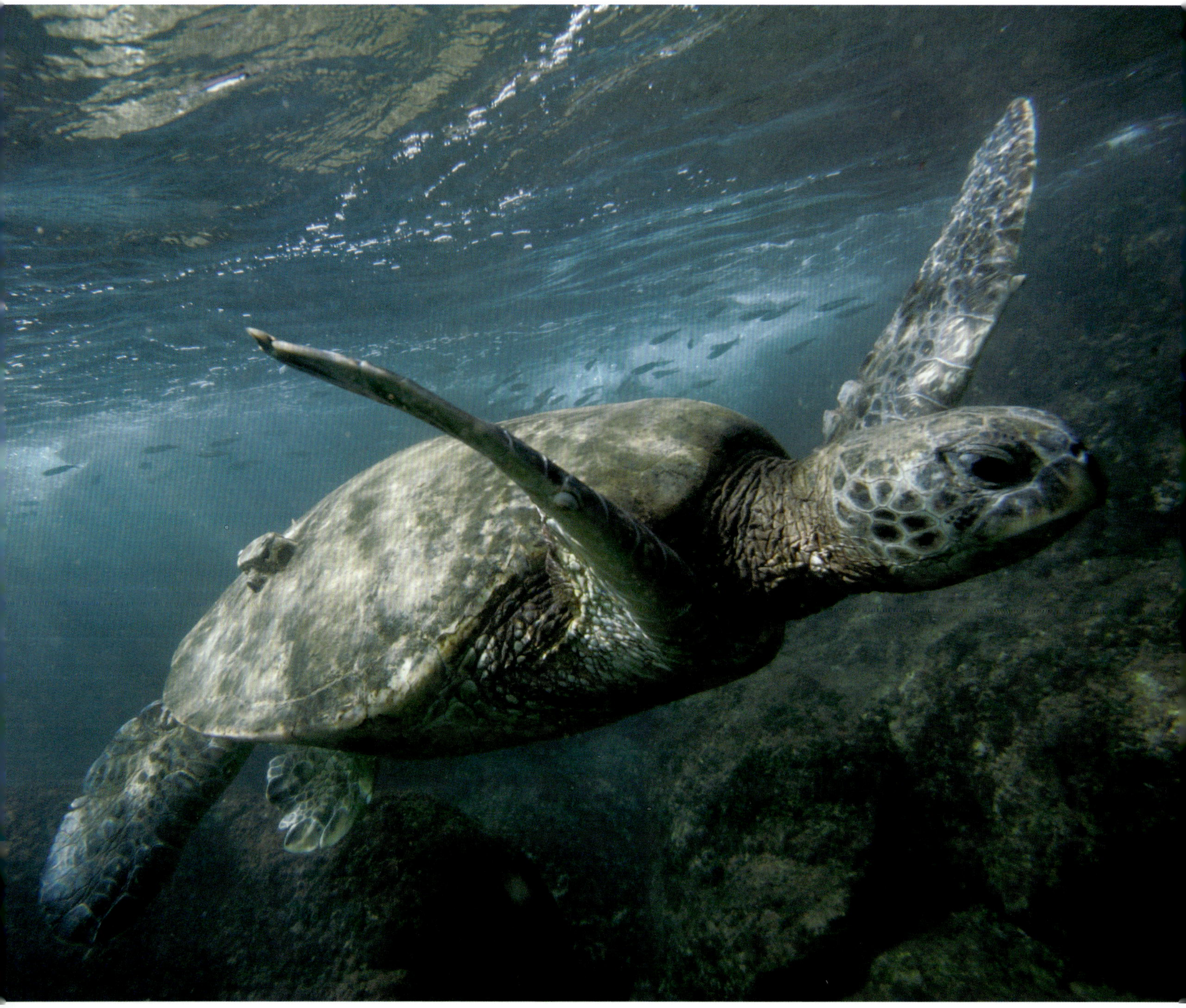

EL VIZCAÍNO WHALE SANCTUARY

The lagoons of Ojo de Liebre and San Ignacio form, with others, a singular marine habitat that begins about halfway down the Baja peninsula in California and stretches right along the Pacific coast. Between December and March, these waters teem with gray whales. They come here to mate and raise their young, after having crossed 8,000 km (5,000 miles) of water from their summer home in the Arctic Bering Sea. Almost half of the world's population of gray whales are born in the waters of Baja California. What's more, five of the world's seven species of sea turtle are found here, among them the endangered green turtle. They come to the long beaches to deposit their eggs. For almost 200 bird species – among them many endemic ones – the coastal areas are an important place for survival. They are also an important wintering place for thousands of migrant species, such as the Pacific Brent goose.

El Vizcaíno's littoral is host not only to gray whales (large image) but also to blue and humpback whales (right). Sickle dunes (right, top) cover the beach.

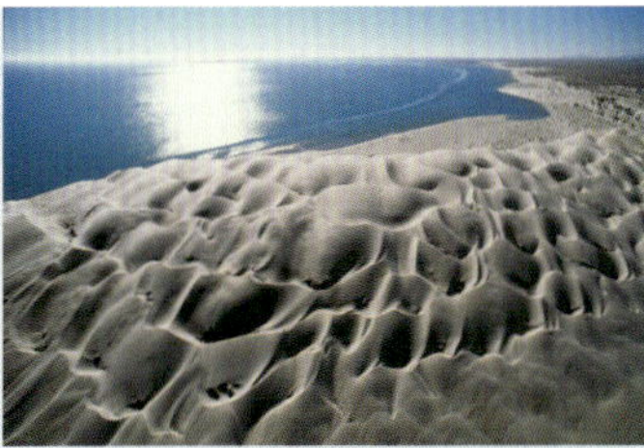

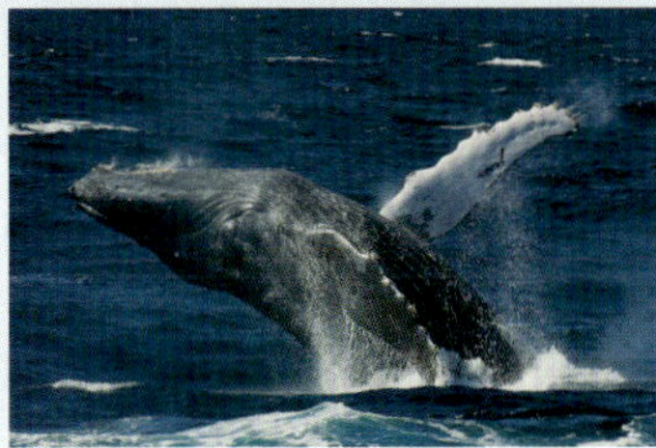

Date of inscription: 1993

Every year, the coastal lagoons of the sanctuary play host to the mating whales and the birth of their calves. Blue whales, humpbacks, seals, sea lions, and elephant seals are also to be found here. Several species of sea turtle lay their eggs on the beaches, and some 200 bird varieties, including many which are endemic, nest or winter here.

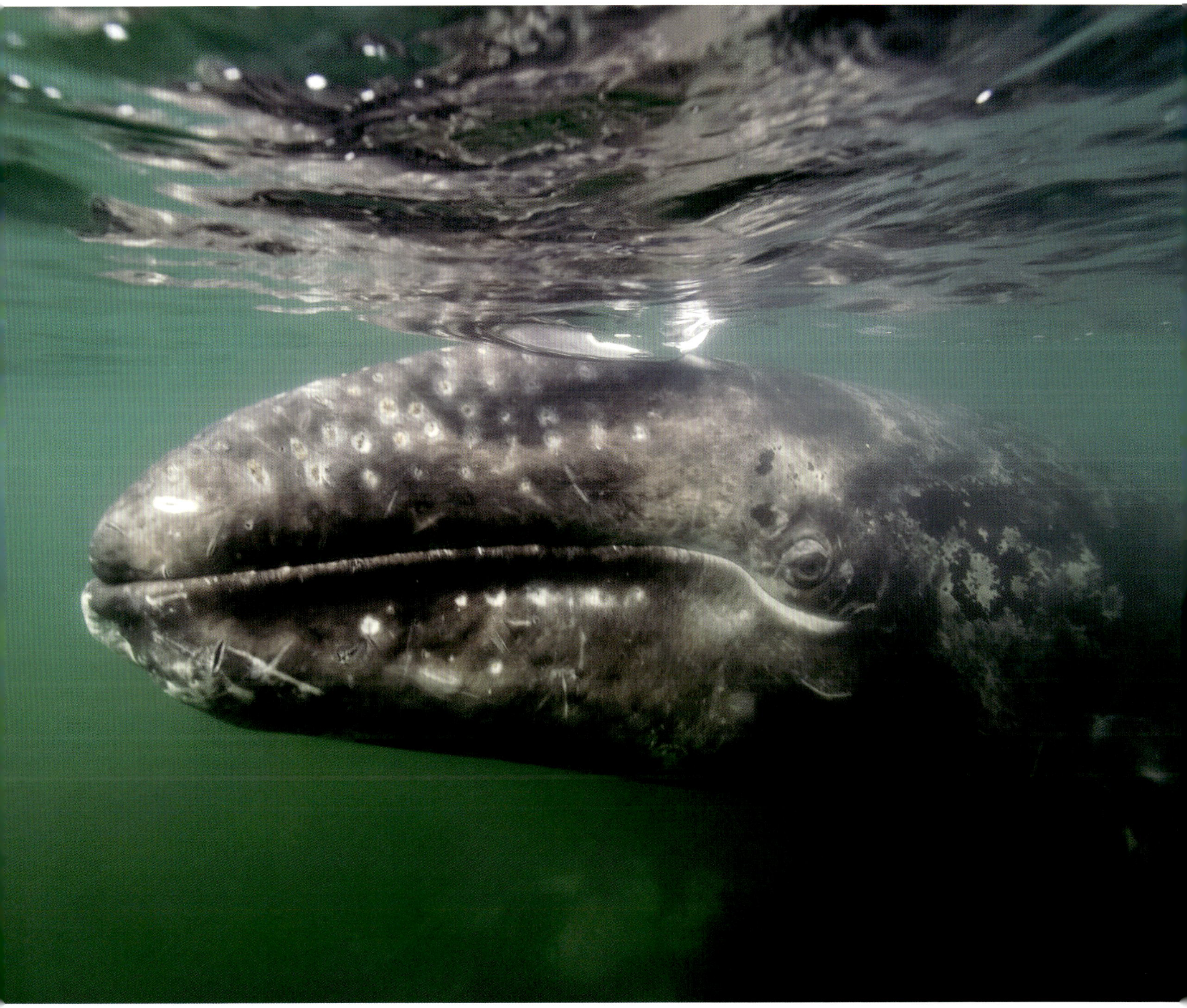

THE ISLANDS AND CONSERVATION AREAS OF THE GULF OF CALIFORNIA

Date of inscription: 2005

The World Heritage Site includes no less than 244 islands, outcrops of rock, and sections of coast, and is a habitat for an incredible variety of flora and fauna.

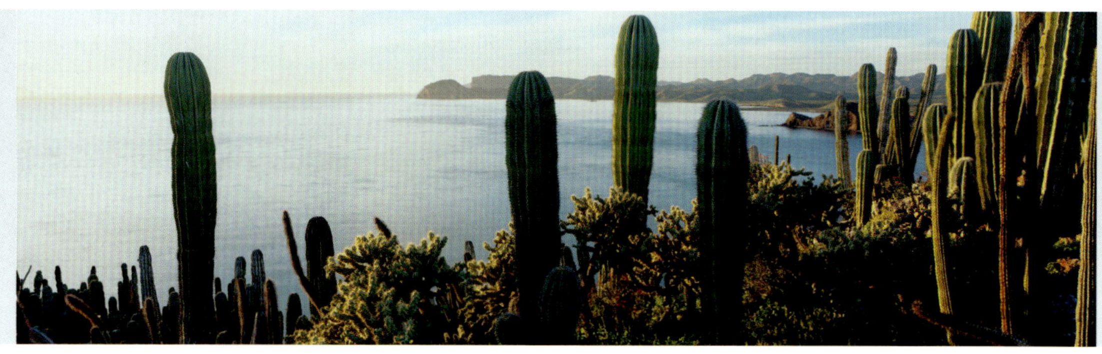

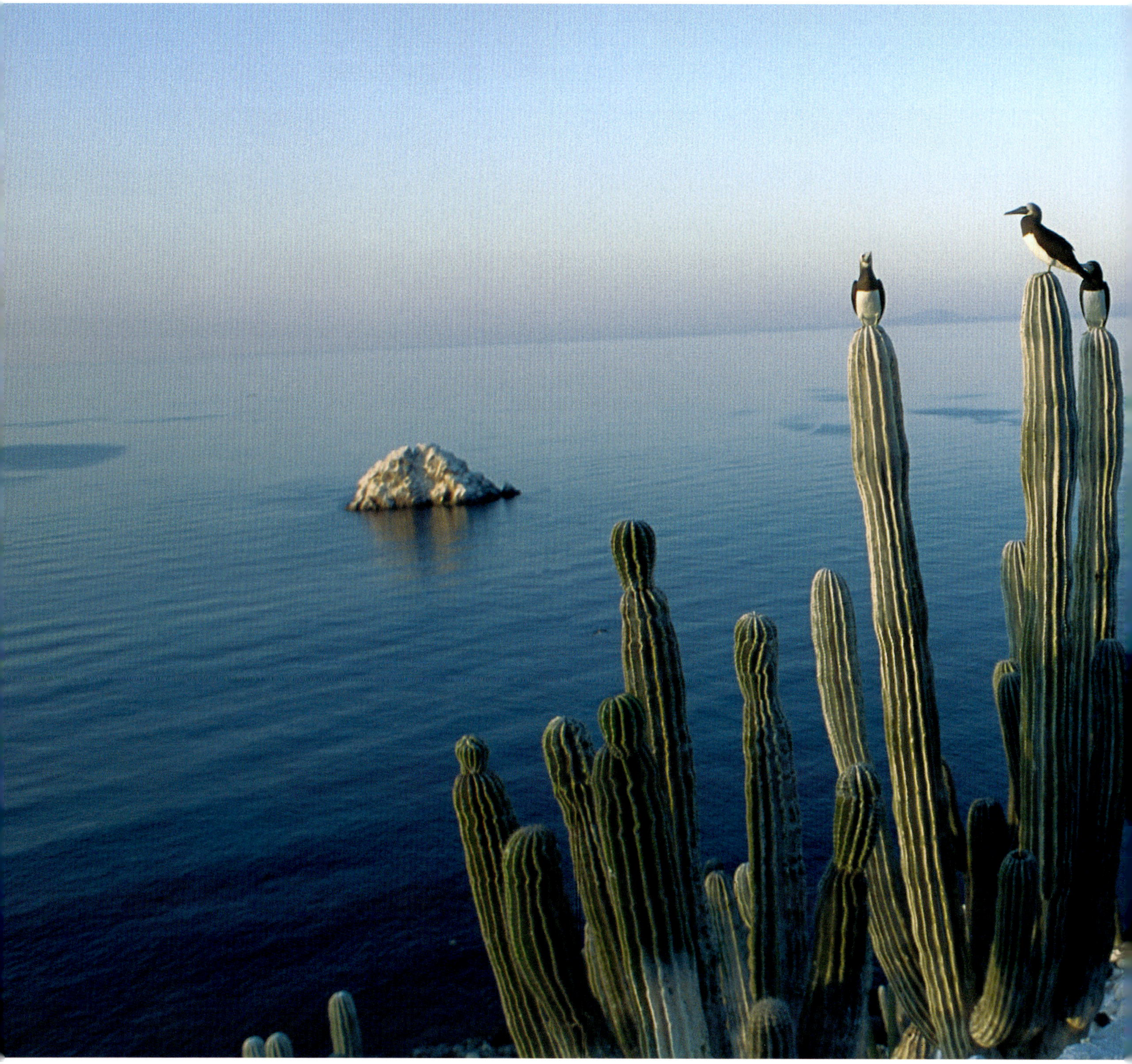

The Gulf of California is 1,100 km long and 90–230 km wide, adjoining the Pacific Ocean and situated between the Mexican west coast and the Baja California peninsula. Nine regions have been placed under protection here, with a total surface area of approximately 18,000 sq. km, of which about three-quarters is marine. From north to south, these regions are: Upper Gulf of California and Colorado River Delta Biosphere Reserve; Islands and Protected Areas of the Gulf of California; the Island of San Pedro Mártir; El Vizcaíno; Bahía de Loreto; Cabo Pulmo; Cabo San Lucas; the Marías Islands and Isabel Island. In the Gulf of California and its islands 200 bird species and 30 species of mammal are found. Of the 891 species of fish in the marine conservation area, 90 are endemic. The vegetation consists of many succulents and cactuses, including some of the world's largest; the Cardon cactus, Pachycereus pringli, for example, can reach a height of 25 m.

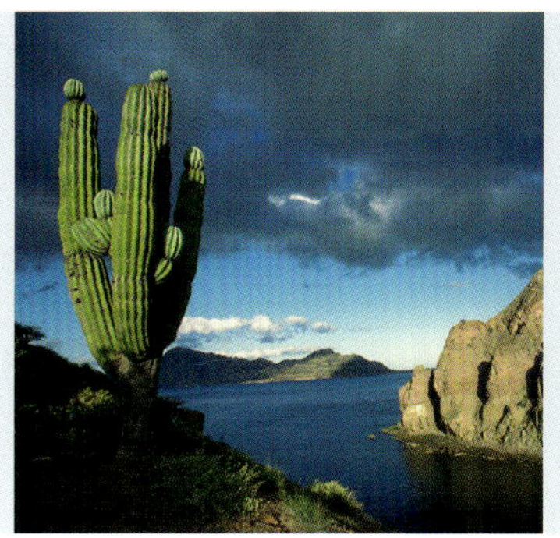

Blue-footed boobies sit unimpressed on top of prickly cacti (large picture), which can grow to gigantic sizes here.

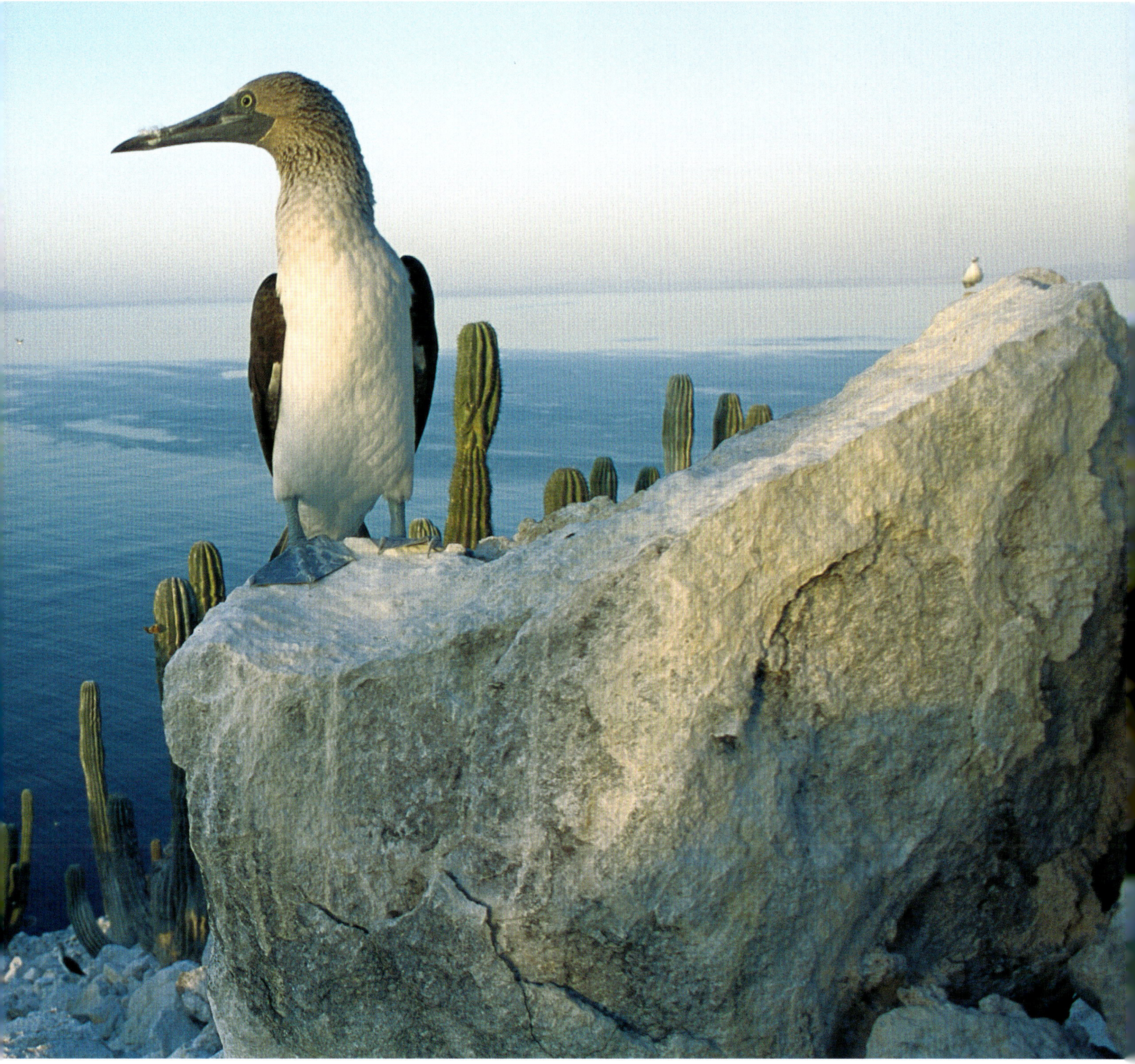

EL PINACATE AND GRAN DESIERTO DE ALTAR BIOSPHERE RESERVE

Date of inscription: 2013

The biosphere reserve comprises numerous different ecosystems of the desert, for example, black lava fields with craters, tall shifting sand dunes and granite hills. Its geological diversity is also reflected in the diversity of its species.

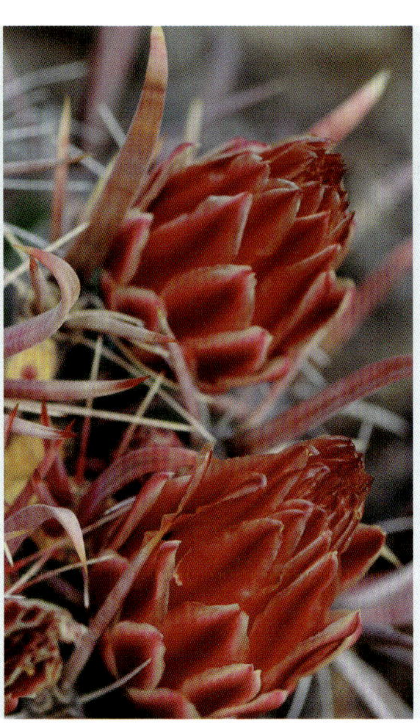

In North America there are four major deserts: the Chihuahuan Desert, the Great Basin, the Mojave Desert and the Sonoran Desert. The latter is especially famous for its large saguaro cacti. The El Pinacate y Gran Desierto de Altar Biosphere Reserve makes up a part of it. It is composed of two different types of landscapes. Pinacate is a currently inactive volcanic area with black and red lava fields. Here you can encounter very diverse geological phenomena, such as a small shield volcano. Most striking and part of El Pinacate's dramatic beauty are ten huge crater lakes caused by an explosion of steam at the contact of groundwater with red-hot magma. In the west, towards the Colorado River and the Gulf of California, there are the ever changing and varied sand dunes of the Altar Desert that can reach up to 200 m (656 ft). Several granite massifs, up to 650 m (2,133 ft) high, rise in between. At this World Natural Heritage site, 540 flowering plants, 200 species of birds and even two endemic species of freshwater fish have been recorded. Its flora and fauna, and volcanic quality make the reserve interesting for scientists.

Dotted across the plain like telegraph poles, the saguaro cacti rise from the ground (large image). The fishhook barrel cactus has beautiful flowers (left).

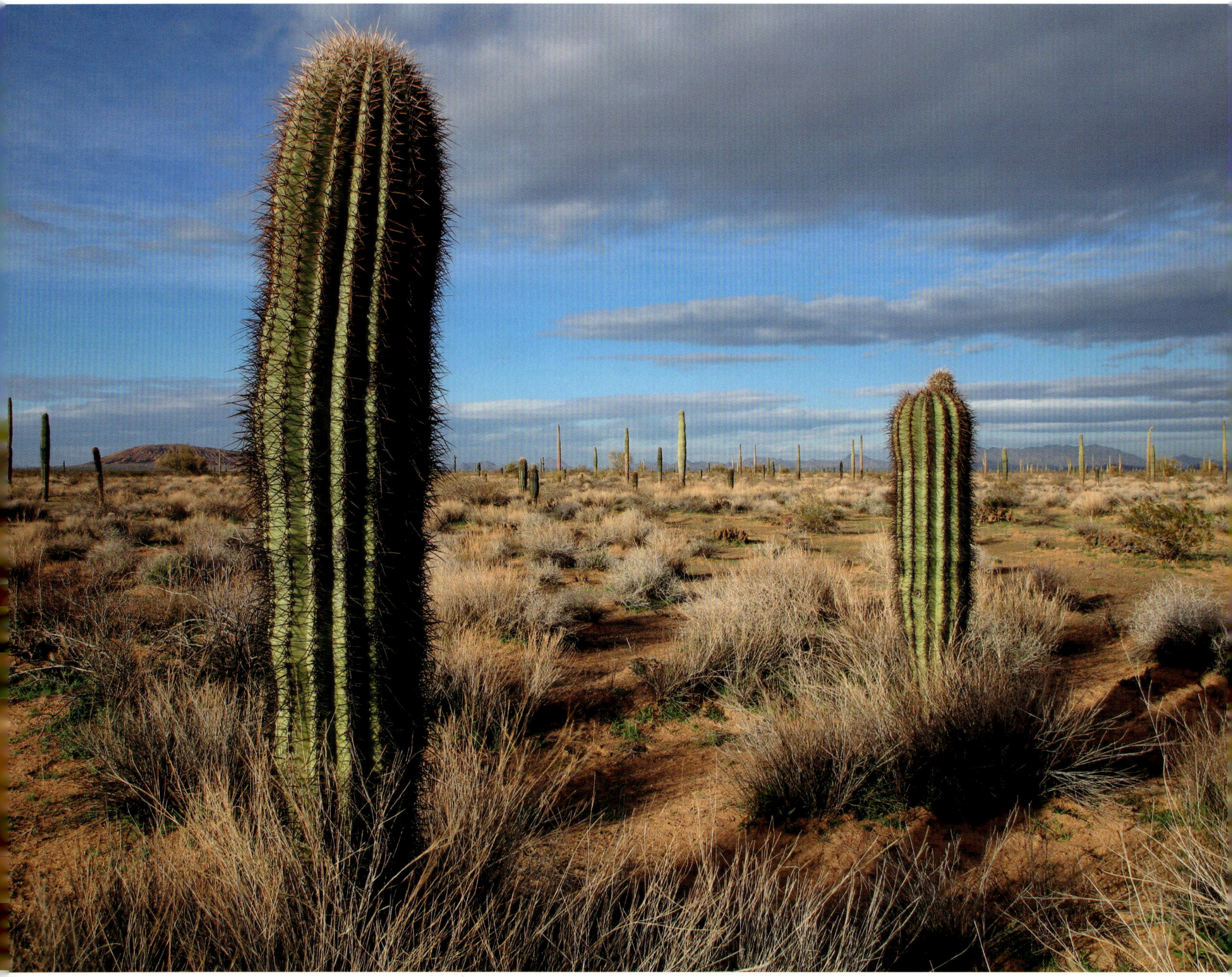

ANCIENT MAYA CITY CALAKMUL, TROPICAL FORESTS OF CAMPECHE

In around AD 300, the Maya began to build stone monuments on which they recorded in hieroglyphs the significant events or achievements of their kings, dating them precisely. These stelae are an important study source for the history of this great Mesoamerican civilization, and in addition they are artworks of a peculiar charm. Approximately 120 stelae have so far been discovered in Calakmul, on the southern Yucatán peninsula, near the Mexican border with Guatemala and Belize. In addition, some pyramidal temples, such as the more than 50-m- (164-ft-) high step pyramid, as well as tombs can also be seen here. A total of more than 5,000 stone buildings along with streets have been discovered, testifying to a highly developed cultural settlement. Calakmul had been forgotten for about a thousand years. Today the former metropolis is of great importance for the study of pre-Columbian cultures in Mexico. The rainforests of Campeche extend from central Mexico to the Panama Canal. They feature a great level of biodiversity, and many endemic animals are at home here.

The main attractions of Calakmul are a multiply overbuilt pyramid known as "Structure II" (below) and the relief stelae. Some trees here are entwined by a vigorous root system (right).

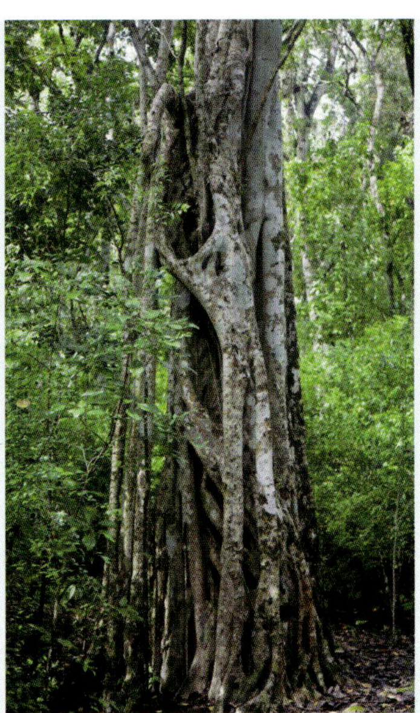

Date of inscription: 2002
Extension: 2014

The Mayan city of Calakmul, located in midst of the tropical rainforest of Yucatán, looks back on a long settlement history. Characteristic of this archaeological site are its large numbers of relief steles. The protected area has been extended to include the rainforest, and the site is now both a cultural and a natural heritage site.

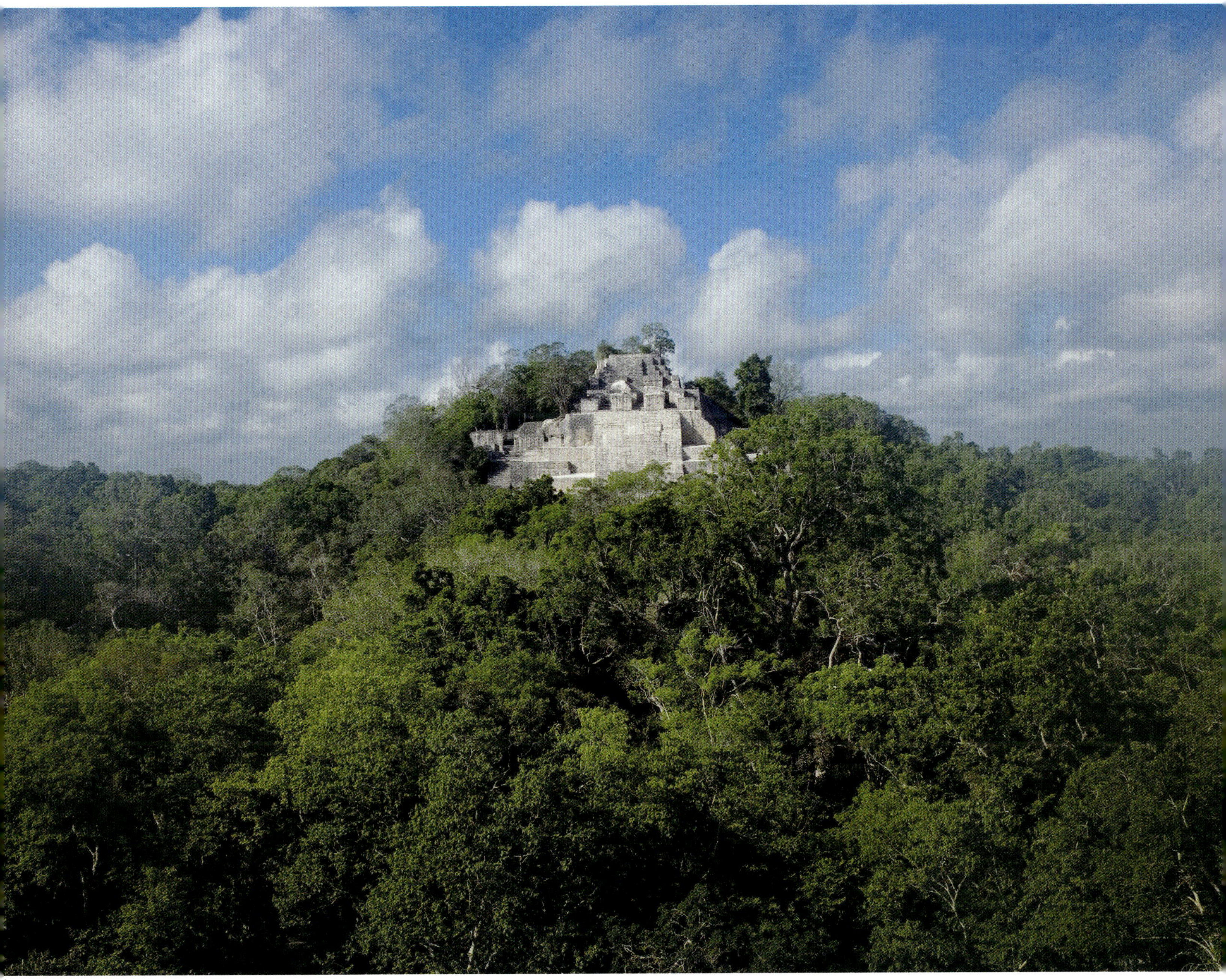

THE MARIPOSA MONARCA BIOSPHERE RESERVE

Date of inscription: 2008

The Mariposa Monarca Biosphere Reserve is located about 100 km (62 miles) north-west of Mexico City. Every year it becomes the home of millions of monarch butterflies which seek out the moderate climate of the Mexican uplands for their winter quarters.

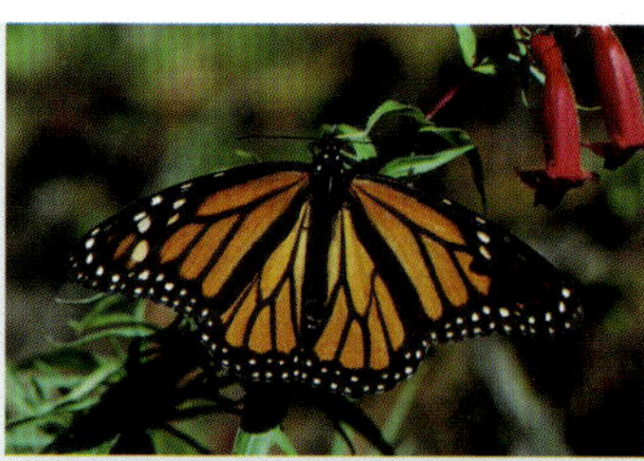

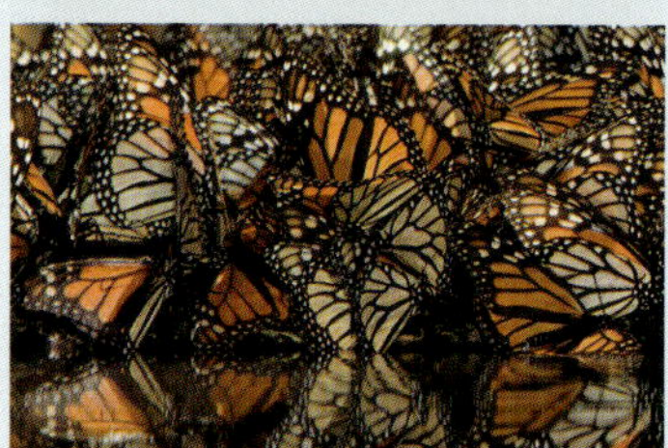

The biosphere reserve covers 56,259 ha (139,000 acres) of montane forest at an elevation of about 3,000 m (9,900 feet) above sea level. It is named after the migratory monarch butterfly, which in the fall travels south for some 4,000 km (2,500 miles) from the USA and Canada to Mexico. Every year, the bare rocks of the Mexican plain are the scene of a fascinating natural spectacle as several hundred million monarch butterflies arrive on the reserve and turn the whole landscape orange. The butterfly's migration is an astounding phenomenon: hatching in North America, the creatures come to Mexico, passing the winter in a kind of suspended animation, and in the spring they return north. Only the fifth generation will return to Mexico. The biosphere reserve was established in the 1980s and houses several sanctuarios, or protected zones, intended to preserve the butterfly's habitat from increasing human settlement and unregulated logging.

The wings of the monarch butterfly (Danaus plexippus) have an orange coloration with black and white markings.

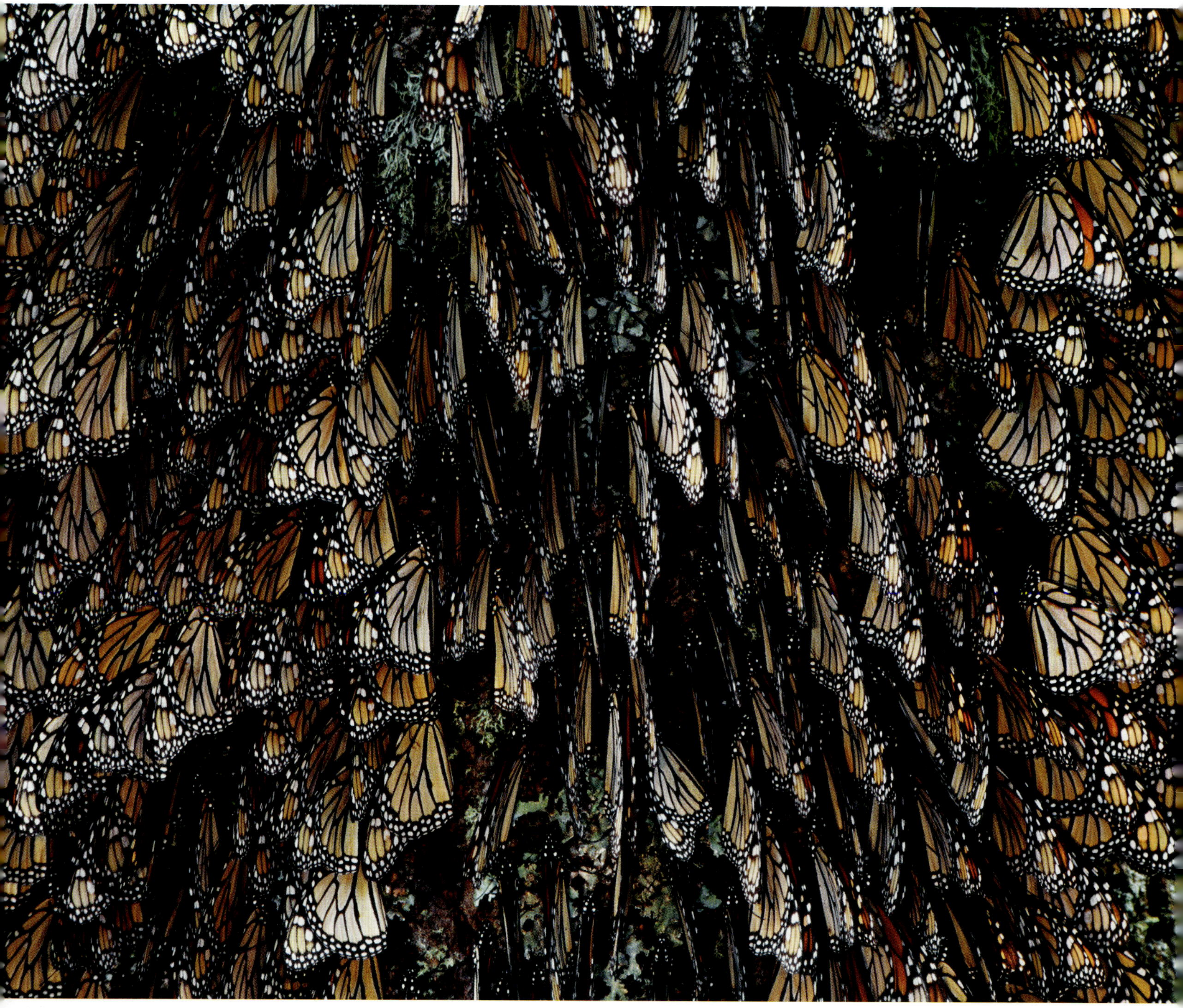

SIAN KA'AN BIOSPHERE RESERVE

Covering a total surface area of more than 5,000 sq. km (1,900 sq. miles) of the eastern Yucatán peninsula, Mexico's largest nature reserve – known in the Mayan language as Sian Ka'an, meaning "a gift from heaven"– offers sublime living conditions for a variety of unique flora and fauna. A big advantage is that only around 2,000 humans live here, mostly in the towns of Punta Allen and Boca Paila. Evergreen, deciduous, coniferous, and rain forests; mangrove swamps, savannah, and flood plains; and 100 km (62 miles) of coral reef and lagoons are a habitat for rare predators such as jaguars, different species of monkey, crocodiles and sea turtles. A quarter of the surface area of the park is taken up by ocean. Some 350 species of bird populate the lagoons, trees, and sky. Sian Ka'an also has a total of 23 archeological sites, with finds from cultures dating as far back as 2,300 years ago. Its diversity is extraordinary and fascinating.

The American white ibis (right) belongs to the family of ibises. Portly crocodiles glide silently through the water (large picture).

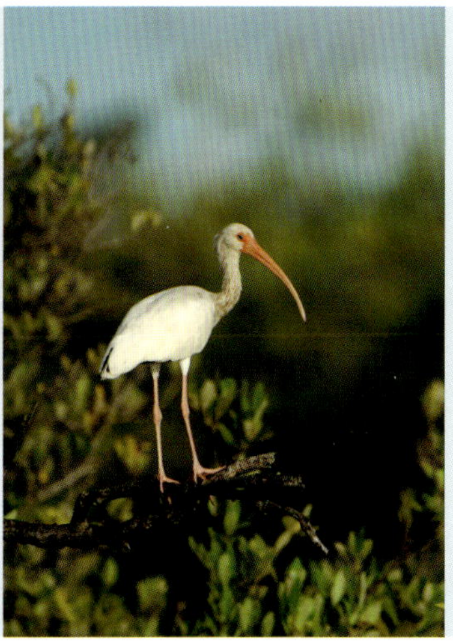

Date of inscription: 1987

This nature reserve on the Caribbean coast of Mexico has a diversity of biotopes, offering ideal living conditions for all kinds of life.

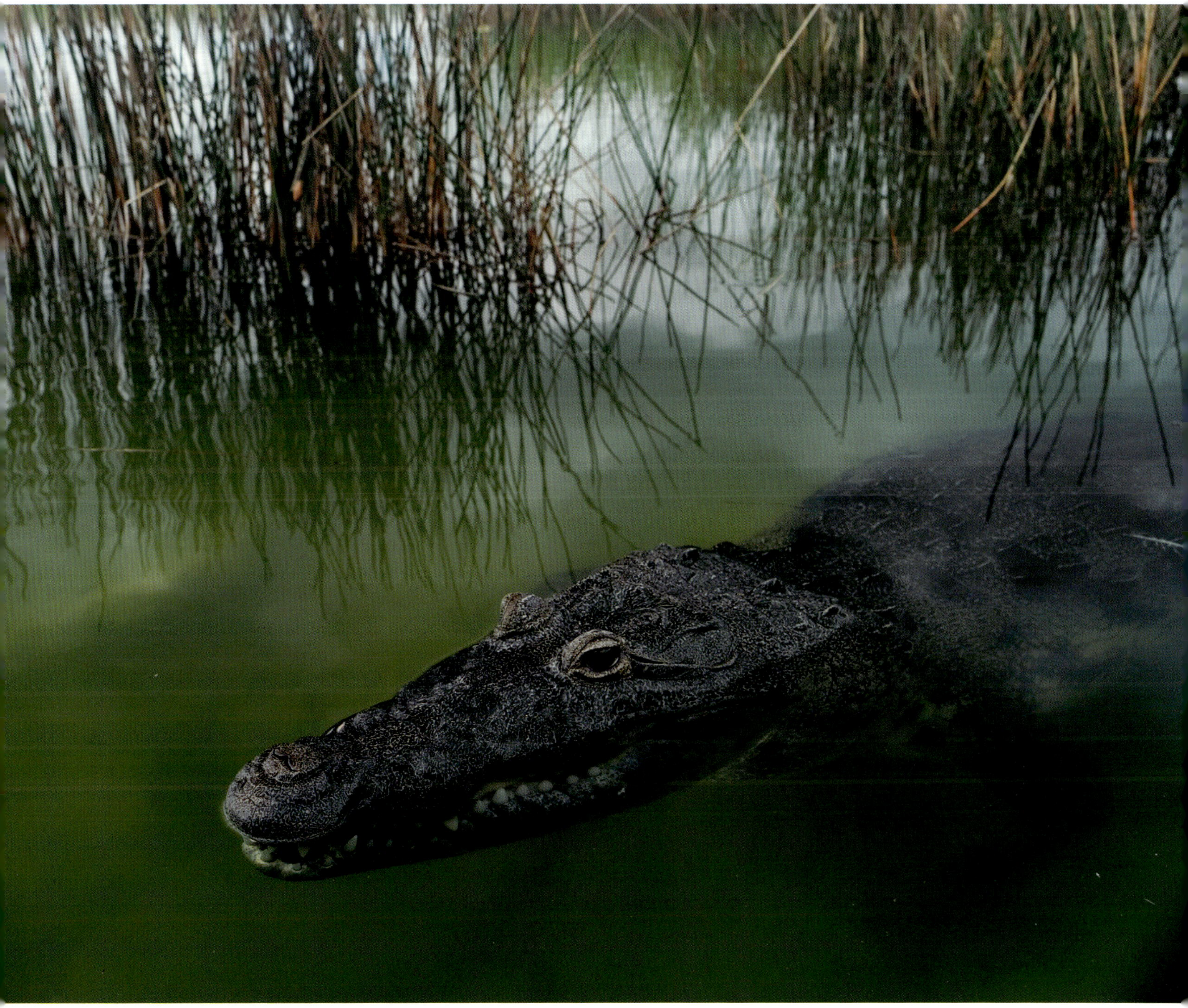

BELIZE BARRIER REEF

Date of inscription: 1996

The longest barrier reef in the northern hemisphere is situated along the edge of the continental shelf off the Belize coast. This unique and vivid underwater paradise is a refuge for many endangered species.

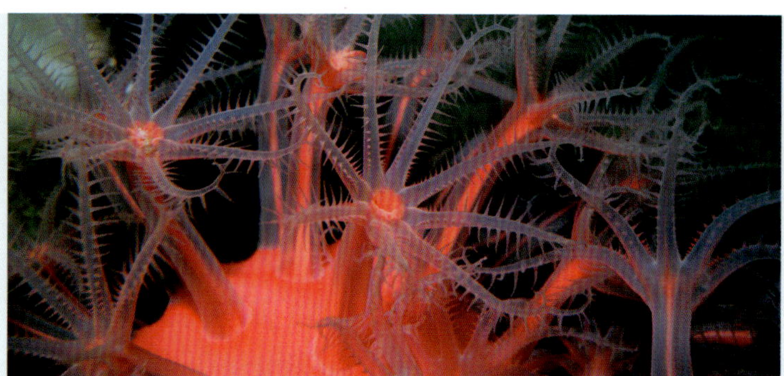

The Atlantic Ocean's largest series of coral reefs forms a highly complex ecosystem. It is composed of over 250 km (155 miles) of barrier reef, three large atolls further offshore, and hundreds of scattered islands known as "Cays," on which 170 plant species grow. Its mangroves, sandy beaches, and lagoons offer ideal living conditions for birds, including endangered species

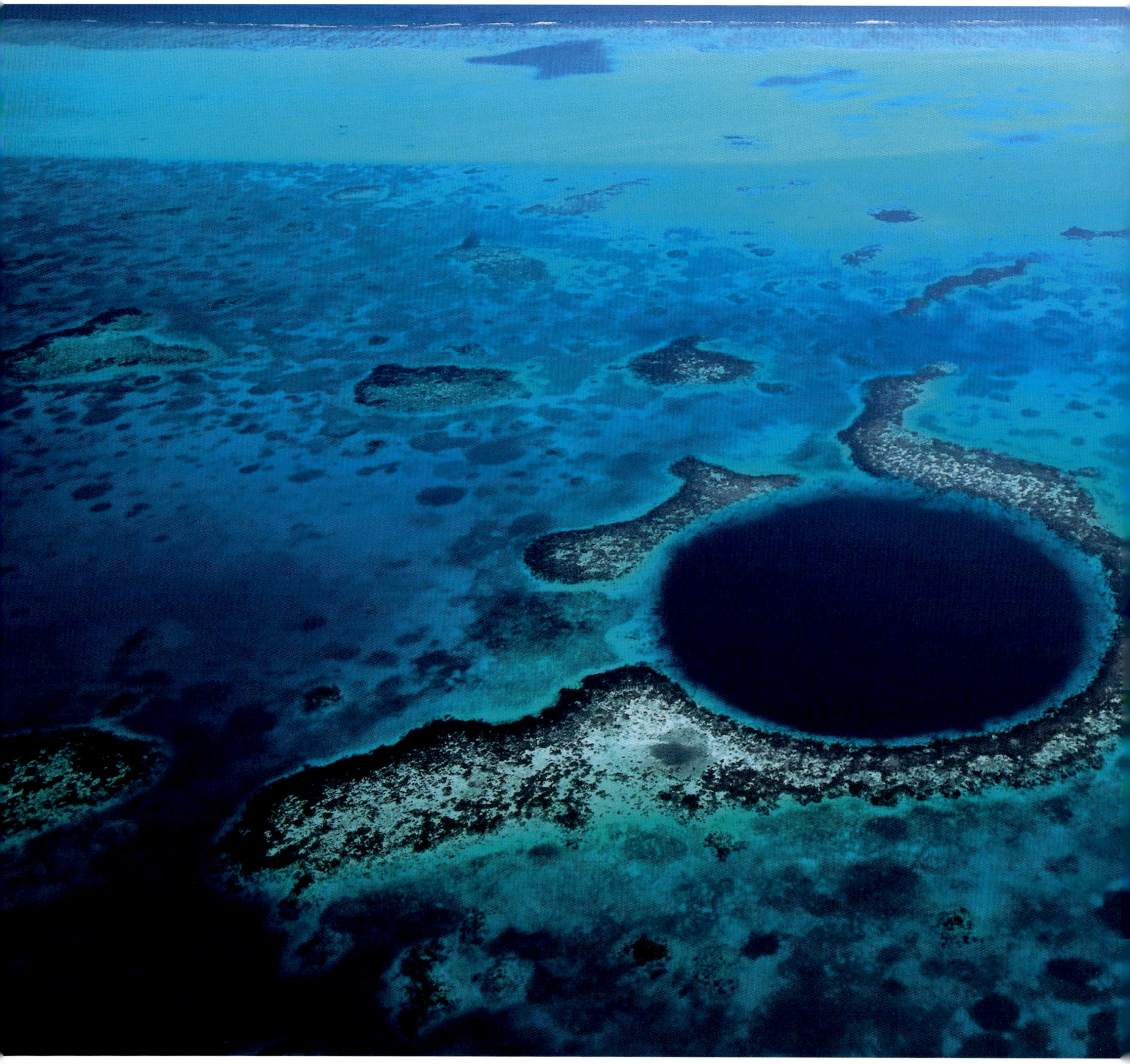

such as the red-footed booby, the magnificent frigate bird, and the lesser noddy.
The World Heritage Site amounts to 1,000 sq. km (390 sq. miles) and consists of seven conservation areas and national parks. It includes various types of reef, made from 65 different varieties of coral. These bizarrely shaped growths and columns are a habitat for innumerable species, including 250 different water plants and 350 molluscs, sponges, and crustaceans, and some 500 species of fish, ranging from eagle rays to groupers. Highly endangered marine animals such as manatees and loggerhead and hawksbill turtles also live in the conservation areas.

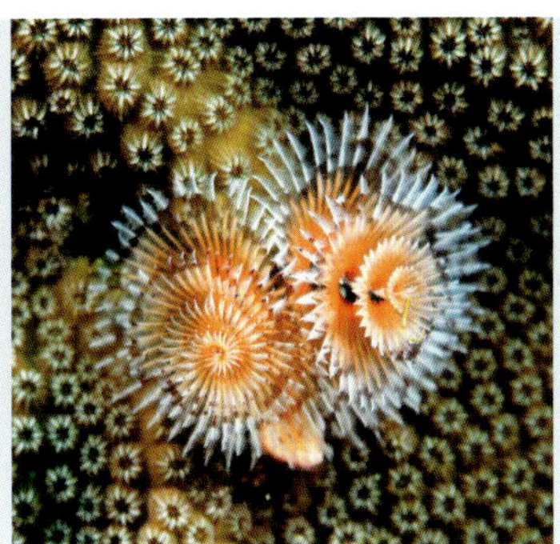

The Blue Hole, some 125 m (400 feet) deep, was created when an underwater cave collapsed (large image) and was filled with water by the rising sea level. It is located close to the Lighthouse Reef and also forms part of the World Heritage site. The underwater world is a paradise of coral beauties.

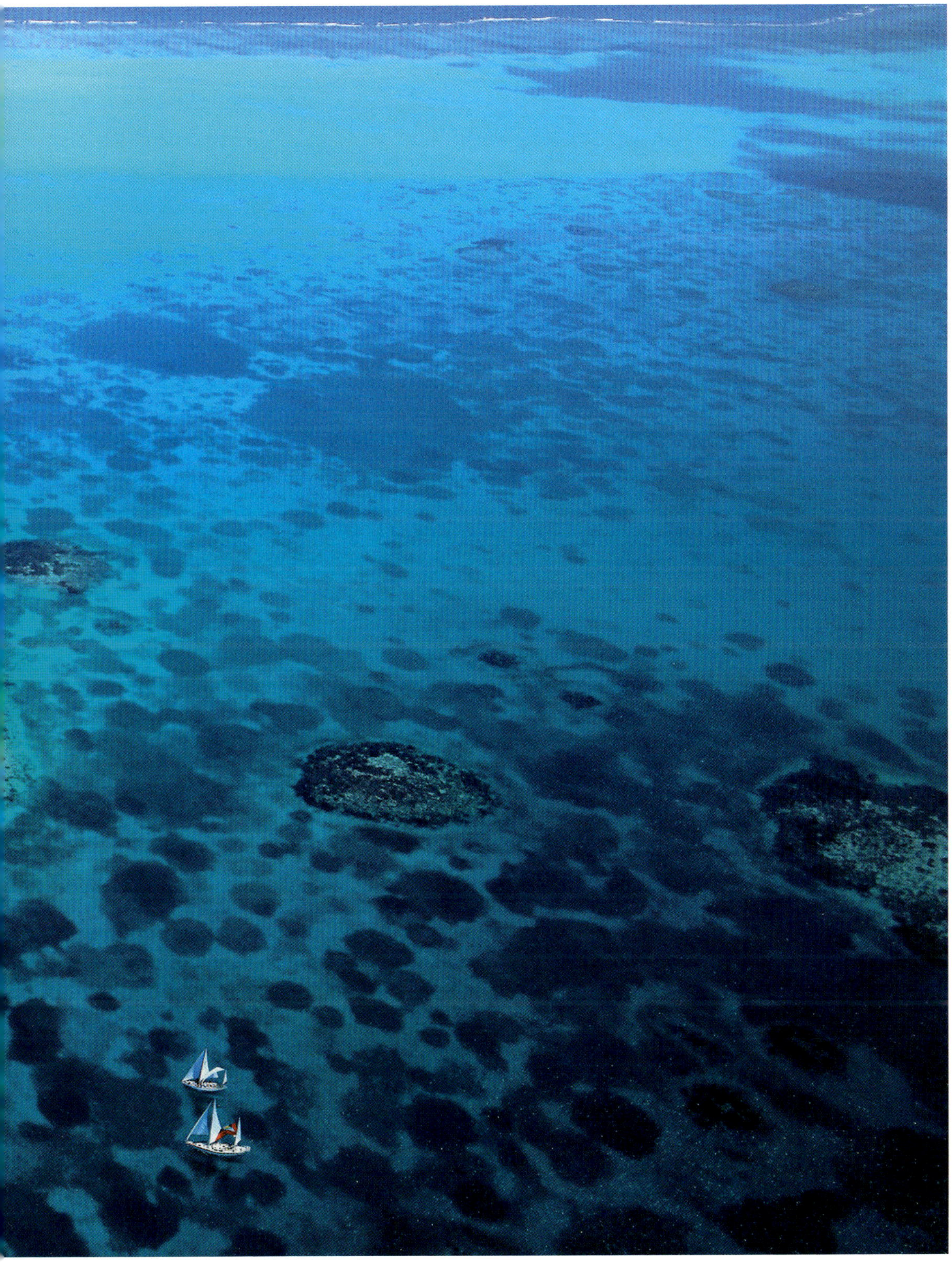

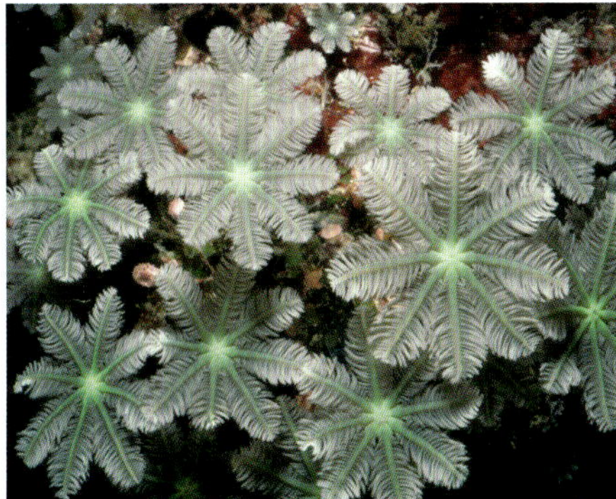

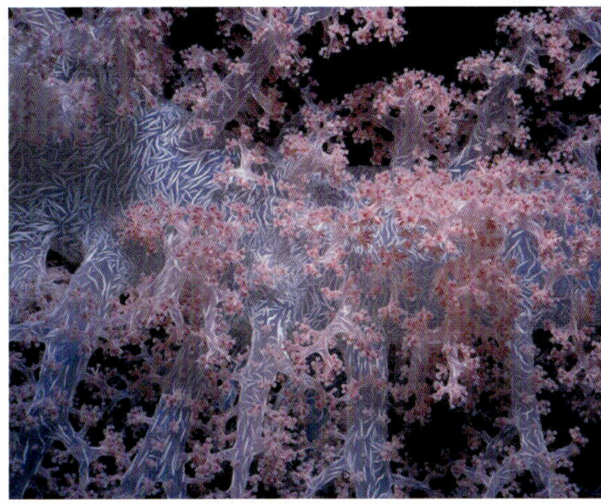

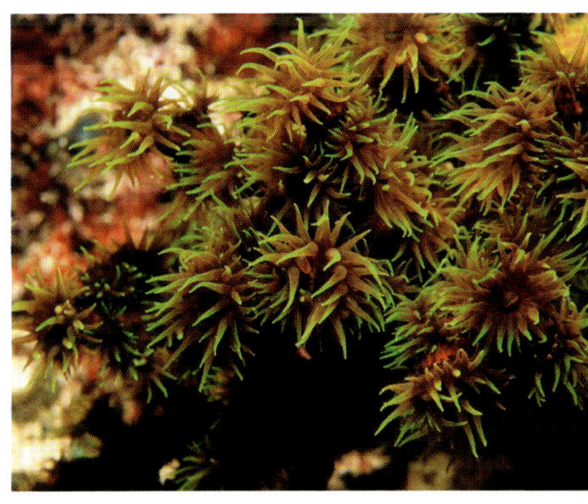

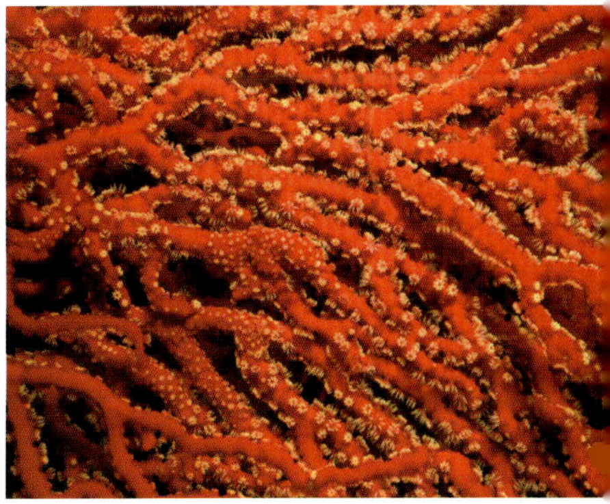

TIK'AL NATIONAL PARK

Date of inscription: 1979

Tik'al, in north-eastern Guatemala, is among the most significant ruins left from the Mayan culture. The earliest settlement of this site in the Petén rainforest was completed by 800 BC. A gigantic complex with temples and palaces was built here in the 3rd century AD.

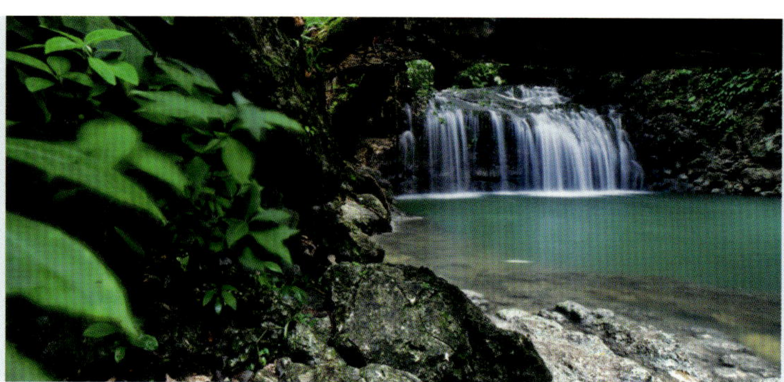

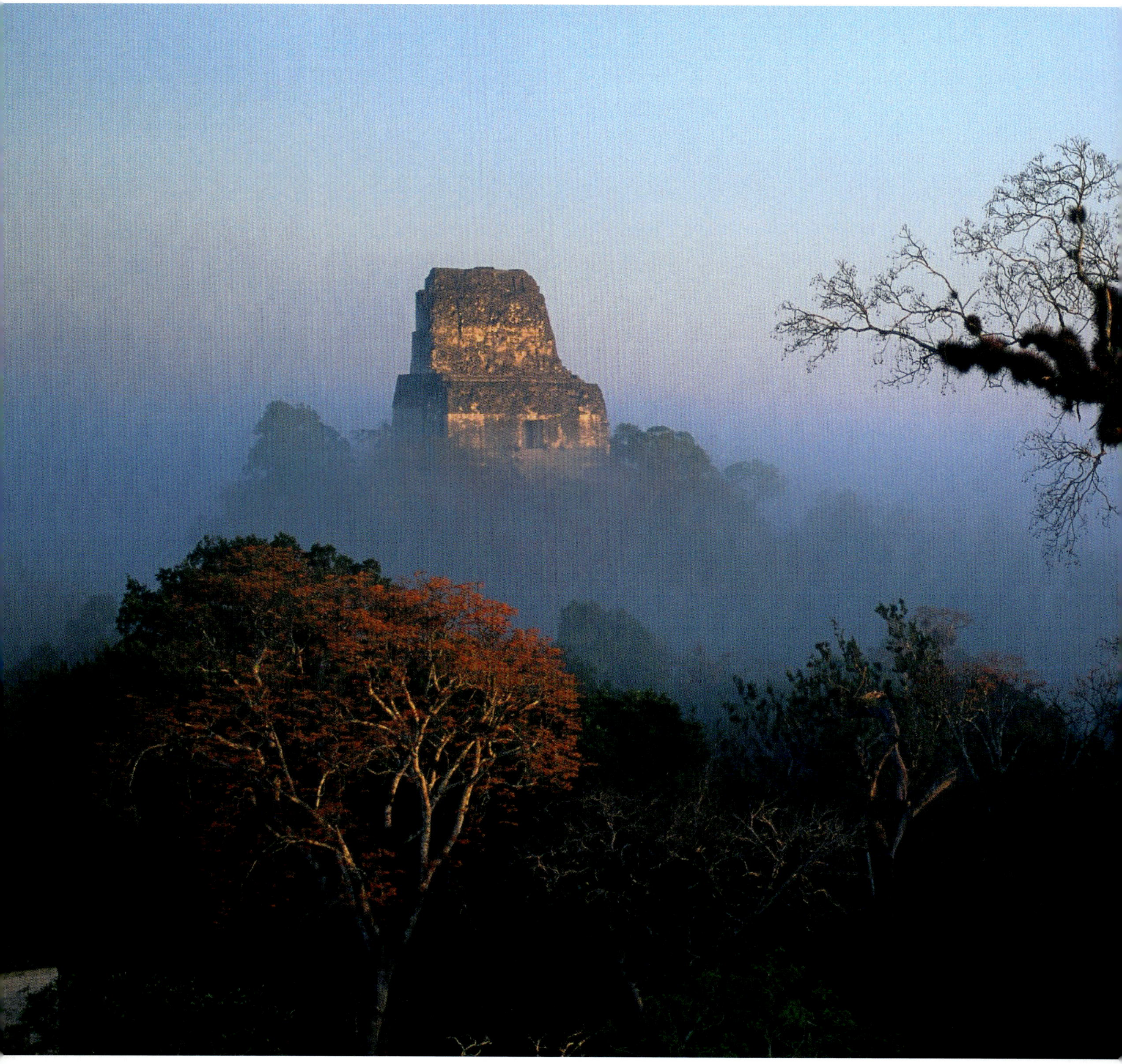

Tik'al is distinct from other Mayan sites in that it is located in the middle of a national park. The park's 600 sq. km (230 sq. miles) of primeval forest are home to howler monkeys, birds, tree frogs, and many other animals. At the height of Tik'al's expansion (AD 550–900), up to 90,000 people lived in this temple city. More than 3,000 structures and edifices have so far been excavated in the 15 sq. km (6 sq. miles) of the heart of the city, including great palaces, simple huts, and games fields. The most spectacular are the five gigantic step pyramid temples; one of these is 65 m (215 feet) tall, and thus is the largest known Mayan structure.

Around AD 800, this cultural complex boasted 12 temples, constructed on a giant platform. Near these monumental buildings archeologists have uncovered numerous tools and religious objects, as well as a series of valuable grave goods.

No significant building work was attempted in Tik'al from the 9th century, and the city was finally deserted during the 10th century. It is a spectacluar site.

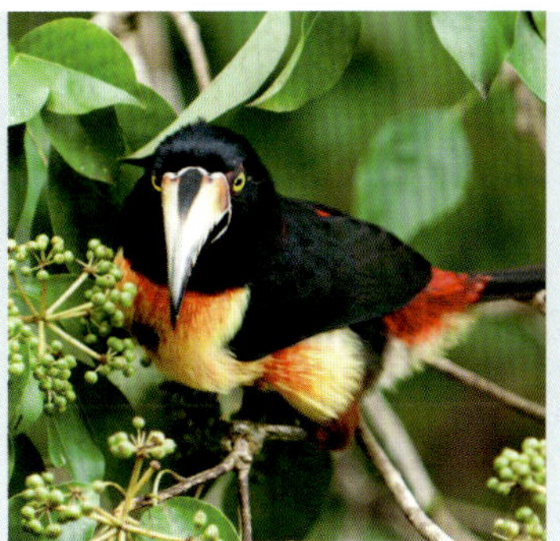

The contours of a monumental pyramid temple are glimpsed as an unreal silhouette through the mists of the Petén rainforest in Guatemala (large image left). Some waterfalls, like the Los Siete Altares, criss-cross the landscape (far left). Also at home here are, among others, the nasua (below) and numerous exotic birds such as the collared aracari (left).

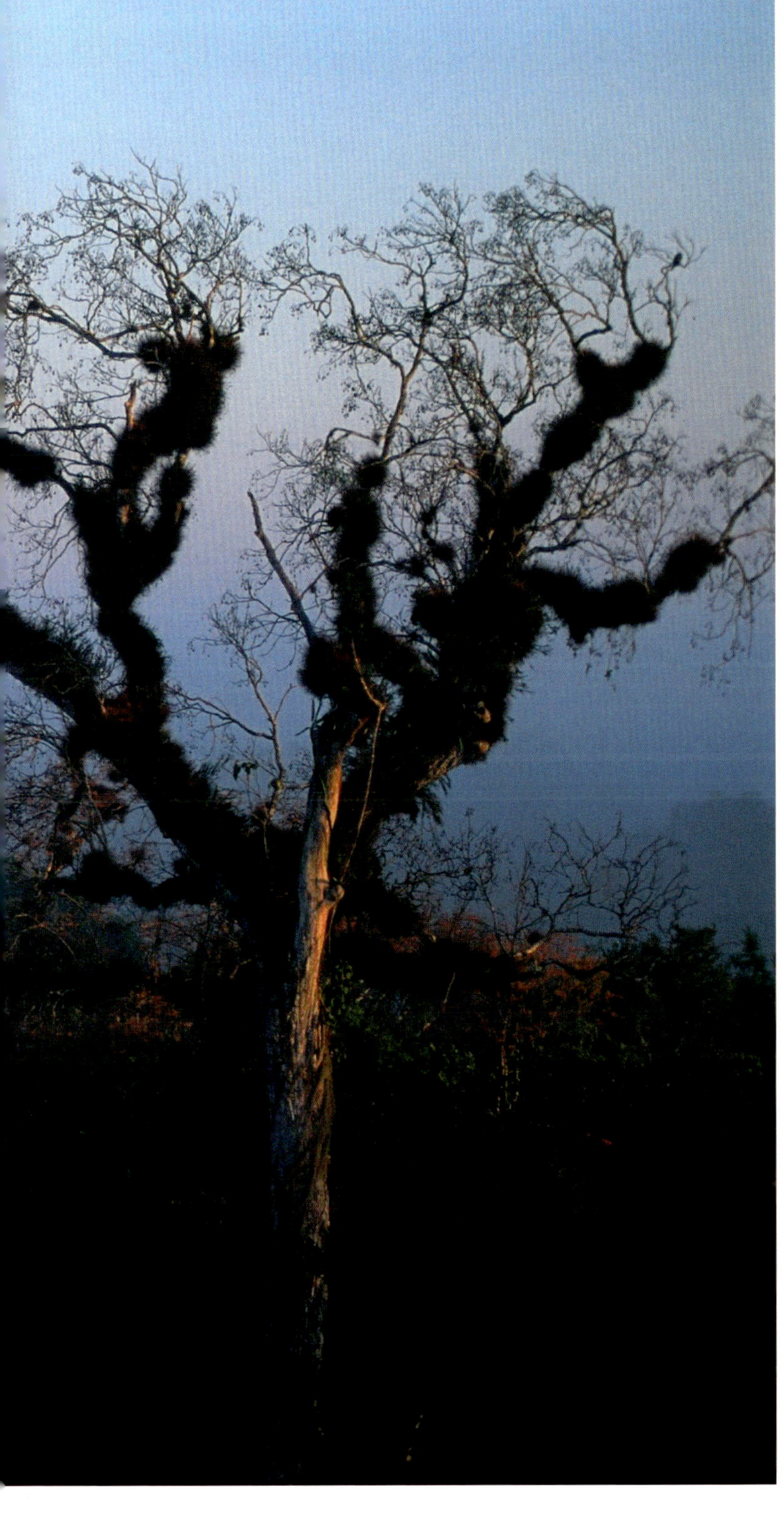

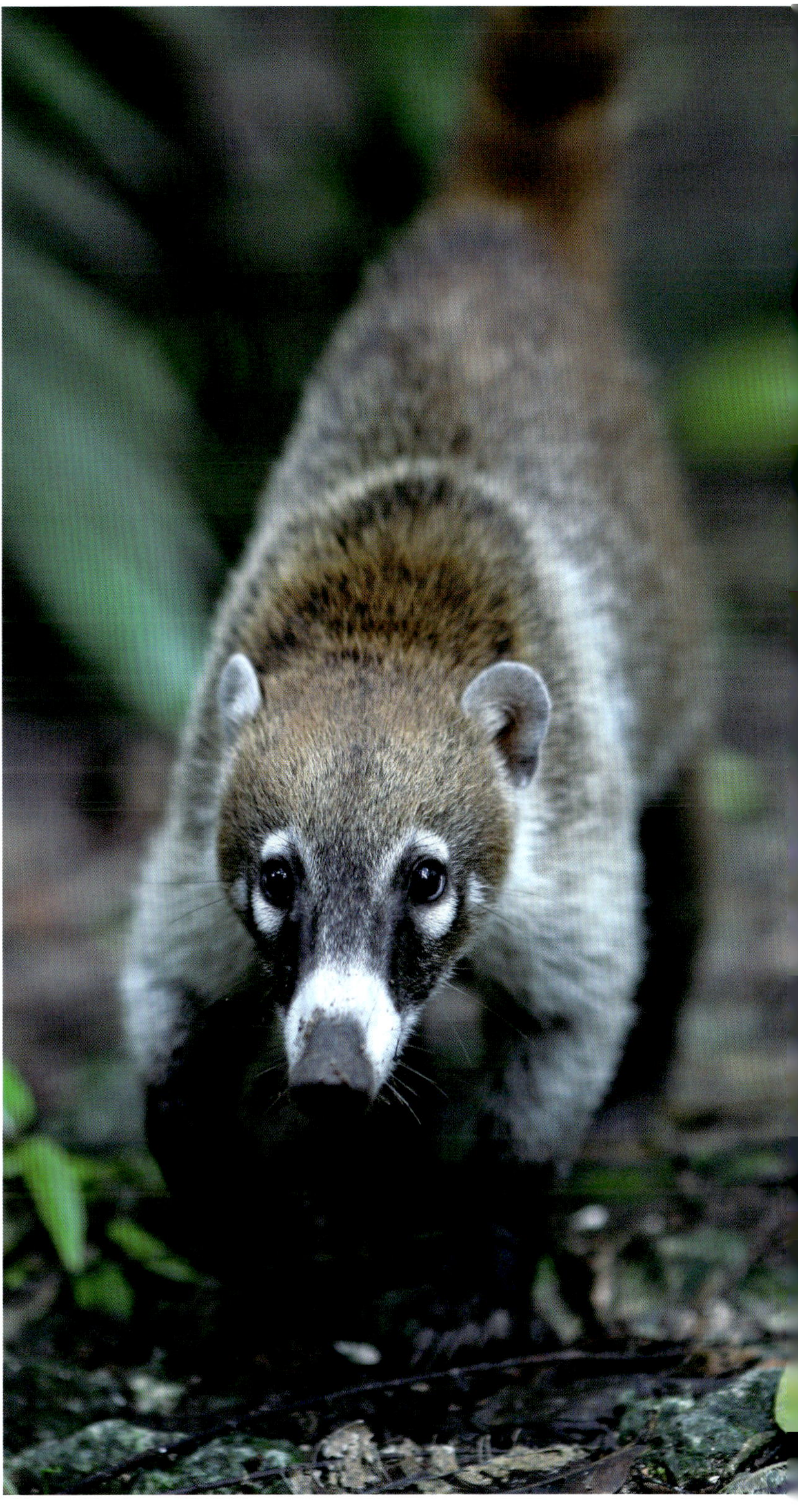

RÍO PLÁTANO BIOSPHERE RESERVE

Date of inscription: 1982

This biosphere reserve in the Río Plátano contains a considerable portion of the world's second-largest continuous area of rainforest. Due to its varied ecosystems, it houses a fantastic wealth of animal and plant life.

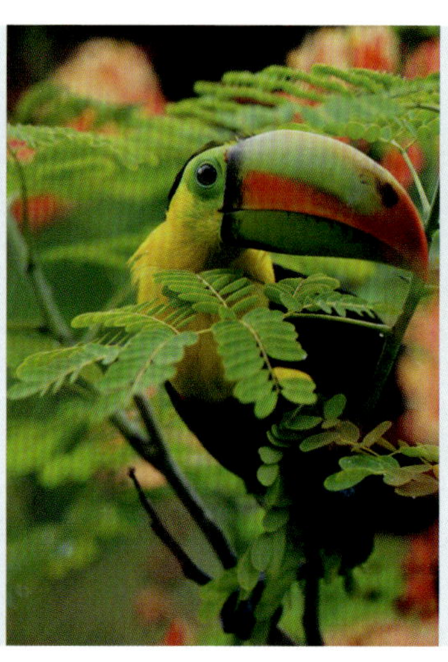

The biosphere reserve covers 8,300 sq. km (3,200 sq. miles) of the Río Plátano, from the north coast to an elevation of 1,300 m (4,250 feet) in the interior of Honduras. Behind untouched sandy beaches on the coast lie lagoons and mangrove forests, coastal savannah with beaksedge and other marsh plants, and palms and umbrella pines. Further into the interior, there is tropical and subtropical rainforest, and all the diversity that these bring. Numerous trees grow here, from the Spanish cedar to mahogany, balsa, and sandalwood. The reserve is home to jaguars, pumas, ocelots, king vultures and harpy eagles, manatees, tapirs, pakas, and several species of monkey. This sparsely populated region is home to only a few thousand people – the indigenous Miskito, Pech, and Tawahka, the Garifuna (an ethnic group with Caribbean and African roots), and mestizos. Moreover, there archeological sites to be found on the reserve, bearing traces of both Mayan and another unknown pre-Columbian culture.

In the woods live keel-billed toucan (left) and the three-toed sloth (large picture).

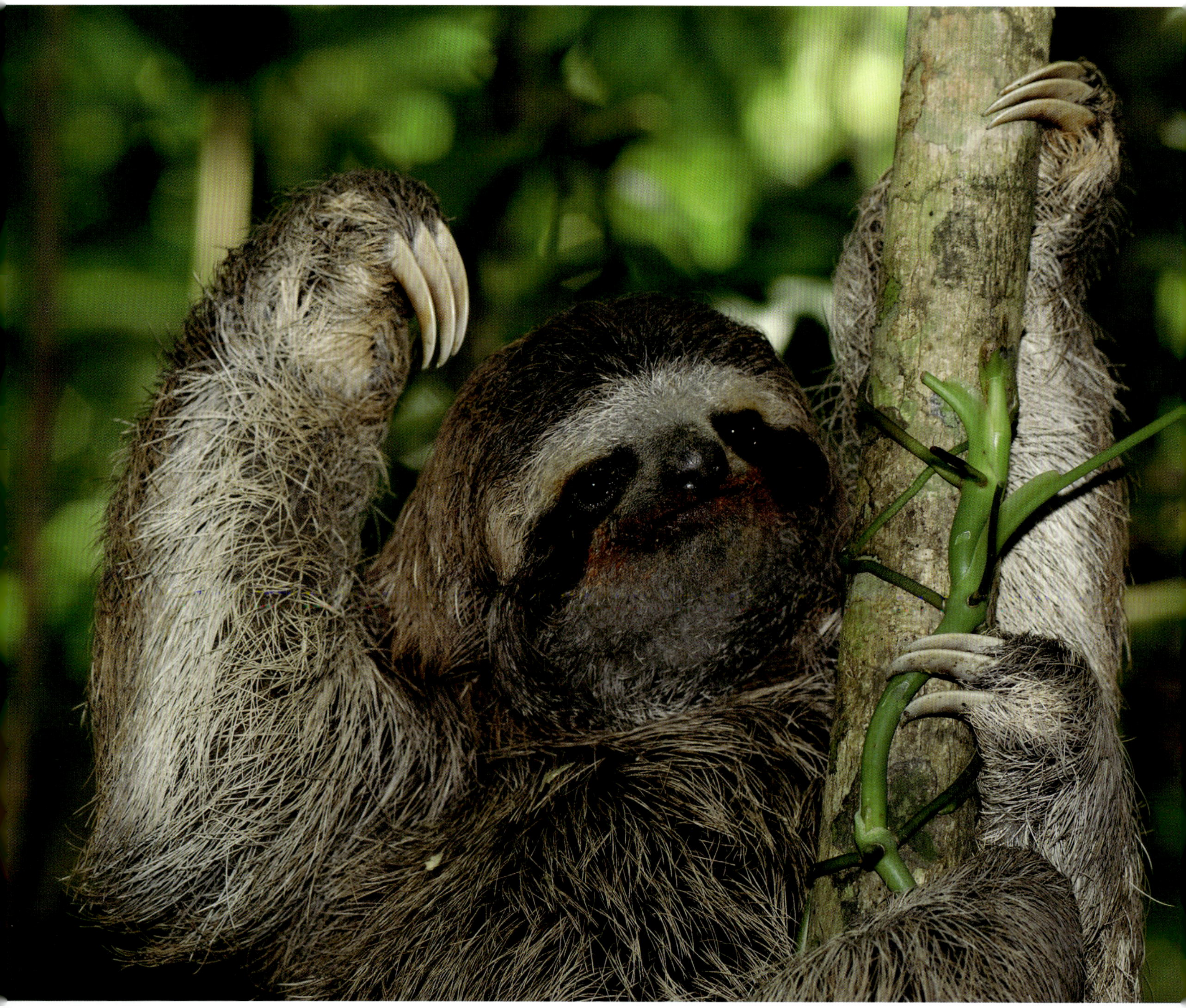

COCOS ISLAND NATIONAL PARK

Legend has it that infamous pirates buried treasure on Cocos Island in the 17th and 18th centuries – although no trace of any has yet been found. The treasure that this island, situated 550 km (340 miles) south-west of the coast of Costa Rica, definitely does have to offer lies in its tropical rainforest. The 24 sq. km island offers a diverse panorama of steep crags growing from the sea, waterfalls, and summits overgrown by the jungle. Due to its remote location, numerous endemic species have evolved here, such as the huriki tree (Sacoglottis holdridgei). In addition, three bird, two reptile, and more than 60 insect species are found only here. Some 100 sq. km (40 sq. miles) of coastal waters around the island also belong to the national park, and these contain large fringing reefs, with 32 species of coral and a wealth of marine life – dolphins, different species of shark and manta rays.

Red-footed boobies (right) nest in the trees. Underwater you will encounter exotic species such as the red-lipped batfish (large picture).

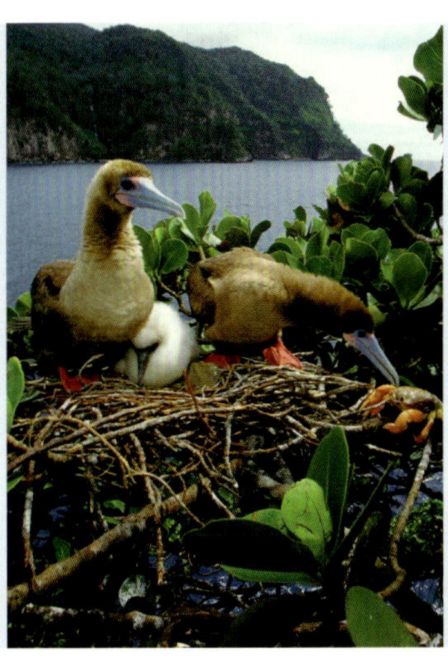

Date of inscription: 1997
Extension: 2002

Cocos is the only island in the East Pacific to be covered in tropical rainforest. Lying far from the mainland, it has evolved singular flora and fauna.

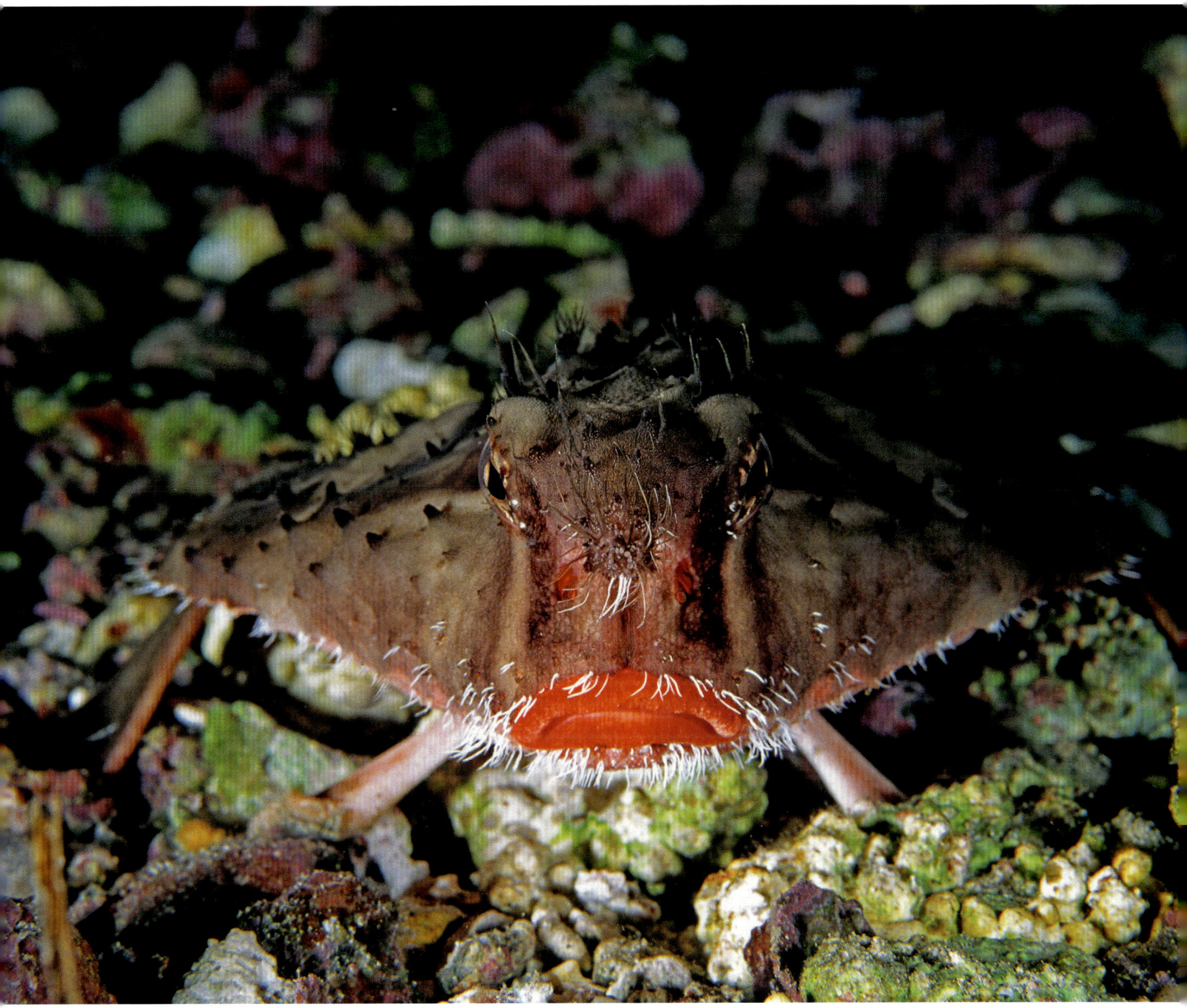

GUANACASTE CONSERVATION AREA

Date of inscription: 1999
Extension: 2004

This extensive conservation area in north-western Costa Rica allows the observation of important ecological processes on land and in the coastal waters. The area is a habitat of many rare species.

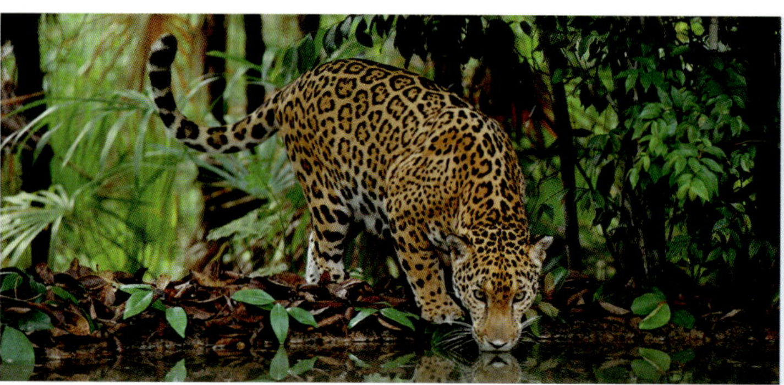

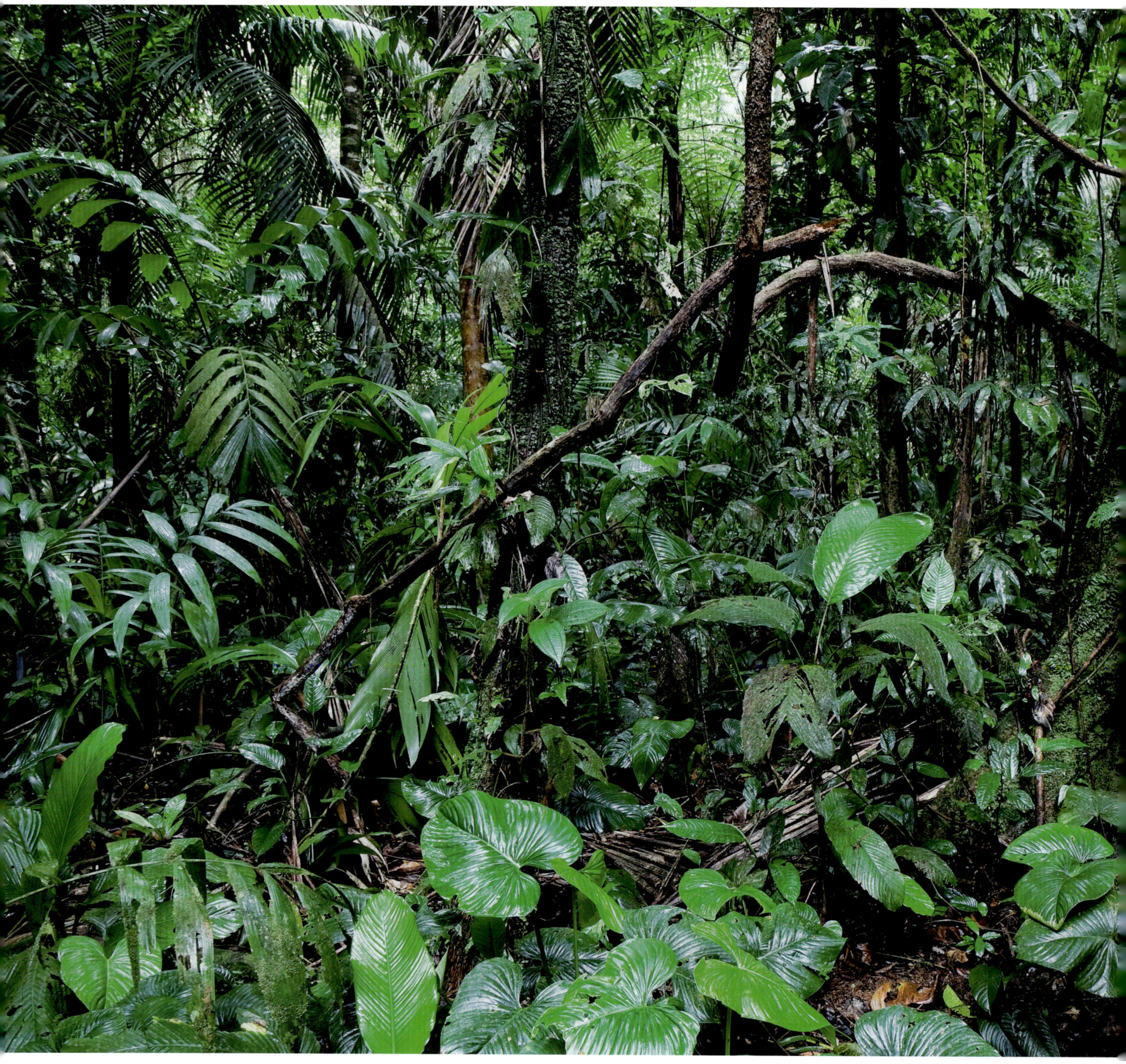

This area of 1,000 sq. km (386 sq. miles) in north-western Costa Rica consists of three national parks and several smaller conservation areas. It extends from the Pacific coast across the 2,000-m (6,600-foot) high mountains of the interior to the lowlands on the Caribbean side. Guanacaste encompasses coastal waters, islands, sandy beaches, and rocky coastland, as well as streams and rivers in the mountainous and volcanic landscape of the interior, including the still active composite volcano, Rincón de la Vieja.

No less than 37 wetlands are to be found here, along with mangroves and a tropical rainforest, whose trees shed their leaves in the hot season. This, the last great intact area of tropical dry forest remaining in Central America, is one of the largest protected forest areas in the world. In total, some 230,000 species flourish in the various ecosystems. This impressive diversity is due to Guanacaste's location in a biogeographical area encompassing both neotropic and neoarctic life from South and North America.

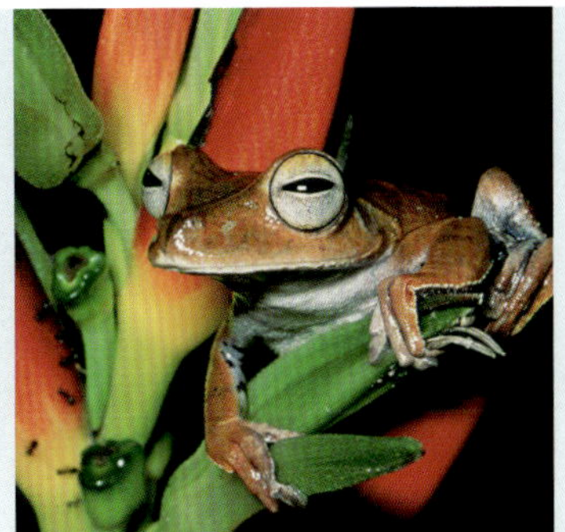

The world is colourful in Costa Rica: A tree frog sitting on a heliconia flower (left); a hummingbird sucks nectar; tamanduas are a genus of anteaters; an eyelash viper snakes through the magnificent foliage (picture series from the top). Far left: the elegantly marked jaguar.

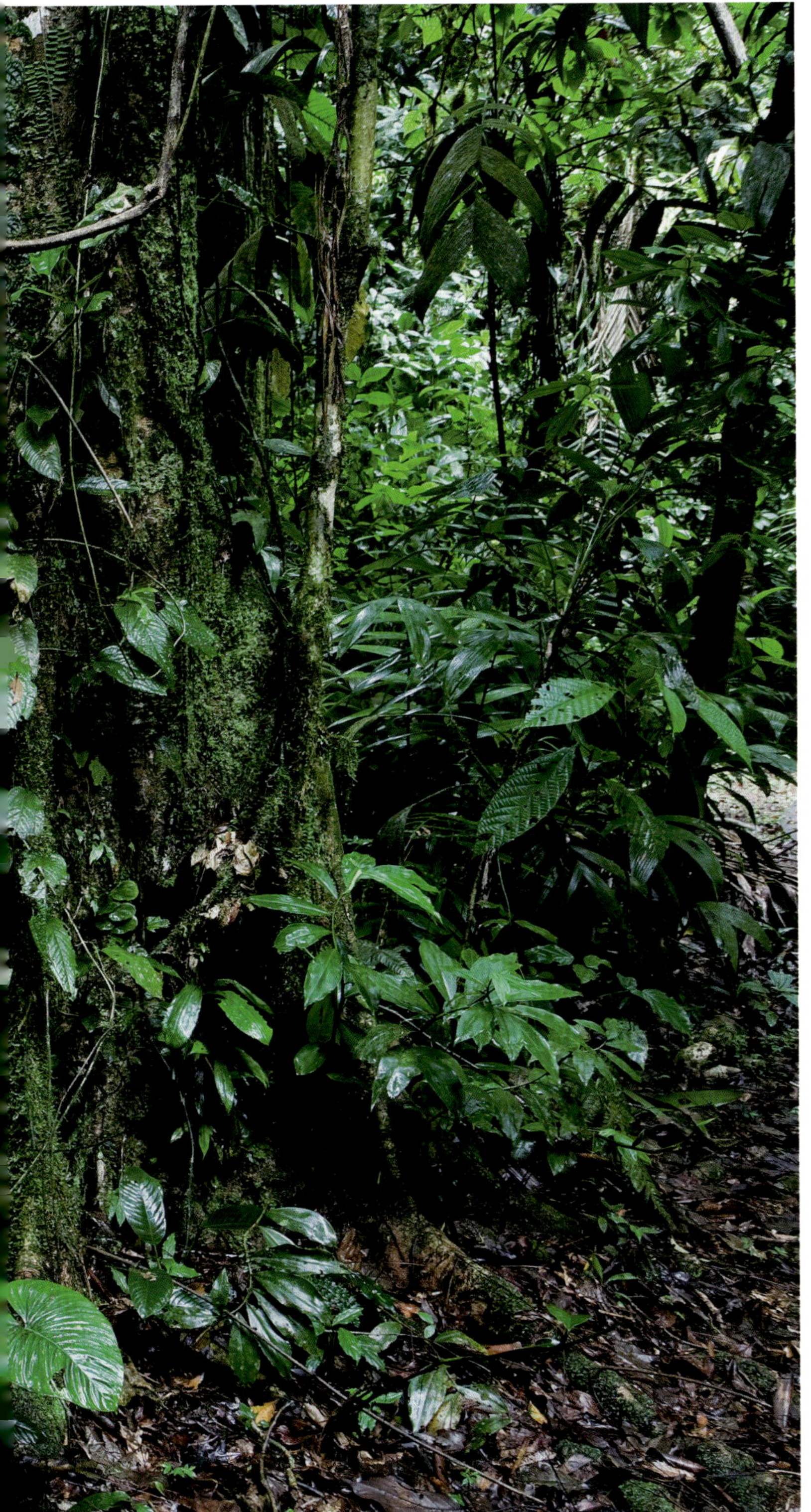

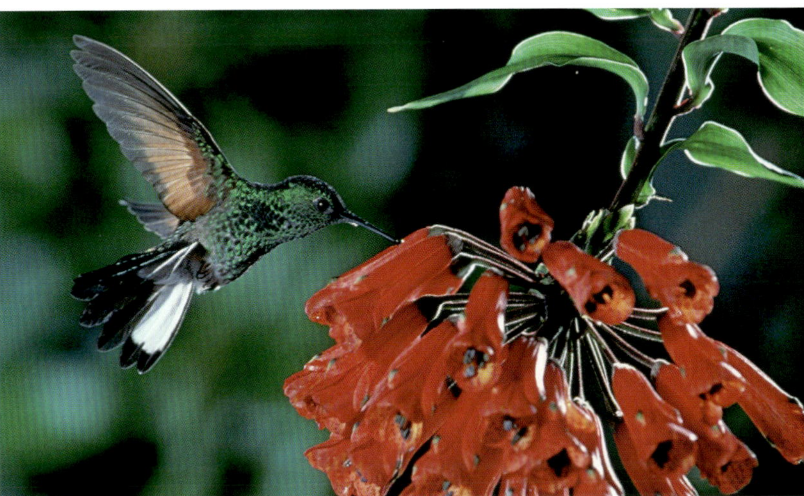

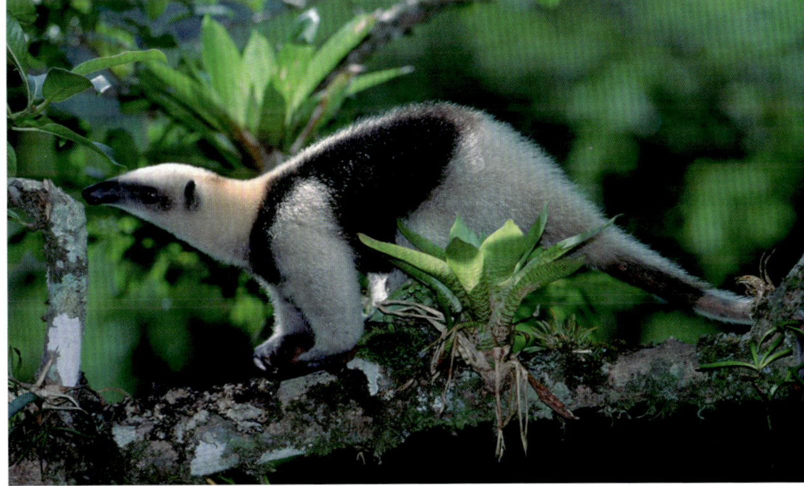

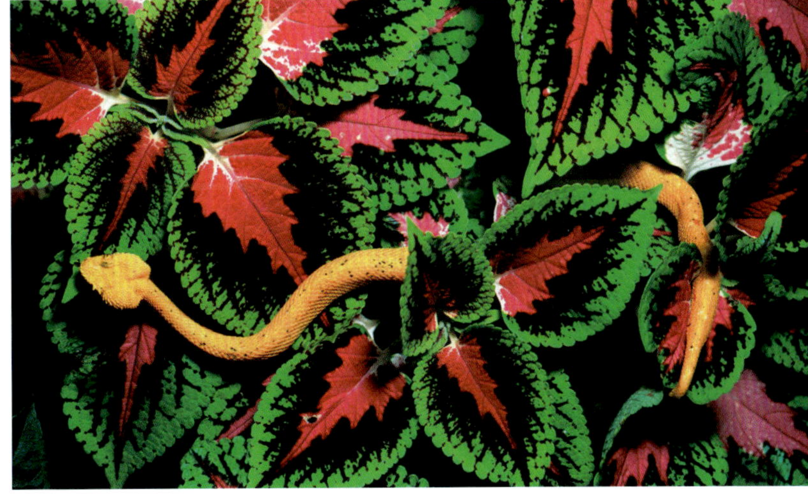

TALAMANCA RANGE AND LA AMISTAD NATIONAL PARK

Date of inscription: 1983
Extension: 1990

This international conservation area, shared between Costa Rica and Panama, is home to a greatest diversity of life.

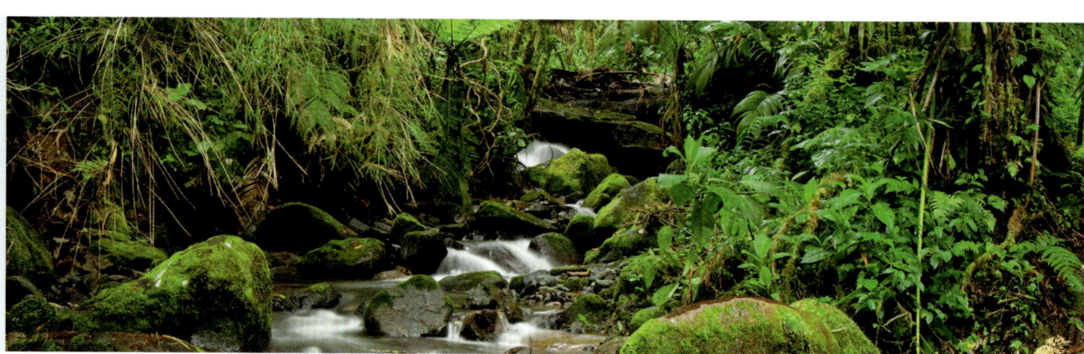

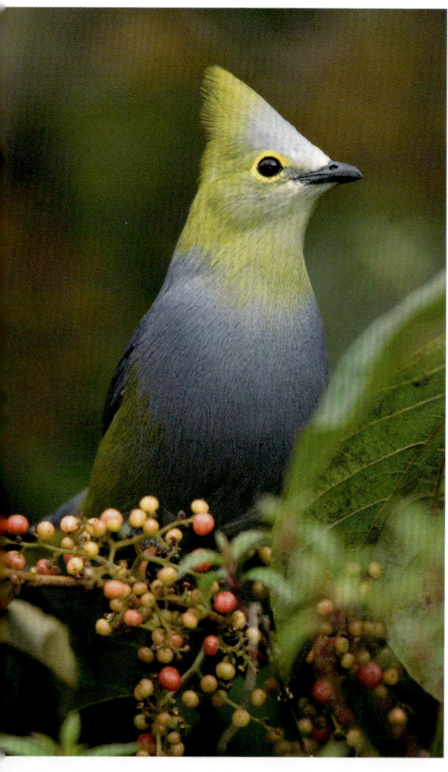

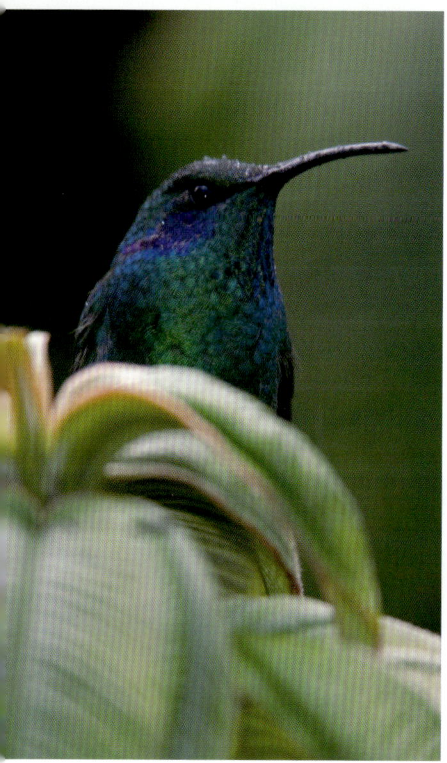

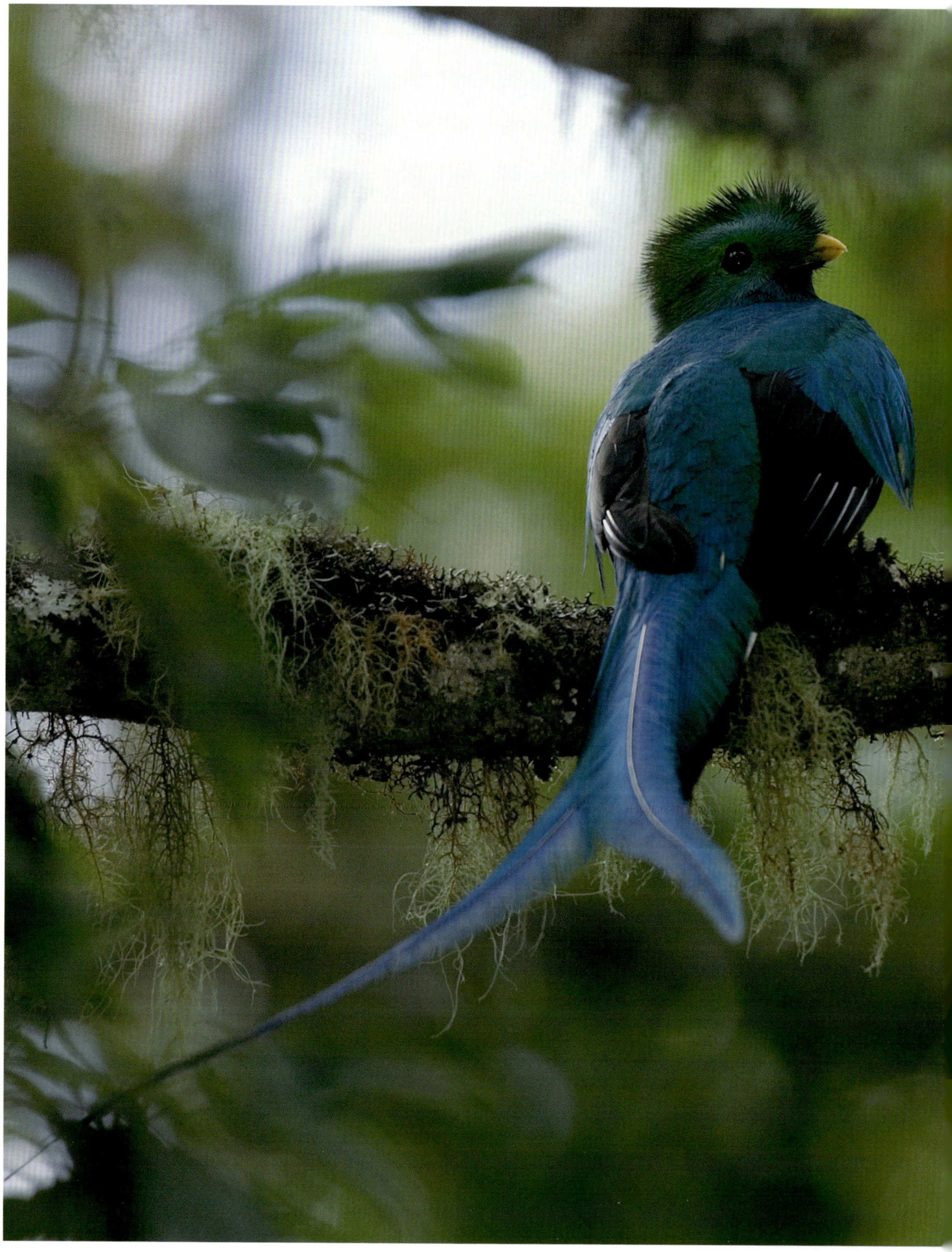

This unique conservation area covers 8,000 sq. km (3,100 sq. miles) of the central Cordillera de Talamanca, stretching from the south of Costa Rica into the west of Panama. A tremendous range of scenery and habitats for wildlife is to be found at elevations that vary from sea level up to some 3,800 m (12,600 feet). The greater part of the reserve is covered in tropical rainforest, which has been growing here for 25,000 years. At elevations higher than the lowland plains there are cloud forests and areas of Páramo with bushes and grasses, as well as areas of evergreen oaks, moorland, and lakes. Due to its topographic and climatic variation, not to mention its geographical situation at the intersection of North and South America, the park boasts a diversity of animal and plant life.

Archeological finds suggest the possibility of human habitation here dating back millennia, but this research is still in its infancy. Today, around 10,000 members of the indigenous Teribe, Guaymi, Bribri, and Cabecar tribal groups live in reservations on the range.

The colourful birdlife in Talamanca comprises, among others, grey silky flycatchers and sparkling violetears (far left top and bottom), grey-tailed mountaingems (bottom right) and quetzals (large picture and right, top). The latter were once hunted for their beautiful tail feathers, but today they are protected. Left: the Chiriqui Viejo River.

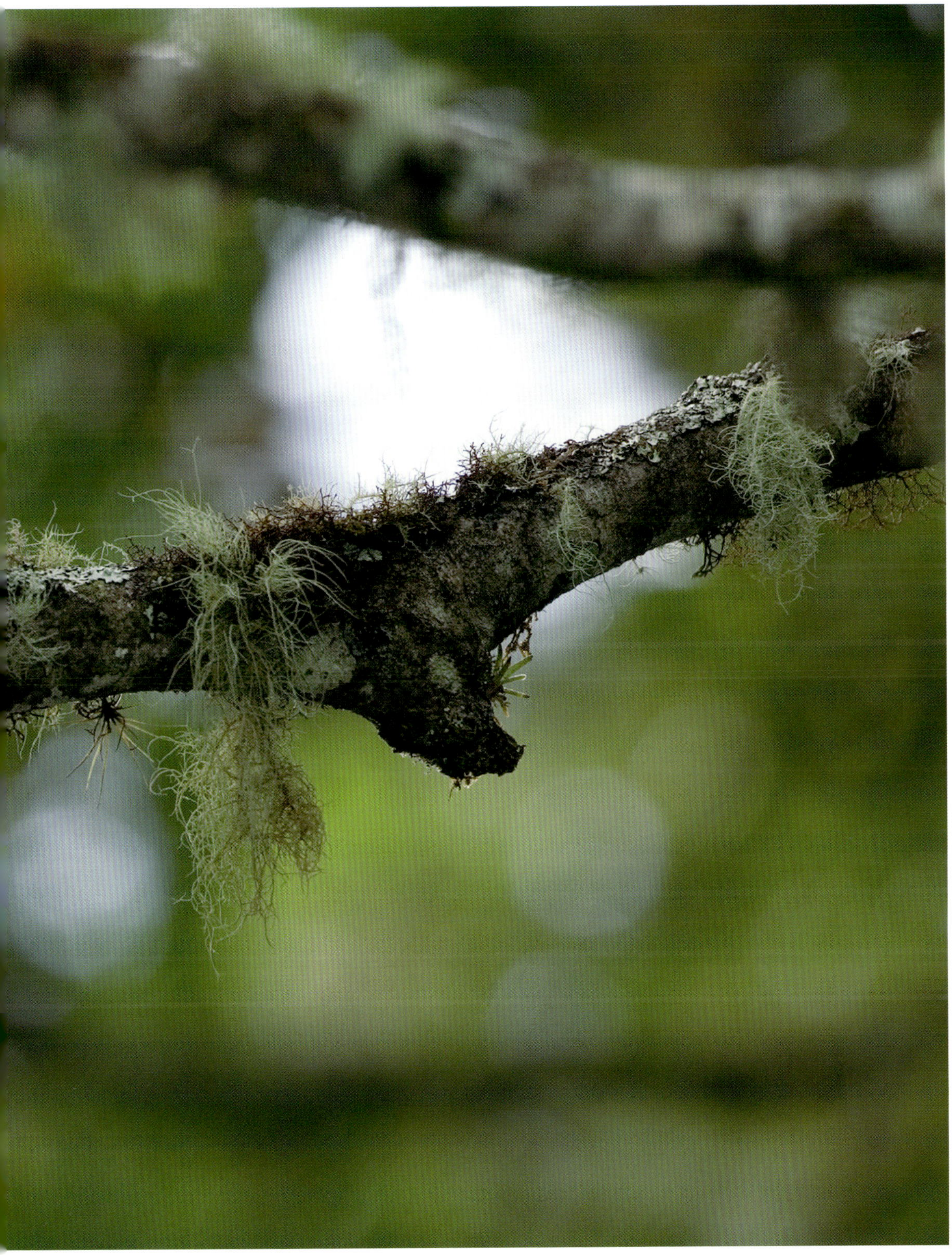

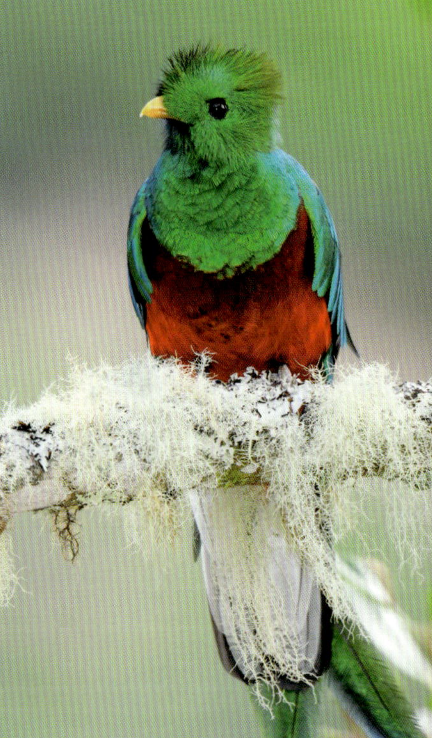

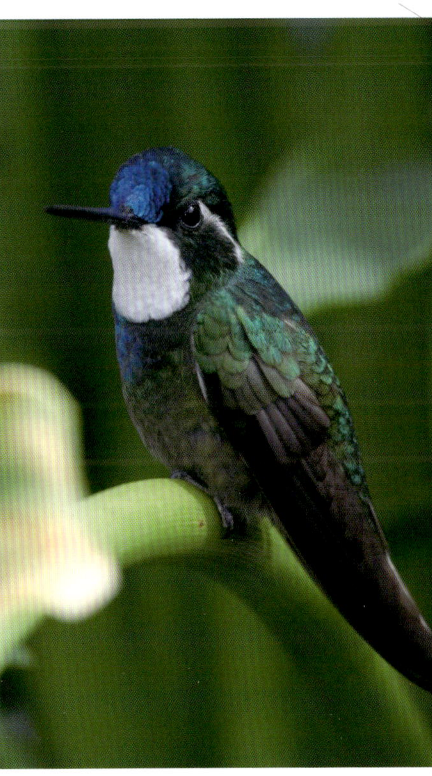

COIBA NATIONAL PARK AND SPECIAL ZONE OF MARINE PROTECTION

Date of inscription: 2005

This conservation area, consisting of Pacific islands spared the storms and temperature variations associated with El Niño, has retained a great variety of species.

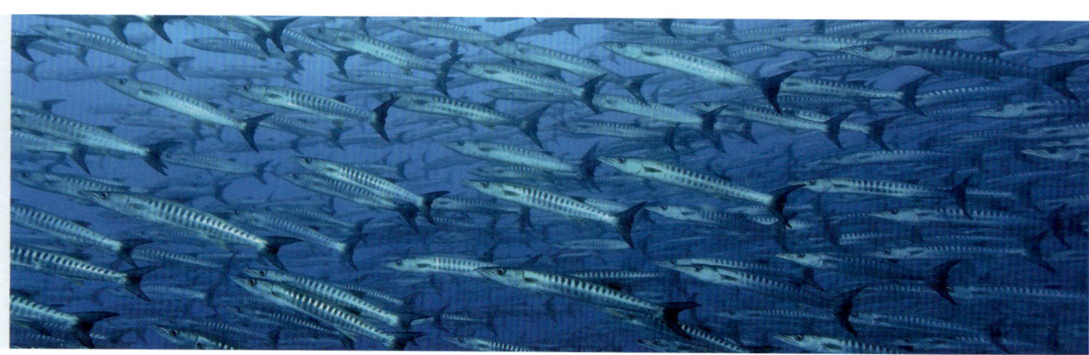

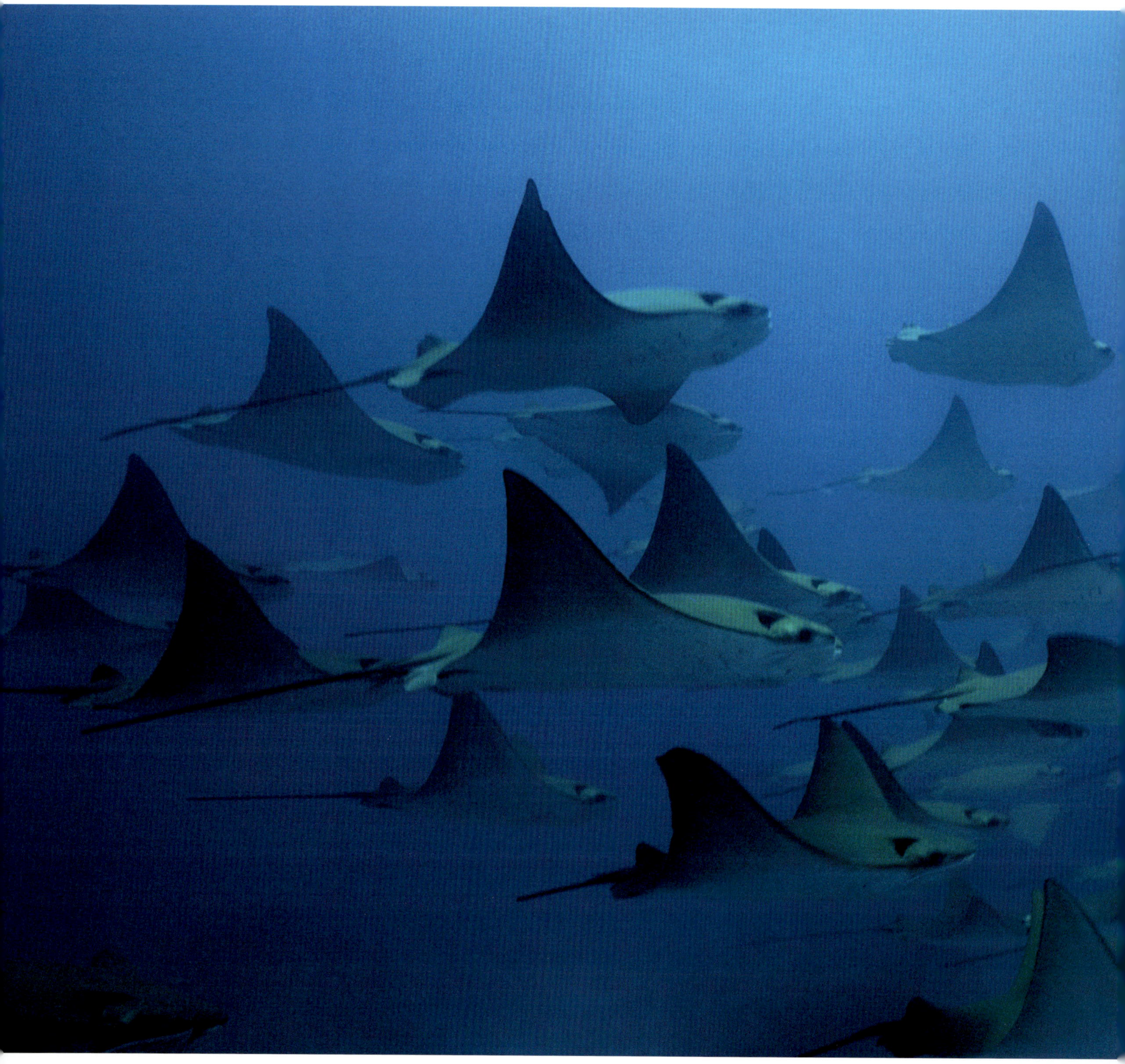

The establishment of 4,000 sq. km of the south-west coast of Panama as a national park has protected not only the rainforest of the island of Coiba, but also a further 38 smaller islands in the Gulf of Chiriquí and the immediately surrounding ocean. The islands, which have been separated from the mainland for millennia, are of great interest to naturalists because of the evolution of various unique species and subspecies here. Among these endemic forms are rodents like the Coiban agouti, as well as several subspecies of howler monkey, opossum, and white-tailed deer. Coiba is also a last refuge for various endangered species that have died out in other areas of Panama, such as the crested eagle and the scarlet macaw. The marine areas of the park are especially rich in animal life, and house the Ensenada Maria Reef, which, at 160 hectares, is the second-largest reef system in the Central East Pacific. More than 750 varieties of sea life have so far been recorded in this important refuge for marine mammals and deep sea fish, including more than 30 varieties of shark and around 20 species of dolphins and whales.

The underwater world reveals a great diversity of marine and reef residents. Shoals of eagle rays (large picture) and pelican barracudas (left) cross the ocean. Cardinalfishes, hawkfishes, pufferfishes and blennies, which like to hide in their "home" buried up to their heads, live on the ocean floor (picture series, from the top).

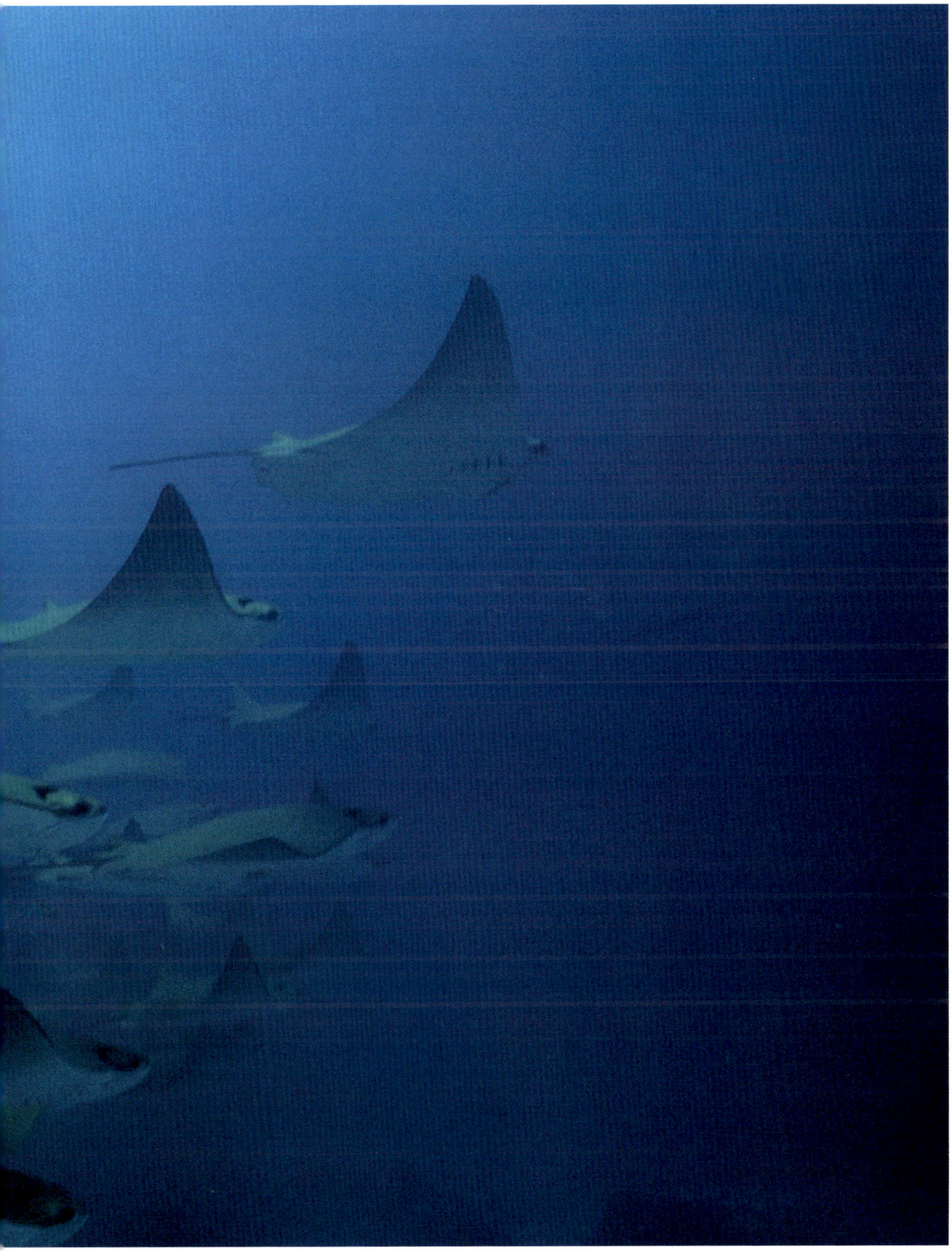

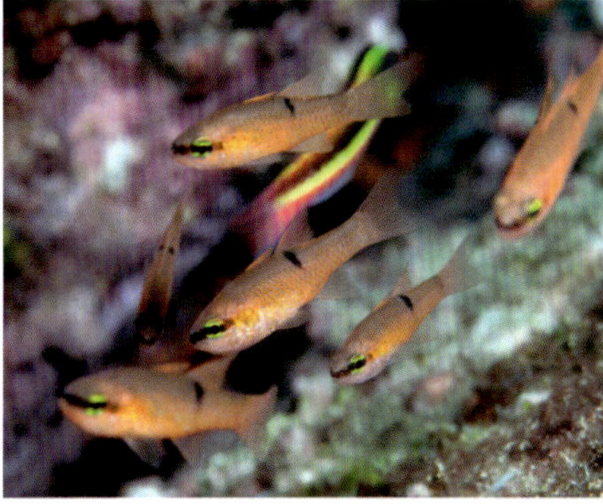

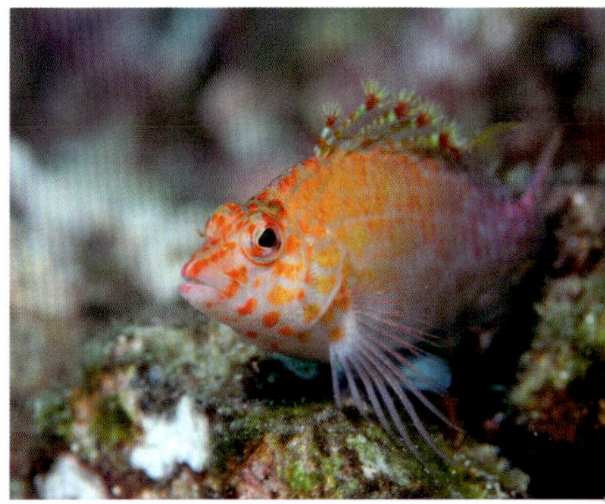

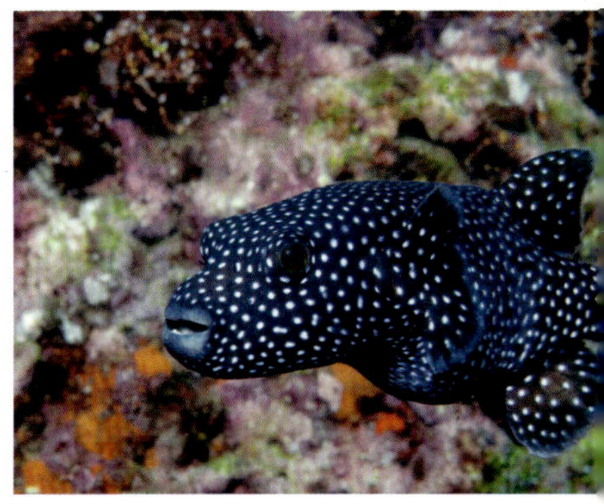

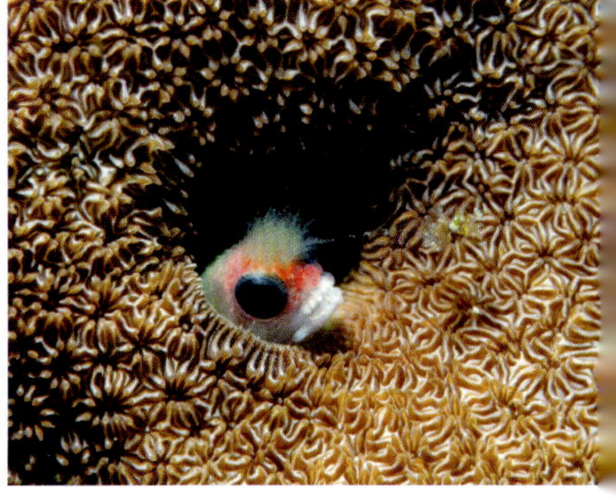

DARIÉN NATIONAL PARK

Date of inscription: 1981

Until recently, the extent of the biodiversity of this enormous tropical wilderness could only be guessed at. Scientists have conjectured that thousands of species remain to be recorded in Darién.

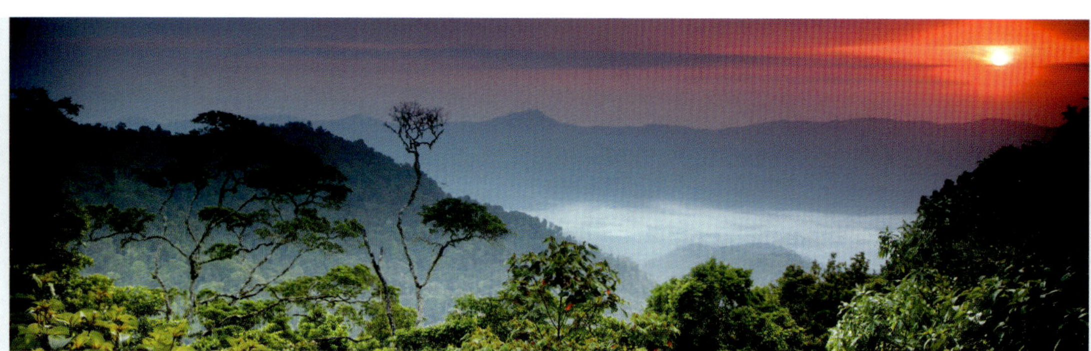

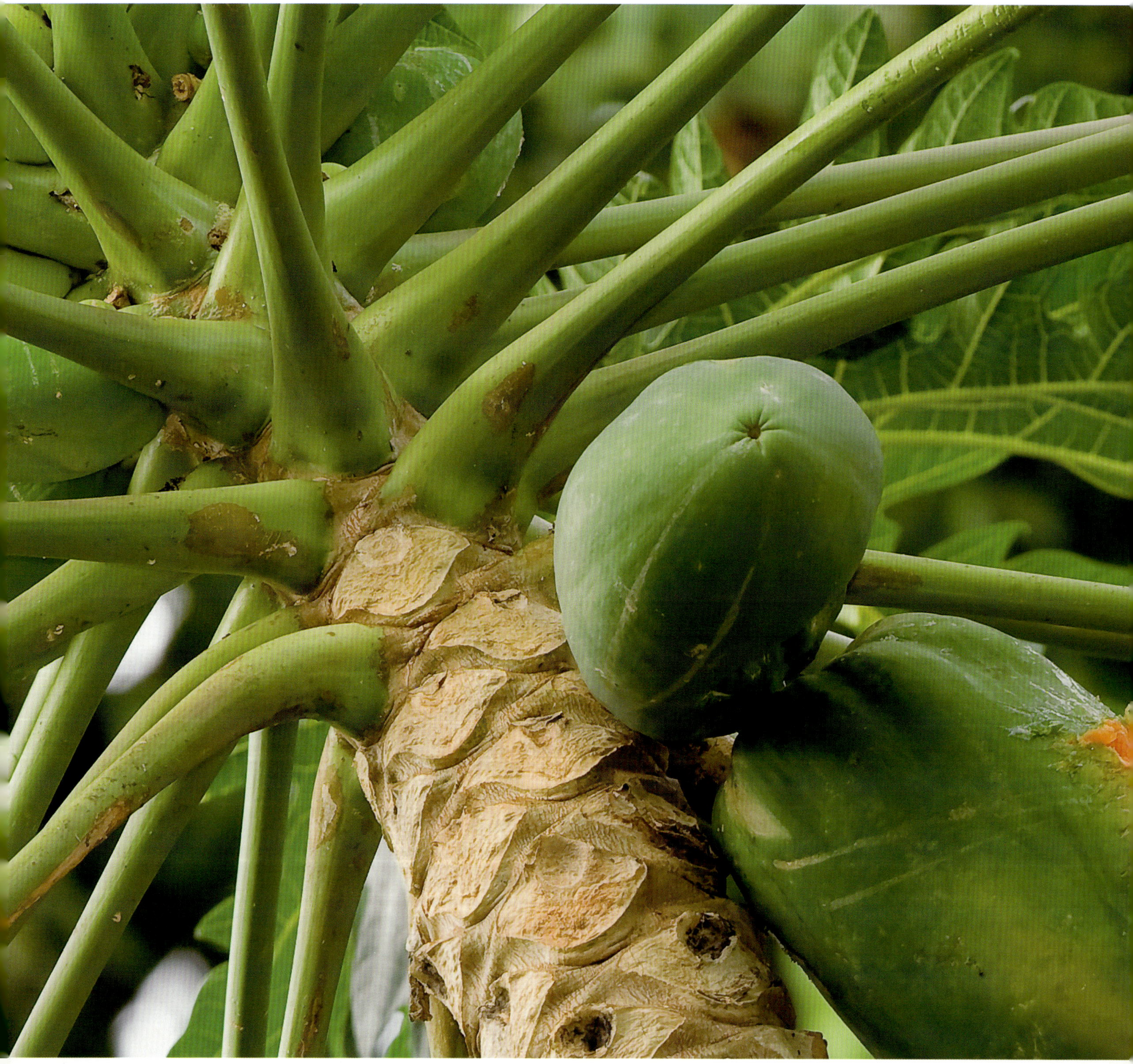

This biosphere reserve in eastern Panama covers 6,000 sq. km (2,300 sq. miles) and stretches from the Pacific coast to the 1,800-m (5,950- foot) high mountains of the Caribbean coast whose highest peak is the Cerro Tacarcuma with 1845 m. The reserve encompasses the most diverse range of habitats, from sandy and rocky beaches, through mangrove intertidal flats, to various types of rainforest. Its ecosystems are considered the most varied in tropical America. Here rare orchids flourish as well as 40 different kinds of endemic plants. This wealth of habitats, and especially the park's situation at the meeting point of the furthest ranges of both South and North American species, ensure fantastic biodiversity. As many as 450 different inidgenous species of bird are to be found here, and five of them are endemic. Species that are threatened with extinction like the harpy, tapir, jaguar and cougar find refuge in the Darién. Some areas of the park are inhabited by members of the indigenous Kuna, Emberá, and Wounaan tribal groups.

The Cerro Pirre is 1,425 m (4,675 feet) high; at sunset you can enjoy a fantastic view of the valley (left). The Swainson's toucan (large picture) feeds mainly on fruits. It uses its large beak to regulate its body temperature.

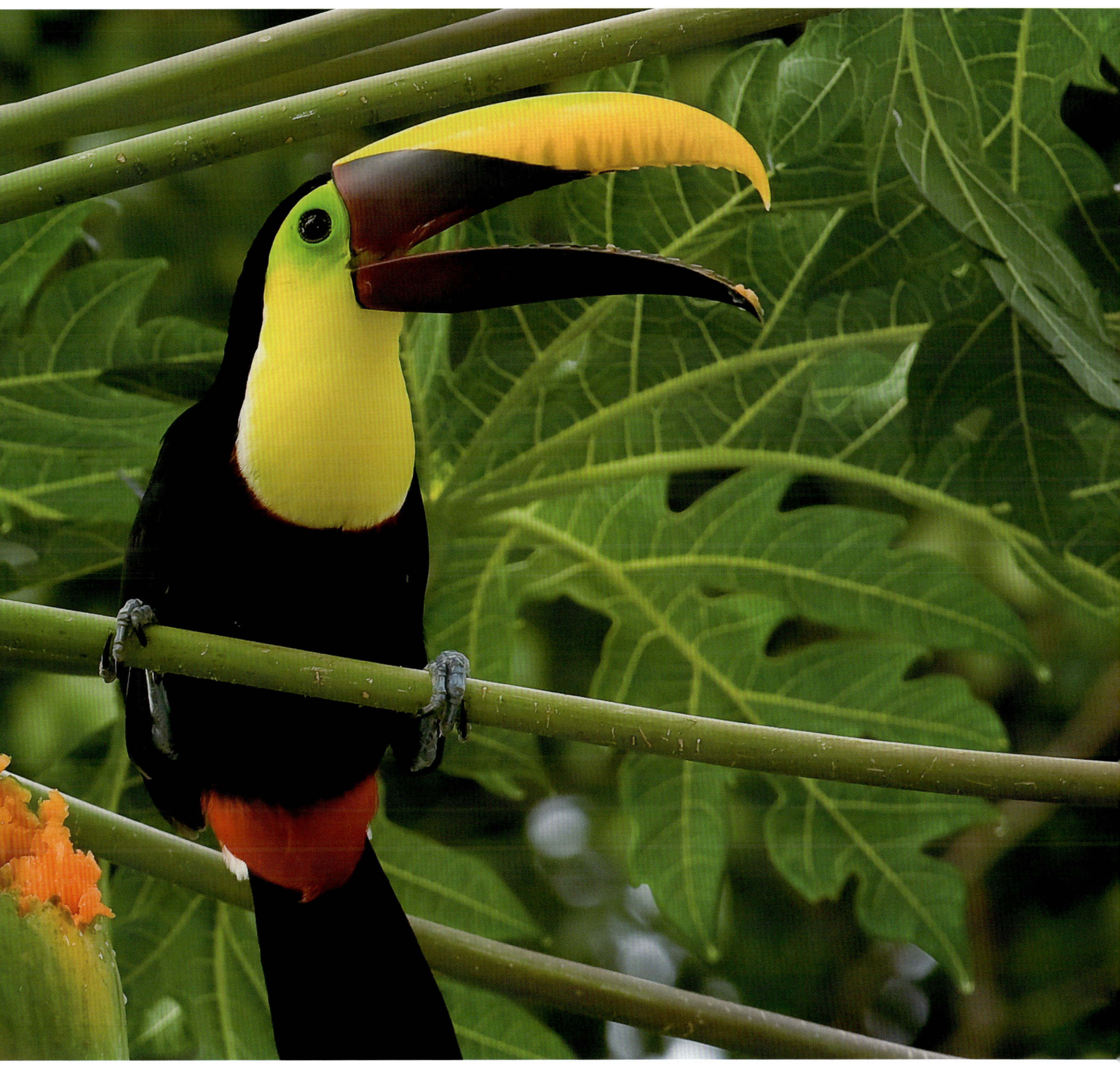

DESEMBARCO DEL GRANMA NATIONAL PARK

Date of inscription: 1999

These singular limestone formations, arranged like terraces at the edge of the Sierra Maestra, provide an important habitat for many rare land and marine species.

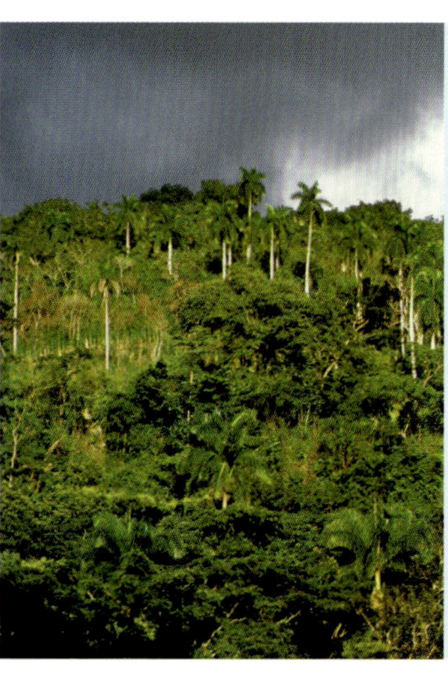

The national park was named after the yacht on which Fidel Castro, Che Guevara, and 81 companions made landfall at Las Coloradas in Cuba to overthrow the Batista dictatorship in 1956. This unique coastal karst landscape of caves and canyons, surrounding Cabo Cruz, is one of the best-preserved of its kind in the world. It consists of limestone terraces, rising up to 360 m above sea level and continue beneath the surface. The total protected surface area amounts to 400 sq. km and lies at the still active convergence of the Caribbean and North American continental plates. More than 500 plant species have been recorded so far, of which some 60 percent are unique. The animal world is equally diverse. A series of caves, used by the pre-Columbian Taino people for ritual purposes, are of cultural and historical interest.

The Cuban Revolution took its course when the yacht "Granma" arrived at this coast (left). The protection of the area is necessary because of obvious weathering processes. In the water, among others, live the fascinating manatees (large picture).

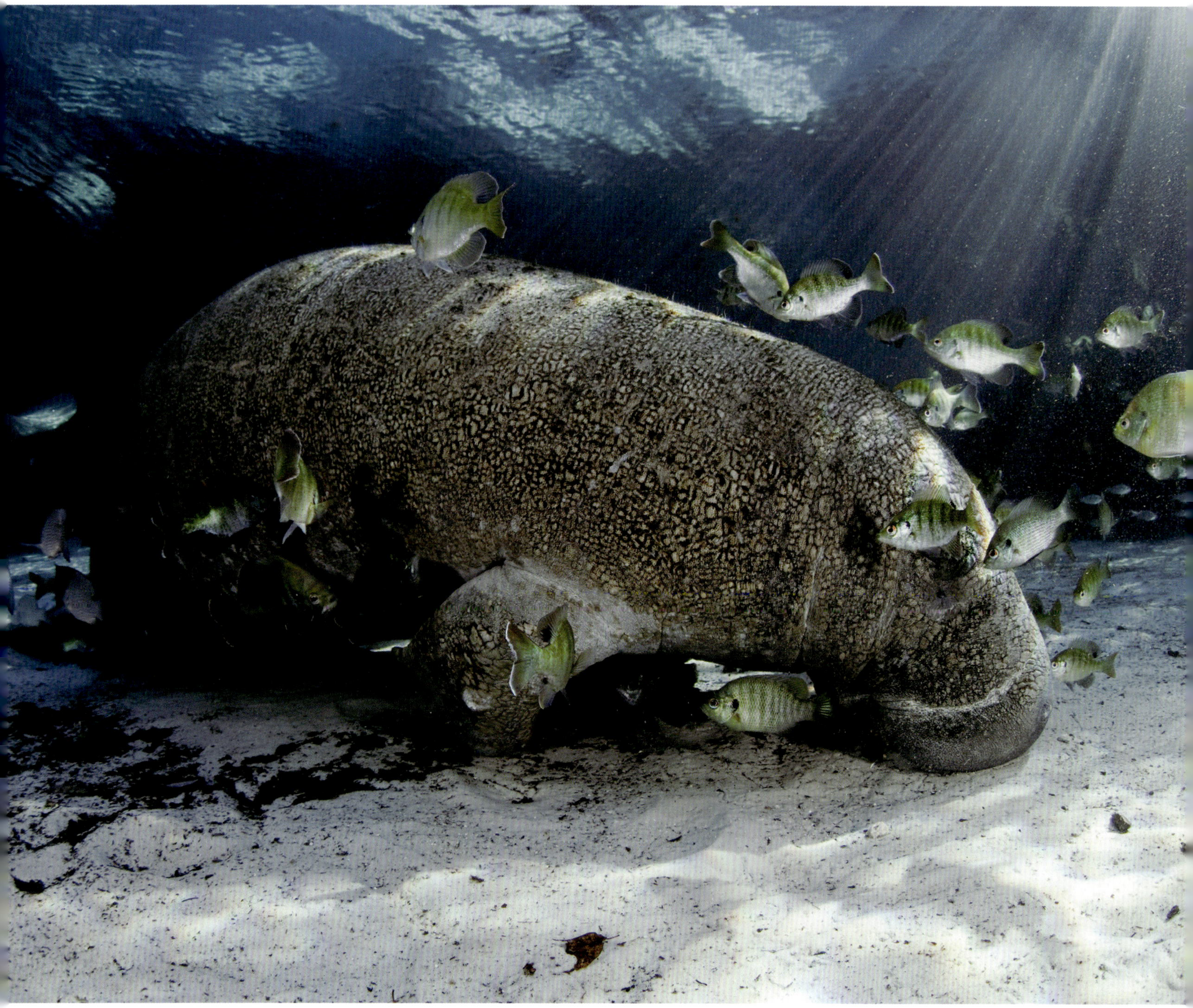

ALEJANDRO DE HUMBOLDT NATIONAL PARK

This national park, situated to the north-west of the eponymous town in the Alturas de Baracoa mountains, is largely given over for use as a biosphere reserve. Its 700 sq. km (270 sq. miles), of which 20 sq. km (8 sq. miles) are marine, boast a particularly rich diversity of ecosystems: a coastal region of coral reefs and mangroves, housing a reasonably large population of otherwise endangered manatees; wetland forests; and a mountainous region surrounding the 1,168-m (3,830-foot) high El Toldo, with its considerable stands of the endemic Cuban pine, one of more than 400 species found exclusively here, the "Noah's Ark of the Caribbean." These statistics better those of previous "centers of endemism," such as the Galápagos Islands, by several orders of magnitude. The national park was named after the famous German explorer Alexander von Humboldt, who spent a total of four and a half months in Cuba between 1801 and 1804.

The Cuban amazon (large picture) and the bee hummingbird (right) occur only here. The latter is regarded as the smallest hummingbird in the world.

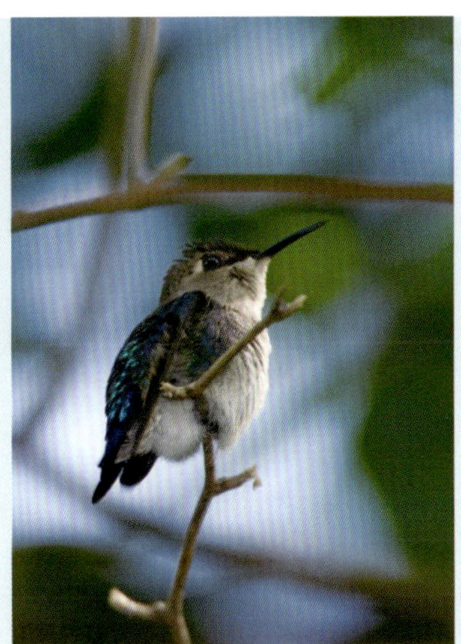

Date of inscription: 2001

The relatively undeveloped eastern side of Cuba still retains fantastic natural landscapes. These – such as in the Alejandro de Humboldt National Park – represent probably the last refuge for many of the island's unique species.

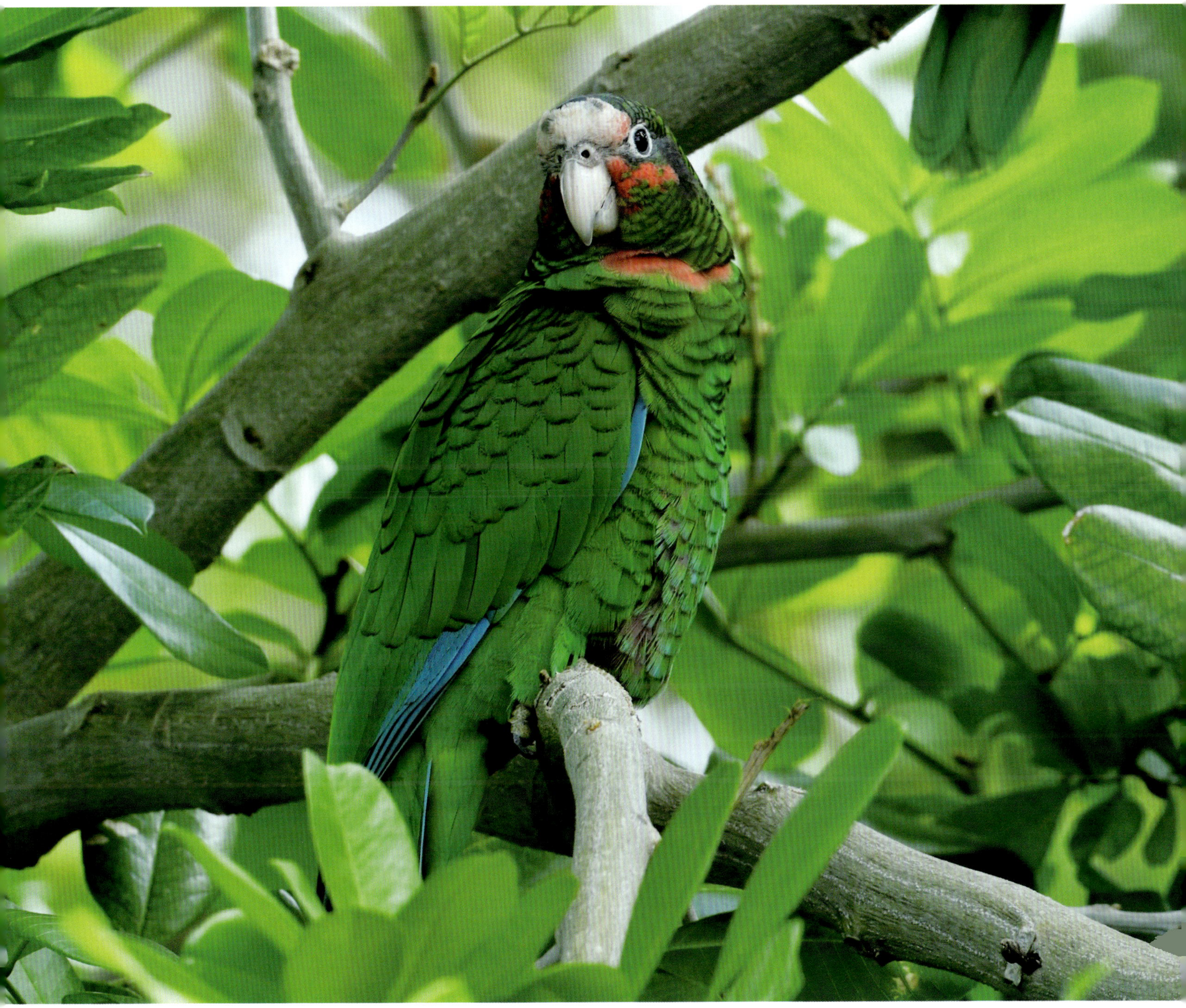

BLUE AND JOHN CROW MOUNTAINS

Date of inscription: 2015

Jamaica was inscribed for the first time in the list of World Heritage sites with its Cultural and Natural site, Blue and John Crow Mountains. Aside from the lush mountain rainforests, harbouring a fantastic flora and fauna, the heritage of the Maroon people (Black Africans who were enslaved in Jamaica as plantation workers) is now under the protection of UNESCO.

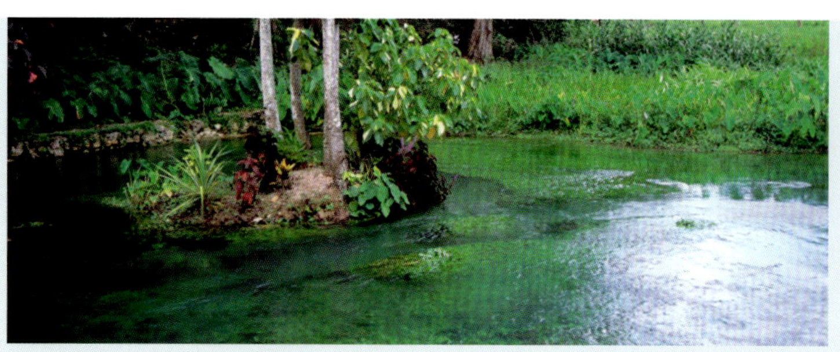

The Blue Mountains are the highest mountain chain in Jamaica, featuring peaks of more than 2,200 m (7,218 feet). Together with the adjoining John Crow Mountains, they form the largest national park in the country, which covers approximately one-fifth of the entire landmass of the Caribbean island. Thanks to the unusually high number of endemic species living here, the Blue Mountains are one of the global hotspots of biodiversity. In the tropical mountain rainforest flourish rare tree species, mosses, ferns, bromeliads and orchids. Many amphibian, bird and mammal species, which are endangered elsewhere in the world, also live here. The WWF regards the Blue Mountains as one of the "Global 200 Priority Ecoregions" – the biologically most valuable habitats on Earth. Yet the Blue Mountains are also of great importance in cultural terms: They are closely linked with the history of the Maroon people and their freedom fight against slavery. The Maroons organized their resistance again the British colonial forces in the inaccessible mountain forests.

A blue mist covers the mountain chains, especially at dawn and dusk (large picture). Cold Spring (top) is home to beautiful gardens.

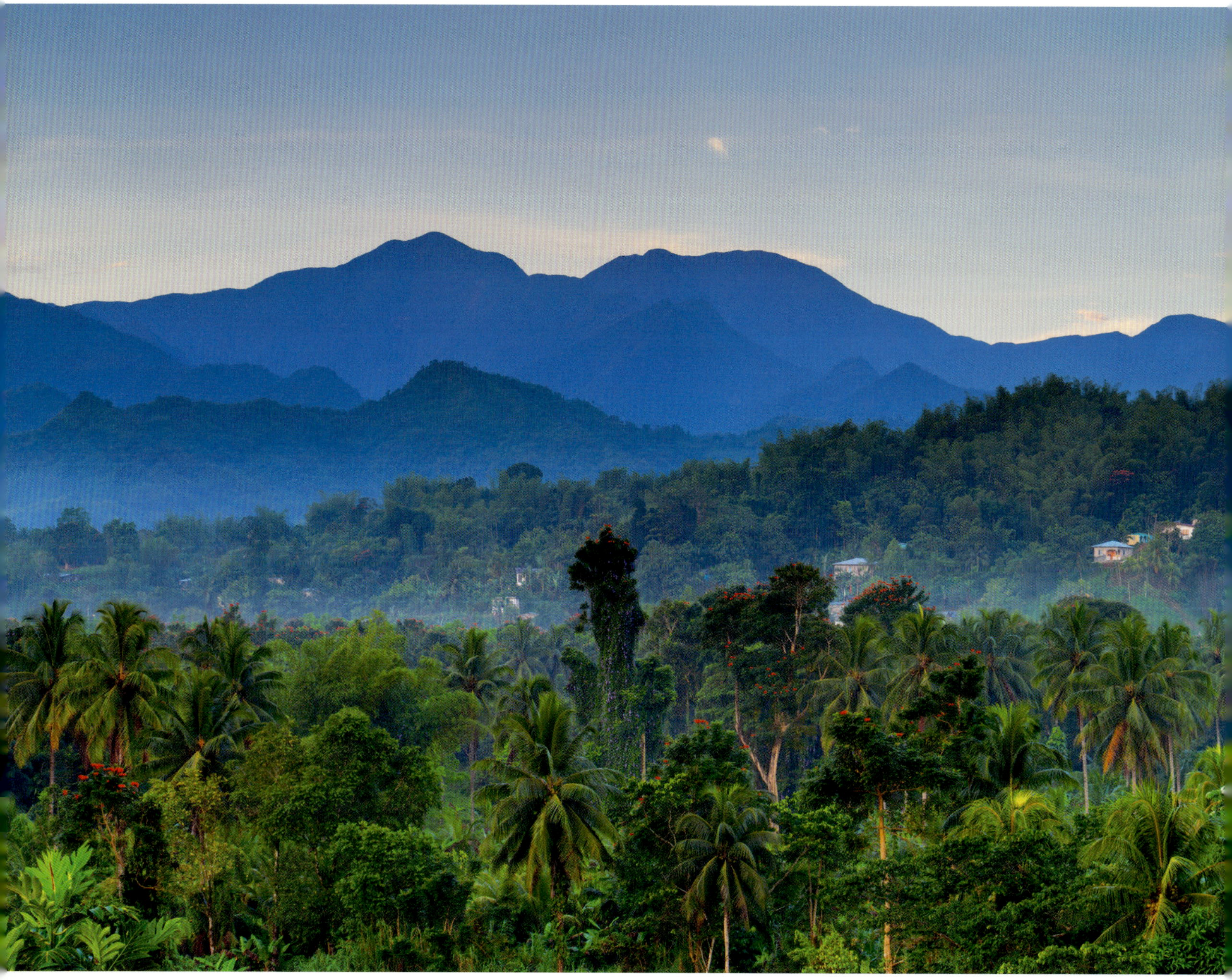

MORNE TROIS PITONS NATIONAL PARK

The Morne Trois Pitons National Park was established in 1975, and the rain and cloud forests, lakes and waterfalls on its 70 sq. km (27 sq. miles) provide a habitat for a variety of animal and plant life. 21 plant species have been recorded in the national park which only exist in this ecological niche Some 150 bird species inhabit the forests, among them a species of parrots that is critically endangered. The various volcanic phenomena observable in the vicinity of the still active Morne Trois Pitons volcano are of breathtaking beauty; there are hot springs, around 50 fumaroles, and five active volcanic craters in between rugged rocks and heavily vegetated ravines. Hot mud bubbles in a boiling lake, and the aptly named "Emerald Pool" owes its extraordinary coloration to elemental processes taking place in the bowels of the earth. Due to its volcanic features the national park is of great scientific interest and the perfect area to study active geomorphological processes.

Fumaroles, such as these in the Valley of Desolation, betray the volcanic origins of the Morne Trois Pitons National Park landscape. The other predominant element is water, in the form of lakes and waterfalls, as here at the Trafalgar Falls in the Roseau valley (below).

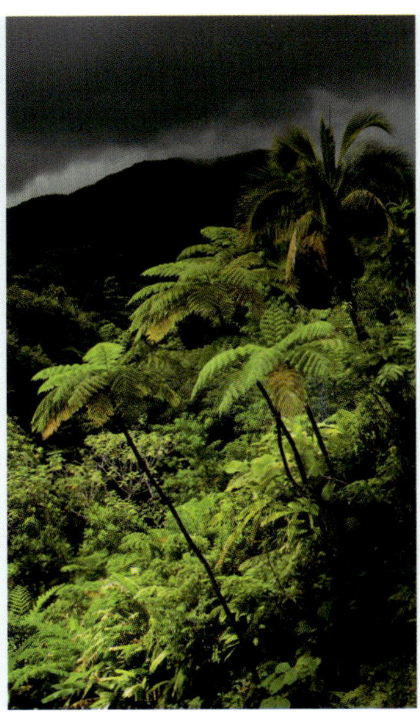

Date of inscription: 1997

Morne Trois Pitons Park in Dominica, lying at the foot of the 1,342-m (4,400-foot) high mountain after which it is named, has enchantingly diverse tropical forests and all kinds of volcanic phenomena.

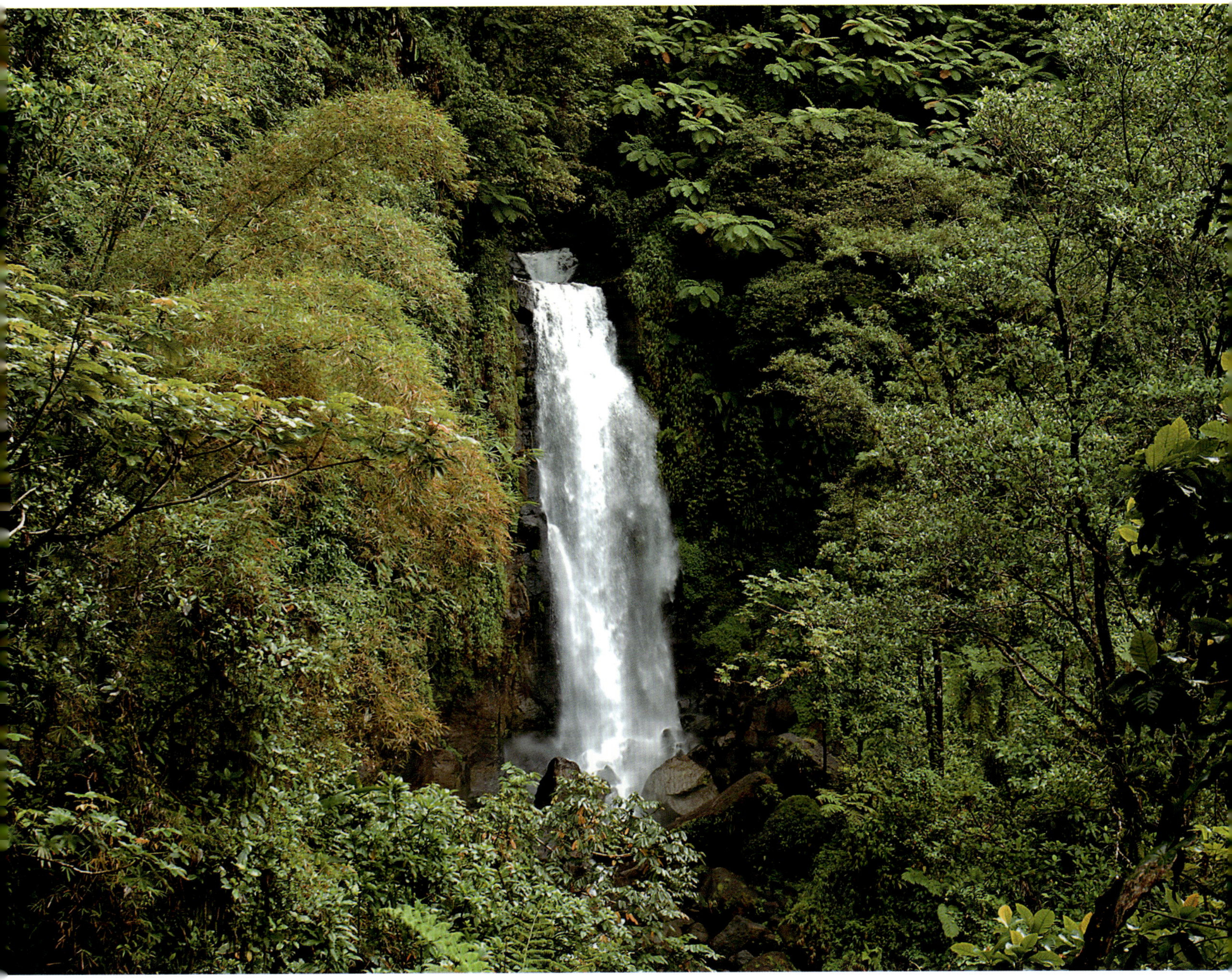

PITONS NATURE RESERVE

Date of inscription: 2004

Rising from the sea and connected by a ridge, these two domed volcanic peaks on the Caribbean island of St Lucia, both above 700 m (2,300 feet), are known as the Pitons.

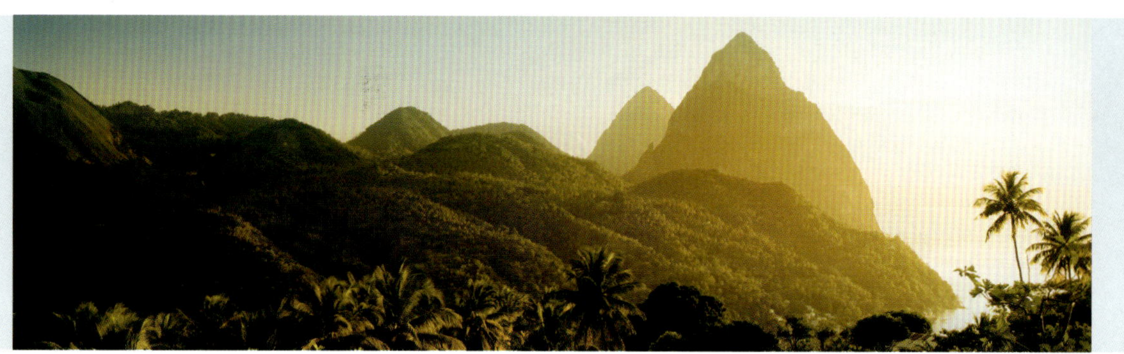

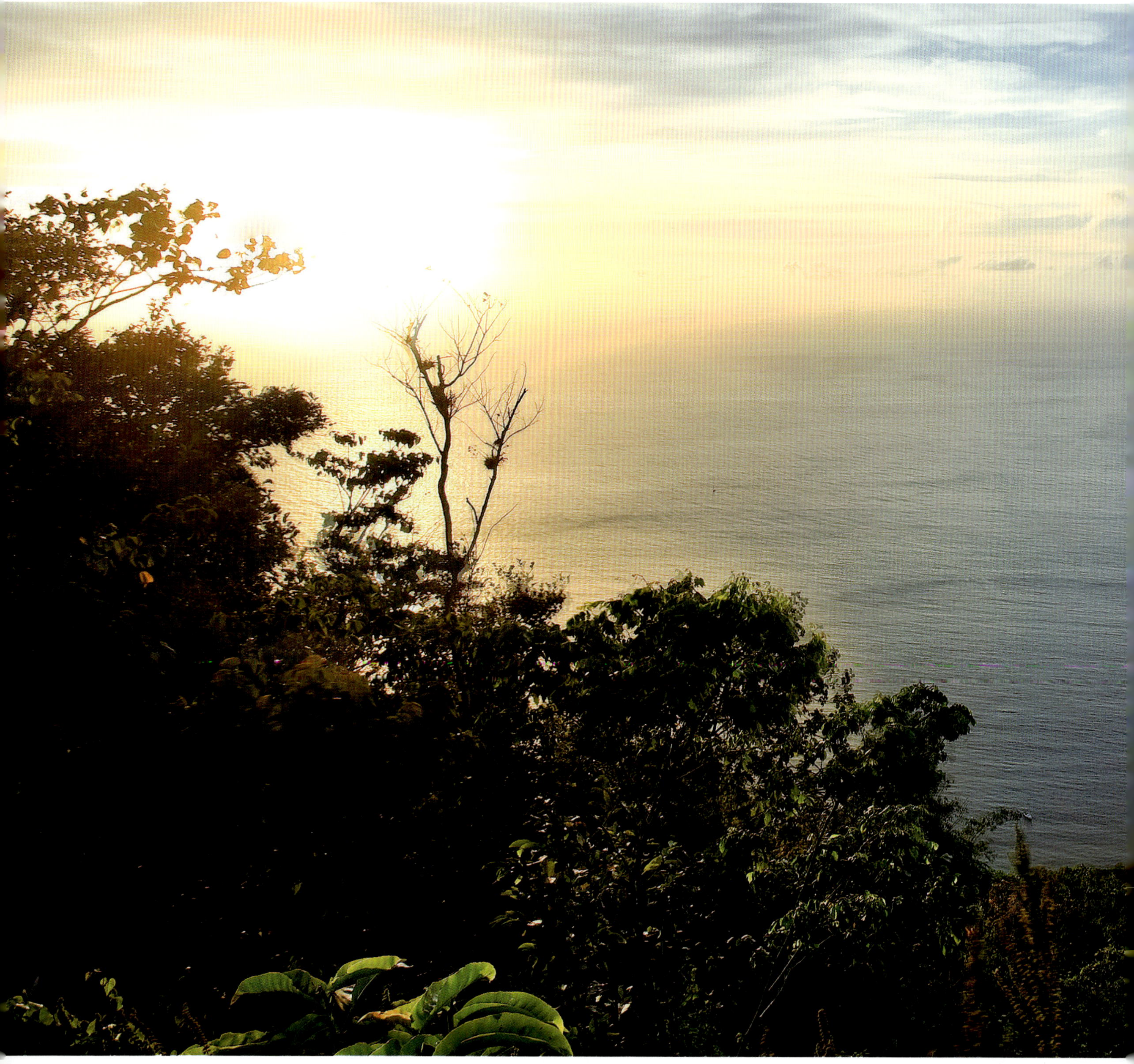

The World Heritage Site includes an area of 30 sq. km (12 sq. miles) at the south-western end of the island, near Soufrière. This is composed of the peaks of Gros Piton (770 m, 2,525 feet) and Petit Piton (743 m, 2,440 feet), the mountain ridge connecting these, a Solfatara field of fumaroles and hot springs, and the adjoining areas of ocean. Up to 60 percent of the underwater region was once covered with coral, but in 1999 Hurricane Lenny destroyed much of this. The establishment of no-fishing zones has given the area some relief, and the waters around the Pitons are now among the most richly stocked in the Caribbean. The different species recorded include 170 fish, 60 jellyfish, 14 sponges, 11 echinoderms, 15 arthropods, and eight annelids.

The predominant vegetation on the mainland is tropical rainforest, with small areas of tropical dry forest. Gros Piton is home to 150 recorded plant species, and Petit Piton about a hundred. Some 30 bird species are also to be found here, of which five are endemic.

The domed double peaks of the Gros and Petit Pitons are an easily visible landmark in the Lesser Antilles. In geological terms, the two peaks are extinct volcanoes.

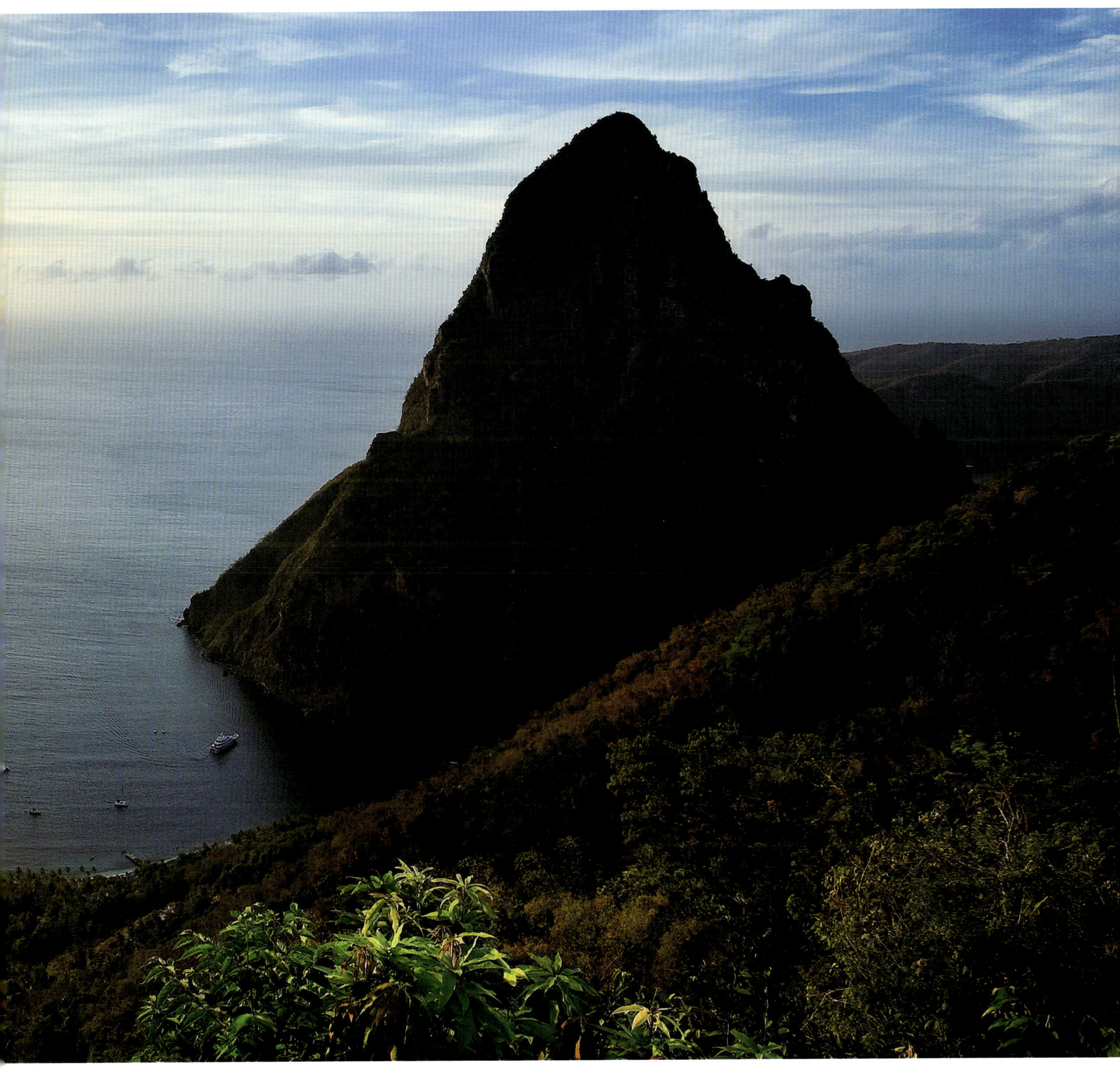

The protected Canaima National Park is located in the south-east of Venezuela. A highlight of the park is the spectacular Salto Ángel, or Angel Falls (large picture). Recognized as the tallest free-falling waterfall in the world, it was named after its (second) discoverer, Jimmie Angel. Guanacas (right), members of the family of camelids, live on the South American plateau.

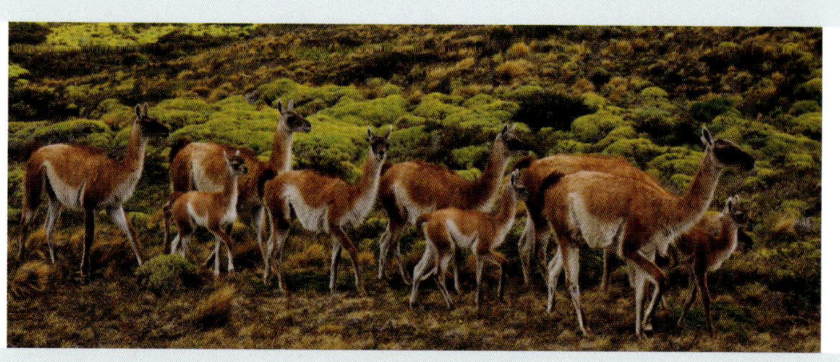

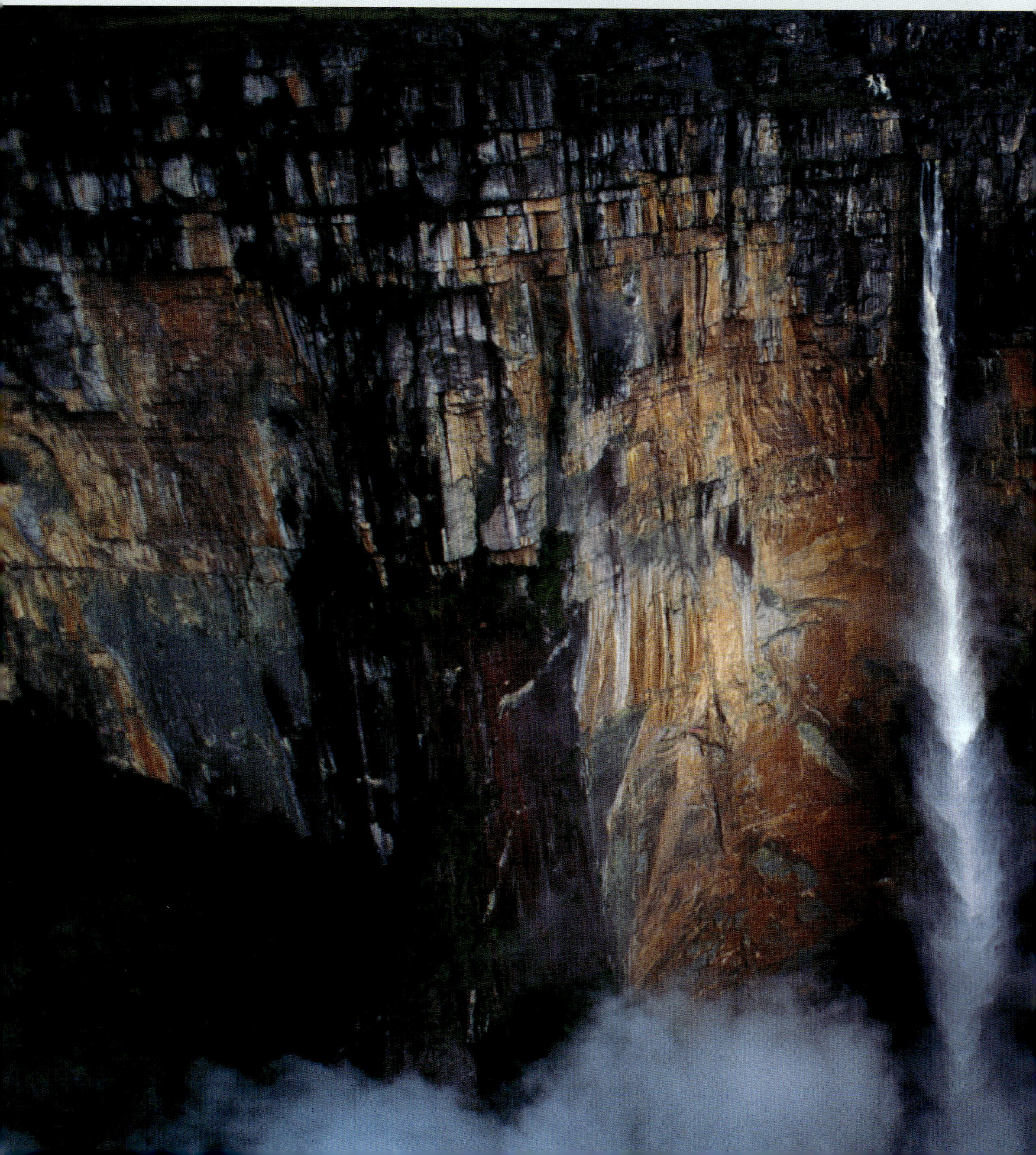

SOUTH AMERICA

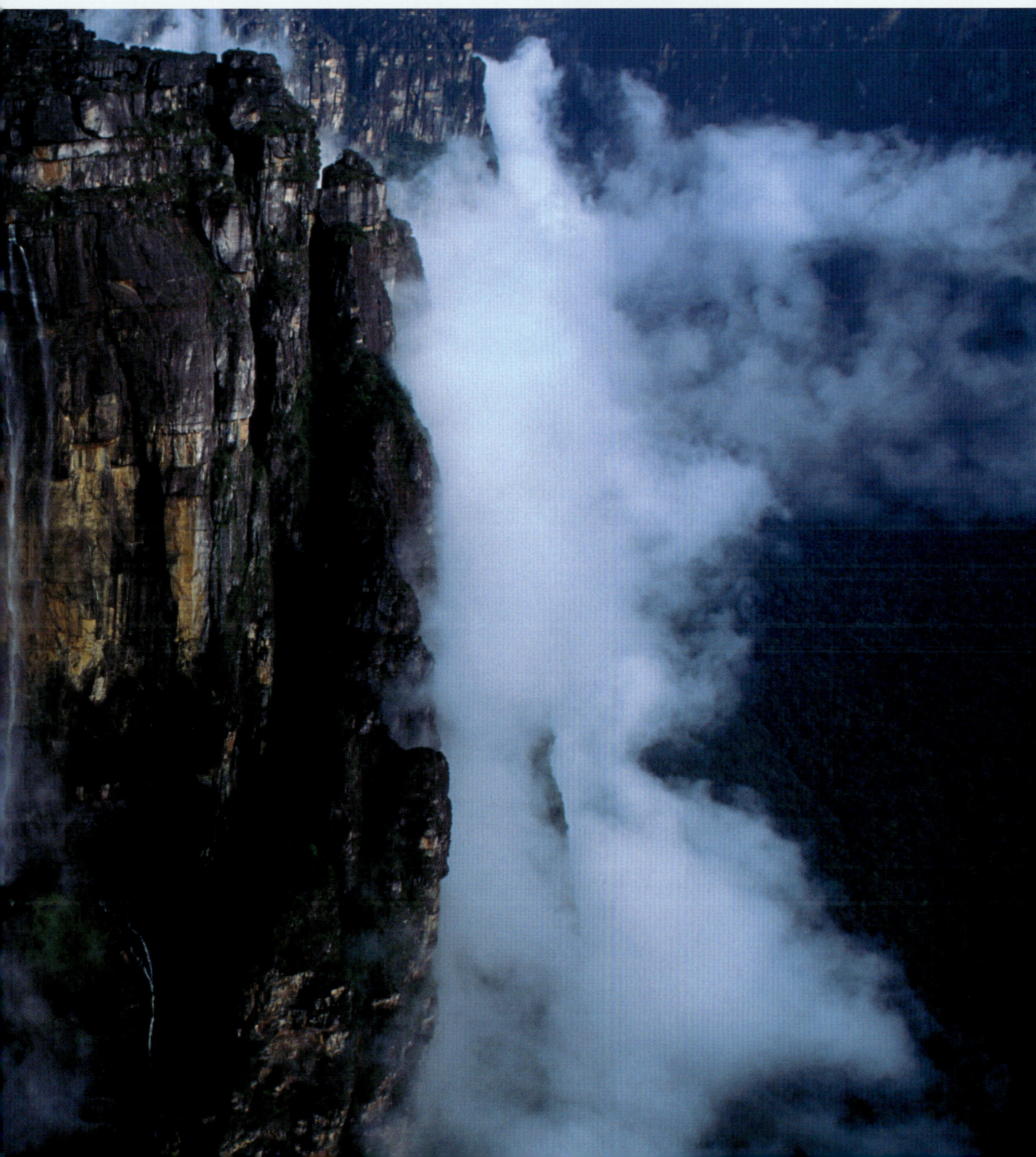

LOS KATÍOS NATIONAL PARK

Date of inscription: 1994

The national park in north-western Columbia, on the Panamanian border, is composed of low hills, rainforest, and swamps. This remote region provides a protected habitat for endangered species and numerous endemic plants.

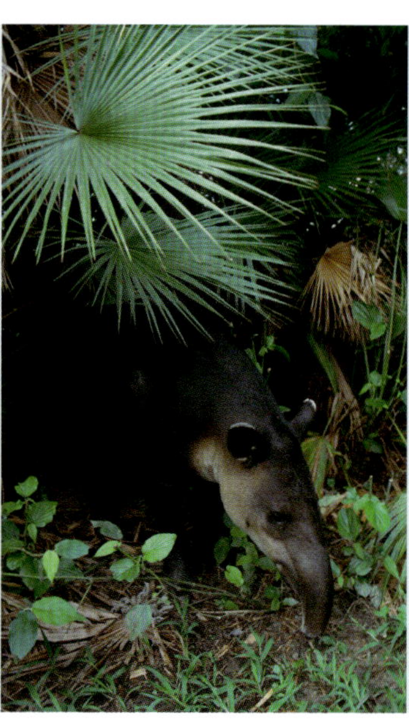

The national park has a total surface area of 720 sq. km (280 sq. miles), of which the eastern section encloses large parts of the swampy area surrounding the mouth of the Atrato river at the Gulf of Darién. The western sec-tion includes the jagged hill chain of the Serranía del Darién, a spur of the Western Andes Cordillera. Due to the high annual precipitation, which averages 3,000 mm (120 inches), extensive areas of swamp and rainforest have been able to evolve, and a variety of valuable timber grows here, such as balsa wood and rubber trees.

The inaccessibility of this primary forest has assured the survival of its varied plant life, much of which is endemic. It has also benefited the animal life; the forest is home to big cats, such as pumas and jaguars, but also to giant anteaters, tapirs, sloths, and various species of monkeys, including howlers, capuchins, and brown woolly monkeys. There are also animals that otherwise only occur in Central America, such as the turkey-like gray-headed chachalaca.

The grey-headed chachalacas (large picture) are approximately 50-cm- (20-inch-) tall birds, which assemble in the treetops in small flocks. The Central American tapir (left) is a relatively large member of the tapir species.

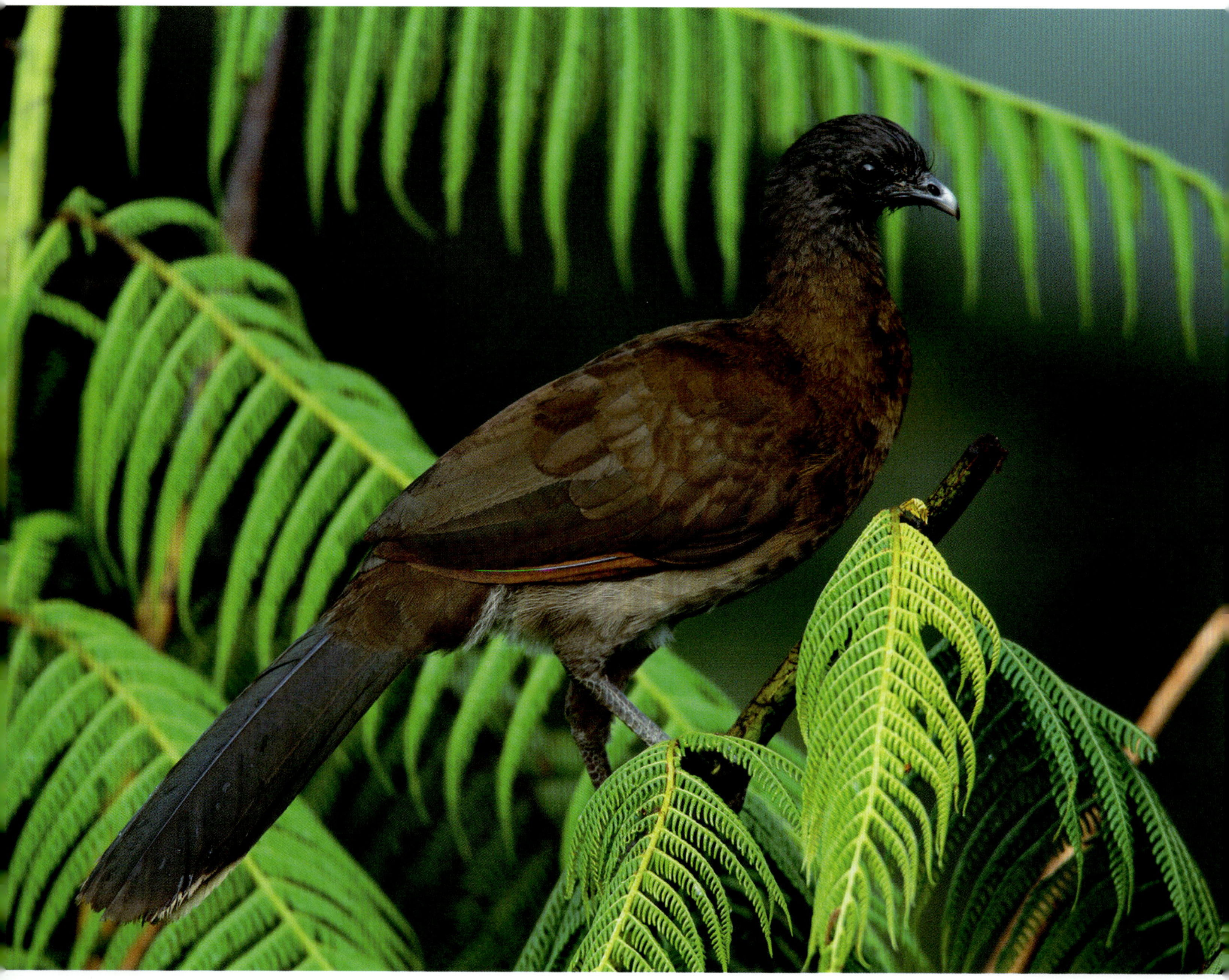

MALPELO NATURE RESERVE

The island of Malpelo, measuring only 3.5 km across, lies in the Pacific, 500 km off the Columbian coast. Malpelo is part of a marine corridor connecting a series of World Heritage Sites, including the Galápagos Island (Ecuador), Coiba (Panama), and Cocos Island (Costa Rica). The island is the tip of the Malpelo ridge, and the seabed surrounding it can reach a depth of 3,400 m. Due to its varied underwater landscape of high cliffs and vertiginous drops, deep canyons and caves, the waters around Malpelo are a popular spot for divers. The confluence of several ocean currents and the nature of the seabed here have conspired to create an exceptionally complex and rich ecosystem. The waters are a breeding ground for many marine animals. Shark species are especially numerous. In addition, there are eagle and manta rays, seahorses, tuna, barracuda, bonitos, and snappers. The park is also a refuge for sea turtles and endemic starfish. The island is a breeding ground for numerous seabirds, including swallow-tailed gulls and Galapagos petrels. The world's largest colony of masked booby, with over 40,000 specimens, is also notable.

Around 200 species of fish live in this underwater world, including the cheeky blennies (right) and lots of snapper shoals (below).

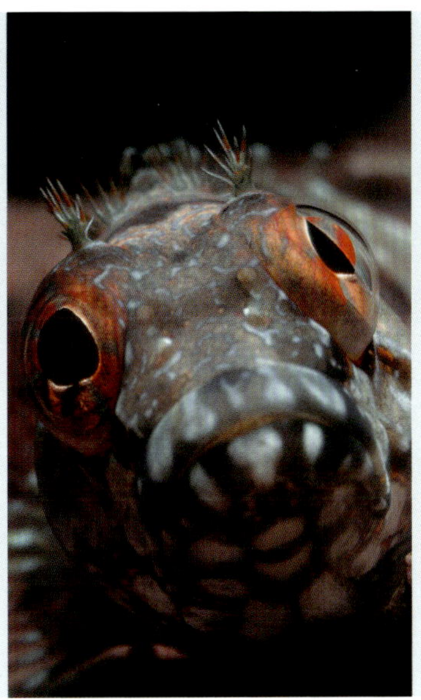

Date of inscription: 2006

This reserve in the tropical East Pacific, which includes the remote island of Malpelo and approximately 8,500 sq. km (3,200 sq. miles) of protected ocean, is home to numerous endangered marine animals.

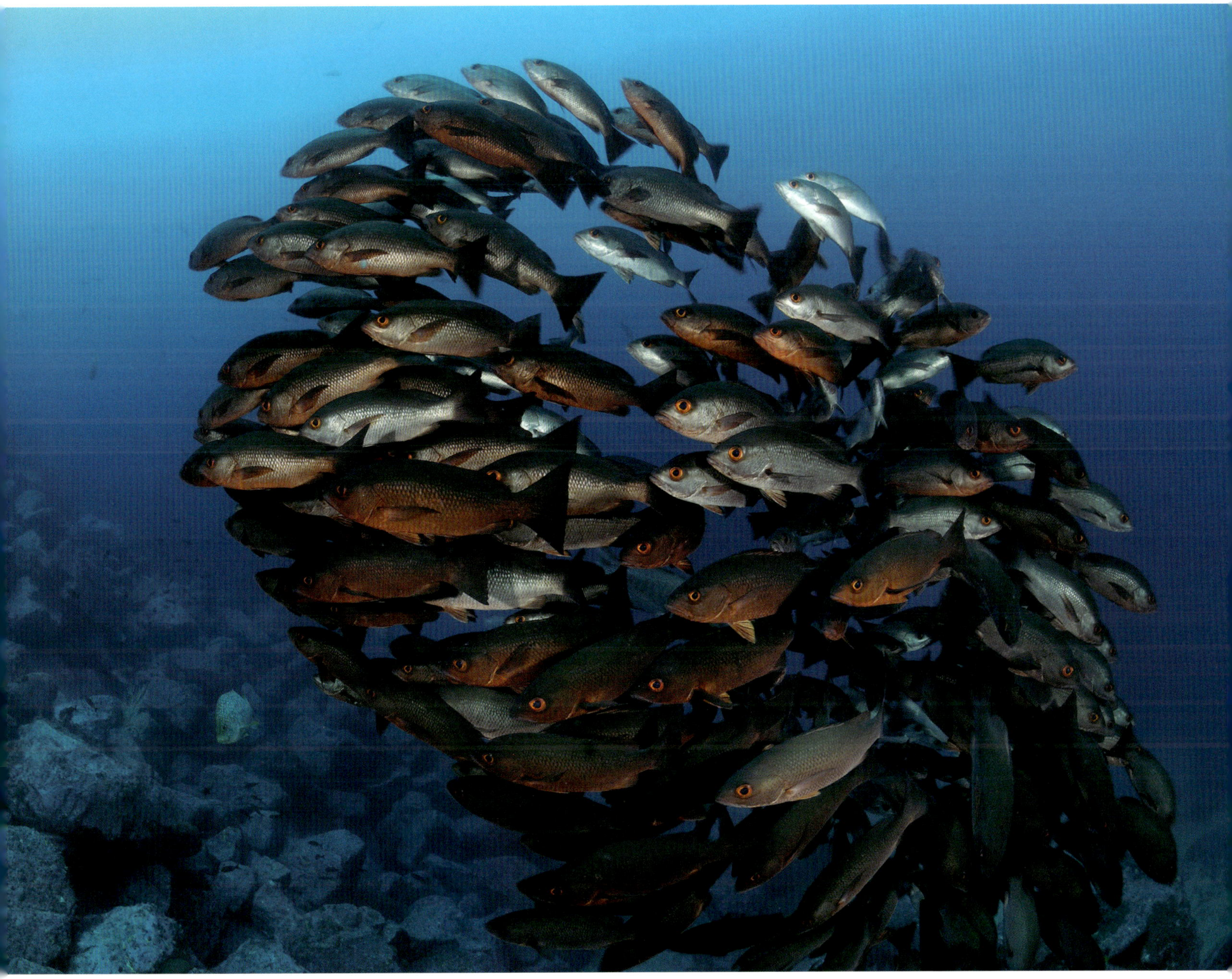

GALÁPAGOS ISLANDS NATIONAL PARK

Date of inscription: 1978
Extended: 2001

The volcanic islands of the Galápagos archipelago present a uniquely living picture of evolution as a result of their isolated situation.

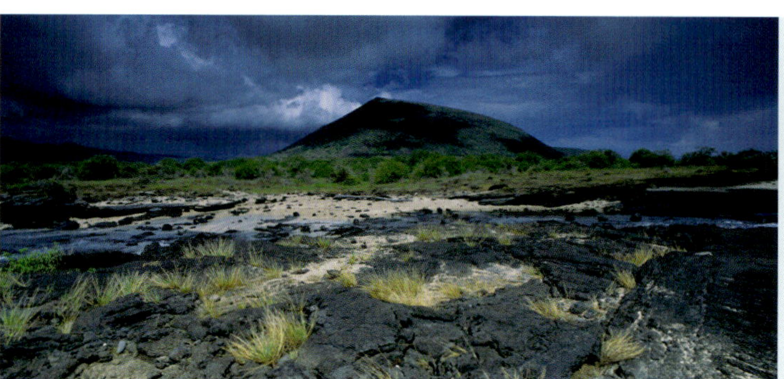

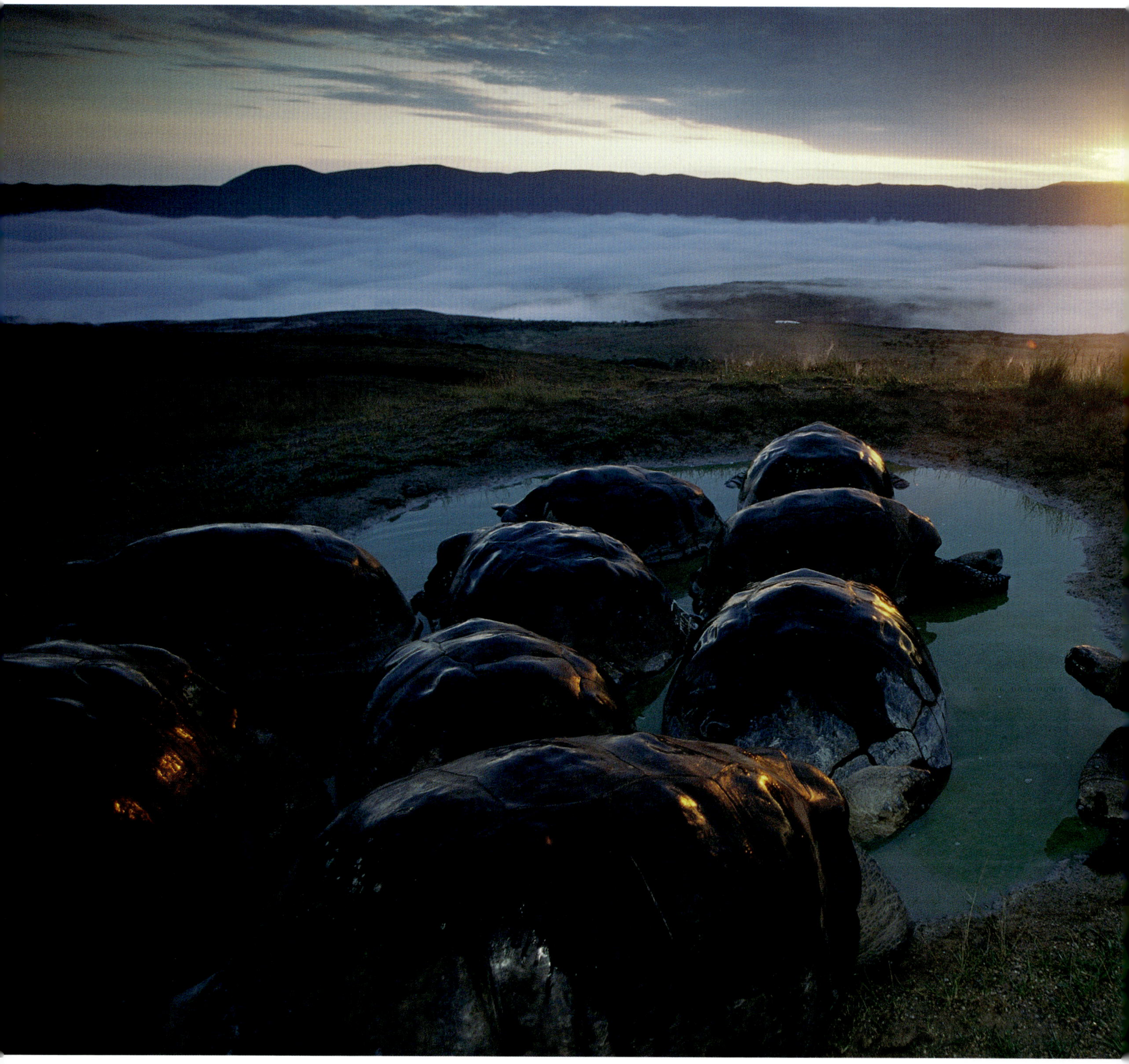

About 1,000 km off the west coast of Ecuador, in the middle of the Pacific, there is a hotspot where molten magma is forced out of the earth's interior to the surface, and a spectacular archipelago of twelve large and over a hundred smaller volcanic islands has arisen. The oldest islands arose 2.4 to 3 million years ago. The archipelago is affected by three great ocean currents, including the cold Humboldt Current, bringing water from the icy polar regions. These ocean currents brought life to the Galápagos from tropical and subtropical regions of Central and South America, and also from the Indo-Pacific Ocean, turning the islands into a crucible of the most diverse species. Their geographical remoteness offered plant and animal life ideal conditions for independent evolution. Charles Darwin's visit in 1835 brought international fame to the islands. His observations of species of finch that were almost identical, yet had developed different shapes of beak depending on the environment of the islands on which they lived, led Darwin to important conclusions in the development of his theory of evolution. The Galápagos Archipelago is a paradise for reptiles and birds, although few mammals have found their way here. Most of the animal life on the islands is endemic. Among the more spectacular residents are the flightless cormorant, the Galápagos land iguana, the marine iguana, and the Galápagos giant tortoise. The national park comprises 90 percent of the Galápagos islands' surface area and an area of protected ocean.

A living archive of evolutionary history: the Galápagos giant tortoises (large picture); a Darwin's finch sucking nectar from a cactus flower; a Galápagos land iguana, which is endemic here; and red rock crabs (picture series from the top). Left: the popular Isla de San Salva.

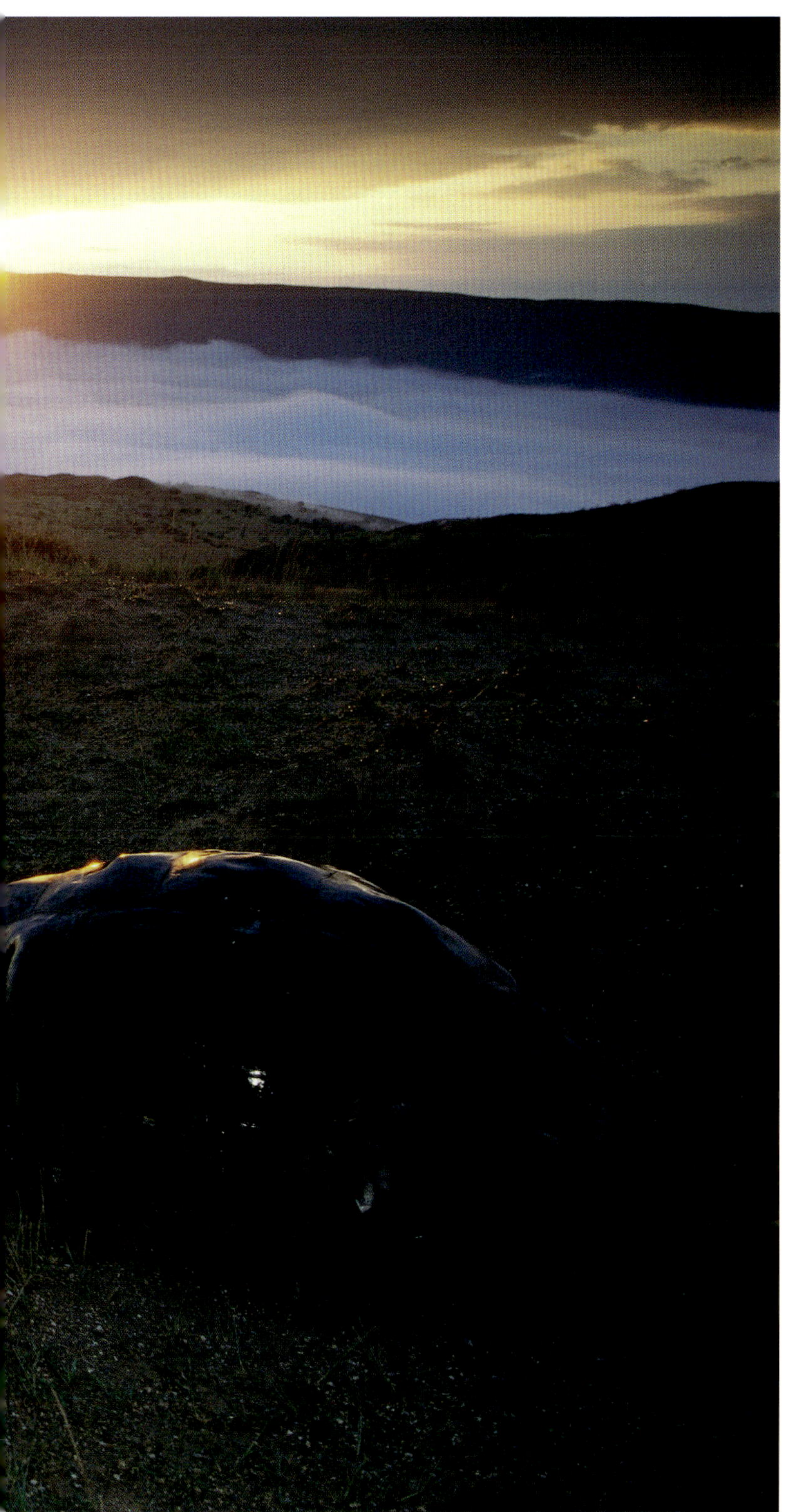

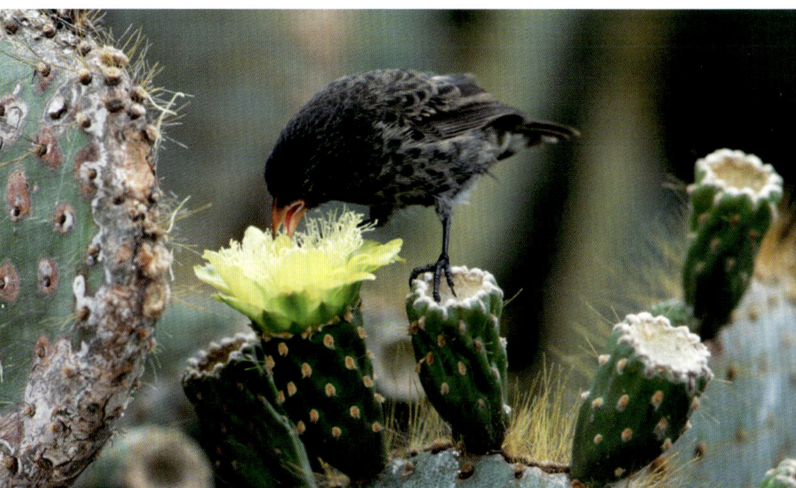

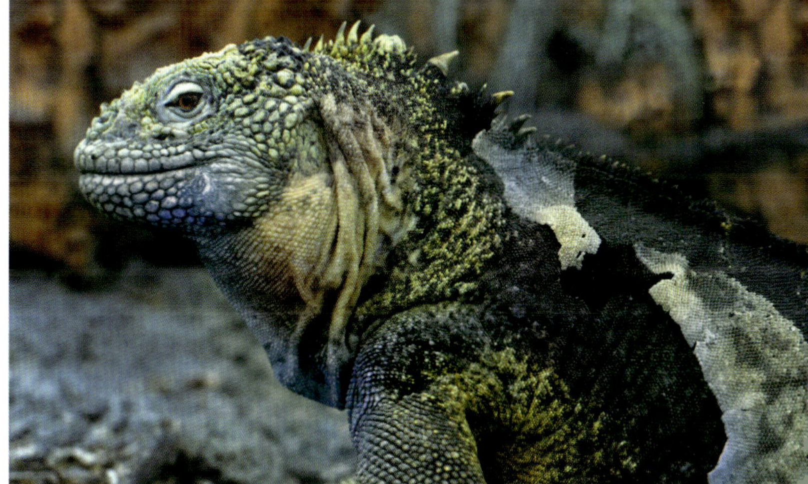

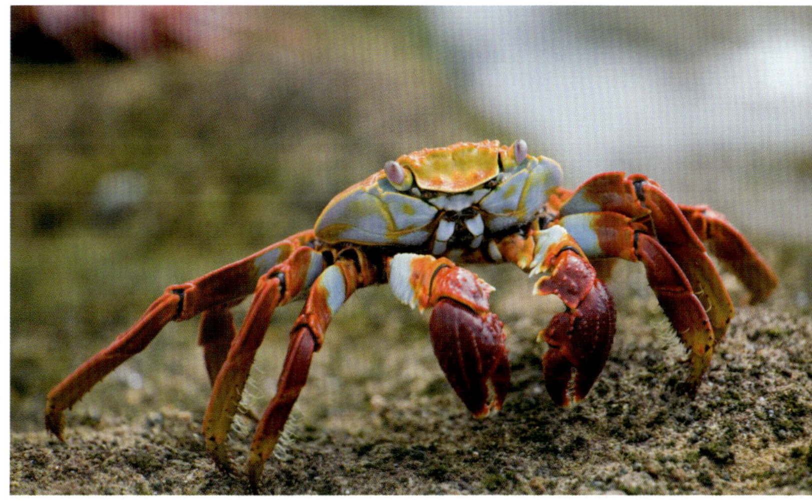

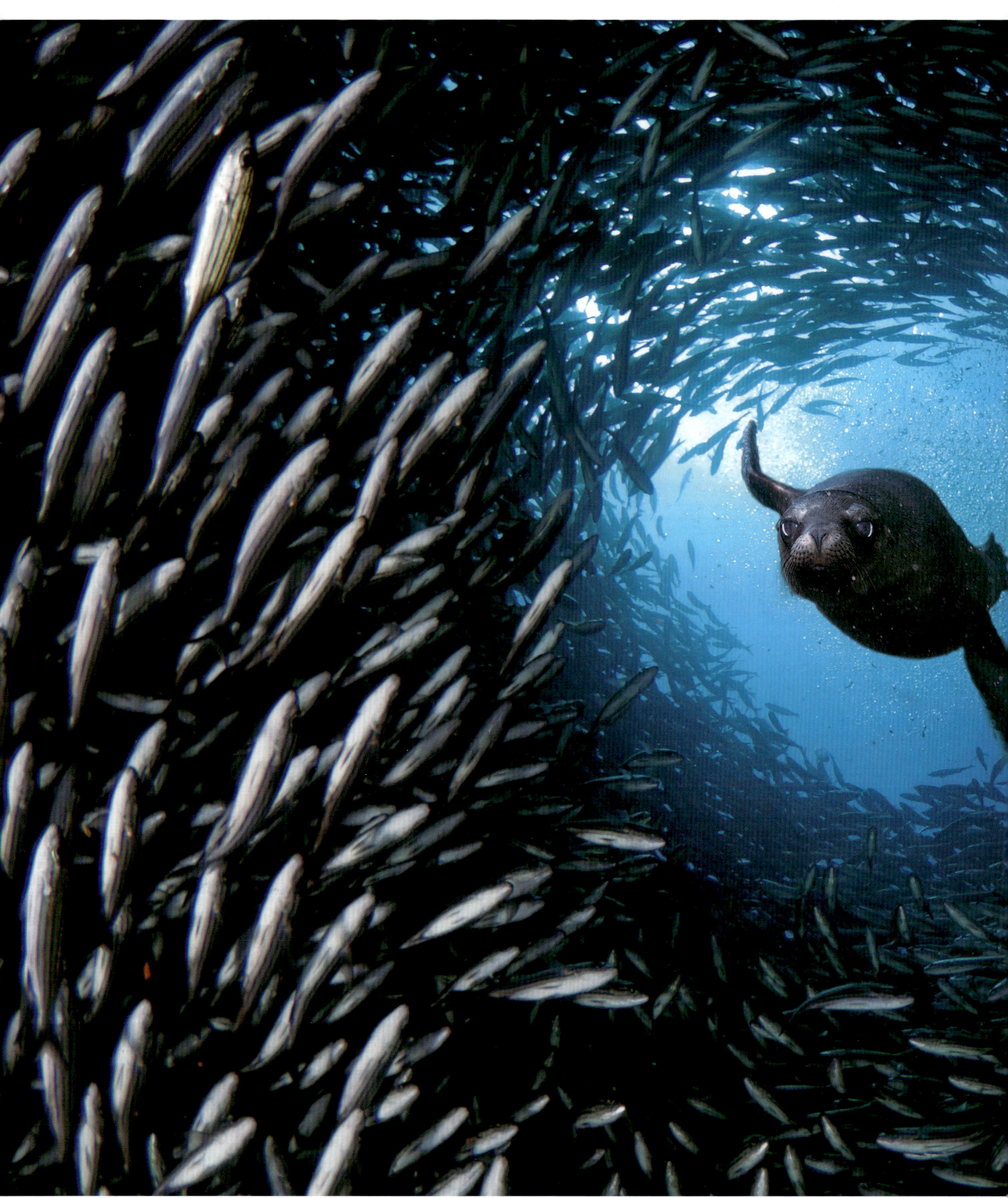

The Galápagos sea lion is another animal endemic to the islands, although it has similarities with other species of sea lion. It stays primarily on the beaches, but is also considered a very skillful swimmer. Sea lions go in search of food in the water and only in daytime; their diet may include small fish like these black-striped salema.

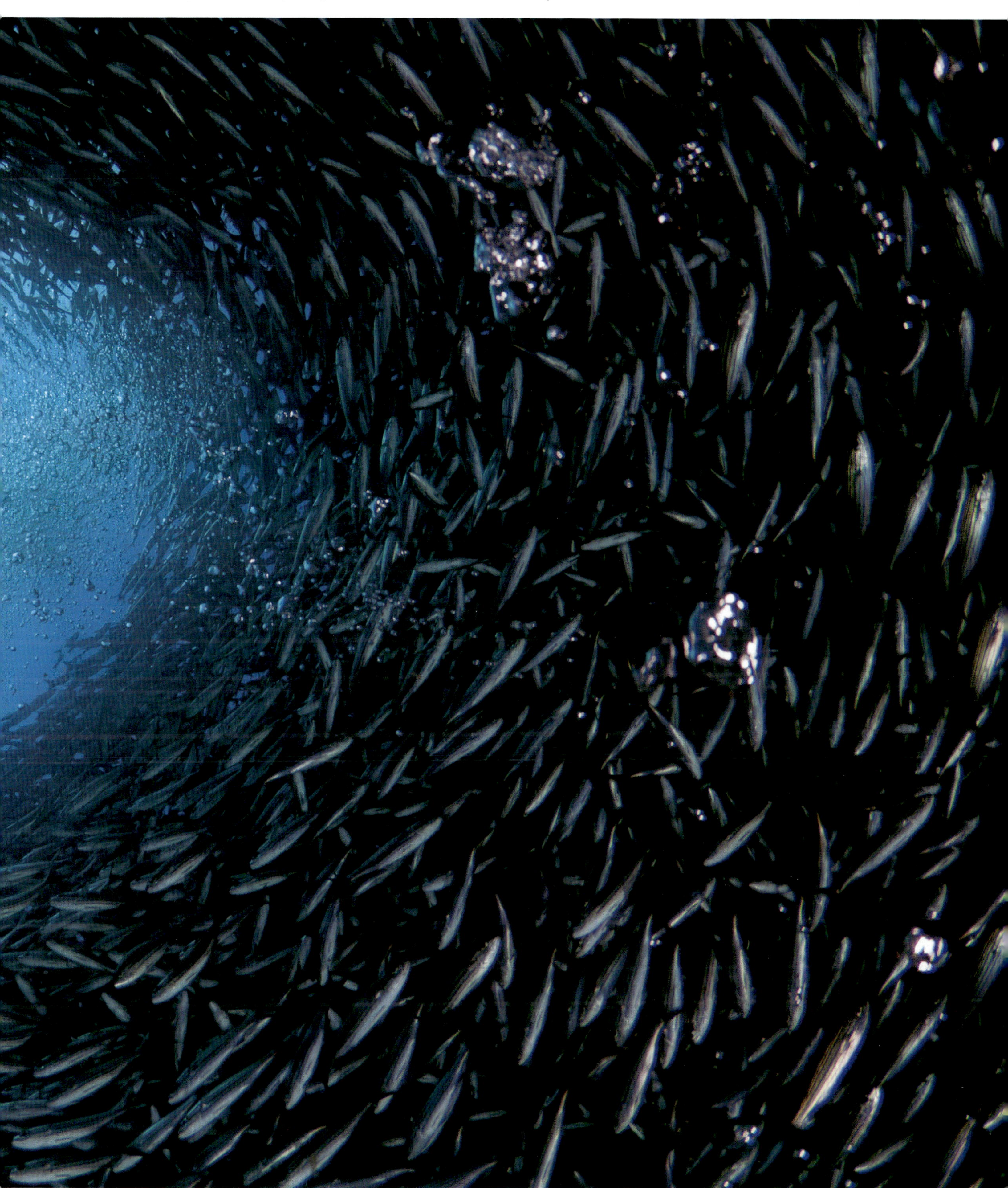

SANGAY NATIONAL PARK

Date of inscription: 1983

Sangay National Park is situated in the middle of the Ecuadorian Andes. Two still-active volcanoes add to the particular charm of the landscape, which is a habitat for rare plant and animal life.

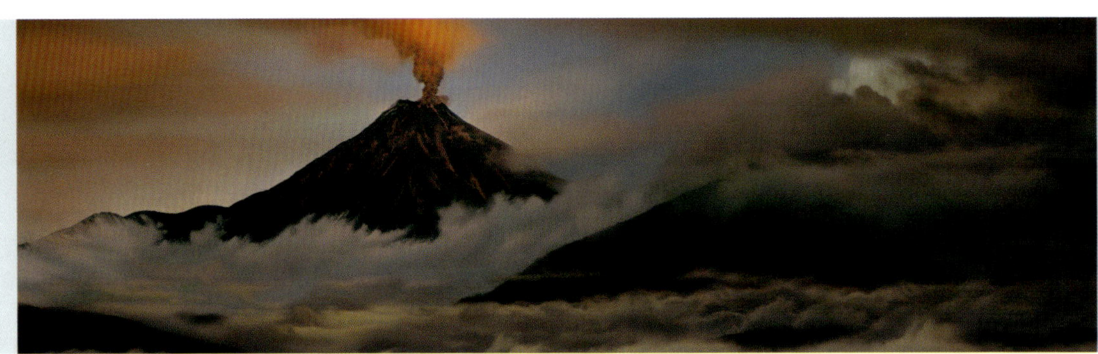

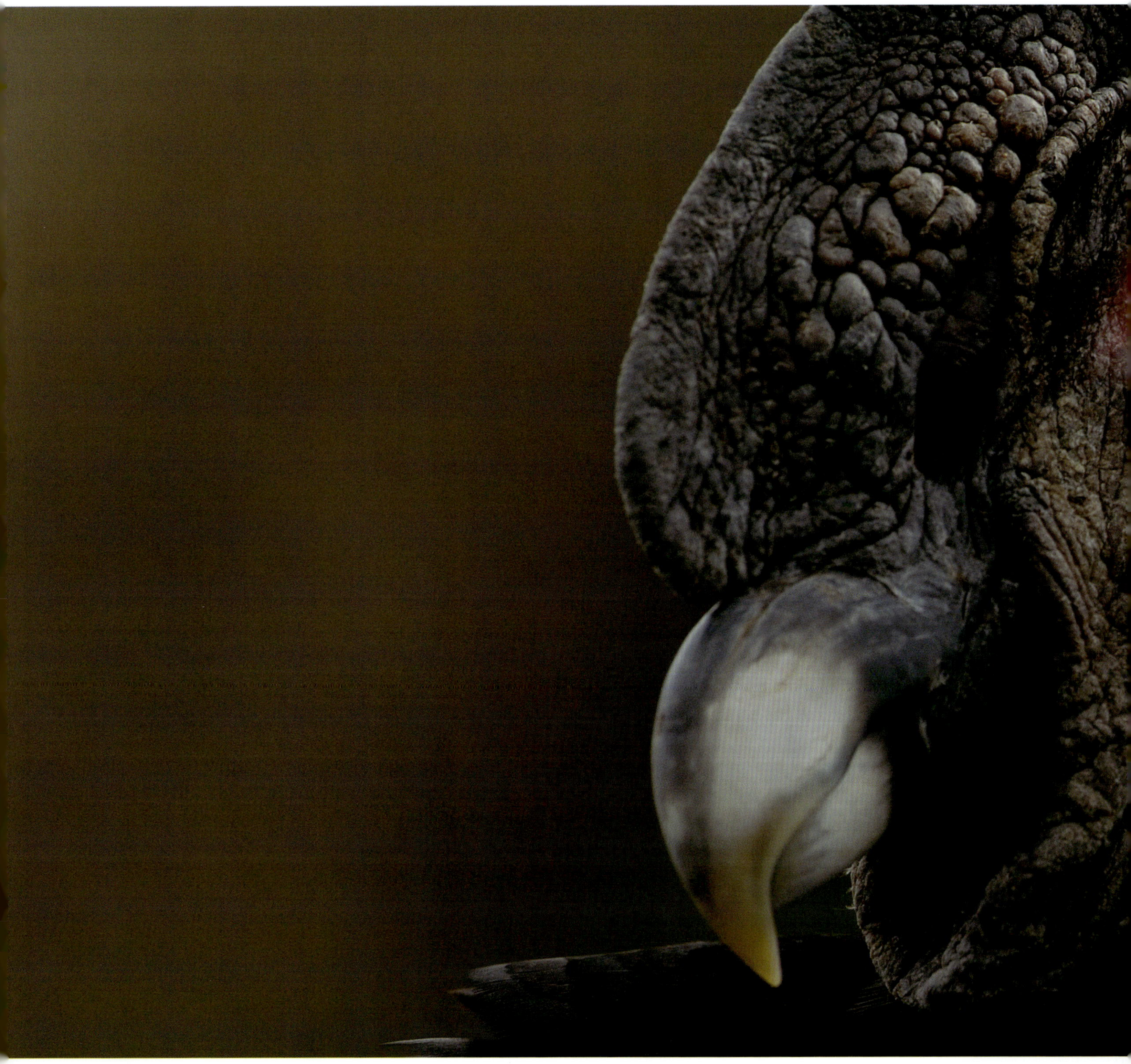

Barely accessible, the Sangay National Park includes three distinct zones: the volcanic High Andes, at elevations of 2,000 to 5,000 m (6,600 to 16,400 feet); the eastern foothills at between 1,000 and 2,000 m (3,300 to 6,600 feet); and the alluvial fan that lies at their foot. The central uplands are dominated by two active volcanoes – Sangay (5,230 m, 17,160 feet) and Tungurahua (5,016 m, 16,500 feet) – and the extinct El Altar (5,319 m, 17,450 feet). The successive bands of vegetation change with elevation – subtropical rainforest merges into lower montane rainforest above 2,000 m (6,600 feet), in turn being replaced by wild Páramo grasslands above 4,500 m (14,750 feet). Above 4,800 m (15,750 feet) is a zone of eternal snow. Animal and plant life gain advantage from the isolation of this primeval landscape. More than 3,000 plant species have been recorded in the national park, and the number of bird species is estimated at between four and five hundred. Many mammals roam the ancient forest, including mountain tapirs, giant otters, spectacled bears, pumas, jaguars, and ocelots.

Tungurahua has undergone periods of strong volcanic activity, for example between 1916 and 1925. It has been active again since 1999 (left). The rare Andean condor (large picture) is both a revered heraldic animal of several South American countries, and an extremely rare and little researched bird species.

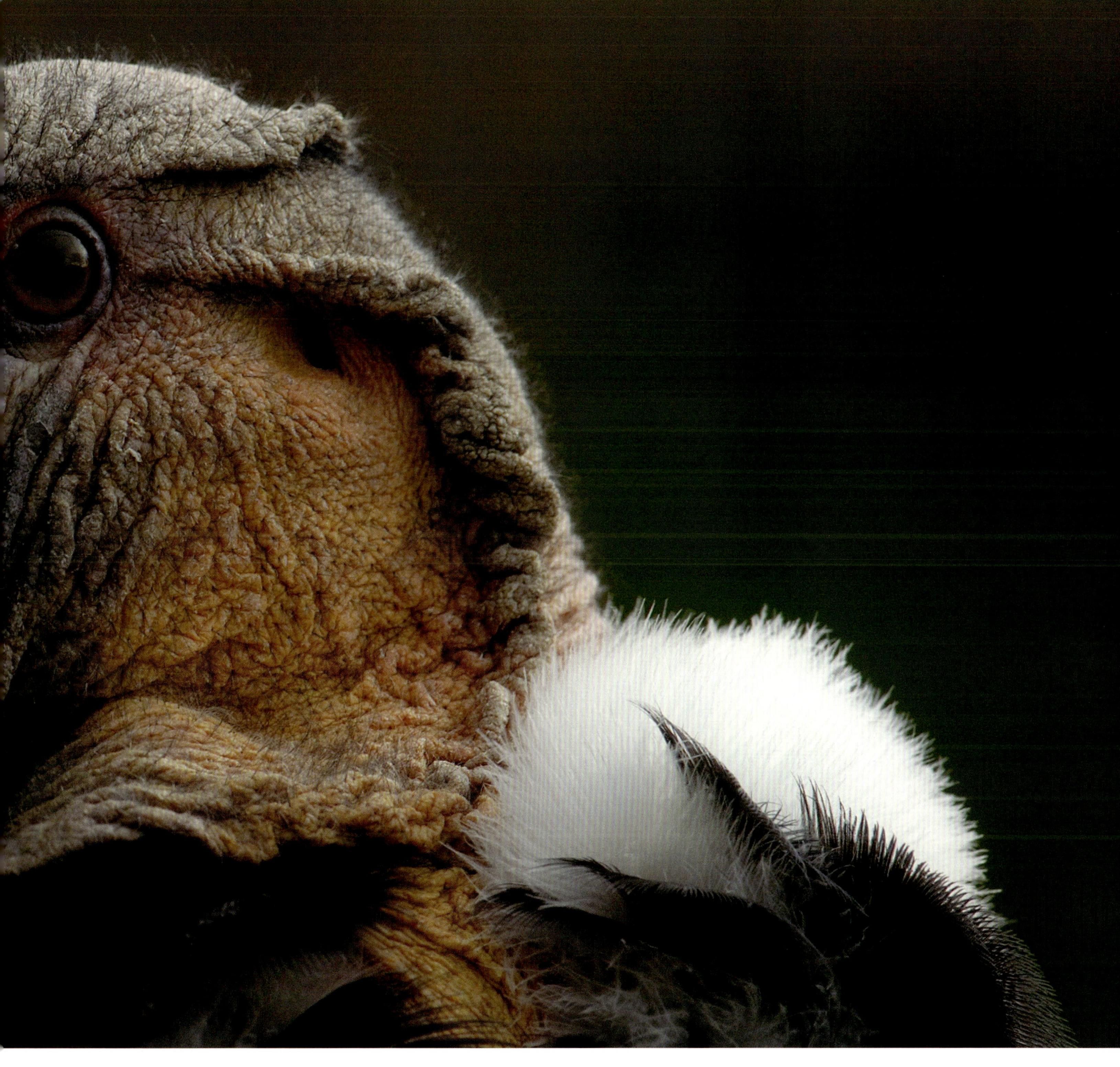

HUASCARÁN NATIONAL PARK

Date of inscription: 1985

Punctuated by the snowy peaks of the Cordillera Blanca, the national park can reach elevations of 6,000 m (19,700 feet). Its gorges and glacial lakes reveal sites of extraordinary natural beauty and are home to much rare animal and plant life.

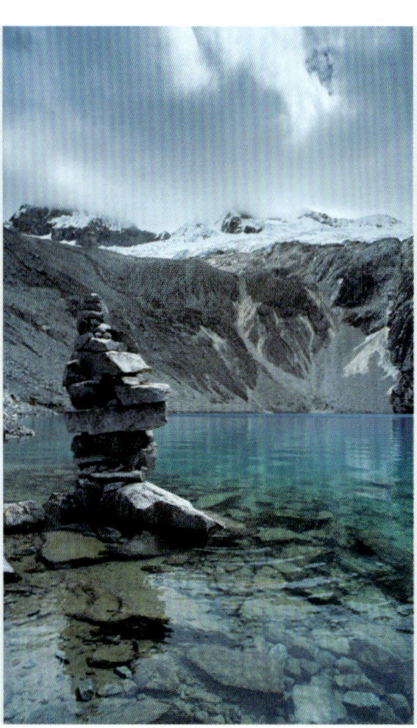

The snow-capped summit of the 6,768-m (22,200-foot) high Nevado Huascarán, Peru's highest mountain, towers majestically over the national park that has taken its name. The scenery of the Cordillera Blanca, with its gigantic glaciers, silent mountain lakes, deep gorges, and roaring streams is a fascinating prospect. The Huascarán is just one of 27 peaks measured here above 6,000 m (19,700 feet), and these are flanked by 30 glaciers and 127 glacial lakes. The average temperature is 3° C, although in winter the thermometer can drop to –30° C. Nonetheless, vegetation grows here at elevations up to 4,000 m (13,200 feet), including rare cactus species and the world's largest bromelia, Puya raimondii. The mammals living in the park, such as the spectacled bear, the puma, the vikunja, the white-tailed deer, and the Peruvian guemal, have adapted ideally to the conditions of this bare and mountainous world. Of the hundred or so species of bird living in the park, the puna hawk, the Andean condor, and the picaflor, the world's largest hummingbird, are the most spectacular.

The crystal-clear Laguna 69 mountain lake (left) lies at the foot of the Nevados Pisco. Despite a difference in altitude of around 1,000 m (3,280 feet) to the Nevado Huascaran (below), it is nevertheless considered a great challenge to climb.

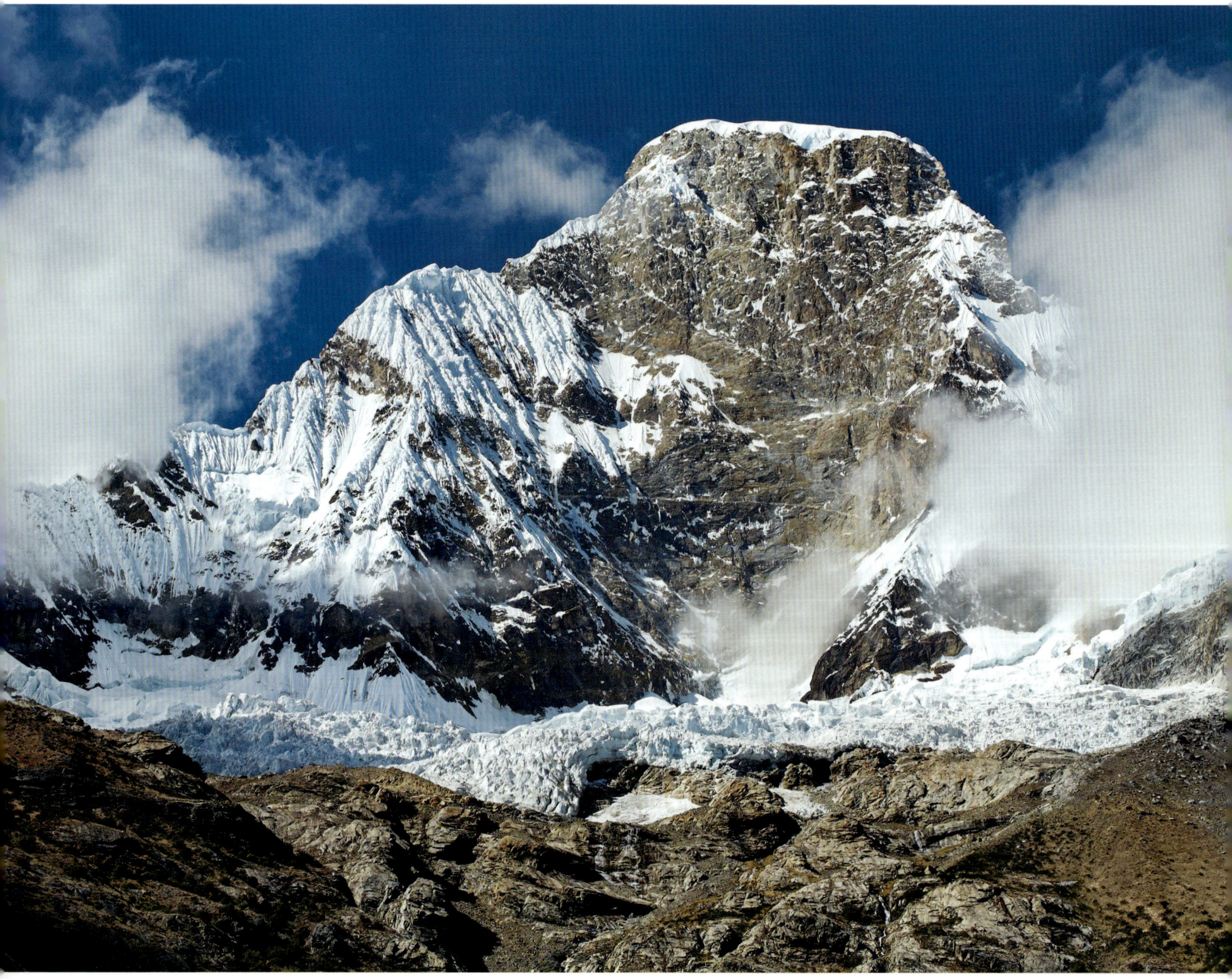

RÍO ABISEO NATIONAL PARK

In 1983, a national park of 2,700 sq. km (1,050 sq. miles) was established on the eastern slope of the central cordillera in northern Peru. It was intended primarily to protect the extraordinary flora and fauna found in the local cloud forest; much of the plant and animal life here is endemic – among it 15 different species of batrachians who call the park home Moreover, it was a minor scientific sensation when the Peruvian yellow-tailed woolly monkey, once thought extinct, was discovered living here a few years ago. The North Andean deer, and the red howler monkey, who are both threatened with extinction, also find refuge in the national park. Since 1985, archeologists have excavated a total of 36 building complexes, dating from the time of the Inca empire. They were discovered in the thick jungle of the conservation area, at elevations between 2,500 and 4,000 m (8,200 and 13,200 feet). The findings are especially precious because they bear witness to an epoch of about 8000 years of Peruvian pre- and early history.

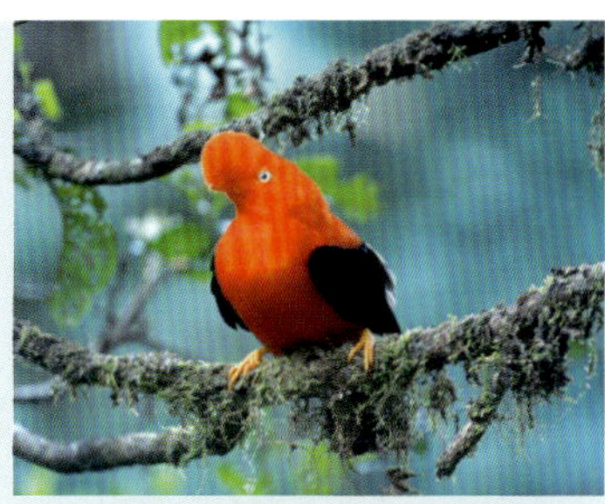

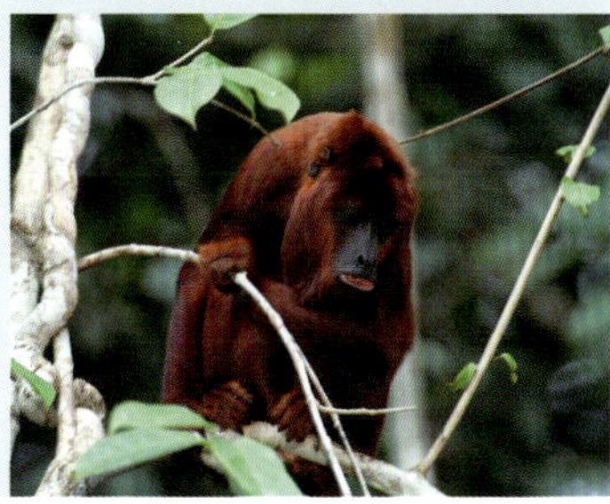

The Río Abiseo National Park is a refuge for many species, including the red howler monkey (right), the king vulture (below), and the Andean cock-of-the-rock, the Peruvian national bird (top).

Date of inscription: 1990
Extended: 1992

Along with its Páramo grassland, the national park boasts stretches of primary cloud forest which served as a refuge for many plants during the last ice age. Numerous ruins from pre-Columbian times have been found in the middle of the forest.

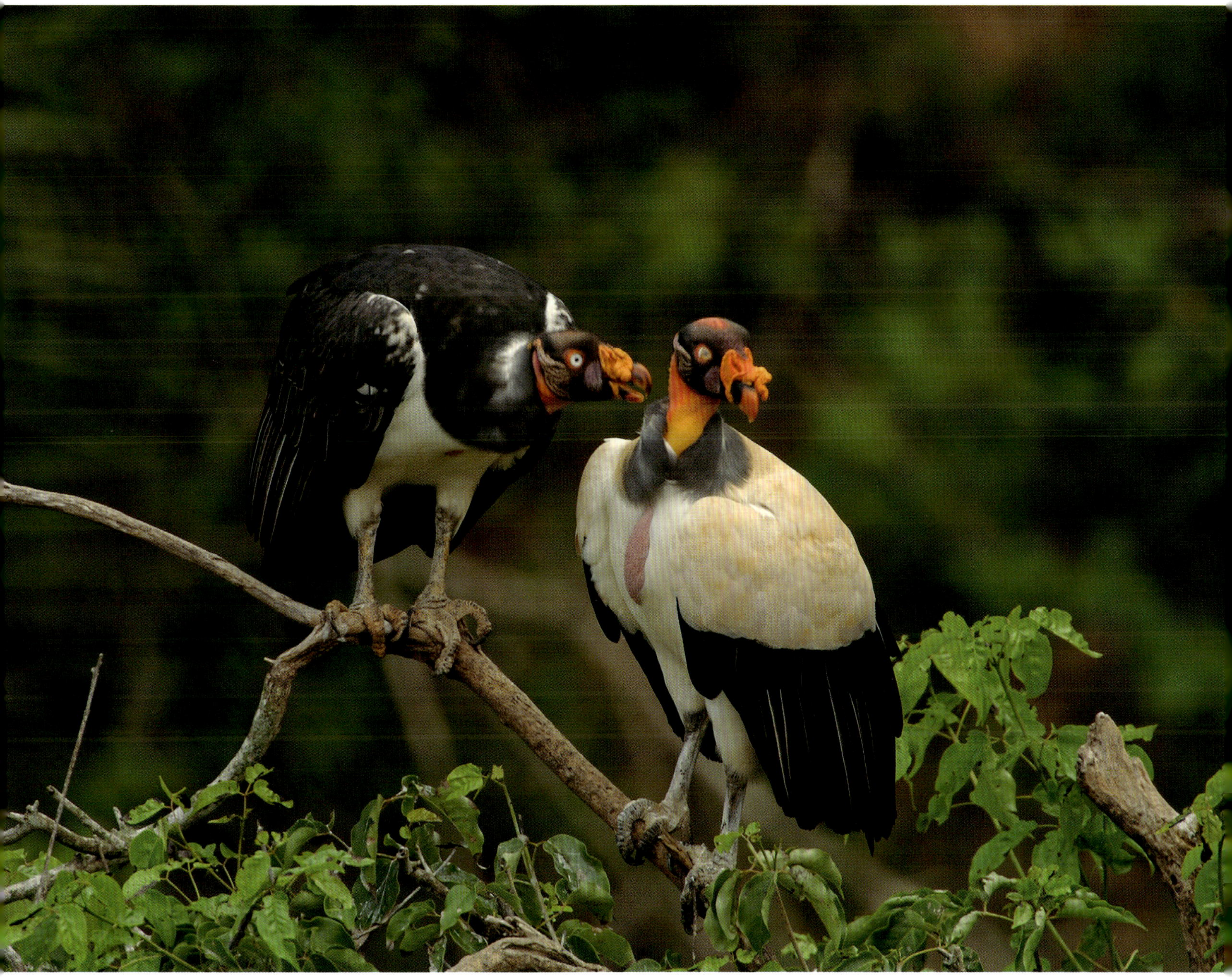

MACHU PICCHU

Date of inscription: 1983

Situated in the middle of a landscape of high mountains, Macchu Picchu, rediscovered at the beginning of the 20th century, is probably the most impressive and best-preserved Inca city ruin, and is also one of the most important archeological sites in South America.

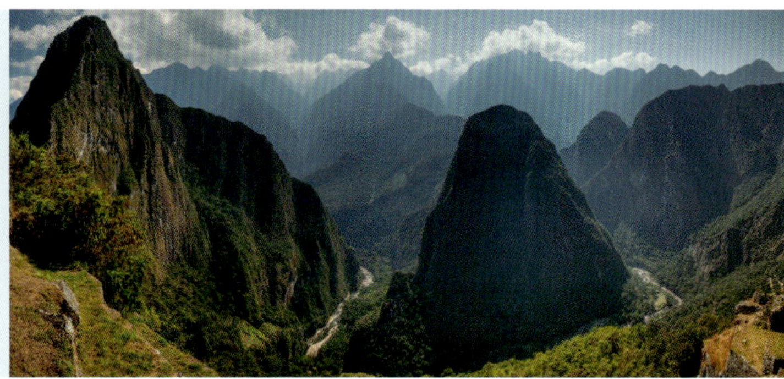

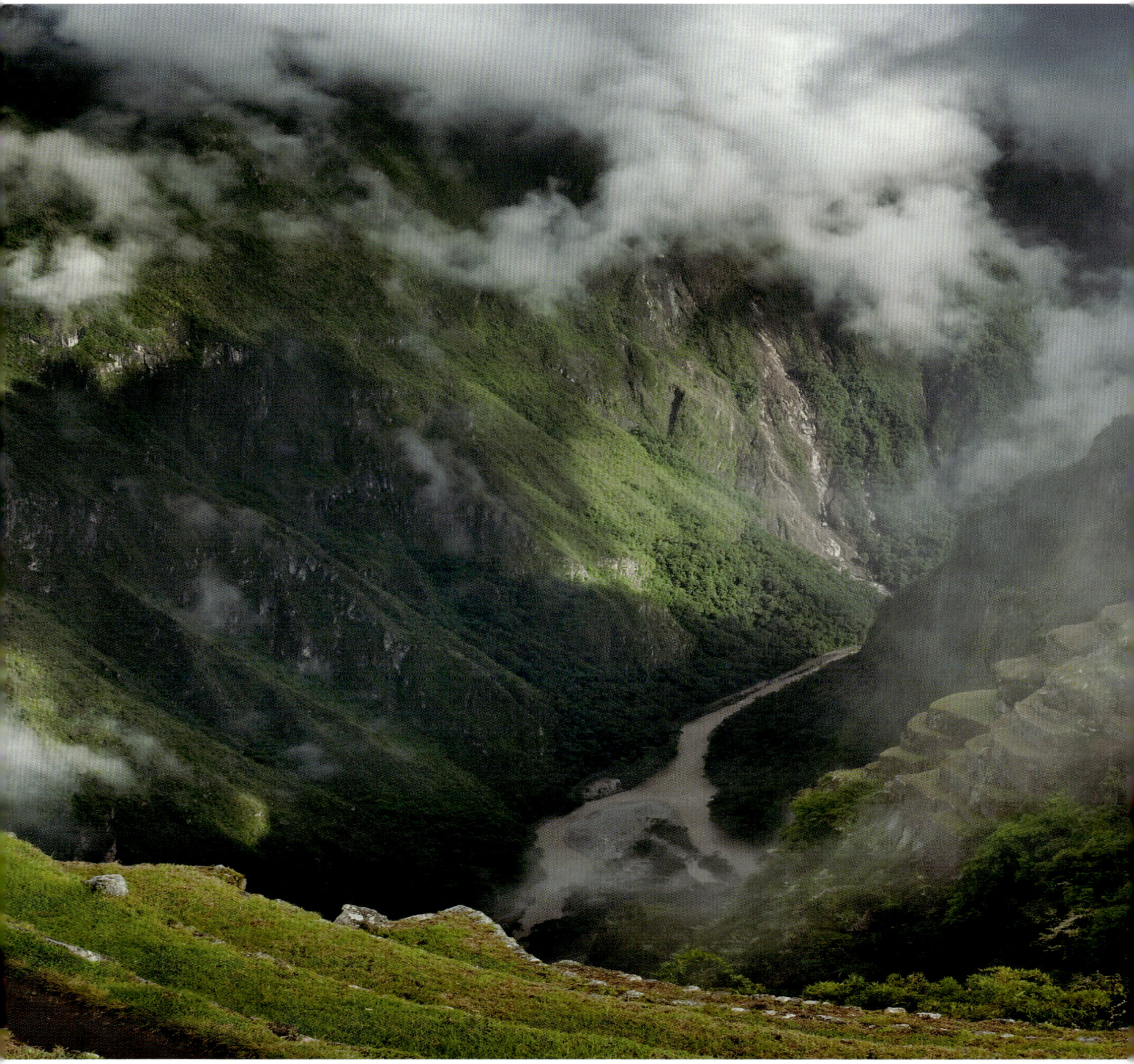

In 1911, an American, Hiram Bingham, became the first white man to set eyes on this spectacular Inca city. Drawing on its location beneath Huayna Picchu, the "young peak," he christened the site Macchu Picchu, the "old peak." Everything seems strange in this Inca city, hidden in the tropical mountain forest on the eastern slopes of the Andes and clinging like an eagle's eyrie to a flattened mountain-top at an elevation of 2,430 m (7,970 feet). This settlement, situated above the Río Urubamba valley, is fascinating not just because of its well-preserved buildings, but also because of the unique interplay of architecture and nature – the buildings fit perfectly into the unevenness of the terrain. There is still speculation today about the importance of this town, which was never recorded or apparently even noticed by the Spanish conquistadors; it may perhaps represent an attempt by the Incas to colonize the eastern slopes of the Andes. All that is certain is that it was constructed around 1450, and already deserted only a century later. The site is divided into two areas: a farmed zone, with terraced agricultural land on the mountain's slopes fed by a cunning irrigation system, and an unfortified municipal area consisting of palaces, temples, and dwellings. Among the most important monuments are the Round Tower, the Temple of the Sun, and the Room of Three Windows.

Ringed by mighty mountains, the "Forgotten City," Macchu Picchu, is one of the most impressive examples of architecture incorporated into its surrounding environment. The Inca settlement was laid out on several levels on a high plateau around 1450. Left: Between Machu Picchu and the ruins lie Huayna Picchu and the Urubamba Valley.

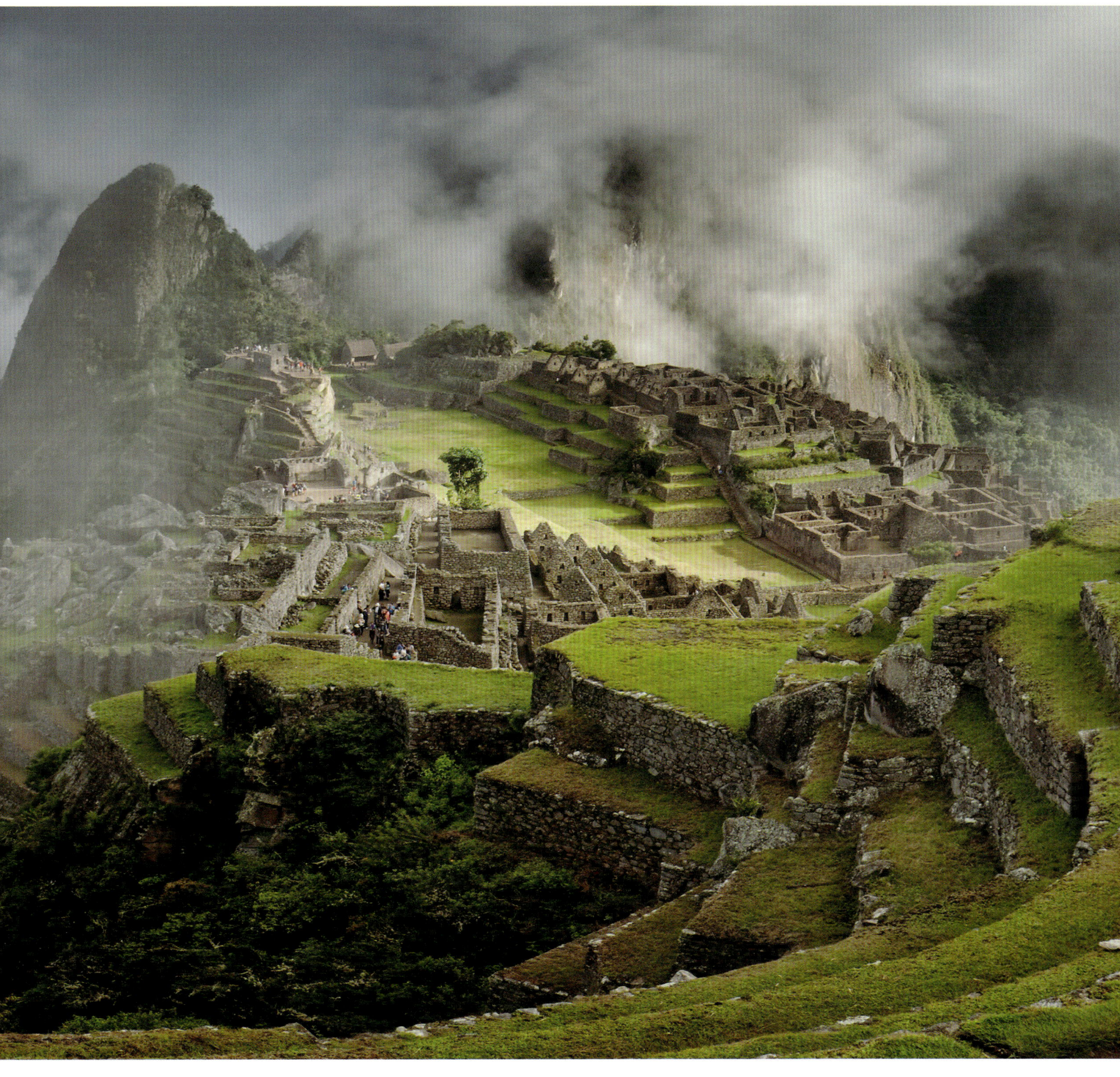

MANÚ NATIONAL PARK

Date of inscription: 1987

This remote park, situated on the eastern slope of the Andes towards the Amazon lowlands, is a region of superlatives, with countless species of plant and animal life. A few indigenous Indians still live here, hunting and farming using traditional methods.

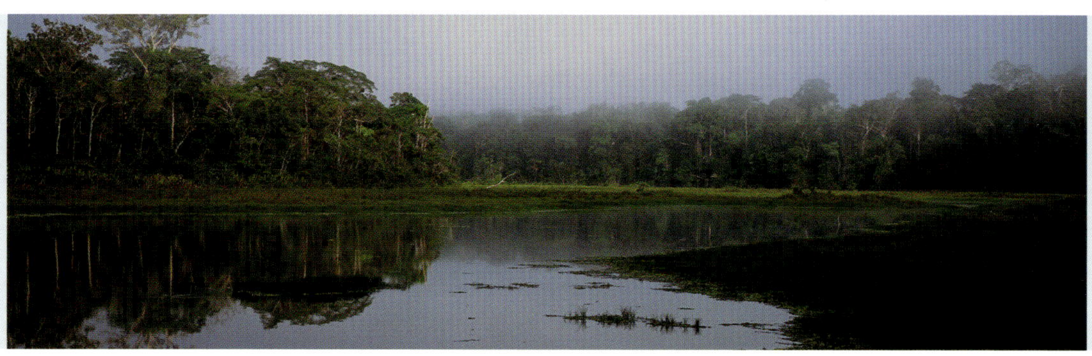

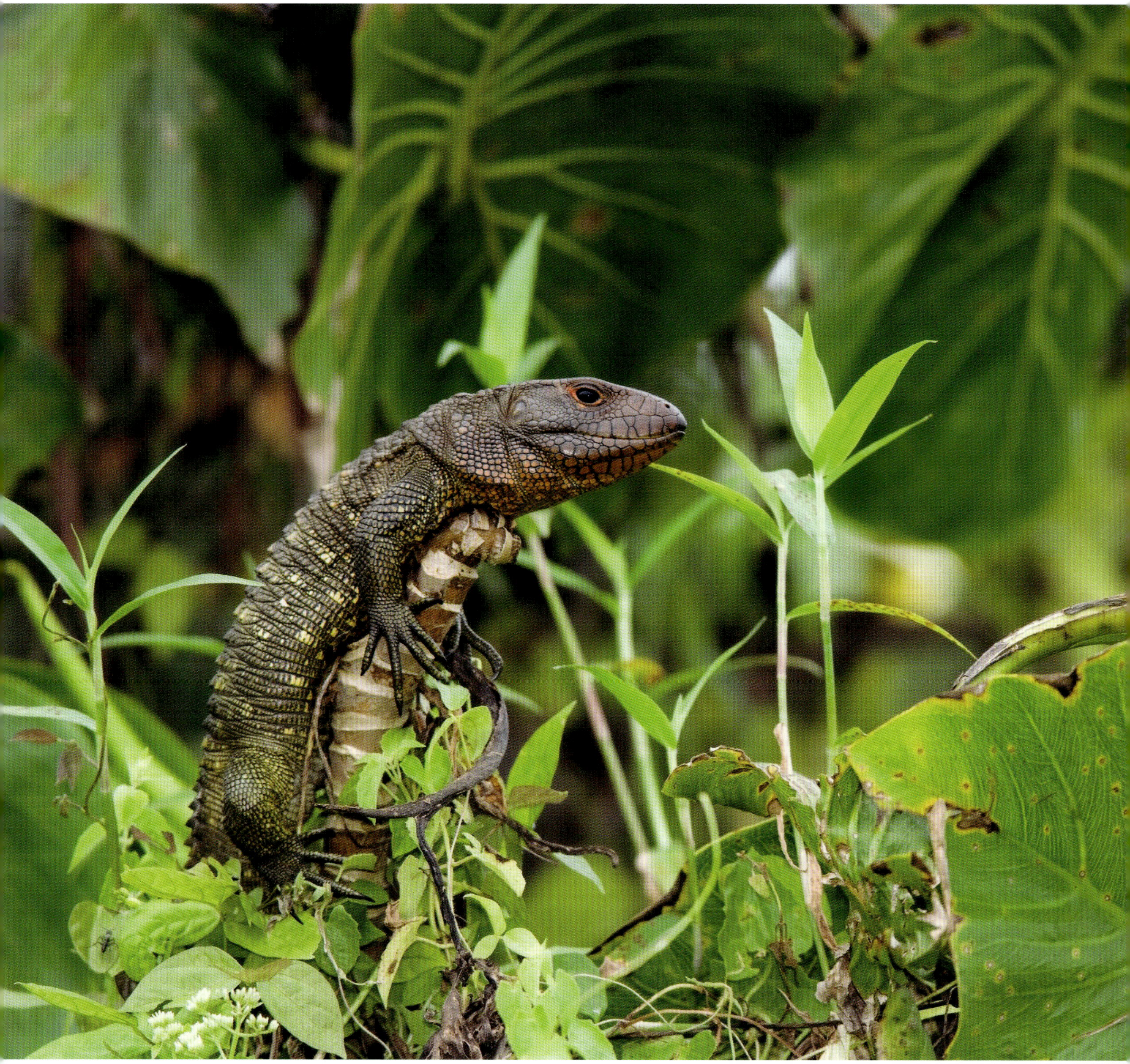

Established in 1973, Peru's second largest national park has an area of 15,000 sq. km (5,800 sq. miles) and is situated at elevations that range from 150 to 4,200 m (500 to 13,900 feet). The park includes the entire catchment basin of the Río Manú, a tributary of the Amazon, in addition to sections of the Río Alto Madre de Dios basin. The conservation area consists of flood plains, hills, and mountains, and the vegetation ranges from tropical rainforest through tropical montane forest to the Puna grasslands. This area, still largely undisturbed, is a true paradise for animals, with over a thousand bird species and 200 mammals, such as the many varieties of parrot and the giant otter, which can reach up to 2 m (7 feet) in length and is threatened with extinction. Even the river terrapin, long since extinct elsewhere, has found a home here. Hanging from trees, three-toed sloths doze upside-down. Other typical South American animals to be found here include the jaguar, the giant armadillo, and the coati. It is also hard to overlook the estimated 15,000 plant species, including 18 different varieties of fig alone.

Primates are represented in the park in large numbers, but the area is also a protected refuge for other mammals and reptiles. Clockwise from below: woolly monkey, squirrel monkey, ocelot, the marten-like jaguarundi, black-mantled tamarin and crested owl. Large picture: the northern caiman lizard; left: Otorongo Lake.

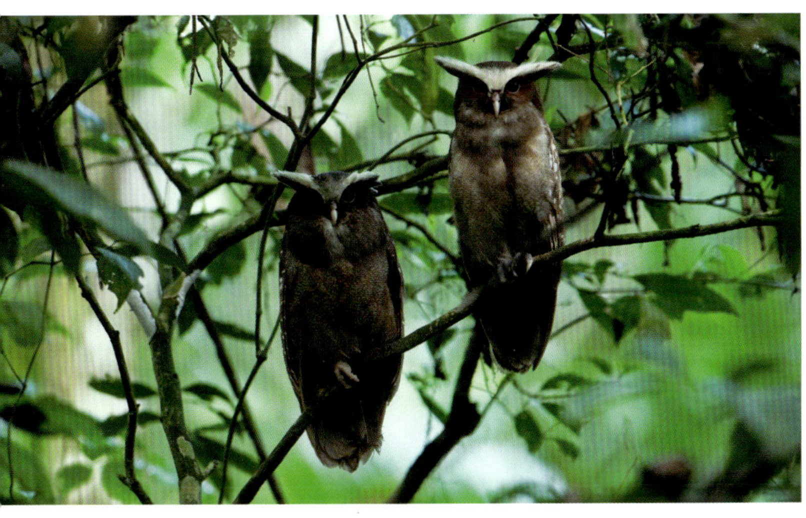

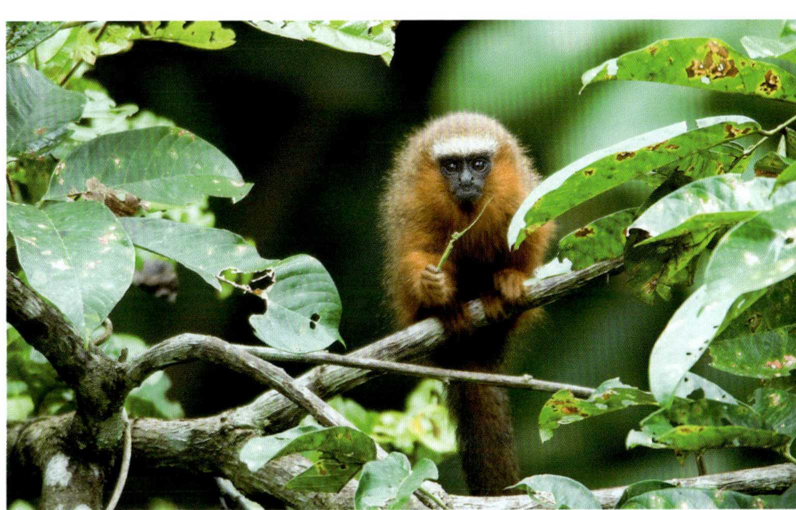

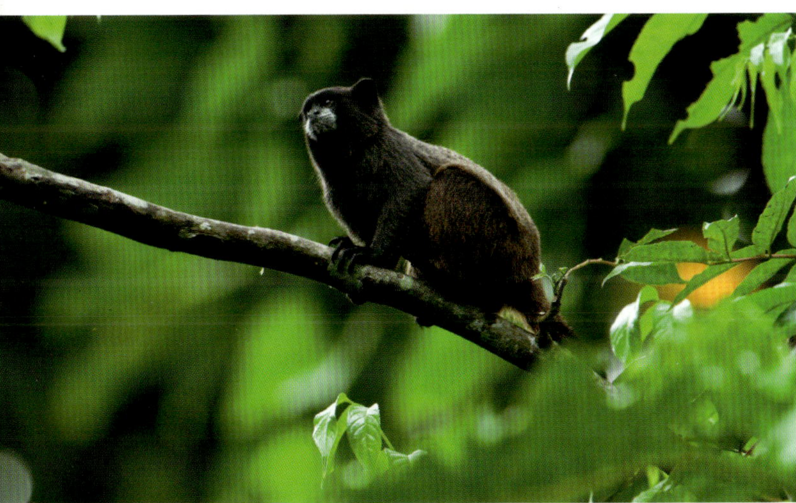

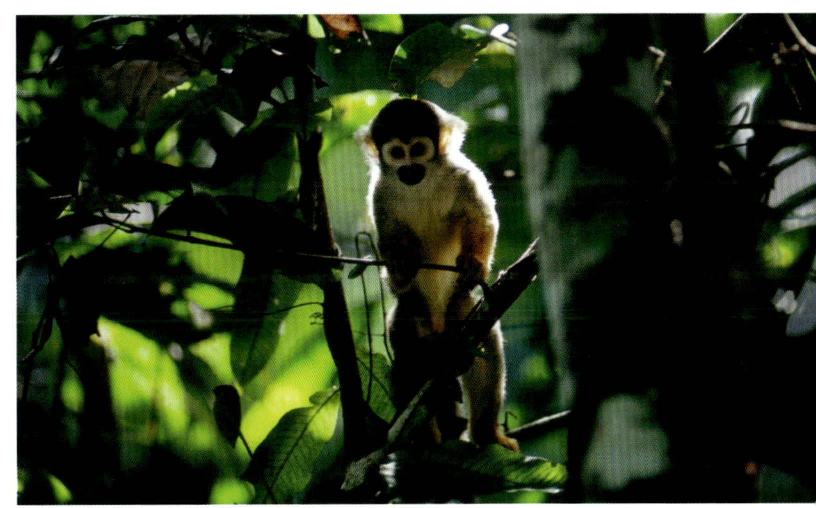

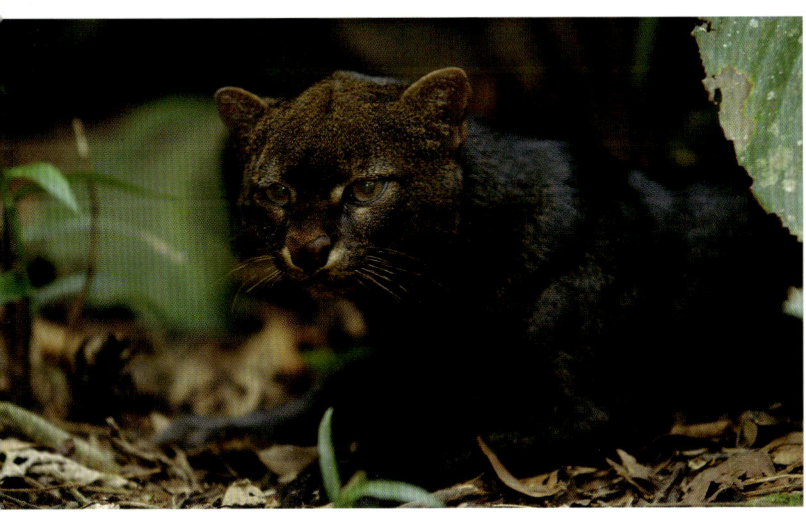

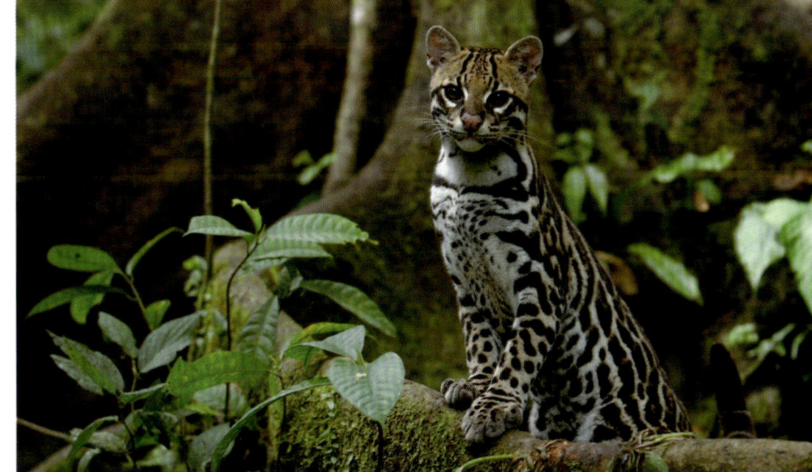

NOEL KEMPFF MERCADO NATIONAL PARK

Date of inscription: 2000

The national park, one of the largest and most continuous in Bolivia, lies on the Brazilian border in the west of the Amazon basin, and is home to an incredible variety of plant and animal life.

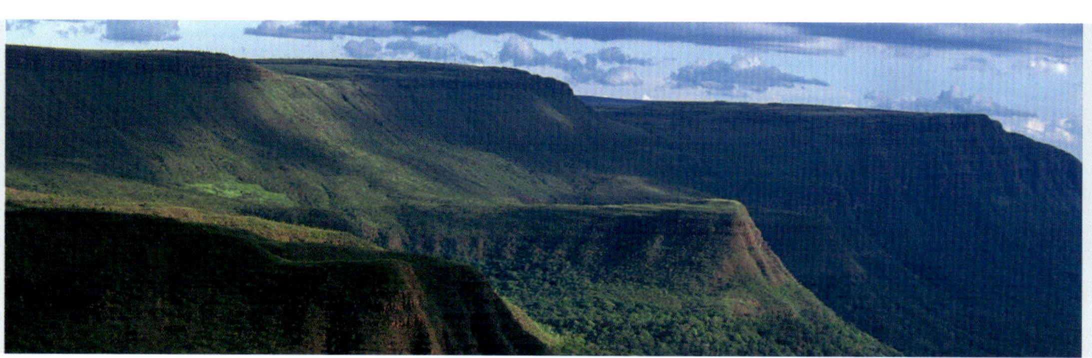

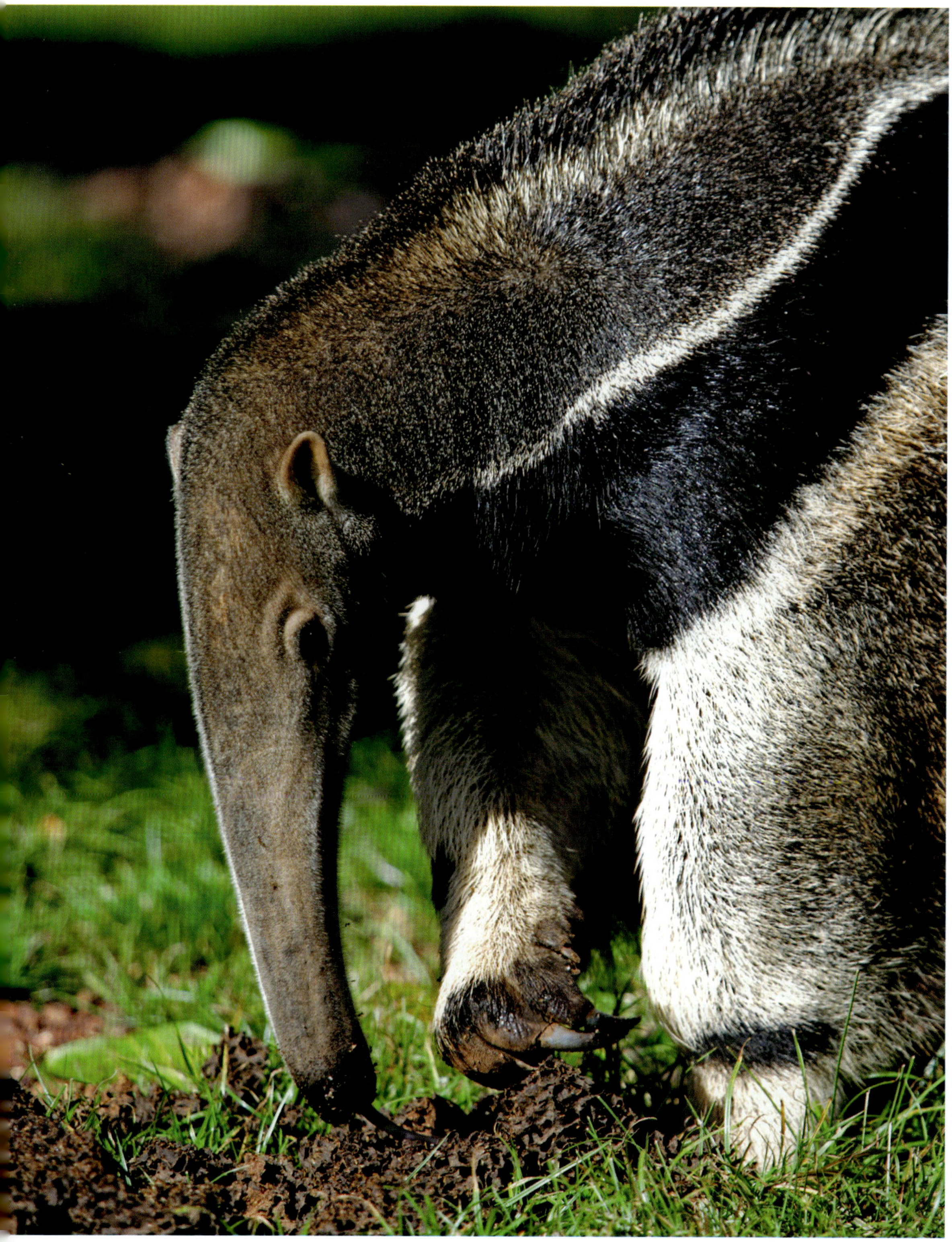

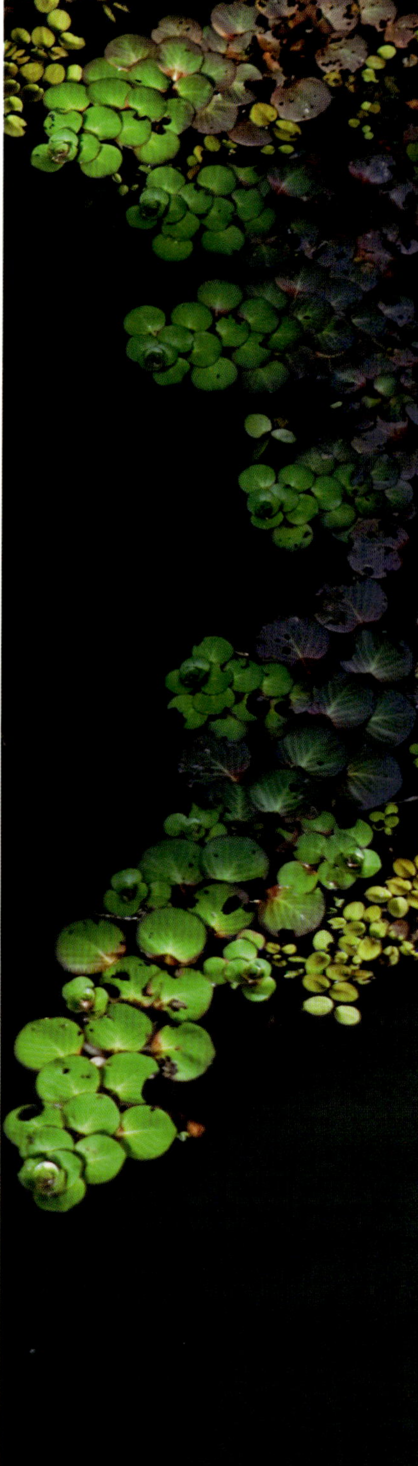

This national park of over 15,000 sq. km (5,800 sq. miles), encompassing both the Huanchaca plateau and its surrounding lowlands, ranges in elevation between 200 and 1,000 m (650 and 3,300 feet). It includes five separate ecosystems: the tropical rainforest of Amazonia, seasonally flooding savannah, deciduous dry forest and montane forest, areas of thorny scrub forest, and extensive swamps and flood plains. This diverse vegetation houses correspondingly varied plant and animal life. The number of plant species alone in the park has been estimated at around 4,000.

Before his brutal murder at the hands of drug smugglers in 1986, the Bolivian naturalist, Noel Kempff Mercado, after whom the national park is named, had begun recording the giant biosystem. More than 600 bird species and 150 mammals and reptiles have been identified, including Gould's toucanet, the hyacinthine macaw, the Amazon river dolphin, the maned wolf, and the giant anteater, in addition to jaguars, pumas, giant otters, numerous monkeys, giant river turtles, and the black caiman.

The rainforest spreads out beneath the steep edges of the Huanchaca plateau (left). The giant anteater lives in the savannah part of the park, and feeds almost exclusively on ants and termites (below left). Reaching a length of up to 6 m (20 feet), South America's largest reptile, the black caiman, has found a home in the park's rivers (below).

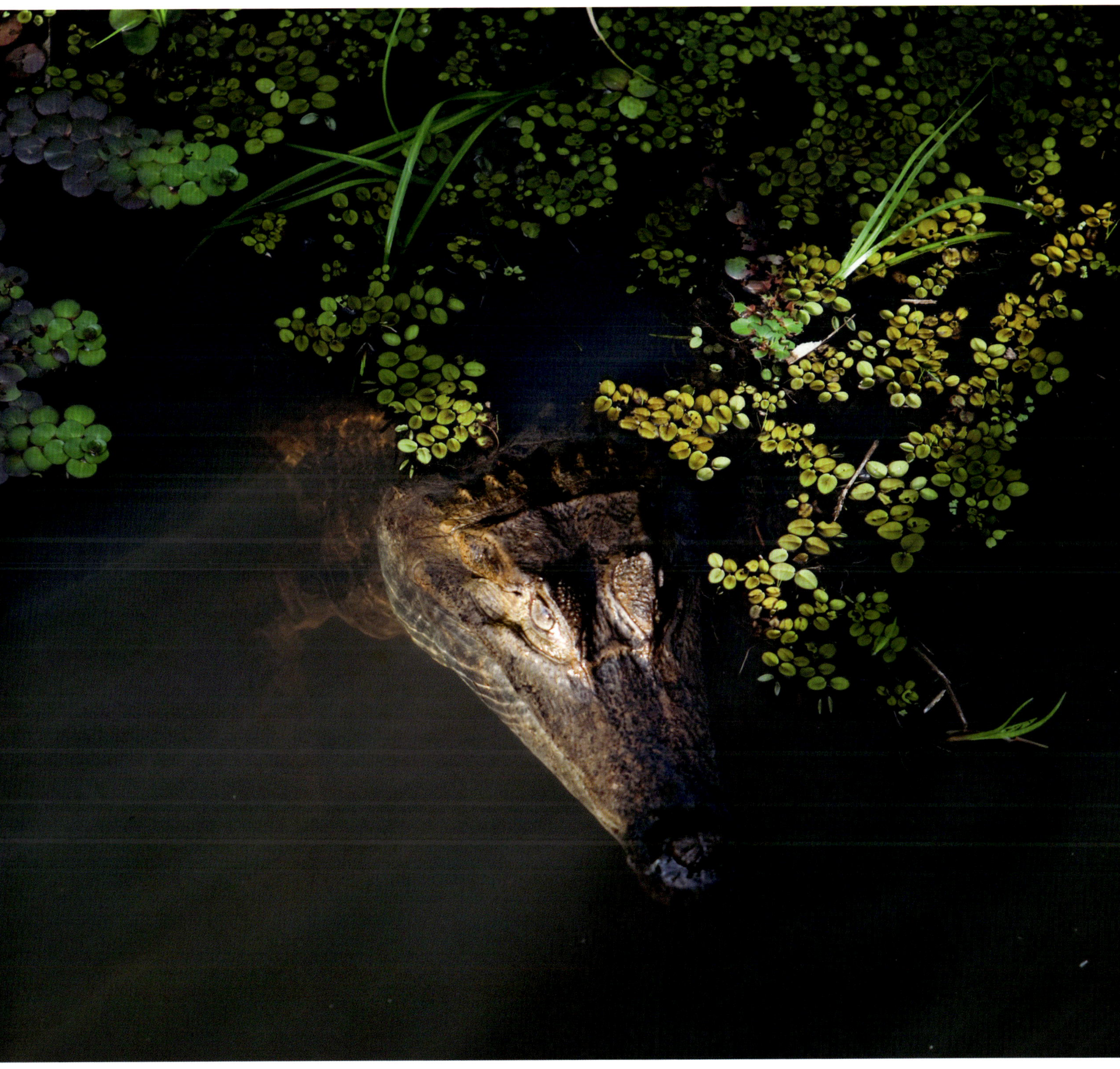

CANAIMA NATIONAL PARK

Date of inscription: 1994

With its mighty mesas and the world's highest waterfall, the Salto Angel, the Gran Sabana is one of the world's most beautiful areas. It is also a habitat for innumerable plant species.

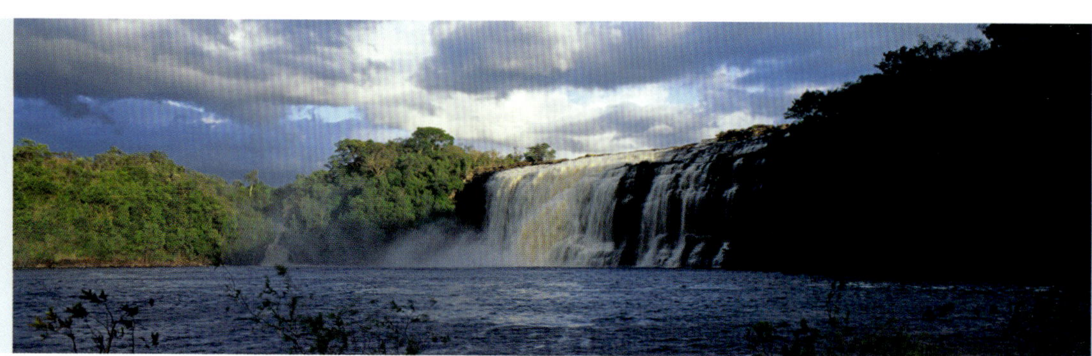

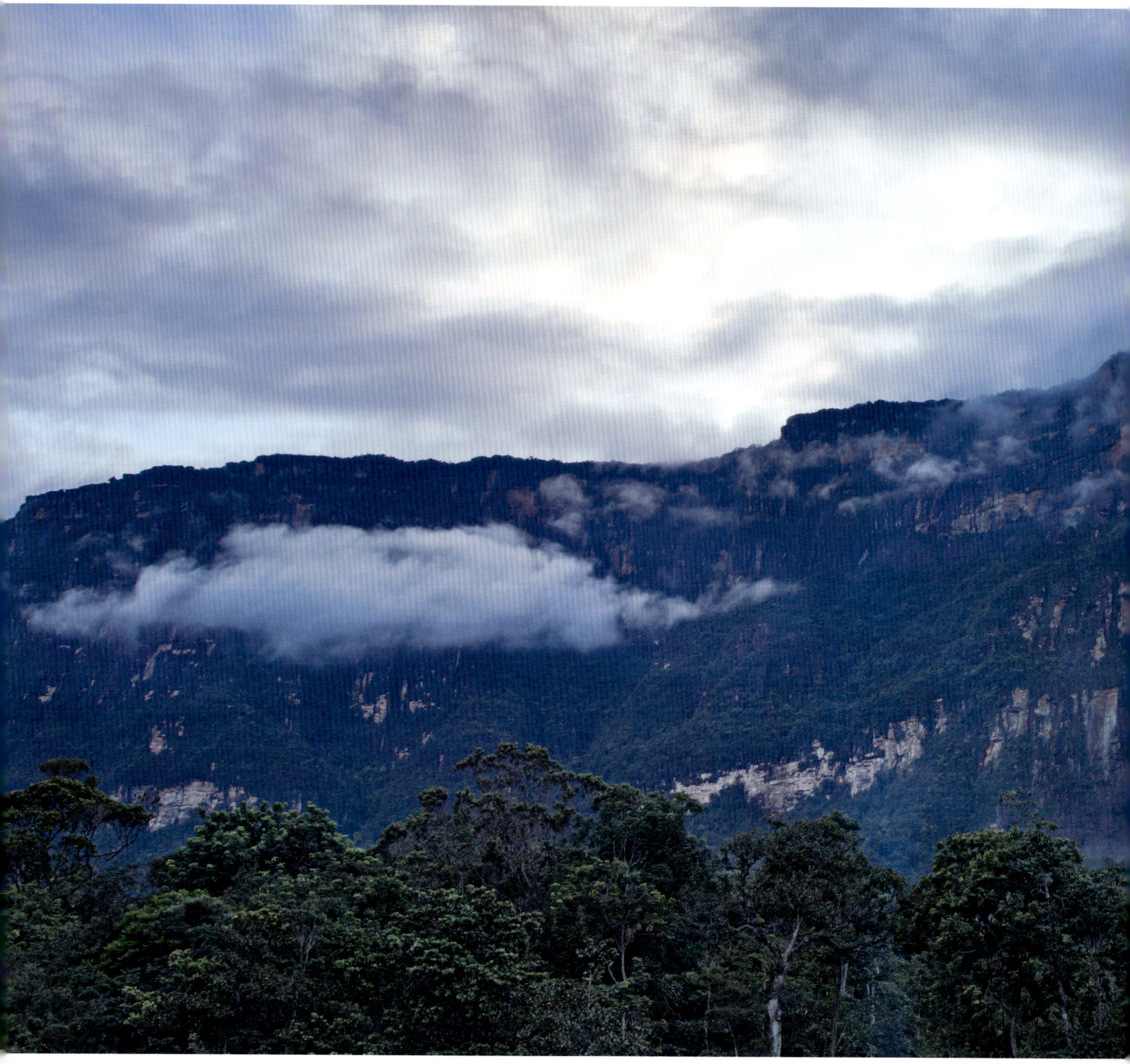

In the language of the local Kamarokoto people, Canaima represents a dark deity, uniting all evil in itself. In contrast, Venezuela's second largest national park (30,000 sq. km) is representative of nothing but overwhelming natural beauty. Situated in the south-east of the country, near the Guyanese and Brazilian borders, the park encompasses the incomparable landscape of the Gran Sabana. Nestling in dense vegetation, a host of spectacular waterfalls, including the Salto Angel, the Salto Kukenam, and the Canaima Lagoon rapids, crash dramatically into the depths. It is thought that some 3,000 to 5,000 flowering plants and ferns grow here, of which many are endemic; besides the savannah, there is also impenetrable montane forest and scrubland. Unique pioneer vegetation has evolved on the many mesas, with numerous species of carnivorous plants. There is also an impressive diversity of orchid species. Around 550 bird species live here, while mammals such as the giant anteater, the giant armadillo, the giant otter, the bush dog, and the oncilla roam the forest floor.

The Salto Angel falls 1,000 m (3,300 feet) from the north-eastern flank of the Auyán Tepui (large image). There is a variety of plant and animal life in the region, with orchids and bromeliads (2nd and 4th image). Howler monkeys and capuchin monkeys (1st and 3rd image) are at home here. Left: the Sapo Falls.

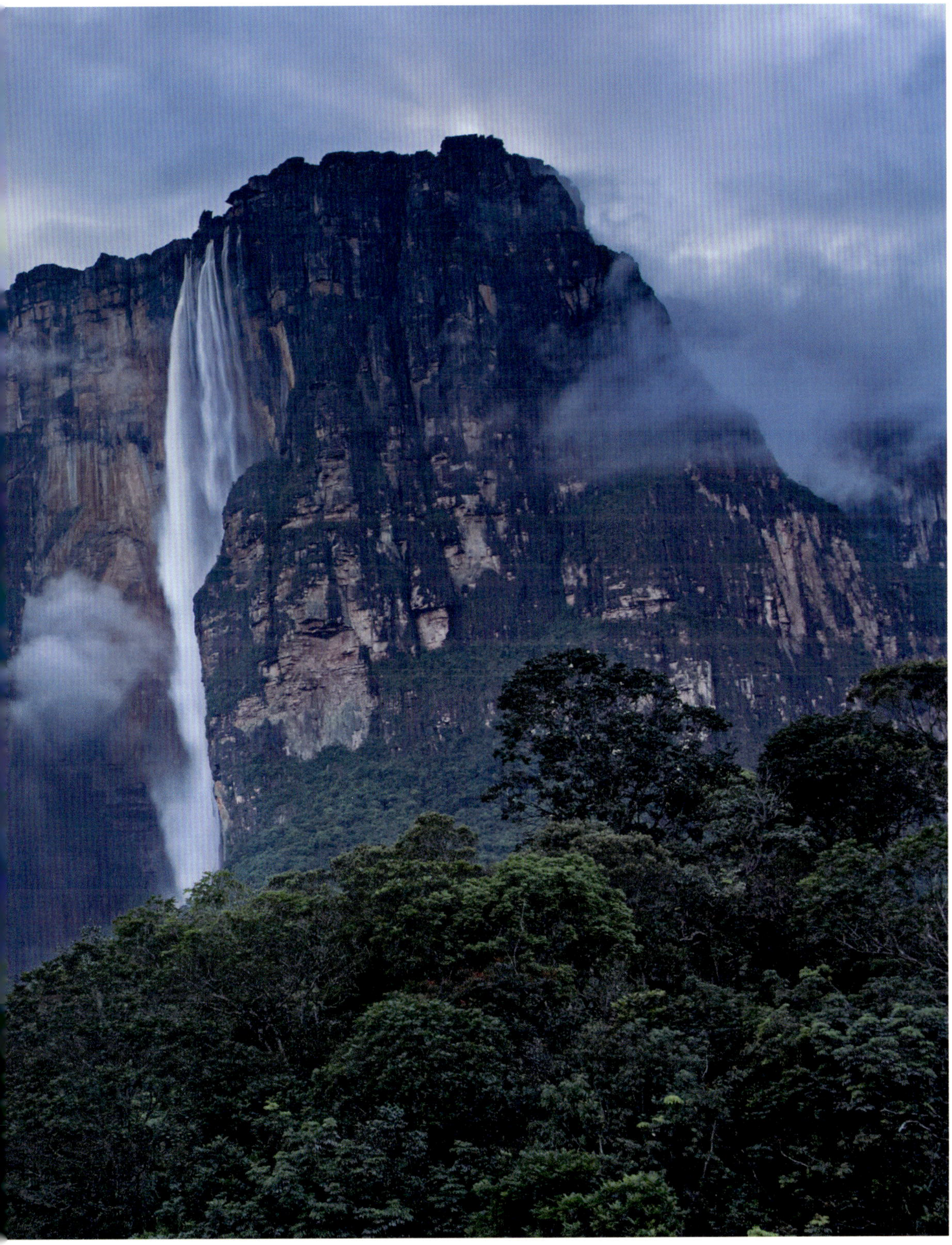

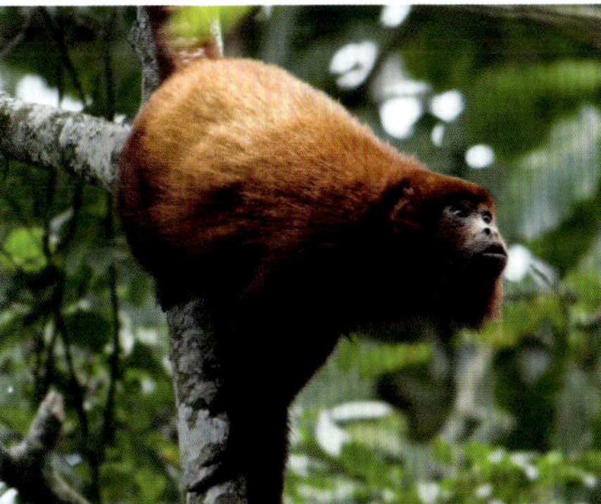

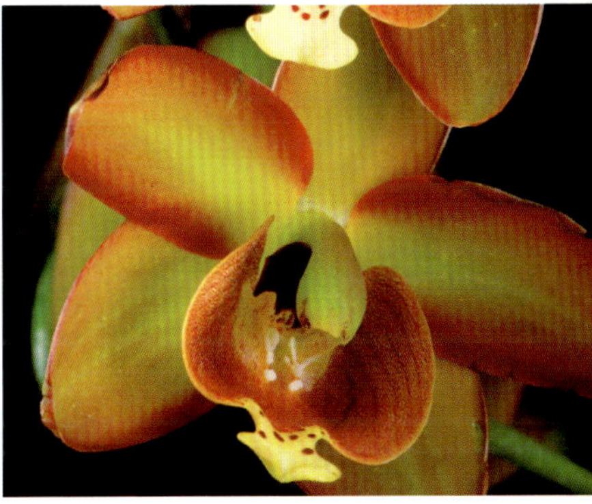

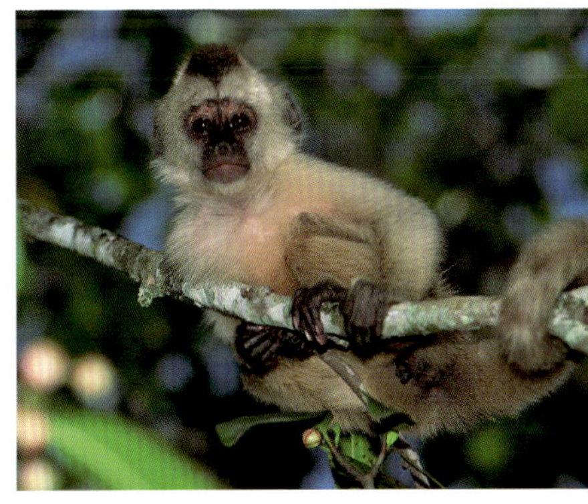

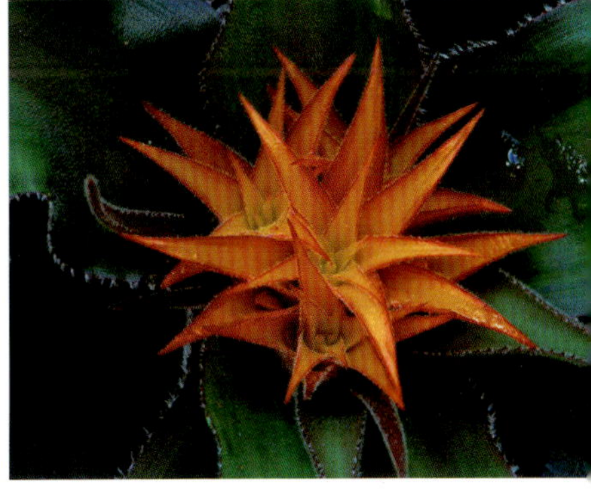

CENTRAL SURINAME NATURE RESERVE

Date of inscription: 2000

This enormous nature reserve encompasses the untouched tropical rainforest of the Guiana Shield and includes an enormous number of plant and animal species, of which many are endemic.

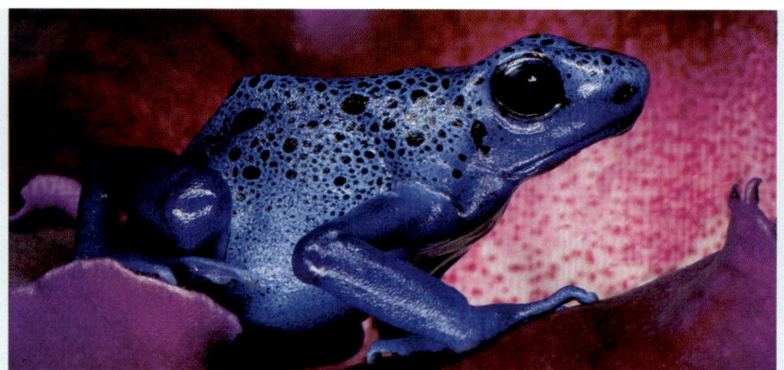

Over two billion years old and dating back to the Precambrian, the Guiana Shield craton of the South American continental plate in north-east South America is one of the oldest formations on earth. Primeval rainforest – largely inaccessible wilderness and still unexplored – covers around 150,000 sq. km (58,000 sq. miles). In 1998, Suriname's three most important conservation

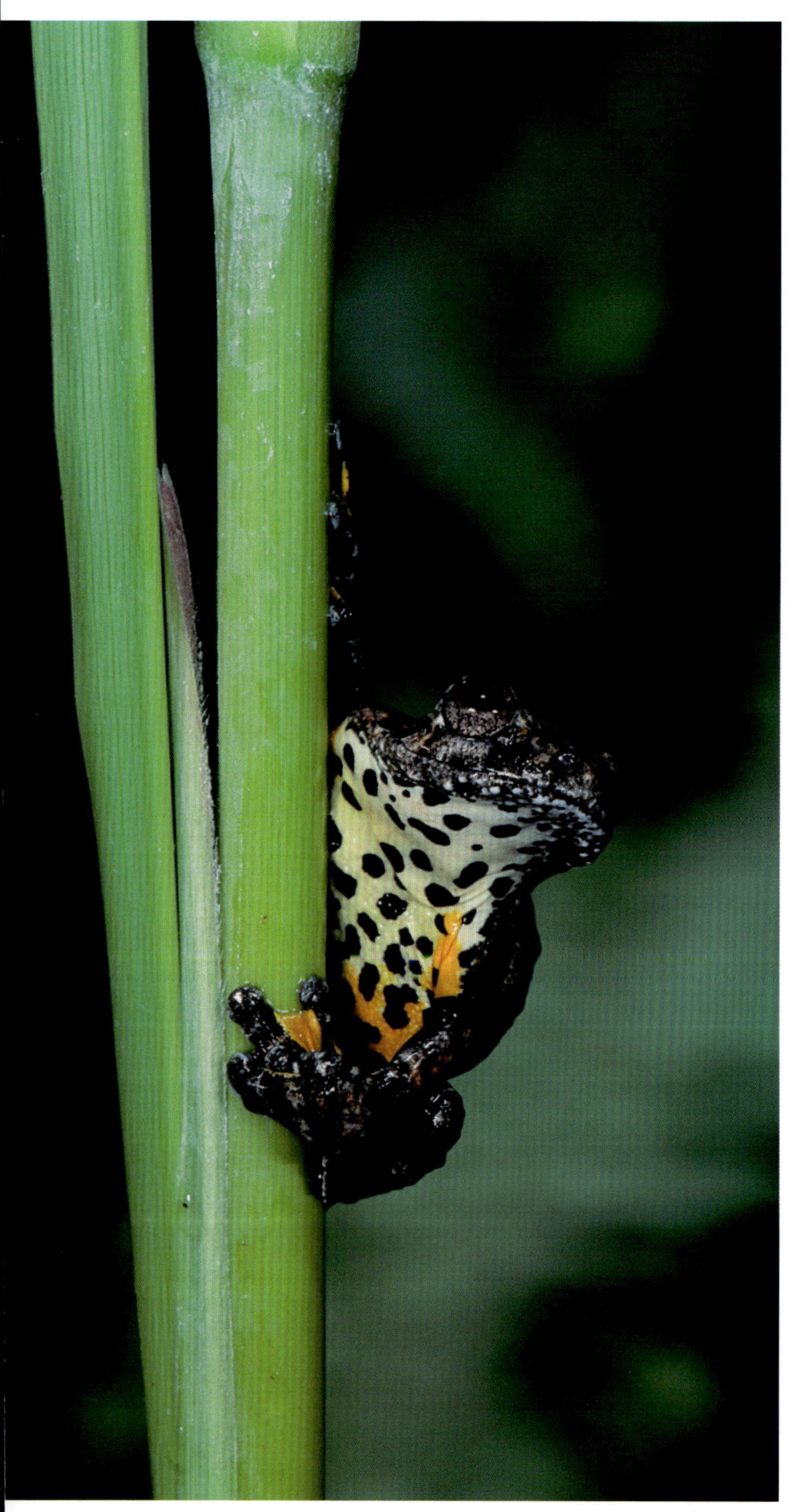

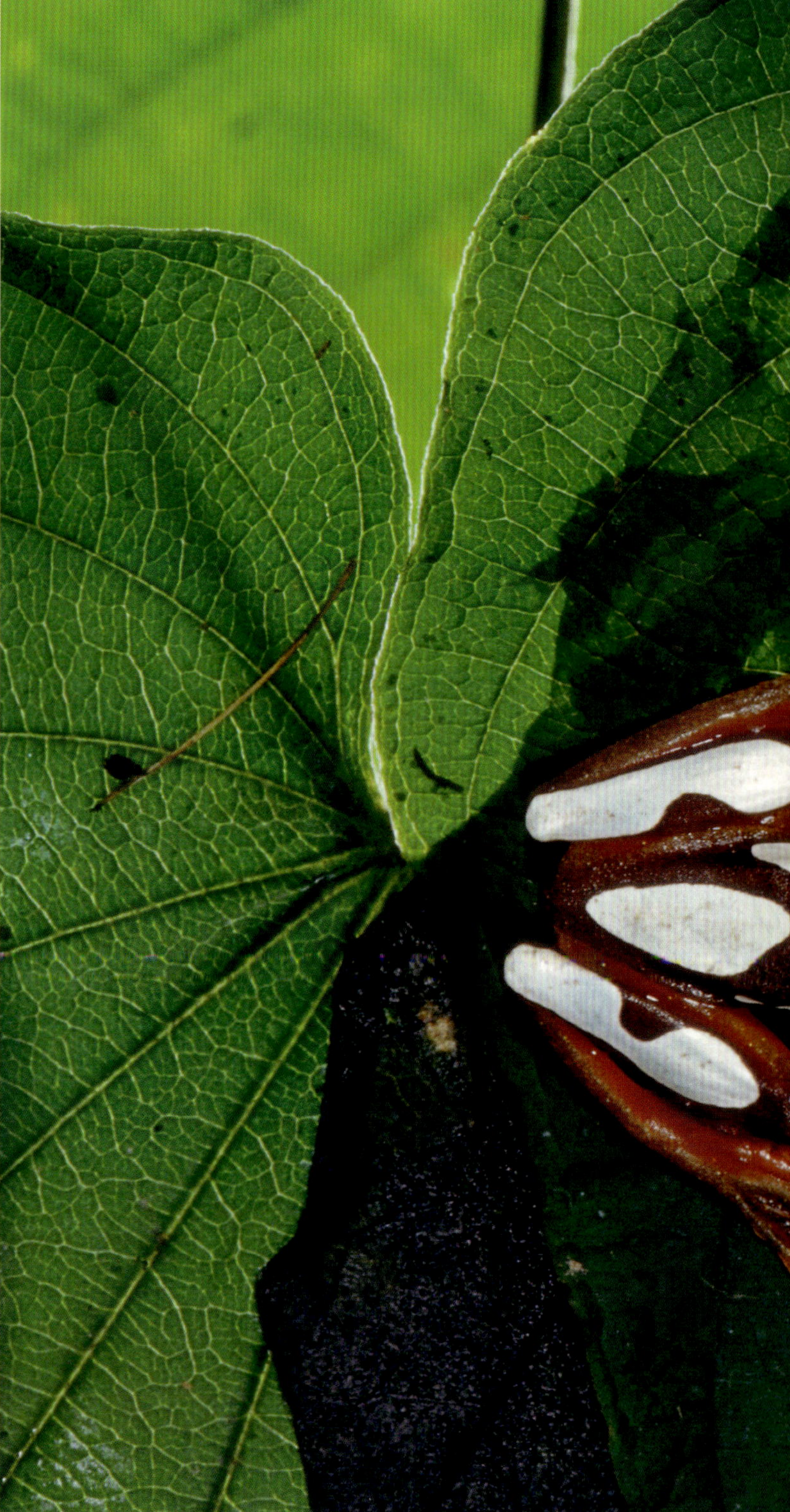

areas were combined into a corridor of 16,000 sq. km (6,200 sq. miles), to be called the Central Nature Reserve. The area encompasses about 11 percent of Suriname's sovereign territory and includes the upper catchment basin of the Coppename river. Among its broad range of landscape formations are table-like mesas, which towers 350 m (1,150 feet) over the surrounding rainforest.The conservation area has an impressive variety of plant life; 6,000 species have been recorded in the dense forests of the mountains and lowlands. Besides the rainforest, there is also wetland forest and savannah, while dry vegetation grows on granite extrusions.

The animal life on the reserve is extraordinarily diverse: 700 different birds, nearly 2,000 mammals, 150 reptiles, and 100 amphibians have been cataloged. The rivers teem with nearly 500 fish species, and, most unusually, no less than eight primate species have found a habitat in Raleigh Vallen National Park, one of the three central reservations.

Indigenous people use the poison secreted by the colourful frogs to hunt small animals. In fact, however, it is the frog's defence against its enemies. Left: blue poison arrow frog. Not all the bright frogs are poisonous: below, from left: marbled tree frog; clown tree frogs.

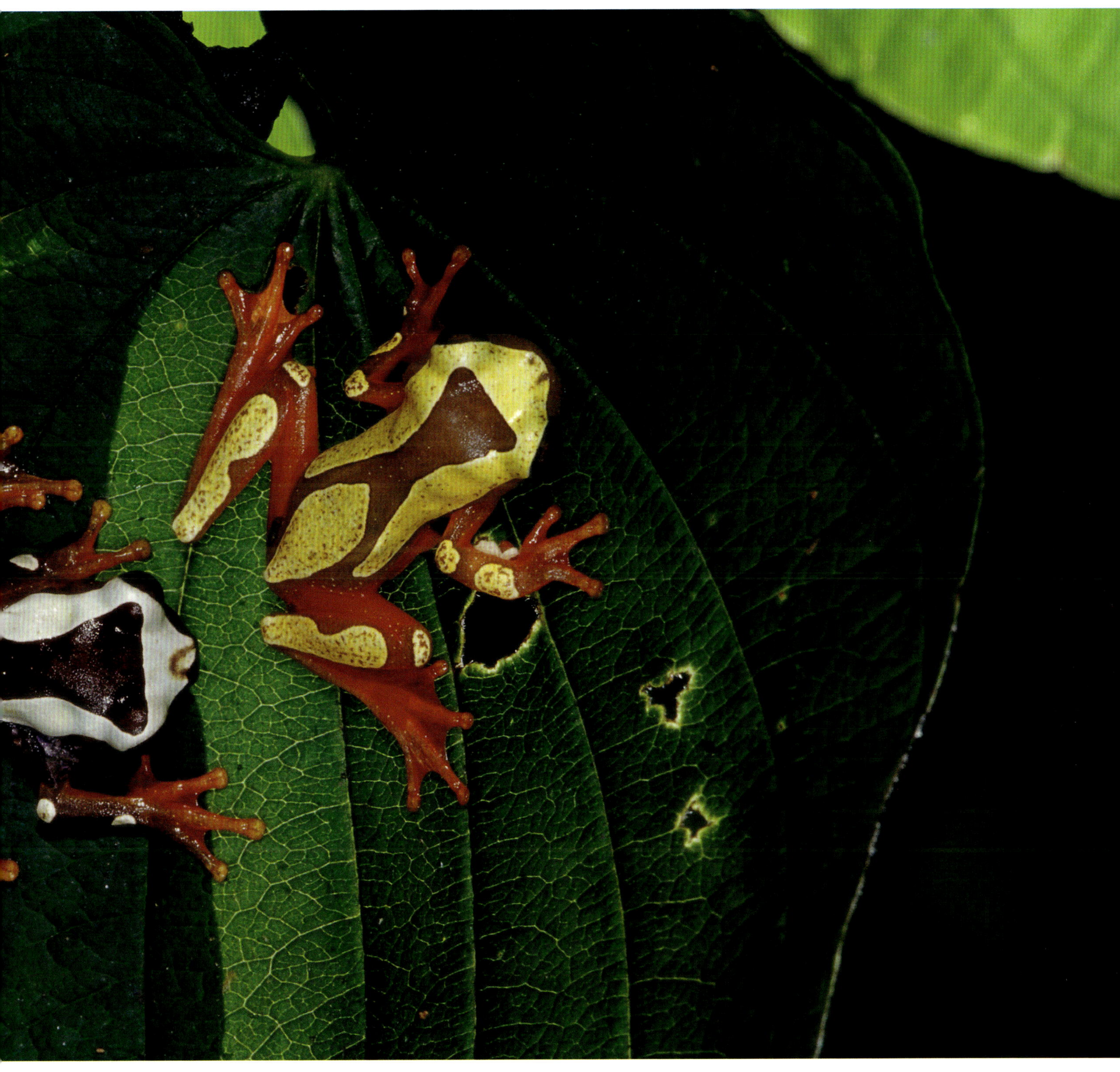

CENTRAL AMAZON CONSERVATION COMPLEX

Date of inscription: 2000
Extended: 2003

The largest conservation area in the Amazon basin includes the Jaú National Park, the Mamirauá and Amanã Nature Reserves, and the Anavilhanas Ecological Station.

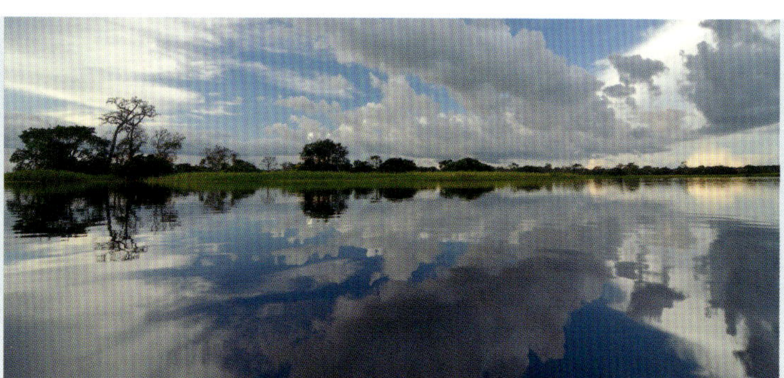

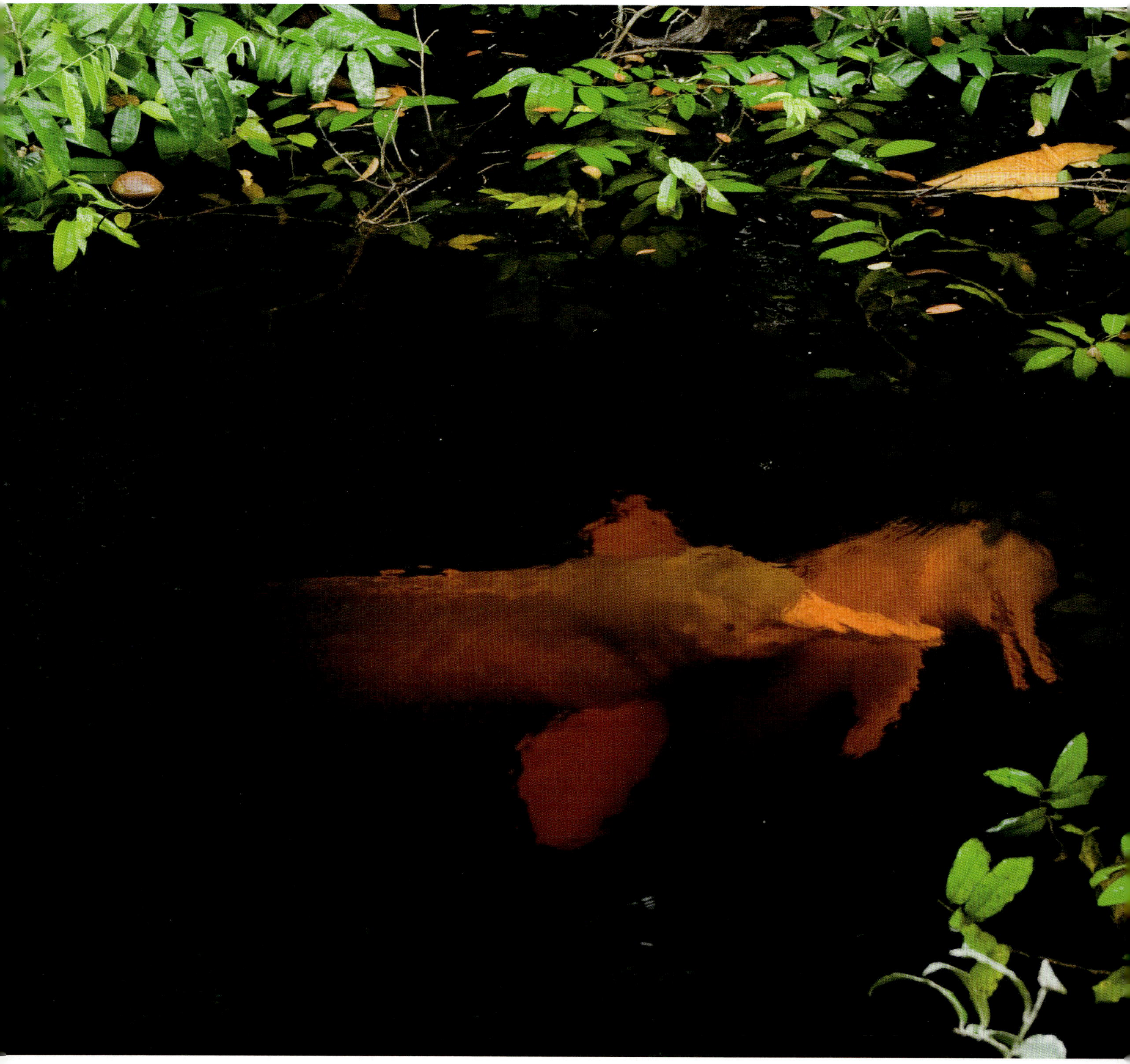

This gigantic rainforest park is situated about 200 km north-west of Manaus. The heart of the area is the Jaú National Park, covering the complete catchment basin of the Río Jaú up to its confluence with the Río Negro. In 2000, the reserve was inscribed as a World Heritage Site, and in 2003 was expanded to more than 60,000 sq. km under the name Complexão de Conservação del Amazonas Central. The Jaú and Negro rivers together form a blackwater ecosystem. The rivers' seasonal change in water level has given rise to the Igapó inundated forest area. Blackwater rivers have a dark coloration, due to dissolved tannins and organic precipitates, and contain little sediment. Inhabitants of such waters include giant otters, river manatees, South American river turtles, and black caimans. In the Mamirauá reserve there are extensive whitewater flood plains ("várzea") with nutrient-rich soils – whitewater rivers have turbid waters, rich in light minerals in suspension. The conservation area is home to 120 different mammals, including the pink and gray river dolphins, more than 450 birds, and 300 fish.

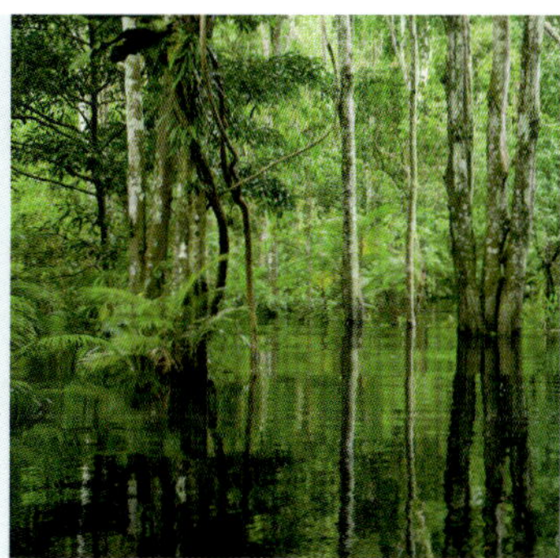

The trees and the dense shrubbery provide shelter and a habitat for nasua, hoatzin, squirrel monkeys and tapirs (picture series from the top). The orange-pink-coloured Amazon river dolphins (large picture) are a marvellous sight.

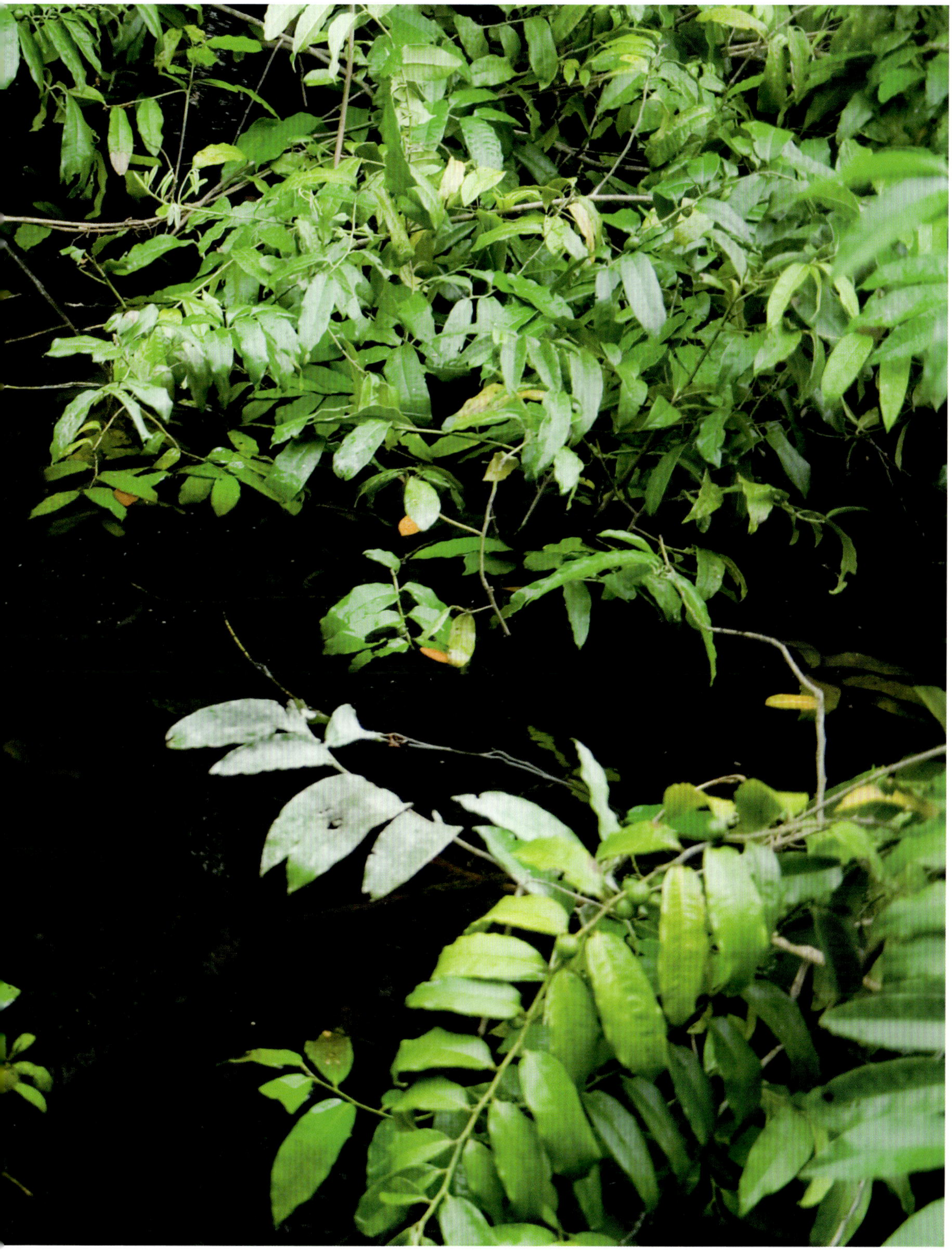

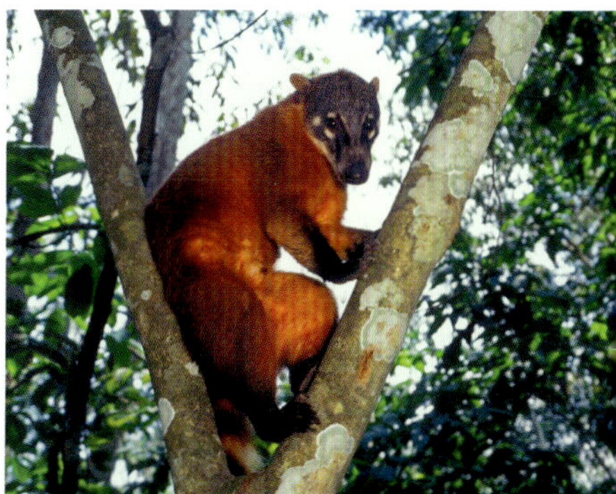

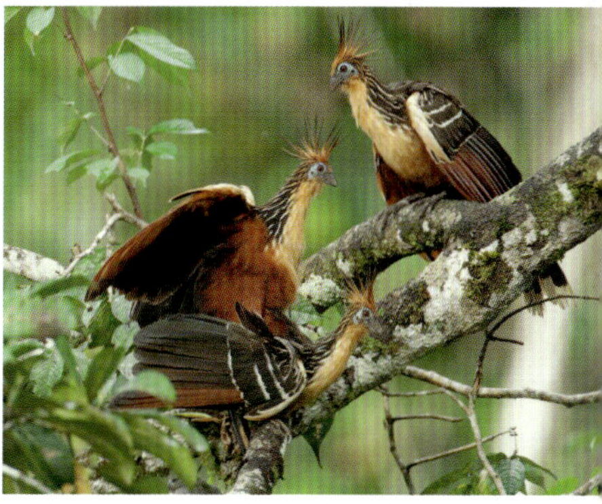

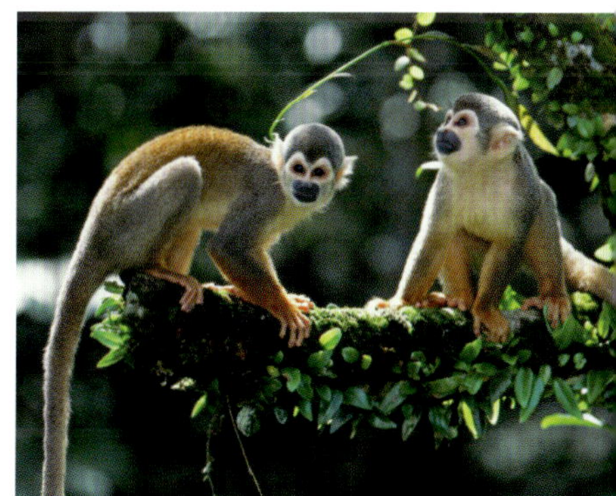

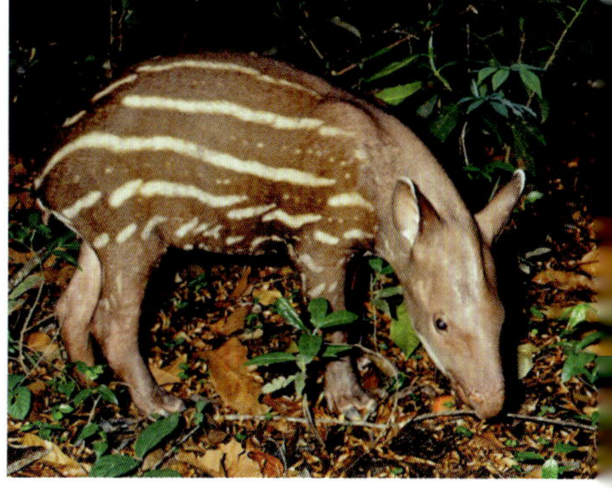

DISCOVERY COAST ATLANTIC RAINFOREST RESERVES

Date of inscription: 1999

The Discovery Coast Atlantic Rainforest Reserves are just part of one of the largest and best-preserved ecosystems of its kind, and home to many rare and endemic species.

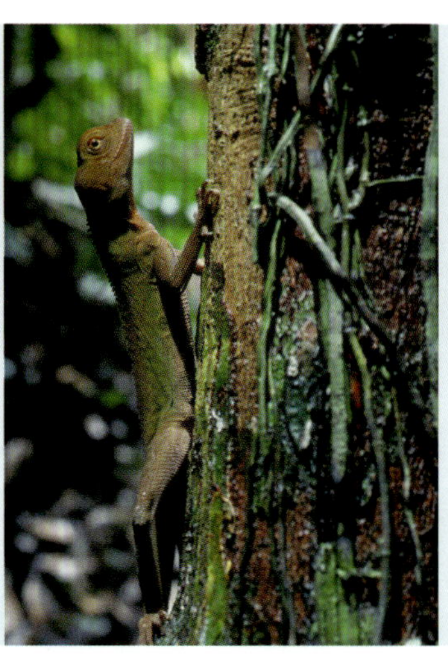

Brazil's Atlantic rainforest extends along the coast from the state of Bahía in the north to Río Grande do Sul in the south. Its dense vegetation is largely composed of 20- to 30-m high trees, on which grow orchids and bromelias. The poor light penetrating the canopy to the forest floor allows for only sparse undergrowth. The biodiversity and evolutionary history of these forests is of great scientific interest, not least as many of the plant species here are endemic. Studies have shown that in Bahía, 458 varieties of tree grow in a single hectare.

It boasts eight protected forest and bush reserves, all part of the northern section of the Atlantic rainforest. The Reservas Biológicas of Una and Sooretama, the Reservas Particulares de Patrimônio Natural of Pau Brasil, Veracruz, and Linhares, together with the national parks of Pau Brasil, Monte Pascual (whith its 536-m mountain of the same name), and Descobrimento.

An Argentine anole, perfectly camouflaged, climbs up a tree (left). Below: The jaguar carefully examines the lie of the land before leaving its hiding place.

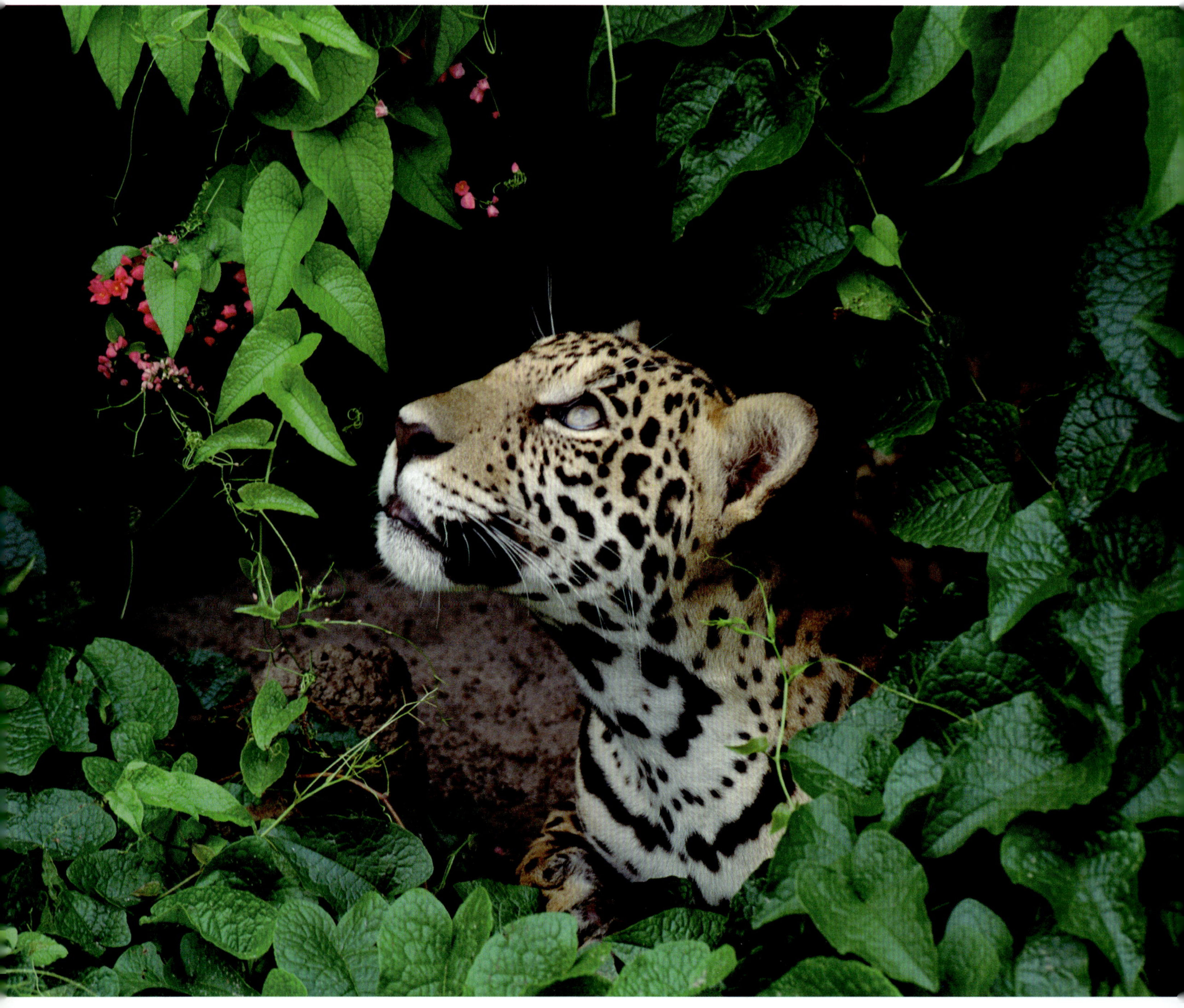

CHAPADA DOS VEADEIROS AND EMAS NATIONAL PARKS

With an area of about two million sq. km, the Cerrado is Brazil's second-largest ecosystem. Despite its rather dry climate and arid soils, it has the greatest biodiversity of any of the tropical savannahs. The Cerrado is located in Brazil's uplands, and large portions of the region feature high plateaus, punctuated by abrupt ravines and river valleys. The Chapada dos Veadeiros National Park covers a total area of 2,400 sq. km and covers the highest points of the Cerrado, providing a home for numerous rare species, including wild deer, monkeys, and king vultures. A total of 45 different mammals and 300 birds have been recorded, as well as about 1,000 butterflies. Emas National Park, covering a total area of 1,300 sq. km, was named after its population of rheas ("ema" in Portuguese). During the breeding season, the mating call of the male, which sounds like "nandu," can be heard far and wide. The open grassland with its termite hills is also an ideal habitat for giant anteaters.

Termite mounds (top) and waterfalls are typical features in the national parks. Right: the endemic pampas deer.

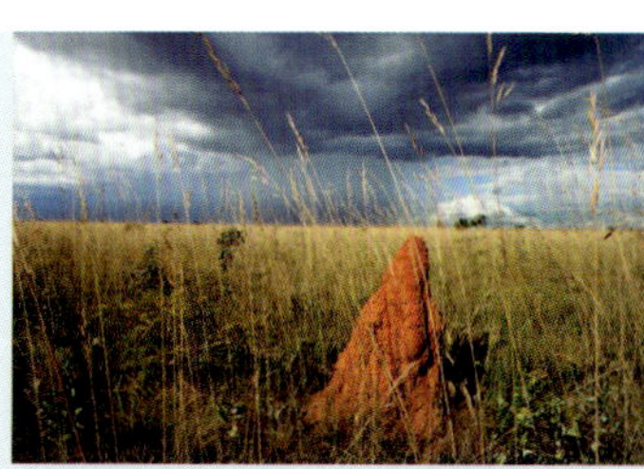

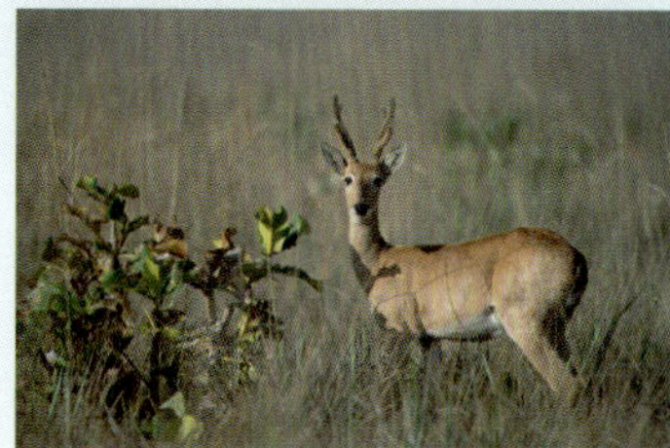

Date of inscription: 2001

Both Chapada dos Veadeiros and Emas National Parks in the state of Goiás are part of the Campos Cerrados, the midwestern Brazilian savannah.

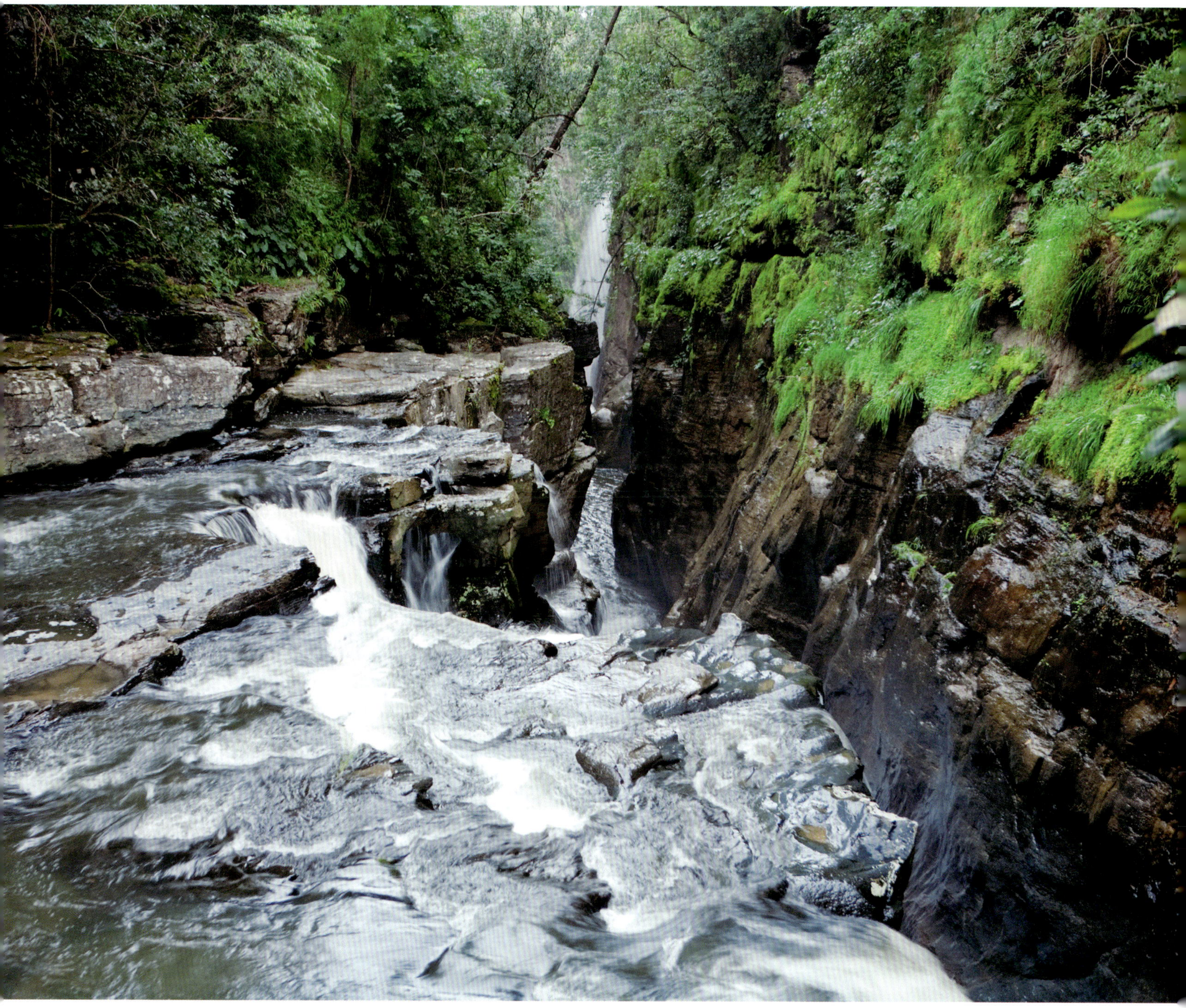

SOUTH-EAST ATLANTIC FORESTS

Date of inscription: 1999

The Atlantic rainforests in this reserve are among the largest and best-preserved in south-east Brazil. The enormous range of species that lives here are testament to the evolutionary history of this part of South America.

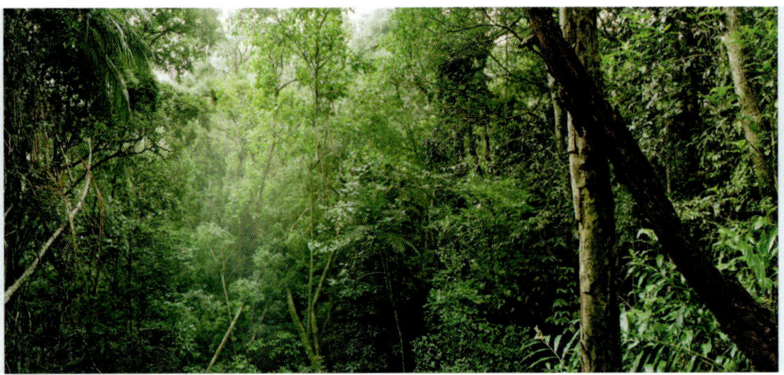

Brazil's Atlantic rainforests are considered endangered: only 7 percent of the original extent of the forests remains. A large part of these remnants grow in the south-east of the country, in the states of Paraná and São Paulo. Large parts of the rainforests of the Discovery Coast in north-east Brazil also enjoy World Heritage status.

The Atlantic forests grow in a stunning

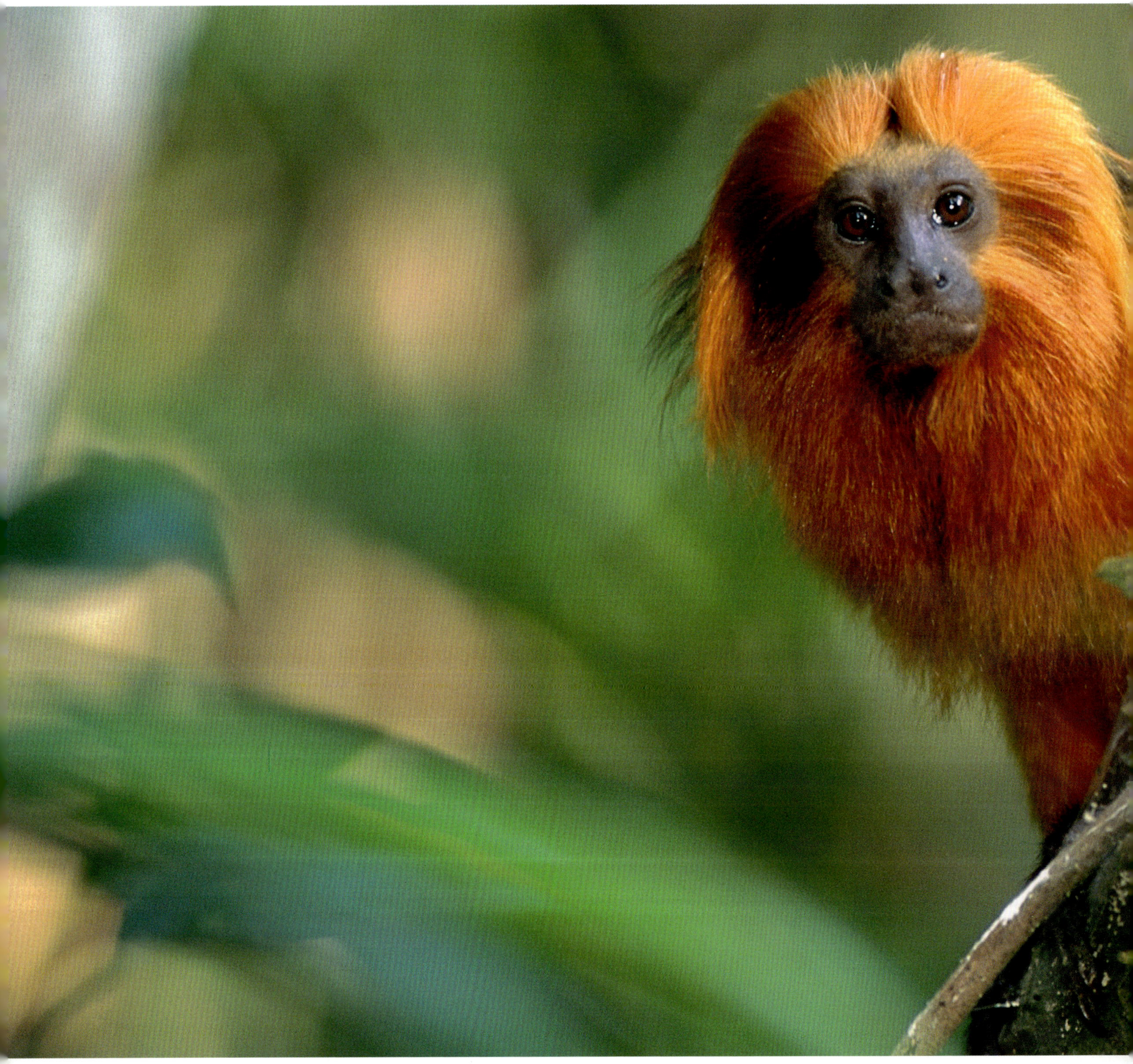

landscape that alternates between forested mountains, fast-flowing rivers, high waterfalls, and shallow swamps. Many rare and endemic plants grow in the 25 conservation areas, which together cover an area of about 5,000 sq. km (1,900 sq. miles). In some areas as many as 450 different tree species per hectare (2.5 acres) have been recorded, a botanical biodiversity greater even than that found in Amazonia.

The animal life in the forest reserves is equally varied, and includes some 120 different mammals (including jaguars, otters, and anteaters) as well as about 350 bird species.

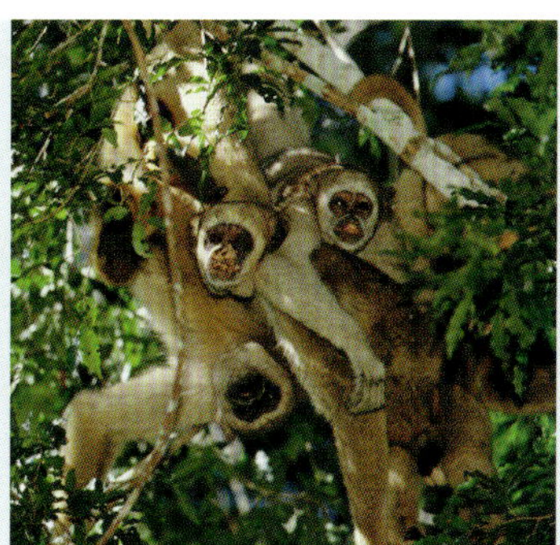

Although the upper canopy of the rainforest develops luxuriant foliage, the lack of light on the forest floor means that only sparse vegetation can grow here. Rare and absolutely worthy of protection: the northern muriqui (left) and the golden lion tamarin (large picture).

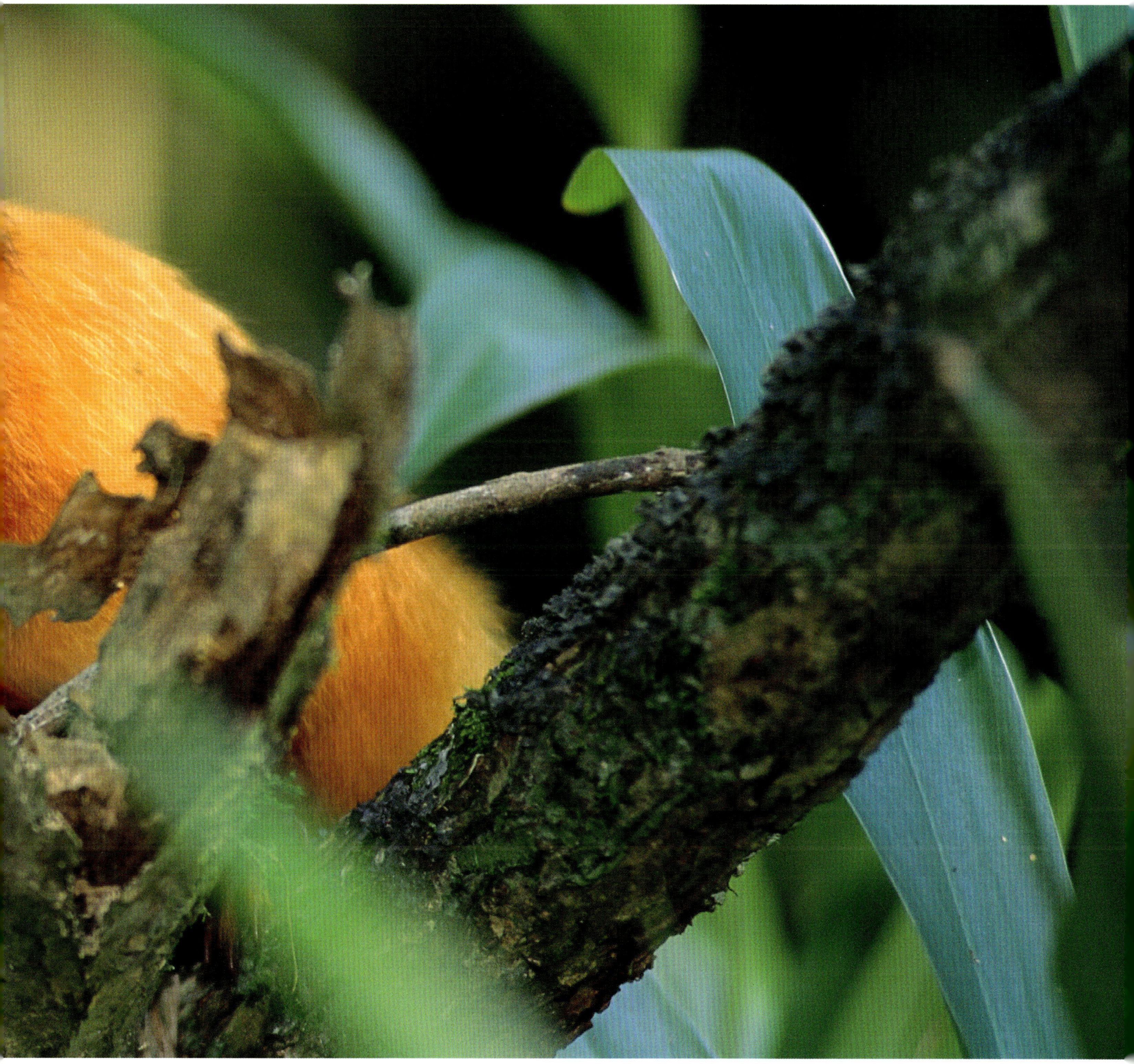

PANTANAL CONSERVATION AREA

Date of inscription: 2000

The Pantanal is one of the world's largest freshwater wetlands and boasts spectacular biodiversity.

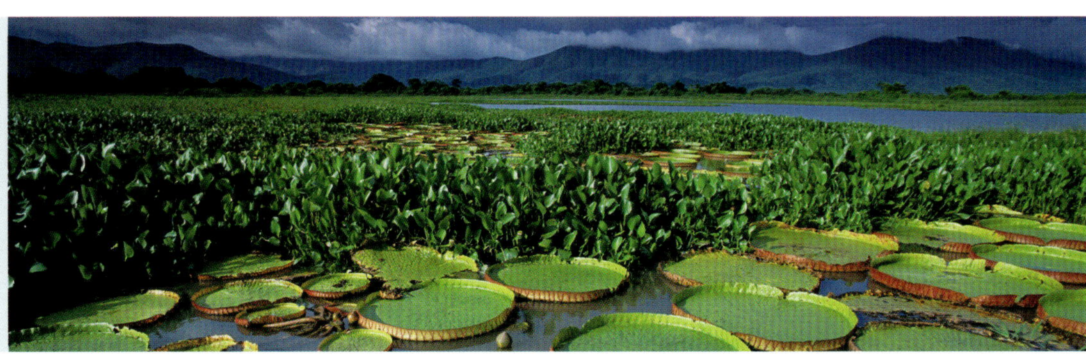

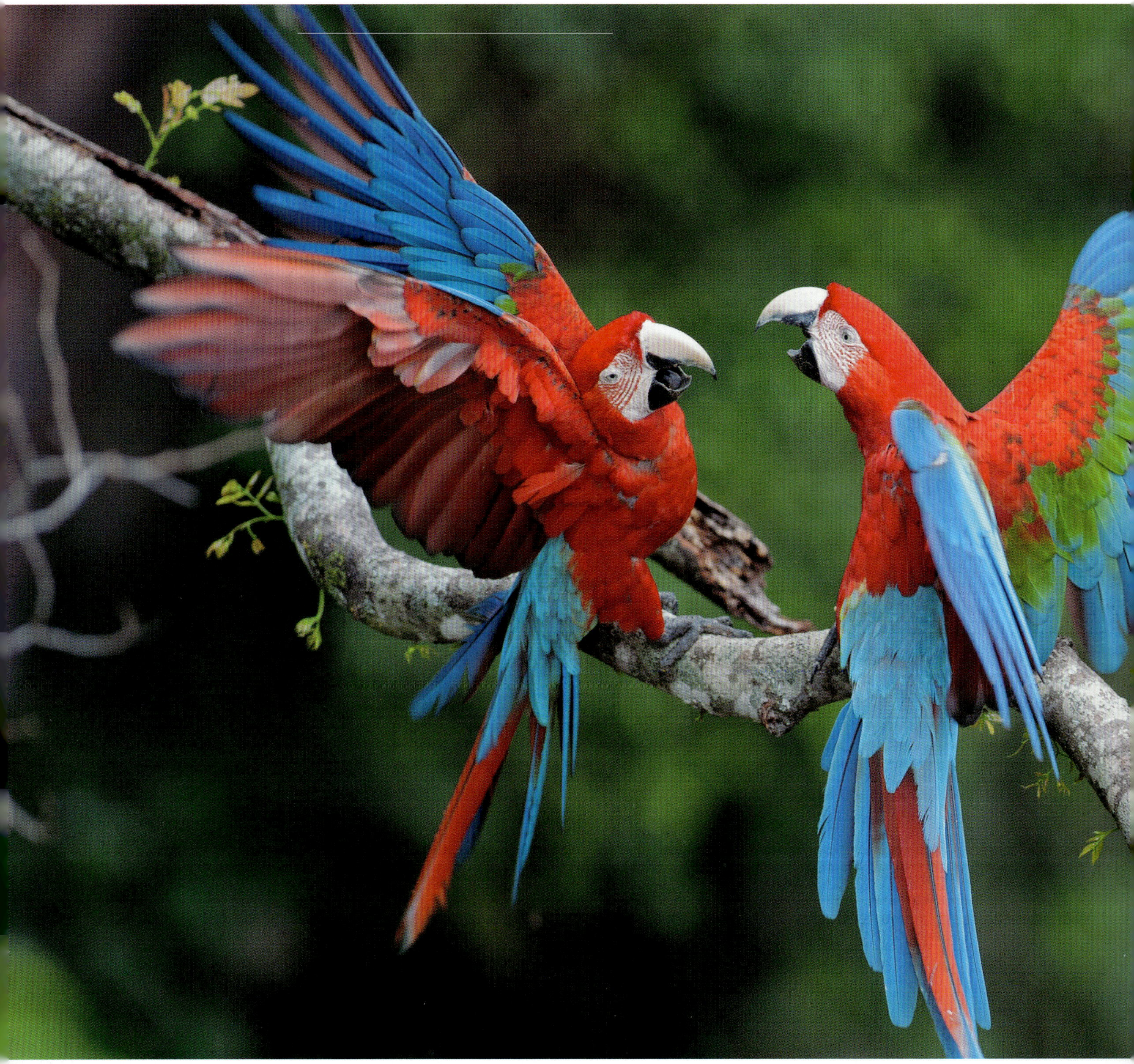

The Pantanal wetlands extend across the far south-west of Brazil, near the Bolivian and Paraguayan borders. From November to April, torrential summer downpours flood the Río Cuiabá and Río Paraguay river systems, a low plain three times the size of Costa Rica, forming an enormous, irregular body of water with shallow lakes, swamps, and flooded morasses. Four conservation areas here have been inscribed as World Heritage Sites, with a combined total area of around 2,000 sq. km (770 sq. miles). The annual floods function as a natural control mechanism, determining the supply, cleaning, and exchange of groundwater and rainwater. The sediment and nutrients transported by the floodwater allow healthy grassland to grow up during the drier winter, when the waters recede between the end of April and October. During these months, Pantanal's unique scenery looks particularly spectacular, steaming in the heat beneath a usually misty sky. The conservation area remains partially inundated during the dry season, making it a refuge for fauna.

Water is the characteristic element of the Pantanal. The flowers and leaves of the Santa Cruz water lily (Victoria cruziana) spread widely across the surface of the water (left). Black howlers, capybara and caimans (picture series, from the top) love hiding in swampy areas. Large picture: excited green-winged macaws.

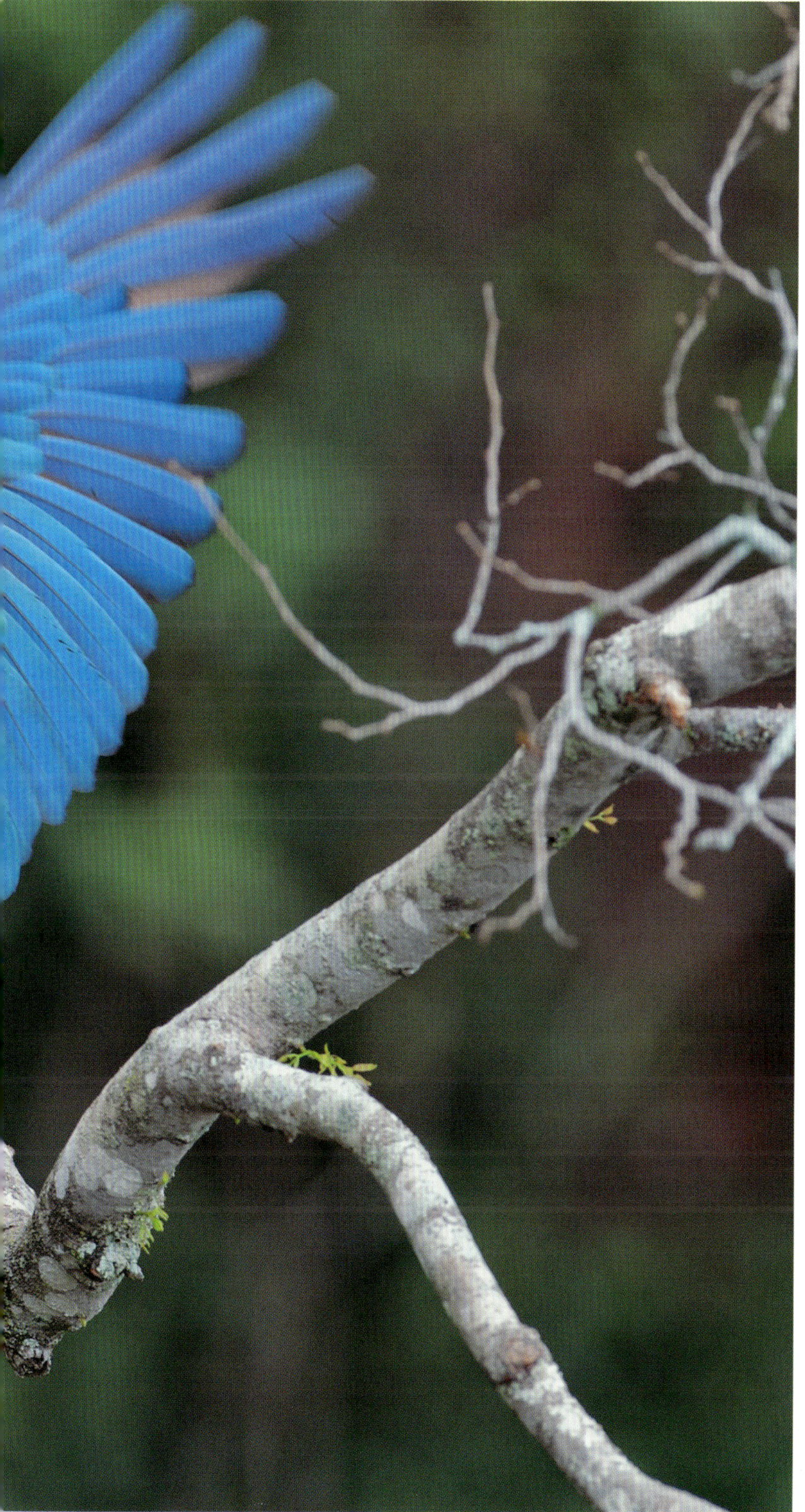

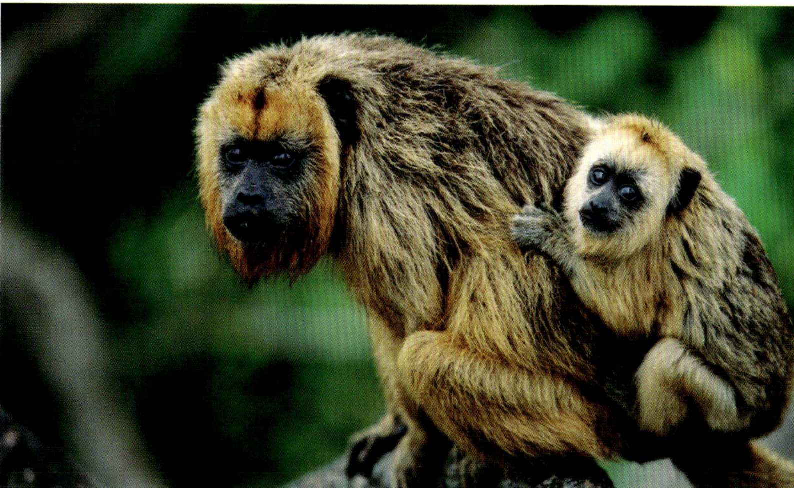

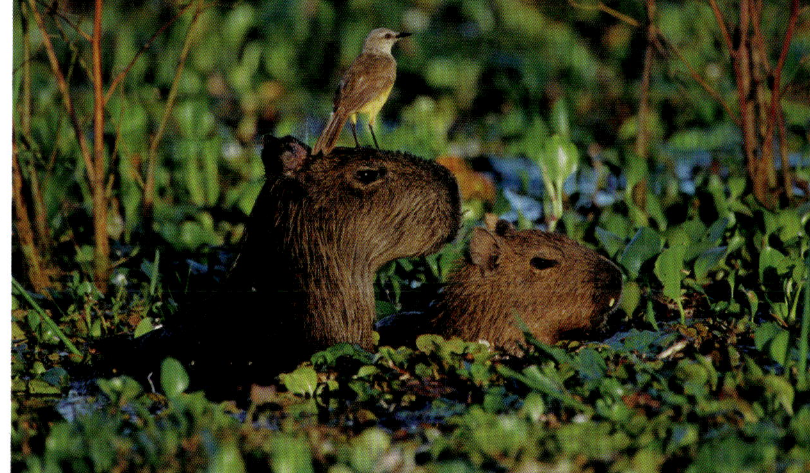

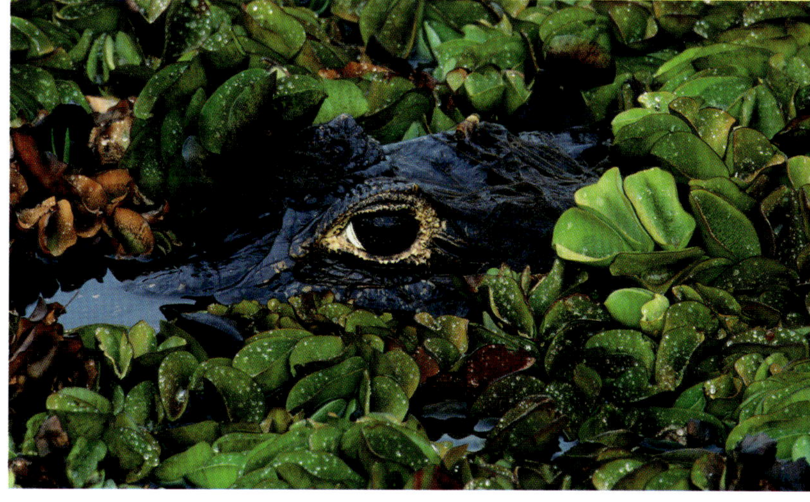

FERNANDO DE NORONHA AND ATOL DAS ROCAS RESERVES

Date of inscription: 2001

This island group, 500 km (310 miles) north-east of Recife, reveals an extraordinary wealth of animal life, with dolphins, sharks, sea turtles, and countless seabirds.

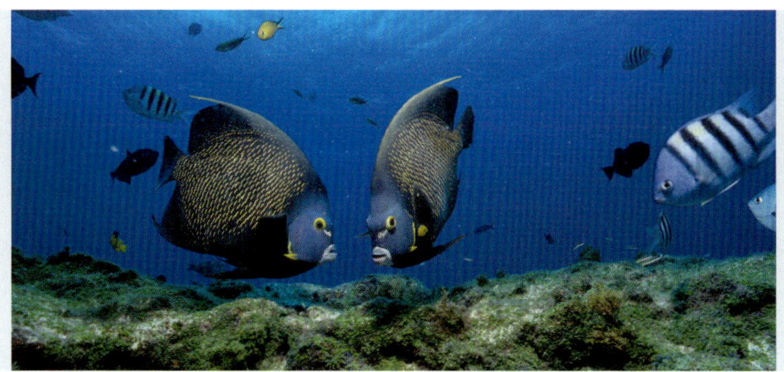

The island reserves of Fernando de Noronha and Atol das Rocas are situated only a few degrees south of the equator, where the cold waters of the South Atlantic meet warm equatorial ocean currents. Fernando de Noronha, the main island, is a volcanic formation, covered in unique island forest and surrounded by a group of 21 satellite islands.

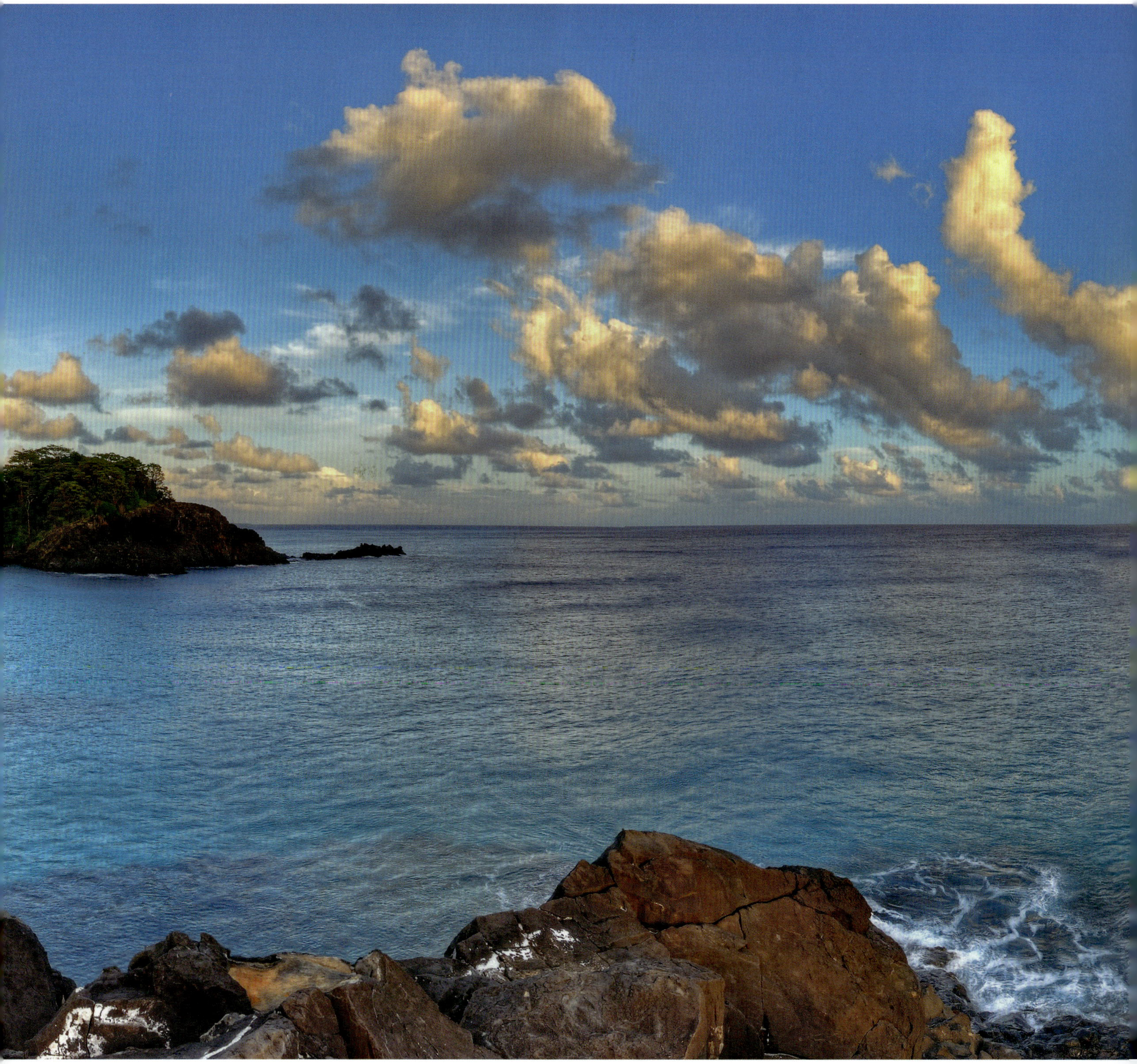

The Rocas Atoll consists of coral reefs that have formed around the summits of an underwater mountain range.
The basins and shallow lagoons of this, the only atoll in the South Atlantic, offer a fascinating natural spectacle at low tide, when a natural aquarium is formed. The island reserve also includes a marine conservation area of extraordinarily rich biodiversity. The nutrient-rich coastal waters round the island group, teeming with tuna, billfish, cetaceans, sharks, and rare sea turtles such as the loggerhead, are used by many fish species as a spawning and feeding ground. The islands of this South Atlantic archipelago are also the most important staging post for many whales on their annual migration from north to south and back again. There are more dolphins resident in the Baía dos Golfinhos than anywhere else on earth. The islands are also a habitat for innumerable tropical seabirds, including many migratory species. The tiny Rocas Atoll alone is home to 150,000 birds. At low tide the atoll reveals a spectacular seascape of lagoons and tidal pools seething with fish.

The bays of Fernando do Noronha Island with their luminous turquoise coastal waters offer ideal conditions for numerous animals (large picture). Above the ocean floor, the beautifully marked French angelfish cavort, among others (left).

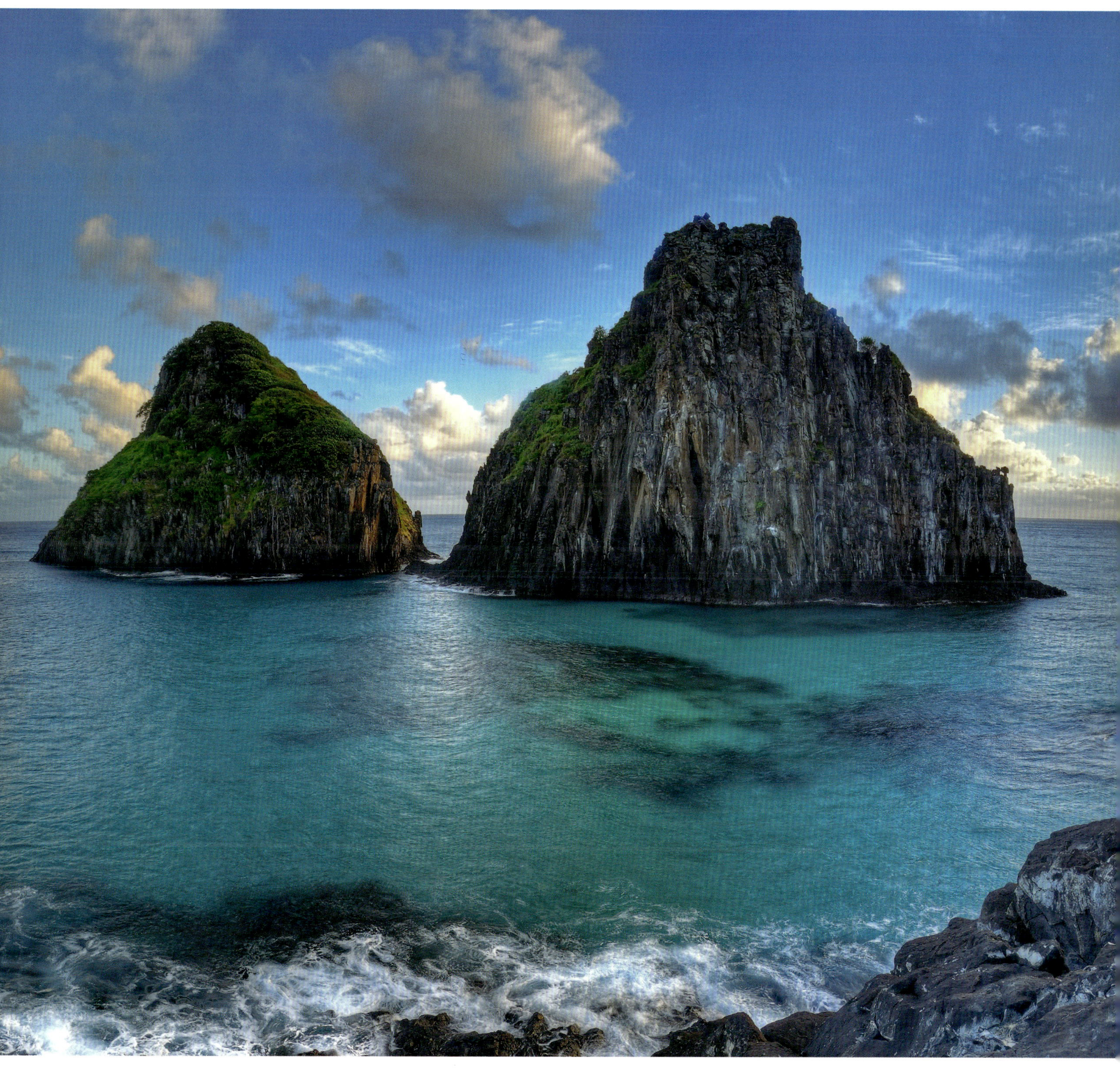

IGUAÇU NATIONAL PARK

Date of inscription: 1986

The Iguaçu Falls are among the biggest and most impressive on earth. This natural monument and its species-rich surroundings were brought under protection through the combining of two parks, one in Brazil and one in Argentina.

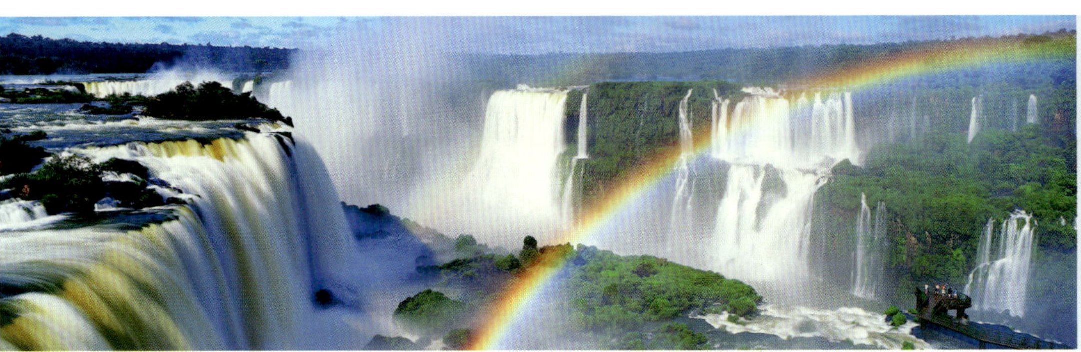

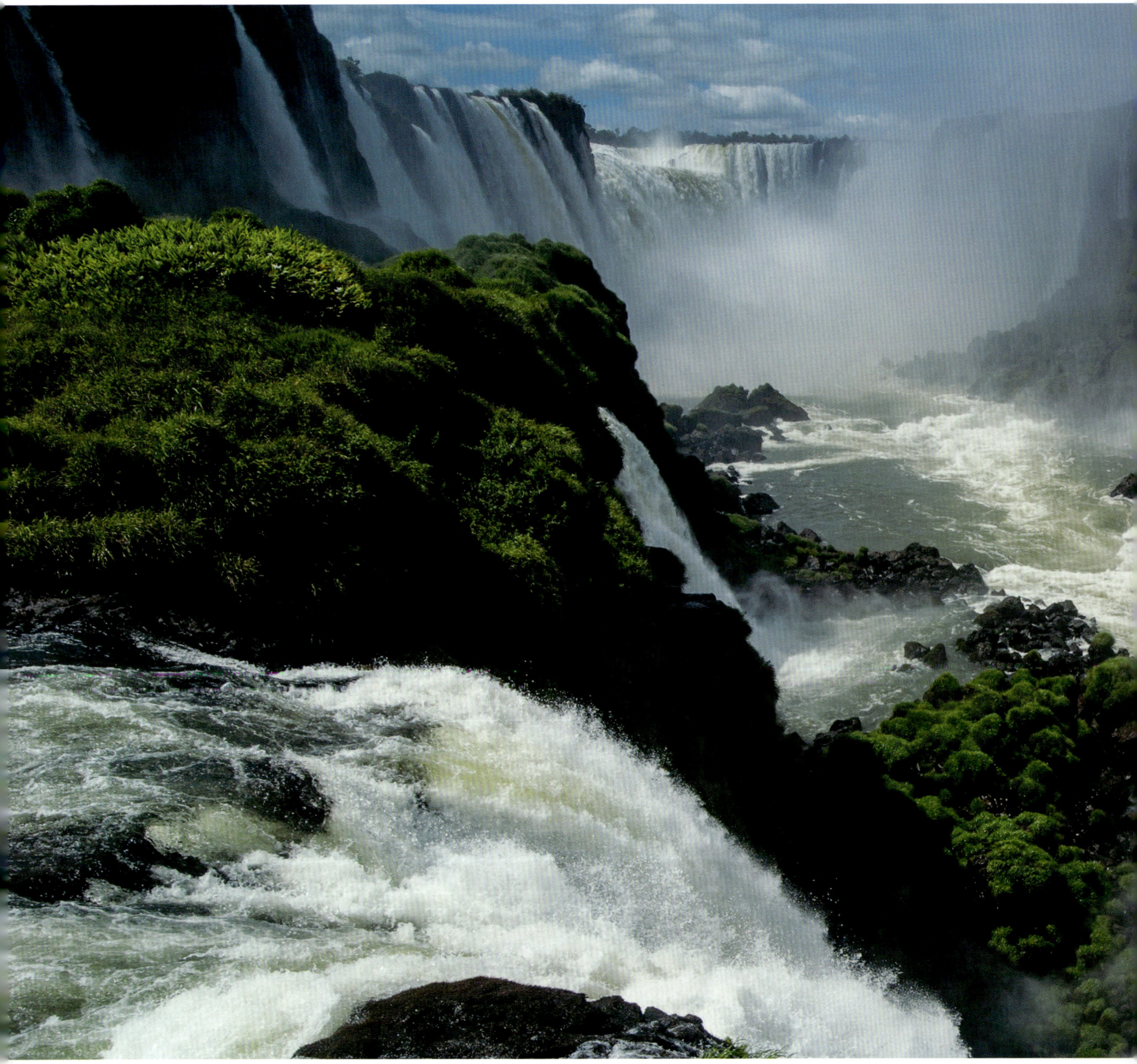

You hear the waterfall at the border of Brazil, Argentina, and Paraguay long before you see it; first, a soft gurgling, which then quickly swells to a deafening rumbling and thundering. Flanked by dense tropical vegetation, the Iguaçu river – known in Argentina as the Iguazú – has already reached a width of almost a kilometer (half a mile) as it approaches the horseshoe-shaped falls. The foaming masses of water then cross a 2,700-m (9,000-foot) wide lip of rock, falling into the chasm with limitless force – a superlative natural spectacle. More than 270 individual waterfalls have been counted here.

The park, which covers a total area of 1,700 sq. km (660 sq. miles) on the Brazilian side, is a refuge for many endangered plant and animal species. Parrots and nothuras fly in the shade of the trees, and swifts build their nests in rock fissures between the waterfalls. The luxuriant rainforests are inhabited by ocelots, jaguars, howler monkeys, tapirs, giant anteaters, and peccaries, and the now rare giant otter hunts for fish in the troubled waters of the plunge pools.

The water drops more than 80 m (265 feet) into the depths. Individual waterfalls are separated by small rock outcrops. Sunlight breaks through the mist and spray and creates magical rainbows (both images).

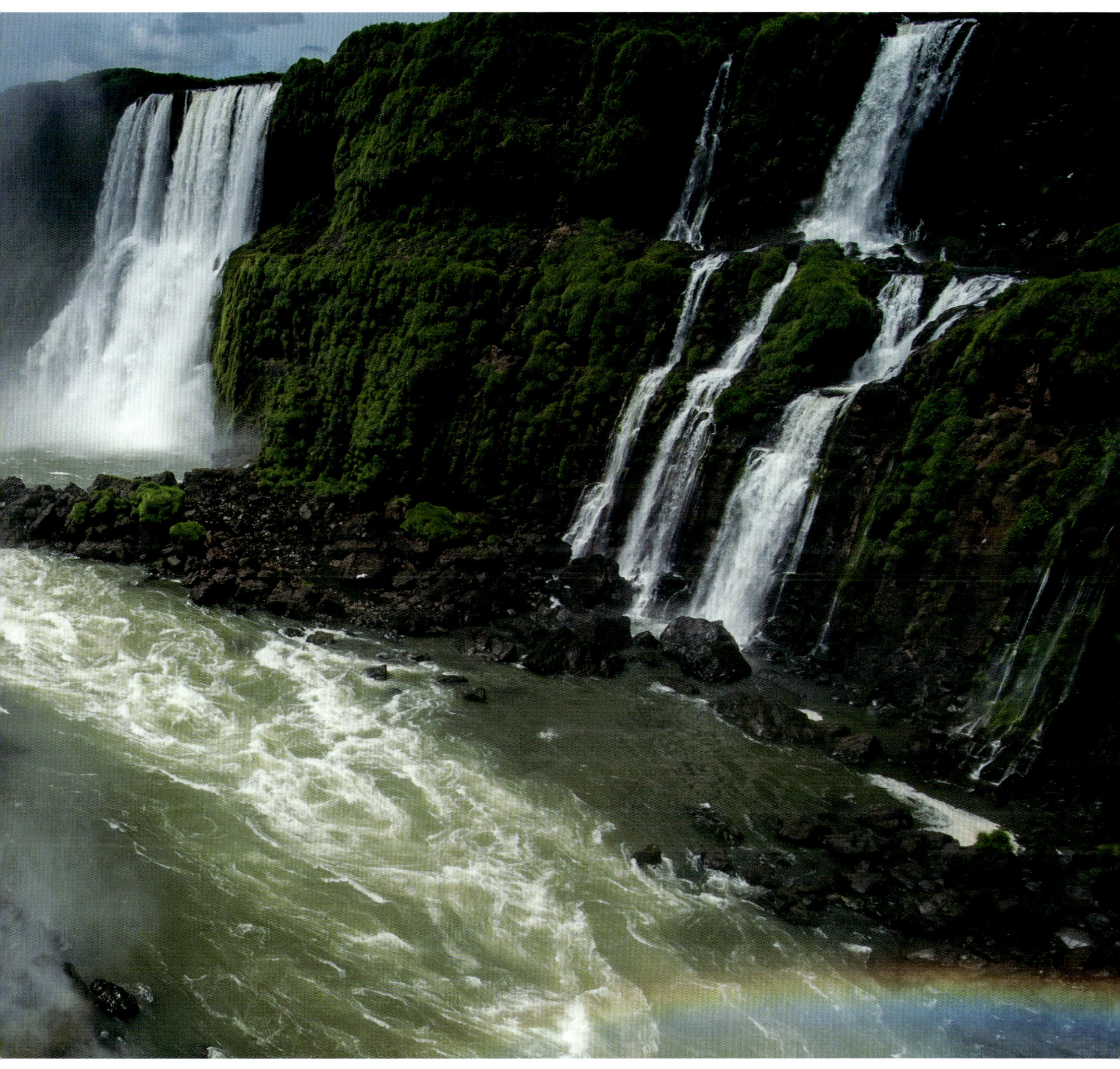

ISCHIGUALASTO AND TALAMPAYA NATURAL PARKS

Date of inscription: 2000

The world's most complete stratified fossil record from the Triassic is to be found in these two neighboring nature parks in western Argentina.

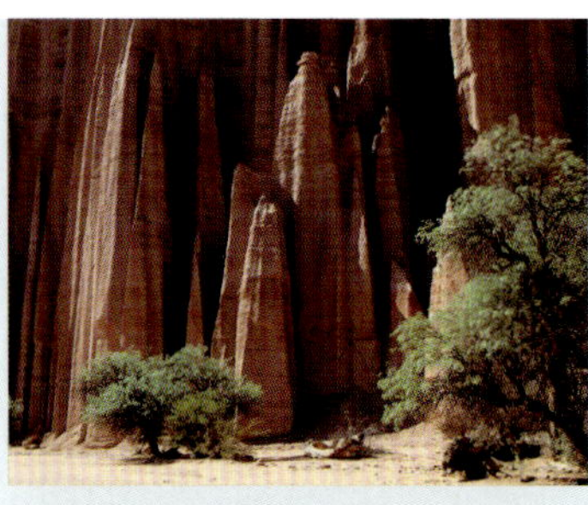

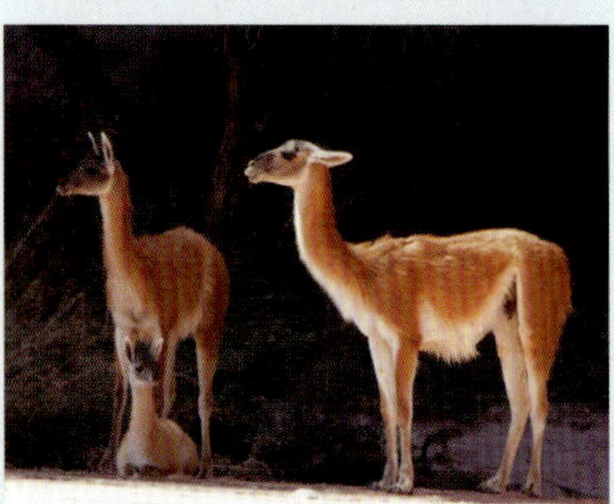

The Valle de la Luna, an extended, desert-like valley about 400 km northwest of Córdoba, near the Chilean border, was researched by paleontologists from the 1950s. The two parks, Ischigualasto Provincial Park and Talampaya, combined form a continuous area of 2,750 sq. km. When the Andes rose from the earth's crust 60 million years ago, they radically changed the environmental conditions. In Talampaya, erosion, nature's sculptor, shaped dark brown and green rocks, columns, and thin obelisks, strewing them across the brick-red, sandy ground and low scrubland, as if thrown by a giant's hand. Neatly separated rock strata in steep cliffs and petrified forests in both parks are open books for geologists and paleontologists, revealing an almost complete evolutionary history of the area, stretching back to the Triassic era. Along with dinosaur bones, paleontologists have excavated fossil remains of 55 other vertebrates and more than 100 plant species. Numerous pre-Columbian rock paintings in Ischigualasto and especially Talampaya are of cultural and historical interest.

Steep canyons where the rocks grow out of the ground like a cathedral (top left) and unique polished rock pillars (large picture) characterize the Talampaya Park. Left: Guanacos are the wild forefathers of domesticated llamas.

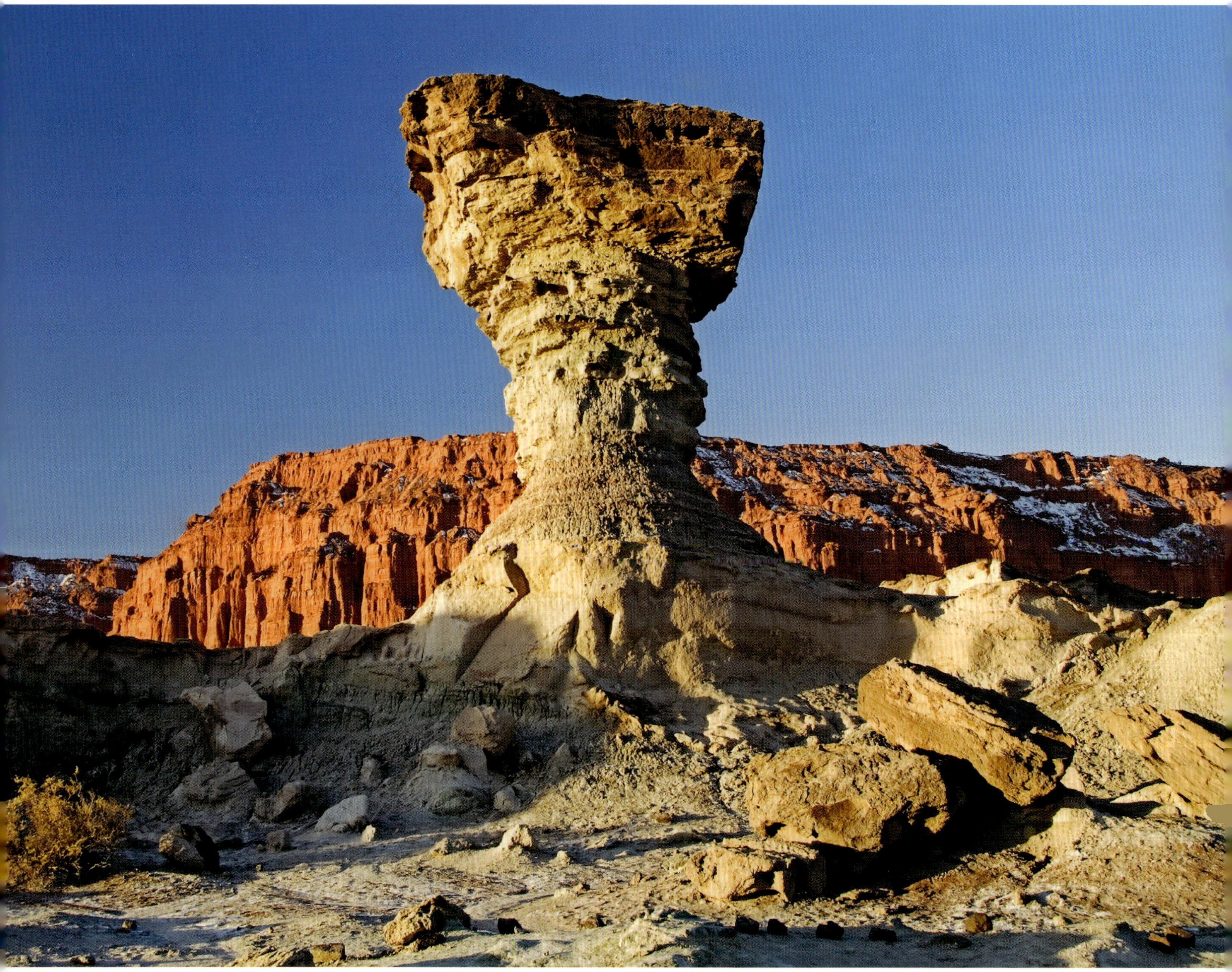

THE VALDÉS PENINSULA

The Ameghino isthmus, 30 km long but only 5–10 km wide, connects the largest Argentinian peninsula to the mainland, and is surrounded by waters that are a habitat for several species of marine mammal, which breed here every year. The southern right whale was hunted almost to extinction, with populations declining every year, but these 14-m long giants, which can weigh 35 metric tons, have since found a safe refuge in the Valdés peninsula, where they congregate at the beginning of every spring, remaining until December. An enormous elephant seal colony is to be found in a protected area of the Punta Norte, the northern extremity of the peninsula. These imposing animals are the largest members of the seal family. A colony of sealions is protected on Cape Punta Delgada. Orcas are a natural enemy of the sealion, and they have developed particular techniques to hunt these animals, even straying close to the shore to catch their prey. There are also Magellan penguins on Valdés, and 180 other bird species, of which many are seabirds.

South American sea lions, also known as southern or Patagonian sea lions, have a protected refuge here on the coast and between the rocky coves. They were long hunted for their skins and their oil was also used commercially.

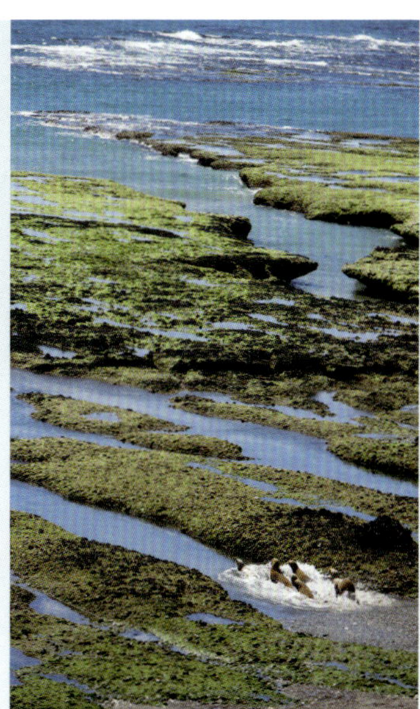

Date of inscription: 1999

The entirety of this 3,600 sq. km (1,390 sq. mile) peninsula mid-way along the Atlantic coast of Argentina is designated as a World Heritage Site. It offers a protected living environment for sea mammals in particular.

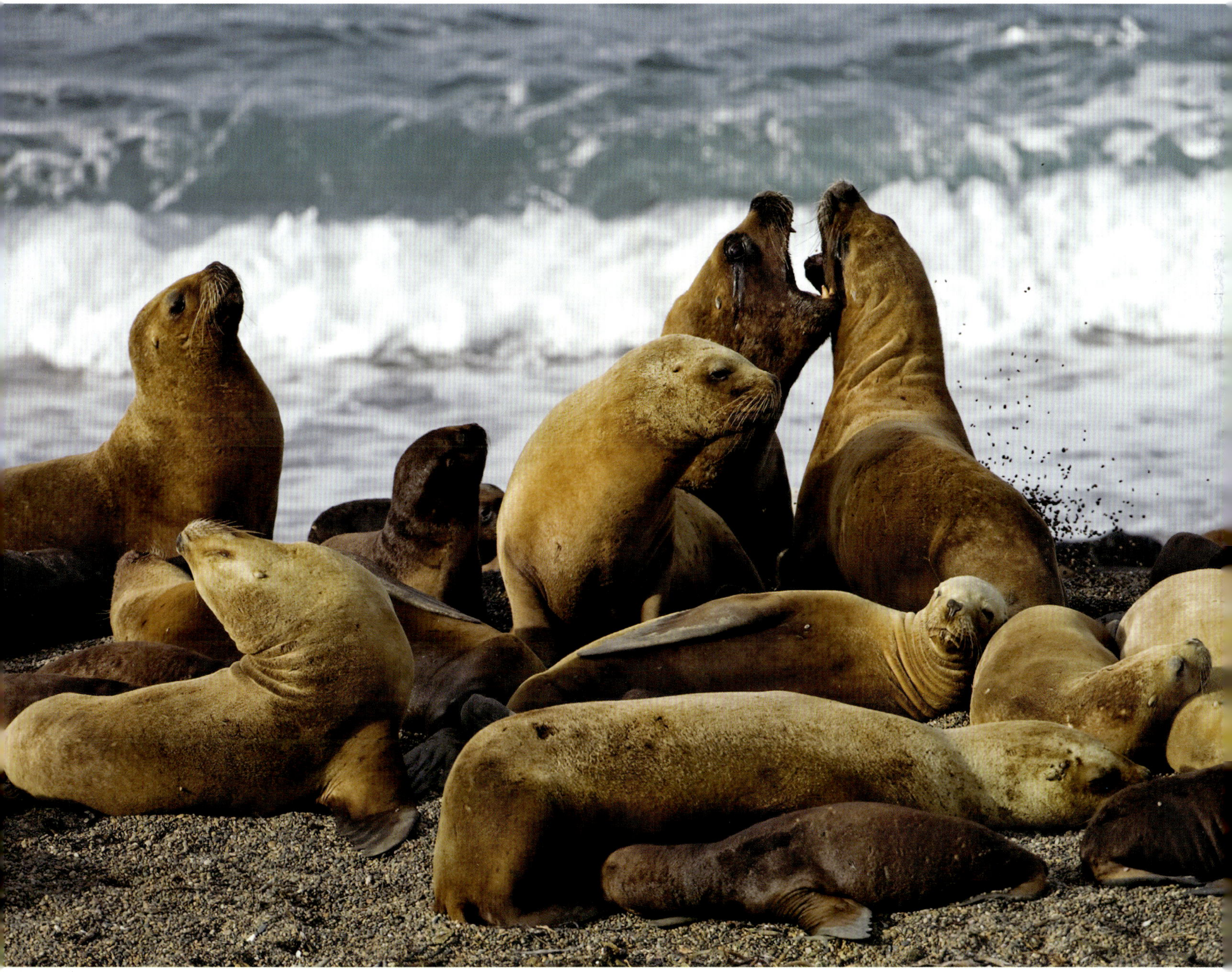

LOS GLACIARES NATIONAL PARK

Date of inscription: 1981

The 4,500 sq. km (1,800 sq. miles) of this national park are situated in the heart of the Patagonian Andes, next to the Chilean border, and boast extraordinary scenic beauty, with spectacular mountains, glaciers, and lakes.

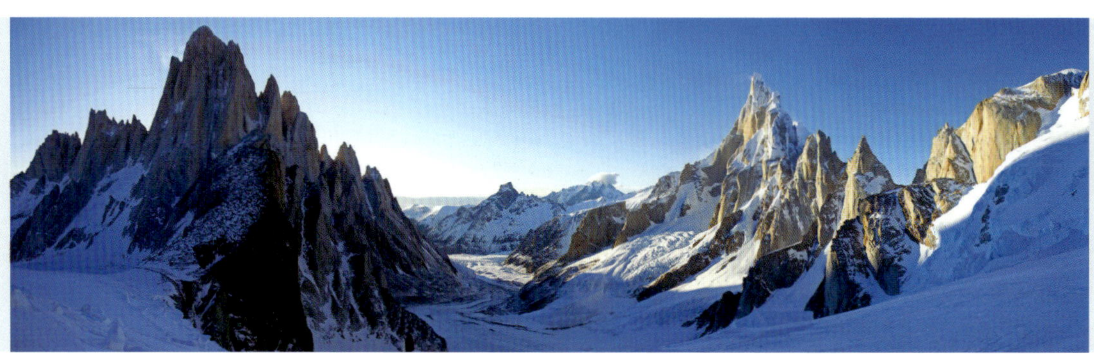

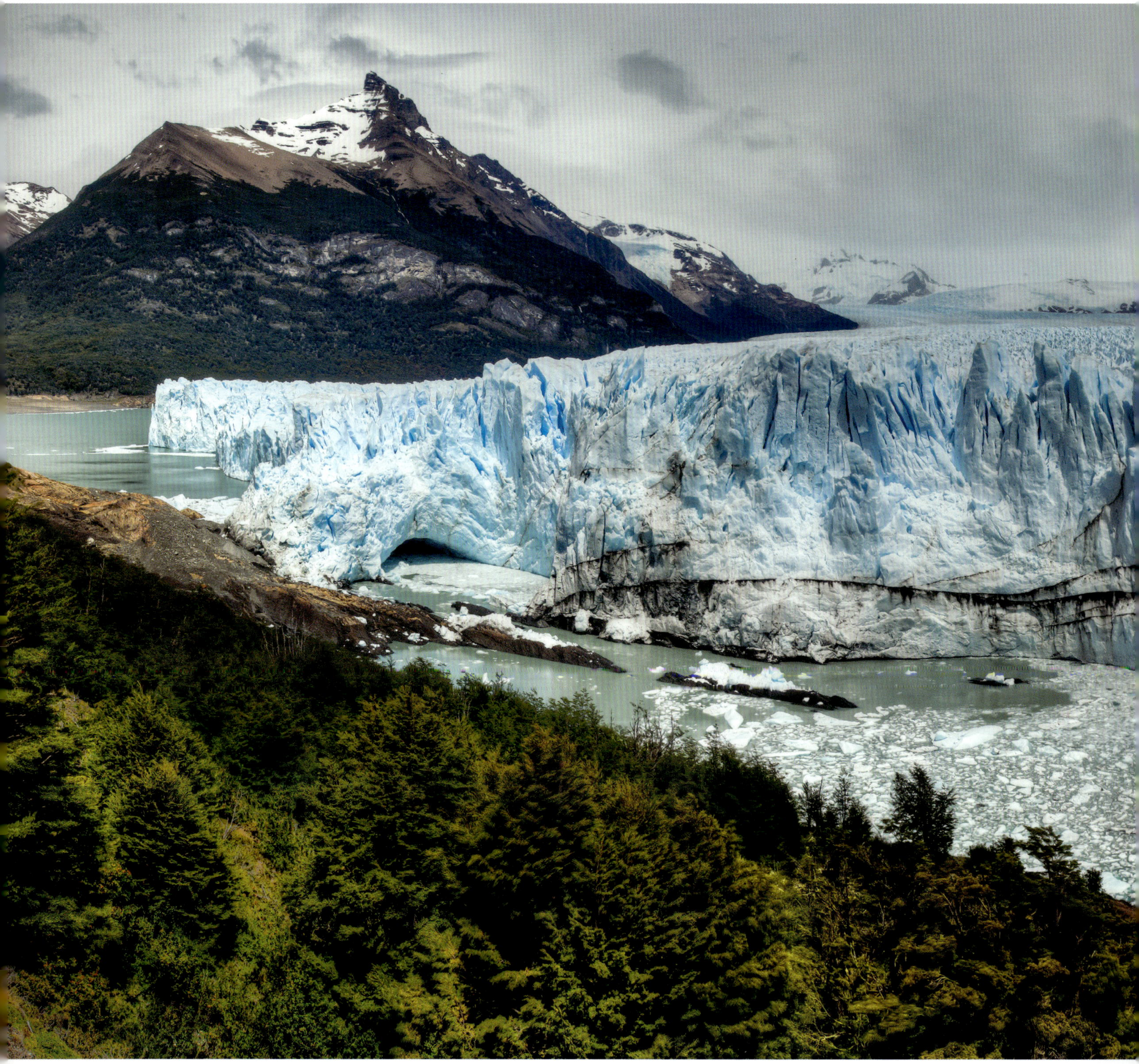

The national park's 13 glaciers form just a part of the extensive Patagonian ice field, which is composed of 47 large glaciers and is the largest continuous mass of ice outside the Antarctic, with a total surface area of 15,000 sq. km (5,800 sq. miles). There are a further 200 smaller glaciers which are not directly connected to the ice field.

The best-known of these is the Perito Moreno glacier, 30 km (19 miles) long and 5 km (3 miles) wide, which "calves" into Lago Argentino. As one of the few glaciers left in the world that is not retreating, it gradually pushes its terminus out as a kind of peninsula, cutting off a spur of the lake every three or four years. The water level here then rises by up to 30 m (100 feet) and, when the wall of ice can no longer stand the intense pressure, an impressive natural spectacle occurs as the dammed-up water ruptures a section of the glacier terminus and floods into the other part of the lake. The Uppsala and Spegazzini glaciers are also a part of this primeval, glacial world. The scenic high points of the granite summits of Cerro Torre and Monte Fitz Roy, both over 3,000 m (9,900 feet) high and challenging climbs, lie in the northern part of the national park, not far from Lago Viedma.

The terminus of the Perito Moreno glacier towers up to 60 m (200 feet) above Lago Argentino (below). Left: the superb panorama of Monte Fitz Roy and Cerro Torre.

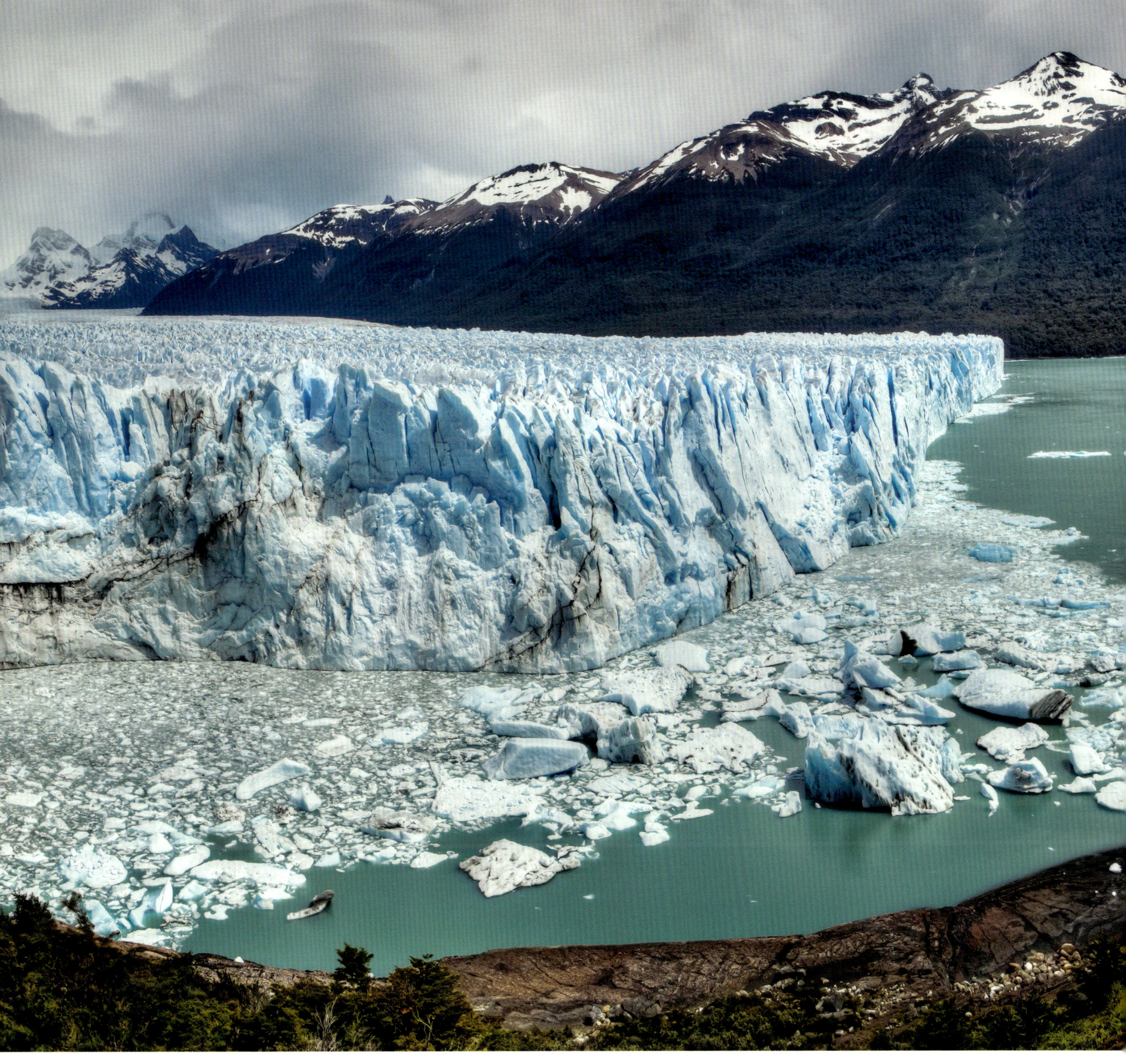

INDEX

The index below makes it easy for you to quickly find all the listed World Natural Heritage sites on the maps of the atlas section. The first number indicates the page on which to find a site, the subsequent combination of letters and numbers gives you the coordinates on the map.

Europe

Asia

Australia/Oceania

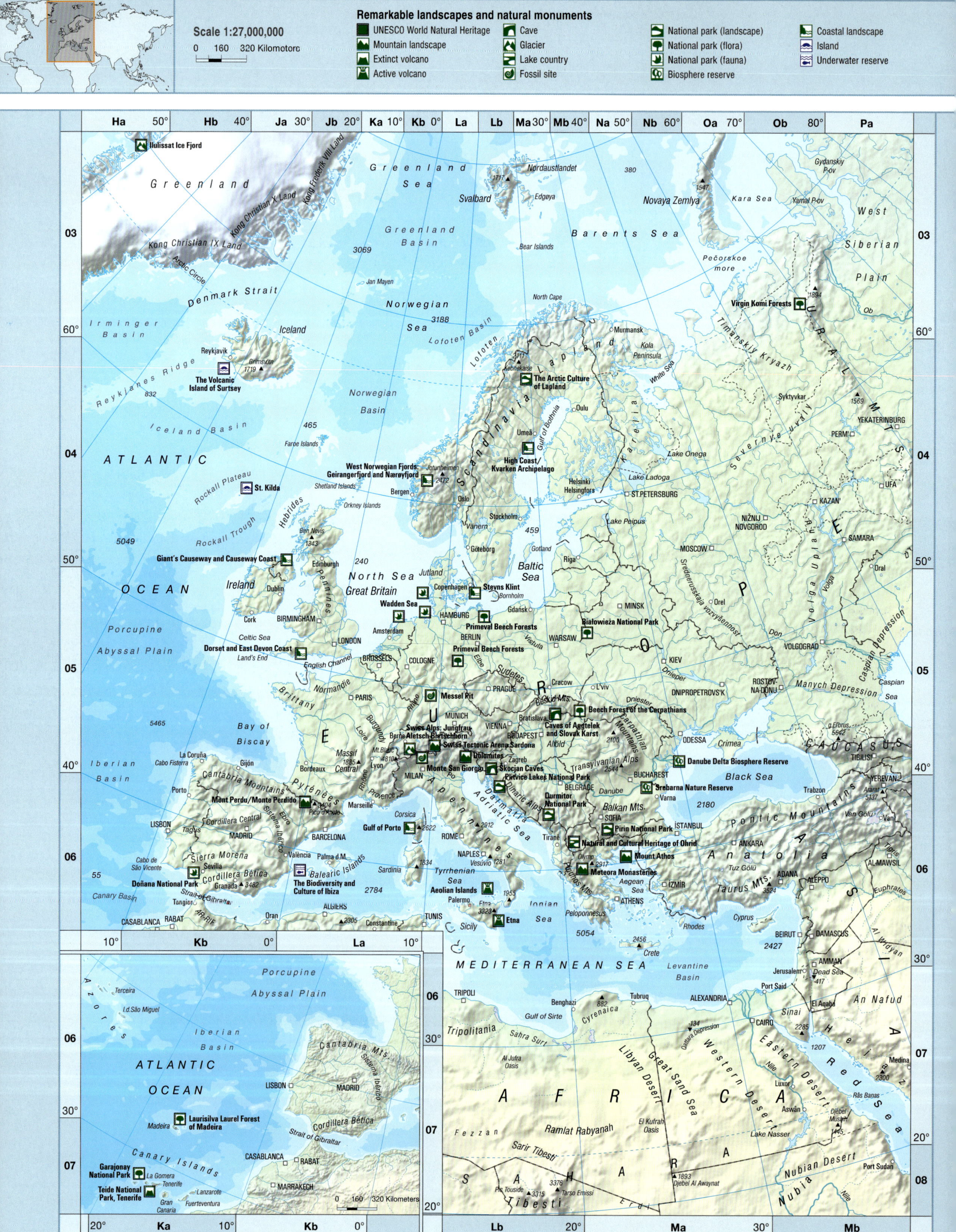
Scale 1:27,000,000
0 160 320 Kilometers
Remarkable landscapes and natural monuments
UNESCO World Natural Heritage
Mountain landscape
Extinct volcano
Active volcano
Cave
Glacier
Lake country
Fossil site
National park (landscape)
National park (flora)
National park (fauna)
Biosphere reserve
Coastal landscape
Island
Underwater reserve
Ilulissat Ice Fjord
Greenland
Greenland Sea
Svalbard
Nordaustlandet
Novaya Zemlya
Kara Sea
Barents Sea
Greenland Basin
Kong Christian IX Land
Kong Christian X Land
Kong Frederik VIII Land
Denmark Strait
Arctic Circle
Jan Mayen
Norwegian Sea
Bear Islands
North Cape
Irminger Basin
Iceland
Reykjavik
The Volcanic Island of Surtsey
Reykjanes Ridge
Iceland Basin
Norwegian Basin
Lofoten Basin
Lofoten
Scandinavia
Lapland
The Arctic Culture of Lapland
Murmansk
Kola Peninsula
White Sea
Virgin Komi Forests
Timanskiy Kryazh
Pečorskoe more
West Siberian Plain
Yamal Pov
Gydanskiy Pov
URAL MTS
Severnye Uvaly
Syktyvkar
YEKATERINBURG
PERM
UFA
KAZAN
SAMARA
ATLANTIC OCEAN
Faroe Islands
Rockall Plateau
Rockall Trough
St. Kilda
Hebrides
West Norwegian Fjords: Geirangerfjord and Nærøyfjord
Shetland Islands
Orkney Islands
Bergen
Oslo
Stockholm
High Coast/ Kvarken Archipelago
Gulf of Bothnia
Umeå
Oulu
Karelia
Lake Onega
Lake Ladoga
Helsinki Helsingfors
ST. PETERSBURG
Lake Peipus
NIŽNIJ NOVGOROD
MOSCOW
Giant's Causeway and Causeway Coast
Ben Nevis
Edinburgh
Pennines
Ireland
Dublin
Cork
Great Britain
North Sea
Jutland
Copenhagen
Stevns Klint
Bornholm
Baltic Sea
Gotland
Göteborg
Riga
Wadden Sea
HAMBURG
BIRMINGHAM
LONDON
Amsterdam
Primeval Beech Forests
Białowieża National Park
MINSK
Porcupine Abyssal Plain
Celtic Sea
Dorset and East Devon Coast
Land's End
English Channel
BRUSSELS
COLOGNE
BERLIN
Gdańsk
WARSAW
Vistula
KIEV
Dnieper
VOLGOGRAD
Don
Volga
Volga Upland
Srednerusskaja vozvyšennost'
Caspian Depression
Caspian Sea
Manych Depression
ROSTOV-NA-DONU
DNIPROPETROVS'K
EUROPE
Normandie
Brittany
PARIS
Messel Pit
Rhine
Elbe
Sudetes
PRAGUE
Cracow
L'viv
Dniester
Beskid Mts.
Beech Forest of the Carpathians
Carpathian Mountains
MUNICH
VIENNA
Bratislava
BUDAPEST
Caves of Aggtelek and Slovak Karst
Alföld
ODESSA
Crimea
Bay of Biscay
Burgundy
Loire
Massif Central
Swiss Alps: Jungfrau-Aletsch-Bietschhorn
Swiss Tectonic Arena Sardona
Bern
Mt. Blanc
Lyon
Dolomites
Zagreb
Monte San Giorgio
Škocjan Caves
Plitvice Lakes National Park
Transylvanian Alps
BUCHAREST
Danube Delta Biosphere Reserve
Black Sea
Caucasus
Elbrus
TBILISI
YEREVAN
Ararat
La Coruña
Gijón
Cabo Fisterra
Cantabria Mountains
Bordeaux
Pyrénées
Rhône
MILAN
Po
Provence
Marseille
Apennines
Dalmatia
Adriatic Sea
Dinaric Alps
BELGRADE
Danube
Durmitor National Park
Srebarna Nature Reserve
Varna
Balkan Mts.
SOFIA
Pirin National Park
ISTANBUL
Pontic Mountains
Trabzon
Van Gölü
Porto
Mont Perdu/Monte Perdido
Pico d'Aneto
Ebro
Sistema Ibérico
Cordillera Central
LISBON
Tagus
MADRID
BARCELONA
Corsica
Gulf of Porto
ROME
Tirane
Natural and Cultural Heritage of Ohrid
Mount Athos
ANKARA
Anatolia
Iberian Basin
Sierra Morena
Sevilla
Cordillera Bética
Granada
Doñana National Park
Cabo de São Vicente
Valencia
Palma d.M.
Balearic Islands
The Biodiversity and Culture of Ibiza
Sardinia
Tyrrhenian Sea
NAPLES
Vesuvio
Olymp
Meteora Monasteries
Aegean Sea
IZMIR
Taurus Mts.
Tuz Gölü
ADANA
ALEPPO
Euphrates
Tigris
AL MAWSIL
Canary Basin
Strait of Gibraltar
Tangier
Er Rif
CASABLANCA
RABAT
Oran
ALGIERS
Constantine
TUNIS
Aeolian Islands
Palermo
Etna
Sicily
Ionian Sea
Pindus Mts.
ATHENS
Peloponnesus
Rhodes
Cyprus
BEIRUT
DAMASCUS
Crete
MEDITERRANEAN SEA
Levantine Basin
Jerusalem
AMMAN
Dead Sea
Port Said
TRIPOLI
Benghazi
Tubruq
ALEXANDRIA
Cyrenaica
Gulf of Sirte
Tripolitania
Sahra Surt
Al Jufra Oasis
Qattara Depression
CAIRO
Sinai
El Aqaba
An Nafud
Libyan Desert
Great Sand Sea
Western Desert
Eastern Desert
Nile
Luxor
Aswân
Red Sea
Hejaz
Medina
Râs Banas
Djebel Mushaq
Lake Nasser
AFRICA
Fezzan
Ramlat Rabyanah
El Kufrah Oasis
Sarir Tibesti
SAHARA
Tibesti
Pic Tousidé
Tarso Emissi
Erdi
Djebel Al Awaynat
Nubian Desert
Nubia
Port Sudan
Porcupine Abyssal Plain
Azores
Terceira
I.d.São Miguel
Iberian Basin
Cantabria Mts.
Sistema Ibérico
ATLANTIC OCEAN
LISBON
MADRID
Laurisilva Laurel Forest of Madeira
Madeira
Cordillera Bética
Strait of Gibraltar
Canary Islands
CASABLANCA
RABAT
MARRAKECH
Garajonay National Park
La Gomera
Tenerife
Teide National Park, Tenerife
Lanzarote
Gran Canaria
Fuerteventura
0 160 320 Kilometers

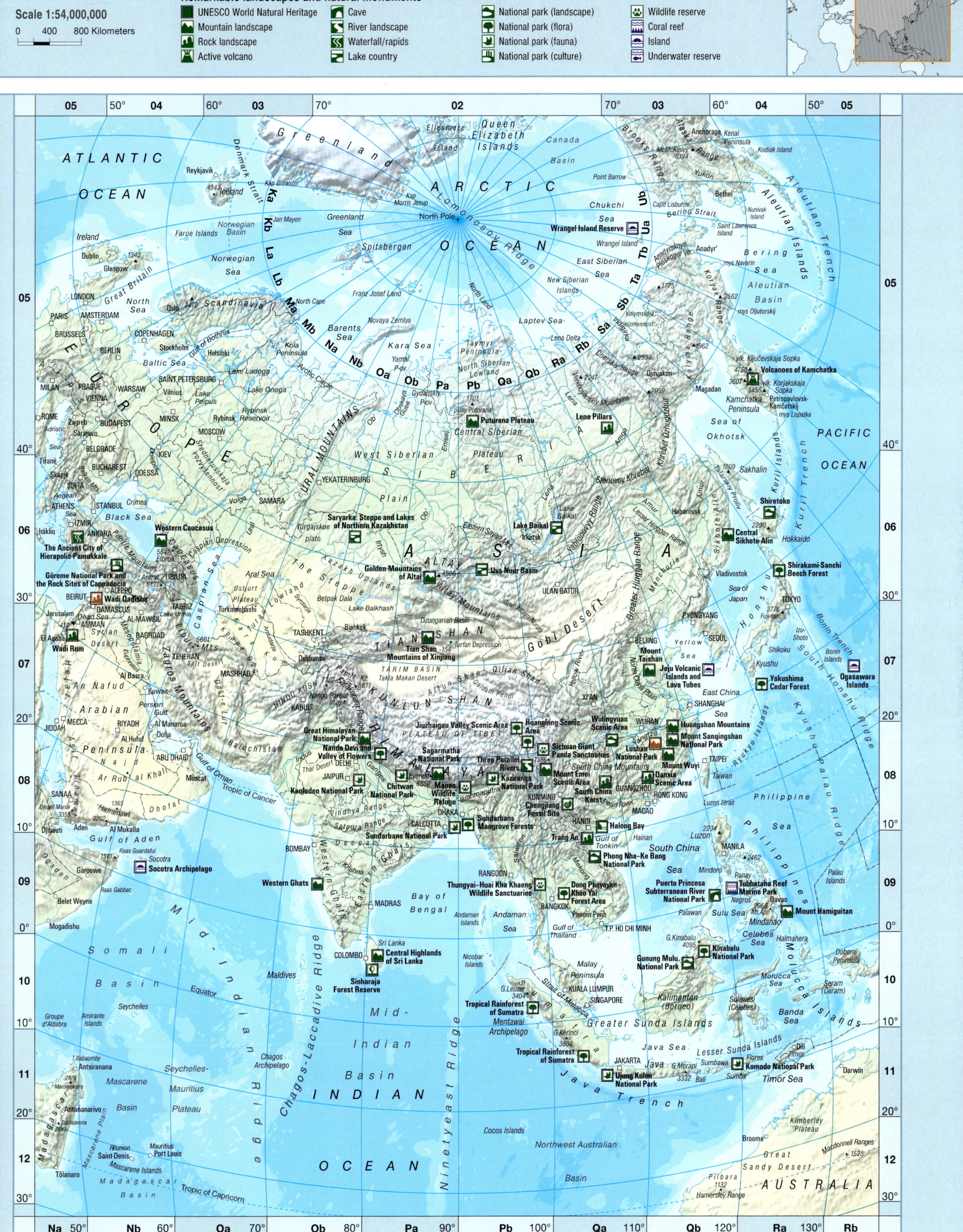

Scale 1:54,000,000
0 400 800 Kilometers
Remarkable landscapes and natural monuments
UNESCO World Natural Heritage
Mountain landscape
Rock landscape
Active volcano
Cave
River landscape
Waterfall/rapids
Lake country
National park (landscape)
National park (flora)
National park (fauna)
National park (culture)
Wildlife reserve
Coral reef
Island
Underwater reserve
ATLANTIC OCEAN
ARCTIC OCEAN
PACIFIC OCEAN
INDIAN OCEAN
EUROPE
ASIA
AUSTRALIA
Wrangel Island Reserve
Volcanoes of Kamchatka
Putorana Plateau
Lena Pillars
Western Caucasus
Saryarka: Steppe and Lakes of Northern Kazakhstan
Lake Baikal
Central Sikhote-Alin
Shiretoko
The Ancient City of Hierapolis-Pamukkale
Göreme National Park and the Rock Sites of Cappadocia
Golden Mountains of Altai
Uvs Nuur Basin
Shirakami-Sanchi Beech Forest
Wadi Qadisha
Wadi Rum
Tian Shan Mountains of Xinjiang
Mount Taishan
Jeju Volcanic Islands and Lava Tubes
Yakushima Cedar Forest
Ogasawara Islands
Great Himalayan National Park
Nanda Devi and Valley of Flowers
Jiuzhaigou Valley Scenic Area
Huanglong Scenic Area
Wulingyuan Scenic Area
Huangshan Mountains
Mount Sanqingshan National Park
Sichuan Giant Panda Sanctuaries
Lushan National Park
Sagarmatha National Park
Three Parallel Rivers
Mount Wuyi
Keoladeo National Park
Chitwan National Park
Manas Wildlife Refuge
Kaziranga National Park
Mount Emei Scenic Area
South China Karst
Danxia Scenic Area
Chengjiang Fossil Site
Sundarbans Mangrove Forests
Sundarbans National Park
Halong Bay
Phong Nha-Ke Bang National Park
Socotra Archipelago
Western Ghats
Thungyai-Huai Kha Khaeng Wildlife Sanctuaries
Dong Phayayen-Khao Yai Forest Area
Puerto Princesa Subterranean River National Park
Tubbataha Reef Marine Park
Mount Hamiguitan
Central Highlands of Sri Lanka
Sinharaja Forest Reserve
Kinabalu National Park
Gunung Mulu National Park
Tropical Rainforest of Sumatra
Ujung Kulon National Park
Komodo National Park

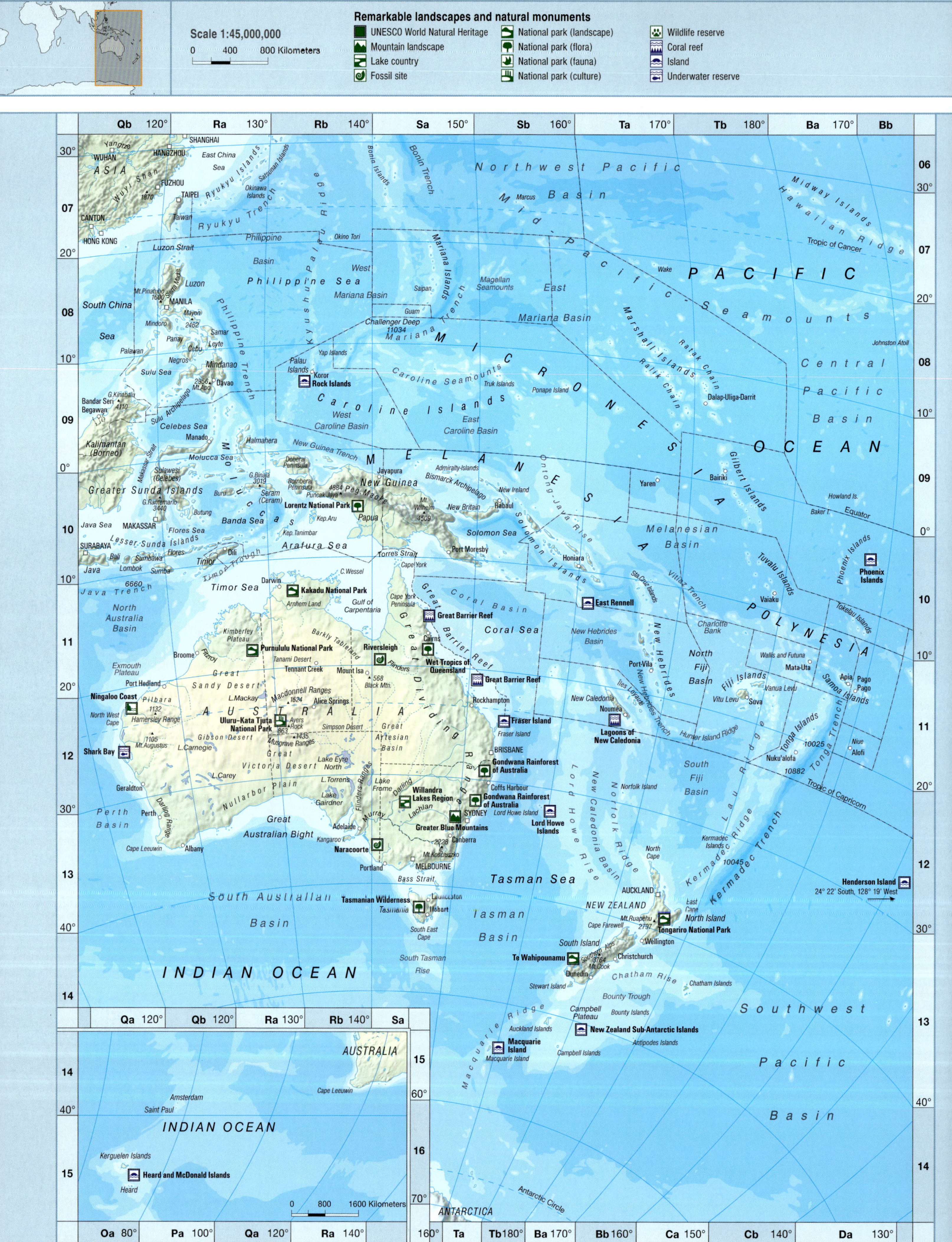

Scale 1:45,000,000
0 400 800 Kilometers
Remarkable landscapes and natural monuments
UNESCO World Natural Heritage
Mountain landscape
Lake country
Fossil site
National park (landscape)
National park (flora)
National park (fauna)
National park (culture)
Wildlife reserve
Coral reef
Island
Underwater reserve
Northwest Pacific Basin
Mid-Pacific Seamounts
PACIFIC OCEAN
Central Pacific Basin
MICRONESIA
MELANESIA
POLYNESIA
Philippine Sea
West Mariana Basin
East Mariana Basin
Challenger Deep 11034
Mariana Trench
Caroline Islands
West Caroline Basin
East Caroline Basin
Rock Islands
Lorentz National Park
New Guinea
Papua
Arafura Sea
Timor Sea
Coral Sea
Coral Basin
Solomon Sea
Melanesian Basin
Kakadu National Park
Purnululu National Park
Riversleigh
Wet Tropics of Queensland
Great Barrier Reef
Ningaloo Coast
Uluru-Kata Tjuta National Park
Shark Bay
Fraser Island
Gondwana Rainforest of Australia
Willandra Lakes Region
Greater Blue Mountains
Lord Howe Islands
Naracoorte
Tasmanian Wilderness
East Rennell
Lagoons of New Caledonia
Phoenix Islands
Henderson Island
24° 22' South, 128° 19' West
Tongariro National Park
Te Wahipounamu
New Zealand Sub-Antarctic Islands
Macquarie Island
AUSTRALIA
Great Australian Bight
Tasman Sea
Tasman Basin
South Australian Basin
INDIAN OCEAN
NEW ZEALAND
North Island
South Island
Southwest Pacific Basin
Heard and McDonald Islands
0 800 1600 Kilometers
ANTARCTICA
Antarctic Circle
Tropic of Cancer
Tropic of Capricorn
Equator

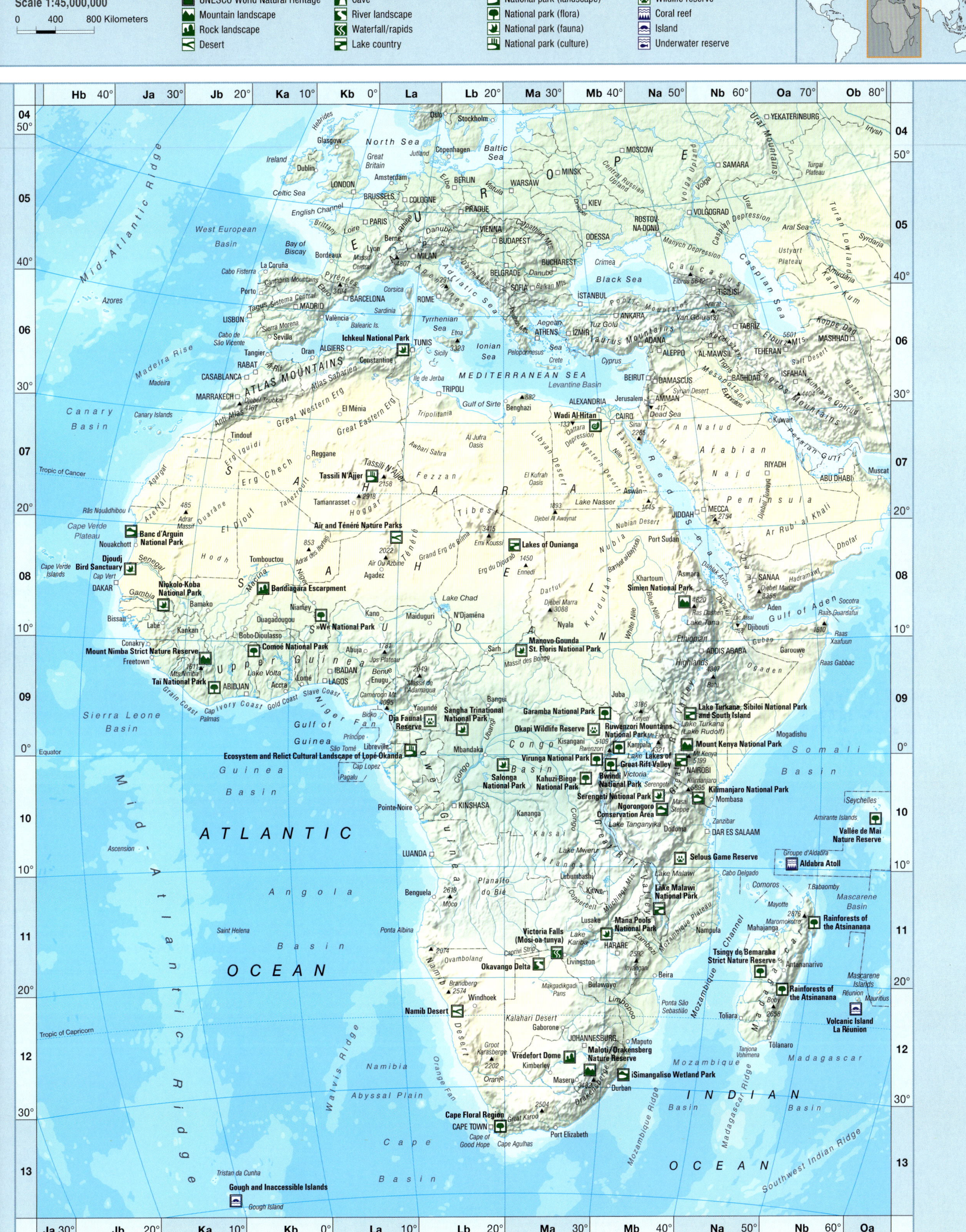

Scale 1:45,000,000
0 400 800 Kilometers
Remarkable landscapes and natural monuments
UNESCO World Natural Heritage
Mountain landscape
Rock landscape
Desert
Cave
River landscape
Waterfall/rapids
Lake country
National park (landscape)
National park (flora)
National park (fauna)
National park (culture)
Wildlife reserve
Coral reef
Island
Underwater reserve
Banc d'Arguin National Park
Djoudj Bird Sanctuary
Niokolo-Koba National Park
Bandiagara Escarpment
Mount Nimba Strict Nature Reserve
Comoé National Park
Tai National Park
"W" National Park
Air and Ténéré Nature Parks
Tassili N'Ajjer
Ichkeul National Park
Wadi Al-Hitan
Lakes of Ounianga
Manovo-Gounda St. Floris National Park
Simien National Park
Lake Turkana, Sibiloi National Park and South Island
Mount Kenya National Park
Garamba National Park
Okapi Wildlife Reserve
Ruwenzori Mountains National Park
Lakes of Great Rift Valley
Virunga National Park
Bwindi National Park
Kahuzi-Biega National Park
Salonga National Park
Sangha Trinational National Park
Dja Faunal Reserve
Ecosystem and Relict Cultural Landscape of Lopé-Okanda
Serengeti National Park
Ngorongoro Conservation Area
Kilimanjaro National Park
Selous Game Reserve
Lake Malawi National Park
Mana Pools National Park
Victoria Falls (Mosi-oa-tunya)
Okavango Delta
Namib Desert
Vredefort Dome
Maloti/Drakensberg Nature Reserve
iSimangaliso Wetland Park
Cape Floral Region
Aldabra Atoll
Vallée de Mai Nature Reserve
Rainforests of the Atsinanana
Tsingy de Bemaraha Strict Nature Reserve
Volcanic Island La Réunion
Gough and Inaccessible Islands
ATLANTIC OCEAN
INDIAN OCEAN
MEDITERRANEAN SEA
ATLAS MOUNTAINS
SAHARA
EUROPE
Mid-Atlantic Ridge
Tropic of Cancer
Equator
Tropic of Capricorn

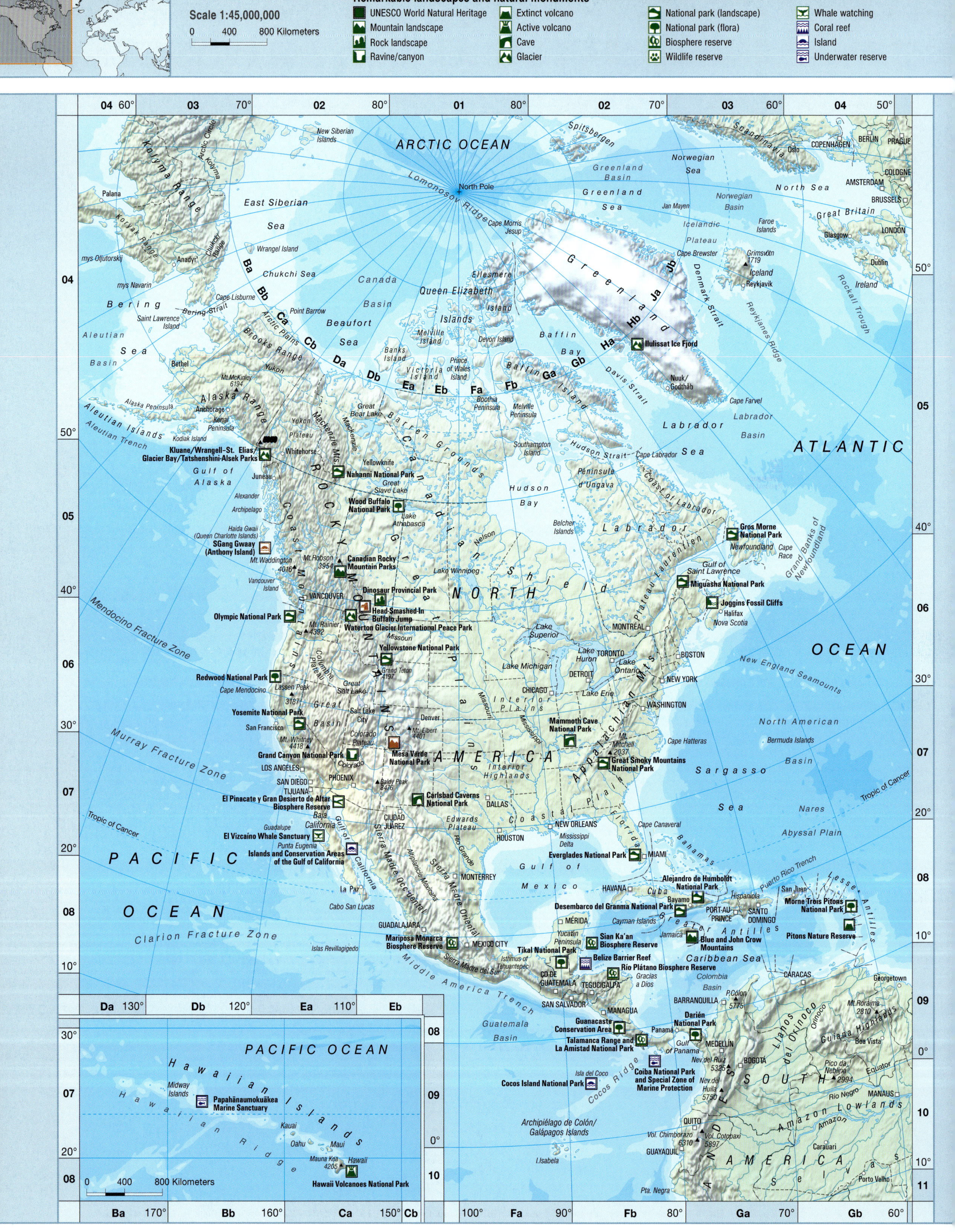
Scale 1:45,000,000
Remarkable landscapes and natural monuments
UNESCO World Natural Heritage
Mountain landscape
Rock landscape
Ravine/canyon
Extinct volcano
Active volcano
Cave
Glacier
National park (landscape)
National park (flora)
Biosphere reserve
Wildlife reserve
Whale watching
Coral reef
Island
Underwater reserve
ARCTIC OCEAN
PACIFIC OCEAN
ATLANTIC OCEAN
NORTH AMERICA
Kluane/Wrangell-St. Elias/Glacier Bay/Tatshenshini-Alsek Parks
Nahanni National Park
Wood Buffalo National Park
SGang Gwaay (Anthony Island)
Canadian Rocky Mountain Parks
Dinosaur Provincial Park
Head-Smashed-In Buffalo Jump
Waterton Glacier International Peace Park
Olympic National Park
Yellowstone National Park
Redwood National Park
Yosemite National Park
Grand Canyon National Park
Mesa Verde National Park
Carlsbad Caverns National Park
El Pinacate y Gran Desierto de Altar Biosphere Reserve
El Vizcaino Whale Sanctuary
Islands and Conservation Areas of the Gulf of California
Mammoth Cave National Park
Great Smoky Mountains National Park
Everglades National Park
Gros Morne National Park
Miguasha National Park
Joggins Fossil Cliffs
Ilulissat Ice Fjord
Alejandro de Humboldt National Park
Desembarco del Granma National Park
Blue and John Crow Mountains
Morne Trois Pitons National Park
Pitons Nature Reserve
Sian Ka'an Biosphere Reserve
Belize Barrier Reef
Rio Plátano Biosphere Reserve
Tikal National Park
Mariposa Monarca Biosphere Reserve
Guanacaste Conservation Area
Talamanca Range and La Amistad National Park
Darién National Park
Coiba National Park and Special Zone of Marine Protection
Cocos Island National Park
Papahānaumokuākea Marine Sanctuary
Hawaii Volcanoes National Park
Hawaiian Islands

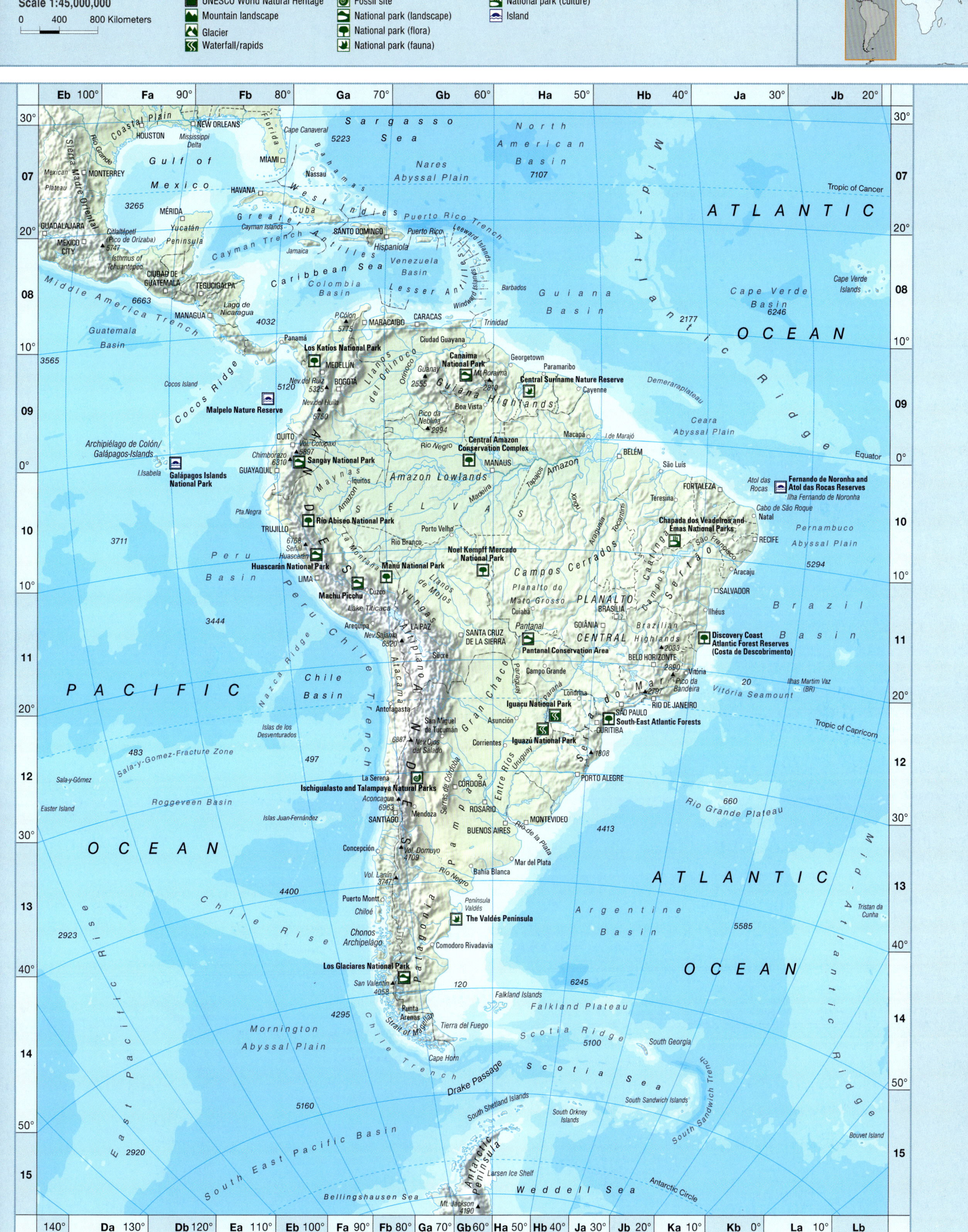
Scale 1:45,000,000
0 400 800 Kilometers
Remarkable landscapes and natural monuments
UNESCO World Natural Heritage
Mountain landscape
Glacier
Waterfall/rapids
Fossil site
National park (landscape)
National park (flora)
National park (fauna)
National park (culture)
Island
Sargasso Sea
North American Basin
Nares Abyssal Plain
Gulf of Mexico
Caribbean Sea
Colombia Basin
Venezuela Basin
Guiana Basin
Puerto Rico Trench
Cayman Trench
Middle America Trench
Guatemala Basin
Cocos Ridge
ATLANTIC OCEAN
Cape Verde Basin
Cape Verde Islands
Mid-Atlantic Ridge
Ceara Abyssal Plain
Demerara plateau
Tropic of Cancer
Equator
Tropic of Capricorn
Los Katios National Park
Canaima National Park
Central Suriname Nature Reserve
Malpelo Nature Reserve
Galápagos Islands National Park
Archipiélago de Colón/ Galápagos-Islands
Sangay National Park
Central Amazon Conservation Complex
Amazon Lowlands
Rio Abiseo National Park
Huascarán National Park
Machu Picchu
Manú National Park
Noel Kempff Mercado National Park
Fernando de Noronha and Atol das Rocas Reserves
Chapada dos Veadeiros and Emas National Parks
Pernambuco Abyssal Plain
Campos Cerrados
Planalto do Mato Grosso
Brazilian Highlands
Pantanal Conservation Area
Discovery Coast Atlantic Forest Reserves (Costa de Descobrimento)
Brazil Basin
Vitória Seamount
Iguaçu National Park
Iguazú National Park
South-East Atlantic Forests
Peru Basin
Peru-Chile Trench
Nazca Ridge
Chile Basin
PACIFIC OCEAN
Sala-y-Gomez-Fracture Zone
Roggeveen Basin
Ischigualasto and Talampaya Natural Parks
Rio Grande Plateau
The Valdés Peninsula
Argentine Basin
Chile Rise
Los Glaciares National Park
Falkland Islands
Falkland Plateau
Scotia Ridge
Scotia Sea
South Georgia
South Sandwich Islands
South Sandwich Trench
Drake Passage
Mornington Abyssal Plain
East Pacific Rise
South East Pacific Basin
Bellingshausen Sea
Weddell Sea
Antarctic Peninsula
Antarctic Circle
Cape Horn
Tierra del Fuego

PICTURE CREDITS

Abbreviations:
C Corbis
M Mauritius
G Getty

Pictures:
Cover: Great Barrier Reef, Australia, P. 2/3: Plitvice Lakes, Croatia; P.4/5: Sumatra Rhinocerus; P.6/7: Ayers Rock, Australia; P.8/9: Dead Vlei, Namibia
Picture Credits:
Cover: C/George Steinmetz;
P.002-003 Look/Rainer Mirau; P.004-005 C/Cyril Ruoso; P.006-007 C/Giles Bracher; P.008-009 G/Chris Simpson; P.010 M/Bernd Zoller; P.010-011 M/Alamy; P.012 C/Pierre Vauthey; P.012 G/Ernst Haas; P.012-013 A/Arctic Images; P.014 Look/age fotostock; P.014-015 G/Karsten Bidstrup; P.016 G/Sven Zacek; P.016-017 G/Sven Zacek; P.017 Look/NordicPhotos; P.018 G/Panoramic Images; P.018-019 G/Altrendo Panoramic; P.020 Look/Konrad Wothe; P.020-021 M/Evelyn Mazanke; P.021 M/Alamy; P.022 G/Michael Schwab; P.022-023 C/Paul Souders; P.024 C/Steve Austin; P.024-025 C/Jim Richardson; P.025 C/Andy Rouse; P.026 Look/age fotostock; P.026-027 Look/age fotostock; P.027 G//Martin Brent; P.028 G/Guy Edwardes; P.028-029 Premium; P.030 C/Tui De Roy; P.030 C/Tui De Roy; P.031 C/Sebastian Kennerknecht; P.031 C/Wolfgang Kaehler; P.032 M/Alamy; P.032-033 M/ANP Photo; P.033 M/ANP Photo; P.033 M/ANP Photo; P.033 M/ANP Photo; P.033 M/United Archives; P.034 M/Alamy; P.034-035 M/Alamy; P.035 M/Alamy; P.036 Look/Konrad Wothe; P.036 Look/Konrad Wothe; P.036 Look/Konrad Wothe; P.037 Look/Franz Marc Frei; P.037 Look/Jan Greune; P.038 C/NASA; P.038 M/Author's Image; P.039 M/Alamy; P.040 Look/Heinz Wohner; P.040 Look/Sabine Lubenow; P.040 Look/Ulf Boettcher; P.041 G/Manuel Gutjahr; P.041 G/Ronald Wittek; P.041 Look/Sabine Lubenow; P.042 M/Andreas Jäkel; P.042-043 C/Frank Lukasseck; P.043 Look/Konrad Wothe; P.044 C/Jonathan Blair; P.044-045 H. & D. Zielske; P.045 C/Jonathan Blair; P.045 C/Jonathan Blair; P.046 G/Dan Tucker; P.046-047 M/Alamy; P.048 M/Michael Szönyi; P.048-049 C/Michael Szönyi; P.048-049 C/Michael Szönyi; P.049 C/Nathan Benn; P.050 C/Grzegorz Lesniewski; P.050-051 C/Raymond Gehman; P.051 C/D. Sheldon; P.051 C/Staffan Widstrand; P.052 M/Thomas Hintze; P.052 M/Wild Wonders of Europe; P.053 Look/age fotostock; P.053 Look/age fotostock; P.053 C/Carmen Redondo; P.054 C/Konrad Wothe; P.054 M/Alamy; P.054 M/Alamy; P.055 M/imagebroker.net; P.055 G/rusm; P.055 G/martovskiy.ru; P.056 C/Grand Tour Collection; P.056-057 C/Mauricio Abreu; P.057 G/Guillermo Casas Baruque; P.057 G/BenC; P.057 G/David Santiago Garcia; P.057 G/Patricio Robles Gil; P.058 C/Ben Welsh; P.058-059 C/Ramon Navarro; P.059 G/Richard Kemp; P.059 G/Martin Zalba; P.059 C/Ramon Navarro; P.059 C/Ramon Navarro; P.059 M/Alamy; P.060 Look/Jan Greune; P.060-061 Look/age fotostock; P.062 G/Images Etc Ltd; P.062-063 C/Guido Cozzi; P.064 C/Guido Cozzi; P.064 M/Alamy; P.064 M/Alamy; P.065 G/Franco Banfi; P.065 C/Cyril Ruoso; P.066 Look/Andreas Strauß; P.066-067 Look/Andreas Strauß; P.067 G/Stefano Rossi; P.067 Look/Andreas Strauß; P.067 Look/Andreas Strauß; P.068-069 Look/Tobias Richter; P.070 G/David Trood; P.070-071 C/Alessandro Saffo; P.071 C/Martin Rietze; P.072 C/Frank Lukasseck; P.072-073 G/Stocktrek Images; P.074 C/Guy Edwardes; P.074 Look/Günther Bayerl; P.074-075 C/Bob Krist; P.075 C/Michael Runkel; P.076 M/Rainer Mirau; P.076-077 C/Jose Fuste Raga; P.077 Look/Rainer Mirau; P.078 Look/Günther Bayerl; P.078-079 Look/Günther Bayerl; P.079 Look/Günther Bayerl; P.080 G/Tony Eveling; P.080-081 C/Peter Langer; P.081 C/Christophe Boisvieux; P.081 M/ Adrian C. Nitu; P.082 M/Alamy; P.082-083 C/Michele Falzone; P.084 A/Stelian Porojnicu; P.084-085 C/Philippe Caron; P.085 G/Martin Zwick; P.085 G/Danita Delimont; P.085 C/Ed Kashi; P.085 M/Alamy; P.085 M/Alamy; P.086 G/Sue Flood; P.086 M/Alamy; P.087 C/Cyril Ruoso; P.087 A/LJS-photography; P.088 M/Alamy; P.088-089 G/Steven Ruiter; P.090 C/Serguei Fomine; P.090 C/Konstantin Mikhailov; P.090 G/Randy Olson; P.091 C/Serguei Fomine; P.091 C/Konstantin Mikhailov; P.091 M/Bluegreen Pictures; P.092 M/Alamy; P.092-093 C/Konstantin Mikhailov; P.094 Look/Per-Andre Hoffmann; P.094-095 Look/age fotostock; P.095 C/Konrad Wothe; P.096-097 C/Tom Brakefield; P.096-097 M/Konstantin Mikhail; P.097 C/David Ponton; P.098 C/Gabrielle & Michel Therin-Weise; P.098-099 Look/Minden Pictures; P.100 Look/Minden Pictures; P.100-101 C/Serguei Fomine; P.101 C/Randy Olson; P.101 C/Sergey Gorshkov; P.101 C/Martin Rietze; P.101 C/Yann Arthus-Bertrand; P.102 Look/age fotostock; P.102-103 M/Alamy; P.104 G/Panoramic Images; P.104-105 Look/Rainer Mirau; P.106 Look/Günther Bayerl; P.106-107 C/O. Alamany & E. Vicens; P.106-107 C/Hans P. Szyszka; P.108 G/jcarillet; P.108 M/Alamy; P.109 Look/age fotostock; P.109 M/Egmont Strigl; P.110 M/Alamy; P.110-111 M/Alamy; P.111 G/Patrick Palmen; P.111 M/John Holmes; P.111 M/Neil Bowman; P.112 C/Joson Photography; P.112 M/Cultura; P.114 G/Richard I'Anson; P.114 G/De Agostini Picture Library; P.114-115 M/Alamy; P.115 M/Alamy; P.115 M/Alamy; P.116-117 C/Dietmar Nill; P.118 C/Christian Hütter; P.118-119 M/Alamy; P.119 C/Christian Hütter; P.119 C/Christian Hütter; P.119 M/age; P.119 M/age; P.119 C/Staffan Widstrand; P.120 G/Dr. Anirban Sinha; P.120-121 G/Ann & Steve Toon; P.121 Look/age fotostock; P.122 G/Anup Shah; P.122-123 C/Anup Shah; P.123 C/Ann & Steve Toon; P.123 C/Nigel Pavitt; P.123 C/Bernard Castelein; P.123 G/Ann & Steve Toon; P.124 G/Murali Aithal; P.124 G; P.124 C/Patricio Robles Gil; P.124 M/Olaf Krüger; P.124-125 C/Anup Shah; P.125 G/Jayaprakash; P.125 C/Frans Lanting; P.125 C/Anup Shah; P.126 G/Pallab Seth; P.126 G/Pallab Seth; P.127 G/Shahnewaz Karim; P.127 G/Farhana Jenny; P.128 C/Kevin Schafer; P.128 C/Rob Francis; P.128 M/Robert Harding; P.128 M/Westend61; P.128 M/Alamy; P.128 M/Alamy; P.128 M/Alamy; P.129 G/Nigel Pavitt; P.129 G/Nigel Pavitt; P.129 G/Nigel Pavitt; P.129 G/www.Wildlifepictures.se; P.129 Look/Kay Maeritz; P.129 Look/Kay Maeritz; P.130 M/Alamy; P.130-131 C/Wolfram Cüppers; P.131 Look/Brown Cannon; P.131 M/Wolfram Cüppers; P.131 M/Alamy; P.132 G/Panorama Media; P.132 G/View Stock; P.132-133 G/Feng Wei; P.133 C/Blue Jean Images; P.134 G/Universal Stopping Point Photography; P.134 G/Christian Kober; P.135 G/Allister Chiong; P.135 C/Imagemore Co. ; P.136 G/David H. Collier; P.136-137 G/Adam Jones; P.138 Look/age fotostock; P.138-139 C/Bruno Morandi; P.139 G/rusm; P.140 C/Frank Krahmer; P.140-141 C/Roland Gerth; P.141 C/Liu Liqun; P.142-143 C/Topic Photo Agency; P.144 C/Frank Krahmer; P.144-145 M/SuperStock; P.145 C/Frank Krahmer; P.146 Look/age fotostock; P.146-147 Look/Minden Pictures; P.148 Look/Karl Johaentges; P.148-149 Look/Karl Johaentges; P.150 C/Liu Jian Ming; P.150-151 C/Redlink; P.151 C/Liu Liqun; P.152 C/Frank Krahmer; P.152-153 C/Roland Gerth; P.154 G/Steve Peterson Photography; P.154-155 Ifa/Int Stock ; P.156 C/xinhua; P.156-157 C/Astock; P.156-157 C/Astock; P.158 C/Wong Adam; P.158 C/John Wang; P.159 C/Qin Qing; P.159 C/Imaginechina; P.160 G/Jon Hicks; P.160-161 G/Colin Monteath; P.162 G/James Warwick; P.162-163 C/Wolfgang Kaehler; P.164 C/Topic Photo Agency; P.164 Look/EuroCreon; P.165 C/Jeremy Woodhouse ; P.165 M/Diversion; P.165 M/Diversion; P.166 C/Mamoru Muto; P.166 M/Jeff Tzu-chao Lin; P.167 G/Karin Slade; P.167 C/B.Schmid; P.167 C/Cyril Ruoso; P.167 C/Cyril Ruoso; P.167 C/amanaimages; P.167 Look/Minden Pictures; P.168-169 G/Shayne Hill Xtreme Visuals; P.170 C/Aflo; P.170-171 C/amanaimages; P.171 C/Hiroya Minakuchi; P.171 C/Hiroya Minakuchi; P.171 C/Hiroya Minakuchi; P.172 M/Alamy; P.172-173 M/Alamy; P.173 M/Photoshot Creative; P.174 C/Thomas Marent; P.174-175 G/Kanate Chainapong; P.175 G/Gary Lewis; P.175 C/Eddi Boehnke; P.175 G/Art Wolfe; P.176 C/Daniele Falletta; P.176-177 C/Daniele Falletta; P.177 C/Daniele Falletta; P.178 Look/Arnt Haug; P.178 C/S P; P.179 C/Chien C. Lee; P.179 C/Mark Moffett; P.180 M/Alamy; P.180-181 G/Klaus Nigge; P.181 C/Romeo Ranoco; P.181 C/Romeo Ranoco ; P.181 C/Bruno Morandi; P.182 G/Jeff Hunter; P.182-183 G/Borut Furlan; P.183 G/David Fleetham; P.183 G/Jeff Hunter; P.183 G/Jeff Hunter; P.183 C/Dave Fleetham; P.184 G/Jeff BrownPhoto Images; P.184-185 G/Gerry Ellis ; P.185 G/Martin Cohen; P.185 G/W K Fletcher; P.185 G/W K Fletcher; P.185 G/W K Fletcher; P.185 C/Thomas Marent; P.185 C/Ch'ien Lee; P.186 G/Robbie Shone; P.186-187 G/Ch'ien Lee; P.187 G/Martin Cohen; P.187 G/Ch'ien Lee; P.187 C/Thomas Marent; P.187 C/Chien C. Lee; P.187 C/Chien C. Lee; P.187 C/Chien Lee; P.188 C/Anup Shah; P.188-189 C/Anup Shah; P.189 C/Fadil; P.190 G/Cyril Ruoso; P.190-191 G/Theo Allofs; P.192 C/Martin Rietze; P.192 C/Martin Rietze; P.192 M/Prisma; P.193 C/Konrad Wothe; P.193 C/Gerry Ellis; P.194 C/moodboard; P.194-195 C/Theo Allofs; P.196 C/Steve Parish; P.196-197 C/W. Perry Conway; P.197 G/Auscape / UIG; P.197 C/Jason Edwards; P.197 C/Jean-Paul Ferrero; P.197 C/Wayne Lawler; P.198-199 C/Nature Connect; P.200 G/Peter Walton Photography; P.200-201 C/Jochen Schlenker; P.202 G/Sara Winter; P.202 G/Doug Perrine; P.203 G/Franco Banfi; P.203 G/Satellite Aerial Images ; P.203 M/Alamy; P.204 Premium/Image State; P.204-205 C/Paul A. Souders; P.206 G/Andrew Watson; P.206-207 Look/Konrad Wothe; P.208 M/Alamy; P.208-209 C/Konrad Wothe; P.209 C/Konrad Wothe; P.209 C/Konrad Wothe; P.209 M/Alamy; P.209 C/Konrad Wothe; P.210 G/Panoramic Images; P.210-211 G/Peter Walton; P.211 G/Ignacio Palacios; P.211 C/Black Flying Fox; P.211 C/Thomas Marent; P.211 G/Roy Toft; P.212 M/Alamy; P.212-213 M/Alamy; P.214 G/Sara Winter; P.214-215 G/Neal Pritchard; P.216 C/Peter Essick; P.216-217 G/Panoramic Images; P.217 C/Shin Yoshino; P.218 C/Steve Parish Publishing; P.218-219 C/George Steinmetz; P.220-221 G/Rodger Klein; P.222 C/Michael Amendolia; P.222-223 G/Peter Walton Photography; P.223 Look/Holger Leue; P.224 Look/Guenther Bayerl; P.224-225 C/Grant Dixon ; P.225 C/Craig Lamotte; P.225 C/Dave Watts; P.225 C/D. Parer & E. Parer-Cook; P.225 C/D. Parer & E. Parer-Cook; P.225 M/imagebroker; P.226 G/Ignacio Palacios; P.226 G/Hatty Gottschalk; P.227 C/Tui De Roy; P.227 M/Alamy; P.228 C; P.228-229 M/Malcolm Schuyl; P.229 M/Mint Images Ltd.; P.230 G/Byron Tanaphol Prukston; P.230-231 C/Roland Gerth; P.231 G/Holger Leue; P.232 C/Maurizio Rellini; P.232-233 C/Colin Monteath; P.234 C/Colin Monteath; P.234-235 G/Julie Fletcher; P.235 G/Yi Jiang; P.236 G/Christopher Chan; P.236-237 C/Colin Monteath; P.237 G/Jeffrey Conley; P.238 C/Yva Momatiuk & John Eastcott; P.238-239 G/Colin Monteath; P.239 Look/age fotostock; P.240 C/Tui De Roy; P.240-241 C/Tui De Roy; P.241 Look/age fotostock; P.241 Look/age fotostock; P.241 G/Tui De Roy; P.241 G/Ingrid Visser; P.242 C/Keren Su; P.242 C/Christopher Ward; P.243 C/Chris Newbert; P.243 C/Hans Leijnse; P.244 M/Alamy; P.244-245 M/Alamy; P.245 C/Jeff Foott; P.246 C/Martin Harvey; P.246-247 C/Martin Harvey; P.248 G/Franck Guiziou; P.248-249 C/Sebastien Cailleux; P.250 C/Daniele Occhiato; P.250 M/Alamy; P.251 M/Jeff Tzu-chao Lin; P.251 M /Jeff Tzu-chao Lin; P.252 Look/Photononstop; P.252 Look/Photononstop; P.253 G/David Kerkhoff; P.253 G/DEA/L.Romano; P.254 L/Michael Martin; P.254-255 L/Michael Martin; P.256 C/Anup Shah; P.256-257 C/Frans Lanting; P.258 C/George Steinmetz; P.258 G/Philippe Bourseiller; P.259 G/Photononstop; P.259 C/Aldo Pavan; P.260 C/Frans Lanting; P.260 C/Frans Lanting; P.261 C/Martin Harvey; P.261 M/Minden Pictures; P.261 M/Minden Pictures; P.262 C/Nigel Pavitt; P.262-263 M/Alamy; P.264 G/Michael K. Nichols; P.264-265 C/Cyril Ruoso; P.265 C/Piotr Naskrecki; P.265 C/David A. Northcott; P.266 C/Anup Shah; P.266 M/Alamy; P.267 G/Michael Nichols; P.267 C/Karl Ammann; P.268-269 M/Gerard Lacz; P.270 C/Fiona Rogers; P.270-271 G/Dr. John Michael Fay; P.272 G/Cyril Ruoso; P.272 C/Cyril Ruoso; P.272 C/David A. Northcott; P.273 G/Anup Shah; P.273 G/Anup Shah; P.273 G/Nigel Pavitt; P.274 C/Anup Shah; P.274-275 G/Ian Nichols; P.275 G/Anup Shah; P.276 C/Flavio Pagani; P.276 C/Ijaz Bhatti; P.277 C/Frans Lanting; P.277 C/David Fettes; P.278 G/Randy Olson; P.278-279 M/Alamy; P.279 M/Alamy; P.280 G/Anup Shah; P.280 C/Frans Lanting; P.281 G/Anup Shah; P.281 M/Alamy; P.282 C/Last Refuge; P.282-283 C/Carsten Peter; P.283 G/Rebecca Yale; P.284 M/age; P.284-285 G/Harry Hook; P.285 C/Anup Shah; P.285 C/Anup Shah; P.285 A/Papilio ; P.286 M/Alamy; P.286-287 Look/age fotostock; P.287 C/Paul Souders; P.287 M/age; P.288 Look/age fotostock; P.288-289 M/age; P.289 G/Nigel Pavitt; P.289 G/Martin Zwick; P.289 Look/age fotostock; P.289 C/Eddi Boehnke; P.289 C/Thomas Marent; P.289 C/Gerry Ellis; P.289 A/Arco Images GmbH; P.290 C/Martin Harvey; P.290-291 G/Richard Du Toit; P.291 G/Nigel Pavitt; P.292 G/Nigel Pavitt; P.292-293 C/Tui De Roy; P.293 G/Gerard Soury; P.293 G/Gerard Soury; P.293 C/Tui De Roy; P.293 C/Tui De Roy; P.294 G/Paul & Paveena Mckenzie; P.294-295 G/Nigel Pavitt; P.294-295 C/Nigel Pavitt; P.296 G/Robin Moore; P.296-297 C/Jim Zuckerman; P.297 G/Paul Souders; P.297 C/ Paul Souders; P.297 M/Alamy; P.297 M/Alamy; P.298 G/Nicholas Parfitt; P.298-299 C/Frans Lanting; P.299 C/Remi Benali; P.300 G/Johnathan Ampersand Esper; P.300-301 C/DLILLC; P.302 G/Nigel Pavitt; P.302-303 G/Michael Poliza; P.304 Look/age fotostock; P.304-305 G/Steve Corner; P.305 Look/age fotostock; P.306 Look/age fotostock; P.306 C/David Fettes; P.307 C/Ben Cranke; P.307 G/Shaen Adey; P.307 M/Alamy; P.307 M/Alamy; P.307 M/Alamy; P.307 M/Alamy; P.308 C/Martin Harvey; P.308-309 G/Sergey Gorshkov; P.309 W. Kunth; P.310 C/Richard Du Toit; P.310-311 C/Martin Harvey; P.311 C/George Steinmetz; P.311 C/George Steinmetz; P.311 C/Richard Du Toit; P.312 C/Tim Hauf; P.312-313 SPL / Agentur Focus; P.314 G/Hugh Mackintosh; P.314-315 G/George Brits; P.316 C/Tim Hauf; P.316-317 C/Jelger Herder; P.317 G/Peter Chadwick; P.317 G/George Brits; P.317 G/Juergen Ritterbach; P.317 G/Martin Harvey; P.318 G/Martin Harvey; P.318-319 C/Steve & Ann Toon; P.319 G/Lanz von Horsten; P.319 G/Ariadne Van Zandbergen; P.319 G/Michael & Patricia Fogden; P.319 G/Tim Jackson; P.320 C/Alex Hyde; P.320-321 C/Nick Garbutt; P.321 C/Thomas Marent; P.321 C/Thomas Marent; P.321 C/Thomas Marent; P.321 C/Nick Garbutt; P.321 C/Thorsten Negro; P.322 C/Konrad Wothe; P.322-323 C/Thomas Marent; P.323 C/Frans Lanting; P.323 C/Thomas Marent; P.323 C/Konrad Wothe; P.323 A/The Africa Image Library; P.323 C/Chris Hellier; P.324 G/Ralph Lee Hopkins; P.324 C/Martin Moxter; P.325 M/Alamy; P.325 M/Alamy; P.326 C/Sumio Harada; P.326-327 C/Michele Falzone; P.328 C/Michael P.Quinton; P.328-329 C/Ron Erwin; P.330 C/Jochen Schlenker; P.330 G/Robert Postma; P.331 C/Matthias Breiter; P.331 G/Art Wolfe; P.332 G/Gerald & Buff Corsi ; P.332 G/Gerald & Buff Corsi ; P.332 G/Gerald & Buff Corsi ; P.332 G/Ernest Manewal; P.332 G/Danita Delimont; P.333 G/Glenn Oakley; P.333 Look/Design Pics; P.333 M/Minden Pictures; P.334 C/Peter Mather; P.334-335 C/Peter Mather; P.336 C/Russ Heinl; P.336 M/Alamy; P.337 C/Stuart McCall; P.337 C/Ron Watts; P.338 C/Scott Dimond; P.338-339 C/Jochen Schlenker; P.340 C/Paul Horsley; P.340-341 C/Clarke Wiebe; P.341 C/Clarke Wiebe; P.342 C/Darwin Wiggett; P.342 C/Yves Marcoux; P.343 C/Thomas Kitchin & Victoria Hurst; P.343 C/Sam Chrysanthou; P.344 G/David Nunuk; P.344-345 C/Michael Wheatley; P.345 C/Michael Wheatley; P.346 C/Jochen Schlenker; P.346-347 C/Robert Postma; P.347 C/Carson Ganci; P.348 C/Richard Berry; P.348-349 C/Destinations; P.350 C/Russ Heinl; P.350 C/Darwin Wiggett; P.351 C/Eryk Jaegermann; P.351 C/Ron Erwin; P.351 C/Ron Erwin; P.352 G/Philippe Henry; P.352-353 G/Dale Wilson; P.354 C/John Cancalosi; P.354 C/Jonathan Blair; P.354 C/Wolfgang Kaehler; P.355 M/Alamy; P.355 M/Alamy; P.356 G/Michael Melford; P.356-357 G/Rolf Hicker; P.358 C/Steven Kazlowski; P.358-359 Christian Heeb; P.359 G/Macduff Everton; P.359 C/James Randkle; P.359 G/Cornelia & Ramon Doerr; P.360 C/Randall Levensaler Photography; P.360-361 G/Panoramic Images; P.361 G/Rich Reid; P.362 C/Momatiuk - Eastcott; P.362-363 Huber/Susanne Kremer ; P.364-365 C/Momatiuk - Eastcott; P.366 C/Jeff Vanuga; P.366-367 G/Jeffrey Murray; P.368-369 M/Alamy; P.370 C/Stephen Alvarez; P.370-371 G/Jeffrey Murray; P.372 C/George H.H. Huey; P.372-373 C/George H.H. Huey; P.374 G/Steven Kazlowski; P.374 Look/NordicPhotos; P.375 G/Stephen Alvarez; P.375 C/David Muench; P.376 C/Donald M. Jones; P.376-377 G/Panoramic Images; P.377 C/Natural Selection Robert Cable; P.378 G/Panoramic Images; P.378-379 G/Panoramic Images; P.379 G/Raul Touzon; P.379 C/Raymond Gehman; P.379 M/Alamy; P.380 G/Richard A Cooke III; P.380-381 G/Art Wolfe; P.381 C/Frans Lanting; P.382 C/Hugh Gentry; P.382 M/Alamy; P.382 M/Alamy; P.383 G/Michael P.Nolan; P.383 G/Kevin Schafer; P.383 C/George Steinmetz; P.384 C/George H. H. Huey; P.384-385 G/Patricio Robles Gil ; P.385 G/Tui de Roy ; P.386 G/Feargus Cooney; P.386 C/Cyril Ruoso; P.387 M/Science Source; P.387 M/Alamy; P.388 C/Ingo Arndt; P.388 C/Thomas Marent; P.388 C/Ocean ; P.389 G/Danita Delimont; P.389 C/Oliver Lucanus; P.390 A/Mark Conlin; P.390-391 Huber/Giovanni; P.391 C/Stuart Westmorland; P.391 C/Paul Souders; P.391 C/Jeffrey L. Rotman; P.391 C/Jeffrey L. Rotman; P.391 C/Jeffrey L. Rotman; P.392 G/Diego Lezama; P.392-393 M/age; P.393 M/Alamy; P.393 M/Alamy; P.394 G/Stuart Westmorland; P.394 C/Thomas Marent; P.395 G/Franco Banfi; P.395 G/Mark Conlin; P.396 C/Frans Lanting; P.396-397 C/Konrad Wothe; P.397 C/Norbert Wu; P.397 C/Michael & Patricia Fogden; P.397 C/Michael & Patricia Fogden; P.397 C/Michael & Patricia Fogden; P.398 G/Roy Toft; P.398 G/Roy Toft; P.398 G/Alfredo Maiquez; P.398-399 G/Roy Toft; P.399 G/Roy Toft; P.399 G/Thomas Chamberlin; P.400 M/Alamy; P.400-401 M/Alamy; P.401 M/Alamy; P.401 M/Alamy; P.401 M/Alamy; P.401 M/Alamy; P.402 M/Oyvind Martinsen; P.402-403 G/Gregory Basco ; P.404 C/David Fleetham; P.404 M/Alamy; P.405 C/Philip Friskorn; P.405 M/Alamy; P.406: M/Alamy; P.406: C/ Doug Pearson; P.407 G/Banana Pancake; P.407 G/Jens Kuhfs; P.408 G/Justin Foulkes; P.408-409 G/Michele Falzone; P.410 C/Colin Monteath; P.410-411 M/Alamy; P.412 C/Kevin Schafer; P.412 C/Tom Vezo ; P.413 G/WaterFrame ; P.413 G/WaterFrame ; P.414 C/Hubert Stadler; P.414-415 C/Tui de Roy ; P.415 C/DLILLC; P.415 Look/Per-Andre Hoffmann; P.415 C/Kevin Schafer; P.416-417 G/David Fleetham; P.418 Look/Per-Andre Hoffmann; P.418-419 C/Pete Oxford; P.420 M/Alamy; P.420 M/Alamy; P.421 C/Thomas Marent; P.421 C/Pete Oxford; P.421 M/Alamy; P.422 C/Colin Monteath; P.422-423 C/Patrick J. Endres; P.424 G/Pete Oxford ; P.424 M/Alamy; P.425 G/Gregory MD.; P.425 C/Lars-Olof Johansson; P.425 C/Pete Oxford; P.425 C/Pete Oxford; P.425 C/Pete Oxford; P.425 C/Pete Oxford ; P.426 M/Jurgen & Christine Sohns; P.426 C/Pablo Corral Vega; P.426-427 Look/Holger Leue; P.428 M/Alamy; P.428-429 C/Jane Sweeney ; P.429 C/Thomas Marent ; P.429 C/Mark Moffett; P.429 C/Kevin Schafer; P.429 M/Alamy; P.430 C/Jim Zuckerman; P.430 C/David A. Northcott; P.431 C/David A. Northcott; P.432 M/Harald von Radebre; P.432-433 C/Kevin Schafer; P.433 C/Murray Cooper; P.433 C/Kevin Schafer; P.433 Look/Minden Pictures; P.433 M/Alamy; P.433 M/Alamy; P.434 Look/Minden Pictures; P.434 M/Alamy; P.435 C/Luciano Candisani; P.435 C/Tui De Roy; P.435 C/Alex Robinson; P.436 C/Macduff Everton; P.436-437 C/Luciano Candisani; P.437 M/Minden Pictures; P.438 C/Theo Allofs; P.438-439 C/Kevin Schafer; P.439 G/Theo Allofs; P.439 C/Theo Allofs; P.439 C/Gavriel Jecan; P.440 C/Luciano Candisani; P.440-441 G/Roberto Peradotto; P.442 C/Jeremy Woodhouse; P.442-443 C/Michael Runkel; P.444 C/Philippe Widling; P.444 C/Peter Langer; P.444 C/Hubert Stadler; P.445 Look/Holger Leue; P.445 M/Christian Heinrich; P.446 C/Jonathan Griffith; P.446-447 C/Colin Monteath.

IMPRINT

MONACO BOOKS is an imprint of
© 2015/2016 Kunth Verlag GmbH & Co KG, München

For distribution please contact:
Monaco Books
c/o Kunth Verlag GmbH & Co KG, München
Königinstr. 11
80539 München
Tel. +49.89.45 80 20-0
Fax +49.89.45 80 20-21
www.kunth-verlag.de
www.monacobooks.com
info@kunth-verlag.de

Translation: JMS Books LLP; Sylvia Goulding
Text: Natascha Albus, Heike Barnitzke, Catrin Barnsteiner, Monika Baumüller, Gesa Bock, Arno Breckner, Klaus Dammann, Klaus A. Dietsch, Michael Elser, Dietmar Falk, Werner Fiederer, Robert Fischer, Petra Frese, Ute Friesen, Winfried Gerhards, Martina Gschließer, Ulrike Köppchen, Dr. Steffen Krämer, Brigitte Lotz, Angela Meißner, Werner Morgenrath, Norbert Pautner, Dr. Ulrike Prinz, Dr. Jürgen Rapp, Ingrid Reuter, André Ruo, Monika Sattrasai, Dr. Susanne Scheffler-Gerken, Dr. Hans-Wilm Schütte, Eckard Schuster, Ingrid Suvak, Dr. Marcus Würmli

Printed in Romania